Handbook of Machine and Computer Vision

Handbook of Machine and Computer Vision

The Guide for Developers and Users

Edited by Alexander Hornberg

Second, Revised and Updated Edition

Editor

Alexander Hornberg
Hochschule Esslingen
University of Applied Sciences
Campus Göppingen
Fakultät Mechatronik und Elektrotechnik
Robert-Bosch-Straße 1
73037 Göppingen
Germany

All books published by **Wiley-VCH** are carefully produced. Nevertheless, authors, editors, and publisher do not warrant the information contained in these books, including this book, to be free of errors. Readers are advised to keep in mind that statements, data, illustrations, procedural details or other items may inadvertently be inaccurate.

Library of Congress Card No.: applied for

British Library Cataloguing-in-Publication Data
A catalogue record for this book is available from the British Library.

Bibliographic information published by the Deutsche Nationalbibliothek
The Deutsche Nationalbibliothek lists this publication in the Deutsche Nationalbibliografie; detailed bibliographic data are available on the Internet at <http://dnb.d-nb.de>.

© 2017 Wiley-VCH Verlag GmbH & Co. KGaA, Boschstr. 12, 69469 Weinheim, Germany

All rights reserved (including those of translation into other languages). No part of this book may be reproduced in any form – by photoprinting, microfilm, or any other means – nor transmitted or translated into a machine language without written permission from the publishers. Registered names, trademarks, etc. used in this book, even when not specifically marked as such, are not to be considered unprotected by law.

Print ISBN: 978-3-527-41339-3
ePDF ISBN: 978-3-527-41343-0
ePub ISBN: 978-3-527-41341-6
Mobi ISBN: 978-3-527-41342-3
oBook ISBN: 978-3-527-41340-9

Cover Design Formgeber, Mannheim
Typesetting SPi Global, Chennai, India
Printing and Binding betz-druck GmbH, Deutschland

Printed on acid-free paper

Contents

Preface Second Edition *xxiii*
Preface First Edition *xxv*
List of Contributors *xxvii*

1   **Processing of Information in the Human Visual System** *1*
Frank Schaeffel
1.1   Preface *1*
1.2   Design and Structure of the Eye *1*
1.3   Optical Aberrations and Consequences for Visual Performance *3*
1.4   Chromatic Aberration *10*
1.5   Neural Adaptation to Monochromatic Aberrations *11*
1.6   Optimizing Retinal Processing with Limited Cell Numbers, Space, and Energy *11*
1.7   Adaptation to Different Light Levels *12*
1.8   Rod and Cone Responses *14*
1.9   Spiking and Coding *16*
1.10   Temporal and Spatial Performance *17*
1.11   ON/OFF Structure, Division of the Whole Illuminance Amplitude *18*
1.12   Consequences of the Rod and Cone Diversity on Retinal Wiring *18*
1.13   Motion Sensitivity in the Retina *19*
1.14   Visual Information Processing in Higher Centers *20*
1.14.1   Morphology *21*
1.14.2   Functional Aspects – Receptive Field Structures and Cortical Modules *22*
1.15   Effects of Attention *23*
1.16   Color Vision, Color Constancy, and Color Contrast *23*
1.17   Depth Perception *25*
1.18   Adaptation in the Visual System to Color, Spatial, and Temporal Contrast *26*
1.19   Conclusions *26*
       Acknowledgements *28*
       References *28*

2		**Introduction to Building a Machine Vision Inspection** *31*
		Axel Telljohann
2.1		Preface *31*
2.2		Specifying a Machine Vision System *32*
2.2.1		Task and Benefit *32*
2.2.2		Parts *33*
2.2.2.1		Different Part Types *33*
2.2.3		Part Presentation *33*
2.2.4		Performance Requirements *34*
2.2.4.1		Accuracy *34*
2.2.4.2		Time Performance *34*
2.2.5		Information Interfaces *34*
2.2.6		Installation Space *35*
2.2.7		Environment *35*
2.2.8		Checklist *35*
2.3		Designing a Machine Vision System *36*
2.3.1		Camera Type *36*
2.3.2		Field of View *37*
2.3.3		Resolution *38*
2.3.3.1		Camera Sensor Resolution *38*
2.3.3.2		Spatial Resolution *38*
2.3.3.3		Measurement Accuracy *38*
2.3.3.4		Calculation of Resolution *39*
2.3.3.5		Resolution for a Line Scan Camera *39*
2.3.4		Choice of Camera, Frame Grabber, and Hardware Platform *40*
2.3.4.1		Camera Model *40*
2.3.4.2		Frame Grabber *40*
2.3.4.3		Pixel Rate *40*
2.3.4.4		Hardware Platform *41*
2.3.5		Lens Design *41*
2.3.5.1		Focal Length *42*
2.3.5.2		Lens Flange Focal Distance *43*
2.3.5.3		Extension Tubes *43*
2.3.5.4		Lens Diameter and Sensor Size *43*
2.3.5.5		Sensor Resolution and Lens Quality *43*
2.3.6		Choice of Illumination *44*
2.3.6.1		Concept: Maximize Contrast *44*
2.3.6.2		Illumination Setups *44*
2.3.6.3		Light Sources *45*
2.3.6.4		Approach to the Optimum Setup *45*
2.3.6.5		Interfering Lighting *46*
2.3.7		Mechanical Design *46*
2.3.8		Electrical Design *46*
2.3.9		Software *46*
2.3.9.1		Software Library *47*
2.3.9.2		Software Structure *47*
2.3.9.3		General Topics *48*
2.4		Costs *48*

2.5	Words on Project Realization	49
2.5.1	Development and Installation	49
2.5.2	Test Run and Acceptance Test	49
2.5.3	Training and Documentation	50
2.6	Examples	50
2.6.1	Diameter Inspection of Rivets	50
2.6.1.1	Task	50
2.6.1.2	Specification	51
2.6.1.3	Design	51
2.6.2	Tubing Inspection	55
2.6.2.1	Task	55
2.6.2.2	Specification	55
2.6.2.3	Design	56

3	**Lighting in Machine Vision**	**63**
	Irmgard Jahr	
3.1	Introduction	63
3.1.1	Prologue	63
3.1.2	The Involvement of Lighting in the Complex Machine Vision Solution	63
3.2	Demands on Machine Vision lighting	67
3.3	Light used in Machine Vision	70
3.3.1	What is Light? Axioms of Light	70
3.3.2	Light and Light Perception	73
3.3.3	Light Sources for Machine Vision	76
3.3.3.1	Incandescent Lamps/Halogen Lamps	77
3.3.3.2	Metal Vapor Lamps	78
3.3.3.3	Xenon Lamps	79
3.3.3.4	Fluorescent Lamps	81
3.3.3.5	LEDs (Light Emitting Diodes)	82
3.3.3.6	Lasers	85
3.3.4	The Light Sources in Comparison	86
3.3.5	Considerations for Light Sources: Lifetime, Aging, Drift	86
3.3.5.1	Lifetime	86
3.3.5.2	Aging and Drift	88
3.4	Interaction of Test Object and Light	91
3.4.1	Risk Factor Test Object	91
3.4.1.1	What Does the Test Object do With the Incoming Light?	92
3.4.1.2	Reflection/Reflectance/Scattering	92
3.4.1.3	Total Reflection	95
3.4.1.4	Transmission/Transmittance	96
3.4.1.5	Absorption/Absorbance	97
3.4.1.6	Diffraction	99
3.4.1.7	Refraction	100
3.4.2	Light Color and Part Color	101
3.4.2.1	Visible Light (VIS) – Monochromatic Light	101
3.4.2.2	Visible Light (VIS) – White Light	103
3.4.2.3	Infrared Light (IR)	104
3.4.2.4	Ultraviolet (UV) Light	106

3.4.2.5	Polarized Light *107*	
3.5	Basic Rules and Laws of Light Distribution *109*	
3.5.1	Basic Physical Quantities of Light *110*	
3.5.2	The Photometric Inverse Square Law *111*	
3.5.3	The Constancy of Luminance *113*	
3.5.4	What Light Arrives at the Sensor – Light Transmission Through the Lens *114*	
3.5.5	Light Distribution of Lighting Components *115*	
3.5.6	Contrast *118*	
3.5.7	Exposure *120*	
3.6	Light Filters *121*	
3.6.1	Characteristic Values of Light Filters *121*	
3.6.2	Influences of Light Filters on the Optical Path *123*	
3.6.3	Types of Light Filters *124*	
3.6.4	Anti-Reflective Coatings (AR) *126*	
3.6.5	Light Filters for Machine Vision *127*	
3.6.5.1	UV Blocking Filter *127*	
3.6.5.2	Daylight Suppression Filter *128*	
3.6.5.3	IR Suppression Filter *128*	
3.6.5.4	Neutral Filter/Neutral Density Filter/Gray Filter *129*	
3.6.5.5	Polarization Filter *130*	
3.6.5.6	Color Filters *130*	
3.6.5.7	Filter Combinations *131*	
3.7	Lighting Techniques and Their Use *131*	
3.7.1	How to Find a Suitable Lighting? *131*	
3.7.2	Planning the Lighting Solution – Influence Factors *133*	
3.7.3	Lighting Systematics *135*	
3.7.3.1	Directional Properties of the Light *135*	
3.7.3.2	Arrangement of the Lighting *138*	
3.7.3.3	Properties of the Illuminated Field *138*	
3.7.4	The Lighting Techniques in Detail *140*	
3.7.4.1	Diffuse Bright Field Incident Light (No. 1, Table 3.14) *140*	
3.7.4.2	Directed Bright Field Incident Light (No. 2, Table 3.14) *142*	
3.7.4.3	Telecentric Bright Field Incident Light (No. 3, Table 3.14) *143*	
3.7.4.4	Structured Bright Field Incident Light (No. 4, Table 3.14) *145*	
3.7.4.5	Diffuse Directed Partial Bright Field Incident Light (Nos. 1 and 2, Table 3.14) *148*	
3.7.4.6	Diffuse/Directed Dark Field Incident Light (Nos. 5 and 6, Table 3.14) *152*	
3.7.4.7	The Limits of the Incident Lighting *154*	
3.7.4.8	Diffuse Bright Field Transmitted Lighting (No. 7, Table 3.14) *155*	
3.7.4.9	Directed Bright Field Transmitted Lighting (No. 8, Table 3.14) *157*	
3.7.4.10	Telecentric Bright Field Transmitted Lighting (No. 9, Table 3.14) *158*	
3.7.4.11	Diffuse/Directed Transmitted Dark Field Lighting (Nos. 10 and 11, Table 3.14) *161*	
3.7.5	Combined Lighting Techniques *162*	
3.8	Lighting Control *163*	

3.8.1	Reasons for Light Control – The Environmental Industrial Conditions *164*	
3.8.2	Electrical Control *164*	
3.8.2.1	Stable Operation *164*	
3.8.2.2	Brightness Control *166*	
3.8.2.3	Temporal Control: Static-Pulse-Flash *167*	
3.8.2.4	Some Considerations for the Use of Flash Light *168*	
3.8.2.5	Temporal and Local Control: Adaptive Lighting *171*	
3.8.3	Geometrical Control *173*	
3.8.3.1	Lighting from Large Distances *173*	
3.8.3.2	Light Deflection *175*	
3.8.4	Suppression of Ambient and Extraneous Light – Measures for a Stable Lighting *175*	
3.9	Lighting Perspectives for the Future *176*	
	References *177*	
4	**Optical Systems in Machine Vision** *179*	
	Karl Lenhardt	
4.1	A Look at the Foundations of Geometrical Optics *179*	
4.1.1	From Electrodynamics to Light Rays *179*	
4.1.2	Basic Laws of Geometrical Optics *181*	
4.2	Gaussian Optics *183*	
4.2.1	Reflection and Refraction at the Boundary between two Media *183*	
4.2.2	Linearizing the Law of Refraction – The Paraxial Approximation *185*	
4.2.3	Basic Optical Conventions *186*	
4.2.3.1	Definitions for Image Orientations *186*	
4.2.3.2	Definition of the Magnification Ratio β *186*	
4.2.3.3	Real and Virtual Objects and Images *187*	
4.2.3.4	*Tilt Rule* for the Evaluation of Image Orientations by Reflection *188*	
4.2.4	Cardinal Elements of a Lens in Gaussian Optics *189*	
4.2.4.1	Focal Lengths f and f' *192*	
4.2.4.2	Convention *192*	
4.2.5	Thin Lens Approximation *193*	
4.2.6	Beam-Converging and Beam-Diverging Lenses *193*	
4.2.7	Graphical Image Constructions *195*	
4.2.7.1	Beam-Converging Lenses *195*	
4.2.7.2	Beam-Diverging Lenses *195*	
4.2.8	Imaging Equations and Their Related Coordinate Systems *195*	
4.2.8.1	Reciprocity Equation *196*	
4.2.8.2	Newton's Equations *197*	
4.2.8.3	General Imaging Equation *198*	
4.2.8.4	Axial Magnification Ratio *200*	
4.2.9	Overlapping of Object and Image Space *200*	
4.2.10	Focal Length, Lateral Magnification, and the Field of View *200*	
4.2.11	Systems of Lenses *202*	
4.2.12	Consequences of the Finite Extension of Ray Pencils *205*	

4.2.12.1	Effects of Limitations of the Ray Pencils 205
4.2.12.2	Several Limiting Openings 207
4.2.12.3	Characterizing the Limits of Ray Pencils 210
4.2.12.4	Relation to the Linear Camera Model 212
4.2.13	Geometrical Depth of Field and Depth of Focus 214
4.2.13.1	Depth of Field as a Function of the Object Distance p 215
4.2.13.2	Depth of Field as a Function of β 216
4.2.13.3	Hyperfocal Distance 217
4.2.13.4	Permissible Size for the Circle of Confusion d' 218
4.2.14	Laws of Central Projection–Telecentric System 219
4.2.14.1	Introduction to the Laws of Perspective 219
4.2.14.2	Central Projection from Infinity – Telecentric Perspective 228
4.3	Wave Nature of Light 235
4.3.1	Introduction 235
4.3.2	Rayleigh–Sommerfeld Diffraction Integral 236
4.3.3	Further Approximations to the Huygens–Fresnel Principle 238
4.3.3.1	Fresnel's Approximation 239
4.3.4	Impulse Response of an Aberration-Free Optical System 241
4.3.4.1	Case of Circular Aperture, Object Point on the Optical Axis 243
4.3.5	Intensity Distribution in the Neighborhood of the Geometrical Focus 244
4.3.5.1	Special Cases 246
4.3.6	Extension of the Point Spread Function in a Defocused Image Plane 248
4.3.7	Consequences for the Depth of Field Considerations 249
4.3.7.1	Diffraction and Permissible Circle of Confusion 249
4.3.7.2	Extension of the Point Spread Function at the Limits of the Depth of Focus 250
4.3.7.3	Useful Effective f-Number 251
4.4	Information Theoretical Treatment of Image Transfer and Storage 252
4.4.1	Physical Systems as Linear Invariant Filters 252
4.4.1.1	Invariant Linear Systems 255
4.4.1.2	Note to the Representation of Harmonic Waves 259
4.4.2	Optical Transfer Function (OTF) and the Meaning of Spatial Frequency 260
4.4.2.1	Note on the Relation Between the Elementary Functions in the Two Representation Domains 261
4.4.3	Extension to the Two-Dimensional Case 261
4.4.3.1	Interpretation of Spatial Frequency Components (r, s) 261
4.4.3.2	Reduction to One-Dimensional Representations 262
4.4.4	Impulse Response and MTF for Semiconductor Imaging Devices 265
4.4.5	Transmission Chain 267
4.4.6	Aliasing Effect and the Space-Variant Nature of Aliasing 267
4.4.6.1	Space-Variant Nature of Aliasing 274
4.5	Criteria for Image Quality 277

4.5.1	Gaussian Data *277*	
4.5.2	Overview on Aberrations of the Third Order *277*	
4.5.2.1	Monochromatic Aberrations of the Third Order (Seidel Aberrations) *278*	
4.5.2.2	Chromatic Aberrations *278*	
4.5.3	Image Quality in the Space Domain: PSF, LSF, ESF, and Distortion *278*	
4.5.3.1	Distortion *280*	
4.5.4	Image Quality in the Spatial Frequency Domain: MTF *281*	
4.5.4.1	Parameters that Influence the Modulation Transfer Function *282*	
4.5.5	Other Image Quality Parameters *283*	
4.5.5.1	Relative Illumination (Relative Irradiance) *283*	
4.5.5.2	Deviation from Telecentricity (for Telecentric Lenses only) *284*	
4.5.6	Manufacturing Tolerances and Image Quality *284*	
4.5.6.1	Measurement Errors due to Mechanical Inaccuracies of the Camera System *285*	
4.6	Practical Aspects: How to Specify Optics According to the Application Requirements? *285*	
4.6.1	Example for the Calculation of an Imaging Constellation *287*	
	References *289*	
5	**Camera Calibration** *291*	
	Robert Godding	
5.1	Introduction *291*	
5.2	Terminology *292*	
5.2.1	Camera, Camera System *292*	
5.2.2	Coordinate Systems *292*	
5.2.3	Interior Orientation and Calibration *293*	
5.2.4	Exterior and Relative Orientation *293*	
5.2.5	System Calibration *293*	
5.3	Physical Effects *293*	
5.3.1	Optical System *293*	
5.3.2	Camera and Sensor Stability *294*	
5.3.3	Signal Processing and Transfer *294*	
5.4	Mathematical Calibration Model *295*	
5.4.1	Central Projection *295*	
5.4.2	Camera Model *295*	
5.4.3	Focal Length and Principal Point *297*	
5.4.4	Distortion and Affinity *297*	
5.4.5	Radial Symmetrical Distortion *297*	
5.4.6	Radial Asymmetrical and Tangential Distortion *299*	
5.4.7	Affinity and Nonorthogonality *299*	
5.4.8	Variant Camera Parameters *299*	
5.4.9	Sensor Flatness *301*	
5.4.10	Other Parameters *301*	
5.5	Calibration and Orientation Techniques *302*	
5.5.1	In the Laboratory *302*	

5.5.2	Using Bundle Adjustment to Determine Camera Parameters	302
5.5.2.1	Calibration Based Exclusively on Image Information	302
5.5.2.2	Calibration and Orientation with Additional Object Information	304
5.5.2.3	Extended System Calibration	307
5.5.3	Other Techniques	307
5.6	Verification of Calibration Results	308
5.7	Applications	309
5.7.1	Applications with Simultaneous Calibration	309
5.7.2	Applications with Precalibrated Cameras	311
5.7.2.1	Tube Measurement within a Measurement Cell	311
5.7.2.2	Online Measurements in the Field of Car Safety	312
5.7.2.3	High Resolution 3D Scanning with White Light Scanners	312
5.7.2.4	Other Applications	313
	References	314
6	**Camera Systems in Machine Vision**	**317**
	Horst Mattfeldt	
6.1	Camera Technology	317
6.1.1	History in Brief	317
6.1.2	Machine Vision versus Closed Circuit TeleVision (CCTV)	317
6.2	Sensor Technologies	319
6.2.1	Spatial Differentiation: 1D and 2D	319
6.2.2	CCD Technology	320
6.2.2.1	Interline Transfer	321
6.2.2.2	Progressive Scan Interline Transfer	321
6.2.2.3	Interlaced Scan Readout	322
6.2.2.4	Enhancing Frame Rate by Multitap Sensors	324
6.2.2.5	SONY HAD Technology	325
6.2.2.6	SONY SuperHAD (II) and ExViewHAD (II) Technology	325
6.2.2.7	CCD Image Artifacts	326
6.2.2.8	Blooming	326
6.2.2.9	Smear	326
6.2.3	CMOS Image Sensor	328
6.2.3.1	Advantages of CMOS Sensor	328
6.2.3.2	CMOS Sensor Shutter Concepts	331
6.2.3.3	Performance Comparison of CMOS versus CCD	336
6.2.3.4	Integration Complexity of CCD versus CMOS Camera Technology	336
6.2.3.5	CMOS Sensor Sensitivity Enhancements	337
6.2.4	MATRIX VISION Available Cameras	338
6.2.4.1	Why So Many Different Models? How to Choose Among These?	338
6.2.4.2	Resolution and Video Standards	338
6.2.4.3	Sensor Sizes and Dimensions	344
6.3	Block Diagrams and Their Description	344
6.3.1	Block Diagram of SONY Progressive Scan Analog Camera	345

6.3.1.1	CCD Read Out Clocks	345
6.3.1.2	CCD Binning Mode	345
6.3.1.3	Spectral Sensitivity	348
6.3.1.4	Analog Signal Processing	348
6.3.1.5	Camera and Frame Grabber	350
6.3.2	Block Diagram of Color Camera with Digital Image Processing	350
6.3.2.1	Bayer™ Complementary Color Filter Array	351
6.3.2.2	Complementary Color Filters Spectral Sensitivity	351
6.3.2.3	Generation of Color Signals	351
6.4	mvBlueCOUGAR-X Line of Cameras	354
6.4.1	Black and White Digital Camera mvBlueCOUGAR-X Camera Series	355
6.4.1.1	Gray Level Sensor and Processing	355
6.4.2	Color Camera mvBlueCOUGAR-X Family	356
6.4.2.1	Analog Processing	356
6.4.2.2	Analog Front End (AFE)	357
6.4.2.3	A/D Conversion	357
6.4.2.4	One-Chip Color Processing	359
6.4.2.5	Inputting Time Stamp Data into Data Stream	361
6.4.2.6	Statistics Engine for White Balance and Auto Features	361
6.4.2.7	Image Memory	361
6.4.2.8	Lookup Table (LUT) and Gamma Function	362
6.4.2.9	Shading Correction	365
6.4.2.10	Reducing Noise by Adaptive Recursive Frame Averaging	366
6.4.2.11	Color Interpolation	367
6.4.2.12	Color Correction	368
6.4.2.13	RGB → YUV Conversion	370
6.4.3	Controlling Image Capture	371
6.4.4	Acquisition and Trigger Modes	371
6.4.4.1	Sequencer	374
6.4.4.2	Latency and Jitter Aspects	375
6.4.4.3	Action Commands	375
6.4.4.4	Scheduled Action Command	377
6.4.5	Data Transmission	377
6.4.5.1	GigE Vision and GVSP	378
6.4.5.2	USB3 Vision	380
6.4.6	Pixel Data	380
6.4.7	Camera Connection	381
6.4.8	Operating the Camera	381
6.4.9	HiRose Jack Pin Assignment	382
6.4.10	Sensor Frame Rates and Bandwidth	382
6.5	Configuration of a GigE Vision Camera	384
6.6	Qualifying Cameras and Noise Measurement (Dr. Gert Ferrano MV)	386
6.6.1	Explanation of the Most Important Measurements	388
6.6.1.1	Linearity Curve	388
6.6.1.2	Photon Transfer Curve	388

6.7	Camera Noise (by Henning Haider AVT, Updated by Author) *391*	
6.7.1	Photon Noise *391*	
6.7.2	Dark Current Noise *391*	
6.7.3	Fixed Pattern Noise (FPN) *392*	
6.7.4	Photo Response Non Uniformity (PRNU) *392*	
6.7.5	Reset Noise *392*	
6.7.6	1/f Noise (Amplifier Noise) *392*	
6.7.7	Quantization Noise *392*	
6.7.8	Noise Floor *393*	
6.7.9	Dynamic Range *393*	
6.7.10	Signal to Noise Ratio *393*	
6.7.11	Example 1: SONY IMX-174 Sensor (mvBlueFOX3-2024) *394*	
6.7.12	Example 2: CMOSIS CMV2000 (mvBlueCOUGAR-X104) *394*	
6.8	Useful Links and Literature *394*	
6.9	Digital Interfaces *395*	

7 Smart Camera and Vision Systems Design *399*
Howard D. Gray and Nate Holmes

7.1	Introduction to Vision System Design *399*	
7.2	Definitions *400*	
7.3	Smart Cameras *403*	
7.3.1	Applications *403*	
7.3.2	Component Parts *404*	
7.3.2.1	Processors *404*	
7.3.2.2	FPGA Processing *406*	
7.3.2.3	Memory and Storage *407*	
7.3.2.4	Operating Systems *408*	
7.3.2.5	Image Sensors *409*	
7.3.2.6	Inputs and Outputs *410*	
7.3.2.7	Other Interfaces *412*	
7.3.2.8	Timers and Counters *413*	
7.3.3	Programming and Configuring *413*	
7.3.3.1	Scripting *413*	
7.3.3.2	High-Level Languages *414*	
7.3.3.3	Third-Party Tools *416*	
7.3.4	Environment *416*	
7.3.4.1	Power Dissipation *416*	
7.3.4.2	Ingress Protection *417*	
7.4	Vision Sensors *418*	
7.4.1	Applications *419*	
7.4.2	Component Parts *420*	
7.4.3	Programming and Configuring *420*	
7.4.4	Environment *421*	
7.5	Embedded Vision Systems *421*	
7.5.1	Applications *424*	
7.5.1.1	Multi-Camera Applications *424*	

7.5.1.2	Closed Loop Control Applications 424
7.5.2	Component Parts 425
7.5.3	Programming and Configuring 425
7.5.4	Environment 425
7.6	Conclusion 425
	References 426
	Further Reading 429

8	**Camera Computer Interfaces** 431
	Nate Holmes
8.1	Overview 431
8.2	Camera Buses 432
8.2.1	Software Standards 433
8.2.1.1	GenICam 433
8.2.1.2	IIDC2 434
8.2.2	Analog Camera Buses (Legacy) 435
8.2.2.1	Analog Video Signal 436
8.2.2.2	Interlaced Video 436
8.2.2.3	Progressive Scan Video 436
8.2.2.4	Timing Signals 437
8.2.2.5	Analog Image Acquisition 437
8.2.2.6	S-Video 438
8.2.2.7	RGB 438
8.2.2.8	Analog Connectors 439
8.2.3	Parallel Digital Camera Buses (Legacy) 439
8.2.3.1	Digital Video Transmission 439
8.2.3.2	Taps 440
8.2.3.3	Differential Signaling 441
8.2.3.4	Line Scan 441
8.2.3.5	Parallel Digital Connectors 441
8.2.4	IEEE 1394 (FireWire) (Legacy) 442
8.2.4.1	IEEE 1394 for Machine Vision 445
8.2.5	Camera Link 449
8.2.5.1	Camera Link Signals 450
8.2.5.2	Camera Link Connectors 451
8.2.6	Camera Link HS 451
8.2.7	CoaXPress 452
8.2.8	USB (USB3 Vision) 452
8.2.8.1	USB for Machine Vision 454
8.2.9	Gigabit Ethernet (GigE Vision) 455
8.2.9.1	Gigabit Ethernet for Machine Vision 456
8.2.9.2	GigE Vision Device Discovery 456
8.2.9.3	GigE Vision Control Protocol (GVCP) 456
8.2.9.4	GenICam 457
8.2.9.5	GigE Vision Stream Protocol (GVSP) 457
8.2.9.6	Packet Loss and Resends 457
8.2.10	Future Standards Development 458

8.3	Choosing a Camera Bus	459
8.3.1	Bandwidth	459
8.3.2	Resolution	459
8.3.3	Frame Rate	460
8.3.4	Cables	460
8.3.5	Line Scan	460
8.3.6	Reliability	460
8.3.7	Summary of Camera Bus Specifications	461
8.3.8	Sample Use Cases	461
8.3.8.1	Manufacturing Inspection	461
8.3.8.2	LCD Inspection	462
8.3.8.3	Security	463
8.4	Computer Buses	463
8.4.1	ISA/EISA	463
8.4.2	PCI/CompactPCI/PXI	464
8.4.3	PCI-X	466
8.4.4	PCI Express/CompactPCI Express/PXI Express	467
8.4.5	Throughput	469
8.4.6	Prevalence and Lifetime	471
8.4.6.1	Cost	471
8.5	Choosing a Computer Bus	471
8.5.1	Determine Throughput Requirements	471
8.5.2	Applying the Throughput Requirements	473
8.6	Driver Software	473
8.6.1	Application Programming Interface	475
8.6.2	Supported Platforms	477
8.6.3	Performance	477
8.6.4	Utility Functions	478
8.6.5	Acquisition Mode	479
8.6.5.1	Snap	479
8.6.5.2	Grab	479
8.6.5.3	Sequence	480
8.6.5.4	Ring	481
8.6.6	Image Representation	482
8.6.6.1	Image Representation in Memory	482
8.6.7	Bayer Color Encoding	485
8.6.7.1	Image Representation on Disk	487
8.6.8	Image Display	487
8.6.8.1	Understanding Display Modes	488
8.6.8.2	Palettes	489
8.6.8.3	Nondestructive Overlays	490
8.7	Features of a Machine Vision System	491
8.7.1	Image Reconstruction	491
8.7.2	Timing and Triggering	492
8.7.3	Memory Handling	494
8.7.4	Additional Features	496
8.7.4.1	Look-Up Tables	497

8.7.4.2	Region of Interest	499
8.7.4.3	Color Space Conversion	499
8.7.4.4	Shading Correction	501
8.8	Summary	501
	References	502

9 Machine Vision Algorithms 505
Carsten Steger

9.1	Fundamental Data Structures	505
9.1.1	Images	505
9.1.2	Regions	506
9.1.3	Subpixel-Precise Contours	508
9.2	Image Enhancement	509
9.2.1	Gray Value Transformations	509
9.2.2	Radiometric Calibration	512
9.2.3	Image Smoothing	517
9.2.4	Fourier Transform	528
9.3	Geometric Transformations	532
9.3.1	Affine Transformations	532
9.3.2	Projective Transformations	533
9.3.3	Image Transformations	534
9.3.4	Polar Transformations	538
9.4	Image Segmentation	540
9.4.1	Thresholding	540
9.4.2	Extraction of Connected Components	548
9.4.3	Subpixel-Precise Thresholding	550
9.5	Feature Extraction	552
9.5.1	Region Features	552
9.5.2	Gray Value Features	556
9.5.3	Contour Features	559
9.6	Morphology	560
9.6.1	Region Morphology	561
9.6.2	Gray Value Morphology	575
9.7	Edge Extraction	579
9.7.1	Definition of Edges in One and Two Dimensions	579
9.7.2	1D Edge Extraction	583
9.7.3	2D Edge Extraction	589
9.7.4	Accuracy of Edges	596
9.8	Segmentation and Fitting of Geometric Primitives	602
9.8.1	Fitting Lines	603
9.8.2	Fitting Circles	607
9.8.3	Fitting Ellipses	608
9.8.4	Segmentation of Contours into Lines, Circles, and Ellipses	609
9.9	Camera Calibration	613
9.9.1	Camera Models for Area Scan Cameras	614
9.9.2	Camera Model for Line Scan Cameras	618
9.9.3	Calibration Process	622

9.9.4	World Coordinates from Single Images	626
9.9.5	Accuracy of the Camera Parameters	629
9.10	Stereo Reconstruction	631
9.10.1	Stereo Geometry	632
9.10.2	Stereo Matching	639
9.11	Template Matching	643
9.11.1	Gray-Value-Based Template Matching	644
9.11.2	Matching Using Image Pyramids	649
9.11.3	Subpixel-Accurate Gray-Value-Based Matching	652
9.11.4	Template Matching with Rotations and Scalings	653
9.11.5	Robust Template Matching	654
9.12	Optical Character Recognition	672
9.12.1	Character Segmentation	672
9.12.2	Feature Extraction	674
9.12.3	Classification	676
	References	690

10 Machine Vision in Manufacturing 699
Peter Waszkewitz

10.1	Introduction	699
10.1.1	The Machine Vision Market	699
10.2	Application Categories	701
10.2.1	Types of Tasks	701
10.2.2	Types of Production	703
10.2.2.1	Discrete Unit Production Versus Continuous Flow	703
10.2.2.2	Job-Shop Production Versus Mass Production	704
10.2.3	Types of Evaluations	704
10.2.4	Value-Adding Machine Vision	705
10.3	System Categories	706
10.3.1	Common Types of Systems	707
10.3.2	Sensors	707
10.3.3	Vision Sensors	708
10.3.4	Compact Systems	709
10.3.5	Vision Controllers	710
10.3.6	PC-Based Systems	710
10.3.6.1	Library-Based Systems	711
10.3.6.2	Application-Package-Based Systems	712
10.3.6.3	Library-Based Application Packages	713
10.3.7	Excursion: Embedded Image Processing	713
10.3.8	Summary	714
10.4	Integration and Interfaces	715
10.4.1	Standardization	715
10.4.2	Interfaces	716
10.5	Mechanical Interfaces	716
10.5.1	Dimensions and Fixation	717
10.5.2	Working Distances	718
10.5.3	Position Tolerances	718

10.5.4	Forced Constraints	*719*
10.5.5	Additional Sensor Requirements	*719*
10.5.6	Additional Motion Requirements	*720*
10.5.7	Environmental Conditions	*721*
10.5.8	Reproducibility	*722*
10.5.9	Gauge Capability	*723*
10.6	Electrical Interfaces	*725*
10.6.1	Wiring and Movement	*726*
10.6.2	Power Supply	*726*
10.6.3	Internal Data Connections	*727*
10.6.4	External Data Connections	*729*
10.7	Information Interfaces	*729*
10.7.1	Interfaces and Standardization	*730*
10.7.2	Traceability	*730*
10.7.3	Types of Data and Data Transport	*731*
10.7.4	Control Signals	*731*
10.7.5	Result and Parameter Data	*732*
10.7.6	Mass Data	*733*
10.7.7	Digital I/O	*733*
10.7.8	Field Bus	*733*
10.7.9	Serial Interfaces	*734*
10.7.10	Network	*734*
10.7.10.1	Standard Ethernet–TCP/IP	*734*
10.7.10.2	OPC UA and Industry 4.0	*735*
10.7.10.3	Ethernet-Based Field Bus/Real-Time Ethernet	*735*
10.7.11	Files	*736*
10.7.12	Time and Integrity Considerations	*736*
10.8	Temporal Interfaces	*738*
10.8.1	Discrete Motion Production	*738*
10.8.2	Continuous Motion Production	*740*
10.8.3	Line-Scan Processing	*743*
10.9	Human–Machine Interfaces	*745*
10.9.1	Interfaces for Engineering Vision Systems	*746*
10.9.2	Runtime Interface	*747*
10.9.2.1	Using the PLC HMI for Machine Vision	*749*
10.9.3	Remote Maintenance	*750*
10.9.3.1	Safety Precaution: No Movements	*751*
10.9.4	Offline Setup	*751*
10.10	3D Systems	*753*
10.10.1	Dimensionality and Representation	*753*
10.10.1.1	Dimensionality	*753*
10.10.1.2	2.5D and 3D	*754*
10.10.1.3	Point Clouds and Registration	*755*
10.10.1.4	Representation	*757*
10.10.2	3D Data Acquisition	*757*
10.10.2.1	Passive Methods	*758*
10.10.2.2	Active Methods	*759*

10.10.3 Applications *764*
10.10.3.1 Identification *765*
10.10.3.2 Completeness Check *765*
10.10.3.3 Object and Pose Recognition *766*
10.10.3.4 Shape and Dimension Applications *767*
10.10.3.5 Surface Inspection *769*
10.10.3.6 Robotics *770*
10.10.4 Conclusion *771*
10.11 Industrial Case Studies *772*
10.11.1 Glue Check Under UV Light *772*
10.11.1.1 Task *772*
10.11.1.2 Solution *773*
10.11.1.3 Equipment *773*
10.11.1.4 Algorithms *774*
10.11.1.5 Key Points *774*
10.11.2 Completeness Check *774*
10.11.2.1 Task *774*
10.11.2.2 Solution *774*
10.11.2.3 Key Point: Mechanical Setup *775*
10.11.2.4 Equipment *775*
10.11.2.5 Algorithms *775*
10.11.3 Multiple Position and Completeness Check *776*
10.11.3.1 Task *776*
10.11.3.2 Solution *776*
10.11.3.3 Key Point: Cycle Time *778*
10.11.3.4 Equipment *778*
10.11.3.5 Algorithms *779*
10.11.4 Pin-Type Verification *779*
10.11.4.1 Task *779*
10.11.4.2 Solution *779*
10.11.4.3 Key Point: Self-Test *781*
10.11.4.4 Equipment *781*
10.11.4.5 Algorithms *781*
10.11.5 Robot Guidance *781*
10.11.5.1 Task *781*
10.11.5.2 Solution *782*
10.11.5.3 Key Point: Calibration *782*
10.11.5.4 Key Point: Communication *783*
10.11.5.5 Equipment *784*
10.11.5.6 Algorithms *784*
10.11.6 Type and Result Data Management *784*
10.11.6.1 Task *784*
10.11.6.2 Solution *785*
10.11.6.3 Key Point: Type Data *785*
10.11.6.4 Key Point: Result Data *785*
10.11.6.5 Equipment *786*
10.11.7 Dimensional Check for Process Control *786*

10.11.7.1 Task *786*
10.11.7.2 Solution *787*
10.11.7.3 Equipment *787*
10.11.7.4 Algorithms *788*
10.11.8 Ceramic Surface Check *788*
10.11.8.1 Task *788*
10.11.8.2 Solution *788*
10.11.8.3 Equipment *789*
10.12 Constraints and Conditions *789*
10.12.1 Inspection Task Requirements *789*
10.12.2 Circumstantial Requirements *790*
10.12.2.1 Cost *791*
10.12.2.2 Automation Environment *791*
10.12.2.3 Organizational Environment *792*
10.12.3 Refinements *793*
10.12.4 Limits and Prospects *794*
References *796*

Appendix *801*

Index *805*

Preface Second Edition

The concept of the first edition (see preface of the first edition) was taken up favorably by the reader, so that in the fundamental structure no change was needed.

Supplements and clarifications were effectively carried out. In the second edition, newer developments in the area of 3D vision and embedded vision systems (embedded camera) were added. These modifications can be found in an additional chapter "Smart Camera and Vision Systems Design" and in the supplements of other chapters.

Finally, my thanks goes to the authors who did really a hard job to realize the second edition and the professionals at Wiley, in particular Nina Stadthaus and Dr. Martin Preuß who were responsible for the second edition.

Plochingen, January 2017   *Alexander Hornberg*

Preface First Edition

Why a Further Book on Machine Vision?

Writing another book about machine vision (or image processing) was initially thought to be unnecessary. The search for a book that describes the whole information processing chain was unsuccessful, because most of the books deal predominantly with the algorithms of image processing, which is an important part of a machine vision application. Those books do not insist that a digital image of the real part of the world has to be acquired which has some important properties:

- High contrast
- High resolution.

The success of developing a machine vision system depends on the understanding of all parts of the imaging chain. The charm and the complexity of machine vision lies in the range of the specialized engineering fields involved in it, namely

- mechanical engineering
- electrical engineering
- optical engineering
- software engineering

each of which struggles for a primary role. The interdisciplinary thought is the base for the successful development of a machine vision application. Today, we have a new term for this field of engineering called *mechatronics*. This situation determines the difficulties and the possibilities of machine vision inspection.

The book is written for users and developers who have little familiarity with machine vision technology and want to gain further insights into how to develop a machine vision inspection system in industrial field.

The goal of the book is to present all elements of the information processing chain (see Chapters 3–8) in a manner such that even a nonspecialist (e.g., a system integrator or a user) can understand the meaning and functions of all these elements.

Chapter 1, "Processing of Information in the Human Visual System," may at first glance seem irrelevant to the subject of the book. Yet, for understanding the problems and methods of machine vision systems, it is useful to know some of the properties of the human eye. There are many similarities between the human eye and a digital camera with its lens. Also the items *color* and *color models* have their roots in the visual optics.

Chapter 2, "Introduction to Building a Machine Vision Inspection," gives a first overview and an introduction of what the user has to do when he/she wants to build a machine vision inspection. The goal is to give an assistance and a guideline for the first few steps. Of course, the individual practice can skip it.

Chapters 3–8 treat different elements of the information processing chain (Figure 1) in detail.

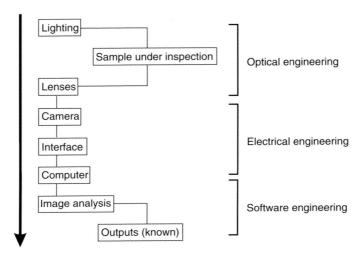

Figure 1 Information processing chain.

- Lighting (Chapter 3)
- Lenses (Chapter 4)
- Camera Calibration (Chapter 5)
- Camera (Chapter 6)
- Camera Computer Interfaces (Chapter 7)
- Algorithms (Chapter 8).

The last chapter, "Machine Vision in Manufacturing," concludes the loop to Chapter 2 and demonstrates the application of machine vision inspection in the industrial sector.

Finally, I would like to express my special thanks to the respected authors and their companies for their great engagement in making this book possible and Wiley-VCH for giving me an opportunity to present my understanding of machine vision to an international audience. In particular, I would like to thank Dr. Thoß and Mrs. Werner for their commitment and patience.

Plochingen, December 2005 *Alexander Hornberg*

List of Contributors

Robert Godding
AICON 3D Systems GmbH
Biberweg 30 C
38122 Braunschweig
Germany

Howard D. Gray
MATRIX Vision GmbH
Talstraße 16
D-71570 Oppenweiler
Germany

Nate Holmes
National Instruments
11500 N. Mopac Expwy.
Austin, TX 78759
USA

Irmgard Jahr
Vision & Control GmbH
Mittelbergstraße 16
D-98527 Suhl
Germany

Karl Lenhardt
Jos. Schneider Optische Werke GmbH
Ringstraße 132
55543 Bad Kreuznach
Germany

Horst Mattfeldt
MATRIX VISION
Talstrasse 16
71570 Oppenweiler
Germany

Frank Schaeffel
Sektion für Neurobiologie des Auges
Forschungsinstitut für
Augenheilkunde
Universitätsklinikum Tübingen
Calwerstrasse 7/1
72076 Tübingen
Germany

Carsten Steger
MVTec Software GmbH
Arnulfstraße 205
80634 München
Germany

Axel Telljohann
Consulting Team Machine Vision
(CTMV)
CTMV GmbH & Co. KG
Schwarzwaldstraße 7a
75173 Pforzheim
Germany

Peter Waszkewitz
Robert Bosch GmbH
Robert-Bosch-Platz 1.
70839 Gerlingen-Schillerhöhe
Germany

1

Processing of Information in the Human Visual System
Frank Schaeffel

Sektion für Neurobiologie des Auges, Forschungsinstitut für Augenheilkunde, Universitätsklinikum Tübingen, Calwerstrasse 7/1, 72076 Tübingen, Germany

1.1 Preface

To gather as much necessary information as possible of the visual world, and neglect as much unnecessary information as possible, the visual system has undergone an impressive optimization in the course of evolution, which is fascinating in each detail that is examined. A few aspects will be described in this chapter. Similar limitations may exist in machine vision, and comparisons to the solutions developed in the visual system in the course of 5 billion years of evolution might provide some insights.

1.2 Design and Structure of the Eye

As in any camera, the *first step in vision* is the projection of the visual scene on an array of photodetectors. In the vertebrate *camera eye*, this is achieved by the cornea and lens in the eye (Figure 1.1) which transmit the light in the visible part of the spectrum, 400–780 nm, by 60–70%. Another 20–30% is lost as a result of scattering in the ocular media. Only about 10% is finally absorbed by the photoreceptor pigment [1]. Because of the content of proteins, both cornea and the lens absorb in the ultraviolet, and because of the water content, the transmission is blocked in the far infrared. The cornea consists of a *thick* central layer – the stroma – which is sandwiched between two semipermeable membranes (total thickness 0.5 mm). It is composed of collagen fibrils, with mucopolysaccharides filling the space between the fibrils. Water content is tightly regulated to 75–80%, and clouding occurs if it changes beyond these limits. The crystalline lens is built up from proteins, called crystallines, which are characterized by their water solubility. The proteins in the periphery have high solubility, but those in the center are largely insoluble. The vertebrate lens is characterized by its continuous growth throughout life, with the older cells residing in the central core, the nucleus. With age, the lens becomes increasingly rigid and immobile and the ability to change its shape and focal length to accommodate for close viewing distances disappears – a disturbing experience for people around 45 who now need reading

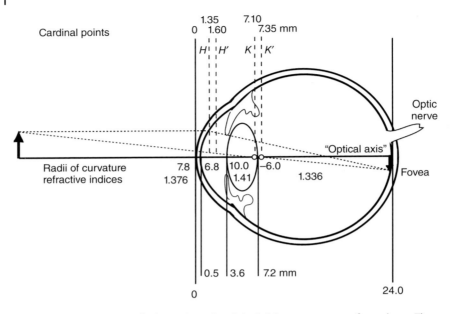

Figure 1.1 Dimensions and schematic optics of the left human eye, seen from above. The anterior corneal surface is traditionally set to coordinate zero. All positions are given in millimeters, relative to the anterior corneal surface (drawing not to scale). The refracting surfaces are approximated by spheres so that their radii of curvatures can be defined. The cardinal points of the optical system, shown on the top, are valid only for rays close to the optical axis (*Gaussian approximation*). The focal length of the eye in the vitreous (the posterior focal length) is 24.0 mm − H = 22.65 mm. The nodal points K and K′ permit us to calculate the retinal image magnification. In the first approximation, the posterior nodal distance (*PND*, which is the distance K to the focal point at the retina) determines the linear distance on the retina for a given visual angle. In the human eye, this distance is about 24.0 mm − 7.3 mm = 16.7 mm. One degree in the visual field maps on the retina to 16.7 tan(1°) = 290 μm. Given that the foveal photoreceptors are 2 μm thick, 140 receptors are sampling 1° in the visual field, which leads to a maximum resolution of 70 cycles per degree. The schematic eye by Gullstrand represents an *average eye*. The variability in natural eyes is so large that it does not make sense to provide average numbers on dimensions with several digits. Refractive indices, however, are surprisingly similar among different eyes. The index of the lens (here homogenous model, $n = 1.41$) is not real but calculated to produce a lens power that makes the eye emmetropic. In a real eye, the lens has a gradient index (see text).

glasses (presbyopia). Accommodation is an active neuromuscular deformation of the crystalline lens that changes focal length from 53 mm to 32 mm in young adults.

Both media have higher refractive index than the water-like solutions in which they are embedded (tear film − on the corneal surface, aqueous − the liquid in the anterior chamber between the cornea and the lens, and vitreous humor − the gel-like material filling the vitreous chamber between the lens and the retina, Figure 1.1). Because of their almost spherical surfaces, the anterior cornea and both surfaces of the lens have positive refractive power with a combined optical focal length of 22.6 mm. This matches almost perfectly (with a tolerance 1/10 of a millimeter) the distance from the first principal plane (Figure 1.1, *H*) to the photoreceptor layer in the retina. Accordingly, the projected image from a distant object is in focus when accommodation is relaxed. This optimal optical condition is called emmetropia but, in 30% of the population in industrialized countries, the eye has grown too long so that the image is in front of the retina even with accommodation completely relaxed (myopia).

The projected image is first analyzed by the retina in the back of the eye. For developmental reasons, the retina in all vertebrate eyes is *inverted*. This means that the photoreceptor cells, located at the backside of the retina, are pointing away from the incoming light. Therefore, the light has to pass through the retina (about a fifth of a millimeter thick) before it can be detected. To reduce scatter, the retina is highly translucent, and the nerve fibers that cross on the vitreal side, from where the light comes in, to the optic nerve head are not surrounded by myelin, a fat-containing sheet that normally insulates spiking axons (see below). Scattering in retinal tissue still seems to be a problem because, in the region of the highest spatial resolution, namely the fovea, the cells are pushed to the side. Accordingly, the fovea in the vertebrate eye can be recognized as a pit. However, many vertebrates do not have a fovea [2]; they have then lower visual acuity but their acuity can remain similar over large regions of the visual field, which is then usually either combined with high motion sensitivity (i.e., rabbit) or high light sensitivity at dusk (crepuscular mammals). It is striking that the retina in all vertebrates has a similar three-layered structure (Figure 1.9), with similar thickness. This makes it likely that the functional constraints were similar. The function of the retina will be described in the following.

The *optical axis* of the eye is not perfectly defined because the cornea and lens are not perfectly rotationally symmetrical and also are not centered on one axis. Nevertheless, even though one could imagine that the image quality is best close to the optical axis, it turns out that the human fovea is not centered in the globe (Figure 1.2). In fact, it is displaced to the temporal retina by an angle κ, ranging in different subjects from 0° to 11° but highly correlated in both eyes. Apparently, a few degrees away from the optical axis, the optical image quality is still good enough not to limit visual acuity in the fovea.

1.3 Optical Aberrations and Consequences for Visual Performance

One would imagine that the optical quality of the cornea and lens must limit the visual acuity since the biological material is mechanically not as stable and the surfaces are much more variable than in technical glass lenses. However, this is not true. In daylight, pupil sizes <2.5 mm constitute the optics of the human eye close to the diffraction limit (further improvement is physically not possible because of the wave properties of light). An eye is said to be diffraction-limited when the ratio of the area under its modulation transfer function (MTF; Figure 1.3) and the area under the diffraction-limited MTF (Strehl *ratio*) is higher than 0.8 (Marcos [3], Rayleigh *criterion*). With a 2 mm pupil, diffraction cuts off all spatial frequencies (SFs) higher than 62 cycles

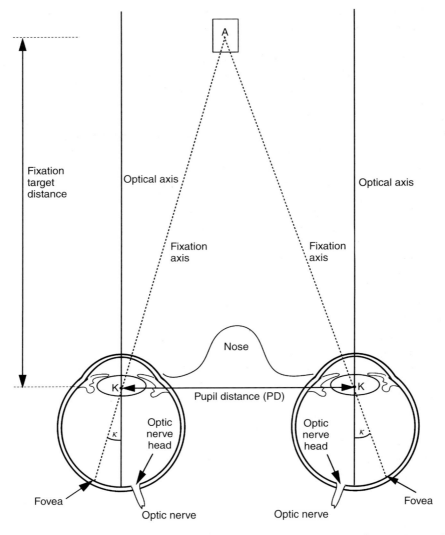

Figure 1.2 Binocular geometry of human eyes, seen from above. Since the fovea is temporally displaced with regard to the optical axis by the angle κ, the optical axes of the eyes do not reflect the direction of fixation. κ is highly variable among eyes, ranging from 0° to 11°, with an average of 3.5°. In the illustrated case, the fixation target is at a distance for which the optical axes happen to be parallel and straight. The distance of the fixation target for which this is true can be easily calculated: for an angle κ of 4°, and a pupil distance of 64 mm, this condition would be met if the fixation target is at 32 mm/tan(4°), or 457.6 mm. The optic nerve head (also called the *optic disk*, or *blind spot*, the position at which the axons of the retinal ganglion cells leave the eye) is nasally displaced relative to the optical axis. The respective angle is in a similar range as κ. Under natural viewing conditions, the fixation angles must be extremely precise since double vision will be experienced if the fixation lines do not exactly cross on the fixation target – the tolerance is only a few minutes of arc).

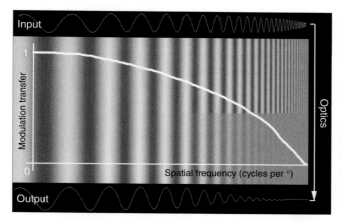

Figure 1.3 Spatial information in an image can be reconstructed as a linear superposition of sine wave components (spatial frequencies) with different amplitudes and phases (Fourier components). Low spatial frequencies (SFs) are generally available with high contrast in the natural visual environment, whereas the contrast declines for higher SFs, generally proportional to 1/SF (input). Because of optical imperfections and diffraction, the image on the retina does not retain the input contrast at high SFs. The decline of *modulation transfer*, the ratio of the output to input contrast, is described by the modulation transfer function (MTF, thick white line). At around 60 cycles per degree, the optical modulation transfer of the human eye reaches zero, with small pupil sizes due to diffraction and with larger pupils due to optical imperfections. These factors limit our contrast sensitivity at high spatial frequencies, even though the retina extracts surprisingly much information from the low-contrast images of high SFs, by building small receptive fields for foveal ganglion cells with antagonistic ON/OFF center/surround organization.

per degree – a limit that is very close to the maximum behavioral resolution achieved by human subjects. By the way, diffraction-limited optics is achieved only in some birds and primates, although it has been recently claimed that also an alert cat has diffraction-limited optics [4]. A number of tricks are used to reduce the aberrations that are inherent in spherical surfaces: the corneal surface is, in fact, clearly aspheric, flattening out to the periphery, and the vertebrate lens is always a *gradient index structure*, with the refractive index continuously increasing from the periphery to the center. Therefore, peripheral rays are bent less than central rays, which compensates for the steeper angles that the rays encounter if they hit a spherical surface in the periphery. The gradient index of the lens reduces its spherical aberration from more than 12 diopters (for an assumed homogenous lens) to less than 1 diopter (for a gradient index lens). Furthermore, the optical aberrations seem to be under tight control (although it remains uncertain whether this control is visual [5]). The remaining aberrations of the cornea and the lens tend to cancel each other, and this is true, at least, for astigmatism, horizontal coma, and spherical aberration [6, 7]. However, aberrations have also advantages: they increase the depth of field by 0.3 D, apparently without reducing visual acuity; there is no strong correlation between the amount of aberrations of subjects and their letter acuity. They also reduce the required precision of accommodation, in particular, during reading [8]. It is questionable whether optical correction of higher order aberrations by refractive surgery or individually designed spectacle lenses would further improve acuity

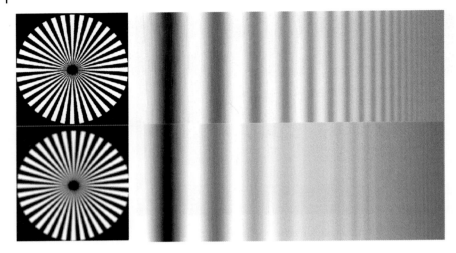

Figure 1.4 Spurious resolution. The modulation transfer function (Figure 1.3) shows oscillations beyond the cutoff spatial frequency, which show up in defocused gratings as contrast reversals. On the left, a circular grating shows the contrast reversals at the higher spatial frequencies in the center (top: in focus, below: defocused). On the right, the grating shown in Figure 1.3 was defocused. Note the lack of contrast at the first transition to zero contrast, and the repeated subsequent contrast reversals. Note also that defocusing has little effect on low spatial frequencies.

for high-contrast letters in young subjects, creating an *eagle's eye*. It is, however, clear that an extended MTF can enhance the contrast sensitivity at high SFs. Correcting aberrations might also be useful in older subjects, since it is known that monochromatic aberrations increase by a factor of 2 with age [9]. Aberrations may also be useful for other reasons; they could provide directionality cues for accommodation [10] and, perhaps, for emmetropization.

In a healthy emmetropic young eye, the optical MTF (Figure 1.3) appears to be adapted to the sampling interval of the photoreceptors.

Contrast modulation reaches zero at SFs of around 60 cycles per degree, and the foveal photoreceptor sampling interval is in the range of 2 µm. Since 1° in the visual field is mapped on a 0.29 mm linear distance on the retina, the highest detectable SF could be about 290/4 µm or about 70 cycles per degree. The MTF shows that the contrast of these high spatial frequencies in the retinal image approaches zero (Figure 1.3). With defocus, the MTF drops rapidly. Interestingly, it does not stop at zero modulation transfer, but rather continues to oscillate (although with low amplitude) around the abscissa. This gives rise to the so-called *spurious resolution*; defocused gratings can still be detected beyond the cutoff SF, although in part with reversed contrast (Figure 1.4).

The sampling interval of the photoreceptors increases rapidly over the first few degrees away from the fovea, and visual acuity declines (Figure 1.5), both because rods are added to the lattice, which increases the distances between individual cones and because their cone diameters increase. In addition, many cones converge on one ganglion cell. Furthermore, only the foveal cones have *private lines* to a single ganglion cell (Figure 1.9).

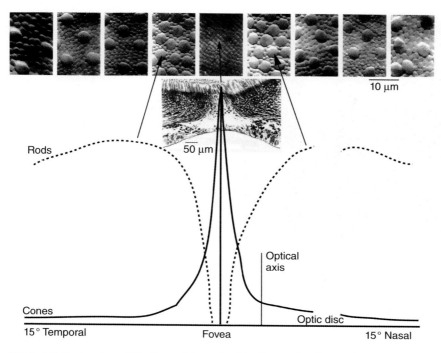

Figure 1.5 Regional specializations of the retina. The fovea is free from rods, and L and M cones are packed as tightly as possible (reaching a density of 200 000 mm^{-2} – histology on top replotted after [11]). In the fovea, the retinal layers are pushed to the side to reduce scattering of light that has reached the photoreceptors – resulting in the foveal pit. Rods reach a peak density of 130 000 mm^{-2} at 3° away from the fovea. Accordingly, a faint star can be seen only if it is not fixated. As a result of the drop in cone densities and due to increasing convergence of cone signals, visual acuity drops even faster: at 10°, visual acuity is only about 20% of the foveal peak. Angular positions relative to the fovea vary between individuals and are therefore approximate. (Adapted from Curcio et al. 1990 [11].)

Because the optical quality does not decline as fast in the periphery as the spatial resolution of the neural network, the retinal image is undersampled. If the receptor mosaic were regular, like in the fovea, stripes that are narrower than the resolution limit would cause spatial illusions (*Moiré* patterns, Figure 1.6). Since the receptor mosaic is not so regular in the peripheral retina, this causes just spatial noise. Moiré patterns are, however, visible in the fovea if a grating is imaged, which is beyond the resolution limit. This can be done by presenting two laser beams in the pupil, which show interference [12].

Moiré patterns are explained from the Shannon's sampling theorem, which states that regularly spaced samples can be resolved only when the sampling rate is equal to or higher than twice the highest spatial frequency; that is, to resolve the samples, between each receptor that is stimulated, there must be one that is not stimulated. The highest SF that can be resolved by the photoreceptor mosaic (*Nyquist limit*) is half the sampling frequency. In the fovea, the highest possible spatial sampling is achieved. Higher photoreceptor densities are not possible for the following reason: Because the inner segments of the photoreceptors have

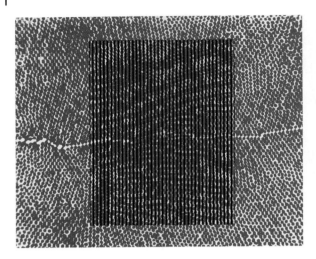

Figure 1.6 Aliasing (undersampling) and Moiré patterns. If a grating is imaged on the photoreceptor array, and the sampling interval of the receptors is larger than half the spatial wavelength of the grating, patterns appear. The photoreceptor lattice (left) is from a histological section of a monkey's retina. If laser interferometry is used to image fine gratings with spatial frequency beyond the resolution limit on the fovea of human subjects, the subjects see Moiré patterns, which are drawn on the right. (Adapted from Williams 1985 [12]. Reproduced with permission of Elsevier.)

higher refractive indices than their surroundings, they act as light guides. But if they become very thin, they show properties of waveguides. When their diameter approaches the wavelength of light, energy starts to *leak out* [13], causing increased optical crosstalk with neighboring photoreceptors. As it is, about 5% of the energy is lost, which seems acceptable. But if the thickness (and the sampling interval) is further reduced to 1 μm, already 50% is lost.

Since the photoreceptor sampling interval cannot be decreased, the only way to increase visual acuity is to enlarge the globe and, accordingly, the PND and the retinal image. This solution was adopted in the eagle's eye, with an axial length of 36 mm, which is the highest spatial acuity in the animal kingdom (grating acuity 135 cycles per degree [14]).

Figure 1.7 Chromatic aberration and some of its effects on vision. Because of the increase in the refractive indices of the ocular media with decreasing wavelength, the eyes become more myopic in the blue. (a) The chromatic aberration function shows that the chromatic defocus between L and M cones is quite small (about a quarter of a diopter) but close to 1 D for the S cone. (b) Because of transverse chromatic aberration, rays of different wavelengths that enter the pupil reach the retina normally not in the same position. If a red line and green line are imaged on the retina through selected parts of the pupil, and the subject can align them via a joystick, the *achromatic axis* can be determined. Light of different wavelengths entering the eye along the achromatic axis is imaged at the same retinal position (although with a wavelength-dependent focus). (c) Because of longitudinal chromatic aberration, light of different wavelengths is focused in different planes. Accordingly, myopic subjects (with too long eyes) see best in the red and hyperopic subjects (with too short eyes) best in the blue.

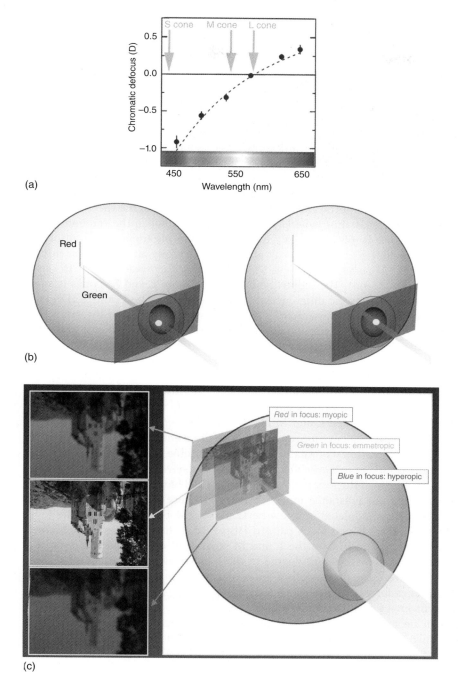

1.4 Chromatic Aberration

In addition to monochromatic aberrations (those aberrations that persist in monochromatic light), there is also chromatic aberration that results from dispersion of the optical media, that is, due to the wavelength-dependent refractive index. In technical optical systems, lenses with different refractive indices are combined in such a way that the focal length does not vary much across the visible spectrum. In natural eyes, no attempt is made to optically balance chromatic aberration. Neural image processing makes it possible for us to be unaware of chromatic image degradation under normal viewing conditions, and, in addition, there are morphological adaptations in the retina. Inspection of the chromatic aberration function in the human eye (Marcos *et al.* [15]; Figure 1.7a) shows that a large dioptric change occurs in the blue end of the spectrum (about 1D from 570 to 450 nm), whereas the change is smaller in the red end (about 0.5 D from 570 to 680 nm). We have three cone photopigments, absorbing at *long* wavelengths (*L cones*, peak absorption typically at 565 nm), at *middle* wavelengths (*M cones*, typically at 535 nm), or at *short* wavelengths (*S cones*, typically at 440 nm). The dioptric difference between L and M cones is small (S0.2D) but the dioptric differences to the S cones are significant (>1D). It is, therefore, impossible to see sharply with all three cone types at the same time (Figure 1.7c). A *white* point of light is, therefore, imaged in the fovea as a circle with a diameter of up to 100 cone diameters, with a 6 mm pupil. Perhaps, as a consequence, the S cone system was removed from the highacuity region of the central 0.5° of the fovea (the foveola); one cannot focus them anyway and they would only occupy space that is better used to pack the M and L cones more densely, to achieve best sampling. High-acuity tasks are then performed only with the combined L and M cones. The *blue information* is continuously *filled in* because small eye movements enable the stimulation of the parafoveal S cones. Therefore, this scotoma is normally not visible, similar to the blind spot, where the optic nerve leaves the eye – surprising, given that the blind spot has 5× the diameter of the fovea. Nevertheless, a small blue spot viewed on a yellow background from a distance appears black, and a blue field of about 440 nm that is sinusoidally modulated at a few hertz makes the blue scotoma in the fovea visible as a star-shaped black pattern [16]. Also in the periphery, the S cones sample more coarsely than the L and M cones and reach a maximum spatial resolution of 5–6 cycles per degree in the parafoveal region at about 2° away from the fovea. The dispersion of the ocular media produces not only different focal planes for each wavelength (*longitudinal chromatic aberration*) but also different image magnifications (*transverse chromatic aberration*). Accordingly, a point on an object's surface is imaged in the different focal planes along a line only in the *achromatic axis* of the eye (which can be psychophysically determined; Figure 1.7b). Even a few degrees away from the achromatic axis, blue light emerging from an object point will be focused closer to achromatic axis than red light. In particular, since the fovea is usually neither in the optical axis nor in the achromatic axis (see above), the images for red and blue are also laterally displaced with respect to each other. With a difference in image magnification of 3%, a κ of 3.5°, and a linear image magnification of 290 μm per degree, the linear displacement would be 3.5 μm × 290 μm × 0.03 μm or 30 μm, which is about the distance from one S cone to the next. Human subjects are not aware of this difference in magnification, and the rescaling of the *blue versus the red image* by neural processing seems to occur without effort.

1.5 Neural Adaptation to Monochromatic Aberrations

The neural image processor in the retina and cortex can relatively easily adapt to the changes of aberrations and field distortions. This can be seen in spectacle wearers. Even though spectacles, in particular progressive addition lenses, cause complex field distortions and additional aberrations, such as astigmatism and coma in the periphery, the wearer is usually not aware of these optical problems, already after a few days. The necessary neural image transformations are impressive. Nevertheless, it is realized that the individual visual system is best trained to the natural aberrations of the eye, even though it can learn to achieve a similar acuity if the same aberrations are experimentally rotated [17]. One of the underlying mechanisms is *contrast adaptation*. If all visible spatial frequencies are imaged on the retina with similar contrast (Figure 1.3), it can be seen that the contrast sensitivity varies with spatial frequency. The highest sensitivity is achieved at 5 cycles per second. However, the contrast sensitivity at each spatial frequency is continuously readjusted according to how much contrast is available at a given spatial frequency. If the contrast is low, the sensitivity increases, and vice versa. This way, the maximum information can be transmitted with a limited total channel capacity. Contrast adaptation also accounts for the striking observation that a defocused image (lacking high contrast at higher spatial frequencies) appears sharper after a while (Webster *et al.* [18]; see Movie, Nature Neuroscience[1]). If myopic subjects take their glasses off, they initially experience very poor visual acuity, but some improvement occurs over the first few minutes without glasses. These changes are not optical but neuronal. Contrast adaptation occurs both in the retina and the cortex [19].

1.6 Optimizing Retinal Processing with Limited Cell Numbers, Space, and Energy

A striking observation is that only the visual system has extensive peripheral neural preprocessing, which starts already at the photoreceptors. Although the retina is a part of the brain, it is not immediately obvious why the nerves from the photoreceptors do not project directly to the central nervous system, as in other sensory organs. The reason is probably that the amount of information provided by the photoreceptors is just too much to be transmitted through the optic nerve (about 1 million fibers) without previous filtering [20].

There are about 125 million photoreceptors, and their information supply converges into 1 million ganglion cells, which send their axons through the optic

---

1 http://www.nature.com/neuro/journal/v5/n9/suppinfo/nn906_S1.html.

nerve to the brain (Figure 1.11). In the optic nerve, the visual information is more compressed than ever before, or after. It follows then why the optic nerve cannot be made any thicker, with more fibers, so that extensive information compression would be unnecessary. The reason appears to be that the visual cortex can process high-spatial-acuity information only from a small part of the visual field. As it is, the foveal region occupies already 50% of the cortical area, and processing the whole visual field of 180° would require a cortex perhaps *as large as a classroom*. On the other hand, confining high acuity to a small part of the visual field requires extensive scanning through eye (or head) movements. A thicker optic nerve would impair such eye movements and it would also increase the size of the blind spot. Eye movements occupy considerable processing capacity in the brain since they are extremely fast and precisely programmed (e.g., the tolerance for errors in the angular position of the eye with binocular foveal fixation is only a few minutes of arc – otherwise, one would see double images). But this seems to require still less capacity than required for extending the foveal area.

1.7 Adaptation to Different Light Levels

The first challenge that the retina has to deal with is the extreme range of ambient illuminances. Between a cloudy night and a sunny day at the beach, illuminance varies by a factor of about 8 log units. Without adaptation, a receptor (and also a charge-coupled device (CCD) photodetector or a film) can respond to 1.5 or 2 log units of brightness differences. This is usually sufficient because natural contrasts in a visual scene are rarely higher. But if the receptors are not able to shift and flatten their response curves during light adaptation (Figure 1.8), they would saturate very soon if the ambient illuminance increases, and the contrast of the image would decline to zero. So, the major role of adaptation is to prevent saturation.

It is clear that light/dark adaptation has to occur either before reception or in the photoreceptors. It is not possible to generate an image with spatial contrast if the photoreceptors are saturated. In the visual system, some adjustment occurs through the size of the pupil, which can vary from 2 to 8 mm in young subjects (a factor of 16, or little more than 1 log unit). It is clear that the remaining 8 log units have to be covered. In vertebrates, this is done by dividing the illuminance range into two parts, the scotopic part, where rod photoreceptors determine our vision, and the photopic part, where the cones take over. There is a range in between where both rods and cones respond, and this is called the mesopic range. Both rods and cones can shift their response curves from higher to lower sensitivity. This is done by changing the gain of the biochemical phototransduction cascade in the photoreceptor cells, which converts the energy of a photon of light that is caught by the photopigment into an electrical signal at the photoreceptor membrane. Adaptation occurs by changes in the intracellular calcium concentration, which, in turn, affects the gain of at least three steps in the cascade (Figure 1.8). Strikingly, photoreceptors hyperpolarize in response to a light excitation and basically show an inverted response, compared to other neurons.

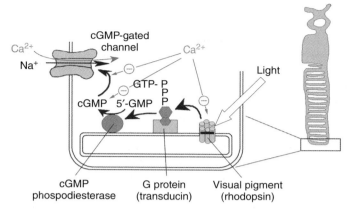

Figure 1.8 Principle of the phototransduction cascade and the role of calcium in light/dark adaptation in a rod photoreceptor. The pigment molecule embedded in the outer segment disk membrane of the photoreceptor, consisting of a protein (opsin) and retinal (an aldehyde), absorbs a photon and converts it into an activated state which can stimulate a G protein (transducin in rods). Transducin, in turn, activates an enzyme, cGMP phosphodiesterase, which catalyzes the breakdown of cGMP to 5′-GMP. cGMP has a key role in phototransduction. To open the *cGMP-gated cation channels*, three cGMP molecules have to bind to the channel protein. Therefore, if cGMP is removed by cGMP phosphodiesterase, the channels cannot be kept open. The Na^+ influx stops (which depolarizes the cell against its normal resting potential), and the membrane potential moves to its resting potential; this means hyperpolarization. When the channels are closed during illumination, the intracellular calcium levels decline. This removes the inhibitory effects of calcium on (i) the cGMP binding on the channel, (ii) the resynthesis pathway of cGMP, and (iii) the resynthesis of rhodopsin. All three steps reduce the gain of the phototransduction cascade (*light adaptation*). It should be noted that complete dark or light adaptation is slow: it takes up to 1 h.

This inverted response is energetically costly, since it means that *dark* represents the adequate stimulus, with a constant high release of the transmitter glutamate from the presynaptic terminals, with a high rate of resynthesis. Glutamate release is controlled by intracellular calcium, with high release at high calcium levels, and vice versa. If the light is switched on, the cation channels in the outer segment cell membrane close, which causes a constant influx of positive ions into the outer segment, and thereby effects its depolarization. Why the photoreceptors respond to light, the adequate stimulus, in an inverted manner, has not been convincingly explained.

The inverted response makes it necessary to reverse the voltage changes at a number of synapses in the retina. Normally, the signal for excitation of a spiking neuron is depolarization, not hyperpolarization. In fact, already at the first synapse in the retina, the photoreceptor terminals, the transmitter glutamate can either induce depolarization of the postsynaptic membrane (OFF bipolar cells) or hyperpolarization (ON bipolar cells), depending on the type of receptors that bind glutamate (OFF: ionotropic AMPA/Kainate receptor; ON: metabotropic mGluR6 receptor).

1.8 Rod and Cone Responses

Rod photoreceptors can reach the maximum possible sensitivity: they show a significant transient hyperpolarization in response to the absorption of a single photon. Photons reach the retina in a star light like rain hits a paved road. Not every rod receives a photon and not every paved stone is hit by a rain drop. Accordingly, the image is *noisy* (Figure 1.9, top).

The probability of catching a certain number of photons during the integration time is described by Poisson statistics, and the standard deviation is the square root of the number of photons caught per unit time. Therefore, the signal-to-noise ratio can be calculated as the square root of the number of photons divided by the number of photons. If 100 photons are absorbed during integration time of the rod (about 200 ms), only changes in contrast that are larger than 10% can be detected. Low-contrast detection requires many photons: to distinguish contrasts of 1%, at least 10 000 photons must be absorbed during the integration time [20].

Another limiting factor is thermal noise. The rhodopsin molecule has an average lifetime of 300 years at 37 °C, but when it decays, rod photoreceptors cannot distinguish between a photon absorption and spontaneous decay. Because of the abundance of rhodopsin in the photoreceptors, 10^6 decays occur spontaneously each second. Thermal noise matches photon noise in a clear star night. If rhodopsin decays only 1 log unit faster, our threshold sensitivity would rise by 3 log units.

With increasing ambient illuminance, rods continue to give binary responses (either hyperpolarization or not) over the first 3 log units [20]. If brightness further increases, in the mesopic range, the degree of hyperpolarization of the rod membrane increases linearly with the number of photons caught during the integration time, up to about 20 photons. At about 100 photons, the rods saturate, although adaptation can reduce their sensitivity so that a graded response is possible up to 1000 photons. Cones take over at 100 photons per integration time (here only a few milliseconds), and only at this number their

Figure 1.9 Photon responses of rods and cones. From complete darkness to a moon-lit night, rods respond to single photons: their signals are binary (either *yes* or *no*). Because not every rod can catch a photon (here illustrated as small white ellipses), and because photons come in randomly as predicted by a Poisson distribution, the image appears noisy and has low spatial resolution and little contrast. Even if it is 1000 times brighter (a bright moon-lit night), rods do not catch several photons during their integration time of 100–200 ms and they cannot summate responses. Until up to 100 photons per integration time, they show linear summation, but their response curve is still corrupted by single photon events. Beyond 100 photons per integration time, rods show light adaptation (see Figure 1.8). At 1000 photons/integration time, they are saturated and silent. Cones take over, and they work best above 1000 photons per integration time. Because cone gather their signal from so many photons, photon noise is not important and their response to brightness changes is smooth and gradual. If the number of photon rises further, the sensitivity of the cone phototransduction cascade is reduced by light adaptation, and their response curve is shifted to higher light levels. Similar to rods, they can respond over a range of about 4 log units of ambient illuminance change.

1.8 Rod and Cone Responses

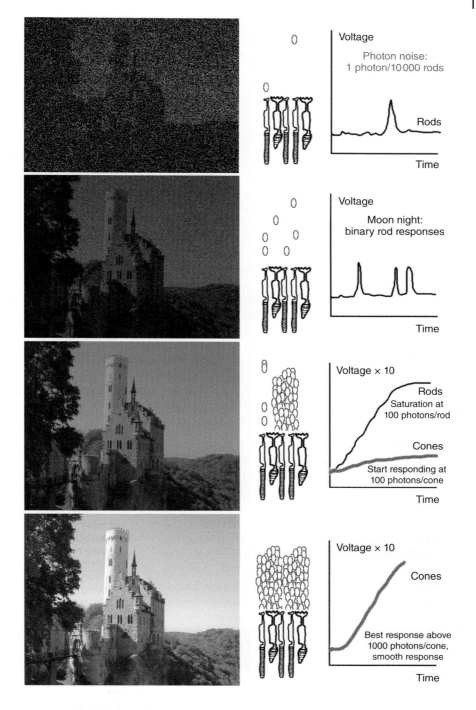

response rises above the dark noise. They work best at 1000 photons or more. In summary, rods' responses are always corrupted by photon noise, whereas cones respond in a smooth, graded manner, and their responses contain more bits (Figure 1.9, bottom). Generally, the response function of sensory organs is logarithmic, which means that for a weak stimulus a small change in stimulus strength is detectable, whereas for a strong stimulus the change must be larger to be detected (Weber's law: detectable stimulus strength difference proportional to stimulus strength).

Since rods are hunting *each photon*, they occupy, in most mammals, as much territory of the retinal area as possible (>95%), whereas cones, which are not limited by photon noise, are densely packed only in the fovea where they permit high spatial sampling. Rods were left out because they would increase the foveal sampling intervals of the M and L cones.

To match the *information channel capacity* of rods and cones to the available information, the rod axons are thin and the terminal synapses small, with only about 80 transmitter vesicles released per second, and with only one region of transmitter release (*active zone*), whereas the cone axon is thick, with up to 1500 vesicles released per second, and a synapse (*cone pedicle*) which is perhaps the most complicated synapse in the whole nervous system. It makes contacts with several hundred other retinal neurons (horizontal and bipolar cells) and has a typical appearance (the *cone pedicle*). The signal is diverged into 10 parallel channels [20], 5 ON- and 5 OFF-type bipolar cells. Rather than using one broadband *super channel*, 10 parallel channels are used, each with a different bandwidth. The separation into different channels is thought to occur because (i) different aspects of visual processing can be separated into different pathways already at an early level and (ii) such a *broadband superchannel* cannot be made because of the limited range of possible spike frequencies (see the next section).

1.9 Spiking and Coding

In electronic devices, electrical signals can be transmitted either in an analog or a binary manner. In fact, both types are also realized in the nervous system. Short-distance signal transmission, like through the dendrites to the cell body of neurons, occurs via an electronically propagating depolarization of the membrane. For long-distance travel, the electronic signals become too degraded and lose their reliability. Therefore, binary coding (*0 or 1*), as used in action potentials, is used, which is much more resistant to degradation. At the root of the neuron's axon, and along the axon, voltage-dependent sodium channels are expressed, which are necessary for the generation of action potentials (*spikes*). Action potentials are rapid and transient depolarizations of the membrane, which travel with high speed (up to 120 m s^{-1}) along the fibers. The level of excitation is now encoded in the frequency of the spikes. Because of a recovery phase after each spike of about 2 ms, the maximum frequency is limited to about 500 Hz. This means that the dynamic range is limited. Because, even with a constant stimulus, the spike frequency displays some noise, the response functions of the neurons have no *steps*. It turns out that noisy signals are a common feature in the nervous system, and high precision is achieved by parallel channels, if necessary (probability summation), or by temporal summation. The signal-to-noise ratio, when a difference in stimulus strength should be detected, is determined by the standard deviation of the firing rate. If the firing rate varies little with constant stimulation (small standard deviation), a small change would be detectable, but if it varies much (large standard deviation), only large differences are detected. The signal-to-noise ratio can be calculated from the differences in spike rates at both stimulus strengths divided by the standard deviation of spike rates (assuming that the standard deviation is similar in both cases). Summation of several channels is not always possible: sometimes decisions need to be made based on the signals from only two cells, for instance, when two spots are resolved that are at the resolution limit of the foveal cones and, accordingly, two retinal ganglion cells.

In the retina, most neuron are nonspiking. This is possible because the distances are short and the signals can be finely graded – *the retina is a tonic machine*. Only at the output side, mostly in ganglion cells (but also in a few amacrine cells), the signals are converted into spikes, which can then travel down the long axons, a few centimeters, to the first relay station, the lateral geniculus (LGN, Figure 1.11). Since ganglion cells can be excited and inhibited (since they can generate ON or OFF responses), it is necessary that they have a baseline spontaneous spike activity (ranging from 5 to 200 Hz). It is clear that those ganglion cells with high spontaneous activity can encode smaller changes in stimulus strength than those with low activity.

1.10 Temporal and Spatial Performance

The temporal resolution of the retina is ultimately limited by the integration time of the photoreceptors. The integration time, in turn, determines the light sensitivity of the receptors. Rods have longer integration time (200 ms) and, accordingly, have lower flicker fusion frequencies (up to 10 Hz). Cones, with integrations times of 20 ms, can resolve stroboscopic flicker light of up to 55 Hz. But under normal viewing conditions, the flicker fusion frequency is much lower, 16–20 Hz. If it were 55 Hz, watching TV would be disturbing. The European TV or video format has a frame rate of 25 Hz, but two frames with half vertical resolution, presented alternatingly at 50 Hz, are interlaced to prevent the flicker from being seen.

The complete description of the eye's spatial performance is the contrast sensitivity function. This function describes the contrast sensitivity (1/contrast threshold) as a function of the SF. It is clear that contrast sensitivity must decline with increasing SF, just based on the optics of the eye: the higher the SF, the less the contrast preserved in its retinal image, due to aberrations and diffraction (the MTF, Figure 1.3). Even if the neural processor in the retina has the same contrast sensitivity, its sensitivity would decline in a psychophysical measurement. On the other hand, it is not trivial that contrast sensitivity also declines in the low-SF range. This decline is determined by neural processing: there are no such large ON/OFF receptive fields to provide high sensitivity to low SFs. This represents probably an adaptation on the abundance of low SFs in natural scenes. It has been shown that the energy at SFs falls off with about 1/SF [21]. The peak of the contrast sensitivity function moves to lower SFs with declining retinal illuminance. At daylight, the peak contrast sensitivity is at 5 cycles per degree. Here, brightness differences of only 1/200 (0.5% spatial frequencies of 50–60 cycles per degree. However, due to the striking feature of the optical transfer function (the first Bessel function), the MTF shows a number of phase reversals beyond the *cutoff frequency* at which the contrast first declines to zero (Figure 1.4). Therefore, it may be possible to detect a grating even though its spatial frequency is higher than the cutoff frequency, even though it may have reversed contrast. For this reason, grating acuity is not the best measure of spatial vision, in particular with defocus [22].

1.11 ON/OFF Structure, Division of the Whole Illuminance Amplitude

Perhaps because no important information is contained in absolute brightness values in the visual environment, the visual system has confined its processing almost exclusively to differences – spatial and temporal contrasts. Recording from neurons along the visual pathways shows that the cells have structured *receptive fields* – defined angular positions in the visual field where they respond to the stimulation. The receptive fields are initially circular (retina, lateral geniculate (LGN), striated cortex) but become later elongated at higher cortical areas, and finally larger and may even cover the whole visual field (e.g., neurons that recognize highly specific features, like a face). Receptive fields in the retina and LGN are organized in an ON center – OFF surround structure, or vice versa. If a small spot of light is projected on to the center of an ON center ganglion cell, the cell fires vigorously, but if the surround also is illuminated, the response returns to baseline activity. If only the surround is illuminated, the cell's activity is reduced below the resting level. From the structure of the receptive fields, it is already clear that homogenously illuminated surfaces without structure are poor stimuli for our visual system; *the inside of a form does not excite our brain* (David Hubel).

Dividing the processing into ON and OFF channels, starting from an intermediate activity level, has also the advantage that the dynamic range of the responses can be expanded. It is surprising that OFF ganglion cells have smaller dendritic fields and denser sampling arrays than the ON cells. This asymmetry seems to correspond to an asymmetric distribution of negative and positive contrasts in natural images [23].

1.12 Consequences of the Rod and Cone Diversity on Retinal Wiring

Since the illuminance range is divided by the visual system into a scotopic and a photopic range, and both are not used at the same time, it would be a waste to use separate lines in the rod and cone pathway. In fact, there is no rod OFF bipolar cell at all, and the rod ON pathway has no individual ganglion cells. Rather, the rods are piggy-packed on the cone circuitry at low light levels via the A2 amacrine

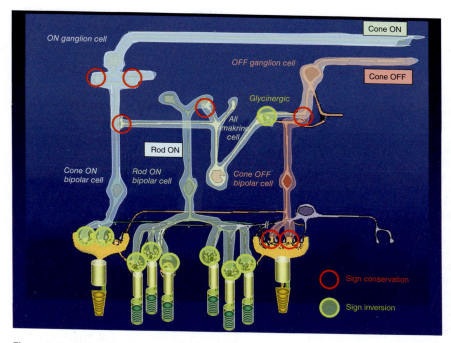

Figure 1.10 Rod and cone pathways and ON/OFF channels. To make the system more sensitive to differences rather than to absolute brightness, the image on the retina is analyzed by an ON/OFF system, that is, cells that respond preferably by changes in brightness in either direction. The division into these two major channels occurs already at the first synapse, the photoreceptor *endfoot*. Because the photoreceptors can hyperpolarize only in response to illumination, the subsequent cells must be either depolarized (*excited*) or hyperpolarized (*inhibited*). This means that the signal must either be inverted (*ON channel*) or conserved (*OFF channel*). It is shown how the signals change their signs along the processing pathway. Since rods and cones respond to different illuminance ranges, it would be a waste of space and energy to give both of them separate lines. In fact, the rods have only the first cells, the rod ON bipolar cell, which then *jumps* on the cone pathways via the *AII amacrine cell*; they are not used by the cones at low light. Rods do not have their own OFF bipolar cell. Cones, with the need for coding small differences in brightness with high resolution and with large information content, have two separate lines (*ON* and *OFF*) to increase information capacity.

cells (Figure 1.10) (at least 40 amacrine cell types have been classified on the basis of their morphological appearance, their transmitters, and their electrical responses). Since the information contained in the cone signals is much richer (since it is not limited by photon noise), the neurons that carry their information have thicker axons and much more synapses. They also have higher spike rates and contain more mitochondria – the energy sources of the cell.

1.13 Motion Sensitivity in the Retina

The ability to detect motion, and in particular its direction, is present already not only at the amacrine cell level in the retina but also in many neurons of the cerebral cortex. Typically, motion-selective cells fire strongly when an edge moves across their receptive field in the *preferred direction*, and they are

Figure 1.11 Feed-forward projections from the eyes to the brain and topographic mapping. In each eye, the visual field on the left and right of the fovea (the cut goes right through the fovea!) projects on to different cortical hemispheres: the ipsilateral retina projects on to the ipsilateral visual cortex, and the contralateral retina crosses the contralateral cortex (*hemi-field crossing* in the optic chiasma). The first synapse of the retinal ganglion cells is in the lateral geniculate nucleus (LGN), but information from the left (L) and right (R) eye remains strictly separated. The LGN consists of six layers; layers 1 and 2 are primarily occupied by the magnocellular pathway, and 3–6 by the parvocellular pathway. Information from both eyes comes first together in the visual cortex, area 17, layers 2 and 3, and a strict topographic projection is preserved (follow the color-coded maps of the visual field areas (b)). The wiring in A17 (c) has been extensively studied, in particular by the Nobel Prize winners Hubel and Wiesel (1981). The input from the LGN ends in layer 4C alpha (magnocellular) and 4C beta (parvocellular) and layers 1–3 (koniocellular). These cells project further into the *blobs*, cytochromoxidase-rich peg-shaped regions (pink spots in (c)). The innervation has a remarkable repetitive pattern; parallel to the cortical surface, the preferred orientation for bars presented in the receptive field of the cells shifts continuously in angle (illustrated by color-coded orientation angles on top of the tissue segment shown in (c)). Furthermore, the regions where the contra or ipsilateral eye has input into layer 4 interchange in a striking pattern. A17 is the cortical input layer with mostly *simple cells*, that is, cells that respond to bars and edges with defined directions of movements. At higher centers (a), two streams can be identified on the basis of single cell recordings and functional imaging with new imaging techniques (functional magnetic resonance imaging, fMRI): a *dorsal stream*, concerned about motion and depth (*where?* stream) and a ventral stream concerned about object features, shape color, structure (*what? stream*). Feedback projections are not shown, and only the major projections are shown.

---

inhibited or even silent when the motion is in the *null direction*. The illusion of motion can be provoked by stimulating briefly at two different positions in the receptive field, with a short time delay, and this illusion appears to work both during electrophysiological recordings at the cellular level and psychophysically. It was concluded that excitation evoked by motion in the preferred direction must reach the ganglion cell before inhibition can cancel it; and inhibition evoked by motion in the null direction must arrive before excitation can cancel it. The asymmetric signal transmission speed was assumed to result from morphologically asymmetric input of the so-called starburst amacrine cells to the directionally sensitive ganglion cells, although neither the developmental mechanism for the asymmetric connections nor the role of the involved transmitters, acetylcholine, and gamma-aminobutyric acid (GABA) is completely understood [24].

1.14 Visual Information Processing in Higher Centers

About 15 types of ganglion cells can be classified in the retina, and they are characterized by different morphologies, bandwidths, and response characteristics. The underlying hypothesis is that each part of the visual field is sampled by a group of ganglion cells that process different aspects of the visual information – how many aspects there are is not exactly known but the number should be between 3 and 20 [25].

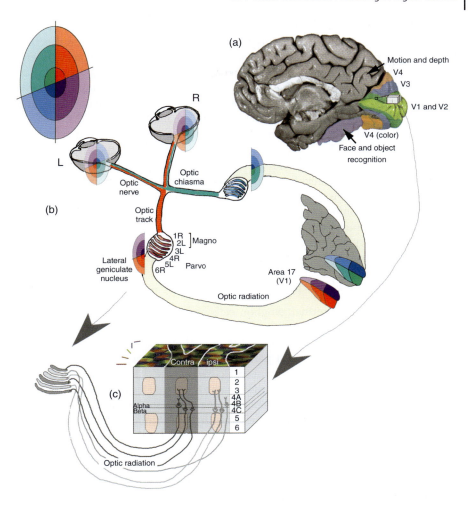

1.14.1 Morphology

Researchers have always attempted to divide the visual pathways into functionally different channels. This is more successful in the initial steps, up to the primary cortex, but the separation of the pathways becomes more diffuse in higher centers. Three pathways were identified: the magnocellular, parvocellular, and koniocellular pathways. The magnocellular pathway is basically a luminance channel with low spatial acuity, large receptive fields of ganglion cells, high motion sensitivity, and high contrast sensitivity under scotopic conditions but with little or no spectral opponency. It is relayed in the LGN in the two basal layers 1 and 2 (1: contralateral eye, 2: ipsilateral eye (Figure 1.11)), and makes 10% of the LGN population. The parvocellular pathway is the high spatial acuity channel, with low temporal resolution and smaller receptive fields of ganglion cells, low contrast sensitivity under scotopic conditions, but with color opponency. It is relayed in layers 3–6 (layers 4 and 6 contralateral, 3 and 5 ipsilateral) and makes

80% of the LGN population. The koniocellular pathway is specific for blue–yellow opponency and large receptive fields of ganglion cells, but no distinct projection to the LGN layers (*intercalated projection*), making 10% of the optic nerve fibers. The separation of these pathways is preserved to the primary visual cortex, also called V1 or area A17. Here, the M cells project onto layer $4C\alpha$ and the P cells onto layer $4C\beta$. The koniocellular pathway feeds into the upper layers (1–3), and there into the cytochrome oxidase-rich regions, the *blobs* (Figure 1.11).

Collaterals of M and P cells also project onto layer 6 from where they project back to the LGN; feedback is one of the common features in the visual system: apparently, the selected input can be shaped, depending on the demand of the unit that sends the feedback. For instance, feedback seems to enhance the resolution of an earlier level to the pattern isolated by the higher level [26], for instance, by enhancing the inhibitory surround in the receptive field of a cell. The feedback seems to be extremely well developed: only 10% of the input in the LGN comes from the periphery, the retina, while the corticofugal feedback connections make up to 30% of its input.

1.14.2 Functional Aspects – Receptive Field Structures and Cortical Modules

The receptive fields of retinal ganglion cells and cells in the LGN are concentric with a typical ON-center/OFF surround structure, or vice versa. At the level of V1, receptive fields become elongated, and they respond best to elongated moving slits, bars, or edges at a particular orientation, but the excitatory and inhibitory regions are no longer concentric (*simple cells*). Different cells require different orientations, and the response can be improved if the stimulus moves in the preferred direction. These cells can now be stimulated through either eye; in fact, the primary visual cortex is the first level at which binocularly driven cells are found. There are also *complex cells* that are selective for the position and orientation of an edge, but they have no longer excitatory or inhibitory regions. In the topographic representations of the visual field in the visual system, the receptive field sizes generally increase with the distance from the fovea. They also increase with hierarchic level of the brain area, and the stimuli that are necessary to excite the cells become increasingly specific. A common view is (Figure 1.10) that there are two major *streams* of information processing from the visual cortex: a dorsal stream that processes predominantly the *where* aspects of an object (location in space, depth, movement), and a ventral stream that processes the *what* aspects (shape, color, details). The P stream is assumed to feed predominantly into the *what* stream, and the M stream more into the *where* pathway. A current view is that the ventral *what* stream is actually responsible for *seeing*, whereas the dorsal *where* stream is only necessary for the direction of attention and for the control of visually guided movements [27]. Along the ventral *what* stream, cells that are extremely specific for certain features of the visual stimuli are found: for instance, they may respond only to faces or even to facial expressions, and this happens largely independently from shading and the visual angle of presentation – a demanding task also in machine vision. The receptive fields of cells that respond to faces may cover the entire visual field, but already in area MT, the major motion processing center in the *dorsal stream*, the receptive field sizes are 10 times as large as in V1.

Hubel and Wiesel won the Nobel Prize (1981) also for their discovery of the modular organization of the striate cortex (Figure 1.11c). There are topographically arranged units with 0.5 mm diameter, which contain the following subunits: (i) a column of cells with a defined orientation selectivity (*orientation column*); (ii) peg-shaped structures that extend through layers 2 and 3 and stain heavily for cytochrome oxidase, a mitochondrial enzyme linked to metabolic activity (*blobs*, assumed to be involved in color processing, with predominant input from the koniocellular stream); and (iii) two ocular dominance columns, with preferential input from either eye (*ocular dominance column*). These units repeat one after the other, and the preferred orientation (see Figure 1.11c) smoothly rotates until a 180° reversal is achieved after about 3/4 mm. A unit with a complete set of orientations has been termed a *hypercolumn*.

Topographic representation of the visual world occurs in the visual system at many levels: first, certainly, in the retina, but then also in the LGN, in the different cortical layers, the superior colliculus and the motion processing center area MT (V4), and others.

1.15 Effects of Attention

Most observations suggest that attention alters the sensitivity of neurons without affecting their stimulus preferences [28]. Only some neurons in V1 are modulated by attention; others ignore it, and some respond exclusively when the stimulus is attended. The influence of attention increases with cortical hierarchy, perhaps also with increasing feature specificity of the cells. Effects of attention can be measured, for instance, by training a monkey to fixate a red or green spot. A neuron, for instance in area V4, is recorded, and the receptive field is mapped. A red or green stimulus, or nothing (e.g., a bar) appears in the receptive field. The monkey is trained to respond if the stimulus color matches the color of the fixation spot or not. In this kind of experiment, the responses of the V4 cell can be compared with different levels of attention and different stimuli.

Attention may also change the synchrony of neuronal signals in the visual cortex, although it is not yet studied how synchrony affects the strength of the neural responses. If attention can shape the responses of neurons to better performance, the question arises why all neurons are not at maximum sensitivity at all times. Presumably, the sensitivity is set to produce an appropriate balance between false alarms about the presence of a stimulus and failure to detect it [28].

1.16 Color Vision, Color Constancy, and Color Contrast

Both the location of the absorption peak of the photopigment and the number of photons that arrive determine the probability that a photon is caught by the photoreceptor. These two variables cannot be separated because the photoreceptor is only a *photon counter*. For the same reason, a single photoreceptor type also cannot provide information on the light intensity. Only the sum of the responses from several receptor types can provide this information, whereas the differences between their responses provide information on the spectral composition of the light reflected from an object and its *color*. For this purpose, photoreceptors have photopigments with different spectral absorptions. Most mammals, including male new-world primates, are dichromatic, indicating that they have only two cone pigments. Only old-world monkeys and humans are regularly trichromatic, but fish, reptiles, and birds may even be tetrachromatic.

Perhaps because the spectral absorbance curves of the photopigments are wide, and there is particularly much overlap in the spectra of the L and M cones with high correlations in the signals, fine wavelength discrimination (as present in our visual system, best performance at about 550 and 470 nm with a detection of only 1 or 2 nm difference) can be achieved only by antagonistic circuitry. Already at the level of the ganglion cells, the initial three spectral sensitivities of the cones are recombined into three mechanisms: (i) a luminance channel, which consists of the added $L + M$ signals, (ii) an $L - M$ color opponent channel where the difference between the signals from L and M cones is taken to compute the red–green component of a stimulus; and (iii) an $S - (L + M)$ channel where the sum of the L and M cone signals is subtracted from the S cone signal to compute the blue–yellow variation of the stimulus. These three channels represent the *cardinal directions in the color space* pathways.

The so-called magnocellular pathway (large *magnocellular* ganglion cells projecting on to the bottom two layers in the LGN) is most sensitive to luminance information, with high contrast sensitivity, low spatial resolution, and no color sensitivity. In the parvocellular pathway (small *parvocellular* ganglion cells, projecting to the upper four layers of the LGN), the red–green information is transmitted, and in the koniocellular pathway (intermediate ganglion cell sizes to all LGH layers), the blue–yellow information is transmitted.

Up to the LGN, it seems to be possible to define cell classes with different functions, but later, in the cortex, this becomes increasingly diffuse. Considerable efforts have been devoted to link the structural differences to functional differences, looking for *the cell type* that processes *color or form, or motion*, or locating *the brain area* that processes a certain aspect of a stimulus. However, the more experiments are done, the less clear becomes the link between the function, position, and structure, and it seems as if most cells in the central visual system have access to most features of a stimulus and that there is no complete segregation of processing aspects. These so-called multiplexing properties are found in cortical neurons as early as in V1.

Also, color processing does not seem to occur independently of the form [29]. For instance, patients with normal photopigments but with loss of color vision due to accidental damage of the cortex (*acquired achromatopsia*) may see objects without color but may still have near-normal sensitivity to chromatic gratings [30].

The color of an object is determined by the proportion of light that it reflects at a given wavelength, which is described by the spectral reflectance function. Color vision is confounded by the spectral composition of a light source. For instance, if the light source includes more light of long wavelengths, the L cones absorb more photons and this should cause a reddish impression of the scene. However, this does not usually happen because the effect of illumination is successfully compensated by the visual system (*color constancy*). Color constancy is not only locally controlled at the receptoral level, since the spectral composition of the light at distant regions in the visual field changes the local spectral sensitivity function.

Analogous to luminance contrasts, which were best detected by ON center/OFF surround cells (or vice versa), color contrasts would be best detected by cells that have antagonistic red–green mechanisms (e.g., +L −M) both in the center and surround, and measure the differences between the center and surround (*double opponent cells*). Such cells, with concentric receptive fields, have been found in the primary visual cortex of monkeys. If their receptive fields are larger, they could also mediate color constancy over extended regions in the visual field.

1.17 Depth Perception

The visual system uses several independent cues to determine the distance of objects in depth. These can be divided into monocular and binocular cues. Monocular depth estimations are typically possible from motion parallax, familiar size, shading, perspective, and – to a minor extent and only for close distances – from the level of accommodation necessary to focus an object. The major depth cue, however, is binocular and results from the fact that both eyes see an object at a different angle. Accordingly, the retinal images best match at the fixation point, that is, the images in the fovea. The peripheral parts of the images do not match; they show *disparity* (Figure 1.3). Rather than producing the impression of double images (*diplopia*), the cortex has some tolerance to these non-corresponding images and can still place them together. But the differences are recognized, which provides a highly sensitive mechanism for depth detection, called *stereopsis*. The two most striking features of stereopsis are that (i) it does not require object recognition but rather works also on Julesz's random dot patterns, and (ii) the difference between the images in both retinas is detected that are smaller than the diameter of a photoreceptor: stereopsis involves a *hyperacuity*. This is necessary, for instance, to insert a thread through a needle's eye. Considering that the visual processing may be based on displacements of less than a photoreceptor's diameter, it is even more striking that displacement of *blue versus red images*, equivalent to about 15 photoreceptor diameters (Figure 1.7), remains undetected.

Disparity-sensitive neurons have been extensively recorded not only in the visual cortex in V1 but also in V2 and the motion areas in the dorsal stream. Cells can be classified as *near cells*, which respond best to crossed disparities, and *far cells* that respond best to uncrossed disparities. Both these types are most frequent in the motion areas, whereas cells that respond best to zero disparity (*zero-disparity cells*) are abundant in areas V1 and V2 (Figure 1.11).

1.18 Adaptation in the Visual System to Color, Spatial, and Temporal Contrast

One of the most striking features of neural processing in our visual system is that the gains for all aspects of vision are continuously adapted. The most immediate adaptation is light/dark adaptation, independently in each photoreceptor, but this adaptation in cones modifies their relative weight and, therefore, also color vision. Not only the receptors adapt but also higher processing steps in the visual system (review [31]). A few examples are that there are (i) motion adaptation (after the train stops, the environment appears to move in the opposite direction); (ii) tilt adaptation (after one looks at tilted bars, vertical bars appear to be tilted in the opposite direction); (iii) contrast adaptation (after prolonged viewing of a high-contrast grating, the sensitivity for detection of similar gratings is severely reduced – this also affects the impression of *sharpness* of an image); (iv) adaptation to scaling (if one looks at a face in which the distance between the eyes is artificially reduced, the *control face* appears to have a larger interocular distance, the *face-distortion aftereffect*; and (v) adaptation to optical aberrations and field distortions of the image on the retina, which are well known to spectacle wearers. Recovery in most of these adaptations is generally in the range of seconds, but extended exposure may also cause extended changes in perception. A most striking example here is that wearing red or green spectacles for 3 or 4 days will shift the ratio of the red–green (L–M cone) weighting also for several days [32]. That the weighting of the different cone inputs can be extremely shifted (perhaps also adapted) could explain why subjects with very different L/M cone ratios (naturally occurring variability: $0.25:1$ to $9:1$) can all have normal color vision. Selective adaptation of color channels can also nicely be seen at the homepage of Professor Michael Bach, http://www.michaelbach.de/ot/col_rapidAfterimage/.

1.19 Conclusions

The most striking features of the natural visual system are the extreme plasticity of image processing and the apparent optimal use of energy, space, and cell numbers.

1) To prevent saturation of photoreceptors over a range of possible ambient illuminances of, at least, 8 log units, in the presence of only about 2 log units of simultaneous contrast in natural scenes, their response curves are shifted by altering the gain of the phototransduction cascade. Furthermore, the retina divides the entire illuminance range into two, the low-illuminance range, where rods respond, and the high-illuminance range, where cones take over. To save energy and wire volume in the retina, both photoreceptors use the same circuitry, and their inputs to these circuits are automatically switched over by synaptic plasticity, although, as in most cases in nature, with a smooth transition.

2) Cable capacity is matched to information content, and multiple parallel channels with different bandwidths are used, if necessary, in the case of cones to make it possible to transmit all relevant information.
3) There is extensive image preprocessing directly in the initial light sensor, namely the retina. This is necessary because 125 million photoreceptors converge into an optic nerve with only about 1 million lines and also because the information from the cones is too much to be fully processed by the cortex. For the same reason, high-acuity information is processed only in the central 1° of the visual field, and this limitation is compensated by eye movements. The spatial resolution here is as good as physically possible for the given eye size of 24 mm, since diffraction at the pupil and the waveguide properties of the cones preclude denser spatial sampling. The preprocessing in the retina focuses on temporal and spatial brightness differences, and spatial and temporal bandpass filtering, by building antagonistic receptive field structures of the output cells of the retina (ON/OFF, color opponency, motion selectivity with preferred direction), to enhance sensitivity to small changes. By matching the sensitivity to the available stimulus strength, maximum information is extracted; for example, contrast sensitivity is continuously adapted at each spatial frequency to make optimal use of the stimulus contrast.
4) Rescaling the retinal image, or compensating for local distortions or optical aberrations, seems to occur largely without effort – a most impressive performance.
5) Depth is determined from several monocular cues, but the most powerful mechanism is stereopsis, derived from binocular disparity. Stereopsis does not require object recognition and works on random dot stereograms; it is impressive how corresponding dots in the two retinal images are identified, and it demonstrates extensive parallel comparisons over a wide range of the visual field.
6) In the cortex, different aspects of the image are initially analyzed at each position in the visual field (small receptive fields of the respective neurons). Later, the trigger features of the cells become more and more specific and the receptive field sizes increase. Cells can be recorded in higher cortical centers that are selective for faces and expressions, and that retain their selectivity for these stimuli at different illuminations. How this information is extracted is not yet clear.
7) An unsolved problem is how and where all the separately processed features finally converge to provide the complete picture of a visual object (the *binding problem*).
8) It is interesting to note that there is an extensive description of the neural responses in the visual system (i.e., retinal ganglion cells) to stimulation with light spots and simple patterns, but no one would dare to describe the visual scene given only a recording of the optic nerve trains. *Natural vision has not been the focus of much research* [33]. It seems that there is need for more research on the responses of the cells in the visual system with natural stimulation.

Acknowledgements

I am grateful to Annette Werner, Howard C. Howland, Marita Feldkaemper, and Mahmound Youness for reading and commenting on an earlier version of this manuscript.

References

Material that is covered by most common text books on the visual system is not referenced.

1 Rodieck, R.W. (1973) *The Vertebrate Retina*, Freeman, San Francisco, CA.
2 Hughes, A. (1977) The topography of vision in mammals of contrasting life styles: comparative optics and retinal organization, in *Handbook of Sensory Physiology*, vol. **VII/5**, Part A (ed. F Crecitelli), Springer-Verlag, Berlin, pp. 615–637.
3 Marcos, S. (2003) Image quality of the human eye. *Int. Ophthalmol. Clin.*, **43**, 43–62.
4 Huxlin, K.R., Yoon, G., Nagy, J., Poster, J., and Williams, D. (2004) Monochromatic ocular wavefront aberrations in the awake-behaving cat. *Vis. Res.*, **44**, 2159–2169.
5 Howland, H.C. (2005) Allometry and scaling of wave aberrations of eyes. *Vis. Res.*, **45**, 1091–1093.
6 Artal, P., Guirao, A., Berrio, E., and Williams, D.R. (2001) Compensation of corneal aberrations by the internal optics of the human eye. *J. Vis.*, **1**, 1–8.
7 Kelly, J.C., Mihahsi, T., and Howland, H.C. (2004) Compensation of corneal horizontal/vertical astigmatism, lateral coma, and spherical aberration by the internal optics of the eye. *J. Vis.*, **4**, 262–271.
8 Collins, M.J., Buehren, T., and Iskander, D.R. (2006) Retinal image quality, reading and myopia. *Vis. Res.*, **46**, 196–215.
9 Guirao, A., Gonzalez, C., Redono, M., Geraghty, E., Norrby, S., and Artal, P. (1999) Average optical performance of the human eye as a function of age in a normal population. *Invest. Ophthalmol. Vis. Sci.*, **40**, 203–213.
10 Wilson, B.J., Decker, K.E., and Roorda, A. (1992) Monochromatic aberrations provide an odd-error cue to focus direction. *J. Opt. Soc. Am. A*, **19**, 833–839.
11 Curcio, C.A., Sloan, K.R., Kalina, R.E., and Hendrikson, A.E. (1990) Human photoreceptor topography. *J. Comput. Neurol.*, **292**, 497–523.
12 Williams, D.R. (1985) Aliasing in human foveal vision. *Vis. Res.*, **25**, 195–205.
13 Kirschfeld, K. (1983) Are photoreceptors optimal? *Trends Neurosci.*, **6**, 97–101.
14 Reymond, L. (1985) Spatial visual acuity of the eagle Aquila audax: a behavioral, optical and anatomical investigation. *Vis. Res.*, **25**, 1477–1491.
15 Marcos, S., Burns, S.A., Moreno-Barriusop, E., and Navarro, R. (1999) A new approach to the study of ocular chromatic aberrations. *Vis. Res.*, **39**, 4309–4323.

16 Magnussen, S., Spillmann, L., Sturzel, F., and Werner, J.S. (2001) Filling-in of the foveal blue scotoma. *Vis. Res.*, **41**, 2961–2971.
17 Artal, P., Fernandez, E.J., Singer, B., Manzamera, S., and Williams, D.R. (2004) Neural compensation for the eye's optical aberrations. *J. Vis.*, **4**, 281–287.
18 Webster, M.A., Georgeson, M.A., and Webster, S.M. (2002) Neural adjustments to image blur. *Nat. Neurosci.*, **5**, 839–840.
19 Heinrichs, T.S. and Bach, M. (2001) Contrast adaptation in human retina and cortex. *Invest. Ophthalmol. Vis. Sci.*, **42**, 2721–2727.
20 Sterling, P. (2003) How retinal circuits optimize the transfer of visual information, in *The Visual Neurosciences*, vol. **1** (eds LM Chalupa and JS Werner), MIT Press, Cambridge, MA, pp. 234–259.
21 Field, D.J. and Brady, N. (1997) Visual sensitivity, blur and sources of variability in the amplitude spectra of antural scenes. *Vis. Res.*, **37**, 3367–3383.
22 Gislen, A. and Gislen, L. (2004) On the optical theory of underwater vision in humans. *J. Opt. Soc. Am. A*, **21**, 2061–2064.
23 Ratliff, L., Sterling, P., and Balasubramanian, V. (2005) Negative contrasts predominate in natural images. *Invest. Ophthalmol. Vis. Sci.*, **46** (Suppl.), 4685 (ARVO abstract).
24 Sterling, P. (2002) How neurons compute direction. *Nature*, **420**, 375–376.
25 Kaplan, E. (2003) The M, P, and K pathways of the primate visual system, in *The Visual Neurosciences*, vol. **1** (eds LM Chalupa and JS Werner), MIT Press, Cambridge, MA, pp. 481–493.
26 Silito, A.M. and Jones, H.E. (2003) Feedback systems in visual processing, in *The Visual Neurosciences*, vol. **1** (eds LM Chalupa and JS Werner), MIT Press, Cambridge, MA, pp. 609–624.
27 Movshon, J.A. (2005) Parallel visual cortical processing in primates. *Invest. Ophthalmol. Vis. Sci.*, **46** (Suppl.), 3584 (ARVO abstract).
28 Maunsell, J.H.R. (2003) The role of attention in visual cerebral cortex, in *The Visual Neurosciences*, vol. **2** (eds LM Chalupa and JS Werner), MIT Press, Cambridge, MA, pp. 1538–1545.
29 Werner, A. (2003) The spatial tuning of chromatic adaptation. *Vis. Res.*, **43**, 1611–1623.
30 Gegenfurtner, K. (2003) The processing of color in extrastriate cortex, in *The Visual Neurosciences*, vol. **2** (eds LM Chalupa and JS Werner), MIT Press, Cambridge, MA, pp. 1017–1028.
31 Webster, M.A. (2003) Pattern-selective adaptation in color and form perception, in *The Visual Neurosciences*, vol. **2** (eds LM Chalupa and JS Werner), MIT Press, Cambridge, MA, pp. 936–947.
32 Neitz, J., Carroll, J., Yamauchi, Y., Neitz, M., and Williams, D.R. (2002) Color perception is mediated by a plastic neural mechanisms that is adjustable in adults. *Neuron*, **35**, 783–792.
33 Meister, M. and Berry, M.J. II, (1999) The neural code of the retina. *Neuron*, **22**, 435–450.

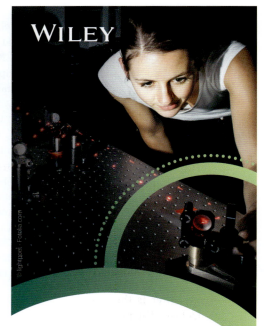

2

Introduction to Building a Machine Vision Inspection

Axel Telljohann

Consulting Team Machine Vision (CTMV), CTMV GmbH & Co. KG, Schwarzwaldstraße 7a, 75173 Pforzheim, Germany

2.1 Preface

This chapter is the introduction to the basics for designing a machine vision inspection. The next chapters give a detailed description of different terms such as lighting, optics, cameras, interfaces, algorithms, and the application of these components to the machine vision system in the environment of manufacturing.

Now, the following sections focus on how to solve a concrete vision task in practice and which steps have to be taken on the road toward achieving successful industrial application.

This roadmap provides a basis for the major decisions that have to be made for a design. It also calls attention to the optimum sequence in realizing a system. It is based on Consulting Team Machine Vision's (CTMV's) long-time experience in designing machine vision systems and displays their method of approaching a vision task.

The sequence of a project realization can be seen as follows:

1) specification of the task
2) design of the system
3) calculation of costs
4) development and installation of the system.

A successful design is based on a detailed *specification*. The task and the environment need to be described. Often, ambient influences such as mechanical tolerances and sometimes even the task are not specified precisely. This might be caused either by a lack of knowledge about these factors or by the misconception that image processing is mainly done by software and thus can be changed easily. Even though software is easy to modify, the consequence of an insufficient specification is a hazard to an effective project workflow. Section 2.2 briefly describes the information that is necessary for a design.

Besides the specification, it is essential to provide a set of sample parts that covers error-free as well as error parts as such being in the range between just good and already inaccurate. These parts are required to design the illumination, to determine the required resolution, and to get an impression of the diversity of feature changes.

As for the *design*, Section 2.3 provides the guideline for the crucial steps, such as

- choosing the camera scan type
- determining the field of view
- calculating the resolution
- choosing a lens
- selecting a camera model, frame grabber, and hardware platform
- selecting the illumination
- addressing the aspects of mechanical and electrical interfaces
- designing and choosing the software.

If the system is designed, *costs* can be evaluated for hardware and software. Furthermore, the required effort for development and installation can be estimated so that a *project plan* including costs can be created. Section 2.4 briefly focuses on the costs for a vision system.

Finally, the project development can be launched; Section 2.5 addresses issues for the successful development and installation of vision systems.

This chapter concludes with the presentation of two examples as realized by Consulting Team Machine Vision (CTMV). The steps of specification and design are displayed on the basis of these projects.

2.2 Specifying a Machine Vision System

Before launching a vision project, the task and conditions need to be evaluated. As for the conditions, a part description as well as requirements of speed and accuracy need to be defined.

This section describes the essential subjects for designing a machine vision system. These topics should be summarized by a system specification in written form. In combination with sample parts this document displays the initial situation. Change requests, which might occur during project realization, can then be checked with the initial setup and can be added to the requirements list. Thus, this outline provides an overview of the system's requirements and potentials to both the user and the developer. Furthermore, this specification provides the basis for the acceptance test.

2.2.1 Task and Benefit

Certainly, the task and the benefit are the most important topics of the specification. This part needs to cover the requirements of the system. Any operation performed and result generated by the system needs to be defined, including the expected accuracy. What is the inspection about? Which measurements have to be performed? As described in Chapter 10, the task type can be categorized, which gives the system a brief title.

The present method of the operation is key to gathering more information about the task and to estimate the benefit. The advantages of a machine vision system can be multiple, for instance: the task is performed with a higher precision or a 100% inline inspection of every part might be possible where random examination used to be the predominant method.

The sum of these benefits justifies the expenses for a vision system. If a cost justification is done by an ROI calculation, these benefits are fundamental to evaluate the budget or the point of time when the system is profitable.

2.2.2 Parts

As mentioned above, a precise description of the parts and a sufficient set of samples are necessary for the outline. The following characteristics and their range of diversity need to be specified:

- discrete parts or endless material (i.e., paper or woven goods)
- minimum and maximum dimensions
- changes in shape
- description of the features that have to be extracted
- changes of these features concerning error parts and common product variation
- surface finish
- color
- corrosion, oil films, or adhesives
- changes due to part handling, that is, labels, fingerprints.

A key feature of vision systems is their ability to operate without the need of touching the parts. Nevertheless, for sensitive test parts, a damage caused by lamp heat or radiation should be checked as well as their compatibility to part handling.

2.2.2.1 Different Part Types

The different part types need a detailed description. What features differ in which way, for instance, dimensions, shape, or color?

With greater variety, type handling becomes more important. The question of how to enable the software to deal with new types will find different answers for a small range of types in comparison to larger ranges. For a vision system that frequently has to cope with new types, it can be essential to enable the user to learn new parts instead of requiring a vision specialist. Besides the difference of the parts it is important to know whether the production is organized as a mixed type or as a batch production. For the latter, the system might not need to identify the part type before inspection, which in most cases will save computation time.

2.2.3 Part Presentation

As for part presentation, the crucial factors are part motion, positioning tolerances, and the number of parts in view.

Regarding part motion, the following options are possible:

- indexed positioning
- continuous movement.

For indexed positioning, the time when the part stops needs to be defined, as it influences the image acquisition time. For a continuous movement, speed and acceleration are the key features for image acquisition.

As for positioning, the tolerances need to be known in translation and rotation. The sum of these tolerances will affect the field of view and depth of view.

If there is more than one part in view, the following topics are important:

- number of parts in view
- overlapping parts
- touching parts.

The main concern with overlapping or touching parts is that the features are not fully visible. For contour-based algorithms used for the outer part's shape, touching and overlapping parts can be a serious problem.

2.2.4 Performance Requirements

The performance requirements can be seen in the aspects of

- accuracy and
- time performance.

2.2.4.1 Accuracy
The necessary accuracy needs to be defined, as it influences the required resolution.

2.2.4.2 Time Performance
Since a vision system usually is one link in the production chain, its task has to be finished within a specified time. The requirements regarding processing time will influence the choice of the hardware platform and will eventually limit the possibility of using certain algorithms.

For the specification, the following times have to be defined:

- cycle time
- start of acquisition
- maximum processing time
- number of production cycles from inspection to result using (for result buffering).

The last topic can be an issue if the part is handled on a conveyor belt and the inspection result is not used straight away, but at a certain distance, as depicted in Figure 2.1.

For the first case, the processing must be finished within one cycle. For the second case, the results have to be latched; in which case, only the mean computation time must be less than the cycle time.

2.2.5 Information Interfaces

As a vision system usually is not a stand-alone system, it will use interfaces in its environment. These can be human machine interfaces to handle the system by

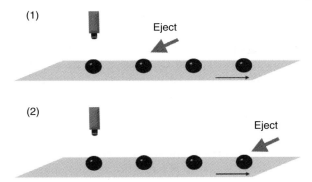

Figure 2.1 Requirements on the processing time.

an operator such as TCP/IP, fieldbus, serial or digital-I/O interfaces for machine to machine communication. Additionally, databases, protocols, or log files are common methods of saving and passing information.

Interfaces are most commonly used for

- user interface for handling and visualizing results
- declaration of the current part type
- start of the inspection
- setting results
- storage of results or inspection data in log files or databases
- generation of inspection protocols for storage or printout.

2.2.6 Installation Space

For installing the equipment, the installation space needs to be evaluated. The possibility of aligning the illumination and the camera has to be checked. Is an insight into the inspection scene possible? What variations are possible for minimum and maximum distances between the part and the camera? Furthermore, the distance between the camera and the processing unit needs to be checked for the required cable length.

2.2.7 Environment

Besides the space, the environment needs to be checked for

- ambient light
- dirt or dust that the equipment needs to be protected from
- shock or vibration that affects the part of the equipment
- heat or cold
- necessity of a certain protection class
- availability of power supply.

2.2.8 Checklist

To gather the information required for designing a machine vision system, a checklist can be used (with kind permission from CTMV). This document can be found in the appendix. It can also be downloaded from www.ctmv.de.

2.3 Designing a Machine Vision System

At this point, the information about the task, the parts, and the miscellaneous topics is available and the project can be designed on this basis. This section provides a guideline for designing a vision project. In general, this will provide a reasonable method for the procedure, although there will be exceptions.

2.3.1 Camera Type

Choosing an area or line scan camera is a fundamental decision for the design. It influences the choice of hardware and the image acquisition. 3D techniques are not covered by this guideline as their range and variety are too great.

For line scan cameras, the following sections will use the labeling of directions as shown in Figure 2.2.

Area cameras are more common in automation and provide advantages in comparison to line scan cameras. Setting up an area camera usually is easier as a movement of the part or the camera is not required. Adjusting a line scan camera in a nonmoving arrangement by using a line profile though can be a challenging task. Besides the setup, the triggering of a line scan camera requires detailed attention. In general, line scan cameras and frame grabbers are more expensive than area cameras.

Why choose line scan cameras then? Using line scan techniques offers higher resolutions in both cross direction and scan direction, where the resolution is defined by the scan rate. Depending on the frame grabber, the use of line scan cameras allows the processing of a continuous image data stream in contrast to single frames captured by area cameras. For applications, such as web inspection, processing a continuous stream offers the advantage that the inspected endless material is not separated into single frames for the image processing. Using area scan cameras instead would implicate the necessity of composing frames or merging defects that are partly visible in two frames.

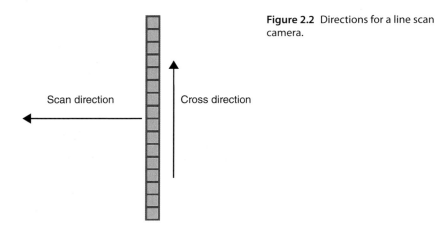

Figure 2.2 Directions for a line scan camera.

For moving parts it might be consequential to use line scan cameras – a classical application used for inspecting the surface of a rotating cylinder.

According to this, the choice between an area and a line scan camera can be made. As for verifying whether the necessary resolution can be achieved by area cameras, the resolution calculation that is addressed later on is required in this step already. Besides the selection of the camera technique, the choice of the camera model is done afterward.

A detailed description of camera technologies can be found in Chapter 6.

2.3.2 Field of View

The field of view is determined by the following factors:

- maximum part size
- maximum variation of part presentation in translation and orientation
- margin as an offset to part size
- aspect ratio of the camera sensor.

As referred in Figure 2.3, the black part labeled 1 displays the maximum part size. Due to positioning, the part can exceed the maximum variation as shown with the gray part, labeled 2. Frame 3 leads to the size determined by the maximum part size plus the maximum positioning tolerance.

Frame 4 is defined by the additional needs of a margin between the part and the image. For the image processing, it might be necessary to provide space between the part and the image edges. Furthermore, for maintenance and installing the camera it is convenient to admit a certain tolerance in positioning.

Frame 4 is the desired field of view. However, the calculated field of view needs to be adapted regarding the camera's sensor resolution. Most area cameras provide an aspect ratio of 4 : 3.

Thus, for every direction the field of view can be calculated as

$$\text{FOV} = \text{maximum part size} + \text{tolerance in positioning} + \text{margin} \\ + \text{adaption to the aspect ratio of the camera sensor} \quad (2.1)$$

Figure 2.3 Field of view.

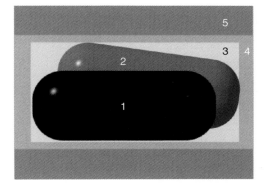

2.3.3 Resolution

If it comes to resolution, the following distinction is necessary:

- camera sensor resolution
- spatial resolution
- measurement accuracy.

2.3.3.1 Camera Sensor Resolution

The number of columns and rows that a camera provides is specified by the internal sensor. It is measured in pixels. For line scan cameras, the resolution is defined for one dimension only. Besides the number of pixels, the size of one pixel – the cell size – is required for the lens design.

2.3.3.2 Spatial Resolution

This is a matter of direct mapping of real-world objects to the image sensor. It can be measured in millimeter per pixel. The resolution is dependent on the camera sensor and the field of view; the mapping is done by the lens.

It has to be considered that some area cameras do not provide square pixels, so that the resulting spatial resolution is not equal in the horizontal and vertical directions. For line scan cameras, the lens determines the resolution in cross directions. In scan direction, the resolution is dependent on the scan rate and speed.

2.3.3.3 Measurement Accuracy

This is the overall performance of the system – the smallest feature that can be measured. Depending on the software algorithm, the measurement accuracy can be different from the spatial resolution.

For the image processing, the contrast of the feature as well as the software algorithms decides whether a feature is measurable. If the contrast of small defects is poor, the software might not be able to detect a single pixel defect; four or five pixels might be necessary then. On the other hand, model algorithms, such as circle fitting, and subpixeling allow higher measurement accuracies than spatial resolution. The following table presents an overview of algorithms and the accuracy that can be expected. Certainly, these values are dependent on the algorithm used and the image quality.

Algorithm	Accuracy in pixel
Edge detection	1/3
Blob	3
Pattern matching	1

Thus, the spatial resolution that is necessary to achieve a measurement accuracy depends on the feature contrast and the software algorithms.

2.3.3.4 Calculation of Resolution

For choosing a camera model, the required resolution has to be determined. Therefore, the size of the smallest feature that has to be inspected and the number of pixels to map this feature are crucial. The necessary spatial resolution are evaluated as follows:

$$Rs = FOV/Rc \qquad (2.2)$$
$$Rc = FOV/Rs \qquad (2.3)$$

Name	Variable	Unit
Camera resolution	Rc	pixel
Spatial resolution	Rs	mm/pixel
Field of view	FOV	mm
Size of the smallest feature	Sf	mm
Number of pixels to map the smallest feature	Nf	pixel

The necessary spatial resolution can be calculated as follows:

$$Rs = \frac{Sf}{Nf} \qquad (2.4)$$

If the field of view is known, the camera resolution can be evaluated as

$$Rc = \frac{FOV}{Rs} = FOV \cdot \frac{Nf}{Sf} \qquad (2.5)$$

This calculation has to be performed for both horizontal and vertical directions. For an area camera this is done in a straightforward manner. However, the aspect ratio of the camera sensor has to be considered.

2.3.3.5 Resolution for a Line Scan Camera

For a line scan camera, the resolution in cross direction can be calculated as above. In scan direction, the resolution defines the necessary scan rate – dependent on the speed – as follows:

$$fs = v/Rs \qquad (2.6)$$
$$ts = 1/fs \qquad (2.7)$$

Name	Variable	Unit
Spatial resolution	Rs	mm per pixel
Relative speed	v	mm s^{-1}
Line frequency	fs	Hz
Scan time	ts	s per scan

2.3.4 Choice of Camera, Frame Grabber, and Hardware Platform

At this point, the camera scan type and the required resolution are known so that an adequate camera model can be chosen. The decisions about the camera model, the frame grabber, and the hardware platform are interacting and basically done in one step.

2.3.4.1 Camera Model

As the camera scan type is defined, further requirements can be checked, such as

- color sensor
- interface technology
- progressive scan for area cameras
- packaging size
- price and availability.

2.3.4.2 Frame Grabber

The camera model affects the frame grabber choice and vice versa. Obviously, the interfaces need to be compatible. Furthermore, the following topics should be considered:

- compatibility with the pixel rate
- compatibility with the software library
- number of cameras that can be addressed
- utilities to control the camera via the frame grabber
- timing and triggering of the camera
- availability of on-board processing
- availability of general purpose I/O
- price and availability.

2.3.4.3 Pixel Rate

The topic addressed above is the pixel rate. This is the speed of imaging in terms of pixels per second. For an area camera, the pixel rate can be determined as

$$PR = Rc_{hor} \cdot Rc_{ver} \cdot fr + \text{overhead} \qquad (2.8)$$

Name	Variable	Unit
Pixel rate	PR	pixel/s
Camera resolution horizontal	Rc_{hor}	pixel
Camera resolution vertical	Rc_{ver}	pixel
Frame rate	fr	Hz
Camera resolution	Rc	pixel
Line frequency	fs	Hz

An overhead of 10–20% should be considered due to additional bus transfer. For a line scan camera, the calculation is similar:

$$PR = Rc \cdot fs + \text{overhead} \tag{2.9}$$

The pixel rate has to be handled by the camera, the frame grabber, and the processing platform. For the grabber and the computer, the sum of the pixel rates of all cameras is essential. As a guideline, the following figures can be used:

Bus technology	Maximum bandwidth for application in megabyte per second
PCI	96
PCI-Express	250 per lane
	(lanes can be combined to increase bandwidth)
IEEE 1394	32
Camera Link	max 680 for full frame Camera Link

2.3.4.4 Hardware Platform

As for the hardware platform, a decision can be made between smart cameras, compact vision systems, or PC-based systems. Costs and performance are diverging. Essential topics for choosing the hardware platform are as follows:

- *Compatibility with frame grabber*
- *Operating system*. Obviously, the software library has to be supported. A crucial factor isthe decision whether a real-time operating system is mandatory. This might be the case for high-speed applications.
- As for the operating system and software, also the *development process* has to be considered. The hardware platform should provide easy handling for development and maintenance.
- If an operator needs to set up the system frequently, the platform should provide *means for a user-friendly human machine interface*.
- *Processing load*. The hardware platform has to handle the pixel rate and the processing load. For high-speed or multiple camera applications, compact systems might be overstrained.
- *Miscellaneous points*, such as available interfaces, memory, packaging size, price, and availability.

2.3.5 Lens Design

As the field of view and the camera resolution are known, the lens can be chosen. An important parameter for the lens design is the standoff distance. In general, using greater distances will increase the image quality. The available space should be used to obtain an appropriate standoff distance. This distance is used to calculate the focal length. A detailed discussion can be found in Chapter 4.

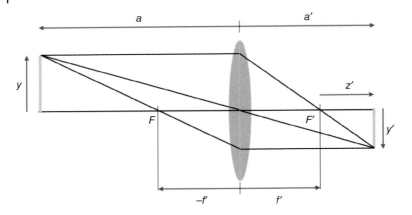

Figure 2.4 Model of a thin lens.

2.3.5.1 Focal Length

On the basis of thin lenses, the focal length f' can be determined. Even though this formula is not correct for a set of thick lenses that camera lenses are made of, it provides a reasonable indication for choosing the focal length. Figure 2.4 displays a thin lens model (see also Section 4.2.5) used for calculation. The optical convention is the same as explained in Section 4.2.3 . A real-world object with the size y is mapped by the lens to an image object of the size y'.

The standoff distance $a < 0$ is a function of the focal length $f' > 0$ and the distance $a' > 0$ between the lens and the image sensor (4.20):

$$\frac{1}{f'} = \frac{1}{a'} - \frac{1}{a} \tag{2.10}$$

The magnification β is determined by (4.23)

$$\beta = \frac{y'}{y} = \frac{a'}{a}. \tag{2.11}$$

Considering that the field of view is mapped to the size of the image sensor, the magnification can also be evaluated by

$$\beta = -\frac{\text{sensor size}}{\text{FOV}}. \tag{2.12}$$

So

$$f' = a \cdot \frac{\beta}{1 - \beta}. \tag{2.13}$$

Hence, for calculating the focal length f', the magnification β and the standoff distance a are necessary. Using an appropriate standoff distance a, formula (2.13) provides a lens focal length. Standard lenses are available with focal lengths such as 8, 16, 25, 35, 50 mm, or greater. Thus, a selection has to be done within this range. After choosing a lens with the focal length that is closest to the calculated value, the resulting standoff distance a can be evaluated by (4.20)

$$a = f' \cdot \frac{1 - \beta}{\beta}. \tag{2.14}$$

Referring to Figure 2.4, the lens extension z' – the distance between the focal point of the lens and the sensor plane (see Section 4.2.8.2) – can be calculated as (4.24)

$$z' = a' - f' = -f' \cdot \beta. \tag{2.15}$$

In addition to the focal length, the following characteristics have to be considered.

2.3.5.2 Lens Flange Focal Distance

This is the distance between the lens mount face and the image plane. There are standardized dimensions; the most common are as follows:

Mount	Size (mm)
C-Mount	17.526
CS-Mount	12.526
Nikon F-Mount	46.5

As seen from the camera perspective, the mount size determines the shortest possible distance between the lens and the image sensor. For a CS-Mount camera any C-Mount lens can be used by inserting a 5 mm extension tube. However, a C-Mount camera cannot be used with a CS-Mount lens. F-Mount is commonly used for line scan cameras.

2.3.5.3 Extension Tubes

For a focused image, decreasing the standoff distance a between the object and the lens results in an increasing focus distance a'. The magnification is also increased. The lens extension l can be increased using the focus adjustment of the lens. If the distance cannot be increased, extension tubes can be used to focus close objects. As a result, the depth of view is decreased. For higher magnifications, such as from 0.4 to 4, macro lenses offer better image quality.

2.3.5.4 Lens Diameter and Sensor Size

Sensor sizes vary; they are categorized in sizes of 1/3 in., 1/2 in., 2/3 in., and 1 in.. The size is not a precise dimension but determines that the sensor lies within a circle of the named diameter.

In addition, for lenses a maximum sensor format is specified. The choice of lens and camera sensor must be suitable. Using a 1 in. sensor with a 2/3 in. lens results in a poorly illuminated sensor; low light and aberration will be an issue. On the other hand, using a lens that is specified for a 1 in. sensor in combination with a 2/3 in. sensor is possible (Figure 2.5).

2.3.5.5 Sensor Resolution and Lens Quality

As for high resolution cameras, the requirements on the lens are higher than those for standard cameras. Using a low-budget lens might lead to poor image quality for high-resolution sensors, whereas the quality is acceptable for lower resolutions.

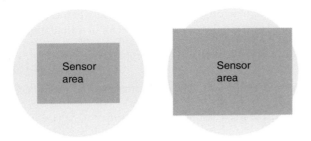

Figure 2.5 Areas illuminated by the lens and camera; the left side displays an appropriate choice.

2.3.6 Choice of Illumination

Illumination for a machine vision system is an individual selection of the optimum concept. Finding the best setup usually is a result of experiments based on a theoretical approach. This section provides an overview of the factors that can be changed and the general illumination concepts, such as back-front lighting. A detailed description of lighting can be found in Chapter 3.

2.3.6.1 Concept: Maximize Contrast

The illumination concept determines the quality of the feature signals in the image. The features need to be presented with a maximum of contrast. The challenge of illumination is to increase the signal to noise ratio, and to emphasize and expose these features to maximize the contrast.

Any effort invested in the optimum illumination concept will increase the system's inspection performance and reliability; it will also decrease the complexity of the software. What means are available to increase the contrast?

- An essential factor is the *direction* of light. It can diffuse from all directions or directed from a range of angles.
- The *light spectrum* also influences the contrast. Effects such as fluorescence or the influence of infrared or ultraviolet light should be checked as well as optical filters. For color applications, the light spectrum needs to be verified for usability; white LEDs for instance usually do not provide a homogeneous spectrum.
- *Polarization*. The effect of polarization increases the contrast between object areas that directly reflect light in comparison to diffuse reflection. Polarization will show an effect on surfaces, such as metal or glass.

2.3.6.2 Illumination Setups

The main setups in illumination are

- backlight and
- frontlight.

Backlight usually is realized in a back-illuminated panel. Common light sources are LEDs and fluorescent tubes. They are available in a wide range of sizes and intensities. This backlight can diffuse; it provides light from a wide range of angles.

A further technique is the condenser illumination; a condenser lens is used to focus the backlight in the direction of the camera. This lighting provides a telecentric path of rays and, therefore, is used for measurement tasks.

For *frontlight*, different techniques can be listed:

- *Diffused light*. This light is provided from all angles. The commonly used diffuse lights are dome lights with different diameters. They often come with an LED illumination inside the dome.
- *Directed light*. This light is provided from a range of angles. This can be ring lights or line lights.
- *Confocal frontlight*. Beam splitters make the light come from the direction of the camera's optical axis.
- *Bright field*. This is a variety of directed light. This light is supplied in a way that it is reflected by the part's surface into the camera. The surface appears bright in the image; part regions that do not reflect light appear dark.
- *Dark field*. This is another variety of directed light where the reflected light of the part is directed away from the camera. The surface then appears dark in the image; irregular part regions reflect light and appear bright.

2.3.6.3 Light Sources
Common light sources are as follows:

- *Fluorescent tubes*. These tubes are available in ring and straight forms; the ring form does not provide a continuous light ring, as the tube needs to be mounted. Essential for machine vision applications is an electrical high frequency setup. If the tube is used with a 50 Hz setup, intensity oscillation will be visible in the images.
- *Halogen and xenon lamps*. These lights run on direct-current voltage; thus, a light oscillation is not an issue. Halogen lights are often used in combination with fiber glass and different attachment caps, such as lines or rings. Xenon lamps are used for flash-light applications.
- *LED*. LED lights are becoming more and more important in machine vision. Advantages of LEDs are the use of direct-current voltage, a long life that exceeds the durability of halogen and fluorescent tubes by multiples. Due to their size, they come in smaller packaging sizes and usually do not need further electrical components. Flashing can easily be realized with LEDs; the light intensity can be increased compared to continuous operation.
- *Laser*. Laser light is used for special applications, such as triangulation.

2.3.6.4 Approach to the Optimum Setup
For finding the optimum setup, a theoretical idea is adjuvant rather than trying. Nevertheless, a confirmation of the setup based on experiments with sample parts is mandatory. Using a camera is not obligatory as for the first step; it can be replaced by the human eye. If at all a camera is required, an area scan camera is recommended due to easier handling. For finding illumination angles, it might be helpful to use a single discrete lamp and then proceed with a choice of suitable lamps.

The alignment of light, the part, and the camera needs to be documented. To balance between similar setups, images have to be captured and compared for the maximum contrast. Furthermore, a compatibility with the mechanical environment needs to be checked before proceeding.

2.3.6.5 Interfering Lighting

When inspecting a number of features, different illumination setups might be required. The influences of different lamps on the images have to be checked. To avoid interfering, a spatial separation can be achieved by using different camera stations. Then, the part is imaged with different sets of cameras and illuminations. Furthermore, a separation in time is possible; images of different cameras are taken sequentially, whereas only the lamp required for the imaging camera is switched on. Another solution is the use of different colors for the cameras. This can be achieved by colored lamps in combination with color filters for the camera that belongs to the lamp.

2.3.7 Mechanical Design

As the cameras, lenses, standoff distances, and illumination devices are determined, the mechanical conditions can be defined. As for mounting of cameras and lights the adjustment is important for installation, operation, and maintenance. The devices have to be protected against vibration or shock. In some cases a mechanical decoupling might be necessary.

The position of cameras and lights should be changed easily. However, after alignment, the devices must not be moved by operators. An easy positioning is achieved by a setup that allows the crucial degrees of freedom to be adjusted separately from each other. If the camera has to be adopted to different standoff distances, a linear stage might be easier in handling than changing the lens focus.

2.3.8 Electrical Design

For the electrical design the power supply is specified. If a certain protection class is necessary, the housing of cameras and illumination need to be adequate. The length of the cables as well as their laying, including the minimum tolerable bend radius, needs to be considered. The following table provides an overview of the specified cable lengths. Using repeaters or optical links can increase the lengths. For digital busses, such as Camera Link or IEEE 1394, the length is also dependent on the bandwidth.

System	Specified cable length (m)
Camera Link	10
IEEE 1394	4.5
Analog	up to 15

2.3.9 Software

As for software, two steps have to be performed:

- selection of a software library
- design and implementation of the application-specific software.

In most cases, not all software functions are programmed by the developer; software libraries or packages are used, which provide image-processing algorithms.

2.3.9.1 Software Library
When selecting a software library, the functionality should be considered; therefore, it is necessary to have a basic concept of the crucial algorithms in mind, which have to be used. Obviously, the software needs to be compatible with the hardware used for imaging as well as with the operating system.

Furthermore, the level of development is important. The machine vision market offers software packages that are configurable; without the need for programming, an application can be realized. Often, these packages are combined with the required hardware.

For more complex tasks, the means of changing algorithms and procedures might not be sufficient. In this case, a programmable software package provides the options to adapt the software to the application needs. The integration is more complex as more programming is involved; the software structure has to be programmed.

The highest level of programming and flexibility offers an application programming interface (API). This is a set of functions that have to be combined with an application software.

2.3.9.2 Software Structure
The software structure and the algorithms used are highly dependent on the vision task. A general guideline cannot be provided. However, for most applications, the software for the image-processing routines follows a structure as follows:

- image acquisition
- preprocessing
- feature localization
- feature extraction
- feature interpretation
- generation of results
- handling interfaces.

Obviously, the sequence starts with the acquisition of images. Certain requirements, such as triggering or addressing flash units, might have to be met.

If the image or the images are acquired, they might have to be preprocessed. Commonly used are filters, such as mean filters or shading. Shading is an important issue to overcome nonhomogeneous illumination scenes. Depending on the hardware, shading can be realized in a camera, respectively, the grabber, or in software. Preprocessing usually consumes plenty of computation time and should only be used if mandatory.

Due to the tolerances in positioning, the position of the features needs to be localized. Based on the position, regions of interest (ROIs) can be defined. In contrast to processing the entire image, ROIs offer the possibility of processing local image areas; computation time can be economically used.

Feature extraction addresses the basic algorithms to present features for an interpretation. Basic algorithms are blob analysis, texture analysis, pattern match, or edge detection – often in combination with geometric fitting.

Feature interpretation basically accomplishes the vision task – a measurement is gauged, a verification is done, and a code is read.

The generation of results is the next step. Depending on the feature interpretation, the results can be compared to tolerances; the part can be an error or an error-free part.

Handling of interfaces addresses means, such as digital-I/O, data logging, or visualization.

2.3.9.3 General Topics

The software should cover requirements for easy handling of the vision system:

- *Visualization* of live images for all cameras
- Possibility of *image saving*
- *Maintenance modus*. Camera and illumination need to be aligned, image contrast needs to be tested, and a camera calibration might be necessary. The software needs to meet these requirements for easy handling and maintenance.
- *Log files* for the system state. The system state and any error occurred while processing parts should be logged in a file for the developer. Software errors sometimes are hard to reproduce; in this case, a log file might lead to the reasons.
- Detailed *visualization* of the image processing. Subsequent processing steps should be displayed in the user interface. This provides the possibility of estimating the processing reliability and reasons for failures.
- Crucial *processing parameters*, such as thresholds, should be accessible from the user interface for a comfortable system adaption.

2.4 Costs

Before launching the project, the costs have to be evaluated. They can be classified as the initial development costs and the operating costs. The development costs consist of expenses for

- project management
- base design
- hardware components
- software licenses
- software development
- installation
- test runs, feasibility tests, and acceptance test
- training
- documentation.

If more than one system is manufactured, the costs for the subsequent systems will be less than that for the prototype; base design, software development, feasibility test, and documentation are not required.

As for the operating costs, the following factors should be considered:

- maintenance, such as cleaning of the optical equipment
- change of equipment, such as lamps
- utility, for instance, electrical power or compressed air if needed
- costs for system modification due to product changes.

2.5 Words on Project Realization

The sequence of a project realization usually is as follows:

1) specification
2) design
3) purchase of hardware and software
4) development
5) installation
6) test runs
7) acceptance test
8) Training and documentation.

Specification and design are addressed above.

2.5.1 Development and Installation

As known from experience, it is advisable to split the installation into two parts. The first part focuses on the setup of the components. As soon as they are available, the installation can be done at the designated location. Even though the software is not fully developed, this early project step is required to check for reliability and image quality

The image quality can be tested directly in the production environment. Therefore, the system needs a basic software for image grabbing, triggering, and image saving. The reliability of the system in terms of triggering and imaging can be checked. At this point, the system comes across influences that have not been or could not be specified. This might be part vibration or electrical interference.

In general, this is a fundamental step in a vision project:

- getting familiar with the imaging routine,
- getting to know the influences of the production process, and
- approving the desired image quality.

Before proceeding, problems with these factors need to be resolved. For the software development, sample images should be gathered as they are imaged with the chosen equipment.

2.5.2 Test Run and Acceptance Test

The software needs to be tested and optimized until the specifications are met. Depending on the complexity of the system, a couple of test and optimization sequences should be expected.

Due to a successful project workflow, an acceptance test states that the system works regarding the requirements.

2.5.3 Training and Documentation

Finally, a documentation and detailed training of operators are mandatory to accomplish the project. A documentation should cover the following points:

- system specification
- handling and usage of the system, and hardware and software handbook
- maintenance
- spare-part list as well as a recommendation of anticipated parts to hold on stack (i.e., lamps)
- mechanical drawings
- circuit diagram
- handbooks of the used components, that is, cameras.

2.6 Examples

Two applications, as realized by CTMV, are displayed as practical examples.

2.6.1 Diameter Inspection of Rivets

2.6.1.1 Task

In the production of floating bearings, the bearing and the shafts are riveted. Due to material and processing influences, the diameter of the rivet needs to be inspected. Every rivet has to be checked (Figure 2.6).

Figure 2.6 Bearing with rivet and disk.

2.6.1.2 Specification

- *Task and benefit.* The diameters of two similar rivets have to be inspected; the task can be categorized into a measurement application. The 100% inspection of every part has to be performed inline. The nominal size of the rivet is 3.5 mm, and the required accuracy is 0.1 mm. The inspection used to be performed manually.
- *Parts.* The nominal size of the rivets lies in a range of 3–4 mm; it is placed in front of a disk. The surface color of the disk might change due to material changes. The rivet material does not change. The bearings can be covered with an oil film.
- *Part positioning.* The positioning is indexed by the use of an automated belt. The parts are presented without overlap. The tolerance of part positioning is less than ±1 mm across the optical axis and ±0.1 mm in the direction of the optical axis. The belt stops for 1.5 s. Part vibration might be an issue. The belt control can provide a 24 V signal for triggering the cameras. There is only one part type to inspect.
- *Performance requirements.* The diameter of the rivet needs to be measured with an accuracy of 0.1 mm. The processing result has to be presented immediately. The maximum processing time is 2 s; the cycle time is 2.5 s.
- *Information interfaces.* The inspection result is passed using a 24 V signal, indicating an error part. The measurement results need to be visualized.
- *Installation space.* A direct insight into the rivet is possible. The maximum space for installing equipment is 500 mm. The distance between the cameras and the computer is 5 m. A certain protection class is not necessary.

2.6.1.3 Design

1) *Camera type.* As the part positioning is indexed and the rivet can be imaged with one frame, area cameras are used.
2) *Field of view.* Referring to Equation 2.1 the field of view is calculated as

$$\text{FOV} = \text{maximum part size} + \text{tolerance in positioning} + \text{margin} + \text{adaption to aspect ratio of camera sensor}$$

In this case, the following values are specified:

Maximum part size (mm)	4
Tolerance in positioning (mm)	1
Margin (mm)	2
Aspect ratio	4 : 3

Hence, the field of view is calculated as

$$\text{FOV}_{\text{ver}} = 4 \text{ mm} + 1 \text{ mm} + 2 \text{ mm} = 7 \text{ mm}$$

As the aspect ratio of the camera sensor is 4:3, the field of view in the horizontal direction is adapted to

$$\text{FOV}_{\text{hor}} = 7 \text{ mm} \cdot \frac{4}{3} = 9.33 \text{ mm}$$

Thus, the field of view is determined to be 9.33 mm × 7 mm.

3) *Resolution.* As the field of view and the accuracy of the measurement are known, the necessary sensor resolution can be calculated as follows (referring to (2.5)):

$$Rc = \frac{\text{FOV}}{Rs} = \text{FOV}\frac{Nf}{Sf}$$

The diameter will be measured using an edge detection and a subsequent circle fitting. Hence, the number of pixels for the smallest feature can be 1/3 pixel. Due to changing disk material the edges of the rivet can be low in contrast. Hence, the number of pixels for the smallest feature is set to 1 pixel. The size of the smallest feature is 0.1 mm.

The horizontal and vertical resolutions can be evaluated as:

$$Rc_{\text{hor}} = 7 \text{ mm} \cdot \frac{1 \text{ pixel}}{0.1 \text{ mm}} = 70 \text{ pixels}$$

$$Rc_{\text{ver}} = 9.33 \text{ mm} \cdot \frac{1 \text{ pixel}}{0.1 \text{ mm}} = 93.3 \text{ pixels}$$

4) *Choice of camera, frame grabber, and hardware platform.* Due to these values, a standard VGA camera can be chosen. As described in Section 2.3.4, the choice of camera, frame grabber, and hardware platform are dependent on each other and basically done within one step. As a hardware platform, a National Instruments Compact Vision System NI CVS 1454 is chosen, since it combines an embedded high-performance processor, direct IEEE 1394 connection, TCP/IP interface, and the use of a powerful software library. For visualization, a computer monitor can be connected. As for the camera, an AVT Marlin F-033B IEEE 1394 CCD camera is used. It provides a camera resolution of 656 × 494 pixels. The choices of IEEE 1394 and the compact vision system save costs for a frame grabber and additional hardware.

5) *Lens design.* As a precise mass is to be measured and the part moves in the direction of the optical axis, a telecentric lens is chosen. For choosing a telecentric lens, the key factors are field of view and magnification rather than the focal length. The field of view was determined to be 9.33 mm. Hence, a lens with a field of view of 10.7 mm was chosen. The standoff distance is specified to be 100 mm.

Thus, the spatial resolution is

$$Rs = \frac{\text{FOV}}{Rc} = \frac{10.7 \text{ mm}}{656 \text{ pixels}} = 0.016 \frac{\text{mm}}{\text{pixel}}.$$

6) *Choice of illumination.* The rivet has a convex shape, as depicted in Figure 2.7. To illuminate the outer edges of the shape, a dome is chosen as diffuse frontlight. The setup of a camera, its illumination, and the part are displayed in

Figure 2.7 Bearing, rivet, and disk in lateral view.

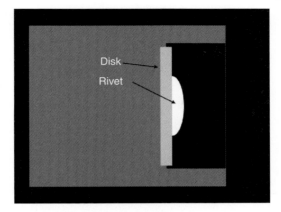

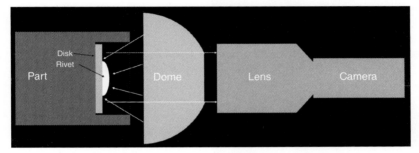

Figure 2.8 Setup of part, illumination, and camera.

Figure 2.8. Regarding the longevity, an LED illumination was preferred. As depicted in Figure 2.8, the diameter needs to have a certain size to illuminate the rivet properly. A dome was chosen with a diameter of 100 mm.

7) *Mechanical design.* For the mechanical design, no particularities have to be considered. The cameras and light domes are mounted on aluminum profiles for easy adjustment.
8) *Electrical design.* As power supply, only 24 V is necessary for the compact vision system and the illumination. The cameras are supplied via the IEEE 1394 connection.
9) *Software.* For the software library, National Instruments LabVIEW, and Imaq Vision are chosen as they provide a powerful image-processing functionality and short implementation efforts.

As mentioned in Section 2.3.9, the software is structured in

- image acquisition
- preprocessing
- feature localization
- feature extraction
- feature interpretation
- generation of results
- handling interfaces.

Figure 2.9 Rivet and disk as imaged by the system.

Figure 2.10 Feature localization by thresholding and blob analysis.

The image acquisition is done by a simultaneous external triggering of the cameras. No preprocessing is used.

Figure 2.9 shows the rivet as depicted by the system.

The feature localization is done by thresholding the image for a blob analysis. Figure 2.10 displays the thresholded image. The center of the greatest blob is used as a feature center position.

For the feature extraction, a circular edge detection and circle fitting are performed as displayed in Figure 2.11.

The feature interpretation and generation of results are performed by comparing the diameter to the defined tolerances. Depending on the result, a digital output is set.

The user interface is designed to display the images of both cameras. Furthermore, the processing results, such as feature localization and interpretation, are displayed (Figure 2.12).

Figure 2.11 Circular edge detection and subsequent circle fitting.

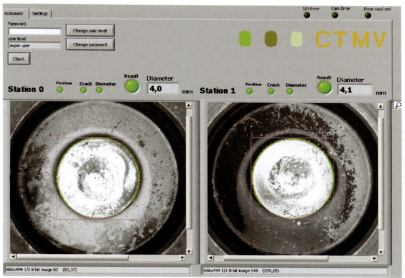

Figure 2.12 User interface for the rivet inspection.

2.6.2 Tubing Inspection

2.6.2.1 Task

While producing tubings for sophisticated applications, defects such as particles and material drops, can be a quality issue. A vision system for an inline tubing inspection was realized by CTMV.

2.6.2.2 Specification
- *Task and benefit.* As mentioned above, an inline inspection for the named defects has to be realized. The smallest defect that has to be detected has a size of 0.08 mm. The defects are classified into different classes regarding

defect type and size. For each class, tolerances can be defined as for the size and frequency of occurrence. For instance, particles are tolerable if their size is between 0.1 and 0.2 mm and not more than 5 defects per 1 m of tube are detected.

An inspection protocol is necessary, which displays the defects, their ongoing meter from the inspection start, size, and image. Additionally, these data have to be provided for an online access from remote computers over the TCP/IP protocol. The inspection is performed manually.

- *Parts.* The tube diameter varies between 5 and 32 mm. The tubes are transparent. A diameter change can be addressed to the system. The tube's surface is free of dirt or adhesives; color changes are not expected.
- *Part positioning.* The tubes are produced in a horizontal movement with a maximum speed of $3\,\text{m}\,\text{min}^{-1}$. The position tolerance in the cross direction is 0.5 mm.
- *Performance requirements.* The smallest defect size that has to be detected is 0.08 mm. The processing time is defined as a function of processing speed. An image needs to be processed before the next acquisition is accomplished.
- *Information interfaces.* As mentioned above, a user interface for controlling and setting the tube diameter, an inspection protocol for printout and storage, and an online access to the defect data over a TCP/IP connection is required.
- *Installation space.* A direct insight into the tube is possible. The maximum distance from the tube center is 400 mm. In the direction of movement, a distance of 700 mm can be used for the system. The distance between the cameras and the computer is 3 m. The components should be covered from dripping water.

2.6.2.3 Design

1) *Camera type.* As the tube is moving and a rather high resolution will be mandatory, a line scan setup is preferred. To cover 360° of the perimeter, at least six cameras have to be used. At this point, a cost calculation of six line scan cameras, an adequate number of frame grabbers, and processing hardware are displayed; the costs exceed the budget.
   Hence, area cameras have to be used. For acquiring single frames, camera triggering, and merging of defects, which are partly visible in two or more images, will be an issue.
2) *Field of view.* When using six cameras, each camera needs to cover a field of view of the radius' size, as depicted in Figure 2.13.
   The maximum diameter is specified to be 32 mm and the radius to be 16 mm. The positioning tolerance is less than 0.5 mm. Hence, the required field of view for one camera can be calculated as

$$FOV = \text{maximum part size} + \text{tolerance in positioning} + \text{margin}$$
$$+ \text{adaption to aspect ratio of camera sensor}$$

$$FOV_{hor} = 16\,\text{mm} + 0.5\,\text{mm} + 1\,\text{mm} = 17.5\,\text{mm}$$

Figure 2.13 Required field of view when using six cameras.

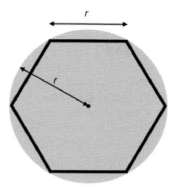

Figure 2.14 Positioning of the camera.

Using an area camera with a sensor ratio of $4:3$, the vertical field of view is determined as

$$\text{FOV}_{\text{vert}} = \text{FOV}_{\text{hor}} \cdot \frac{3}{4} = 17.5 \text{ mm} \cdot \frac{3}{4} = 13.125 \text{ mm}$$

Hence, the field of view is calculated to be 17.5 mm × 13.125 mm. The camera is mounted as depicted in Figure 2.14.

3) *Resolution.* The size of the smallest defect is defined as 0.08 mm. As the processing routine will be based on blob analysis, at least three pixels should be used to map the smallest defect. Hence, a spatial resolution of 0.027 mm per pixel is required.

With the field of view, the camera resolution can be calculated to be

$$Rc = \frac{\text{FOV}}{Rs} = \frac{17.5 \text{ mm}}{0.027 \text{ mm/ pixel}} = 656 \text{ pixels}$$

4) *Choice of camera, frame grabber, and hardware platform.* Due to these values, a standard VGA camera can be chosen. A camera interface technique, IEEE 1394, is chosen due to an easy integration and low costs in comparison to systems such as Camera Link. The choice is made for a Basler 601f CMOS camera with a sensor resolution of 656 × 491 pixels.

Using 656 pixels to map the 17.5 mm FOV, the resulting spatial resolution is

$$Rs = \frac{\text{FOV}}{Rc} = \frac{17.5 \text{ mm}}{656 \text{ pixels}} = 0.027 \text{ mm/ pixel}$$

The smallest defect of 0.08 mm then is mapped with three pixels.

A 19 in. Windows XP-based computer is used as hardware platform. The cameras are connected to two National Instruments PCI-8254R boards with a reconfigurable I/O and IEEE 1394 connectivity.

5) *Lens design.* The maximum distance from the tube center is defined as 400 mm. The magnification can be calculated as

$$\beta = -\frac{\text{sensor size}}{\text{FOV}} = -\frac{6.49 \text{ mm}}{17.5 \text{ mm}} = -0.371.$$

The sensor size results from the multiplication of the cell size of 9.9 μm per pixel and the sensor resolution of 656 pixels.

Using the magnification and the maximum distance from the tube center of 400 mm subtracted by a value of 200 mm for the camera and lens, the focal length can be calculated as

$$f' = a \cdot \frac{\beta}{1-\beta} = 200 \text{ mm} \frac{0.371}{1+0.371} = 54.1 \text{ mm}$$

The choice is made for a 50 mm lens.

The resulting standoff distance d is

$$a = f' \cdot \frac{1-\beta}{\beta} = 50 \text{ mm} \cdot \frac{1+0.371}{-0.371} = -184.8 \text{ mm}$$

As referred to (2.15), the lens extension l can be evaluated to

$$l = a' - f' = -f \cdot \beta = 50 \text{ mm} \cdot 0.371 = 18.55 \text{ mm}$$

As this distance cannot be realized by focus adjustment, an extension tube of 15 mm is used.

6) *Choice of illumination.* As the tube is translucent, a diffuse backlight is used. Defects appear dark then. As the shutter time needs to be set to a low value, high intensities are required. The time the tube takes to move a distance of 1 pixel in the image is calculated as

$$t = \frac{Rs}{v}$$

where v is the speed (3 m min^{-1} = 50 mm s^{-1}) and Rs is the spatial resolution scan direction.

Hence

$$t = \frac{0.027 \text{ mm per pixel}}{50 \text{ mm s}^{-1}} = 540 \text{ μs}$$

The choice is made for a high power LED backlight with a size of 50 mm × 50 mm. Due to the intensity, a flash operation is not necessary.

7) *Mechanical design.* For the mechanical design, the mounting of the cameras and lights needs to be considered. Since different illuminations could interfere with each other, the sets of camera and light are positioned in a row. The setup for one camera is depicted in Figure 2.15. As the equipment has to be covered from dripping water, the lights and cameras are mounted in housings, and so is the computer.

8) *Electrical design.* The cable length is below 4.5 m and within the IEEE 1394 specification.

9) *Software.* For the software library, a CTMV software package was programmed using Microsoft Visual C#. For image acquisition the API of National Instruments Imaq for IEEE 1394 was chosen.

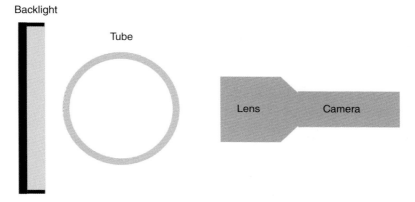

Figure 2.15 Lateral view of one set of camera and light.

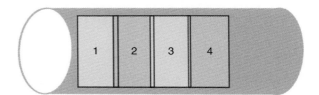

Figure 2.16 Frames, as captured by one camera.

For *image acquisition*, the cameras have to be triggered to capture the frames with a defined overlap of 2 mm. Figure 2.16 displays four subsequent frames as imaged by one camera.

For triggering, a rotary encoder is used, which indicates the tube movement (Figure 2.17). The encoder signals are connected to a specially designed input of the frame grabber. Using an FPGA counter, the trigger signal is created by a card and set to the camera. The application software on the host computer does not handle the triggering; it is done by the FPGA. This saves computation time and guarantees high reliability of the triggering process.

Since the tubes are curved, a homogeneous light uniformity in the image is not present. Figure 2.18 displays an image of a tube. To achieve uniformity for the latter inspection, a shading is used. The teach-in is done at the start of the inspection; the reference is a mean computation of several images.

The feature localization and segmentation is done by thresholding. Since shading is used, an adaption of the threshold for different tubes is not mandatory.

Figure 2.17 Generating trigger signals using a rotary encoder.

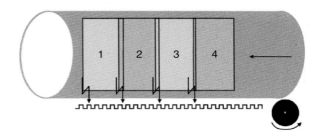

Figure 2.18 Tube, as imaged by the system.

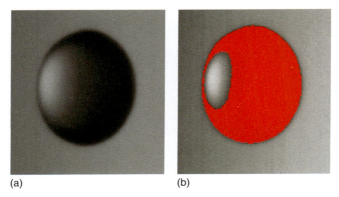

Figure 2.19 (a) Defect as imaged. (b) Defect as thresholded by the system.

Figure 2.19a,b displays a defect in the original image and as segmented by thresholding.

After segmentation, feature interpretation is done by blob analysis. Every blob is measured in height, width, and area. Furthermore, it is classified into the defect classes, such as particles and drops. For measurement, it has to be

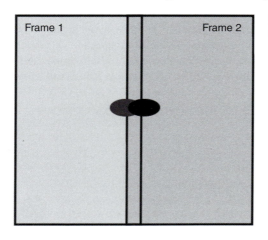

Figure 2.20 Merging defects, which are partly visible in two frames.

checked whether the defect is visible in more than one frame and, therefore, has to be merged due to a correct measurement. Figure 2.20 displays the situation.

After measurement and classification, the defect is added to the appropriate defect class. If the number of tolerated defects exceeds the defined tolerance, an error signal is set.

Furthermore, an entry in the defect logging database including width, height, and an image of the defect is performed.

3

Lighting in Machine Vision
Irmgard Jahr

Vision & Control GmbH, Mittelbergstraße 16, D-98527 Suhl, Germany

3.1 Introduction

3.1.1 Prologue

One simple part and a hand full of lighting techniques (e.g., Figures 3.1 and 3.2). And everyone looks different. However, there still remain many questions, some of which are

- What do you prefer to see?
- What shall the vision system see?
- What do you need to see? What does the vision system need to see?
- How do you emphasize this? How does the vision system emphasize this?
- Where are the limits?
- Does it work stable in practice?
- What are the components used?
- What light sources are in use?
- What are their advantages and disadvantages?

Questions over questions. But on the first view everything seemed to be very simple: it is all only made by light, basically caused by the presence of light. But many people do not know how to do that. For them light is a closed book.

The reader's mission is to learn, how to illuminate, that some features appear dark and others bright. But everything as desired (see Figure 3.3)!

The aim of this chapter is to teach the reader to recognize, for example, why the background is dark, why the lettering is dark or how can I avoid from hot spots. They shall understand how light works.

3.1.2 The Involvement of Lighting in the Complex Machine Vision Solution

In the beginning there was light.

Not only from a historical view, but also from the view of Machine Vision People, this is one of the most important proverbs. Let us consider this: photography means *writing with light*. And one can consider Machine Vision as an (extended) contemporary further development of photography. So, the light is the base of

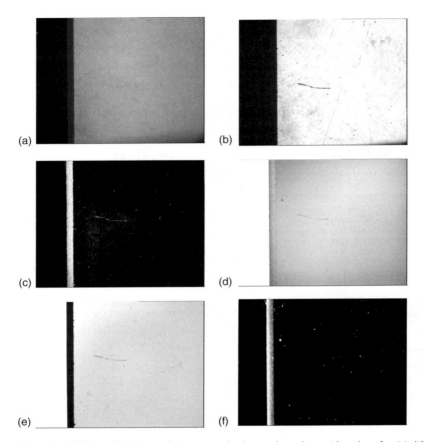

Figure 3.1 Different lighting techniques applied on a glass plate with a chamfer: (a) diffuse incident bright field lighting, (b) telecentric incident bright field lighting, (c) directed incident dark field lighting, (d) diffuse transmitted bright field lighting, (e) telecentric transmitted bright field, lighting, (f) directed transmitted dark field lighting.

Figure 3.2 Glass plate with a chamfer in the familiar view of the human eye.

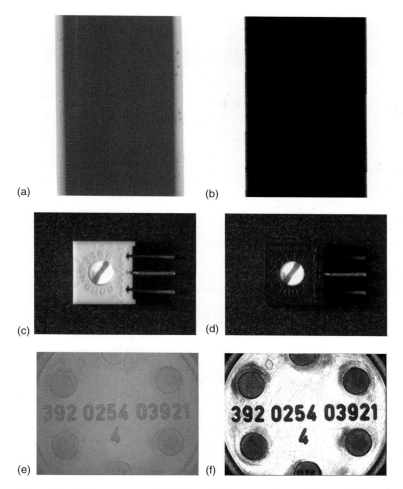

Figure 3.3 Different parts under different lighting conditions. (a) Metal bolt with diffuse backlight, (b) metal bolt with telecentric backlight, (c) blue potentiometer under blue light, (d) blue potentiometer under yellow light, (e) cap with diffuse lighting, (f) cap with directed lighting.

Machine Vision. It does not only mean *writing with light*, but also *working with light* as their information carrier.

You may ask: why the light? A vision system consists of much more parts than a *lamp*! True, but all information that is processed comes from the light. The light information is the origin. The lighting is as important as the optics, because it carries the primary information. To do image processing mathematically, the brightness values of the object and the background have to differ. Contrast, brightness and darkness, shadows, textures, reflexes, and streaks are necessary. And all this is done by light. That is why the experts know that two-third of a robust Machine Vision solution is lighting.

Let me express in this way: garbage in – garbage out. Where none takes care of the lighting design, none should be surprised about worse results delivered by

3 Lighting in Machine Vision

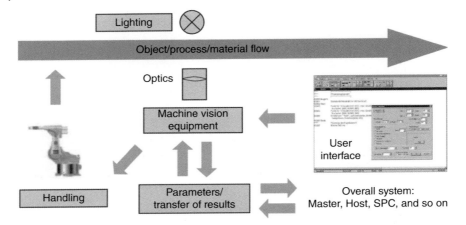

Figure 3.4 Basic structure of a Machine Vision solution and main parts of a vision system.

the vision system. No brightness and contrast – no algorithm will find the edges. What are a few hours to plan the lighting solution and a few hundreds of dollars for a professional lighting against a few man-weeks of software engineering to save the consequences of bad lighting. And after that there still remains a lot of unsteadiness.

To systematically search for a matching lighting saves real money, time, and nerves!

Knowing the main parts of a vision system, one fact is obvious: Machine Vision is a complex teamwork of totally different technical disciplines that are involved (see Figure 3.4). And depending on the discipline you are qualified in the sight can be a totally different one. If you are right in the middle, the view for the entirety can be lost. The same applies to Machine Vision. It is a synthesis technology, consisting of

- lighting
- optics
- hardware (electronics/photonics)
- software engineering.

These are the core disciplines. But Machine Vision is always embedded in

- automation
- mechanical engineering
- connected with the information technology
- electrical engineering.

In this delicate mixture the lighting is the key. However, on the other hand, to find one lighting solution we cannot divide the lighting from the rest of the vision system. All parts are in interaction (see Figure 3.5). If you change something in the lighting design, other parameters of the vision system also change. There are many feedbacks. The lighting determines other parts of the vision system (optics, sensor, hardware, software).

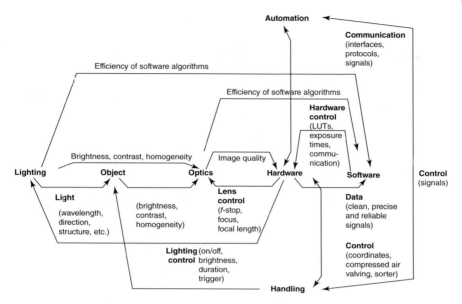

Figure 3.5 Some interactions of the components of a Machine Vision system (selection, not complete).

The intention of this chapter is to give you an approach to solve lighting problems. It was made with the view to the practical everyday life in the factory floor of Machine Vision.

3.2 Demands on Machine Vision lighting

A Machine Vision lighting for industrial applications is not only a *lamp* but also more than only a cluster of LEDs. Against the expectations of an uninitiated user there are a few important aspects to pay attention to (see Figure 3.6) [24].

State-of-the-art Machine Vision illumination components for industrial use are complex technical systems consisting of

- light sources
- mechanical adjustment elements
- light guiding optical elements
- stabilizing, controlling, and interface electronics
- if necessary, software (firmware)
- stable and mountable housing
- robust cabling.

All these features are necessary to form a device that resists the adverse environmental conditions of the industrial floor.

The demands of industrial lighting components are manifold. Partly they are opposing and challenge the developers. Not all criteria are always necessary:

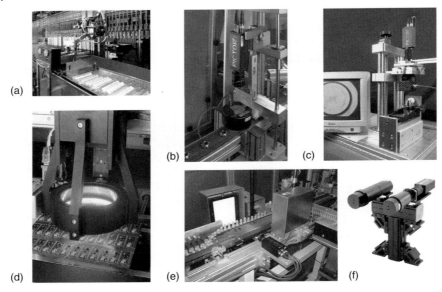

Figure 3.6 Examples for the variance of Machine Vision lighting. (a) Illumination of the calibration process for medical thermometers. Demands: robustness, brightness, homogeneity, and protection against vibrations and splashes of water. (b) Illumination of mechanical parts, running on a dirty and dark conveyor belt. Demands: robustness, tough mounting points, brightness, protection against dust, protection against voltage peaks. (c) Precise illumination for measurement of milled parts. Demands: obvious mounting areas for adjustment, brightness, homogeneity. (d) Lighting stack of a free adaptable combination of red and IR light in an automat for circuit board inspection. Demands: brightness control of different parts of the illuminations using standard interfaces, brightness, shock and vibration protection. (e) Lighting plates for inspection in the food industry. Demands: homogeneity, wide range voltage input, defined temperature management. (f) Telecentric lighting and optics' components for highly precise measurements of optically unfavorable (shiny) parts. Demands: stable assembly with option to adjust, homogeneity, stabilization, possibility to flash. (www.vision-control.com).

Demands of optical features:

- wavelength (light color):
  - defined and constant distribution, especially for color image processing
  - no (low) aging
  - no (low) drift caused by temperature
  - no differences from device to device
- brightness:
  - defined and constant
  - no (low) aging
  - no (low) drift caused by temperature
  - no differences from device to device
- homogenous or defined, known and repeatable brightness profile
- only one component for static, pulsed and flash light
- possibility of flashing independent of the illumination wavelength

- bright and powerful, but not dangerous (lasers and in some cases LEDs can also cause damages to the human eye retina).

Demands of electrical features:

- operation with no dangerous low voltage
- wide range voltage input with stabilization for typical industrial voltages between 10 and 30 V DC
- protection against wrong connection
- different controlling/operation modes (static, pulsed, flash, programmable)
- process interfacing: standard interfaces such as PLC inputs/outputs, data interfaces with USB or Ethernet (if necessary).
- simple storage and adjustment of operating parameters (see Figure 3.7)
- all controlling circuitry included in the housing
- temperature management to avoid overheating
- flexible and tough cables for operation in robotics with a high resistance against bending stress.

Demands of mechanical features:

- mechanically robust, packed in black anodized aluminum housing or industrial polyamide
- diverse and solid mounting points for a firm fixing and adjustment (see Figure 3.8)
- protection of all elements against vibrations and strong acceleration (lighting in robotics can be stressed up to 10 g or >100 m s^{-2})!
- dust and splash water protection.

Above all stands, the demand for an easy and fast installation without additional components, such as mechanical adaptors or holders, electrical convertors, or boxes. Further, the compliance with national and international standards such as CE, IP, radiation protection degree, and so forth is needed [25].

Figure 3.7 Elements to adjust lighting characteristics (brightness and flash duration) on a telecentric backlight directly on the lighting component. All electronics are included. (www.vision-control.com.)

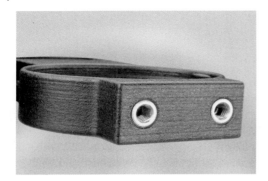

Figure 3.8 Robust mounting threads for a tough fixing and adjustment. (www.vision-control.com.)

Industrial users usually accept a 10 000 h (longer than a year) minimum life and operation time of the light sources. Only this is the base for short downtimes and low maintenance. This fact often limits the choice of a matching lighting component.

It is expected from the users that standard components are in use. This is meant not only for the light source but also for the complete lighting. These components should be – if sometimes necessary – replaced very fast. A supplier with an ISO9001:2000 certificate and a wide distributor network can guarantee a fast spare part delivery even after many years.

3.3 Light used in Machine Vision

3.3.1 What is Light? Axioms of Light

Light as the information carrier of all visual information and Machine Vision is based on electromagnetic waves. Light means a limited sector of the electromagnetic spectrum. The range of light waves extends from wavelengths of 15 nm to 1 mm (see Table 3.1). It can be divided into three general ranges:

UV (ultraviolet light):   From 15 nm to 380 nm

VIS (visible light):   From 380 nm to 780 nm

IR (infrared light):   From 780 nm to 1 mm

At the lower limit it is related to the X-rays and at the upper limit it is related to the microwaves. Most Machine Vision applications use the range of VIS and the near IR. Some applications extend the use of light to the near UV. But this needs special image sensors.

The range of visible light that is accessible to man contains the whole spectra of colors from blue to red. A more or less mixture of all colors (with changing quantities) appears as white to the human eye.

It is a philosophical question what light is – waves or particles? Using the property of waves it can be handled with the theory of electrical engineering. The physical optics accomplishes it. This allows us to explain the effects of diffraction, polarization, and interference.

Table 3.1 The spectrum of light according to DIN 5031 [28].

		Range	Wavelength λ (nm)	Frequency f (Hz)
UV	UV-C	VUV/vacuum UV	100–200	3×10^{15}
		FUV/far UV	200–280	
	UV-B	Middle UV	280–315	
	UV-A	Near UV	315–380	7.9×10^{14}
VIS		Violet	380–424	7.9×10^{14}
		Blue	424–486	
		Blue green	486–517	
		Green	517–527	
		Yellow green	527–575	
		Yellow	575–585	
		Orange	585–647	
		Red	647–780	3.85×10^{14}
IR	IR-A	NIR/near IR	780–1400	
	IR-B		1400–3000	
	IR-C	MIR/middle IR	3000–50 000	
		FIR/far IR	50 000–1 000 000	3.0×10^{11}

Using the property of particles, the photons act as carriers of energy. To illustrate the energy of photons, it is mentioned that a laser of 1 mW power emits approximately 10^{16} photons s^{-1}.

The direction of propagation of the photons (this is the direction of the normals of the wave fronts too) is symbolized by the *light rays* that use the geometrical optics. Single light rays practically do not occur. That is why usually it is spoken of as light ray bundles. The ray model is a clear and simple one for the explanation of lighting in Machine Vision.

Light is always in the form of both wave and particle. This is expressed as the so-called *wave–particle dualism*. Depending on the effect that is to be Explained, the property of wave or particle can be used.

To explain the effects of lighting and optics, some axioms (established hypothesises) for the light are made:

- light is an electromagnetic wave (with an electric and a magnetic component)
- light propagates in straight lines in homogenous and isotrope media
- there is no interaction between light of different light sources
- refraction and reflection occur at boundaries
- the velocity of propagation is dependent on the crossed medium
- the propagation velocity of light is $c = \lambda \cdot f$ with λ being the wavelength and f the frequency of light.

The velocity of light propagation depends on the medium, where the light passes through. The *absolute speed* of 299 792 km s^{-1} reaches the light only in the vacuum. In all other medium light propagates more slowly. This should

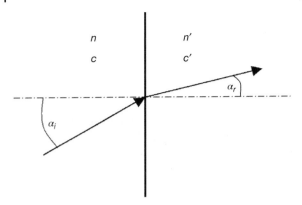

Figure 3.9 Refraction: refractive indices, angles, and velocities.

be considered when other materials are inserted in the optical path. Changed distances are the consequence. The propagation velocity is connected with the refraction law of the optics (see Figure 3.9):

$$n \sin \alpha_i = n' \sin \alpha_r$$

and

$$\frac{\sin \alpha_i}{\sin \alpha_r} = \frac{c_0}{c'}$$

where

n, n' is the refraction index of the medium,
n_0 is the refraction index in the vacuum = 1,
c, c' is the velocity of light in the medium,
c_0 is the velocity of light in the vacuum,
α_i is the entrance angle,
α_r is the exit angle.

According to $n = c_0/c$, Table 3.2 of refraction indices and velocity speeds can be made.

Table 3.2 Typical refraction indices of optical materials and accompanying light propagation velocity.

Refraction index n	Velocity c (km s^{-1})
1.0	299 792
1.3	230 609
1.5	199 861
1.7	176 348
1.9	157 785

3.3.2 Light and Light Perception

For simplification, the following viewings disregard that the imaging objective influences the spectral composition of the passing light to the image sensor. Each objective has its specific spectral transmission that changes the composition of light (see Chapter 4).

Starting from the spectral perception of light, solid state image sensor materials of Machine Vision cameras and the human eye have different perceptions of light. The spectral response of the human eye covers the range of light between 380 and 780 nm and is described by the so-called $V(\lambda)$ curve (for daylight perception). This curve is the base for the calculation of all photometric units such as luminous intensity, luminous flux, and so forth (see Section 3.5).

The light perception of Machine Vision cameras differs from that of the human eye. In most cases, Machine Vision uses light with wavelengths between 380 and 1100 nm (from blue light to near infrared). This is caused by the reception and spectral response of the imagers. The precise dependence is caused by the donation of the solid state material of the imager. The data sheet of the image sensor used in the camera informs about this.

A solid state imager with a sensitivity as shown in Figure 3.10 can only output a weighted brightness information per pixel. One single pixel is not able to determine colors.

To interpret and determine colors, it is necessary to combine the information of three (or four) pixels with different color perceptions. Red, green, and blue (RGB) or the complementary colors cyan yellow and magenta are typical triples to determine the color values.

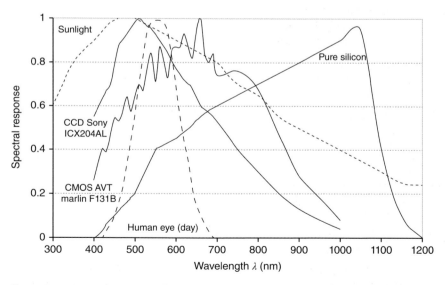

Figure 3.10 Spectral response of the human eye, typical monochrome CCD image sensor (Sony ICX204AL), typical monochrome CMOS image sensor (camera AVT Marlin F131B). For demonstration, the spectral emission of the sun is also presented.

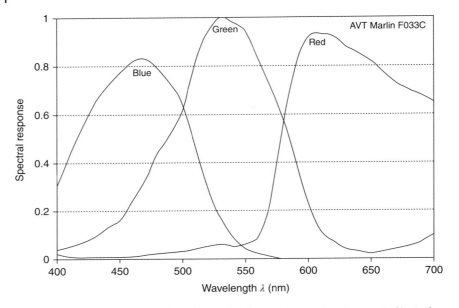

Figure 3.11 Spectral response of the three color channels (caused by the mosaic filter) of a typical one-chip-color CCD image sensor (camera AVT Marlin F033C).

In practice, this is realized with micro-optical mosaic filters for single chip color cameras (see Figure 3.11). These color filters cover the single pixels inside the image sensor with a special pattern (e.g., the Bayer pattern) and make them spectrally sensitive (one-chip-color camera).

Another construction uses three separate sensors. Each sensor is made sensitive for only one color (RGB). The information of all three sensors is correlated and delivers the color information (3-CCD-cameras).

The brightness perception of the sensor is one side. The other side is the spectral supply that the light sources emit. Figure 3.12 shows typical spectral supply of different LEDs.

The interaction between lighting and receiver means that only a useful coordination of the light source and the sensor gives the base for a contrastful image with a large gray level difference. This makes sure that the following components in the signal chain of the vision system can operate optimally and work reliably in the machine.

The following example shows the brightness perception of a CCD imager combined with different typical colored LED light sources (see Figure 3.12). The approximation of a Gaussian spectral light distribution is only valid for single-colored LEDs. For white LEDs there is no simple approximation.

The power of light sources is usually given in data sheets by their luminous intensity/radiant intensity. In simplification, it represents the area below the relevant curve, multiplied with a constant, that represents the power of the light source without considering the sensitivity of the sensor. It is pointed out that the brightness reception of the sensor and the human eye is different (see Figure 3.10).

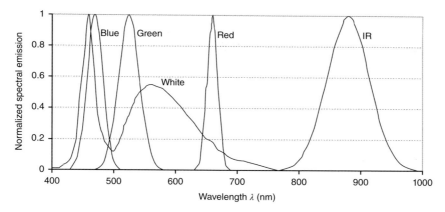

Figure 3.12 Normalized light emission of different colored LEDs.

The result of the evaluation of the brightness by the CCD imager (sensitivity see Figure 3.10) is obtained by some calculations and conversions in [1] and appears as in Table 3.3.

It is realized that a difference occurs between the catalog values of luminous intensity (made for the human eye)/radiant intensity and the evaluated radiation by the sensor.

The red LED produces the largest gray value on a CCD sensor, although the luminous intensity (for the human eye) is not the greatest.

On the other hand, the white LED with the largest luminous intensity of 5100 mcd produces only a medium gray value. This is caused by the difference of the value of luminous intensity with the evaluation of the $V(\lambda)$ curve of the human eye and the perception by a CCD sensor.

Even the infrared LED with its low sensor relevant radiant intensity produces a considerable gray value due to its wide half-width wavelength.

Table 3.3 Brightness perception of typical colored 5 mm LEDs.

	Values from catalog				Measured gray values
LED color	Luminous radiant intensity (values from data sheet)	Peak wave length λ_p (nm) (see Figure 3.12)	Half width wavelength radiant intensity $\Delta\lambda_{1/2}$ (nm)	Calculated sensor relevant I_{CCD} (mW sr^{-1}) from the CCD sensor	
Blue	$I_v = 760$ mcd	470	30	10.2	232
Green	$I_v = 2400$ mcd	525	40	4.77	129
Red	$I_v = 2700$ mcd	660	20	33.5	378
White	$I_v = 5100$ mcd	$x = 0.31$, $y = 0.32$		13.8	246
IR	$I_e = 25$ mW sr^{-1}	880	80	3.3	120

Transformation of the catalog data into sensor relevant values.

These considerations must be made for each sensor – LED combination for finding a new effective way to illuminate most brightness. However, still a few more interactions of light and test object influence the choice of lighting component.

3.3.3 Light Sources for Machine Vision

The basic element of lighting components are the light sources. The built-in light source influences very much the whole lighting setup.

A practical classification of light sources can be made based on the kind of conversion of light. Only these kinds of light sources that are typical for use in Machine Vision are mentioned in this publication.

a) Temperature radiators

The incandescent emission of these radiators (lamps) produces a mixture of wavelengths and continuous spectrum. The efficiency for a solid state imager is low, because only a part of the emitted spectrum is used. Temperature radiators need a high operation temperature, the higher they are the more effective (T^4) and whiter they radiate. The radiation maximum shifts to shorter wavelength if it is hot (*Wien's shifting law*). These radiators provide a simple mode of operation.

b) Luminescence radiators

These are LEDs, lasers. They emit light in a selective and limited spectral band. The efficiency is high (with a adapted receiver) due to the selective emission. At low temperatures, these light sources work most efficiently. Some of them have complex modes of operation.

Concerning the converted light power all light sources are comparable by their efficiency, their light output. The theoretical maximum is 683 lumen per Watt from monochromatic green light (555 nm). For white light, the theoretical maximum is 225 lm W^{-1}. The efficiency of real light sources is shown in Table 3.4.

Within the next few years, it is targeted to increase the luminous efficiency of colored LEDs to 300 lm W^{-1}. Thus, the LED will be the most efficient light source known.

Table 3.4 Real light sources and their *luminous efficiency* (as of the 2003) [2].

Lamp type	Luminous efficiency (lm W^{-1})
Na-vapor lamp	To 200
Metal halide lamps	To 100
Xenon lamps	To 60
Fluorescent lamps	40–100
Halogen lamps	To 35
Incandescent lamps	10–20
Colored LED	To 55 (red-range)
White LED	To 25

3.3.3.1 Incandescent Lamps/Halogen Lamps

These lamps in their classical form use tungsten filament for the incandescent emission. The wide band emission of radiation (from UV to IR, see Figure 3.13) causes that only about 7% of the energy are converted into visible light. The consequence is bad efficiency.

To achieve a high luminous flux, the filament must be as hot as possible, that is, must be driven with a higher voltage than recommendable. But heat is a contraproductive factor for the lifetime of an incandescent lamp. So, they always work in the compromise between intensity and lifetime. The dependences of a typical halogen lamp [4] are as follows:

$$\text{lifetime}: \quad t = t_0(U/U_0)^{-1.2}$$
$$\text{luminous flux}: \quad \Phi = \Phi_0(U/U_0)^{3.2}$$
$$\text{color temperature}: \quad T = T_0(U/U_0)^{0.37}$$

with

- t_0 being the rated lifetime,
- L_0 the rated luminous flux,
- T_0 the rated color temperature,
- U_0 the rated voltage,
- U the operating voltage.

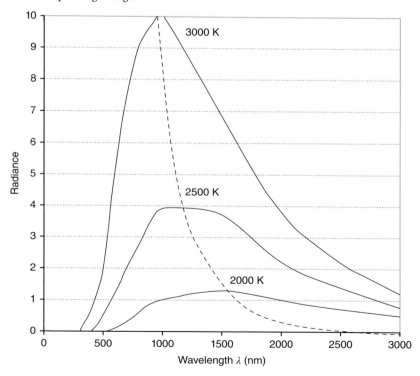

Figure 3.13 Wavelength composition of emitted light in dependence of the temperature of the radiator (radiance over wavelength) [3].

The exponential dependence of the luminous flux makes clear that halogen light sources can only be driven with a stabilized power supply. Unstabilized voltage sources pass through an increased change of the luminous flux.

Halogen lamps have filled the lamp bulb with halogen gas. This takes care of a limited darkening process along the lifetime and also doubles the luminance. The tungsten vapor during the emission again settles at the filament and not at the glass bulb. But the halogen cycle works only between 70% and 105% of the rated voltage. Halogen lamps are usually built in cold light sources. To improve the light output, these lamps are equipped with a cold mirror on the backside to reflect the visible light to the fiber bundle coupling. The IR radiation passes the cold light mirror backward.

Advantages

- bright light sources
- continuous spectrum (VIS: white light with color temperature 3000–3400 K)
- operation with low voltage
- works in hot environment too (up to 300°C).

Disadvantages

- typical lifetimes: 300–2000 h (very short!)
- high-power halogen lamps have much shorter lifetimes
- large fall off in brightness (drift)
- sensitivity to vibration
- delay on switching on and off makes it applicable only for statical light
- operating voltage fluctuations are directly passed through to brightness changes – need of a powerful stabilization
- in some cases, protection measures are necessary – depending on the glass bulb (quartz glass or hard glass) UV light is emitted (with quartz glass)
- large and heavy when built in a tough casing
- needs additional fiber optics to form the light (~40% loss of light output (incoupling, transfer of light))
- produces much heat.

Considerations for Machine Vision

- useful for color applications, good color rendering
- does not meet industrial demands for a lighting

3.3.3.2 Metal Vapor Lamps

These kinds of gas discharging lamps work very efficiently with a high yield of light. The metal vapor inside is used to produce a vapor pressure that is necessary for the gas discharge.

The application in Machine Vision is also rare because of the large amount of heat that is to lead away. Metal vapor lamps are usually built in cold light sources.

Advantages

- very bright
- cold light (high color temperature).

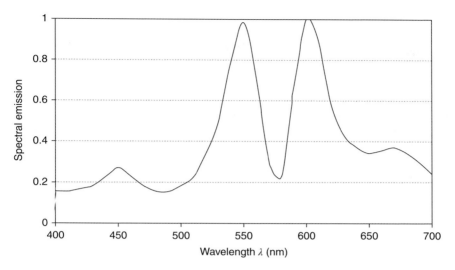

Figure 3.14 Spectral emission of a metal vapor lamp.

Disadvantages

- lifetime limited, approximately 10 000 h
- brightness adaptation only optically feasible
- working with high voltage up to 30 kV – protective measures are necessary
- lamp bulbs are under high pressure
- UV quantity in the spectra
- single spectral bands used (see Figure 3.14) can cause problems for color rendering
- very expensive
- limited temperature range (typically 10–40 °C)
- produces heat
- warm running necessary.

Considerations for Machine Vision

- seldom used
- restricted suitability for industrial applications.

3.3.3.3 Xenon Lamps

These discharging lamps are available in both, for continuous and flash operation. Xenon flash lamp generators are preferred for Machine Vision. They are usually for the illumination of fast running processes because of their high intensity. To *freeze* motion they are able to produce very short flashes with up to 250 000 cd intensity that can still be seen in a 20 km distance.

The wavelength spectrum covers a range from below 150 nm to greater than 6 μm (see Figure 3.15). Xenon flash lamps provide an almost continuous spectrum of wave lengths in the visible region. This leads to a balanced white light that makes additional color balancing filters generally not necessary.

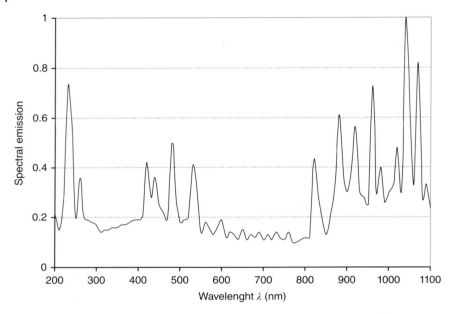

Figure 3.15 Typical spectral emission of a xenon flash lamp. The wide spectral distribution brings good color balance.

In contrast to a tungsten halogen lamp that produces a temporal continuous energy, the energy of the xenon lamp can be concentrated in high power flashes. The differences are considerable. In contrast to a 150 W tungsten halogen lamp with 1.2×10^{-2} lm luminous flux produces a 43 W xenon flash light 4 lumens luminous flux [5].

Xenon flash lamps use sensible glass tubes that need housing and further an expensive control circuitry that is built in unwieldy boxes. Some little application uses the direct light from the flash tube; usually the emitted light is coupled into fiber optics to form the light.

Advantages

- extremely bright
- high color temperature (5500–12 000 K), very white, best color rendering
- flashable with flash duration of 1–20 μs (short arc models), 30 μs to several milliseconds (long arc models)
- high flash rate with up to 200 (1000 with decreasing flash energy) flashes per second
- lifetime of up to 10^8 flashes.

Disadvantages

- protection measures needed, because of the use of high voltage
- EMC problems caused by strong electrical pulses to control the light source
- expensive, costly electronics
- bulky, needs a light generator box

- unflexible shape (flash bulb with a reflector) or requirement of additional fiber optics (~40% loss of light caused by incoupling and transfer of light)
- flash to flash variation of intensity (<10%)
- aging: intensity after a few million flashes can be down to 50%.

Considerations for Machine Vision

- useful for color image processing where much light is needed
- useful for fast running processes
- reservations for industrial use because of operation conditions.

3.3.3.4 Fluorescent Lamps

Fluorescent lamps are discharging lamps that are known from lighting of rooms. Their efficiency is better than that of incandescent lamps. A different distribution of spectra can be chosen due to different coatings of the lamp tubes inside. Customary catalog of fluorescent lamp suppliers inform about the widespread possibilities. These coatings ensure that the UV radiation that is produced by the evaporated mercury inside the tube converts into visible light (see Figure 3.16).

Fluorescent lamps are driven with alternating current (AC). The change of the current direction is converted into a flickering of light with the double frequency of the supplying voltage, because the luminants inside the tubes continue to glow for a maximal time of 1/1000 s. To avoid brightness interferences between fluorescent light and image acquisition frequency, it is necessary to use HF-ballasts (22 kHz or more are advisable). Without this measure, variations of brightness from image to image up to total darkness can occur for the worst case.

Fluorescent lamps are popular for low-cost solutions and for achieving a homogenous lighting from a distance.

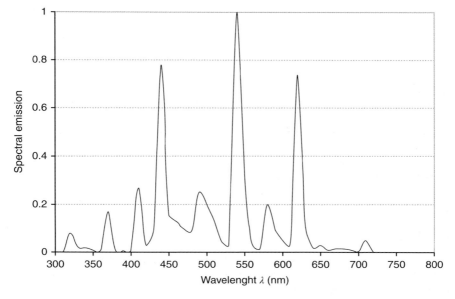

Figure 3.16 Typical spectral emission of an HF driven fluorescent ring light.

Advantages

- cheap
- different color temperatures for selection (3000–6000 K)
- able to illuminate large areas.

Disadvantages

- inflexible, limited fixed shapes of the light source (line, ring)
- reduced working lifetime 5000–12 000 h, small ring lights only 2500 h
- HF-ballast necessary (possible EMC problems)
- single spectral bands
- large temperature drift
- only applicable for static light, no flash
- rapid aging (after 12 000 h approximately 50% of the brightness from beginning)
- warm running necessary.

Considerations for Machine Vision

- use for illumination of large areas
- low-cost solutions (with all the disadvantages)
- use of electronic HF-ballast is necessary.

3.3.3.5 LEDs (Light Emitting Diodes)

The progress in materials and electronics technology pushes the triumphant advances of the LED technology. One can say that nowadays LED lighting is the standard lighting of Machine Vision. This development was driven by the demands of the automotive industry for tough, cheap, reliable, and powerful light sources.

LEDs are small and very robust light sources and emit cold light with a narrow half-width of wavelength of approximately 30 nm (see Figure 3.12), which means almost monochromatic light. They are powerful with an efficiency of optical power of up to 55 lm W^{-1}, tendency strongly increasing.

The lifetime for LEDs differs strongly depending on the color, measurement conditions, environmental conditions, design, manufacturer, and so forth. For monochromatic LEDs it is supposed that they achieve average lifetimes under optimal conditions between 100 000 and 200 000 h, while white LEDs achieve partially much less. These data of single LEDs do not have to do with the lifetime of an industrial lighting component [6] (see Section 3.5.3.1).

The color of the emitted light depends on the substrate of the p–n transition inside the LED. Many colors are possible (see Table 3.5).

Since a few years, direct white LEDs are available. They compete more and more with traditional white light sources. What was possible before only with a triple of closely mounted red, green, and blue LEDs (Multiled) is now possible in one chip. From their nature are white LEDs blue light emitting LEDs covered with a yellow illuminant. The yellow pigments that are embedded in a transparent synthetic resin result in emitted white light. Depending on the stability of the production

Table 3.5 Some solid state materials and their emitted center wavelength in LEDs.

Color	λ_c (nm)	Material
White	$x = 0.32$, $y = 0.31$	InGaN
Blue	470	InGaN
Blue-green	505	InGaN
Green	528	InGaN
Green	570	GaAlP
Yellow	587	InGaAlP
Amber	615	InGaAlP
Orange	606	InGaAlP
Red	633	InGaAlP
Hyper-red	645	GaAlAs
Red	645	GaAlP
IR	950	GaAlAs

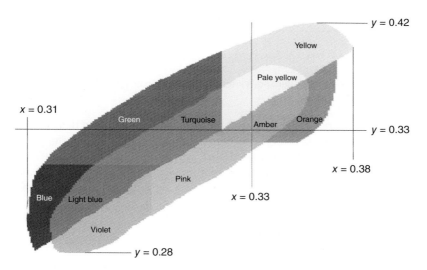

Figure 3.17 Distribution and span of hues of white LEDs. Use for color classification and sorting of white LEDs [7]. x and y are color coordinates.

of the yellow pigments different hues are achievable or disturb application that need stable color conditions (see Figure 3.17).

LEDs can operate with up to a 10-fold current overload if they are pulsed for a short time. The result can be up to 10-fold higher intensity of light emission (infrared). White LEDs can achieve an up to six times higher intensity in this operation mode (see Figure 3.18). The real increase of light emission depends on the used substrate (color) of the LED.

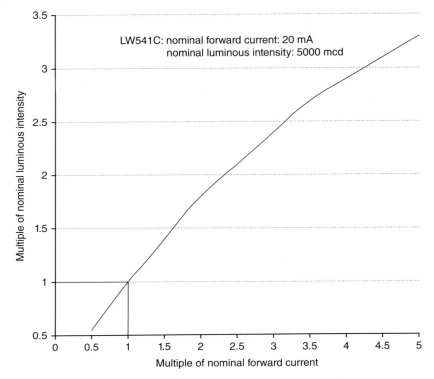

Figure 3.18 Example for a current–luminous intensity relationship of a white LED. (Data sheet LW541C OSRAM semiconductors.)

Note for this operation that the allowed pulse-duty factor to avoid the thermal destruction of the LED has to be kept. For the operation of LEDs in the pulse mode no aging is noted even after a few 10 millions of flashes! [23]

The different sizes and small designs (5 mm, 3 mm, SMD types, LED on Chip, etc.) inspire developers of Machine Vision lighting to various lighting components.

Advantages

- particularly suitable for industry
- lifetime >20 000 to >100 000 h. Strongly depending on operation conditions.
- vibration insensitive/shock resistant, survive higher G-forces
- nearly monochromatic or white light
- small temperature drift (time, temperature) of brightness
- ideal electrical controllability
- fast reaction down to <1 μs
- flash light is possible in all colors and IR
- free design of lighting shapes, all lighting techniques are possible
- lighting with mixed colors possible
- low power consumption and low emergence of heat
- no maintenance necessary

- low voltage means low danger
- low space necessary.

Disadvantages

- aging of white LEDs changes color coordinates (hue and color temperature)
- white LEDs not homogenous to manufacture (sorting LEDs required regarding center wavelength, optical power, color coordinates)
- not yet as bright as halogen lamps (state 2004)
- maximum operation temperature of 60 °C, otherwise strongly increased aging.

Considerations for Machine Vision

- equipped with those features LEDs are ideal light sources for Machine Vision
- the progress in LED technology will also inspire Machine Vision.

3.3.3.6 Lasers

Laser light sources are relatively seldom used in Machine Vision. If so, only lasers based on laser diode modules are applied, no solid state or gas lasers. Characterizing facts are

- highly concentrated energy
- emission of coherent light
- emission of real monochromatic light
- point-shaped origin of light.

The highly concentrated energy makes it possible to work with an optical power of only a few milliwatts to achieve considerable brightness on the camera sensor. On the other hand, the concentrated energy is an obstacle for the use. Many safety measures are taken to protect the human eye and body from the danger of concentrated radiation.

Laser light sources are classified into laser protection classes (see [8]). These classes describe the protection measures in dependence from the power and wavelength used. This explains the aversion of many companies to forbid the use of lasers in any kind in their production lines.

The emission of coherent light is an optical phenomenon based on the emission of light waves of only one wavelength (monochromatic) in phase. The superposition of many of these waves leads to the appearance of interference and with that to the characteristic speckle patterns. The speckle patterns appear as local and temporal unregular and changing patterns of brighter and darker points. This appears even with a defocused imaging optics or with a beam shaping optics in front of the laser light source (see Figure 3.19). The speckle patterns prevent the correct function of most image processing algorithms.

To avoid this, one can destroy the coherence of the laser using a fiber coupling into a multimode fiber. This is expensive and needs high precision for manufacturing.

Using a beam shaping optics, laser lighting can produce the best possible parallel light (beam expanders). Using diffractive gratings manifold light structures for projection can be produced (see Section 3.7.4.4).

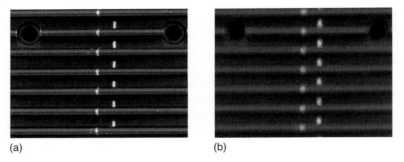

Figure 3.19 Illumination of a structured surface with a laser line: (a) with focused imaging objective, (b) with unfocused imaging objective. Clearly perceptible in both cases is the pepper–salt pattern of the light line caused by speckles.

Electrically seen are laser diodes easy to handle but they need a specialized drive. They can be driven in cw (continuous wave) mode or can be modulated up to a few megahertz. They are very sensitive against electrostatic discharging and optical overload. That is why they need an integrated monitor (photo)diode to control the optical output.

Advantages

- special and different light shapes achievable
- emission of almost perfect parallel light possible
- highly intense.

Disadvantages

- protection measure needed
- nonhomogenous illumination because of speckles
- used only for special procedure in Machine Vision.

Considerations for Machine Vision

- reservation because of danger for man
- useful for some application in 3D.

3.3.4 The Light Sources in Comparison

The mesh diagram (see Figure 3.20) shows the suitability of different light sources for Machine Vision. A larger area typifies a better matching.

3.3.5 Considerations for Light Sources: Lifetime, Aging, Drift

3.3.5.1 Lifetime

The industrial use of light sources implies that they work when built in a complete lighting device. Thus, the lifetime does not only mean the lifetime of the light source but also the lifetime of all cooperating electronic and thermal effective components under harsh industrial conditions. And this is usually much less than

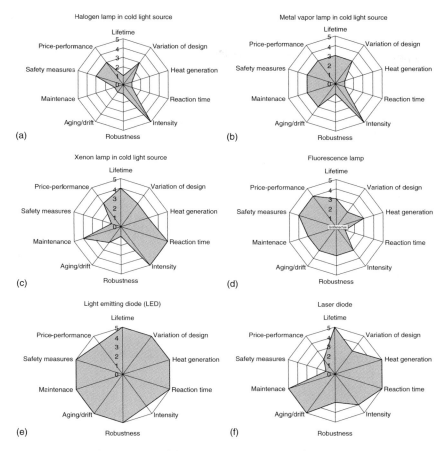

Figure 3.20 (a)–(f) How much of the requirements a lighting has to meet to be used in Machine Vision? Assessments are made from 1 = bad to 5 = very good.

only the lifetime of the light source that is measured under optimal conditions. That is why diverge the lifetime data from only the light source and from the complete lighting component.

If we keep in mind that all data of lifetime are statistical values (MTBF – mean time between failure), we feel that the nominal values provide a rather vague information of how long an illumination device will work (see Table 3.6).

To talk about lifetime of lighting also means to talk about the reliability and availability of the complete vision system. Lighting as the core component and information carrier of the vision system decides fundamentally on the function of the whole machine. False economy for lighting components can cause high costs:

a) preventive maintenance to replace short-lived light sources cyclically
b) unforeseen failure of the machine/system with all possible consequences.

Table 3.6 Lifetime in hours, days, month, years.

	Life time		
Hours	Days (approx.)	Month (approx.)	Years (approx.)
500	21	0.7	0.06
1 000	42	1.5	0.10
5 000	208	6.7	0.60
10 000	416	31.4	1.10
20 000	833	26.9	2.20
50 000	2 083	67.2	5.60
100 000	4 166	134.4	11.2

Both include

- costs for replaced components
- costs for downtime of the machine (system)
- labor costs for maintenance
- delay time costs to maintenance, delay time costs to delivery of the replacement part (for b).

This should also be considered while selecting a lighting component.

3.3.5.2 Aging and Drift

The light emission of light sources is based on chemical compounds that have characteristic aging behavior in their substantial structure. This temporal influences on the emission of light is called aging. Depending on the kind of light source this aging can be totally different. It is important to know this behavior to limit or to compensate it.

Almost all image processing algorithms are based on brightness and contrast in the image with relatively constant values. Aging light sources are changing the brightness and contrast. The allowed value of this change depends on the used algorithms. Some algorithms are very sensitive, while others are more tolerant. Measurements, tests, or calculations by the software engineers can give information about these dependences related to the software.

Measurement application with Machine Vision, in particular, needs stable lighting for stable images. This is an indispensable condition to maintain the accuracy of detection.

Aging is usually sped up by temperature. For most light sources a long-term operation with overtemperature will shorten the lifetime and/or the brightness. Thermal processes or even passed time changes the chemical structure of the radiant materials irreversibly. The consequences are lower or changed emission of light.

For LEDs this has an effect on the maximum of brightness (monochromatic LEDs) or on the brightness, color distribution, and color temperature (white

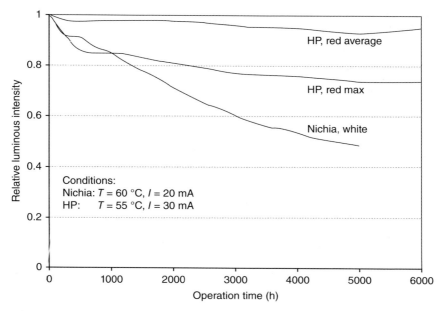

Figure 3.21 Aging of different LEDs [9].

LEDs). Especially, the conversion layer of white LEDs tends to intensify aging at higher temperatures (see Figure 3.21).

A typical temporal course of aging of an LED related to the luminous intensity is given by

$$I(t) = I_0 \exp(-t/t_s)$$

with

- I_0 being the luminous intensity at the beginning of the operation,
- t the operation time, and
- t_s the aging constant [7]

  (144 270 h for 50% brightness after 100 000 h operation).

To avoid this, lighting components need a temperature compensation to bring down the temperature of the sensitive components as much as possible (see Figure 3.22). The colder the chips the better the stability. Well-planned constructions of lighting components bear that in mind. The electrical and mechanical-thermal construction ensures that all temperature-sensitive elements work at critical temperatures, particularly the light sources. In some cases airflows can help to reduce their warming.

LED light sources work most effectively if they are cold, which means below a temperature of approximately 60 °C. The concrete temperature depends on the substrate and LED type. If LEDs warm up more, it is observed that the brightness decreases by 1% for each degree increase of temperature [6]. That is why the thermal compensation of lighting is very important and is a distinguishing feature for robust and long-lived lighting components.

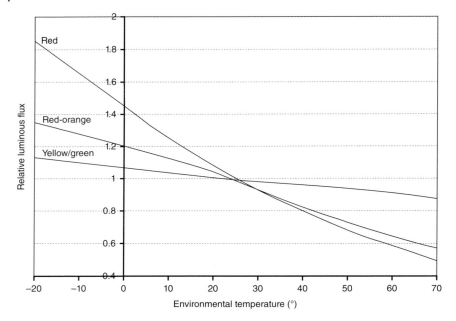

Figure 3.22 Brightness behavior of LEDs depending on environmental temperature.

A very simple possibility of avoiding overheating is to switch on the light source only, when the camera acquires an image. Rest of time the lighting is switched off.

Working with LED in flash operation mode means to avoid from aging too. A flashed LED does not age over a few million flashes in compliance with a pulse-duty factor of 1 : 10 minimum (flash duration: rest) and a maximum flash duration of <10 μs (average value). This operation mode prolongs the lifetime of the LED light source to the maximum.

Rule of the thumb:

A recommended setting of brightness of a light source is 50%. This optimizes the lifetime and minimizes aging.

Even in short time periods the intensity of lighting changes. This drift is caused by warming up the light source/controlling electronics. Depending on the light source this behavior totally differs. For temperature radiators, it is known that their power of radiation increases with increasing temperature.

Fluorescent lamps need a warm operating temperature. That is why they deliver lower light output in a cold environment. On the other hand, they need a lead time to warm up to achieve the rated light intensity. After further warming decreases the intensity (see Figure 3.23).

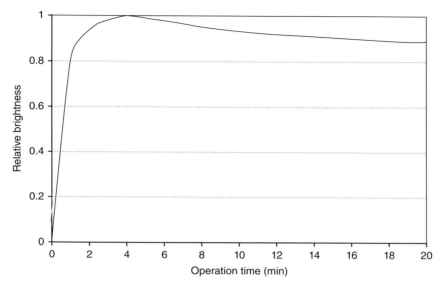

Figure 3.23 Time dependence of brightness of a typical fluorescent lamp PL-S11W/840/4P [Philips].

3.4 Interaction of Test Object and Light

3.4.1 Risk Factor Test Object

Light begins to work for Machine Vision when it starts interacting with the test object. And instantly the test object becomes the decisive but not the predictable component. What are the problems that the test object brings along?

Above all, there are no constant optical properties. We should consider that the optical inspection with Machine Vision is not limited to only parts with stable optical characteristics. Parts with totally different or changing properties can occur such as plastic molding parts of different color. For the functions of the parts may mean nothing, but for the function of the vision system that can mean everything.

The classical dilemma of Machine Vision is to know only a little or almost nothing about the optical properties of the test object. Most of the parts are not even specified for those properties. This means almost to work with a *black box* part.

A few properties of test objects that have an influence on the possibilities of optical inspection are shown in Table 3.7.

Often, even the customer cannot foresee the changes of these properties, because he is dependent on his contractors and usually he does not know the technological processes behind. So, the test object remains the primary risk factor. The risk factors can be limited by using a matching lighting.

Table 3.7 Properties of test objects that influence the vision system inspection.

Factor group	Influence factor	Possible reasons for the change in properties
Optical factors	Part color	Changed material or material mixture
	Pattern	Changed tool quality
	Reflection	Changed material, material mixture, manufacturing method
	Scattering	Changed material, material mixture, surface finish
	Transmission	changed material or material mixture
	Absorption	Changed material or material mixture
Mechanical factors	Shape of edge	New and worn tools (i.e., cutting tool)
	Surface geometry	New and worn tools (i.e., cutting tool)
	Surface imperfections	New and worn tools (i.e., cutting tool), changed contractor
	Surface roughness	Changed tool quality
	Chatter marks	Worn tool
	Surface finish	Changed contractor
Chemical factors	Corrosion	Different reflection
	Oil film	Protection from corrosion needed
	Release agent	Changed manufacturing method

3.4.1.1 What Does the Test Object do With the Incoming Light?

Light that enters the test object is divided into three fundamental parts (see Figure 3.24):

- the light quantity that is reflected by the test object – the reflection R
- the light quantity that passes the test object – the transmission T
- the light quantity that is absorbed by the test object – the absorption A.

In accordance with the energy conservation law, is the sum of all three parts:

$$R + T + A = 100\%$$

Above all, these material specific characteristic values of the test object depend on the wavelength and incident angle but a few more influencing factors are known. A real test object is always an unknown mixture of reflection, absorption, and transmission. The effect of fluorescence is not considered in this place.

3.4.1.2 Reflection/Reflectance/Scattering

The reflected light is essentially optically shaping the part in Machine Vision. Reflection means the deviation of light at surfaces and interfaces of materials with different refraction indices. It forms the basis for imaging in mirrors and prisms. According to the reflection law (see Section 3.1) the light is basically reflected from the part where the incident and reflected light rays are in the same plane.

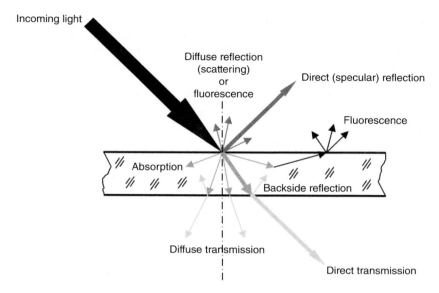

Figure 3.24 Quantities of the incoming light at the test object and their distribution.

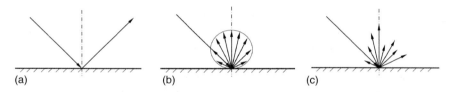

Figure 3.25 Different qualities of surfaces and their influence on the distribution of the reflected light. (a) Directed reflection, (b) regular diffuse reflection, (c) irregular diffuse (mixed) reflection.

After reflection, the reflected light has changed the direction of oscillation. It is polarized (see Section 3.4.2.5).

Usually, the parts from Machine Vision are located in air that the angle of incidence is equal to the angle of reflection. The geometrical macro structure of the test object generally determines where the light is reflected (see Figure 3.25). But the geometrical microstructure (surface quality and roughness) influences how the light is reflected. The surface will diffuse or scatter the light and determines the light distribution after reflection. Different reflecting characteristics of the test object occur in different gray values in the image. This fact is the main reason for problems of malfunctioning of vision systems.

The condition for a directed reflection is a smooth surface with a peak-to-valley-height smaller than $\lambda/4$ (The Rayleigh condition). If the peak-to-valley-height is larger than this, the light is diffusely reflected, it is scattered. The directional properties of a reflecting surface depend on the material and above all from the surface treatment. A polished one will have other reflecting properties than a milled surface, a grinded surface others than a painted.

Depending on these different possible light distributions only a smaller amount of light energy is reflected backward to the camera's lens. The rest is distributed into the whole area surrounding the reflecting surface. The reflected light energy can be strongly reduced. Details have to be checked from part to part and from application to application.

Information about the general degree of reflection gives the material characteristic value reflectance R that expresses the relationship between reflected and incident luminous flux:

$$R = \Phi_r/\Phi_0$$

where Φ_r is the reflected luminous flux and Φ_0 is the incident luminous flux (see Figure 3.8).

The reflectance depends on factors such as material, wavelength/color temperature, polarization of light, angle of incidence of light, and so forth (see Figure 3.26).

An extended view to the reflection properties gives the characteristic value *glossfactor* that expresses the ratio of directed to diffuse reflection. A high gloss factor means a large amount of direct reflection.

These values can be taken for an approximate calculation of the light reflected toward the lens and the sensor.

> From an incoming illuminance of 100 lx (from the light source) to a nickel surface only 45–63 lx are reflected toward the camera. The efficiency of the lighting is drastically reduced.

Transparent materials do not reflect only on the surface. They tend to reflect at the backside too (see Figure 3.24). The consequences are backside reflections in the form of double images or ghost images. For targeted reflection using only thin

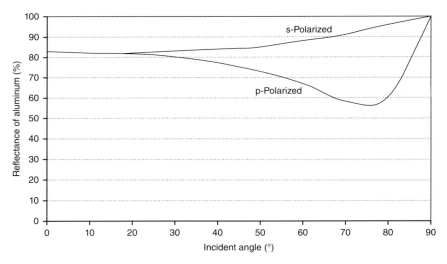

Figure 3.26 Dependence of the incident angle of light – reflectance for a polished aluminum mirror surface.

film materials can avoid this or it can be reduced with anti-reflection coatings if possible.

That can be useful for special measurement methods with Machine Vision; for example, the measurement of thickness of glass plates using the double images of a laser point. With a known angle of incidence into the glass plate, the thickness evaluating the distance between the incoming spot and the reflected one can be measured.

Last but not least it affects the shape of the test object on the reflected light. A sharp-edged and a rounded-edged part possess totally different reflection properties. So, the shape of the material edges essentially determines the light that reaches the camera lens and the sensor (see Figure 3.27).

Even chemical processes (surface treatment, corrosion, corrosion protection) influence the reflection. They change the reflectance.

Note this if getting parts from different suppliers that use different manufacturing and surface treatment procedures. Parts that are stored in a humid or chemical aggressive environment can corrode. They will look principally different to parts from the (perfect) pilot production.

Parts that are treated with anti-corrosive agents change their reflective properties too. The difference among a clean metal part, a metal part with an oil film or a wax covered metal part is only mentioned.

> *Tip*
>
> Take two sample test objects as (visually) different in reflecting as possible. Determine the difference in the reflected light of both parts using the vision system and compare gray values. How do the parameters vary? Do they both fulfill the needs for safe function of the software? If not, change the lighting and/or lighting method!

> *Tip*
>
> Take the reflections at the test object into consideration according to the reflection law. Think of the micro- and/or macrostructure of the part. Position the light source(s) in such a way that the light is reflected into the camera. Try it from different positions so long as you get the reflexes in the desired places.

3.4.1.3 Total Reflection

A special phenomenon on reflecting parts (e.g., transparent glass and plastics) is the total reflection. Above a marginal angle α_l some materials reflect completely.

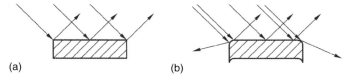

(a) (b)

Figure 3.27 Light reflection from a stamped metal part: (a) stamped with a new cutting tool and (b) stamped with a wear out cutting tool. The light distribution changes totally due to the different shape.

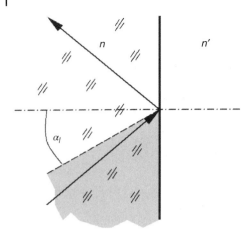

Figure 3.28 Total reflection can be found only in the gray area. At smaller angles the transparent material is only refracting the light.

This occurs for example on surfaces of water, glass, and plastics and can be profitable when used for the reflection of light inside prisms and fiberglass.

The condition for this is an angle of incident light being larger than the marginal angle α_l and a transition of the refraction indices from a higher to a lower value (see Figure 3.28).

$$\alpha_l = \arcsin(n'/n)$$

where n is the refraction index before reflection and n' is the refraction index of the adjacent medium.

Typical values of the marginal angles are

48.7° for a transition of water ($n = 1.33$) against air ($n' = 1$)
41.8° for a transition of an average optical glass ($n = 1.5$) against air ($n' = 1$)
62.5° for a transition of an average optical glass ($n = 1.5$) against water ($n' = 1.33$).

Tip

Note the total reflection when inspecting transparent parts. Changed viewing angle or lighting angle can abolish or let appear the total reflection.

3.4.1.4 Transmission/Transmittance

Another part of light can pass the test object. The material specific value to characterize this is the transmission (see Figures 3.24 and 3.29).

For backlight, applications mean the amount of light passing through the object that produces brightness for the test object at the imager during transmission (see Figure 3.30). The higher the transmission, the brighter the part occurs. Possibly a high transmission of the part is not desirable, because it prevents a necessary contrast between the bright background (from lighting) and dark test object.

For front light, applications mean the loss of brightness during transmission. The incoming light is not reflected to the camera sites as desired. It is not usable for the camera because it passes the object.

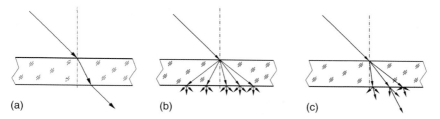

(a)   (b)   (c)

Figure 3.29 Different qualities of transparent materials and their influence on the distribution of the transmitted light, (a) directed transmission, (b) diffuse transmission, (c) irregular diffuse (mixed) transmission.

Figure 3.30 Image of directed and diffuse transmission: round glass block with chamfer. In the middle the light is directly transmitted. An annulus around shows diffused and strongly reduced transmission caused by the rough surface of the chamfer. Lighting component: telecentric lighting.

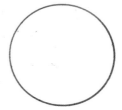

Information about the degree of transmission gives the material characteristic value transmittance T:

$$T = \Phi_t/\Phi_0$$

where Φ_t is the transmitted luminous flux and Φ_0 is the incident luminous flux.

The transmittance depends above all on the illuminated material, wavelength/color temperature, polarization of light, angle of incidence of light, and so forth. Some average values for transmittance are shown in Table 3.8.

These values can be taken for approximately calculating the transmitted light through the test object.

> From a generated luminance in a diffuse light source of $4000 \, \text{cd m}^{-2}$ still remain approximately $2000 \, \text{cd m}^{-2}$ after passing a part of white plastics with 3 mm thickness.

But transmission does not only occur from the test objects but also from inserted optical filters. Apart from the spectral influence on the light information they reduce the transmission of light (see Section 3.6.1).

3.4.1.5 Absorption/Absorbance

The third part of light energy that influences the light distribution of the test object is the absorption. Light is absorbed by opaque and transparent objects too. This portion of light is changed into warmth in the test object. To foresee the amount of absorbed light energy is difficult, because it depends on many imponderable and material factors that cannotbe determined easily.

To determine these factors, an approximate value can be derived from converting the starting formula

$$R + T + A = 100\% \quad \text{to absorbance} \quad A = 100\% - R - T$$

Table 3.8 Average reflectance, transmission, absorbance of materials for white light (color temperature 3000 K).

Material	Reflectance	Absorbance	Transmission
Aluminum, polished	0.6–0.72	0.28–0.4	
Aluminum, polished and anodized (nature)	0.75–0.9	0.1–0.25	
Aluminum, frosted	0.55–0.6	0.4–0.45	
Aluminum foil	0.8–0.87	0.13–0.2	
Brass, polished	0.61–0.62	0.39–0.38	
Brass, frosted	0.52–0.55	0.45–0.48	
Brick	0.15–0.4		
Chrome, polished	0.6–0.7	0.3–0.4	
Chrome, frosted	0.4–0.45	0.55–0.6	
Color paint			
White	0.7–0.85	0.15–0.3	
Cream	0.56–0.72	0.28–0.44	
Yellow	0.48–0.52	0.48–0.52	
Brown	0.27–0.41	0.59–0.73	
Green	0.12–0.2	0.8–0.88	
Blue	0.07–0.1	0.9–0.93	
Red	0.1–0.27	0.73–0.9	
Copper, polished	0.48–0.6	0.4–0.52	
Cotton, white	0.3–0.4	0.23–0.4	0.25–0.4
Earth, damp	Approx. 0.07		
Enamel, white	0.65–0.8	0.2–0.35	
Glass aluminum mirror	0.9–0.94	0.06–0.1	
Glass, clear (1–4 mm thick)	0.06–0.08	0.02–0.04	0.9–0.92
Glass, frosted (2–3 mm thick)	0.07–0.2	0.05–0.17	0.63–0.88
Glass, opal (2–4 mm thick)	0.31–0.57	0.03–0.31	0.12–0.66
Grass	Approx. 0.06		
Granite	0.1–0.2		
Marble	0.6–0.65		
Nickel, polished	0.53–0.63	0.37–0.47	
Nickel, frosted	0.45–0.55	0.45–0.55	
Paper	0.6–0.85	0.05–0.39	0.05–0.41
Plaster	0.2–0.55		
Plastics, white (2–3 mm thick)	0.2–0.4	0.1–0.2	0.4–0.6
Sandstone	0.15–0.4		
Silk, white	0.25–0.38	0.01–0.06	
Silver, polished	0.85–0.94	0.06–0.15	

Table 3.8 (Continued)

Material	Reflectance	Absorbance	Transmission
Skin, untanned	Approx. 0.45		
Snow	0.65–0.75		
Steel, polished	0.55–0.6	0.4–0.45	
Tin plate	0.67–0.69	0.31–0.33	
Velvet, black	0.02–0.1	0.9–0.98	
Wood bright	To 0.4	To 0.6	
Wood dark	From 0.07	From 0.93	

Perpendicular incidence of light [10].

Some guide numbers for the absorbance are given in Table 3.8. Note that this part of light is not at all usable for lighting purposes.

3.4.1.6 Diffraction

One axiom of light is the straight propagation within a homogenous medium. But light as an electromagnetic phenomenon can look behind the test object into the geometrical shadow area. If a light wave touches the edge of an object, the light wave is diffracted. That means it changes the direction of propagation. Because light always consists of bundles of light rays, interference happens. This is known from specific diffraction patterns (see Figure 3.31).

The size of diffraction effects proportionally depends on the used illumination wavelength. The smaller the used wavelength, the smaller the width of the diffraction patterns. This means that a reduction of the illumination wavelength from IR (typically 880 nm) to blue light (typically 450 nm) can reduce the diffraction effects to almost half.

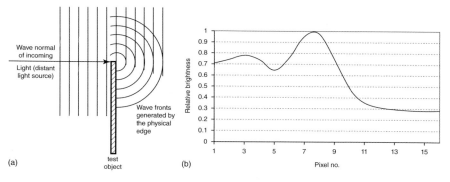

Figure 3.31 (a) Principle of diffraction with interference of waves touching a body. The incoming wave interferes with the new created wave from the physical edge of the test object. This results in typical diffraction patterns, (b) gray value distribution of a real edge with notable diffraction. Image scale of 5 : 1 in combination with a telecentric backlighting of 450 nm wavelength. Pixel resolution is 1.5 µm per pixel.

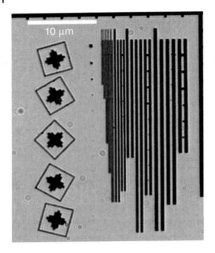

Figure 3.32 Diffraction on dust spots and geometrical structures (chrome on glass) at a test chart for photolithography. The pixel resolution of 0.688 μm per pixel is on the resolution limit for visible light. Diffraction limits the detectability.

Diffraction will be notable for Machine Vision applications with monochromatic light and image scales larger than $3:1$. For smaller image scales it only distorts the width and shape of the gray value/brightness transition of the edge. If diffraction is notable, it is necessary to check the image processing software. How the edge detection is done and how does the software treat the diffraction patterns? Will the edge be found in the right place? Is the edge location reliable? (see Figure 3.32) Maximum gradient algorithms can help there.

White light as a mixture of different wavelengths does not produce diffraction. The mix prevents the occurrence of diffraction. The results are blurred edges in comparison to the best possible edge in monochromatic light.

Diffraction occurs at each material edge that the light touches. These edges can be

- the test object (distorts gray value transitions in the image)
- dust spots on the lens, sensor, ... (enlarges the dust spots)
- f-stops, lens mounting (reduces the resolution of the objective).

3.4.1.7 Refraction

If the test object is transparent and a backlight application is used, refraction can occur. Basically, it is connected to the refraction law (see Section 3.3.1). The refraction indices are listed in the relevant optical literature.

If light passes a boundary between two transparent materials with different refraction indices (propagation velocities), the light propagation direction is deviated. What is useful for the function of all lenses can cause problems and surprises for illumination and imaging the test object (see Figure 3.33).

Tip

If you are working with transparent test objects it can be helpful to approximately do ray tracing from the light source through the test object, through the objective to the camera sensor. It shows the change in the propagation of light depending on the geometry of the included test object.

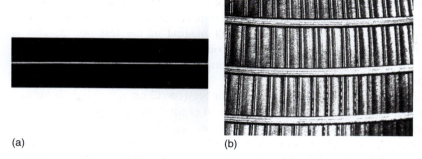

(a)   (b)

Figure 3.33 Change of light propagation in transparent test objects in telecentric backlight, (a) glass rod, (b) curved transparent plastic body. Curved transparent objects act like optical elements and refracted light. A parallel glass plate would not influence the brightness, it would appear homogenously bright.

3.4.2 Light Color and Part Color

3.4.2.1 Visible Light (VIS) – Monochromatic Light

Why does light occur in a special color? Because it consists of a limited range or of a special spectrum of wavelengths.

Why does the test object occur in their specific color if it is illuminated with white light? Because it reflects only the range of light wave of their own color and absorbs or transmits the rest. A blue body, for example, reflects only the light waves of blue light and absorbs the others.

Accordingly, it is most effective (brightest!) to illuminate a blue part with blue light and a red part with red light, and so forth.

On the other hand, there are colors – those which are best possibly extinct–the so-called complementary colors. Illuminating a part with their complementary color it will appear dark (see Figure 3.34).

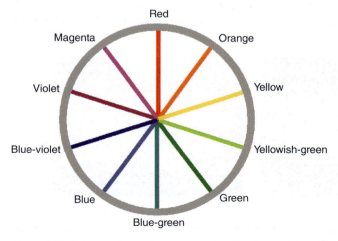

Figure 3.34 Colors and complementary colors. On the opposite side of the circle can be read the complementary color.

Monochrome cameras have an enormous effect on the gray value produced in the imaging sensor. Knowing these connections it is possible to emphasize or suppress colors for a contrastful imaging of the test object. This is valid if the test object has a constant color (see Figure 3.34). On the other hand, the color perception of the imaging sensor influences the result (see Section 3.3.1).

Color cameras will produce a mixed color between illumination light color and part color. In this case, things get difficult to predict the resulting hue, because this depends on many material specific factors.

In some Machine Vision applications the part color is permanently changing. For these parts, white light is the best alternative, because it does not suppress or emphasize any colors. In that case, it will be necessary for the settings of the software to find those tolerant parameters that make it possible to detect parts of all colors (see Figures 3.35 and 3.36).

The color of incident light can be mixed (additive mix) using the three basic colors red, green, blue (RGB). In the illumination plane, a new mixed light color is made, brighter than the initial brightnesses (see Table. 3.9).

Some new imaging objectives for extremely large fields are adapted to the use of monochromatic light. Due to the built-in lenses and the color correction it is necessary to use these objectives with monochromatic light to achieve best imaging results. White light would decrease the imaging power of these objectives because of chromatic aberrations.

Usually, the imaging objectives of Machine Vision work with monochromatic and white light as well. Nevertheless, it should be considered that a change of the illumination wavelength can also change working distances. Particularly for large image scales (magnifications larger than 1) the illumination wavelength notably determines the working distance. This is based on the variable refraction index of the lenses inside the imaging objective that depends on the wavelength (dispersion). Shorter wavelength (UV, blue) are more refracted than longer (red, IR). This means shorter working distances for UV/blue light than for red/IR light. The consequence is to adapt focus when changing the illumination wavelength.

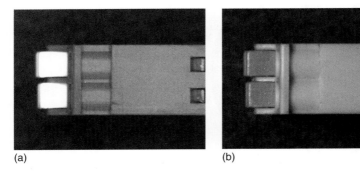

Figure 3.35 Yellow-greenish connection block with orange terminals, (a) illuminated with red light, (b) illuminated with green light.

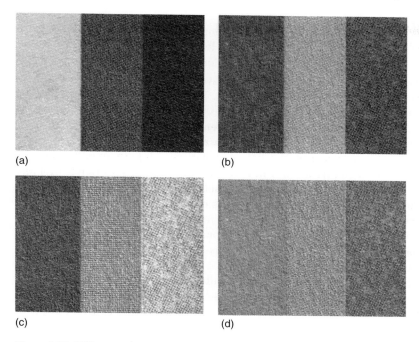

Figure 3.36 Different color perceptions caused by different illumination colors. The color bars are red, green, blue (from left to right), (a) red illumination, (b) green illumination, (c) blue illumination, (d) white illumination.

Table 3.9 Additive mixed illumination colors.

Intensities Blue (%)	Green (%)	Red (%)	Additive mix color
100	100	100	White
100	100	0	Cyan
100	0	100	Magenta
0	100	100	Yellow
100	50	50	Unsaturated blue
0	50	100	Orange
50	100	0	Blue green
100	50	0	Green blue
100	0	50	Violet
50	50	0	Dark blue green

3.4.2.2 Visible Light (VIS) – White Light

The most natural light is white light as a melange of (all) visible light wavelengths (colors) (see Figure 3.10). Some classical light sources produce it directly by their principle of origin.

Above all, white light is used

- either for the inspection of colored parts with monochrome cameras
- or for color image processing.

Frequently white light is the only alternative to get a grip on the processing of incidental but different colored test objects. This happens typically in industrial production processes, if the part color does not play a role for the function of the part, but parts are delivered from different suppliers and the hue of the part changes caused by the compound of the raw materials.

Related to monochrome Machine Vision solutions colored light of small wavelength ranges will emphasize or tone down single colors (see Section 3.4.2.1 and Figure 3.36). This produces high contrasts between parts of different colors.

Illumination with white light produces as moderate as possible contrasts. To work with white light is the compromise to work with different colored test objects. This leads to finding parameters for a reliable working software. If the fitting parameters could not be found it is wise to change the monochrome camera into a color camera.

In color Machine Vision applications, white light is necessary to reproduce a realistic color perception for the vision system. To get reliable results in these applications, it is important to acquaint oneself with the theory of colors, a special field of optics.

In 2005 approximately only 5–10% of all Machine Vision applications were color applications. However, the number of color application are expected to become proportionally more.

3.4.2.3 Infrared Light (IR)

Traditional Machine Vision uses IR light in the wavelength range from 780 to 1000 nm due to the sensitivity and common use of CCD and CMOS sensors. Longer wavelengths are processed with special thermal imagers for temperature measurements.

To work with IR illumination means to use all the considerations for radiometric values and not for photometric values (see Section 3.5.1).

However, it is known that IR is not so effective to the sensor from their spectral response (see Figure 3.10). Nevertheless, IR light is favorably used in some applications. It is not visible to the human eye and does not disturb the worker (see below). Furthermore, IR light penetrates the silicon substrate of the imager and produces blurred images due to induced charges. The consequence are images with lower contrast.

Together with a daylight suppression, filter or bandpass filter IR illumination can avoid from extraneous (visible) light (see Sections 3.6.5.2 and 3.6.5.7). On the other hand, IR lighting based on LED is particularly effective in fast running applications where short (down to 1 µs duration) and high-energy flash light is needed.

Some details of test objects are viewable only with IR light. It is possible to see the minute details. Particularly, the color reproduction is not reproducible. Objects that are colored in white light could be transparent to IR light (see Figures 3.37 and 3.38). Objects that are dark in white light can reflect IR light

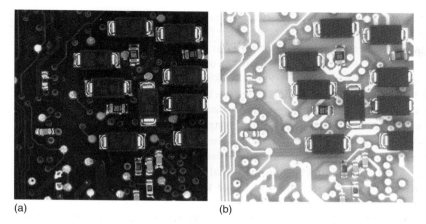

(a)   (b)

Figure 3.37 Circuit board with dark green solder resist, illuminated in red (a) and IR, 880 nm (b). The IR light passes the solder resist almost without loss and is reflected on the surface of the supporting material of the circuit board.

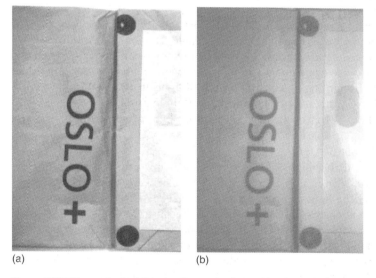

(a)   (b)

Figure 3.38 To see the *invisible* detail: panel opening in a vacuum cleaner bag, (a) illuminated with white light, (b) illuminated with the IR light. It is to recognize how the IR light makes the contrast of a green printing worse.

and be bright. Rules to determine cannot be designated. Nothing is predictable. To check the color reproduction under IR illumination there is only one way and that is the experiment.

From object to object, from pigment to pigment, the reflecting and absorbing properties of parts illuminated with IR light can change for some of them such as

- painted surfaces
- ink on printed materials
- color pigments in plastic materials.

Natural materials interact with infrared light too. The *Wood effect* is responsible for the bright appearance of leafs, because the chlorophyll is transparent for IR light, and the infrared light is reflected at air bubbles on the underside of leafs.

Note the influence of infrared light on the used imaging objective. Not all lenses (glass sorts) are highly transparent for the IR light. Some of them reduce the passing IR light. To check this, evaluate the spectral transmission of the objective.

Most imaging objectives for Machine Vision use transmit IR light without a remarkable loss of intensity up to a wavelength of 900 nm.

The interaction of the test object and the light causes diffraction at the test object edges. This appears particularly at large magnifications of the objective. The size of diffraction effects is proportional to the used wavelength. The longer the wavelength of the IR light the larger the diffraction effects (see Section 3.4.1.6).

Some information for eye protection. Due to the enormous radiation power of LED, nowadays there are some rules to be considered when using IR light. Preliminary remark: IR light, which is much more intense than LEDs can produce, is part of the spectrum of the sunlight. It can be found only in combination with the visible light [31].

But LED lighting is often used in relatively dark factory halls which means that the iris of the human eye is open. Incident isolated IR light from a lighting does not close it like visible light does. So, the full radiation can pass and reach the retina. This can cause eye damages. For the safety of all persons working in the environment of IR lighting it is best to switch IR lighting on and off only for the time it is needed. So that nobody is exposed to IR light durably.

The standard EN 171 gives further information about eye protection.

3.4.2.4 Ultraviolet (UV) Light

Ultraviolet light on the opposite side of the spectrum uses wavelength below 380 nm. Machine Vision applications with UV light were made relatively seldom in the past. The light sources were unwieldy, expensive, and inflexible and the cameras are expensive (specialized sensors, because the conventionally used silicon is not sensitive to UV). On the other hand, the contact with UV light implies some danger for the operator (human eye and skin). Current developments in LED technology make it possible to produce small, flexible, and easily controllable light sources in the range of UV-A light (typical 370 nm with a narrow half-wave bandwidth of 10–12 nm). This will inspire Machine Vision applications for the future.

Two general classes of application of UV illumination are given:

- direct UV illumination in combination with an UV-sensitive camera
- fluorescence caused by illumination with UV light.

UV illumination for observation with an UV-sensitive camera needs special sensors. These sensors use a fluorescence layer at the front glass of the imager to convert the UV light into visible light (e.g., a Lumogen conversion layer converts wavelength from 190 to 380 nm into visible light). Disadvantages of these sensors (layers) are aging and high costs.

Some kind of test objects produce fluorescence by themselves under an UV light illumination. This effect converts the incoming UV light on the object (short wavelength <380 nm) into an emission of visible light from the part (longer wavelength >380 nm). This effect is seen in fluorescence paint illuminated with *black light* or whitener in washing powder or paper illuminated with daylight (with quantity of UV light).

For the color rendering, similar relations are valid as known from IR light. Only experiments can give information about the suitability of UV light for the concrete test object.

Note the influence of the used imaging objectives in interaction with UV light. Not all lenses (glass sorts) are transparent for UV light. Some of them block the UV light. To check this, evaluate the spectral transmission of the objective.

However, consider the protection measures for the human eye and skin using UV too.

3.4.2.5 Polarized Light

The effects of polarization can be explained only by the wave character of light. Almost all light sources emit unpolarized (natural) light (LEDs, incandescent lamps, fluorescent lamps). This means that the light contains light waves that oscillate in all directions around the normal propagation direction (see Figure 3.39). Only special lasers with Brewster windows can directly emit polarized light.

Polarization occurs only on smooth surfaces. On these surfaces, polarization can be produced. The degree of polarization depends on the material and on the incident angle of light for reflection. On the other hand, change transmitting materials the polarization (test objects, light filters).

Different types of polarization can occur: linear, circular, elliptical (see Figure 3.39). Machine Vision typically uses two types of application of polarization:

1) polarized illumination to take advantage of the polarizing properties of the test object in combination with a polarizing light filter in front of the imaging objective (see Fig 3.40)
2) suppression of reflexes from unpolarized illumination reflected from the object using only one polarizing light filter in front of the imaging objective.

Polarized illumination can be achieved using a polarization filter (linear, circular or elliptical) in front of the light source (see Figure 3.40). These light filters act as the *polarizer* and produce polarized light (possible in white, monochromatic, band of wavelengths). Not all wavelengths can be polarized by commercial polarizers. For the IR light it is a problem.

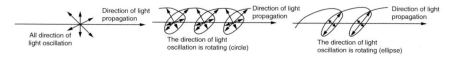

Figure 3.39 Unpolarized, linear, circular, and elliptical polarized light.

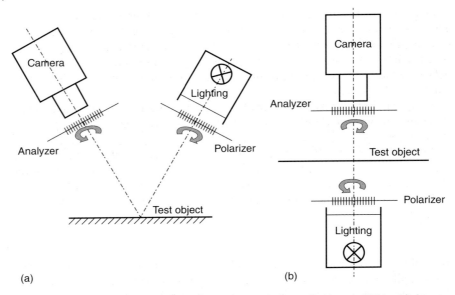

Figure 3.40 Principle of polarizer and analyzer: (a) top light application and (b) backlight application.

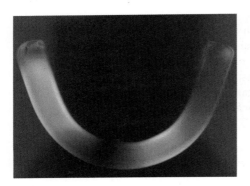

Figure 3.41 Example for polarization with transmission: the Glass handle of a cup. The transparent glass part between two crossed linear polarizing filters change the polarization direction as a result of stretched and pressed particles inside the glass. Mechanical tension becomes viewable with the principle of tension optics.

After leaving, the lighting enables the polarized light to interact with the test object (transmission or reflection), which changes the polarizing properties in relation to the incoming light. To grasp this in front of the camera objective is mounted another polarizing filter, the *analyzer*. Depending on the rotation of this filter the incoming polarized light from the test object is analyzed (see Figures 3.40 and 3.41).

The removal of surface reflexes from some materials for example glass, metal, plastic, and so on, can be made using unpolarized light with only one polarization filter in front of the imaging objective. The surface of the test object polarizes depending on the refraction index of the irradiated material. It is possible to analyze it with a polarization filter (see Figures 3.40a and 3.42). Under some conditions (material, incident/reflecting angle of light, wave length), it is possible to prevent from disturbing reflections (see Figure 3.43).

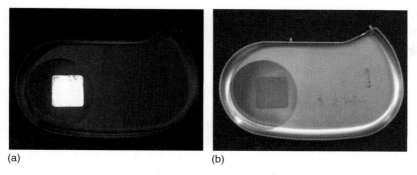

(a) (b)

Figure 3.42 Polarized incident light in combination with polarizing filter in front of the camera. (a) The transparent plastic label inside a stainless steel housing of a pacemaker is viewable because it turns the polarization different from the steel surface. (b) In comparison, the same part without polarized light.

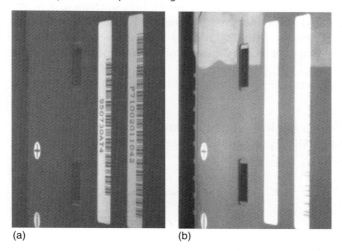

(a) (b)

Figure 3.43 Larger polarization effects tend to occur especially on electrically nonconduction materials: barcode reading of lacquered batteries, (a) with polarization filter, (b) without polarization filter.

Smaller polarization effects occur on surfaces of electrically conductive materials such as shiny metal parts. Among other things, the differences of polarization effects between conductive and nonconductive materials are usable to suppress the influence of oil films (corrosion protection on metal parts) for the nontactile measurement with Machine Vision.

It goes beyond the scope of this chapter to explain more about polarization. It is a much more complex effect and can be basically looked up from the optical literature.

3.5 Basic Rules and Laws of Light Distribution

To work effectively with light means to know basically a few rules and laws. This makes possible to selectively control the light and maximizes the effects of the used illumination. This chapter gives a short overview of some influencing factors.

3.5.1 Basic Physical Quantities of Light

To describe the properties of light and light distribution one can generally use the radiometric quantities. This covers the whole range of the light from 15 nm to 800 μm wavelength. If the light is evaluated by a receiver (sensor, eye) with a characteristic spectral response (e.g., $V(\lambda)$ – curve with sensitivity from 380 to 780 nm (see Section 3.3.2) – one can use the photometric quantities. This paper pays attention only to some of the photometric quantities that represent the visible range of light. The UV and IR light are not considered.

Origin of all photometrics related to the International System of Units (SI) is the luminous intensity with the unit candela (cd) (see Figure 3.44). Today, 1 cd is defined as the luminous intensity that a monochromatic light source with $f = 540$ THz (555 nm (green light)) emits (into all directions) with a radiant intensity of $1/683$ W sr^{-1} (Watts per steradian) (see Figure 3.45). To illustrate a practical comparison, 1 cd corresponds approximately to the luminous intensity of one candle light.

Characteristics mostly used for the power of lighting components in Machine Vision are

- the illuminance E for the incident light, ring lights, dark field ring lights
- the luminance L for backlights such as diffuse backlights or luminous objects.

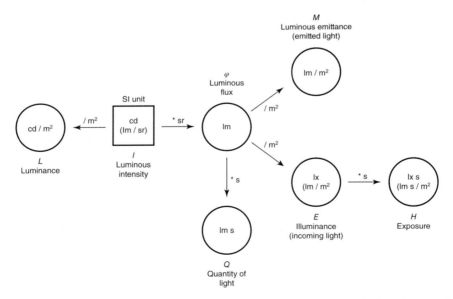

Figure 3.44 Schematic connection between SI unit luminous intensity and other photometric quantities of lighting engineering. More about lighting units and basics can be found in [11, 12].

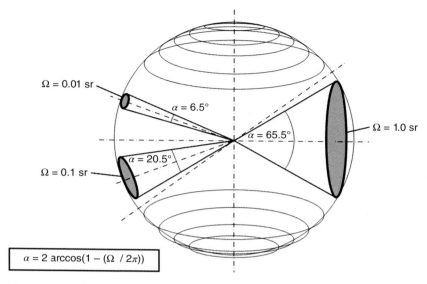

Figure 3.45 Definition of the solid angle Ω with unit steradian (sr). A light source that emits light into all directions (full sphere) covers 4π sr, a half sphere $2\pi 2$ sr. One steradian (sr) solid angle includes a cone with 65.5° plane angle.

3.5.2 The Photometric Inverse Square Law

Photometric inverse square law is relevant to anyone working with top light. The statement of this law is that the illuminance E on the surface of the test object decreases with the reciprocal of the square of the distance d (see Figure 3.46).

$$E \sim 1/d^2$$

with

E being illuminance at the object and
d the distance lighting – object.

In a practical usable approximation, $E = I/d^2$ [13] with I -luminous intensity of the light source. Note that the distance between the test object and the observing camera with objective does not influence the brightness at the image sensor of the camera! This distance influences only the optical parameters of the image.

The connection between illuminance and distance is exactly valid only for a point-shaped light source. In approximation it can also be used for two-dimensional light sources (see Table 3.10).

An approximation example: an incident area lighting illuminates the surface of a test object with an illuminance of 10 000 lx at a distance of 100 mm. The distance of the lighting component is doubled to 200 mm. As a consequence, the illuminance at the test objects surface decreases down to 2500 lx. That is only caused by the change of distance.

But this is only half the truth. Not all the incoming light on the part surface reaches the sensor too. The reflectance, absorbance, and transmittance at the

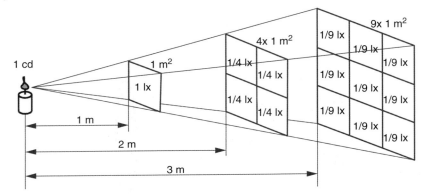

Figure 3.46 Course of the illuminance at the object depends on the distance of the lighting due to the photometric inverse square law.

Table 3.10 Relative error Δ for a circular Lambert radiator (d – distance lighting – object; r – radius of the light source (radiator)).

r/d	Δ (%)
3	10
5	3.8
10	1
15	0.44
30	0.1

object (see Section 3.4) reduce the available light on it's path through the imaging object towards the image sensor.

Tip

To minimize the impact of the photometric inverse square law, try to mount the lighting components for top light applications as near as possible to the test object. Note the effects caused by the brightness distribution of the lighting.

The practical consequences of this effect are far-reaching. Caused by the mechanical construction of the machine or environmental limitations it is not always possible to mount the lighting as near as possible to the test object. Consequences for the practical application can be found in Section 3.8.3.

Dynamical effects happen if the distance between the test object and lighting changes from part to part. This occurs due to handling and feed equipment irregularities (e.g., part on a conveyor belt) and leads to changing brightness in

3.5.3 The Constancy of Luminance

The incoming light from a light source generates an illuminance E_{ob} on the surface of the test object. Multiplied with the reflectance ρ of the object results in a luminance of the object L_{ob}. The object shines with the luminance L_{ob} (see Figure 3.47):

$$L_{ob} = E_{ob} \cdot \rho$$

where

L_{ob} is the resulting luminance of the object,
E_{ob} is the incoming illuminance at the object, and
ρ is the reflectance of the object.

The characteristic value of a backlight is the luminance L too. It shines itself with a luminance. The consequence of the above equation means that this is independent of the distance.

In contrast to the illuminance, the luminance is not dependent on the distance. The luminance is constant in the optical pass of the vision system.

Practically, this means that

- for top light applications with fixed distance lighting – test object:
  No changes of brightness at the test object, neither from short or long camera distances, nor from short or long focal distances of the imaging objective.
- for backlight applications (see Figure 3.48):
  No change of brightness of the lighting independent of the distance from the object to the imaging objective.

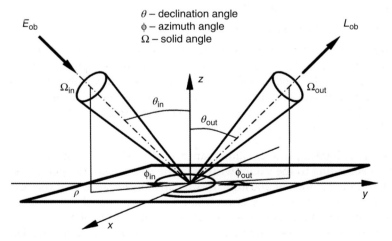

Figure 3.47 Conversion of illuminance into luminance [14].

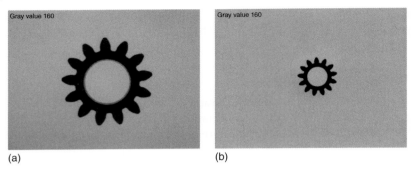

Figure 3.48 Identical luminance (gray value) on the part surface, (a) Imaged with a short working distance of the objective, (b) imaged with a long working distance.

3.5.4 What Light Arrives at the Sensor – Light Transmission Through the Lens

The following viewings are made without considering the natural vignetting (*cosine to the power of 4-law*) of the imaging objective. A homogenous light distribution at the image sensor plane is assumed. To simplify the relations, a perpendicular view to the object and a relative long working distance in relation to the field of view is supposed.

With some approximations [13] is the illuminance E_{sensor}:

$$E_{\text{sensor}} = E_{\text{ob}} \cdot \rho \cdot \frac{\tau}{4k^2}$$

with

E_{ob} the incoming illuminance at the object,
ρ the reflectance of the object,
τ the transmittance of light through the objective,
(medium value $\tau \sim 0.9$ for an average imaging objective with anti-reflective coating), and
k the f-stop number at the imaging objective.

The illuminance E_{sensor} arriving at the image sensor is not dependent on any distances and can be directly controlled by the f-stop of the imaging objective and the illuminance of the used lighting. Imaging objectives with anti-reflective coatings can help to increase the throughput of light through the lenses (transmission τ). The following example shows how a camera can be checked for the usability with regard to the sensor sensitivity.

> An incident lighting has an illuminance of 10 000 lx at a distance of 100 mm according to the values written in the data sheet. The lighting is mounted in a distance of 200 mm. This means on the surface of the test object come in 2500 lx (see Section 3.5.2). Let us say that the test object is made of aluminum. The reflectance (see Table 3.8) is approximately $\rho = 0.6$. According to an estimated transmittance of the imaging objective of $\tau = 0.9$ (anti-reflex coated objective) and a f-stop setting of $k = 8$ (read

from the imaging objective) all values for the approximate calculation are given.

Using the above equation, the illuminance that arrives at the sensor is 5.27 lx. The intended fictitious camera has a minimal sensitivity of 0.3 lx (value from the data sheet of the camera). This means that there is about 17 times more light than minimum necessary. Under these conditions the lighting should be right dimensioned.

Tip

The lighting should produce, at a minimum, a 10 times higher illuminance at the sensor than the documented minimal sensitivity from the data sheet of the imaging sensor/camera. This ensures a reliable function even under changing industrial conditions.

In some data sheets the information about the minimal sensitivity is mentioned using the value of the *exposure H*. To get the needed illuminance it is necessary to divide this value by the exposure time (integration time, shutter time) to get the minimal illuminance at the imaging sensor.

The viewings in this paragraph are only approximate. For an exact View, the following should be considered:

illuminance from lighting, f-stop number, wavelength of lighting, incident angle of light, type of lighting (diffuse, direct, telecentric, structured), reflectance of the test object, transmittance of the imaging objective, perspective characteristics of the used objective (entocentric, telecentric, hypercentric), inserted light filters (in the camera too), and so forth.

3.5.5 Light Distribution of Lighting Components

The distribution of illuminance and luminance in the object plane plays is fundamental for the analysis with image processing algorithms.

The conventional aim is to achieve a homogenous, temporal, and spatial constant lighting or at least a predictable and constant distribution of brightness (structured lighting). Such conditions make the software easier, and the application more reliable and stable.

Different types of lighting, different models, and different lighting techniques produce different characteristic light distribution and brightness profiles. But even for one lighting component the light distribution can change with the distance, incident angle, and direction. That is why data sheets can only tell a part of the whole light characteristics.

The reasons for inhomogenous lighting can be caused by

- the principle of the lighting technique
- the quality of the lighting component (low-cost components tend to poor light distribution)
- wrong application of the lighting
- strongly changing properties of the test object.

The graphical expression of luminance distribution depending on the viewing angle is the luminance indicatrix. It shows the connection between the luminance and observation direction. For a Lambert radiator the luminance indicatrix looks like a half sphere [15]. Other lighting components possess directed radiation characteristics in some other shapes.

Backlights are often characterized only with a perpendicular view to the light emitting surface. The distribution of the luminance gives information about the homogeneity.

Incident light is usually characterized in a similar way. It shines perpendicular to a surface where the illuminance is measured (see Figure 3.49).

Other light sources with special shapes produce characteristic illumination profiles independent of the distance to the test object. Some typical brightness profiles are shown in Figure 3.50.

Avoid to prove this directly with the vision system. Many influencing factors are added to this case. Especially the natural vignetting of the imaging objective will falsify the result. These measurements can be made only with specialized instruments.

It is to be seen that the light distribution of light sources can be totally different depending on the selected light source and the desired purpose. The art is to find the light source that emphasizes the necessary details as best as possible. In addition, the light distribution can differ for various designs. One model of a ring light with a constant diameter and working distance lights up totally different with fresnel lens, with a diffuser, or without an additional element. All these factors influence the lighting result.

The drop of brightness caused by the lighting (see Figure 3.50) can cause software problems. A decrease of 40% means a drop from a gray value of 230 to a gray value of 138. Is the software able to tolerate such large differences? Some inhomogeneities of lighting can be compensated using the shading correction function of the image processing software.

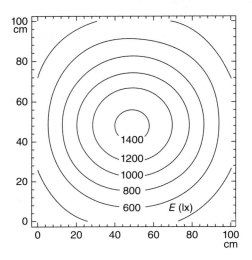

Figure 3.49 Distribution of the illuminance in 0.5 m distance of a commercial fluorescence light source with two compact radiators of each 11 W. (www.vision-control.com.)

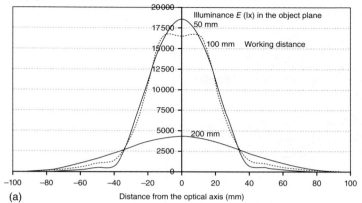

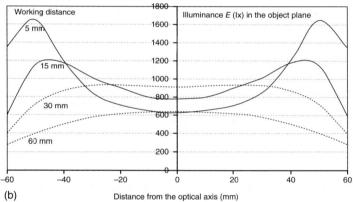

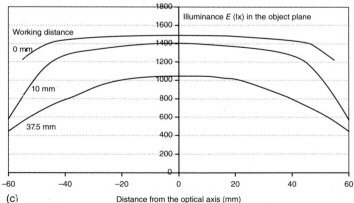

Figure 3.50 Exemplary distributions of illuminances, (a) ring light with fresnel lens, (b) dark field ring light, (c) shadow-free lighting. (www.vision-control.com.)

Figure 3.51 Brightness profile of a lighting to compensate natural vignetting of an imaging objective.

Sometimes a deliberated inhomogenous light distribution is used to compensate other effects like the natural vignetting from the optics. This decrease of illuminance toward the edges of the image can be compensated in a plane, for example, with a dark field ring light that is brighter in the outer illuminated areas (see Figures 3.50 and 3.51).

Some new possibilities in technology (small discrete light sources, progress in information technology) permit us to control the well-defined distribution of light. These so-called *adaptive lighting* allow us to control each single light source (LED) in intensity and time, even with changing distribution in real time. This makes it possible to compensate inhomogeneities in a very sensitive way (see Section 3.8.2.5).

3.5.6 Contrast

All Machine Vision applications are influenced by the contrast. A good contrast at the object and the image sensor respectively is the base that the algorithms of the image processing software can work. No contrast means no usable information. The contrast is the direct consequence of lighting.

Contrast in the classical definition stands in the context of the human perception and is related to absolute values of luminances:

$$K = (L_{max} - L_{min})/(L_{max} + L_{min})$$

with

- K being the contrast for human perception/interpretation,
- L_{max} the maximal luminance at the object (top light),
      or at the lighting (backlight) and
- L_{min} the minimal luminance at the object.

Some simple calculations show that the contrast is higher if the luminances found are larger. In comparison, the contrast in images for digital interpretation K_{dig} is defined by the absolute gray value difference within the image (area of interest/relevant image area):

$$K_{dig} = G_{max} - G_{min}$$

3.5 Basic Rules and Laws of Light Distribution

with

K_{dig} being the contrast in digital images/gray value difference,
G_{max} the maximal gray value, and
G_{min} the minimal gray value.

Table 3.11 shows the comparison of contrasts K and K_{dig} (values from gray values taken as luminance values) from Figure 3.52.

The better the contrast, the more reliable are the results of the software (see Figure 3.53). There is no rule to predict which contrast is necessary, because it depends on the function and the built-in algorithms. Some algorithms (gradient algorithm for edge detection) are known, which can still work with contrasts of 3 (from 255) gray values. Some others need gray value differences of more than 30.

Tip

Image processing algorithms work more precisely at contrastful images. Further, the processing time decreases for a few algorithms if they can work on contrastful images. And not at least is the processing of contrastful images more reliable.

All efforts to maximize the contrast should be considered to avoid from saturation. The maximal brightness that is found in the image (if necessary only in a relevant area, see Figure 3.54) should be not more than 90% of the maximum value. For a camera with 8 bit gray value resolution means a maximal gray value of 230. At gray values of 255 (for 8 bit), the image information is lost and no result can be calculated. Depending on the oversize of light and sensor principle even

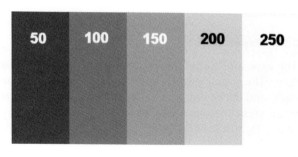

Figure 3.52 Gray bars with constant gray value differences of 50. That means a constant contrast K_{dig} of 50 from bar to bar. Note the seemingly decreasing contrast from left to right at assessment with the human eye.

Table 3.11 Contrast comparison of K and K_{dig}.

Transition from gray value to gray value		K	K_{dig}
50	100	0.33	50
100	150	0.2	50
150	200	0.14	50
200	250	0.11	50

The values for K correspond with their decreasing course to the human perception.

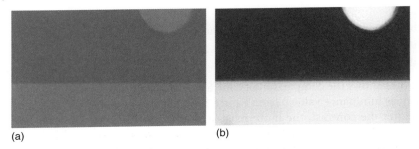

Figure 3.53 Images of one part: (a) imaged with poor contrast and (b) imaged with strong contrast.

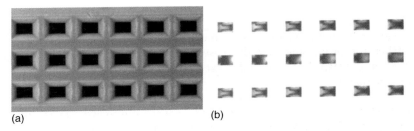

Figure 3.54 Connector housing with inside contact springs, (a) without saturation. There is nothing to recognize in the holes, (b) local overexposure of the housing makes the connector springs viewable.

the image information in the neighborhood can be destroyed by flooding charges (for a CCD).

3.5.7 Exposure

The exposure forms the connection between lighting, time, and camera hardware. The almost general goal will be to generate images with sufficient contrast (light and dark), not over-exposed and not under-exposed. This can be achieved in different manners. The *exposure* opens different possibilities of getting the same brightness in the image. Exposure means in simplification

$$H = E \cdot t$$

with

- H being the exposure,
- E the illumination at the test object, and
- t the exposure time/shutter time.

A constant exposure can be achieved with different boundary conditions. Some of them are

- double (half) exposure time and half (double) illuminance (power) of lighting
- open (close) one f-stop number of the objective and half (double) illuminance (power) of lighting

- insert (remove) a 2 × neutral filter and double (half) illuminance (power) of lighting.

All these parameters can also be used in combinations. Further, allow these variations to use brighter or darker lighting and compensate this. To play with the parameters of exposure means to know more about the application. Note that changes in exposure time have an effect on the motional blurring of moving parts. Changes of the f-stop have effects on depth of focus, aberrations, and more (see Chapter 4 also).

Tip

Consider the boundary conditions for every application before choosing a lighting. What is possible?

- long or short exposure time (still standing/moving test object)
- small/large f-stop number (small/large depth of focus needed)
- or both.

These facts will influence the needed illuminance/luminance, which means lighting power! Table 3.12 shows the example of constant exposure for all combinations of f-stop and exposure time.

Note that the combination of f-stop number 16 together with a 1/3200 s exposure time needs a 64 times brighter lighting. This is usually limited by the limits of lighting power.

3.6 Light Filters

Light filters are optical elements that influence the light path and remove unwanted or unused parts of light. With their effect, they are a bridge between optics and lighting.

3.6.1 Characteristic Values of Light Filters

Besides geometrical values such as socket thread, diameter and height of light filters are characterized by few values [16]. Here, only the general values are introduced (see Figure 3.55):

Table 3.12 Example for constant exposure with time and f-stop variations.

f-Stop	2	2.8	4	5.6	8	11	16
Exposure time (s)	1/3200	1/1600	1/800	1/400	1/200	1/100	1/50
Depth of focus	Small						Large
Sensitivity to movement/vibration	Small						Large

f-Stop number and exposure time determine the possible applications. If the combination of a large f-stop number and a short exposure time is needed the only way is to increase the lighting power. Each step (one f-stop number more or halfen the exposure time) means to double the light emission.

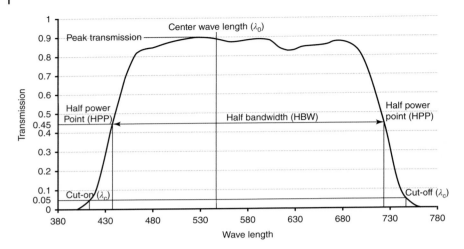

Figure 3.55 Major characteristics of light filters.

Transmission (T). Relation from passing light energy and incoming light energy (see Section 3.4.1.4). Sometimes, the average transmission is indicated for a limited wavelength ranges.

Cutoff/cuton wavelength (λ_c). The wavelength specifies the location of the transition from high (low) transmission to low (high) transmission. This term is often used for specifying the wavelength location of a short-wavelength/long-wavelength pass filter. The criterion of 5% absolute transmission describes the wavelength.

Half-power points (*HPP*). The wavelength at which a filter transmits one-half of its peak transmission. (For a bandpass with peak transmission of 70%, the HPP are at 35% transmission.)

Center wavelength (λ_0). For bandpass filters $2\lambda_1\lambda_2/(\lambda_1 + \lambda_2)$: can be applied, where λ_1 and λ_2 are the bandpass HPP. This is not the simple arithmetical average.

Bandwidth (*BW*). The width of a bandpass filter between specific absolute transmission points. Usually for this, the HPP are used. Then it is called half-bandwidth (HBW).

The transmission properties of light filters can be found in different descriptions (see Table 3.13):

- filter diagrams for filters with wavelength-dependent transmission
- filter prolongation factors for edge filters
- values for optical density for edge and neutral filters.

Filter diagrams usually show in logarithmic dependence the transmission of light relative to the wavelength. They are used for wavelength-sensitive filters. It has to be read from the diagram how much light the filter blocks for a defined wavelength range.

Table 3.13 Light transmission through filters: connection between filter factor, optical density, and f-stop-difference of the lens.

Light transmission T	Filter factor for exposure time (without change of f-stop no.)	Optical density D	Number of f-stops to open to compensate intensity difference (without change of exposure time)
50% or 0.5	2	0.3	1
25% or 0.25	4	0.6	2
12.5% or 0.125	8	0.9	3
6.25% or 0.0625	16	1.2	4
...	...	...	...
0.1% or 0.00962	1000(1024)	3.0	10

Filters without/low spectral response are described by their filter factor. This is an average value how much the exposure has to be prolonged to achieve the same brightness in the image as without the light filter. If there are several filters in use as a stack the densities have to be multiplied to get the total density.

A third description of the loss of intensity of light filters is the optical density D. It is the logarithmic reciprocal of the transmission T. The definition is $D = \log 1/T$.

Filters can be used in stacks. If more than one filter is used the filter factors are multiplied or the optical densities are added.

> Stack of two light filters with 50% and 25% transmittance.
> Calculation with filter factors 2 and 4 → 2 × 4 = 8
> Calculation with optical density 0.3 and 0.6 → 0.3 + 0.6 = 0.9

3.6.2 Influences of Light Filters on the Optical Path

All light filters are active optical elements and act like a plain parallel glass plate and lengthen the optical path length. The consequences are longer working distances of the imaging objective. This effect can be particularly strong depending on the place where the light filter is inserted/removed.

Rule of the thumb

As an approximation for an average optical glass (refraction index $n = 1.5$) applies:

Filter in front of lens: increase of working distance = Glass thickness/3
Filter in front of sensor: increase of working distance
 = Glass thickness/$3\beta^2$

with β being the image scale of the used imaging objective [3].

Tip

Consider the change of the working distance if a light filter is removed (IR cutting filter from a camera for an application with IR lighting) or inserted (daylight cutting filter to suppress ambient light). This can cause strong effects to the construction/distances of the machine where the camera is built-in.

All inserted light filters not only change the optical path, but also cause artificial astigmatism (aberration). A light filter that is tilted in relation to the optical axis additionally causes a parallel offset of the optical axis because of the refraction on the glass plate surfaces (see Figure 3.56). For large image scales this can be significant. The connection is for small angles (the paraxial area) [3]:

$$v = \frac{n-1}{n} \cdot d \cdot \varepsilon$$

with

- v being the parallel offset,
- n the refractive index of the filter,
- d the thickness of the filter, and
- ε the twisting angle of the filter

3.6.3 Types of Light Filters

Light filters can be divided into three main classes by their principle of extinction:

Absorbing filters [17]:

- extinct wavelength ranges by absorbing light

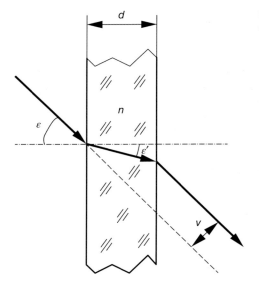

Figure 3.56 Parallel offset of the optical axis caused by a tilted light filter.

- can be made of colored glass, with a gelatine layer between two transparent glass plates or plastic plates (limited optical quality! – streaks, different thicknesses, etc.)
- provide wide bands of transmission (not so exact)
- are available in many hues and made from standard optical glasses
- can be made of fluorescent dyes too (conversion: *new colors for old*)
- are cost effective, mounted in sockets with standardized threads and made by many manufacturers.

Interference filters [18]:

- extinct wavelength ranges by interference of light
- use thin metal or dielectric films ($\lambda/4$ thickness) on transparent glass plates
- provide narrow bands of transmission (very accurate)
- are working very effectively. But, the smaller the bandwidth the larger the loss of transmission even in the pass range: 5 nm bandwidth means 70% loss of transmission, 10 nm: 50%, 20 nm: 10%.
- available for many center wavelengths in small intervals
- are expensive and usually not easy to handle for Machine Vision (square glass plates without socket).

Polarization filters

- extinct light with defined directions of oscillation. Light with defined oscillation directions can pass.
- are made of crystal or synthetic materials that are stretched (to align the molecules) to get the directional properties
- available as thin films, glass filters. Plastic plates are more suitable for large areas (only to use in the lighting light path)
- work relatively independent of wavelength within a wide bandwidth
- mounted in sockets with standardized threads
- are turnable to adjust the polarization.

Absorbing and interference light filters can be divided into four main classes by their range of extinction of wavelengths [16]:

Short-wavelength pass filters (SWP). Filters that transmit light at wavelengths shorter than the cut-off. Light at wavelengths longer than the cut-off wavelength is attenuated.

Long-wavelength pass filters (LWP). Filters that transmit light at wavelengths longer than the cut-on. Light at wavelengths shorter than the cut-on is attenuated.

Bandpass filters (BP). Filters that transmit light energy only within a selected band of wavelengths. Two classes are given: narrow or wide band-pass filters. A detailed description of function is written in [4].

Neutral density filters. Filters that are relatively little selective to a wavelength range and serve to suppress a defined amount of light. They are characterized by their optical density (see Table 3.13).

Note that some light filters have a limited wavelength range where they work.

3.6.4 Anti-Reflective Coatings (AR)

Every transition of light between two media with different refractive indices such as air and glass causes a loss of light energy. The incident light is reflected from each uncoated average glass surface with an approximate reflectance of 4% (exactly that depends on wavelength, incident angle of light, etc.) (see Figure 3.57).

For a filter glass plate this means loss of intensity too. Simultaneously, this is connected with a worsening of the image quality (loss of contrast, milky images, ghost images) caused by multiple reflections inside the glass (see Figure 3.24, backside reflections).

This fact is significant for single lenses, complete objectives and for light filters too. That is why qualitatively better light filters are coated with anti-reflective coatings made from dielectric thin films of $\lambda/2$ thickness. Single- or multi-layer coatings (metal oxides, CaF_2) are applied to improve the image quality.

Because of the necessary thickness of $\lambda/2$ that is required for the anti-reflective coating, it is necessary to use different anti-reflective layers for a high qualitative dereflection. Each of them is applied for one narrow wavelength band. The so-called multi-coated lenses and filters are expensive. A good compromise for Machine Vision is the use of single-layer coatings made from calcium fluoride (CaF_2) (see Table 3.14).

Regarding the employment of light filters as the front element and interface to the industrial environment in Machine Vision applications there are needs to ensure durability. Besides their optical function, the coatings have to

- protect the glass surface of the filter/lens
- be nonabrasive
- be noncorroding.

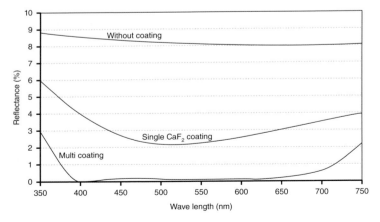

Figure 3.57 Typical course of reflectances of an uncoated, single coated (CaF_2 coating) and multi-coated glass plate (average optical glass, transitions air–glass–air) in dependence of the wavelength [17].

Table 3.14 Classification of lighting techniques: systematic overview [27].

Light direction field characteristics	Incident lighting		Transmitted lighting	
	Bright field	Dark field	Bright field	Dark field
Directional properties	Diffuse (1)	Diffuse (5)	Diffuse (7)	Diffuse (10)
	Directed (2)	Directed (6)	Directed (8)	Directed (11)
	Telecentric (3)	–	Telecentric (9)	–
	Structured (4)	–	–	–

The name of the technique is to read from bottom to top.

3.6.5 Light Filters for Machine Vision

3.6.5.1 UV Blocking Filter

This long-wavelength pass filter blocks the UV part of the light spectrum. Since most of the image sensors of Machine Vision (CCD or CMOS) are not sensitive in the UV range of light they almost do not influence the image brightness. The visible light can pass more than 90%, which means that there is no noticeable prolonging factor. The cut-on wavelength depends on the filter model and is typically about 380 nm.

UV blocking filters (see Figure 3.58) are used as

- protective screens against dirt
- protection of the front lens against cleaning with polluted clothes
- as mechanical barriers against unintentional strokes.

Tip

Use generally a UV blocking filter as a seal of the imaging objective. It is cost effective and protects the costly lens from the rough environmental conditions of the industrial floor.

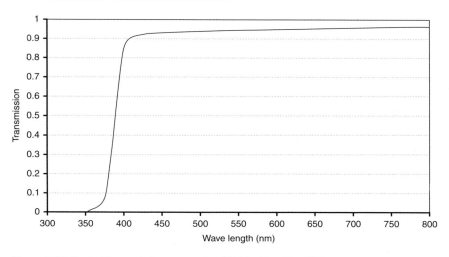

Figure 3.58 Typical transmission curve of an UV blocking filter [17].

3.6.5.2 Daylight Suppression Filter

This long-wavelength pass filter blocks the visible light of the spectrum or their parts. Near-infrared light can pass. Since most of the image sensors of Machine Vision (CCD or CMOS) are sensitive in the range of near-infrared light, only this part of light can be used when applying a daylight suppression filter. The cut-on wavelength is model specific. Typical for Machine Vision are cut-on wavelength from about 780 nm.

Daylight suppression filters (see Figure 3.59) are used

- for IR lighting applications
- for independence from extraneous light (lighting of the factory hall) in combination with an IR lighting (needs coordination of cut-on wavelength and wavelength of the lighting).

Note: Remove the IR suppression filter from the camera before using a daylight suppression filter! Otherwise no light can pass to the image sensor, because both filter characteristics overlap.

If sunlight is part of the ambient light the effect of daylight suppression filters can be strongly limited, because the incoming sunlight contains quantities of the IR light too. These quantities can be partially larger than the IR-lighting itself (typically, LED lighting with their narrow bandwidth of light emission). In these cases, there will be no effect of daylight suppression filters. The use of the filter is practical in factory halls with artificial light.

For a better suppression of sunlight it is recommended to use a filter combination (see Section 3.6.5.7).

3.6.5.3 IR Suppression Filter

This wide band pass filter lets the visible light to pass and blocks the UV light and IR light alike. Many Machine Vision cameras contain these filters to improve the

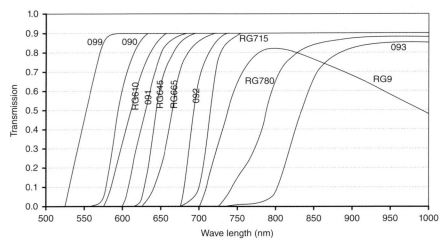

Figure 3.59 Typical transmission curves of different filter glass sorts of daylight suppression filters [19].

image quality for the visible light, because IR light penetrates deep into the silicon substrate of the image sensors and causes blurred and contrastless images.

Usually, the IR suppression filters are separate filters and are removable from the camera (reddish-green-coated glass in front of the sensor chip) for applications with IR light. In some cases, the cover glass of the sensor chip is directly coated with the IR suppression layer.

IR suppression filters are in use not only in monochrome cameras but also in color cameras. They ensure that the IR light does not influence the brightness of the single-color pixels (RGB) in a different manner. Thus, the brightness offset for the whole color triples is the same.

IR suppression filters are used

- to achieve contrastful and sharp images (in visible light)
- to suppress uncontrolled influence of the IR light
- to remove brightness offset for color pixels in color cameras.

Note: For IR applications the IR suppression filter must be removed! An application with IR lighting is impossible, if the cover glass of the sensor chip is coated with the IR suppression filter layer (see Figure 3.60). Furthermore, the removal of the IR suppression filter causes changes in the working distance of the imaging objective (see Section 3.6.2).

3.6.5.4 Neutral Filter/Neutral Density Filter/Gray Filter

These unselective light filters reduce the luminous flux (relatively) independent of the wavelengths used. The degree of reduction is specified by the density or the prolongation factor. They are available in different densities (usually with prolongation factors from 2 to 1000) (see above) (Figure 3.61). Neutral filters are used

- if there is too much light (too bright light source)
- to reduce the light intensity without change of the f-stop number (for objectives with fix f-stop respectively with no change of depth of focus!)

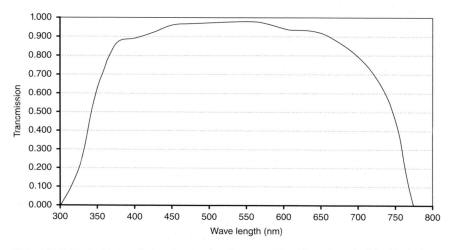

Figure 3.60 Typical transmission curves of an IR suppression filter glass used for Machine Vision [17].

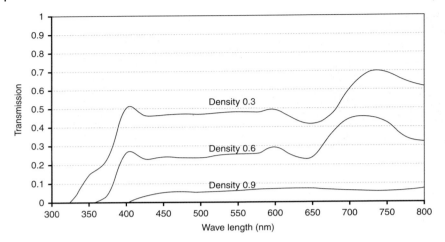

Figure 3.61 Typical transmission curves of neutral filters with different densities [17].

- to reduce the light intensity without change of exposure time (no change of motional blurring).

3.6.5.5 Polarization Filter

Polarization filters are color neutral. They extract light components with special polarization properties: linear, circular, or elliptical polarized light (see Section 3.4.2.5). To achieve the right polarization it is necessary to turn (and fix!) the filter in the socket. Typical filter prolongation factors are between 2.3 and 2.8 depending on the angle of rotation. Caused by the used polarizing materials many polarization filters do not work in IR light – see the data sheet. Polarization filters are used

- to suppress reflections
- for special analysis techniques (tension optics)
- for polarizing lighting components
- to adjust infinitely variable brightness (two stacked linear polarizing filters) without any change of f-stop or exposure time.

3.6.5.6 Color Filters

Color filters are realized as long-wavelength pass filters or as bandpass filters. In the color that they appear to the human eye, most light energy can pass.

The use of color filters is limited to monochrome image sensors/cameras, because they distort the color information. The course of transmission of these filters is individual, and is dependent on the wavelength and the optical glass used.

Color filters in combination with white light result in similar effects from contrast as the use of colored light (see Section 3.4.2 cont.). The disadvantage of this construction is that the color filter reduces the radiation of the light source with the filter. It is better to use a light source that already emits effectively in the desired wavelength band.

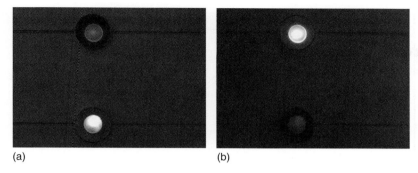

(a)   (b)

Figure 3.62 Plausibility check of orange (top position) and green (bottom position) LEDs: (a) with green bandpass color filter; (b) with orange color glass filter.

A light filter with the same color as the part produces a bright part, and a light filter with complementary color produces a dark part (see Section 3.4.2). Color filters (see Figures 3.59 and 3.62) are used

- inside color image sensor chips (mosaic filter) to achieve a defined and narrow spectral response of the RGB pixels
- to emphasize or suppress colored image information.

3.6.5.7 Filter Combinations

Light filters can be stacked or combined, one on the lighting and the other in front of the imaging objective, and so forth. The overall effect is to combine different filter characteristics.

As an example hereinafter the combination of a short-wavelength pass filter and a long-wavelength pass filter is explained. The combination simulates a bandpass filter.

An effective suppression of daylight for Machine Vision applications – better than with an IR suppression filter – can be achieved using the camera built-in IR suppression filter – this removes disturbing IR-light. The combination with a red color long-wavelength pass filter 090 (see Figure 3.59) in front of the imaging objective removes the visible light with a shorter wavelength. The result is a filter characteristic of a band pass filter (see Figure 3.63) but much cheaper.

If the selected lighting emits within the center wavelength of this band pass, an almost perfect suppression of ambient light is realized. The used lighting will have a much higher light output in this narrow band than the ambient light (usually white light as a mixture of different wavelengths). For the example described in Figure 3.63, a red light with a 660 nm center wavelength will fit the requirements.

In addition, this is particularly effective because the imaging sensors are more sensitive in this wavelength range than in the IR.

3.7 Lighting Techniques and Their Use

3.7.1 How to Find a Suitable Lighting?

This will be the most important question of an engineer who has to select a right lighting setup for the Machine Vision application. Probably he remembers

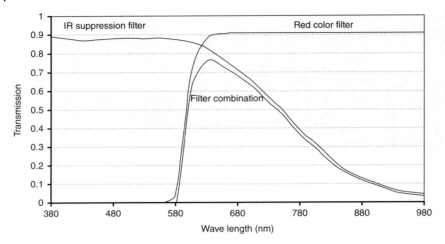

Figure 3.63 Transmission characteristics of an IR suppression filter and a red color filter and the resulting characteristics of their combination.

some clever Machine Vision proverbs such as "better to light than write (software)," "avoid garbage in (bad lighting) that causes *garbage* out (bad result)," "create the BEST image first," and so forth. The general aim will be

- to maximize the contrast of features of interest
- to minimize the contrast of all others
- to minimize external influences.

To get an approach for the selection of lighting a general comparison of human and machine perception of visual information is made.

Human beings possess a biological vision system capable of learning combined with a skilled handling system with all degrees of freedom. Identification of a defect is known from their term and from recollection. The part and the viewer move around until the required lighting is obtained and the feature can be seen, even under the most inadequate lighting conditions. And the more each part is inspected the ability to recognize (cognitive vision) increases – the man learns from experience.

A Machine Vision system usually owns static performance data: predetermined position for image acquisition and predetermined position of lighting, limited range of motion, predetermined functionality of the software. Under these limitations the result shall be found to be reliable, precise, and stable. This is the chance for lighting to compensate all those shortcomings and result in finding the best possible lighting.

A good starting point for all viewings to select a lighting is the lighting perception with the human eye. Although the biological vision is not comparable with a Machine Vision system it can give first clues for lighting, even if it is known that a man cannot see some details that the machine can see and vice versa. Some exceptions are given where the first check from the eye will fail:

- too small details (not resolvable by the eye)

- lighting in a wavelength range where the eye is not sensitive (UV and IR)
- lighting with flash light or lighting of fast running parts.

Tip

Observe the object with the human eye using different lighting techniques. What cannot be illuminated viewable for the human eye that is (usually) not viewable for the machine too.

A strategy to find a right lighting can be to think backward. Think of these questions before:

"What I am looking for?,""How should the lighting be moved to produce light or shadow at the part in the right place.?""What lights or shadows are disturbing?,""Where do they come from?,""How do I have to modify the lighting to emphasize or suppress these effects?"

To get the first ideas for lighting imagine where I have to put the light that produces the reflexes in the places where I expect it. How large must be the lighting to obtain this? Keep to the basic rules of light propagation: reflection and scattering. The surface angles determine very roughly, where the light is reflected and must be positioned in order to properly illuminate an object. So you get the first approximation for the setup.

Tip

An overall lighting is not always possible (with only one or even more lighting components), because light works according to the superposition principle. Different lighting overlay. The consequence is low contrast.

That is why divide the complex lighting task into single jobs with single components. Possibly a few images have to grabbed sequentially, each with another lighting method and component. Try to optimize, what lighting is combinable without mutual influence.

Nevertheless, find a right lighting that depends on a multitude of factors. A few standard solutions are possible. However, the lighting still depends on many factors. It is a mixture of systematics, experience, and trial and error.

3.7.2 Planning the Lighting Solution – Influence Factors

Frequently, the practically possible lighting setup differs from the solution found either from experiments or from theory. It depends on many factors besides the inherent lighting characteristics of the component itself. Not each lighting technique found can be put into practice. The environment of the vision system, the machine, and the interfaces are restricting and interacting. Those factors can be

The lighting component itself:

- light source properties (see Sections 3.3–3.5)
- power and heat generation (refrigeration necessary)
- available size of illuminated area.

The properties of the test object (see Section 3.4).

***Lighting environment*:**

- ambient/extraneous light (constant, changing)
- preferred wavelengths (e.g., pharmaceutical applications: IR light)
- interactions with the background (constant, changing).

***Machine Vision hardware*:**

- possible operation mode of lighting: static, pulse, or flash
- possible synchronization of lighting (trigger of flash, switch on/off, brightness control)
- possible operation mode of the camera: short time/long time shutter
- necessary intensity on the image sensor of the camera (power of lighting)
- spectral sensitivity of the image sensor of the camera (see Section 3.3)
- need of stabilized power supply for lighting.

***Machine Vision software*:**

- supported synchronization of lighting (trigger of flash, switch on/off, brightness control)
- necessary minimum gray value contrast
- necessary/tolerable edge widths
- necessary homogeneity of light
- useable/necessary algorithms.

***Imaging optics*:**

- spectral transmission of the imaging objective
- working distance of the imaging objective (determines power of lighting needed)
- f-number of the imaging objective (determines the position, where the lighting is mounted)
- use of light filters.

***Machine environment*:**

- limitations of the space available
- necessary distances, angles, directions of lighting
- vibrations that forbid the use of some light sources (e.g., halogen lamps)
- cable specifications (bending-change strength).

***Customer requirements*:**

- compliance of standards
- company internal forbidden/unwanted components like lasers
- prescribed wavelengths from special branches
- prescribed maintenance intervals/lifetime demands
- costs.

All these exemplary factors demonstrate that good initial considerations and good contacts with the design engineer of the whole machine helps us to avoid nasty surprises. The design engineer has to put your lighting setup into action at the machine. For an early intervention, it is important to coordinate all actions that could have an influence on the lighting. Remember: The design engineer is the master of space and arrangement at the machine!

3.7.3 Lighting Systematics

Above all, the following prior criteria are helpful to systematize lighting techniques for practical use (see Table 3.14 and Figure 3.64) [26]:

- directional properties of lighting
- direction of the arrangement of lighting
- characteristics of the illuminated field.

3.7.3.1 Directional Properties of the Light

The directional properties of light give the base for the interaction of the lighting component with reflective, transmitting, and scattering properties of the test object. They are divided into diffuse, directed, telecentric, and structured properties.

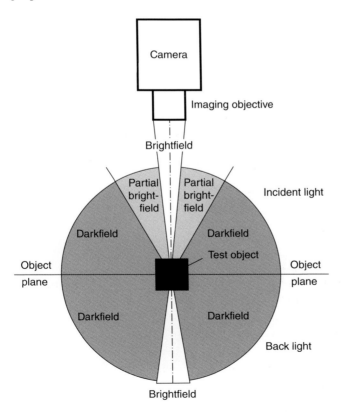

Figure 3.64 Classification of lighting techniques: spatial arrangement of the lighting.

136 | *3 Lighting in Machine Vision*

Diffuse lighting does not have the preferred direction of light emission. The light leaves the emitting surface in each direction. Frequently, the light emission obeys the rules of a Lambert radiator. This means that the luminance indicatrix of a plane light source forms a half sphere (Figure 3.65) and the luminance is independent of the viewing direction.

These lighting need no special precautions or preferential directions for installation. For the function it is important to achieve local homogeneity on the part. The illuminated area is directly defined by the size of the luminous field of the diffuse lighting.

The general use of diffuse lighting is to obtain even lighting conditions.

Directed lighting have radiation characteristics that can vary widely (Figure 3.66). Already the directive characteristics of the single light sources can vary as also the characteristics of clusters of light sources. Generally produce lighting components with overlapping of multiple light sources produce a better light intensity and homogeneity.

Note that for the installation shifting and tilting of the illumination or the object has a strong influence on the brightness and contrast in the image due to the directionality.

The general use of directed lighting is to show edges and surface structures by reflection or shadowing. Even strong contrasts that are desired for lighting pre-processing can be achieved.

Telecentric lighting are special forms of directed lighting with extremely strong directional characteristics by means of an optical system in front of the light source. Due to the arrangement of the light source (typically LED with a mounted pin-hole aperture) in the focal plane of the optics they produce parallel chief rays.

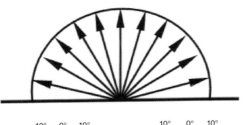

Figure 3.65 Luminance indicatrix of a Lambert radiator. Most diffuse area lighting reacts like a Lambert radiator.

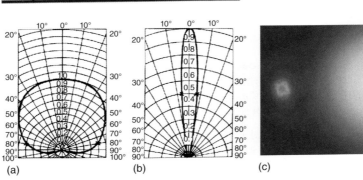

Figure 3.66 Brightness distribution of LEDs (luminance indicatrix) with different directive properties, (a) cardioid characteristics, (b) beam shaping characteristics, (c) brightness distribution on the surface of an object. Left: from a single LED. Right: from an LED cluster.

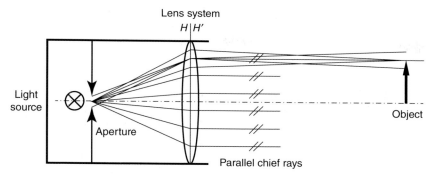

Figure 3.67 Principle function of a telecentric lighting.

Telecentric lighting is not parallel lighting, as the light source is not infinitely small. Parallel, convergent, and divergent light rays contribute to illumination (Figure 3.67).

Telecentric lighting are not as sensitive against vibration and adjustment like parallel lighting. And even if they are not fully aligned with a telecentric objective the principle of telecentry still works, but the brightness distribution becomes inhomogenous. That is why it is ensured that telecentric components are stable and defined mounted.

Telecentric lighting works only in combination with telecentric objectives. If this is not taken into account, the view from an entocentric objective (objective with prespective properties) into a telecentric lighting shows only a spot. For, the objective seems to be the lighting in infinity – as the name *telecentric* already says.

Though the telecentric lighting uses only one single LED it is much more brighter than a diffuse transmitted lighting that is using many LEDs. This happens because the light source of a telecentric lighting emits the light only in the direction where it is needed.

Telecentric lighting on the basis of LED produces incoherent light. This means the avoidance of speckles (intensity differences from lasers made by interferences of waves from same wavelength and same phase).

Telecentric lighting is mostly in use for transmitted light applications. Different wavelengths (light color) are

- red light for a maximum of brightness (most imagers have a maximum of sensitivity of red light)
- blue light for a maximum of accuracy (size of diffraction effects is proportional to the wavelength)
- IR light for lighting with reduced extraneous light
- IR flash for very short and bright flashes in fast processes.

A specific feature besides the directional properties of light is structured lighting. Superimposed to the direction the light can carry various geometrical bright-dark structures some of which are

- single points
- grids of points (point arrays)
- single lines

- groups of parallel lines
- grids of squared lines
- single circles
- concentric rings
- single squares
- concentric squares.

The methods of production of these geometrical structures are manifold. From slides, templates, masks, through LCD projectors and laser diodes with diffraction or interference gratings or intelligent adaptive lighting, with LED everything is possible.

The general use of the structured light is to project the structure onto the test object. The knowledge of the light pattern and the comparison with the distorted pattern gives detailed information about the 3D structure and the topography of the part.

3.7.3.2 Arrangement of the Lighting

Incident lighting affects the test object from the same side like the imaging objective. The reference line is the optical axis of the imaging objective. From there with ±90° the range of incident light encloses. The dividing plane is the object plane (see Figure 3.64). The function needs incident light reflections or at least scattering of the test objective for imaging. Most Machine Vision application must work with the incident light, because frequently the backlight construction is impossible by the mechanical structure of the machine.

Transmitted lighting (backlighting) is positioned at the opposite side of the object plane contrary to the imaging system (see Figure 3.64).

Transmitted lighting creates sharp and contrastful contours for opaque or low transparent parts. Transparent parts can appear different depending on the lighting technique.

> *Tip*
>
> Only a few Machine Vision applications can work with transmitted lighting. If so, do not position the part directly on the light emitting surface of the lighting. In time the surface will be scratched and scraped. Take care for a position of the lighting away from the object. This ensures that dust and dirt on the lighting surface is not imaged (out of focus) and cannot disturb the evaluation of the software.

3.7.3.3 Properties of the Illuminated Field

The *brightfield illumination* is named after the brightness appearance of the filed of view (see Figure 3.64). The field of view is directly illuminated by the lighting – it is bright. It is bright from the incident and the reflected light of a perfect test object (see Figure 3.68) or directly from the transmitted lighting. Disturbing structures such as defects, scratches, or flaws (incident light) or the test object itself (transmitted light) appear dark. Because of the bright illuminated field

Figure 3.68 Bright field reflections from a glass surface. The flawless surface appears bright; engraved scratches are dark.

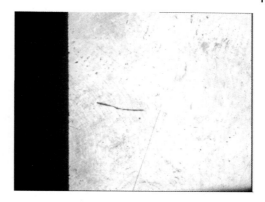

Figure 3.69 Partial brightfield illumination on a brushed part.

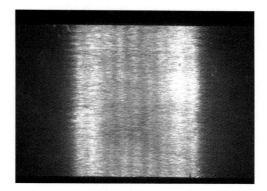

applications with bright field illumination are usually unsensitive to extraneous light.

Partial bright field illuminations are those illuminations that are located at the transition between bright field and dark field illumination (see Figure 3.64). There is no clear dividing line/limiting angles between both. This determines the surface roughness of the test object. A typical clue for a partial bright field illumination is that the image appears as a bright field image and the local arrangement means a dark field lighting. The limits are given at the transition from reflecting light (bright field) to scattering light (dark field) on the surface of the test object (see Figure 3.69). Frequently used components for partial bright field illuminations are ring lights.

Darkfield illumination describes the field brightness of a flawless field of view that is not directly illuminated by the lighting. It remains dark (see Figure 3.70). No light from the lighting is directly reflected into the imaging objective. The only light that can pass the lens is the scattered light from the surface of the test object. As a consequence, homogenous objects appear dark and defects, scratches textures, dust, and so forth appear bright.

Figure 3.70 Darkfield illumination with test object, mirror bar. Only the dust corns and the grinded edges of the mirror bar scatter light.

3.7.4 The Lighting Techniques in Detail

3.7.4.1 Diffuse Bright Field Incident Light (No. 1, Table 3.14)

This lighting technique is used for

- homogenous lighting of weakly structured and slightly uneven little formed parts
- specular parts
- opaque/transparent parts (with well reflecting surface)
- creation of low glare
- suppression of small surface structures, for example, machining and tool marks, diffuse surfaces
- low contrast at edges
- smaller contrasts on surfaces of translucent materials.

Arrangement

The lighting technique can be achieved with

- coaxial diffuse light, the so-called diffuse on axis light
- tilted camera and tilted diffuse area lighting component.

Coaxial light means that the light passes the same optical path like the image information through the imaging objective. It is necessary to use some kind of beam splitter (foil, plate, or prism cube). Usually, these components divide the transmitted and reflected light into 50/50 parts for lighting purposes. An inherent characteristic is the appearance of ghost images (double images) from the front and back surface and lower contrast. With some optical efforts this can be compensated.

The light efficiency of coaxial light is very poor. Caused by their principle (2 times passing the 50/50 beam splitter) less than 1/4 intensity of the light source can reach the camera sensor. In reality it is much less because of the limited reflectance of the test objects. That is why this kind of lighting works fairly well only with extreme powerful light sources and/or good reflecting test objects.

The units for coaxial lighting are mounted between imaging objective and test object. They can be mounted directly in front of the lens or separately.

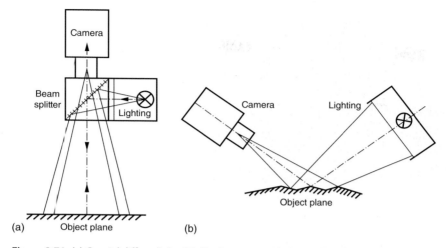

Figure 3.71 (a) Coaxial diffuse light, (b) tilted camera and tilted diffuse light.

In most cases these components reduce the working distance of the imaging objective (not, if built in the objective). Note that the necessary size of the light source increases with a larger viewing angle of the used imaging objective (see Figure 3.71a). Worst case is that the field of view will not be completely illuminated.

For the use of tilted lighting it is noted that the reflection law lies down where the lighting has to be positioned. On the other hand, the viewing angle of the imaging objective determines the size and distance of the lighting (perspective effect, see Figure 3.71b). The more distant the lighting, the larger the size of the lighting has to be. And the more powerful – note the photometric inverse square law! (see Figure 3.72)

Components

- beamsplitter units with connected diffuse area lighting
- diffuse area lighting.

How to select?

1) Determine the light color: note the interaction with the part color.
2) Determine the lighting size:
   a) the beam splitter lays down the usable lighting size by the field of view of the imaging objective
   b) approximately 5 mm wider than the field of view. For entocentric objectives note the effect of the perspective/viewing angle of the imaging objective. In this case, the size depends on the distance of the lighting to the test object.
3) Determine the performance of the controlling technique
4) Select from catalog.

Figure 3.72 The diffuse incident lighting levels differences of brightness from tooling marks on the test object surface: chip sticked on to an aluminum sheet.

3.7.4.2 Directed Bright Field Incident Light (No. 2, Table 3.14)

Directed bright field incident light is similar to the diffuse bright field incident light. But the directional characteristic of light leads to the use for

- even illumination of parts with diffusely reflecting surfaces
- conscious utilization of reflections
- reflectant flat surfaces and deep cavities.

Arrangement

The lighting technique can be achieved with

- coaxial directed light/directed on axis light (see Figure 3.73a)
- a tilted direct area lighting component (see Figure 3.73b).

To arrange coaxial directed light, it is necessary to ensure that the optical path of the imaging objective is almost perpendicular to the surface details that shall be bright. Deviations of angles of a few degrees are possible depending on the size of the illumination and the surface quality of the test object.

The arrangement of tilted direct area lighting components is strongly connected with the reflecting properties of the test object, light direction, height, and angle.

Set up and selection are similar to diffuse bright field incident light (see Section 3.7.4.1).

Components

- directed area lighting with and without polarizers
- special design as line lights to emphasize line-shaped information
- beamsplitter units with connected directed area lighting

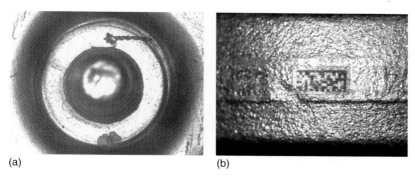

Figure 3.73 (a) Surface check of an interference fit-pin connection with coaxial incident bright field lighting, (b) data matrix code is recognizable at rough casting parts with directed incident light.

Examples:

3.7.4.3 Telecentric Bright Field Incident Light (No. 3, Table 3.14)

One can consider the telecentric brightfield incident light as a special and extreme case of the directed bright field incident light (see Section 3.7.4.2). It can be used only under some conditions:

- check for even very small surface imperfections and inhomogeneities of specular parts: surface defects show up clearly as dark areas.

This lighting technique only works in combination with a telecentric imaging objective.

Arrangement

The lighting technique can be achieved with

- coaxial telecentric light/telecentric on axis light (see Figure 3.74)
- a tilted telecentric lighting component.

This lighting technique needs mechanically stable conditions. The preferential direction of telecentric light causes the extreme sensitivity of this lighting technique against changes in rotation of the part. Bear in mind that if the part tilts with an angle α, referring to the reflection law, the light will be deflected with the double angle 2α.

For coaxial telecentric lighting it is important to hold the reflecting surface of the test object at exactly 90° to the optical axis of the imaging objective. Already a small deviation or a slightly arched test object will result in failure. The size of the tolerated angle depends on the degree of parallelity of the telecentric light and the quality of the telecentric objective. Typical tolerated angles for tilting are 0.5–1.5°.

Furthermore, telecentric incident light is attached to the condition of smooth and shiny surfaces. Roughness destroys the telecentric light by scattering. After this diffusion the amount of reflected light toward the lens is much too small and the image is dark.

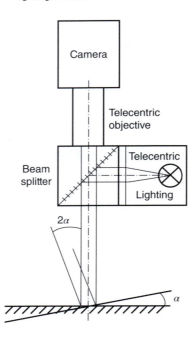

Figure 3.74 Influence of a tilting object using coaxial telecentric bright field incident light.

Figure 3.75 Combination of a telecentric lighting (right bottom) with a beam splitter unit (middle) and a telecentric objective (cylinder left). (www.vision-control.com.)

Components

- telecentric lighting
- beamsplitter units with connected telecentric lighting (see Figure 3.75).

How to select?

1) Determine light color: note the interaction with the part color.
2) Determine lighting size: the beam splitter lays down the lighting size by the field of view of the imaging objective

3) Determine the performance of the controlling technique
4) Select from catalog.

The example for telecentric bright field incident lighting is shown in Figure 3.76.

3.7.4.4 Structured Bright Field Incident Light (No. 4, Table 3.14)

Structure lighting is used to check 3D surface information with a projected light pattern. The projected light on a nontransparent surface allows us to achieve three-dimensional information using a two-dimensional sensor. By means of light pattern one can

- check the presence of three-dimensional parts
- measure the height of one point
- measure the macroscopic height distribution along a line
- measure the microscopic roughness along a line
- measure the complete topography/flatness of a part.

The interpretation is done by mathematically comparing the projected light structure with the deformed light structure at the surface topography of the object [20].

The discipline of structured lighting is widely split up. Many different principles are known. Common for all is that they are number crunching and need specialized algorithms for processing.

The achievable accuracy of the depth information depends on many factors such as lighting technique, camera resolution, and analyzing software and others. Generally, the resolution can be increased by using the approach of coded light. The principle can be found in the relevant literature.

Even transparent materials can be checked with structured light. The projection of light patterns on known shaped transparent materials produces predictable (multiple) reflections inside the materials. What is disturbing for the light path through imaging elements (see Section 3.4 – anti-reflective coatings) is useful for the point-shaped 3D – measurement of transparent parts. From this it is possible to determine measures in-depth like

- thicknesses of a wall
- parallelity of planes (wedge angle)
- using the effect of multiple and backside reflections.

Figure 3.76 Highly specular surface with engraved characters. Only at the perfect reflecting surface parts the image is bright. Disturbing structures destroy the telecentric characteristics of light. So the characters appear dark.

Arrangement

Conditions for the application of structured lighting are that

- the inspected parts have scattering and nonspecular surfaces (for surface measures)
- the inspected parts have reflecting back surface (for transparent materials)
- the inspected parts do not contain viewable undercuts (for inspection of the whole topography). Test objects with undercuts make it impossible to assign the projected lines from the lighting to the interpreted lines on the part.

Three basic light structures and principles are used:

3.7.4.4.1 Zero-Dimensional Light Structure (Point-Shaped) The projection of a light point leads to the principle of triangulation. The local drift of the position of the projected light point depending on the height of the test object gives a point-shaped information (see Figure 3.77).

A setup made with a telecentric objective takes care of simple mathematical relations using only angular functions.

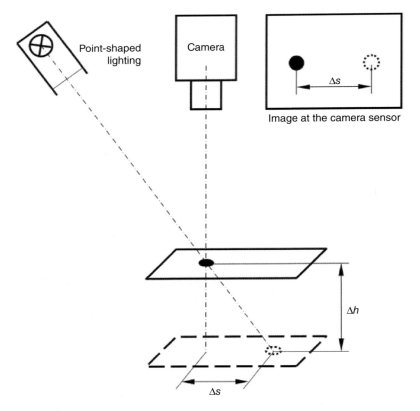

Figure 3.77 Principle of triangulation.

For Machine Vision the triangulation plays only a subordinated role as an additional information to a complex two-dimensional measuring job. The setup with a Machine Vision system only for a point-shaped height information is too costly.

For that purpose, complete triangulation sensors are manufactured as small automation devices (triangulation head) comprising a point-shaped light source (usually laser), an imaging optics, a light sensitive receiver (position sensitive device (PSD) or CCD/CMOS sensor), and an evaluating electronics. The output signal can be digital or analog. The working distances and measurement ranges cover the range from millimeters up to meters. Depending on the measurement ranges and working distances accuracies down to 0.01 mm are possible.

A good height resolution of this method can be achieved with a

- short working distance
- wide basic distance/angle (distance between lighting and receiver)
- small measuring range
- highly resolving imaging sensor
- highly resolving evaluating software
- constant reflective/scattering optical properties of the test object.

3.7.4.4.2 One-Dimensional Light Structure (Line) The projection of a light line leads to the principle of the so-called *light-slit method*. The deformation of a straight line projected at an angle on a surface gives information about the height along a *section* on the surface of the test object (see Figure 3.78).

The principle was introduced by Schmaltz many decades ago for the visual measurement of the microscopical surface roughnesses of parts. Today it can be used for the check of *sections* of larger parts too.

3.7.4.4.3 Two-Dimensional Light Structures (Line-Grid-Shaped) The projection of multiple parallel lines or other two-dimensional light structures allows the evaluation of complete surfaces (see Figure 3.79). Many different procedures are known from the literature. For the calculation of the height properties of the complete surfaces (topography) complex mathematical algorithms are in use.

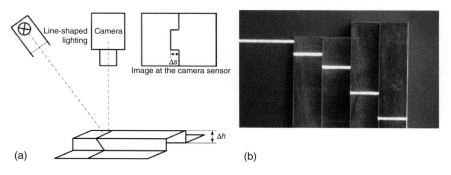

Figure 3.78 (a) Principle of the light-slit method, (b) application of the light-slit method for the height measurement of stacked blocks.

148 | *3 Lighting in Machine Vision*

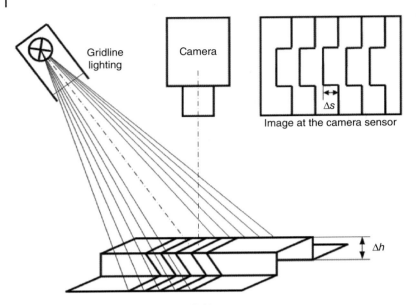

Figure 3.79 Principle of multiple parallel lines.

Components

- diode lasers with beam shaping optics of various shapes provide almost distance-independent measures of light geometry with structure widths down to 0.05 mm.
- LCD projectors with adaptable light and intelligent sequences of light Structures.

3.7.4.5 Diffuse Directed Partial Bright Field Incident Light (Nos. 1 and 2, Table 3.14)

This group of lighting can be considered as a sub-category of bright field incident light, because the result at the imaging sensor looks similar. The effects are made by the scattering surface of the part.

From the exact definition (see Section 3.7.3.3) it is an actual dark field illumination. Partial bright field lighting is used for

- homogenous illumination of three-dimensional parts
- illumination of larger parts with wavy or crushed surface
- emphasizing cracks at angled convex and concave surfaces
- selected lighting to produce shadows from edges and steps
- reduction of shadows and softening of textures on even surfaces
- minimization of the influence of fissures, dust and faults.

Arrangements and Components

The result of this lighting technique strongly depends on materials, positions, and angles (see Figure 3.80). With reference to the reflection law, one can adapt the

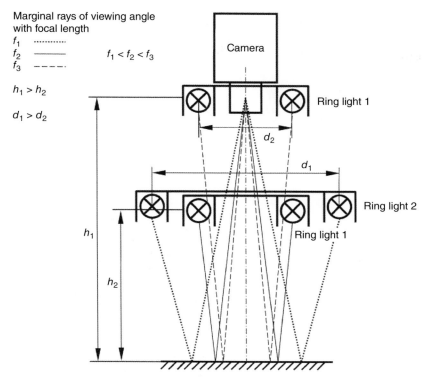

Figure 3.80 Relationships for distances, angles, and focal lengths of partial bright field components.

brightness and brightness distribution on the illuminated surface in combination with

- moving the lighting along the optical axis (changing distance)
- choosing light directions of the component (directed light, directed light with fresnel lens, diffuse light)
- choosing the light emitting diameter of the component
- changing the focal length of the imaging objective.

3.7.4.5.1 Ring Lights The use of ring lights combined with diffuse reflecting/scattering surfaces are a common and universal lighting technique for partial bright field illumination. Depending on the parts, geometrical shadows can occur. To control the light distribution, models are available with direct light emission, with included fresnel lenses, with diffusors, and with polarizing filters (see Figure 3.81).

3.7.4.5.2 Lighting with Through-Camera View This kind of lighting is the plane extension of conventional ring lights but the emitting light surface is much larger. This ensures that even slightly crushed surfaces are illuminated homogenously.

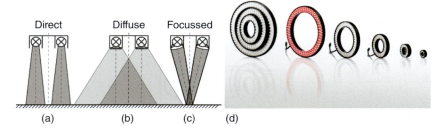

Figure 3.81 Light emission from ring lights, (a) direct emission, (b) diffused emission, (c) focused emission, (d) different models of LED ring lights. (www.vision-control.com.)

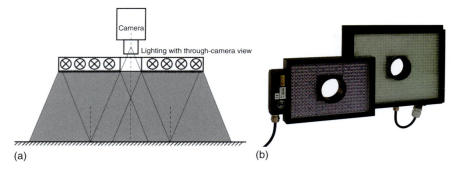

Figure 3.82 (a) Principle of a lighting with through-camera view. (b) Lighting component with through-camera view. (www.vision-control.com.)

For scattering surfaces, directed light emitting models can be used and for greater uneven and moderately formed parts the diffuse light emitting models.

Typical application of lighting with through-camera view are in robotics and the packing industry (see Figure 3.82).

3.7.4.5.3 Superdiffuse Ring Lights and Shadow-Free Lighting   The most extreme case of a diffuse incident lighting is a shadow-free lighting. These lighting components are not only extended in the plane but also in depth. This makes sure that structures in depth are illuminated too. The light emitting area is represented from almost the whole half-space of incident light (see Figure 3.64). This can be achieved by an emitting cylinder with a special reflecting covering area or with a half-sphere construction, the so-called cloudy day illumination or a dome lighting. This provides light from all angles of the top half sphere (see Figure 3.83).

Furthermore, these lighting are characterized by a hole in the top of the camera to look through. Especially shiny parts will answer this construction with a dark spot in the center of the image (the camera observes itself). To avoid this one can combine a shadow-free lighting with a brightness adjusted coaxial incident bright field lighting (see Section 3.7.4.1) that compensates the dark spot from the camera side.

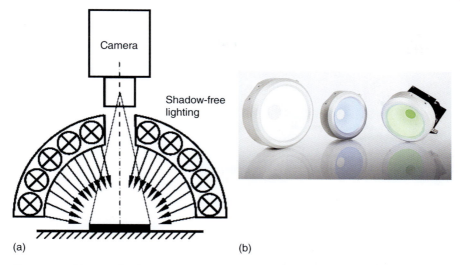

Figure 3.83 (a) Principle of a shadow-free lighting, (b) dome light components. (www.vision-control.com.)

Shadow-free lighting is used for homogenous lighting of larger uneven and heavily formed and deformed parts. There is no hard influence of reflection or scattering: the overlay of the macrostructure (the shape of the object) and microstructure (surface imperfections) superimposes and the homogeneity increases more with every diffuse reflection. Almost each object can be illuminated homogenously. This eliminates shades and reflections, smoothes the textures, and diminishes the influence of dust, reliefs, and curvatures.

This kind of lighting technique needs to be very close to the object in order to the function based on their principle.

How to select?

1) preliminary selection of ring light, lighting with through-camera view, superdiffuse or shadow-free lighting
2) determine light color: note the interaction with the part color.
3) determine lighting size
   a) ring lights, lighting with through-camera view, superdiffuse lighting: note the reflections (micro and macro). Where must the lighting be positioned that the reflected light meets the viewing angle of the imaging objective? Take the whole light emitting area into account (see Figure 3.80).
   b) shadow-free lighting: ensure that a very short working distance is possible. Choose the diameter of lighting no larger than half of the the cylinder or half sphere. Prefer longer focal length for better homogeneity on the edges of the field of view.
4) Determine the performance of the controlling technique
5) Select from catalog.

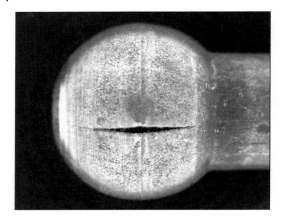

Figure 3.84 Detection of cracks in a forged shiny ball joint for steering systems. The use of a shadow-free lighting is the only way to check these safety relevant parts with a step-by-step rotation of only three steps of 120°.

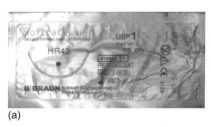
(a)

(b)

Figure 3.85 Reading characters on knitted surfaces, (a) conventional diffuse lighting with low and strongly changing contrasts, (b) shadow-free lighting ensures a contrastful and homogenous image.

The examples are shown in Figures 3.84 and 3.85.

3.7.4.6 Diffuse/Directed Dark Field Incident Light (Nos. 5 and 6, Table 3.14)

Dark field incident light is created if the lighting is positioned in a place that the imaging objective cannot see. A perfect even surface will appear dark and only elevations and deepenings appear bright due to scattering (see Figure 3.70).

Scattering and diffuse reflecting surfaces produce lower contrasts than a shiny or specular one. In addition, the dark field lighting technique is sensitive against dust, dirt, and fibers. These disturbances appear in the same way like structures. Dark field incident light is used for the following:

- emphasizing contours, shapes, structures, textures, edges
- emphasizing structural imperfections (scratches, corrugations, cracks)
- emphasizing single details
- surface defect detection
- make viewable embossed or engraved contours like characters of OCR/OCV
- lighting with high contrast at opaque objects; especially flat ones gives the silhouette/contour of the object
- translucent objects: they become transparent and the upper and lower surfaces cannot be separated
- creating contrast with embossed or engraved surfaces and for distinguishing surfaces of differing texture (laser-etched symbology).

Arrangement

The arrangement of dark field lighting components is strongly connected with the reflecting properties of the test object, the light direction, height, and angle. The farther the object, the smaller the dark fieldeffect appears (see Figure 3.86). That is the reason why dark field illuminations work always with short distances to the part (down to a few millimeters).

The width of the dark field effect (bright lines and areas) depends on the quality of the edges and the degree of the direction of light [29]. A sharp physical edge produces a thin reflected light line in cooperation with a directed dark field illumination. A well-rounded edge will produce a broad one (see Figure 3.87). That is the span. On the other hand, the width of the light emitting ring determines the width of the bright line. Narrow rings produce thin lines and wide rings produce broad lines.

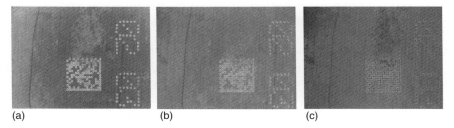

Figure 3.86 The effect of dark field illumination in dependence of different distances to a test object with needled data matrix codes. (a) Lighting is laying on the part surface. (b) 15 mm distance. (c) 30 mm distance.

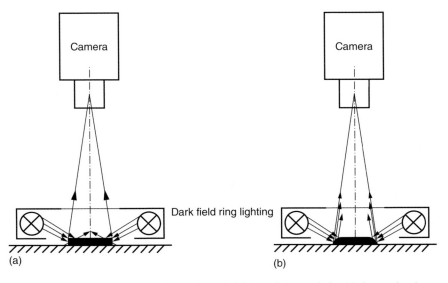

Figure 3.87 Principle and path of rays of a dark field incident ring light, (a) sharp edged part, (b) well-rounded edged part.

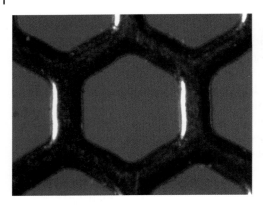

Figure 3.88 Streaking light from left. The directed area lighting component at large angle emphasizes left vertical edges using the dark field effect.

Conventionally, the dark field illumination components are realized as ring lights for a rotation-independent lighting. If the rotation of the part is known, a directed lighting component can be used for the technique of dark field lighting too. The so-called streaking light works as a dark field lighting too (see Figure 3.88).

A possibility of adapting the structure of a dark field ring light to the necessities of the shape of the test object is to use an adaptive lighting (see Section 3.8.2.5). Sectors can be switched on or off or the illuminating sector can walk around.

Tip

Directed dark field incident light is often used for surface inspections. The dark field effect of scattering light will be better when light with shorter wavelength is used. That is why a blue lighting will emphasize scratches better than a red one.

Components

- specialized dark field ring lights
- directed area lighting (for streaking light)
- spot lights (for streaking light).

How to select?

- Ensure that a short/very short working distance is possible.
- Determine light color: note the interaction with the part color.
- Determine the illuminated area
- Determine the performance of the controlling technique
- Select from catalog.

The examples are shown in Figure 3.89.

3.7.4.7 The Limits of the Incident Lighting

The application of incident light is connected with a few limitations. This should be known to avoid from bad surprises. All incident lighting live from the reflecting and scattering properties and the shape and outer contour of the part. Note

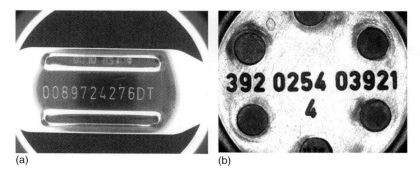

(a) (b)

Figure 3.89 (a) Engraved numbers in a specular metal plate, (b) embossed characters on a plastic part.

that all checked parts are different and – imperfect! The consequences are no perfect reflections, no perfect scattering as estimated, and no realistic shape or contour as expected!

Some of the influencing factors of edges found in different places can be (see Section 3.4.1):

- changed manufacturing procedure
- different position/rotation of parts (varying reflections or scattering)
- wear out (cutting) tools (see Figure 3.27)
- instable porous surfaces
- torn edges
- rounded edges
- contamination.

Example stamped parts: parts that are cut with a new and a wear out cutting tool look totally different (edges). The mechanical function of the part for the end user may be right, but the light reflecting properties with the incident light are drastically different.

All this and much more influences on the place where transitions of brightness are found in the image. Note this fact and take it into consideration when ascertaining if measurement with the incident light is required (see Figure 3.90).

Tip

Avoid using the incident light for measuring jobs with Machine Vision in any case. The accuracy of measurement obtainable within the range of several to a great many pixels is totally dependent on the microgeometry of the part. (see [19, Bl. 6.1, p. 10])

3.7.4.8 Diffuse Bright Field Transmitted Lighting (No. 7, Table 3.14)

This lighting technique provides good contrastful images. It finds use as follows:

- in opaque parts
- flat to very flat parts gives almost perfect transition from bright to dark (foils, seals, stampings).

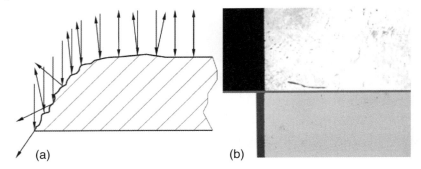

Figure 3.90 (a) Course of parallel incident light at a typically shaped edge (microstructure: broken edge) not all light can return to the objective on the top, (b) apparent differences at one part (glass plate with chamfer) illuminated with incident light (top) and transmitted light (bottom). With incident light the complete part is not viewable.

Transparent parts give lower contrasts. The more transparent the parts are the smaller the contrasts become. Three-dimensional parts can cause problems due to reflections from the side wall areas. This results in edge transitions with shapes that are difficult to interpret from the software.

Arrangement

The mounting is directly on the opposite side of the imaging objective (see Figure 3.91). No special requirements for the orientation of the lighting are needed. The distance between part and lighting should be larger than the depth of focus (no imaging of dirt and dust).

Components

Diffuse area lighting (see Section 3.7.4.1).

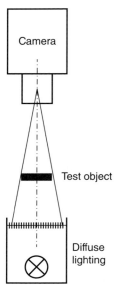

Figure 3.91 Principle of diffuse bright field transmitted lighting.

How to select?

1) determine light color: monochrome camera: color almost does not matter – Note the spectral response for the brightest appearing color. Color camera: white.
2) determine lighting size: Approximately 5 mm wider than the field of view. For entocentric objectives note the effect of perspective/viewing angle of the imaging objective. In this case the size depends on the distance of the lighting to the test object.
3) Determine the performance of the controlling technique
4) Select from catalog.

The examples are shown in Figure 3.92.

3.7.4.9 Directed Bright Field Transmitted Lighting (No. 8, Table 3.14)

This relatively seldom used lighting technique needs translucent parts to homogenize the light. Otherwise, the structure of the light source(s) overlays the test object structure. It makes use of different material distributions inside the part (see Figure 3.93). It can be used for

- checking the completeness of translucent parts
- targeted lighting of deep holes, small slits, and clefts where diffuse or telecentric lighting fails.

Arrangement

Ensure that the light sources inside the lighting component are not viewable for the camera. Avoid overexposure!

Components

Directed area lighting (see Section 3.7.4.2).

How to select?

1) Determine light color: For translucent parts use the same color as the part. These wavelengths can pass best. For holes and clefts use the most effective wavelength to the sensor.

(a)

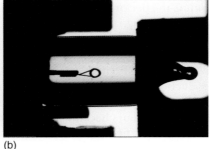
(b)

Figure 3.92 (a) Lead frame silhouette, (b) inspection of a filament inside the glass bulb.

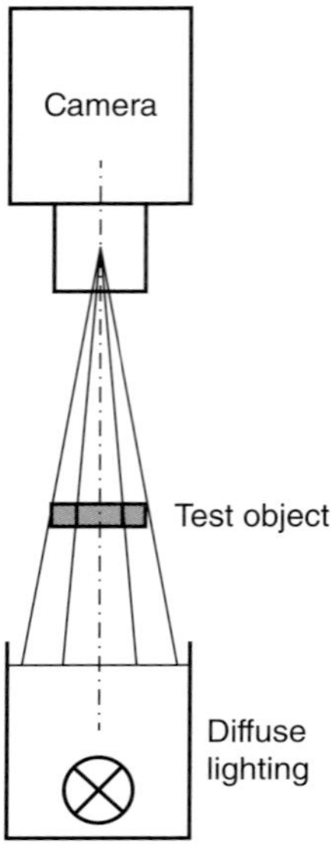

Figure 3.93 Principle of directed bright field transmitted lighting.

Figure 3.94 Green diffuse transparent molded packaging part illuminates from back with a green directed bright field transmitted lighting to check the completeness of molding. This lighting technique gives a much more contrastful image than the incident light.

2) Determine lighting size: Approximately 5 mm wider than the field of view. For entocentric objectives note the effect of perspective/viewing angle of the imaging objective. In this case, the size depends on the distance of the lighting to the test object.
3) Determine the performance of the controlling technique
4) Select from catalog.

The example is shown in Figure 3.94.

3.7.4.10 Telecentric Bright Field Transmitted Lighting (No. 9, Table 3.14)

This introduction of this lighting technique in the beginning of the 1990s revolutionized the accuracy of Machine Vision. The imaging of extremely well-shaped silhouettes and contours became possible. Together with telecentric objectives, the telecentric bright field transmitted lighting can be used for

- contrastful illumination of transparent to opaque 3D objects
- providing sharp edges even from shiny spherical and cylindrical parts

- applications where accuracy and reliability of results is needed
- very good suppression of extraneous light
- very homogenous and high contrasted illumination of transparent and opaque parts.

Arrangement

Telecentric lighting can work only in combination with a telecentric lens (see Section 3.7.3.1). A parallel assembly of both (objective and lighting) is needed. Deviations of approximately $< \pm 1°$ are typically allowed. Connected with this demand is to ensure that the components are mounted vibration free.

The distance between telecentric objective and telecentric lighting does not matter. The distance between the test object and telecentric lighting should be adjusted so that no dust at the lens surface of the lighting is viewable (distance approximately 3× larger than the depth of focus of the objective).

Figures 3.95 and 3.96 demonstrate the effect of conventional lighting components in comparison with telecentric lighting. The right coordination of the lighting and imaging system apertures determines the position of the edge. Telecentric lighting ensures independent edge location.

Occasional problems crop up with lighting for parallel walled parts. If the wall is shiny and the part axis is not parallelly arranged to the axis of the imaging objective disturbing reflections can occur. In some cases help the change of the lighting method and the use of diffuse lighting.

If the part is tilted, even the use of telecentric components does not help to avoid measuring errors. Only the projection of the part is viewable (see Figure 3.97). The deviation depends on the depth of the part and the tilting angle.

Flat parts:

Following Abbe's comparator, principle errors of the second order will occur. Seemingly, the parts become smaller if they are tilted (see Figure 3.97a):

$$L = L_0 - [L_0(1 - \cos \alpha)]$$

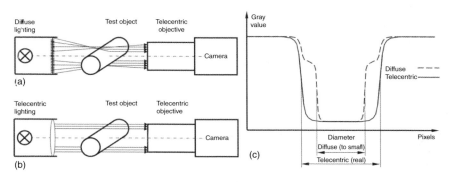

Figure 3.95 Course of light on the surface of a shiny cylinder: (a) with diffuse transmitted light, (b) with telecentric transmitted light, and (c) course of gray values at the image sensor.

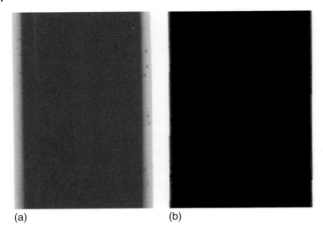

Figure 3.96 Shiny cylindrical metal part imaged with a telecentric objective. (a) With diffuse transmitted lighting: the large lighting aperture causes undefinable brightness transitions depending on surface quality, lighting size, and lighting distance. (b) With telecentric lighting: the small lighting aperture guarantees sharp and well-shaped edges for precise and reliable edge detection.

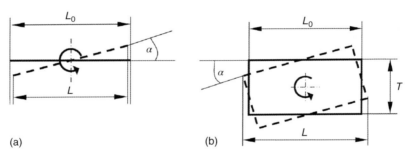

Figure 3.97 Tilting and projection leads to changed results in the projection. (a) Flat part (2D). (b) Deep part (3D).

with

L_0 being the original length of the part,
L the apparent length, and
α the tilting angle.

For Machine Vision, applications can be neglected angles $< |3°|$.

Deep parts:

In this case, errors of the first order occur. Seemingly the parts become larger if they are tilted (see Figure 3.97b):

$$L = L_0 - [L_0(1 - \cos \alpha)] + T \sin \alpha$$

with

- L_0 being the original length of the part,
- L the apparent length,
- T the depth of the part, and
- α the tilting angle.

This effect is also present for small angles and becomes larger with an increasing depth of the object. The consequence for the brightness transition at the sensor are unsymmetrical edges (note the processing by the software).

Components

Telecentric lighting (see Figure 3.98)

How to select?

1) Determine light color
   (see Section 3.7.3.1). Color cameras should use white light.
2) Determine lighting size
   corresponding to the field of view of the telecentric objective. Note that the size has to be larger than the outside measures of the test object (parallel chief rays).
3) Determine the performance of the controlling technique.
4) Select from catalog.

Examples are shown in Figure 3.99.

3.7.4.11 Diffuse/Directed Transmitted Dark Field Lighting (Nos. 10 and 11, Table 3.14)

This lighting technique works only for transparent or strongly translucent parts. To see the bright reflexes at the edges of the backside it is necessary that the

Figure 3.98 Telecentric lighting components of different sizes. (www.vision-control.com.)

Figure 3.99 (a) Quality check for a shiny milled part. (b) Diameter measurement of glass rods. (c) Check of completeness of sinter parts.

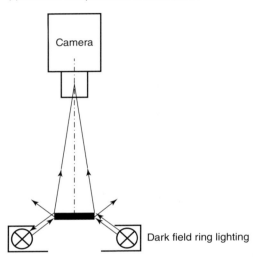

Figure 3.100 Principle of diffuse/directed transmitted dark field lighting.

lighting components are mounted behind the part and the light can pass the part. These are the conditions for the function (see Figure 3.100). Otherwise, this method does not work.

It is applicable to similar kind of parts like for diffuse or directed incident dark field lighting (Section 3.7.4.6). Only the structures at the backside of the part become visible.

Arrangement, Components, How to Select?

Same statements as diffuse/directed incident dark field lighting (Section 3.7.4.6).

3.7.5 Combined Lighting Techniques

The lighting techniques mentioned above are systematically derived from all feasible arrangements of the practice. Each lighting technique was regarded individually.

Realistic parts from industrial processes are often complex. The necessary areas to illuminate covers. However, some lighting techniques are mutually exclusive, or they include different features that cannot be illuminated with only one lighting or one lighting technique.

In those cases it is impossible to apply a pure lighting technique. Compromises and combinations must be made.

a) *Individual lighting for each feature.*
   The simplest but neat variation is to use individual and separate lighting for each feature. It is costly and takes time, because all features are processed one after the other. This is only possible if there are no time limitations. Image acquisition with many cameras or moving the camera with a handling system is necessary for optimal optical and lighting conditions.
b) *Classify lighting situations.*
   More effective is it to use one lighting technique for all similar lighting situations. Image acquisition in combination with a handling system is needed. Repetition must be made for the other lighting techniques in the same manner. It is as time consuming as the variation (a).
c) *Different lighting techniques in sequence.*
   Use a long exposure time and switch through sequentially all necessary lighting within the exposure time of one image. This method is applicable only if all used lighting techniques are feasible in one view.
d) *Change the lighting technique within the lighting component.*
   Use of an adaptive lighting (see Section 3.8.2.5) that can change the light structure and direction sequentially from image acquisition to image acquisition or within one image acquisition.

To select the best variation from (a) to (d) note the mutual influence of lighting. To use all lighting techniques together is impossible almost in every case.

And the rest of lighting jobs? Some lighting problems are not solvable. They cannot be solved, particularly if the expected lighting technique is refused under the predetermined mechanical and arrangement conditions. For example, it is impossible to apply a dark field illumination if the minimal possible distance from the object to the lighting is, let us say, 200 mm.

Among the experts are the well-known *challenge cups*. These are jobs that circulate in the market and come up from time to time, because nobody could solve the problem. Unexperienced personal will try many times and put in much energy, time, and money to find a way. Frustration will be the result. But to recognize the limits is not to learn – it is only to experience.

However, keep in mind the high performance of the human eye. And again and again the lighting engineer will ask the question: *Why does the machine not see what I can see?*

3.8 Lighting Control

Deduced from the demands on Machine Vision lighting (see Section 3.2) and the outstanding properties of LEDs for an easy lighting control (see Section 3.3.3.5) the following comments are made for LED lighting components. In some points they can be transferred to other kind of lighting.

3.8.1 Reasons for Light Control – The Environmental Industrial Conditions

Besides emphasizing on desired details, the aim of a Machine Vision lighting is to be, as much as possible, independent of disturbing and influencing factors (see Section 3.7.2). Many of them can be lined out by controlling the lighting such as

- voltage variations (instable light)
- machines running with asynchronous cycle times (triggering lighting)
- fast running machines (avoid motional blurring with flash light)
- inspection of different parts/changing the light distribution (adaption of light to the part)
- coordination of different lighting (switchable lighting)
- switching of dangerous lighting
- dynamic response (no delay or afterglow allowed)
- adaption to space limitations (using deflection, long distances)
- disturbing light (reflexes, ambient light).

3.8.2 Electrical Control

3.8.2.1 Stable Operation

Only in a few cases single LEDs work in lighting components such as in telecentric lighting or coaxial lighting for microscope. But even these LEDs need stable operation.

The required high luminances and illuminances require interconnection of many LEDs. Note that the large area lighting need a few hundred up to a few thousands of LEDs.

If LEDs are combined in series connection typical voltages in industry from 12 to 24 V are rapidly exceeded. This limits the length of the chains, because all LEDs operating with the same current brightness differences occur due to different forward currents of each LED. One single-defect LED puts the whole LED chain out of action. A positive feature of this are small operating currents.

If LEDs are working in parallel connection rapidly high currents occur. The nonlinear characteristics of the LEDs cause additional problems for a homogenous brightness. Small operating voltages are advantageous.

It is an art to find a matching combination of series (chains) and their parallel connections. Different possibilities are given (see Figure 3.101):

1) serial connection
2) parallel connection of single LEDs without series resistor
    - used for low-cost lighting
    - strong inhomogeneity of brightness
3) parallel connection of chains with resistor
    - compensation of different currents possible.

Different LED substrates (LED colors) have different current–voltage characteristics. This makes it impossible to work with those constructions in a color mixed mode (see Figure 3.102).

Additionally, the manufacturing data of the LEDs are not stable so that they even differ in their forward voltage for one model (see Figure 3.103):

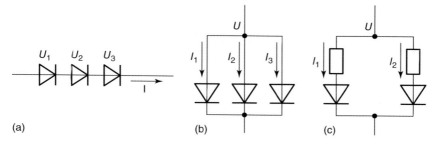

Figure 3.101 Possible LED connection: (a) series connection, (b) parallel connection, (c) parallel connection with series resistors.

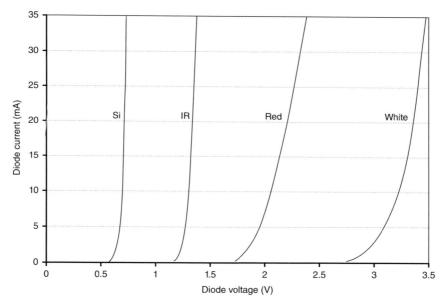

Figure 3.102 Current–voltage characteristics of different LED substrates (colors).

To know this structure gives the best base for a defined control. LED lighting with defined control use classified and sorted LEDs (according to the characteristics). This is expensive but precise. Furthermore, an individual series resistor per chain is integrated. This limits small differences of the forward voltage but produces additional dissipation power and, therefore, heat. A wide voltage range input 10–30 V DC rounds up the stabilization.

Knowing the condition that LEDs work most effectively if they are cold and that overheating reduces the lifetime and increases aging and brightness drift (see Section 3.3.5.2 and Figure 3.22), it is desirable that lighting operates cold. This can be achieved with a built-in current control circuitry. This compensates the loss of brightness caused by increasing temperature. So, the current control works as a brightness control and is the basic equipment for all controllable lighting.

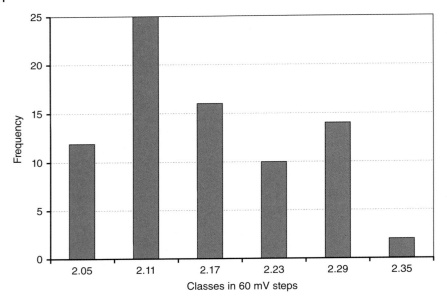

Figure 3.103 Classes of forward voltages for red LEDs [6].

Tip

Details about the quality of the temperature compensation and thus for a stable function gives the temperature coefficient of the illuminance (incident light) or the luminance (transmitted light). A good lighting for industrial use should have a coefficient of only a few tenth percent per Kelvin $(-0.4\%, \ldots, 0.4\%/\mathrm{K})$.

Many simple casted LED arrays without housing do not use a controlling circuitry, a thermal compensation, or overvoltage protection. The consequence is that each small change of the supplying voltage is passed through directly in a change of brightness. These lighting need a good stabilized and costly power supply.

The application is to recommend to refrigerate these lighting and to use it only in a switch mode. The continuous operation with full capacity slowly destroys the lighting.

3.8.2.2 Brightness Control

To adapt the brightness on the test object, it is necessary to adjust the brightness of the lighting. This does not mean a change of the supplying voltage. For industrial use this must be done on a separate input. Basically, two possibilities are in use:

- brightness adjustment with potentiometer. This can be done manually.
- brightness adjustment with typical voltages between 0 and 10V DC.

This needs an additional controlling voltage. 0V means dark and 10V means maximum brightness. So the lighting can be controlled (brighter, darker) and more. They can be switched on/off from a distance. For steady maximal light output the controlling input channel can be connected with the supplying voltage level. Most lighting permits this.

Typical delay times from connecting the controlling voltage to the light effect are a few milliseconds. Using the power supply input for switching on/off this takes approximately 10–20 times more.

3.8.2.3 Temporal Control: Static-Pulse-Flash

Due to their electrical properties, LEDs can be modulated up to the megahertz range. Independent of the adjustment of brightness they can operate in three different operation modes:

- *Static mode*: the LED current either changes slowly or not at all.
- *Pulse mode*: switching the LED with nominal current in time periods >100 µs.
- *Flash mode*: overload the LED for very short time periods <100 µs with up to 10-fold nominal current (see Figure 3.17). Some models allow flash times of smaller than 0.5 µs. The controlling unit ensures the right pulse duty factor to protect the LED chip from thermal destruction.

The lighting component for *static lighting* is simply made with or without a current/voltage stabilization. If they are misused to switch that can cause delay time from switching to full/no brightness of a few up to a few hundred milliseconds. The concrete value depends on the model.

Pulsed lighting or controlled lighting are equipped with a separate pulse input. The included controlling electronics ensures a fast reaction from pulse to light. Typical delay times are in the range of microseconds. Minimal light pulse widths of 10 µs are possible. The triggering pulse can use TTL or PLC level.

Flash lighting electronics are more complex. A few of flash lighting components use a constant power integral circuitry. This means a constant exposure independent of the chosen flash time. The shorter the flash, the more powerful it must be. The adjustment of the flash time can be fixed, adjustable with potentiometer, with DIL switches or with a bus interface connection. Flash times shorter than 5 µs make great demands on the energy storage in the lighting and the driving electronics and make those components very expensive apart from the ambitious synchronization that is needed to coordinate all optical hardware and software processes and EMC problems.

Typical delay times from flash trigger impulse to light are 10 µs. Trigger impulses use TTL or PLC level. The controlling unit includes a circuitry to keep the requirements for the pulse-duty factor. This ensures stable lighting and protect the LEDs. Typical are 100 Hz for full load. The temporal variation from one flash to the next is less than a microsecond.

The construction of flash lighting components can be different. Some of them have built-in flash controller, and some of them use external control boxes. The disadvantages of external controllers are the influence of interferences and additional delays.

Some demands that one should make on flash lighting:

- short delay, raise, fall times inside the flash
- flash recurrence rate > frame rate of the used camera

- EMC capable
- long lifetime
- low loss of brightness beyond the lifetime (no compensation possible!)
- changeable flash time at constant light energy
- changeable flash brightness without change of flash time.

Modern lighting components allow all operation modes in one lighting component. The operation modes (static, pulse, flash) are electrically adjustable even during operation. The brightness control can be made with a bus interface, digital, analog, or manual. Some components save the lighting settings even at a power failure. An integrated temperature/current measurement at the LED module provides the automatic tracking of optical power parameters.

3.8.2.4 Some Considerations for the Use of Flash Light

The short light pulse width of flash lighting makes them an excellent choice for applications where stop motion is required, such as for high-speed inspections. A flash lighting can be used to *freeze* a part on a production line as it passes under a camera for inspection. The consistency at which the flash lighting can be triggered is also a major benefit in these applications (see Figure 3.104).

The use of flash light enables shorter exposure times (down to $1/200\,000$ s) than the preset from the imaging sensor (typically $1/30\,000–1/60\,000$ s) is given. Furthermore, it is possible to flash into the standard exposure time for sensors that do not have a shutter. Sensors with rolling shutter technology are not suitable for the combination with flash lights – progressive scans are required for that.

Last but not least are flash lighting (and short exposure times) suitable to suppress the influence of ambient light. This needs a few times higher light energy of the flash than the ambient light.

From the theory, it can be seen that flash applications are possible for both, for incident and transmitted light. Note the reflectance of the test object (see Section 3.4.1.2). The limited reflectance of many real parts makes it impossible to use the incident flash light. The amount of the reflected light is simply too small. Flash light applications with the transmitted light work generally reliably.

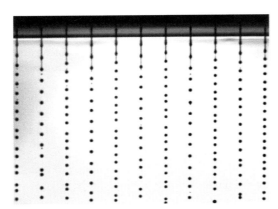

Figure 3.104 Edge triggering with very low delay times allow us to achieve flashes from 0.5 to 100 μs that are able to image blur free object speeds up to $30\,\mathrm{m\,s^{-1}}$. The image shows ink drops that are injected under high pressure.

3.8 Lighting Control

Motional blurring is the effect that the part moves during the exposure or flash time. It can be caused by

- movement of the part during the exposure time
- movement of the camera during the exposure time (vibrations)
- too long exposure time
- too long illumination time (flash time).

Tip

In general, a motional blurring of one pixel in the image is accepted for sharp imaging (exceptions possible).

The size of motional blurring can be determined by

$$\text{MB} = s_{\text{exp}}/\text{PR} = s_{\text{exp}} \cdot \frac{\text{no. of pixels}}{\text{FOV}}$$

with

MB	being the motional blurring in the image,
s_{exp}	the movement of the part during the exposure time/flash time,
PR	the pixel resolution,
no. of pixels	the used number of pixels of the sensor, in the direction of the movement of the part, and
FOV	the length of the field of view of the camera in the direction of the movement of the part.

The above formula illustrates that a better pixel resolution makes an application more sensitive against motional blurring. To avoid this is to shorten the exposure time and/or the flash time.

A remark on brightnesses. Based on the demand for a constant exposure $H = E \cdot t$ (see Section 3.5.7) it is necessary for reaching the same brightness in the image to increase drastically the lighting power (illuminance E) if a flash lighting is used. To generate the same brightness in the image (constant f-stop number), the following exemplary relations are valid:

	Exposure time/flash time	Necessary illuminance (for the time of exposure)
Static light	1/50 s = 20 ms	2000 lx
Flash light	1/20 000 s = 50 µs	800 000 lx

The example shows that the need for such high illuminances can be satisfied only for short times and only from flash light sources.

The demands for enough flash light energy are often connected with the demands for a large depth of focus (see Chapter 4). The connections are shown in Table 3.12 in Section 3.5.7. A stronger closed f-stop for a larger depth of focus will again increase the demand for more light. One larger f-stop number means the need for the double amount of light.

The synchronization of flash lighting is a complex field connected with the cooperation of

- trigger sensors and PLC of the machine
- vision system
- flash lighting
- camera
- software.

These connections do not make it easy to investigate problems. Components are often made by different manufacturers and the necessary information of the internal function of the components is not available. That is why only a few influencing factors can be considered at this point. Condition is a precise enough positioning of the test part. The worst case conditions for the whole machine should be considered.

Three synchronization possibilities are given as follows:

a) flash time > shutter time → safe, but loss of light energy,
b) flash time = shutter time → not stable working by varying time components,
c) flash time < shutter time → most effective, but needs perfect synchronization.
Case (c) is the most interference free (and demanding). The light pulse has to flash match into the short time window of the light sensitive phase of the imaging sensor (shutter time).

Figure 3.105 shows a typical succession of processes that are to synchronize. A trigger pulse is given from a sensor in the machine. This information is transferred through the PLC (delay!) to the trigger input of the vision system. The vision system processes this information with their software (delay!) and sends a trigger pulse to the flash light (or to the PLC that triggers the flash light (delay!)). Considering the delays up to the start of the light sensitive phase of the camera the image acquisition (including short shutter time) is started. After finishing the light emission of the flash light the camera shutter is closed.

To achieve stable time conditions for synchronization it is necessary to know the time response of the whole system. Especially unregular processes causes problems of synchronization. This includes the mechanical synchronization of the machine too. Reasons for time problems can be

- variable/unknown moments of the trigger impulses
- undefined time response of the controlling unit (PLC, etc.)
- variable/unknown delay times (vision system, flash lighting, camera, PLC)
- variable/unknown flash times (flash duration, constancy)
- variable/unknown shutter times (camera)
- start of image acquisition to early or to late (vision system, camera)
- variable/unknown signal runtimes in the machine.

To get down to bedrock the problems of synchronization it needs special equipment (oscilloscope, optical detectors (for short light pulses), background information to the components and …perseverance.

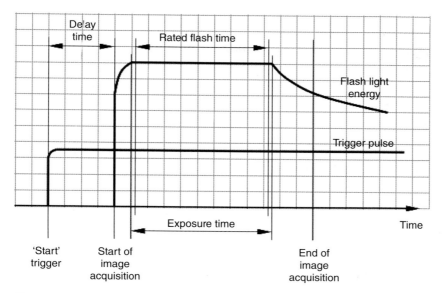

Figure 3.105 Time diagram of the connected processes during flash light synchronization.

How to select a flash lighting? – A rough estimation:

1) Find a matching lighting technique (see Section 3.7):
   lighting check with static light: possible or impossible?
2) Determine light color:
   note the interaction with the part color.
3) Determine lighting size
4) Lighting component available as pulsed or flash model?
5) Time and brightness considerations (strongly depends on design):
   incident light with flash light: shorter flash times than 1/10 000 s are mostly problematic
   incident light with pulsed light: shorter flash times than 1/2000 s are mostly problematic
   transmitted light with flash light: possible up to 1/200 000 s
   transmitted light with pulsed light: approximately possible up to 1/20 000 s
6) Flash repetition rate attainable (strongly depends on design)
7) Select from catalog.

3.8.2.5 Temporal and Local Control: Adaptive Lighting

Traditional lighting components suffer from the fact that they are selected for one special purpose. Once selected only little possibilities modify the use.

Adaptive lighting extends these possibilities. Temporal, local, and spectral are all participating light sources (above all LEDs) separately controllable per software [21]. The individual adjustment of local illumination parameters (duration and moment of emission, brightness, wavelength) provides application of specific lighting. This leads to the following advantages:

- different lighting modes in one lighting (static, pulsed, flash)
- very fast automatic lighting control
- state enquiry possible (e.g., failure check for single LEDs)
- simple adaptation of lighting to changing products
- treating the lighting component as an automation device
- no sensitive electromechanical adjustment elements

Some examples for the wide use of adaptive lighting are

- compensation of the natural vignetting of objectives ($\cos^4$ brightness decrease, see Figure 3.108a)
- avoidance of reflections from the test object (see Figure 3.108c)
- homogenous lighting of three-dimensional structured objects (see Figure 3.108b)
- light structures for transmitted lighting
- adaptation of the illuminating wavelength/color mixture to the color of the test object.

Adaptive lighting are based on complex drives (see Figure 3.106). They are equipped with wide range voltage input, they are switchable and flashable. Flash times and brightnesses can be saved resident in a memory. Basic structures are adaptive base modules (ABM) with on-board-electronics including interface for control per software or keystroke. The base modules can be combined just as you like. This opens up total new possibilities to combine them in (almost) every shape and realize all lighting techniques.

The temporal and local and brightness control of each single LED is done with pulse width modulation (PWM).

Above all there are two procedures for the input of the lighting parameters (light patterns and times) for adaptive lighting:

- *manually by keystroke*: using the keys at the housing of the adaptive lighting components
- *by programming* (see Figure 3.107): this can be done from a user interface or directly from a vision system.

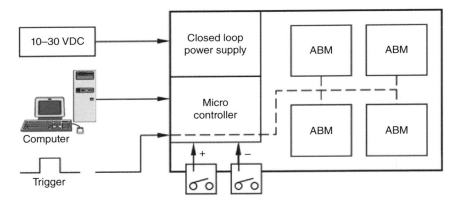

Figure 3.106 Block diagram of adaptive lighting.

3.8 Lighting Control

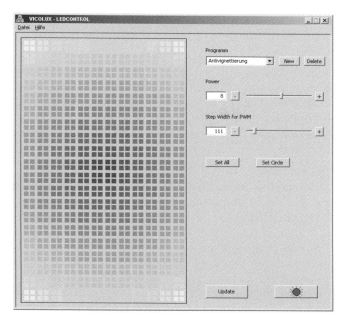

Figure 3.107 Windows user interface for programming an adaptive lighting. The brightness and flash duration of each single LED can be selected and adjusted by a mouse click. The demonstrated light pattern can be used for vignetting compensation. (www.vision-control.com.)

(a)   (b)   (c)

Figure 3.108 Different programming examples of a diffuse adaptive area lighting: (a) correction of natural vignetting of an objective, (b) and (c) compensation of reflexes at shiny parts. (www.vision-control.com.)

During operation the light pattern information is sent from the vision system to the adaptive lighting through an USB or Ethernet interface.

All kind of lighting components can be designed as adaptive lighting. Tendencies for the future are adaptive lighting that adapts automatically to the lighting situation (Figure 3.108).

3.8.3 Geometrical Control

3.8.3.1 Lighting from Large Distances

Except the fact that some lighting techniques need special distances and strongly determine the image of the test object (see Section 3.7), two general lighting situations influence the lighting from large distances:

a) incident light
   or
b) backlight

For the use of the incident light shows the existence of the photometric inverse square law (see Section 3.5.2) that it is a difficult assignment to illuminate a part from large distances. In addition some of the lighting techniques cannot work from a distance by their principle.

If they can work by their principle, the effect of darkening for larger distances can be compensated as follows:

- Use of a more powerful lighting.
  Note: To compensate the reciprocal square reduction it is necessary to increase the power exponential! For the replacement consider the limits of different light sources. Not all substitute light sources allow all kinds of lighting techniques!
- Opening the f-stop from the imaging objective.
  To open the f-stop one step means that the double luminous flux can pass the objective. Two f-stop steps mean four times more luminous flux and so forth. Use this option only if the application allows the subsequent change (reduction) of the depth of focus.
- Extending the exposure time of the camera.
  To double the exposure time means that the double quantity of light can be collected from the image sensor.
  Use this option only if the motional blurring of the test object at the image sensor is smaller.
- Removing light absorbing filters if possible (think of the optical consequences).
- Using another wavelength of light that is more effective for the image sensor (see Section 3.3.2).
  Note the effects that happen in interaction with the test object (see Section 3.4).
- Using a objective with a higher light intensity.
  This option is effective only if the application can work with a open f-stop at the objective. Note that the depth of focus is reduced in this case as much as possible.
- Using a higher sensitive camera.
- Increasing the gain of the camera (notably noise, nonlinearities, etc.)
- Using highly robust software algorithms that can process a wide range of gray values.
- Using another lighting technique if all mentioned above measures do not help.

For backlight applications, a longer distance between lighting and test object does not have an influence on the image brightness because of the constancy of luminance. Prolonging the distance of the lighting can have an effect on

- the complete illumination of the field of view of the camera objective when using a lens with perspective properties. Compensate it with a larger lighting component.
- changed reflections at the test object because of three-dimensional structure of the part (interaction part – light).

3.8.3.2 Light Deflection

Not all applications and machine environments possess a simple structure. They are adapted to complex industrial manufacturing processes. Machine Vision is usually only an add-on device that controls. The consequence for mounting the components is often a limited space.

It is known from the lighting techniques (see Section 3.7) that some of them need space. Other lighting components are bulky itself caused by their optical principle (e.g., telecentric lighting).

To mediate between both, demands from lighting and machine too one can use deflection units for some lighting. They operate with mirrors or prisms and work follow the optical principles of reflection.

Deflection units are front end elements of lighting and thus the interface to the rough environment of the industrial floor. That is why they should be easy-care and robust. Prisms meet these demands more than mirrors.

Prisms:

The glass surface of a prism is an ideal front seal for the lighting. There are no problems in cleaning them. They are easy to install if they are built in prism deflection units. The compact size makes them match even under limited space conditions. Referring to the reflection law depends their size on the illuminated field and light emitting angle of the lighting (note that the total reflection of a prism is limited by a critical angle). Mostly they are used for a 90° beam deflection.

Prisms are more costly and more heavy than mirrors.

Mirrors:

The cheap and easy availability of mirrors makes them seemingly applicable for Machine Vision. However, one should evade the application of mirrors in the industrial floor wherever possible.

1) To avoid ghost images and low contrast only surface mirrors should be used. But these mirrors have extremely sensitive surfaces against mechanical and chemical stress.
2) To remove dust is a problem. Frequently mirrors are built in constructions with cavities that attract dust. On the other hand, dust should be only blown away to save the mirror surface (see Section 3.1).
3) Because mirrors are no standard components (they are cut on request) there are no standardized holders and adjustable frames. Each mounting is a costly handicraft.
4) Vibrations and not precise positioning have a multiple higher influence on the beam deflection than at prisms.

3.8.4 Suppression of Ambient and Extraneous Light – Measures for a Stable Lighting

The industrial floor of Machine Vision does not provide an ideal lighting environment as in the lab. The tested lighting from the lab does not work automatically in the factory floor too. This plastically demonstrates the difference between theory and practice. The biggest and imponderable influence comes from ambient and extraneous light. It can be static (illumination from factory hall) or dynamic (incoming sunlight through windows).

The first condition to minimize the influence of ambient light is to choose as powerful a lighting as possible referred to as a right selected lighting technique. The aim is that the calculated lighting power (in the spectral band considered) is mightier than the ambient light.

If this is guaranteed, it can be tried to minimize the influence of the ambient light by

- choosing a shorter exposure time
- choosing a larger f-stop number
- choosing a flash lighting
- choosing all these measures together.

Tip

For a first approximation check the ambient and extraneous lighting conditions at the place where the vision system is later mounted. Check it by measuring with a vision system too, not only by your subjective eye. Get a feeling for the amount of the ambient light. Take this into consideration when choosing a lighting technique, lighting components, and software algorithms. Some options for that are automatically denied.

Suppress the influence of ambient light using monochromatic or infrared light in combination with light filters (see Section 3.6).

A simple but very effective method is to enclose the camera – optics – lighting unit with an opaque housing. This is a tried and tested method that is used by prestigious companies to achieve the as best possible ambient/extraneous light suppression that works under every condition. If it is not clear where the machine later is installed this method will be the most secure.

First of all, the ambient light is the most important source of lighting disturbances. But to ensure stable lighting conditions a few other measures have to take into consideration too:

- an electrically and optically stabilized lighting component (see Section 3.8.2)
- operate the lighting in the middle of the characteristics. This provides power reserves to compensate other influences
- no (low) aging and drift (see Section 3.3.5.2) that ensure no change of materials (change of hue of the light source, diffusors, etc.)
- mechanical stable mounting of the lighting to avoid vibrations and change of adjustment.

3.9 Lighting Perspectives for the Future

The fast development of small, discrete, and powerful semiconductor light sources have drastically sped up the present developments of Machine Vision lighting. This process will continue. It is assumed that within the next 3–5 years LEDs are so powerful that they can completely substitute all usual incandescent lamps for indoor and car applications.

This will have a big effect on Machine Vision lighting. All known lighting components from today will be equipped with those new light sources. "Too dark light" will be an episode of the past. Even the light critical applications of line scan cameras will work with LEDs.

New technologies and materials such as OLEDs (organic light emitting diodes) and electro-luminescent foils will influence the design of lighting components. The technical problems of limited lifetime and low efficiency will be soon overcome. A cold lighting that is like a thin film, dimmable, and cuttable with a scissors will provide a perfect adaptation to the lighting job.

Today, reliable LEDs with UV emissions too are available. Built in all known lighting components open a few new applications where UV light is needed.

The fact that Machine Vision conquers more and more branches will drive the development of industrial compliant lighting with robust construction, assembly areas, and wiring. This will lead to standards for Machine Vision lighting components.

State-of-the-art lighting components are needed for shaping light optical components too. Machine Vision lighting technology directly benefits from new developments of optics e.g. microprism foils or specially for LED-use moulded plastic lenses.

The interaction between Machine Vision hardware, image processing software, and lighting hardware will make possible to use adaptive lighting that adapt their light emission, pattern, and sequences themselves. Smarter software algorithms will provide an automatic closed-loop control of lighting to achieve the optimal image. This will lead to standardized protocols for light control. Especially the robotic technology will benefit from this new approach.

Lighting as a long time neglected discipline of Machine Vision has become a driving force. As a consequence, the Smart Cameras will get siblings: Smart Lighting will change the future applications of Machine Vision.

References

1 Schuster, N. and Hotop, M. (2000) Spektrale Wirksamkeit von Lichtemitterdioden fuer CCD-Matrizen, msr-Magazin, 10/2000.
2 3M, OPTICAL SYSTEMS DIV. (2004) *The Photonics Handbook*, Laurin Publishing, Pittsfield, MA, p. 272.
3 Naumann, H. (1987) *Bauelemente der Optik, Hanser*, Hanser.
4 Muehlemann, M. (2004) *Tungsten Halogen: When Economy, Reliability Count, The Photonics Handbook*, Laurin Publishing, Pittsfield, MA.
5 Jacobsen, D. and Katzman, P. (2001) Benefits of Xenon Technology for Machine Vision Illumination, Perkin Elmer Optoelectronics, Santa Clara, CA.
6 Piske, C. (2003) Statische und dynamische Ansteuerung von LED's für ortsaufgelöste, adaptive Flächenbeleuchtungen in der industriellen Bildverarbeitung, Diplomarbeit, FH Lübeck.

7 Study of color fidelity of white LEDs, company paper Vision & Control GmbH.
8 DIN EN 60825-1:1994 Laser protection classes.
9 (2004) Machine Vision Lighting: A First-order Consideration, The Photonics Handbook, Schott North America.
10 Phillipow, E. (1982) *Taschenbuch Elektrotechnik*, Bd. **6**, Verlag Technik, Berlin.
11 Baer, R. (1996) *Beleuchtungstechnik – Grundlagen*, Verlag Technik, Berlin.
12 Hentschel, H.-J. (1994) *Licht und Beleuchtung*, Hüthig Verlag, Heidelberg.
13 Jahr, I. (1991) *Opto-elektronisches Messen und Erkennen zur Qualitätssicherung*, course documentation, Haus der Technik, Essen.
14 Nehse, U. (2001) Beleuchtungs- und Fokusregelungen für die objektivierte optische Präzisionsantastung in der Koordinatenmesstechnik. Dissertation, TU Ilmenau, Fakultät für Maschinenau.
15 Jahr, I. (2003) *Lexikon der industriellen Bildverarbeitung*, Spurbuchverlag, Baunach.
16 JDS Uniphase, OCLI Products. (2004) *Filters: Glossary, Equations, Parameters, The Photonics Handbook*, Laurin Publishing, Pittsfield, MA, p. H-304.
17 Filter catalogue, Heliopan Lichtfilter-Technik, Graefeling.
18 Johnson, R.L. (2004) *Bandpass Filters: The Transistor's Optical Cousin, The Photonics Handbook 2004*, Laurin Publishing, Pittsfield, MA.
19 Filter catalogue, B+W Filter, Bad Kreuznach.
20 Ahlers, R.-J. (Hrsg.) (2000) 3D-Bildaufnahme mit programmierbaren optischen Lichtgittern, in *Handbuch der Bildverarbeitung*, Expert-Verlag, Renningen-Malmsheim.
21 Jahr, I. (2003) *Adaptive Beleuchtungen*, Vortrag, 23, Heidelberger Bildverarbeitungsforum.
22 Aging considerations of LEDs, company paper Vision & Control GmbH.
23 Vision Academy Erfurt, teaching material (2015) Demands on industrial vision components system, www.vision-academy.org (accessed 25 October 2016).
24 Vision and Control Suhl, Information and images from the catalogue 'Vision & Control components system 2015' www.vision-control.com (accessed 25 October 2016).
25 Vision Academy Erfurt, Course documentations (2015), Expert training Image acquisition, www.vision-academy.org, (accessed 25 October 2016).
26 Vision Academy Erfurt, Training scripts (2015) 'Lighting engineering', www.vision-academy.org, (accessed 25 October 2016).
27 DIN 5031, Strahlungsphysik im optischen Bereich und Lichttechnik, Teil 7, Benennung der Wellenlängenbereiche.
28 VDI Richtlinie 2617, Koordinatenmessgeräte mit optischer Antastung, Bl. 6.1, S. 10.
29 European Standard Persönlicher Augenschutz – Infrarotschutzfilter – Transmissionsanforderungen und empfohlene Anwendung.

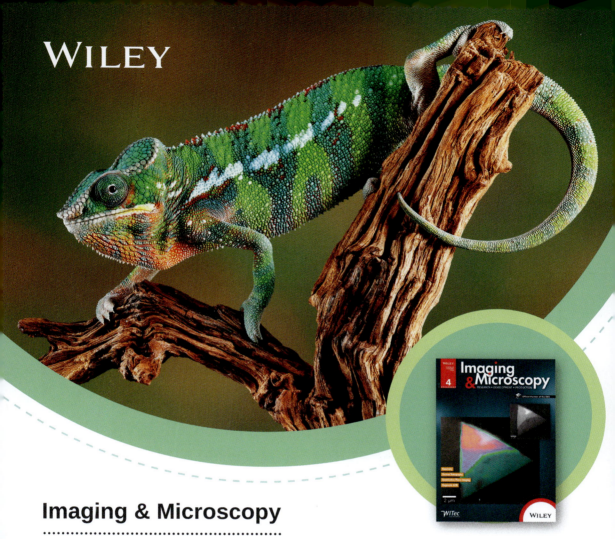

Imaging & Microscopy

Adept at Adapting to your Wishes

Imaging & Microscopy – is an imaging magazine …

… dedicated to delivering your message to a pan-European audience of 18,000 users and decision-makers in industrial and academic research. Our readers are key decision makers and/or individuals who are in the position to recommend or influence the purchase of products and services within their organization. Whether your goal is to Build Brands, Drive Traffic or Generate Leads, Imaging & Microscopy can support you individually with whatever you need.

Dr. Stefanie Krauth (Sales Manager)
Wiley-VCH Verlag GmbH & Co. KGaA
Tel.: +49 (0) 6201 606 728
stefanie.krauth@wiley.com

www.imaging-git.com

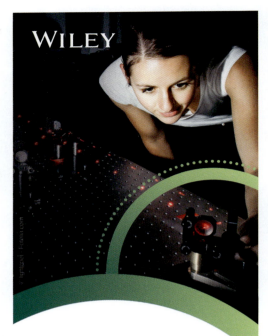

4

Optical Systems in Machine Vision
Karl Lenhardt

Jos. Schneider Optische Werke GmbH, Ringstraße 132, 55543 Bad Kreuznach, Germany

4.1 A Look at the Foundations of Geometrical Optics

4.1.1 From Electrodynamics to Light Rays

The optical system transmits information such as intensity distribution, color distribution, forms, and structures into the image space. This information is finally stored in a single plane, called the image plane.

The usual and most simple treatment of this information transmission – or *imaging* – is accomplished with the help of *light rays*. With their introduction, and with the knowledge of the laws of reflection and refraction, one arrives at the field of geometrical optics, in which the object – image relations follow from purely geometrical considerations.

Now, the concept of light rays is a pure hypothetical assumption, which is well suited to work in a first approximation. According to classical physics, light consists of electromagnetic waves of a certain wavelength range:

light = electromagnetic waves with wavelengths $\lambda = 380$–780 nm (1 nm = 10^{-9} m)

In order to give a general survey on the underlying principles, we will give a very short outline on the approximations that result in the idea of light rays.

The propagation of electromagnetic waves is described by electrodynamics and, in particular, by Maxwell's equations. These are a set of vectorial, linear, and partial differential equations. They play the role of an axiomatic system, similar to Newton's axioms in mechanics. From this set of axioms, one may – at least in principle – calculate all macroscopic phenomena. In the absence of charges and currents in space, they may be simplified to the wave equation.

Wave equation in a homogeneous medium is given by

$$\Delta \vec{E} - \frac{\epsilon \cdot \mu}{c_0^2} \cdot \frac{\partial^2 \vec{E}}{\partial t^2} = \vec{0} \qquad (4.1)$$

where $\vec{E}$ = electric field vector, Δ = Laplace operator, ε = dielectric constant, μ = magnetic permeability, c_0 = velocity of light in vacuum ($\approx 3 \times 10^8$ m s^{-1})

$$c = \frac{c_0}{\sqrt{\varepsilon \cdot \mu}} = \text{velocity of light in matter}$$

An analogous equation holds for the magnetic field vector $\vec{H}$.

Now the wavelength in the visible region of the electromagnetic spectrum is very small compared to other optical dimensions. Therefore, one may neglect the wave nature in many cases and arrive, to a first approximation, at the propagation laws if one performs the limiting case

$$\lambda \rightarrow 0$$

in the wave equation. Mathematically, this results in the Eikonal equation, which is a partial differential equation of the first order.

This limiting case ($\lambda \rightarrow 0$) is known as the relm of *geometrical optics*, because in this approximation the optical laws may be formulated by pure geometrical considerations.

From the Eikonal equation one may derive an integral equation, the so-called *Fermat principle*:

> Among all possible ray paths between points P_1 and P_2, light rays always choose that which makes the product of the refractive index and geometrical path a minimum.

Wave equation → Eikonal equation → Fermat's principle

The Fermat principle is, by the way, in complete analogy with the Hamiltonian principle in classical mechanics, and, in the same way, the Eikonal equation corresponds to the Hamilton–Jacobi differential equation in mechanics. From a formal point of view, light rays may therefore be interpreted as particle rays; in fact, this has been the interpretation by Isaac Newton!

The conclusions from the limiting case $\lambda \rightarrow 0$ for homogeneous media are twofold:

1) Four basic laws of geometrical optics follow from it.
2) Light rays may be defined as the orthogonal trajectories of the wavefronts and correspond to the direction of energy flow (Pointing vector).

The four basic laws of geometrical optics will be dealt with in the next section; here we will give some simple interpretations for wavefronts and light rays.

Example 4.1 Point-like light source – spherical wavefronts (Figure 4.1)

The light rays – being orthogonal to the spherical wavefront – form a homocentric pencil, which means that they all intersect at one single point.

Example 4.2 Plane wavefronts – light source at infinity (Figure 4.2)

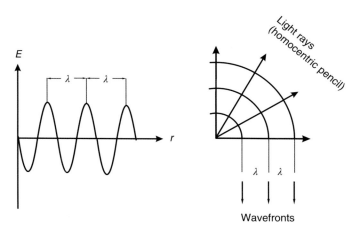

Figure 4.1 Spherical wavefronts and light rays.

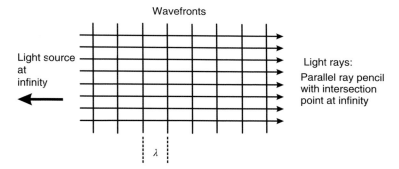

Figure 4.2 Plane wavefronts and a parallel light-ray bundle.

The light rays – orthogonal to the plane wavefronts – now form a parallel bundle, which is also homocentric because there is one single intersection point at infinity.

4.1.2 Basic Laws of Geometrical Optics

The four basic laws of geometrical optics may be described as follows:

1) Rectilinear propagation of light rays in homogeneous media
2) Undisturbed superposition of light rays
3) Law of reflection
4) Law of refraction.

The laws of reflection and refraction will be dealt with in Section 4.2.

The rectilinear propagation and undisturbed superposition of light rays are very easily demonstrated by a pinhole camera (camera obscura, Figure 4.3).

Light rays from different object points propagate rectilinearly through a very small hole until they reach the image plane. They intersect at the pinhole with undisturbed superposition.

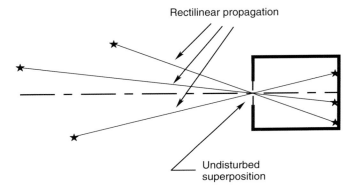

Figure 4.3 Pinhole camera.

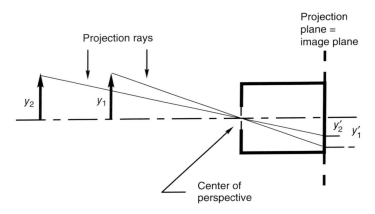

Figure 4.4 Central projection.

Image formation is done by *central projection* (Figure 4.4):

The pinhole acts as the center of perspective, the projection plane is the image plane, and the projecting rays are the light rays. The image y' will become smaller and smaller when the objects y are more and more distant from the projection center. In the limiting case of a vanishingly small pinhole, this corresponds to the linear camera model in digital image processing. This model may be described mathematically by a projective transformation with rotational symmetry. Points in the object space are associated with the corresponding points in the image plane by a linear transformation. Geometrically, one may construct this image formation in central projection just as with the pinhole camera: lines joining the object point, the projection center P, and intersecting the projection plane (image plane, sensor plane). The intersection point represents the image point corresponding to the object point (Figure 4.5).

This model is therefore represented by the projection center and the position of the image plane relative to it. This position is given by the distance c to the projection center (*camera constant*) and by the intersection point of the normal

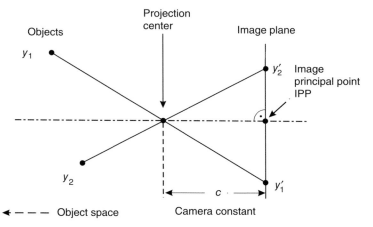

Figure 4.5 Linear camera model.

to the image plane through the projection center, sometimes called *the image principal point*.

As may be seen, this is linear image formation: straight lines in the object space are mapped to straight lines in the image plane. However, this imagery is not uniquely reversible. To each object point, there exists a unique image point, but to one single image point there correspond an infinite number of object points, namely those lying on the projection ray.

The question arises how and to what approximation this linear camera model may by realized by systems with the nonvanishing pinhole diameter, since the energy transport of electromagnetic waves requires a finite entrance opening of the optical system. We have to postpone this question until Section 4.2.12.4, and will deal first with the second set of the basic laws of geometrical optics, namely the laws of reflection and refraction.

4.2 Gaussian Optics

4.2.1 Reflection and Refraction at the Boundary between two Media

We will deal with the boundary between two transparent (nonabsorbing) media. The propagation speed of light in matter (c) is always smaller than that in vacuum (c_0). The frequency v will be the same, so the wavelength λ will become smaller in matter. The refractive index n of a certain medium is defined as the ratio of the light velocity in vacuum (c_0) to that in the medium (c), and hence it is always >1.

$$n = \frac{c_0}{c} \qquad (4.2)$$

With the refractive indices or the light velocities in different media, one may deduce the law of refraction. When a light ray meets a plane boundary between two media, it will be split into a reflected ray and a transmitted (refracted) one. Incident, refracted, and reflected rays lie within one plane, which contains also

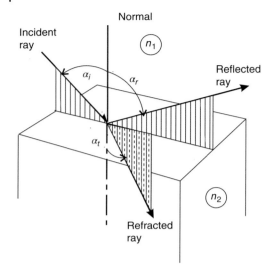

Figure 4.6 Laws of reflection and refraction.

the normal to the plane boundary between the two media (Figure 4.6).

$$\alpha_i = -\alpha_r \quad \text{law of reflection} \tag{4.3}$$

$$n_1 \sin \alpha_i = n_2 \sin \alpha_t \quad \text{law of refraction} \tag{4.4}$$

The propagation velocity c of light depends on the wavelength λ, and therefore the refractive index n is a function of the wavelength.

$$n = n(\lambda) \tag{4.5}$$

This is known as the *dispersion of light*. According to the law of refraction, the change of direction of a light ray at the boundary will be different for different wavelengths. White light, which is a mixture of different wavelengths, will split up by refraction into different wavelengths or colors (Figure 4.7).

As Equation 4.4 shows, the law of refraction is nonlinear. Thus we may not expect to get a linear transformation (especially a central projection) when we image with light rays through lenses.

It may be shown that, with arbitrarily formed refracting surfaces, no imaging of the points in the object space to the corresponding points in an image space is possible, in general.

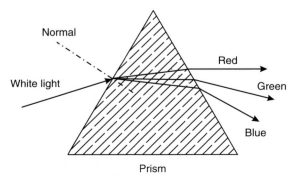

Figure 4.7 Dispersion of white light by a prism.

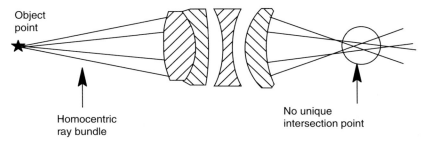

Figure 4.8 Ray pencils in the image space.

This means that a homocentric pencil of rays originating from an object point will not be transformed into a homocentric pencil of rays converging to a single point in the image space (Figure 4.8).

There is no unambiguous correspondence between the object and image points. The next section shows how one can solve this pitfall.

4.2.2 Linearizing the Law of Refraction – The Paraxial Approximation

The region where the light rays intersect in Figure 4.8 will become smaller as the incident angle between the rays and the normal to the surface becomes smaller. This will lead to a further approximation in geometrical optics.

If we develop the trigonometric sine function of Equation 4.4 into a power series, that is

$$\sin \alpha = \alpha - \frac{\alpha^3}{3!} + \frac{\alpha^5}{5!} - \cdots \tag{4.6}$$

and if we choose the incidence angle α so small that we may restrict ourselves to the first term of the series within a good approximation, then we may linearize the law of refraction. From

$$n_1 \sin \alpha_1 = n_2 \sin \alpha_2$$

we get

$$n_1 \alpha_1 = n_2 \alpha_2 \tag{4.7}$$

This is the case of *Gaussian optics*. It may be shown then that, with a system of centered spherical surfaces (e.g., two spherical surfaces that form a lens), one has a unique and reversible correspondence between the object points and the corresponding image points. The axis of symmetry is the *optical axis*, which is the line that joins all centers (vertices) of the spherical surfaces (Figure 4.9).

The validity of this approximation is restricted to a small region around the optical axis, called the *paraxial region*. For angles $\alpha \leq 7°$, the difference between the sine function and the arc of the angle α is 1%.

Gaussian optics is therefore the *ideal for all optical imaging* and serves as a reference for real physical imaging. All deviations thereof are termed *aberrations* (deviations from Gaussian optics). It should be pointed out that these aberrations are not due to manufacturing tolerances, but to the physical law of refraction.

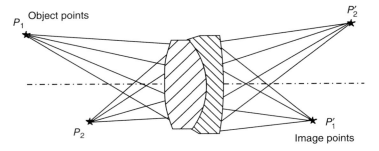

Figure 4.9 Imaging with the linearized law of refraction.

A large amount of the effort of optical designers goes to enlarging the paraxial region so that it may be useful for practical applications. In this case, a single lens will no longer be sufficient, and the cost will rise depending on the requirements on the image quality (Section 4.5).

Before we deal with the laws of imaging in the paraxial region, we have to introduce some basic optical conventions.

4.2.3 Basic Optical Conventions

4.2.3.1 Definitions for Image Orientations

The images through the optical system have, in general, a different orientation compared to that of the object. This image orientation may be defined with the help of an asymmetrical object, for instance, with the character of the number 1 in Figure 4.10.

Important: for the definition of image orientations, one has to look against the direction of light.

4.2.3.2 Definition of the Magnification Ratio β

The magnification ratio is defined as the ratio of image size to object size (Figure 4.11).

$$\beta = \frac{\text{image size}}{\text{object size}} = \frac{y'}{y} \tag{4.8}$$

Hence, this is a linear ratio (not by areas).

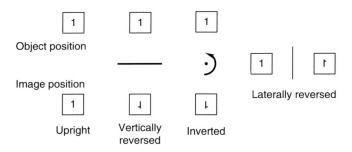

Figure 4.10 Definitions for image orientations.

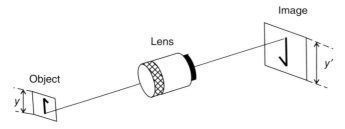

Figure 4.11 Definition of the magnification ratio β.

4.2.3.3 Real and Virtual Objects and Images

A *real object or image* really exists; the image may be captured, for instance, by a screen. A real image point is given by the intersection point of a converging homocentric ray pencil.

A *virtual image* exists only seemingly; the eye or a camera locates the image at this position, but it cannot be captured on a screen.

Example 4.3 Imaging by a mirror (Figure 4.12). The eye *does not know* anything about reflection; it extends the rays backwards until the common intersection point of the pencil. Virtual image points are the result of ray pencils extended backward. There is no real intersection point; the point is virtual.

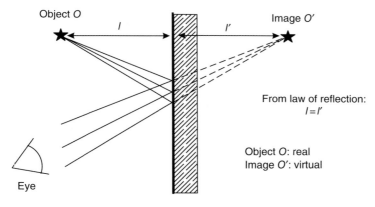

Figure 4.12 Virtual image by reflection.

Now we consider *virtual objects*. They may occur when imaging through optical systems with several components such that the image of the first component serves as the object for the following optical component. If the intermediate image is virtual, this will be a *virtual object* for imaging at the following component.

Example 4.4 Taking an image with a camera over a mirror (Figure 4.13). The real object O gives a virtual image by the mirror. This virtual image O' is an object for imaging with the lens of the camera, so it is a virtual object. The final image is again real and located in the sensor plane.

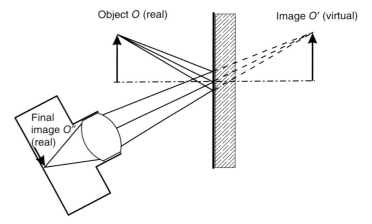

Figure 4.13 Image by a mirror followed by a camera.

Example 4.5 Imaging with a lens followed by a mirror (Figure 4.14). The image by the lens is an object for the following imaging at the mirror. But this mirror is located in front of the normally real image by the lens! So the intermediate image does not really exist. It *would* be there if the mirror did not exist. Hence this intermediate image is a virtual object for the imaging at the mirror. The final image is again real.

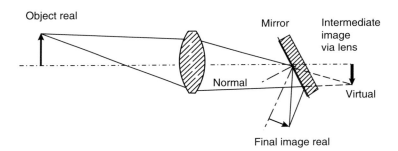

Figure 4.14 Virtual object.

4.2.3.4 *Tilt Rule* for the Evaluation of Image Orientations by Reflection

From the law of reflection, one gets the following simple procedure for the evaluation of image orientations (Figure 4.15):

We take an asymmetric object, for instance, the character 1, and push it along the light ray and tilt it toward the surface of the mirror. Then we turn it in the shortest way perpendicular to the light ray. If we look against the direction of light, we will see a vertically reversed image.

This rule is very useful if one has to consider many reflections. As an asymmetric object, one may take, for instance, a ball pen.

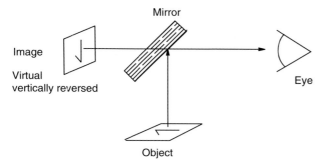

Figure 4.15 Tilt rule.

Example 4.6 For two reflections (Figure 4.16).

Even number of reflections: the image is upright or inverted
Odd number of reflections: the image is vertically reversed or laterally reversed.

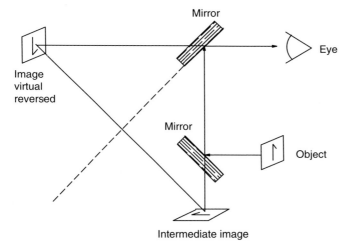

Figure 4.16 Image position with two reflections.

4.2.4 Cardinal Elements of a Lens in Gaussian Optics

A parallel pencil of rays, which may be realized by a light source at infinity, passing through a converging lens will intersect at a single point, which is the image-side focal point F' of the lens. A typical and well-known example is the *burning glass*, which collects the rays coming from the sun at its focal point. The sun is practically an object at infinity (Figure 4.17).

Hereafter, we will denote image-side entities always with a prime. In just the same way, one may define an object-side focal point F (Figure 4.18).

The location on the optical axis where a point-like light source gives, after passing through the lens, a parallel bundle of rays will be called the object-side focal

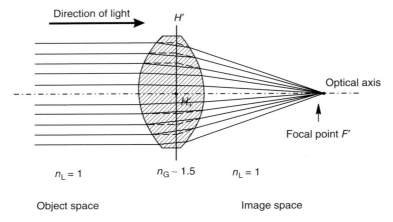

Figure 4.17 Definition of the image-side focal point F' and the principal plane H'.

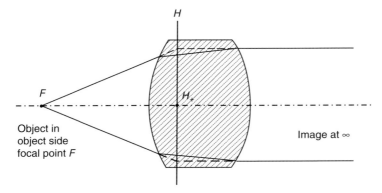

Figure 4.18 Definition of the object-side focal point F and the object-side principal plane H.

point F. For practical reasons, we enlarge the paraxial region, which means that the linear law of refraction is valid in the whole space, which is the idealized assumption of Gaussian optics.

If we extend in Figures 4.16 and 4.17 the incident rays forward and the refracted rays backward (against the direction of light), then all the intersection points will lie in two planes, the object- and image-side principal planes H and H', respectively. The intersection of these two planes with the optical axis is the object- and image-side principal point H_+ and H'_+. All the refractive power seems thus to be concentrated in the principal planes of the lens. In this way, they may be a replacement for the refracting spherical surfaces if we do not consider the real ray path within the lens. If one knows the position of H, H' and F, F', then the imaging through the lens is completely determined. In order to see this, we have to consider some further important properties of the principal planes.

> Principal planes are conjugate planes with the magnification ratio of +1. Conjugate planes or points are those that may be imaged on to each other.

If one could place an object on the object-side principal plane (e.g., a virtual object!), then the image would lie in the image-side principal plane with the same magnitude ($\beta = +1$).

Note 4.1 *The focal points F and F' are not conjugate to each other. Conjugate points are, for instance, $-\infty$ and F'. This is an important exception from the general convention that conjugate entities are denoted by the same symbol, without the prime in the object space and with the prime in the image space.*

For a lens that is surrounded by the same optical medium on both sides, we further have the following rule:

A ray passing through the point H_+ will leave the lens parallel to it and originating from H'_+.

In the following, we always consider optical systems in air.

These rules will be made evident in Section 4.2.9, where we deal with the imaging equations and their related coordinate systems.

With these properties of the principal planes and those of the focal points (the ray parallel to the optical axis will pass through F' and the ray through F will leave the lens parallel to the optical axis), we may determine the image of an object without knowing the real form of the lens. In order to fix the position and magnitude of an image, we select three distinct rays from the homocentric bundle of an object point (Figure 4.19). Considering the property $\beta = +1$ for all points on the object-side principal plane, all the rays between H and H' must be parallel to the optical axis.

Ray 1 Parallel to the optical axis, must pass through F'.

Ray 2 Passing through the point F, must be parallel to the optical axis.

Ray 3 Passing through H_+ must leave the lens parallel to it and passing through H'_+ (additional).

Since the points H_+, H'_+, and F, F' completely determine the imaging situation in Gaussian optics, these points are called the *cardinal elements*.

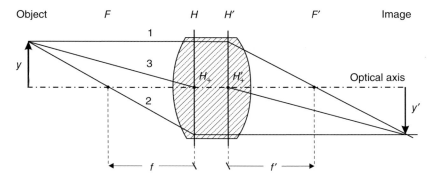

Figure 4.19 Graphical construction of the image position.

4.2.4.1 Focal Lengths f and f'

The directed distances from H_+ to F and from H'_+ to F' are called the object-side focal length f and the image-side focal length f', respectively. As a general convention, we assume that the light rays pass from left to right in our drawings. If the directed distance $\overrightarrow{H_+F}$ is against the direction of light, then f will be negative, and if the directed distance $\overrightarrow{H'_+F'}$ is in the direction of light, then f' will be positive, and vice versa.

The positions of the cardinal elements with respect to the geometrical dimensions of the lens depend on their thickness d, refractive index n, and the radii r_1 and r_2 of the spherical refractive surfaces 1 and 2. Here we will restrict ourselves to the pure presentation of the formula (without proof). Once we know the position of the cardinal elements with respect to the lens geometry, we do not need the lens geometry itself in Gaussian optics.

First, we have to describe the geometry of the lens and the corresponding conventions (Figure 4.20).

4.2.4.2 Convention

1) Direction of light from left to right (positive z-axis).
2) S_1, S_2 vertices of the refracting surfaces 1 and 2.
3) Surface numbering is in the direction of light.
4) M_1, M_2 centers of the refracting spherical surfaces.
5) Radii of curvature. These are directed distances from S to M; $\vec{r} = \overrightarrow{SM}$, positive in the direction of light, negative against it. In Figure 4.20, we have $r_1 > 0$, $r_2 < 0$.
6) d is the thickness of the lens, $d = \overline{S_1 S_2}$ and is always positive, because the refracting surfaces are numbered in the direction of light.

The position of the cardinal elements is described by the distances from the vertices S_1, S_2; they are taken with reference to the coordinate systems y_1, s_1, y'_2, s'_2. Looking in the direction of light, objects or images on the left of the optical axis are positive ($+y_1, y'_2$ directions), while on the right-hand side of the optical axis

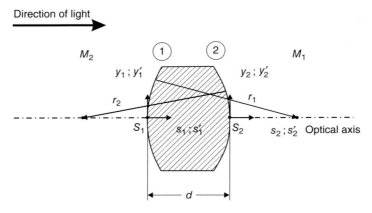

Figure 4.20 Geometry of the thick lens.

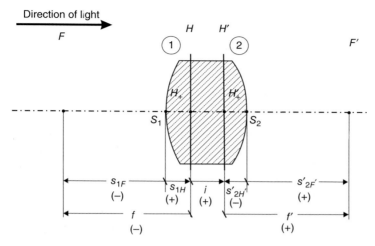

Figure 4.21 Position of the cardinal elements.

they are negative (Figure 4.21).

$$f' = \frac{r_1 \cdot r_2 \cdot n}{(n-1) \cdot R}, \quad f = -f' \tag{4.9}$$

$$R = n \cdot (r_2 - r_1) + d \cdot (n-1) \tag{4.10}$$

$$s'_{2H'} = -\frac{r_2 \cdot d}{R}, \quad s_{1H} = -\frac{r_1 \cdot d}{R} \tag{4.11}$$

$$s'_{2F'} = f'\left(1 - \frac{(n-1) \cdot d}{n \cdot r_1}\right), \quad s_{1F} = -f'\left(1 + \frac{(n-1) \cdot d}{n \cdot r_2}\right) \tag{4.12}$$

$$i = d\left(1 - \frac{r_2 - r_1}{R}\right) \tag{4.13}$$

4.2.5 Thin Lens Approximation

If the thickness of the lens is small compared to other dimensions of the imaging situation (radii, focal length, object distance), we may set $d = 0$ (thin lens approximation). In this case, we obtain from Equations 4.9–4.13

$$R = n(r_2 - r_1) \tag{4.14}$$

$$f' = \frac{r_1 r_2}{(n-1) \cdot (r_2 - r_1)} \tag{4.15}$$

$$s_{1H} = s'_{2H'} = i = 0 \tag{4.16}$$

The principal planes coincide, and the lens is replaced by a single refracting surface. The ray through the principal point $H_+ = H'_+$ passes straight through (Figure 4.22).

4.2.6 Beam-Converging and Beam-Diverging Lenses

If in the formula for the focal length we have $r_1 > 0$ and $r_2 < 0$, we get $f' > 0$ and $f < 0$. The image-side focal point F' then is on the right-hand side of the lens,

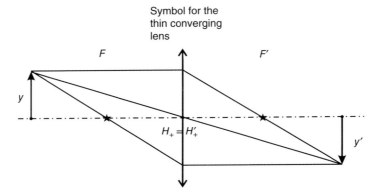

Figure 4.22 Image construction with a thin lens.

and F is on the left. The lens is beam-converging, and the image construction is as shown in Figure 4.19.

Another situation arises if $r_1 < 0$ and $r_2 > 0$ (Figure 4.23).

Here one has $f' < 0$ and $f > 0$. The image side focal point F' is now in front of the lens (taken in the direction of light); the lens is beam-diverging (Figure 4.24).

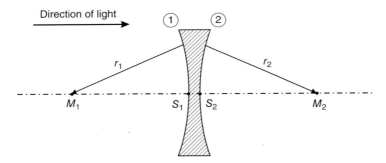

Figure 4.23 Beam-diverging lens.

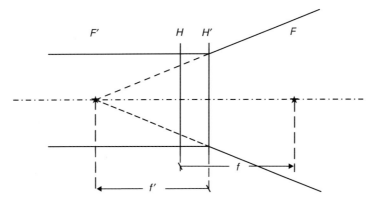

Figure 4.24 Position of the image-side focal point F' for a beam-diverging lens.

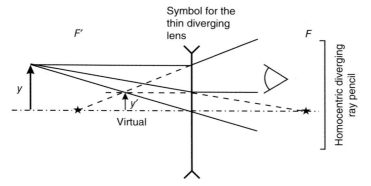

Figure 4.25 Image construction with a thin beam-diverging lens.

The direction of rays incident parallel to the optical axis after refraction is such that the backward extension passes through F'! The image-side focal length is negative. The imaging through a thin beam-diverging lens is as shown in Figure 4.25.

4.2.7 Graphical Image Constructions

4.2.7.1 Beam-Converging Lenses
Figures 4.26–4.28.

4.2.7.2 Beam-Diverging Lenses
See Figures 4.29 and 4.30.

4.2.8 Imaging Equations and Their Related Coordinate Systems

There are different possibilities for the formulation of imaging equations and, correspondingly, different sets of coordinate systems related to them.

Figure 4.26 Real object, real image.

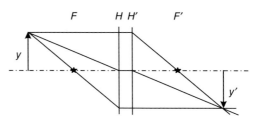

Figure 4.27 Real object, virtual image.

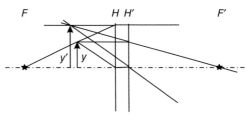

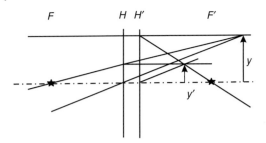

Figure 4.28 Virtual object, real image.

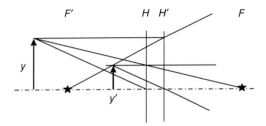

Figure 4.29 Real object, virtual image.

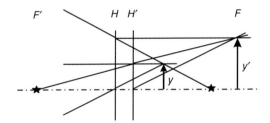

Figure 4.30 Virtual object, real image.

4.2.8.1 Reciprocity Equation

Here, the object- and image-side coordinate systems (Figure 4.31) are located in the principal planes.

From geometrical considerations and with the sign conventions, one has

$$\frac{-y'}{y} = \frac{-f}{-(a-f)} \quad \text{on the object side and} \tag{4.17}$$

$$\frac{-y'}{y} = \frac{a'-f'}{f'} \quad \text{on the image side} \tag{4.18}$$

Equating the right-hand sides of (4.17) and (4.18) gives

$$\frac{f'}{a'} + \frac{f}{a} = 1 \tag{4.19}$$

and with $f = -f'$

$$\frac{1}{a'} - \frac{1}{a} = \frac{1}{f'} \tag{4.20}$$

With $\beta = y'/y$, we get from Equation 4.17

$$a = f\left(1 - \frac{1}{\beta}\right) \tag{4.21}$$

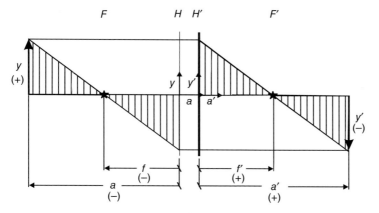

Figure 4.31 Derivation of the reciprocity equation.

and from Equation 4.18

$$a' = f'(1 - \beta) \tag{4.22}$$

and finally from (4.21) and (4.22)

$$\beta = \frac{a'}{a} \tag{4.23}$$

4.2.8.2 Newton's Equations

Here, the origins of the object- and image-side coordinate systems are located at the object- and image-side focal points, respectively (Figure 4.32).

From geometrical considerations, we get

$$-\frac{y'}{y} = \frac{-f}{-z} \quad \text{on the object side and} \tag{4.24}$$

$$-\frac{y'}{y} = \frac{z'}{f'} \quad \text{on the image side} \tag{4.25}$$

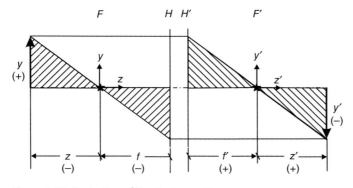

Figure 4.32 Derivation of Newton's equations.

This gives

$$\beta = -\frac{f}{z} \quad \text{on the object side,}$$

$$\beta = -\frac{z'}{f'} \quad \text{on the image side, finally} \tag{4.26}$$

$$z \cdot z' = f \cdot f'$$

and from Equation 4.26

$$\beta = \sqrt{-\frac{z'}{z}} \tag{4.27}$$

where z and z' are the Newton coordinates of the conjugate points O and O', respectively. The advantage of the Newton equations lies in the fact that there are no reciprocal quantities and one may perform algebraic calculations in a somewhat easier way.

4.2.8.2.1 Position of the Positive Principal Points H_+, H'_+:
For the conjugated points H_+ and H'_+, we have by definition $\beta = +1$. With Newton's equations, we therefore get the positions of these points:

$$\begin{aligned} z_{H_+} &= -f \\ z'_{H'_+} &= -f' \end{aligned} \tag{4.28}$$

4.2.8.2.2 Position of the Negative Principal Points H_-, H'_-:
The conjugate points for which the magnification ratio β is equal to -1 are called negative principal points H_-, H'_-.

The image has thus the same size as the object, but is inverted. From Newton's equations with $\beta = -1$

$$\begin{aligned} z_{H_-} &= +f \\ z'_{H'_-} &= +f' \end{aligned} \tag{4.29}$$

The object and image are located at twice the focal lengths $(2f)$ and $(2f')$ respectively, measured from the corresponding principal planes H and H'. The image is real and inverted.

4.2.8.3 General Imaging Equation

A more general applicable imaging equation is obtained when the origins of the object- and image-side coordinate systems lie in two conjugate but otherwise arbitrarily selected points P and P' in the object and image space. In Section 4.2.12, we will use these equations with P and P' lying in the entrance and exit pupil of the optical system, respectively. Here we give the general derivation (Figure 4.33).

From Figure 4.33, we have

$$z = p + z_P \quad p = z - z_P \quad z_P = (\overrightarrow{FP})_z \tag{4.30}$$

$$z' = p' + z'_{P'} \quad p' = z' - z'_{P'} \quad z'_{P'} = (\overrightarrow{F'P'})_z \tag{4.31}$$

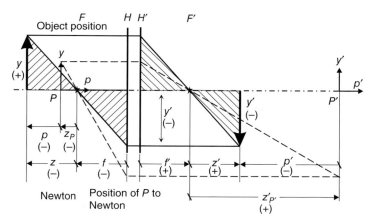

Figure 4.33 General imaging equation.

With Newton's equations, we have

$$z \cdot z' = f \cdot f' = (p + z_P) \cdot (p' + z'_{P'}) \tag{4.32}$$

$$z_P \cdot z'_{P'} = f \cdot f' \quad (P \text{ and } P' \text{ are conjugate}) \tag{4.33}$$

$$\beta_z = -\frac{z'}{f'} = -\frac{f}{z} \qquad z = -\frac{f}{\beta_z} \qquad z' = -\beta_z \cdot f' \tag{4.34}$$

$$\beta_p = -\frac{z'_{P'}}{f'} = -\frac{f}{z_P} \qquad z_P = -\frac{f}{\beta_p} \qquad z'_{P'} = -\beta_p \cdot f' \tag{4.35}$$

Equations 4.30 and 4.31 when substituted into Equations 4.34 and 4.35 give

$$p = f'\left(\frac{1}{\beta_z} - \frac{1}{\beta_p}\right) \tag{4.36}$$

$$p' = f'(\beta_p - \beta_z) \tag{4.37}$$

$$\frac{p'}{p} = \beta_p \cdot \beta_z \tag{4.38}$$

From Equations 4.32 and 4.33, we have

$$(p + z_P) \cdot (p' + z'_{P'}) = z_P \cdot z'_{P'} \tag{4.39}$$

and from this

$$\frac{z_P}{p} + \frac{z'_{P'}}{p'} + 1 = 0 \tag{4.40}$$

With Equations 4.35 and 4.34, namely $z_P = f/\beta_p$ and $z'_{P'} = -\beta_p \cdot f'$, we get

$$-\frac{\beta_p \cdot f'}{p'} = -\frac{f'}{\beta_p \cdot p} - 1 \tag{4.41}$$

$$\frac{\beta_p}{p'} = \frac{1}{\beta_p \cdot p} + \frac{1}{f'} \tag{4.42}$$

This is the analogous version of the reciprocal equation (4.20) where the origins of the coordinate systems are now generalized to two conjugate but otherwise arbitrary points P and P'.

If these points coincide with the positive principal points H_+ and H'_+ with $\beta_p = +1$, then we come back to the reciprocal equation

$$\frac{\beta_p}{p'} = \frac{1}{\beta_p \beta} + \frac{1}{f'} \xrightarrow{\beta_p = +1} \frac{1}{p'} = \frac{1}{p} + \frac{1}{f'} \tag{4.43}$$

With the notation $p' = a', p = a$, Equation 4.43 changes to Equation 4.20. Later (Section 4.2.13) we will use these imaging equations under the assumption $P =$ entrance pupil, and $P' =$ exit pupil. Then β_p will be the *pupil magnification ratio*.

4.2.8.4 Axial Magnification Ratio

The axial magnification ratio is defined as the ratio of the axial displacement of an image if the object is displaced by a small distance.

$$\text{Axial magnification ratio: } \alpha = \frac{dz'}{dz} \approx \frac{\Delta z'}{\Delta z} \tag{4.44}$$

From Newton's equation (4.26), we have

$$z' = \frac{f \cdot f'}{z} \quad \Rightarrow \quad \frac{dz'}{dz} = -\frac{f \cdot f'}{z^2} \tag{4.45}$$

and with $\beta = -f/z$ and $f' = -f$, this results in

$$\alpha = \beta^2 \tag{4.46}$$

4.2.9 Overlapping of Object and Image Space

From the results of Section 4.2.8, we may conclude the following:

> Imaging with a lens is unidirectional. A displacement of the object along the optical axis results in a displacement of the image in the same direction. With the object and image distances a and a' according to the reciprocal equation, we get the following situations:
>
> $a < 0$ real object $a' < 0$ virtual image
> $a > 0$ vitual object $a' > 0$ real image

As shown in Figure 4.34, the object and image space *penetrate each other completely*. In the axial direction, we have certain stretchings and compressions.

The object and image space are thus not defined geometrically but by the fact that the object space is defined *before the imaging* and the *image space after the imaging* at the optical system.

4.2.10 Focal Length, Lateral Magnification, and the Field of View

From Newton's equations, namely Equation 4.26, we may see that with a constant object distance, the magnification ratio $|\beta|$ becomes larger with a longer focal length of the lens. As a convention, a *normal focal length* is that which is equal to the diagonal of the image format (Table 4.1).

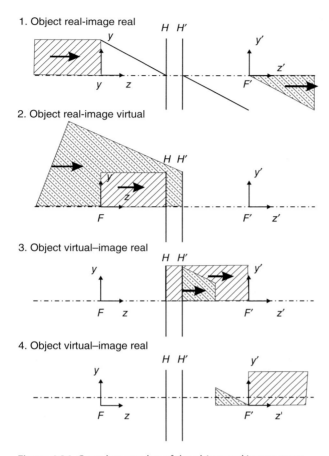

Figure 4.34 Complete overlap of the object and image space.

Table 4.1 Normal focal lengths for different image formats.

Image format	Normal focal length (mm)
16 mm film	20
24×36 mm²	45–50
60×60 mm²	75–80
60×70 mm²	90
60×90 mm²	105
90×120 mm²	135–150

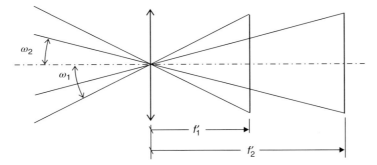

Figure 4.35 Object-side field angle ω and focal length.

Table 4.2 Classification of optical systems according to the object-side field angle ω.

Tele lens, extreme focal length lens	$2\omega < 20°$
Long focal length lens	$20° < 2\omega < 40°$
Normal focal length lens	$40° < 2\omega < 55°$
Wide angle lens	$2\omega > 55°$

Longer focal length lenses will give a larger magnification ratio (*larger images*). Correspondingly, the object extension, which belongs to a certain image format conjugate to it, is smaller. This means that the object-side field angle becomes smaller (Figure 4.35).

According to DIN 19040, one has the following classification of object field angles and focal lengths (Table 4.2).

Remark 4.2 *The object-side field angle is taken here with reference to the object-side principal point H_+. In Section 4.2.13, we will see that it is more meaningful to refer this angle with respect to the center of the entrance pupil (EP). In that case, this angle will be called the* object-side pupil field angle ω_p. *Only in the special case of infinite object distance will the principal point H_+ related field angle ω and the entrance pupil related field angle ω_p be the same.*

4.2.11 Systems of Lenses

In Section 4.2.5, we replaced a lens, which consists of two spherical refracting surfaces, by the principal planes H and H' and the corresponding focal points F and F'. In this way, the imaging properties of the lens are completely fixed as long as we do not consider the real ray path within the lens.

In the same manner, we may represent a *system of lenses* by their overall principal planes H_t, H'_t, and their corresponding overall focal points F_t and F'_t (the index t stands for the total system).

We will demonstrate this by a graphical construction of these overall cardinal elements in the example of a system of two thin lenses. The extension to

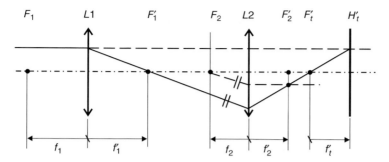

Figure 4.36 Graphical construction of the overall cardinal elements.

an arbitrary number of thick lenses is straightforward, but no principally new insight would be gained by doing so. The basic idea behind this is that most of the renowned optical manufacturers present the Gaussian data of their optical systems in their data sheets. So we may limit ourselves to the overall cardinal elements of a certain optical system when dealing with object-to-image relationships, as long as we are not interested in the real ray paths within that optical system.

Figure 4.36 shows a system of two thin lenses of which we want to determine the overall cardinal elements graphically.

We are given the principal points and focal points of the two single thin lenses. The direction of a light ray incident parallel to the optical axis will be constructed after passing each single lens up to the intersection point with the optical axis. This will give the overall image-side focal point F'_t. In the same way, a light ray parallel to the optical axis but with opposite direction will give the overall object-side focal point F_t. The intersection points of the backward-extended finally broken rays with the forward-extended incident rays will give the overall principal planes H_t and H'_t, respectively.

With this procedure, the question arises how we may find out the direction of the ray refracted at the second lens. This is shown for the image-side cardinal elements of the system in Figure 4.37.

The ray refracted at $L1$ (not shown in the figure) will give an intersection point with the object-side focal plane of $L2$. All rays that originate from this point would leave the lens $L2$ parallel to each other because they originate from a point on the focal plane. Within this ray pencil, there is a ray passing through $H_{2+} = H'_{2+}$ and

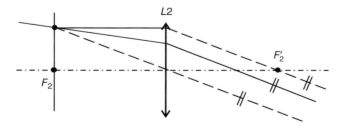

Figure 4.37 Construction of the ray direction refracted at $L2$.

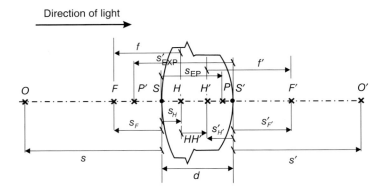

Figure 4.38 Conventions for describing the Gaussian data of an optical system: for example, s_F and $s'_{F'}$ are the z-coordinates (in the light direction) of the points F and F' related to the origins S and S', respectively.

consequently leaves the thin lens $L2$ undeviated. This gives the direction of the real beam after refraction at $L2$.

The Gaussian data of an optical system are given with reference to two coordinate systems, the first being in the vertex of the first lens surface. This describes the object-side entities. The second coordinate system has its origin in the last surface of the last lens of the system and describes the image-side Gaussian entities. We will describe this with reference to the German standard DIN 1335 since no international standard on this subject exists (Figure 4.38).

As an example, we take a real optical system, the Xenoplan 1.4/17 mm from Schneider Kreuznach, to show the cardinal elements (Table 4.3):

Note 4.3 *In the same way as we described the overall Gaussian data of an optical system, one may apply the above considerations to some components of the system. It turns out that this is very useful for systems with two principal components in order to understand the particular constellation and properties of such systems. Among those are, for example, telecentric systems, retrofocus systems, tele objective systems, and others. We will come back to this point in Section 4.2.14.*

Table 4.3 Gaussian data of a real lens system.

Focal length	$f' = 17.57$ mm
Back focal distance	$s'_{F'} = 13.16$ mm
Front focal distance	$s_F = 6.1$ mm
Image side principle point distance	$s'_{H'} = -4.41$ mm
Principal plane distance	$i = HH' = -3.16$ mm
Entrance pupil distance	$s_{EP} = 12.04$ mm
Exit pupil distance	$s'_{EXP} = -38.91$ mm
Pupil magnification ratio	$\beta_p = 2.96$
f/number	$f/nr = 1.4$
Distance of the first lens surface to the last lens surface	$d = 24.93$ mm

Example 4.7 We calculate the missing lens data f, s_H, and $i_p = PP'$ using the lens data of Table 4.3.

$$f = -f' = -17.57 \text{ mm}$$
$$s'_{H'} = s'_{F'} - f' = 13.16 \text{ mm} - 17.57 \text{ mm} = -4.41 \text{ mm}$$
$$s_H = s_F - f = 6.1 \text{ mm} + 17.57 \text{ mm} = 23.67 \text{ mm}$$
$$s_H = d - i + s'_{H'} = 24.93 \text{ mm} + 3.16 \text{ mm} - 4.41 \text{ mm} = 23.68 \text{ mm}$$
$$i_p = d - s_{EP} + s'_{EXP} = 24.93 \text{ mm} - 12.04 \text{ mm} - 38.91 \text{ mm} = -26.02 \text{ mm}$$

The difference of the results of s_H is due to a rounding effect. We recognize that the data of $s'_{H'}$ and i in Table 4.3 are obsolete if we know s_F and d.

4.2.12 Consequences of the Finite Extension of Ray Pencils

4.2.12.1 Effects of Limitations of the Ray Pencils

Up to now, we used three distinct rays to construct the images from the homocentric ray pencils originating from the object points:

1) Ray parallel to the optical axis
2) Ray through the object-side focal point F
3) Ray passing through the principal points H_+, H'_+.

We could do this because in Gaussian optics there is a one-to-one relationship between the object space and image space: a homocentric, diverging ray pencil originating from an object point will intersect in a single point, namely the image point. In reality, however, the ray pencils will be limited by some finite openings, for instance, the border of lenses or some mechanical components. It may therefore be that the selected rays for image construction do not belong to this limited ray pencil. But because these rays *would intersect at the same image point*, we may use them nevertheless for the image construction (Figure 4.39).

However, these limitations of the ray pencils have other effects, which are of utmost importance for the imaging. In order to show this, we use a very simple

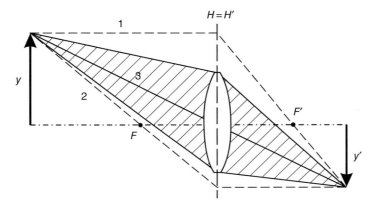

Figure 4.39 Limitation of ray pencils.

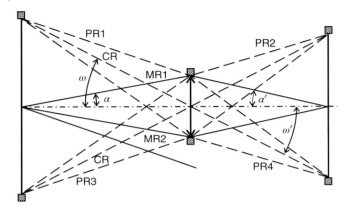

Figure 4.40 Limitation of ray pencils in a simplified camera.

example of a thin lens with finite extension and at a certain distance an image plane also with finite extension, Figure 4.40.

Only a limited number of ray pencils originating from the object points will contribute to the imaging, namely those rays passing through the aperture of the lens. Since this limited ray pencil corresponds to a certain fraction of the spherical wave emitted by the object point, only a fraction of the energy flow will be transmitted. This means that the finite extension of the lens limits the brightness of the image. We therefore call it an *aperture stop* because it limits the angle of the ray pencil that is responsible for the image brightness.

But in our imaging device there is yet another limiting opening, namely the one in the image plane. Only that region in the object space may be imaged (sharply) onto the finite image plane which is *conjugate* to this limited field. In this way, the limited image plane restricts the extension of the image and object field. It is therefore called a *field stop*. However, this field stop need not necessarily be located in the image plane. With a slide projector, this opening is realized by the mask of the slide and hence lies in the object plane.

We thus have identified two important effects of stops:

Aperture stops have influences on the image brightness.
    Field stops limit the extensions of the object and image field.

Under the concept of stops, we always will understand real (physically limiting) openings as, for example, openings in mechanical parts, the edges of lenses, the edges of mirrors, and so on.

There are still other effects of stops on imaging, which will be partly discussed in the following sections. If, for instance, the stops are very small, then the approximation of geometrical optics (*light rays!*) will be invalid, and one has to consider the wave nature of light. This will have consequences for the image sharpness and resolution (Section 4.3).

Table 4.4 shows other important influences of stops on the imaging.

Finally, in this section we have to give some definitions for those rays that limit the ray pencils.

Table 4.4 Influences of stops in the ray path.

Aperture stops	Image brightness, depth of field
Very small aperture stops	Diffraction (image sharpness, resolution)
Field stops	Limitation of the field of view
Other (undesired) stops	Vignetting
Position and size of aperture stops	Influence on aberrations (e.g., distortion)

Rays that limit the homocentric pencil for object points on the optical axis will be called *marginal rays* (MRs). The angle α of the half-cone with respect to the optical axis is a measure for this homocentric ray pencil.

Rays that limit the field of view are called *chief rays* (CRs) (or *principal rays*). These rays proceed from the edge of the object field via the center of the aperture stop up to the edge of the image field. They are the central rays for the ray pencil emerging from this object point. The corresponding angle ω with reference to the optical axis represents the field of view:

ω = object side field of view

ω' = image side field of view

Rays from object points at the edge of the object field that limit these ray bundles are called *pharoid rays* (PRs). They are analogous to the marginal rays (for object points on the optical axis) and thus determine the image brightness for points at the edge of the field of view.

Note 4.4 *By our definition, pharoid rays are conjugate rays, which means they correspond to the same ray pencil.*

Sometimes rays 1–4 of Figure 4.40, which characterize the totality of all rays passing through the optical system, are called pharoid rays. In that case, these rays are, of course, not conjugate rays.

Summary 4.1

Marginal ray (MR). It passes from the center of the object to the edges of the aperture stop and to the center of the image.
Chief ray (CR). It passes from the edges of the object to the center of the aperture stop to the edges of the image.
Pharoid ray (PR). It passes from the edges of the object to the edges of the aperture stop up to the edges of the image.

4.2.12.2 Several Limiting Openings

The very simple model of ray pencil limitations introduced in the last section must now be extended to more realistic situations. In real optical systems, there are several lenses with finite extensions such as the lens barrel and the iris diaphragm as limiting openings. It seems difficult to decide which of these

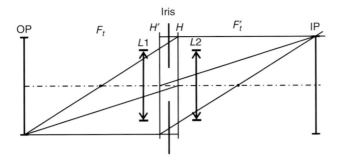

Figure 4.41 Example for ray pencil limitations.

stops is responsible for the image brightness and which one determines the field of view. In order to decide on this, we introduce a more realistic example: The optical system may consist of two thin lenses and an iris diaphragm in between. The image plane (IP) shall again be limited according to the image format (Figure 4.41)

In Figure 4.41, we also introduced the cardinal elements H, H', F, F' of the system. These may be constructed by the rules introduced in Section 4.2.11. From these cardinal elements, the position and size of the object plane (OP; which is conjugate to the IP) were found.

In order to decide which of the stops really limit the ray pencils, we use a simple trick: if a limiting stop is touched in the object space by a ray, then also the image of this stop in the image space will be touched by the corresponding ray, since the object and image are conjugate to each other. The same is also valid for the opposite direction of light. Hence, we will image all the limiting stops into the object space (from right to left). From the center of the object plane we look at all these stops (or images of stops in the object space) and may now decide which one is the smallest. This stop will limit the ray pencil for an object point on the optical axis in the object space and act as an *aperture stop*. However, since this must not only necessarily be a physical stop but may also be an image of such a stop in the object space, we call it the *entrance pupil* (EP). This is shown in Figure 4.42.

All the limiting stops or the images of these that lie in the object space are drawn with thick lines (object plane OP, $L1, L2'_O, I'_O$). From these stops, the image of the iris in the object space (I'_O) is the smallest opening viewed from the point O. This image is virtual *and lies in the object space*, since it was imaged via $L1$ to the left. *Object and image space intersect each other here!* This is the *entrance pupil* (EP) of the system. The image of the EP in the image space (or the image of the iris I via $L2$, which turns out to be the same) is then the *exit pupil* (EXP) and limits the ray pencil in the image space. EXP is also virtual. The iris I itself is hence the aperture stop and at the same time the *intermediate pupil* in an intermediate image space and is, of course, a real (physical) opening.

All the limiting stops in the image space or the *images* of stops in the image space are drawn with dashed lines. If one has already fixed the EP, we must not construct all these images but only the image of EP in the image space, which is then the EXP.

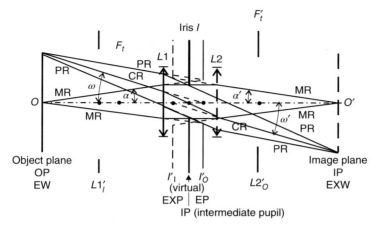

Figure 4.42 Concept of pupils and windows.

The same considerations are valid for stops that limit the field of view. In order to find these, one looks from the center of the EP into the object space. The smallest opening with respect to the center of EP is then the *object field stop*. But since this need not necessarily be a physical stop, we generalize it to the concept of *windows*. Hence this opening is called the *entrance window* (EW). The image of the EW in the image space is the *exit window* (EXW).

The concept of aperture and field stops from the simple constellation of Figure 4.40 has thus been generalized to the concept of pupils and windows. Of course, we still may speak of the aperture stop if this physical opening or an image of it in the object space acts as EP. The same considerations apply for the field stops.

For the limiting rays of the pencils, the same rules apply as in Section 4.2.12.1, with the generalization that the concept of aperture stops and field stops will be replaced by pupils and windows. If there exist intermediate pupils and windows, they have to be incorporated in the order in which the light rays touch them. Virtual pupils and windows are not really touched by the limiting rays but only by their (virtual) extensions. With the example of Figure 4.42, we have the following definitions:

Marginal ray (MR). Center of EW to the edges of EP (real up to $L1$, then virtual, since EP is virtual). From $L1$ to the edges of the intermediate pupil (IP) up to $L2$ (real since IP is real). From $L2$ to the center of EXW. The backward extensions of these rays touch virtually the edges of EXP.

Chief rays (CRs). Edges of EW to $L1$ and to the center of EP (real up to $L1$, then virtual, since EP is virtual). From $L1$ to the center of IP up to $L2$ (real since IP is real). From $L2$ to the edges of EXW. The backward extensions of these rays touch virtually the center of EXP.

Pharoid rays (PRs). Edges of EW to $L1$ and to the edges of EP (real up to $L1$, then virtual, since EP is virtual). From $L1$ to the edges of IP up to $L2$ (real since IP is real). From $L2$ to the edges of EXW. The backward extensions of these rays touch virtually the edges of the EXP. The virtual PRs are drawn only partly

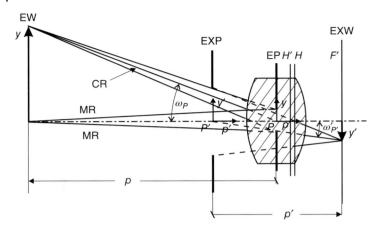

Figure 4.43 Ray pencils for a real optical system.

since they lie near the real rays. Furthermore, the intermediate window (image of EXW at $L2$) is not taken into consideration.

Finally, we will show the limitations for the ray pencils of a real optical system. In Table 4.3 we give all the relevant Gaussian data for this system, Figure 4.43.

The object and image space intersect each other! EXP, for instance, is geometrically in front of the optical system but belongs to the image space since it is the image of the iris imaged through the optical system into the image space (virtual image!).

4.2.12.3 Characterizing the Limits of Ray Pencils

For systems with a fixed object distance, the extension of the ray pencil which corresponds to the marginal rays may be characterized by the angle α of Figure 4.43, or more distinctly by the *numerical aperture A*

$$A = n \sin \alpha \quad (n = 1 \text{ for systems in air}) \tag{4.47}$$

In many cases, the object distance is variable or very large; then it makes no sense to characterize the ray pencil by the angle α. In this case one uses the *f-number*

$$f/nr = \frac{f'}{\text{diameter EP}} \tag{4.48}$$

Relation between f/nr and numerical aperture A:

$$f/nr = \frac{1}{2A} \tag{4.49}$$

The extension of the object field is characterized by the object-side field angle ω_P. It is given by the angle of the *chief rays* with respect to the optical axis. These chief rays pass from the edges of the windows to the centers of the pupils. On the object side, this angle is denoted by ω_P and on the image side by $\omega'_{P'}$. Since the corresponding ray pencils are limited by the pupils, the chief ray will be the central ray of the pencil. Because of the finite extension of the pencils, only one distinct object plane will be imaged sharply onto the image plane. All object points in

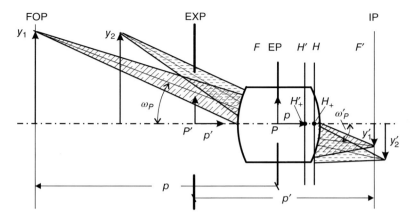

Figure 4.44 Chief rays as centers of the circle of confusion.

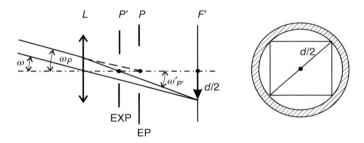

Figure 4.45 Field angles ω and ω_p, $\omega'_{p'}$ for infinite object distance.

front or behind this *focusing plane* (FOP) will be imaged as a circle of confusion, the center of which is given by the intersection point of the chief ray with the image plane, Figure 4.44.

Thus, it is more appropriate to use the chief rays for the characterization of the field of view and *not* the principal *point* rays (Section 4.2.10). The angle ω for the principal *point* rays is, in general, different from ω_p for the object-side chief ray. Only for the case of infinitely distant objects are these two angles equal in magnitude (Figure 4.45).

The extension of the image field is mostly characterized by the image circle diameter d. The image circle is, however, not sharply limited, but the brightness decreases toward the border, and in the peripheral zone the image is unsharp because of aberrations (deviations from Gaussian optics).

4.2.12.3.1 Imaging Equation with the Coordinate Systems in the Center of the Pupils
In the general imaging equations of Section 4.2.8, we now choose as the two conjugate points for the coordinate systems the center P of the entrance pupil on the object side and the center P' of the exit pupil on the image side. The magnification ratio between these conjugate points is then a *pupil magnification ratio*

$$\beta_p = \frac{\text{diameter EXP}}{\text{diameter EP}} = \frac{\varnothing_{EXP}}{\varnothing_{EP}} \qquad (4.50)$$

The imaging equations related to the centers of the pupils are then given by

$$p' = f'(\beta_p - \beta) \quad \text{distance EXP-image} \tag{4.51}$$

$$p = f'\left(\frac{1}{\beta} - \frac{1}{\beta_p}\right) \quad \text{distance EP-object} \tag{4.52}$$

$$\frac{p'}{p} = \beta_p \cdot \beta \quad \text{magnification ratios} \tag{4.53}$$

$$\frac{\beta_p}{p'} = \frac{1}{\beta_p \cdot p} + \frac{1}{f'} \quad \text{imaging equation} \tag{4.54}$$

4.2.12.3.2 Relation Between Object- and Image-Side Pupil Field Angles From Figure 4.43, we have

$$\tan \omega_P = \frac{y}{p} \quad \text{on the object side and} \tag{4.55}$$

$$\tan \omega'_{P'} = \frac{y'}{p'} \quad \text{on the image side} \tag{4.56}$$

Thus

$$\frac{\tan \omega_P}{\tan \omega'_{P'}} = \frac{y \cdot p'}{p \cdot y'} \tag{4.57}$$

with Equation 4.53 and

$$\frac{y}{y'} = \frac{1}{\beta} \tag{4.58}$$

One finally has

$$\frac{\tan \omega_P}{\tan \omega'_{P'}} = \beta_p \tag{4.59}$$

If $\beta_p \neq +1$, then ω_P and $\omega'_{P'}$ will be different, as in Figure 4.42, where $\beta_p \approx 3$!

4.2.12.4 Relation to the Linear Camera Model

We now may answer the question of Section 4.1.2 on how the linear camera model is related to Gaussian optics. From the results of the last section, we have the following statements:

1) The chief rays (CRs) are the projection rays.
2) There exist *two* projection centers, one in the center of the entrance pupil (*P*) for the object side, and one in the center of the exit pupil (*P′*) on the image side.

In order to reconstruct the objects from the image coordinates, one has to reconstruct the object-side field angles. But this may not be done with *P′* as the projection center because the chief ray angles ω_P and $\omega'_{P'}$ are in general different.

One rather has to choose the projection center on the image side such that the angles to the image points are the same as those from the center of the entrance

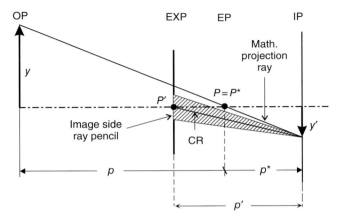

Figure 4.46 Projection model and Gaussian optics.

pupil P to the object points. We denote this image-side projection center by P^* with a distance c to the image plane. Then we require

$$\omega_P = \omega'_{P^*} \quad \text{or} \quad \frac{y}{p} = \tan(\omega_P) = \tan(\omega'_{P^*}) = \frac{y'}{c} \tag{4.60}$$

This gives

$$c = \frac{y'}{y} \cdot p = \beta \cdot p \tag{4.61}$$

This equation describes nothing but a *scaling of the projection distance on the image side*. Since the image is changed by a factor β with respect to the object, we have to change the distance of the projection center as well by the same factor in order to arrive at the same projection angle. This gives the connection to the linear camera model.

The common projection center is $P = P^*$ (P = center of EP) and the distance to the image plane is the camera constant c.

$$c = \beta \cdot p = f' \left(1 - \frac{\beta}{\beta_p}\right) \tag{4.62}$$

In photography, this distance is called the *correct perspective viewing distance*. Figure 4.46 illustrates this fact.

Note 4.5 *In order to avoid misunderstandings, we point out that, when dealing with error consideration with variations of the imaging parameters (e.g., variation of image position), one always has to take into consideration the real optical ray pencils. The projection rays of Figure 4.46 are purely fictive entities on the image side.*

Finally, we make the following comment concerning the limitations of ray pencils in Gaussian approximation:

Remark 4.6 *Against this model of Gaussian ray pencil limitation, one may argue that the pupil aberrations (deviation of real rays from Gaussian optics) are in general large and thus the Gaussian model may not be valid in reality. But, indeed, we used only the centers of the pupils in order to derive the projection model. If one introduces canonical coordinates according to Hopkins [1], one may treat the ray pencil limitation and thus the projection model even for aberrated systems in a strictly analogous way. The pupils are then reference spheres, and the wavefront aberrations of real systems are calculated relative to them. The reduced pupil coordinates will then describe the extensions of the ray pencils and are – independent of the chief ray angle – unit circles. For a detailed treatment, we refer to [1].*

4.2.13 Geometrical Depth of Field and Depth of Focus

As a consequence of the finite extension of the ray pencils, only a particular plane of the object space (the focusing plane FP) will be imaged sharply onto the image plane. All other object points in front and behind the focusing plane will be imaged more or less unsharply. The diameters of these circles of confusion depend on the extension of the ray pencils, Figure 4.47.

d is the diameter of the circle of confusion in the object space. The index f means **f**ar point and index n is for **n**ear point. First we consider the situation in

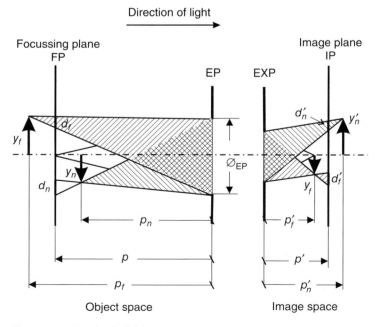

Figure 4.47 Depth of a field.

the object space. By geometric considerations, we have

$$\frac{\varnothing_{EP}}{-p_f} = \frac{d_f}{-(p_f - p)} \qquad (4.63)$$

or

$$p_f = \frac{p \cdot \varnothing_{EP}}{\varnothing_{EP} - d_f} \qquad (4.64)$$

Multiplying the numerator and denominator with β, we get

$$d'_f = -\beta \cdot d_f \qquad (4.65)$$

$$p_f = \frac{\beta \cdot p \cdot \varnothing_{EP}}{\beta \cdot \varnothing_{EP} + d'_f} \qquad (4.66)$$

and in the same way for the near point

$$p_n = \frac{\beta \cdot p \cdot \varnothing_{EP}}{\beta \cdot \varnothing_{EP} - d'_n} \qquad (4.67)$$

In the following, we set $d' = d'_f = d'_n$ with d' as the permissible circle of confusion in the image plane. From these relations, we may now calculate the depth of field as a function of the object distance or, alternatively, as a function of the magnification ratio β.

4.2.13.1 Depth of Field as a Function of the Object Distance p

With the imaging equation (4.52) solved for p and with Equation 4.48 for f/nr, we get from Equations 4.66 and 4.67

$$p_{f,n} = \frac{f'^2 \cdot p}{f'^2 \pm d' \cdot \left(p + \frac{f'}{\beta_p}\right) \cdot (f/nr)} \qquad (4.68)$$

$$T = p_f - p_n = \frac{2p \cdot f'^2 \cdot d' \cdot (f/nr) \cdot \left(p + \frac{f'}{\beta_p}\right)}{f'^4 - d'^2 \cdot (f/nr)^2 \cdot \left(p + \frac{f'}{\beta_p}\right)^2} \qquad (4.69)$$

These equations are exact within the scope of Gaussian optics.

4.2.13.1.1 Approximation 1 Let

$$p \geq 10 \cdot \frac{f'}{\beta_p} \qquad (4.70)$$

Then we have from Equations 4.68 and 4.69

$$p_{f,n} \approx \frac{f'^2}{f'_2 \pm p \cdot d' \cdot (f/nr)} \qquad (4.71)$$

$$T \approx \frac{2 \cdot f'^2 \cdot f/nr \cdot d' \cdot p^2}{f'^4 - (f/nr)^2 \cdot d'^2 \cdot p^2} \qquad (4.72)$$

4.2.13.1.2 Approximation 2
In addition, we require

$$f'^4 \geq 10 \cdot p^2 \cdot (f/nr)^2 \cdot d'^2 \qquad (4.73)$$

Then

$$T \approx \frac{2 \cdot (f/nr) \cdot d' \cdot p^2}{f'^2} \qquad (4.74)$$

Within the validity of this approximation, the depth of field T is inversely proportional to the square of the focal length (*with a constant object distance p*). Reducing the focal length by a factor of 2 will enlarge the depth of field by a factor of 4.

Example 4.8 For the validity of Equation 4.74: With $d' = 33$ µm and $f/nr = 8$, we get for

$f' = 100$ mm $\quad 1 \text{ m} \leq p \leq 12 \text{ m}$
$f' = 50$ mm $\quad 0.5 \text{ m} \leq p \leq 3 \text{ m}$
$f' = 35$ mm $\quad 0.35 \text{ m} \leq p \leq 1.5 \text{ m}$

4.2.13.2 Depth of Field as a Function of β
We replace p in Equation 4.68 with Equation 4.52 and introduce f/nr. Then

$$p_{f,n} = \frac{f'^2 \left(1 - \frac{\beta}{\beta_p}\right)}{f' \cdot \beta \pm (f/nr) \cdot d'} \qquad (4.75)$$

and

$$T = \frac{2 \cdot \left(1 - \frac{\beta}{\beta_p}\right) \cdot (f/nr) \cdot d'}{\beta^2 + \frac{(f/nr)^2 \cdot d'^2}{f'^2}} \qquad (4.76)$$

These equations are exact within the scope of Gaussian optics.

4.2.13.2.1 Approximation
We require

$$\beta^2 \geq 10 \cdot \frac{(f/nr)^2 \cdot d'^2}{f'^2} \qquad (4.77)$$

and introduce the *effective f-number*

$$(f/nr)_e = (f/nr) \cdot \left(1 - \frac{\beta}{\beta_p}\right)$$

Then

$$T \approx \frac{2 \cdot (f/nr)_e \cdot d'}{\beta^2} \qquad (4.78)$$

Within the validity of this approximation, the depth of field T is independent of the focal length (with equal β). For the *depth of focus T*, we have

$$T' \approx \beta^2 \cdot T \qquad (4.79)$$
$$T' = 2 \cdot (f/nr)_e \cdot d' \qquad (4.80)$$

Example 4.9 For the range of validity

$$d' = 33 \text{ μm } (35 \text{ mm format}) \quad f' = 50 \text{ mm}, \quad f/nr = 16, \quad |\beta| \geq \frac{1}{30}$$

$$d' = 100 \text{ μm } (9 \times 12 \text{ cm}^2) \quad f' = 150 \text{ mm}, \quad f/nr = 16, \quad |\beta| \geq \frac{1}{30}$$

4.2.13.3 Hyperfocal Distance

In some cases, one has to image objects at (nearly) infinity and, in the same Case, some other objects that are at a finite distance in the foreground. Then it will not be useful to adjust the object distance at infinity. One rather has to adjust the distance such that the far distance p_f of the depth of field is at infinity. This is called the *hyperfocal distance* p_∞. From Equation 4.75, we see that for $p_f = \infty$ the denominator must vanish, which means

$$\beta_\infty = -\frac{(f/nr) \cdot d'}{f'} \tag{4.81}$$

and from Newton's equations we have

$$\beta_\infty = \frac{z'_\infty}{f'} \tag{4.82}$$

Thus

$$z'_\infty = (f/nr) \cdot d' \tag{4.83}$$

where z'_∞ is the Newton image-side coordinate, counting from F'. For the object plane conjugate to this, we again have with Newton's equations

$$z_\infty = -\frac{(f')^2}{(f/nr) \cdot d'} \tag{4.84}$$

For the pupil coordinates p_∞, p'_∞ (with reference to the pupils), we see from Equation 4.68 that the denominator must vanish and we get

$$p_\infty = -\frac{(f')^2}{(f/nr) \cdot d'} - \frac{f'}{\beta_p} = z_\infty - \frac{f'}{\beta_p} \tag{4.85}$$

and with Equation 4.52

$$p'_\infty = (f/nr) \cdot d' + f' \cdot \beta_p = z'_\infty + f' \cdot \beta_p \tag{4.86}$$

Figure 4.48 gives an illustration of the Newton and pupil coordinates.

Finally, we are interested at the *near limit* of the hyperfocal depth of field. With Equation 4.75 and the minus sign in the denominator and Equation 4.81, we get

$$p_n = -\frac{(f')^2}{2 \cdot (f/nr) \cdot d'} - \frac{f'}{2\beta_p} \tag{4.87}$$

and comparing it with (4.85)

$$p_n = \frac{p_\infty}{2} \tag{4.88}$$

The near limit of the hyperfocal depth of field is thus half of the hyperfocal distance p_∞!

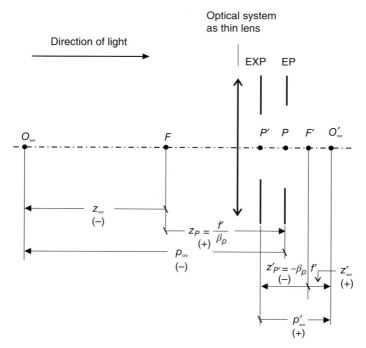

Figure 4.48 Relations between the Newton and pupil coordinates: $z_P = FP = f'/\beta_p$, $z'_{P'} = F'P' = -\beta_p f'$.

For the near limit of the depth of focus, we start with Equation 4.81 and with

$$p = z - \frac{f'}{\beta_p}, \quad z \cdot z' = -f'^2 \tag{4.89}$$

One has

$$z'_n = 2 \cdot z'_\infty \left[\frac{1}{1 + \frac{\beta_\infty}{\beta_p}} \right] \tag{4.90}$$

Usually

$$\beta_\infty = -\frac{(f/nr) \cdot d'}{f'} \ll \beta_p \tag{4.91}$$

which leads to the approximation

$$z'_n \approx 2 \cdot z'_\infty \tag{4.92}$$

4.2.13.4 Permissible Size for the Circle of Confusion d'

The permissible size for the circle of confusion depends on the resolution capability of the detector. For visual applications, this is the eye with a resolving power of approximately 1.5'. Together with the correct perspective viewing distance, this would give the size d' for the circle of confusion.

Table 4.5 Standard diameters for the permissible circle of confusion for different image formats.

Format	90 × 120	60 × 90	60 × 60	45 × 60	24 × 36	18 × 24	7.5 × 10.5	3.6 × 4.8
Diagonal (mm)	150	108	85	75	43	30	13	6
$d' = \dfrac{\text{diag}}{1500}$	0.1 mm	72 µm	57 µm	50 µm	29 µm	20 µm	9 µm	4 µm
d'_N stand.	0.1 mm	75 µm	60 µm	50 µm	33 µm	25 µm	15 µm	10 µm
Δ in %	0	−4	−5	0	−12	−20	−40	−60
β for enlarging to diag. 150 mm	1	1.39	1.76	2	3.49	5	11.5	25
Viewing angle for $d'_N \cdot \beta$ from 250 mm	1′23″	1′26″	1′27″	1′23″	1′35″	1′43″	2′23″	3′26″

Moving pictures less critical

But usually one does not look at an image with this distance, for instance taken with a telephoto lens, but much closer. The reason is that the eye may detect some details that could not be seen in the object only if the viewing angle is larger than that to the object. With the correct perspective viewing distance, we have however the same angle.

It thus makes sense to connect the viewing distance with the final image format. Because a larger taking (format) requires only a smaller magnification for the final print than a smaller taking format, the permissible size for the circle of confusion may be larger for the larger sensor (format).

The starting point for the evaluation is an image format of 9×12 cm², which is observed at the standardized viewing distance of 25 cm without magnification. For the permissible circle of confusion, we then have

$$d' \approx \frac{\text{sensor diagonal}}{1500} = \frac{150}{1500} = 0.1 \text{ mm} \tag{4.93}$$

From the standardized viewing distance (5/3 of image diagonal), this corresponds to an angle of 1.5′, which is the resolving power of the eye. The values of d' for other sensor formats follow from Equation 3.93 with the corresponding image diagonal. For small diagonals, d' will become smaller but the viewing angle will be approximately the same, Table 4.5 (see Tables 4.6 and 4.7).

4.2.14 Laws of Central Projection–Telecentric System

4.2.14.1 Introduction to the Laws of Perspective

It is a well-known fact that extreme tele and wide angle photos show very different impressions of spatial depth. When taking pictures with extreme telephoto lenses (long focal length lenses), the impression of spatial depth in the image seems to be very flat, whereas with extreme wide angle lenses (short focal lengths), the spatial depth seems to be exaggerated. As an example, we look at the two photos of a checker board (Figure 4.49).

Table 4.6 Summary of the formulae for the depth of field and depth of focus.

	Depth of field as function of	
Distance p		**Magnification ratio β**

Geometrically exact:

$$T = \frac{2p \cdot f'^2 \cdot d' \cdot (f/nr) \cdot \left(p + \frac{f'}{\beta_p}\right)}{f'^4 - d'^2 \cdot (f/nr)^2 \cdot \left(\beta + \frac{f'}{\beta_p}\right)^2}$$

$$p_{f,n} = \frac{p \cdot f'^2}{f'^2 \pm d' \cdot (f/nr) \cdot \left(p + \frac{f'}{\beta_p}\right)}$$

Approximation 1: $p < 10\, f'/\beta_p$

$$T \approx \frac{2f'^2 \cdot (f/nr) \cdot d' \cdot p^2}{f'^4 - (f/nr)^2 \cdot d'^2 \cdot p^2}$$

$$p_{f,n} \approx \frac{f'^2}{f'^2 \pm p \cdot d' \cdot (f/nr)}$$

Approximation 2:
$10 f'/\beta_p < p < f'/3(f/nr)d'$

$$T \approx \frac{2(f/nr) \cdot d' \cdot p^2}{f'^2}$$

$$T = \frac{2 \cdot \left(1 - \frac{\beta}{\beta_p}\right) \cdot (f/nr) \cdot d'}{\beta^2 + \frac{(f/nr)^2 \cdot d'^2}{f'^2}}$$

$$p_{f,n} = \frac{f'^2 \left(1 - \frac{\beta}{\beta_p}\right)}{f' \cdot \beta \pm (f/nr) \cdot d'}$$

Approximation: $\beta^2 \geq 10 \cdot \frac{(f/nr)^2 \cdot d'^2}{f'^2}$

$$T \approx \frac{2 \cdot (f/nr)_e \cdot d'}{\beta^2}$$

$$T' \approx \beta^2 \cdot T = 2 \cdot (f/nr)_e \cdot d'$$

Table 4.7 Summary of the formulae for the hyperfocal distance.

	Hyperfocal distance	
Newton coordinates		**Pupil coordinates**

Exact $z_\infty = \dfrac{f'^2}{(f/nr) \cdot d'}$

$z'_\infty = (f/nr) \cdot d'$

$z_n = \dfrac{1}{2}\left(z_\infty + \dfrac{f'}{\beta_p}\right)$

$z'_n = 2z'_\infty \dfrac{1}{1 - \dfrac{(f/nr) \cdot d'}{f' \cdot \beta_p}}$

Approximation: $(f/nr) \cdot d' \leq \dfrac{1}{10} f' \cdot \beta_p$

$z'_n = 2 \cdot z'_\infty$

$p_\infty = z_\infty - \dfrac{f'}{\beta_p}$

$p'_\infty = z'_\infty + \beta_p f'$

$p_n = \dfrac{p_\infty}{2}$

$p'_n = z'_n + \beta_p \cdot f'$

$p'_n = 2z_\infty + \beta_p \cdot f'$

Figure 4.49 Wide angle and tele perspective.

Both photos have been taken with a small format camera (24 mm × 36 mm), the left one with a moderately wide angle lens (focal length 35 mm) and the right one with a telephoto lens of 200 mm focal length. In both Pictures, the foreground (e.g., the front edge of the checker board) has almost the same size. In order to realize this, one has to approach the object very closely with the wide angle lens (~35 cm). With the telephoto lens, however, the distance has to be very large (~2 m).

One may clearly observe that with the wide angle lens the chess figures, which were arranged in equally spaced rows, seem to become rapidly smaller, thus giving the impression of large spatial depth. In contrast, with the telephoto lens picture, the checker figures seem to reduce very little, thus leading to the impression that the spatial depth is much lower. What are the reasons for these different impressions of the same object?

In order to give a clear understanding for these reasons, we look away from all laws of optical imaging by lenses and look at the particularly simple case of a pinhole camera (*camera obscura*).

We call the distance between the pinhole and the image plane the *image width* p'. With this pinhole camera, we want to image different regularly spaced objects of the same size into the image plane.

Figure 4.50 shows a side view of this arrangement.

Each object point, for example, also the top of the objects – shown by the arrows – will emit a bundle of rays. But only one single ray of this bundle will pass through the pinhole onto the image plane. Thus, this indicates the top of the

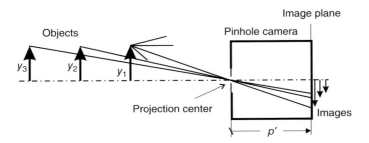

Figure 4.50 Imaging with a pinhole camera.

object in the image and hence its size. All other rays of this object point are of no interest for this image.

In this manner, if we construct the images of all objects, we will see that the images will become smaller and smaller the more distant the object is from the pinhole. The pinhole is the center at which all imaging rays cross each other. Therefore we will call it the *projection center*.

> To summarize, *the farther the object is located from the projection centre, the smaller is the image. This kind of imaging is called* **entocentric perspective**.

The characteristic feature of this arrangement is that, viewed in the direction where the light travels, we have first the object, then the projection centre, and, finally, the image plane. The objects are situated at a finite distance *in front* of the projection center.

But now, what are the reasons for the different impressions of spatial depth? With the wide angle lens, the distance to the first object y is small, whereas with the tele-lens this distance is considerably larger by a factor of 6. We shall simulate this situation now with the help of our pinhole camera (Figure 4.51).

The picture on the top (case (a)) shows the same situation as in Figure 4.50. In the picture at the bottom (case (b)), the distance to the first object is however 3.5 times larger. In order to image the first object y_1 with the same size as in case (a), we have to expand the image distance by the same factor 3.5 correspondingly. We now see that the three objects y_1, y_2, y_3 have nearly of the same size as with the telephoto lens of Figure 4.49. Whereas in case (a) the image y'_3 is roughly half the size of the image y'_1, in case (b) it is three-quarters of that size. There would have been no change in the *ratio* of the image sizes if the image distance p' in case (b) were the same as in case (a); only the total image size would become smaller and could be enlarged to the same size.

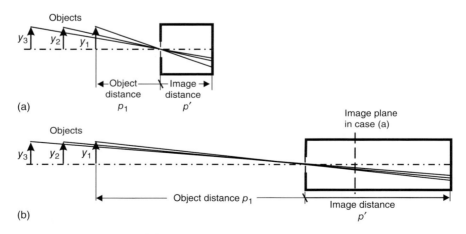

Figure 4.51 Imaging with different object distances.

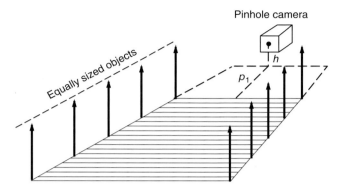

Figure 4.52 Positional arrangement of the objects in space.

Conclusion 4.7 *The only thing that is important for the* ratio *of the image sizes is the distance of the objects from the projection center.*

To gain a clearer picture of the resulting spatial depth impression, we have to arrange the object scene in space, as shown in Figure 4.52.

Here we have two rows of equally sized and equally spaced objects (arrows). We may imagine the objects to be the checker figures of Figure 4.49. The pinhole camera is located centrally and horizontally in between the two object rows at a distance p_1 and height h relative to the objects. For the construction of the images taken with different object distance p_1, we choose to view this scene from above. This is shown in Figure 4.53.

Here, the objects are represented by circles (view from above) and are situated on the dashed background plane. The pinhole camera is shown by its projection center and its image plane. The image plane is perpendicular to the plane of the paper, and is therefore only seen as a straight line. The projection rays (view from above) are shown only for one row of the objects for the sake of clarity and not to overload the drawings.

The two parallel straight lines on which the objects are positioned intersect each other at infinity. Where is this point located in the image plane? It is given by the ray with the same direction as the two parallel straight lines passing through the projection center and cutting the image plane.

If we tilt the image plane toward the plane of the paper, we may now reconstruct all the images.

The horizon line (skyline) is to be found at an image height h' as the image of the height h of the pinhole camera above the ground. The point of intersection of the two parallel lines at infinity is located in the image plane on this horizon and is the *far point F for this direction*. We transfer now all the intersection points of the projection rays with the perpendicular image plane onto the tilted image plane. The connecting line between the intersection point of the nearest object projection ray and the far point gives the direction of convergence of the two parallel object lines in the image. In this way, we may construct all the images of different objects. If we now finally rotate the image by 180° and remove all

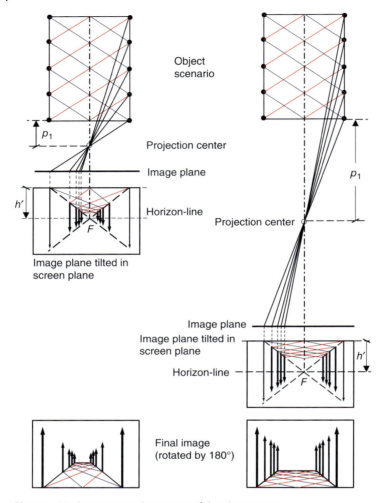

Figure 4.53 Constructing the images of the object scene.

auxiliary lines, we then see very clearly the effect of different perspectives for the two object distances. This is in good agreement with the photo of the introductory example (Figure 4.49).

Imagine now we want to measure the heights of different objects from their images. This proves to be impossible because equally sized objects have different image sizes depending on the object distance which is unknown in general. The requirement would be that the images should be mapped with a constant size ratio to the objects. Only in this case would equally sized objects give equally sized images, independent of the object distance.

In order to see what this requirement implies, we will investigate the image size *ratios* of equally sized objects under the influence of the object distance (Figure 4.54).

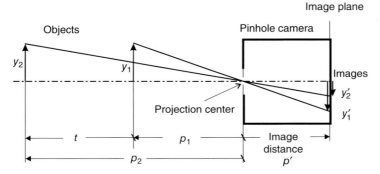

Figure 4.54 Image size ratio and object distance.

From Figure 4.54

$$\frac{y'_1}{y_1} = \frac{p'}{p_1} \quad \text{and} \quad \frac{y'_2}{y_2} = \frac{p'}{p_2} \tag{4.94}$$

The image size ratio y'_1/y'_2 will be called m. Dividing the first equation by the second and knowing that $y_1 = y_2$ will result in the following:

$$\frac{y'_1}{y'_2} = m = \frac{p_2}{p_1} \tag{4.95}$$

The image sizes of equally sized objects are inversely proportional to the corresponding object distances.

In addition to

$$t = p_2 - p_1 = y'_1 \cdot m - y'_1 \tag{4.96}$$

we have

$$p_1 = \frac{t}{m-1}, \quad p_2 = \frac{t \cdot m}{m-1} \tag{4.97}$$

If now p_1 becomes larger and larger, the ratio

$$\frac{p_2}{p_1} = \frac{p_1 + t}{p_1} \tag{4.98}$$

approaches 1, and hence also the image size ratio y'_1/y'_2. In the limit, as p_1 reaches infinity, the image size ratio will be exactly 1.

This is the case of *telecentric perspective*:

> The projection center is at infinity, and all equally sized objects have the same image size.

Of course, we may not realize this in practice with a pinhole camera, since the image distance p' would also go to infinity. But with an optical trick we may transform the projection center into infinity without reducing the image sizes to zero. In front of the pinhole camera, we position a lens in such a way that the pinhole lies at the (image-side) focal point of this lens (see Figure 4.55).

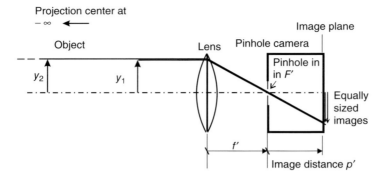

Figure 4.55 Object-side telecentric perspective.

The image of the pinhole imaged by the lens onto the left side in the object space is now situated at infinity. Only those rays parallel to the axis of symmetry of the pinhole camera will pass through the pinhole, because it lies at the image-side focal point of the lens. That is why all equally sized objects will be imaged with equal size onto the image plane.

As a consequence of the imaging of the pinhole, we now have *two projection centers*, one on the object side (which lies at infinity) and other on the side of the images, which lies at a finite distance p' in front of the image plane. Therefore this arrangement is called *object-side telecentric perspective*.

If the pinhole is positioned with regard to the lens in such a way that its image (in object space on the left) is situated at a finite distance in front of the objects, the case of *hypercentric perspective* is realized (see Figure 4.56).

The projecting rays (passing through the pinhole) now have such a direction that their backward extensions pass through the object-side projection center.

All equally sized objects will now be imaged with larger size, the farther they are from the pinhole camera. Thus we may look *around the corner*!

At the end of this section we will show some examples that are of interest for optical measurement techniques. The object is a plug-in with many equally sized pins. Figure 4.57 shows two pictures taken with a 2/3 in. CCD camera and two different lenses.

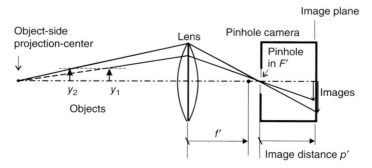

Figure 4.56 Hypercentric perspective.

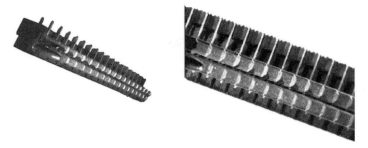

Figure 4.57 Entocentric and telecentric perspective.

The left side picture is taken with a lens with a focal length of 12 mm (this corresponds roughly to a standard lens of 50 mm focal length for the format 36 mm × 24 mm). Here we clearly see the perspective convergence of parallel lines, which is totally unsuitable for measurement purposes. On the other hand, the telecentric picture on the right, which is taken from the same position, shows all the pins with equal size and is thus suited for measurement purposes.

Perspective convergence is true not only for horizontal views into the object space but also for views from the top of the objects. This is shown for the same plug-in in Figure 4.58.

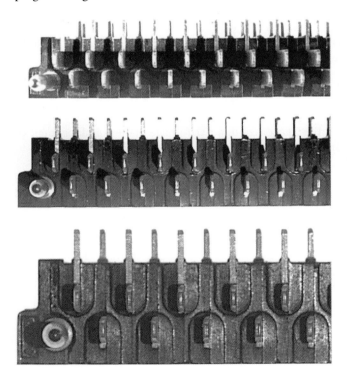

Figure 4.58 Viewing direction from the top of the object.

The picture with the standard lens ($f' = 12$ mm) shows only one pin exactly from top (it is the fourth, counted from left). All others show the left or right sidewalls of the pins. For the picture with a 3× telephoto lens ($f' = 35$ mm), this effect is already diminished. But only the picture taken with a telecentric lens clearly shows all pins exactly from the top. In this case, the measurement of the distance of all the pins is possible.

4.2.14.2 Central Projection from Infinity – Telecentric Perspective

4.2.14.2.1 Object-Side Telecentric Systems

Limitation of Ray Bundles As has been shown in Section 4.2.12.4, there are two projection centers with Gaussian optics: the center P of the entrance pupil in object space, and the center P' of the exit pupil in image space. Hence, for object-side telecentric systems the object-side projection center P (and therefore the entrance pupil) has to be at infinity (cf. Section 4.2.14.1).

In the simplest case – which we choose for didactic reasons – this may be done by positioning the aperture stop at the image-side focal point of the system. The aperture stop is then the exit pupil (EXP). The entrance pupil (EP) is the image of the aperture stop in the object space, which is situated at infinity and is infinitely large. For the pupil magnification ratio, we therefore have

$$\beta_p = \frac{\varnothing_{EXP}}{\varnothing_{EP}} = 0 \tag{4.99}$$

(Figure 4.59).

The chief rays (blue) are parallel to the optical axis (virtual from the direction of the center EP – dashed), and pass through the edge of the object to the lens, from there to the center of EXP, and finally to the edge of the image.

This chief ray is the same for all equally sized objects (y_1, y_2) regardless of their axial position, and it intersects the fixed image plane at one single point. For the object y_2, it is (in a first approximation) the central ray of the circle of confusion.

> The result is that the image size in a *fixed* image plane is independent of the object distance.

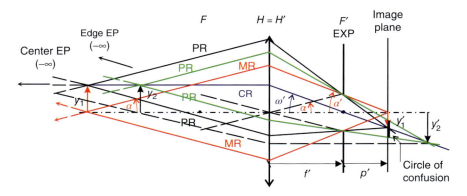

Figure 4.59 Principle of object-side telecentric imaging.

The marginal rays (MRs; red) and the pharoid rays (PRs; black and green) have an aperture angle α that depends on the diameter of the aperture stop AS (=EXP). Here we may see the characteristic limitation for imaging with telecentric systems:

> The diameter of the optical system (in the present case, the lens) must at least be as large as the object size plus the size determined by the aperture angle of the beams.

The imaging equations now become

$$p' = -f' \cdot \beta \quad \text{(counted from EXP)} \tag{4.100}$$

$$p = \infty \quad \text{(counted from EP)} \tag{4.101}$$

$$\beta_p = \frac{\tan \omega_p}{\tan \omega'_{p'}} = 0 \Rightarrow \varnothing_{EP} = \infty \tag{4.102}$$

$$c = f' \cdot \left(1 - \frac{\beta}{\beta_p}\right) = \infty \quad \text{(camera constant)} \tag{4.103}$$

The f-number $f/nr = f'/\varnothing_{EP}$ is now formally 0 and $1/\beta_p$ approaches infinity. Therefore, the usual expression for the depth of field will be undetermined. We may, however, transform the equation

$$T = \frac{2d' \cdot (f/nr) \cdot \left(1 - \frac{\beta}{\beta_p}\right)}{\beta^2}$$

$$= \frac{2d' \cdot f' \cdot \left(\frac{1}{\varnothing_{EP}} - \frac{\beta}{\varnothing_{AP}}\right)}{\beta^2} \tag{4.104}$$

$$\lim_{\varnothing_{EP} \to \infty} T = \frac{-2 \cdot f'}{\varnothing_{AP}} \cdot \frac{d'}{\beta} \quad \text{from Figure 4.59:} \quad \frac{f'}{\varnothing_{AP}/2} = \sin \alpha \tag{4.105}$$

We have

$$T = -\frac{d'}{\beta \cdot \sin \alpha} \tag{4.106}$$

where $A = \sin(\alpha)$ is the object side numerical aperture. With the sine condition

$$\frac{\sin \alpha}{\sin \alpha'} = -\beta \tag{4.107}$$

we get

$$T = \frac{d'}{\beta^2 \cdot \sin \alpha'} \tag{4.108}$$

$A' = \sin(\alpha')$ = image side numerical aperture.

4.2.14.2.2 Bilateral Telecentric Systems

Afocal systems For bilateral (object *and* image side) telecentric systems, the entrance pupil (EP) and the exit pupil (EXP) have to be at infinity. This we may achieve only with a two-component system, since the aperture stop has to be imaged in the object space as well as in the image space to infinity. It follows that the image-side focal point of the first component must coincide with the object-side focal point of the second component ($F_1' = F_2$). According to Section 4.2.11 (system of lenses), we may represent the two components of the system by two thin lenses in a first approximation.

Such systems are called afocal systems since the object- and image-side focal points (F, F') for the complete system are at infinity now. Figure 4.60 shows the case of two components $L1, L2$ with positive power.

A ray parallel to the optical axis leaves the system also parallel to the optical axis. The intersection point lies at infinity; this is the image-side focal point F' of the system. The same is true for the object-side focal point F of the system (afocal means *without focal points*). A typical example of an afocal system with two components of positive power is the *Keplerian telescope*. Objects that practically lie at infinity will be imaged by this system again at infinity. The images are observed behind the second component with the relaxed eye (looking at infinity). Figure 4.61 shows this for an object point at the edge of the object (e.g., the edge of the moon's disk).

The clear aperture of the first component ($L1$ = telescope lens) now acts as the entrance pupil (EP) of the system. The image of EP, imaged by the second component ($L2$ = eye-piece), is the exit pupil (EXP) in the image space (dashed black lines).

The object point at infinity sends a parallel pencil of rays at the field angle ω_P into the component $L1$. $L1$ produces the intermediate image y' at the image-side focal plane F_1'. At the same time, this is the object-side focal plane for component $L2$. Hence this intermediate image is again imaged to infinity by the second

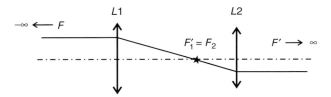

Figure 4.60 Afocal systems.

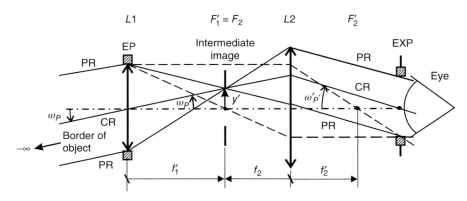

Figure 4.61 Kepler telescope.

component $L2$ with a field angle of $\omega'_{p'}$. The eye is positioned at the exit pupil EXP and observes the image without focusing under the field angle $\omega'_{p'}$. Since the object and the image are situated at infinity (and are infinitely large), the magnification ratio is undetermined. In this case, for the apparent magnification of the image, it depends on how much the tangent of the viewing angle $\omega'_{p'}$ has been changed compared to the observation of the object without telescope from the place of the entrance pupil (tangent of viewing angle ω_P). In this way, the telescope magnification is defined:

The telescope magnification V_F is the ratio of the viewing angle ($\tan\omega'_{p'}$) with the instrument to the viewing angle ($\tan\omega_P$) without the instrument.

$$V_F = \frac{\text{tangent of the viewing angle } \omega'_{p'} \text{ with instrument}}{\text{tangent of the viewing angle } \omega_P \text{ without instrument}} \quad (4.109)$$

From Figure 4.61

$$\tan\omega_P = \frac{y'}{f'_1} \quad (4.110)$$

$$\tan\omega'_{p'} = \frac{y'}{f_2} = -\frac{y'}{f'_2} \quad (4.111)$$

Hence the telescope magnification V_F is given by

$$V_F = -\frac{f'_1}{f'_2} \quad (4.112)$$

With a large focal length f'_1 and an eye piece with focal length f'_2, we will get a large magnification of the viewing angles. This is the main purpose of the Keplerian telescope.

Imaging with Afocal Systems at Finite Distances With afocal systems, one may, however, not only observe objects at infinity but also create real images at a finite position. This is true in the case of a contactless optical measurement technique and has been the main reason for choosing the Keplerian telescope as a starting point.

In order to generate real images with afocal systems, we have to consider the following fact: we will get real final images only when the intermediate image of the first component is *not* situated in the region between $F'_1 = F_2$ and the second component. Otherwise, the second component would act as a magnifying lupe and the final image would be virtual. This is explained in Figure 4.62.

The object is now situated between the object-side focal points F_1 and $L1$. Because of this, the intermediate image y' is virtual and is located in front of the object. This virtual intermediate image is then transformed by $L2$ into the real final image y''.

For the mathematical treatment of the imaging procedure, we now apply Newton imaging equations one after another to components $L1$ and $L2$.

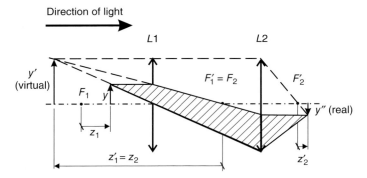

Figure 4.62 Real final images with afocal systems.

Intermediate image at component $L1$:

$$\beta_1 = -\frac{z_1'}{f_1'} = -\frac{f_1}{z_1} \tag{4.113}$$

This intermediate image acts as an object for the imaging at the second component $L2$ (in Figure 4.62). The intermediate image is virtual, and hence for the second component a *virtual object*!

With the relation

$$F_1' = F_2 \quad \text{(afocal system)} \tag{4.114}$$

we have

$$z_2 = z_1' \tag{4.115}$$

For imaging at the second component ($L2$)

$$\beta_2 = -\frac{f_2}{z_2} = -\frac{z_2'}{f_2'} \tag{4.116}$$

The overall magnification ratio is

$$\beta = \beta_1 \cdot \beta_2 \tag{4.117}$$

$$\beta = -\frac{z_1'}{f_1'} \cdot \left(\frac{f_2}{z_2}\right) \tag{4.118}$$

With $z_1' = z_2$ and $f_2 = -f_2'$, this gives

$$\beta = -\frac{f_2'}{f_1'} \tag{4.119}$$

With the telescope magnification V_F

$$\beta = \frac{1}{V_F} \tag{4.120}$$

The overall magnification ratio is independent of the object position (characterized by z_1) and constant.

This is valid – in contrast to the object-side telecentric imaging (where the image size has been constant only for a *fixed* image plane, cf. Section 4.2.14.2.1) – *for all image planes* conjugate to different object planes. If the image plane is slightly tilted, there is – to a first approximation – no change in the image size, because the image-side chief ray is parallel to the optical axis. The image size error produced by the tilt angle depends only on the cosine of this angle.

The *image positions* may be calculated with the help of the second form of the Newton equations:

$$z_1 = \frac{f_1' \cdot f_1}{z_1'}, \quad z_2' = \frac{f_2' \cdot f_2}{z_2} \tag{4.121}$$

Dividing the second equation by the first one yields

$$\frac{z_2'}{z_1} = \frac{f_2' \cdot f_2}{f_1' \cdot f_1} \cdot \frac{z_1'}{z_2} \tag{4.122}$$

With $z_1' = z_2$, we have

$$z_2' = \frac{f_2' \cdot f_2}{f_1' \cdot f_1} \cdot z_1 = (-\beta)^2 \cdot z_1 = \beta^2 \cdot z_1 \tag{4.123}$$

For the *axial* magnification ratio α, we have

$$\alpha = \frac{dz_2'}{dz_1} = \beta^2 = \text{const} \tag{4.124}$$

Limitation of Ray Bundles We now position the aperture stop (AS) at $F_1' = F_2$. The entrance pupil (EP; as the image of the aperture stop in the object space) is now situated at $(-)$ infinity, and the exit pupil (EXP; as the image of the aperture stop in the final image space) is situated at $(+)$ infinity. With that, we may construct the ray pencil limitations as in Figure 4.63.

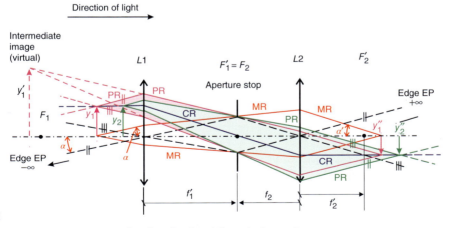

Figure 4.63 Limitation of ray bundles for a bilateral telecentric system.

The *principal rays* MR (blue) are again the projection rays and represent the central ray of the imaging ray pencils. They start parallel to the optical axis (coming virtually from the direction of the center of EP at infinity – dashed), pass through the edges of the objects y_1 and y_2 up to component $L1$ and from there through the center of the aperture stop (which is conjugate to EP, EXP) to component $L2$, and finally proceed parallel to the optical axis to the edge of the images and point virtually to the center of EXP at infinity (dashed).

The *marginal rays* (MRs; red) have an aperture angle α that depends on the diameter of the aperture stop. They start at the axial object point (pointing backward virtually to edge of EP) up to $L1$, from there to the edge of the aperture stop up to component $L2$, and proceed finally to the image (pointing virtually to the edge of EXP at infinity).

The *pharoid rays* PS (pink and green) also have an aperture angle α. They come virtually from the edge of EP (dashed) to the edge of the objects, from there real up to component $L1$, then through the edge of the aperture stop up to $L2$, and finally to the edge of the image (pointing virtually to the edge of EXP at infinity-dashed).

> Here we may see, again, very clearly that because of the bilateral Telecentricity, equally sized objects will give equally sized images, even for different image planes.

Pupil Magnification Ratio β_p Since EP and EXP are at infinity (and are infinitely large), we may not use the term *magnification ratio* but should speak correctly of the pupil magnification β_p. The principal rays of the Keplerian telescope (cf. Figure 4.61) are now the marginal rays of the bilateral telecentric system, since the positions of pupils and objects/images have been interchanged. Therefore, we may define the pupil magnification β_p in a way analogous to the telescope magnification V_F:

$$\beta_p = \frac{\text{tangent of marginal ray } \alpha' \text{ of EXP}}{\text{tangent of marginal ray } \alpha \text{ of EP}} = \frac{\tan \omega'_F}{\tan \omega_F} = V_F \tag{4.125}$$

$$\beta_p = \frac{\tan \alpha'}{\tan \alpha} = \frac{\frac{1}{2}\varnothing_{AB}}{f_2} \cdot \frac{f'_1}{\frac{1}{2}\varnothing_{AB}} = -\frac{f'_1}{f'_2} = V_F \tag{4.126}$$

Depth of Field The starting point is the formula that expresses the depth of field as a function of the magnification ratio β (cf. Section 4.2.13.2).

$$T = \frac{2 \cdot d'}{\beta^2} \cdot (f/nr)_e \tag{4.127}$$

We have

$$(f/nr)_e = \frac{f'}{\varnothing_{EP}} \left(1 - \frac{\beta}{\beta_p}\right) \tag{4.128}$$

$$\frac{(f/nr)_e}{\beta} = \frac{f'}{\varnothing_{EP}} \cdot \left(\frac{1}{\beta} - \frac{1}{\beta_p}\right) = \frac{p}{\varnothing_{EP}} \tag{4.129}$$

Hence

$$T = \frac{2 \cdot d'}{\beta} \cdot \frac{(f/nr)_e}{\beta} = \frac{2 \cdot d'}{\beta} \cdot \frac{p}{\varnothing_{EP}} = \frac{d'}{\beta} \cdot \frac{z_p}{\varnothing_{EP}} \quad (4.130)$$

with

$$\lim_{p \to \infty} \frac{\varnothing_{EP}}{z_p} = \sin \alpha \quad (4.131)$$

This gives for the object-side *depth of field*:

$$T = \frac{d'}{\beta \cdot \sin \alpha} \quad (4.132)$$

with

$$\frac{\sin \alpha'}{\sin \alpha} = \frac{1}{\beta} \quad \text{and} \quad T' = \beta^2 \cdot T \quad (4.133)$$

We have

$$T' = \frac{d'}{\sin \alpha'} \quad (4.134)$$

4.3 Wave Nature of Light

4.3.1 Introduction

We come back to the starting point of geometrical optics: because of the very small wavelength of light ($\lambda \approx 0.5$ µm), we introduced in the wave equation (4.1) the limiting case $\lambda \to 0$ as an approximation. This resulted in the Eikonal equation and the concept of light rays.

As a further approximation, we introduced for the paraxial region the *Gaussian optics*: the homocentric ray pencil from a certain object point is transferred to a homocentric ray pencil converging at a well-defined image *point*.

This is valid only under the assumption that the spatial dimensions are large compared to the wavelength of light. If one looks at regions on the order of the magnitude of the wavelength in the neighborhood of the image "point" or at the limits of the geometrical shadow, then the limiting case $\lambda \to 0$ is invalid and geometrical optics is no longer meaningful.

Since this wave propagation is in general not rectilinear as required by the light rays, it is termed as *diffraction*.

First investigations on the propagation of waves were undertaken by Christian Huygens (1678!). He postulated that each point on a wavefront is the source of a secondary spherical wave. Then the wavefront at a later time will be given by the envelope of all the secondary wavelets (Figure 4.64).

With these assumption, he was, however, not able to give a satisfactory explanation of the wave propagation. Much later (1818), Augustin Fresnel introduced Young's principle of interference in diffraction theory. In this way, he

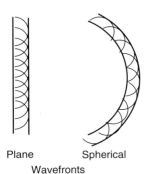

Figure 4.64 Reconstruction of the wavefront by secondary wavelets.

Plane   Spherical
   Wavefronts

could calculate the diffraction phenomenon with good accuracy. However, he had to introduce some strange assumptions on the Huygens wavelets:

1) The phase of the wavelets differs by $\pi/2$ from the original wave front at this point.
2) The amplitude is proportional to $1/\lambda$.
3) There exists an obliquity factor.

These assumptions could be confirmed by Kirchhoff (1882) and Sommerfeld (1894) in the development of a scalar diffraction theory.

4.3.2 Rayleigh–Sommerfeld Diffraction Integral

As implied by the wave equation (4.1), the electric disturbance is a vectorial quantity. We neglect this vectorial nature by dealing with one component only. This scalar theory will give accurate results only if the following conditions are met:

1) The diffracting aperture must be large compared to the wavelength.
2) The diffracted field must not be observed too close to the aperture.

In any case, all polarization phenomena are neglected, since these essentially depend on the vectorial nature of light. We then may write the field amplitude for a monochromatic wave as

$$u(\vec{r}, t) = U_0(\vec{r}) \cos[2\pi v t + \phi(\vec{r})] \tag{4.135}$$

where $U_0(\vec{r})$ and $\phi(\vec{r})$ are the amplitude and phase of the wave at position $\vec{r}$, respectively. This may be expressed in an exponential form as

$$u(\vec{r}, t) = \mathrm{Re}\left[U_0(\vec{r}) \cdot e^{i[2\pi v t + \phi(\vec{r})]}\right] = \mathrm{Re}\left[U(\vec{r}) \cdot e^{i 2\pi v t}\right] \tag{4.136}$$

where Re means the real part, and $U(\vec{r})$ is the complex amplitude and a function of the position $\vec{r}(x, y, z)$.

The real disturbance $u(\vec{r}, t)$ must satisfy the scalar wave equation

$$\Delta u - \frac{1}{c^2}\frac{\partial^2 u}{\partial t^2} = 0 \tag{4.137}$$

Substituting (4.136) in (4.137) with $c = \lambda \cdot v$ gives

$$\Delta U + \frac{4\pi^2}{\lambda^2} U = 0 \tag{4.138}$$

With

$$|\vec{k}|^2 = k^2 = \frac{4\pi^2}{\lambda^2}, \quad k = \text{wave number} \qquad (4.139)$$

one has

$$\Delta U(\vec{r}) + k^2 U(\vec{r}) = 0 \qquad (4.140)$$

This is the time-independent Helmholtz equation. Only the relative phases of the wave are of importance, not the absolute phases given by t since a monochromatic wave exhibits absolutely synchronous time behavior at all points of space. The particular solutions of Equation 4.140 are as follows:

1) Plane wave in the x-direction:

$$U(x) = U_0 \, e^{-ikx} \qquad (4.141)$$

2) Spherical wave:

$$U(|\vec{r}|) = \frac{U_0}{r} \cdot e^{-ikr} \qquad (4.142)$$

We shortly describe the conditions that lead to the Rayleigh–Sommerfeld formulation of scalar diffraction

1) With the Helmholtz equation (4.140)
2) With Greens theorem of vector analysis and
3) With the appropriate boundary conditions (the Greens function introduced by Sommerfeld without discrepancy).

One gets the amplitude of the wave at a point $P(\vec{r}_0)$ behind an aperture of an infinite opaque screen as a superposition of spherical waves that originate from the wavefront in the diffracting aperture, Figure 4.65.

The diffraction integral has the form

$$U(\vec{r}_0) = -\frac{1}{i\lambda} \iint_S U(\vec{r}_1) \frac{e^{-i\vec{k}\cdot(\vec{r}_0-\vec{r}_1)}}{|\vec{r}_0-\vec{r}_1|} \cos(\vec{n}, \vec{r}_0 - \vec{r}_1) dS \qquad (4.143)$$

The integration has to be taken over the whole surface S of the aperture.

Figure 4.65 Diffraction by a plane screen.

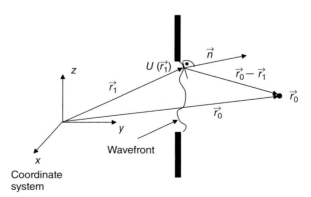

The first factor under the integral is the (complex) amplitude of the incident wavefront at point $\vec{r}_1$; the second factor is the spherical wave.

The following conditions must hold:

1) The amplitude of the wave immediately behind the limiting aperture is zero, whereas within the aperture it remains undisturbed.
2) The distance of the observation point $\vec{r}_0$ from the screen is very large compared to the wavelength: $|\vec{r}_0 - \vec{r}_1| \gg \lambda$.

Equation 4.143 gives the explanation for the seemingly arbitrary assumptions of Fresnel:

1) phase advance of the secondary wavelets by

$$-\frac{1}{i} = +i = e^{+i\frac{\pi}{2}}$$

2) amplitudes proportional to $1/\lambda$
3) obliquity factor as the cosine between the normal $\vec{n}$ of the wavefront at $\vec{r}_1$ and $\vec{r}_0 - \vec{r}_1$ as the direction of the point $U(\vec{r}_0)$ viewed from $\vec{r}_1$:

$$\cos(\vec{n}, \vec{r}_0 - \vec{r}_1)$$

Note 4.8 *The diffraction integral may be interpreted as a* **superposition integral** *of linear system theory (refer to Section 4.4)*

$$U(\vec{r}_0) = \iint_S U(\vec{r}_1) h(\vec{r}_0, \vec{r}_1) dS \qquad (4.144)$$

with

$$h(\vec{r}_0, \vec{r}_1) = -\frac{1}{i\lambda} \frac{e^{-i\vec{k}\cdot(\vec{r}_0 - \vec{r})}}{|\vec{r}_0 - \vec{r}_1|} \cos(\vec{n}, \vec{r}_0 - \vec{r}_1) \qquad (4.145)$$

as impulse response of the system of wave propagation. The impulse response corresponds to the Huygens elementary waves or: the response of the system of wave propagation to a point-like excitation is a spherical wave.

4.3.3 Further Approximations to the Huygens–Fresnel Principle

We make the following assumptions:

1) Plane diffracting aperture Σ
2) Plane observation surface B parallel to it
3) Distance z between these two planes much larger than the dimensions of Σ and B

$$z \gg \text{dimension of } \Sigma$$
$$z \gg \text{dimension of } B$$

(Figure 4.66).

Figure 4.66 Geometry of the diffraction constellation.

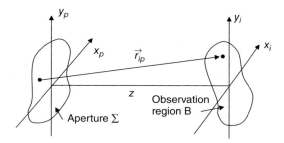

This gives

$$\cos(\vec{n}, \vec{r}_{ip}) \approx 1,$$

with an accuracy of 1% for an angle of 8°. Then the diffraction integral will give

$$U(x_i, y_i) = -\frac{1}{i\lambda} \iint_{\mathbb{R}^2} P(x_p, y_p) \cdot U(x_p, y_p) \cdot \frac{e^{-i\vec{k}\cdot\vec{r}_{ip}}}{r_{ip}} dx_p\, dy_p \qquad (4.146)$$

The function $P(x_p, y_p)$ takes into consideration the boundary conditions

$$P(x_p, y_p) = \begin{cases} 1 \text{ within the diffracting aperture} \\ 0 \text{ outside the diffracting aperture} \end{cases}$$

With our geometrical assumptions 1–3, we may replace $\vec{r}_{ip} = \vec{r}_0 - \vec{r}_1$ in the denominator of the third factor in the integral equation (4.146) by z, but *not* in the exponent of the third factor since $|\vec{k}|$ is a large number $|\vec{k}| = \frac{2\pi}{\lambda}$ and the phase error would be much larger than 2π.

4.3.3.1 Fresnel's Approximation

The expression in the exponent will be developed into a power series as

$$r_{ip} = \sqrt{z^2 + (x_i - x_p)^2 + (y_i - y_p)^2} = z\sqrt{1 + \left(\frac{x_i - x_p}{z}\right)^2 + \left(\frac{y_i - y_p}{z}\right)^2} \qquad (4.147)$$

With

$$\sqrt{(1+b)} = 1 + \frac{1}{2}b - \frac{1}{8}b^2 + \cdots \qquad (|b| < 1)$$

we get

$$z\sqrt{1 + \left(\frac{x_i - x_p}{z}\right)^2 + \left(\frac{y_i - y_p}{z}\right)^2} \approx z\left[1 + \frac{1}{2}\left(\frac{x_i - x_p}{z}\right)^2 + \left(\frac{1}{2}\frac{y_i - y_p}{z}\right)^2\right] \qquad (4.148)$$

and the diffraction integral will become

$$U(x_i, y_i) = -\frac{e^{ikz}}{i\lambda z} \iint_{\mathbb{R}^2} P(x_p, y_p) U(x_p, y_p) e^{i\frac{k}{2z}[(x_i - x_p)^2 + (y_i - y_p)^2]} dx_p\, dy_p \qquad (4.149)$$

If we expand the quadratic terms in the exponent, we get

$$U(x_i, y_i) \cdot e^{-i\frac{\pi}{\lambda z}(x_i^2 + y_i^2)}$$
$$= c \iint_{\mathbb{R}^2} P(x_p, y_p) U(x_p, y_p) e^{i\frac{\pi}{\lambda z}(x_p^2 + y_p^2)} e^{-i\frac{2\pi}{\lambda z}(x_i x_p + y_i y_p)} \, dx_p \, dy_p \qquad (4.150)$$

with c a complex factor.

4.3.3.1.1 Interpretation of Equation 4.150
Apart from the corresponding phase factors $-i\frac{k}{2z}(x_i^2 + y_i^2)$ and $+i\frac{k}{2z}(x_p^2 + y_p^2)$, which appear as factors for the diffracted and incident wave, the complex amplitude in the plane z is given by a *Fourier transform* of the wave in plane $z = 0$ where the spatial frequencies r and s have to be taken as

$$r = \frac{x_i}{\lambda \cdot z}, \quad s = \frac{y_i}{\lambda \cdot z} \qquad (4.151)$$

in order to get correct units in the image plane. (For the meaning of spatial frequencies, see Section 4.4.)

The mentioned phase factors may be interpreted as optical path difference, so that the corresponding wavefronts will be curved surfaces. The deviation of the wavefront from the x–y plane for each point is equal to the path difference introduced by the phase factors. For the image plane

$$e^{-i\frac{\pi}{\lambda}\left(\frac{x_i^2 + y_i^2}{z}\right)} = e^{+i\frac{\pi}{\lambda}c} \quad (c = \text{constant}) \qquad (4.152)$$

and one has

$$z = -\frac{1}{c}(x_i^2 + y_i^2) \qquad (4.153)$$

This is a rotation paraboloid opened in the $-z$-direction. In the same way, for the plane $z = 0$ (index p) one gets a rotation paraboloid opened in the $+z$-direction.

However, we know that these paraboloids are quadratic approximations to spherical surfaces!

If, therefore, the complex amplitude of the incident wave is given on a spherical surface, then the complex amplitude of the diffracted wavefront is also given on a spherical surface by simple Fourier transformation.

4.3.3.1.2 The Fraunhofer Approximation
An even simpler expression for the diffraction pattern is obtained if one chooses more stringent approximations than those of the Fresnel case.

If we assume

$$z \gg \frac{k(x_p^2 + y_p^2)_{\max}}{z} \quad \text{and} \quad z \gg \frac{k(x_i^2 + y_i^2)_{\max}}{2} \qquad (4.154)$$

then

$$U(x_i, y_i) = c \iint_{\mathbb{R}^2} U(x_p, y_p) e^{-i\frac{2\pi}{\lambda z}(x_p x_i + y_p y_i)} \, dx_p \, dy_p \qquad (4.155)$$

This is simply the Fourier transform of the aperture distribution evaluated at spatial frequencies $r = x_i/\lambda z, s = y_i/\lambda z$.

The requirement of the Fraunhofer approximation is quite stringent; However, one may observe such diffraction patterns at a distance closer than required by Equation 4.154 if the aperture is illuminated by a spherical converging wave or if an (ideal) lens is positioned between the aperture and the observing plane.

4.3.4 Impulse Response of an Aberration-Free Optical System

An ideal lens, which fulfils completely the laws of Gaussian optics, will transfer a diverging homocentric ray pencil (with its intersection point at a certain object point) into a converging homocentric pencil with its intersection point at the ideal (Gaussian) image point.

As pointed out in Section 4.1.1, light rays are the orthogonal trajectories of the wavefronts. Thus for a homocentric pencil of rays, the corresponding wavefronts are spherical with their center at the intersection point of the homocentric ray pencil. Such a system, which converts a diverging spherical wave into a converging spherical wave, will be called *diffraction-limited*.

Speaking in terms of imaging, a diverging spherical wave originating from a certain object point and traveling to the entrance pupil will be transformed by the diffraction-limited optical system into a converging spherical wave originating from the exit pupil and traveling toward the ideal image point, Figure 4.67.

The problem of finding the impulse response (for the diffraction-limited optical system) may thus be dealt with in three steps:

1) The impulse response of the system of wave propagation to a point-like disturbance (object point) is a spherical wave, namely a Huygens elementary wave as shown in Section 4.3.3.

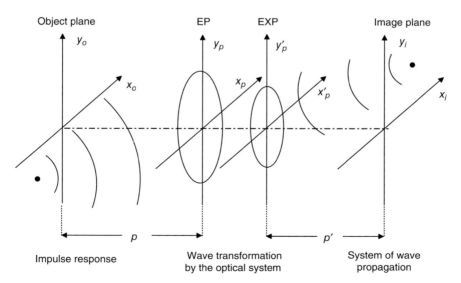

Figure 4.67 Imaging situation for a diffraction-limited optical system.

2) This wave enters the optical system and will be transformed in an ideal manner. This transformation by the diffraction-limited system must be formulated mathematically.
3) The spherical wave originating from and limited by the exit pupil will be dealt within the Fresnel approximation in order to end with the amplitude distribution in the image plane.

This point of view, that is, to consider the wave propagation from the finite exit pupil, was introduced by Rayleigh (1896) and is essentially equivalent to the considerations of Abbe (1873), who analyzed the relations in the finite entrance pupil. We will consider the three indicated steps now.

1) *Impulse response*
According to Section 4.3.3, and with reference to Figure 4.67, we have for the impulse response in Fresnel approximation

$$U_{EP}(x_p, y_p) = -\frac{1}{i\lambda p} e^{-i\frac{k}{2p}[(x_p-x_0)^2+(y_p-y_0)^2]} \qquad (4.156)$$

2) *Ideal lens transformation $t_l(x_p, y_p)$*
This transformation will be given as a result only; detailed considerations may be found in [2].

$$t_l(x_p, y_p) = c\, P(x_p\beta_p, y_p\beta_p) \cdot e^{+i\frac{k\beta_p^2}{2z'_{p'}}(x_p^2+y_p^2)} \qquad (4.157)$$

with

$$P(x_p\beta_p, y_p\beta_p) = \begin{cases} 1 & \text{inside the pupil} \\ 0 & \text{outside the pupil} \end{cases}$$

and

β_p = pupil magnification ratio

$z'_{p'} = (\overrightarrow{F'P'})_z$ distance from the focal point F' of the lens to the center of the exit pupil (Equation 4.31)

3) *Amplitude distribution in the image plane*
The diffraction integral in the Fresnel approximation for our constellation is

$$U(x_i, y_i) = \frac{1}{i\lambda p'} \iint_{\mathbb{R}^2} U(x'_p, y'_p) e^{i\frac{k}{2p'}[(x_i-\beta_p x_p)^2+(y_i-\beta_p y'_p)^2]} dx'_p\, dy'_p \qquad (4.158)$$

with

$$U(x'_p, y'_p) = U_{EP}(x_p, y_p)\, t_l(x_p, y_p)$$

Substituting from Equations 4.156 and 4.157 into Equation 4.158 gives

$$U(x_i, y_i) = \frac{1}{\lambda^2 \cdot p \cdot p'} \exp\left\{i \cdot \frac{k}{2p'}(x_i^2+y_i^2)\right\} \exp\left\{-\frac{ik}{2p}(x_o^2+y_o^2)\right\}$$

$$\cdot \iint_{\mathbb{R}^2} P(x_p\beta_p, y_p\beta_p) \exp\left\{\frac{ik}{2}\left(\frac{\beta_p^2}{z'_{p'}} - \frac{1}{p} + \frac{\beta_p^2}{p'}\right)(x_p^2+y_p^2)\right\} \qquad (4.159)$$

$$\cdot \exp\left\{ik\left[\left(\frac{x_o}{p} - \frac{\beta_p x_i}{p'}\right)x_p + \left(\frac{y_o}{p} - \frac{\beta_p \cdot y_i}{p'}\right)y_p\right]\right\} dx_p\, dy_p$$

The first two exponential terms are independent of the pupil's coordinates and could therefore be drawn in front of the integral. They may again be interpreted as phase curvatures over the object and image plane in the sense that they will vanish if one takes as image and object surfaces the corresponding spherical surfaces. In the case of incoherent imaging, the system is linear with respect to intensities, which means to the square of the modulus of the complex amplitude. In this case, these terms may also be omitted for the transmission between object and image planes.

The third exponential term vanishes because the position of the image plane has been chosen according to the imaging equations of Gaussian optics:

From Equation 4.35

$$z'_{p'} = -\beta_p f' \quad (4.160)$$

and the third exponential term may be written as

$$\frac{ik\beta_p}{2}\left(\frac{\beta_p}{p'} - \frac{1}{\beta_p\, p} - \frac{1}{f'}\right) = 0 \quad (4.161)$$

The bracketed term vanishes because of the imaging equation (4.42).

Thus the impulse response of the diffraction-limited optical system is given by

$$U(x_i, y_i) = h(x_i, y_i, x_0, y_0) = \frac{1}{\lambda^2 pp'}\iint_{\mathbb{R}^2} P(x_p\beta_p, y_p\beta_p) \quad (4.162)$$

$$\cdot \exp\left\{ik\left[\left(\frac{x_0}{p} - \frac{\beta_p x_i}{p'}\right)x_p + \left(\frac{y_0}{p} - \frac{\beta_p y_i}{p'}\right)y_p\right]\right\} dx_p\, dy_p$$

and with Equation 4.38

$$\frac{p'}{p} = \beta_p\, \beta$$

we finally have

$$h(x_i, y_i, x_0, y_0) = \frac{1}{\lambda^2 \cdot p \cdot p'}\iint_{\mathbb{R}^2} P(x_p\beta_p, y_p\beta_p) \quad (4.163)$$

$$\cdot \exp\left\{-i\frac{k\cdot\beta_p}{p'}[(x_i - \beta x_0)x_p + (y_i - \beta y_0)y_p]\right\} dx_p\, dy_p$$

The impulse response (point spread function) is given by the Fourier transform of the pupil function with the center of the image at

$$x_i = \beta x_0, \quad y_i = \beta y_0$$

4.3.4.1 Case of Circular Aperture, Object Point on the Optical Axis

For circular apertures (as is usual in optics), it is useful to introduce polar coordinates in the pupil and image planes. We just give the result for the intensity

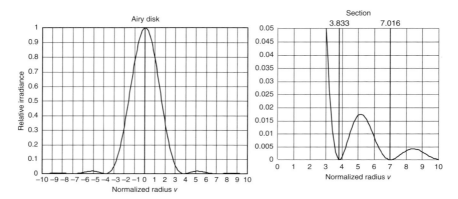

Figure 4.68 Airy disk in geometrical focus, $v = \frac{\pi r}{\lambda f / nr}$.

distribution in the image plane of a diffraction-limited optical system; details are given in [3].

$$I = \left[\frac{2J_1(v)}{v}\right]^2 \qquad (4.164)$$

where J_1 is the Bessel function of the first order,

$$v = \frac{2\pi}{\lambda} \sin \alpha r = \frac{\pi}{\lambda (f/nr)_e} r \qquad (4.165)$$

$$r = \sqrt{x'^2 + y'^2} \qquad (4.166)$$

This is the well-known *Airy disk*, which is rotationally symmetric and depends only on the numerical aperture $\sin \alpha$ (or the effective f/nr) and on wavelength λ.

Figure 4.68 shows a cross-section of the Airy disk for the normalized radius v. The extension of the central disk up to the first minimum is given by

$$r_0 = 1.22 \cdot \lambda \cdot (f/nr)_e \qquad (4.167)$$

This is usually taken as the radius of the diffraction disk. In this area, one has 85% of the total radiant flux. The first bright ring has 7% of total flux.

4.3.5 Intensity Distribution in the Neighborhood of the Geometrical Focus

The problem of finding the intensity distribution in the region near the geometrical focus was first dealt by Lommel [4] and Struve [5]. In what Follows, we will give a short outline based on [6]. It will be useful to introduce reduced coordinates. Instead of r and z, we use

$$v = k \sin \alpha r \quad \text{(as with the Airy disc)} \qquad (4.168)$$
$$u = k \sin^2 \alpha z \qquad (4.169)$$

and

$$\sin \alpha = \frac{1}{2 \cdot (f/nr)_e} \tag{4.170}$$

Then the intensity distribution near the Gaussian image plane may be described by two equivalent expressions:

$$I(u, v) = \left(\frac{2}{u}\right)^2 [U_1^2(u, v) + U_2^2(u, v)] \cdot I_0 \tag{4.171}$$

and

$$I(u, v) = \left(\frac{2}{u}\right)^2 \left[1 + V_0^2(u, v) + V_1^2(u, v)\right.$$

$$- 2V_0(u, v) \cos\left[\frac{1}{2}\left(u + \frac{v^2}{u}\right)\right] \tag{4.172}$$

$$\left. - 2V_1(u, v) \sin\left[\frac{1}{2}\left(u + \frac{v^2}{u}\right)\right]\right] I_0$$

U_n and V_n are the so-called *Lommel functions,* an infinite series of Bessel functions, defined as follows:

$$U_n(u, v) = \sum_{s=0}^{\infty} (-1)^s \left(\frac{u}{v}\right)^{n+2s} J_{n+2s}(v) \tag{4.173}$$

$$V_n(u, v) = \sum_{s=0}^{\infty} (-1)^s \left(\frac{v}{u}\right)^{n+2s} J_{n+2s}(v) \tag{4.174}$$

I_0 is the intensity in the geometrical focus $u = v = 0$.

Equation 4.171 converges for points

$$\frac{u}{v} = \sin \alpha \frac{z}{r} < 1$$

This means that, when the observation point is within the geometrical shadow region, Equation 4.172 converges for points

$$\frac{u}{v} > 1$$

that is, for points in the geometrically illuminated region. For points on the shadow limit, we have $u = v$.

From these equations and using the properties of the Lommel functions, one may derive the following conclusions:

1) The intensity distribution is rotationally symmetric around the u-axis (and hence around the z-axis).
2) The intensity distribution near the focus is symmetrical with respect to the geometrical image plane.

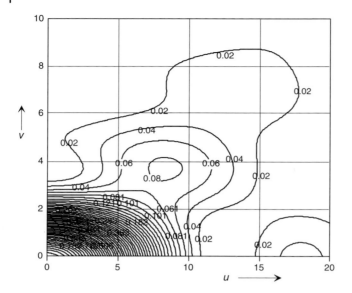

Figure 4.69 Isophotes of intensity distribution near the focus.

Figure 4.69 shows the intensity distribution as lines of constant intensity for the upper right half of the light pencils only (because of the mentioned symmetry properties).

4.3.5.1 Special Cases

From Equations 4.171 and 4.172, for $u = 0$ (geometrical focal plane) one has

$$\lim_{u \to 0} \left[\frac{U_1(u,v)}{u} \right] = \frac{J_1(v)}{v}, \quad \lim_{u \to 0} \left[\frac{U_2(u,v)}{u} \right] = 0$$

which gives

$$I(0,v) = \left[\frac{2J_1(v)}{v} \right]^2$$

which is the intensity distribution of the *Airy disk*.

Furthermore, from Equation 4.172 one may derive the *intensity distribution along the optical axis*. For $v = 0$ (i.e., $r = 0$), it is

$$V_0(u,0) = 1 \quad \text{and} \quad V_1(u,0) = 0 \tag{4.175}$$

and the intensity is

$$I(u,0) = \frac{4}{u^2} \left[2 - 2\cos\frac{u}{2} \right] \tag{4.176}$$

which gives

$$I(u,0) = \left\{ \frac{\sin\frac{u}{4}}{\frac{u}{4}} \right\}^2 = \left[\operatorname{sinc}\frac{u}{4} \right]^2 \tag{4.177}$$

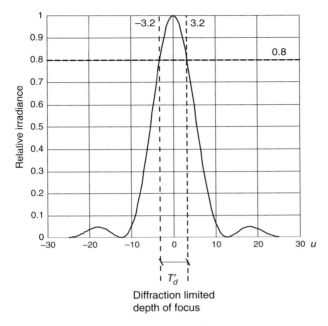

Figure 4.70 Intensity distribution of a diffraction-limited system along the optical axis.

The result is that the maximum intensity of the point spread function changes with defocusing (along the optical axis) with a sinc-square function. The first minimum is at

$$u = 4\pi$$

in agreement with the isophotes of Figure 4.69. Figure 4.70 shows the intensity distribution along the optical axis.

The ratio of the maximum intensity of the defocused point spread function to that of the Gaussian image plane is a special case of the *Strehl ratio*.

It may be shown that with pure defocusing, a Strehl ratio of 80% corresponds to a wavefront aberration (deviation from the Gaussian reference sphere) of $\lambda/4$. This value for the Strehl ratio is thus equivalent to the Rayleigh criterion and is considered to be the permissible defocusing tolerance for diffraction-limited systems.

The sinc²-function of Equation 4.177 decreases by 20% for $u \approx 3.2$. Thus one has for the diffraction-limited depth of focus with

$$z = \frac{\lambda}{2\pi} \frac{1}{\sin^2 \alpha} u, \quad \frac{1}{\sin \alpha} = 2(f/nr)_e \qquad (4.178)$$

and with

$$u \approx \pm 3.2 \qquad (4.179)$$

$$\Delta z' = \pm 3.2 \frac{\lambda}{2\pi} \frac{1}{\sin^2 \alpha} \qquad (4.180)$$

or

$$\Delta z' \approx \pm 2\lambda (f/nr)_e^2 \qquad (4.181)$$

4.3.6 Extension of the Point Spread Function in a Defocused Image Plane

Equation 4.181 gives the limits of defocusing at which the point spread function may still be considered for practical purposes as diffraction-limited. Then the question arises immediately: what extension does the point spread function have at these limits? In order to decide this, we need a suitable criterion for that extension. For the Gaussian image plane, this criterion was the radius r_0 of the central disk, which includes 85% of the total intensity flux. We generalize this and define it as follows:

> The extension of the point spread function in a defocused image plane is given by the radius that includes 85% of the total intensity.

Then the above question may be reformulated as follows:

> What are the limits of the point spread function as a function of defocusing and when will they coincide with the geometrical shadow limits – defined by the homocentric ray pencil?

This problem may be solved by the integration of Equations 4.171 and 4.172 over v. We only show the results in the form of contour line plots of fractions of the total energy, in Figure 4.71.

The extension of the point spread function as a function of defocusing u is given as defined above by the value 0.85 (the thick broken line in Figure 4.71).

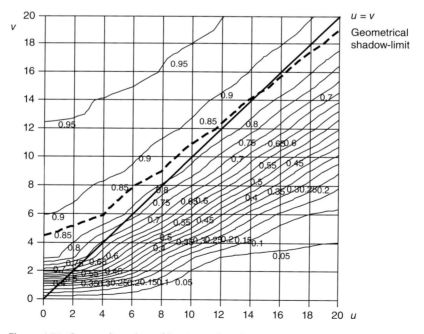

Figure 4.71 Contour line plots of fractions of total energy.

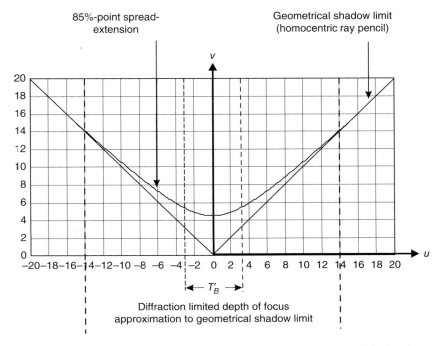

Figure 4.72 Approximation of the point spread extension and geometrical shadow limit.

The geometrical shadow limit (limit of the Gaussian ray pencil) is given by $u = v$, which is the thick straight line.

In Figure 4.72, the 0.85 line is approximated by a hyperbolic function.

We may draw the following conclusions from this approximation:

1) The extension of the point spread function is always larger than or equal to the geometrical shadow limit.
2) The geometrical shadow limit is reached for $u \approx 14$.
3) For the extension of the point spread functions and the corresponding defocusing values in the focal plane ($u = 0$), at the diffraction limit ($u \approx 3.2$) and at the approximation to the geometrical shadow limit ($u \approx 14$), we get with

$$r = \frac{\lambda (f/nr)_e}{\pi} v, \quad z' = \frac{2\lambda (f/nr)_e}{\pi} u \tag{4.182}$$

Table 4.8.

4.3.7 Consequences for the Depth of Field Considerations

4.3.7.1 Diffraction and Permissible Circle of Confusion

The diameter of the diffraction point spread function approximates the geometrical shadow limit at $u = v \approx 14$. This gives

$$d'_s = 9 \cdot \lambda \cdot (f/nr)_e \quad \text{(index } s \text{ for shadow)} \tag{4.183}$$

Table 4.8 Diffraction-limited point spread extension in three different image planes.

	u	z'	v	r	r/r_0
Focus	0	0	3.83	$r_0 = 1.22\lambda(f/nr)_e$	1
Diffraction limit	$u_d \approx 3.2$	$z_d = 2\lambda(f/nr)_e^2$	$v_d \approx 5.5$	$r_d \approx 1.9\lambda(f/nr)_e$	~1.43
Shadow limit	$u_s \approx 14$	$z_s = 8.9\lambda(f/nr)_e^2$	$v_s \approx 14$	$r_s \approx 4.45\lambda(f/nr)_e$	~3.6

Table 4.9 Maximum permissible f-number for purely geometric calculations.

d'_G (µm)	150	100	75	60	50	33	25
Maximum $(f/nr)_e$	33	22	16	13	11	7.3	5.6

Thus there is an upper limit for the f-number in order not to exceed the diameter d'_G of the permissible circle of confusion:

$$(f/nr)_e \leq \frac{d'_G}{4.5} \tag{4.184}$$

for $\lambda = 0.5$ µm and d'_G in micrometers.

Table 4.9 shows the maximum effective f-number for different circles of confusion at which one may calculate with geometrical optics.

4.3.7.2 Extension of the Point Spread Function at the Limits of the Depth of Focus

The 85% point spread extension as a function of defocusing has been approximated in Section 4.3.5 by a hyperbolic function. This function is

$$v = \sqrt{u^2 + 4.5^2} \tag{4.185}$$

and

$$u = \frac{2\pi}{\lambda}\sin^2\alpha \quad \Delta z' = \frac{\pi}{(f/nr)_e^2} \cdot \Delta z' \quad (\lambda = 0.5 \text{ µm}) \tag{4.186}$$

where $\Delta z'$ is the deviation from the Gaussian image plane. On the other hand, for the limits of the geometrical depth of focus, we have by Equation 4.80 with $\Delta z' = T'/2$

$$\Delta z' = (f/nr)_e \cdot d'_G \tag{4.187}$$

Thus

$$u = \frac{\pi \cdot d'_G}{(f/nr)_e} \quad (d'_G \text{ in µm}) \tag{4.188}$$

For the coordinate v, according to Equation 4.165

$$v = \frac{\pi \cdot r_d}{\lambda \cdot (f/nr)_e}, \quad r_d = \frac{d'_d}{2} \tag{4.189}$$

$$v = \frac{\pi \cdot d'_d}{(f/nr)_e} \quad (\lambda = 0.5 \text{ µm}; \quad d'_d \text{ in µm}) \tag{4.190}$$

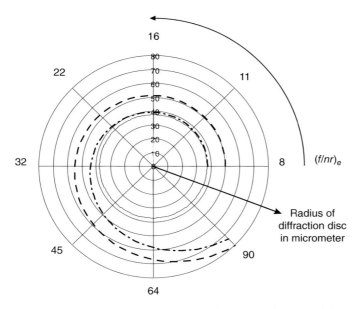

Figure 4.73 Extension of the point spread function at the limits of the geometrical depth of focus.

or

$$d'_d = \frac{(f/nr)_e}{\pi} \cdot v \tag{4.191}$$

With the hyperbolic equation (4.185)

$$d'_d = \frac{(f/nr)_e}{\pi} \cdot \sqrt{u^2 + 4.5^2} \tag{4.192}$$

and with u according to Equation 4.188, finally

$$d'_d \approx \sqrt{d'^2_G + 2(f/nr)^2_e} \tag{4.193}$$

Figure 4.73 shows d'_d as a function of the effective f-number for $d'_G = 75$ and 100 μm.

4.3.7.3 Useful Effective f-Number

For rather large magnification ratios β (because of $(f/nr)_e = (f/nr) \cdot \left(1 - \frac{\beta}{\beta_p}\right)$) and with small image formats, one exceeds quickly the limit

$$(f/nr)_e \leq \frac{d'_G}{4.5}$$

Then one should work with the useful effective f-number $(f/nr)_{eu}$, which gives at the *diffraction-limited* depth of focus a point spread diameter equal to the permissible circle of confusion

$$2r_d = 3.8 \cdot \lambda \cdot (f/nr)_{eu} = d'_G \tag{4.194}$$

$$(f/nr)_{eu} = \frac{d'_G}{1.9} \quad (\lambda = 0.5 \text{ μm})$$

Table 4.10 Diffraction and depth of focus.

Point spread function in geom. image plane	$d'_d = 2.44\lambda(f/nr)_e$
Diffraction limited depth of focus	$\Delta z' = \pm 2\lambda(f/nr)_e^2$
Maximum eff. f/nr for geometrical considerations	$(f/nr)_e \leqq d'_G/4.5$
85% intensity diameter for point spread function at the limits of geom. depth of focus	$d'_d \approx \sqrt{d_G^2 + 2(f/nr)_e^2}$
Usable effective f-number corresponding diffraction limited depth of focus	$(f/nr)_{eu} = d'_G/1.9$
	$T'_d = \pm 2\lambda \cdot (f/nr)_{eu}^2$

Then the depth of focus is equal to the diffraction-limited depth of focus (see Table 4.10):

$$T'_d = \pm 2 \cdot \lambda \cdot (f/nr)_{eu}^2 \qquad (4.195)$$

Example 4.10

$$d'_G = 33 \text{ µm}, \quad (f/nr)_{eu} = 18, \quad \beta_p \approx 1, \quad \beta = -1$$

$$(f/nr)_e = (f/nr) \cdot \left(1 - \frac{\beta}{\beta_p}\right) = 2 \cdot (f/nr)$$

$$(f/nr)_u = \frac{1}{2}(f/nr)_{eu} \approx 9$$

$$T'_d \approx \pm 0.32 \text{ mm!}.$$

4.4 Information Theoretical Treatment of Image Transfer and Storage

Having supplemented the model of geometrical optics (and in particular that of Gaussian optics) by the scalar wave theory, we now proceed with the important topic of information theoretical aspects, not only for information transfer but also for storage of information with digital imaging devices. In the first step, we will introduce the general concept of physical systems as linear invariant filters.

4.4.1 Physical Systems as Linear Invariant Filters

A physical system in general may be interpreted as the transformation of an input function into an output function. This physical system may act by totally different principles. We have the following examples:

- Electrical networks: here the entrance and output functions are real functions of voltage or currents of the one-dimensional real variable t (time).
- Optical imaging systems, where, in the case of incoherent radiation, the input and output functions are real positive quantities (intensities) of two independent variables, the space coordinates u and v.

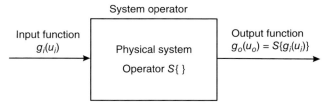

Figure 4.74 Physical system as a mathematical operator.

It turns out that there is a close analogy between these two systems. We restrict ourselves to *deterministic* (non-statistical) systems, which means that a certain input function will be transformed into an unambiguous output function. Then the system may be represented by a *black box* and its action may be described by a mathematical operator $S\{\ \}$, which acts on the input function and thereby produces the output function (Figure 4.74).

An important subclass of the deterministic systems is *linear systems*. Linear systems exhibit the properties of *additivity* and *homogeneity*, independent of their physical nature. Here, additivity means that the response of the system to a sum of input functions is given by the sum of the corresponding output functions:

$$S\{g_{i1}(u_i) + g_{i2}(u_i) + \cdots\} = S\{g_{i1}(u_i)\} + S\{g_{i2}(u_i)\} + \cdots \quad (4.196)$$

Homogeneity is the property that the response to an input function that is multiplied by a constant is given by the product of the constant c with the response to the input function:

$$S\{c \cdot g_i(u_i)\} = c \cdot S\{g_i(u_i)\} = c \cdot g_o(u_o) \quad (4.197)$$

These two properties may be combined to the *linearity* of the system:

$$S\{c_1 g_{i1}(u_i) + c_2 g_{i2}(u_i) + \cdots\} = c_1 \cdot S\{g_{i1}(u_i)\} + c_2 \cdot S\{g_{i2}(u_i)\} + \cdots \quad (4.198)$$

Linearity of the system = additivity + homogeneity

In optics, the linearity of the system is given by the fact that the propagation of waves is described by the wave equation, which is a *linear* partial differential equation. For these, a superposition principle is valid, which means that the sum and multiple of a solution is again a solution of the differential equation and thus expresses nothing but the linearity of the system.

With the mentioned properties of linear systems, one may decompose a complicated input function into simpler elementary functions. As an input function we take a sharp (idealized) impulse. With electrical networks, where the independent variable is the time t, this corresponds to an impulse-like voltage peak at a certain *time*. In optics, the independent variable is the spatial coordinate u (for the sake of simplicity we consider first a one-dimensional situation). Here, the idealized impulse is strictly a point-like object at a certain *position*.

Mathematically, this idealized impulse may be represented by Dirac's δ-function. This function represents an infinitely sharp impulse with the following

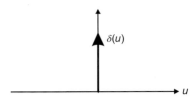

Figure 4.75 Dirac impulse.

properties:

$$\delta(u) = \begin{cases} 0 & (u \neq 0) \\ \infty & (u = 0) \end{cases} \quad (4.199)$$

and

$$\int_{-\infty}^{+\infty} \delta(u) \, du = 1 \quad (4.200)$$

(Figure 4.75).

One more important property of the δ-function is the shifting property:

$$\int_{-\infty}^{+\infty} f(u) \cdot \delta(u - u_1) \, du = f(u_1) \quad (4.201)$$

The integral produces the value of the function $f(u)$ at position u_1 of the shifted δ-function (Figure 4.76).

With this, one may decompose an input signal g_i into an infinitely dense series of δ-functions, weighted with $g_i(\xi)$:

$$g_i(u_i) = \left\{ \int_{-\infty}^{+\infty} g_i(\xi) \cdot \delta(u_i - \xi) \, d\xi \right\} \quad (\xi = \text{auxiliary variable}) \quad (4.202)$$

The output function as the systems response is then

$$g_o(u_o) = S \left\{ \int_{-\infty}^{+\infty} g_i(\xi) \cdot \delta(u_i - \xi) \, d\xi \right\} \quad (4.203)$$

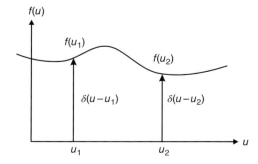

Figure 4.76 Shifting property of the δ-function.

Here, $g_i(\xi)$ are nothing but the weighting coefficients for the shifted Dirac impulses. Because of the linearity of the system, we may then write

$$g_o(u_o) = \int_{-\infty}^{+\infty} g_i(\xi) S\{\delta(u_i - \xi)\} d\xi \qquad (4.204)$$

The response of the system S at position u_o of the output to a Dirac impulse with coordinate ξ at the input can be expressed as

$$h(u_o, \xi) = S\{\delta(u_i - \xi)\} \qquad (4.205)$$

This is the *impulse response* of the system.

The response of the system to a complicated input function is then given by the following fundamental expression:

$$g_o(u_o) = \int_{-\infty}^{+\infty} g_i(\xi) \cdot h(u_o, \xi) d\xi \quad \text{(superposition integral)} \qquad (4.206)$$

The superposition integral describes the important fact that a linear system is completely characterized by its response to a unit impulse (impulse response).

However, in order to describe the output of the system completely, we must know the impulse response for all possible positions (i.e., for all possible values of the independent variable) of the input pulse. An important subclass of linear systems are those systems for which the impulse response is independent of the absolute position of the input impulse.

4.4.1.1 Invariant Linear Systems

In order to introduce the concept of invariant linear systems, we start from an electrical network (Figure 4.77).

Here, the impulse response at time t_o to an impulse at time t_i depends only on the *time difference* $(t_o - t_i)$. At a later time t'_o, we will get the same response to an impulse at the input at time t'_i if the difference $t'_o - t'_i$ is the same. Here we have a *time-invariant* system.

In optics we use, instead of the time coordinate, a (normalized) spatial coordinate u (all considerations are one-dimensional for the moment). Then *space invariance* means that the intensity distribution in the image of a point-like object

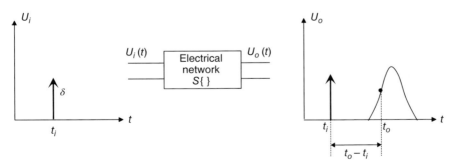

Figure 4.77 Electrical networks as invariant systems.

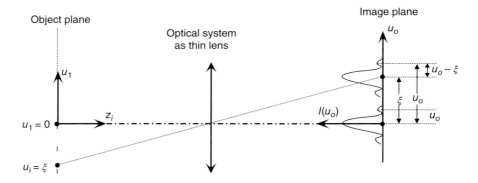

Figure 4.78 Space invariance with optical systems.

depends only on the distance $(u_o - u_i)$ and not on the absolute position of the object point in the object plane (Figure 4.78).

In optics, space invariance is called the isoplanasic condition. The intensity distribution in the image of a point (the so-called point spread function (PSF)) is the same, independent of its position in the image plane. The impulse response and output function in Equations 4.205 and 4.206 may now be written as

$$h(u_o, \xi) = h(u_o - \xi) \tag{4.207}$$

$$g_o(u_o) = \int_{-\infty}^{+\infty} g_i(\xi) h(u_o - \xi) d\xi \tag{4.208}$$

Under the condition of space invariance, the superposition integral will be simplified to a *convolution integral*, which is a convolution between the input function (object function) and the impulse response (point spread function). Equation 4.208 may be written symbolically as

$$g_o = g_i * h \tag{4.209}$$

The condition of space invariance is fulfilled in optics only for limited spatial regions, namely the *isoplanatic regions*. Optical systems are in general rotationally symmetric and therefore the impulse response (PSF) is constant for a certain distance from the center of the image, which is the intersection point of the optical axis with the image plane. This means that the impulse response is invariant for an image circle with a given image height $\xi = h'$ (Figure 4.79).

If we change the radius h' of the image circle gradually, then the PSF will change continuously as a function of h'. Within a small region $\Delta h'$, we may treat the PSF as being independent of h'.

During manufacturing, there will be tolerances for the constructional parameters of the optical system. These tolerances may destroy the rotational symmetry. Then the isoplanatic regions will be restricted to certain sectors of the image circle area (Figure 4.80).

Then one has to measure the impulse response (PSF) for each isoplanatic region!

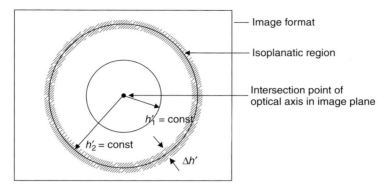

Figure 4.79 Isoplanatic regions for rotationally symmetric optical systems.

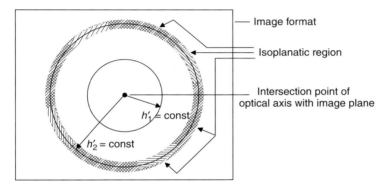

Figure 4.80 Isoplanatic regions with a decentered optical system.

Definition 4.9 The isoplanatic region of an optical system is the spatial region where the impulse response (PSF) is constant within the measurement accuracy.

Within an isoplanatic region, the system is completely described by the convolution of the input function with the corresponding impulse response.

For the convolution integral, there is a theorem of Fourier analysis:

A convolution of two functions in the spatial domain corresponds – after a Fourier transformation (FT) – to a multiplication of the transformed functions in the frequency domain, Equation 4.210 :

$$\begin{aligned} \text{if} \quad & g_a(u_a) = g(u) * h(u) \\ \text{and} \quad & FT^-\{g(u)\} = G(r), \quad FT^-\{h(u)\} = H(r) \\ \text{then} \quad & FT^-\{g_a(u_a)\} = G_a(r) = G(r) \cdot H(r). \end{aligned} \quad (4.210)$$

For the principles of Fourier theory, see [7–9]. The Fourier transform is defined as

$$F(r) = FT^-\{f(u)\} = \int_{-\infty}^{+\infty} f(u)e^{-i2\pi ur}\, du \qquad (4.211)$$

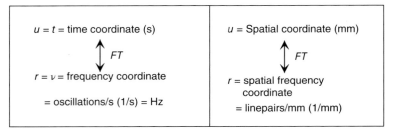

Figure 4.81 Transition to different representation domains.

and the inverse transform is

$$f(u) = FT^+\{F(r)\} = \int_{-\infty}^{+\infty} F(r)e^{+i2\pi ur}\,dr \quad (4.212)$$

The Fourier transform is to be understood as an integral operator that acts on a function $f(u)$ of the independent variable u (e.g., space – or time – coordinate) and transforms it into a function in the frequency domain, with the independent variable r.

With Fourier transformation, we thus make a transition to another *representation* of the same physical system in some other *representation space* (Figure 4.81).

As Equation 4.212 shows, we may interpret the Fourier transform as an alternative decomposition of the function $f(u)$ into other elementary functions.

Example 4.11 Time function $f(t)$:

$$f(t) = \int_{-\infty}^{+\infty} F(\nu)e^{i2\pi\nu t}\,d\nu \quad (4.213)$$

A *well behaved* function of time may be decomposed into an infinitely dense sum (integral) of harmonic vibrations. Each harmonic component is weighted with a factor $F(\nu)$, which is uniquely determined by $f(t)$.

Example 4.12 Space function $f(u)$: In this case we have, from Equation 4.212

$$f(u) = \int_{-\infty}^{+\infty} F(r)e^{i2\pi ur}\,dr \quad (4.214)$$

An intensity distribution in the object may be decomposed into an infinite sum of *harmonic waves*. Each wave is weighted with a certain factor $F(r)$, which is uniquely determined by $f(u)$. The alternative elementary functions are, in this case, the harmonic waves with the spatial frequencies r. (Harmonic intensity distribution with period $1/r$.)

Figure 4.82 Harmonic wave as a component n of the Fourier integral, Equation 4.214.

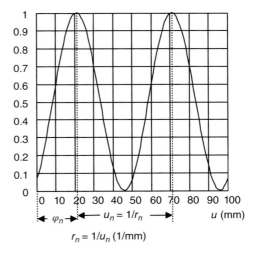

4.4.1.2 Note to the Representation of Harmonic Waves

We take two components of Equation 4.214 with spatial frequency r_n and write them as

$$a_n \cdot e^{i2\pi r_n u} \quad \text{and} \quad a_{-n} \cdot e^{-i2\pi r_n u} \tag{4.215}$$

a_n and a_{-n} are conjugate complex since $f(u)$ is real:

$$a_n = c_n e^{+i\varphi_n}, \quad a_{-n} = c_n e^{-i\varphi_n} \tag{4.216}$$

with

$$\cos \alpha = \frac{1}{2}(e^{+i\alpha} + e^{-i\alpha})$$

We have

$$\frac{1}{2}[a_n e^{+i2\pi r_n u} + a_{-n} e^{-i2\pi r_n u}] = \frac{1}{2} c_n \cdot [e^{+i(2\pi r_n u + \varphi_n)} + e^{-i(2\pi r_n u + \varphi_n)}]$$
$$= c_n \cdot \cos(2\pi r_n u + \varphi_n) \tag{4.217}$$

This is a harmonic wave with period $u_n = \frac{1}{r_n}$ and phase shift φ_n, Figure 4.82. With the convolution theorem, we now have

$$g_o(u) = g_i(u) * h(u)$$
$$\text{FT} \downarrow \quad \text{FT} \downarrow \quad \text{FT} \downarrow \tag{4.218}$$
$$G_o(r) = G_i(r) \cdot H(r)$$

A convolution in the space domain u corresponds to a multiplication in the frequency domain r. The Fourier transform of the impulse response $h(u)$ is the *transfer function* $H(r)$ of the system (of the isoplanatic region).

$$H(r) = \int_{-\infty}^{+\infty} h(u) e^{-i2\pi r u} \, du \tag{4.219}$$

$$h(r) \xleftrightarrow{+FT-} H(r) \tag{4.220}$$

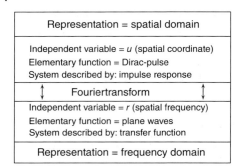

Figure 4.83 Relationship between the two representations for optical systems.

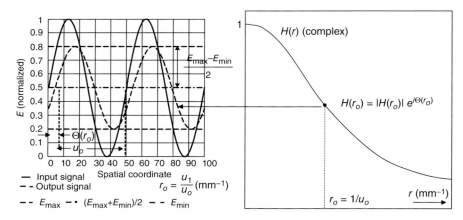

Figure 4.84 Optical transfer function and the effect on a plane wave component at frequency r_o.

$G_i(r)$ is the decomposition of the object function $g_i(u)$ into a sum of harmonic waves (angular spectrum of plane waves).

Figure 4.83 gives an overview on the two representation domains.

4.4.2 Optical Transfer Function (OTF) and the Meaning of Spatial Frequency

Equation 4.218 means that the convolution in the spatial domain may be transformed – by application of the Fourier transform – into a simple multiplication in the spatial frequency domain. The elementary functions are then the complex exponential functions, which may be interpreted as harmonic waves. The system acts on the components (elementary functions) by multiplying each with a complex number $H(r)$, hence with the transfer function at coordinate r. The action of the system is thus restricted to a change of amplitude and to a phase shift of the waves, Figure 4.84.

The transfer function is thus a (complex) low-pass filter. The amplitude is attenuated *but the frequency and mean intensity remain the same.* Additionally, the wave will suffer a phase change.

$$\text{mean intensity} = \frac{E_{\max} + E_{\min}}{2} \tag{4.221}$$

$$\text{amplitude} = \frac{E_{\max} - E_{\min}}{2} \tag{4.222}$$

4.4 Information Theoretical Treatment of Image Transfer and Storage

$$\text{modulation} = \frac{\text{amplitude}}{\text{mean intensity}} = \frac{E_{\max} - E_{\min}}{E_{\max} + E_{\min}} \quad (4.223)$$

$$= |H(r_o)| = \text{MTF}$$

$$\text{phase shift} = \arctan\left[\frac{\text{imaginary part of } H(r_o)}{\text{real part of } H(r_o)}\right] \quad (4.224)$$

$$= \Theta(r_o) = \text{PTF}$$

Therefore, we may decompose the complex optical transfer function (OTF) into a modulation transfer function (MTF) as magnitude and into a phase transfer function (PTF) as the phase of the complex transfer function.

4.4.2.1 Note on the Relation Between the Elementary Functions in the Two Representation Domains

The Fourier transform of the Dirac pulse (which is the elementary function in the space domain) is a constant in spatial frequency domain, Figure 4.85.

In the frequency domain, all the harmonic waves are present with the same magnitude. The totality of all these waves in the frequency domain corresponds to the Dirac pulse in the spatial domain.

The δ-function is thus the sample signal for the optical system, and the Fourier transform of the impulse response (PSF) will determine to what extent the harmonic waves will be attenuated and shifted.

4.4.3 Extension to the Two-Dimensional Case

4.4.3.1 Interpretation of Spatial Frequency Components (r, s)

The response of the optical system to a Dirac impulse in the two-dimensional object plane is a two-dimensional intensity distribution $I(u, v)$. This is the PSF depending on the spatial coordinates u, v in the image plane.

The optical transfer function (OTF) is then the two-dimensional Fourier transform of the PSF depending on the two independent variables, the spatial frequencies r and s with units linepairs per millimeter.

$$\text{OTF}(r, s) = \iint_{\mathbb{R}^2} I(u, v) e^{-i 2\pi (ur + vs)} \, du \, dv \quad (4.225)$$

$$I(u, v) = \iint_{\mathbb{R}^2} \text{OTF}(r, s) e^{+i 2\pi (ur + vs)} \, dr \, ds \quad (4.226)$$

Figure 4.85 Fourier transform of the Dirac pulse.

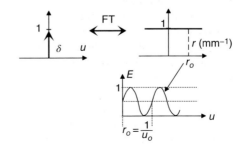

Symbolically:

$$\mathrm{OTF}(r, s) \xleftrightarrow{-\,FT+} I(u, v) \qquad (4.227)$$

What is the meaning of two-dimensional spatial frequencies? In order to answer this, we look at one single elementary wave of the form

$$e^{i2\pi(ur_0 + vs_0)} \qquad (4.228)$$

The real part is

$$I(u, v) = \cos[2\pi(ur_0 + vs_0)] \qquad (4.229)$$

The imaginary part introduces a phase shift of the wave, as shown in Section 4.4.2 for the one-dimensional case. We will omit it here for simplicity.

The function $I(u, v)$ represents a two-dimensional cosine intensity distribution. For each frequency pair (r_0, s_0) (which is represented in the Fourier plane by a point with coordinates (r_0, s_0)), the positions of the constant phase are given by

$$u \cdot r_0 + v \cdot s_0 = \mathrm{const} + n \quad (n = 0, 1, \ldots) \qquad (4.230)$$

or

$$v = -\frac{r_0}{s_0} \cdot u + \frac{\mathrm{const} + n}{s_0} \qquad (4.231)$$

There is a periodicity with 2π, and the positions of equal phase are straight lines with the slope

$$\tan \alpha = -\frac{r_0}{s_0} \qquad (4.232)$$

Thus this elementary function represents a plane wave with the normal direction

$$\tan \Theta = \frac{s_0}{r_0} \qquad (4.233)$$

since the normal vector is perpendicular to the lines of constant phase. The length L of a period of the wave is

$$\frac{1}{L} = \sqrt{r_0^2 + s_0^2} \qquad (4.234)$$

(Figure 4.86).

Figure 4.87 finally gives an overview on the relationships between the two representation domains.

Figure 4.87a is a contour line image (lines of constant intensity) of the two-dimensional PSF, and Figure 4.87b is the corresponding contour line image (lines of constant MTF) in the spatial frequency domain. Each point r_0, s_0 in the frequency domain corresponds to a plane wave in the spatial domain, and vice versa.

4.4.3.2 Reduction to One-Dimensional Representations

A two-dimensional (2D) Fourier transform is numerically tedious, and in most cases it will be sufficient to characterize the 2D OTF by two cross-sections.

Figure 4.86 Plane wave with spatial frequency components r_0, s_0.

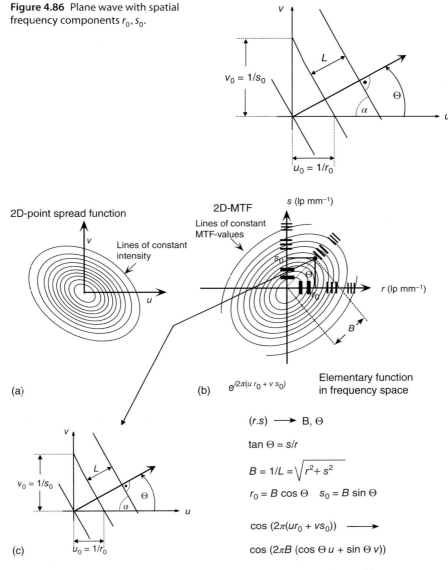

Figure 4.87 Relationships between the representations in space and spatial frequency domain.

A cross-section through MTF(r, s) is given by the Fourier transform of an intensity distribution that is obtained by integration of the 2D PSF perpendicular to the direction of the cross-section.

We demonstrate this by the example of a cross-section along the r-axis ($s = 0$):

$$\text{OTF}(r, s)|_{s=0} = \text{OTF}(r) = \iint_{\mathbb{R}^2} I(u, v) e^{-i2\pi(ru+sv)} \, du \, dv \bigg|_{s=0} \qquad (4.235)$$

$$\text{OTF}(r) = \int_{-\infty}^{+\infty} \left[\int_{-\infty}^{+\infty} I(u,v) dv \right] e^{-i2\pi ru} \, du \qquad (4.236)$$

$$\text{OTF}(r) = \int_{-\infty}^{+\infty} L(u) e^{-i2\pi ru} \, du \qquad (4.237)$$

with

$$L(u) = \int_{-\infty}^{+\infty} I(u,v) dv \qquad (4.238)$$

as integration of the PSF intensity along the v direction. $L(u)$ is called the *line spread function* (LSF).

It may be shown that the same is true for any cross-section with the direction α.

A scan of the 2D PSF with a narrow slit and detection of the resulting intensity results in an integration in the direction of the slit.

The slit scans the PSF perpendicular to its extension and thus gives the line spread function $L(u)$. If the slit is oriented tangential to the image circle with radius h' (this means in the direction u), then the scan direction is perpendicular, in the direction of v. The integration of the 2D PSF is in direction u, and after Fourier transformation of this line spread function one gets spatial frequencies with the lines of constant phase being *tangential* to the image circle and the direction of the cross-section of the 2D OTF being perpendicular to the slit, which is in the direction of scan, Figure 4.88.

An analogous situation arises for the orientation of the slit perpendicular to the image circle, in the v-direction. The scan direction is then the u-direction, and after Fourier transformation one has spatial frequencies with lines of constant phase in the radial direction to the image circle.

In order to characterize the transfer function of an optical system, one usually takes these two directions of cross-sections. Then the MTF for tangential structures is plotted as a function of spatial frequency (for each isoplanatic region) with dashed lines and that for radial structures in full lines, see Figure 4.88.

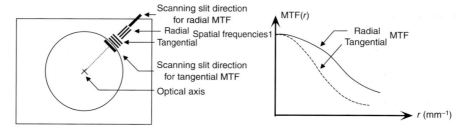

Figure 4.88 Radial and tangential spatial frequencies and the corresponding cross-sections of the transfer function.

4.4.4 Impulse Response and MTF for Semiconductor Imaging Devices

We consider the impulse response of a single pixel. Within the sensitive area of this pixel – which must not coincide with its geometrical extension – the response to a Dirac impulse at position ξ in the form of the electrical signal is given by the pixel sensitivity function $S(\xi)$, Figure 4.89.

The impulse response within the sensitive area of a pixel is thus space-variant and the system is not space-invariant in the sub-pixel region (Section 4.4.6). A complete description of the system is possible only if one knows the impulse response for *all* values of ξ within the sensitive area. This is given by the pixel sensitivity function $S(\xi)$. In what follows, we assume that all pixels of the sensor have the same sensitivity function $S(\xi)$, which means that the system is completely described by $S(\xi)$ and the pixel distance d. How does this affect the output function of the linear system (semiconductor imaging device)?

Figure 4.90 shows the imaging constellation.

We assume the optical system to be ideal in the sense of Gaussian optics, which means that the image in the sensor plane is geometrically similar and each object

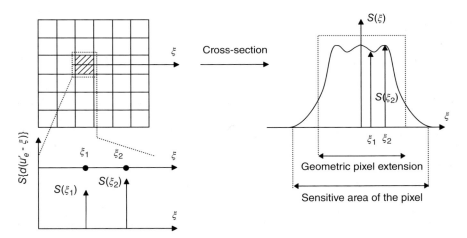

Figure 4.89 Pixel sensitivity function.

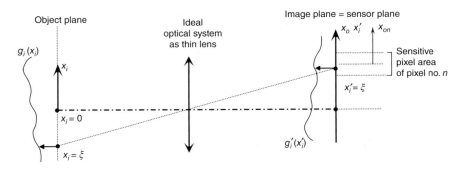

Figure 4.90 Output function of the linear system.

point will be imaged to an exact point. By this assumption, we may neglect the influence of the optical transfer function of the lens; we will take this into consideration in Section 4.4.5.

The image is reversed and changed by the magnification ratio $\beta < 0$. In order to describe the input function in the plane of the sensor, we have to introduce a coordinate transformation:

$$x'_i = \beta \cdot x_i \tag{4.239}$$
$$g_i(x_i) \rightarrow g'_i(x'_i) \tag{4.240}$$

The weighting of the object function $g'(x'_i)$ with the pixel sensitivity function and integration will give the output function of the nth pixel at position x_{on}.

$$g_o(x_{on}) = \int_{\xi=x_{on}-d/2}^{x_{on}+d/2} g'_i(\xi) \cdot S(\xi) d\xi \tag{4.241}$$

This could be, for instance, the response at the output of the horizontal shift register of a CCD for pixel number n in kilo-electrons.

If we shift the pixel continuously along the coordinate x_o, then the output function will be

$$g_o(x_o) = \int_{\xi=x_o-d/2}^{x_o+d/2} g'_i(\xi) \cdot S(x_o - \xi) d\xi = \int_{-\infty}^{+\infty} g'_i(\xi) \cdot S(x_o - \xi) d\xi \tag{4.242}$$

This is a convolution of the object function $g'_i(\xi)$ with the pixel sensitivity function $S(\xi)$, Figure 4.91.

Although we assumed the same sensitivity function $S(\xi)$ for all pixels, the output function $g_o(x_o)$ is not space-invariant in the sub-pixel region ($0 \leq \varphi \leq d$), as shown in Figure 4.91:

$$g_o(x_o = n \cdot d) \neq g_o(x_o = n \cdot d + \varphi) \tag{4.243}$$

The output signal of the system consists of a Dirac comb, weighted by the convolution function, the amplitudes of this Dirac comb *not* being space-invariant in the sub-pixel region. The consequences will be dealt with in Section 4.4.6.

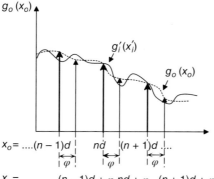

Figure 4.91 Convolution with the pixel sensitivity function.

The transfer function of the pixel system array follows from Equation 4.242 with the convolution theorem.

$$g_o(x) = g'_i(x) * S(x)$$
$$\updownarrow \text{FT} \quad \updownarrow \text{FT} \quad \updownarrow \text{FT} \hspace{4cm} (4.244)$$
$$G_o(r) = G'_i(r) \cdot \text{MTF}_{\text{sen}}(r)$$

Here, the Fourier transform of the pixel sensitivity function is the *transfer function of the pixel*.

4.4.5 Transmission Chain

With the concept of the pixel transfer function, one may formulate now the imaging and optoelectronic conversion of an object scene as an *incoherent* transmission chain. Incoherent in this context means that the system is linear with respect to *intensities*.

The total transfer function is equal to the product of the single transfer functions of the members of the transmission chain (with incoherent coupling), Figure 4.92.

The spatial distribution of the image information is transformed by the image sensor into a temporal variation of a signal (video signal). There is a one-to-one correspondence between spatial and temporal frequencies. For the standardized video signal, for instance, the limiting frequency of 5 MHz corresponds to the use of a 2/3 in. image sensor to a spatial frequency of 30 lp mm^{-1}. The reconstruction function represents further steps of information processing up to the final image. These may contain analog devices, analog-to-digital conversion, digital image processing, and digital-to-analog conversion for the display device.

4.4.6 Aliasing Effect and the Space-Variant Nature of Aliasing

We will investigate the requirements and limits for the application of semiconductor imaging devices. A Dirac impulse in the object plane is imaged by the optical system (PSF) onto the sensor. In order to simplify the considerations, we take a linear sensor array, such as a line scan sensor. This consists of a linear arrangement of light-sensitive surfaces (pixel) with typical dimensions of 2.5–25 µm. The

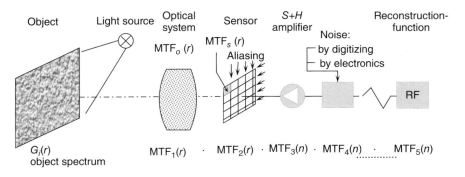

Figure 4.92 Transmission chain.

incident photons generate electrical charges that accumulate during the exposure time, which are then read out of the device by trigger pulses via a shift register.

The intensity distribution over a single pixel will be spatially integrated by the sensitive area of the pixel. In our one-dimensional case, this would be the sensitivity function $S(u)$. For simplicity, we assume $S(u)$ to be a rectangular function with width b. The pixel distance is denoted by d.

The spatial integration by the pixels may be modeled by a convolution between the one-dimensional line spread function $h(u)$ with the rectangular sensitivity function [rect($1/b$)]. This is shown in Figure 4.93. Since the pixels are located at discrete distances d, one has to multiply the convolved function $\tilde{h}(u)$ with a Dirac comb with distances d (Figure 4.94).

Figures 4.95 and 4.96 show the same situation in the spatial frequency domain with the independent variable r (mm^{-1}). The modulus of the Fourier transform of $h(u)$ is the modulation transfer function MTF$_o$ of the optical system. According to the convolution theorem of Fourier theory, a convolution in the spatial domain corresponds to a multiplication of the Fourier transforms in the spatial frequency domain. The Fourier transform of the rectangular sensitivity function is a sinc

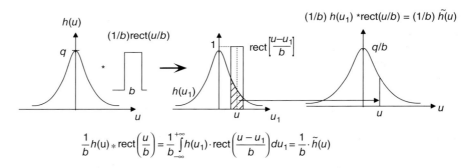

$h(u)$ is area normalized, the factor $1/b$ is introduced because of the normalization of the MTF

Figure 4.93 Convolution of the impulse response with the rectangular sensitivity function of the pixel.

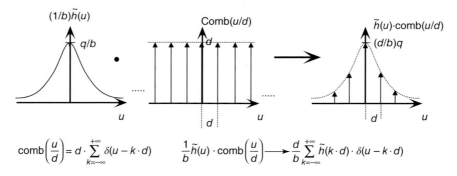

Figure 4.94 Discretizing with pixel distance d.

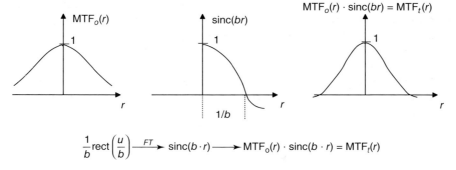

Figure 4.95 Multiplication of the transfer functions.

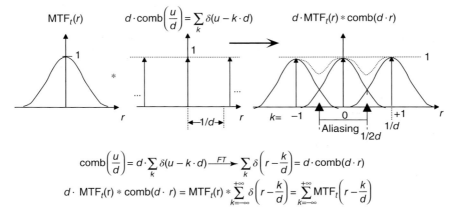

Figure 4.96 Convolution with Dirac comb in the spatial frequency domain.

function with the first zero value at $r = 1/b$. This value will become larger for smaller values of b.

More General: The Fourier transform of the pixel sensitivity function $S(u)$ is the optical transfer function of the line-scan array and is a multiplicative factor for the total transfer function $\mathrm{MTF}_t(r)$.

Figure 4.96 shows the influence of the discrete pixel distances d in the spatial frequency domain. Now, a multiplication in the spatial domain corresponds to a convolution with the Fourier-transformed Dirac comb in the frequency domain. This is again a Dirac comb with distances $1/d$. The effect is a periodic repetition of the total transfer function $\mathrm{MTF}_t(r)$. These functions will overlap each other in certain regions and give rise to incorrect MTF values. This phenomenon is called *aliasing effect* (crosstalk) and may be reduced only with smaller pixel distances d ($1/d$ becomes larger).

For band-limited systems, which means systems where the MTF is zero above a certain highest spatial frequency, the aliasing effect may be avoided completely if one scans at double the rate of the highest spatial frequency (Nyquist sampling theorem).

Now one has to take into account the finite length of the line scan array. In the spatial domain, this means that we have to multiply the function $\tilde{h}(u)\mathrm{comb}(u/d)$ with a rectangular function of width L, Figure 4.97.

The result in the spatial frequency domain is now a convolution with a small sinc function, with first zero at $1/L$ and L large, Figure 4.98.

The last step has nothing to do with the aliasing problem, but we will Introduce it in order to get a discrete spatial frequency spectrum, which is then a discrete Fourier transform.

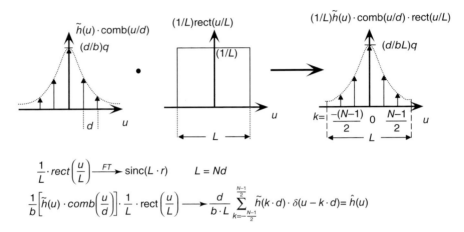

Figure 4.97 Limitation of the impulse response by the length of the array: in spatial domain.

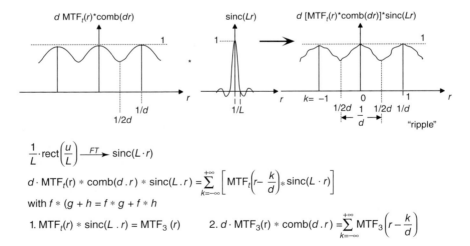

Figure 4.98 Limitation of the impulse response by the length of the array: in the spatial frequency domain.

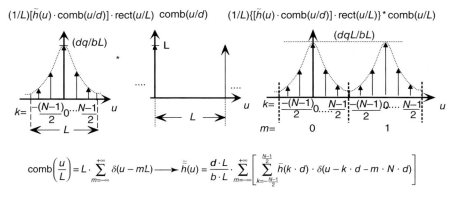

Figure 4.99 Periodic repetition in the spatial domain u with basic period L.

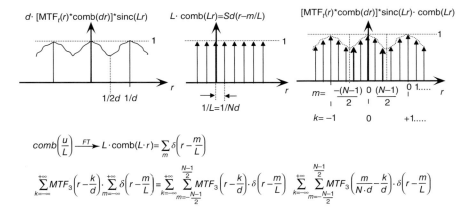

Figure 4.100 Discretization in the spatial frequency domain (discrete Fourier transform).

This will be done by introducing a periodic repetition of the function in the spatial domain. The basic period is the discrete function array, which is cropped with the length L (Figure 4.97). Convolution with a Dirac comb with impulse distances L gives the desired result. One basic period has thus N Dirac impulses with distance d and $L = N \cdot d$, Figure 4.99.

Transferring to the spatial frequency domain gives a multiplication with a Dirac comb with impulse distance $1/L = 1/Nd$. Since the extension of one basic period in the spatial frequency domain is $1/d$, one has again N Dirac impulses within that period, as in the spatial domain, Figure 4.100.

This final function represents a discrete Fourier transform of the impulse response function generated by the line scan array.

Summary 4.2 Because of the periodic scanning with the pixel distance d, there is a periodic repetition of the total transfer function in the spatial frequency domain with distance $1/d$. Since the transfer function in optics is band-limited only at very high spatial frequencies, there exist crosstalks of the higher terms with the basic term for spatial frequencies less than the Nyquist frequency $1/(2d)$. Since the object spectrum is also not band-limited, these crosstalk terms (which may be interpreted as a mirror image of the basic term with respect to the Nyquist frequency) represent parasitic lower frequency terms within the Nyquist bandpass. These crosstalks must therefore be interpreted as *additive noise, which depends on the spatial frequency*.

In this context, we cite from the paper of Park and Rahman [10]:

The folklore that sampling effects are important only if the scene is *periodic* is false. (Note: in this case one will see disturbing Moiré effects.) It is certainly true that sampling effects are most *evident* if the scene has small periodic features, for example, a bar target whose frequency is close to the Nyquist frequency, because in that case familiar obvious sampling artefacts are produced. It is wrong, however, to conclude that the absence of such obvious visual artifacts proves the absence of sampling effects. However, except in special *periodic* cases, aliasing may not be recognized as such because sampling effects are largely indistinguishable from other possible sources of noise.

In this paper, we argue that for the purposes of system design and digital image processing, aliasing should be treated as scene-dependent additive noise.

Example 4.13 A real CCD imaging sensor

- Pixel numbers: 2000×3000
- Pixel dimensions (b): 12 μm × 12 μm
- Pixel distance (d): 12 μm

The sensor format corresponds to 35 mm film: 24×36 mm². To simplify, we assume again that the sensitivity function is rectangular:

$$S(u) = \text{rect}\left(\frac{u}{b}\right)$$

Then the transfer function of the CCD is a sinc function. The Nyquist frequency is at 41 lp mm^{-1}. The first zero for the pixel MTF is at $r \approx 83$ lp mm^{-1}, and the modulation at 40 lp mm^{-1} is 66%. A good optical system may have a modulation of 60% at 40 lp mm^{-1}. Then the total transfer function at 40 lp mm^{-1} is 40%.

If one enlarges the sensor format to a final print of DIN A4 and looks at this print at a distance of 250 mm, then the eye may not resolve more than 6 lp mm^{-1}. If we transfer this with the corresponding magnification ratio to the image side, this gives a frequency of 40 lp mm^{-1}, which corresponds roughly to the Nyquist frequency of the sensor. Here we have to account for considerable aliasing, and the sensor is not well suited for the required image quality (Figure 4.101).

4.4 Information Theoretical Treatment of Image Transfer and Storage | 273

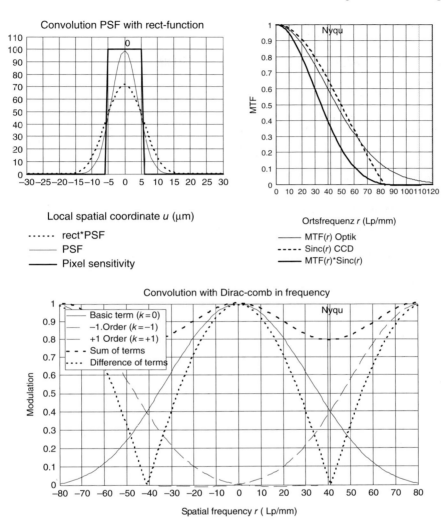

Figure 4.101 PSF, MTF, and aliasing, Example 1.

Example 4.14

Hypothetical sensor (future generation?)
- Pixel numbers: 4000×6000
- Pixel dimensions (b): $6\,\mu m \times 6\,\mu m$
- Pixel distance (d): $6\,\mu m$
- image format: $24 \times 36\,mm^2$

Sensor transfer function
- First zero position of MTF at: $167\,lp\,mm^{-1}$
- MTF at $40\,lp\,mm^{-1}$: 91% (~80% with realistic $S(u)$)
- MTF at the Nyquist frequency ($83\,lp\,mm^{-1}$): 66%

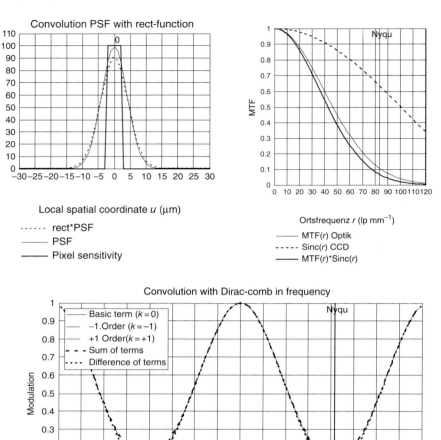

Figure 4.102 PSF, MTF, and aliasing for a hypothetical sensor optic combination (Example 2).

Optical system transfer function (modeled as the Gaussian function)
- Specified as in example 1: $r = 40$ lp mm^{-1}, MTF $= 60\%$
- This gives (according to Gauss function): $r = 83$ lp mm^{-1}, MTF $= 11\%$

Total transfer function
- MTF at 40 lp mm^{-1}: ~50%
- MTF at 83 lp mm^{-1}: ~6%

Conclusion: This sensor would fulfill the quality requirements Completely; even the enlargement for the final print could be higher (up to 30 cm × 40 cm for $r_{max} = 70$ lp mm^{-1}), Figure 4.102.

4.4.6.1 Space-Variant Nature of Aliasing

Up to now, we made some simplifying assumptions when dealing with the effects of discrete sampling by the pixel structure: on one hand, we approximated the pixel sensitivity by a rectangular function, and on the other hand we did not take into account how a small local shift of the input function (or of the sensor, which is the same) affects the Fourier transform.

The latter will be investigated in detail now, and we assume again the one-dimensional case for simplicity.

The impulse response function of the optical system is again $h(u)$. This will be convolved with the finite pixel sensitivity function as before (giving $\tilde{h}(u)$) and then multiplied with a Dirac comb of distance d. But now we introduce a small displacement φ of the Dirac comb with respect to the impulse response $h(u)$:

$$\text{comb}\left(\frac{u}{d}\right) = \sum_{k=-\infty}^{+\infty} \delta(u - k \cdot d - \varphi) \tag{4.245}$$

Because of the periodic nature of the scanning, we may restrict ourselves to the values of φ

$$0 \leq \varphi \leq d \tag{4.246}$$

This gives

$$\tilde{h}(u)\text{comb}\left(\frac{u}{d}\right) = [h(u) * S(u)] \cdot \left[\sum_{k=-\infty}^{+\infty} \delta(u - k \cdot d - \varphi)\right] \tag{4.247}$$

According to the shift theorem of Fourier analysis, the Fourier transform is given by

$$FT\left\{\tilde{h}(u)\text{comb}\left(\frac{u}{d}\right)\right\} = FT\{\tilde{h}(u)\} * \sum_{k} \delta\left(r - \frac{k}{d}\right) e^{i2\pi \varphi r} \tag{4.248}$$

The Fourier transform of $\tilde{h}(u)$ is again

$$FT\{\tilde{h}(u)\} = \text{MTF}_o(r) \cdot \text{sinc}(b \cdot r) = \text{MTF}_t(r)$$

From (4.248)

$$\text{MTF}_t(r) * \sum_{k=-\infty}^{+\infty} \delta\left(r - \frac{k}{d}\right) e^{i2\pi \varphi k/d} = \text{MTF}_t\left(r - \frac{k}{d}\right) e^{i2\pi \varphi k/d} \tag{4.249}$$

To the relative shift in the spatial domain there corresponds now a phase term in the spatial frequency domain r. Figure 4.103 shows this situation for the special case of a *symmetric* PSF, which gives, by Fourier transformation, a *real* OTF ($\text{MTF}_t(r)$).

With the introduction of a small shift φ in the spatial domain, the replica functions ($\pm k$) in the spatial frequency domain rotate about the r-axis anticlockwise for ($+k$) and clockwise for ($-k$), with larger angles as k becomes larger. In the overlapping region, the functions will be added by their real and imaginary parts separately. But since the real and imaginary parts depend on the rotation angle and hence on the shift φ, *also the sum in the overlapping region will critically depend on the shift φ in the spatial frequency domain!*

In other words

> even for very small shifts ($\varphi < d$), the optical transfer function is *no longer space-invariant* in the overlapping region and the isoplanatic condition is violated. The reason for this is – as shown – the aliasing effect with the finite pixel distance d.

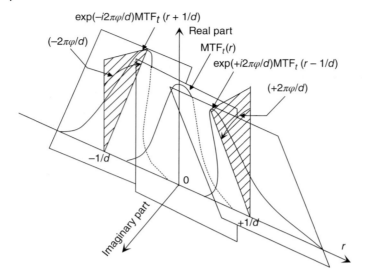

Figure 4.103 Space-variant nature of aliasing.

Thus we have to redefine the isoplanatic condition [11]:

> An imaging system is called isoplanatic if the Fourier transform of the impulse response is independent of the position of the impulse in the object plane.

In the same way, we have to redefine the isoplanatic condition in the spatial frequency domain:

> The isoplanatic region of an imaging system is the region where the Fourier transform of the impulse response may be considered as constant within the measurement accuracy, if the point-like light source in the image plane is shifted within the range $\varphi \leq d$.

Within the validity of the so-defined isoplanatic region, the multiplication rule for the OTF of incoherently coupled systems is valid.

Since an aliased system may not completely be described by the Fourier transform of the impulse response, one has to give additionally a measure for the aliasing effect.

There are several possibilities of defining such a measure. ISO 15529 [12] introduces three different measures:

1) Aliasing function
2) Aliasing ratio
3) Aliasing potential

1) *Aliasing function* AF(r):
   The difference between the highest and lowest values of $|\text{MTF}_t(r)|$ when a shift $0 \leq \varphi \leq d$ is introduced.

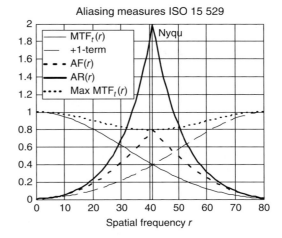

Figure 4.104 Aliasing measures for the constellation of Figure 4.101.

2) *Aliasing ratio* AR(r):
The ratio of AF(r) to $|MTF_t(r)|_{AV}$ where $|MTF_t(r)|_{AV}$ is the average of the highest and lowest values of $|MTF_t(r)|$ as a shift ($0 \leq \varphi \leq d$) is introduced. AR(r) can be considered as a measure of the noise-to-signal ratio, where AF(r) is a measure of the noise component and $|MTF_t(r)|_{AV}$ is a measure of the signal.

3) *Aliasing potential AP*
The ratio of the area under $MTF_t(r)$ from $r = r_N$ to $r = 2r_N$ Nyquist frequency).

Figure 4.104 shows the aliasing measures AF(r) and AR(r) for the constellation given in Figure 4.101. The aliasing potential in this case is

$$AP \approx 18.5\%$$

4.5 Criteria for Image Quality

4.5.1 Gaussian Data

These data are the *backbone* of an optical system because we will count them to the image quality data. In Section 4.2.11 we gave an overview on the most important data, in Table 4.3.

4.5.2 Overview on Aberrations of the Third Order

In Section 4.2.2, we introduced Gaussian optics by linearizing the law of refraction. In the development of the sine function (4.6)

$$\sin \alpha = \alpha - \frac{\alpha^3}{3!} + \frac{\alpha^5}{5!} - \cdots$$

we restricted ourselves to the first member as the linear term.

If one now takes into account the second member additionally, which is of third order, then a detailed analysis shows [13] that certain basic types of deviation from Gaussian optics will occur. Since Gaussian optics is ideal for optical imaging, these types are called *aberrations* (deviations from Gaussian optics) of the third order.

We will only mention them briefly because for the end user of optical systems the quality criteria given in the following sections are of more importance.

4.5.2.1 Monochromatic Aberrations of the Third Order (Seidel Aberrations)
- Spherical aberration
- Astigmatism
- Coma
- Field curvature
- Distortion.

The first three of the above have influence on the form and extent of the PSF; the last two represent a deviation of the position of the PSF with respect to Gaussian optics.

4.5.2.2 Chromatic Aberrations
Another group of aberrations is concerned with dispersion, that is, the dependence of the refractive index with wavelength. This is already true for the Gaussian quantities, so that these aberrations are termed *primary chromatic aberrations*. These are

- Longitudinal chromatic aberration
- Lateral chromatic aberrations.

Longitudinal chromatic aberrations result in an axial shift of the image point for different wavelengths. Lateral chromatic aberrations are concerned with the chief ray, which is now different for different wavelengths. This results in a lateral shift of the image point for a wavelength λ with respect to the position for a certain reference wavelength λ_0.

In addition, all monochromatic aberrations depend on the refractive index and thus also on the wavelength. The result is that one has a chromatic variation of all monochromatic aberrations (*chromatic aberrations of higher order*).

4.5.3 Image Quality in the Space Domain: PSF, LSF, ESF, and Distortion

For the end user, the effects of aberrations on the PSF, the LSF, and the edge spread function (ESF), as well as on the deviation of the image position with respect to Gaussian optics (distortion) are by far more important than the aberrations themselves. All these quantities depend on the local coordinates u, v in the space domain.

However, it is not very easy to handle 2D quantities such as the PSF. For most applications, it is sufficient to consider 1D LSFs as introduced in Section 4.4.3.2. The LSF is the integration of the 2D PSF in a certain direction, Figure 4.105:

$$LSF(u) = \int_{-\infty}^{+\infty} PSF(u, v) dv \qquad (4.250)$$

The origin of the LSF is chosen so as to define the radiometric center. This is true if the ordinate divides the LSF into two equal areas (Figure 4.105).

Figure 4.105 Line spread function $LSF(u)$.

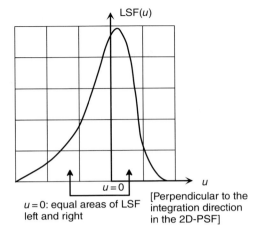

Figure 4.106 Integration directions for LSFs.

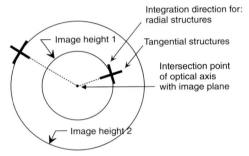

In order to have a more complete characterization of the PSF, one takes two LSFs with two integration directions perpendicular to each other, one in the radial direction (for tangential structures) and the other in the tangential direction (for radial structures) to the image circle, Figure 4.106.

From the viewpoint of application, there is a further important object structure, namely the ESF. This is the image of an ideal edge, that is, a sudden dark-to-light transition. The transition in the image of such an ideal edge will be more or less continuous, since the LSF has finite extension.

Indeed, the ESF is connected with the LSF as shown in Figure 4.107.

The area of the LSF up to the coordinate u_1 is A_1 and is equal to the value of the ESF at this coordinate u_1. This is valid for all values of u. Therefore, the final value of the ESF represents the total area of the LSF, and the value at $u = 0$ is half of the total area according to the definition of the coordinate origin of the LSF. Usually, the LSF is normalized to unit area so that the value of ESF at $u = 0$ is $1/2$.

$$\mathrm{ESF}(u) = \int_{-\infty}^{u} LSF(u) du \qquad (4.251)$$

Sub-pixel edge detection is a standard procedure in digital image processing and is used to locate the position of objects. Therefore, it is important to know the profile of the ESF, and even more important to know the variation of the

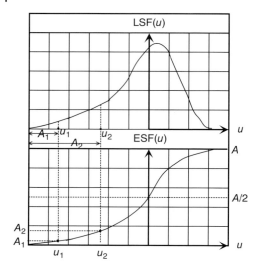

Figure 4.107 Relation between LSF and ESF.

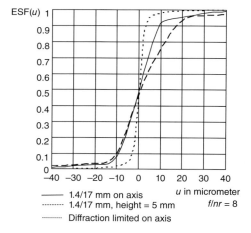

Figure 4.108 Different edge spread functions (ESFs).

ESF with image height and orientation of the edge. Therefore, it is not so much important to have a steep gradient, but rather it is important to have a uniform ESF over image height and orientation. Figure 4.108 shows the ESF of a perfect (diffraction-limited) system, as well as those of our sample lens 1.4/17 mm (on axis and for the image height of 5 mm for $f/nr = 8$). The radial ESF for the image height of 5 mm is practically identical to the ESF on axis, and is therefore omitted.

4.5.3.1 Distortion

Distortion is the geometric deviation of the image point with respect to the ideal position of Gaussian optics (offence against the linear camera model). Since the optical system is nominally rotationally symmetric, the theoretical distortion is also the same [14]. Thus it will be sufficient to plot distortion as a function of the image height h'.

$$D(h') = \frac{h'_D - h'_G}{h'_G} \cdot 100(\%) \tag{4.252}$$

Figure 4.109 Distortion over the relative image height.

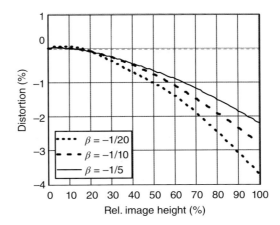

with

h'_D = distorted image position

h'_G = Gaussian image position

Figure 4.109 shows the distortion of the lens 1.4/17 for different magnification ratios over the relative image height.

Because of manufacturing tolerances of real optical systems, there will be centering errors that destroy the nominal rotational symmetry. In photogrammetry, this real distortion will be calibrated with the help of a power series expansion. For very high accuracy (in the micrometer range), a power series with only two coefficients is not sufficient, not even for the reconstruction of nominal distortion! Other forms for the representation of the distortion function may be more efficient (with fewer coefficient than in a power series).

4.5.4 Image Quality in the Spatial Frequency Domain: MTF

The functions PSF(u, v) and LSF(u) in the space domain have their counterparts in the spatial frequency domain, the 2D OTF (as 2D Fourier transform of the PSF) and the 1D OTF (as the Fourier transform of the LSF). The modulus of the OTF is the modulation transfer function MTF, which describes the modulation in the image plane as a function of the line pairs per millimeter, see Section 4.4.3 and Figure 4.110.

The modulation becomes lower for finer structures (larger number of line pairs per millimeter) and will be zero for a certain number of line pairs per millimeter. Hence the optical system is essentially a low-pass filter. For the impression of sharpness, however, this limit (*resolution limit*) is not a good measure. More important is a high modulation over the entire frequency range, *up to a frequency limit that depends on the application*.

As we have shown in Section 3.4.6, because of the regularly spaced pixel structure of the sensor, there exists a highest spatial frequency r_N (*Nyquist frequency*), where for higher frequencies the image information will be falsified and leads to

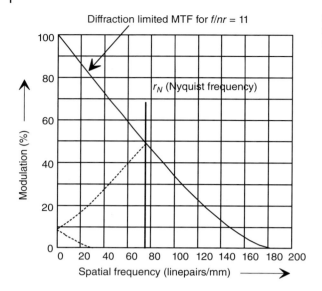

Figure 4.110 Modulation as a function of spatial frequency.

a spatial-frequency-dependent additive noise.

$$r_N = \frac{1}{2d} \quad \text{example } d = 7\ \mu\text{m}, \quad r_N = 72\ \text{lp mm}^{-1}$$

(see Figure 4.110).

It thus *makes no sense* to require a high modulation at the Nyquist frequency, since this will only enlarge the additive noise!

4.5.4.1 Parameters that Influence the Modulation Transfer Function

One MTF is only valid for a certain isoplanatic region, and one has to plot several MTF curves in order to characterize the optical system. Therefore, one uses a different representation in which the modulation is plotted over the image height for some meaningful spatial frequencies as parameter, Figure 4.111.

This representation is normally used in data sheets and corresponds to the international standards ISO 9334 [15] and ISO 9335 [16] full lines to the radial one. Furthermore, the MTF depends on the f-number, on the magnification ratio, and – very important – on the spectral weighting function within the used wavelength region.

> *Without the information on spectral weighting, the MTF data are meaningless!*

For wide angle lenses with large pupil field angles ω_p, the MTF for radial orientation decreases with the cosine of the *object-side* field angle ω_p and for tangential orientation with the third power of ω_p ($\cos^3\omega_p$).

The examples in Figure 4.111 are for a perfect (diffraction-limited) lens for 30 lp mm^{-1} and $f/nr = 8$ (thin lines) and for our sample lens 1.4/17 mm (thick lines) for radial (full lines) and tangential (dashed lines) orientations.

Figure 4.111 MTF as a function of image height.

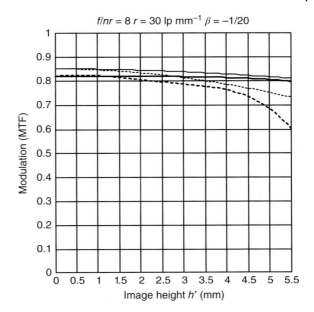

4.5.5 Other Image Quality Parameters

4.5.5.1 Relative Illumination (Relative Irradiance)

The decrease of illumination with the image height h' depends on several components: the basic term is a decrease with the forth power of the cosine of the *object-side* field angle ω_p ($\cos^4$-law, sometimes called *natural vignetting*) [17]. This effect may be changed by distortion and by pupil aberrations (area of the entrance pupil changes with the field angle ω_p). On the other hand, the light cones may be reduced by mechanical parts of the lens barrel or by the diameter of the lenses, which gives an additional decrease of illumination (*mechanical vignetting*). This effect will be reduced when stopping down the lens aperture and vanishes in general when stopping down by two to three f/numbers. Figure 4.112a shows the $\cos^4\omega_p$-law and Figure 4.112b our sample lens 1.4/17 mm for three magnification ratios and f-numbers 1.4 and 4.

4.5.5.1.1 Spectral Transmittance The absorption of optical glasses and the residual reflections at the lens surfaces are responsible for wavelength-dependent light losses [18]. The residual reflections may be reduced by antireflection coatings (evaporation with thin dielectric layers). Figure 4.113 shows the spectral transmittance of our sample lens 1.4/17 mm as a function of wavelength.

If one wants to use the whole spectral sensitivity range of semiconductor imaging sensors (~400–1000 nm) one has to use lenses with sufficient spectral transmission over this region and also sufficient image quality. Usual antireflection coatings, as for photographic lenses, are designed for the visible region only and show transmission-*reducing* properties in the near infrared. Because of this, the rays will suffer multiple reflection within the optical system, which may cause undesired ghost images, secondary iris spots, and veiling glare.

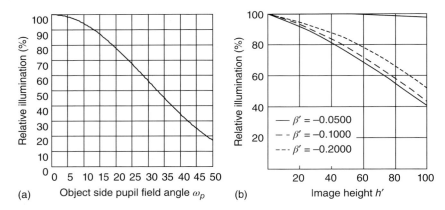

Figure 4.112 (a) Natural vignetting and (b) relative illumination for the lens 1.4/17 mm.

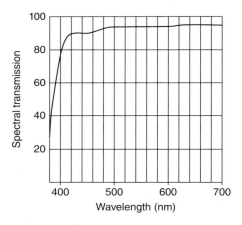

Figure 4.113 Spectral transmittance.

4.5.5.2 Deviation from Telecentricity (for Telecentric Lenses only)

Figure 4.114 shows an example for a bilateral telecentric lens. The deviations are given in micrometers over the relative image height for a variation in object position of ±1 mm. The parameters are three different object-to-image distances. The deviations are shown for the object side as well as for the image side. The latter are practically zero here.

4.5.6 Manufacturing Tolerances and Image Quality

Manufacturing is inevitably connected with tolerances. For the manufacturing of lenses, these are typically as follows:

- Deviations from the spherical surfaces of lenses (measured in $\lambda/2$ units)
- Thickness tolerances for lenses and air gaps (typically 0.01–0.1 mm)
- Lateral displacement of lenses (typically 5–100 µm)
- Tilt of the lens surfaces (typically 0.5–5 arcmin)
- Refractive index tolerances of optical glasses.

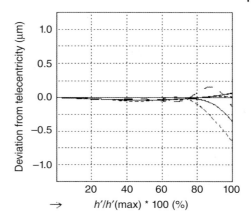

Figure 4.114 Deviation from telecentricity.

Here, the interaction between mechanics (lens barrel) and optics (lens elements) is most important. Image quality parameters are differently sensitive to these tolerances. Table 4.11 gives a rough classification of the sensitivity of the quality parameters on manufacturing tolerances, as well as some typical values one has to account for. Of course, these depend on the practical application and the manufacturing efforts. Lenses for amateur photography show much higher quality fluctuations than special optical systems, for semiconductor production for instance. Correspondingly, the costs may differ by several orders of magnitude. The table is valid for near-professional photo quality [19].

4.5.6.1 Measurement Errors due to Mechanical Inaccuracies of the Camera System

The corresponding influences may be mentioned here only by some headings. Nevertheless they are as important as the variation of optical quality parameters, for example, for contactless measurement techniques [20], Table 4.12.

4.6 Practical Aspects: How to Specify Optics According to the Application Requirements?

Not every optical system may be used for all applications.

A universal optical system does not exist!

Therefore one has to specify the most important parameters in order to find the best suited optics for the particular application – also with regard to cost versus performance.

Most of these parameters are fixed by the geometrical imaging situation and by some spatial restrictions. Other parameters are defined by the used image sensor as well as by the light source/filter combination. The following gives a list of the most important parameters.

Table 4.11 Sensitivity of optical quality parameters to manufacturing tolerances.

Parameter		Sensitivity				Remarks/typical deviations
		++	+	−	−−	
1	Focal length			X		Typ. 1% max. of nominal value 5% max. according to standard [19] caused by mechanical inaccuracies of the iris Standard [19]: up to 50% depending on f-number!
2	Relative aperture			X		
3	f-number		X			
4	ESF	X				Depending on spatial frequency, f-number fixed focal length: 10%
5	MTF	X				Absolute (typically); zoom lenses: 10–20% absolute (typically)
6	Distortion	X				Without special measures: 10–30 μm with special measures: ≤5 μm
7	Relative illumination				X	
8	Spectral transmission				X	Depending on the stability of antireflection manufacturing process

Table 4.12 Influence of mechanical inaccuracies of the camera system.

Cause		Effect
1	Unprecise (non reproducible) image position (e.g., by repetative focussing)	Change of image size (heading: bilateral telecentric lenses)
2	Unprecise object position (e.g., parts tolerances)	Change of image size (heading: object – side telecentric lenses)
3	Image plane tilt (e.g., unprecise sensor position)	Introduction of asymmetrical distortion terms
4	Object plane tilt	Distortion terms, change of image size as 3 and 4
5	Deviation of optical axis from mechanical reference axis ("Bore sight")	

- Object – image distance
- Magnification ratio, which defines the focal length
- Required depth of field
- Relative aperture (f-number), influencing each other
- Minimum relative illumination
- Wavelength range (spectral transmission)

- Maximum permissible distortion
- Minimum MTF values at defined spatial frequencies/image heights
- Environmental influences
  - temperature/humidity
  - mechanical shocks
  - mechanical vibrations
  - dust
  - veiling glare by external light sources
- Mechanical interfaces
  - maximum diameter and length
  - maximum weight
  - interface to the camera (C-mount, D-mount, etc.)

We will explain the procedure with the help of an example:

4.6.1 Example for the Calculation of an Imaging Constellation

1) *Image sensor data*
   - $\frac{1}{2}$ in. FT-CCD, sensor size 4.4×6.6 mm^2
   - pixel distance: 7 µm
   - pixel size 7×7 µm^2
2) *Object data*
   - object distance ≈ 500 mm
   - object size: 90×120 mm^2
   - object depth: 40 mm
3) *Calculation of the magnification ratio and focal length*
   - from object and sensor size:

$$|\beta| = \frac{\text{sensor size}}{\text{object size}} = \frac{4.4 \text{ mm}}{90 \text{ mm}} \approx 1/20$$

$$\beta = -1/20 \quad \text{(inverted image)}$$

   - from object to image distance and from the imaging equation

$$e = f'\left(\frac{1}{\beta} - \frac{1}{\beta_p}\right) \quad (\beta_p \approx 1)$$

$$f' \approx 23 \text{ mm}$$

4) *Calculation of the depth of field*
   - the depth of field is given by the depth of the object and with the depth of field formula:

$$T = \frac{2(f/nr)_e \cdot d'_G}{\beta^2}$$

   - definition of the permissible circle of confusion: for sub-pixel edge detection, the range of the ESF shall be 4–7 pixels:

$$d'_G = 28 \text{ µm} \quad (4 \text{ pixels})$$

Thus

$$(f/nr)_e \geq 3 \cdot \frac{T \cdot \beta^2}{2 \cdot d'_G} = 1.8!$$

- control for the validity of the depth-of-field approximation:

$$|\beta| \geq 3 \cdot \frac{(f/nr) \cdot d'_G}{f'}$$

$$\frac{1}{20} \geq \frac{1}{150} \quad \text{(fulfilled)}$$

- condition for permissible geometrical calculation:

$$(f/nr)_e \leq \frac{2.8}{4.5} \approx 6.2 \quad \text{(fulfilled)}$$

- diffraction-limited disk of confusion:
  - at the limits of the depth of field:

$$d'_d = \sqrt{(d'_G)^2 + 2 \cdot (f/nr)_e^2} \approx 28.5 \, \mu m \quad [(f/nr)_e = 4.0]$$

  - in focus

$$d'_d = 1.22 \cdot (f/nr)_e \approx 5 \, \mu m$$

5) *Definition of image quality parameters*
   - spectral weighting: Vis (380–700 nm) (IR cut-off filter required)
   - Nyquist frequency of the sensor:

   $$r_N \approx 70 \, \text{lp mm}^{-1}$$

   - specification of MTF data:

spatial frequency r (lp mm^{-1})	20	40	60
MTF (%)	≥ 80	≥ 50	≥ 20

   for image heights $h' \leq 3.5$ mm

6) *Specification of distortion*
   - required measurement accuracy in the object: ±0.05 mm
     → absolute distortion in image

   $$|\Delta y'| \leq \frac{0.05}{20} \, \text{mm} = 2.5 \, \mu m$$

   → calibration of distortion required

7) *Comparison with manufacturer's data*
   There exist some simple optical design programs that might facilitate such calculations, for example, [21].
   Figure 4.115 shows schematically the interdependences between the requirements of the optical system and the parameters of the measurement situation.

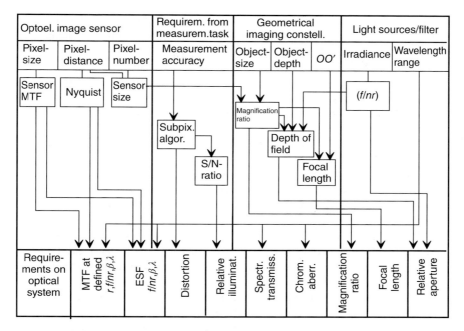

Figure 4.115 Requirements for the optical system depending on the measurement task.

References

1 Hopkins, H.H. (1983) Canonical and real space coordinates in the theory of image formation, in *Applied Optics and Optical Engineering*, vol. IX, Chapter 8 (eds R.R. Shannon and J.C. Wyant), Academic Press, New York.
2 Goodman, J.W. (1968) *Introduction to Fourier Optics*, McGraw-Hill, New York.
3 Born, M. and Wolf, E. (1975) *Principles of Optics*, Chapter 8.5, Pergamon Press, Oxford.
4 Lommel, E. (1995) *Abh. Bayer. Akad.*, **15**, 233. Abth. 2.
5 Struve, H. (1986) *Mém. Acad. de St. Petersbourgh (7)*, **34**, 1.
6 Born, M. and Wolf, E. (1975) *Principles of Optics*, Chapter 8.8, Pergamon Press, Oxford.
7 Brigham, E.O. (1974) *The Fast Fourier Transform*, Prentice-Hall, Englewood Cliffs, NJ.
8 Bracewell, R.N. (1978) *The Fourier Transform and its Applications*, 2nd edn, McGraw-Hill Kogakusha, International student edition.
9 Lighthill, M.J. (1966) *Einführung in die Theorie der Fourieranalysis und der verallgemeinerten Funktionen*, Bibliographisches Institut, Mannheim.
10 Park, S.K. and Rahmen, Z. (1999) Fidelity analysis of sampled imaging systems. *Opt. Eng.*, **38** (5), 786–800.

11 Wittenstein, W., Fontanella, J.C., Newbery, A.R., and Baars, J. (1982) The definition of the OTF and the measurement of aliasing for sampled imaging systems. *Optica Acta*, **29** (1), 41–50.
12 ISO 15529. (2010) Optics and Photonics–Optical Transfer Function–Principles of Measurement of Modulation Transfer Function (MTF) of Sampled Imaging Systems, ISO.
13 Welford, W.T. (1974) *Aberrations of the Symmetrical Optical System*, Academic Press, London.
14 ISO 9039:2008. (2008) Optics and Optical Instruments–Quality Evaluation of Optical Systems–Determination of Distortion, ISO.
15 ISO 9334:2012. (2012) Optics and Optical Instruments–Optical Transfer Function–Definition and Mathematical Relation Ships, ISO.
16 ISO 9335:2012. (2012) Optics and Optical Instruments–Optical Transfer Function–Principles and Procedures of Measurement, ISO.
17 ISO 13653:1996. (1996) Optics and Optical Instruments–General Optical Test Methods–Measurement of the Relative Irradiance in the Image Field, ISO.
18 ISO 8478:1996. (1996) Photography–Camera Lenses–Measurement ISO Spectral Transmittance, ISO.
19 ISO 517:2008. (2008) Photography–Apertures and Related Properties Pertaining to Photographic Lenses–Designations and Measurements, ISO.
20 Schneider Kreuznach. (English version), Optical measurement techniques with telecentric lenses, www.schneiderkreuznach.com/ knowhow/reports (accessed 7 October 2016).
21 Schneider Kreuznach. www.schneiderkreuznach.com/ knowhow/downloads (accessed 7 October 2016).

5
Camera Calibration
Robert Godding

AICON 3D Systems GmbH, Biberweg 30 C, 38122 Braunschweig, Germany

5.1 Introduction

In the past years, the use of optical measurement systems has continuously increased in industrial measurement technology. On the one hand, there are digital cameras (partly with telecentric optics) that are used for the determination of two-dimensional measuring quantities; on the other hand, the 3D measurement technology has greatly come to the fore. Favorable to this development was the improvement of the sensor technology of digital cameras so that nowadays cameras with about 50 megapixels can be used as well as ever faster processors enabling the fast processing of large data quantities.

The mode of operation of the systems, however, greatly differs.

One method consists in using one-camera systems by means of which almost any objects are taken (partially with several hundred images), which are then evaluated offline. Besides, there are numerous systems in use in which a great number of cameras are simultaneously acquiring an object, the evaluation being made online. Due to this, there are rising requirements with respect to the geometrical quality of manufactured parts and most industrial applications require a very high accuracy for evaluation.

This accuracy can only be reached if corresponding mathematical models form the basis of the cameras used for all calculations, that is, all camera and lens parameters are known and are taken in consideration accordingly.

In photogrammetry, the subject of which has been the derivation of three-dimensional measuring quantities from images for many years, intensive work has always been done in the field of camera modeling. In this connection the determination of the significant camera parameters is often referred to as *camera calibration*.

Here, there are basically two approaches. While in some cases the actual object information and the camera parameters can be simultaneously determined with corresponding models (simultaneous calibration), the camera systems are first calibrated separately in other applications. The camera parameters are then assumed to be constant in the latter measurement. Approaches combining both methods are used as well.

In addition, the methods of camera calibration can also be used to obtain quality information of a camera system or information about the measuring accuracy that can be reached by a measuring system.

Methods of calibration and orientation of optical measurement systems are described in the following chapters, focusing primarily on photogrammetric methods since these permit a homologous and highly accurate determination of the parameters required.

5.2 Terminology

The terminology in the following chapters is based on the photogrammetric definitions. Sometimes this terminology differs from the terms that are used in other disciplines, for example, in machine vision.

5.2.1 Camera, Camera System

All mechanical, optical, and electronic components that are necessary to produce an image used for measurement purposes, can be described as a camera or camera system. The camera mainly consists of a lens system (sometimes equipped with an additional filter) on the one side and a sensor on the other side and a mechanical component to connect these two elements. In most cases, these mechanical components are not independent from the camera housing, which can result in instable conditions. For the imaging different digital sensor types (e.g., CMOS and CCD) are used.

In addition, the electronic components, which have an influence on the geometry of the final digital image (e.g., A/D converter), have to be added to the definition of the camera. These components can be outside the camera housing, for example, frame grabbers within the computer systems. Some cameras (especially consumer cameras) perform a kind of image preprocessing within the camera, which cannot be influenced by the user. Even these preprocessing algorithms sometimes have an influence on the geometry of the digital image.

5.2.2 Coordinate Systems

Mainly three kinds of coordinate systems are used for the description of the complete parameter set for calibration. The first coordinate system is a two-dimensional system defined in the sensor plane and is used for the description of the measured image information. This system is often called sensor or image coordinate system.

The second kind of system is used for the description of the camera parameters, it is called the *interior coordinate system*. The last system is a higher-order system, frequently called the world coordinate system or object coordinate system. The last two systems are cartesian, right-handed systems.

5.2.3 Interior Orientation and Calibration

The interior orientation describes all parameters that are necessary for the description of a camera or a camera system itself.

In photogrammetric parlance, calibration refers to the determination of these parameters of interior orientation of individual cameras. The parameters to be found by calibration depend on the type of camera used and on the mathematical camera model, which is used for the description. Various camera models with different numbers of parameters are available. Once the imaging system has been calibrated, measurements can be made after the cameras have been duly oriented.

5.2.4 Exterior and Relative Orientation

The exterior orientation describes the transformation between the coordinate system of the interior orientation (or multiple transformations in case of camera systems with more than one camera) and the world coordinate system.

The relative orientation describes the transformation between different interior coordinate systems in case of a multi-camera configuration.

Both transformations require the determination of three rotational and three translational parameters – that is, a total of six parameters and can be described with 4×4 homogeneous transformation matrices.

5.2.5 System Calibration

In many applications, fixed setups of various sensors are used for the measurement. Examples are online measurement systems in which, for example, several cameras, laser pointers, pattern projectors, rotary stages, and so on, may be used. If the entire system is considered as the actual measurement tool, then the simultaneous calibration and orientation of all the components involved may be defined as the system calibration.

5.3 Physical Effects

5.3.1 Optical System

Practically all lenses have typical radial symmetrical distortions that may greatly vary in magnitude. On the one hand, some lenses used in optical measurement systems are nearly distortion-free [1], while on the other hand, wide-angle lenses, above all, frequently exhibit a distortion of several 100 µm at the edges of the field of view. Fisheye lenses belong to a class of their own; they frequently have extreme distortion at the edges. There are special mathematical models to describe those special lens types [2].

Since radial symmetrical distortion is a function of the lens design, it cannot be considered as an aberration. In contrast to that, centering errors often unavoidable in lens making cause aberrations reflected in radial asymmetrical and tangential distortion components [3]. Additional optical elements in the light path, such as the different kind of filters at the lens and the protective filter at the sensor, also leave their mark on the image and have to be considered in the calibration of a system.

5.3.2 Camera and Sensor Stability

The stability of the camera housing has one of the most important impacts on the measurement accuracy. The lens system and sensor should be in a stable mechanical connection during a measurement or between two calibrations of a system. From the mechanical point of view the best construction may be a direct internal connection between the lens and the sensor which is independent of the outer housing. In addition, this connection can have a provision for mounting the camera on a tripod or carrier. This allows a handling of the camera without too much influence on the stability of the interior orientation.

These ideal conditions are not realized for most of the cameras, which are used for measurement purposes. Normally there is a connection between the lens or sensor and the outer housing so that a rough camera handling can influence the interior orientation. Besides, the sensor is often not fixed well enough to the housing so that a small movement between the sensor and the lens is possible. An influence of thermal effects caused by electronic elements is also possible.

Due to their design, digital sensors usually offer high geometrical accuracy [4]. On the other hand, sensors have become larger in size. Digital full format sensors with sizes of 24 mm × 36 mm and larger are commonly used for measurement purposes. Most camera models imply the planarity of the sensor, which normally cannot be guaranteed for larger sensors.

5.3.3 Signal Processing and Transfer

When evaluating an imaging system, its sensor should be assessed in conjunction with all additional electronic devices, for example, necessary frame grabbers. Geometrical errors of different magnitude may occur during A/D conversion of the video signal, depending on the type of synchronization, especially if a pixel-synchronous signal transfer from camera to image storage is not guaranteed [5]. However, in the case of a pixel-synchronous data readout, the additional transfer of the pixel clock pulse ensures that each sensor element will precisely match a picture element in the image storage. Most of the currently used cameras work with digital data transfer, for example, with Camera Link, IEEE 1394, GigE, or USB2/3 [6] and, therefore, a lot of problems (pixel shift, timing problems) are not relevant. Very high accuracy has been proved for these types of cameras. However, even with this type of transfer the square shape of individual pixels cannot be taken for granted. As with any kind of synchronization, most sensor-storage combinations make it necessary to consider an affinity factor; in other words, the pixels may have different extensions in the direction of lines and columns. Especially, some consumer or professional still video cameras are provided with special sensor types (e.g., no square pixels) and an integrated computation system. Even those sensors must be considered in a mathematical model.

5.4 Mathematical Calibration Model

5.4.1 Central Projection

In principle, image acquisition by an optical system can be described by the mathematical rules of central perspective. According to these, an object is imaged in a plane so that the object points P_i and the corresponding image points P'_i are located on straight lines through the perspective center O_j (Figure 5.1). The following holds under idealized conditions for the formation of a point image in the image plane

$$\begin{bmatrix} x_{ij} \\ y_{ij} \end{bmatrix} = \frac{-c}{Z^*_{ij}} \begin{bmatrix} X^*_{ij} \\ Y^*_{ij} \end{bmatrix} \tag{5.1}$$

with

$$\begin{bmatrix} X^*_{ij} \\ Y^*_{ij} \\ Z^*_{ij} \end{bmatrix} = D(\omega, \varphi, \kappa)_j \begin{bmatrix} X_i - X_{oj} \\ Y_i - Y_{oj} \\ Z_i - Z_{oj} \end{bmatrix} \tag{5.2}$$

where

X_i, Y_i, Z_i are the coordinates of an object point P_i in the object coordinate system K,

XO_j, YO_j, ZO_j the coordinates of the perspective center O_j in the object coordinate system K,

$X^*_{ij}, Y^*_{ij}, Z^*_{ij}$ the coordinates of the object point P_i in the coordinate system K^*_j,

x_{ij}, y_{ij} the coordinates of the image point in the image coordinate system K_B, and

$D(\omega, \varphi, \kappa)_j$ the rotation matrix between K and K^*_j as well as,

c the distance between perspective center and image plane,

the system K^*_j being parallel to the system K_B with the origin in the perspective center O_j [8].

The above representation splits up the optics in such a manner that in (i) it is primarily the image space (interior) parameters and in (ii) primarily the object space (exterior) parameters – that is, the parameters of exterior orientation – that take effect.

This ideal concept is not attained in reality where a multitude of influences are encountered due to the different components of the imaging system. These can be modeled as deviations from the strict central perspective. The following section describes various approaches to mathematical camera models.

5.4.2 Camera Model

When optical systems are used for measurement, modeling the entire process of image formation is decisive for the accuracy to be attained. In case of systems with active illumination, basically the same ideas apply to projection systems for which models can be set up similarly to imaging systems. That may be important for the calibration of white light scanners, where the projector can be one main part of the measurement unit and has to be calibrated also with high accuracy.

5 Camera Calibration

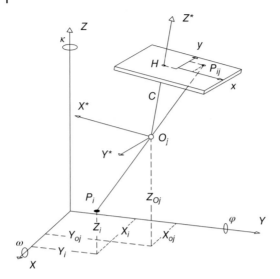

Figure 5.1 Principle of central perspective [7].

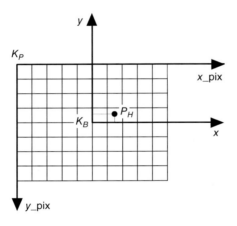

Figure 5.2 Sensor coordinate system.

The basic coordinate system for the complete description is the image coordinate system K_B in the image plane of the camera. In electro-optical cameras, this image plane is defined by the sensor plane. Here, it is entirely sufficient to place the origin of the image coordinate system in the center of the digital images in the storage (Figure 5.2). The centering of the image coordinate system is advantageous to the determination of the distortion parameters, which is described later.

Since the pixel interval in column direction in the storage is equal to the interval of the corresponding sensor elements, the unit "pixel in column direction" may serve as a unit of measure in the image space. All parameters of interior orientation can be directly computed in this unit, without conversion to metric values.

The transformation between a pixel and a metric coordinate system (which sometimes is used to have units independently from the pixel size) is very simple

$$x_{ij\_pix} = x_{ij} \times Fx + Tx \tag{5.3}$$
$$y_{ij\_pix} = Ty - y_{ij} \times Fy \tag{5.4}$$

where Tx and Ty are half of the sensor resolution in x and y and Fx and Fy are calculated from the quotient of the sensor resolution and the sensor size in x and y.

5.4.3 Focal Length and Principal Point

The reference axis for the camera model is not the optical axis in its physical sense, but a principal ray through the perspective center O_j which is perpendicular to the image plane defined above and intersects the latter at the principal point P_H (x_H, y_H). The perspective center O_j is located at the distance c_k (also known as *calibrated focal length*) perpendicularly in front of the principal point [9].

The original formulation of Equation 5.1 is thus expanded as follows:

$$\begin{bmatrix} x_{ij} \\ y_{ij} \end{bmatrix} = \frac{-c_k}{Z_{ij}^*} \begin{bmatrix} X_{ij}^* \\ Y_{ij}^* \end{bmatrix} + \begin{bmatrix} x_H \\ y_H \end{bmatrix} \tag{5.5}$$

5.4.4 Distortion and Affinity

The following additional correction function can be applied to Equation 5.5 for radial symmetrical, radial asymmetrical, and tangential distortion.

$$\begin{bmatrix} x_{ij} \\ y_{ij} \end{bmatrix} = \frac{-c_k}{Z_{ij}^*} \begin{bmatrix} X_{ij}^* \\ Y_{ij}^* \end{bmatrix} + \begin{bmatrix} x_H \\ y_H \end{bmatrix} + \begin{bmatrix} dx(V,A) \\ dy(V,A) \end{bmatrix} \tag{5.6}$$

dx and dy may now be defined differently, depending on the type of camera used, and are made up of the following different components:

$$dx = dx_{sym} + dx_{asy} + dx_{aff} \tag{5.7}$$
$$dy = dy_{sym} + dy_{asy} + dy_{aff} \tag{5.8}$$

5.4.5 Radial Symmetrical Distortion

The radial symmetrical distortion typical of a lens can generally be expressed with sufficient accuracy by a polynomial of odd powers of the image radius (x_{ij} and y_{ij} are henceforth called x and y for the sake of simplicity):

$$dr_{sym} = A_1(r^3 - r_0^2 r) + A_2(r^5 - r_0^4 r) + A_3(r^7 - r_0^6 r) \tag{5.9}$$

where

dr_{sym} is the radial symmetrical distortion correction,
r the image radius from $r^2 = x^2 + y^2$,
A_1, A_2, A_3 the polynomial coefficients, and
r_0 the second zero crossing of the distortion curve,

5 Camera Calibration

so that we obtain

$$dx_{sym} = \frac{dr_{sym}}{r} x \qquad (5.10)$$

$$dy_{sym} = \frac{dr_{sym}}{r} y \qquad (5.11)$$

A polynomial with two coefficients is generally sufficient to describe radial symmetrical distortion. Expanding this distortion model, it is possible to describe even lenses with pronounced departure from perspective projection (e.g., fisheye lenses) with sufficient accuracy [10]; in the case of very pronounced distortion it is advisable to introduce an additional point of symmetry P_S (x_S, y_S). Figure 5.3 shows a typical distortion curve.

For numerical stabilization and far-reaching avoidance of correlations between the coefficients of the distortion function and the calibrated focal lengths, a linear component of the distortion curve is split off by specifying a second zero crossing [11].

Lenz [12] proposes a different formulation for determining radial symmetrical distortion, which includes only one coefficient. We thus obtain the following formula:

$$dr_{sym} = r \frac{1 - \sqrt{1 - 4Kr^2}}{1 + \sqrt{1 - 4Kr^2}} \qquad (5.12)$$

where K is the distortion coefficient to be determined.

The basic approach from [13], which is used from a lot of applications in machine vision, uses two coefficients k_1 and k_2 for the description of the radial

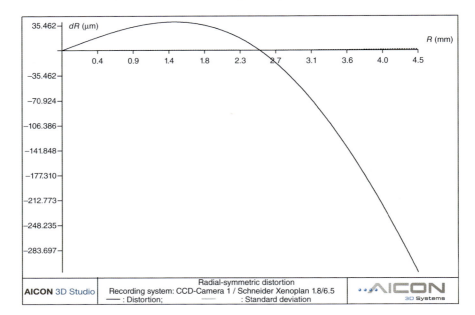

Figure 5.3 Typical distortion curve of a lens.

distortion. Nevertheless, to obtain high accuracy results it is necessary to take into account additional effects of asymmetric distortions.

5.4.6 Radial Asymmetrical and Tangential Distortion

To cover radial asymmetrical and tangential distortion, various different formulations are possible. Based on [14], these distortion components may be formulated as follows [3]:

$$dx_{asy} = B_1(r^2 + 2x^2) + 2B_2 xy \tag{5.13}$$

$$dy_{asy} = B_2(r^2 + 2y^2) + 2B_1 xy \tag{5.14}$$

In other words, these effects are always described with the two additional parameters B_1 and B_2.

This formulation is expanded by Brown [15], who adds parameters to describe overall image deformation or the lack of image plane flatness.

$$\begin{aligned}dx_{asy} = &\,(D_1(x^2 - y^2) + D_2 x^2 y^2 + D3(x^4 - y^4))x/c_k \\ &+ E_1 xy + E_2 y^2 + E_3 x^2 y + E_4 xy^2 + E_5 x^2 y^2\end{aligned} \tag{5.15}$$

$$\begin{aligned}dy_{asy} = &\,(D_1(x^2 - y^2) + D_2 x^2 y^2 + D3(x^4 - y^4))y/c_k \\ &+ E_6 xy + E_7 x^2 + E_8 x^2 y + E_9 xy^2 + E_{10} x^2 y^2\end{aligned} \tag{5.16}$$

In view of the large number of coefficients, however, this formulation implies a certain risk of too many parameters. Moreover, since this model was primarily developed for large-format analog imaging systems, some of the parameters cannot be directly interpreted for applications using digital imaging systems. Equations 5.8 and 5.9 are generally sufficient to describe asymmetrical effects. Figure 5.4 shows typical effects for radial symmetrical and tangential distortion.

5.4.7 Affinity and Nonorthogonality

The differences in length and width of the pixels in the image storage caused by synchronization can be taken into account by an affinity factor. In addition, an affinity direction may be determined, which primarily describes the orthogonality of the axes of the image coordinate system K_B. An example may be a line scanner that does not move perpendicularly to the line direction. These two effects can be considered as follows:

$$dx_{aff} = C_1 x + C_2 y \tag{5.17}$$

$$dy_{aff} = 0 \tag{5.18}$$

Figure 5.5 gives an example of the effect of affinity.

5.4.8 Variant Camera Parameters

In particular for cameras with mechanical instabilities or thermal problems it can be helpful to use special mathematical models, which allow some parameters to be variant during the measurement. That implies that those parameters are different for each image during a measurement process, while other parameters are assumed as stable.

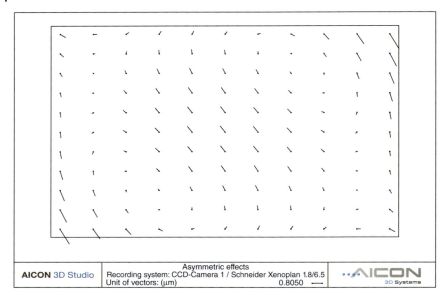

Figure 5.4 Radial symmetrical and tangential distortion.

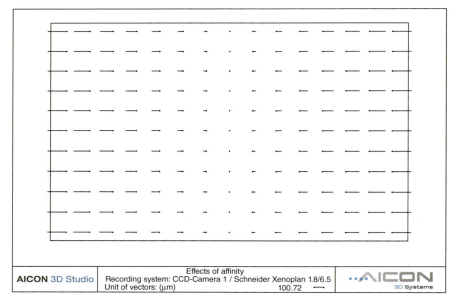

Figure 5.5 Effects of affinity.

A usual practice in that case is setting the focal length c_k and the coordinates of the principle point x_H and y_H as variant parameters for each image. That strategy is only possible for special applications, for example, photogrammetric measurements with a lot of images. In those cases it is possible to get results with high accuracy, in spite of problems with mechanical instabilities [16].

5.4.9 Sensor Flatness

The above described mathematical model is based on a plane sensor, which cannot be implied in reality, especially for cameras with a large sensor format. In order to compensate for those effects a finite-elements correction grid based on anchor points can be used, which is described by Hastedt *et al.* [17]. The sensor is subdivided by a rectangular grid and for each node of the grid corrections are computed so that each measured coordinate can be improved by the interpolated corrections. Figure 5.6 shows a typical correction grid for a high-resolution camera (Mamiya DCS 645, sensor size 36 mm × 36 mm). It could be shown that the use of such models can improve the accuracy of 3D coordinates significantly.

5.4.10 Other Parameters

The introduction of additional parameters may be of interest and can improve the accuracy for special applications. Dold [18] and Fraser and Shortis [19] describe formulations that also make allowance for distance-related components of distortion within the photographic field. However, these are primarily effective with medium and large image formats and the corresponding lenses and are of only minor importance for the wide field of digital uses.

Gerdes *et al.* [20] use a different camera model in which two additional parameters have to be determined for the oblique position of the sensor.

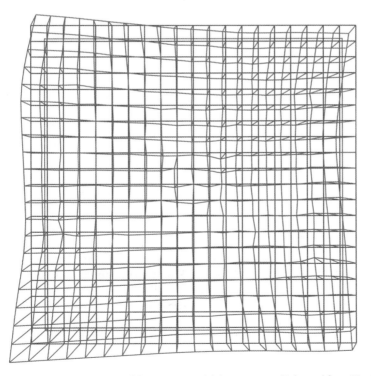

Figure 5.6 Correction grid for a camera with large sensor. (Adapted from Hastedt *et al.* 2002 [17].)

5.5 Calibration and Orientation Techniques

5.5.1 In the Laboratory

Distortion parameters can be determined in the laboratory under clearly defined conditions. That possibility is often used for the calibration of high-resolution cameras for aerial photogrammetry [21].

In the goniometer method, a highly precise grid plate is positioned in the image plane of a camera. Then the goniometer is used to measure the grid intersections from the object side and to determine the corresponding angles. Distortion values can then be obtained by comparing the nominal and actual values.

In the collimator technique, test patterns are projected onto the image plane by several collimators set up at defined angles to each other. Here too, the parameters of interior orientation can be obtained by a comparison between nominal and actual values, though only for cameras focused on infinity [9].

Apart from this restriction, there are more reasons speaking against the use of the aforementioned laboratory techniques for calibrating digital imaging systems, including the following:

The scope of equipment required is high.
The interior orientation of standard industrial cameras normally used is not stable, requiring regular recalibration by the user.
Interior orientation including distortion varies at different focus and aperture settings so that calibration under practical conditions appears more appropriate.
There should be a possibility of evaluating and recalibrating optical measurement systems on the measurement side to avoid system maintenance costs that are too high.

5.5.2 Using Bundle Adjustment to Determine Camera Parameters

All parameters required for calibration and orientation may be obtained by means of photogrammetric bundle adjustment. In bundle adjustment, two so-called observation equations are set up for each point measured in an image, based on Equations 5.2 and 5.4. The total of all equations for the image points of all corresponding object points results in a system that makes it possible to determine the unknown parameters [22]. Since this is a nonlinear system of equations, approximate values for all unknown parameters are necessary. The computation is made iteratively by the method of least squares, the unknowns being determined in such a way that the squares of deviations are minimized at the image coordinates observed. Newer approaches such as balanced parameter estimation work with modern algorithms [23]. Bundle adjustment thus allows simultaneous determination of the unknown object coordinates, exterior orientation, and interior orientation with all relevant system parameters of the imaging system. In addition, standard deviations are computed for all parameters, which give a measure of the quality of the imaging system.

5.5.2.1 Calibration Based Exclusively on Image Information

This method is particularly well suited for calibrating individual imaging systems. It requires a survey of a field of points in a geometrically stable photogrammetric

Figure 5.7 Reference plate for camera calibration.

assembly. The points need not include any points with known object coordinates (control points); the coordinates of all points need only be known approximately [22]. It is, however, necessary that the point field is stable for the duration of image acquisition. Likewise, the scale of the point field has no effect on the determination of the desired image space parameters. Figure 5.7 shows a point field suitable for calibration.

The accuracy of the system studied can be judged from the residual mismatches of the image coordinates as well as the standard deviation of the unit of weight after adjustment (Figure 5.8). The effect of synchronization errors, for example, becomes immediately apparent, for instance by larger residual mismatches of different magnitude in line and column direction.

Figure 5.9 gives a diagrammatic view of the minimum setup for surveying a point array with which the aforementioned system parameters can be determined. The array may be a three-dimensional test field with a sufficient number of properly distributed, circular targets. This test field is first recorded in three frontal images, with camera and field at an angle of 100^g for determining affinity and 200^g for determining the location of the principal point. In addition, four convergent images of the test field are used to give the assembly the necessary geometric stability for determining the object coordinates and to minimize correlations with exterior orientation.

Optimum use of the image format is a precondition for the determination of distortion parameters. However, this requirement does not need to be satisfied for all individual images. It is sufficient if the image points of all images cover the format uniformly and completely.

If this setup is followed, seven images will be obtained roughly as shown in Figure 5.10, their outer frame standing for the image format, the inner frame for the image of the square test field, and the arrow head for the position of the test field. It is generally preferable to rotate the test field with the aid of a suitable suspension in front of the camera instead of moving the camera for image acquisition. Complete, commercially available software packages

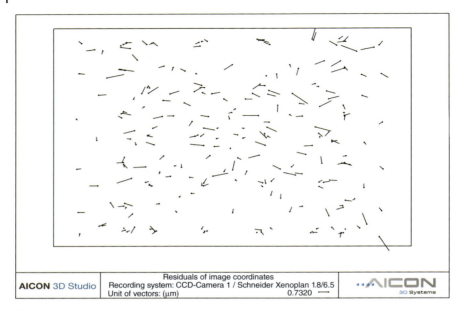

Figure 5.8 Residual after bundle adjustment.

offer far-reaching automated processes for the described calibration task, in most cases using special coded targets for an automatic point number determination.

5.5.2.2 Calibration and Orientation with Additional Object Information

Once the interior orientation of an imaging system has been calibrated, its orientation can be found by resection in space. The latter may be seen as a special bundle adjustment in which the parameters of interior orientation and the object coordinates are known. This requires a minimum of three control points in space, the object coordinates of which in the world coordinate system are known and

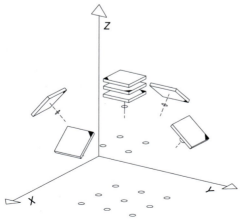

Figure 5.9 Imaging setup for calibration [1].

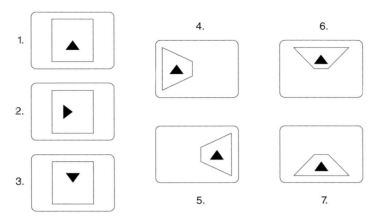

Figure 5.10 Positions of reference plate during calibration.

the image points of which have been measured with the imaging system to be oriented.

In addition to a simple orientation, a complete calibration of an imaging system is also possible with a single image. However, since a single image does not allow the object coordinates to be determined, suitable information within the object has to be available in the form of a three-dimensional control point array [24]. Today, such reference fields can be easily constructed by using carbon fiber elements. In any case, the control pattern should completely fill the measurement range of the cameras to be calibrated and oriented to ensure good agreement between the calibration and measurement volumes.

The effort is considerably smaller if several images are available. For a two-image assembly and one camera, a spatial array of points that need to be approximately known only, plus several known distances (scales) as additional information distributed in the object space will be sufficient, similar to Section 5.5.2.1. In an ideal case, one scale on the camera axis, another one perpendicular to it, and two oblique scales in two perpendicular planes parallel to the camera axis are required (Figure 5.11). This will considerably reduce the effort on the object side, since the creation and checking of scales is much simpler than that of an extensive three-dimensional array of control points.

A similar setup is possible if the double-image assembly is recorded with several cameras instead of just one. This is, in principle, the case with online measurement systems. An additional scale is then required in the foreground of the object space, bringing the total number of scales to five (Figure 5.12).

If at least one of the two cameras can be rolled, the oblique scales can be dispensed with, provided that the rolled image is used for calibration [24].

The setups described are applicable to more than two cameras as well. In other words, all cameras of a measurement system can be calibrated if the above mentioned conditions are created for each of the cameras. At least two cameras have to be calibrated in common, with the scales set up as described. Simultaneous calibration of all cameras is also possible, but then the scale information must be

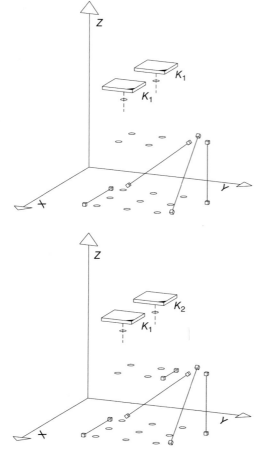

Figure 5.11 Scale setup for calibrating one camera.

Figure 5.12 Scale setup for calibrating two cameras.

simultaneously available to all the cameras. If all cameras are also to be calibrated in common, this will have to be done via common points.

With digital, multi-camera-online systems another calibration method is possible, which is based on the above described theory. It is possible to make the calibration only with one scale, which is moved in front of the measurement system. It is important, that the scale covers all directions in 3d space. The scale bar should be positioned parallel and rectangular to the image planes. For each position, images with all cameras are recorded and the image coordinates are measured. For each camera, all measured image coordinates are subsumed in one image so that we get one virtual image for each camera with the coordinates of all measurements. If raw calibration values are known, approximate object coordinates can be computed. Together with the knowledge of the distance of the scale (which is known for each snap of the system) enough information for the calibration is available. Figure 5.13 shows a calibrated scale bar with four targets, which allows a measurement from different directions.

Figure 5.13 Principle of plumb-line method.

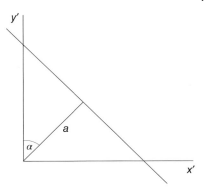

5.5.2.3 Extended System Calibration

As we have seen from the last sections, a joint calibration and orientation of all cameras involved and thus the calibration of the entire system is possible if certain conditions are met. With the aid of bundle adjustment, the two problems can be solved jointly with a suitable array of control points or a spatial point array of unknown coordinates plus additional scales. The cameras then already are in measurement position during calibration. Possible correlations between the exterior and interior orientations required are thus neutralized because the calibration setup is identical to the measurement setup.

Apart from the imaging systems, other components can be calibrated and oriented within the framework of system calibration. Godding and Luhmann [25] describe a technique in which a suitable procedure in an online measurement system allows both the interior and exterior orientation of the cameras involved as well as the orientation of a rotary stage to be determined with the aid of a spatial point array and additional scales. The calibration of a line projector within a measurement system using photogrammetric techniques was, presented by Strutz [26].

The calibration of a recording system with one camera and four mirrors is described in [27]. This system generates an optical measurement system with four virtual cameras. The advantage of the setup is that, especially in the case of high speed image recording, the accuracy of a determination of 3D coordinates is not influenced by synchronization errors from different cameras. This principle allows a much cheaper solution than using four single cameras.

5.5.3 Other Techniques

Based on the fact that straight lines in the object space have to be reproduced as straight lines in the image, the so-called plumb-line method serves to determine distortion. The method is based on the fact that the calibrated focal length and the principal point location are known [28].

According to Figure 5.13, each of the straight-line points imaged are governed by the relationship

$$x' \sin \alpha + y' \cos \alpha = a \qquad (5.19)$$

where x' and y' can be expressed as follows:

$$x' = x_{ij} + dx_{\text{sym}} + dx_{\text{asy}} \tag{5.20}$$

$$y' = y_{ij} + dy_{\text{sym}} + dy_{\text{asy}} \tag{5.21}$$

dx_{sym}, dy_{sym}, dx_{asy}, dy_{asy} corresponding to the formulations in Equations 5.10, 5.11, 5.13–5.16. It is an advantage of this method that, assuming suitable selection of the straight lines in the object, a large number of observations are available for determining distortion, measurement of the straight lines in the image lending itself to automation. A disadvantage is the fact that simultaneous determination of all relevant parameters of interior orientation is impossible.

Lenz [12] presented a method in which an imaging system was likewise calibrated and oriented in several steps. The method requires a plane test field with known coordinates, which generally should not be oriented parallel to the image plane. Modeling radial symmetrical distortion with only one coefficient and neglecting asymmetrical effects allows the calibration to be based entirely on linear models. Since these do not need to be resolved interactively, the method is very fast. It is a disadvantage, however, that here too it is impossible to determine all the parameters simultaneously and that, for example, the location of the principal point and the pixel affinity have to be determined externally.

Gerdes et al. [20] describe a method permitting cameras to be calibrated and oriented with the aid of parallel straight lines projected onto the image. A cube of known dimensions is required for the purpose as a calibrating medium. Vanishing points and vanishing lines can be computed from the cube edges projected onto the image and are used to determine the unknown parameters.

A frequently used formulation for determining the parameters of exterior and interior orientation is the method of direct linear transformation (DLT) first proposed by Abdel-Aziz and Karara [29]. This establishes a linear relationship between image and object points. The original imaging equation is converted to a transformation with 11 parameters that initially have no physical importance. By introducing additional conditions between these coefficients it is then possible to derive the parameters of interior and exterior orientation, including the introduction of distortion models [30]. Since the linear formulation of DLT can be solved directly, without approximations for the unknowns, the technique is frequently used to determine approximations for bundle adjustment. The method requires a spatial test field with a minimum of six known control points, a sufficient number of additional points being needed to determine distortion. However, if more images are to be used to determine interior orientation or object coordinates, nonlinear models will have to be used here too.

Other direct solutions for the problems of calibration and orientation based on the methods of projective geometry and DLT and attractive for the applications of machine vision are shown by Förstner [31].

5.6 Verification of Calibration Results

After the calibration and orientation has been made, the system is ready for measuring. The final acceptance and verification of the measurement system can be done according to the German guideline VDI 2634 [32] by measuring a spatial

Figure 5.14 Spatial test object for VDI 2634 test.

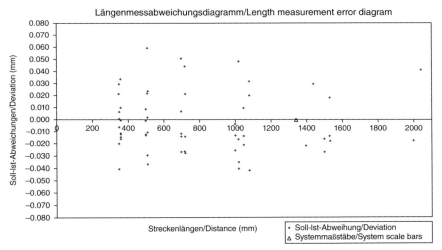

Figure 5.15 Length measurement error diagram.

object with a range of 2 m × 2 m × 1.5 m with at least seven different measuring lines distributed in a specific manner [33]. The measuring lines are realized, for example, by highly accurate carbon fiber scales with some external calibrated distances (e.g., by a coordinate measuring machine (CMM)). The accuracy of the system can be verified by a comparison between the measured and the nominal values of the distances so that the quality of the optical measurement system is reflected by the error of the length measurement. Figure 5.14 shows a spatial test object for a verification test, Figure 5.15 a typical result.

5.7 Applications

5.7.1 Applications with Simultaneous Calibration

The imaging setup for many photogrammetric applications allows a simultaneous calibration of cameras. It is an advantage of this solution that no additional effort

Figure 5.16 Photogrammetric deformation measurement of a crashed car.

is required for an external calibration of the cameras and that current camera data for the instant of exposure can be determined by bundle adjustment. This procedure, however, is possible only if the evaluation software offers the option of simultaneous calibration. As an example, let us look at the measurement of a car for the determination of deformations during a crash test (Figure 5.16).

A total of 80 photos were taken before and after the crash with a professional camera (Figure 5.17) with a resolution of approximately 4000×3000 sensor elements. The AICON 3D Studio software was used for the complete evaluation [34]. This allows the fully automatic determination of 3D coordinates, starting with the measurement of image points right up to computation of all unknown parameters. In addition to target sizes and the 3D coordinates of all measured points in the world coordinate system, these include the camera parameters and all camera stations. For the evaluation of the crash test a complete deformation

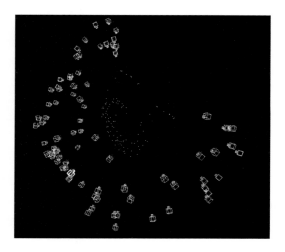

Figure 5.17 Camera positions for crash car measurement.

analysis was made within the software. For this example the coordinates have an RMS value of approximately 0.04 mm in each of the three coordinate axes.

Most photogrammetric applications for high-precision 3D industrial metrology work are based on simultaneous calibration. All parameters of interior and exterior orientation are computed in parallel to the 3D coordinates. Numerous other uses can be found in the aviation industry (measuring aircraft components and fixtures), in the aeronautical industry (measuring satellites and antennas), in shipbuilding, and in civil engineering (measuring of tunnels).

5.7.2 Applications with Precalibrated Cameras

5.7.2.1 Tube Measurement within a Measurement Cell

Some applications are running in an environment with fixed cameras; nevertheless, these camera systems have to be calibrated and the calibration has to be checked to ensure reliable measurement results.

One example of such a system is the TubeInspect system, a measurement system which incorporates advanced technology for the high-precision measurement of tubes, the determination of set up, and correction data and quality assurance of different kind of tubes [34]. The system acquires the tube with 16 high-resolution cameras (GigE), which are firmly mounted on a stable steel frame. All cameras are pre-calibrated. The calibration and orientation is checked with 30 illuminated reference targets with known positions, which cover the whole measuring space (Figure 5.18). If the system recognizes a significant difference between nominal and measured values, a new calibration of some interior orientation or a new camera orientation is made automatically. With that calibration strategy it is possible to obtain accuracies up to 0.1 mm within a measurement range of 2500 mm × 1250 mm × 700 mm.

Figure 5.18 Tube inspection system with fixed cameras and reference points.

Figure 5.19 Online measurement system with three cameras.

5.7.2.2 Online Measurements in the Field of Car Safety

Another example of a measurement system with precalibrated cameras is an online positioning system with two or more cameras. Such systems are used for positioning tasks, for example, in car safety applications. One task is the positioning of dummies before a crash test is conducted [34].

Some high resolution cameras (GigE) are mounted on a stable base beam. The system can be mounted to a workstation cart and can easily be moved to different measurement locations. If the system detects deviations during the measurement that are too high a new system orientation may be necessary, which can be done by the user on the test location directly with a carbon fiber reference plate or a carbon scale bar (Figure 5.19).

5.7.2.3 High Resolution 3D Scanning with White Light Scanners

If surface measurement with high accuracy and very dense resolution is required, the measurement systems are combined with projector units displaying different kinds of patterns onto an object.

Advanced topometrical systems are using a two camera setup with an additional pattern projector. An asymmetrical projector positioning even offers the possibility of integrating three triangulation angles in only one system setup. The system configuration includes an intelligent data management selecting those 3D data recorded with the largest triangulation angle, thus offering best data quality and reliability. In case the corresponding object area is captured by only one camera, the smaller triangulation angles are used to calculate the 3D data. To work with all these options requires the calibration of cameras and projector.

Most of the topometrical systems based on structured light techniques are use either a random pattern or a fringe projection technique. The random patterns are analyzed by spatial correlation techniques that result in a strong low-pass filtering (smoothing) of the calculated 3D data. On the other hand, these techniques are instantaneous, because the data acquisition can be based on only one image acquisition of both cameras [35].

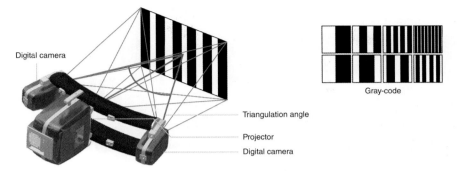

Figure 5.20 Principle of fringe projection.

High-definition fringe projection techniques of white light scanners are mainly based on phase shift technology. Instead of recording only one image, a sequence of fringe patterns is projected and captured (Figure 5.20). The main advantages of this technique are:

- Separation of fringes and background structure by basic arithmetic operations
- Calculation of the local phase φ of the fringes with highest accuracy and without using spatial correlation algorithms
- Easy determination of data reliability (fringe contrast).

Fringe projection systems are widely used for the determination of surfaces, for example, in cultural heritage measurements [36]. On the other hand, the number of industrial applications is increasing constantly. White light scanners are employed for tasks in geometric dimensioning and tolerancing (GD&T), inspection, and reverse engineering. All applications need a simple and fast system calibration. In most cases, calibration with reference plates is a common method. For automated measurement processes, the calibration is fully integrated into the measurement sequences, that is, a manual calibration is not required.

To work with a fully calibrated color digital projection unit to display the fringe pattern provides additional advantages [34]: After measuring the 3D surface and evaluating the target data (e.g., differences between nominal CAD data and measurement), the results can be projected back onto the measuring object (Figure 5.21). In this case, the calibrated measurement device is also used for the accurate visualization of results, because the computed 3D data are exactly projected onto the object surface by using the calibrated parameters for the positioning and the lens distortion parameters of the projector.

5.7.2.4 Other Applications

Other photogrammetric applications for the 3D capture of objects can be found, for example, in accident photography and in architecture. In these fields, scale drawings or rectified scale photos (orthophotos) are primarily obtained from the digital images. The cameras used are generally calibrated for different focus settings using the methods described above. Special metric lenses, which guarantee reproducible focus setting by mechanical click stops of the focusing ring, keep the

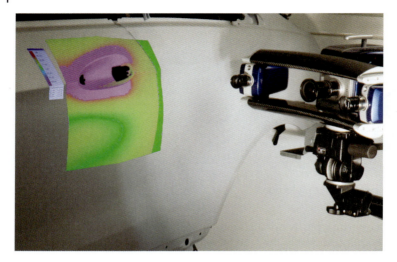

Figure 5.21 White light scanner with digital color projection unit.

interior orientation constant for prolonged periods. The data of interior orientation are entered in the software and thus used for plotting and all computations. This guarantees high-precision 3D plotting with minimum expense in the phase of image acquisition. Other applications can be found in [37, 38].

References

1 Godding, R. (1993) Ein photogrammetrisches Verfahren zur Überprüfung und Kalibrierung digitaler Bildaufnahmesysteme. *Z. Photogramm. Fernerkund.*, **2/93**, 82–90.
2 Schwalbe, E. (2005) Geometric modelling and calibration of fisheye lens camera systems. Presented at 2nd Panoramic Photogrammetry Workshop. International Archives of Photogrammetry, Remote Sensing and Spatial Information Sciences, Vol. XXXVI, Part 5/W8.
3 Brown, D.C. (1966) Decentering distortion of lenses. *Photogramm. Eng.*, **32** (3), 444–462.
4 Lenz, R. (1988) Zur Genauigkeit der Videometrie mit CCD-Sensoren. Informatik Fachberichte 180. 10th DAGM Symposium, Zurich, Switzerland, pp. 179–189.
5 Bösemann, W., Godding, R., and Riechmann, W. (1990) Photogrammetric investigation of CCD cameras. ISPRS Symposium, Commission V. Close-Range Photogrammetry Meets Machine Vision, Zurich, Switzerland, Proceedings of SPIE, Vol. 1395, pp. 119–126.
6 Godding, R. (2005) *Integration aktueller Kamerasensorik in optischen Messsystemen*, Band **14**, Publikationen der Deutschen Gesellschaft für Photogrammetrie, Fernerkundung und Geoinformation, Potsdam, pp. 255–262.

7 Dold, J. (1994) Photogrammetrie, in *Vermessungsverfahren im Maschinen- und Anlagenbau* (ed. W. Schwarz), Schriftenreihe des Deutschen Vereins für Vermessungswesen DVW.
8 Wester-Ebbinghaus, W. (1989) Mehrbild-Photogrammetrie – Räumliche Triangulation mit Richtungsbündeln. Symposium Bildverarbeitung '89. Technische Akademie Esslingen, pp. 25.1–25.13.
9 Rüger, W., Pietschner, J., and Regensburger, K. (1978) *Photogrammetrie – Verfahren und Geräte*, VEB Verlag für Bauwesen, Berlin.
10 Schneider, D., Schwalbe, E., and Maas, H.-G. (2009) Validation of geometric models of fisheye lenses. *ISPRS J. Photogramm. Remote Sens.*, **64** (3), 259–266.
11 Wester-Ebbinghaus, W. (1980) Photographisch-numerische Bestimmung der geometrischen Abbildungseigenschaften eines optischen Systems. *Optik*, **3**, 253–259.
12 Lenz, R. (1987) Linsenfehlerkorrigierte Eichung von Halbleiterkameras mit Standardobjektiven für hochgenaue 3D-Messungen in Echtzeit. Informatik Fachberichte 149. 9th DAGM Symposium Brunswick, pp. 212–216.
13 Zhang, Z. (2000) A flexible new technique for camera calibration. *IEEE Trans. Pattern Anal. Mach. Intell.*, **22** (1), 1330–1334.
14 Conrady, A. (1919) Decentered lens systems. *Mon. Not. R. Astron. Soc.*, **79**, 384–390.
15 Brown, D.C. (1976) The bundle adjustment – progress and perspectives. International Archives of Photogrammetry 21(III). Paper 303041, Helsinki, Finland.
16 Maas, H.-G. (1998) *Ein Ansatz zur Selbstkalibrierung von Kameras mit instabiler innerer Orientierung*, Band **7**, Publikationen der DGPF, München.
17 Hastedt, H., Luhmann, T., and Tecklenburg, W. (2002) Image-variant interior orientation and sensor modelling of high-quality digital cameras. ISPRS Symposium Commission V, Corfu, Greece.
18 Dold, J. (1997) *Ein hybrides photogrammetrisches Industriemeßsystem höchster Genauigkeit und seine Überprüfung*, Heft 54, Schriftenreihe Universität der Bundeswehr, München.
19 Fraser, C. and Shortis, M. (1992) Variation of distortion within the photographic field. *Photogramm. Eng. Remote Sens.*, **58** (6), 851–855.
20 Gerdes, R., Otterbach, R., and Kammüller, R. (1993) Kalibrierung eines digitalen Bildverarbeitungssystems mit CCD-Kamera. *Tech. Mess.*, **60** (6), 256–261.
21 Schuster, R. and Braunecker, B. (2000) Calibration of the LH systems ADS40 airborne digital sensor. International Archives of Photogrammetry and Remote Sensing, Vol. 33, Part B1, 19th ISPRS Congress, Amsterdam, Netherlands, pp. 288–294.
22 Wester-Ebbinghaus, W. (1985) Bündeltriangulation mit gemeinsamer Ausgleichung photogrammetrischer und geodätischer Beobachtungen. *Z. Vermessungswesen*, **3**, 101–111.
23 Fellbaum, M. (1996) PROMPT – a new bundle adjustment program using combined parameter estimation. International Archives of Photogrammetry and Remote Sensing, Vol. XXXI, Part B3, pp. 192–196.

24 Wester-Ebbinghaus, W. (1985) Verfahren zur Feldkalibrierung von photogrammetrischen Aufnahmekammern im Nahbereich. DGK-Reihe B, No. 275, pp. 106–114.
25 Godding, R. and Luhmann, T. (1992) Calibration and accuracy assessment of a multi-sensor online photogrammetric system. International Archives of Photogrammetry and Remote Sensing. Commission V. Vol. XXIX, 17th ISPRS Congress, Washington, DC, pp. 24–29.
26 Strutz, T. (1993) Ein genaues aktives optisches Triangulationsverfahren zur Oberflächenvermessung. Thesis. Magdeburg Technical University.
27 Putze, T. (2005) Geometric modelling and calibration of a virtual four-headed high speed camera-mirror system for 3-d motion analysis applications. Optical 3D Measurement Techniques VII, Vol. 2, Vienna, Austria, 2005, pp. 167–174.
28 Fryer, J. (1989) Camera calibration in non-topographic photogrammetry, in *Handbook of Non-Topographic Photogrammetry*, 2nd edn, American Society of Photogrammetry and Remote Sensing, pp. 51–69.
29 Abdel-Aziz, Y.J. and Karara, H.M. (1971) Direct linear transformation from comparator coordinates into object space coordinates in close-range photogrammetry. Symposium of the American Society of Photogrammetry on Close-Range Photogrammetry, Falls Church, VA.
30 Bopp, H. and Kraus, H. (1978) Ein Orientierungs- und Kalibrierungsverfahren für nichttopographische Anwendungen der Photogrammetrie. Allgemeine Vermessungs-Nachrichten (AVN) 5/87, pp. 182–188.
31 Förstner, W. (2000) New orientation procedures. International Archives of Photogrammetry and Remote Sensing 3A, 19th ISPRS Congress, Amsterdam, Netherlands, pp. 297–304.
32 VDI (2000) *Optische 3D-Messsysteme. VDI/VDE-Richtlinie 2634, Blatt 1-2*, Beuth Verlag, Berlin.
33 Luhmann, T. and Wendt, K. (2000) Recommendations for an acceptance and verification test of optical 3D measurement systems. International Archives of Photogrammetry and Remote Sensing, Vol. 33/5, 19th ISPRS Congress, Amsterdam, Netherlands, pp. 493–499.
34 AICON (2015) www.aicon3d.com (accessed 08 December 2015).
35 Breuckmann, B. (1993) *Bildverarbeitung und Optische Messtechnik in der industriellen Praxis*, Franzis Verlag, München.
36 Breuckmann, B. (2014) 25 years of high definition 3D scanning: history, state of the art, outlook. 2014 Proceedings of the EVA London 2014 on Electronic Visualisation and the Arts, London, UK, pp. 262–266.
37 Luhmann, T. (2002) *Nahbereichsphotogrammetrie in der Praxis – Beispiele und Problemlösungen*, Wichmann Verlag, Heidelberg.
38 Luhmann, T. (2014) *Close-Range Photogrammetry and 3D Imaging*, 2nd edn, Walter de Gruyter, Berlin, Boston, MA.

WILEY

Light at Work

PhotonicsViews.com
The international news platform for industry and research in
- Optics
- Photonics
- Laser Technology

PhotonicsViews.com

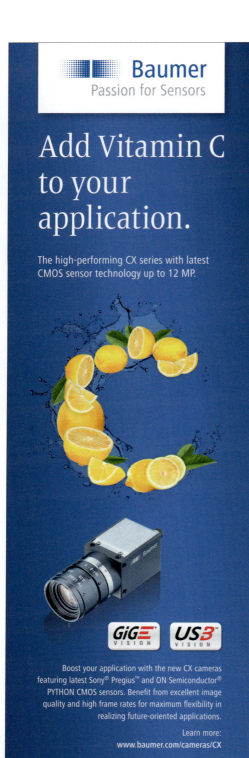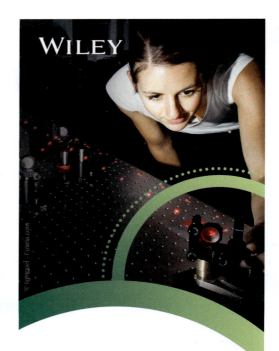

6

Camera Systems in Machine Vision
Horst Mattfeldt

MATRIX VISION, Talstrasse 16, 71570 Oppenweiler, Germany

6.1 Camera Technology

6.1.1 History in Brief

Historically, the mechanical scanning of two-dimensional images by rotating disk with spiral holes (Figure 6.1) (by Paul Nipkow of Berlin) was overcome in the early 1930s by electronic scanning methods with the help of electron tubes.

Manfred von Ardenne and Vladimir Zworykin were the first to demonstrate "television" (Figure 6.2).

Scanning and amplifying tubes dominated until they were smoothly replaced by transistors in the 1960s. First the amplifiers became solid state.

The invention of integrated circuits then in the 1970s led to the development of a silicon scanning technology.

Firstly, CCDs (charge couple devices, to be explained later), became popular in the early 1970s and, at the time of writing, still have a relatively high market share in terms of units sold of ~20% in the machine vision market and 10% in the global sensor market (according to http://info.adimec.com/blogposts/bid/39656/CCD-vs-CMOS-Image-Sensors-in-Machine-Vision-Cameras).

In the past 10 years, there has been a second popular technique gaining ground for image sensors, based on CMOS (complementary metal oxide semiconductor) technology, showing a high momentum of technological innovation.

Almost every camera that we use today in our electronic lifestyle is based on CMOS imagers.

At the time of writing, SONY announced that it will stop producing CCDs in the year 2025.

6.1.2 Machine Vision versus Closed Circuit TeleVision (CCTV)

First let us try to differentiate a machine vision camera from a standard (Closed circuit Television → CCTV) camera.

- Mechanically, a machine vision camera preferably does not have an integrated lens but a standardized adapter with a distance of 17.526 mm (12.5 mm in the

Figure 6.1 Nipkow Scheibe. (BR-online.)

Figure 6.2 Video camera in the mid-1930s. (BR-online.)

case of a CS-Mount) from sensor to thread (called *C-Mount*) to put different characteristic lenses on.
- The housing should be robust and equipped with various mounting possibilities so that it can be coupled very flexibly with the housing machine or equipment.
- The connectors should be standardized and lockable.
- Electrically it should accept external synchronization as well as internal operation.
- It should work in continuous modes but it should also accept external trigger/strobing so that the image output can be synchronized to moving objects.
- It should be quick enough to follow the trigger frequency in the case of higher speed application.
- Electrical parameters, like mode or gain and exposure time (electronic shutter) should be changeable, either by potentiometer and DIP-switches or preferably by software.
- Image output must be stable with no amplitude fading or weakening or image jitter over time and temperature.
- Preferably, the machine vision camera should digitize the image in the camera itself and output the video signal as a digital stream of numbers to achieve a pixel- synchronous representation of the image pixel in the computer memory.
- Generally, machine vision cameras do not compress the image (by means of algorithms such as JPEG or MPEG or H264) to reduce the amount of data to be transmitted.

Thus we see that there is not one dominating criterion but a smooth gradation from a machine vision to a CCTV camera. The latter will benefit from the ability to output the best image, no matter what lighting and ambient conditions (at day/night, sunlight).

This imposes an enormous challenge on automatic image control loops in the camera, on the capabilities of the sensor itself, and on the use of special lenses, whereas a machine vision camera works preferably under controlled lighting environment.

This is true even with the most recent advances in adaptive machine vision algorithms able to compensate for lighting changes.

Sometimes based on requirements, machine vision applications can use economical CCTV (board level) cameras; but generally the more demanding the application, the higher the request for a true machine vision camera.

6.2 Sensor Technologies

The essential and most important part of a camera is the sensor, which is used for the generation of the image. Trivial? The sensor is the eye of the camera.

The camera's eye has the task of capturing the image and translating it into information, which can either be preprocessed in the camera, or transmitted to a host and processed and displayed on a monitor.

This is of course easier said than done: The human eye uses

- a spatially ultrahigh resolution, and
- a parallel (nontemporally scanning) image capturing scheme,

which is by far too complicated to be copied even with today's technology.

Thus, the compromises for "industrial eyes" are the following:

- Limited resolution in pixels (picture elements) for both spatial dimensions (preferably with equal spacing ($\rightarrow$ square pixels)).
- Scanning temporally with defined frames per second suitable to follow the motion of the object or the changes of the objects.
- Serialization of the sensor's pixel output, be it analog or digital.

6.2.1 Spatial Differentiation: 1D and 2D

Here we first discriminate between one-dimensional and two-dimensional image sensors.

The 1D sensor is a line sensor, whereas a 2D is an area sensor (consequently, a light barrier should be named a 0D sensor!).

Although an image is two-dimensional, having a discrete height and width, one can also think of it in terms of an endless image having only a defined width but unknown or unlimited height.

An example for the latter is an image of a wooden board, whose height varies with the height of the tree it is being cut off from.

A line image sensor will be advantageous here because it will scan the width of the image line by line while the wooden board is moved (preferably with constant or known velocity!) under the optics. The wooden board's end also limits the height of the image.

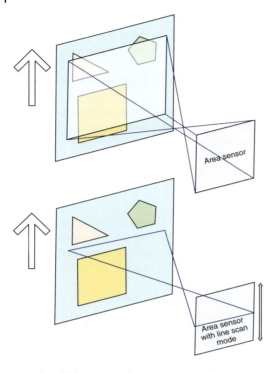

Figure 6.3 Switching between area scan and line scan mode.

It should be noted that with new advances in CMOS sensor technology, sensors that can be switched between line scan and area scan mode are available, such as the EV76C560 from the company E2V.

The image in Figure 6.3 highlights these modes to the extent that it is even possible to select the line that is used in line scan mode.

Because line scan cameras expose and read out per line (whereas area scan cameras expose all lines at the same time and then read out the lines) they require much more light (and/or would need bigger pixels) to collect more photons if a high line rate is required. Line scan cameras are not detailed further due to their lower market importance though.

6.2.2 CCD Technology

CCDs, invented by American Bell laboratories in the 1960s (for analog storage and shift registers!) became the dominant scanning device because silicon is also light sensitive.

In a CCD, the photo effect is used to generate electrons out of photons, this charge is collected and held in virtual tiny buckets forming individual picture elements (pixels). Using various gating clocks it is possible to move this charge serially toward the output of the device (usually one), where it is converted into a current or voltage.

Currently, SONY of Japan and ON Semiconductor (formerly Truesense, formerly KODAK) of USA are important CCD manufacturers in terms of volume, followed by a few others.

The technology for 2D image sensors, adopted by these various manufacturers, has emerged and diversified into various technological and architectural substructures.

The differences arise in the way the lines are scanned and charge storage is handled and outputted.

Each substructure will be explained shortly with its main advantages and disadvantages, which are summarized from the machine vision point of view as follows:

- Full frame
- Frame transfer sensor.

While the above two principles are of importance for scientific cameras, the latter principles are widely used in machine vision and described in more detail.

- *Interline transfer*
  - Interlaced scan interline transfer
  - Progressive scan interline transfer.

6.2.2.1 Interline Transfer

Interline technology splits into two subcategories, depending on the way the lines are read out:

- Progressive scan readout
- Interlaced scan readout
  - Field integration
  - Frame integration.

6.2.2.2 Progressive Scan Interline Transfer

Progressive scan is straightforward but nevertheless, it is the latest development in CCD: Each light sensitive pixel has its storage companion, which again reduces the fill factor and sensitivity a bit, but there are sophisticated microlenses to compensate for this drawback. With the shift pulse the charge of each pixel in each line is transferred, making the time between two shift pulses the frame time and usually also the shutter time. Most progressive scan sensors have square pixels, which enables an easy transformation between pixel count and distance measurement without x–y calibration.

The picture illustrates the principle: In each picture each pixel's storage can be placed (with the charge transfer command) into the respective vertical storage register, which can hold the charge of all lines (Figure 6.4).

Very advantageous here is the fact, that after a shift command, the sensor pixel can be kept in a reset state so that the integration can start (virtually the shutter can be electronically opened) by a control signal. This gives control over the integration time, so that

- moving objects do not blur (more light is needed!);
- moving objects are shuttered precisely from image to image at the same position and are not "jumping";

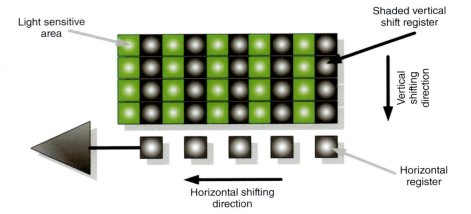

Figure 6.4 Progressive scan interline transfer.

- auto shutter can be built so that the image brightness becomes less dependent on the illumination.

Pro: Electronic (asynchronous) shutter
Suitable for stationary and moving industrial applications
No flash needed
No mechanical/LCD-shutter.

Con: Lower fill factor
Lower sensitivity (microlenses improve this feature)
Lower IR sensitivity.

6.2.2.3 Interlaced Scan Readout

Interlaced is still the standard video technology in use for more than 70 years.

Interlaced stands for the fact that an image is scanned and displayed consecutively by two half images called *fields* where one field displays the odd lines, and the other displays the even lines, simply because at the beginning it was not possible to speed up with all lines and frame rates. The first field, drawn in solid black starts with half-a-line, whereas the second field (dashed) starts with a full line (Figure 6.5).

The flyback (of the electron beam of the CRT or tube) is drawn in gray. The vertical flyback is shown in principle; it actually goes zigzag, because it takes more line times.

While the above description explains the historical aspects of interlaced scanning the advantage on the CCD architecture is mainly that it requires only one vertical shift register element per two pixel elements.

6.2.2.3.1 Field Integration
This mode combines the charge of two vertical pixels.

Usually one-chip complementary color cameras must (and b/w color cameras can) add the content of two adjacent lines together to derive the color information (and to increase the sensitivity).

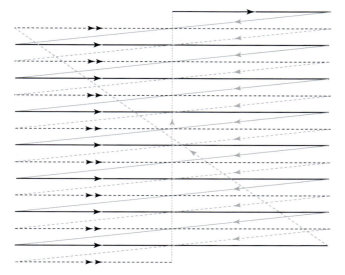

Figure 6.5 Interlaced scanning scheme.

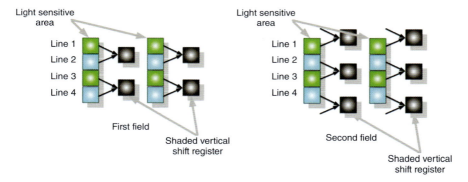

Figure 6.6 Interlaced sensor with field integration.

In the first field, for example, line one and two are added, while in the second field, two and three are added as shown in Figure 6.6.

With this field integration mode it is also possible to benefit from an electronic shutter.

The drawback is the loss in vertical resolution because adding two lines together is also effectively a low pass filter.

6.2.2.3.2 Frame Integration The other method is called *frame integration*: The advantage is the higher vertical resolution. Because the integration of the two fields overlap, it is possible to use a flash and to freeze an image in full vertical resolution. An electronic shutter is not possible in this mode (Figure 6.7).

Depending on their horizontal resolution, interlaced sensors may have rectangular pixels dimensions (e.g., $9.8\,\mu m \times 6.3\,\mu m$), opting for high sensitivity

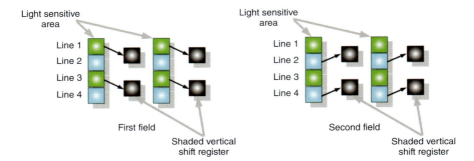

Figure 6.7 Interlaced sensor with frame integration.

Table 6.1 Summary and comparison of modes.

	Progressive scan noninterlaced	Interlaced	
		Field integration	Frame integration
Vertical resolution	Good	Lower	Good
Temporal resolution	Good	Good	Lower

but making either rescaling or calibration efforts necessary for dimensional measurement machine vision tasks.

Compare the CCD readout technologies with the help of Table 6.1.

As a conclusion, progressive scan is the best compromise for most of the applications because it is the most flexible.

Machine vision systems (frame grabber, displays) favor progressive cameras, because they make the conversion from interlaced to progressive obsolete.

6.2.2.4 Enhancing Frame Rate by Multitap Sensors

CCD sensors circuitries have limits in terms of pixel clock frequencies in the range of 60 MHz. On the other hand, it is possible to create small pixels and increase the resolution to about 30 Megapixels.

To overcome the drop in frame rate (2 fps in the above example), manufacturers use multiplex readout schemes, such as dual or quad tap readout.

An example is shown in the picture in Figure 6.8: It shows the structure of, for example, SONY ICX834 which is a 1/2/4 tap 12 Megapixels sensor achieving up to 15 fps.

It can be seen that we have now two horizontal shift registers on the top and bottom of the image. Each shift register has two output stages on the left and the right side of the image.

Either the camera or the frame grabber or the host computer needs to take care of the necessary horizontal and vertical flipping of the image quadlets, so that finally the image is correctly reconstructed.

The corresponding readout scheme is in quadlets according to the next illustration (Figure 6.9).

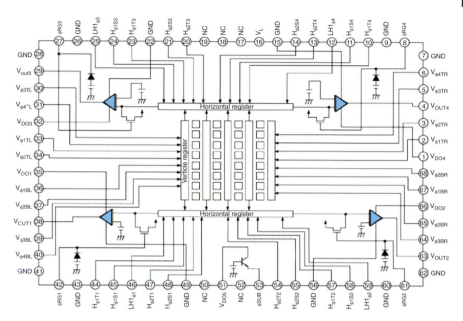

Figure 6.8 Quad tap CCD sensor (SONY).

Figure 6.9 Tap arrangement (shown with taps misbalanced on purpose).

It should be also noted that although there are highly integrated multi analog front end (AFE) circuitries available, the power consumption of a quad tap image head will be higher and it needs a careful analog/digital gain/offset adjustment tap balance to make the tap borders invisible.

6.2.2.5 SONY HAD Technology

HAD (hole accumulation diode) is a SONY term for the silicon structure of the CCD.

The image in Figure 6.10 (by SONY) illustrates the concept: Note that microlenses on top of each pixel focus the light, such that it is concentrated on the light sensitive part but not hitting the transfer section, which considerably enhances the sensitivity.

6.2.2.6 SONY SuperHAD (II) and ExViewHAD (II) Technology

These terms stand for improvements in the structure of the lens, so that a higher sensitivity both in visible and IR (ExView) regions are achieved.

The image (by SONY) shows the differences (Figure 6.11).

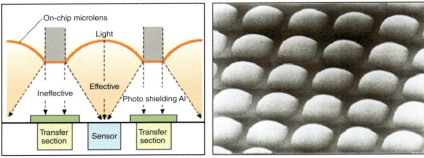

Figure 6.10 HAD principle of SONY CCD sensors. (Courtesy by SONY.)

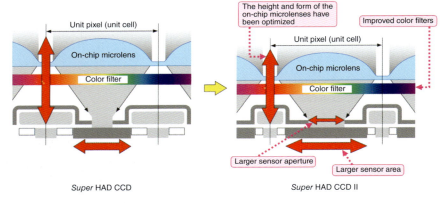

Figure 6.11 Super HAD (II) principle of SONY CCD sensors. (Courtesy by SONY.)

6.2.2.7 CCD Image Artifacts

Although this technology has been specially optimized over decades for perfect image generation, it may suffer from some general image artifacts.

6.2.2.8 Blooming

When a CCD gets excessively saturated by extremely bright objects, it may show blooming. This is when the charge cannot be held at an individual pixel's place but floods over the array (Figure 6.12).

6.2.2.9 Smear

Smear can be seen as a vertical line, usually above and under a bright spot in an image. This is due to "cross talk" of electrons moving from the pixel to the vertical shift register, while the image is shifted out (Figure 6.13).

Smear is affected by the ratio of the readout time versus the shutter (integration) time.

Short shutter times and/or long readout times increase smear.

Figure 6.12 Blooming due to excessive sunlight hitting the CCD sensor.

Figure 6.13 Smear of CCD image sensor due to bright spot.

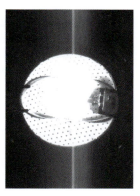

The following two methods are helpful for reducing smear:

Using of mechanical shutters can block the light after the exposure time, while the image is shifted. Alternatively, the use of a flash is recommended so that it dominates over the ambient light.

Multitap sensors identify themselves in the way they are susceptible to smear: A bright spot in the top half: smear goes to the top (due to the direction the image is shifted out); bright spot in the bottom half: Smear goes to the bottom (Figure 6.14).

Figure 6.14 Dual tap sensor smear appearance.

6.2.3 CMOS Image Sensor

CMOS image sensors are newer although the underlying technology is not new. Only the use of CMOS silicon for imaging purposes has seen a lot of progress over the past decade.

The basic principle is also the photovoltaic effect. While the CCD holds and moves the charge per pixel to one (or more) output amplifier(s), the CMOS sensor usually converts the charge to voltage already in the pixel (Voltage domain pixel). By crossbar addressing and switching, the voltage can be read out of the sensing area.

The two technologies are compared in Table 6.2.

Recently SONY introduced a charge domain CMOS pixel architecture which integrates some CCD technology elements in CMOS sensors, resulting in very high dynamic range and very low dark noise.

6.2.3.1 Advantages of CMOS Sensor

Because CMOS is basically used in digital circuits, it is obvious that analog to digital conversion, addressing, windowing, gain and offset adjustments, and smart preprocessing functions can be easily added to the chip, aiming for the ultimate goal of a camera on a chip.

Surveillance cameras are already reaching this goal, but machine vision is a few steps behind. A higher level of integration is one aim; lower power consumption (a 3rd to a 10th) is the other.

6.2.3.1.1 High Dynamic Range (HDR) By using variable logarithmic photodiodes (LinLog™ Photonfocus) or multiple reset thresholds (knee points) some manufacturers, such as OnSEmi, CMOSIS, E2V can achieve up to 120 dB (compared to 60–80 dB for CCD) in intra-scene dynamic range.

The graph (by MATRIX VISION) of the signal level output versus total integration time shows the behavior of two knee points (Figure 6.15).

The thresholds S1 and S2 are configured at 33% and 66% relative brightness.

Table 6.2 CCD versus CMOS comparison by OnSemi (formerly Cypress/FillFactory).

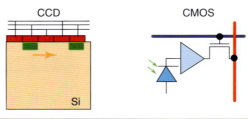

	CCD	CMOS
Photodetection	Buried diode	Photodiode
Technology	Nonstandard	Standard
Charge conversion	At output	In pixel
Readout	Changed transfer	Voltage multiplexing
Supply and biasing	Multiple supplies needed	Single supply

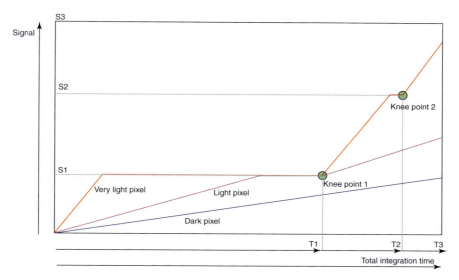

Figure 6.15 Integration time for different light pixels with two knee points for an OnSemi MT9V034 sensor.

A very light pixel (red) reaches threshold S1 early within exposure time period 1 and is clipped there.

For the second and much shorter integration time T2 (~4% of total) the very bright pixel also reaches limit S2.

A light pixel (purple) reaches the limit S1 later in time but does not reach limit S2; whereas a darker pixel (blue) does not reach S1 at all.

Within the very short period T3 (~1% of total) all three pixels reach their final signal level.

The result of this process is that the very light pixel requires 100 times higher brightness to reach final signal compared to linear, representing at least a 20 dB high dynamic range (HDR).

The resulting sensitivity shows these two knee points at the set signal levels (Figure 6.16).

The next screenshot shows a practical example, taken with USB2 camera mvBlueFOX-200W using viewer program mvPropView (Figure 6.17).

Please note that exposure times can only be changed in line length units resulting in wavy response.

Figure 6.18 shows an image in linear mode on the left and another image with one additional knee point to increase the intra-scene dynamic on the right.

6.2.3.1.2 Readout Schemes and Effects on Windowing (Area of Interest) and Frame Rate

There are basically two readout architectures for CMOS sensors:

The conventional one uses a column/row addressing scheme for reading out the active pixel array (via correlated double sampling (CDS) stages) into one ADC (Analog Digital Converter).

As a positive side effect, these sensors usually increase their frame rate by reading out fewer pixels both in the vertical and horizontal dimension.

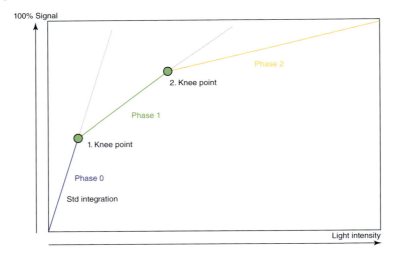

Figure 6.16 Nonlinear response curve with two knee points for an OnSemi MT9V034 sensor.

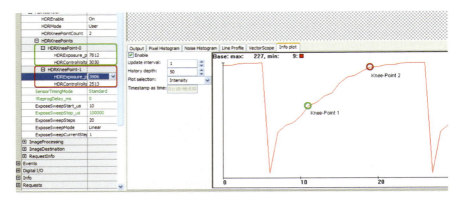

Figure 6.17 Practical response curve with two knee points for an OnSemi MT9V034 sensor.

The consequence is that the ADC has to run at pixel frequency, which may limit conversion accuracy to usually 10 bit while still generating high frequency sideband noise.

A typical architecture (according to a technical paper of SONY) is shown in Figure 6.19.

6.2.3.1.3 Column Parallel Readout Schemes A typical architecture (according to a technical paper of SONY) is shown in Figure 6.20.

We have now as many ADCs as we have columns. This reduces the conversion speed to line frequency enabling "simpler" yet more accurate ADC conversion techniques and also shifting ADC noise spectrum drastically to lower frequencies.

The general concept of using multiplexed LVDS (low voltage differential signaling) output channels (up to 32 output channels) makes it possible to achieve an

Figure 6.18 High dynamic range mode with one knee point.

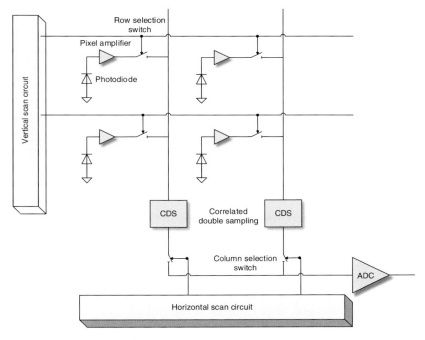

Figure 6.19 Conventional CMOS readout architecture (according to SONY).

extremely high pixel rate of more than 8 Gigapixel s^{-1} with frame rates of several 1000 fps.

This makes CMOS sensors very qualified for high-speed imaging systems.

6.2.3.2 CMOS Sensor Shutter Concepts

Every pixel of a CMOS imager consists of several transistors.

A pixel is called *active* (APS) when it comes combined with an amplifier. It needs a minimum of three transistors for an APS. In machine vision, it is useful to have an electronic shutter.

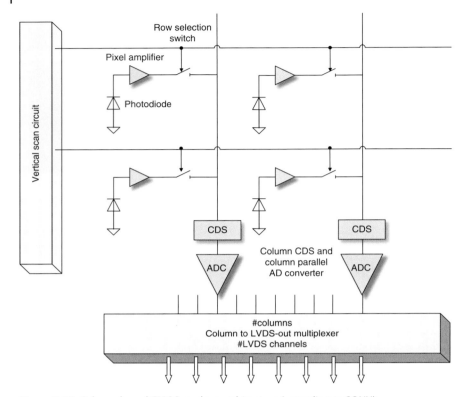

Figure 6.20 Column-based CMOS readout architecture (according to SONY).

Even with the simplest three-transistor pixel it is possible to have an electronic shutter in the so-called rolling (curtain) shutter architecture (see Figure 6.21). The image is reset line by line a configurable time before reading the respective line. The time difference between resetting and reading is the integration or shutter (or exposure) time.

This may be perfect for stationary applications, but it can introduce severe artifacts for moving applications, as can be seen in Figure 6.22.

On the right the blades of the fan are scanned by a rolling shutter creating extreme deformation to them, while on the left they have been scanned with a global (synchronous for all pixels or snapshot) shutter.

The left image also shows the effect of Photonfocus' LinLogtechnology to enhance the dynamic range.

A variant of the rolling shutter pixel architecture enables a global reset for all pixels, followed by the readout in a consecutive manner.

This is called *Global Reset Release Shutter* (Figure 6.23).

Integration time in this mode is the sum of blue and red time and is, therefore, different for every row.

Using a flash in the blue period, it is possible to freeze an image with no rolling shutter artifacts, assuming that ambient light is not an issue or a mechanical shutter is used to close the light after the flash.

6.2 Sensor Technologies | 333

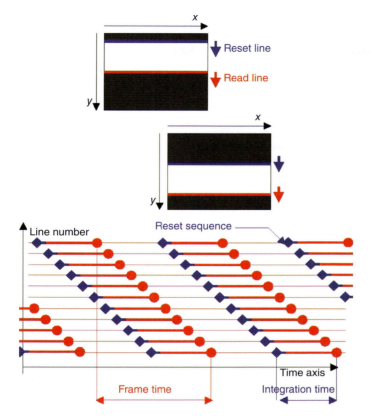

Figure 6.21 Rolling shutter visualization (by OnSemi).

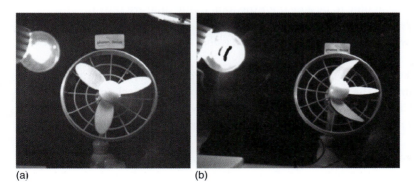

Figure 6.22 Rolling shutter (b) versus global shutter (a). (Courtesy by Photonfocus.)

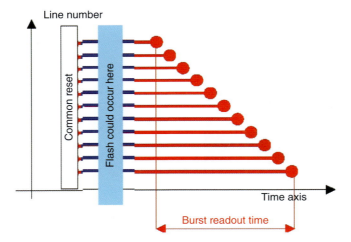

Figure 6.23 Global reset release schematics (OnSemi).

The need for a true global shutter makes at least a fourth transistor necessary for the global resetting of every pixel. With every additional transistor potentially reducing the fill factor (the ratio between the photodiode area vs the total pixel area) as a side effect, sensitivity may decrease or structural fixed pattern noise (FPN) may increase. The next image shows the structure of one of the first sensors with a global shutter, the IBIS5 pixel by FillFactory (Figure 6.24).

Even with this four transistor cell, in global shutter mode, the sensor can either integrate or readout at a time. This possibility has a clear impact on the achievable frame rate that will go down when the shutter time goes up. This is explained in Figure 6.25 where the constant frame readout time in red and the variable integration time in blue to be added for the total frame time are shown.

The *interleaving* of integration of a new frame, while reading out the actual one, possible with a CCD, also called *pipelined global shutter*, again requires additional circuitry.

To make things even more complicated, other important sensor performance aspects impact the sensor pixel design such as reducing pixel noise (reset noise, FPN by CDS or dual CDS) and the goal to achieve a good *global shutter efficiency* (or a low *parasitic light sensitivity*) while maintaining high sensitivity.

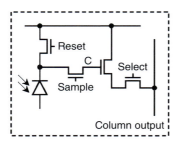

Figure 6.24 Active pixel structure (by Cypress/FillFactory).

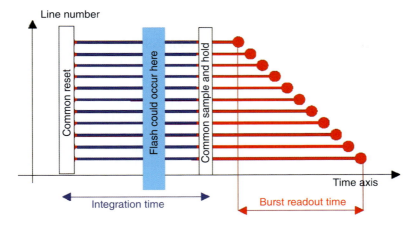

Figure 6.25 Serialization of integration and readout (OnSemi).

Shutter efficiency describes how well the sensor is able to keep ambient light from integrating after the electronic shutter is closed.

This is especially important at short exposure times and high ambient light situations.

A sensor, which is not applicable for an application, may present blurred moving contours or a vertical gradient with increasing FPN due to saturation effects in the pixel memory.

A brute force test can be executed by pointing a (CMOS-) camera without a lens toward an appropriate light source and simultaneously closing its electronic shutter (exposure) register as much as possible.

Assuming that one could close the shutter to say 10 µs or even less and one gets a dark image, the PLS is high.

Sensors with worse PLS showing artifacts in this test can be used in flash light applications with less ambient light outside the flash.

At the time of writing the technical progress led to several different pixel designs with as much as eight transistors per pixel plus two voltage-based sample and hold stages in the form of capacitors (C1 and C2) at company CMOSIS.

This pixel architecture is shown in Figure 6.26.

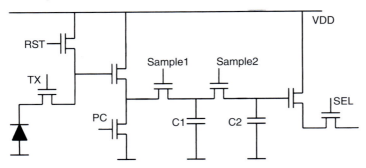

Figure 6.26 CMV2000/4000 pixel architecture (by CMOSIS).

This results in the highest frame rate and shutter efficiency with a good sensitivity and low noise. SONY, as mentioned, invented a charge-based pipelined global shutter pixel (called *Pregius*™) with the focus on extremely low noise and highest full well capacity resulting in a CCD- like performance in terms of dynamic range and also very high speed with 6.5 transistors per pixel.

6.2.3.3 Performance Comparison of CMOS versus CCD

While in the past there was a clear difference in image performance, it is no longer true today. It is believed that CMOS can cope with CCD and overhaul in terms of frame rate, so it will become the dominating sensor technology in the future.

Table 6.3 highlights some important performance figures. Details on how to achieve these figures are explained in this chapter.

6.2.3.4 Integration Complexity of CCD versus CMOS Camera Technology

One clear advantage of CMOS technology is the higher level of integration.

With CMOS it is possible to integrate

- The AFE (Analog Front End) preprocessing functionality,
- The timing generator on the sensor,
- The ADC.

achieving more compact solutions with less power consumption.

This integration is depicted in Figure 6.27.

On the left you see that a CCD camera has most of the building blocks separate, whereas on the right the blocks are part of the CMOS sensor itself.

Today, modern CMOS sensors differ by their built-in preprocessing (smart) functions, so it is worth trying to get a data sheet of the sensor and see what features of the sensor found its way in the camera that you are interested in.

Table 6.3 Comparison of sensor performance data.

Manufacturer	OnSemi	E2V	CMOSIS	SONY	SONY	SONY
Type	M021	76C560	CMV2000	IMX174	ICX445	ICX674
Technology	CMOS	CMOS	CMOS	CMOS	CCD	CCD
Pixel size (µm)	3.75	5.3	5.5	5.9	3.75	4.5
Trans./pixel[a]	5?	5	8	6.5	na	na
Resolution ($H \times V$)	1280 × 960	1280 × 1024	2048 × 1088	1920 × 1214	1280 × 960	1936 × 1460
Full well	5300e$^-$	9600e	9800e	32 000e	9600e	15 400e
Dynamic (dB)	55	53 (GS)	57	73.5	61	60.5
SNR (dB)	37	40	40	45	40	42
Dark noise	8e$^-$	21e$^-$	13e$^-$	6e$^-$	7.7e$^-$	14e$^-$
PLS[a]	1 : <300	1 : 3000[b]	1 : 50 000	1 : 48 000	Smear?	Smear?
Frame rate	45	60	340	164	22/31	64
Relative price[c]	1	2.5	10	9	2	22

a) Data from manufacturer.
b) http://image-sensors-world.blogspot.de/2009/09/e2v-launches-13mp-cmos-sensor.html.
c) Volume sensor price.

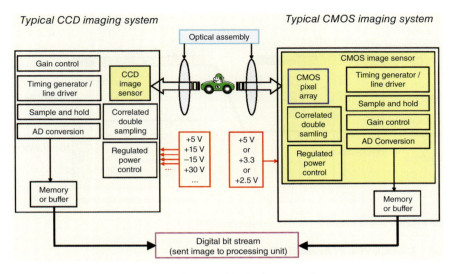

Figure 6.27 CCD and CMOS camera building blocks (by OnSemi).

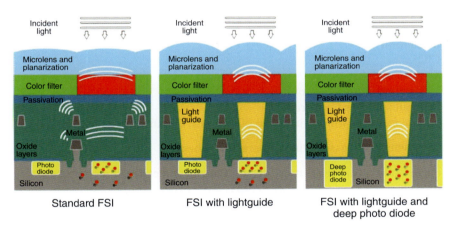

Figure 6.28 Sensitivity enhancements using standard front side illumination structures (by OnSemi).

6.2.3.5 CMOS Sensor Sensitivity Enhancements

Several different strategies are required to increase sensitivity with shrinking pixel size.

OnSemi's Aptina, sensors use light guides to direct the light to the photodiode as the picture in Figure 6.28 shows.

On the other hand, SONY and others (e.g., OmniVision) use the so-called back side illumination (BSI) structure to achieve the same goal.

The image in Figure 6.29 depicts this structure.

At the time of writing, no BSI CMOS sensor with global shutter was available.

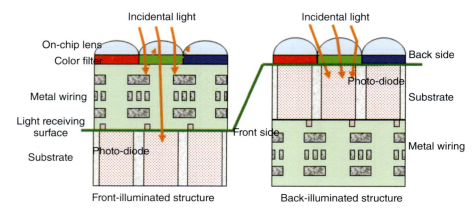

Figure 6.29 FSI and BSI structure comparison (by SONY).

6.2.4 MATRIX VISION Available Cameras

See Table 6.4.

6.2.4.1 Why So Many Different Models? How to Choose Among These?
Sensors differ roughly in

- Resolution
- Chip size
- Sensitivity
- Spectral response: color or b/w
- Readout speed or frame rate
- Special features (windowing (area of interest), binning (sub sampling)).

Every sensor and associating camera has its best fit:

- Higher resolution shows more details, but can make the camera less sensitive (pixel is smaller) or more costly (chip is more expensive).
- Bigger pixels on the other hand have higher sensitivity and fewer pixels per image can be read out faster so that the frame rate is higher.
- It is generally recommended to make the resolution only as high as necessary.
- More pixels need usually more processing power/time.
- The effective pixel size goes along with inherent ability to collect more electrons, which is a prerequisite, together with low noise electronics, for good dynamic range, and high sensitivity.

6.2.4.2 Resolution and Video Standards
Class follows the nomenclature in the PC industry:

VGA resolution is standard and similar to EIA (RS170) TV video standard used in USA and Japan. SVGA resolution is similar to PAL (CCIR) standard used in Europe and many parts in the world. The higher resolution PC standards have no analog in TV standards and can be used further with varying frame frequencies.

Table 6.4 Cameras available from MATRIX Vision.

Product	Interface	Resolution	FPS	Type	Gray/color	Size (in.)	Sensor	Trigger-shutter
mvBlueFOX Family								
BF-(M)120	USB 2.0	640 × 480	60	CCD	G/C	1/4	Sony ICX098	Pipel. global
BF-(M)120a	USB 2.0	640 × 480	100	CCD	G/C	1/3	Sony ICX424	Pipel. global
BF-(M)121	USB 2.0	1024 × 768	39	CCD	G/C	1/3	Sony ICX204	Pipel. global
BF-(M)123	USB 2.0	1360 × 1024	20	CCD	G/C	1/2	Sony ICX267	Pipel. global
BF-(M)124	USB 2.0	1600 × 1200	16	CCD	G/C	1/1.8	Sony ICX274	Pipel. global
BF-(M)100w	USB 2.0	752 × 480	90	CMOS	G/C	1/3	OnSemi MT9V034	Global
BF-(M)102a	USB 2.0	1280 × 1024	25	CMOS	G	1/2	OnSemi MT9M001	Rolling
BF-(M)105	USB 2.0	2592 × 1944	5.8	CMOS	G/C	1/2.5	OnSemi MT9P031	Rolling/GRR
BF-ML/IGC200w	USB 2.0	752 × 480	90	CMOS	G/C	1/3	OnSemi MT9V034	Global
BF-ML/IGC202a	USB 2.0	1280 × 1024	25	CMOS	G	1/2	OnSemi MT9M001	Rolling
BF-ML/IGC202b	USB 2.0	1280 × 960	24.6	CMOS	G/C	1/3	OnSemi MT9M021	Global
BF-ML/IGC202d	USB 2.0	1280 × 960	24.6	CMOS	G/C	1/3	OnSemi MT9M034	Rolling
BF-ML/IGC205	USB 2.0	2592 × 1944	5.8	CMOS	G/C	1/2.5	OnSemi MT9P031	Rolling/GRR

(continued overleaf)

Table 6.4 (Continued)

Product	Interface	Resolution	FPS	Type	Gray/color	Size (in.)	Sensor	Trigger-shutter
mvBlueCOUGAR-X Family (GigE Vision compliant)								
BC-X120a	GigE	640 × 480	104	CCD	G/C	1/3	Sony ICX424	Pipel. global
BC-X120b	GigE	640 × 480	104	CCD	G/C	1/2	Sony ICX414	Pipel. global
BC-X120d	GigE	776 × 580	87	CCD	G/C	1/2	Sony ICX415	Pipel. global
BC-X122	GigE	1280 × 960	31	CCD	G/C	1/3	Sony ICX445	Pipel. global
BC-X123	GigE	1360 × 1024	30	CCD	G/C	1/2	Sony ICX445	Pipel. global
BC-X124	GigE	1600 × 1200	28	CCD	G/C	1/1.8	Sony ICX274	Pipel. global
BC-X125a	GigE	2448 × 2050	10	CCD	G/C	2/3	Sony ICX655	Pipel. global
BC-X225	GigE	2448 × 2050	16	CCD	G/C	2/3	Sony ICX625	Pipel. global
BC-X100w	GigE	752 × 480	117	CMOS	G/C	1/3	OnSemi MT9V034	Global
BC-X102b	GigE	1280 × 960	40.6	CMOS	G/C	1/3	OnSemi MT9M021	Global
BC-X102d	GigE	1280 × 960	40.6	CMOS	G/C	1/3	OnSemi MT9M034	Rolling
BC-X102e	GigE	1280 × 1024	60	CMOS	G/C	1/1.8	e2v EV76C560	Global
BC-X102eGE	GigE	1280 × 1024	60	CMOS	G (IR)	1/1.8	e2v EV76C661	Global
BC-X104	GigE	2048 × 1088	34.8	CMOS	G/C	2/3	CMOSIS CMV2000	Pipel. global
BC-X104b	GigE	2048 × 2048	18.5	CMOS	G/C	1	CMOSIS CMV4000	Pipel. global
BC-X104e	GigE	1600 × 1200	41.4	CMOS	G/C	1/1.8	e2v EV76C570	Pipel. global
BC-X104f	GigE	1936 × 1214	41	CMOS	G/C	1/1.2	Sony IMX249	Pipel. global

Model	Interface	Resolution		Type		Size	Sensor	Shutter
BC-X105	GigE	2592 × 1944	14.4	CMOS	G/C	1/2.5	OnSemi MT9P031	Rolling/GRR
BC-X1010	GigE	3856 × 2764	8.7	CMOS	G/C	1/2.3	OnSemi MT9J003	Rolling/GRR
mvBlueCOUGAR-XD Family (GigE Vision compliant)								
BC-XD104	Dual GigE	2048 × 1088	270	CMOS	G/C	2/3	CMOSIS CMV2000	Pipel. global
BC-XD204	Dual GigE	2048 × 1088	52	CMOS	G/C	2/3	CMOSIS CMV2000	Pipel. global
BC-XD104a12	Dual GigE	2048 × 1088	270	CMOS	G (IR)	2/3	CMV2000-2E12	Pipel. global
BC-XD104b	Dual GigE	2048 × 2048	140	CMOS	G/C	1	CMOSIS CMV4000	Pipel. global
BC-XD204b	Dual GigE	2048 × 2048	27	CMOS	G/C	1	CMOSIS CMV4000	Pipel. global
BC-XD104d	Dual GigE	1936 × 1214	128	CMOS	G/C	1/1.2	Sony IMX174	Pipel. global
BC-XD124a	Dual GigE	1936 × 1460	64.5	CCD	G/C	2/3	Sony ICX674	Pipel. global
BC-XD126	Dual GigE	2752 × 2208	33	CCD	G/C	1	Sony ICX694	Pipel. global
BC-XD126a	Dual GigE	2752 × 2208	16.5	CCD	G/C	1	Sony ICX695	Pipel. global
BC-XD129	Dual GigE	3384 × 2712	22.2	CCD	G/C	1	Sony ICX814	Pipel. global
BC-XD129a	Dual GigE	3384 × 2712	11.2	CCD	G/C	1	Sony ICX815	Pipel. global

(continued overleaf)

Table 6.4 (Continued)

Product	Interface	Resolution	FPS	Type	Gray/color	Size (in.)	Sensor	Trigger-shutter
BC-XD1212	Dual GigE	4250 × 2838	15	CCD	G/C	1	Sony ICX834	Pipel. global
BC-XD1212a	Dual GigE	4250 × 2838	9	CCD	G/C	1	Sony ICX834	Pipel. global
mvBlueFOX3 Family (USB3 Vision compliant)								
BF3-(M)1012b	USB 2/3.0	1280 × 960	45	CMOS	G/C	1/3	OnSemi MT9M031	Global
BF3-(M)1012d	USB 2/3.0	1280 × 960	45	CMOS	G/C	1/3	OnSemi MT9M034	Rolling
BF3-(M)1013	USB 2/3.0	1280 × 1024	60	CMOS	G/C	1/1.8	e2v EV76C560	Global
BF3-(M)1013GE	USB 2/3.0	1280 × 1024	60	CMOS	G	1/1.8	e2v EV76C661	Global
BF3-(M)1020	USB 2/3.0	1600 × 1200	51.7	CMOS	G/C	1/1.8	e2v EV76C570	Global
BF3-(M)1020a	USB 2/3.0	1600 × 1200	60	CMOS	G/C	1/1.8	e2v EV76C570	Global
BF3-(M)1031	USB 2/3.0	2048 × 1536	21	CMOS	C	1/3	OnSemi AR0331	Rolling
BF3-(M)1100	USB 2/3.0	3856 × 2764	7.3	CMOS	G/C	1/2.3	OnSemi MT9J003	Rolling/GRR
BF3-2024	USB 2/3.0	1936 × 1214	163	CMOS	G/C	1/1.2	Sony IMX174	Pipel. global
BF3-2024a	USB 2/3.0	1936 × 1214	41	CMOS	G/C	1/1.2	Sony IMX249	Pipel. global
BF3-2032	USB 2/3.0	2064 × 1544	120	CMOS	G/C	1/1.8	Sony IMX252	Pipel. global
BF3-2051	USB 2/3.0	2464 × 2056	75	CMOS	G/C	2/3	Sony IMX250	Pipel. global

Table 6.5 Video class, resolution, and format aspect ratios.

			Format ratio: 5:4 (1.25:1)				
				SXGA			QSXGA
				1280 × 1024			2560 × 2048
			Format ratio: 4:3 (1.33:1) standard TV format				
		SVGA	XGA	SXGA-	SXGA+	UXGA	QXGA
QVGA	VGA	PAL (CCIR)					
320 × 240	640 × 480	768 × 576	800 × 600	1024 × 768	1280 × 960	1400 × 1050	1600 × 1200	2048 × 1536
			Format ratio: 8:5 (1.6:1)				
			WXGA	WXGA+	WSXGA+	WUXGA	WQXGA
CGA			1280 × 800	1440 × 900	1680 × 1050	1920 × 1200	2560 × 1600
320 × 200							
			Format ratio: 16:9 (1.77:1)				
			WVGA	HD 720		HD 1080	UHD (4k)
			854 × 480	1280 × 720		1920 × 1080	3840 × 2160

The next image lists most of the existing abbreviations and resolutions (Table 6.5).

On the other hand, there are sensors available which differ from this list or extend it.

6.2.4.3 Sensor Sizes and Dimensions

Sensor sizes are given mostly in fractions of inches but also in millimeters.

However that the dimension in millimeter is smaller than in inches is confusing This is (another) historic relict of the image tube days.

A tube with a diameter of half an inch, which is ~12 mm, had a usable image area of 6.4 mm × 6.8 mm, which gives a diameter of 8 mm.

Dimensions of some other common imager sizes are shown in the images in (Figure 6.30).

Aspect ratio is usually 4 × 3 ($H \times V$); other areas of interest can be created by windowing techniques in the camera, assuming the sensor supporting it, otherwise in the system.

6.3 Block Diagrams and Their Description

There is presumably no single camera for all conceivable applications, but there are (usually confusingly many) choices of different camera types and technologies.

Consequently, the intention of this chapter is to help the reader to choose a camera, which has the ideal performance and price match for the intended application.

Apart from the sensor, various types of cameras differ in the way they process and output the image data from the sensor.

Three groups of cameras were created and reference candidates for every group were chosen:

- Progressive scan analog image processing with analog output, mostly with black and white cameras

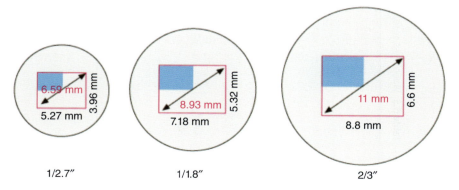

Figure 6.30 Sensor sizes.

- SONY XC-HR57/58
- Digital image processing with analog output, mostly with color cameras
  - SONY Color Camera building blocks
- Digital image processing with digital output (b/w and color)
  - Digital output to be RS422
  - USB 2.0
  - Camera link
  - Gigabit Ethernet (GigE Vision compliant)
  - USB 3.0 (USB3 Vision compliant).

Based on the data from the sensor to the output, specific blocks are needed and described in more detail in the paragraphs to follow.

The block diagrams illustrate the data paths.

6.3.1 Block Diagram of SONY Progressive Scan Analog Camera

See Figure 6.31.

6.3.1.1 CCD Read Out Clocks

This camera uses a *progressive scan* b/w CCD-sensor, which means that all lines are output consecutively in one image. (This is in contrast to the so-called *interlaced* scan sensors where odd and even lines are output in subsequent half images (fields) and interleaved with the help of the idleness of the eye or knitting facilities in the frame grabber.)

The following image with information from the SONY sensor's data sheet gives an overview (Figure 6.32).

There are separate drivers for the horizontal ($H_{\Phi 1}$, $H_{\Phi 2}$, and ΦRG) and vertical clocks ($V_{\Phi 1}$, $V_{\Phi 2}$, and $V_{\Phi 3}$) needed to drive a CCD sensor.

The charge from all pixels is shifted with the SG-pulse (a special condition of the V-pulses) into the vertical shift register (which terminates the shutter/exposure and thus separates the images).

The SG pulse occurs at a defined line count within the vertical interval but is a very short signal. After the shifting a new image exposure could immediately begin, which makes the pipelining nature a basic feature of an interline CCD. The actual exposure begin is controlled with the ΦSUB pulse, which acts as a (asynchronous) reset.

With the help of three different phased clocks, the charge is "jostled" to the horizontal shift register, which effectively holds one complete line of pixels.

This line of pixels is then moved with pixel clock frequency to the output amplifier, which is reset after every pixel.

The complete timing is controlled by an ASIC (application specific integrated circuit), called *adequately timing generator*.

6.3.1.2 CCD Binning Mode

The example camera supports vertical binning, which is done by reading out the sensor in a special shifting mode.

While the normal image readout is a sequence of

$$\text{V-Shift} \rightarrow \text{H-Shift} \rightarrow \text{V-Shift},$$

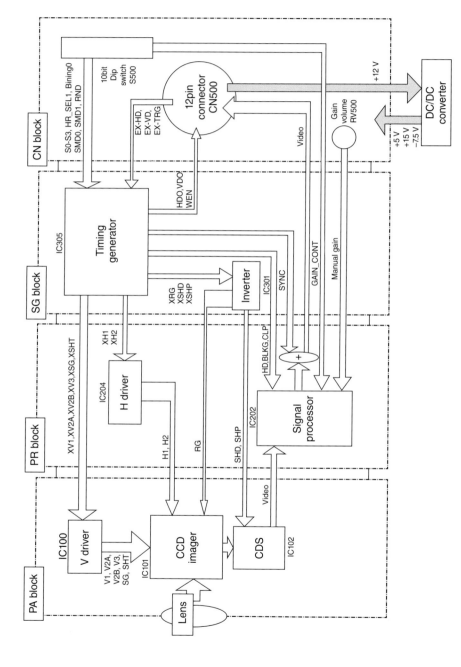

Figure 6.31 Block Diagram of SONY Progressive Scan Analog Camera.

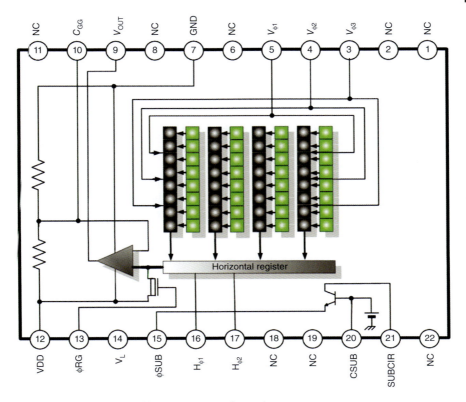

Figure 6.32 SONY ICX415AL sensor structural overview.

Figure 6.33 Vertical binning.

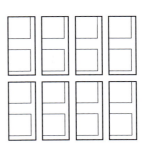

Vertical binning can be made by

V-Shift → V-Shift → H-Shift sequence.

This adds the charge of two vertically adjacent pixels together in the horizontal register, creating a vertical binning effect.

Vertical binning increases the light sensitivity of the camera by a factor of 2. At the same time, this normally improves signal to noise ratio by about 3 dB (Figure 6.33).

This almost doubles the vertical frequency but also changes the image ratio.

6 Camera Systems in Machine Vision

Vertically shifting out more than one line and finally dumping that charge away can also be used for windowing (area of interest) functionality.

Dumping is also faster, so that the frame frequency goes up as a side effect.

The data sheets of the individual cameras tell, how fast exactly for what model and what mode.

6.3.1.3 Spectral Sensitivity

The spectral sensitivity of this camera is given by the following screenshot, taken from the camera's manual. It also illustrates that there is considerable sensitivity in the IR spectrum, as well as in the UV.

In combination with the lens it can be necessary to block the IR spectrum with an IR-Cut filter so that it does not reach the sensor when the application works with the visible spectrum or to block the visible spectrum when the application works in the IR spectrum.

Although this reduces overall sensitivity it can, depending on the lens, contribute to contrast and sharpness in the image just because some lenses may need different focal adjustments for the two spectra.

Using the UV spectrum requires special (and rather expensive) UV lenses, made of quartz glass and is nevertheless limited by the cover glass of the sensor, which would have to be removed with extraordinary diligence (Figure 6.34).

It should be noted that generally the signal of a CCD-imager is an analog signal in terms of levels; it is discrete only in terms of spatial quantization in the form of pixels.

6.3.1.4 Analog Signal Processing

The CDS (Correlated Double Sampling) block is an important block in all CCD (and CMOS as well!) cameras and is used for the elimination of certain noise components. Description (by Analog Devices) gives a substantial explanation as shown in the picture in Figure 6.35.

By taking two different samples in time of the CCD signal, one at the reset level and one at the signal level and subtracting them, any noise source that is correlated to the two samples will be removed.

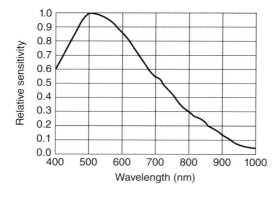

Figure 6.34 Relative spectral sensitivity of SONY XC-HR57/58, taken from a technical manual of SONY.

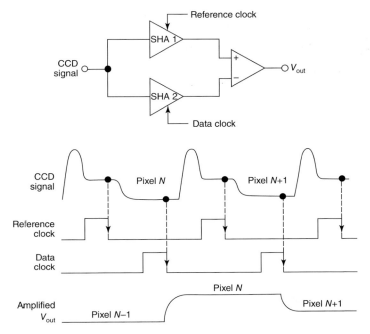

Figure 6.35 CDS processing (Analog Devices).

A slowly varying noise source that is not correlated will be reduced in magnitude. Noise introduced in the output stage of the CCD consists primarily of kT/C noise from the charge-sensing node, and $1/f$ and white noise from the output amplifier.

The kT/C noise from the reset switch's ON-resistance is sampled on the Sense node, where it remains until the next pixel. It will be present during both the reference and data levels, so it is correlated within 1 pixel period and will be removed by the CDS.

The CDS will also attenuate the $1/f$ noise from the output amplifier, because the frequency response of the CDS falls off with decreasing frequency. Low-frequency noise introduced prior to the CDS from power supplies and by temperature drifts will also be attenuated by the CDS. However, wideband noise introduced by the CCD will not be reduced by the CDS.

Further analog signal processing comprises low pass filtering, eliminating the pixel clock, manual and or automatic gain/shutter, and optional gamma enhancement, to accommodate the nonlinear display curve of some displays all of which are carried out in one single IC, significantly called the *signal processor*.

The video signal is then completed by the sync impulses and fed to a 75-Ω line driver, so that effectively one single wire carries all the information needed for (continuous) display of video.

Fed from external single 12 V DC, a low-noise DC–DC converter is used to generate the three different voltages, which are needed in this camera to drive the CCD and the glue logic.

Figure 6.36 Photo of extremely small SONY XC-ES50 camera.

Depending on the sensor, up to seven different voltages need to be generated in some CCD-cameras, making the power supply quite complex and power consumption an issue.

6.3.1.5 Camera and Frame Grabber

For more advanced modes, like external trigger or multicamera modes, additional signal exchange with the frame grabber comes into play:

Most machine vision cameras offer two different modes for the adaptation to frame grabbers. The camera can run as a *master* supplying video and synchronization signals via the standardized 12-pin HiRose connector so that the frame grabber is the slave having to synchronize with its *PLL* (phase locked loop) to the horizontal and vertical timing of the camera.

Alternatively, the frame grabber is the master synchronizing the camera.

The latter is easier when you have more cameras connected which all act as slaves synchronized to the frame grabber.

The camera's timing generator needs to adapt this situation by either inputting or outputting synchronization signals HD (horizontal drive) and VD (vertical drive).

When the camera is master and runs in, for example, external trigger shutter mode, it signalizes with the so-called WEN impulse when a valid image is output. This is important for the frame grabber, to grab the right image (e.g., corresponding to a flash).

Because of the complexity of certain modes, make sure that the frame grabber supports the camera in the desired mode and have a look into the technical manual to reassure yourself.

Due to the high component integration, it is currently possible to build these cameras in very miniaturized dimensions, for example, in a square of only 29 mm × 29 mm × 32 mm (exclusive C-Mount and lens). An example is the interlaced camera SONY XC-ES50 (Figure 6.36).

6.3.2 Block Diagram of Color Camera with Digital Image Processing

The block diagram of a highly integrated solution of SONY, comprising of only three chips for a one-chip (interlaced) color camera shows the hybrid nature of most color cameras nowadays: Image processing is done after analog to digital conversion in sophisticated video-DSP, outputting either analog reconstructed video or digital signals directly for flexible connectivity to displays or computers (Figure 6.37).

6.3.2.1 Bayer™ Complementary Color Filter Array

To start with the color sensor, it needs to be mentioned that most one-chip color sensors (be it CCD and CMOS) use the concept proposed by Bryce E. Bayer of KODAK, who got a patent 40 years ago on the idea of placing selectively transmissive filters on top of the pixels of a b/w sensor, such that each filter occurs regularly and repeatedly.

This is called the *BAYER™ pattern*.

Interlaced color sensors mostly use complementary color filters cyan (Cy), yellow (Ye), magenta (Mg), and green (G), instead of the primary color filters (red, green, blue). It is also important that the order of Mg and G is altered for every second line (Figure 6.38).

6.3.2.2 Complementary Color Filters Spectral Sensitivity

The main advantage of using complementary color filters is that this enhances the sensitivity compared to using primary color (RGB) filters. The following screenshot is of a typical interlaced color sensor (ICX418Q) from SONY.

It shows the transmission curves of the four color filters (yellow, cyan, magenta, and green) relative to the visible spectrum of the human eye, which ranges roughly from 400 to 700 nm.

It can be seen that especially yellow and magenta is transmissive over almost half of the visible spectrum, so that lesser energy is filtered out than with RGB primary color filter, where roughly 2/3 of the energy is filtered out per primary color.

As magenta is not a spectral color (but a mixture of red and blue) the curve shows two maxima (Figure 6.39).

The fourth color green is beneficial for color resolution and gamut.

6.3.2.3 Generation of Color Signals

The output signal Luminance (Y) and the two chrominance (C) signals (R−Y) and (B−Y) can be generated relatively easy by vertically averaging the charges of two adjacent lines in the analog domain (by *field readout* of the CCD).

It is now important that due to the changed ordering of Mg and G in every second line, the vertical averaging of the first two adjacent lines gives:

$$(Cy + Mg) \text{ and } (Ye + G),$$

and the second two lines give:

$$(Cy + G) \text{ and } (Ye + Mg)$$

As an approximation by SONY, the Y signal is created by adding horizontally adjacent pixels, and the chroma signal is generated by subtracting these adjacent pixel signals.

$$Y = 1/2 * (2B + 3G + 2R) = 1/2 * ((G + Cy) + (Mg + Ye));$$

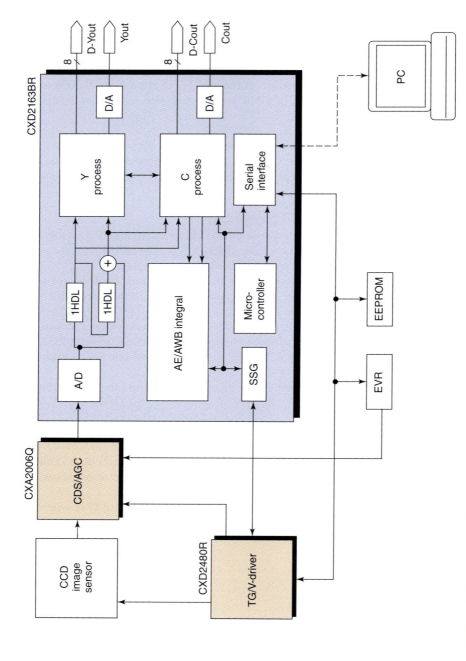

Figure 6.37 Block diagram of a SONY color camera.

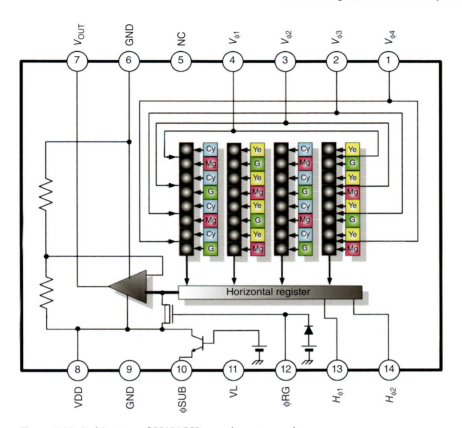

Figure 6.38 Architecture of SONY CCD complementary color sensor.

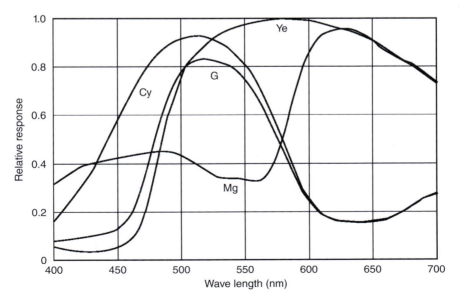

Figure 6.39 SONY ICX254AK spectral sensitivity (according to datasheet of SONY semiconductor corporation) for CyYeMgG complementary color filter array.

with $(R + G) = Ye; (R + B) = Mg; (G + B) = Cy$

$$R - Y = (2R - G) = ((Mg + Ye) - (G + Cy))$$

is used for the second chroma (color difference) signal.

For the first line pair, the Y signal is formed from these signals as follows:

$$Y = 1/2 * ((G + Ye) + (Mg + Cy)) = 1/2 * (2B + 3G + 2R)$$

This is balanced since it is formed in the same way as for the first line pair.
Similarly, the first chroma (color difference) signal is approximated as follows:

$$-(B - Y) = -(2B - G) = (G + Ye) - (Mg + Cy)$$

In other words, the two chroma signals can be alternately retrieved from the sequence of lines from $R - Y$ and $-(B - Y)$.

This is also true for the second field.

Complementary filtering is thus a way to achieve higher sensitivity at a slight expense of color resolution.

Keeping luminance (Y) and color information separate, as this example shows, is beneficial for the video quality because cross-color and cross-luminance effects ($\rightarrow$ the colored stripes in some patterned jacket of some news anchorman) are greatly reduced.

This is of even bigger importance, because the chipset can do extensive horizontal and vertical aperture correction for detail enhancement, as seen in the block diagram by the integrated two video delay lines.

The image is output, either analog or digital, again demonstrating the hybrid nature of this architecture.

With the capability of internal and external synchronization, this architecture is well suitable for many applications not only in surveillance but also in machine vision.

External asynchronous image triggering is though not possible, indicating the need for more flexible camera architecture for the challenging machine vision applications.

6.4 mvBlueCOUGAR-X Line of Cameras

The block diagrams of the mvBlueCOUGAR cameras are examples of digital cameras with Gigabit Ethernet interface with the following design goals:

- Modular concept regarding the sensors, both CCD and CMOS, so that a family of products can be built
- Flexible hardware concept by the use of a combination of powerful FPGA-based microprocessor and FPGA (field programmable gate array)
- Smart real-time image preprocessing functions
- Buying out functionality of the frame grabber, which becomes obsolete by the GigE Vision (GenICam) interface

- Variable IO interface with or without POE (Power over Ethernet)
  - High power outputs (24 V@700 mA)
  - Standard Hirose™ and RJ-45 or Industrial M12 connectors
- Best possible image quality
- Best value for money.

Going through the building blocks, we learn how the design goals were finally met.

We start with the sensor as the most important part, floating down with the data toward the output.

6.4.1 Black and White Digital Camera mvBlueCOUGAR-X Camera Series

Figure 6.40.

6.4.1.1 Gray Level Sensor and Processing

Gray cameras are equipped with monochrome CCD or CMOS sensors. Typical spectral sensitivity is shown below for, for example, SONY ICX415 (Figure 6.41).

Overlaid in red is the spectrum of the IR-Cutfilter with an edge frequency of 645 nm.

The contrary DL-Cutfilter with an edge frequency of 730 nm is drawn in blue.

Both b/w as well as color camera are usually equipped with an IR cut filter in order to keep unwanted IR energy from hitting the sensor.

Specific applications may require another spectral characteristic, for example, with less steeper curves, lower transmission loss in the passing region and/or shifted to longer wavelength.

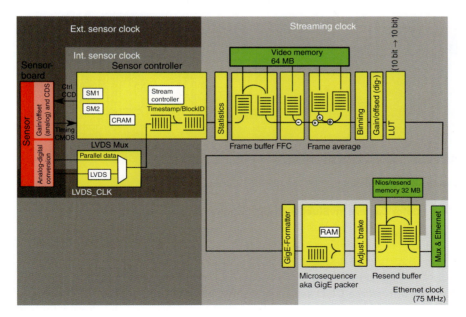

Figure 6.40 Block diagram b/w camera.

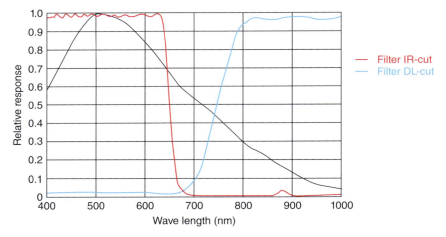

Figure 6.41 Spectral sensitivity of mvBlueCOUGAR-X120DG without cut filter and optics.

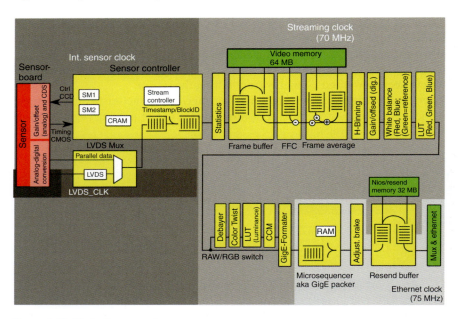

Figure 6.42 Block diagram color camera.

6.4.2 Color Camera mvBlueCOUGAR-X Family

See Figure 6.42.

6.4.2.1 Analog Processing

The signal from the CCD sensor first must be processed in the analog domain, before it gets converted to digital numbers. Processing is slightly different for b/w and one-chip-color sensors.

6.4.2.2 Analog Front End (AFE)

CCD sensors output analog signals pixel per pixel. The AFE subsumes the analog circuitry with optional color preprocessing and high qualitative digitizing, including analog/digital black level clamping in one chip.

Next to the sensor the AFE is crucial for the performance of a digital camera.

Analog Devices manufactures them in a broad range, ideally suited for this task.

CMOS sensors usually have a higher integration level and have this functionality built in the sensor itself, making an external AFE obsolete.

The diagram illustrated in Figure 6.43 is taken from the datasheet of such an AFE and illustrates the details.

The analog signal, coming in pulse amplitude modulation from the sensor is in the form of the BAYER™ color pattern sequence in the case of color. It is initially clamped to restore a DC level to fit for the analog circuits, processed in the already discussed CDS before further amplification and digitization.

An example of a real signal from a CCD sensor, clocked at 24 MHz, is shown in Figure 6.44.

V_{out} is the output of CCD video, HL is the pixel clock. RG is the pixel reset signal.

Actual AFEs have detailed possibility to shift and adjust relative signal positions.

SHD (Data) and SHP (Reference) illustrate the sample positions for the CDS stage.

6.4.2.3 A/D Conversion

As mentioned earlier, the A/D conversion is another crucial part of the AFE.

Selection criteria are as follows:

- Bit depth: 8, 10, 12–14 bit
- High dynamic and accuracy, no missing codes
- Low noise
- Good linearity (differential (DNL) and incremental (INL))
- High pixel clock frequency, suitable for the sensor's speed
- Low power consumption
- Small physical size.

Clearly, the AFE must not limit the performance of the sensor. This forces the pixel clock to match at least that of the sensor.

This calls for up to 66 MHz for certain cameras.

We then have to guarantee that the potential dynamic of the sensor is not sacrificed by insufficient bit depth, which in turn calls quickly for up to 14 bits, knowing that some digital calculations (e.g., shading correction) will have to multiply the digital signal by, for example, a factor of 2 thus leading to missing codes, when there is no reserve in bit depth.

Finally, the AFE must not add noise to the sensor's signal. A SNR (signal to noise ratio) of at least 72 dB is required for this.

Low power consumption and a small physical size are required to build a small footprint camera, which stays cool so that it has a long lifetime.

It is a generally accepted fact in electronics that the average lifetime drops by 50% for a temperature rise of 10°.

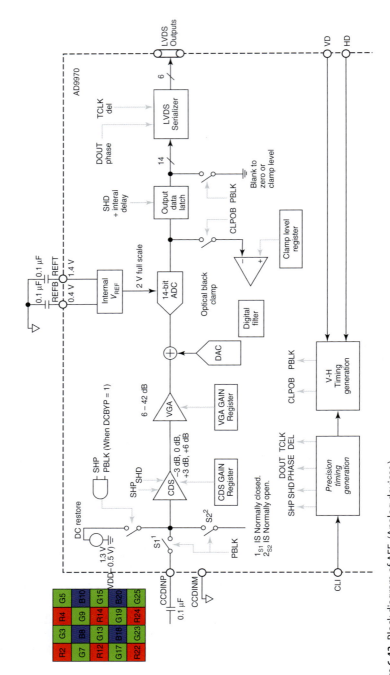

Figure 6.43 Block diagram of AFE. (Analog devices.)

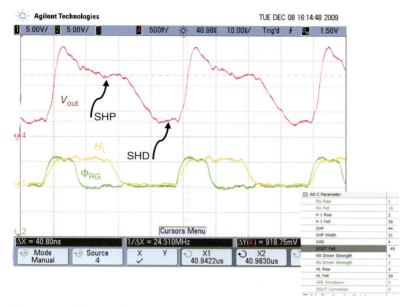

Figure 6.44 CCD signal entering CDS stage.

6.4.2.4 One-Chip Color Processing

To start with color processing, it needs to be again mentioned that most one-chip color sensors (be it CCD and CMOS) use the concept proposed by Bryce E. Bayer of KODAK, who got a patent 40 years ago for his idea of placing selectively transmissive filters on top of the pixels of a b/w sensor, such that each filter occurs repeatedly with the luminance (greenish) filter dominating. This is called the *BAYER pattern*. Here we use the variant, which uses the so-called *primary colors*, Red, Green, and Blue, according to the Tristimulus theory of Color Perception, shown below. We notice that the structure follows insights into the physiology of the eye that it is advantageous for a good image reconstruction to have higher luminance than chrominance resolution. So, the green filter dominates because it dominates in luminance (Y) as stated in the known formula for Y (Figure 6.45):

$$Y = 0.3 \cdot R + 0.59 \cdot G + 0.11 \cdot B$$

The following screenshot shows the spectral sensitivity of a sensor with primary color filter array, such as used in the mvBlueCOUGAR-120aC (Figure 6.46).

It can be seen that each of the three primary color filter filters out almost 2/3 of the visible spectrum per color, resulting in lower sensitivity of a color camera compared to that of b/w for the same light exposure.

The fact that probably not all colors are (correctly) displayed due to RGB filter maxima different to those of the eye or the display calls for additional color correction matrices, is one of the smart functionalities of the MATRIX VISION camera family.

MATRIX VISION cameras use bilinear color interpolation, which is explained later in this chapter.

6 Camera Systems in Machine Vision

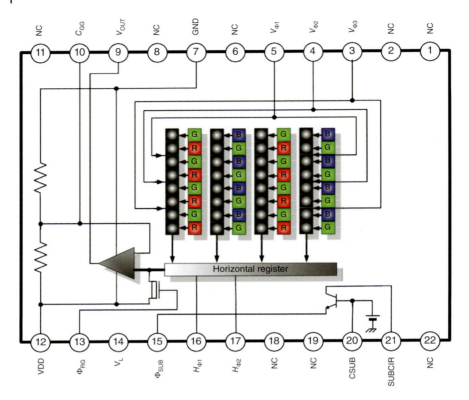

Figure 6.45 Architecture of SONY CCD primary color sensor.

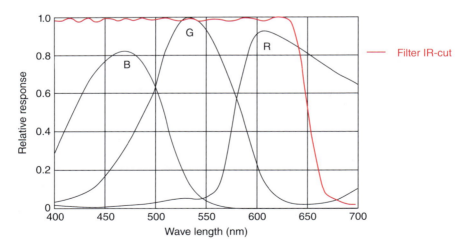

Figure 6.46 Spectral sensitivity of ICX415Q without cut filter and optics.

6.4.2.5 Inputting Time Stamp Data into Data Stream

As an important step for an industrial camera, a camera-generated time stamp with microseconds precision and a block_ID number is added to the image for identification purposes.

It should be noted that it is part of the GigE Vision standard development to have this time stamp synchronized with real world clock and to keep it automatically synchronized by means of the IEEE 1588 network standards.

This enables applications like multicamera synchronization or "scheduled action commands" modes (command (all) camera(s) to trigger at a defined moment in future time) without external hardware trigger wiring.

6.4.2.6 Statistics Engine for White Balance and Auto Features

Next to sensor data output follows the statistics engine as part of the FPGA. It generates histogram data of RGB values over the whole image or selectable parts of it.

Based on the assumption that "the world is gray" the camera can selectively amplify Red and Blue channels with full 12–14 bit depth digitally for an automatic or one push white balance in the camera until the mean histogram values are equal.

This avoids possible missing codes that can occur if you do this on the host at transmission bit depth (say 8 bit only).

This algorithm holds well for most scenery, and fails only when there is only one color in the scene, because this color will desaturate.

This is demonstrated in the two pictures in Figure 6.47.

The histogram is created over the full AOI and shows mean values R/G/B of 100/98/102.

The same scene with a histogram over the upper three colored rows shows very similar mean values in R/G/B of 97/94/96 (Figure 6.48).

The same histogram can also be used for auto exposure and auto gain algorithms.

Optionally the area where the histogram is computed can be user selected, so that one can exclude, for example, the upper area from being taken into account for AEC and AGC (e.g., exclude sky in image).

6.4.2.7 Image Memory

Normally, images are captured and transported in consecutively pipelined steps. The image is exposed, read out from the sensor, digitized, and sent over the interface in packets, depending on the interface.

Because many modern interfaces (such as Gigabit Ethernet or USB) do not have guaranteed bandwidth (as was the case with ISO transmission in FireWire) an image buffer in a camera is almost mandatory.

For example, with GigE Vision, one piece of an image is the so-called MTU (maximum transmission unit) in bytes, which is by default 1500 to say 9000 bytes/frame (aka jumbo packets).

So, assume that the network is temporarily not available: Usually, it is hard to impossible to hold the sensor readout and continue some time later without image degradation or corruption.

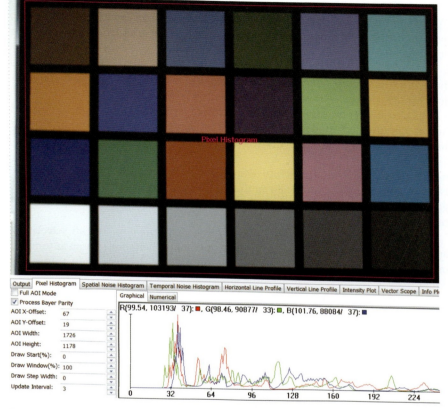

Figure 6.47 Histogram of Gretag MC-Beth color chart with full AOI.

Normally, this image needs to be thrown away, which is a severe problem in most machine vision applications.

The memory is arranged in a FIFO (First in First out) manner. This makes addressing for individual images unnecessary.

Nowadays, memory in a camera can be of size of several Megabytes (64–256 MB at MV) and can probably perform faster than the interface. If, on the other hand, the sensor can also readout faster this enables

- high speed burst mode buffer functionality;
- short time slow motion recording;
- record mode with pretrigger functionality.

It is very important to state that this memory must not introduce general latency time in the transmission path, which means that by design it is usually bypassed in normal mode.

6.4.2.8 Lookup Table (LUT) and Gamma Function

MATRIX VISION cameras provide the functionality of user-defined lookup table (LUT). The use of this LUT allows any function (in the form Output = F (Input))

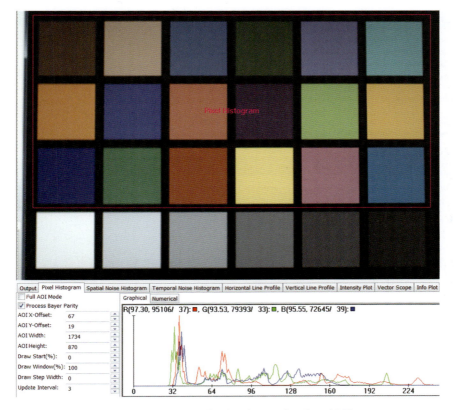

Figure 6.48 Histogram of Gretag MC-Beth color chart with reduced AOI.

to be stored in the camera's RAM and to apply it on the individual pixels of an image at run-time.

Think of a RAM-LUT in the following way: The address lines of the RAM are connected to the incoming digital data, these in turn point to the values of functions which are calculated offline, for example, with the wizard or a spreadsheet program. This function needs to be loaded into the camera's RAM before use.

One example of using a LUT is the flexible Gamma LUT:

$$Y = (1 + \gamma\alpha) * X\hat{\,}(1/\gamma) - \gamma\alpha$$

Gamma signal enhancement is known as compensation for the nonlinear brightness response of many displays, for example, CRT or TFT monitors. The lookup table converts the 10 or 12 most significant bits (MSBs) from the digitizer to 9 or 10 bits.

It can equally be used as a dynamic compression tool to compress the say 12 bit sensor data into 8 bit for transmission.

The advantage of having a LUT in the camera lies in the fact that preprocessing is possible at higher bit depth, having less missing codes in the transmission path.

MATRIX VISION's viewer PropView offers a Wizard for convenient LUT definition, which supports the basic GigE Vision structure of an array of indexed value (Figure 6.49).

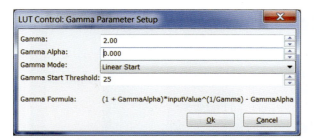

Figure 6.49 Programmable LUT: Gamma.

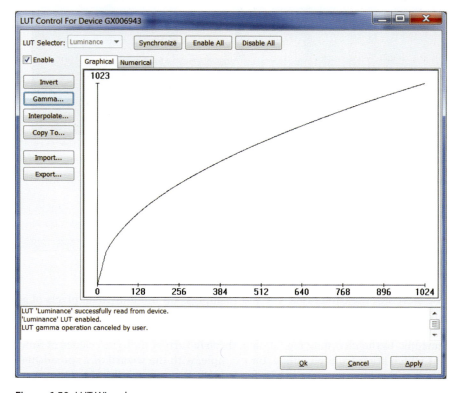

Figure 6.50 LUT Wizard.

The wizard window is shown in the screenshot in Figure 6.50. It can be seen that this flexible tool allows

- free selection of gamma;
- free selection of a linear starting function to reduce dark noise;
- gamma alpha: Individual offset before Gamma function starts.

But even more specific contrast variations, such as

- Threshold (binarization): $Y = 0\ (x < A);\ 1023,$
- Windowing: $Y = 1023\ (A < X < B);\ 0,$
- Inversion: $Y = 1023 - X,$

- Negative offset: $Y = X - \text{Offset}$,
- Digital gain: $Y = X(X < 1024);\ 1023$,

are very simple to generate offline with the help of import and export functions.

6.4.2.9 Shading Correction

Shading correction is used to compensate for nonhomogeneities caused by lighting or optical characteristics within specified ranges.

To correct an image, a multiplier is calculated between 0 and 8 for each pixel, this allows for shading to be compensated.

All this processing is done in real-time in the FPGA at full bit depth of the camera and is thus another example of a "smart feature."

The camera allows correction data to be generated automatically in the camera itself.

Upon generation of the shading image in the camera, it can be stored in the camera or uploaded to the host computer for nonvolatile storage purposes.

The process of automatic generation of correction data is described in Figure 6.51.

On the image above you see the source image of a background with nonuniform illumination.

By defocusing the lens, high-frequency image data is to be removed from the source image, and is not to be included in the shading image.

After the start of automatic generation, the camera pulls in a configurable number of frames. The mean value for the image is calculated followed by the correction image with the corresponding multiplication factors to bring each pixel to this mean value.

After the lens has been focused again the image below is generated, now with a uniform gradient (Figure 6.52).

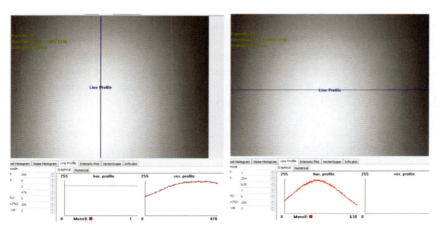

Figure 6.51 Shading correction: *Source*: image with nonuniform illumination – horizontal/vertical line profile.

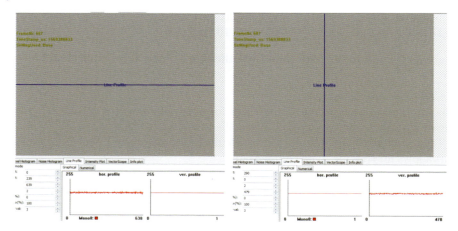

Figure 6.52 Example of shaded image.

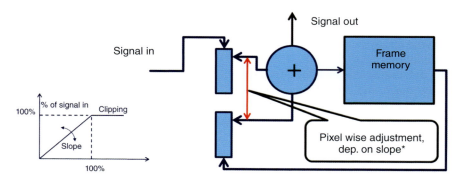

Figure 6.53 Running image average.

6.4.2.10 Reducing Noise by Adaptive Recursive Frame Averaging

Another quite impressive example for FPGA-based preprocessing is frame averaging.

It is instantly clear that averaging of images in the camera is possible if the camera is equipped with flexible and fast memory. Averaging only two images already improves the SNR by 3 dB assuming that the dominating source of noise is random noise such as photon shot noise, dark noise of sensor, or digitization noise of ADC. On the other hand, simple averaging will introduce motion artifacts.

The following known principle of an adaptive noise reduction is implemented in the FPGA of several MATRIX VISION cameras (Figure 6.53).

Consider that pixel for pixel the deviation in gray level of *signal in* versus signal from frame memory is calculated. The incoming signal and the averaged signal are added in an inverse proportional way illustrated by two potentiometers. (The more incoming signal the less averaged signal.)

This characteristic is controlled by a slope parameter so that, for example, 10% difference in pixel value leads to say 95% signal in and 5% of averaged signal. With this parameter one can control noise reduction at the expense of motion artifacts.

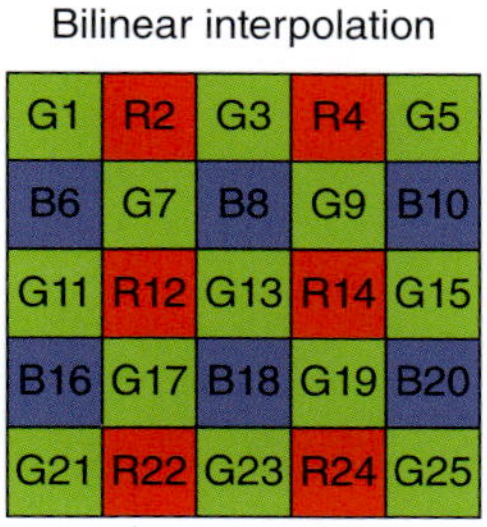

Figure 6.54 Bayer demosaicing using bilinear interpolation.

Bilinear interpolation

G1	R2	G3	R4	G5
B6	G7	B8	G9	B10
G11	R12	G13	R14	G15
B16	G17	B18	G19	B20
G21	R22	G23	R24	G25

6.4.2.11 Color Interpolation

As already mentioned the color sensors capture the color information via so-called primary color (R-G-B) filters placed over the individual pixels in a "BAYER mosaic" layout. An effective Bayer → RGB color interpolation is implemented in many MV color cameras.

Color processing can be switched on or bypassed by using the appropriate pixel format.

- RAW-mode is primarily used to
  - save bandwidths on the bus;
  - achieve higher frame rates;
  - use different BAYER demosaicing algorithms on the PC.
- Camera based color processing is primarily used
  - to reduce CPU load on the host while preserving best image preprocessing quality;
  - reduce image latency.

The purpose of the color interpolation is the generation of one red, green, and blue value for each pixel.

The MATRIX VISION cameras use a modified bilinear interpolation as described below (Figure 6.54).

Consider generation of green pixel at position G7:

$$G7\_new = 0.5 * G7 + 0.5 * (G1 + G3 + G11 + G13)/4$$

This compensates for slightly different green filters that can sometimes occur in the red blue rows, whereas $G8 = (G3 + G7 + G9 + G13)/4$.

Interpolation of red and blue pixels at a green pixel position use:

$$B7 = (B6 + B8)/2; \quad R7 = (R2 + R12)/2$$

Interpolation of red and blue pixels at a blue/red pixel position use:

$$R8 = (R2 + R4 + R12 + R14)/4; \quad B12 = (B6 + B8 + B16 + B18)/4$$

Advantage of bilinear demosaicing is less false colors at contours at a slight expense of sharpness.

Bayer demosaicing inherently introduces color alias effects at horizontal and vertical borders, which cannot be completely suppressed. There are many algorithms known with different complexities, some clearly overriding FPGA resources.

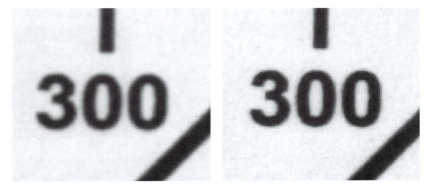

Figure 6.55 Color alias due to Bayer demosaicing: (a) Bilinear and (b) adaptive edge sensing.

The photos below show alias occurring at a three pixel wide contour (Figure 6.55).

With adaptive (edge interpreting) techniques in the host PC, it is possible to achieve almost perfect contours while using RAW image from the camera at the expense of CPU load and latency.

6.4.2.12 Color Correction

So far we have described the spectral sensitivity of image sensors, which are used in our cameras. Now we discuss the optimization in order to adapt them to the human eye and the different displays.

The next image is a superposition of a sensor characteristic (dotted) and the two degree human eyes cone spectral sensitivity as published here: http://cvrl.ucl.ac.uk/cones.htm (Figure 6.56).

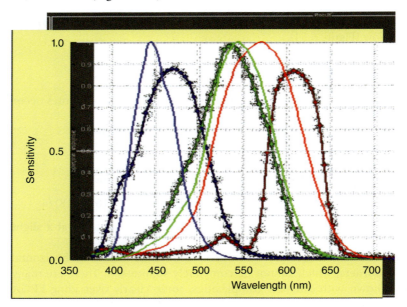

Figure 6.56 Spectral sensitivity of image sensor and human cone sensitivity overlaid.

Figure 6.57 Example matrix for a specific SONY color CCD.

$$\begin{pmatrix} X \\ Y \\ Z \end{pmatrix} = \begin{bmatrix} 0{,}65724 & 0{,}26420 & 0{,}07857 \\ 0{,}23601 & 0{,}92376 & -0{,}15977 \\ 0{,}07757 & -0{,}31273 & 1{,}23516 \end{bmatrix} * \begin{pmatrix} R \\ G \\ B \end{pmatrix}$$

It can be seen that the maxima differ mainly at red and blue in frequency.

With matrix multiplication it is possible to improve this behavior considerably.

Sensor specific coefficients C_{xy} are scientifically generated to ensure that GretagMacbeth™ ColorChecker® – colors are displayed with highest color fidelity and color balance while preserving the white point (WPPLS matrix). The matrix above shifts and adjusts both red and blue sensor maximum to match the human cone as closest as possible (Figure 6.57).

We still have to solve the display part of the improvement.

We have to take into account that displays today differ quite largely in their color gamut, which is the amount of colors and brightness they can display.

This is shown in the graphic in Figure 6.58.

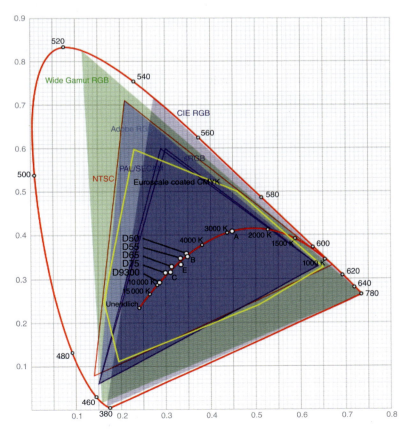

Figure 6.58 Color gamut of different display technologies. (https://en.wikipedia.org/wiki/SRGB#/media/File:CIE1931xy_gamut_comparison.svg. Used under CC BY-SA 3.0 https://creativecommons.org/licenses/by-sa/3.0/.)

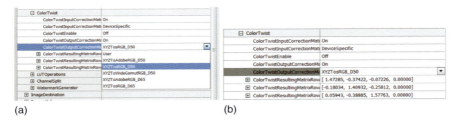

Figure 6.59 (a) Selection of display and (b) resulting matrix.

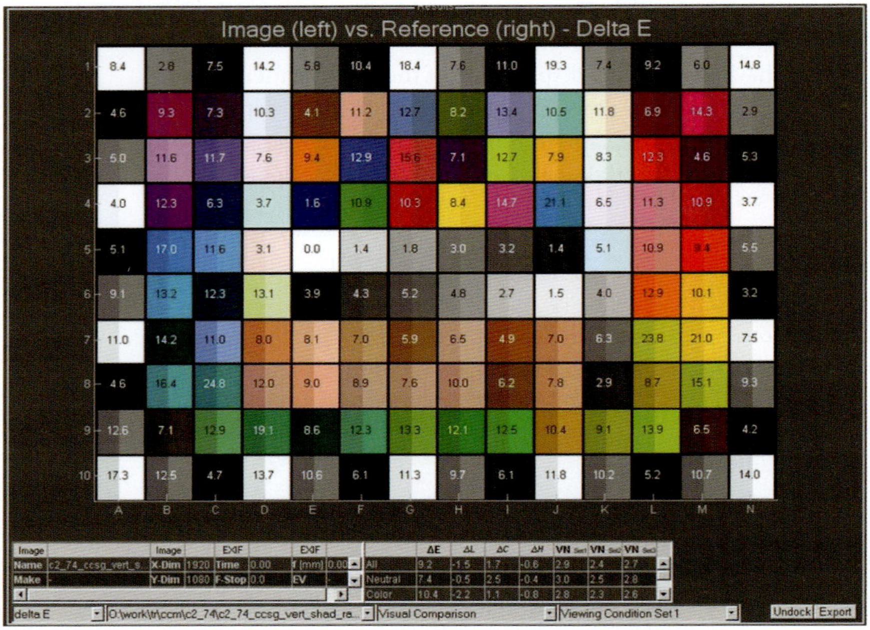

Figure 6.60 Image with CCM: deltaE visualized.

Using MV's viewer PropView or image acquisition frame work called *ImpactAcquire* it is possible to conveniently combine these matrix multiplications by selecting the desired display gamut as shown in Figure 6.59.

As a result, this procedure lowers the deltaE (difference of displayed color vs correct color) color error by roughly a factor of 2 and results in very low color errors as displayed in the image in Figure 6.60.

6.4.2.13 RGB → YUV Conversion

The conversion from RGB to YUV is made using the following formulae:

$$Y = 0.299 \cdot R + 0.587 \cdot G + 0.114 \cdot B$$
$$U = (-0.147 \cdot R - 0.289 \cdot G + 0.436 \cdot B) + 128$$
$$V = (0.615 \cdot R - 0.515 \cdot G - 0.100 \cdot B) + 128$$

Color space YUV is helpful to reduce bandwidth in transmission and for certain color-based inspection tasks, where luminance and color signals have to be independent of each other.

Please note: The term *YUV color space* is typically an incorrect usage of the Y'CbCr color space. (Legacy from IIDC standard.) Signal range is full scale (0–255).

6.4.3 Controlling Image Capture

The cameras support the Exposure modes specified in GigE Visions and GenICam's standard feature naming convention (SFNC) specification. For models with a global shutter, all pixels are exposed to the light at the same moment and for the same time span.

These exposure modes are mostly as follows:

- Timed (sets exposure time by register value) and
- Trigger width (sets exposure time by the time the trigger signal is high or low, depending on trigger selector).

In continuous modes, the exposure begins timely before the image is latched and read out, thus acting in a frame-synchronous way.

Combined with an external trigger or a software trigger event, it becomes asynchronous in the sense that individual images are exposed and recorded only whenever this trigger event or edge or level occurs. This ensures that even fast moving objects can be grabbed at the same position in the image and with minimal image blur.

Latency and jitter and complexity depend highly on the method of triggering.

- A hardware trigger is the most precise, but it requires feeding the trigger signal to a pin of the HiRose connector and configuring of this input accordingly. Latency and jitter is in the range of a few microseconds, depending on input circuitry and the time it takes to reset the sensor for the new image only.
- A software command from the application does not require any wiring but has the largest latency and jitter due to application latency and jitter (operating system and load dependant) and the individual command decoding time in the camera. Generally, as a rule of thumb, it can be in the range of several milliseconds and may differ among the connected cameras.
- Using the so-called software action command, latency, and jitter can be lowered and made the same for all cameras connected due to broadcast nature of the command and a more efficient decoding of the command in the camera. Latency and jitter can thus be brought much closer to the hardware figures.

6.4.4 Acquisition and Trigger Modes

A basic external trigger scenario is shown now:

- The camera waits for a rising edge at line4, which is the first input (blue).
- It holds the shutter (exposure) open as long as the external signal is high (trigger width) (drawn in red).
- The start of exposure is delayed by 500 µs.

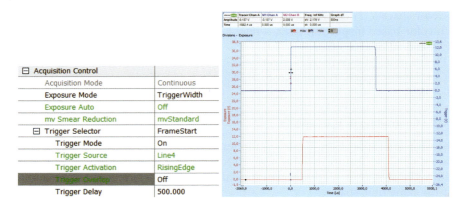

Figure 6.61 Hardware trigger mode of FrameStart and Exposure Mode TriggerWidth with Trigger Delay.

This way one external signal can be used to trigger a camera and control its exposure, just as with analog industrial cameras (Figure 6.61).

As mentioned already the source of an image trigger can be a variety of hardware sources, internally generated signals, or software signals including action commands.

Having this flexibility customers can

- connect cameras directly with rotary encoders;
- generate pulses with the help of timers and counters;
- generate sequences of different exposure times (see also sequencer mode) which are exactly changing from trigger to trigger;
- directly drive high power flashing LEDs (Figure 6.62).

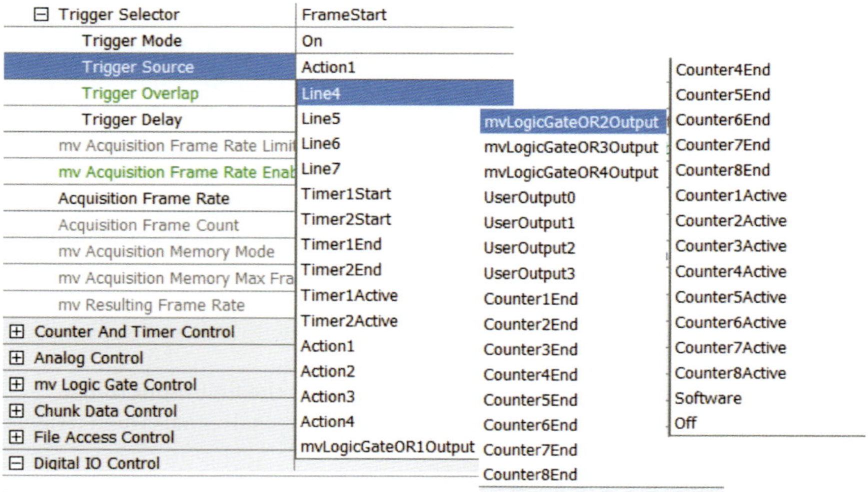

Figure 6.62 Trigger source selection overview.

The following shows a more trigger complicated *FrameBurstStart* scenario:

- The camera waits for *one* rising edge at line4, which is the first input.
- It then starts precisely and records and outputs five images each exposed by 1000 μs. The images are set to be grabbed with a frequency of 40 fps.
- Alternatively, certain high speed camera models can record an amount of images at maximum sensor frequency into its internal buffer regardless of transmission limits (Burst mode buffer). This allows slow motion image sequence generation (Figures 6.63 and 6.64).

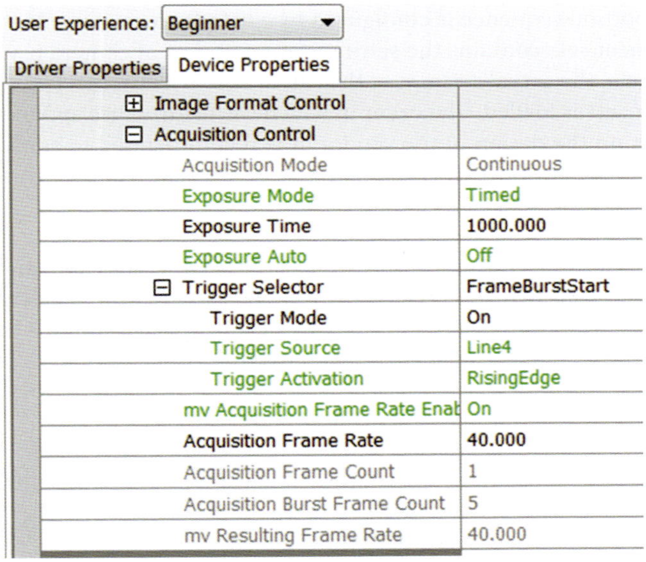

User Experience: Beginner
Driver Properties
Device Properties
Image Format Control
Acquisition Control
Acquisition Mode
Continuous
Exposure Mode
Timed
Exposure Time
1000.000
Exposure Auto
Off
Trigger Selector
FrameBurstStart
Trigger Mode
On
Trigger Source
Line4
Trigger Activation
RisingEdge
mv Acquisition Frame Rate Enat
On
Acquisition Frame Rate
40.000
Acquisition Frame Count
1
Acquisition Burst Frame Count
5
mv Resulting Frame Rate
40.000

Figure 6.63 Setting up a frame burst of 5 images from one external trigger.

Divisions - Exposure
Exposure (V)
Trigger (V)
Time (ms)

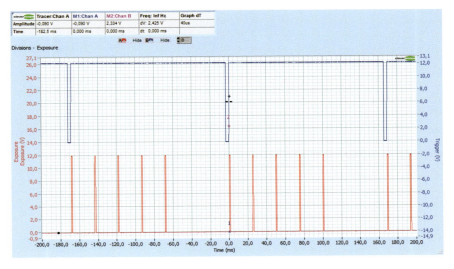

Figure 6.64 Frame burst trigger mode.

6.4.4.1 Sequencer

The purpose of a sequencer is to allow the user of a camera to define a series of feature sets for image acquisition, which can consecutively be activated during the acquisition by the camera.

For example, change exposure time or other image-related parameters in a defined and strict sequence from image to image.

Although there is a concept of event messages sent by the camera to notify a host of internal state changes in the camera (such as exposure ended…) changing image-related properties can perform either slowly or is complicated to impossible when trying to do this timely from a usually non-real-time host program.

Accordingly, the proposed sequence is configured by a list of parameter sets.

Each of these sequencer sets contains the settings for a number of camera features. Similar to user sets, the actual settings of the camera are overwritten when one of these sequencer sets is loaded. The order in which the features are applied to the camera depends on the design of the vendor. It is recommended to apply all the image related settings to the camera offline, before the first frame of this sequence is captured.

The next screenshot shows a simple example.

The camera is triggered externally and a sequence of three different exposure times (1000, 10 000, and 20 000 μs) was created before. The camera now toggles, regardless of the trigger frequency, between these three exposures automatically with no commands needed from the host side (Figure 6.65).

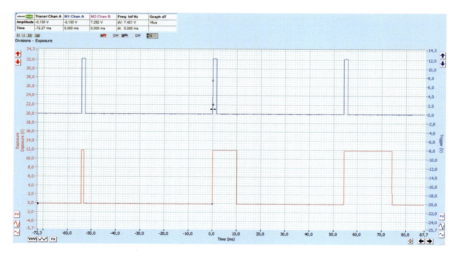

Figure 6.65 Sequence with three different exposure times.

Application scenarios for different exposure times are in surveillance to further increase dynamic range or the creation of HDR images.

6.4.4.2 Latency and Jitter Aspects

The following section describes the time response of the camera using a single frame (One Shot) command.

In the case of a hardware trigger, the One Shot command decoding is skipped so that the camera reacts almost immediately to the trigger edge.

Latency can be separated into:

- *Hardware trigger latency*: Delay of input circuitry (~20 µs) plus 2 µs sensor reset (CCD); CMOS: sensor dependant
- *Sensor latency*: 1 image readout time plus exposure time
- *Sensor jitter*: 1 pixel clock (if sensor is idle) or 1 horizontal line (overlapped readout)
- *Camera processing latency*:
  - *Stream controller:* ~20 sensor clocks
  - *Frame buffer:* ~3.6 µs
  - *Resend buffer:* ~1.8 µs
  - *Ethernet latency*: ~MTU * 8 ns.

It can be seen that in total the delay is dominated by the sensor. There is no conceptual delay by the frame buffer or the fact that the camera "is digital."

On the host side there is time needed to build the image in the memory, depending on preprocessing stages, like color, bit depth, LUT, and other steps. This can be in the range of 10 µs < latency > 100 ms.

It should be noted that in the case of displaying an image on a TFT, the monitor itself is another source of significant delay (in the range of several frames), due to display image processing.

6.4.4.3 Action Commands

GigE Vision specifies so called action commands to trigger an action in multiple devices at roughly the same time. Together with POE this can make additional power and I/O wiring obsolete and achieve a one-camera-one-cable solution.

Due to the nature of Ethernet, this is not as precise as a hardware trigger since different network segments can have different latencies. Nevertheless, in a switched network, the resulting jitter is acceptable for a broad range of applications and this scheme provides a convenient way to synchronize devices by means of a software command.

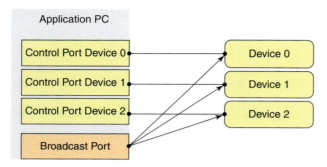

Figure 6.66 Action command sent as broadcast to all devices in the subnet.

Action commands can be unicasted or broadcasted by applications with either exclusive, write or read (only when the device is configured accordingly) access to the device. They can be used, for example, to

- increment or reset counters;
- reset timers;
- act as trigger sources.

The most typical scenario is when an application wants to trigger a simultaneous action on multiple devices. This case is shown in Figure 6.66. It is assumed that all cameras are connected and configured, for example, via a switch to appear in the same subnet. The application fires a broadcast action command that will reach all the devices on the subnet.

However, action commands can also be used by secondary applications. This can be even another device (a camera or a suitable I/O device) on the same subnet. This is depicted in Figure 6.67.

Upon reception of an action command, the device will decode the information to identify which internal action signal is requested. An action signal is a device internal signal that can be used as a trigger for functional units inside the device (e.g., a frame trigger). It can be routed to all signal sinks of the device.

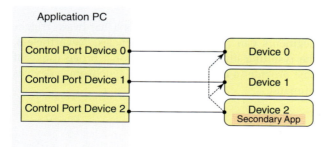

Figure 6.67 Action command using secondary application to send broadcast to all devices in the subnet.

Each action command message contains information for the device to validate the requested operation:

1) device_key to authorize the action on this device;
2) group_key to define a group of devices on which actions have to be executed;
3) group_mask to be used to filter out some of these devices from the group.

6.4.4.4 Scheduled Action Command

Scheduled action commands provide a way to trigger actions in a device at a specific time in the future. The typical use case is depicted in Figure 6.68.

The transmitter of an action command records the exact time, when the source signal is asserted (External signal). This time t_0 is incremented by a delta time Δt_L and transmitted in an action command to the receivers. The delta time Δt_L has to be larger than the longest possible transmission and processing latency of the action command in the network.

If the packet passes the action command filters in the receiver, then the action signal is put into a time queue (the depth of this queue is indicated by the ActionQueueSize property).

When the time of the local clock is greater or equal to the time of an action signal in the queue, the signal is removed from the queue and asserted. Combined with the timestamp precision of IEEE 1588 which can be sub-microseconds, a Scheduled Action Command provides a way to allow low-jitter software trigger. If the sender of an action command is not capable to set a future time into the packet, the action command has a flag to fall back to legacy mode (bit 0 of the flag field). In this mode the signal is asserted the moment the packet passes the action command filters.

Scheduled action commands are not supported by every device. A device supporting scheduled action commands should also support time stamp synchronization based on IEEE 1588. At the time of writing, both features were under development at MATRIX VISION.

6.4.5 Data Transmission

This section describes the data transmission as per Standards *GigE Vision* and *UBS3 Vision*. It is common sense that these standards currently belong to the most important ones in the machine vision industry.

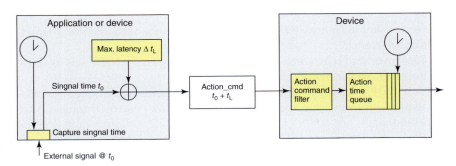

Figure 6.68 Principle of scheduled action commands.

Depending on the interface, pixel data are transmitted as

- UDP (User Datagram Protocol) data packets for GVSP (*GigE Vision Stream Protocol*)
- Bulk data (in most implementations) for USB3.

It is worth noticing that these formats do not guarantee isochronous timing (as with IEEE 1394).

6.4.5.1 GigE Vision and GVSP

GigE Vision is designed to make use of GigE technology for industrial digital cameras.

The standard comprises of four main elements:

- *Device discovery*:
  - IP configuration, initiated by the device using DHCP, LLA, persistent address
  - Device enumeration, initiated by the application on the host.
- *Two* protocols, embedded in UDP/IP packets (because of their lower overhead):
  GVCP (*GigE Vision Control Protocol*)
  GVSP (*GigE Vision Streaming Protocol*)
- An *XML* – camera description file (GenICam)

GenICam itself is a standard to define camera behavior.

The idea is to have a machine readable camera manual (this is the XML-file, which can be stored in the device, delivered as file or accessible by web-link.

Not only available for GigE Vision but also for USB3 Vision.

One has to be GenICam compliant to promote GigE-Vision compliance.

GenICam Is divided into three parts:

- *GenAPI*: Camera configuration
- *SFNC*: Standard Feature Naming Convention: recommended names and types for common features; (*PFNC*: pixel format naming convention)
- *GenTL*: Agnostic (= interface independent) Transport-layer for communication and image acquisition
  Using GenTL, a USB3 camera and an GigE-camera could be used in the very same application.

The screenshot in Figure 6.69 shows how GVSP is embedded into the IP (Internet Protocol) frame.

Protocol overhead is between 1% and 5%, depending on the MTU setting. UDP was chosen for performance reasons.

Because UDP is unreliable, GVSP provides mechanisms to guarantee the reliability of packet transmission and to ensure minimal flow control (through GVCP and Resend).

Finally image data is sent as GVSP data to the network interface.

6.4 mvBlueCOUGAR-X Line of Cameras

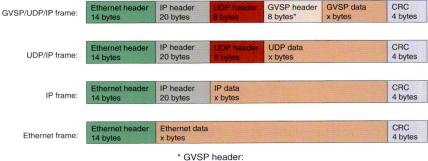

Figure 6.69 GVSP.

It is important that performance optimizations in terms of

- jumbo packets,
- interrupt moderation settings

are set in the driver settings, so that the amount of image data per IP frame is maximized (to say 9 k Byte instead of 1.5 kB as default).

This lowers the #interrupts by the driver and the CPU load.

With GigE up to 120 MB s^{-1} data is usually possible, depending on chipset.

GigE Vision also offers the possibility to group interfaces via so called LAG (link aggregation grouping).

MvBlueCOUGAR-XD cameras consequently offer dual network ports and can thus transport up to 240 MB s^{-1} of image data over up to 100 m cable distance.

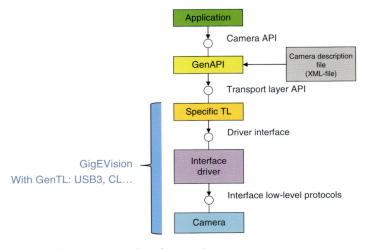

Figure 6.70 Layer protocols and interaction.

6.4.5.2 USB3 Vision

USB3 Vision bases also on the GenICam standard. The next screenshot shows how this all interacts (Figure 6.70):

USB3 offers with

- Up to 400 MB s^{-1} interface bandwidth,
- Backwards compatibility with USB2,
- A better protocol (less polling needed),
- More bus power (4.5 W), and
- Efficient methods to reduce CPU load for image transfer (Zero Copy mechanism: Only the first and the last packet per image generate interrupts, the data is transferred via DMA into the computer's memory) and the standard USB3 Vision ideal preconditions for camera interfaces.

MATRIX VISION offers a USB3 Vision compliant mvBlueFOX3 camera family.

6.4.6 Pixel Data

GigE Vision and the later defined PFNC define dozens of different pixel formats including custom defined ones.

MATRIX VISION cameras support a very large subgroup of these.

The color and gray camera formats supported by the cameras at the time of writing are shown in Table 6.6.

The term *BAYER* indicates, that the camera outputs RAW BAYER data and the two letters indicate the color sequence, followed by the bit depth.

All other formats indicate that the camera is doing color processing.

For compatibility reasons RGB8Packed (GigE Vision 1.x legacy) and RGB8 (GeV 2.0) formats appear twice. As mentioned in Section 6.4.2.11, color processing in the camera increases bandwidth to be seen in byte per pixel.

Table 6.6 Pixel formats supported by MATRIX VISION.

Device name	Pixel format	Byte per pixel
mvBlueCOUGAR-X(D)xxxyC	• BayerBG8	1
	• BayerBG12Packed	1.5
	• BayerBG10	2
	• BayerBG12	2
	• BayerBG16	2
	• RGB8Packed (RGB8)	3
	• BGR8Packed (BGR8)	3
	• BGRA8Packed (BGRA8)	4
	• BGR10V2Packed (RGB10p32)	4
	• YUV422Packed (YUV422_8_UYVY)	2
	• YUV422_YUYVPacked (YUV422_8)	2
	• YUV444Packed (YUV8_UYV)	3
mvBlueCOUGAR-X(D)xxxyG	• Mono8	1
	• Mono10	2
	• Mono12	2
	• Mono14	2
	• Mono16	2
	• Mono12Packed	1.5

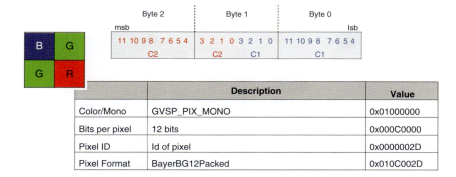

	Description	Value
Color/Mono	GVSP_PIX_MONO	0x01000000
Bits per pixel	12 bits	0x000C0000
Pixel ID	Id of pixel	0x0000002D
Pixel Format	BayerBG12Packed	0x010C002D

Figure 6.71 Pixel format BayerBG12Packed and data example.

For example, BayerBG12Packed (packed as Mono12Packed) is defined as follows:

By default little-endian is to be used; this means Byte 0 is sent first on the wire, followed by Byte 1 (Figure 6.71).

6.4.7 Camera Connection

Gigabit Ethernet and USB 2/3 offer different connection possibilities, some of them shown in the pictures below (Figure 6.72).

A clear advantage of GigE is the very long cable distance of up to 100 m, which gives unique ranging options.

Copper cables for USB 2/3 are more limited in length, in practice very good cable quality is required for 8 m distance. Active repeaters can increase length up to ~15 m.

There are glass optical fiber (GOF) solutions for USB 3 available to bridge distances of 100 m, as well as so called active optical cables (AOCs) which have the conversion chips integrated in the connectors itself. These offer nice and stable solutions to bridge distances of up to 100 m together without distributing the GND, which could introduce stability problems.

6.4.8 Operating the Camera

Gigabit Ethernet cameras require separate power (in the industrial range of 12–24 V DC) on the HiRose connector or the camera option POE. The latter requires more expensive POE switches or power inserters on the other hand.

6 Camera Systems in Machine Vision

Figure 6.72 Upper left: Industrial M12 option with x-coded GigE and IO; lower left: mini USB2; lower middle: USB2 Type B; upper middle: RJ45 and HiRose; upper right: micro USB3; lower right: dual RJ45 plus dual HiRose (motorized lens control) and video lens control.

USB 3 cameras can either be bus powered or also externally powered if their power consumption exceeds the limits of 4.5 W (or 2.5 W in USB 2 compatible mode).

6.4.9 HiRose Jack Pin Assignment

The HiRose plug is also designed for industrial use and in addition to providing access to the digital inputs and outputs on the camera; it also provides a RS232 serial interface. The following diagram shows the pinning of a Standard mvBlueCOUGAR-X as viewed in pin direction. Separate power is not needed in the case of cameras with POE option and for USB3 cameras when bus powered. In any case separate power connection is required to drive the outputs (Figure 6.73 and Table 6.7).

6.4.10 Sensor Frame Rates and Bandwidth

In this chapter we discuss the calculation of sensor frame rates and the resulting bandwidth requirements.

A modern CMOS sensor such as the SONY Pregius™ IMX174 can be driven in various configurations, modes, and clocks.

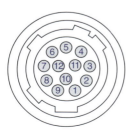

Figure 6.73 HiRose connector pin assignment.

Table 6.7 HiRose pinning.

Pin	Signal	Use	Pin	Signal	Use
1	GND	Power GND	7	Opto GND	Common GND for inputs
2	V_{IN} +12 to +24 V	Power supply for camera	8	RS232_RX	
3	DigOut3 12–24 V	wxPropView numbering: line3	9	RS232_TX	
4	Opto DigIn0 3.3–24 V	line4	10	+24V_HSD	12.24 V supply for the outputs
5	DigOut2	line2	11	Opto DigIn1 3.3–24 V	line5
6	DigOut0	line0	12	Opto DigOut1 12–24 V	line1

Table 6.8 Constants for calculating the frame time.

Name	Value
Internal line length	462
Vertical blank lines	37
Sensor in clock	74.25 (@50 MHz pixel clock)
	37.125 (@25 MHz pixel clock)
Number of LVDS	8

To calculate the maximum frames per second (FPS_{max}) in free running mode we need the following formula and values as per camera manual (Table 6.8):

$$\text{Frame Time} = \frac{\text{Internal Line Length} * 8}{\text{Sensor In Clock} * \text{\#Of LVDS}} * \frac{(\text{Image Height} + \text{Vertical Blank Lines})}{1000} \quad (6.1)$$

Equation 6.1: frame time calculation.

If now the exposure time < frame time, we get:

$$FPS_{max} = \frac{1}{\text{Frame Time}}$$

In our example the sensor can achieve 164 fps (in 8/10 bit mode readout), leading to

$$1936 \times 1214 * 164 = 387 \text{ MB s}^{-1}$$

In Mono8 transmission already.

Acquisition Control	
Acquisition Mode	Continuous
Exposure Mode	Timed
Exposure Time	20000.000
Exposure Auto	Off
⊞ Trigger Selector	FrameStart
mv Acquisition Frame Rate Lim	mvDeviceLinkThroughput
mv Acquisition Frame Rate En	Off
Acquisition Frame Count	1
mv Acquisition Memory Mode	Default
mv Acquisition Memory Max F	0
mv Resulting Frame Rate	41.100

Figure 6.74 mv Resulting Frame Rate.

While this is at the edge of the USB 3 transmission chip (Cypress FX3) used in the camera, it is well above the capabilities of GigE or dual GigE.

MATRIX VISION cameras offer an automatic property mv Resulting Frame Rate to recalculate the achievable frame rate based on actual settings such as pixel clock, exposure time, image format, and mode.

The image above shows the relevant screenshot for the sensor IMX249 which is a #LVDS-limited version (#LVDS = 2) of the IMX174: This limits the frame rate to ~41 fps and the bandwidth to 97 MB s^{-1} (Figure 6.74).

6.5 Configuration of a GigE Vision Camera

As we have already mentioned, it is mainly the task of the GenApi specification within GenICam to configure the camera.

The key idea is to make camera manufacturers provide machine readable versions of the manuals for their cameras. These *camera description files* contain all of the required information to automatically map a camera's *features* to its *registers*.

A typical feature would be the camera's gain and the user's attempt might be, for example, to set *Gain* = 42. Using GenICam, a piece of generic software will be able to read the camera's description file and figure out that setting the *Gain* to 42 means writing a value of 0×2A to a register located at 0×0815. Other tasks involved might be to check in advance whether the camera possesses a *Gain* feature and to check whether the new value is consistent with the allowed *Gain* range.

Note that adding a new feature to a camera just means extending the camera's description file, thus making the new feature immediately available to all GenI-Cam aware applications (GenICam Standard v2.0 page 6).

Effectively this makes the knowledge of a register layout for users and customers obsolete. That is explained below with the help of the temperature feature in the camera:

The GenICam description below finds its representation in the xml-file, which is part of the camera and finally the image viewer (or any application), makes this property accessible without knowing further details (Figure 6.75).

6.5 Configuration of a GigE Vision Camera

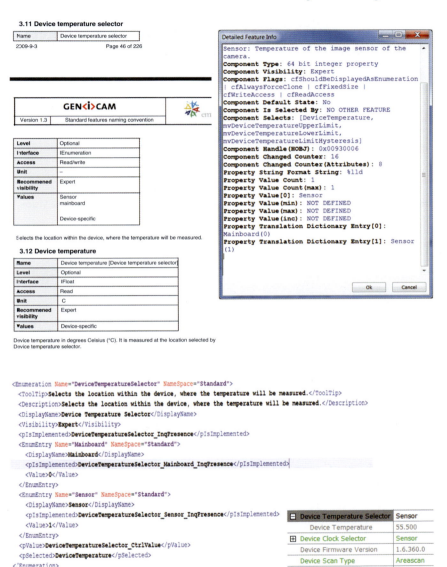

Figure 6.75 Device temperature selector: GenICam definition; XML-description; detailed feature info in impact acquire and how it appears in PropView.

This abstraction greatly facilitates the usage of even complex cameras and features.

This is believed to be one source of success that GigE Vision and USB 3 Vision compliant cameras found their way into numerous third party image libraries and applications such as the brands shown in Figure 6.76 and many more to come.

6 Camera Systems in Machine Vision

Figure 6.76 Icons of machine vision software libraries which are supported by Matrix-Vision cameras.

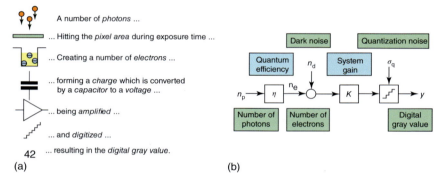

Figure 6.77 (a) Physical model of a camera and (b) mathematical model of a camera. (EMVA1288 standard.)

6.6 Qualifying Cameras and Noise Measurement (Dr. Gert Ferrano MV)

The important requirement of a camera is the more or less identical reproduction of a light signal. A *linear* increase of light intensity has to produce the same *linear* increase of gray values for each pixel.

Together with the maximum number of stored electrons (the so called full well capacity), signal to noise ratio, sensitivity, and dynamic range can be calculated.

The output signal of any camera is more or less distorted by additional noise produced by different noise sources.

The image above shows the physical and mathematical model of a (linear) camera according to EMVA1288 standard (Figure 6.77).

The first idea to measure noise could be a constant light input to the pixels and measure the output.

However, the only noise which cannot be avoided due to natural laws is photon shot noise. This noise follows fundamental laws described by quantum theory.

$V(i) = \text{Mean}(i)$ Variance of a signal is equal to the mean value.

So if we cannot avoid this kind of noise, we use it as a measurement method.

Practically we send a noisy light signal with different mean values to a sensor (or a camera) and measure the output noise. Then the output has to follow above mentioned equation. If the noise is larger than the theoretical value this extra noise was added by the camera and characterizes the camera quality.

Noise can be separated into a static part, which is the same in every image and dynamic part, changing from image to image.

Static part is caused by different sensitivity levels of pixels background structures in the dark and some reasons more. The good thing concerning this part is the fact, that it can be measured and compensated by software.

Dynamic noise cannot be compensated by calculation; it only can be avoided by optimizing the camera.

So nearly every noise measurement method captures multiple images of an evenly distributed light standard at different light levels.

Mean($I_n(x,y)$) is a mean image of many images at one light level and represents static noise.

Var($I_n(x,y)$) is the variance of an image and can be calculated easily, using the formula:

Var($I_n(x,y) - I_m(x,y)$) = 2 * Var($I_{nm}(x,y)$) or the variance of a difference is twice the variance of an image.

One of these measurement methods is defined by EMVA1288 standard. It defines a illumination setup with homogenous illumination directly on the sensor. The aperture angle is 1/8.

Intensity can be controlled by change of exposure time and stable light or variation of light and constant exposure time of the camera. All light intensities are measured, using a calibrated photodiode. By means of this measurement gray values can be correlated to number of photons or physical light values.

So two measurement curves are produced:

$G = \text{func}(N_{photons})$ linearity curve, gray values as a function of number of photons

Var(G) = func(Mean(G)) photon transfer curve, variance as function of mean value.

The photon transfer curve is very sensitive to camera defects and can be analyzed by pure visual inspection.

Other values like SNR or dynamic range are calculated from measured values.

This is explained in Chapter 6.7.

For the end user a standard like EMVA1288 enables to compare cameras of different producers, without knowing the insides of the camera.

Either the camera manufacturer uses a unit, accepted by EMVA1288 or the user builds his own unit.

Hardware and software is described in the standard papers. For acceptance a data set is available. With this data set own software has to produce defined results within also defined limits.

6.6.1 Explanation of the Most Important Measurements

Within the next pages the most important measurements and image checks for camera users are explained. The measurements follow EMVA1288 standard. There are further values measured, which are very important for a more detailed camera analysis. The following selection gives a first immediate qualification of a camera.

6.6.1.1 Linearity Curve

The linearity curve (of IMX-174 sensor in an mvBlueCOUGAR-X104dG) shows the direct response in gray values on photon input of a camera. Ideally, it is a straight line from minimum to maximum (Figure 6.78).

In case of early saturation of a camera, the curve shows nonlinear behavior at high end. The example Figure 6.79 is used from EMVA1288 documentation.

6.6.1.2 Photon Transfer Curve

Due to the large range, the linearity curve is not so sensitive to small errors.

If any, these could be seen very clearly within the photon transfer curve. Again, camera is mvBlueCOUGAR-X104dG (Figure 6.80).

Two examples from EMVA1288 documentation show possible errors:
Influence of nonlinearity (Figure 6.81);
Influence of bad ADC (Figure 6.82).

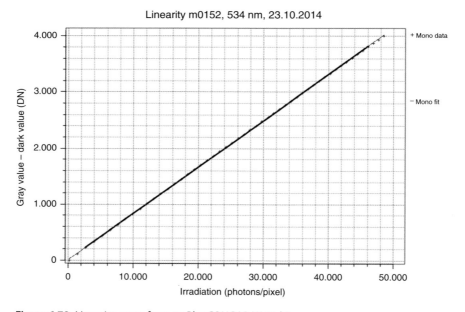

Figure 6.78 Linearity curve from mvBlueCOUGAR-X104dG.

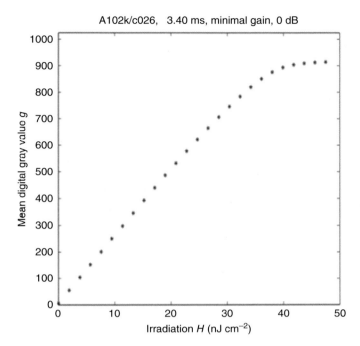

Figure 6.79 Linearity curve with saturation.

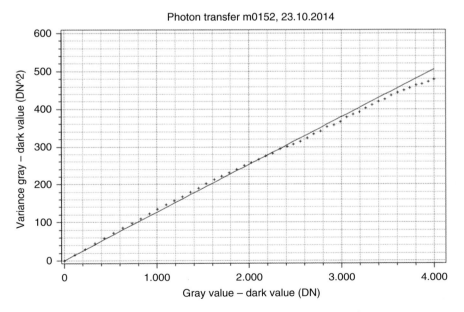

Figure 6.80 Photon transfer response function of mvBlueCOUGAR-X104dG.

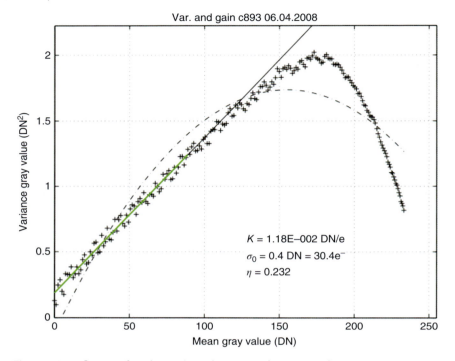

Figure 6.81 Influence of nonlinearity on photon transfer response function.

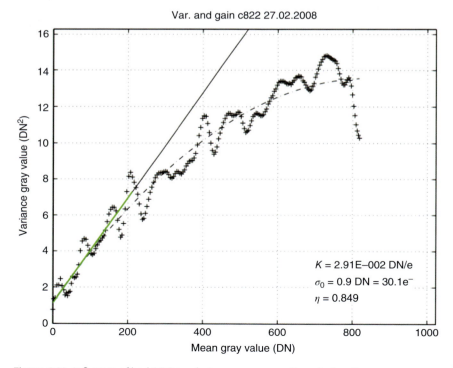

Figure 6.82 Influence of bad ADC on photon response nonlinearity function.

6.7 Camera Noise (by Henning Haider AVT, Updated by Author)

Various different noise sources contribute at different stages in a CCD or CMOS camera to an overall total, appearing at the output of a digital camera.

The following image details the various noise sources. All noise sources are to be added in their quadrature (Figure 6.83).

6.7.1 Photon Noise

As mentioned already earlier, photons generate electrons in the photodiode on a statistical base because of their quantum nature.

That means the count of electrons differs from image to image according to the so-called Poisson distribution.

Noise n in (count of electrons root mean square (rms)) is equal to the square root of the mean N of the generated count of electrons N_{photon}. The maximum of the generated photons is expressed as N_{well}, which is the full well capacity.

$$n_{photon} = \sqrt{N_{photon}} \text{ (e}^- \text{ rms)} \qquad (6.2)$$

Equation 6.2: photon generated noise.

6.7.2 Dark Current Noise

Temperature in silicon material generates a flow of electrons, the so-called dark current, depending on the process and temperature. For CCD sensors, the current is typically much lower than for CMOS sensors. Nevertheless, it doubles per 7–9 °C and it adds up to the photon created electrons in the pixels and the shift registers thus limiting their capacity.

With CMOS sensors this can even limit longer integration times, because the sensor can reach saturation due to the dark current. Its nature is also statistical, so that the following formula applies:

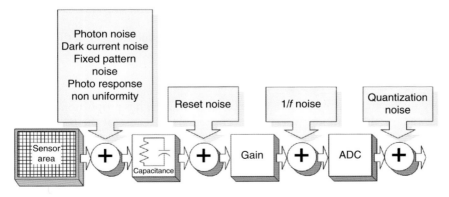

Figure 6.83 Different noise components and their location.

Noise n in (electrons rms) is equal to the square root of the mean N of the dark current electrons:

$$n_{\text{dark}} = \sqrt{N_{\text{dark}}} \quad (e^- \text{ rms}) \tag{6.3}$$

Equation 6.3: dark signal generated noise.

6.7.3 Fixed Pattern Noise (FPN)

Related with the dark current is its electrical behavior to be regionally different on the sensor. This introduces a structural spatial noise component, called *fixed pattern noise*, although it is not meant to be temporal, visible with low illumination conditions.

FPN is typically more dominant with CMOS sensors than with CCD, where it can be ignored mostly.

This noise n_{fpn} (%) is usually quantified in % of the mean dark level.

6.7.4 Photo Response Non Uniformity (PRNU)

Due to local differences in the pixel the count of electrons for a given illumination is not perfectly the same. Every pixel has a slightly different photon to electron response characteristics. Again this is a structural spatial noise component, measured in % n_{prnu} (%) of the maximum signal level.

6.7.5 Reset Noise

Reading out a pixel requires the conversion of the charge into a voltage. This is done via destructive readout with a capacitance, which is reset after the actual pixel value is sampled. Again we have here a variance in the reset level from pixel to pixel, depending on the absolute temperature T and the capacitance C according to the following formula, with q being the elementary charge and k the Boltzmann constant:

$$n_{\text{reset}} = \frac{\sqrt{k \cdot T \cdot C}}{q} \quad (e^- \text{ rms}) \tag{6.4}$$

Equation 6.4: reset noise.

This component can be ignored with CCD sensors due to CDS in the analog front end, as discussed earlier.

6.7.6 1/f Noise (Amplifier Noise)

Every analog amplifier contains a noise component, which is proportional to $1/f$.

Nowadays, this component can be neglected also because of the use of CDS signal preprocessing.

6.7.7 Quantization Noise

Quantization noise is a side effect in the conversion of an analog signal to a digital number. It occurs due to the uncertainty in the switching from one step to the other, usually in the middle of one step.

Obviously it can be made smaller by a larger amount of bits and quantization steps.

Assuming a sawtooth shape of the quantization error, in terms of noise electrons it can be expressed with $N_{electron}$ = count of signal electrons and N = # bits as:

$$n_{adc} = \frac{N_{electron}}{2^N \cdot \sqrt{12}} \quad (\text{e}^- \text{ rms}) \tag{6.5}$$

Equation 6.5: quantization noise.

Normally, quantization is smaller than the noise floor, so that it can be ignored.

6.7.8 Noise Floor

It can be seen from above that the total noise of a camera has a component, which is dependent on the wanted signal, and one component independent of the wanted signal, called the *noise floor*. The noise floor sets the lower limit for the sensitivity of a camera.

The noise floor can be given as:

$$n_{floor} = \sqrt{n_{dark}^2 + n_{fpn}^2} = \sqrt{N_{dark} + n_{fpn}^2} \quad (\text{e}^- \text{ rms}) \tag{6.6}$$

Equation 6.6: noise floor.

6.7.9 Dynamic Range

The dynamic range of a camera is the quotient of wanted signal to ground floor.

$$\text{DNR} = \frac{N_{photon} - N_{dark}}{\sqrt{n_{dark}^2 + n_{fpn}^2}} = \frac{N_{photon} - N_{dark}}{\sqrt{N_{dark} + n_{fpn}^2}} \tag{6.7}$$

Equation 6.7: dynamic range of a camera.

The DNR of a sensor is given related to the maximum signal as:

$$\text{DNR}_{sensor} = \frac{N_{well} - N_{dark}}{\sqrt{N_{dark} + n_{fpn}^2}} \tag{6.8}$$

Equation 6.8: dynamic range of a sensor.

6.7.10 Signal to Noise Ratio

The signal to noise ratio of a camera is the quotient between the total signal and the total noise and could be given as:

$$\text{SNR} = \frac{N_{photon} + N_{dark}}{\sqrt{n_{photon}^2 + N_{dark} + n_{fpn}^2 + n_{prnu}^2 + n_{reset}^2 + n_{adc}^2}} \tag{6.9}$$

Equation 6.9: SNR of a camera.

Simplified by elimination of dark current component via clamping:

$$\text{SNR} = \frac{N_\text{photon}}{\sqrt{N_\text{photon} + N_\text{dark} + n_\text{fpn}{}^2 + n_\text{prnu}{}^2 + n_\text{reset}{}^2 + n_\text{adc}{}^2}} \qquad (6.10)$$

Equation 6.10: simplified SNR of a camera.

Related to the maximum of the sensor:

$$\text{SNR} = \frac{N_\text{well}}{\sqrt{N_\text{well} + N_\text{dark} + n_\text{fpn}{}^2 + n_\text{prnu}{}^2 + n_\text{reset}{}^2 + n_\text{adc}{}^2}} \qquad (6.11)$$

Equation 6.11: simplified SNR of a sensor.

6.7.11 Example 1: SONY IMX-174 Sensor (mvBlueFOX3-2024)

$N_\text{well} = 31\,900\,\text{e}^-$ (own measurements according EMVA1288)
$n_\text{readout} = 5.9\,\text{e}^-$ (own measurements according EMVA1288).

$$\text{DNR} = \frac{31\,900}{5.9} = 5407 = 74.6\,\text{dB} \approx 12.4\,\text{bit}$$
$$\text{SNR} = \frac{31\,900}{\sqrt{31\,900 + 35}} = 178.5 = 45\,\text{dB} \approx 7.5\,\text{bit}$$

6.7.12 Example 2: CMOSIS CMV2000 (mvBlueCOUGAR-X104)

$N_\text{well} \approx 9700\,\text{e}^-$ (own measurements according EMVA1288)
$n_\text{readout} \approx 13\,\text{e}^-$ (own measurements according EMVA1288).

$$\text{DNR} = \frac{9700}{13} = 746 = 57.5\,\text{dB} \approx 9.5\,\text{bit}$$
$$\text{SNR} = \frac{9700}{\sqrt{9700 + 169}} = 97.6 = 39.8\,\text{dB} \approx 6.6\,\text{bit}$$

6.8 Useful Links and Literature

www.cmosis.com – CMOS image sensors
www.framos.de – Image sensors and components
www.atdelectronique.de – Image sensors and components
http://www.emva.org/cms/index.php?idcat=26 – EMVA1288 Standard
http://www.visiononline.org/vision-standards-details.cfm?type=5 – GigE Vision
http://www.visiononline.org/vision-standards-details.cfm?type=11 – USB3 Vision
http://www.emva.org/cms/index.php?idcat=27 – GenICam standard

www.onsemi.com – CCD/CMOS sensors
www.photonfocus.com – Photonfocus CMOS sensors
http://www.sony.net/Products/SC-HP/ – SONY semiconductor
http://www.cs.rit.edu/~ncs/color/ – Information about color
http://www.matrix-vision.com – Homepage of MATRIX VISION
http://www.matrix-vision.com/manuals/ – Manuals of MATRIX VISION
http://damien.douxchamps.net/ieee1394/cameras/search/m/ – List of USB3 cameras
Holst, G.C. (1996) *CCD Arrays, Cameras, and Displays*, SPIE Press.
Theuwissen, A.E. (2014) Seminar on Solid State Imaging Technologies, Harvest imaging.

6.9 Digital Interfaces

Today, more than a handful of rivaling digital interfaces is on the market.

In principle, any interface able to deal with the amount of data of an uncompressed digital video stream, is a candidate.

The requirements can be summarized and prioritized as follows:

- Bandwidth requirement >10 MB s^{-1} per camera in VGA, b/w @ 30 fps
- Secure protocol (HW/SW)
- Robust electrical interface, able to bridge distances of 3–30 m (100 m)
- No image loss
- Low CPU consumption for image acquisition and transfer
- Low latency
- Multicamera support
- Open (vendor independent) standardization for the protocol.

Clearly, *1394a* was pioneering the terrain and together with *1394b* was gaining considerable market share and spread. However, at the time of writing it is clear that this standard is no longer developed for future and faster versions.

USB 2.0 has also proven that it can handle the amount of data, needed to transmit raw, uncompressed digital images into the memory of the PC.

Gigabit Ethernet demonstrated its ability to transport video data over the network architecture with the increase of the network bandwidth. Together with the very well accepted standards GigE Vision and GenICam it is today the interface with the biggest potential and growth rate.

USB 3.0 recently increased 10-fold the performance of USB 2.0 together with overcoming some shortcuts in the architecture. The corresponding camera standard USB3 Vision twins seamlessly with GigE Vision ensuring USB 3.0 is an almost ideal high bandwidth interface for industrial cameras. At the time of writing, UB3.1 was already moving into silicon, with again more than doubling the bandwidth.

Table 6.9 Digital interface comparison.

Interface	IEEE 1394a	USB 2.0	IEEE 1394B	Gigabit ethernet (802.3AB)	Camera link	USB 3.0
Maximum bit rate (Mbps)	400	480	800	1000	>2000	5000
Isochronous (video) mode	Yes	Yes	Yes	No	Yes	Yes
Bandwidth/total usable bandwidth (MB s^{-1})	Video: 32 (80%) Total: 40	45 (90%)	Video: 64 (80%) Total: 80	120	255 (base) 680 (full)	~400
Topology	Peer-to-peer	Master–slave, OTG (On the go)	Peer-to-peer	Networked, P2P	Master–slave	Enhanced master–slave
Single cable distance in copper or other media	4.5 m, worst case; 10 m, typical camera application; 300 m GOF	5–8 m	8 m copper; 300 m GOF	25 m, 100 m (CAT5)	10 m	3 m worst case, 8 m possible; GOF: >100 m
Max. distance copper using repeaters (m)	70	30	70	n.a	30	~15
Bus power	Up to 1.5 A and 36 V	Up to 0.5 A and 5 V	Up to 1.5 A and 36 V	Default: none; power over ethernet (POE)	Default: none; power over CL (POCL)	Up to 0.9 A and 5 V
Motherboard support	Many	Virtually all	Rare	Virtually all	None	Virtually all
CPU load	Very low	Low	Very low	Low to middle	n.a.	Very low
OS support	Windows, Linux	Windows, Linux	Windows, Linux	Windows, Linux	Depending on vendor	Windows, Linux
Main applications	Multimedia electronics	PC-centric serial Input/output	Multimedia electronics	Networking	High speed camera interface	PC-centric serial input/output
Camera standard	IIDC V1.3	None (?)	IIDC V1.31	GigE Vision; GenICam	CL	USB3 Vision
Devices per Bus	63; 4 (8) simultaneous/card, according to 4 (8) DMA's type	Theoretically:127; in practice: <32	63; 4 simult./card, according to 4 DMA's type	Dependent on software and available bandwidth	1 per interface	Theoretically: 255; in practice: <32

All of the above are interfaces, which were not primarily designed for digital camera interfaces, but adopted for this use.

Camera link is today probably the only open digital interface of relevance, which was developed specifically for use in digital image transfer.

It can be said that depending on the application the user has the freedom of choice.

An overview of the important facts and figures are given in Table 6.9.

7

Smart Camera and Vision Systems Design

Howard D. Gray[1] and Nate Holmes[2]

[1] MATRIX Vision GmbH, Talstraße 16, D-71570 Oppenweiler, Germany
[2] National Instruments, 11500 N. Mopac Expwy., Austin, TX 78759, USA

7.1 Introduction to Vision System Design

The design and selection of a vision system involves considering both the hardware and software architecture of the system and how they are to be combined to meet the requirements of an application. As you can see from the diagram of a typical vision application development workflow, this can be a very iterative process (Figure 7.1).

It is iterative because in many ways vision application design is still more of an art than a science. That is, the image content is dependent on complex variables that cannot at this time be modeled and simulated accurately enough to enable design without empirical data. The lighting, lens, and sensor selection all contribute to image content in complex and nuanced ways. The resulting image content and variability will determine what type and complexity of vision algorithms are necessary to achieve satisfactory inspection results, and then the final system for deployment is often chosen based on processing capability to return results in an adequate amount of time, as well as optimizing for space, cost, ease-of-use, maintainability, and other factors. The result is a trial and error approach with vision integrators maintaining "vision labs" full of various lighting, lenses, and vision systems to prototype solutions. Great value is correspondingly placed on experience in the vision integration business, as this experience, versus an inexperienced system designer, will often manifest as a significant savings on the cost and time of a particular project.

Any given application will have multiple requirements that determine appropriate hardware and software selection: size, cost, weight, and physical environment will all play a role. Machine vision processing task(s), speed required, and what other tasks such as input and output (I/O), synchronization, or motion control that the system is tasked with will also play a role. What type of SW architecture will be deployed to the system? What are the processing requirements? Does the system have to be flexible enough to be frequently updated and mass deployed, or will it be a "one off" system for research or

Handbook of Machine and Computer Vision: The Guide for Developers and Users,
Second Edition. Edited by Alexander Hornberg.
© 2017 Wiley-VCH Verlag GmbH & Co. KGaA. Published 2017 by Wiley-VCH Verlag GmbH & Co. KGaA.

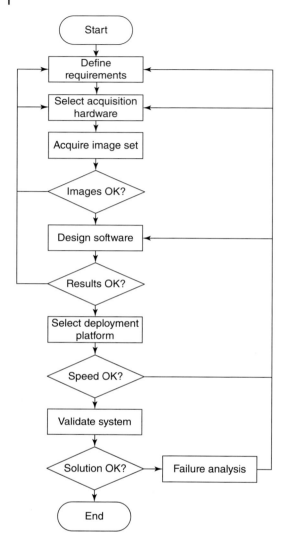

Figure 7.1 Workflow diagram demonstrating the iterative nature of typical vision application design.

a laboratory application? All of these questions will contribute to the design engineer's choice of vision system.

7.2 Definitions

The rise of low-cost heterogeneous deployment platforms and the ability for vision algorithms to be deployed across different hardware architectures has resulted in the emergence of different types of vision hardware to meet varying application needs.

Most articles about vision sensors, smart cameras, or embedded vision systems start with a definition of these terms. For example, in *Smart Cameras*, we find interpretations in Chapter 1 and again in Chapter 2 [1, 2]. The Automated

Imaging Association's (AIA's) Glossary of Machine Vision Terms [3] contains the following, authoritative definitions:

> Vision sensor: A lower-end smart camera. A smart camera with less flexibility and programmability that is usually intended for less demanding applications.
> Smart camera: A complete or near complete vision system contained in the camera body itself ... At a minimum a Smart Camera combines a camera with image processing and MV[1] related programs within the same housing. A smart camera is functionally equivalent to an Embedded Vision Processor. Sometimes smart cameras are called "intelligent cameras" and "Vision Sensors." The term *Vision Sensor* tends to apply to a lower-end Smart Camera.
> Embedded vision processor: configuration of machine vision equipment where a camera is tethered to a specialized, mini-computer (not a PC[2]). Unlike the Smart Camera, the computer power for processing images is external to the camera's housing.

All three terms refer to complete vision systems, that is, equipment incorporating one or more cameras and including hardware and/or software capable of implementing complete machine vision applications. The differences come in the components used in the design.

A vision system aims to tap the image data at source, to analyze this data, and to pass on a result or at least a preprocessed or smaller amount of visual information. In these days of increasingly large image sensor formats, this difference to a camera without intelligence is significant; using a vision system can avoid passing large amounts of unprocessed information from the source to a processing system – data which, in many cases, is destined to be discarded by that processing system. In turn, this allows a significant reduction in the bandwidth required by the transport mechanism, simplifying the infrastructure and reducing the costs.

A practical example is a smart camera that is able to extract the coordinates of objects from an image. Only these coordinates are transferred via a network instead of each and every captured image. In the first case, the information content may be measured in a few bytes, but in the second the infrastructure must be able to handle megabytes of data per second.

Many typical applications, such as bar code and data matrix reading, shape and color recognition, or measurement, may be realized using smart cameras, vision sensors, or embedded vision systems. So how does a system planner decide which type of system to use?

In fact, one main difference between a smart camera and vision sensor is the way it is intended to be *reused*. There is a clue in the AIA glossary [3]; the terms *less flexibility* and *programmability* for vision sensors are mentioned. So let us add some explanations based on these terms to illustrate their use in this chapter:

- Smart cameras are multipurpose devices and are often supplied without a fixed or default function. They must be reprogrammed using a system that may

---

1 Machine vision.
2 Personal computer.

resemble a high-level scripting or programming language or another flexible method.
- Vision sensors are single-purpose, off-the-shelf devices. They may be reconfigured to serve a new purpose or parameters may be adjusted, but they may lack the flexibility to implement new machine vision applications not envisaged by the manufacturer. Since vision sensors are designed for specific tasks they may contain specially designed hardware in field-programmable gate arrays (FPGAs) or application-specific integrated circuits (ASICs) and be very good at these tasks. By including only the electrical interfaces really needed it should be possible to build vision sensors physically smaller (and cheaper) than those in smart cameras. If the range of applications is finite and known by the manufacturer it is easier to supply the sensor with an appropriate, built-in lighting system.
- Embedded vision processors or systems are usually more flexible in their programmability as smart cameras. Configuration or programming takes place on the embedded computer, perhaps like any other PC. In applications where cable lengths between embedded computer and camera are unimportant, where the processing unit hardware is robust enough to be located near to the application itself and where physical size is less important, these systems provide a viable alternative to both smart cameras and vision sensors.

Boundaries between the types of systems are being blurred as vision suppliers seek the right mix of price/performance for application niches and utilize new and ever improving technology. It can be helpful to view the available options on a spectrum (see Figure 7.2), with generally accepted system types shown:

1) Vision sensors
2) Smart cameras
3) Embedded vision systems.

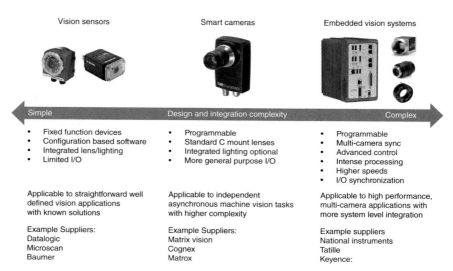

Figure 7.2 Overview of choices for building vision systems.

For each type of machine vision system we will discuss accepted industry definitions, a short history, considerations when choosing between them, and which applications are particularly suited to each type. The information in this chapter is intended to help shorten development time and reduce the number of design iterations necessary in designing a system by providing guidance on which system architectures and characteristics are best suited for particular applications.

7.3 Smart Cameras

Many of the design characteristics for smart cameras apply equally to the design of vision sensors and embedded vision systems. We start by taking a look at some typical design parameters for smart cameras and later highlight the similarities and differences for the other categories.

Figure 7.3 shows a typical smart camera in a compact housing with C-mount lens. As can be inferred from the size of the lens in the image, the dimensions of this casing are small (specifically 65 mm × 100 mm × 40 mm without the lens and cables), yet it contains a complete camera and embedded computer. The following sections explain the technologies used for specific parts of this and similar products and illustrate the design decisions that need to be made when developing such products.

7.3.1 Applications

Smart cameras are used in machine vision applications where the presence of long cables, physically large computing units, and the transfer or large amounts of image data is difficult or impossible due to space restrictions or reliability concerns. Smart cameras can represent an advantage compared with the total costs of separate PCs, cameras, and software. Since the computing power of a single

Figure 7.3 MATRIX VISION mvBlueGEMINI. (Photo courtesy of MATRIX VISION GmbH.)

smart camera is likely to be less than of a PC, some applications must be ruled out on the grounds of complexity.

Typical smart camera applications include the following:

- Bar code and data matrix reading. Printed or stamped codes with different positions, sizes, and rotations
- Optical character recognition (OCR) including learning of new fonts
- Quality checks for completeness in manufacturing, for example, surface quality
- Position and measurement of object parts (absolute length, angles)
- Counting or classifying objects according to shape or color
- Sorting and control of robots
- Crowd or traffic surveillance
- Reading and comparing biometric information.

7.3.2 Component Parts

For an explanation of the component parts of a smart camera that follows please refer to Figure 7.4.

7.3.2.1 Processors

In order to process programming instructions intelligibly a processing unit of some kind is needed. The processor often consists of a standard central processing unit (CPU), similar to that found in a PC system or mobile device. Some devices make use of a digital signal processor (DSP) or have a combination of CPU, DSP, and/or graphics processing unit (GPU).

A number of distinct generations of smart camera processors have been noted [4]. The first recognizable smart cameras in the 1990s were based on DSP technology, the second generation on PC architectures, specifically x86 processors. The need for small, powerful, low-power processors for smart phones, and other mobile devices toward the end of the decade ending 2010 affected smart camera design too. The currently dominant CPUs in this market are based on ARM® technology. Intel's multicore devices, formerly code-named "Bay Trail" and based on Intel® Atom™ technology for notebooks and tablets, are also being used in smart camera designs.

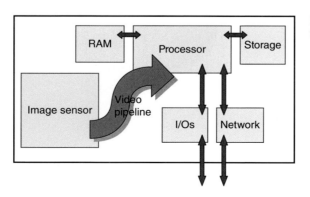

Figure 7.4 Block diagram of a typical smart camera.

Table 7.1 Example processor architectures used in smart cameras.

Processor	Type	Example smart camera	Operating system	Product launch
Analog Devices ADSP2181, 32 MHz	DSP	VC11, Vision Components GmbH [6]	Real-time	1996
PowerPC™, 133–400 MHz	CPU	mvBlueLYNX, MATRIX VISION GmbH [7]	Linux®	2002
PowerPC™, 400–533 MHz	CPU	NI 1722/1742, National Instruments [8]	—	2007
Analog Devices Blackfin® ADSP-BF537, 500 MHz	DSP	LeanXcam, Supercomputing Systems AG [9]	μClinux	2008
Intel® Atom™ (Z530), 1.6 GHz	CPU	Iris GT, Matrox Imaging [10]	Embedded Microsoft® Windows® (various)	2008
Texas Instruments OMAP™ 3750, 1 GHz	CPU/DSP/ GPU Hybrid	mvBlueLYNX-X, MATRIX VISION GmbH [11]	Linux®	2010
Texas Instruments TMS320C64xx, 400 MHz	DSP	VC4012nano, Vision Components GmbH [12]	VC real-time (VCRT)	2010
Xilinx Zynq®, 800 MHz/1 GHz, dual-core	FPGA/SoC	RazerCam, EVT Eye Vision Technology GmbH [13]	Linux®	2014
Altera Cyclone® V, 800 MHz, dual-core	FPGA/SoC	mvBlueGEMINI, MATRIX VISION GmbH [14]	Linux®	2015

Recently, affordable combinations of FPGA and CPU have become available, notably from Xilinx Zynq® and Altera Cyclone V series. For camera designs that previously required separate FPGAs these system-on-chip (SoC) devices can now offer many similar features to the two-chip designs but now combined in a single package. This is not only an advantage in terms of the overall size of the design and lower power requirements but also provides very high bandwidths between FPGA and CPU (typically 5–10 GB s^{-1} [5]).

Table 7.1 shows examples of processing units used in smart cameras over the past two decades.

For the developer of a smart camera the factors involved in the choice of processor include the following:

- The speed or performance and/or the number of parallel cores
- Peripheral components and bus systems supported by the processor
- The architecture and, therefore, the operating systems (OSs) supported
- Cost
- Software development – are cross-compiler or "native" development tools and equipment needed?

- Power requirements, possible heat dissipation methods, and environmental conditions, for example, ambient temperature
- Types of volatile and nonvolatile memory available
- Video pipeline – how are image sensors controlled and how are image data to be saved in memory or accessed by the processor, for example, DMA (direct memory access)? Some embedded processors actually include camera ports and video pipelines. In other designs the pipeline will need to be implemented using external logic, for example, FPGAs.

For the end user of a smart camera or a vision system planner the significance of some of the above factors clearly depends on the usage scenario; for example, the environmental conditions. Other factors may be not so obvious. For example,

- The implementation of the video pipeline is probably an internal or proprietary detail and not useful in the comparison of smart camera products. More obviously important is the resultant range of image sensors available from the manufacturer.
- Good speed or performance of the camera is a universally required feature, and, incidentally, one of the more difficult to quantify for a programmable camera.
- Power requirements are likely to be important to the end user because a smart camera represents a significant advantage in this area over more conventional, PC-based machine vision systems. More information about power requirements and restrictions is to be found in Section 7.3.4.1.

7.3.2.2 FPGA Processing

As mentioned above, the advent of FPGA SoC devices has spawned a number of new smart camera designs. In fact, FPGAs have been used for a number of years to support the integration of image sensors or to facilitate real-time I/Os, as mentioned in Section 7.3.2.6, albeit as devices separate from the CPU.

A vision system with the ability to reprogram FPGA devices with components able to preprocess image data, or in another way to support the particular machine vision algorithm being used for an application, could have significant advantages of overall speed and deterministic behavior compared to systems based only on conventional CPUs. Examples of tasks that could be performed in this way are, the compression of images for transmission to a monitoring system, or the extraction of coordinates for candidate objects within image data. In the latter case, algorithms running as software on the CPU do not need to search through the whole image data for objects but, instead, can start processing the candidates directly.

Since programming FPGAs is not necessarily a core skill associated with image processing expertise, a number of ways exist to speed up the implementation of machine vision algorithms in FPGA fabric. For Xilinx FPGAs and for the Xilinx Zynq® series of FPGA/SoCs it is possible to use Silicon Software's Visual Applets [15] software to program FPGA content using a graphical front end. Another option is the LabVIEW Graphical programming environment from National Instruments, which includes a high level vision algorithm development tool called Vision Assistant that can be used to estimate resource utilization and script code that can be directly complied for Xilinx FPGAs. Smart cameras based on this FPGA technology, such as the EVT RazerCam or Tattile cameras using EVT EyeVision 3.0, are able to make use of this method to add hardware acceleration to user applications [16].

An alternative and promising solution may be to use OpenCL™, which the Khronos® Group describes as an "open standard for parallel programming of heterogeneous systems" [17]. Altera claims that its Cyclone V SoC Development Kit is the first conformant OpenCL software development kit (SDK) for FPGAs [18]. Using it, machine vision algorithms, written and tested on a CPU or GPU system, can be converted into a compatible form for direct use in the FPGA fabric. This new feature, previously only available for high-end devices, has the potential to give huge speed advantages to machine vision applications.

7.3.2.3 Memory and Storage

Irrespective of the processor used in a smart camera the OS and video pipeline will need volatile random access memory (RAM) to store and process image data. Typical technologies used for the memory include double data rate 2 (DDR2) and double data rate 3 (DDR3) and a total capacity of between 64 MB and 2 GB. Fast RAM is a power-hungry component that needs significant physical space inside the camera, which places a natural limit on the total memory. As mentioned in Section 7.3.2.5, the amount of memory needed beyond the normal requirements of the OS can be significant for large image sensor formats.

In addition to RAM, non-volatile storage will be required in order to contain the OS, application, and configuration. In an embedded design this is usually provided by a form of flash memory that retains its contents without a power supply. The technology used can be discrete NOR or NAND devices or a combination with controller in the form of a memory card. Examples include: Secure Digital (SD), MultiMediaCard (MMC), embedded MultiMediaCard (eMMC), or solid state disk (SSD). Once again, the availability of large flash-based devices can be attributed to the advances in the market for mobile equipment. Hard disks as storage medium are no longer used in modern smart cameras since they have moving parts and are less likely to survive shocks and vibrations in a harsh, industrial environment.

It is important to note that the use of flash memory can lead to problems if an end user is unaware of its limitations. The lifetime of each memory cell is limited to a finite number of programming and erase cycles (typically several hundred thousand cycles). This makes it unwise to use flash storage to store images or to log data continually. A compromising solution may have to be found, for example, storing data in RAM and transferring only essential information to flash memory at intervals or using the network to export data to external storage devices. Memory devices with a built-in controller implement sophisticated mechanisms designed to prolong the life of flash memory and to allow a standard file system to be used by the OS. Some embedded OSs make use of specialist flash file systems that implement wear leveling algorithms to distribute data evenly over all the memory cells when using discrete flash devices without their own controller. The Linux® kernel provides, for example, the "Journaling Flash File System" (JFFS/JFFS2) and other solutions, such as "Yet Another Flash File System" (YAFFS), are available too.

Exactly which method is used in a smart camera and whether restrictions or recommendations exist for the use of flash memory is important information that ideally should be available to end users of the camera.

7.3.2.4 Operating Systems

Designers of smart cameras have used a wide range of OSs in their products. For any given processor a smart camera designer may have a choice of OSs, both commercial and freely available. The more specialized a processor, the smaller will be the choice of OSs. It follows that CPU-type processors allow more choice of OS than DSPs. However, a DSP's OS may be developed by the processor manufacturer itself. Using this "insider knowledge" the manufacturer is able to extract the highest possible performance from its own hardware.

The OS itself may be hidden from and be unimportant to the user if the camera is merely configured via a web interface or other similar tools. However, when advanced programming skills are required many users prefer a camera that recognizably runs the same OS as their desktop PC. Some users have already built up considerable knowledge of image processing algorithms and have a tried-and-tested library which they would like to continue to use with a smart camera. If this library is in turn dependent on commercial products that are available only for particular OSs, software compatibility with other systems, previous products, or with proprietary machine vision libraries may dictate the optimal OS which, in turn, will restrict the choice of processor architecture. For example, the use a commercial machine vision library that is available only for current versions of the Windows® OS will effectively limit the choice of architecture to x86 or ARM® processors. Linux® has traditionally been more flexible with support for x86, ARM®, PowerPC®, and many others. Neither of these OSs are likely to be used in a smart camera that contains a DSP as its only processing unit, although versions of the Linux® kernel have been ported to DSPs [19].

7.3.2.4.1 Real-Time Operating Systems

An OS is defined as real-time if the maximum time for a known operation is deterministic – an output is guaranteed within a known time. Traditional OSs used on desktop PCs or for server systems do not fulfill this requirement but can come very close to it; close enough to make their use in a smart camera system feasible, especially if specialized hardware (e.g., a FPGA) is used to handle critical I/O signals without intervention by the CPU or OS.

The Open Source Automation Development Lab (OSADL) [20] supports the integration of real-time patches into the Linux® kernel through sponsorship provided by membership fees and provides testing facilities for members. In January 2015 it announced [21] it had raised a further €250 000 to continue its integration policy so it now seems likely that the mainstream Linux® kernel will be supplied with improved real-time features in the future. Before this announcement the future of the real-time patch set was uncertain.

A further possibility is the combination of standard OS and real-time scheduler. Effectively, the whole OS becomes a pre-emptive process, that is, it is executed with a lower priority than other real-time tasks that are used for the most demanding operations. Commercial schedulers of this type are available for Windows®, for example, Interval Zero's RTX and RTX64 products [22]. For Linux®, a number of open source projects aim to provide a separate real-time scheduler. Examples include The Real Time Application Interface (RTAI) [23] and Xenomai [24].

Examples of tasks performed by a smart camera requiring near real-time facilities are as follows:

- Input signals used as a trigger for capturing images
- Output signals used to control an external flash light, synchronized with image capture
- Other signals dependent on accurate timers within the smart camera.

7.3.2.4.2 Updates Processor-based cameras are complex systems: it is unrealistic to expect OSs and applications to be completely free of programming errors. Therefore, it is extremely likely that a smart camera manufacturer will need to provide software and firmware updates from time to time. In this way, new features may also be added or security problems in the OS itself, corrected. The majority of smart cameras used in manufacturing processes are unlikely to have a direct, unprotected connection with the Internet but they may well be accessed by normal PCs, which in turn do have Internet access. Arguably, cameras most at risk from security issues are those with a similar architecture and identical OS to that of standard PCs. Cameras with specialized processors or OS are not as widespread and unlikely to be targeted.

The designer of a smart camera needs to decide on an update policy and the user needs to know the answers to these basic questions:

- Will security updates to the OS be made available for the camera? For how long?
- Will feature updates be possible?
- How easy is it to apply an update once a camera is *in situ* in an application?
- Does the manufacturer offer support for cameras that an end user has decided not to update?

7.3.2.5 Image Sensors

The differences between complementary metal-oxide-semiconductor (CMOS) and charge-coupled device (CCD) sensors have been explained in other chapters in this book. Of course, all the criteria used in the choice of image sensors for other cameras apply equally to smart cameras. For the smart camera designer the electrical interface (serial, parallel, low-voltage differential signaling LVDS, etc.) to the image sensor and other control buses such as I-squared-C (I^2C) or serial peripheral interface (SPI) are important and must be adequately supported by the CPU and the software.

The characteristics of the image sensor; its size in mega pixels or line length for line scan sensors, its maximum frame rate, and so on, are major factors in the design of the smart camera electronics. Processing very high-resolution images, particularly in color, requires extremely powerful hardware and software but it is not only the processing power that needs to be considered. Despite the recent advances in embedded processors, the restrictions on space and cooling possibilities in an embedded system place an upper limit on other hardware components that are not present in desktop systems. Consider a typical color area sensor with around 5 million pixels (e.g., Aptina MT9P031 with a resolution of 2592×1944) and a smart camera required to hold, say, 30 color images in volatile memory (RAM). The majority of image processing libraries will need color data in its component parts of red, green, and blue (RGB) so the smart camera will need to convert each image into an RGB format. Assuming that each color component part is the same size as the raw image before color extraction, the total amount of RAM needed to hold 30 color images and the original data can, therefore, be calculated:

$$\begin{aligned} \text{RAM requirement} &= \text{number of images} \\ &\quad \times ((\text{size of one color component} \times 3) \\ &\quad + \text{size of raw image}) \\ &= 30 \times ((5\,\text{MB} \times 3) + 5\,\text{MB}) \\ &= 30 \times 20\,\text{MB} \\ &= 600\,\text{MB} \end{aligned}$$

Allowing for the RAM requirements of the OS itself the smart camera will need around 1 GB of volatile memory in this configuration; a typical upper limit for a high-end smart camera today. By comparison a modern desktop computer is usually fitted with at least 4 GB of RAM and has extension slots available for more memory.

For the developers and users of smart cameras the factors involved in the choice of image sensor include the following:

- The size in mega pixels – that is, the resolution in pixels
- The theoretical speed of image acquisition from the sensor, as specified by the manufacturer
- The technology used for the sensor (CMOS, CCD, shutter type, etc.)
- The quality characteristics of the sensor (signal-to-noise ratios, sensitivity, dynamic range, bad-pixel quota, fixed-pattern noise, etc.)
- The maximum possible throughput of image data with the processor in the camera given the required complexity of the algorithms used to process images.

7.3.2.6 Inputs and Outputs

Since a smart camera is capable of processing images and making decisions based on the content it also needs to be able to signal the decision made to the outside world. A signal that merely turns on an alarm lamp does not need to be particularly fast; a real-time output is not needed here. But typically, in a quality control process, an output signal will indicate that a failed part is to be removed from the production line. In a fast-moving process such a signal will be required within milliseconds of the decision. Here, it may be necessary to support the CPU with dedicated hardware or FPGA logic to ensure that once the decision has been made no further nondeterministic delays ensue.

Some smart camera models reserve particular outputs for controlling external lighting and may have a standardized connector for lighting too.

Similarly, input signals are needed to trigger image acquisition within microseconds of an external event. It may be tempting to consider using the processor, with its almost unlimited possibilities, to program logic combinations in order to generate output signals or make use of combined input signals. However, it may be important to reserve the processor for image processing tasks and leave time-critical signaling to hardware or FPGA logic, without intervention from the processor. Cameras with dedicated trigger inputs are common; some models allow all inputs to be used for this function.

When comparing the characteristics of smart camera I/Os it is therefore important to consider how many signals are needed for real-time and how many for normal signal operation.

Users of smart cameras will be interested in the answers to many of the following questions about the I/Os of a smart camera being evaluated:

- How many real-time and normal I/Os are available and are these fixed or more flexible with bidirectional circuitry?
- How deterministic are the real-time I/Os? Can an exact timing relationship to an image sensor event, for example, exposure time, be programmed?
- What is the electrical load that can be driven by outputs, both individually and in total for the camera?
- What is the switching voltage level for the inputs – programmable logic controller (PLC) levels, transistor–transistor logic (TTL), or programmable by the user?
- Does the application require electrically isolated I/Os? Are they protected against short circuit or reversed connections?
- Is there a requirement for differential inputs, for example, to reduce the interference on long signal lines?
- Are signals from position encoders with phase-shifted outputs to be used as smart camera inputs? Can the camera interpret the directional information from such signals correctly?
- Can output signals be generated by chains of logic, by combination with other signals or with timers and counters? Can input signals be used as part of such chains in order to trigger an internal event?

7.3.2.6.1 Field Buses The ability to integrate a smart camera into an industrial process controlled by a PLC is a worthwhile goal. Since machine vision systems are used in industrial environments it is becoming increasingly common to find industrial standard buses and protocols in use with smart cameras. Protocols based on industrial Ethernet stacks appear to be replacing older systems that use RS485 or similar serial-bus technology [25]. Smart cameras, with their inherent networking capabilities, are predestined to be used to implement industrial Ethernet field buses.

At the very least, these protocols allow a PLC to start or stop a preprogrammed machine vision task running on the smart camera or to allow signaling from

Table 7.2 Common field bus protocols.

Name	Type
PROFINET	Industrial Ethernet
Ethernet/IP	Industrial Ethernet
EtherCAT	Industrial Ethernet
MODBUS/TCP	Industrial Ethernet
MODBUS	Serial
PROFIBUS	Serial
CANbus	Serial
IO-Link	Serial

the camera to other devices in the process. Complete integration of the smart camera's programming interface into the control program of the PLC remains, for the moment, a difficult task. Programming smart cameras often still requires a detailed knowledge of machine vision in order to solve a visual inspection or measurement task. According to participants in a podium discussion at the SPS Drives trade fair in November 2014, many conventional or graphical programming interfaces used to generate an application for the camera are not yet compatible with PLC programming and many PLC programmers lack explicit machine vision knowledge [26].

The multitude of different standards available makes a detailed analysis here difficult. There are strong regional differences in the distribution of particular protocol standards worldwide so we will restrict ourselves to listing a table of common standards that are likely to be available in smart cameras now or in the near future (Table 7.2).

Table 7.2 shows examples of common field bus protocols that may be available in smart cameras.

N.B. Gateway products exist to convert from one field bus protocol to another so that the absence of support for a particular protocol in a smart camera may not exclude its use from a given automation process, as long as an appropriate gateway is used.

7.3.2.7 Other Interfaces

Smart cameras may be fitted with other interfaces beyond the standard I/O signals and an Ethernet interface. Examples include USB host and USB on-the-go (OTG) interfaces. A camera with a USB host interface emulates a PC. Host interfaces are used to connect USB peripheral equipment such as a computer mouse or keyboard. External USB mass storage is also usable with a host interface. A camera with a USB OTG interface is, itself, a peripheral device, for example, implements a mass storage device to allow direct access to internal storage. With OTG it is also possible to use point-to-point serial and network protocols via the physical USB medium, for example, for debugging purposes or configuration of the Ethernet network.

Cameras with video outputs for the direct connection of monitors with a Video Graphic Array (VGA), Digital Video Interface (DVI), or High-Definition Multimedia Interface (HDMI) connector are available.

Monitor, mouse, and keyboard allow display and control of the OS (e.g., Windows®) or the application. The monitor may be needed to display the live image seen by the camera, for example, when setting up lens and lighting when the complete image is not transferred via the network.

Other interfaces, no longer as common in PC systems, are serial ports conforming to RS232, RS485, or RS422 standards.

7.3.2.8 Timers and Counters

An important feature of cameras used for machine vision is the inclusion of accurate hardware timers and counters. Timers may be considered to be a special case of counters that are supplied with a clock signal running at a known frequency. Counters may be incremented or decremented using signals from an application or potentially asynchronously from an external source via an input. Timers and counters are often implemented in FPGA fabric so that they can be combined with the logic used for triggers or to generate accurate output signals.

- The smart camera's programming interface should include the ability to use built-in timers and counters and allow for their use with I/O signals.

7.3.3 Programming and Configuring

A smart camera's programming interface is arguably the most important aspect involved in the selection of the camera. The amount of time needed and the level of skills involved are essential factors involved in the cost of setting up a machine vision system. If use of a smart camera requires new or different programming skills than those already in use in an organization it may be necessary to recruit new staff or to outsource programming to specialist companies.

Ideally, a smart camera will be programmed or configured using a skill, an OS, or a library already well known from previous products or experience. By reusing tried-and-tested methods ported from more traditional machine vision systems, an end user can significantly reduce the time and effort needed to solve a problem. Alternatively, the smart camera itself must provide an intuitive interface able to be used by people who are not experts in the choice or implementation of image processing algorithms.

In the following sections we will describe a number of different ways to program or to configure smart cameras and provide examples of products using these methods.

7.3.3.1 Scripting

Scripting means the use of a high-level programming language used for a run-time environment that interprets the script directly, that is, it avoids the use of a compiler stage.

Scripts have the advantages of a rapid prototyping system, that is, the effect of changes in the script can be tested immediately after a change is made. By the use of different but compatible interpreters for PC and smart camera systems it is possible to use identical scripts on both systems. The run-time interpreters abstract the hardware and hide the differences from the user. Some smart cameras will allow the creation and editing of scripts directly on the camera without the use of a PC as a development system. Sometimes scripts are created by hand using a text editor or they will be the result of a semi-automated process, for example, a visual programming environment.

Compared to a compiled binary application, a traditional, interpreted script may show a speed disadvantage due to the overheads of the interpreter.

An example of a scripting system used in machine vision is MVTec's Embedded HALCON using its *HDevEngine* product [27]. Examples of smart camera systems supported are listed on the MVTec website [28].

7.3.3.2 High-Level Languages

High-level programming languages used in machine vision include C, C++, Java, C#, or other languages implemented with the .NET framework. Although it is beyond the scope of this book to discuss the comparative advantages or disadvantages of individual programming languages it is important to note that the language itself will significantly determine the work flow for programming a smart camera. Here we describe a number of different work-flow methods.

7.3.3.2.1 Cross-Compiling In the case of traditional, compiled languages such as C or C++, compiler and linker may not necessarily be installed on the camera itself. This is due to the limited storage specifications of an embedded system and the speed at which complex applications need to be compiled. It is therefore not uncommon for a smart camera manufacturer to supply a "cross-compiler" suitable for use on a conventional PC – the host system. Here, all the advantages of an integrated development environment (IDE), large volatile memory, and powerful processor are harnessed to enable an application to be quickly written and compiled. The resulting binary files are often unusable on the PC itself, as it may use a different CPU or OS, so they need to be transferred to the camera – the target system – before being tested. IDEs such as Eclipse [29] largely automate the process of integrating a cross-compiler and downloading compiled code to a target system. Even remote debugging of an application is possible within Eclipse.

Of course, as embedded processors approach the performance values previously only reached by desktop systems, running graphical IDEs, and compiling natively on the host system (i.e., the camera itself) is becoming increasingly common. This implies, however, that the camera itself has all the interfaces needed to emulate a small PC, for example, connections for mouse, keyboard, and for a monitor. Once development of a machine vision application has been completed, these interfaces may well remain unnecessary and unused, as well as occupying valuable space for connectors or increasing the power consumption of the smart camera.

7.3.3.2.2 Java and .NET In Java, the source code is converted to byte code which is then converted within a machine-specific Java virtual machine (JVM) by a "just-in-time" (JIT) compiler at run-time. In C# the .NET framework converts the source code to an intermediate form, the common intermediate language (CIL) and the common language runtime (CLR) creates machine-specific code at run-time. Both languages include garbage collection systems designed to make memory management easier and safer but the unpredictability [30] of the time requirements needed for the garbage collector should be seriously investigated if deterministic processing is required. Both have the advantage of portability of the executable code. It should be possible to create a single binary application on one system, for example, a PC, and then transfer it without change to a smart camera where it will work too. In reality the specific differences in hardware (e.g., I/Os) between a PC and a smart camera may make using identical binaries difficult.

7.3.3.2.3 Visual Programming Visual programming involves the end user of a computer system constructing applications using graphical elements. Since the nature of a machine vision system involves a large visual content it very much makes sense to allow a user to see what the camera sees and to allow selection of artifacts, regions, and objects within the camera image during the programming stage. The effects of processing the image or the objects can then be shown to the user who can make corrections or add further processing steps. By adding the possibility to control I/Os, lighting and other peripheral parts of the camera or to determine actions based on results, an approach to programming based on problem-solving rather than image-processing theory is possible. Thus, a visual programming technique to the configuration of a smart camera has long been requested by end users.

However, the challenges for the designer to incorporate an intuitive, graphical programming interface into a smart camera are extremely complex. At the underlying level a first-class image processing library is necessary to process the images. The camera will need to be able to display not only the scene involved but acceptable, easily identifiable graphical elements. The actual programming of an application will require a pointing device like a mouse to drag and drop elements and possibly a keyboard to enter textual information such as parameters.

A host PC usually has all the prerequisites for visual programming: a mouse, keyboard, graphical display, and a powerful processor for controlling a complex, graphical application. This approach has been used by smart camera manufacturers such as Matrox [31] and National Instruments [32]. If the camera can supply live images during the programming process the result of visual programming can be a script, as noted above, or a binary application that can be transferred to the smart camera.

Just as the development of smart phones and tablets has created spin-off technology in the form of embedded processors suitable for smart cameras, web-based control of devices has resulted in the need for more powerful web-technologies. Examples include the development of extensive Java Script libraries, a technology that has its roots in the original Netscape browser and was first standardized in 1998 [33]. Another standard, HTML5 [34], aims to improve multimedia support in browsers and includes the WebSocket API [35] for two-way communications between a web server and browser.

Smart cameras usually come with the prerequisites needed to implement browser-based configuration and control:

- Ethernet network support, often 1000BASE-T/IEEE 802.3ab "Gigabit" Ethernet
- OSs with complete TCP/IP stacks
- The ability to make use of modern web servers supporting the WebSocket API.

A major advantage of this approach is that no software other than a standard browser is needed on the PC used to configure or monitor the smart camera, as long as standardized, nonproprietary technologies are used. Equally important: by making use of the powerful CPU and GPU technology contained in a modern desktop PC, the work-intensive display of graphical information is not handled by the smart camera, leaving its resources free to handle real-time machine vision tasks.

An example of a smart camera using web-based configuration is the MATRIX VISION mvBlueGEMINI [14].

7.3.3.3 Third-Party Tools

In addition to tools specifically designed by camera manufacturers for their own products a number of third-party tools and libraries exist. One, MVTec's HALCON, has already been mentioned because it has been explicitly ported to several smart cameras.

Libraries may be available in source-code, particularly if the smart camera has an open OS such as Linux®. An example of this type of library is "Open Source Computer Vision" (OpenCV) [36]. In theory, given sufficient information from the camera manufacturer and an adequate SDK an end user can build and use such libraries without explicit support from the manufacturer.

A camera that uses the Windows® OS and a CPU based on Intel's x86 architecture can often be used just like a Windows® PC, that is, commercial machine vision libraries may be installed in binary form. For example, the discontinued Ximea CURRERA-R smart camera, using Windows® and an Intel® Atom™ x86 Z530 CPU, was able to support the full PC version of HALCON, Cognex® VisionPro®, MathWorks MATLAB®, Matrox MIL, and National Instruments LabVIEW, amongst others [37].

7.3.4 Environment

7.3.4.1 Power Dissipation

Power dissipation has already been mentioned in Section 7.3.2.1 since the main source of power dissipation is normally the most complex device – the processor or an FPGA. However, care must be taken when comparing manufacturers' data sheets for such devices. A typical scenario for a smart camera being used for machine vision in a manufacturing process is 100% CPU load, 24 h a day, 7 days a week. Therefore, power figures referring to terms such as "typical power dissipation" (TDP) or "scenario power dissipation" (SDP) depend on the exact definition of these terms, sadly often lacking. In fact, CPUs designed explicitly for smart phones and mobile devices will have power requirements based on a completely different scenario than that common in machine vision because the power-hungry components of a smart phone, the display, and the wireless connection, are only used intermittently.

The term *Green Automation* has been adopted by smart camera manufacturers wishing to highlight the advantages of embedded vision systems in terms of energy conservation.

Strongly related to the power requirements is the maximum ambient temperature for the machine vision system as part of the designated application. Consider the following real example.

A small smart camera in a metal casing (zinc die-cast with a size of 100 mm × 50 mm × 40 mm) has a thermal resistance of $4.15\,\text{K}\,\text{W}^{-1}$. The electronics within the camera generate approximately 7 W of thermal energy resulting in a temperature difference across the casing of:

$$4.15\,\text{K}\,\text{W}^{-1} \times 7\,\text{W} = 29\,\text{K}$$

With an ambient temperature of 23 °C the temperature of the outside of the case is measured to be 49 °C after an appropriately long settling time. A camera this hot is already uncomfortable to be held in the hand. Far more important is the fact that the inside temperature of the camera is likely to be nearly 30 °C higher.

Clearly, the camera in the above example will need to be redesigned with a different material (e.g., aluminum) to reduce the thermal resistance or to use sophisticated passive components such as heat sinks or heat pipes in order to be used at higher ambient temperatures, otherwise the temperature within the casing will exceed the nominal limits for many components being used. Even if the manufacturer has chosen the majority of electronic components to conform to military grade use, most commercial image sensors are simply not specified to work at these high temperatures. The result will be higher noise levels in the image data and shorter component lifetimes. In this example it would also seem appropriate to try to reduce the power dissipated by the camera. By halving the thermal resistance and reducing the power requirements to 5 W, the temperature difference across the casing will be reduced to around 10 °C.

Machine vision systems based on desktop PCs do not have this problem – they will, of course, contain a number of fans and ventilation slots. However, active cooling methods with moving parts are unlikely to be popular in many situations where a smart camera is used since they are likely to be considerably less reliable than passive methods.

Implementing very low power devices opens up new possibilities for reducing cabling, for example, a smart camera with a power requirement of only 5 W may be designed with a Power-over-Ethernet (PoE) option that uses existing Ethernet cables for the network and power supply.

7.3.4.2 Ingress Protection

One of the major advantages of smart cameras over PC-based systems is the ability to deploy them in harsh environments. Here, the ingress protection (IP) class of the casing plays an important role when choosing a smart camera. The IP class defines whether the internal electronics are protected against moisture or dust

Table 7.3 IP classes commonly used for smart cameras.

IP class	Protection against ...
IP30	Objects >2.5 mm, not protected against harmful ingress of water
IP40	Objects >1 mm, not protected against harmful ingress of water
IP51	Dust protected, dripping water
IP65	Dust tight, water jets
IP67	Dust tight, immersion up to 1 m
IP68	Dust tight, immersion beyond 1 m

Figure 7.5 IP67 and standard Ethernet connectors. (Photo: Gray.)

and are regulated by the international ANSI/IEC standard number 60529 [38]. Table 7.3 shows examples of IP classes commonly available in commercial smart cameras. An important fact to note is that a higher IP class will usually require appropriate connectors and cables. These are likely to be more expensive than standard equipment. Figure 7.5 shows a circular (M12) x-coded Ethernet connector certified to IP67 and the equivalent, standard RJ-45 network plug. The IP67 version is considerably more expensive than the standard connector.

Even if the application environment does not require a high IP class for the smart camera the extra costs for specialist cables may adversely affect the total project budget.

7.4 Vision Sensors

Figure 7.6 shows a vision sensor with programming device, mounted and used in a typical application. The device has a built-in lens and lighting but is nevertheless smaller than a typical smart camera (specifically 50 mm × 50 mm × 40 mm without cables). A separate viewing and configuring device is available (shown in the image), making the use of a PC unnecessary. This vision sensor is also typical in that it is available in a number of different variations. For example, there is a model specifically for code reading and one fitted with infra-red lighting [39]. If the end user has a requirement that can be met with one of these options off-the-shelf

Figure 7.6 BVS-E vision sensor. (Photo courtesy of Balluff GmbH.)

there is no need to invest in extra software packages, making the vision sensor an economic alternative to a programmable smart camera.

Since smart cameras and vision sensors are very closely related, in the following sections we will restrict ourselves to mentioning only the differences between the two categories or highlighting similarities when they are especially relevant to vision sensors.

7.4.1 Applications

Typical vision sensor camera applications are those that require less computing power, have less available physical space or will be controlled by operators less skilled in machine vision than for smart camera applications. Complex or unusual applications are not usually realized with vision sensors for the simple fact that manufacturers concentrate on implementing the most common requirements for the mass market. Users requiring more flexibility are expected to use more expensive smart camera models.

Essentially, the same list of examples of smart camera applications can be applied to vision sensors. If the device has been specially designed for one of these tasks its performance may even be better than a flexible smart camera. However, if the processing unit is not as powerful, only simplified versions of these application types may be possible. Please compare with the smart camera, Section 7.3.1.

- Bar code and data matrix reading. Printed or stamped codes, possibly with known position, size, and rotation
- Simple OCR for known fonts
- Identification of parts for simple sorting
- Elementary quality checks for completeness in manufacturing, for example, fill-level control, presence of all component parts
- Counting or classifying objects according to shape or color

- Replacement for other sensors such as photoelectric barriers
- Machine vision applications where small size and low weight requirements are combined with difficult accessibility for cables, for example, movable robots and robotic arms.

7.4.2 Component Parts

Despite the possible differences in application fit, the basic hardware of vision sensors resembles that of smart cameras.

A processor capable of being programmed and able to implement machine vision algorithms is essential, whether as a separate CPU or DSP or integrated into another device with its own video pipeline. FPGAs or FPGA/SoCs are also a possibility here since they are available in many different combinations: the number of logic gates in the FPGA fabric and the number and speed of CPU kernels can be scaled down to the minimum necessary to implement specific machine vision applications without essentially changing the hardware or software design structure.

Likewise, memory and storage requirements can be reduced and unnecessary interfaces removed if a known set of machine vision applications are available.

The choice of image sensors is likely to be smaller and reduced resolutions common, since the basic processing power of vision sensor may prohibit handling large amounts of data. For example, while image sensors with 5 megapixels (i.e., 2592×1944 pixels) are found in smart cameras, vision sensors may use VGA formats (i.e., 640×480 pixels) and less complex optics.

Some form of I/O lines will still be necessary in order to trigger image acquisition or signal results. A network interface may not be strictly necessary or may be implemented at lower speeds. The simpler field bus protocols, better suited to signaling sensor results (e.g., IO-Link) are likely to become available to facilitate integration of vision sensors into industrial processes.

7.4.3 Programming and Configuring

If a user of vision sensors is assumed to be less skilled in machine vision applications than a smart camera user it follows that the configuration interface should be simpler to operate. For some applications fewer parameters are presented to the user.

A vision sensor built with a single purpose in mind may contain comparatively simple application software, but if the vision sensor is not going to be unduly restricted in its field of operation, this means, paradoxically, that the software built into the device might need to be more intelligent and more complex to design than for a smart camera – the built-in intelligence needs to replace the missing machine vision knowledge of the user. Given the restrictions on performance, size, and cost presented to a vision sensor designer, requiring more intelligence represents a design challenge. Vision sensor manufacturers solve this conundrum by placing restrictions elsewhere, normally by implementing only a limited number of fixed applications, allowing only one type of application to be "loaded" into the vision sensor at one time, or requiring a separate device for configuring than the one used to program the vision sensor.

7.4.4 Environment

The environmental considerations for vision sensors are very similar to or even more demanding than those for smart cameras. As vision sensors tend to be smaller than smart cameras they may be located closer to potentially hazardous processes and farther away from people. A casing with a very small volume, that nevertheless still contains a complex microprocessor system, is difficult to keep cool and more difficult to repair.

7.5 Embedded Vision Systems

Embedded vision systems differ from smart cameras and vision sensors in that the vision processing and I/O are physically separated from the camera by a cable and the camera sends images back to the embedded vision system over a standard digital bus via an imaging communication standard like USB3 Vision or GigE Vision. Separating the computational unit and I/O from the camera, lens, and lighting has a few drawbacks but provides for several advantages relative to smart cameras and vision sensors that make it appealing for high performance, specialized, or multi-camera systems.

The advantages of the embedded vision system approach are higher performance processing, multi-camera connectivity, quantity and variety of I/O, flexibility in component selection, and flexibility in system integration. The tradeoffs for these advantages are that embedded vision systems are typically more complex to set up and program, and are more expensive than smart cameras or vision sensors.

- *Higher performance processing*: The larger size and heat dissipation capabilities found in embedded vision systems allow for the use of higher performance processors, more memory, and more disk space. Most embedded vision systems at the time of this writing incorporate an Intel® Core™ i7 class multi-core processor @ 2+ GHz, 4 or 8 GB DDR3 RAM, and 32 or 64 GB SSD.
- *Multi-camera connectivity*: Embedded vision systems typically have 4+ GigE camera ports and 2+ USB 3.0 camera ports for connectivity to multiple cameras, networks, and peripherals. Combined with the higher performance processing, a single embedded vision system can replace multiple smart cameras and/or vision sensors in a system as long as the allowed cable lengths between camera and embedded system are acceptable. Typical limits are ~3 m for USB 3.0, ~50 m for GigE. These distances will vary considerably depending on electromagnetic compatibilty (EMC) environmental conditions, cable and connection quality, and parts used in the interface on the embedded vision system. These distances can be extended through the use of active cables at the expense of higher cost/size of the cable. Using a single consolidated embedded vision system with multiple cameras makes sense when information from these cameras needs to be consolidated to make pass/fail or inspection decisions. It can also be more cost-effective for multi-camera systems, especially for a larger number of cameras, as the processing is consolidated and more efficiently utilized than in the distributed processing model necessary with multiple smart cameras.

- *Quantity and variety of I/O*: The reasoning here is similar to that for the processor selection: a larger size and bigger thermal capacity mean many more options for the included I/O. A typical I/O set is represented by that included on the NI Compact Vision System (CVS):
  eight ISO input (0–24 V, 100 kHz)
  eight ISO output (5–24 V, 20 kHz)
  eight bidirectional TTL (0–5 V, 2 MHz)
  two bidirectional (differential or single-ended) (0–5.5 V, 5 MHz).
  In the case of the NI CVS this I/O is all routed through a user-programmable FPGA. The unit ships with a default FPGA personality for common inspection I/O tasks, but also allows users to customize that personality or write their own to enable application specific high-performance I/O capabilities. Some embedded vision systems come with expansion slots (typically some form of PCIe) to add additional I/O cards as necessary.
- *Flexibility in component selection*: Embedded vision systems allow for the most flexibility in component selection. They are designed to work with any standard cameras that comply to industry camera bus specifications. Industrial cameras usually come with a much wider selection of image sensors and with a more rapid release cycle with the newest sensors as compared to vision sensors and smart cameras. You can also choose to incorporate line scan cameras, specialty short wave infrared (SWIR) or thermal cameras, or any other camera that you can find that conforms to the USB3 or GigE Vision standards. There is corresponding flexibility in lens and lighting choices. Lighting and lens vendors carry hundreds of standard products in their catalogs, and even still, a large percentage of their business involves customized products for specific applications. Vision sensors and smart cameras are designed for the majority of cases. For applications outside those use cases, an embedded vision system paired with separate camera, lens, and lighting components from a mix of vendors is the usual system architecture.
- *Flexibility in system integration*: If necessary, embedded vision systems give system designers the ability to more closely couple sub-systems in a machine than vision sensors or smart cameras. Vision sensors and smart cameras process results onboard, and then send results either as a digital trigger, or as a value over a network bus to a PLC or industrial PC (IPC), which then takes appropriate action based on its programming (often some type of state machine logic). While sufficient for many applications, this architecture of separate vision system and machine controller can represent a big challenge for those applications that need higher performance, specialized processing, or more integration. Embedded vision systems allow for I/O processing, multi-camera processing, motion controller integration, data decimation, web servers, direct human machine interface (HMI) connectivity, and more to facilitate system consolidation and integration for these more challenging applications.

An embedded vision system is often compared to a desktop PC during the system selection process. While similar in terms of computing power, an embedded vision system (or Industrial PC with integrated frame grabber) has some key differences that set it apart. The below mentioned differences all boil down to more rugged equipment that is more reliable and able to stand up to deployment in a variety of factory floor situations for much longer than a standard consumer/business grade PC. Often the term MTBF "mean time between failure" is brought up when considering the difference in "uptime" between an embedded vision system and a standard PC. Factors that contribute to giving embedded vision systems generally much higher reliability and longevity include:

- *Fanless design and greater temperature range specifications*: A system fan is a key point of failure in a computing system, especially in long-term deployments and in the less-than-sterile factory floor setting. Fanned systems deployed in such settings come with a recommended maintenance/replacement schedule that adds to total cost of ownership of the system and increases the risk of a failure. Fanless embedded vision systems are designed with industrial components with wider operational temperature range ratings and remove the fan as a point of failure.
- *Better shock and vibration ratings and testing*: Embedded systems manufacturers typically put their equipment through a more rigorous testing and qualification plan that includes different shock and vibration requirements not required of standard PCs. To meet these requirements, different printed circuit board layout and/or manufacturing processes may be employed.
- *Full bandwidth on each camera port*: Embedded vision systems are designed to sustain full bus bandwidth from each individual USB3 or GigE port to stream lots of data from multiple cameras. Consumer USB and GigE ports are typically multiplexed (multiple ports share bandwidth) as they are intended for the much lighter/intermittent data throughput requirements from peripherals and networked storage devices. Embedded vision system GigE ports also typically timing and synchronization capabilities such as the IEEE 1588 precision time protocol (PTP) that are not generally supported on standard PCs.
- *SLC versus MLC memory solid state memory*: Consumer grade devices use MLC (multi-level cell) memory to allow for a higher data density with just a small increase in cost and size. However, this comes with trade-offs in terms of reliability and performance. Embedded vision systems (along with military, avionics, and other industrial applications) will often use SLC (single-level cell) memory for added performance and reliability because of the increased cost of amending failure and bad/corrupted data in these applications [40].
- *Built-in hardware defined I/O for timing, triggering, and signaling*: The I/O on embedded vision systems will be designed for connection to 24 V I/O industrial sensors/relays, quadrature encoders, and camera triggers. It is often backed by an FPGA to implement custom I/O behavior in the device firmware for common machine vision application tasks such as recording position of a quadrature encoder and queuing a trigger pulse at a set distance down the line to trigger an ejection mechanism [41].

An example of an embedded vision system is the CVS from National Instruments [42] shown in Figure 7.5. This product can be configured with a real-time OS based on Linux® or Windows® and contains a quad-core Intel® Atom™ processor. It is supplied with considerably more RAM (e.g., 4 GB) and the casing is

Figure 7.7 NI compact vision system. (Photo courtesy of National Instruments.)

larger than our example smart camera (specifically 130 mm × 108 mm × 61 mm without camera heads and cables) (Figure 7.7).

7.5.1 Applications

The list of potential applications for an embedded vision system includes all of the possible areas mentioned in Section 7.3.1 for a smart camera. The higher processing power and larger I/O set of an embedded vision system will open up new opportunities in the high-end range of applications or for time-critical situations. The increased physical size and thermal envelope may preclude it from others. Specific areas where embedded vision systems are applicable are for high camera count applications and vision-guided motion or closed loop control based on vision results.

7.5.1.1 Multi-Camera Applications

Some applications, for example, in automotive or electronics manufacturing, employ many cameras for different types of inspection or inspection at different parts of a manufacturing cell. Often, this is a sequential process where not all the cameras are in operation concurrently. These types of applications could be solved with a network of Smart Cameras connected to the automation bus in the system to pass inspection results, but the smart cameras would sit idle for a majority of the total automation process time. A potential alternative is to use multiple standard GigE or USB3 cameras connected back to a single embedded vision system. The higher power processing available in an embedded vision system can handle concurrent acquisition and inspection, correlation of results, and the relevant I/O for timing and triggering of different parts of the system. In this case, even though the unit cost of the embedded vision system is greater than that for a smart camera, the total system cost could be less because of the consolidation and increased utility of the available processing power [43].

7.5.1.2 Closed Loop Control Applications

Another class of applications where embedded vision systems are employed are those that require some sort of closed loop control between the vision system and I/O to complete a task. Vision-guided motion falls into this category, as does correlating vision measurements with specialty sensors, analog I/O, or measurements outside the typical I/O set of a smart camera or vision sensor. Some embedded vision systems have the capability to integrate a motion controller on the same processor as the vision processing, and thus close the control loop to pass position or velocity setpoints to the motion controller. Other configurations involve connecting EtherCAT motion drives directly to an embedded vision system. These configurations can be used in web inspection/alignment applications or in path following applications like using a robotic arm or gantry to apply adhesive/sealant to a part with a variable profile. An example of closed loop control with I/O would be an alignment process where the output of the vision system is not a pass/fail decision or a digital I/O (DIO) trigger but an analog signal or digitized value that is proportional to the "error" measured using machine vision algorithms to derive information from the source images. The error signal is then used as an input to a PID (proportional-integral-derivative) or model-based control algorithm to control a process.

7.5.2 Component Parts

An embedded vision system consists of a self-contained processing unit and a separate camera or cameras. All of the criteria for design decisions mentioned for smart cameras apply equally to these systems. By making use of standard camera interfaces such as USB3 Vision or GigE Vision a wide range of cameras from different manufacturers will give the end user more flexibility in a single system than with a smart camera or vision sensor series, with their limited number of sensor options. Higher power processing elements and a wider range/quantity of I/O are also available.

7.5.3 Programming and Configuring

Programming and configuration concepts known from the PC and general embedded systems worlds are usually used for embedded vision systems. In the example CVS system, National Instrument's LabVIEW development environment is used.

7.5.4 Environment

Despite the rugged casing, some embedded vision systems may have to be located away from hazardous areas due to physical size and weight or lower IP classes. In this case, the maximum length of the cables between the computing unit and the cameras may become significant and should be carefully considered at the design stage.

A processor system that is more powerful than that used in a small smart camera is likely to generate more heat, but the larger casing can be equipped with adequate passive cooling systems to allow a similar range of ambient temperatures to that allowed for the smaller devices. A typical temperature range for embedded vision systems is 0–55 °C.

7.6 Conclusion

We have seen that the skills involved in designing or just deploying vision systems of any kind are related more to microelectronics and computing systems than to machine vision themes. These systems are smaller versions of more traditional, PC-based designs that use standard cameras but they contain components and interfaces suited to the conditions prevailing directly at the point of interest in an application. They are robust and may contain sophisticated software that, for the end user, reduces the complexity of solving problems with machine vision.

Placing the computer and camera together can reduce the intricacy of the data transmission infrastructure and make servicing or replacement of individual units easier. However, the computing power of small devices sets a natural limit on the speed or complexity of machine vision applications realizable with these systems.

Having decided that a vision system is a viable possibility for a particular application it should be possible to decide on which category – smart camera, vision sensor, or embedded vision system – best suits the application and then to compare the key features of commercial products. Alternatively, developers wanting to build their own custom system from component parts should now have a list of key decisions that need to be made in order to create a successful product.

As far as the future is concerned, as faster and more powerful CPUs and other devices are developed to keep pace with the worldwide demand for mobile equipment, the spin-off technology is likely to make its way into smart cameras and other vision systems – vision systems will get faster and smaller. The way these systems are configured or programmed will also need to be simplified if they are to establish themselves successfully for automation – a PLC programmer, who is capable of integrating a complex machine like a robot into an industrial process, also needs to be able to add vision components in the same way without having to understand all the details of machine vision. The physical interface between the vision system and the automation process is likely to be an industrial Ethernet protocol.

References

1 Belbachir, A.N. and Göbel, P.M. (2010) in *Smart Cameras* (ed. A.N. Belbachir), Springer Science+Business Media LLC, New York, pp. 3–4.
2 Shi, Y. and Real, D.F. (2010) in *Smart Cameras* (ed. A.N. Belbachir), Springer Science+Business Media LLC, New York, pp. 21–23.
3 Automated Imaging Association (2012). Glossary of Machine Vision Terms, http://www.visiononline.org/market-data.cfm?id=73 (accessed 28 April 2015).
4 Dawson, B. Smart Cameras (2014): Yesterday, Today and Tomorrow, http://www.qualitymag.com/articles/91857-smart-cameras-yesterday-today-and-tomorrow (accessed 28 April 2015).
5 Altera (2013) Architecture Matters: Choosing the Right SoC FPGA for Your Application, White paper WP-01202-1.0, http://www.altera.com/literature/wp/wp-01202-embedded-system-soc-design-considerations.pdf (accessed 28 April 2015).

6 Vision Components GmbH (2003) Technical Documentation VC11, VC38, VC65, VC67, http://www.machine-vision.de/documents-flyer-sheets-of-machine-vision-products?task=document.viewdoc&id=149 (accessed 28 April 2015).
7 MATRIX VISION GmbH (2002–2011) mvBlueLYNX, http://www.matrix-vision.com/smart-camera-with-video-sensor-mvbluelynx.html (accessed 28 April 2015).
8 National Instruments Newsletter (Q4 2007), http://www.ni.com/pdf/newsletters/us/q4_07_inl_final.pdf (accessed 28 April 2015).
9 Super Computing Systems (2008–2015). The leanXcam Datasheet, http://www.scs.ch/en/ueber-scs/departments/johannes-gassner/leanxcam.html (accessed 28 April 2015).
10 Matrox Imaging (2009) Smart Cameras, http://www.matrox.com/imaging/en/products/smart_cameras/ (accessed 28 April 2015).
11 MATRIX VISION GmbH (2010–2016) Versatile Smart Camera of the Next Generation – mvBlueLYNX-X, http://www.matrix-vision.com/smart-vision-sensor-mvbluelynx-x.html (accessed 28 April 2015).
12 Vision Components GmbH (2010–2016) VC4012 Nano Data Sheet, http://www.vision-components.com/en/products/smart-cameras/oem-gehaeusekameras/vc-nano/ (accessed 28 April 2015).
13 EVT Eye Vision Technology GmbH (2015) RazerCam, http://www.evt-web.com/en/products/smart-cameras/razercam/ (accessed 28 April 2015).
14 MATRIX VISION GmbH (2015) mvBlueGEMINI – Compact Application Camera, http://www.matrix-vision.com/smart-cam-compact-application-camera.html (accessed 28 April 2015).
15 Silicon Software GmbH (2006–2016) VisualApplets, https://silicon.software/products/visual-applets/ (accessed 15 December 2016).
16 EVT Eye Vision Technology GmbH (2014). EyeVision 3.0 with VisualApplets – A Speedboost for Smart Cameras, http://www.evt-web.com/en/current-issues/news/newsdetails/?tx_ttnews%5Btt_news%5D=348&cHash=f1cf2ede125d77094c3edb921af2dfbf (accessed 28 April 2015).
17 Khronos Group (2016) OpenCL – The open standard for parallel programming of heterogeneous systems, https://www.khronos.org/opencl/ (accessed 28 April 2015).
18 Altera SDK for OpenCL is First in Industry to Achieve Khronos Conformance for FPGAs (2013), http://www.prnewswire.com/news-releases/altera-sdk-for-opencl-is-first-in-industry-to-achieve-khronos-conformance-for-fpgas-227993801.html (accessed 28 April 2015).
19 ADI Linux Kernel – Linux Kernel Port for the ADI's Blackfin and Future Processors (2005–2016), http://sourceforge.net/projects/adi-linux/ (accessed 28 April 2015).
20 Open Source Automation Development Lab (OSADL), https://www.osadl.org/ (accessed 28 April 2015).

21 elektroniknet.de (2015) Etappensieg für Echtzeit-Linux (German language), http://www.elektroniknet.de/embedded/sonstiges/artikel/116408/ (accessed 28 April 2015).
22 IntervalZero (2013–2016) RTOS Platform Vision, http://www.intervalzero.com/products/rtos-platform-vision/ (accessed 28 April 2015).
23 RTAI, https://www.rtai.org/ (accessed 28 April 2015).
24 Xenomai, http://xenomai.org/ (accessed 28 April 2015).
25 HMS Industrial Networks GmbH Markttrends (2015): Industrielle Kommunikation (German language), http://www.anybus.de/technologie/technologie_trends.shtml (accessed 28 April 2015).
26 VDMA-Podiumsdiskussion SPS & Bildverarbeitung (2014): Wie geht es weiter? (German language audio), http://ea.vdma.org/documents/266693/6614459/VDMA_SPS_und_Bildverarbeitung.MP3 (accessed 28 April 2015).
27 MVTec Software GmbH (2013–2016) HDevEngine, http://www.halcon.com/halcon/hdevelop/hdevengine.html (access 28 April 2015).
28 MVTec Software GmbH (2014–2016) Embedded HALCON, http://www.halcon.com/embedded/ (accessed 28 April 2015).
29 Eclipse IDE. https://eclipse.org/ (accessed 28 April 2015).
30 Hunter, A. (2009) Understanding Garbage Collection in.NET, https://www.simple-talk.com/dotnet/.net-framework/understanding-garbage-collection-in-.net/ (accessed 28 April 2015).
31 Matrox Design Assistant, http://www.matrox.com/imaging/en/products/smart_cameras/iris_gt_da/ (accessed 28 April 2015).
32 National Instruments (2015), What is NI Vision? http://www.ni.com/vision/whatis/ (accessed 28 April 2015).
33 ISO ISO/IEC 16262:1998. *ECMAScript Language Specification*, http://www.iso.org/iso/home/store/catalogue_ics/catalogue_detail_ics.htm?csnumber=29696 (accessed 28 April 2015).
34 World Wide Web Consortium (W3C) (2014), HTML5, http://www.w3.org/TR/html5/ (accessed 28 April 2015).
35 World Wide Web Consortium (W3C) (2012), The WebSocket API, http://www.w3.org/TR/websockets/ (accessed 28 April 2015).
36 Open Source Computer Vision (OpenCV), Home page, http://opencv.org/ (accessed 28 April 2015).
37 Ximea GmbH. CURRERA-R: Machine Vision Smart Camera with PC Inside, http://www.ximea.com/en/machine-vision/smart-camera (accessed 28 April 2015).
38 ANSI ANSI/IEC 60529–2004. (2004) *Degrees of Protection Provided by Enclosures (IP Code)*, National Electrical Manufacturers Association, Rosslyn, VA, http://www.nema.org/Standards/Pages/American-National-Standard-for-Degrees-of-Protection-Provided-by-Enclosures.aspx (accessed 28 April 2015).
39 Balluff GmbH (2012–2016) Overview|Vision Sensors, http://www.balluff.com/balluff/MDE/en/products/overview-vision-sensors.jsp (accessed 28 April 2015).
40 EE Times. (2012) SLC vs MLC: Which Works Best for High-Reliability Applications? http://www.eetimes.com/document.asp?doc_id=1279762&page_number=4 (accessed 2 December 2015).

41 National Instruments (2013) Using Vision RIO to Synchronize Vision and I/O with Queued Pulses, http://www.ni.com/white-paper/14599/en/ (accessed 3 December 2015).
42 National Instruments (2013). What is the NI Compact Vision System? http://www.ni.com/vision/systems/cvs (accessed 28 April 2015).
43 A3 Business Forum (2014) Opportunities and Challenges for Vision Technology in Automotive Manufacturing Applications, Steve Jones, General Motors, & Frank Maslar, Ford Motor (presented January 2014).

Further Reading

Readers interested in a direct comparison of three different types of smart camera architectures are referred to:

Malik, A., Thörnberg, B., and Kumar, P. (2013) Comparison of three smart camera architectures for real-time machine vision system, pages 1–3, 10. *Int. J. Adv. Rob. Syst.*, http://www.intechopen.com/download/pdf/45942 (accessed 28 April 2015). Further information about field bus protocols may be found at various websites as listed below:

CANbus. http://www.can-cia.org/index.php?id=can (accessed 28 April 2015).
EtherCAT. http://www.ethercat.org (accessed 28 April 2015).
Ethernet/IP. http://www.odva.org/ (accessed 28 April 2015).
IO-Link. http://www.io-link.com (accessed 28 April 2015).
MODBUS & MODBUS/TCP. http://www.modbus.org (accessed 28 April 2015).
PROFIBUS & PROFINET. http://www.profibus.com/ (accessed 28 April 2015).

8

Camera Computer Interfaces

Nate Holmes

National Instruments, 11500 N. Mopac Expwy., Austin TX 78759, USA

8.1 Overview

Machine vision acquisition architectures come in many different forms, but they all have the same end goal. That goal is to get image data from a physical sensor into a processing unit that can process the image and initiate an action. This goal is the same for personal computer (PC)-based machine vision systems, embedded compact vision systems, and smart cameras.

All physical architectures have the same starting point and ending point: you have a sensor on one end and a processing unit on the other.

The focus of this chapter is on the camera bus, the interface device, the computer bus, and the driver software. When designing your machine vision system, you will need to make decisions and tradeoffs based on the strengths and weaknesses of each of these components.

The camera bus section discusses the most popular mechanisms for getting data from a camera to the interface device. Each camera bus has its own strengths and weaknesses. The section explores the very different approaches used in machine vision, and the evolution from the analog approach to vision-specific digital buses to leveraging cost-effective commercial digital buses.

The interface device connects the camera bus and the computer bus. The interface device is necessary because the camera does not directly output data in the same format that the computer uses internally. Even if the camera bus and the computer bus use the same protocol, an interface device is still needed to physically convert data from the cable to the motherboard. Machine vision interface devices vary in price, complexity, and performance. Interface devices that are specifically designed for machine vision, commonly referred to as *frame grabbers*, include many convenient features such as triggering support, image reconstruction, and preprocessing. General-purpose interface devices such as the universal serial bus (USB) and gigabit ethernet are so simple that the interface device consists of no more than a connector and a microchip, leaving the necessary machine vision features to either the camera or the host processor.

As technology has evolved over the years, so have the computer buses. This section discusses the buses that have defined the decades, such as Industry

Standard Architecture (ISA), Peripheral Component Interconnect (PCI), and PCI Express as well as the intermediate buses such as Extended Industry Standard Architecture (EISA), 64-bit PCI, and PCI-X. This section also explores how each of these buses paved the way for PC-based machine vision.

The chapter concludes with a discussion on driver software. The driver software is responsible for getting images from the camera into the computer. The software does this by interacting directly with the interface device. It also serves as the interface between the programmer and the machine vision system. In addition to receiving images from the camera, the driver software also provides many convenient features such as software mechanisms for controlling the camera, for displaying images, and for transferring images to the disk for later viewing or processing.

After reading this chapter, you will have a thorough understanding of the image acquisition component of a machine vision system. You will be able to evaluate your application needs and pick the right camera bus, interface device, and computer bus for your application. This knowledge will help you ensure that you meet your image acquisition form factor and performance goals without over-engineering your vision system.

8.2 Camera Buses

The first machine vision systems used analog signals to send images from a camera to an acquisition device. For more than 50 years, analog video signal standards have helped ensure compatibility among a wide range of cameras, monitors, and frame grabbers. A camera from any manufacturer would likely work with a frame grabber from another manufacturer, provided the cameras use one of the standard video formats. The same video standards that promoted nearly universal compatibility also limited the performance of the camera for some applications. These common standards also diminished the ability of camera companies to differentiate their products. Since the development of analog video standards, several additional buses of interest for machine vision applications were developed for transmitting image data. When digital technology became available, there was a proliferation of proprietary parallel digital interfaces in the 1990s that caused confusion because of widely varying implementations and little or no interoperability. FireWire/IEEE 1394 was introduced by Apple Inc. in 1987 as a general data transfer bus that could be utilized in vision applications, and Camera Link was developed specifically for machine vision and introduced in 2000 to bring standardization to the many varying parallel digital implementations out there. Since then, both approaches (specialized vision buses and adopting standards based on commercially available general-purposes buses) have been progressing. GigE Vision and USB3 Vision standards both utilize technologies well established in other markets and, through the introduction of additional specifications in recent years, have been adapted specifically for machine vision applications. CoaXPress and Camera Link HS (CLHS) were developed concurrently and specifically to be high-bandwidth deterministic buses specific to vision applications. GigE Vision was released in 2006, and was followed by CoaXPress in 2009, CLHS in 2012, and USB3 Vision in 2013.

In recent years, there has been a big push for standardization of camera buses across the industry. In 2009, the three leading vision associations (Automated Imaging Association (AIA), European Machine Vision Association (EMVA), and Japan Industrial Imaging Association (JIIA)) agreed to cooperate in the development and management of vision standards through a cooperative agreement and initiative called "G3." VDMA (Verband Deutscher Maschinen- und Anlagenbau, German Engineering Association) and CMVU (China Machine Vision Union) have since joined the G3 effort. The Future Standards Forum (FSF) was established under G3 to provide standards oversight and strategic guidance in the development of standards and to minimize the creation of conflicting standards within the machine vision industry. An early significant accomplishment was the publication of the "Global Machine Vision Interface Standards" brochure to give end users a comprehensive and unbiased reference and comparison between standards and serves much the same purpose as the camera buses section of this chapter. Currently, the AIA hosts the GigE Vision, Camera Link and CLHS, and USB3 Vision standards. EMVA hosts the 1288 and GenICam standards. JIIA hosts CoaXPress and various lens mount standards. The "Global Machine Vision Interface Standards" brochure as well as more information on each standard (specs, committee members, meetings, versions, etc.) can be found at the respective trade association websites.

- AIA-Advancing Vision + Imaging (AIA) (http://www.visiononline.org/vision-standards.cfm)
- European Machine Vision Association (EMVA) (http://www.emva.org/cms/index.php?idcat=23&lang=1)
- Japan Industrial Imaging Association (JIIA) (http://jiia.org/en/standardization/outline/).

The following sections describe each camera bus. Analog, parallel-digital, and FireWire are now considered legacy camera buses and are no longer recommended for new designs. A summary is included, as understanding the evolution of camera bus technology is instructive in considering the currently available buses and standardization efforts.

8.2.1 Software Standards

8.2.1.1 GenICam

Machine vision cameras are becoming increasingly sophisticated and can do much more than return an image. With onboard reconfigurable FPGAs (field-programmable gate arrays) to implement camera firmware, camera manufactures have the ability to put a lot of functionality right on the camera. Processing the image and appending the results to the image data stream, controlling external hardware, and doing the real-time part of the application have become common tasks for machine vision cameras. As a result, the programming interface for cameras has become more and more complex.

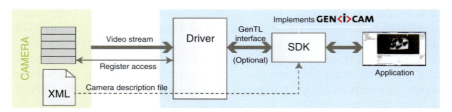

Figure 8.1 Components of the GenICam Standard. GenICam version 1.0 released in late 2006, version 2.0 in 2009, and 2015 version 3.0 release [1].

The goal of GenICam™ is to provide a generic programming interface for cameras no matter what interface technology (GigE Vision, USB3 Vision, CoaXPress, CLHS, Camera Link, 1394 DCAM, etc.) they are using or what features they are implementing. With GenICam, the application programming interface (API) should be always the same. This allows for much more efficient integration of cameras into larger applications and reuse of knowledge and code across applications. The GenICam standard is maintained by the EMVA.

The GenICam™ standard consists of multiple modules according to the main tasks to be solved:

Generic transport layer (GenTL) standardizes the transport layer programming interface. This allows enumerating cameras, accessing camera registers, streaming data, and delivering asynchronous events. Since GenTL is a fairly low level interface, end users usually rely on a software development kit (SDK) instead of directly using GenTL. GenTL's main purpose is to ensure drivers and SDKs from different vendors work seamlessly together.

Generic application programming interface (GenApi) standardizes the format of the camera self-description file. This file lists all of the features that are implemented by the camera (standard and custom) and defines their mapping to the camera's registers. The file format is based on XML and thus readable by humans. Typically, this file is stored in the camera firmware and is retrieved by the SDK when the camera is first connected to a system.

Standard feature naming convention (SFNC) standardizes the name, type, meaning, and use of camera features in the camera self-description file. This ensures that cameras from different vendors always use the same names for the same provided functionality.

Generic control protocol (GenCP) standardizes packet layout for the control protocol and is used by interface standards to reuse parts of the control path implementation (Figure 8.1).

8.2.1.2 IIDC2

The IIDC2 standard, which is a successor to IIDC for FireWire cameras, defines a flexible-fixed camera control register layout. All details are defined for how each feature, such as exposure time, is mapped to the register space, representing a very simple approach to camera control (Figure 8.2).

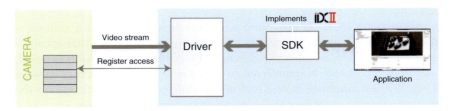

Figure 8.2 Components of the IIDC2 Standard [1].

IIDC2 aims to be

- Easy to implement and use
- Accessible to camera control registers
- Expandable for vendor-specific functions
- A common controlling method for all cameras
- Usable on IEEE 1394, but also on USB3 Vision, CoaXPress, and future interfaces
- Able to be mapped to a GenICam interface.

The standard offers an easy method for controlling cameras by only reading/writing registers directly inside the camera. All information regarding camera functionality is in the camera control registers. Users can determine supported features by reading the registers.

The register mapping works as a semi-fixed method, meaning a fixed mapping for accessibility and a free mapping for expandability. The camera functions are categorized into basic functions (fixed register layout and its behavior) and expanded functions. Functions can be added freely by the vendor, its register layout is selectable from the list in the specification, and its behavior is vendor-specific. When using IIDC2 registers with GenICam, the camera description file can be common for all cameras because the IIDC2 register layout is defined in the specification [1]. The IIDC2 standard is maintained by JIIA.

8.2.2 Analog Camera Buses (Legacy)

Industrial analog cameras use a coaxial cable to transmit an analog video signal from the camera to an image acquisition device or monitor. The analog video signal transmitted by the camera uses the same composite video formats used by TV stations to broadcast video signals around the world. For color video signals, there are two main video standards: National Television Systems Committee (NTSC) and Phase Alternative Line (PAL). NTSC was more common in North America and Japan, and PAL was more common in Europe. For monochrome video signals, the two main video standards were Electronic Industries Association (EIA) RS-170 and Consultative Committee for International Radio (CCIR). RS-170 was common in North America and CCIR was common in Europe. Analog television broadcasting is now considered a legacy technology. Most of the developed world has switched or is in the process of switching to digital television [2].

8.2.2.1 Analog Video Signal

The analog video signal is generated when the image sensor in a camera is scanned. The image sensor is a matrix of photosensitive elements that accumulates an electric charge when exposed to light. Once the image sensor is exposed, the accumulated charge is transferred to an array of linked capacitors called a *shift register*. An amplifier at one end of the shift converts the charge on the capacitor to voltage and drives the voltage onto a coaxial video cable.

Charges are sent to the amplifier as the image sensor is scanned. This creates a continuous analog voltage waveform on the video cable. The amplitude of the video signal at some point in time represents the luminance, or brightness, of a particular pixel. Before each line of video, a signal known as the *back porch* is generated. The back porch signal is used as a reference by the receiver to restore any DC components from the AC-coupled video signal. The period when the DC components are removed is called the *clamping interval*.

Color information, or chroma, can be transmitted along the same coaxial cable with a monochrome video signal. The chroma signal is created by modulating two quadrature components onto a carrier frequency. The phase and amplitude of these components represent the color content of each pixel. The chroma is added to the luminance signal to create a color composite video signal.

8.2.2.2 Interlaced Video

According to the composite video format, an image frame is transmitted as two independent fields. One field contains all the odd lines, and the other contains all the even lines. When two independent fields are used to transmit an image, it is called *interlaced video transfer*. Figure 8.3 shows a diagram of an interlaced video frame. In the RS-170 interlaced video format, frames are transmitted at 30 Hz, but the fields are updated every 60 Hz. The effect of interlaced video transfer is that the human eye perceives a 60-Hz video update rate when watching a monitor, as opposed to the true 30-Hz full image update rate.

8.2.2.3 Progressive Scan Video

Although interlaced video can deceive the human eye into seeing a higher video update rate, the reconstructed image of a moving object looks blurred when viewed as a single frame. This is because the odd and even lines were exposed

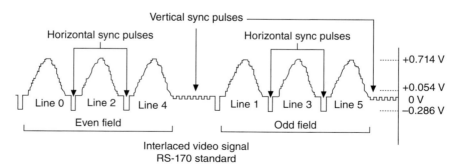

Figure 8.3 Interlaced video frame.

at different times. Progressive scan cameras are designed to eliminate motion blurring. Such cameras expose and scan the entire image sensor without interlacing even and odd lines. The result is improved performance for applications where the objects are constantly moving.

8.2.2.4 Timing Signals

In addition to video data, composite video signals also carry synchronization signals to designate the beginning of a field or line. A horizontal synchronization (Hsync) pulse is generated at the beginning of a line, and is seen as a negative-going pulse in the video stream. A vertical synchronization (Vsync) pulse is a negative-going pulse that designates the beginning of a field. Figure 8.4 illustrates a composite video signal.

The color burst is a timing signal used to decode color information from a video waveform. The color burst appears on the back porch, at the beginning of each line. It is a sinusoid whose frequency is equal to that of the chroma carrier signal. The color burst is used as a phase reference to demodulate the quadrature-encoded chroma signal.

The RS-170 video standard uses a 640 × 480 frame size. Seven-hundred and eighty discrete pixel values are transmitted between Hsync pulses, and 640 of the pixel values transmitted are active image pixels that make up a full line of video. The remaining pixels are referred to as *line blanking pixels* and are unused. There are 525 lines per frame, and 480 of the lines contain active image data. The remaining lines are called *frame blanking lines* and are unused. Table 8.1 lists the specifications for the most common analog video standards.

8.2.2.5 Analog Image Acquisition

Analog image acquisition boards, commonly referred to as *frame grabbers*, typically use a sync separator to detect these timing signals and extract them from the video data stream. A phase-lock loop (PLL) synchronizes with the extracted Vsync and Hsync signals and generates a pixel clock, which is used to sample the video data. The pixel clock frequency of an RS-170 video signal is 12.27 MHz.

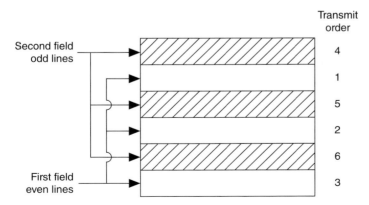

Figure 8.4 Composite video signal.

Table 8.1 Analog video standards.

Standard	Type	Frame size (pixels)	Frame rate (frames per second)	Line rate (lines per second)
NTSC	Color	640 × 480	29.97	15 734
PAL	Color	768 × 576	25.00	15 625
RS-170	Black and white	640 × 480	30.00	15 750
CCIR	Black and white	768 × 576	25.00	15 625

A DC restore clamps to the back porch DC reference signal at the beginning of a line. An analog-to-digital converter (ADC) then samples the analog video signal on each pixel clock cycle, generating discrete digital pixel values. The digital pixels are transferred across the computer bus and reconstructed on a frame in the system memory.

For color analog frame grabbers, the chroma signal is separated from the luminance signal with an analog filter. The two signals are sampled simultaneously by separate ADCs. Digital processing then converts the chrominance and luminance values into red, green, and blue (RGB) intensity components. These values are then transferred across the computer bus into the system memory. Most color image processing algorithms use the RGB or hue, saturation, and luminance (HSL) color formats.

8.2.2.6 S-Video

Combining the chroma and luminance signals on the same wire causes problems for applications that require high resolution, accuracy, and signal integrity. Sometimes, the higher frequency chroma signal bleeds into the luminance spectrum and appears as noise in the acquired image.

To improve color composite video transmission, a new standard was developed called S-Video. S-Video uses the same timing and synchronization signals as composite video, but uses two independent wires to transmit the chroma and luminance signals. S-Video is rarely used in commercial or machine vision applications today.

8.2.2.7 RGB

RGB cameras encode color information as RGB components before transmitting the video signal across the cable. These components are transmitted on three different coaxial cables in parallel. Like the luminance value of a composite video signal, a voltage on the coaxial wire represents the intensity value of each component. Vsync and Hsync timing signals are typically added to one of the three component signals for synchronization.

Since there is no high-frequency chroma signal present in RGB video signals, the signal integrity of each component is better than that of a composite video signal. The video signal is transmitted in RGB color format, so there is no need for digital processing on the acquisition board. However, since there are three

Figure 8.5 (a) BNC connector and (b) S-video connector.

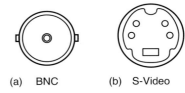

(a) BNC   (b) S-Video

different analog signals, the acquisition hardware must have three ADCs to sample a single video signal.

8.2.2.8 Analog Connectors

Composite video signals are transmitted on shielded coaxial cables. A standard BNC connector is commonly used for machine vision applications. RGB video transfer also uses coaxial cables and BNC connectors for each component video signal. The S-Video standard defines a special connector and cable for video transfer. Figure 8.5a shows a BNC connector and Figure 8.5b shows an S-Video connector.

8.2.3 Parallel Digital Camera Buses (Legacy)

As higher resolution camera sensors were developed, the limits of composite video were exceeded. As an alternative, camera manufacturers turned to digital video. In digital video, the analog video signal from the camera sensor is converted to a digital signal within the camera and sent to the image acquisition device in digital format.

To transmit digital video signals, custom-shielded cables were designed that bundle many conductors in parallel, each providing a separate stream of digital data. This allows the guaranteed transmission of data at very high speeds with high immunity to noise.

8.2.3.1 Digital Video Transmission

In composite video transmission, the Vsync and Hsync timing signals are embedded in the analog video signal and extracted using a PLL on the frame grabber. In most digital video transmission schemes, timing signals are sent on separate conductors in parallel with the video data signals. The Vsync signal is replaced with frame valid, which is asserted for the duration of a video frame. The Hsync signal is replaced with line valid, which is asserted for the duration of a video line. The pixel clock signal is generated by the camera and sent as a separate parallel signal, instead of being generated by the PLL on the frame grabber. All digital signals are transmitted from the camera at the same time as the pixel clock.

After the camera sensor is exposed, it must be scanned, one pixel at a time. Analog voltages from the sensor are converted to digital pixel values and sent one after the other along the parallel cable. Typically, each data wire within a cable is dedicated to a particular bit of the pixel value. For example, a camera sensor that is sampled with a 10-bit ADC requires a cable with 10 parallel data wires. Figure 8.6 shows the timing diagram for a parallel digital camera and the pixel locations on the image sensor. Two frames are read out. Each frame is two

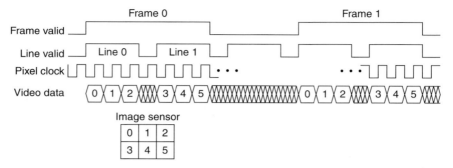

Figure 8.6 Parallel digital timing diagram.

lines high and three pixels wide. The image sensor is scanned from upper-left to bottom-right.

8.2.3.2 Taps

As larger and faster sensors were developed, it became necessary to scan two, four, or even eight pixels at a time. Multiple pixels are sent down the parallel video cable in separate digital streams called *taps*. The scanning order and direction for camera sensors vary depending on the camera. Frame grabber companies rely on the camera manufacturer to indicate the scanning order and direction for multiple-tap cameras so that images can be properly reconstructed in computer memory.

In Figure 8.7, the image sensor is split into four quadrants, each corresponding to a different tap. Each tap is scanned from the middle of the sensor outward. Pixel 0 from each tap is transmitted at the same time, then pixel 1, and so on. If the bit depth of each pixel is 8 bits, this tap configuration requires a cable with 32 parallel wires, plus 3 additional wires for the timing signals. The frame grabber samples all 32 signals on every pixel clock cycle and stores the values in memory. Typically, the image is reconstructed in the frame grabber memory as a contiguous image, upper-left to bottom-right, before being sent across the computer bus.

Multiple taps can also be used to transmit color video signals. Pixels from color image sensors are typically represented by three independent 8-bit RGB components. Together, these three components represent any 24-bit color. Pixels are transmitted one per pixel clock on three different taps. Each tap carries an 8-bit RGB component value.

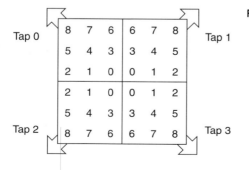

Figure 8.7 Image sensor taps.

8.2.3.3 Differential Signaling

The earliest cameras transmitted digital video using transistor–transistor logic (TTL) signaling. The limits of clock speed and cable length quickly forced manufacturers to consider a standard for differential signaling. RS-422 and RS-644 low-voltage differential signaling (LVDS) were developed, and quickly adopted, as standards for digital video transmission. Differential signaling has better noise immunity, which allows for longer cable lengths, and can be run at much higher rates. However, a twisted pair of wires is now required for each digital data stream, doubling the number of wires in the cable and increasing cable cost.

8.2.3.4 Line Scan

Most image sensors are two dimensional, having a matrix of pixels arranged in rows and columns. Light reflected from a three-dimensional object is projected onto the sensor, and each pixel samples the light from a small region within the camera's field of view. Two-dimensional sensors are an ideal geometry for capturing images of stationary objects, but blurring occurs if the object is moving. This is because it usually takes many milliseconds to expose the entire sensor, during which time the object would have moved. Special lighting and high-speed exposure can help the situation, but some applications use another kind of image sensor.

Applications that typically involve imaging a continuous object that is always moving in the same direction are known as *web inspections*. One example is a paper mill inspection system. Paper continuously rolls along a conveyor belt and is inspected by a vision system. The conveyor belt never stops, so the image sensor must be exposed very quickly. Furthermore, there are no breaks in the paper, so it must be imaged as one continuous object.

Line scan sensors are sensors designed specifically to solve web applications. These sensors are unique because they have only a single row of pixels. Since they are one-dimensional sensors, objects must be scanned one line at a time by moving the object past a stationary sensor. One line is exposed, sampled, and transmitted at a time. The frame grabber builds a two-dimensional image by stacking consecutive lines on top of each other in the system memory. The image height is theoretically infinite, since the image is continuous. Image blur is significantly reduced with a line scan camera because only one line is exposed at a time. Figure 8.8 illustrates a line scan sensor imaging a continuous paper reel moving along a conveyor.

8.2.3.5 Parallel Digital Connectors

Before any official standard for digital video could be put in place, camera vendors adopted their own proprietary formats for encoding analog camera sensor signals into digital video streams. Frame grabber manufacturers struggled to keep up with an ever-growing number of available formats. A list of compatible cameras and frame grabbers had to be maintained by each manufacturer, and custom cables had to be developed for a particular combination.

Since there was no early standard to mandate the transmission of digital video, camera and frame grabber manufacturers used an assortment of different high-density connectors for parallel digital connectivity. Custom cables were

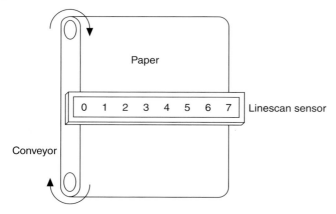

Figure 8.8 Paper inspection using a line scan sensor.

required to interface a specific camera with a particular frame grabber. Some commonly used connectors are shown in Figure 8.9a–f.

8.2.4 IEEE 1394 (FireWire) (Legacy)

The initial IEEE 1394 specification was released in December 1995. Unlike USB, IEEE 1394 was never intended for basic computer peripherals. The initial speed of IEEE 1394 was 100 Mbps, compared to the 1.5 Mbps of a USB at the time. This higher bandwidth was better suited for devices such as cameras and hard drives.

The plug and play feature is another benefit of IEEE 1394. With plug and play, users can add and remove devices without restarting the computer. When a device is added, the device announces its presence to the host computer. At this point, the operating system (OS) can launch the correct driver and any applications associated with the device.

IEEE 1394 has power on the cable. Low-power devices can draw power off the IEEE 1394 bus without the need for an external power source. High-power devices still require an external power source.

There are several different connectors available with IEEE 1394 devices. For IEEE 1394a, there are six-pin and four-pin connectors. The six-pin connector, shown in Figure 8.10a, is commonly found on most IEEE 1394 devices and provides power over the cable. The smaller four-pin connector, shown in Figure 8.10b, is occasionally found on older laptops and does not provide power over the cable. There is also a latching six-pin connector, shown in Figure 8.10c. This connector is suitable for industrial applications where cables should not be able to be easily unplugged. IEEE 1394b has a nine-pin connector, shown in Figure 8.10d, which supersedes the six-pin connector. The nine-pin connector can be used in beta or bilingual applications. IEEE 1394b connectors are dedicated to running at 800 Mbps, while bilingual cables can interoperate with IEEE 1394a devices at 400 Mbps. Additionally, IEEE 1394b also specifies a fiber optic connector, shown in Figure 8.10e, which is useful for applications that require longer cable lengths.

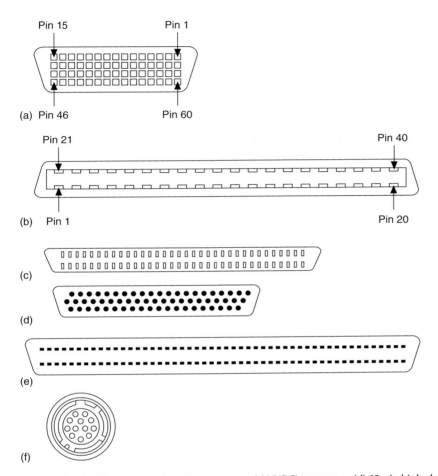

Figure 8.9 (a) DVI connector, (b) MDR connector, (c) VHDCI connector, (d) 62-pin high-density DSUB connector, (e) 100-pin SCSI connector, and (f) 12-pin Hirose connector.

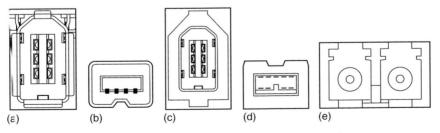

Figure 8.10 (a) IEEE 1394 six-pin connector, (b) IEEE 1394 four-pin connector, (c) IEEE 1394 latched six-pin connector, (d) IEEE 1394 nine-pin connector, and (e) IEEE 1394 fiber connector.

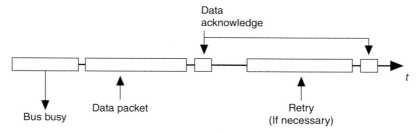

Figure 8.11 Asynchronous transfer.

IEEE 1394 defines two modes of data transfer – asynchronous and isochronous. Both types of data transfers can occur simultaneously on the same network. The IEEE 1394 specification assigns 20% of the available bandwidth to asynchronous communication and 80% to isochronous communication.

Asynchronous data transfer guarantees that all data is transferred correctly by means of a data acknowledge packet from the recipient. If a device is set up for asynchronous transfer, and does not get a data acknowledge packet after sending data, the device retries the command. This mode of data transfer guarantees that data has been transmitted, but because retries are a possibility, there is no guarantee of bandwidth. Figure 8.11 illustrates asynchronous transfer.

The following is an example of guaranteed data integrity, but not bandwidth. Assume there are 10 devices on the bus. Nine of the devices are slow and need 100 kB s^{-1}. One is fast and requires 6 MB s^{-1}. The total amount of data that needs to be transported is approximately 7 MB s^{-1}. At first glance, you may think that this setup would not be a problem for a bus that can support 50 MB s^{-1}. However, in asynchronous transfer mode, IEEE 1394 uses round-robin bus access. Assume that size of each packet size is 1024 bytes, and each device takes 25 µs to transfer its data. Every 250 µs, the fast device is allowed to send its 1024-byte packet, giving a throughput of only 4 MB s^{-1}. In this scenario, all of the data from the device would not be transferred.

Isochronous data transfer guarantees bandwidth but not data integrity. As each device is connected to the bus, the devices request bandwidth on the bus. The amount of bandwidth the device requests is determined by the packet size of the device. The bus is divided into 125-µs cycles. Each cycle begins with an asynchronous cycle start packet. Devices that have requested isochronous bandwidth are guaranteed a single packet during each cycle. Once the packets are sent from each device, the remainder of the cycle is left for any other asynchronous transfers that need to take place. Overall, ~80% of each cycle is dedicated to isochronous data transfers. Because the recipient does not acknowledge that it has received a packet, there is no guarantee that the data made it across the bus. However, data received at one end is guaranteed to be in time with the data transmitted. In most cases, particularly those configurations that have only two devices on the bus, the transmission is successful. Figure 8.12 illustrates isochronous transfer.

IEEE 1394 devices may be capable of transferring data at certain rates, but since isochronous transfer splits this up into cycles, the actual throughput is calculated differently. Since every cycle of isochronous transfer is 125 µs, you will have

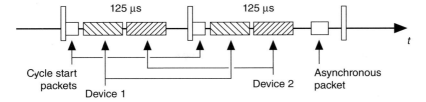

Figure 8.12 Isochronous transfer.

Table 8.2 IEEE 1394 specification.

Property	Specification
Throughput (Mbps)	400 (IEEE 1394a)
	800 (IEEE 1394b)
Connectors	IEEE 1394a four-pin (no power on bus)
	IEEE 1394a six-pin
	IEEE 1394a six-pin latching
	IEEE 1394b nine-pin
	IEEE 1394b fiber optic
Cables (m)	4.5 (copper twisted pair)
	40 (plastic fiber)
	100 (glass fiber)
	100 (copper Cat5)
Max bus current (mA)	1500 (8–30 V)

8000 cycles in 1 s. Also, each device sends one packet per cycle. Therefore, the throughput in bytes per second can be determined by the packet size of the device in bytes multiplied by 8000.

$$\text{Bytes per second} = (\text{bytes per packet} \times 8000)$$

With IEEE 1394a, isochronous transfers theoretically account for 320 Mbps. In practice, the bus can transfer a maximum of 4096 bytes every 125 μs, which is closer to 250 Mbps of bandwidth. With IEEE 1394b, the practical maximum doubles to 8192 bytes every 125 μs, or 500 Mbps of bandwidth. There is almost zero transfer overhead, as isochronous headers are stripped in hardware and the payload is transferred directly into the system memory. Table 8.2 lists specifications for IEEE 1394.

8.2.4.1 IEEE 1394 for Machine Vision

The IIDC specification used for FireWire cameras uses asynchronous transfers for camera query and control and isochronous transfers for video transfer. The IIDC specification scales well between a single fast acquisition and several slower acquisitions. An IEEE 1394b system is capable of supporting a single 640 × 480, 8-bit camera running at 200 fps, or three 640 × 480, 8-bit cameras running at

Table 8.3 Maximum packer size at various bus speeds.

Bus speed (Mbps)	Maximum packet size (bytes)
100	1024
200	2048
400	4096
800	8192

66 fps. An IEEE 1394a system is capable of running at 100 fps on a single camera or at 33 fps on three identical cameras.

The maximum packet size differs according to bus transfer speed. Table 8.3 shows the relationship between bus speed and maximum packet size.

Cameras are forced to work within the maximum packet size. When configuring an IEEE 1394 acquisition, it is important to consider the number of cameras and the frame rate for each camera. For faster but fewer cameras, increase the isochronous packet size for the best performance. For more but slower cameras, decrease the packet size. A camera typically generates fewer large packets to transfer over the IEEE 1394 bus. These modes have high frame rates, but do not share the bus well with many cameras. Figure 8.13 shows an example of isochronous transfer using large packets.

Alternatively, a camera can generate a larger number of smaller packets to transfer the same amount of data. While the frame rate is slower, it does allow more cameras to simultaneously transfer data. Figure 8.14 shows an example of isochronous transfer using small packets.

The IIDC specification allows partial images to be transferred across the IEEE 1394 bus. A user can define a subregion of the full image size, shown in Figure 8.15. The benefit of this is that you have better control over the amount of data that can be transferred across the bus. Additionally, you also have more granular control of the individual packet size of an acquisition. You can optimize for either speed or shared bandwidth, depending on your needs.

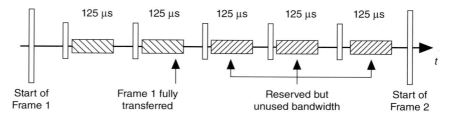

Figure 8.13 Isochronous transfer using large data packets.

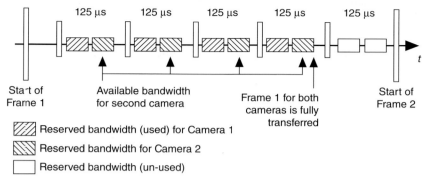

Figure 8.14 Isochronous transfer using small data packets.

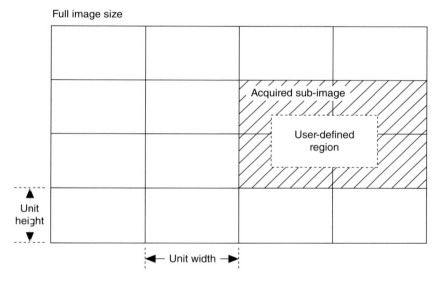

Figure 8.15 Defining subregions in an image.

Consider the following example: You wish to inspect a small region of interest (ROI) as quickly as possible. Using one of the standard video modes in the IIDC specification would not be sufficient. The standard video modes transfer the full image size in various fixed frame rates. With partially scanned images, you can select only the desired region of the image. Additionally, you can maximize the packet size for the acquisition. Now you can acquire a small region at several hundred frames per second.

A typical IIDC camera has memory on the camera. The camera sensor is exposed and scanned into the onboard memory. Some cameras implement a transform/correction on the image at this time. The complete image is typically transferred one or two scan lines at a time. Each segment of data is combined with an isochronous header to form an isochronous packet, shown in Figure 8.16. The packets are transferred every 125 s. The packet headers are verified and

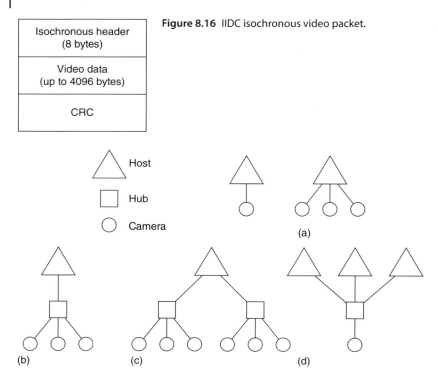

Figure 8.16 IIDC isochronous video packet.

Figure 8.17 Common IEEE 1394 network topologies.

stripped before the data is transferred into the system memory. The frame is complete when the last packet of an image is transferred into the system memory. Onboard camera memory allows a camera to expose the next frame while transferring the current frame to the host computer.

Configuring the IEEE 1394 network topology is very important for proper acquisition of a machine vision application. Ideally, you want to create the shortest possible path for the data in order to minimize data loss. Longer cables and breaks in the cable can cause signal degradation and other noise-related issues. Figure 8.17 shows some of the common network topologies used with IEEE 1394.

The most basic setup, Figure 8.17a, is one or more cameras directly connected to an IEEE 1394 interface card. This topology is probably the one most commonly used. Most IEEE 1394 interface cards have three ports, which is well suited to the number of cameras that can be used simultaneously without violating the bandwidth limitations of the IEEE 1394.

An IEEE 1394 hub can be added to the topology above (Figure 8.17b). The hub connects several cameras to a single IEEE 1394 port. Additionally, the hub extends the tethered range of cameras connected to the host computer.

Certain applications require more than three cameras on a single host computer (Figure 8.17c). It is important to note that many IEEE 1394 host controllers cannot sustain more than four simultaneous isochronous receives. This limits a user to four simultaneously acquiring cameras per interface card. You can add another IEEE 1394 interface card to the system, but you should be cautious of exceeding the host computer bus bandwidth. Plugging several PCI IEEE 1394 adapters into a host computer and running each interface at the full IEEE 1394 bandwidth of 50 MB s^{-1} might saturate the PCI bandwidth limit of 133 MB s^{-1}.

Isochronous transfers are inherently broadcast transfers. To monitor a single camera from several host computers, connect a single camera to an IEEE 1394 hub (Figure 8.17d). Connect the hub to several different host computers. One of the host computers will be the designated controller for starting and stopping acquisitions while receiving video data. The remaining computers will be listening stations to receive video data.

In recent years, both GigE Vision and USB3 Vision have taken much of the market share away from FireWire. Some of the key advantages such as power over the bus and plug-and-play functionality are now offered with GigE Vision and USB3 Vision, and at higher bus speeds. FireWire is also less available commercially, with the consumer market consolidating on USB3 "SuperSpeed" ports and ethernet connectivity.

8.2.5 Camera Link

The cost of custom cables and the broad range of digital transmission formats were the driving force behind the development of a standard for high-speed transmission of digital video. The AIA standard is known as *Camera Link* was released in 2000. Revision 1.1 was adopted in 2004, version 1.2 in 2007, and version 2.0 in November 2011. The Camera Link specification defines the cable, connector, and signal functionality. Any camera that complies with the Camera Link specification should work with any frame grabber that is also Camera Link compliant.

The Camera Link standard replaces expensive custom cables with a single, low-cost, standard cable with fewer wires. Special components on the camera are used to serialize 28 parallel TTL signals into 4 high-speed differential pairs, which are transmitted across the cable. A similar component is used on the frame grabber to de-serialize the data stream into parallel TTL signals. This reduces cable size and cost, and increases noise immunity and maximum cable length. Camera Link is a non-packet-based protocol (as opposed to recent USB3 and GigE Vision standards) and remains the simplest camera bus.

The Camera Link specification has come a long way in standardizing digital video transmission by defining the cable, the connector, and the signal functionality. However, Camera Link still leaves many aspects of the camera–frame grabber interface un-addressed. Tap configurations, for example, were not defined in the initial release of the Camera Link specification. The frame grabber must be configured to properly reconstruct image data from a particular camera. The tap configuration of one camera may not even be supported by a particular frame grabber, although both are compliant with the Camera Link specification.

Although serial signals are defined on the cable pin-out, the specific serial commands for setting exposure, gain, and offset, for example, are not defined by the specification. The frame grabber driver software must be configured to accommodate a particular camera's serial commands. Control signals are also provided on the Camera Link cable for triggering and timing, but many manufacturers provide separate connectors for advanced triggering capabilities. The Camera Link specification now includes optional GenICam support for plug-and-play compatibility and to address some of these concerns.

8.2.5.1 Camera Link Signals

The Camera Link specification allows three levels of support: base, medium, and full configuration. A base configuration camera uses one cable, one connector, and one serializer chip. Four TTL signals are used for timing, and 24 are used for data transfer, or three 8-bit taps. The serializer components run at up to 85 MHz, providing up to 255 MB s^{-1} of video throughput.

The timing signals include frame valid, line valid, data valid, and reserved. Frame valid and line valid are used the same way as in parallel digital transmission. The data valid signal asserts for each valid pixel. It can be de-asserted to indicate that a particular clock cycle should not be sampled. The reserved signal functionality is left to the camera manufacturer. Figure 8.18 shows the Camera Link timing signals for an image sensor with two lines, each three pixels wide. Notice that data valid de-asserts for one clock cycle between pixel 1 and pixel 2, making that sample invalid.

In addition to the data and timing signals, the TTL pixel clock is also converted into a fifth differential pair and transmitted along with the data. Camera configuration is supported through two serial data lines for communication to a universal asynchronous receiver transmitter (UART). Four additional timing and triggering lines run from the frame grabber to the camera for precise exposure control. The serial and timing signals are also transmitted as differential pairs to provide higher speed and increased noise immunity. The connector and the cable pin-out are defined by the Camera Link specification for all the timing, data, serial, and trigger signals.

Medium configuration was added to the Camera Link specification as an extra layer of support to increase video throughput. Twenty-four additional data signals are added for medium configuration to support a total of six 8-bit taps. At 85 MHz, medium configuration Camera Link supports a maximum throughput

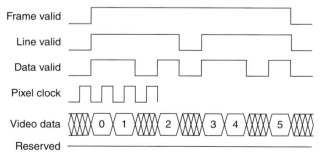

Figure 8.18 Camera link timing diagram.

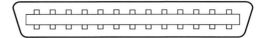

Figure 8.19 Camera link connector.

of $510\,\text{MB}\,\text{s}^{-1}$. Two serializer components are required to accommodate the additional data lines. Full configuration Camera Link uses three serializer components and two separate Camera Link cables for a total of ten 8-bit taps and a maximum throughput of $680\,\text{MB}\,\text{s}^{-1}$. Pixel data-bit positions for each configuration are defined by the Camera Link specification. There is now also an 80-bit configuration that allows a maximum throughput of $850\,\text{MB}\,\text{s}^{-1}$.

8.2.5.2 Camera Link Connectors

The Camera Link connector is defined in the specification as a 26-pin MDR connector from the 3M Corporation, shown in Figure 8.19. This connector was designed specifically for high-speed LVDS signals. The camera and frame grabber connections are female, and the cable connections are male. The Camera Link specification defines a maximum cable length of 10 m. The wires within the cable are insulated, and differential pairs are twisted and individually shielded to provide better noise immunity. An outer shield is added and tied to a chassis ground. Version 2.0 of the specification includes mini Camera Link connectors (SDR, HDR 26-pin) and power over Camera Link (PoCL).

8.2.6 Camera Link HS

The CLHS standard was released in 2012 and is overseen by the AIA. It does not extend the functionality of Camera Link (it is not backward compatible with Camera Link) but is instead a new and separate standard. The standard provides scalable bandwidths from 300 to $16\,000\,\text{MB}\,\text{s}^{-1}$ ($2.1\,\text{GB}\,\text{s}^{-1}$ per cable and up to eight cables) to meet the needs of applications using high-resolution and high-speed sensors. The interface defines the handling of video data, real-time triggers, and various command-and-control instructions. The CLHS spec also offers an intellectual property (IP) core solution that implements the message layer of the CLHS standard to support the implementation on cameras and frame grabbers.

Information sent using the CLHS interface is divided into packets of various types: trigger, GPIO, ack/nack, video, command, and idle. For the M protocol variant, these packets consist of a sequence of data and control characters that are passed between the CLHS IP core and a physical layer device (PHY) using a 9-bit parallel interface. The interface uses 1 bit to indicate whether the word should be interpreted as data or control/status information and the remaining 8 bits to carry information. To facilitate high-speed communication over physical media (such as CX4 copper cabling), physical layer devices are used to encode the 9-bit data bus, serialize it, transmit the high-speed data over some transmission medium, then deserialize and decode the received data at the far end of the link. CLHS uses the 8b/10b encoding/decoding scheme to ensure DC balance of the serial data and to provide sufficient data transition density for proper recovery of embedded clock signals. In implementing these physical layer functions, system designers are typically faced with a choice between custom IC (application-specific integrated circuit (ASIC)) development, using FPGA-integrated SERDES (serializer/de-serializer), or using a discrete SERDES solution [3].

It has a trigger jitter of 3.2 ns and a latency of ~100–300 ns. Because of a high-speed uplink to the camera, CLHS allows frame-by-frame control of an image acquisition. For example, the ROI can be changed each frame of an acquisition [4].

The fiber optic physical layer was chosen because of its low cost, light weight, small diameter, and long-distance capability. It has high bandwidth, extreme flex-life rating, and immunity to electrical noise. CLHS can also use SFP, SFP+, or SFF-8470 connectors (InfiniBand or CX4) [1].

8.2.7 CoaXPress

Imaging sensor size and speed improvements are leading to a huge increase in camera data rate outputs. Users and vendors saw the need to go beyond the capabilities of established interfaces such as Camera Link, GigE Vision, and USB3 Vision. Drivers behind the development of CoaXPress include longer cable lengths and higher data transfer rates. CoaXPress version 1.0 was released in 2011. JIIA is responsible for the maintenance of the standard. The CoaXPress standard was endorsed by the AIA and EMVA to become an official world standard in 2011. Version 1.1 was released in 2013. It is an asymmetric, high-speed, point-to-point serial communication standard scalable over single or multiple coaxial cables. Coaxial cables were specified because of their suitability for high-speed data transmission, immunity to intra-pair skew, good EMI/EMC (electromagnetic interference/electromagnetic compatibility) performance, low cost, and ease of installation and termination. It supports "downlink" speeds from a camera to an interface device of up to 6.25 Gbps per coaxial cable connection, as well as a 20 Mbps uplink for communication and control. Power over the cable is specified at up to 13 W in the standard, and cable lengths of greater than 100 m are possible. CoaXPress uses a 75-Ω coaxial cable as a physical medium. It is a point-to-point scalable interface with a master connection and optional extension connections to increase the bandwidth from a device to a host [1, 5].

8.2.8 USB (USB3 Vision)

The initial USB 1.0 specification was released in November 1995 with a transfer rate of 12 Mbps. USB 2.0 was released in 2001 with transfer rates of 480 Mbps. USB 3.0 was released in 2010 with 5 Gbps transfer speeds (10 times faster than USB 2.0), and is called SuperSpeed USB. USB 3.0 ports are often designated with an "SS" on consumer devices. USB 3.1 was released in July 2013 with transfer rates up to 10 Gbps (called SuperSpeed+) but is not widely adopted yet.

Figure 8.20 (a) USB Type A connector and (b) USB Type B connector.

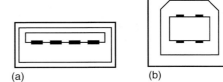

A USB is used to connect external devices to a computer. These external devices include printers, scanners, keyboards, mice, joysticks, audio\video devices, hard drives, and web cams. Prior to USB, a typical PC had the following:

- Two RS-232 serial ports for low-bandwidth peripherals like modems
- One parallel port for high-bandwidth peripherals such as printers
- Two PS/2 connectors for the keyboard and the mouse
- Other plug-in cards such as an audio capture or SCSI card.

Each peripheral used a different connector. Older connectors took up a lot of space at the back of the computer. Older technologies also did not allow you to network peripherals.

A modern PC or laptop typically has between two and four USB ports. Multiple USB peripherals can be connected to a single USB port with an optional USB hub. A USB allows a theoretical maximum of 127 devices on a single port, but in practice a typical USB hub allows 6 devices per port.

Plug-and-play is another benefit of USB. Plug-and-play means that users can add and remove devices without restarting the computer. When a device is added, the device announces its presence to the host computer. At this point, the OS launches the correct driver and any applications associated with the device.

USB has power on the cable. Low power devices, such as a mouse and keyboard, can draw power from the USB bus without needing an external power source. However, high power devices, such as scanners and printers, still require an external power source. The introduction of USB Battery Charging 1.2 specification allows up to 7.5 W of power through USB 3.0. USB is not the ubiquitous connection for charging cell phones and small peripheral devices, typically with the Micro-B connector.

There is more than one basic connector for USB. Most peripherals that plug directly into a host computer use the flat, or Type A, USB connector shown in Figure 8.20a Peripherals that require a separate power cable use a Type A connector on the host side and a square, or Type B, connector on the peripheral side. Figure 8.20b shows a Type B USB connector. The different connector types are intended to prevent incorrect plugging of USB devices.

A USB defines four modes of data transfer – control, bulk, isochronous, and interrupt. All types of data transfers can occur simultaneously on the same network.

Control transfer is used for initial configuration of a device. Bulk transfer is used to move large amounts of data when the bus is not active. Interrupt transfer

Table 8.4 USB specifications.

Property	USB 1.0	USB 2.0	USB 3.0	USB 3.1
Throughput	12 Mbps	480 Mbps	5 Gbps	10 Gbps
Power	2.5 W (at 5 V)	2.5 W (at 5 V)	4.5 W (at 5 V)	4.5 W (at 5 V)

is used to poll peripherals that might need immediate service. Cyclic redundancy check (CRC) error checking is used to ensure that all the packets are transferred correctly.

Isochronous transfer guarantees timely delivery of data. No error correction mechanism is used, so the host must tolerate potentially corrupted data. Up to 90% of the available bandwidth can be allocated for isochronous transfers. Table 8.4 lists the specifications for a USB.

USB 3.0 (super-speed USB) provides many improvements over USB 2.0 and FireWire, including an order of magnitude high bandwidth, better error management, higher power supply, longer cable lengths, and lower latency and jitter times. These benefits, combined with commercial adoption of USB 3.0 with native hardware support across laptops and other computing devices, argues for rapid growth of USB 3.0 connected devices [6].

8.2.8.1 USB for Machine Vision

The one obstruction to the widespread adoption of USB 2.0 for machine vision applications was the lack of a hardware specification for video acquisition devices. Each vendor had to implement their own hardware and software design. Different vendor designs prevented devices from different vendors from working together, and forced users to install device-specific drivers.

To solve the standardization problem on USB, and since USB 3.0 represented such a huge bandwidth improvement, USB3 Vision was ratified in 2013 as a camera bus. It builds on the GenICam standards and borrows much from GigE vision in implementation of the standard. Because of the improvements over USB 2.0 and the bandwidth now eclipsing FireWire and GigE capabilities, USB 3.0 is poised for rapid adoption in the machine vision industry.

The USB3 vision standard is built on the SuperSpeed USB specification, otherwise known as the *USB 3.0 specification*. USB 3.0 is managed by the USB implementers forum (USB-IF) and offers a 400 MB s^{-1} throughput and 4.5 W of power (at 5 V) to the device.

The USB3 Vision standard defines mechanisms for device discovery and identification, control, and image streaming. Hosted by the AIA, the global trade association for the vision and imaging industry, USB3 Vision will allow "plug-and-play" compatibility between a USB3 Vision device and a computer running a standard USB 3.0 interface. USB3 Vision builds off existing standards such as the GigE Vision and standard for gigabit ethernet devices. As such, cameras will have an XML file that defines supported camera features. USB3 Vision will use the GenICam programming interface to allow access to common and also vendor-specific features.

USB3 Vision also permits zero-copy image transfers of image data directly into host memory with no CPU usage. The standard also encompasses specifications for a standardized screw-lock USB 3.0 connector to secure cables to the devices and the host machine [7].

The USB bus is already evolving to USB 3.1, with early devices like the Apple Inc. MacBook adopting the standard. USB 3.1 expands the USB charging profile to 100 W and 10 Gbps. This will enable devices that traditionally had multiple peripheral ports and a separate power port (like the above-mentioned Apple MacBook) to consolidate all I/O and power into one connector. Additionally, the new USB Type C connector is an attempt to solve the near-universal problem of not knowing how to orient a USB Type A connector when plugging it into a port on a device [8].

8.2.9 Gigabit Ethernet (GigE Vision)

The original IEEE 802.3 Ethernet standard was published in 1985. Ethernet was originally developed by the Xerox Corporation in 1970 and initially ran at 10 Mbps. The 100-Mbps fast ethernet protocol was standardized in 1995, and the 1000-Mbps gigabit ethernet protocol in 1998.

The RJ-45 ethernet connector, shown in Figure 8.21, is the standard connector found in most computer systems. The benefit of gigabit ethernet is that it is backward compatible with original and fast ethernet devices using existing connectors and cables. Gigabit ethernet uses the same CSMA/CD protocol as the ethernet.

Unlike a USB or the IEEE 1394, ethernet was not originally intended to connect peripherals. Ethernet does not offer plug-and-play notification. Device discovery requires additional protocols or user intervention. Additionally, no power is provided on the bus. All these shortcomings are planned to be addressed in future revisions of various specifications.

The theoretical maximum bandwidth of the gigabit ethernet is 1000 Mbps. With hardware limitations and software overheads, the practical maximum bandwidth is closer to 800 Mbps. Table 8.5 lists the specifications for the gigabit ethernet.

Ethernet has many derivative protocols like IP, UDP, and TCP, which offer portable transport layers. Each derivative layer is built on top of the previous one. For example, in order to transport user data via UDP, a UDP, IP, and ethernet header must all be calculated and prefixed to the user data.

Figure 8.21 RJ-45 ethernet connector.

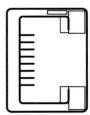

Table 8.5 Gigabit ethernet specification.

Property	Specification
Throughput	1000 Mbps
Connectors	RJ-45
Cables	100 m (copper CAT5)
Max bus current	n/a

8.2.9.1 Gigabit Ethernet for Machine Vision

While ethernet was originally developed for networking computers, it has found some peripheral applications. The high bandwidth and ease of cabling makes the gigabit ethernet an attractive option for industrial cameras.

GigE Vision is probably the most widely adopted vision interface today. It has many benefits:

- Fast data transfer with $125\,\text{MB}\,\text{s}^{-1}$ speeds
- 100 m cable lengths
- Low-cost CAT5e or CAT6 cables and standard connectors
- Scalable to the fast growth of ethernet
- Standard hardware and cabling allows easy low cost integration.

The GigE Vision standard 2.0 was released in November 2011. It includes non-streaming device control for things like lighting controllers and support for 10 GigE ethernet and link aggregation. It also enables the transmission of compressed images (JPEG, JPEG 2000, and H.264), accurate synchronization of multicamera systems through 1588 (PTP) and enhanced support for multitap sensors.

The GigE Vision standard defines the behavior of the host as well as the camera. There are four discrete components to the standard:

8.2.9.2 GigE Vision Device Discovery

When a GigE Vision device is powered on, it attempts to acquire an IP address in the following order: persistent IP, DHCP server, link local addressing.

8.2.9.3 GigE Vision Control Protocol (GVCP)

GigE Vision control protocol (GVCP) allows applications to configure and control a GigE Vision device. The application sends a command using the UDP protocol and waits for an acknowledgment (ACK) from the device before sending the next command. This ACK scheme ensures data integrity. Using this scheme, the application can get and set various attributes on the GigE Vision device, typically a camera.

The GigE Vision standard defines a minimum set of attributes that GigE Vision devices must support. These attributes, such as image width, height, pixel format, and so on, are required to acquire an image from the camera and hence are mandatory. However, a GigE Vision camera can expose attributes beyond the minimal set. These additional attributes must conform to the GenICam standard.

8.2.9.4 GenICam

GenICam provides a unified programming interface for exposing arbitrary attributes in cameras. It uses a computer-readable XML datasheet, provided by the camera manufacturer, to enumerate all the attributes. Each attribute is defined by its name, interface type, unit of measurement, and behavior.

GenICam-compliant XML datasheets eliminate the need for custom camera files for each camera. Instead, the manufacturer can describe all the attributes for the camera in the XML file so that any GigE Vision driver can control the camera. Additionally, the GenICam standard recommends naming conventions for features such as gain, shutter speed, and device model, which are common to most cameras.

8.2.9.5 GigE Vision Stream Protocol (GVSP)

The GigE Vision standard uses UDP packets to stream data from the device to the application. The device includes a GigE Vision header as part of the data packet that identifies the image number, packet number, and the timestamp. The application uses this information to construct the image in user memory.

8.2.9.6 Packet Loss and Resends

Since image data packets are streamed using the UDP protocol, there is no protocol-level handshaking to guarantee packet delivery. Therefore, the GigE Vision standard implements a packet recovery process to ensure that images have no missing data. However, this packet recovery implementation is not required to be GigE Vision compliant. While most cameras will implement packet recovery, some low-end cameras may not implement it.

The GigE Vision header, which is part of the UDP packet, contains the image number, packet number, and timestamp. As packets arrive over the network, the driver transfers the image data within the packet to user memory. When the driver detects that a packet has arrived out of sequence (based on the packet number), it places the packet in kernel mode memory. All subsequent packets are placed in kernel memory until the missing packet arrives. If the missing packet does not arrive within a user-defined time, the driver transmits a resend request for that packet. The driver transfers the packets from kernel memory to user memory when all missing packets have arrived [7].

Configuring the network topology is very important for proper image acquisition in a machine vision application. You should connect the network in such a way as to minimize network collisions and lost packets. Additionally, you should sufficiently shield cameras in an industrially noisy environment. Figure 8.22 shows some of the common topologies used with ethernet networks.

The most basic configuration, shown in Figure 8.22a, is to directly connect a camera to a host computer using a crossover cable. This topology will lead to the least amount of network collisions and lost packets. Having a separate network interface for camera communication and network traffic is essential.

Another configuration, shown in Figure 8.22b, provides a network hub between several cameras and a host computer. The hub should be isolated from any external network. Network collisions can still occur between the connected cameras, but data loss due to lost packets should be minimal.

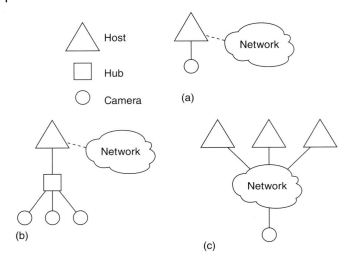

Figure 8.22 Common ethernet topologies.

Yet another possible configuration, shown in Figure 8.22c, involves connecting one or more cameras to an external network. One thing to consider with this configuration is that using an external network will induce more network collisions and lost packets. There is a good chance that packets may become stalled or fragmented before reaching the host computer depending on the surrounding network traffic. One of the benefits to this configuration is that a camera can be placed far away and it does not need to be directly connected to the host computer. Also, a single camera can be shared between several monitoring stations.

8.2.10 Future Standards Development

It appears that the market is still shifting and adapting to the rapid release of new camera bus standards in the past few years. As the bus standards make their way into the market through more vendors offering interfaces and cameras with those standards, vision system designers have more choice than ever before.

USB3 serves the plug-and-play market very well, and will take some share from Camera Link at the lower bandwidths and further obsolete FireWire. The upcoming USB 3.1 release may rapidly accelerate the trend away from Camera Link and toward USB. GigE Vision will remain the most popular bus for networking solutions, and will remain relevant, with advancements in bandwidth and timing capabilities being driven by other industries and by the IEEE. Time-sensitive network (TSN) capabilities for determinism and timing as well as bandwidth improvements to 10 GigE links, if the industry can sufficiently drive down the cost and thermal limitations of the standard, will continue to make GigE Vision a very attractive solution.

CLHS and CoaXPress will duke it out at the high end of the market. Indications are that CoaXPress will emerge as the dominant bus for high-speed/high-throughput applications.

The G3 cooperation between major industry groups will help accelerate and guide the evolution of current vision standards as the technology improves. Standards committee meetings are now co-located, and there is a lot of technology reuse between different standards. The efforts of the G3 will help ensure that the industry does not unnecessarily develop competing standards in parallel, and will help insure that interoperability and compatibility are highly valued. This is good news for integrators and for vendors, as better technology should be standardized and available for implementation at a lower cost by vendors on a faster cadence than has previously been possible.

8.3 Choosing a Camera Bus

Modern machine vision system developers have at least five different camera buses to choose from when designing a system. This section addresses the criteria to consider when choosing a camera bus and identifies which criteria are likely to be the most important for your application.

8.3.1 Bandwidth

The bandwidth, or throughput, of a camera bus is a measure of the rate at which image data is transferred from the camera to the acquisition device. Bandwidth is dictated by the frame rate, image resolution, and amount of data representing one pixel. Eight-bit monochrome images are usually represented by 1 byte per pixel, and 10-bit or larger monochrome images are usually represented by 2 bytes per pixel. Color images are usually transmitted as 1–3 bytes per pixel. Cameras that output data based on some color mosaic pattern, such as Bayer cameras, transmit data exactly in the same manner as monochrome cameras. Some color cameras output data in RGB format, usually as 3 bytes per pixel.

8.3.2 Resolution

Resolution is a measure of the ability of an imaging system to discern detail within a scene. Resolution is determined by many factors including optics, lighting, mechanical configuration, and the camera. For the sake of choosing a suitable imaging bus, only the camera itself has much impact. The resolution of a camera can be described by several measures, but generally the most noted specification is the number of pixels on the charge-coupled device (CCD) or complementary metal–oxide–semiconductor (CMOS) sensor. For area scan cameras, the width and height of the sensor are specified in pixels, while line scan cameras only specify the line width. It is assumed the height of a line scan image is arbitrarily large and limited only by the acquisition device.

Camera specifications such as sensitivity and signal-to-noise ratio impact the quality of the acquired image; however, the resolution is fundamentally limited by the signal format. Several years ago, a system designer might choose the appropriate sensor for an application and be forced to use whichever bus the camera used. With a much larger selection of cameras currently in the market, many sensors are available with a choice of bus technology. Often the same camera model will be offered with the option of GigE or USB 3.0 output.

Ultimately, the choice of a camera bus cannot be made on the basis of resolution alone.

8.3.3 Frame Rate

The maximum frame rate for cameras is limited by the pixel clock rate and related circuitry in the camera and how fast it can put images onto a camera bus. The camera bus components then also have limiting factors in terms of total bandwidth and signaling limitations, which will restrict the bandwidth.

8.3.4 Cables

In the days of parallel digital cameras, cabling was complex, costly, and customized. Since few standards existed for parallel digital cameras, there were a variety of connectors and pin-outs available and users generally did not expect to find an off-the-shelf cable. Because of the parallel data format, cables could have 40 or more wire pairs. Cabling for cameras has been greatly simplified by standardization efforts around the use of low-cost, readily available options. With USB and ethernet in particular, the component cost is further driven down by widespread commercial uses and volumes. Maximum cable lengths vary greatly between camera buses from the point-to-point and relatively short 3–5 m cable lengths of USB to over 5000 m for fiber optic connections for CLHS and GigE. Maximum cable length depends on several factors including the transmitter/receiver circuitry, signal integrity, attenuation characteristics of the cabling, cabling construction quality, and so on. Each bus architecture and physical layer will have limiting factors, and the maximum cable length recommendations have to be made when looking at the combination of factors in the components that make up the acquisition system.

8.3.5 Line Scan

The majority of line scan cameras use Camera Link or GigE connections. The trend in line scan sensors toward longer line lengths and higher rates makes Camera Link a good choice. Current line scan cameras have line lengths up to 12 000 pixels and line rates up to 140 kHz [9].

8.3.6 Reliability

Imaging reliability refers to the ability of an imaging system to guarantee acquisition of every image during an inspection process. In many applications such as manufacturing, inspection, and sorting, it is often important that the imaging system acquire and process every image to guarantee 100% inspection. If a fault occurs that causes the acquisition to miss an image, the user should be notified of the event. Events that can cause a system to miss an image include noise on the trigger lines or spurious trigger signals. In a typical system, an external signal from a part sensing device, such as an optical trigger, is connected to the frame grabber. The frame grabber receives the trigger signal and provides a signal to trigger the camera. Routing the trigger signals through the frame grabber provides advanced timing features, such as delayed or multiple pulse generation, or signal conditioning such as converting a 24-V isolated input to a TTL signal for the camera. The trigger signal also informs the frame grabber that an image is expected. If a trigger is received by the frame grabber and an image is not returned from the camera, the driver software can alert the application of a missed image. A missed image can be caused by an electrical problem or by sending triggers to the camera faster than it can accept them. Unlike Camera Link cameras, USB and GigE cameras are usually triggered directly at the camera. The image acquisition system does not process the trigger and is not aware of the one-to-one relationship between trigger pulses and acquired images. If a GigE camera receives a trigger at an invalid time, the camera ignores the trigger and the acquisition system may not be aware that a part was missed. This is one advantage of a frame-grabber-based machine vision system.

Deterministic image transfer is also important for an image acquisition system. Determinism describes the confidence with which an image will be received within a specified time after a trigger event. The amount of time required to transfer an image will vary based on the camera resolution and the bus bandwidth, but the delay should be predictable. Camera Link, CLHS, USB, and CoaXPress can usually guarantee deterministic timing due to the point-to-point nature of the bus and predictable camera timing. The transfer of data is controlled by the camera, and there is no other data competing for bandwidth on the bus. Although various bus topologies are possible with hubs, each device is reserved a certain amount of bandwidth upon initialization. This allows the camera to send slices of data at known time intervals and transfer the image in a fixed time. Ethernet cameras cannot necessarily guarantee the transfer of an image. Network congestion can cause data packets to be dropped, requiring the data to be resent. This increases the transfer time in an unpredictable manner. In the worst case, some of the image data may never be received. For simple network topologies or point-to-point connections, data transfer should be reliable, but acquiring images over a larger network, where the data must contend with other traffic, can be challenging.

8.3.7 Summary of Camera Bus Specifications

See Figure 8.23.

8.3.8 Sample Use Cases

8.3.8.1 Manufacturing Inspection

The inspection of manufactured goods is increasingly relying on machine vision systems. Verifying the quality of a product or process often includes measuring the size and shape of a part, checking for defects, or searching for the presence of components in an assembly. For example, a company that packages and sells window glass cleaner may need to verify the bottle cap and label placement as well as the fill level in the bottle. All of these tasks can be accomplished using machine vision. In this hypothetical example, the features to inspect are large and the field of view of the camera may only

HARDWARE DIGITAL INTERFACE STANDARD COMPARISON

Name of Standard	IEEE1394 + IIDC	Camera Link	Camera Link HS	CoaXPress	GigE Vision	USB3 Vision
Date of initial release	August 1996	October 2000	May 2012	December 2010	May 2006	January 2013
Current version	version 1.32	version 2.0	version 1.0	version 1.1	version 2.0	version 1.0
Date of latest release	July 2008	February 2012	May 2012	February 2013	November 2011	January 2013
Topology	Daisy chain	Point-to-point	Point-to-point, data splitting	Point-to-point	Point-to-point, network	Point-to-point, tiered-star
Transmission format	Packet-based	Parallel	Packet-based	Packet-based	Packet-based	Packet-based
Image transmission robustness	Error detection only	None	Data retransmission/ Forward error correction	Error detection only	Data retransmission	Data retransmission
Related software standard	Mandatory: IIDC	Optional: GenICam CLProtocol	Mandatory: GenICam GenApi, GenCP, SFNC Optional: GenICam GenTL	Mandatory: GenICam GenApi, GenTL, SFNC Optional: IIDC2	Mandatory: GenICam GenApi, SFNC Optional: GenICam GenTL	Mandatory: GenICam GenApi, GenCP, SFNC Optional: GenICam GenTL, IIDC2
Certification requirements	Self certification	Registration form, self certification	Registration form, compliance matrix	Registration form, electrical/protocol/ Interoperability compliance tests, PlugFest	Registration form, compliance matrix, device validation software, PlugFest	Registration form, compliance matrix, device validation software, electrical compliance tests, PlugFest
Configuration	IEEE1394a (S400) IEEE1394b (S800) / IEEE1394b (S1600)	BASE / MEDIUM/ FULL / 80-bit	C2 / F2 / 8xF2 (splitting)	CXP3 / CXP6 / 4+1 CXP6 (LAG)	1 GigE / 2x1GigE (LAG) / 10 GigE	SuperSpeed 5 Gbits/s
Bandwidth (image data) *: ≤100 Mbytes/s **: ≤200 Mbytes/s ***: ≤500 Mbytes/s ****: ≤1000 Mbytes/s *****: >1000 Mbytes/s	* / **	*** / **** / ****	***** / ***** / *****	*** / **** / *****	** / *** / ****	***
Control channel	Full-duplex, shared with image data	Dedicated serial port	Dedicated uplink, shared downlink	Dedicated uplink, shared downlink	Full-duplex, shared with image data	Full-duplex, shared with image data
Cable types	IEEE 1394	Camera Link	CX4 / Fiber	Coaxial	CAT-5e/6a/7, Fiber / CAT-6a/7, Fiber	SuperSpeed USB
Cable length (passive cable) *: ≤10 meters **: ≤20 meters ***: ≤50 meters ****: ≤120 meters *****: >120 meters	*	*	** / *****	**** / *** / ***	****(CAT-5e/6a/7) *****(Fiber)	* (Copper) **** (Fiber Adapter)
Power over the cable	Mandatory	Optional	None	Mandatory	Optional	Mandatory
Wattage available at camera	45W max (depends on PC)	4W / 8W / 8W	N/A	13W / 52W	13W (IEEE802.3af) 25W (IEEE802.3at)	4.5W
Frame grabber required	No	Yes	Yes	Yes	No	No
Camera trigger input signal	Direct on camera	On camera or from frame grabber	On camera or from frame grabber	On camera or from frame grabber	Direct on camera	Direct on camera
Trigger latency - frame grabber to camera (link latency, protocol overhead only) *: ≥100 µs **: ≥10 µs ***: ≥1 µs ****: ≥100 ns *****: <100 ns	N/A	*****	****	****	N/A	N/A

Figure 8.23 Hardware digital interface standard comparison [1].

be a few inches diagonally. Feature size and field of view are the two system parameters that determine the necessary camera resolution. These inspections could likely be done with a standard-resolution camera. The inspection rate for many applications will be limited by the mechanics of the manufacturing system to considerably less than 30 Hz, and a standard-frame-rate camera is sufficient. Cameras with this frame rate and resolution are available for any of the camera buses, and the decision will be based on other criteria. Cost is almost always critical, and USB3 and GigE Vision each can provide a cost-effective solution.

8.3.8.2 LCD Inspection

Automated optical inspection is used to inspect LCD display panels during manufacturing to provide feedback for process control and to verify the quality of a finished product. Inspecting LCD displays typically requires detecting very small defects over a wide field of view. For example, defects as small as 5 µm must be detected on panels that are often 400 mm wide or more. Field of view and minimum feature size determine the necessary image resolution. Even with the high-resolution cameras currently available, such as 11 megapixel area-scan cameras and 12 K line-scan cameras, multiple images are required for full coverage. The throughput of the inspection system can be linked directly to the throughput of the acquisition. Camera Link, CLHS, or CoaXPress provide the bandwidth necessary for high-resolution and high-speed inspections. High-resolution GigE and USB cameras offer similar sensor sizes and are useful where inspection time is limited by processing time or by other steps in the manufacturing process rather than camera bus throughput.

8.3.8.3 Security

Security and site-monitoring applications present interesting challenges for a camera bus. Typically, several cameras are required, and often they are located at a considerable distance away from each other and from a monitoring/recording station. USB and GigE cameras can be easily networked to accommodate multiple cameras, but the limited cable length can restrict camera placement. Fiber optic extenders are available to extend the range to hundreds of meters, but adding an extender for each camera is a costly and complex solution. Point-to-point connections restrict the number of cameras that can be monitored from one station, and security monitoring typically would not take advantage of the high bandwidth of Camera Link or CoaXPress. GigE cameras are good candidates for this application. They are capable of covering large distances and can be connected in a variety of arrangements, and the inherent networking ability allows many cameras to be controlled and viewed from one station. Connecting multiple cameras reduces the frame rate from each camera, but high frame rates may not be required from all cameras simultaneously.

8.4 Computer Buses

Once you have acquired an image from a camera and sent the image data over the camera bus to an interface device, the data must still travel across a second bus, that is, the internal computer bus, before it can be processed by the computer. The most efficient way to provide data to the processor is to first send the data to memory. Sending the data to memory allows the processor to continue working on other tasks while the data is being prepared for processing. Tight integration between the processor and main memory allows the processor to retrieve image data from memory much faster than retrieving it from another location. Using the wrong computer bus for your application can have significant impact on the overall performance of the system.

The following sections describe the most common computer buses for machine vision applications. There are many variations of these computer buses that offer different throughput, availability, and cost. The peak throughput, prevalence, and costs discussed in this section are for the most common and widely available computer buses. Refer to Figure 8.24 for an overview of common computer buses. In most cases, the peak throughput of a bus will be much higher than the average throughput of the bus, because of the overheads of the bus protocol.

8.4.1 ISA/EISA

When PCs first became widely available, there was no standard internal computer bus, forcing device manufacturers to make multiple versions of their devices with different interfaces for each brand of computer. As computers became common, developing custom devices became less practical, and a number of computer vendors began using a bus originally developed by IBM. The result of this was the ISA bus, introduced in the mid-1980s. Sometimes, ISA buses are referred to by the original IBM name, AT. The ISA bus did not have

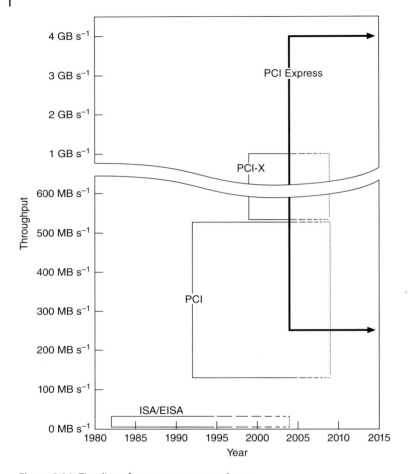

Figure 8.24 Timeline of common computer buses.

an agreed-upon specification and initially suffered from compatibility problems. A few years later, a similar but more fully featured bus was developed called the EISA bus. Depending on the exact version, ISA and EISA buses deliver a peak throughput of 4.7–33 MB s^{-1}. By the late 1990s, the superior performance and prevalence of the PCI bus had largely eclipsed the ISA and the EISA. It remained common, however, for computers to continue to offer EISA buses for use with legacy devices until the introduction of PCI Express. As computer manufacturers have added support for PCI Express, they have generally eliminated support for EISA.

8.4.2 PCI/CompactPCI/PXI

In the early 1990s, Intel developed a standardized bus called the PCI bus. PCI quickly gained acceptance in desktop, workstation, and server computers. PCI provides significantly improved performance over ISA/EISA buses. Initially, PCI offered peak throughput of 132 MB s^{-1} and a data width of 32 bits.

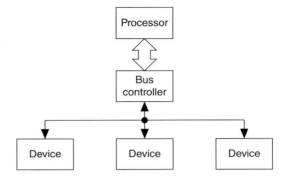

Figure 8.25 Multi-drop bus configuration.

Later, a faster PCI bus was developed by increasing the frequency from 33 to 66 MHz. A second variety increased the data width from 32 to 64 bits. By combining both these changes, PCI offered a peak throughput of 528 MB s^{-1}. Because of higher development and implementation costs, the 64-bit/66-MHz PCI bus has not been as widely adopted as the original PCI implementation. Such PCI buses are primarily limited to high-end computers that require additional performance.

The average throughput that can be achieved with PCI depends significantly on the configuration of the system. With only one device on the bus, the original implementation of PCI offers an average throughput of ~100 MB s^{-1} out of the 132 MB s^{-1} peak throughput. While the bus can achieve 132 MB s^{-1} for short periods, continuous use of the bus will yield ~100 MB s^{-1} due to some of the transfer time being used to prepare for the data transactions. PCI is a type of bus called a *multi-drop bus* because it can accommodate multiple devices. However, adding multiple devices to the PCI bus affects the available throughput. Refer to Figure 8.25 for the diagram of a multi-drop bus configuration.

In a multi-drop bus, all of the devices on the bus share the same physical wires to communicate with the processor and the memory. Because there is only one set of wires, only one device can *talk* at a time. This means that the 100 MB s^{-1} average throughput must be shared among all the devices on the bus. For example, an application that requires two input devices providing data at 80 MB s^{-1} each would not be possible on the 33-MHz/32-bit PCI bus because 2×80 MB s^{-1} = 160 MB s^{-1}, which far exceeds the 100 MB s^{-1} that can be averaged on the PCI bus. In addition, when switching between multiple devices, a larger amount of throughput is required than the sum of the data rates of the two devices because some of the transfer time will be lost due to the time it takes to switch between the two devices. The exact amount of throughput lost to the overheads of switching will depend on your system configuration. Factors such as the amount and timing of data coming in on the two input devices, and the type of chipset used by the computer, all affect the amount of overheads resulting from sharing the bus. Even with the drawback of sharing throughput among all devices, the PCI bus provides sufficient throughput for many machine vision applications.

As PCI became more widespread, extensions were built on top of the original specification to allow PCI to address the needs of specific markets. Two of these extensions, CompactPCI and PCI eXtensions for Instrumentation

(PXI), leveraged the existing PCI standard to address the requirements of test, measurement, and automation applications. Timing and triggering capabilities were added to the standard, and the mechanical design of the bus was changed to create a more rugged enclosure. The electrical interface and protocol from PCI were reused to provide consistency and reduce both development and implementation time and cost for markets not traditionally served by commodity computer technologies.

With the introduction of PCI Express, computer manufacturers have an incentive to reduce or eliminate traditional PCI device slots in new computers because PCI is no longer natively supported by some of the new chipsets required by the latest processors. Motherboard vendors must add additional circuitry to support PCI with these new chipsets, making the motherboard more costly. However, since PCI has a very large installed customer base, the need for a legacy PCI solution will continue for some time.

8.4.3 PCI-X

PCI-X was developed to provide additional data throughput, and address some design challenges associated with the 66-MHz version of the PCI bus. The initial PCI-X specification, released in 1999, allowed bus speeds of up to 133 MHz with a 64-bit data width to achieve up to 1 GB s^{-1} of peak throughput. Like the frequency and width extensions for PCI, PCI-X is primarily found only in server and workstation computers due to the higher implementation cost. Subsequent versions of PCI-X have continued to increase throughput, but they are not widely implemented. Many motherboard manufacturers that offer PCI-X operate the bus at a rate lower than 133 MHz, such as 100 or 66 MHz, because running the bus at 133 MHz limits the motherboard to a single slot per PCI-X bus. Some computer vendors have designed multiple PCI-X buses into the same machine to address this limitation, but doing so further increases the cost of the computer. Running the bus at 100 or 66 MHz reduces the peak throughput to either 800 or 533 MB s^{-1} and allows for two or four device slots per computer.

Like PCI, PCI-X is a multi-drop bus. Offering more than one device slot on the same PCI-X bus does not increase total throughput because the bus resources must be shared between the multiple devices. In order to gain more throughput, an entire second PCI-X bus would have to be connected to the computer chipset. Usually, only the server chipsets support this level of functionality. With multiple devices installed in the same PCI-X bus, the peak throughput that can be maintained by a device using PCI-X is about 75% of the peak bandwidth.

PCI-X does offer backward compatibility with PCI, which allows the use of devices using PCI bus frequencies and protocols in a PCI-X bus. Taking advantage of this functionality by using a PCI device in a PCI-X slot causes all the devices to operate at the lower PCI rate. In this case, there is no value in selecting PCI-X over PCI.

Like PCI, the introduction of PCI Express has given computer manufacturers the incentive to reduce or eliminate PCI-X slots on new motherboards. PCI-X is no longer natively supported by most new processor chipsets that support PCI Express.

8.4.4 PCI Express/CompactPCI Express/PXI Express

PCI Express, sometimes referred to as PCIe, was designed to be scalable from desktop computers to servers. While the underlying hardware implementation of the bus was entirely redesigned, the software interface to PCI Express was kept backward-compatible with that of PCI. This was done to speed up the adoption of PCI Express and allow device manufacturers to leverage their existing software investment.

The most basic implementation of PCI Express uses one set of wires to receive data and a second set to transmit data. This is referred to as an ×1 interface because one set of wires is used in each direction. Unlike PCI, where the 132 MB s^{-1} peak throughput is shared by traffic going both to and from the device, a PCI Express device offers a peak bandwidth of 250 MB s^{-1} per direction for the ×1 interface. This results in a total throughput of 500 MB s^{-1} if the device accesses are evenly divided between sending and receiving data. For most devices, however, this is not the case. For example, the data of a video card is almost entirely sent from the processor to the device and then out the video port. For a frame grabber, the data is almost entirely in the opposite direction – being sent to the processor as it is acquired from a camera. For this reason, throughput numbers for PCI Express are usually quoted as the throughput per direction, and for machine vision applications this will be the most relevant figure.

Like the other buses, PCI Express can deliver its peak throughput only in short bursts. For the ×1 link, the portion of this throughput that can be averaged by the input device can be above 200 MB s^{-1}. The amount of overheads on PCI Express, as a percentage of the peak throughput, is generally larger than that of PCI. This can be particularly true under certain system configurations. One situation that can reduce the average throughput well below 200 MB s^{-1} is when only a few bytes of data are sent at a time. On PCI Express, data is transferred in packets. For each packet, additional information is sent along with the data such as the amount of data in the packet and a checksum. This information is used to ensure reliable transfer to the receiving device, but it uses some of the transfer time. Because the amount of overheads information that must be sent along with each packet is the same regardless of the amount of data in the packet, packets with small amounts of data dramatically reduce the achieved throughput. For most machine vision applications, however, the packet size does not dramatically impact performance.

Unlike the multi-drop buses of PCI and PCI-X, where the bus is shared by all devices, PCI Express is a point-to-point bus designed in a tree topology. Refer to Figure 8.26 for the diagram of a PCI Express point-to-point configuration.

In a PCI Express bus, each device has its own interface to a chip on the motherboard. This interface combines the data from its downstream devices and sends it up the tree until it reaches the access point to the processor and main memory. As long as the available throughput of the connections going toward the processor are well matched to the combined throughput of the branches, individual PCI Express devices can operate simultaneously without significantly impacting the performance of the other devices.

As was the case for increased throughput on the PCI bus, PCI Express also offers increased throughput by increasing the operating frequency and number

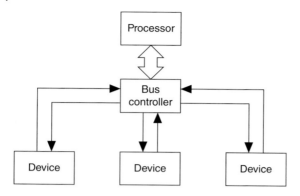

Figure 8.26 Point-to-point bus configuration.

of data bits transferred at a time. Unlike PCI, where the earliest computers only implemented the basic configuration, the initial PCI Express computers included slots that supported different levels of throughput. This was achieved through what PCI Express refers to as scalable widths, allowing the computer vendor to offer slots with different levels of performance. The most common widths in initial PCI Express computers were ×1, ×4, ×8, and ×16. Interfaces of different widths provide additional throughput in multiples of the 250 MB s^{-1} peak and 200 MB s^{-1} average offered by the ×1 configuration. For example, ×16 provides up to 16 times the peak throughput, or about 4 GB s^{-1}. PCI Express technology is constantly evolving. As of this writing, we are on version 4.0 of the PCI Express standard, which uses 128b/130b line coding with a transfer rate of 16 GT s^{-1} and a per-lane bandwidth of 15.75 Gbps as opposed to version 1.0 which provided a transfer rate of 2.5 GT s^{-1} and 2 Gbps.

Because of the variety of PCI Express offerings, some care must be taken to avoid potential pitfalls when combining PCI Express devices and slots. When using a device of a particular width in a slot of a matched width, the situation is straightforward and performance will match the throughput of the common width. If, however, the device and slot are not of the same width, some investigation might be necessary to avoid performance surprises. Refer to Figure 8.27 for a diagram of allowable combinations.

In PCI Express, a device may never be used in a slot of smaller width. For example, a ×4 device will not fit in a ×1 slot. It requires a ×4 slot or larger. The

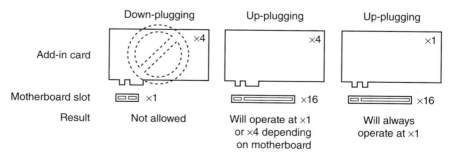

Figure 8.27 PCI Express width interoperability.

opposite configuration, using a device in a larger slot, is called *up-plugging* and is permitted. In this case, however, the motherboard vendor has the freedom to choose whether it will support the device at its full data rate or only at the lowest ×1 rate. This is done to allow motherboard vendors flexibility in controlling costs. Most commonly, it will be desktop computers that limit the device to ×1, whereas workstations and servers support the device at its full rate. Even some desktop machines support the full data rate when a card is used in an up-plugging configuration. If you require the full performance of the device at greater than the ×1 rate, verify with the computer manufacturer that the motherboard will support the device at its full rate in the intended slot.

In addition to the basic data transfer functionality that has been offered by previous buses, PCI Express also promises future capability to add support for a variety of advanced features such as regularly timed transfers. While many of these features were not implemented in the first computers to support PCI Express, they are likely to be added as the bus matures.

As with PCI, variations of PCI Express also serve markets with additional needs such as CompactPCI Express and PXI Express for the test, measurement, and automation markets.

8.4.5 Throughput

When selecting a machine vision system, one of the foremost considerations is how many parts can be inspected per minute. If the application only requires inspections for a limited period and does not require immediate output from the system during the acquisition, the system designer has more flexibility in system selection. In this scenario, the system can lag somewhat behind on transfer and processing during the acquisition as long as it has enough memory to queue up the incoming images until the acquisition is over.

In the case where a certain rate is required indefinitely, all components of the system must, on average, operate at that rate. If any part of the system – the camera, camera bus, input device, computer bus, main memory, or processor – fails to keep pace with the incoming objects, objects will be missed.

Even when components, on average, operate at the required rate, there will often be periods of interruption when operation falls below average. When systems are designed, each component should be so chosen that its performance at least matches the required rate most of the time. In addition, the system should have some excess capacity to allow the system to catch up from periods of interruption. Refer to Figure 8.28 for a depiction of such a system.

The *Ideal* frame of Figure 8.28 shows an example of a system where the computer bus is operating without interruption. As each image arrives, it is immediately transferred to the processor. The *Delay Tolerant* frame shows a more realistic view of a computer bus. Occasionally, another device on the computer bus, perhaps an ethernet interface, interrupts image transfer, causing a delay in the data arriving at the processor's memory. Because this system was designed for headroom in addition to the transfer time required in an ideal situation, it is able to catch up and average the desired inspection rate. If, however, the interruption is for a period that is longer than the processor has

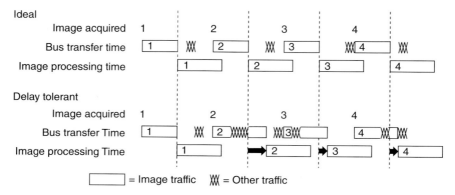

Figure 8.28 Computer buses that tolerate deviation from ideal.

memory for, an inspection can be lost. When only one buffer is available to store images in the processor memory, a loss of inspection happens as soon as a new image starts transferring while the processing on the previous image is not finished. In Figure 8.28, a new image could not be sent to the image location in memory because the processor was still working on the last image.

For the input device and its connection to the computer bus, there are two ways to address this issue. The first solution is to select a bus that either interrupts devices less often or a bus that is fast enough, relative to the required transfer rate, to allow the device to quickly catch up once interruptions are over. The second solution is to choose an input device with large banks of memory to store up images while waiting for access to the bus so that it can withstand the long interruptions of the bus.

When transferring data among devices on the same computer bus, each bus interrupts devices at different times. For example, all PCI and PCI-X devices must share the bus. If more than one device has data to provide at a time, the device must await its turn, causing delays in starting the transfer of data. In PCI Express, each device has its own interface, and it is delayed only when the interface chips between the device and the computer exceed their larger interfaces to the processor. The primary method for ensuring that the inspections are not missed, however, is to select a computer bus that provides ample throughput to allow the bus to catch up once the device is interrupted. In this regard, the examples to follow will help you make this choice for your system.

The option of using large banks of memory is often exercised for acquisitions that only need to run for a predetermined time limit. Using memory to store multiple images before using them is referred to as *image buffering*. Image buffering can be done on the camera, in the input device, or in the main memory. Image buffering in the camera is relatively uncommon because camera manufacturers usually select the camera bus to match the output requirements of the camera. Image buffering in host memory is done because the computer bus is providing image data faster than the processor can process it. Buffering images in the main memory allows images to be queued up for the processor as they become available. This type of buffering will be discussed in section 8.7.3. When buffering at the input device, additional memory in the input device itself is used to withstand delays in the availability of the computer bus.

When using image buffering, it is important to remember that for continuous application, buffering delays the inevitable only if the bus is not fast enough to catch up after interruptions. The system must stay close enough to the average transfer rate so that it never lags behind by more inspections than the number of buffers available. Otherwise, inspections will be missed.

8.4.6 Prevalence and Lifetime

A second important area of consideration during initial system specification is the prevalence and long-term availability of the selected computer bus. Selecting a dying bus limits supplier selection, resulting in difficulties if a decision is made later to deploy additional vision systems on the factory floor, and in the availability of replacement parts. As technologies age, the older technologies tend to become more expensive as they begin their phase-out. Once the technology is no longer available at a reasonable price, the task of adding to an existing line can require an entirely new respecification process.

With the introduction of PCI Express, ISA/EISA, PCI, and PCI-X are no longer commonly available in the latest computers and should not be selected for new systems.

8.4.6.1 Cost

Like the range in cost of the camera bus and its associated input device, the selected computer bus also has a cost impact as part of the overall cost of the computer. The first area of cost impact is the computer that offers the desired bus. Some buses are available in all classes of computers, but if more than one input device is required in the system, a low-end computer might not provide enough slots for the devices, or it might not offer enough throughput for the combined requirements of the two devices. Again, this can force the purchase of a more expensive computer.

The second area of cost impact is in the cost of the input device. The input device will cost more if it offers a large amount of on-board memory for image buffering, due to the selected bus being unable to maintain the required throughput. While all input devices include a small amount of unadvertized memory to deal with limited bus overheads, the amount of memory required to withstand the long periods of interruption typical when operating at a high inspection rate on a multi-drop bus can go into the megabytes or gigabytes, adding significantly to the cost of the device.

8.5 Choosing a Computer Bus

8.5.1 Determine Throughput Requirements

Determining whether or not a particular computer bus will meet an application's needs begins with gathering information about the system requirements. This section will discuss how to quantify requirements and evaluate the computer bus of the selected input device for appropriate throughput.

- *How many inspections per minute does the application require?* This will often be limited by the mechanics of the equipment on the factory floor.
- *Must inspections continue at this rate indefinitely or only for a limited period?* Is it acceptable to miss parts occasionally or must every part be inspected?
- *For the camera that will meet the imaging needs, what will be the width and height of the returned image?* If the application does not require the full width and height offered by the camera, can the image returned by the input device or camera be limited only to what is needed? This can reduce the transfer and processing burden.
- *How many pixels does the camera output simultaneously?* Sometimes this will be called a tap or the number of channels.
- *How many digitized bits are used to represent each pixel?* For digital cameras, this will be included in the camera's specification. Most commonly, a monochrome digital camera will be either 8- or 10-bit. For an RGB camera, this is commonly 8 bits each for RGB. For analog cameras, the digitization of an analog video signal happens at the frame grabber. Some analog frame grabbers might support only 8-bit digitization while others support a selectable number of bits. For IEEE 1394 cameras, this value is often selectable when configuring the camera.
- *How many digitized bits will be transferred across the computer bus by the input device for each pixel?* For applications that involve immediate processing of the acquired image, the data will usually be transferred in a byte- or word-aligned format to allow more efficient access to the data by the processor. If using a 10-bit monochrome camera, it is likely that 16 bits (2 bytes) will be transferred, so that the processor will not have to use processing time to separate out the bits that belong to another pixel from the data that it gets from its memory. Likewise, for immediate processing of data from an RGB camera, transferring the three 8-bit color values is often done as 32 bits (4 bytes) so that the processor does not have to read memory twice if the data for a single pixel straddles multiple memory locations.
- *What bus does the proposed input device use?* For frame grabbers, this will be described as part of the product specifications. For USB or ethernet ports, refer to the documentation for the computer to determine whether the port is integrated into the motherboard. Refer to the device documentation if the device is a plug-in device. Also be careful of interface ports that are internally multiplexed. For instance, an industrial PC vendor could provide four USB 3.0 ports on the machine, but they are internally routed to only two USB controllers, meaning that you must share full USB 3.0 bandwidth between ports. If you require full bandwidth per port, look for a machine that routes each port to it is own controller.
- *Are there any other devices sharing the computer bus?* On some computers, the integrated ethernet port will often share the same PCI bus as the device slots. If the network is connected during your acquisitions, the bus throughput available for imaging can be dramatically reduced.

8.5.2 Applying the Throughput Requirements

With the above information, it is possible to determine the rate at which data must be transferred across the computer bus. While the examples in this section are intended to help you select a computer bus for a system that must run continuously, a similar process is applied to determine throughput needs of a system that will only acquire in bursts.

Consider the following example: A particular application requires 480 inspections per minute that will be continuously acquired and processed. The user's camera evaluation determined that a monochrome camera is needed to produce images that are 1280 pixels × 1024 pixels with 10 bits used to represent each pixel. Two pixels are output by the camera at a time. Because the incoming data is 10 bits, the input device will transfer 2 bytes of data per pixel. Because of the continuous acquisition requirement, the selected computer bus must transfer an average of at least 480 images per minute. Each image will be made up of 1280 × 1024 = 1 310 720 pixels per image and the bus will transfer two bytes for each pixel, 1 310 720 pixels per image × 2 bytes per pixel = 2 621 440 bytes per image. So, with this information, we know how many bytes the bus will have to transfer in each acquisition interval. Combining this information with the number of images the system must transfer per second gives the data rate that the bus must average. Because bus throughput is specified in the amount of data per second, convert the inspections per minute to inspections per second by dividing the 480 images per minute by 60 s min^{-1}. This results in eight images per second. By multiplying the amount of data per image by the number of images per second, you get a data throughput of 2 621 440 bytes per image × 8 images per second = 20 971 520 bytes per second. Bus throughput is usually given in megabits or megabytes per second, so we will need to convert to this format. One thing to remember is that, although kilobytes are usually multiples of 1024 bytes and megabytes are multiples of 1024 kB, when bus speeds are specified in megabytes per second, it is usually in multiples of 1000 kB s^{-1}, which are in turn multiples of 1000 bytes per second. So, to evaluate our calculated value in terms of the megabytes per second used when talking about computer buses, we will use 1000 multiples, which yield 20.97 MB s^{-1}.

Assuming that there are no other devices in the system, the throughput needs of this application can be solved by PCI, PCI-X, or PCI Express. Lifetime and cost will be the factors that drive the decision.

8.6 Driver Software

The most commonly overlooked component of most machine vision systems is the software used to acquire images from your camera. The software that handles this responsibility is typically referred to as *driver software*. To get a clear understanding of driver software and how it pertains to your machine vision

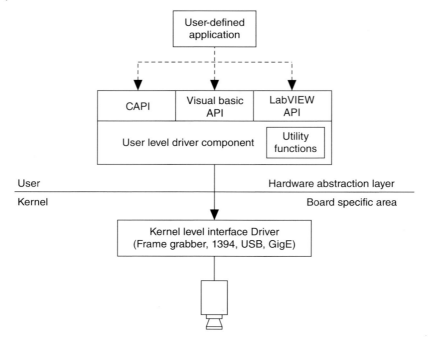

Figure 8.29 Layers of typical driver software architecture.

application, you should have a good understanding of the features of driver software, the acquisition modes possible with driver software, and how images are represented in memory and on disk.

To evaluate any driver software, you should consider the following dimensions: the API, supported platforms, performance, and utility functions.

A typical driver software package has different layers to it, each with a specific responsibility. Figure 8.29 shows each of these layers. For the purposes of this discussion, assume that the OS you are using is a *dual-mode* OS. Windows, Linux, and MacOS are examples of dual-mode OSs. A dual-mode OS means that the time-critical low-level hardware interaction takes place in one partition, known as the *kernel mode*, while the less critical high-level user interaction takes place in another partition, called the *user mode*.

In this type of architecture, the lowest level component is the kernel-level driver. The kernel-level driver is in direct control of the hardware interface regardless of whether the hardware is a frame grabber, IEEE 1394 interface card, USB interface card, or gigabit ethernet card. The kernel level driver manages detection of the hardware on system startup, directly reads and writes registers in the hardware during configuration and operation, and handles the low-level hardware interactions such as servicing interrupts and initiating direct memory access (DMA). The kernel-level driver typically encapsulates the hardware interface device.

The next component is referred to as the *user-level driver*. The user-level driver interacts with the interface hardware through the kernel-level driver and interacts with the user-defined application through the API. Typically, the user-level driver still has fairly intimate knowledge of the interface hardware, but it also has knowledge of the interface hardware being used to connect to a camera. It also understands the concept of an image. The user-level driver manages all the functions of the acquisition that are not time-critical, and offloads the high-priority tasks to the kernel-level driver.

The user-level driver will also expose a set of APIs to the user. The API is the set of functions that programmers have at their disposal for developing an application. An API is specific to a programming language such as C, Visual Basic, or LabVIEW, and an application will use one of the exposed APIs to interface with the user-level driver.

8.6.1 Application Programming Interface

The API is the highest layer of the driver software. The API is the set of functions that programmers have for controlling the interface hardware and the corresponding camera. The API is extremely important because, while the driver can be very powerful and efficient, it is useless unless it exposes those features easily to the programmer through the API.

Most driver software packages will expose more than one API. This is because of the variety of programming languages that programmers use throughout the industry. One of the first things you should look for in a driver software package is whether it has support for the programming environment that you want to use. If there are going to be multiple programmers on the project, it is a good idea to make sure that all the necessary APIs are exposed.

Almost all driver software packages should expose a C API since it is one of the most powerful and well-adopted programming languages in the industry. If you are programming in Visual Basic, you should look for a driver software package that exposes an ActiveX interface. ActiveX is a software model that provides a simple-to-program interface to Visual Basic programmers. This software model (and API) is typically less powerful and less efficient than C. However, in many cases it is sufficient for machine vision applications and provides incredible advantages to developers because of the rapid development of user interfaces and applications.

While C and Visual Basic are well-established programming languages in machine vision, there are a couple of languages that are just starting to emerge. The first is VB.NET from Microsoft. This programming environment is intended to replace Visual Basic, although adoption has been slow. While many machine vision vendors are currently providing VB.NET compatibility through *wrappers*, none is providing native VB.NET controls. In the coming years, some software packages may emerge, but for now Visual Basic is still more widely accepted.

Another exciting programming language for machine vision is LabVIEW. It is only since the late 1990s that LabVIEW has been used in machine vision applications, but the language has been used extensively since the mid-1980s in industries such as test, data acquisition, and instrument control. LabVIEW is becoming popular because of the productivity and power it brings to machine vision. Designing a user interface in LabVIEW is very similar to the Visual Basic experience. However, writing the code is a very intuitive experience. LabVIEW uses visual blocks to represent functions and wires to control program flow. The end result is a code that looks very much like a flowchart, which mirrors the way many engineers think. Since LabVIEW has an optimized compiler, which generates raw machine code, it runs almost as efficiently as C-compiled software.

Regardless of which programming language you use, the two most important features of a good API are intuitive and identifiable function names and multidimensional scalability. Good function names are necessary for rapid code development and easy readability of the code. If the function name maps well to the concept, the programmer can charge ahead without constantly referencing the documentation. The following code snippet provides an example of a good API.

```
/* Initialize variables */
int startNow = TRUE;
int continue = TRUE;
int waitForNext = TRUE;
int resize = TRUE;

/* Open the interface to the camera */
imgInterfaceOpen("img0",\&InterfaceID);

/* Start the image acquisition immediately */
imgGrabSetup(InterfaceID, startNow);

/* Continuously grab the next image and draw it to the
   screen */
while (continue == TRUE)    \{
    imgGrab (InterfaceID, myImage,waitForNext);
    imgDraw (myImage, windowNumber, resize);
\}

/* Close the interface when done */
imgClose (InterfaceID);
```

The first thing you will notice about this API is that it is very intuitive. The actual function names are very descriptive, and someone reading the code can immediately understand what this section of code does even without extensive comments. In this case, we are setting up and initiating a continuous image acquisition with display. First, you initialize resources, next start the acquisition, then copy and display each image, and finally close the resources. Another defining aspect of the API is that each function is easily recognizable as part of this API since all functions have the same prefix. This may seem like an unimportant aspect, but since most applications require linking into multiple APIs, it can be very useful for debugging if you can quickly identify which library a particular function belongs to.

Another important feature of the API is scalability. It is very common for the needs of your application to change between the start of development and the final product. There are multiple dimensions in which you may want to scale your application. For example, you may start out with a low-cost analog-camera-based solution to your problem. However, as you start working on your processing, you may find that you need a higher resolution camera to resolve the features you need to inspect. With a good API, you should be able to change over to a high-resolution Camera Link camera and Camera Link frame grabber without changing your code. You may have a multi-camera application with two frame grabbers and, for cost reasons, want to port it to a single multichannel board. A major hurdle to porting to this new hardware is the need to rewrite the acquisition portion of your application. With a good API, this migration should not require much in the way of code changes.

Lastly, any good scalable API will offer both high-level and low-level options. For example, the above code sample was written with a high-level API. It is very simple for doing common tasks, but does not provide the flexibility that may be needed for accomplishing advanced tasks.

8.6.2 Supported Platforms

Most machine vision applications today run on a PC. There are a number of OSs in use today, and most of them are appropriate for machine vision. Be sure that the hardware you buy has support for the platform that you intend to use for your application. The most prevalent platform is Windows.

A more recent OS to emerge in machine vision is Linux. Linux has proven to be a very popular platform for vision in Europe and is catching on in the United States. Programmers like the open source nature of the OS because it provides transparency to the inner workings of the OS, which can allow developers to work around nuances or bugs that may exist at the lowest levels of the OS. Additionally, Linux is better suited for creating a streamlined environment for machine vision since it is fairly easy to include only the components you need for your solution and none of the additional drivers and utilities that you do not need.

There are also a number of real-time OSs in the market. Real-time OSs such as VxWorks provide a light-weight OS that is extremely reliable and can run on embedded machines consuming very little resources. There are also real-time versions of Linux that are gaining popularity. Many embedded vision systems and smart cameras are now taking advantage of low-power processors and real-time OSs to provide machine vision in a highly reliable, small form factor machine vision solution.

8.6.3 Performance

Machine vision applications are typically some of the most demanding applications for a computer. The reason for this is the large size of the dataset. A typical machine vision image has a resolution of 1024 pixels × 1024 lines, or a total of 1 million pixels. If each of these pixels is represented by 1 byte (8 bits), the total size of the image is 1 MB. You can imagine that an algorithm running on this image to find edges or patterns to execute arithmetic operations on each of these 1 million pixels. Many algorithms even require multiple passes over an image.

If your application intends to run at 30 fps, it is not uncommon for your computer to perform tens of millions of instructions per second just to find your pattern.

Given the intense nature of image processing, it is important to minimize the overheads required in getting the image into the PC. This is the role of an efficient driver and hardware. PC architectures provide a mechanism for interface cards to move data into PC memory without using the processor. This mechanism is called direct memory access or DMA. If your interface and driver support DMA, almost all of the overheads associated with copying data to the PC are handled by the hardware and driver and the CPU is free to process the resulting images.

Since copying the image data into the buffer is now handled without processor involvement, there needs to be some sort of notification to the processor that the image transfer is complete. Without this notification, the application running on the CPU would not know when it is safe to start processing the image. One way to implement this notification is with a polling mechanism. This mechanism consists of a loop that regularly checks a status bit of the hardware to see whether the operation is complete. Polling is not ideal because it requires too much CPU usage to run the loop that reads the status bit. The CPU is too valuable a resource in most machine vision applications to be used in this manner. For this reason, most interfaces use a mechanism called an *interrupt* to let the processor know that an image is complete. When an interrupt asserts, the driver calls an interrupt service routine (ISR) to handle that interrupt. A well-written driver will minimize the amount of work that is done in an ISR so that it does not take valuable cycles away from the CPU until necessary. For example, if a frame grabber asserts an interrupt to signal that a frame has just been captured, an efficient ISR would simply increase a counter marking the count of frame that has arrived and perhaps store off the memory address into which that frame is stored. At a later time, the application can retrieve that image and perform a copy or other operations required to prepare the image for processing. In general, the ISR should defer as much as possible until the application requests that it be done.

Ideally, the basic acquisition of images from an interface should use less than 5% of the CPU. You will sometimes see more CPU usage if the camera outputs compressed data that the computer needs to convert. This is very common with color cameras, which output images in a Bayer or YUV format that need to be uncompressed for processing. If this is a concern, you may need to pay a little more for a camera that does not output compressed image data.

8.6.4 Utility Functions

Along with the basic components required for image acquisition, most drivers include utility functions for displaying and saving images. These features, while not a core part of the driver, are necessary components of a vision application. Display provides feedback that the images have been acquired properly and that the field of view and focus are properly set for your scene. The ability to save images allows you to share images with colleagues as well as record images that can be used to test processing algorithms. Later on in this chapter, we will discuss image display and image files in more depth.

8.6.5 Acquisition Mode

One of the first things a programmer needs to determine is the correct acquisition mode for his or her application. There are two primary dimensions you will need to define in order to ensure that they pick the proper acquisition mode. The first question is whether your application will require a single shot or a continuous acquisition. A single-shot acquisition runs once and then stops. A continuous acquisition will run indefinitely until you stop the acquisition. The second question is whether the application will require a single buffer or multiple buffers. Buffer refers to the memory space used to hold images, and image corresponds to a single frame of data given by the camera. Figure 8.30 shows common names for each acquisition mode and a summary of when to use each one.

8.6.5.1 Snap

The most simple acquisition mode is the snap, which merely acquires a single image into a memory buffer, as shown in Figure 8.31.

The image can be processed further after the acquisition is complete. The snap is useful when you only need to work with a single image: for example, if you want to take a test image of a part to save to disk and use it as a sample image for developing your image processing operation.

Another common use of the snap is to call the acquisition repeatedly in a software-timed loop. This method is inefficient and will not provide accurate timing, but can be useful when you only need to monitor a scene periodically. It is commonly used in monitoring applications, such as in observing a slowly varying temperature on an analog meter.

8.6.5.2 Grab

In the grab acquisition mode, the frame grabber transfers each image into an acquisition buffer in the system memory. It continually overwrites the same buffer

	One shot	Continuous
Single buffer	Snap • Simple programming • One time image capture	Grab • Simple programming • Minimal processing time required • Suitable for display applications
Multi-buffer	Sequence • High speed capture • Any processing done offline • Typically used for capturing an event	Ring • High speed capture • Processing done inline • Provides buffer protection during processing

Figure 8.30 Selecting the right acquisition mode.

Figure 8.31 Snap acquisition.

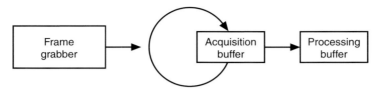

Figure 8.32 Grab acquisition.

with new frames as long as the acquisition is in progress. The buffers are copied as necessary to a separate processing buffer where analysis or display may take place as shown in Figure 8.32.

The grab acquisition is the simplest method of displaying a live image in real time. It is most useful in applications where a visual display is all you need. A typical application might involve monitoring a security gate to allow a guard to recognize and grant access to visitors from a remote location.

In some cases, the single acquisition buffer used in a grab is insufficient. If you are trying to acquire and process every single image, any OS delays can cause frames to be missed. There is also a very short time available for the image to be copied into the processing buffer before the acquisition buffer is overwritten with the next frame. With dynamic scenes, you can clearly see this effect appear as a horizontal discontinuity in the image; one portion of the image comes from the latest frame, while the rest is from the previous frame. In these cases, a ring acquisition is recommended instead.

8.6.5.3 Sequence

A sequence acquisition uses multiple buffers, shown in Figure 8.33, but writes to them only once. The image acquisition stops as soon as each buffer has been filled once.

Sequence acquisition is useful in cases where you need to capture a one-time event that will span over multiple frames. Any processing or display that needs to be done will typically be done after the acquisition is complete. Most applications that use this type of acquisition start the image acquisition on a trigger and then acquire at the maximum camera rate until all buffers are full. An example application would be monitoring a crash test.

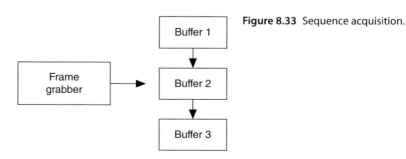

Figure 8.33 Sequence acquisition.

8.6.5.4 Ring

A ring acquisition is the most complex but also the most powerful acquisition mode. A ring uses and recycles multiple buffers in a continuous acquisition. Figure 8.34 shows a ring acquisition.

The interface copies images as they come from the camera into Buffer 1, then Buffer 2, then Buffer 3, and then back to Buffer 1, and so on. Ring acquisition is the safest for robust machine vision applications.

This becomes apparent when we start thinking about adding processing into the equation. Inserting processing could cause problems if the algorithm takes more than one frame period to complete. Figure 8.35 illustrates a ring acquisition with processing.

The image processing for any image can begin as soon as a given image has been completely copied into a buffer. With a multi-buffered approach, processing can safely happen at the same time when the next image is being acquired. This would never be safe with a single-buffered approach.

In a single-buffer approach, if the processing algorithm *blocks* and does not return until complete, the application may miss a frame. If the algorithm returns

Figure 8.34 Ring acquisition.

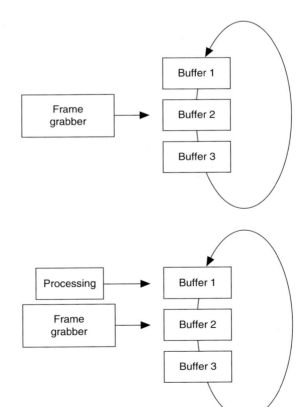

Figure 8.35 Ring acquisition with processing.

immediately but runs in a separate thread, the next iteration of the acquisition loop may overwrite the image that is being processed. The multi-buffered approach ensures that your application can process one image while acquiring another.

The other benefit of ring acquisition is that, if the processing for a particular image takes longer than average to complete, the acquisition can safely jump ahead to the next buffer. On average, however, the processing still does need to keep up with the acquisition. If not, the application will run out of buffers as the acquisition keeps pulling further and further ahead of the processing. However, multiple buffered acquisitions do allow robustness when there is variability in processing time from image to image. This variability typically exists when the time that the algorithm takes to run is data-driven. For example, if the algorithm counts objects and calculates statistics on each object, an image with 1 object will process much faster than an image with 20 objects. Sometimes, the variability has nothing at all to do with the application itself, but with other tasks that the computer must attend to such as running an auto-save or IT-mandated virus scan. A well-written application will have enough buffers in the acquisition list to accommodate the worst case scenarios.

8.6.6 Image Representation

Like everything else in a computer, images are stored as a series of bits. By understanding the bit structure, developers can better optimize their code for space and performance. The following sections discuss how images are stored both in memory and on disk.

8.6.6.1 Image Representation in Memory

An image is a 2D array of values representing light intensity. For the purposes of image processing, the term *image* refers to a digital image. An image is a function of the light intensity $f(x, y)$, where f is the brightness of the point (x, y) and x and y represent the spatial coordinates of a picture element, or pixel. By convention, the spatial reference of the pixel with the coordinates $(0, 0)$ is located at the top-left corner of the image. Notice in Figure 8.36 that the value of x increases on moving from left to right, and the value of y increases from top to bottom.

In digital image processing, an imaging sensor converts an image into a discrete number of pixels. The imaging sensor assigns to each pixel a numeric location and a gray level or color value that specifies the brightness or color of the pixel.

A digitized image has three basic properties: resolution, definition, and number of planes. The spatial resolution of an image is determined by the number of rows and columns of pixels. An image composed of m columns and n rows has a

Figure 8.36 Spatial reference of the (0, 0) pixel.

resolution of $m \times n$. This image has m pixels along its horizontal axis and n pixels along its vertical axis.

The definition of an image indicates the number of shades that you can see in the image. The bit depth of an image is the number of bits used to encode the value of a pixel. For a given bit depth of n, the image has an image definition of 2^n, meaning a pixel can have 2^n different values. For example, if n equals 8 bits, a pixel can have 256 different values ranging from 0 to 255. If n equals 16 bits, a pixel can have 65 536 different values ranging from 0 to 65 535 or from negative 32 768 to 32 767. The manner in which you encode your image depends on the nature of the image acquisition device, the type of image processing you need to use, and the type of analysis you need to perform. For example, 8-bit encoding is sufficient if you need to obtain the shape information of objects in an image. However, if you need to precisely measure the light intensity of an image or a region in an image, you must use 16-bit or floating-point encoding. Use color-encoded images when your machine vision or image processing application depends on the color content of the objects you are inspecting or analyzing.

The number of planes in an image corresponds to the number of arrays of pixels that compose the image. A grayscale or pseudo-color image is composed of one plane, while a true-color image is composed of three planes – one each for the red, blue, and green components. In true-color images, the color component intensities of a pixel are coded into three different values. A color image is the combination of three arrays of pixels corresponding to the RGB components in an RGB image. HSL images are defined by their HSL values.

Most image processing libraries can manipulate both grayscale and color images. Grayscale images can be represented with either 1 or 2 bytes per pixel, and color images can be represented as either RGB or as HSL values. Figure 8.37 shows how many bytes per pixel grayscale and color images use. For an identical spatial resolution, a color image occupies 4 times the memory space of an 8-bit grayscale image.

A grayscale image is composed of a single plane of pixels. Each pixel is encoded using either an 8-bit unsigned integer representing grayscale values between 0 and 255 or a 16-bit signed integer representing grayscale values between 0 and 65 535. Color image pixels are a composite of four values. RGB images store color information using 8 bits each for the RGB planes. HSL images store color information using 8 bits each for HSL. RGB U64 images store color information using 16 bits each for the RGB planes. In the RGB and HSL color models, an additional 8-bit value goes unused. This representation is known as 4×8-bit or 32-bit encoding. In the RGB U64 color model, an additional 16-bit value goes unused. This representation is known as 4×16-bit or 64-bit encoding. Figure 8.38 shows how RGB and HSL store color information.

Figure 8.39 depicts an example of how an image is represented in the system memory. Note that this is only one type of representation, and the actual representation may vary slightly depending on your software package. In addition to the image pixels, the stored image includes additional rows and columns of pixels called the *image border* and the left and right alignments. Specific processing functions involving pixel neighborhood operations use image borders. The alignment regions ensure that the first pixel of the image is 8-byte aligned in memory.

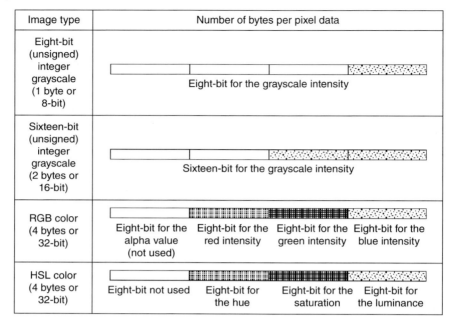

Figure 8.37 Bytes per pixel.

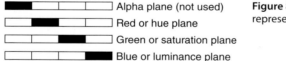

Figure 8.38 RGB and HSL pixel representation.

The size of the alignment blocks depend on the image width and border size. Aligning the image increases processing speed by as much as 30%. The line width is the total number of pixels in a horizontal line of an image, which includes the sum of the horizontal resolution, the image borders, and the left and right alignments. The horizontal resolution and line width may be the same if the horizontal resolution is a multiple of 8 bytes and the border size is 0.

Many image processing functions process a pixel by using the values of its neighbors. A neighbor is a pixel whose value affects the value of a nearby pixel when an image is processed. Pixels along the edge of an image do not have neighbors on all four sides. If you need to use a function that processes pixels based on the value of their neighboring pixels, specify an image border that surrounds the image to account for these outlying pixels. You define the image border by specifying a border size and the values of the border pixels.

The size of the border should accommodate the largest pixel neighborhood required by the function you are using. The size of the neighborhood is specified by the size of a 2D array. For example, if a function uses the eight adjoining neighbors of a pixel for processing, the size of the neighborhood is 3×3, indicating an array with three columns and three rows. Set the border size to be greater than or equal to half the number of rows or columns of the 2D array rounded down to

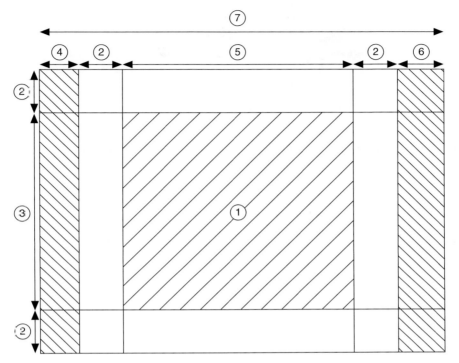

Figure 8.39 Internal image representation: (1) image, (2) image border, (3) vertical resolution, (4) left alignment, (5) should be Horizontal Resolution, (6) right alignment, and (7) line width.

the nearest integer value. For example, if a function uses a 3 × 3 neighborhood, the image should have a border size of at least 1. If a function uses a 5 × 5 neighborhood, the image should have a border size of at least 2.

8.6.7 Bayer Color Encoding

Bayer encoding is a method you can use to produce color images using a single imaging sensor, instead of three individual sensors for the RGB components of light. This technology greatly reduces the cost of cameras. In some higher end cameras, the decoding algorithm is implemented in the camera firmware. This type of implementation guarantees that the decoding works in real time. Other cameras simply output the raw Bayer pattern so that the image you get in memory needs to be decoded by the software to get the expected RGB format.

The Bayer color filter array (CFA) is a primary color mosaic pattern of 50% green, 25% red, and 25% blue pixels. Green pixels comprise half of the total pixels because the human eye gets most of its sharpness information from green light.

Figure 8.40 describes how the Bayer CFA is used in the image acquisition process.

Light travels through the camera lens onto an image sensor that provides one value for each sensor cell. The sensor is an array of tiny light-sensitive diodes called *photosites*. The sensor converts light into electrical charges. The sensor is

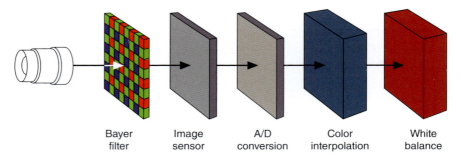

Figure 8.40 Bayer encoding.

covered by the Bayer CFA so that only one color value reaches any given pixel. The raw output is a mosaic of RGB pixels of differing intensities. When the image is captured, the accumulated charge for each cell is read, and analog values are converted to digital pixel values using an ADC.

Color interpolation, sometimes referred to as *demosaicing*, fills in the missing colors. A decoding algorithm determines a value for the RGB components of each pixel in the array by averaging the color values of selected neighboring pixels and producing an estimate of color and intensity. After the interpolation process is complete, the white balancing process further enhances the image by adjusting the red and blue signals to match the green signal in the white areas of the image.

Several decoding algorithms perform color decoding, including nearest neighbor, linear, cubic, and cubic spline interpolations. The following example provides a simple explanation of the interpolation process.

Determine the value of the pixel in the center of the following group:

```
R   G   R
G   B   G
R   G   R
```

These pixels have the following values:

```
200   050   220
060   100   062
196   058   198
```

Neighboring pixels are used to determine the RGB values for the center pixel. The blue component is taken directly from the pixel value, and the green and red components are the average of the surrounding green and red pixels, respectively.

$$R = (200 + 220 + 196 + 198)/4 = 203.5204$$
$$G = (50 + 60 + 62 + 58)/4 = 57.558$$
$$B = 100$$

The final RGB value for the pixel is (204, 58, 100). This process is repeated for each pixel in the image.

White balancing is a method you can use to adjust for different lighting conditions and optical properties of the filter. While the human eye compensates for light with a color bias based on its memory of white, a camera captures the real state of light. Optical properties of the Bayer filter may result in mismatched intensities between the RGB components of the image.

To adjust image colors more closely to the human perception of light, white balancing assumes that, if a white area can be made to look white, the remaining colors will be accurate as well. White balancing involves identifying the portion of an image that is closest to white, adjusting this area to white, and correcting the balance of colors in the remainder of the image based on the white area. You should perform white balancing every time lighting conditions change. Setting the white balance incorrectly can cause color inconsistencies in the image.

The white level defines the brightness of an image after white balancing. The values for the RGB gains are determined by dividing the white level by the mean value of each component color. The maximum white level is 255. If the white level is too high or too low, the image will appear too light or too dark. You can adjust the white level to fine-tune the image brightness.

8.6.7.1 Image Representation on Disk

An image file is composed of a header followed by pixel values. Depending on the file format, the header contains image information about the horizontal and vertical resolution, pixel definition, and the original palette. Image files may also store supplementary information such as calibration, overlays, or timestamps. The following are the common image file formats:

- BMP – the bitmap file format represents most closely the image representation in memory. Bitmap files are uncompressed, so the size on disk will be very near the size in memory. One benefit of the bitmap format is that you do not lose any data when you save your image.
- TIFF – a popular file format for bitmapped graphics that stores the information defining graphical images in discrete blocks called tags. Each tag describes a particular attribute of the image. TIFF files support compressed and noncompressed images.
- PNG – a very flexible file format that supports lossless compression as well as support for 16-bit monochrome images and 64-bit color images. PNG also offers the capability of storing additional image information such as calibration, overlays, or timestamps.
- JPEG – JPEG images offer support for grayscale and color images and a high level of compression. However, this compression is lossy. Once the image is saved, you can never recover all the image information.

Standard formats for 8-bit grayscale and RGB color images are BMP, TIFF, PNG, and JPEG. The standard formats for 16-bit grayscale and 64-bit RGB is PNG.

8.6.8 Image Display

Displaying images is an important component of machine vision applications because it gives you the ability to visualize your data. Image processing and image visualization are distinct and separate elements. Image processing refers to the creation, acquisition, and analysis of images. Image visualization refers to how image data is presented and how you can interact with the visualized images. A typical imaging application uses many images in memory that the application never displays.

Use display functions to visualize your image data, to retrieve generated events and the associated data from an image display environment, to select ROI from an image interactively, and to annotate the image with additional information.

Display functions display images, set attributes of the image display environment, assign color palettes to image display environments, close image display environments, and set up and use an image browser in image display environments. Some ROI functions, a subset of the display functions, interactively define ROIs in image display environments. These ROI functions configure and display different drawing tools, detect draw events, retrieve information about the region drawn on the image display environment, and move and rotate ROIs. Non-destructive overlays display important information on top of an image without changing the values of the image pixels.

8.6.8.1 Understanding Display Modes

One of the key components of displaying images is the display mode that the video adaptor operates. The display mode indicates how many bits specify the color of a pixel on the display screen. Generally, the display mode available from a video adaptor ranges from 8 to 32 bits per pixel, depending on the amount of video memory available on the video adaptor and the screen resolution you choose. If you have an 8-bit display mode, a pixel can be one of 256 different colors. If you have a 16-bit display mode, a pixel can be one of 65 536 colors. In 24- or 32-bit display mode, the color of a pixel on the screen is encoded using 3 or 4 bytes, respectively. In these modes, information is stored using 8 bits each for the RGB components of the pixel. These modes offer the possibility to display about 16.7 million colors.

Understanding your display mode is important to understanding how your software displays the different image types on a screen. Image processing functions often use grayscale images. Because display screen pixels are made of RGB components, the pixels of a grayscale image cannot be rendered directly. In 24- or 32-bit display mode, the display adaptor uses 8 bits to encode a grayscale value, offering 256 gray shades. This color resolution is sufficient to display 8-bit grayscale images. However, higher bit depth images, such as 16-bit grayscale images, are not accurately represented in a 24- or 32-bit display mode. To display a 16-bit grayscale image, either ignore the least significant bits or use a mapping function to convert 16 to 8 bits.

Mapping functions evenly distribute the dynamic range of the 16-bit image to an 8-bit image. The following techniques describe the common ways in which software convert 16-bit images to 8-bit images and display those images using mapping functions.

Full dynamic – the minimum intensity value of the 16-bit image is mapped to 0 and the maximum intensity value is mapped to 255. All other values in the image are mapped between 0 and 255 using the following equation:

$$z = \frac{x-y}{v-y} \times 255$$

where

z	is the 8-bit pixel value
x	is the 16-bit value
y	is the minimum intensity value
v	is the maximum intensity value

The full dynamic mapping method is a good general-purpose method because it ensures the display of the complete dynamic range of the image. Because the minimum and maximum pixel values in an image are used to determine the full dynamic range of that image, the presence of noisy or defective pixels with minimum or maximum values can affect the appearance of the displayed image.

Given range – This technique is similar to the full dynamic method, except that the minimum and maximum values to be mapped to 0 and 255 are user-defined. You can use this method to enhance the contrast of some regions of the image by finding the minimum and maximum values of those regions and computing the histogram of those regions. A histogram of this region shows the minimum and maximum intensities of the pixels. Those values are used to stretch the dynamic range of the entire image.

Downshifts – This technique is based on shifts of the pixel values. This method applies a given number of right shifts to the 16-bit pixel value and displays the least significant bit. This technique truncates some of the lowest bits, which are not displayed. The downshifts method is very fast, but it reduces the real dynamic of the sensor to 8-bit sensor capabilities. It requires knowledge of the bit depth of the imaging sensor that has been used. For example, an image acquired with a 12-bit camera should be visualized using four right shifts in order to display the eight most significant bits acquired with the camera.

8.6.8.2 Palettes

At the time a grayscale image is displayed on the screen, the software converts the value of each pixel of the image into RGB intensities for the corresponding pixel displayed on the screen. This process uses a color table, called a *palette*, which associates a color to each possible grayscale value of an image.

With palettes, you can produce different visual representations of an image without altering the pixel data. Palettes can generate effects such as photonegative displays or color-coded displays. In the latter case, palettes are useful for detailing particular image constituents in which the total number of colors is limited.

Displaying images in different palettes helps to emphasize regions with particular intensities, identify smooth or abrupt gray-level variations, and convey details that might be difficult to perceive in a grayscale image.

For example, the human eye is much more sensitive to small intensity variations in a bright area than in a dark area. Using a color palette may help you distinguish these slight changes.

A palette is a predefined or user-defined array of RGB values. It defines for each possible gray-level value a corresponding color value to render the pixel. The gray-level value of a pixel acts as an address that is indexed into the table, returning three values corresponding to an RGB intensity. This set of RGB values defines a palette in which varying amounts of RGB are mixed to produce a color representation of the value range. Color palettes are composed of 256 RGB elements. A specific color is the result of applying a value between 0 and 255 for each of the three color components. If the RGB components have an identical value, the result is a gray-level pixel value. A gray palette associates different shades of gray with each value to produce a continuous, linear gradation of gray from black to white. You can set up the palette to assign the color black to the value 0 and white to 255, or vice versa. Other palettes can reflect linear or nonlinear gradations going from red to blue, light brown to dark brown, and so on.

8.6.8.3 Nondestructive Overlays

A nondestructive overlay enables you to annotate the display of an image. You can overlay text, lines, points, complex geometric shapes, and bitmaps on top of your image without changing the underlying pixel values in your image; only the display of the image is affected. Figure 8.41 shows how you can use the overlay to depict the orientation of each particle in the image.

You can use nondestructive overlays for many purposes, such as the following:

- Highlighting the location in an image where objects have been detected
- Adding quantitative or qualitative information to the displayed image – like the match score from a pattern matching function
- Displaying ruler grids or alignment marks.

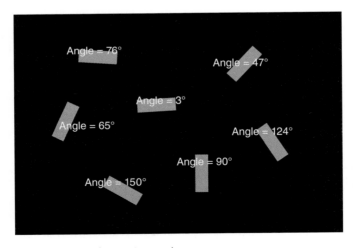

Figure 8.41 Nondestructive overlay.

Overlays do not affect the results of any analysis or processing functions – they affect only the display. The overlay is associated with an image, so there are no special overlay data types. You only need to add the overlay to your image.

8.7 Features of a Machine Vision System

A machine vision system is composed of a camera connected through a camera bus to an interface device, which interacts with the host PC memory through the computer bus. Machine vision systems use certain features to acquire the pixel data from a camera sensor, manipulate the pixel data, and deliver the image of interest to the host PC memory. While the features are common across machine vision applications, they can be implemented in a variety of ways and in any of the major system components. Machine vision systems use image reconstruction, timing and triggering, memory handling, look-up tables (LUT)s, ROIs, color space conversion, and shading correction to manipulate the image data in preparation for image processing. This section provides an introduction to the purpose, functionality, and implementation options for these features.

8.7.1 Image Reconstruction

There is a disparity between the way camera sensors output pixel data and the way that image processing software expects to receive the image data. Camera sensors output individual pixel data rather than the data for a full image. Therefore, you need a way to properly interpret and orient the data so that a recognizable image is available for image processing or display. Image reconstruction refers to the reordering of the sensor data to create the acquired image in the host memory.

Sensors output image data in what is called a *tap* or *channel*. A tap is defined as a group of data lines that acquire one pixel each. A camera that latches only one pixel on the active edge of the pixel clock is known as a *single-tap camera*. Multi-tap cameras acquire multiple pixels on separate data lines that are available on the same active edge of the pixel clock. Using multiple taps greatly increases the camera's acquisition speed and frame rate.

Camera sensors output data in a variety of configurations. A single-tap camera scans data beginning with the top-left pixel and moves to the right before proceeding down to the next line, continuing in this manner until the last line is completed for that frame. The camera then starts acquiring the pixel at the top-left corner of the next frame. In contrast, the data from each tap of a multi-tap camera can be independently acquired using one of several different configurations. Figure 8.42 depicts several of the possible tap configurations machine vision sensors use.

Image reconstruction can occur at any point in the machine vision system. Since the sensor does not output pixel data in order, the pixel data must be directed to the correct location in memory to reconstruct the image.

Image reconstruction requires a large amount of memory to appropriately reorder the image data. To minimize size and cost, cameras rarely provide the memory needed to store pixel data during image reconstruction. Image

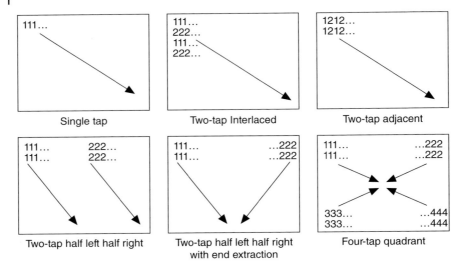

Figure 8.42 Tap configuration.

reconstruction can be implemented with software on the host PC to reorder the pixel data in memory; however, this increases the amount of memory required in the system. Most commonly, a frame grabber interface device provides on-board memory and logic to perform inline reconstruction of the image.

8.7.2 Timing and Triggering

Most machine vision systems rely on timing and triggering features to control and synchronize various parts of the system. Timing is the ability to precisely determine when a measurement is taken. Triggering offers the flexibility to couple timing signals between several channels and devices to provide precise control of signal generation and acquisition timing. In machine vision systems, timing and triggering provide a method to coordinate a vision action or function with events external to the computer, such as sending a pulse to strobe lighting or receiving a pulse from a position sensor to signal the presence of an item on an assembly line.

In the simplest system configurations, a trigger is not used, and the camera acquires images continuously. However, if your application requires only certain images, you can use a trigger to acquire a single frame (or line), start an acquisition, or stop an acquisition. These types of triggers are commonly generated by external devices, such as data acquisition boards, position encoders, strobe lights, or limit switches. Triggering can capture repetitive vision events that occur at unknown intervals by starting an acquisition upon each occurrence of the event.

Several triggering configurations are available to acquire images in a machine vision application. Some cameras are designed to connect directly to the output trigger of an external device. This connectivity is simple; however, this configuration provides limited functionality. Since the trigger is passed directly from the external device to the camera, the way in which the external device outputs the trigger pulse needs to be compatible with the way in which the camera uses

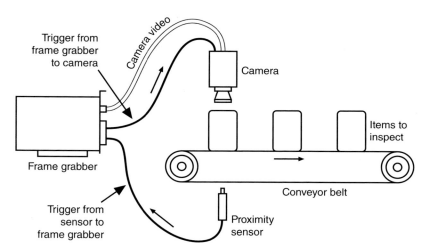

Figure 8.43 Trigger configuration example.

the trigger. Without this compatibility, the camera may not acquire the desired image. Alternatively, the output trigger of an external device can be connected to a frame grabber. The frame grabber receives the external device trigger, programmatically determines the appropriate action for that trigger, and sends out a conditioned trigger to the camera. In response to a trigger, the frame grabber can either take no action (trigger disabled), send a pulse to the camera to start a continuous acquisition, send a pulse to the camera to acquire a single image in response to each trigger received, or perform other trigger conditioning. Figure 8.43 depicts a possible configuration for triggering in a machine vision system. In this configuration, the proximity sensor outputs a trigger when an item moves past the sensor. The trigger is routed to the frame grabber, which sends out a trigger to acquire an image with the camera.

In many cases, trigger conditioning is required to provide camera control and to ensure that the desired images are acquired for your application. There are many types of trigger conditioning to accomplish different types of control for the system. A delay can be inserted between the times when the frame grabber receives a trigger from the external device and sends a trigger out to another device. For example, a delay could be used in a manufacturing conveyor belt system that uses a proximity sensor located at a distance from the camera. The frame grabber receives a trigger when the object passes by the proximity sensor, applies a delay, and sends a trigger to the camera to start the acquisition when the object is in front of the camera. For some applications and cameras, the width of the trigger pulse can define the duration of the exposure for the camera's sensor. For advanced triggering in systems, pattern generation provides synchronization of multiple events using multiple trigger lines, such as camera exposure, lighting, and plunger. A frame grabber can also be programmed to ignore triggers received from the external device. This feature is most useful for ignoring pulses that occur while the camera is still outputting the previous image data.

Ignoring triggers is very useful in applications that use asynchronous reset, a feature provided by many high-end cameras. The term *asynchronous* refers to the fact that the response of the camera to an external input (the trigger) is immediate. This causes the camera to *reset* and capture an image as soon as it receives a trigger. If the frame grabber receives a trigger before the camera completes the transmission of the current frame, the camera resets without completing the current frame, and the application receives a partial frame. For this reason, certain triggers should be ignored to avoid resetting the camera while transmitting data from the previous frame. Additionally, the frame grabber can keep a count of the ignored triggers so that you can determine whether any trigger events did not result in an acquired image.

Applications that use line-scan cameras also benefit from triggering in a machine vision system. In contrast to area-scan cameras that provide images of a set image size, line-scan cameras can theoretically provide a continuous image. For this reason, they are commonly used in document scanning and web inspection applications. The stationary line-scan camera acquires a single line of pixels with each exposure, and the object of interest is moved in front of the camera at a rate compatible with the exposure frequency. Each acquired line is combined with previous lines to build the entire image of the object. A lack of synchronization between the acquisition and the object speed can distort the image. If the object speeds up, the image is stretched. If the belt slows down, the image is compressed. Quadrature encoder triggers account for changes in speed of the object of interest. Frame grabbers can provide additional trigger conditioning by triggering the acquisition at different multiples of the quadrature encoder clicks, giving extra control over the acquisition.

Variable height acquisition (VHA) is often used in line-scan applications where you do not know the exact size of the object you are acquiring. In VHA mode, you can use an external sensor that indicates whether an object is within the field of view to trigger your image acquisition from this object's present/not present signal. The advantage of this mode is that the acquired image has a *variable height*. This guarantees that your object will fit in one image because the acquisition is based on whether the object is present. In contrast, area-scan cameras might acquire only a part of an object because the image size is smaller than the object. Since VHA is an advanced function, it is commonly implemented using triggering with frame grabbers and not with cameras.

Triggering serves an essential role in the integration of machine vision systems. Triggers allow for coordination between vision actions, such as image acquisition, and other events in the system. Frame grabbers provide many benefits in the control and manipulation of triggers through routing and trigger conditioning, which are not available with cameras or software alone.

8.7.3 Memory Handling

Machine vision applications are memory-intensive because of the amount of data involved in image acquisition and processing. For this reason, you need a location to buffer the acquired image data before transferring or processing the data. Without buffering, you can acquire only at the maximum rate supported by the bottleneck of the system (commonly the camera bus or the computer bus bandwidth). If you exceed this maximum rate, you would have a data overflow and frames would be lost. Memory for image buffering can be provided by the camera, interface device, or system memory.

By allocating a sufficient number of buffers in the system memory, you should be able to prevent losing frames even with an arbitrarily large delay caused by limited bus throughput. Unfortunately, that is not exactly true. To illustrate this scenario, compare the architectures of buffering in the system memory versus buffering in onboard memory on a frame grabber. Figure 8.44 depicts an acquisition into the system memory, and Figure 8.45 shows an acquisition into frame grabber memory.

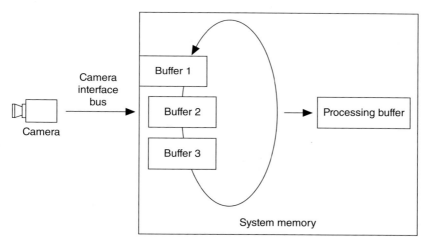

Figure 8.44 Acquiring an image into the system memory.

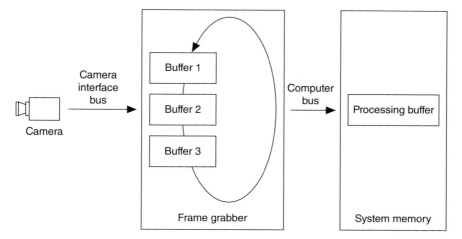

Figure 8.45 Acquiring an image into memory on a frame grabber.

By populating memory on the frame grabber, the user can acquire images from a high-speed event into the onboard memory and then transfer them to the system memory across the PCI bus more slowly. If there is a delay associated with the PCI bus, the OS, or image processing, the onboard buffers will continue to be filled until resources are freed to catch up with the acquisition. Cameras can include memory for buffering; however, buffering is most commonly handled by the frame grabber. Most frame grabbers provide some amount of onboard memory, either in the form of a small first in–first out (FIFO) buffer designed to hold a few video lines (4 kB), or a larger memory space sufficient to hold several images (16–80 MB). Even if the acquisition is configured to go to the system memory, the onboard memory acts as a buffer to absorb the various delays that might be encountered.

In addition to the buffering advantages, onboard memory allows burst acquisitions at very high rates. Some very high speed applications, such as tracking a bullet, require extremely high frame rates for short periods. The PCI bus can only sustain 100 MB s^{-1}, and the frame grabber can be designed to acquire at a much higher rate from the camera (e.g., 32 bits per pixel at 50 MHz resulting in 200 MB s^{-1} of data). Onboard memory allows you to store the image data from a high-speed event on the frame grabber before transferring the data to the system memory across the PCI bus more slowly. As a result, you can bypass the PCI bus limitation for short-duration acquisitions, and guarantee that no frames will be lost until the onboard memory is filled. Using onboard memory is also beneficial when the system memory is limited. In this case, you could acquire the images onto the onboard memory and transfer one buffer at a time into the system memory for processing. This configuration reduces the required system memory because you hold only a single buffer on the host PC at a given time.

Onboard memory can also assist in minimizing the PCI bus traffic used by the machine vision application. Unnecessary traffic across the PCI bus can be avoided by evaluating the processing results of each buffer and discontinuing the transfers as soon as the information of interest has been obtained. Alternatively, the acquisition can store images into onboard memory at the full frame rate and transfer images across the PCI bus only when the user requests them. This solution is commonly used in monitoring applications that do not require every image but do require PCI bandwidth for other data. This provides the most recent image, and the PCI bus is busy with image transfers only when the user requests an image. This results in continuous onboard acquisition, which allows the most immediate response to image requests without taking up unnecessary PCI bandwidth.

8.7.4 Additional Features

While all machine vision systems take advantage of image reconstruction, timing and triggering, and memory handling features, there are several other features available to help manipulate the acquired image data to prepare for image processing. These features are commonly used as preprocessing operations to prepare the image for analysis. These operations include LUTs, ROI, color space conversion, and shading correction.

8.7.4.1 Look-Up Tables

An LUT is a commonly used feature in machine vision systems. LUT transformations are basic image processing functions that improve the contrast and brightness of an image by modifying the dynamic intensity of regions with poor contrast. LUTs efficiently transform one value into another by receiving a pixel value, relating that value to the index of a location in the table, and reassigning the pixel value to the value stored in that table location. Common LUT transformations applied in machine vision applications include data inversion, binarization, contrast enhancement, gamma correction, or other nonlinear transfer functions. Table 8.6 presents an example of a data-inversion LUT for an 8-bit grayscale image type.

Commonly, the LUT index value is directly related to the pixel intensity value. In a data-inversion LUT, the pixel intensity values are reversed; the lowest intensity pixel value (0 or black) is converted to the highest intensity pixel value (255 or white), and the highest intensity pixel value is converted to the lowest pixel intensity value. When constructing an LUT, a specific output value is determined for each index using an equation or other logic. Figure 8.46 illustrates the results of applying various LUT transformations to an image.

Many machine vision applications require manipulation of the image to separate the objects of interest from the background. Binarization, also known as *thresholding*, segments an image into two regions: a particle region and a background region. Binarization is accomplished by selecting a pixel value range, known as the *gray-level interval* or *threshold interval*. Binarization works by setting all image pixels that fall within the threshold interval to white and setting all other image pixels to black. The result is a binary image that can easily undergo additional binary image processing algorithms. Since certain detail may be lost in the image, binarization is commonly used in applications where the outline or shape of objects in the image is of interest for processing.

Often, the brightness of an image does not make full use of the available dynamic range. Contrast enhancement is a simple image processing technique that increases the intensity dynamic of an image. Also known as an *LUT table*, this transfer function increases the contrast by evenly distributing a specified gray-level range over the full gray scale of intensities. For processing,

Table 8.6 Sample data inversion look-up table.

LUT index	LUT output
0	255
1	254
2	253
...	...
253	2
254	1
255	0

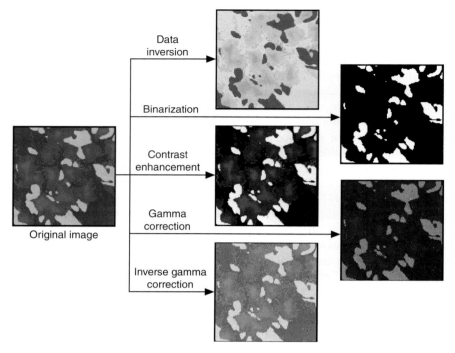

Figure 8.46 Sample transformation using LUTs.

the increased contrast helps in differentiating between the lighter and darker features in the image without losing image details, as happens with binarization.

Gamma correction, or power-of-Y transformation, changes the intensity range of an image by simultaneously adjusting the contrast and brightness of an image. This transformation uses a gamma coefficient Y to control the adjustment. For gamma correction transformations, the higher the gamma coefficient, the higher the intensity correction. Gamma correction enhances high-intensity pixel values by expanding high gray-level ranges while compressing low gray-level ranges. This decreases the overall brightness of an image and increases the contrast in bright areas at the expense of the contrast in dark areas. Inverse gamma correction, or power of 1/Y, enhances the low-intensity pixel values by expanding low gray-level ranges while compressing high gray-level ranges. This increases the overall brightness of an image and increases the contrast in dark areas at the expense of the contrast in bright areas. Gamma correction is commonly used in applications where the intensity range is too large to be stored or displayed.

Data inversion, binarization, contrast enhancement, and gamma correction are just a sample of the transformations that can be performed with LUTs. LUTs are highly customizable, allowing you to create user-defined LUTs to perform other operations such as gain or offset transformations. LUTs provide an efficient way to perform data transformations because the output values are precalculated and stored in the table. Retrieving the table value and processing takes less time than performing the calculation to determine the output value for each pixel in an

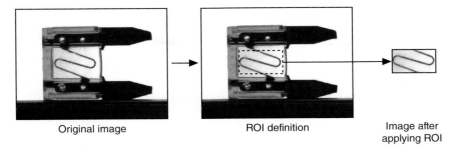

Original image   ROI definition   Image after applying ROI

Figure 8.47 Region of interest.

image. LUTs can be implemented in the hardware to do inline processing of the image, or in the software to process the image after the image is acquired.

8.7.4.2 Region of Interest

A ROI is a user-defined subset of an image. The ROI identifies the areas of interest for machine vision application, and removes the uninteresting image data that is beyond the ROI. Figure 8.47 illustrates the process and the result of defining an ROI.

ROIs can be applied by the camera, the interface device, or the host PC. For cameras and interface devices, an ROI is a hardware-programmable rectangular portion of the acquisition window defining the specific area of the image to acquire. In an ROI acquisition with hardware, only the selected region is transferred across the PCI bus. As a result, defining an ROI increases the sustained frame rate for the system because the image size is smaller and there is less data per acquisition to transfer across the bus. At the host PC, ROIs are the regions of an image in which you want to focus your image processing and analysis. These regions can be defined using standard contours, such as ovals or rectangles, or freehand contours. In software, the user can define one or more regions to be used for analysis. For image processing, applying an ROI reduces the time needed to perform the algorithms because there is less data to process.

8.7.4.3 Color Space Conversion

A color space is a subspace within a 3D coordinate system where each color is represented by a point. You can use color spaces to facilitate the description of colors between persons, machines, or software programs. Most color spaces are geared toward displaying images with hardware, such as color monitors and printers, or toward applications that manipulate color information, such as computer graphics and image processing.

A number of different color spaces are used in various industries and applications. Humans perceive color according to parameters such as brightness, hue, and intensity, while computers perceive color as a combination of RGB. The printing industry uses cyan, magenta, and yellow to specify color. Every time you process color images, you must define a color space. The RGB and HSL color spaces are the most common color spaces used in machine vision applications. Table 8.7 lists and describes common color spaces.

Table 8.7 Common color spaces.

Color space	Description
RGB	Based on red, green, and blue. Used by computers to display images
HSL	Based on hue, saturation, and luminance. Used in image processing applications
CIE	Based on brightness, hue, and colorfulness. Defined by the Commission Internationale de l'Eclairage (International Commission on Illumination) as the different sensations of color that the human brain perceives
CMY	Based on cyan, magenta, and yellow. Used by the printing industry
YIQ	Separates the luminescence information (Y) from the color information (I and Q). Used for TV broadcasting

The RGB color space is the most commonly used color space. The human eye receives color information in separate RGB components through cones, which are the color receptors present in the human eye. These three colors are known as *additive primary colors*. In an additive color system, the human brain processes the three primary light sources and combines them to compose a single color *image*. The three primary color components can combine to reproduce the most possible colors. The RGB space simplifies the design of computer monitors, but it is not ideal for all applications. In the RGB color space, the RGB color components are all necessary to describe a color. Therefore, RGB is not as intuitive as other color spaces.

The HSL color space describes color using the hue component, which makes HSL the best choice for many image processing applications, such as color matching. The HSL color space was developed to put color in terms that are easy for humans to quantify. HSL are characteristics that distinguish one color from another in the HSL space. Hue corresponds to the dominant wavelength of the color. The hue component is a color, such as orange, green, or violet. You can visualize the range of hues as a rainbow. Saturation refers to the amount of white added to the hue and represents the relative purity of a color. A color without any white is fully saturated. The degree of saturation is inversely proportional to the amount of white light added. Colors such as pink, composed of red and white, and lavender, composed of purple and white, are less saturated than red and purple. Brightness embodies the chromatic notion of luminance, or the amplitude or power of light. Chromaticity is the combination of hue and saturation. The relationship between chromaticity and brightness characterizes a color. Systems that manipulate hue use the HSL color space. Overall, two principal factors – the decoupling of the intensity component from the color information and the close relationship between chromaticity and human perception of color – make the HSL space ideal for developing machine vision applications.

Variables, such as the lighting conditions, influence which color space to use in your image processing. If you do not expect the lighting conditions to vary

Figure 8.48 Effects of shading on image processing.

considerably during your application, and you can easily define the colors you are looking for using RGB, use the RGB space. Since the RGB space reproduces an image as you would expect to see it, use the RGB space if you want to display color images but not process them. If you expect the lighting conditions to vary considerably during your color machine vision application, use the HSL color space. The HSL color space provides more accurate color information than the RGB space when running color processing functions, such as color matching or advanced image processing algorithms.

A machine vision application might require conversion between two color spaces. There are standard ways to convert RGB to grayscale and to convert one color space to another. For example, the transformation from RGB to grayscale is linear. Other transformations from one color space to another, such as the conversion of RGB color space to HSL space, are nonlinear because some color spaces represent colors that cannot be represented in the other color space. Color space conversion often occurs in software on the host PC, or in real time on some color frame grabbers, to prepare the image for processing or display.

8.7.4.4 Shading Correction

Differences in the lighting, camera, and geometry of an object can cause shadows in the acquired image. For example, there might be a bright spot in the center of an image, or there could be a gradient from one side of the image to the other. These variations in pixel intensities can hinder the processing of the image. To demonstrate the impact of shading in image processing, Figure 8.48 shows an acquired image and the binarization of that image.

The acquired image is brighter on the left than on the right. When a binarization transformation is applied to the image, some of the image information is lost because of this uneven illumination. Shading correction is an image preprocessing function to compensate for uneven illumination, sensor nonlinearity, or other factors contributing to the shading of the image. There are several techniques and algorithms that can be used to correct image shading. While certain methods are simple to implement in hardware, cameras do not often perform shading correction. Shading correction is most commonly provided by a frame grabber interface device or as a preprocessing algorithm executed in the software of the host PC.

8.8 Summary

Machine vision systems can employ a variety of features to manipulate image data in preparation for image processing and analysis. Image reconstruction, timing and triggering, memory handling, LUTs, ROIs, color space conversion, and shading correction are common features used in machine vision applications. The host PC, interface device, and camera can provide this functionality; however, there are differences in the implementations that make certain solutions preferable to others.

The primary tradeoffs between the implementations are the differences in memory and CPU requirements. Implementing features such as image reconstruction, memory handling, and LUTs in the camera or interface device requires populating memory on the hardware. While onboard memory increases the cost of the hardware, it also provides a higher performance solution. These types of machine vision system features are less expensive to implement with software on the host PC; however, these solutions are more processor-intensive. For these reasons, the best implementation of these features is very system- and application-dependent. Some applications have heavy processing loads, which necessitate efficient methods of image data manipulation. In contrast, other systems have plenty of processing power but require a low-cost solution.

Frame grabber hardware provides the most efficient implementation of these features for machine vision systems. Since frame grabber interface devices are specifically meant for machine vision applications, they can be designed to provide many of the image data manipulation features useful in machine vision applications. It is highly efficient for the frame grabber to implement these features in line with the translation of image data from the camera interface bus protocol to the PC memory protocol. As a result, more system processing power is available for use in image processing and analysis.

Cameras that communicate with the host via a standard computer bus, such as GigE or USB, cannot rely on the interface device to provide these features. Since these buses are not specific to machine vision applications, they do not implement the features required by machine vision applications. Therefore, the implementation of these features becomes the responsibility of the camera or the host software. Many cameras include some amount of onboard memory to buffer for potential bus delays, and some cameras provide ROI control. However, to reduce cost, most cameras leave the majority of machine vision features to the host computer and the software. The resulting system development effort directly relates to the features and ease of use provided by your vision software package. Robust vision software packages will ease your development by providing you with the functions and features needed to quickly get your system up and running.

References

1 AIA, EMVA, JIIA trade associations G3 initative. (2014). *Global Machine Vision Interface Standards, Understanding Today's Digital Camera Interface Options*.
2 Burgess, J. (2015, January). *Throwing the Switch: An Update on the State of the Global Transition to Digital TV Broadcasting*. Retrieved from Center for International Media Assistance (CIMA): http://www.cima.ned.org/resource/

throwing-the-switch-an-update-on-the-state-of-the-global-transition-to-digital-tv-broadcasting/

3 Max Robertson, M. M. (2012, March). *Implementing a CameraLink HS Interface Using the TLK3134*. Retrieved from Texas Instruments: http://www.ti.com/lit/wp/slaa533/slaa533.pdf

4 News. (2012, May). *Camera Link HS standard released*. Retrieved from imveurope: http://www.imveurope.com/news/news_story.php?news_id=925

5 CoaXPress Working Group. (2013, Feburary 21). *CoaXPress Working Group*. Retrieved from JIIA (Japan Industrial Imaging Association): http://jiia.org/en/standard_dl/coaxpress-wg/

6 Gupta, A. (2014, December). *USB 3.0 vs USB 2.0: A quick reference summary for the busy engineer*. Retrieved from Embedded: http://www.embedded.com/design/connectivity/4437961/USB-3-0-vs-USB-2-0--A-quick-reference-summary-for-the-busy-engineer

7 National Instruments. (2013, July 11). *Acquiring from GigE Vision Cameras with Vision Acquisition Software - Part I*. Retrieved from National Instruments: http://www.ni.com/white-paper/5651/en/; National Instruments. (2013, March 28). *NI Announces USB 3.0 Camera Support with NI Vision Acquisition Software August 2013*. Retrieved from National Instruments: http://www.ni.com/white-paper/14308/en/

8 Hruska, J. (2015, March 13). *USB-C vs. USB 3.1: What's the Difference?* Retrieved from ExtremeTech: http://www.extremetech.com/computing/197145-reversible-usb-type-c-finally-on-its-way-alongside-usb-3-1s-10gbit-performance

9 Basler Inc. (n.d.). *Line Scan Camera Selector*. Retrieved from Basler: http://www.baslerweb.com/en/support/tools/camera-selector/line-scan-camera-selector

9

Machine Vision Algorithms

Carsten Steger

MVTec Software GmbH, Arnulfstraße 205, 80634 München, Germany

In the previous chapters, we have examined the different hardware components that are involved in delivering an image to the computer. Each of the components plays an essential role in the machine vision process. For example, illumination is often crucial to bring out the objects we are interested in. Triggered frame grabbers and cameras are essential if the image is to be captured at the right time with the right exposure. Lenses are important for acquiring a sharp and aberration-free image. Nevertheless, none of these components can "see," that is, extract the information we are interested in from the image. This is analogous to human vision. Without our eyes we cannot see. Yet, even with eyes we cannot see anything without our brain. The eye is merely a sensor that delivers data to the brain for interpretation. To this analogy a little further, even if we are myopic, we can still see – only worse. Hence, we can see that the processing of the images delivered to the computer by the sensors is truly the core of machine vision. Consequently, in this chapter, we will discuss the most important machine vision algorithms.

9.1 Fundamental Data Structures

Before we can delve into the study of the machine vision algorithms, we need to examine the fundamental data structures that are involved in machine vision applications. Therefore, in this section we will take a look at the data structures for images, regions, and subpixel-precise contours.

9.1.1 Images

An image is the basic data structure in machine vision, since this is the data that an image acquisition device typically delivers to the computer's memory. As we saw in Chapter 6, a pixel can be regarded as a sample of the energy that falls on the sensor element during the exposure, integrated over the spectral distribution of the light and the spectral response of the sensor. Depending on the camera type, typically the spectral response of the sensor will comprise the entire visible spectrum and optionally a part of the near-infrared spectrum. In this case, the camera will return one sample of the energy per pixel, that is, a single-channel gray value image. RGB cameras, on the other hand, will return three samples per pixel, that is, a three-channel image. These are the two basic types of sensors that are encountered in machine vision applications. However, cameras capable of acquiring images with tens to hundreds of spectral samples per pixel are possible [1, 2]. Therefore, to handle all possible applications, an image can be considered as a set of an arbitrary number of channels.

Intuitively, an image channel can simply be regarded as a two-dimensional (2D) array of numbers. This is also the data structure that is used to represent images in a programming language. Hence, the gray value at the pixel (r, c) can be interpreted as an entry of a matrix: $g = f_{r,c}$. In a more formalized manner, we can regard an image channel f of width w and height h as a function from a rectangular subset $R = \{0, \ldots, h-1\} \times \{0, \ldots, w-1\}$ of the discrete 2D plane $\mathbb{Z}^2$ (i.e., $R \subset \mathbb{Z}^2$) to a real number, that is, $f : R \mapsto \mathbb{R}$, with the gray value g at the pixel position (r, c) defined by $g = f(r, c)$. Likewise, a multichannel image can be regarded as a function $f : R \mapsto \mathbb{R}^n$, where n is the number of channels.

In the above discussion, we have assumed that the gray values are given by real numbers. In almost all cases, the image acquisition device will discretize not only the image spatially but also the gray values to a fixed number of gray levels. In most cases, the gray values will be discretized to 8 bits (1 byte), that is, the set of possible gray values will be $\mathbb{G}_8 = \{0, \ldots, 255\}$. In some cases, a higher bit depth will be used, for example, 10, 12, or even 16 bits. Consequently, to be perfectly accurate, a single-channel image should be regarded as a function $f : R \mapsto \mathbb{G}_b$, where $\mathbb{G}_b = \{0, \ldots, 2^b - 1\}$ is the set of discrete gray values with b bits. However, in many cases this distinction is unimportant, so we will regard an image as a function to the set of real numbers.

Up to now, we have regarded an image as a function that is sampled spatially, because this is the manner in which we receive the image from an image acquisition device. For theoretical considerations, it is sometimes convenient to regard the image as a function in an infinite continuous domain, that is, $f : \mathbb{R}^2 \mapsto \mathbb{R}^n$. We will use this convention occasionally in this chapter. It will be obvious from the context which of the two conventions is used.

9.1.2 Regions

One of the tasks in machine vision is to identify regions in the image that have certain properties, for example, by performing a threshold operation (see Section 9.4). Therefore, at the minimum we need a representation for an arbitrary subset of the pixels in an image. Furthermore, for morphological operations, we will see in Section 9.6.1 that it will be essential that regions can also beyond the image borders to avoid artifacts. Therefore, we define a region as an arbitrary subset of the discrete plane: $R \subset \mathbb{Z}^2$.

The choice of the letter R is intentionally identical to the R that is used in the previous section to denote the rectangle of the image. In many cases, it is extremely useful to restrict the processing to a certain part of the image that is specified by a region of interest (ROI). In this context, we can regard an image as a function from the ROI to a set of numbers, that is, $f : R \mapsto \mathbb{R}^n$. The ROI is sometimes also called the domain of the image because it is the domain of the image function f. We can even unify the two views: we can associate a rectangular ROI with every image that uses the full number of pixels. Therefore, from now on, we will silently assume that every image has an associated ROI, which will be denoted by R.

In Section 9.4.2, we will also see that often we will need to represent multiple objects in an image. Conceptually, this can simply be achieved by considering sets of regions.

From an abstract point of view, it is therefore simple to talk about regions in the image. It is not immediately clear, however, how best to represent regions. Mathematically, we can describe regions as sets, as in the above definition. An equivalent definition is to use the characteristic function of the region:

$$\chi_R(r, c) = \begin{cases} 1, & (r, c) \in R \\ 0, & (r, c) \notin R \end{cases} \tag{9.1}$$

This definition immediately suggests the use of binary images to represent regions. A binary image has a gray value of 0 for points that are not included in the region, and 1 (or any other number different from 0) for points that are included in the region. As an extension to this, we could represent multiple objects in the image as label images, that is, as images in which the gray value encodes the region to which the point belongs. Typically, a label of 0 would be used to represent points that are not included in any region, while numbers > 0 would be used to represent the different regions.

The representation of regions as binary images has one obvious drawback: it needs to store (sometimes very many) points that are not included in the region. Furthermore, the representation is not particularly efficient: we need to store at least 1 bit for every point in the image. Often, the representation actually uses 1 byte per point because it is much easier to access bytes than bits. This representation is also not particularly efficient for runtime purposes: to determine which points are included in the region, we need to perform a test for every point in the binary image. In addition, it is a little awkward to store regions that extend to negative coordinates as binary images, which also leads to cumbersome algorithms. Finally, the representation of multiple regions as label images leads to the fact that overlapping regions cannot be represented, which will cause problems if morphological operations are performed on the regions. Therefore, a representation that only stores the points included in a region in an efficient manner would be very useful.

Table 9.1 shows a small example region. We first note that, either horizontally or vertically, there are extended runs in which adjacent pixels belong to the region. This is typically the case for most regions. We can use this property and store only the necessary data for each run. Since images are typically stored line by line in memory, it is better to use horizontal runs. Therefore, the minimum amount of data for each run is the row coordinate of the run and the start and end columns of the run. This method of storing a region is called a run-length representation or run-length encoding. With this representation, the example region can be stored with just four runs, as shown in Table 9.1. Consequently, the region can also be

Table 9.1 Run-length representation of a region.

Run	Row	Start column	End column
1	1	1	4
2	2	2	2
3	2	4	5
4	3	2	5

regarded as the union of all of its runs:

$$R = \bigcup_{i=1}^{n} \mathbf{r}_i \tag{9.2}$$

Here, $\mathbf{r}_i$ denotes a single run, which can also be regarded as a region. Note that the runs are stored sorted in lexicographic order according to their row and start column coordinates. This means that there is an order of the runs $\mathbf{r}_i = (r_i, cs_i, ce_i)$ in R defined by: $\mathbf{r}_i < \mathbf{r}_j \Leftrightarrow r_i < r_j \vee r_i = r_j \wedge cs_i < cs_j$. This order is crucial for the execution speed of algorithms that use run-length encoded regions.

In the above example, the binary image could be stored with 35 bytes if 1 byte per pixel is used or with 5 bytes if 1 bit per pixel is used. If the coordinates of the region are stored as 2-byte integers, the region can be represented with 24 bytes in the run-length representation. This is already a saving, albeit a small one, compared to binary images stored with 1 byte per pixel, but no saving if the binary image is stored as compactly as possible with 1 bit per pixel. To get an impression of how much this representation really saves, we can note that we are roughly storing the boundary of the region in the run-length representation. On average, the number of points on the boundary of the region will be proportional to the square root of the area of the region. Therefore, we can typically expect a very significant saving from the run-length representation compared to binary images, which must at least store every pixel in the surrounding rectangle of the region. For example, a full rectangular ROI of a $w \times h$ image can be stored with h runs instead of $w \times h$ pixels in a binary image (i.e., wh or $\lceil w/8 \rceil h$ bytes, depending on whether 1 byte or 1 bit per pixel is used). Similarly, a circle with diameter d can be stored with d runs as opposed to at least $d \times d$ pixels. We can see that the run-length representation often leads to an enormous reduction in memory consumption. Furthermore, since this representation only stores the points actually contained in the region, we do not need to perform a test to see whether a point lies in the region or not. These two features can save a significant amount of execution time. Also, with this representation it is straightforward to have regions with negative coordinates. Finally, to represent multiple regions, lists or arrays of run-length encoded regions can be used. Since in this case each region is treated separately, overlapping regions do not pose any problems.

9.1.3 Subpixel-Precise Contours

The data structures we have considered so far are pixel-precise. Often, it is important to extract subpixel-precise data from an image because the application

Figure 9.1 Different subpixel-precise contours. Contour 1 is a closed contour, while contours 2–5 are open contours. Contours 3–5 meet at a junction point.

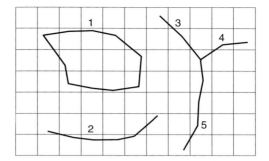

requires an accuracy that is higher than the pixel resolution of the image. The subpixel data can, for example, be extracted with subpixel thresholding (see Section 9.4.3) or subpixel edge extraction (see Section 9.7.3). The results of these operations can be described with subpixel-precise contours. Figure 9.1 displays several example contours. As we can see, the contours can basically be represented as a polygon, that is, an ordered set of control points (r_i, c_i), where the ordering defines which control points are connected to each other. Since the extraction typically is based on the pixel grid, the distance between the control points of the contour is approximately 1 pixel on average. In the computer, the contours are simply represented as arrays of floating-point row and column coordinates. From Figure 9.1, we can also see that there is a rich topology associated with the contours. For example, contours can be closed (contour 1) or open (contours 2–5). Closed contours are usually represented by having the first contour point identical to the last contour point or by a special attribute that is stored with the contour. Furthermore, we can see that several contours can meet at a junction point, for example, contours 3–5. It is sometimes useful to explicitly store this topological information with the contours.

9.2 Image Enhancement

In the preceding chapters, we have seen that we have various means at our disposal to obtain a good image quality. The illumination, lenses, cameras, and frame grabbers (if used) all play a crucial role here. However, although we try very hard to select the best possible hardware setup, sometimes the image quality is not sufficient. Therefore, in this section we will take a look at several common techniques for image enhancement.

9.2.1 Gray Value Transformations

Despite our best efforts in controlling the illumination, in some cases it is necessary to modify the gray values of the image. One of the reasons for this may be a weak contrast. With controlled illumination, this problem usually only occurs locally. Therefore, we may only need to increase the contrast locally. Another possible reason for adjusting the gray values may be that the contrast or brightness of the image has changed from the settings that were in effect when we set up our application. For example, illuminations typically age and produce a weaker contrast after some time.

A gray value transformation can be regarded as a point operation. This means that the transformed gray value $t_{r,c}$ depends only on the gray value $g_{r,c}$ in the input image at the same position: $t_{r,c} = f(g_{r,c})$. Here, $f(g)$ is a function that defines the gray value transformation to apply. Note that the domain and range of $f(g)$ typically are $\mathbb{G}_b$, that is, they are discrete. Therefore, to increase the transformation speed, gray value transformations can be implemented as a look-up table (LUT) by storing the output gray value for each possible input gray value in a table. If we denote the LUT as f_g, we have $t_{r,c} = f_g[g_{r,c}]$, where the [ ] operator denotes the table look-up.

The most important gray value transformation is a linear gray value scaling: $f(g) = ag + b$. If $g \in \mathbb{G}_b$, we need to ensure that the output value is also in $\mathbb{G}_b$. Hence, we must clip and round the output gray value as follows:

$$f(g) = \min(\max(\lfloor ag + b + 0.5 \rfloor, 0), 2^b - 1) \qquad (9.3)$$

For $|a| > 1$, the contrast is increased, while for $|a| < 1$ the contrast is decreased. If $a < 0$, the gray values are inverted. For $b > 0$, the brightness is increased, while for $b < 0$ the brightness is decreased.

Figure 9.2a shows a small part of an image of a printed circuit board (PCB). The entire image was acquired such that the full range of gray values is used. Three components are visible in the image. As we can see, the contrast of the components is not as good as it could be. Figures 9.2b–e show the effect of applying

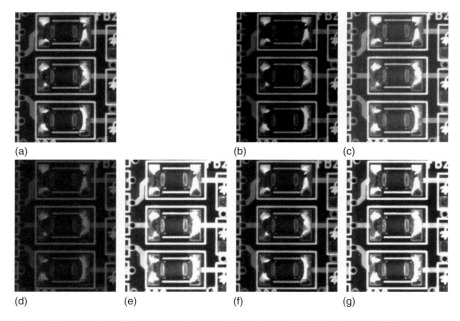

Figure 9.2 Examples of linear gray value transformations. (a) Original image. (b) Decreased brightness ($b = -50$). (c) Increased brightness ($b = 50$). (d) Decreased contrast ($a = 0.5$). (e) Increased contrast ($a = 2$). (f) Gray value normalization. (g) Robust gray value normalization ($p_l = 0, p_u = 0.8$).

a linear gray value transformation with different values for a and b. As we can see from Figure 9.2e, the component can be seen more clearly for $a = 2$.

The parameters of the linear gray value transformation must be selected appropriately for each application and adapted to changed illumination conditions. Since this can be quite cumbersome, ideally we would like to have a method that selects a and b automatically based on the conditions in the image. One obvious method to do this is to select the parameters such that the maximum range of the gray value space $\mathbb{G}_b$ is used. This can be done as follows: let $g_{\min}$ and $g_{\max}$ be the minimum and maximum gray value in the ROI under consideration. Then, the maximum range of gray values will be used if $a = (2^b - 1)/(g_{\max} - g_{\min})$ and $b = -ag_{\min}$. This transformation can be thought of as a normalization of the gray values. Figure 9.2f shows the effect of the gray value normalization of the image in Figure 9.2a. As we can see, the contrast is not much better than in the original image. This happens because there are specular reflections on the solder, which have the maximum gray value, and because there are very dark parts in the image with a gray value of almost 0. Hence, there is not much room to improve the contrast.

The problem with the gray value normalization is that a single pixel with a very bright or dark gray value can prevent us from using the desired gray value range. To get a better understanding of this point, we can take a look at the gray value histogram of the image. The gray value histogram is defined as the frequency with which a particular gray value occurs. Let n be the number of points in the ROI under consideration, and n_i be the number of pixels that have the gray value i. Then, the gray value histogram is a discrete function with domain $\mathbb{G}_b$ that has the values

$$h_i = \frac{n_i}{n} \tag{9.4}$$

In probabilistic terms, the gray value histogram can be regarded as the probability density of the occurrence of gray value i. We can also compute the cumulative histogram of the image as follows:

$$c_i = \sum_{j=0}^{i} h_j \tag{9.5}$$

This corresponds to the probability distribution of the gray values. Figure 9.3 shows the histogram and cumulative histogram of the image in Figure 9.2a. We can see that the specular reflections on the solder create a peak in the histogram at gray value 255. Furthermore, we can see that the smallest gray value in the image is 16. This explains why the gray value normalization did not increase the contrast significantly. We can also see that the dark part of the gray value range contains the most information about the components, while the bright part contains the information corresponding to the specular reflections as well as the printed rectangles on the board. Therefore, to get a more robust gray value normalization, we can simply ignore a part of the histogram that includes a fraction p_l of the darkest gray values and a fraction $1 - p_u$ of the brightest gray values. This can easily be done based on the cumulative histogram by selecting the smallest gray value for which $c_i \geq p_l$ and the largest gray value for which $c_i \leq p_u$. Conceptually,

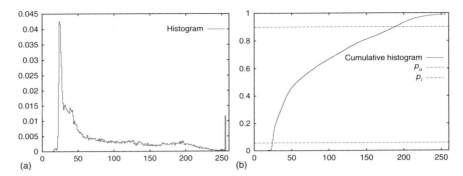

Figure 9.3 (a) Histogram of the image in Figure 9.2a. (b) Corresponding cumulative histogram with probability thresholds p_u and p_l superimposed.

this corresponds to intersecting the cumulative histogram with the lines $p = p_l$ and $p = p_u$. Figure 9.3b shows two example probability thresholds superimposed on the cumulative histogram. For the example image in Figure 9.2a, it is best to ignore only the bright gray values that correspond to the reflections and print on the board to get a robust gray value normalization. Figure 9.2g shows the result that is obtained with $p_l = 0$ and $p_u = 0.8$. As we can see, the contrast of the components is significantly improved.

The robust gray value normalization is an extremely powerful method that is used, for example, as a feature extraction method for optical character recognition (OCR; see Section 9.12), where it can be used to make the OCR features invariant to illumination changes. However, it requires transforming the gray values in the image, which is computationally expensive. If we want to make an algorithm robust to illumination changes, it is often possible to adapt the parameters to the changes in the illumination, for example, as described in Section 9.4.1 for the segmentation of images.

9.2.2 Radiometric Calibration

Many image processing algorithms rely on the fact that there is a linear correspondence between the energy that the sensor collects and the gray value in the image, namely $G = aE + b$, where E is the energy that falls on the sensor and G is the gray value in the image. Ideally, $b = 0$, which means that twice as much energy on the sensor leads to twice the gray value in the image. However, $b = 0$ is not necessary for measurement accuracy. The only requirement is that the correspondence is linear. If the correspondence is nonlinear, the accuracy of the results returned by these algorithms typically will degrade. Examples of this are the subpixel-precise threshold (see Section 9.4.3), the gray value features (see Section 9.5.2), and, most notably, subpixel-precise edge extraction (see Section 9.7, in particular Section 9.7.4). Unfortunately, sometimes the gray value correspondence is nonlinear, that is, either the camera or the analog frame grabber (if used) produces a nonlinear response to the energy. If this is the case, and we want to perform accurate measurements, we must determine the nonlinear response and invert it. If we apply the inverse response to the images,

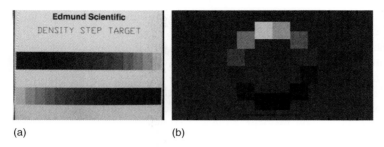

(a) (b)

Figure 9.4 Examples of calibrated density targets that are traditionally used for radiometric calibration in laboratory settings. (a) Density step target (image acquired with a camera with linear response). (b) Twelve-patch ISO 14524 target (image simulated as if acquired with a camera with linear response).

the resulting images will have a linear response. The process of determining the inverse response function is known as *radiometric calibration*.

In laboratory settings, traditionally calibrated targets are used to perform the radiometric calibration. Figure 9.4 displays examples of target types that are commonly used. Consequently, the corresponding algorithms are called chart-based. The procedure is to measure the gray values in the different patches and to compare them to the known reflectance of the patches [3]. This yields a small number of measurements (e.g., 15 independent measurements in the target in Figure 9.4a and 12 in the target in Figure 9.4b), through which a function is fitted, for example, a gamma response function that includes gain and offset, given by

$$f(g) = (a + bg)^\gamma \qquad (9.6)$$

There are several problems with this approach. First of all, it requires a very even illumination throughout the entire field of view in order to be able to determine the gray values of the patches correctly. For example, [3] requires less than 2% variation of the illuminance incident on the calibration target across the entire target. While this may be achievable in laboratory settings, it is much harder to achieve in a production environment, where the calibration often must be performed. Furthermore, effects like vignetting may lead to an apparent light drop-off toward the border, which also prevents the extraction of the correct gray values. This problem is always present, independent of the environment. Another problem is that there is a great variety of target layouts, and hence it is difficult to implement a general algorithm for finding the patches on the targets and to determine their correspondence to the true reflectances. In addition, the reflectances on the targets are often specified as a linear progression in density, which is related exponentially to the reflectance. For example, the targets in Figure 9.4 both have a linear density progression, that is, an exponential gray value progression. This means that the samples for the curve fitting are not evenly distributed, which can cause the fitted response to be less accurate in the parts of the curve that contain the samples with the larger spacing. Finally, the range of functions that can be modeled for the camera response is limited to the single function that is fitted through the data.

Because of the above problems, a radiometric calibration algorithm that does not require any calibration target is highly desirable. These algorithms are called chart-less radiometric calibration. They are based on taking several images of the same scene with different exposures. The exposure can be varied by changing the aperture stop of the lens or by varying the exposure time of the camera. Since the aperture stop can be set less accurately than the exposure time, and since the exposure time of most industrial cameras can be controlled very accurately in software, varying the exposure time is the preferred method of acquiring images with different exposures. The advantages of this approach are that no calibration targets are required and that they do not require an even illumination. Furthermore, the range of possible gray values can be covered with multiple images instead of a single image, as required by the algorithms that use calibration targets. The only requirement on the image content is that there should be no gaps in the histograms of the different images within the gray value range that each image covers. Furthermore, with a little extra effort, even overexposed (i.e., saturated) images can be handled.

To derive an algorithm for chart-less calibration, let us examine what two images with different exposures tell us about the response function. We know that the gray value G in the image is a nonlinear function r of the energy E that falls on the sensor during the exposure e [4]:

$$G = r(eE) \qquad (9.7)$$

Note that e is proportional to the exposure time and also proportional to the area of the entrance pupil of the lens, that is, proportional to $(1/F)^2$, where F is the f-number of the lens. As described previously, in industrial applications we typically leave the aperture stop constant and vary the exposure time. Therefore, we can think of e as the exposure time.

The goal of the radiometric calibration is to determine the inverse response $q = r^{-1}$. The inverse response can be applied to an image via an LUT to achieve a linear response.

Now, let us assume that we have acquired two images with different exposures e_1 and e_2. Hence, we know that $G_1 = r(e_1 E)$ and $G_2 = r(e_2 E)$. By applying the inverse response q to both equations, we obtain $q(G_1) = e_1 E$ and $q(G_2) = e_2 E$. We can now divide the two equations to eliminate the unknown energy E, and obtain

$$\frac{q(G_1)}{q(G_2)} = \frac{e_1}{e_2} = e_{1,2} \qquad (9.8)$$

As we can see, q depends only on the gray values in the images and on the ratio $e_{1,2}$ of the exposures, but not on the exposures e_1 and e_2 themselves. Equation (9.8) is the defining equation for all chart-less radiometric calibration algorithms.

One way to determine q based on equation (9.8) is to discretize q in a LUT. Thus, $q_i = q(G_i)$. To derive a linear algorithm to determine q, we can take logarithms on both sides of equation (9.8) to obtain $\log(q_1/q_2) = \log e_{1,2}$, that is, $\log(q_1) - \log(q_2) = \log e_{1,2}$ [4]. If we set $Q_i = \log(q_i)$ and $E_{1,2} = \log e_{1,2}$, each pixel in the image pair yields one linear equation for the inverse response function Q:

$$Q_1 - Q_2 = E_{1,2} \qquad (9.9)$$

Hence, we obtain a linear equation system $AQ = E$, where Q is a vector of the LUT for the logarithmic inverse response function, while A is a matrix with 256 columns for byte images. Matrices A and E have as many rows as pixels in the image, for example, 307 200 for a 640 × 480 image. Therefore, this equation system is much too large to be solved in an acceptable time. To derive an algorithm that solves the equation system in an acceptable time, we can note that each row of the equation system has the following form:

$$(0 \;\cdots\; 0 \; 1 \; 0 \;\cdots\; 0 \; -1 \; 0 \;\cdots\; 0) \, Q = E_{1,2} \qquad (9.10)$$

The indices of the 1 and −1 entries in the above equation are determined by the gray values in the first and second images. Note that each pair of gray values that occurs multiple times leads to several identical rows in A. Also note that $AQ = E$ is an overdetermined equation system, which can be solved through the normal equations $A^\top A Q = A^\top E$. This means that each row that occurs k times in A will have the weight k in the normal equations. The same behavior is obtained by multiplying the row (9.10) that corresponds to the gray value pair by $\sqrt{k}$ and to include that row only once in A. This typically reduces the number of rows in A from several hundred thousand to a few thousand, and thus makes the solution of the equation system feasible.

The simplest method to determine k is to compute the 2D histogram of the image pair. The 2D histogram determines how often gray value i occurs in the first image while gray value j occurs in the second image at the same position. Hence, for byte images, the 2D histogram is a 256 × 256 image in which the column coordinate indicates the gray value in the first image while the row coordinate indicates the gray value in the second image. It is obvious that the 2D histogram contains the required values of k. We will see examples of 2D histograms in the following.

Note that the discussion so far has assumed that the calibration is performed from a single image pair. It is, however, very simple to include multiple images in the calibration since additional images provide the same type of equations as in (9.10), and can thus simply be added to A. This makes it much easier to cover the entire range of gray values. Thus, we can start with a fully exposed image and successively reduce the exposure time until we reach an image in which the smallest possible gray values are assumed. We could even start with a slightly overexposed image to ensure that the highest gray values are assumed. However, in this case we have to take care that the overexposed (saturated) pixels are excluded from A because they violate the defining equation (9.8). This is a very tricky problem to solve in general, since some cameras exhibit a bizarre saturation behavior. Suffice it to say that for many cameras it is sufficient to exclude pixels with the maximum gray value from A.

Despite the fact that A has many more rows than columns, the solution Q is not uniquely determined because we cannot determine the absolute value of the energy E that falls onto the sensor. Hence, the rank of A is at most 255 for byte images. To solve this problem, we could arbitrarily require $q(255) = 255$, that is, scale the inverse response function such that the maximum gray value range is used. Since the equations are solved in a logarithmic space, it is slightly more convenient to require $q(255) = 1$ and to scale the inverse response to the full gray value range later. With this, we obtain one additional equation of the form

$$(0 \quad \cdots \quad 0 \quad k) \, Q = 0 \tag{9.11}$$

To enforce the constraint $q(255) = 1$, the constant k must be chosen such that equation (9.11) has the same weight as the sum of all other equations (9.10), that is, $k = \sqrt{wh}$, where w and h are the width and height of the image.

Even with this normalization, we still face some practical problems. One problem is that, if the images contain very little noise, equation (9.10) can become decoupled, and hence do not provide a unique solution for Q. Another problem is that, if the possible range of gray values is not completely covered by the images, there are no equations for the range of gray values that are not covered. Hence, the equation system will become singular. Both problems can be solved by introducing smoothness constraints for Q, which couple the equations and enable an extrapolation of Q into the range of gray values that is not covered by the images. The smoothness constraints require that the second derivative of Q should be small. Hence, for byte images they lead to 254 equations of the form

$$(0 \quad \cdots \quad 0 \quad s \quad -2s \quad s \quad 0 \quad \cdots \quad 0) \, Q = 0 \tag{9.12}$$

The parameter s determines the amount of smoothness that is required. Like for equation (9.11), s must be chosen such that equation (9.12) has the same weight as the sum of all the other equations, that is, $s = c\sqrt{wh}$, where c is a small number. Empirically, $c = 4$ works well for a wide range of cameras.

The approach of tabulating the inverse response q has two slight drawbacks. First of all, if the camera has a resolution of more than 8 bits, the equation system and 2D histograms will become very large. Second, the smoothness constraints will lead to straight lines in the logarithmic representation of q, that is, exponential curves in the normal representation of q in the range of gray values that is not covered by the images. Therefore, sometimes it may be preferable to model the inverse response as a polynomial, for example, as in [5]. This model also leads to linear equations for the coefficients of the polynomial. Since polynomials are not very robust in the extrapolation into areas in which no constraints exist, we also have to add smoothness constraints in this case by requiring that the second derivative of the polynomial is small. Because this is done in the original representation of q, the smoothness constraints will extrapolate straight lines into the gray value range that is not covered.

Let us now consider two cameras: one with a linear response, and one with a strong gamma response, that is, with a small γ in equation (9.6), and hence with a large γ in the inverse response q. Figure 9.5 displays the 2D histograms of two images taken with either camera with an exposure ratio of 0.5. Note that in both cases the values in the 2D histogram correspond to a line. The only difference is the slope of the line. A different slope, however, could also be caused by a different exposure ratio. Hence, we can see that it is quite important to know the exposure ratios precisely if we want to perform the radiometric calibration.

To conclude this section, we give two examples of the radiometric calibration. The first camera is a linear camera. Here, five images were acquired with exposure times of 32, 16, 8, 4, and 2 ms, as shown in Figure 9.6a. The calibrated

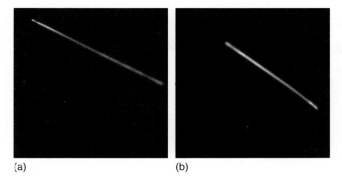

(a) (b)

Figure 9.5 (a) Two-dimensional histogram of two images taken with an exposure ratio of 0.5 with a linear camera. (b) Two-dimensional histogram of two images taken with an exposure ratio of 0.5 with a camera with a strong gamma response curve. For better visualization, the 2D histograms are displayed with a square root LUT. Note that in both cases the values in the 2D histogram correspond to a line. Hence, linear responses cannot be distinguished from gamma responses without knowing the exact exposure ratio.

inverse response curve is shown in Figure 9.6b. Note that the response is linear, but the camera has set a slight offset in the amplifier, which prevents very small gray values from being assumed. The second camera is a camera with a gamma response. In this case, six images were taken with exposure times of 30, 20, 10, 5, 2.5, and 1.25 ms, as shown in Figure 9.6c. The calibrated inverse response curve is shown in Figure 9.6d. Note the strong gamma response of the camera. The 2D histograms in Figure 9.5 were computed from the second and third brightest images in both sequences.

9.2.3 Image Smoothing

Every image contains some degree of noise. For the purposes of this chapter, noise can be regarded as random changes in the gray values, which occur for various reasons, for example, because of the randomness of the photon flux. In most cases, the noise in the image will need to be suppressed by using image smoothing operators.

In a more formalized manner, noise can be regarded as a stationary stochastic process [6]. This means that the true gray value $g_{r,c}$ is disturbed by noise $n_{r,c}$ to get the observed gray value: $\hat{g}_{r,c} = g_{r,c} + n_{r,c}$. We can regard the noise $n_{r,c}$ as a random variable with mean 0 and variance σ^2 for every pixel. We can assume a mean of 0 for the noise because any mean different from 0 would constitute a systematic bias of the observed gray values, which we could not detect anyway. "Stationary" means that the noise does not depend on the position in the image, that is, it is identically distributed for each pixel. In particular, σ^2 is assumed constant throughout the image. The last assumption is a convenient abstraction that does not necessarily hold because the variance of the noise sometimes depends on the gray values in the image. However, we will assume that the noise is always stationary.

Figure 9.7 shows an image of an edge from a real application. The noise is clearly visible in the bright patch in Figure 9.7a and in the horizontal gray value profile

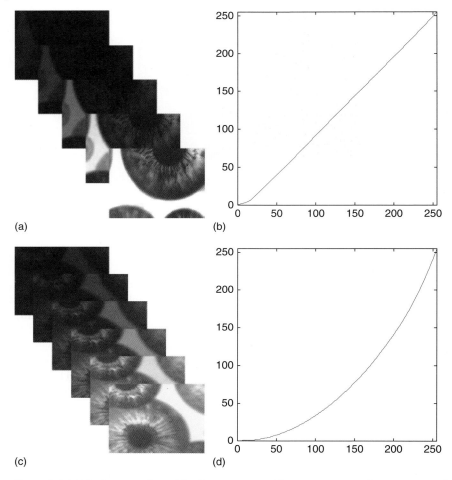

Figure 9.6 (a) Five images taken with a linear camera with exposure times of 32, 16, 8, 4, and 2 ms. (b) Calibrated inverse response curve. Note that the response is linear, but the camera has set a slight offset in the amplifier, which prevents very small gray values from being assumed. (c) Six images taken with a camera with a gamma response with exposure times of 30, 20, 10, 5, 2.5, and 1.25 ms. (d) Calibrated inverse response curve. Note the strong gamma response of the camera.

in Figure 9.7b. Figure 9.7c,d shows the actual noise in the image. How the noise has been calculated is explained below. It can be seen that there is slightly more noise in the dark patch of the image.

With the above discussion in mind, noise suppression can be regarded as a stochastic estimation problem, that is, given the observed noisy gray values $\hat{g}_{r,c}$, we want to estimate the true gray values $g_{r,c}$. An obvious method to reduce the noise is to acquire multiple images of the same scene and to simply average these images. Since the images are taken at different times, we will refer to this method as temporal averaging or the temporal mean. If we acquire n images, the temporal

9.2 Image Enhancement

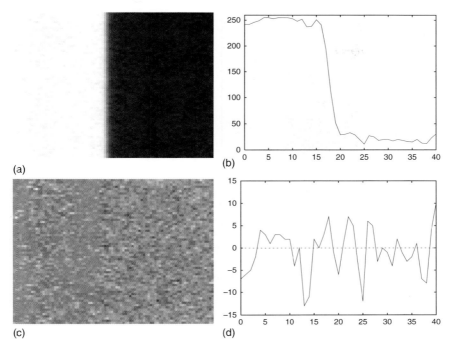

Figure 9.7 (a)Image of an edge. (b) Horizontal gray value profile through the center of the image. (c) Noise in (a) scaled by a factor of 5. (d) Horizontal gray value profile of the noise.

average is given by

$$g_{r,c} = \frac{1}{n} \sum_{i=1}^{n} \hat{g}_{r,c;i} \qquad (9.13)$$

where $\hat{g}_{r,c;i}$ denotes the noisy gray value at position (r, c) in image i. This approach is frequently used in X-ray inspection systems, which inherently produce quite noisy images. From probability theory [6], we know that the variance of the noise is reduced by a factor of n by this estimation: $\sigma_m^2 = \sigma^2/n$. Consequently, the standard deviation of the noise is reduced by a factor of $\sqrt{n}$. Figure 9.8 shows the result of acquiring 20 images of an edge and computing the temporal average. Compared to Figure 9.7a, which shows one of the 20 images, the noise has been reduced by a factor of $\sqrt{20} \approx 4.5$, as can be seen from Figure 9.8b. Since this temporally averaged image is a very good estimate for the true gray values, we can subtract it from any of the images that were used in the averaging to obtain the noise in that image. This is how the image in Figure 9.7c was computed.

One of the drawbacks of the temporal averaging is that we have to acquire multiple images to reduce the noise. This is not very attractive if the speed of the application is important. Therefore, other means for reducing the noise are required in most cases. Ideally, we would like to use only one image to estimate the true gray value. If we turn to the theory of stochastic processes again, we see that the temporal averaging can be replaced with a spatial averaging if the

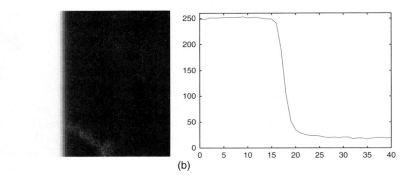

(a) (b)

Figure 9.8 (a) Image of an edge obtained by averaging 20 images of the edge. (b) Horizontal gray value profile through the center of the image.

stochastic process, that is, the image, is ergodic [6]. This is precisely the definition of ergodicity, and we will assume for the moment that it holds for our images. Then, the spatial average or spatial mean can be computed over a window (also called mask) of $(2n + 1) \times (2m + 1)$ pixels as follows:

$$g_{r,c} = \frac{1}{(2n+1)(2m+1)} \sum_{i=-n}^{n} \sum_{j=-m}^{m} \hat{g}_{r-i,c-j} \qquad (9.14)$$

This spatial averaging operation is also called a mean filter. Like in the case of temporal averaging, the noise variance is reduced by a factor that corresponds to the number of measurements that are used to calculate the average, that is, by $(2n + 1)(2m + 1)$. Figure 9.9 shows the result of smoothing the image of Figure 9.7 with a 5×5 mean filter. The standard deviation of the noise is reduced by a factor of 5, which is approximately the same as the temporal averaging in Figure 9.8. However, we can see that the edge is no longer as sharp as with temporal averaging. This happens, of course, because the images are not ergodic in general, but are only in areas of constant intensity. Therefore, in contrast to the temporal mean, the spatial mean filter blurs edges.

In equation (9.14), we have ignored the fact that the image has a finite extent. Therefore, if the mask is close to the image border, it will partially stick out of the

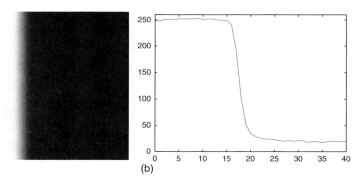

(a) (b)

Figure 9.9 (a) Image of an edge obtained by smoothing the image of Figure 9.7a with a 5×5 mean filter. (b) Horizontal gray value profile through the center of the image.

image, and consequently will access undefined gray values. To solve this problem, several approaches are possible. A very simple approach is to calculate the filter only for pixels for which the mask lies completely within the image. This means that the output image is smaller than the input image, which is not very helpful if multiple filtering operations are applied in sequence. We could also define that the gray values outside the image are 0. For the mean filter, this would mean that the result of the filter would become progressively darker as the pixels get closer to the image border. This is also not desirable. Another approach would be to use the closest gray value on the image border for pixels outside the image. This approach would still create unwanted edges at the image border. Therefore, typically the gray values are mirrored at the image border. This creates the least amount of artifacts in the result.

As was mentioned earlier, noise reduction from a single image is preferable for reasons of speed. Therefore, let us take a look at the number of operations involved in the calculation of the mean filter. If the mean filter is implemented based on equation (9.14), the number of operations will be $(2n+1)(2m+1)$ for each pixel in the image, that is, the calculation will have the complexity $O(whmn)$, where w and h are the width and height of the image, respectively. For $w = 640$, $h = 480$, and $m = n = 5$ (i.e., an 11×11 filter), the algorithm will perform 37 171 200 additions and 307 200 divisions. This is quite a substantial number of operations, so we should try to reduce the operation count as much as possible. One way to do this is to use the associative law of addition of real numbers as follows:

$$g_{r,c} = \frac{1}{(2n+1)(2m+1)} \sum_{i=-n}^{n} \left(\sum_{j=-m}^{m} \hat{g}_{r-i,c-j} \right) \qquad (9.15)$$

This may seem like a trivial observation, but if we look closer we can see that the term in parentheses only needs to be computed once and can be stored, for example, in a temporary image. Effectively, this means that we are first computing the sums in the column direction of the input image, save them in a temporary image, and then compute the sums in the row direction of the temporary image. Hence, the double sum in equation (9.14) of complexity $O(nm)$ is replaced by two sums of total complexity $O(n+m)$. Consequently, the complexity drops from $O(whmn)$ to $O(wh(m+n))$. With the above numbers, now only 6 758 400 additions are required. The above transformation is so important that it has its own name. Whenever a filter calculation allows a decomposition into separate row and column sums, the filter is called separable. It is obviously of great advantage if a filter is separable, and it is often the best speed improvement that can be achieved. In this case, however, it is not the best we can do. Let us take a look at the column sum, that is, the part in parentheses in equation (9.15), and let the result of the column sum be denoted by $t_{r,c}$. Then, we have

$$t_{r,c} = \sum_{j=-m}^{m} \hat{g}_{r,c-j} = t_{r,c-1} + \hat{g}_{r,c+m} - \hat{g}_{r,c-m-1} \qquad (9.16)$$

That is, the sum at position (r, c) can be computed based on the already computed sum at position $(r, c-1)$ with just two additions. The same holds, of course, also for the row sums. The result of this is that we need to compute the complete sum only once for the first column or row, and can then update it very efficiently. With this, the total complexity is $O(wh)$. Note that the mask size does not influence the runtime in this implementation. Again, since this kind of transformation is so important, it has a special name. Whenever a filter can be implemented with this kind of updating scheme based on previously computed values, it is called a recursive filter. For the above example, the mean filter requires just 1 238 880 additions for the entire image. This is more than a factor of 30 faster for this example than the naive implementation based on equation (9.14). Of course, the advantage becomes even bigger for larger mask sizes.

In the above discussion, we have called the process of spatial averaging a mean filter without defining what is meant by the word "filter." We can define a filter as an operation that takes a function as input and produces a function as output. Since images can be regarded as functions (see Section 9.1.1), for our purposes a filter transforms an image into another image.

The mean filter is an instance of a linear filter. Linear filters are characterized by the following property: applying a filter to a linear combination of two input images yields the same result as applying the filter to the two images and then computing the linear combination. If we denote the linear filter by h, and the two images by f and g, we have

$$h\{af(p) + bg(p)\} = ah\{f(p)\} + bh\{g(p)\} \tag{9.17}$$

where $p = (r, c)$ denotes a point in the image and the $\{\ \}$ operator denotes the application of the filter. Linear filters can be computed by a convolution. For a one-dimensional (1D) function on a continuous domain, the convolution is given by

$$f * h = (f * h)(x) = \int_{-\infty}^{\infty} f(t)\, h(x - t)\, dt \tag{9.18}$$

Here, f is the image function and the filter h is specified by another function called the convolution kernel or the filter mask. Similarly, for 2D functions we have

$$f * h = (f * h)(r, c) = \int_{-\infty}^{\infty} \int_{-\infty}^{\infty} f(u, v)\, h(r - u, c - v)\, du\, dv \tag{9.19}$$

For functions with discrete domains, the integrals are replaced by sums:

$$f * h = \sum_{i=-\infty}^{\infty} \sum_{j=-\infty}^{\infty} f_{i,j}\, h_{r-i, c-j} \tag{9.20}$$

The integrals and sums are formally taken over an infinite domain. Of course, to be able to compute the convolution in a finite amount of time, the filter $h_{r,c}$ must be 0 for sufficiently large r and c. For example, the mean filter is given by

$$h_{r,c} = \begin{cases} \dfrac{1}{(2n+1)(2m+1)}, & |r| \leq n \land |c| \leq m \\ 0, & \text{otherwise} \end{cases} \tag{9.21}$$

The notion of separability can be extended for arbitrary, linear filters. If $h(r, c)$ can be decomposed as $h(r, c) = s(r)t(c)$ (or as $h_{r,c} = s_r t_c$), then h is called separable. As for the mean filter, we can factor out s in this case to get a more efficient implementation:

$$f * h = \sum_{i=-n}^{n} \sum_{j=-n}^{n} f_{i,j}\, h_{r-i,c-j} = \sum_{i=-n}^{n} \sum_{j=-n}^{n} f_{i,j}\, s_{r-i}\, t_{c-j}$$
$$= \sum_{i=-n}^{n} s_{r-i} \left(\sum_{j=-n}^{n} f_{i,j}\, t_{c-j} \right)$$
(9.22)

Obviously, separable filters have the same speed advantage as the separable implementation of the mean filter. Therefore, separable filters are preferred over nonseparable filters. There is also a definition for recursive linear filters, which we cannot cover in detail. The interested reader is referred to [7]. Recursive linear filters have the same speed advantage as the recursive implementation of the mean filter, that is, the runtime does not depend on the filter size. Unfortunately, many interesting filters cannot be implemented as recursive filters. Usually they can only be approximated by a recursive filter.

Although the mean filter produces good results, it is not the optimum smoothing filter. To see this, we can note that noise primarily manifests itself as high-frequency fluctuations of the gray values in the image. Ideally, we would like a smoothing filter to remove these high-frequency fluctuations. To see how well the mean filter performs this task, we can examine how the mean filter responds to certain frequencies in the image. The theory of how to do this is provided by the Fourier transform (see Section 9.2.4). Figure 9.10a shows the frequency response of a 3×3 mean filter. In this plot, the row and column coordinates of 0 correspond to a frequency of 0, which represents the medium gray value in the image, while the row and column coordinates of ± 0.5 represent the highest possible frequencies in the image. For example, the frequencies

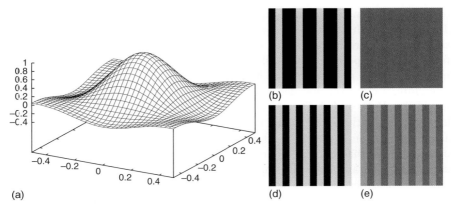

Figure 9.10 (a) Frequency response of the 3×3 mean filter. (b) Image with one-pixel-wide lines spaced three pixels apart. (c) Result of applying the 3×3 mean filter to the image in (b). Note that all the lines have been smoothed out. (d) Image with one-pixel-wide lines spaced two pixels apart. (e) Result of applying the 3×3 mean filter to the image in (d). Note that the lines have not been completely smoothed out, although they have a higher frequency than the lines in (b). Note also that the polarity of the lines has been reversed.

with column coordinate 0 and row coordinate ±0.5 correspond to a grid with alternating one-pixel-wide vertical bright and dark lines. From Figure 9.10a, we can see that the 3 × 3 mean filter removes certain frequencies completely. These are the points for which the response has a value of 0. They occur for relatively high frequencies. However, we can also see that the highest frequencies are not removed completely. To illustrate this, Figure 9.10b shows an image with one-pixel-wide lines spaced three pixels apart. From Figure 9.10c, we can see that this frequency is completely removed by the 3 × 3 mean filter: the output image has a constant gray value. If we change the spacing of the lines to two pixels, as in Figure 9.10d, we can see from Figure 9.10e that this higher frequency is not removed completely. This is an undesirable behavior since it means that noise is not removed completely by the mean filter. Note also that the polarity of the lines has been reversed by the mean filter, which is also undesirable. This is caused by the negative parts of the frequency response. Furthermore, from Figure 9.10a we can see that the frequency response of the mean filter is not rotationally symmetric, that is, it is anisotropic. This means that diagonal structures are smoothed differently than horizontal or vertical structures.

Because the mean filter has the above drawbacks, the question of which smoothing filter is optimal arises. One way to approach this problem is to define certain natural criteria that the smoothing filter should fulfill, and then to search for the filters that fulfill the desired criteria. The first natural criterion is that the filter should be linear. This is natural because we can imagine an image being composed of multiple objects in an additive manner. Hence, the filter output should be a linear combination of the input. Furthermore, the filter should be position-invariant, that is, it should produce the same results no matter where an object is in the image. This is automatically fulfilled for linear filters. Also, we would like the filter to be rotation-invariant, that is, isotropic, so that it produces the same result independent of the orientation of the objects in the image. As we saw previously, the mean filter does not fulfill this criterion. We would also like to control the amount of smoothing (noise reduction) that is being performed. Therefore, the filter should have a parameter t that can be used to control the smoothing, where higher values of t indicate more smoothing. For the mean filter, this corresponds to the mask sizes m and n. We have already seen that the mean filter does not suppress all high frequencies, that is, noise, in the image. Therefore, a criterion that describes the noise suppression of the filter in the image should be added. One such criterion is that, the larger t gets, the more local maxima in the image should be eliminated. This is a very intuitive criterion, as can be seen in Figure 9.7a, where many local maxima due to noise can be detected. Note that, because of linearity, we only need to require maxima to be eliminated. This automatically implies that local minima are eliminated as well. Finally, sometimes we would like to execute the smoothing filter several times in succession. If we do this, we would also have a simple means to predict the result of the combined filtering. Therefore, first filtering with t and then with s should be identical to a single filter operation with $t + s$. It can be shown that, among all smoothing filters, the Gaussian filter is the only one that fulfills all of the above criteria [8]. Other natural criteria for a smoothing filter have been proposed [9–11], which also single out the Gaussian filter as the optimal smoothing filter.

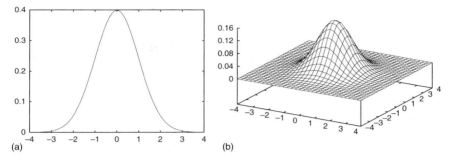

Figure 9.11 (a) One-dimensional Gaussian filter with $\sigma = 1$. (b) Two-dimensional Gaussian filter with $\sigma = 1$.

In one dimension, the Gaussian filter is given by

$$g_\sigma(x) = \frac{1}{\sqrt{2\pi}\sigma} e^{-x^2/(2\sigma^2)} \tag{9.23}$$

This is the function that also defines the probability density of a normally distributed random variable. In two dimensions, the Gaussian filter is given by

$$g_\sigma(r,c) = \frac{1}{2\pi\sigma^2} e^{-(r^2+c^2)/(2\sigma^2)} = \frac{1}{\sqrt{2\pi}\sigma} e^{-r^2/(2\sigma^2)} \frac{1}{\sqrt{2\pi}\sigma} e^{-c^2/(2\sigma^2)} \tag{9.24}$$
$$= g_\sigma(r)g_\sigma(c)$$

Hence, the Gaussian filter is separable. Therefore, it can be computed very efficiently. In fact, it is the only isotropic, separable smoothing filter. Unfortunately, it cannot be implemented recursively. However, some recursive approximations have been proposed [12, 13]. Figure 9.11 shows plots of the 1D and 2D Gaussian filters with $\sigma = 1$. The frequency response of a Gaussian filter is also a Gaussian function, albeit with σ inverted. Therefore, Figure 9.11b also gives a qualitative impression of the frequency response of the Gaussian filter. It can be seen that the Gaussian filter suppresses high frequencies much better than the mean filter.

Like the mean filter, any linear filter will change the variance of the noise in the image. It can be shown that, for a linear filter $h(r, c)$ or $h_{r,c}$, the noise variance is multiplied by the following factor [6]:

$$\int_{-\infty}^{\infty}\int_{-\infty}^{\infty} h(r,c)^2 \, dr \, dc \quad \text{or} \quad \sum_{i=-\infty}^{\infty}\sum_{j=-\infty}^{\infty} h_{r,c}^2 \tag{9.25}$$

For a Gaussian filter, this factor is $1/(4\pi\sigma^2)$. If we compare this to a mean filter with a square mask with parameter n, we see that, to get the same noise reduction with the Gaussian filter, we need to set $\sigma = (2n+1)/(2\sqrt{\pi})$. For example, a 5×5 mean filter has the same noise reduction effect as a Gaussian filter with $\sigma \approx 1.41$.

Figure 9.12 compares the results of the Gaussian filter with those of the mean filter of an equivalent size. For small filter sizes ($\sigma = 1.41$ and 5×5), there is hardly any noticeable difference between the results. However, if larger filter sizes are used, it becomes clear that the mean filter turns the edge into a ramp, leading to a badly defined edge that is also visually quite hard to locate, whereas the

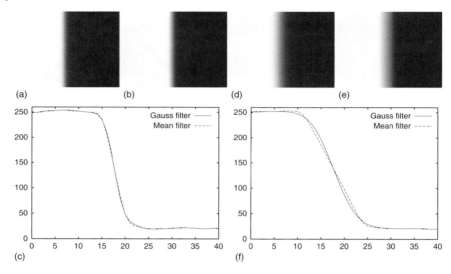

Figure 9.12 Images of an edge obtained by smoothing the image of Figure 9.7a. Results of (a) a Gaussian filter with $\sigma = 1.41$ and (b) a mean filter of size 5×5; and (c) the corresponding gray value profiles. Note that the two filters return very similar results in this example. Results of (d) a Gaussian filter with $\sigma = 3.67$ and (e) a 13×13 mean filter; and (f) the corresponding profiles. Note that the mean filter turns the edge into a ramp, leading to a badly defined edge, whereas the Gaussian filter produces a much sharper edge.

Gaussian filter produces a much sharper edge. Hence, we can see that the Gaussian filter produces better results, and consequently it is usually the preferred smoothing filter if the quality of the results is the primary concern. If speed is the primary concern, then the mean filter is preferable.

We close this section with a nonlinear filter that can also be used for noise suppression. The mean filter is a particular estimator for the mean value of a sample of random values. From probability theory, we know that other estimators are also possible, most notably the median of the samples. The median is defined as the value for which 50% of the values in the probability distribution of the samples are smaller than the median and 50% are larger. From a practical point of view, if the sample set contains n values g_i, $i = 0, \ldots, n - 1$, we sort the values g_i in ascending order to get s_i, and then select the value median $(g_i) = s_{n/2}$. Hence, we can obtain a median filter by calculating the median instead of the mean inside a window around the current pixel. Let W denote the window, for example, a $(2n + 1) \times (2m + 1)$ rectangle as for the mean filter. Then the median filter is given by

$$g_{r,c} = \underset{(i,j) \in W}{\text{median}}\, \hat{g}_{r-i,c-j} \tag{9.26}$$

With sophisticated algorithms, it is possible to obtain a runtime complexity (even for arbitrary mask shapes) that is comparable to that of a separable linear filter: $O(whm)$, where m is the number of horizontal boundary pixels of the mask, that is, the pixels that are at the left or right border of a run of pixels in the

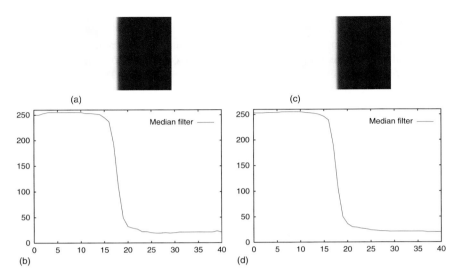

Figure 9.13 Images of an edge obtained by smoothing the image of Figure 9.7a. (a) Result with a median filter of size 5 × 5, and (b) the corresponding gray value profile. (c) Result of a 13 × 13 median filter, and (d) the corresponding profile. Note that the median filter preserves the sharpness of the edge to a great extent.

mask [14, 15]. For rectangular masks, it is possible to construct an algorithm with constant runtime per pixel (analogous to a recursive implementation of a linear filter) [16]. The properties of the median filter are quite difficult to analyze. We can note, however, that it performs no averaging of the input gray values, but simply selects one of them. This can lead to surprising results. For example, the result of applying a 3 × 3 median filter to the image in Figure 9.10b would be a completely black image. Hence, the median filter would remove the bright lines because they cover less than 50% of the window. This property can sometimes be used to remove objects completely from the image. On the other hand, applying a 3 × 3 median filter to the image in Figure 9.10d would swap the bright and dark lines. This result is as undesirable as the result of the mean filter on the same image. On the edge image of Figure 9.7a, the median filter produces quite good results, as can be seen from Figure 9.13. In particular, it should be noted that the median filter preserves the sharpness of the edge even for large filter sizes. However, it cannot be predicted if and how much the position of the edge is changed by the median filter, which is possible for the linear filters. Furthermore, we cannot estimate how much noise is removed by the median filter, in contrast to the linear filters. Therefore, for high-accuracy measurements the Gaussian filter should be used.

Finally, it should be mentioned that the median filter is a special case of the more general class of rank filters. Instead of selecting the median $s_{n/2}$ of the sorted gray values, the rank filter would select the sorted gray value at a particular rank r, that is, s_r. We will see other cases of rank operators in Section 9.6.2.

9.2.4 Fourier Transform

In the previous section, we considered the frequency responses of the mean and Gaussian filters. In this section, we will take a look at the theory that is used to derive the frequency response: the Fourier transform [17, 18]. The Fourier transform of a 1D function $h(x)$ is given by

$$H(f) = \int_{-\infty}^{\infty} h(x) e^{2\pi i f x}\, dx \qquad (9.27)$$

It transforms the function $h(x)$ from the spatial domain into the frequency domain: that is, $h(x)$, a function of the position x, is transformed into $H(f)$, a function of the frequency f. Note that $H(f)$ is in general a complex number. Because of equation (9.27) and the identity $e^{ix} = \cos x + i \sin x$, we can think of $h(x)$ as being composed of sine and cosine waves of different frequencies and different amplitudes. Then $H(f)$ describes precisely which frequency occurs with which amplitude and with which phase (overlaying sine and cosine terms of the same frequency simply leads to a phase-shifted sine wave). The inverse Fourier transform from the frequency domain to the spatial domain is given by

$$h(x) = \int_{-\infty}^{\infty} H(f)\, e^{-2\pi i f x}\, df \qquad (9.28)$$

Because the Fourier transform is invertible, it is best to think of $h(x)$ and $H(f)$ as being two different representations of the same function.

In two dimensions, the Fourier transform and its inverse are given by

$$H(u,v) = \int_{-\infty}^{\infty}\int_{-\infty}^{\infty} h(r,c)\, e^{2\pi i(ur+vc)}\, dr\, dc$$

$$h(r,c) = \int_{-\infty}^{\infty}\int_{-\infty}^{\infty} H(u,v)\, e^{-2\pi i(ur+vc)}\, du\, dv \qquad (9.29)$$

In image processing, $h(r,c)$ is an image, for which the position (r,c) is given in pixels. Consequently, the frequencies (u,v) are given in cycles per pixel.

Among the many interesting properties of the Fourier transform, probably the most interesting one is that a convolution in the spatial domain is transformed into a simple multiplication in the frequency domain: $(g * h)(r,c) \Leftrightarrow G(u,v)H(u,v)$, where the convolution is given by equation (9.19). Hence, a convolution can be performed by transforming the image and the filter into the frequency domain, multiplying the two results, and transforming the result back into the spatial domain.

Note that the convolution attenuates the frequency content $G(u,v)$ of the image $g(r,c)$ by the frequency response $H(u,v)$ of the filter. This justifies the analysis of the smoothing behavior of the mean and Gaussian filters that we have performed in Section 9.2.3. To make this analysis more precise, we can compute the Fourier transform of the mean filter in equation (9.21). It is given by

$$H(u,v) = \frac{1}{(2n+1)(2m+1)} \operatorname{sinc}((2n+1)u)\operatorname{sinc}((2m+1)v) \qquad (9.30)$$

where sinc $x = (\sin \pi x)/(\pi x)$. See Figure 9.10 for a plot of the response of the 3×3 mean filter. Similarly, the Fourier transform of the Gaussian filter in equation (9.24) is given by

$$H(u,v) = e^{-2\pi^2 \sigma^2 (u^2 + v^2)} \tag{9.31}$$

Hence, the Fourier transform of the Gaussian filter is again a Gaussian function, albeit with σ inverted. Note that, in both cases, the frequency response becomes narrower if the filter size is increased. This is a relation that holds in general: $h(x/a) \Leftrightarrow |a| H(af)$.

Another interesting property of the Fourier transform is that it can be used to compute the correlation

$$g \star h = (g \star h)(r, c) = \int_{-\infty}^{\infty} \int_{-\infty}^{\infty} g(r+u, c+v)\, h(u,v)\, du\, dv \tag{9.32}$$

Note that the correlation is very similar to the convolution in equation (9.19). The correlation is given in the frequency domain by $(g \star h)(r,c) \Leftrightarrow G(u,v) H(-u,-v)$. If $h(r,c)$ contains real numbers, which is the case for image processing, then $H(-u,-v) = \overline{H(u,v)}$, where the bar denotes complex conjugation. Hence, $(g \star h)(r,c) \Leftrightarrow G(u,v)\overline{H(u,v)}$.

Up to now, we have assumed that the images are continuous. Real images are, of course, discrete. This trivial observation has profound implications for the result of the Fourier transform. As noted above, the frequency variables u and v are given in cycles per pixel. If a discrete image $h(r,c)$ is transformed, the highest possible frequency for any sine or cosine wave is $1/2$, that is, one cycle per two pixels. The frequency $1/2$ is called the Nyquist critical frequency. Sine or cosine waves with higher frequencies look like sine or cosine waves with correspondingly lower frequencies. For example, a discrete cosine wave with frequency 0.75 looks exactly like a cosine wave with frequency 0.25, as shown in Figure 9.14. Effectively, values of $H(u,v)$ outside the square $[-0.5, 0.5] \times [-0.5, 0.5]$ are mapped to this square by repeated mirroring at the borders of the square. This effect is known as *aliasing*. To avoid aliasing, we must ensure that frequencies higher than the Nyquist critical frequency are removed before the image is

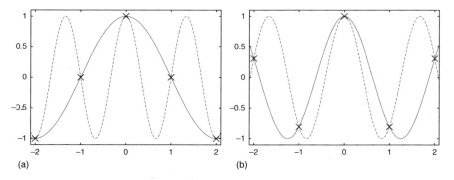

Figure 9.14 Example of aliasing. (a) Two cosine waves, one with a frequency of 0.25 and the other with a frequency of 0.75. (b) Two cosine waves, one with a frequency of 0.4 and the other with a frequency of 0.6. Note that if both functions are sampled at integer positions, denoted by the crosses, the discrete samples will be identical.

sampled. During the image acquisition, this can be achieved by optical low-pass filters in the camera. Aliasing, however, may also occur when an image is scaled down (see Section 9.3.3). Here, it is important to apply smoothing filters before the image is sampled at the lower resolution to ensure that frequencies above the Nyquist critical frequency are removed.

Real images are not only discrete, they are also only defined within a rectangle of dimension $w \times h$, where w is the image width and h is the image height. This means that the Fourier transform is no longer continuous, but can be sampled at discrete frequencies $u_k = k/h$ and $v_l = l/w$. As discussed previously, sampling the Fourier transform is useful only in the Nyquist interval $-1/2 \leq u_k, v_l < 1/2$. With this, the discrete Fourier transform (DFT) is given by

$$H_{k,l} = H(u_k, v_l) = \sum_{r=0}^{h-1} \sum_{c=0}^{w-1} h_{r,c} \, e^{2\pi i (u_k r + v_l c)}$$

$$= \sum_{r=0}^{h-1} \sum_{c=0}^{w-1} h_{r,c} \, e^{2\pi i (kr/h + lc/w)} \tag{9.33}$$

Analogously, the inverse DFT is given by

$$h_{r,c} = \frac{1}{wh} \sum_{k=0}^{h-1} \sum_{l=0}^{w-1} H_{k,l} \, e^{-2\pi i (kr/h + lc/w)} \tag{9.34}$$

As noted previously, conceptually, the frequencies u_k and v_l should be sampled from the interval $(-1/2, 1/2]$, that is, $k = -h/2+1, \ldots, h/2$ and $l = -w/2+1, \ldots, w/2$. Since we want to represent $H_{k,l}$ as an image, the negative coordinates are a little cumbersome. It is easy to see that equations (9.33) and (9.34) are periodic with period h and w. Therefore, we can map the negative frequencies to their positive counterparts: that is, $k = -h/2+1, \ldots, -1$ is mapped to $k = h/2+1, \ldots, h-1$; and likewise for l.

We noted previously that for real images, $H(-u, -v) = \overline{H(u, v)}$. This property still holds for the DFT, with the appropriate change of coordinates as defined above, that is, $H_{h-k, w-l} = \overline{H_{k,l}}$ (for $k, l > 0$). In practice, this means that we do not need to compute and store the complete Fourier transform $H_{k,l}$ because it contains redundant information. It is sufficient to compute and store one half of $H_{k,l}$, for example, the left half. This saves a considerable amount of processing time and memory. This type of Fourier transform is called the real-valued Fourier transform.

To compute the Fourier transform from equations (9.33) and (9.34), it might seem that $O((wh)^2)$ operations are required. This would prevent the Fourier transform from being useful in image processing applications. Fortunately, the Fourier transform can be computed in $O(wh \log (wh))$ operations for $w = 2^n$ and $h = 2^m$ [18] as well as for arbitrary w and h [19]. This fast computation algorithm for the Fourier transform is aptly called the fast Fourier transform (FFT). With self-tuning algorithms [19], the FFT can be computed in real time on standard processors.

As discussed previously, the Fourier transform can be used to compute the convolution with any linear filter in the frequency domain. While this can be used to

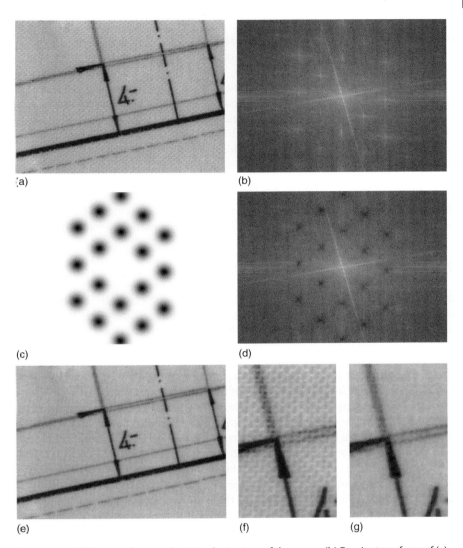

Figure 9.15 (a) Image of a map showing the texture of the paper. (b) Fourier transform of (a). Because of the high dynamic range of the result, $H_{u,v}^{1/16}$ is displayed. Note the distinct peaks in $H_{u,v}$, which correspond to the texture of the paper. (c) Filter $G_{u,v}$ used to remove the frequencies that correspond to the texture. (d) Convolution $H_{u,v}G_{u,v}$. (e) Inverse Fourier transform of (d). (f, g) Detail of (a) and (e), respectively. Note that the texture has been removed.

perform filtering with standard filter masks, for example, the mean or Gaussian filter, typically there is a speed advantage only for relatively large filter masks. The real advantage of using the Fourier transform for filtering lies in the fact that filters can be customized to remove specific frequencies from the image, which occur, for example, for repetitive textures.

Figure 9.15a shows an image of a map. The map is drawn on a highly structured paper that exhibits significant texture. The texture makes the extraction of the data in the map difficult. Figure 9.15b displays the Fourier transform $H_{u,v}$. Note that the Fourier transform is cyclically shifted so that the zero frequency is in the center of the image to show the structure of the data more clearly. Hence, Figure 9.15b displays the frequencies u_k and v_l for $k = -h/2 + 1, \ldots, h/2$ and $l = -w/2 + 1, \ldots, w/2$. Because of the high dynamic range of the result, $H_{u,v}^{1/16}$ is displayed. It can be seen that $H_{u,v}$ contains several highly significant peaks that correspond to the characteristic frequencies of the texture. Furthermore, there are two significant orthogonal lines that correspond to the lines in the map. A filter $G_{u,v}$ that removes the characteristic frequencies of the texture is shown in Figure 9.15c, while the result of the convolution $H_{u,v}G_{u,v}$ in the frequency domain is shown in Figure 9.15d. The result of the inverse Fourier transform, that is, the convolution in the spatial domain, is shown in Figure 9.15e. Figure 9.15f,g shows details of the input and result images, which show that the texture of the paper has been removed. Thus, it is now very easy to extract the map data from the image.

9.3 Geometric Transformations

In many applications, one cannot ensure that the objects to be inspected are always in the same position and orientation in the image. Therefore, the inspection algorithm must be able to cope with these position changes. Hence, one of the problems is to detect the position and orientation, also called the pose, of the objects to be examined. This will be the subject of later sections of this chapter. For the purposes of this section, we assume that we know the pose already. In this case, the simplest procedure to adapt the inspection to a particular pose is to align the ROIs appropriately. For example, if we know that an object is rotated by 45°, we could simply rotate the ROI by 45° before performing the inspection. In some cases, however, the image must be transformed (aligned) to a standard pose before the inspection can be performed. For example, the segmentation of the OCR is much easier if the text is either horizontal or vertical. Another example is the inspection of objects for defects based on a reference image. Here, we also need to align the image of the object to the pose in the reference image, or vice versa. Therefore, in this section we will examine different geometric image transformations that are useful in practice.

9.3.1 Affine Transformations

If the position and rotation of the objects cannot be kept constant with the mechanical setup, we need to correct the rotation and translation of the object. Sometimes the distance of the object to the camera changes, leading to an apparent change in size of the object. These transformations are part of a very useful class of transformations called affine transformations, which are transformations that can be described by the following equation:

$$\begin{pmatrix} \tilde{r} \\ \tilde{c} \end{pmatrix} = \begin{pmatrix} a_{11} & a_{12} \\ a_{21} & a_{22} \end{pmatrix} \begin{pmatrix} r \\ c \end{pmatrix} + \begin{pmatrix} t_r \\ t_c \end{pmatrix} \quad (9.35)$$

Hence, an affine transformation consists of a linear part given by a 2×2 matrix and a translation. The above notation is a little cumbersome, however, since we always have to list the translation separately. To circumvent this, we can use a representation where we extend the coordinates with a third coordinate of 1, which enables us to write the transformation as a simple matrix multiplication:

$$\begin{pmatrix} \tilde{r} \\ \tilde{c} \\ 1 \end{pmatrix} = \begin{pmatrix} a_{11} & a_{12} & a_{13} \\ a_{21} & a_{22} & a_{23} \\ 0 & 0 & 1 \end{pmatrix} \begin{pmatrix} r \\ c \\ 1 \end{pmatrix} \quad (9.36)$$

Note that the translation is represented by the elements a_{13} and a_{23} of the matrix A. This representation with an added redundant third coordinate is called homogeneous coordinates. Similarly, the representation with two coordinates in equation (9.35) is called inhomogeneous coordinates. We will see the true power of the homogeneous representation below. Any affine transformation can be constructed from the following basic transformations, where the last row of the matrix has been omitted:

$$\begin{pmatrix} 1 & 0 & t_r \\ 0 & 1 & t_c \end{pmatrix} \quad \text{Translation} \quad (9.37)$$

$$\begin{pmatrix} s_r & 0 & 0 \\ 0 & s_c & 0 \end{pmatrix} \quad \text{Scaling in row and column direction} \quad (9.38)$$

$$\begin{pmatrix} \cos\alpha & -\sin\alpha & 0 \\ \sin\alpha & \cos\alpha & 0 \end{pmatrix} \quad \text{Rotation by an angle of } \alpha \quad (9.39)$$

$$\begin{pmatrix} \cos\theta & 0 & 0 \\ \sin\theta & 1 & 0 \end{pmatrix} \quad \text{Skew of row axis by an angle of } \theta \quad (9.40)$$

The first three basic transformations need no further explanation. The skew (or slant) is a rotation of only one axis, in this case the row axis. It is quite useful to rectify slanted characters in the OCR.

9.3.2 Projective Transformations

An affine transformation enables us to correct almost all relevant pose variations that an object may undergo. However, sometimes affine transformations are not general enough. If the object in question is able to rotate in three dimensions, it will undergo a general perspective transformation, which is quite hard to correct because of the occlusions that may occur. However, if the object is planar, we can model the transformation of the object by a 2D perspective transformation, which is a special 2D projective transformation [20, 21]. Projective transformations are given by

$$\begin{pmatrix} \tilde{r} \\ \tilde{c} \\ \tilde{w} \end{pmatrix} = \begin{pmatrix} h_{11} & h_{12} & h_{13} \\ h_{21} & h_{22} & h_{23} \\ h_{31} & h_{32} & h_{33} \end{pmatrix} \begin{pmatrix} r \\ c \\ w \end{pmatrix} \quad (9.41)$$

Note the similarity to the affine transformation in equation (9.36). The only changes that were made are that the transformation is now described by a full 3 × 3 matrix and that we have replaced the 1 in the third coordinate with a variable w. This representation is actually the true representation in homogeneous coordinates. It can also be used for affine transformations, which are special projective transformations. With this third coordinate, it is not obvious how we are able to obtain a transformed 2D coordinate, that is, how to compute the corresponding inhomogeneous point. First of all, it must be noted that in homogeneous coordinates all points $p = (r, c, w)^\top$ are only defined up to a scale factor, that is, the vectors p and λp ($\lambda \neq 0$) represent the same 2D point [20, 21]. Consequently, the projective transformation given by the matrix H is also defined only up to a scale factor, and hence has only eight independent parameters. To obtain an inhomogeneous 2D point from the homogeneous representation, we must divide the homogeneous vector by w. This requires $w \neq 0$. Such points are called finite points. Conversely, points with $w = 0$ are called points at infinity because they can be regarded as lying infinitely far away in a certain direction [20, 21].

Since a projective transformation has eight independent parameters, it can be uniquely determined from four corresponding points [20, 21]. This is how the projective transformations will usually be determined in machine vision applications. We will extract four points in an image, which typically represent a rectangle, and will rectify the image so that the four extracted points will be transformed to the four corners of the rectangle, that is, to their corresponding points. Unfortunately, because of space limitations we cannot give the details of how the transformation is computed from the point correspondences. The interested reader is referred to [20, 21].

9.3.3 Image Transformations

After having taken a look at how coordinates can be transformed with affine and projective transformations, we can consider how an image should be transformed. Our first idea might be to go through all the pixels in the input image, to transform their coordinates, and to set the gray value of the transformed point in the output image. Unfortunately, this simple strategy does not work. This can be seen by checking what happens if an image is scaled by a factor of 2: only one-quarter of the pixels in the output image would be set. The correct way to transform an image is to loop through all the pixels in the output image and to calculate the position of the corresponding point in the input image. This is the simplest way to ensure that all relevant pixels in the output image are set. Fortunately, calculating the positions in the original image is simple: we only need to invert the matrix that describes the affine or projective transformation, which results again in an affine or projective transformation.

When the image coordinates are transformed from the output image to the input image, typically not all pixels in the output image transform back to coordinates that lie in the input image. This can be taken into account by computing a suitable ROI for the output image. Furthermore, we see that the resulting coordinates in the input image will typically not be integer coordinates. An example of this is given in Figure 9.16, where the input image is transformed by an affine transformation consisting of a translation, rotation, and scaling. Therefore, the gray values in the output image must be interpolated.

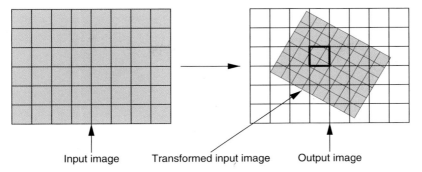

Figure 9.16 Affine transformation of an image. Note that integer coordinates in the output image transform to non-integer coordinates in the original image, and hence must be interpolated.

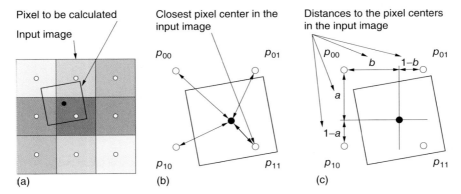

Figure 9.17 (a) A pixel in the output image is transformed back to the input image. Note that the transformed pixel center lies at a non-integer position between four adjacent pixel centers. (b) Nearest-neighbor interpolation determines the closest pixel center in the input image and uses its gray value in the output image. (c) Bilinear interpolation determines the distances to the four adjacent pixel centers and weights their gray values using the distances.

The interpolation can be done in several ways. Figure 9.17a displays a pixel in the output image that has been transformed back to the input image. Note that the transformed pixel center lies on a non-integer position between four adjacent pixel centers. The simplest and fastest interpolation method is to calculate the closest of the four adjacent pixel centers, which only involves rounding the floating-point coordinates of the transformed pixel center, and to use the gray value of the closest pixel in the input image as the gray value of the pixel in the output image, as shown in Figure 9.17b. This interpolation method is called nearest-neighbor interpolation. To see the effect of this interpolation, Figure 9.18a displays an image of a serial number of a bank note, where the characters are not horizontal. Figure 9.18c,d displays the result of rotating the image such that the serial number is horizontal using this interpolation. Note that, because the gray value is taken from the closest pixel center in the input image, the edges of the characters have a jagged appearance, which is undesirable.

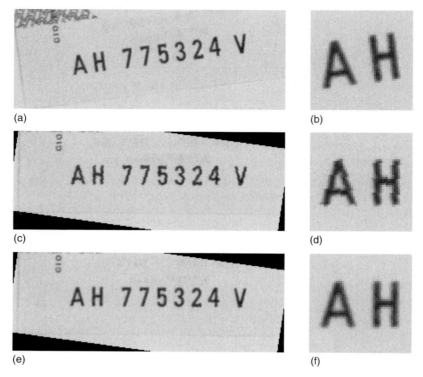

Figure 9.18 (a) Image showing a serial number of a bank note. (b) Detail of (a). (c) Image rotated such that the serial number is horizontal using nearest-neighbor interpolation. (d) Detail of (c). Note the jagged edges of the characters. (e) Image rotated using bilinear interpolation. (f) Detail of (e). Note the smooth edges of the characters.

The reason for the jagged appearance in the result of the nearest-neighbor interpolation is that essentially we are regarding the image as a piecewise constant function: every coordinate that falls within a rectangle of extent ±0.5 in each direction is assigned the same gray value. This leads to discontinuities in the result, which cause the jagged edges. This behavior is especially noticeable if the image is scaled by a factor > 1. To get a better interpolation, we can use more information than the gray value of the closest pixel. From Figure 9.17a, we can see that the transformed pixel center lies in a square of four adjacent pixel centers. Therefore, we can use the four corresponding gray values and weight them appropriately. One way to do this is to use bilinear interpolation, as shown in Figure 9.17c. First, we compute the horizontal and vertical distances of the transformed coordinate to the adjacent pixel centers. Note that these are numbers between 0 and 1. Then, we weight the gray values according to their distances to get the bilinear interpolation:

$$\tilde{g} = b(ag_{11} + (1-a)g_{01}) + (1-b)(ag_{10} + (1-a)g_{00}) \tag{9.42}$$

Figure 9.18e,f displays the result of rotating the image of Figure 9.18a using bilinear interpolation. Note that the edges of the characters now have a very smooth appearance. This much better result more than justifies the longer computation time (typically a factor of around 2).

To conclude the discussion on interpolation, we discuss the effects of scaling an image down. In the bilinear interpolation scheme, we would interpolate from the closest four pixel centers. However, if the image is scaled down, adjacent pixel centers in the output image will not necessarily be close in the input image. Imagine a larger version of the image of Figure 9.10b (one-pixel-wide vertical lines spaced three pixels apart) being scaled down by a factor of 4 using nearest-neighbor interpolation: we would get an image with one-pixel-wide lines that are four pixels apart. This is certainly not what we would expect. For bilinear interpolation, we would get similar unexpected results. If we scale down an image, we are essentially subsampling it. As a consequence, we may obtain aliasing effects (see Section 9.2.4). An example of aliasing can be seen in Figure 9.19. The image in Figure 9.19a is scaled down by a factor of 3 in Figure 9.19c using bilinear interpolation. Note that the stroke widths of the vertical strokes of the letter H, which are equally wide in Figure 9.19a, now appear to be substantially different. This is undesirable. To improve the image transformation, the image

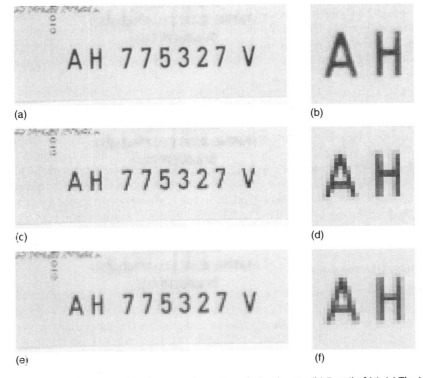

(a)　　　　　　　　　　　　　　　　　　(b)

(c)　　　　　　　　　　　　　　　　　　(d)

(e)　　　　　　　　　　　　　　　　　　(f)

Figure 9.19 (a) Image showing a serial number of a bank note. (b) Detail of (a). (c) The image of (a) scaled down by a factor of 3 using bilinear interpolation. (d) Detail of (c). Note the different stroke widths of the vertical strokes of the letter H. This is caused by aliasing. (e) Result of scaling the image down by integrating a smoothing filter (in this case a mean filter) into the image transformation. (f) Detail of (e).

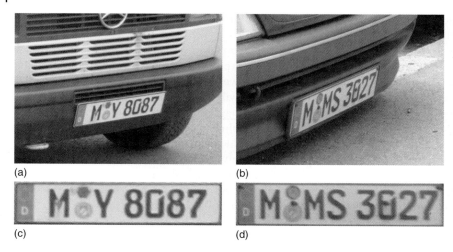

Figure 9.20 (a,b) Images of license plates. (c,d) Result of a projective transformation that rectifies the perspective distortion of the license plates.

must be smoothed before it is scaled down, for example, using a mean or a Gaussian filter. Alternatively, the smoothing can be integrated into the gray value interpolation. Figure 9.19e shows the result of integrating a mean filter into the image transformation. Because of the smoothing, the strokes of the H now have the same width again.

In the above examples, we have seen the usefulness of the affine transformations for rectifying text. Sometimes, an affine transformation is not sufficient for this purpose. Figure 9.20a,b shows two images of license plates on cars. Because the position of the camera with respect to the car could not be controlled in this example, the images of the license plates show severe perspective distortions. Figure 9.20c,d shows the result of applying projective transformations to the images that cut out the license plates and rectify them. Hence, the images in Figure 9.20c,d would result if we had looked at the license plates perpendicularly from in front of the car. Obviously, it is now much easier to segment and read the characters on the license plates.

9.3.4 Polar Transformations

We conclude this section with another very useful geometric transformation: the polar transformation. This transformation is typically used to rectify parts of images that show objects that are circular or that are contained in circular rings in the image. An example is shown in Figure 9.21a. Here, we can see the inner part of a CD that contains a ring with a bar code and some text. To read the bar code, one solution is to rectify the part of the image that contains the bar code. For this purpose, the polar transformation can be used, which converts the image into polar coordinates (d, ϕ), that is, into the distance d to the center of the transformation and the angle ϕ of the vector to the center of the transformation. Let the center of the transformation be given by (m_r, m_c). Then, the polar coordinates

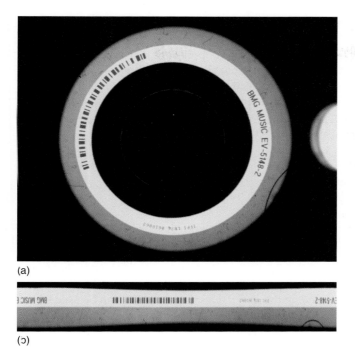

Figure 9.21 (a) Image of the center of a CD showing a circular bar code. (b) Polar transformation of the ring that contains the bar code. Note that the bar code is now straight and horizontal.

of a point (r, c) are given by

$$d = \sqrt{(r - m_r)^2 + (c - m_c)^2}$$
$$\phi = \arctan\left(-\frac{r - m_r}{c - m_c}\right) \quad (9.43)$$

In the calculation of the arc tangent function, the correct quadrant must be used, based on the sign of the two terms in the fraction in the argument of arctan. Note that the transformation of a point into polar coordinates is quite expensive to compute because of the square root and the arc tangent. Fortunately, to transform an image, like for affine and projective transformations, the inverse of the polar transformation is used, which is given by

$$r = m_r - d \sin \phi$$
$$c = m_c + d \cos \phi \quad (9.44)$$

Here, the sines and cosines can be tabulated because they only occur for a finite number of discrete values, and hence only need to be computed once. Therefore, the polar transformation of an image can be computed efficiently. Note that by restricting the ranges of d and ϕ, we can transform arbitrary circular sectors. Figure 9.21b shows the result of transforming a circular ring that contains the bar code in Figure 9.21a. Note that because of the polar transformation the bar code is straight and horizontal, and consequently can be read easily.

9.4 Image Segmentation

In the preceding sections, we have looked at operations that transform an image into another image. These operations do not give us information about the objects in the image. For this purpose, we need to segment the image, that is, extract regions from the image that correspond to the objects we are interested in. More formally, segmentation is an operation that takes an image as input and returns one or more regions or subpixel-precise contours as output.

9.4.1 Thresholding

The simplest segmentation algorithm is to threshold the image. The threshold operation is defined by

$$S = \{(r,c) \in R \mid g_{\min} \leq f_{r,c} \leq g_{\max}\} \qquad (9.45)$$

Hence, the threshold operation selects all points in the ROI R of the image that lie within a specified range of gray values into the output region S. Often, $g_{\min} = 0$ or $g_{\max} = 2^b - 1$ is used. If the illumination can be kept constant, the thresholds $g_{\min}$ and $g_{\max}$ are selected when the system is set up and are never modified. Since the threshold operation is based on the gray values themselves, it can be used whenever the object to be segmented and the background have significantly different gray values.

Figure 9.22a,b shows two images of integrated circuits (ICs) on a PCB with a rectangular ROI overlaid in light gray. The result of thresholding the two images with $g_{\min} = 90$ and $g_{\max} = 255$ is shown in Figure 9.22c,d. Since the illumination is kept constant, the same threshold works for both images. Note also that there are some noisy pixels in the segmented regions. They can be removed, for example,

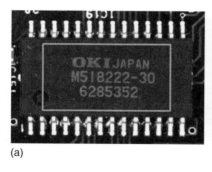
(a)

(b)

(c)   (d)

Figure 9.22 (a,b) Images of prints on ICs with a rectangular ROI overlaid in light gray. (c,d) Result of thresholding the images in (a),(b) with $g_{\min} = 90$ and $g_{\max} = 255$.

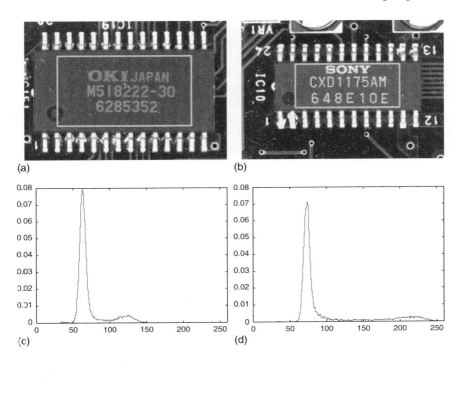

Figure 9.23 (a,b) Images of prints on ICs with a rectangular ROI overlaid in light gray. (c,d) Gray value histogram of the images in (a) and (b) within the respective ROI. (e,f) Result of thresholding the images in (a) and (b) with a threshold selected automatically based on the gray value histogram.

based on their area (see Section 9.5) or based on morphological operations (see Section 9.6).

The constant threshold works well only as long as the gray values of the object and the background do not change. Unfortunately, this occurs less frequently than one would wish, for example, because of changing illumination. Even if the illumination is kept constant, different gray value distributions on similar objects may prevent us from using a constant threshold. Figure 9.23 shows an example of this. In Figure 9.23a,b, two different ICs on the same PCB are shown. Despite the identical illumination, the prints have a substantially different gray value distribution, which will not allow us to use the same threshold for both images. Nevertheless, the print and the background can be separated easily in both cases. Therefore, ideally, we would like to have a method that is able to determine the thresholds automatically. This can be done based on the gray value histogram of the image. Figure 9.23c,d shows the histograms of the images in Figure 9.23a,b. It is obvious that there are two relevant peaks (maxima) in the histograms in both images. The one with the smaller gray value corresponds to the background, while the one with the higher gray value corresponds to the print. Intuitively, a good threshold corresponds to the minimum between the two peaks in the histogram. Unfortunately, neither the two maxima nor the minimum is well defined because of random fluctuations in the gray value histogram. Therefore, to robustly select the threshold that corresponds to the minimum, the histogram must be smoothed, for example, by convolving it with a 1D Gaussian filter. Since it is not clear which σ to use, a good strategy is to smooth the histogram with progressively larger values of σ until two unique maxima with a unique minimum in between are obtained. The result of using this approach to select the threshold automatically is shown in Figure 9.23e,f. As can be seen, for both images suitable thresholds have been selected. This approach of selecting the thresholds is not the only approach. Other approaches are described, for example, in [22, 23]. All these approaches have in common that they are based on the gray value histogram of the image. One example of such a different approach is to assume that the gray values in the foreground and background each have a normal (Gaussian) probability distribution, and to jointly fit two Gaussian densities to the histogram. The threshold is then defined as the gray value for which the two Gaussian densities have equal probabilities. Another approach is to select the threshold by maximizing a measure of separability in gray values of the region and the background [24].

While calculating the thresholds from the histogram often works extremely well, it fails whenever the assumption that there are two peaks in the histogram is violated. One such example is shown in Figure 9.24. Here, the print is so noisy that the gray values of the print are extremely spread out, and consequently there is no discernible peak for the print in the histogram. Another reason for the failure of the desired peak to appear is an inhomogeneous illumination. This typically destroys the relevant peaks or moves them so that they are in the wrong location. An uneven illumination often even prevents us from using a threshold operation altogether because there are no fixed thresholds that work throughout the entire image. Fortunately, often the objects of interest can be characterized by being

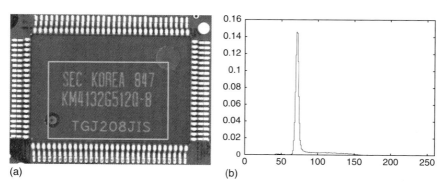

Figure 9.24 (a) Image of a print on an IC with a rectangular ROI overlaid in light gray. (b) Gray value histogram of the image in (a) within the ROI. Note that there are no significant minima and only one significant maximum in the histogram.

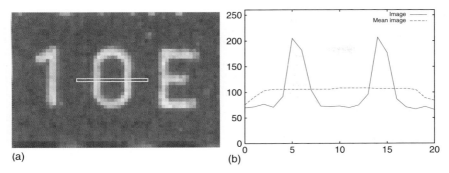

Figure 9.25 (a) Image showing a small part of a print on an IC with a one-pixel-wide horizontal ROI. (b) Gray value profiles of the image and the image smoothed with a 9 × 9 mean filter. Note that the text is substantially brighter than the local background estimated by the mean filter.

locally brighter or darker than their local background. The prints on the ICs we have examined so far are a good example of this. Therefore, instead of specifying global thresholds, we would like to specify by how much a pixel must be brighter or darker than its local background. The only problem we have is how to determine the gray value of the local background. Since a smoothing operation, for example, the mean, Gaussian, or median filter (see Section 9.2.3), calculates an average gray value in a window around the current pixel, we can simply use the filter output as an estimate of the gray value of the local background. The operation of comparing the image to its local background is called a dynamic thresholding operation. Let the image be denoted by $f_{r,c}$ and the smoothed image be denoted by $g_{r,c}$. Then, the dynamic thresholding operation for bright objects is given by

$$S = \{(r, c) \in R \mid f_{r,c} - g_{r,c} \geq g_{\text{diff}}\} \tag{9.46}$$

while the dynamic thresholding operation for dark objects is given by

$$S = \{(r, c) \in R \mid f_{r,c} - g_{r,c} \leq -g_{\text{diff}}\} \tag{9.47}$$

Figure 9.25 gives an example of how the dynamic thresholding works. In Figure 9.25a, a small part of a print on an IC with a one-pixel-wide horizontal ROI is shown. Figure 9.25b displays the gray value profiles of the image and the image smoothed with a 9 × 9 mean filter. It can be seen that the text is substantially brighter than the local background estimated by the mean filter. Therefore, the characters can be segmented easily with the dynamic thresholding operation.

In the dynamic thresholding operation, the size of the smoothing filter determines the size of the objects that can be segmented. If the filter size is too small, the local background will not be estimated well in the center of the objects. As a rule of thumb, the diameter of the mean filter must be larger than the diameter of the objects to be recognized. The same holds for the median filter. An analogous relation exists for the Gaussian filter. Furthermore, in general, if larger filter sizes are chosen for the mean and Gaussian filters, the filter output will be more representative of the local background. For example, for light objects the filter output will become darker within the light objects. For the median filter, this is not true since it will completely eliminate the objects if the filter mask is larger than the diameter of the objects. Hence, the gray values will be representative of the local

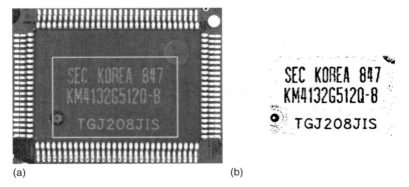

(a)   (b)

Figure 9.26 (a) Image of a print on an IC with a rectangular ROI overlaid in light gray. (b) Result of segmenting the image in (a) with a dynamic thresholding operation with $g_{\text{diff}} = 5$ and a 31×31 mean filter.

background if the filter is sufficiently large. If the gray values in the smoothed image are more representative of the local background, we can typically select a larger threshold g_{diff}, and hence can suppress noise in the segmentation better. However, the filter mask cannot be chosen arbitrarily large because neighboring objects might adversely influence the filter output. Finally, it should be noted that the dynamic thresholding operation returns a segmentation result not only for objects that are brighter or darker than their local background but also at the bright or dark region around edges.

Figure 9.26a again shows the image of Figure 9.24a, which could not be segmented with an automatic threshold. In Figure 9.26b, the result of segmenting the image with a dynamic thresholding operation with $g_{\text{diff}} = 5$ is shown. The local background was obtained with a 31×31 mean filter. Note that the difficult print is segmented very well with the dynamic thresholding.

As described so far, the dynamic thresholding operation can be used to compare the image with its local background, which is obtained by smoothing the image. With a slight modification, the dynamic thresholding operation can also be used to detect errors in an object, for example, for print inspection. Here, the image $g_{r,c}$ is an image of the ideal object, that is, the object without errors; $g_{r,c}$ is called the reference image. To detect deviations from the ideal object, we can simply look for too bright or too dark pixels in the image $f_{r,c}$ by using equation (9.46) or (9.47). Often, we are not interested in whether the pixels are too bright or too dark, but simply in whether they deviate too much from the reference image, that is, the union of equations (9.46) and (9.47), which is given by

$$S = \{(r,c) \in R \mid |f_{r,c} - g_{r,c}| > g_{\text{abs}}\} \tag{9.48}$$

Note that this pixel-by-pixel comparison requires that the image $f_{r,c}$ of the object to check and the reference image $g_{r,c}$ are aligned very accurately to avoid spurious gray value differences that would be interpreted as errors. This can be ensured either by the mechanical setup or by finding the pose of the object in the current image, for example, using template matching (see Section 9.11), and then transforming the image to the pose of the object in the ideal image (see Section 9.3).

This kind of dynamic thresholding operation is very strict on the shape of the objects. For example, if the size of the object increases by half a pixel and the gray value difference between the object and the background is 200, the gray value difference between the current image and the model image will be 100 at the object's edges. This is a significant gray value difference, which would surely be larger than any reasonable g_{abs}. In real applications, however, small variations of the object's shape typically should be tolerated. On the other hand, small gray value changes in the areas where the object's shape does not change should still be recognized as an error. To achieve this behavior, we can introduce a thresholding operation that takes the expected gray value variations in the image into account. Let us denote the permissible variations in the image by $v_{r,c}$. Ideally, we would like to segment the pixels that differ from the reference image by more than the permissible variations:

$$S = \{(r,c) \in R \mid |f_{r,c} - g_{r,c}| > v_{r,c}\} \tag{9.49}$$

The permissible variations can be determined by learning them from a set of training images. For example, if we use n training images of objects with permissible variations, the standard deviation of the gray values of each pixel can be used to derive $v_{r,c}$. If we use n images to define the variations of the ideal object, we might as well use the mean of each pixel to define the reference image $g_{r,c}$ to reduce noise. Of course, the n training images must be aligned with sufficient accuracy. The mean and standard deviation of the n training images are given by

$$\begin{aligned} m_{r,c} &= \frac{1}{n} \sum_{i=1}^{n} g_{r,c;i} \\ s_{r,c} &= \sqrt{\frac{1}{n} \sum_{i=1}^{n} (g_{r,c;i} - m_{r,c})^2} \end{aligned} \tag{9.50}$$

The images $m_{r,c}$ and $s_{r,c}$ model the reference image and the allowed variations of the reference image. Hence, we can call this approach a variation model. Note that $m_{r,c}$ is identical to the temporal average of equation (9.13). To define $v_{r,c}$, ideally we could simply set $v_{r,c}$ to a small multiple c of the standard deviation, that is, $v_{r,c} = cs_{r,c}$, where, for example, $c = 3$. Unfortunately, this approach does not work well if the variations in the training images are extremely small, for example, because the noise in the training images is significantly smaller than in the test images, or because parts of the object are near the saturation limit of the camera. In these cases, it is useful to introduce an absolute threshold a for the variation images, which is used whenever the variations in the training images are very small: $v_{r,c} = \max(a, cs_{r,c})$. As a further generalization, it is sometimes useful to have different thresholds for too bright and too dark pixels. With this, the variation threshold is no longer symmetric with respect to $m_{r,c}$, and we need to introduce two threshold images for the too bright and too dark pixels. If we denote the threshold images by $u_{r,c}$ and $l_{r,c}$, the absolute thresholds by a and b, and the factors for the standard deviations by c and d, the variation model segmentation is given by

$$S = \{(r,c) \in R \mid f_{r,c} < l_{r,c} \vee f_{r,c} > u_{r,c}\} \tag{9.51}$$

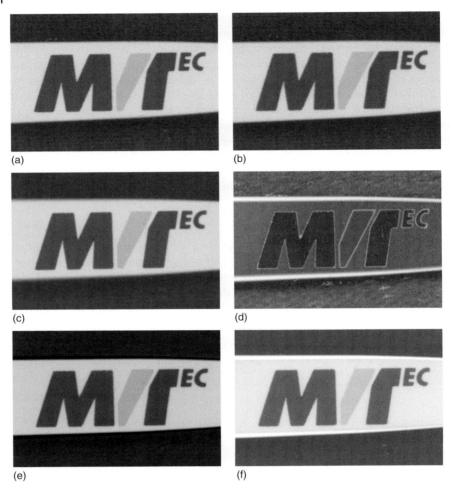

Figure 9.27 (a,b) Two images of a sequence of 15 showing a print on the clip of a pen. Note that the letter V in the MVTec logo moves slightly with respect to the rest of the logo. (c) Reference image $m_{r,c}$ of the variation model computed from the 15 training images. (d) Standard deviation image $s_{r,c}$. For better visibility, $s_{r,c}^{1/4}$ is displayed. (e,f) Minimum and maximum threshold images $u_{r,c}$ and $l_{r,c}$ computed with $a = b = 20$ and $c = d = 3$.

where

$$u_{r,c} = m_{r,c} + \max(a, cs_{r,c})$$
$$l_{r,c} = m_{r,c} - \max(b, ds_{r,c})$$

(9.52)

Figure 9.27a,b displays two images of a sequence of 15 showing a print on the clip of a pen. All images are aligned such that the MVTec logo is in the center of the image. Note that the letter V in the MVTec logo moves with respect to the rest of the logo and that the corners of the letters may change their shape slightly. This happens because of the pad printing technology used to print the logo. The two colors of the logo are printed with two different pads, which can

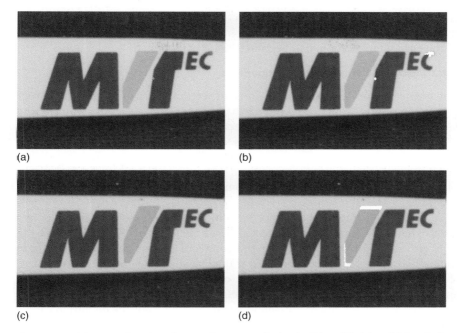

Figure 9.28 (a) Image showing a logo with errors in the letters T (small hole) and C (too little ink). (b) Errors displayed in white, segmented with the variation model of Figure 9.27. (c) Image showing a logo in which the letter V has moved too high and to the right. (d) Segmented errors.

move with respect to each other. Furthermore, the size of the letters may vary because of slightly different pressures with which the pads are pressed onto the clip. To ensure that the logo has been printed correctly, the variation model can be used to determine the mean and variation images shown in Figure 9.27c,d, and from them the threshold images shown in Figure 9.27e,f. Note that the variation is large at the letter V of the logo because this letter may move with respect to the rest of the logo. Also note the large variation at the edges of the clip, which occurs because the logo's position varies on the clip.

Figure 9.28a shows a logo with errors in the letters T (small hole) and C (too little ink). From Figure 9.28b, it can be seen that the two errors can be detected reliably. Figure 9.28c shows a different kind of error: the letter V has moved too high and to the right. This kind of error can also be detected easily, as shown in Figure 9.28d.

As described so far, the variation model requires n training images to construct the reference and variation images. In some applications, however, it is possible to acquire only a single reference image. In these cases, there are two options to create the variation model. The first option is to create artificial variations of the model, for example, by creating translated versions of the reference image. Another option can be derived by noting that the variations are necessarily large at the edges of the object if we allow small size and position tolerances. This can be clearly seen in Figure 9.27d. Consequently, in the absence of training images that show the real variations of the object, a reasonable approximation for $s_{r,c}$ is given by computing the edge amplitude image of the reference image using one of the edge filters described in Section 9.7.3.

9.4.2 Extraction of Connected Components

The segmentation algorithms in the previous section return one region as the segmentation result (recall the definitions in equations (9.45)–(9.47)). Typically, the segmented region contains multiple objects that should be returned individually. For example, in the examples in Figures 9.22–9.26 we are interested in obtaining each character as a separate region. Typically, the objects we are interested in are characterized by forming a connected set of pixels. Hence, to obtain the individual regions we must compute the connected components of the segmented region.

To be able to compute the connected components, we must define when two pixels should be considered connected. On a rectangular pixel grid, there are only two natural options to define the connectivity. The first possibility is to define two pixels as being connected if they have an edge in common, that is, if the pixel is directly above, below, left, or right of the current pixel, as shown in Figure 9.29a. Since each pixel has four connected pixels, this definition is called the 4-connectivity or 4-neighborhood. Alternatively, the definition can be extended to also include the diagonally adjacent pixels, as shown in Figure 9.29b. This definition is called the 8-connectivity or 8-neighborhood.

While these definitions are easy to understand, they cause problematic behavior if the same definition is used on both foreground and background. Figure 9.30 shows some of the problems that occur if 8-connectivity is used for foreground and background. In Figure 9.30a, there is clearly a single line in the foreground, which divides the background into two connected components. This is what we would intuitively expect. However, as Figure 9.30b shows, if the line is slightly rotated, we still obtain a single connected component in the foreground. However, now the background is also a single component. This is quite counterintuitive. Figure 9.30c shows another peculiarity. Again, the foreground region consists of a single connected component. Intuitively, we would say that the region contains a hole. However, the background also is a single connected component, indicating that the region contains no hole. The only remedy for this problem is to use opposite connectivities on the foreground and background. If, for example, 4-connectivity is used for the background in the examples in Figure 9.30, all of the above problems are solved. Likewise, if 4-connectivity is used for the foreground and 8-connectivity for the background, the inconsistencies are avoided.

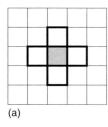 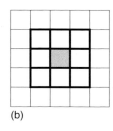

(a) (b)

Figure 9.29 Two possible definitions of connectivity on rectangular pixel grids: (a) 4-connectivity and (b) 8-connectivity.

9.4 Image Segmentation | 549

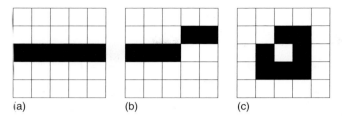

Figure 9.30 Some peculiarities occur when the same connectivity, in this case 8-connectivity, is used for the foreground and background. (a) The single line in the foreground clearly divides the background into two connected components. (b) If the line is very slightly rotated, there is still a single line, but now the background is a single component, which is counterintuitive. (c) The single region in the foreground intuitively contains one hole. However, the background is also a single connected component, indicating that the region has no hole, which is also counterintuitive.

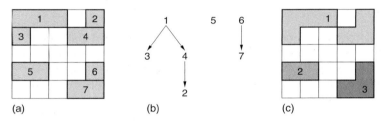

Figure 9.31 (a) Run-length representation of a region containing seven runs. (b) Search tree when performing a depth-first search for the connected components of the region in (a) using 8-connectivity. The numbers indicate the runs. (c) Resulting connected components.

To compute the connected components on the run-length representation of a region, a classical depth-first search can be performed [25]. We can repeatedly search for the first unprocessed run, and then search for overlapping runs in the adjacent rows of the image. The used connectivity determines whether two runs overlap. For 4-connectivity, the runs must at least have one pixel in the same column, while for the 8-connectivity the runs must at least touch diagonally. An example of this procedure is shown in Figure 9.31. The run-length representation of the input region is shown in Figure 9.31a, the search tree for the depth-first search using the 8-connectivity is shown in Figure 9.31b, and the resulting connected components are shown in Figure 9.31c. For the 8-connectivity, three connected components result. If 4-connectivity had been used, four connected components would result.

It should be noted that the connected components can also be computed from the representation of a region as a binary image. The output of this operation is a label image. Therefore, this operation is also called labeling or component labeling. For a description of algorithms that compute the connected components from a binary image, see [22, 23].

To conclude this section, Figure 9.32a,b shows the result of computing the connected components of the regions in Figure 9.23e,f. As can be seen, each character is a connected component. Furthermore, the noisy segmentation results are also returned as separate components. Thus, it is easy to remove them from the segmentation, for example, based on their area.

```
OK  JAPAN                       SONY
M5182 22-30                     CXD117 AM
 6 85352                         648E1 E
```

(a)   (b)

Figure 9.32 (a,b) Result of computing the connected components of the regions in Figure 9.23e,f. The connected components are visualized by using eight different gray values cyclically.

9.4.3 Subpixel-Precise Thresholding

All the thresholding operations we have discussed so far have been pixel-precise. In most cases, this precision is sufficient. However, some applications require a higher accuracy than the pixel grid. Therefore, an algorithm that returns a result with subpixel precision is sometimes required. Obviously, the result of this subpixel-precise thresholding operation cannot be a region, which is only pixel-precise. The appropriate data structure for this purpose therefore is a subpixel-precise contour (see Section 9.1.3). This contour will represent the boundary between regions in the image that have gray values above the gray value threshold g_{sub} and regions that have gray values below g_{sub}. To obtain this boundary, we must convert the discrete representation of the image into a continuous function. This can be done, for example, with bilinear interpolation (see equation (9.42) in Section 9.3.3). Once we have obtained a continuous representation of the image, the subpixel-precise thresholding operation conceptually consists of intersecting the image function $f(r, c)$ with the constant function $g(r, c) = g_{sub}$. Figure 9.33 shows the bilinearly interpolated image $f(r, c)$ in a 2 × 2 block of the four closest pixel centers. The closest pixel centers lie at the corners of the graph. The bottom of the graph shows the intersection curve of the image $f(r, c)$ in this 2 × 2 block with the constant gray value $g_{sub} = 100$. Note that this curve is part of a hyperbola. Since this hyperbolic curve would be quite cumbersome to represent, we can simply substitute it with a straight line segment between the two points where the hyperbola leaves the 2 × 2 block. This line segment constitutes one segment of the subpixel contour we are interested in. Each 2 × 2 block in the image typically contains between zero and two of these line segments. If the 2 × 2 block contains an intersection of two contours, four line segments may occur. To obtain meaningful contours, these segments need to be linked. This can be done by repeatedly selecting the first unprocessed line segment in the image as the first segment of the contour and then tracing the adjacent line segments until the contour closes, reaches the image border, or reaches an intersection point. The result of this linking step typically is closed contours that enclose a region in the image in which the gray values are either larger or smaller than the threshold. Note that, if such a region contains holes, one contour will be created for the outer boundary of the region and one for each hole.

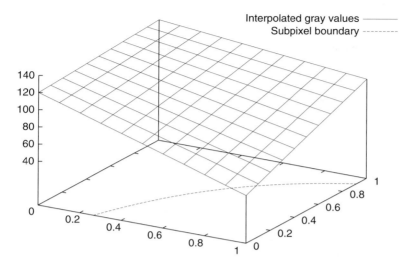

Figure 9.33 The graph shows gray values that are interpolated bilinearly between four pixel centers, lying at the corners of the graph, and the intersection curve with the gray value $g_{sub} = 100$ at the bottom of the graph. This curve (part of a hyperbola) is the boundary between the region with gray values >100 and gray values <100.

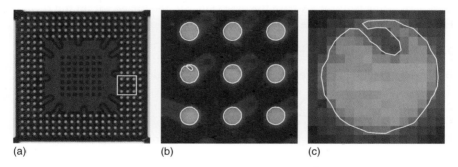

Figure 9.34 (a) Image of a PCB with BGA solder pads. (b) Result of applying a subpixel-precise threshold to the image in (a). The part that is being displayed corresponds to the white rectangle in (a). (c) Detail of the left pad in the center row of (b).

Figure 9.34a shows an image of a PCB that contains a ball grid array (BGA) of solder pads. To ensure good electrical contact, it must be ensured that the pads have the correct shape and position. This requires high accuracy, and, since in this application typically the resolution of the image is small compared to the size of the balls and pads, the segmentation must be performed with subpixel accuracy. Figure 9.34b shows the result of performing a subpixel-precise thresholding operation on the image in Figure 9.34a. To see enough details of the results, the part that corresponds to the white rectangle in Figure 9.34a is displayed. The boundary of the pads is extracted with very good accuracy. Figure 9.34c shows even more detail: the left pad in the center row of Figure 9.34b, which contains an error that must be detected. As can be seen, the subpixel-precise contour correctly captures the erroneous region of the pad. We can also easily see the individual line segments in the subpixel-precise contour and how they are contained in the

2 × 2 pixel blocks. Note that each block lies between four pixel centers. Therefore, the contour's line segments end at the lines that connect the pixel centers. Note also that in this part of the image there is only one block in which two line segments are contained: at the position where the contour enters the error on the pad. All the other blocks contain one or no line segments.

9.5 Feature Extraction

In the previous sections, we have seen how to extract regions or subpixel-precise contours from an image. While the regions and contours are very useful, they may not be sufficient because they contain the raw description of the segmented data. Often, we must select certain regions or contours from the segmentation result, for example, to remove unwanted parts of the segmentation. Furthermore, often we are interested in gauging the objects. In other applications, we might want to classify the objects, for example, in the OCR, to determine the type of the object. All these applications require that we determine one or more characteristic quantities from the regions or contours. The quantities we determine are called features. Typically they are real numbers. The process of determining the features is called feature extraction. There are different kinds of features. Region features are features that can be extracted from the regions themselves. In contrast, gray value features also use the gray values in the image within the region. Finally, contour features are based on the coordinates of the contour.

9.5.1 Region Features

By far the simplest region feature is the area of the region:

$$a = |R| = \sum_{(r,c) \in R} 1 = \sum_{i=1}^{n} ce_i - cs_i + 1 \tag{9.53}$$

Hence, the area a of the region is simply the number of points $|R|$ in the region. If the region is represented as a binary image, the first sum has to be used to compute the area; whereas if a run-length representation is used, the second sum can be used. Recall from equation (9.2) that a region can be regarded as the union of its runs, and the area of a run is extremely simple to compute. Note that the second sum contains many fewer terms than the first sum, as discussed in Section 9.1.2. Hence, the run-length representation of a region will lead to a much faster computation of the area. This is true for almost all region features.

Figure 9.35 shows the result of selecting all regions with an area ≥ 20 from the regions in Figure 9.32a,b. Note that all the characters have been selected, while all noisy segmentation results have been removed. These regions could now be used as input for OCR.

The area is a special case of a more general class of features called the moments of the region. The moment of order (p, q), with $p \geq 0$ and $q \geq 0$, is defined as

$$m_{p,q} = \sum_{(r,c) \in R} r^p c^q \tag{9.54}$$

Note that $m_{0,0}$ is the area of the region. As for the area, simple formulas to compute the moments solely based on the runs can be derived. Hence, the moments can be computed very efficiently in the run-length representation.

(a)   (b)

Figure 9.35 (a,b) Result of selecting regions with an area ≥20 from the regions in Figure 9.32a,b. The connected components are visualized by using eight different gray values cyclically.

The moments in equation (9.54) depend on the size of the region. Often, it is desirable to have features that are invariant to the size of the objects. To obtain such features, we can simply divide the moments by the area of the region if $p + q \geq 1$ to get normalized moments:

$$n_{p,q} = \frac{1}{a} \sum_{(r,c) \in R} r^p c^q \tag{9.55}$$

The most interesting feature that can be derived from the normalized moments is the center of gravity of the region, which is given by $(n_{1,0}, n_{0,1})$. It can be used to describe the position of the region. Note that the center of gravity is a subpixel-precise feature, even though it is computed from pixel-precise data.

The normalized moments depend on the position in the image. Often, it is useful to make the features invariant to the position of the region in the image. This can be done by calculating the moments relative to the center of gravity of the region. These central moments are given by $(p + q \geq 2)$

$$\mu_{p,q} = \frac{1}{a} \sum_{(r,c) \in R} (r - n_{1,0})^p (c - n_{0,1})^q \tag{9.56}$$

Note that they are also normalized. The second central moments $(p + q = 2)$ are particularly interesting. They enable us to define an orientation and an extent for the region. This is done by assuming that the moments of order 1 and 2 of the region were obtained from an ellipse. Then, from these five moments, the five geometric parameters of the ellipse can be derived. Figure 9.36 displays the ellipse's parameters graphically. The center of the ellipse is identical to the center of gravity of the region. The major and minor axes r_1 and r_2 and the angle of the

Figure 9.36 Geometric parameters of an ellipse.

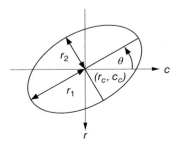

ellipse with respect to the column axis are given by

$$r_1 = \sqrt{2\left(\mu_{2,0} + \mu_{0,2} + \sqrt{(\mu_{2,0} - \mu_{0,2})^2 + 4\mu_{1,1}^2}\right)}$$

$$r_2 = \sqrt{2\left(\mu_{2,0} + \mu_{0,2} - \sqrt{(\mu_{2,0} - \mu_{0,2})^2 + 4\mu_{1,1}^2}\right)} \qquad (9.57)$$

$$\theta = -\frac{1}{2}\arctan\frac{2\mu_{1,1}}{\mu_{0,2} - \mu_{2,0}}$$

For a derivation of these results, see [22] (note that there the diameters are used instead of the radii). From the ellipse parameters, we can derive another very useful feature: the anisometry r_1/r_2. This is scale-invariant and describes how elongated a region is.

The ellipse parameters are extremely useful to determine the orientations and sizes of regions. For example, the angle θ can be used to rectify rotated text. Figure 9.37a shows the result of thresholding the image in Figure 9.18a. The segmentation result is treated as a single region, that is, the connected components have not been computed. Figure 9.37a also displays the ellipse parameters by overlaying the major and minor axes of the equivalent ellipse. Note that the major axis is slightly longer than the region because the equivalent ellipse does not need to have the same area as the region. It only needs to have the same moments of orders 1 and 2. The angle of the major axis is a very good estimate for the rotation of the text. In fact, it has been used to rectify the images in Figure 9.18b,c. Figure 9.37b shows the axes of the characters after the connected components have been computed. Note how well the orientation of the regions corresponds with our intuition.

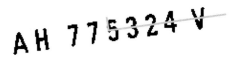

(a)

(b)

Figure 9.37 Result of thresholding the image in Figure 9.18a overlaid with a visualization of the ellipse parameters. The light gray lines represent the major and minor axes of the regions. Their intersection is the center of gravity of the regions. (a) The segmentation is treated as a single region. (b) The connected components of the region are used. The angle of the major axis in (a) has been used to rotate the images in Figure 9.18b,c.

9.5 Feature Extraction

While the ellipse parameters are extremely useful, they have two minor shortcomings. First of all, the orientation can be determined only if $r_1 \neq r_2$. Our first thought might be that this applies only to circles, which have no meaningful orientation anyway. Unfortunately, this is not true. There is a much larger class of objects for which $r_1 = r_2$. All objects that have a fourfold rotational symmetry, such as squares, have $r_1 = r_2$. Hence, their orientation cannot be determined with the ellipse parameters. The second slight problem is that, since the underlying model is an ellipse, the orientation θ can only be determined modulo π (180°). This problem can be solved by determining the point in the region that has the largest distance from the center of gravity and use it to select θ or $\theta + \pi$ as the correct orientation.

In the above discussion, we have used various transformations to make the moment-based features invariant to certain transformations, for example, translation and scaling. Several approaches have been proposed to create moment-based features that are invariant to a larger class of transformations, for example, translation, rotation, and scaling [26] or even general affine transformations [27, 28]. They are primarily used to classify objects.

Apart from the moment-based features, there are several other useful features that are based on the idea of finding an enclosing geometric primitive for the region. Figure 9.38a displays the smallest axis-parallel enclosing rectangle of a region. This rectangle is often also called the bounding box of the region. It can be calculated very easily based on the minimum and maximum row and column coordinates of the region. Based on the parameters of the rectangle, other useful quantities like the width and height of the region and their ratio can be calculated. The parameters of the bounding box are particularly useful if we want to quickly find out whether two regions can intersect. Since the smallest axis-parallel enclosing rectangle sometimes is not very tight, we can also define a smallest enclosing rectangle of arbitrary orientation, as shown in Figure 9.38b. Its computation is much more complicated than the computation of the bounding box, however, so we cannot give details here. An efficient implementation can be found in [29]. Note that an arbitrarily oriented rectangle has the same parameters as an ellipse. Hence, it also enables us to define the position, size, and orientation of a region. Note that, in contrast to the ellipse parameters, a useful orientation for squares is returned. The final useful enclosing primitive is an enclosing circle, as shown in Figure 9.38c. Its computation is also quite complex [30]. It also enables us to define the position and size of a region.

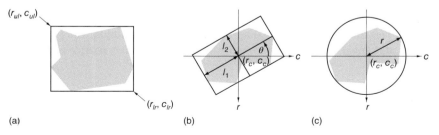

Figure 9.38 (a) Smallest axis-parallel enclosing rectangle of a region. (b) Smallest enclosing rectangle of arbitrary orientation. (c) Smallest enclosing circle.

The computation of the smallest enclosing rectangle of arbitrary orientation and the smallest enclosing circle is based on first computing the convex hull of the region. The convex hull of a set of points, and in particular a region, is the smallest convex set that contains all the points. A set is convex if, for any two points in the set, the straight line between them is completely contained in the set. The convex hull of a set of points can be computed efficiently [31, 32]. The convex hull of a region is often useful to construct ROIs from regions that have been extracted from the image. Based on the convex hull of the region, another useful feature can be defined: the convexity, which is defined as the ratio of the area of the region to the area of its convex hull. It is a feature between 0 and 1 that measures how compact the region is. A convex region has a convexity of 1. The convexity can, for example, be used to remove unwanted segmentation results, which often are highly nonconvex.

Another useful feature of a region is its contour length. To compute it, we need to trace the boundary of the region to get a linked contour of the boundary pixels [22]. Once the contour has been computed, we simply need to sum the Euclidean distances of the contour segments, which are 1 for horizontal and vertical segments and $\sqrt{2}$ for diagonal segments. Based on the contour length l and the area a of the region, we can define another measure for the compactness of a region: $c = l^2/(4\pi a)$. For circular regions, this feature is 1, while all other regions have larger values. The compactness has similar uses as the convexity.

9.5.2 Gray Value Features

We have already seen some gray value features in Section 9.2.1, namely the minimum and maximum gray values within the region:

$$g_{\min} = \min_{(r,c) \in R} g_{r,c}, \quad g_{\max} = \max_{(r,c) \in R} g_{r,c} \qquad (9.58)$$

They are used for the gray value normalization in Section 9.2.1. Another obvious feature is the mean gray value within the region:

$$\bar{g} = \frac{1}{a} \sum_{(r,c) \in R} g_{r,c} \qquad (9.59)$$

Here, a is the area of the region, given by equation (9.53). The mean gray value is a measure of the brightness of the region. A single measurement within a reference region can be used to measure additive brightness changes with respect to the conditions when the system was set up. Two measurements within different reference regions can be used to measure linear brightness changes and thereby to compute a linear gray value transformation (see Section 9.2.1) that compensates the brightness change, or to adapt segmentation thresholds. The mean gray value is a statistical feature. Another statistical feature is the variance of the gray values:

$$s^2 = \frac{1}{a-1} \sum_{(r,c) \in R} (g_{r,c} - \bar{g})^2 \qquad (9.60)$$

and the standard deviation $s = \sqrt{s^2}$. Measuring the mean and standard deviation within a reference region can also be used to construct a linear gray value transformation that compensates brightness changes. The standard deviation can be used to adapt segmentation thresholds. Furthermore, the standard deviation is a measure of the amount of texture that is present within the region.

The gray value histogram (9.4) and the cumulative histogram (9.5), which we have already encountered in Section 9.2.1, are also gray value features. From the histogram, we have already used a feature for the robust contrast normalization: the α-quantile

$$g_\alpha = \min\{g : c_g \geq \alpha\} \tag{9.61}$$

where c_g is defined in equation (9.5). It was used to obtain the robust minimum and maximum gray values in Section 9.2.1. The quantiles were called p_l and p_u there. Note that, for $\alpha = 0.5$, we obtain the median gray value. It has similar uses as the mean gray value.

In the previous section, we have seen that the region's moments are extremely useful features. They can be extended to gray value features in a natural manner. The gray value moment of order (p, q), with $p \geq 0$ and $q \geq 0$, is defined as

$$m_{p,q} = \sum_{(r,c) \in R} g_{r,c}\, r^p c^q \tag{9.62}$$

This is the natural generalization of the region moments because we obtain the region moments from the gray value moments by using the characteristic function χ_R (Equation (9.1)) of the region as the gray values. Like for the region moments, the moment $a = m_{0,0}$ can be regarded as the gray value area of the region. It is actually the "volume" of the gray value function $g_{r,c}$ within the region. Like for the region moments, normalized moments can be defined by

$$n_{p,q} = \frac{1}{a} \sum_{(r,c) \in R} g_{r,c}\, r^p c^q \tag{9.63}$$

The moments $(n_{1,0}, n_{0,1})$ define the gray value center of gravity of the region. With this, central gray value moments can be defined by

$$\mu_{p,q} = \frac{1}{a} \sum_{(r,c) \in R} g_{r,c}\, (r - n_{1,0})^p (c - n_{0,1})^q \tag{9.64}$$

Like for the region moments, based on the second central moments we can define the ellipse parameters, major and minor axes, and the orientation. The formulas are identical to equation (9.57). Furthermore, the anisometry can also be defined identically as for the regions.

All the moment-based gray value features are very similar to their region-based counterparts. Therefore, it is interesting to look at their differences. Like we saw, the gray value moments reduce to the region moments if the characteristic function of the region is used as the gray values. The characteristic function can be interpreted as the membership of a pixel to the region. A membership of 1 means that the pixel belongs to the region, while 0 means that the pixel does not belong to the region. This notion of belonging to the region is crisp: that is, for every pixel a hard decision must be made. Suppose now that, instead of making a hard decision for every pixel, we could make a "soft" or "fuzzy" decision about whether a pixel belongs to the region, and that we encode the degree of belonging to the region by a number $\in [0, 1]$. We can interpret the degree of belonging as a fuzzy membership value, as opposed to the crisp binary membership value. With this, the gray value image can be regarded as a fuzzy set [33]. The advantage of regarding the image as a fuzzy set is that we do not have to make a hard decision about whether a pixel belongs to the object or not. Instead, the fuzzy membership value determines what percentage of the pixel belongs to the object. This

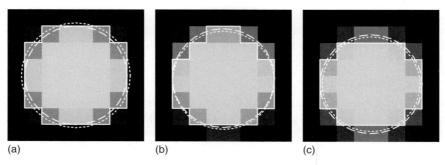

Figure 9.39 Subpixel-precise circle position and area using the gray value and region moments. The image represents a fuzzy membership, scaled to values between 0 and 200. The solid line is the result of segmenting with a membership of 100. The dotted line is a circle that has the same center of gravity and area as the segmented region. The dashed line is a circle that has the same gray value center of gravity and gray value area as the image. (a) Shift: 0; error in the area for the region moments: 13.2%; for the gray value moments: −0.05%. (b) Shift: 5/32 pixel; error in the row coordinate for the region moments: −0.129; for the gray value moments: 0.003. (c) Shift: 1/2 pixel; error in the area for the region moments: −8.0%; for the gray value moments: −0.015%. Note that the gray value moments yield a significantly better accuracy for this small object.

enables us to measure the position and size of the objects much more accurately, especially for small objects, because in the transition zone between the foreground and background there will be some mixed pixels that allow us to capture the geometry of the object more accurately. An example of this is shown in Figure 9.39. Here, a synthetically generated subpixel-precise ideal circle of radius 3 is shifted in subpixel increments. The gray values represent a fuzzy membership, scaled to values between 0 and 200 for display purposes. The figure displays a pixel-precise region, thresholded with a value of 100, which corresponds to a membership above 0.5, as well as two circles that have a center of gravity and area that were obtained from the region and gray value moments. The gray value moments were computed in the entire image. It can be seen that the area and center of gravity are computed much more accurately by the gray value moments because the decision about whether a pixel belongs to the foreground or not has been avoided. In this example, the gray value moments result in an area error that is always smaller than 0.25% and a position error smaller than 1/200 of a pixel. In contrast, the area error for the region moments can be up to 13.2% and the position error can be up to 1/6 of a pixel. Note that both types of moments yield subpixel-accurate measurements. We can see that on ideal data it is possible to obtain an extremely high accuracy with the gray value moments, even for very small objects. On real data, the accuracy will necessarily be somewhat lower. It should also be noted that the accuracy advantage of the gray value moments primarily occurs for small objects. Because the gray value moments must access every pixel within the region, whereas the region moments can be computed solely based on the run-length representation of the region, the region moments can be computed much faster. Hence, the gray moments are typically used only for relatively small regions.

The only question we need to answer is how to define the fuzzy membership value of a pixel. If we assume that the camera has a fill factor of 100% and the

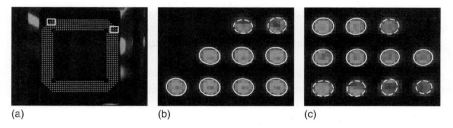

Figure 9.40 (a) Image of a BGA device. The two rectangles correspond to the image parts shown in (b) and (c). The results of inspecting the balls for correct size (gray value area ≥20) and correct gray value anisometry (≤1.25) are visualized in (b) and (c). Correct balls are displayed as solid ellipses, while defective balls are displayed as dashed ellipses.

gray value response of the camera (and analog frame grabber, if used) is linear, the gray value difference of a pixel from the background is proportional to the portion of the object that is covered by the pixel. Consequently, we can define a fuzzy membership relation as follows: every pixel that has a gray value below the background gray value g_{min} has a membership value of 0. Conversely, every pixel that has a gray value above the foreground gray value g_{max} has a membership value of 1. In between, the membership values are interpolated linearly. Since this procedure would require floating-point images, the membership is scaled to an integer image with b bits, typically 8 bits. Consequently, the fuzzy membership relation is a simple linear gray value scaling, as defined in Section 9.2.1. If we scale the fuzzy membership image in this manner, the gray value area needs to be divided by the maximum gray value, for example, 255, to obtain the true area. The normalized and central gray value moments do not need to be modified in this manner since they are, by definition, invariant to a scaling of the gray values.

Figure 9.40 displays a real application where the above principles are used. In Figure 9.40a, a BGA device with solder balls is displayed, along with two rectangles that indicate the image parts shown in Figure 9.40b,c. The image in Figure 9.40a is first transformed into a fuzzy membership image using $g_{min} = 40$ and $g_{max} = 120$ with 8-bit resolution. The individual balls are segmented and then inspected for correct size and shape by using the gray value area and the gray value anisometry. The erroneous balls are displayed with dashed lines. To aid visual interpretation, the ellipses representing the segmented balls are scaled such that they have the same area as the gray value area. This is done because the gray value ellipse parameters typically return an ellipse with a different area than the gray value area, analogous to the region ellipse parameters (see the discussion following equation (9.57) in Section 9.5.1). As can be seen, all the balls that have an erroneous size or shape, indicating partially missing solder, have been correctly detected.

9.5.3 Contour Features

Many of the region features we have discussed in Section 9.5.1 can be transferred to subpixel-precise contour features in a straightforward manner. For example, the length of the subpixel-precise contour is even easier to compute because the contour is already represented explicitly by its control points (r_i, c_i), for $i = 1, \ldots, n$. It is also simple to compute the smallest enclosing axis-parallel rectangle (the bounding box) of the contour. Furthermore, the convex hull of the contour can be computed like for regions [31, 32]. From the convex hull, we can also derive the smallest enclosing circles [30] and the smallest enclosing rectangles of arbitrary orientation [29].

In the previous two sections, we have seen that the moments are extremely useful features. An interesting question, therefore, is whether they can be defined for contours. In particular, it is interesting to see whether a contour has an area. Obviously, for this to be true, the contour must enclose a region, that is, it must be closed and must not intersect itself. To simplify the formulas, let us assume that a closed contour is specified by $(r_1, c_1) = (r_n, c_n)$. Let the subpixel-precise region that the contour encloses be denoted by R. Then, the moment of order (p, q) is defined as

$$m_{p,q} = \iint_{(r,c) \in R} r^p c^q \, dr \, dc \tag{9.65}$$

Like for regions, we can define normalized and central moments. The formulas are identical to equation (9.55) and (9.56) with the sums being replaced by integrals. It can be shown that these moments can be computed solely based on the control points of the contour [34]. For example, the area and center of gravity of the contour are given by

$$a = \frac{1}{2} \sum_{i=1}^{n} r_{i-1} c_i - r_i c_{i-1}$$

$$n_{1,0} = \frac{1}{6a} \sum_{i=1}^{n} (r_{i-1} c_i - r_i c_{i-1})(r_{i-1} + r_i) \tag{9.66}$$

$$n_{0,1} = \frac{1}{6a} \sum_{i=1}^{n} (r_{i-1} c_i - r_i c_{i-1})(c_{i-1} + c_i)$$

Analogous formulas can be derived for the second-order moments. Based on them, we can again compute the ellipse parameters, major axis, minor axis, and orientation. The formulas are identical to equations (9.57). The moment-based contour features can be used for the same purposes as the corresponding region and gray value features. By performing an evaluation similar to that in Figure 9.39, it can be seen that the contour center of gravity and the ellipse parameters are equally as accurate as the gray value center of gravity. The accuracy of the contour area is slightly worse than that of the gray value area because we have approximated the hyperbolic segments with line segments. Since the true contour is a circle, the line segments always lie inside the true circle. Nevertheless, subpixel-thresholding and the contour moments could also have been used to detect the erroneous balls in Figure 9.40.

9.6 Morphology

In Section 9.4, we discussed how to segment regions. We have already seen that segmentation results often contain unwanted noisy parts. Furthermore, sometimes the segmentation will contain parts in which the shape of the object we are interested in has been disturbed, for example, because of reflections. Therefore, often we need to modify the shape of the segmented regions to obtain the desired results. This is the subject of the field of mathematical morphology, which can be defined as a theory for the analysis of spatial structures [35]. For our purposes, mathematical morphology provides a set of extremely useful operations that enable us to modify or describe the shape of objects. Morphological operations can be defined on regions and gray value images. We will discuss both types of operations in this section.

9.6.1 Region Morphology

All region morphology operations can be defined in terms of six very simple operations: union, intersection, difference, complement, translation, and transposition. We will take a brief look at these operations first.

The union of two regions R and S is the set of points that lie in R or in S:

$$R \cup S = \{p \mid p \in R \vee p \in S\} \tag{9.67}$$

One important property of the union is that it is commutative: $R \cup S = S \cup R$. Furthermore, it is associative: $(R \cup S) \cup T = R \cup (S \cup T)$. While this may seem like a trivial observation, it will enable us to derive very efficient implementations for the morphological operations below. The algorithm to compute the union of two binary images is obvious: we simply need to compute the logical OR of the two images. The runtime complexity of this algorithm obviously is $O(wh)$, where w and h are the width and height of the binary image. In the run-length representation, the union can be computed with a lower complexity: $O(n + m)$, where n and m are the number of runs in R and S. The principle of the algorithm is to merge the runs of the two regions while observing the order of the runs (see Section 9.1.2) and then to pack overlapping runs into single runs.

The intersection of two regions R and S is the set of points that lie in R and in S:

$$R \cap S = \{p \mid p \in R \wedge p \in S\} \tag{9.68}$$

Like the union, the intersection is commutative and associative. Again, the algorithm on binary images is obvious: we compute the logical AND of the two images. For the run-length representation, again an algorithm that has complexity $O(n + m)$ can be found.

The difference of two regions R and S is the set of points that lie in R but not in S:

$$R \setminus S = \{p \mid p \in R \wedge p \notin S\} = R \cap \overline{S} \tag{9.69}$$

The difference is neither commutative nor associative. Note that it can be defined in terms of the intersection and the complement of a region R, which is defined as all the points that do not lie in R:

$$\overline{R} = \{p \mid p \notin R\} \tag{9.70}$$

Since the complement of a finite region is infinite, it is impossible to represent it as a binary image. Therefore, for the representation of regions as binary images, it is important to define the operations without the complement. It is, however, possible to represent it as a run-length-encoded region by adding a flag that indicates whether the region or its complement is being stored. This can be used to define a more general set of morphological operations. There is an interesting relation between the number of connected components of the background $|C(\overline{R})|$ and the number of holes of the foreground $|H(R)|$: we have $|C(\overline{R})| = 1 + |H(R)|$. As discussed in Section 9.4.2, complementary connectivities must be used for the foreground and the background for this relation to hold.

Apart from the set operations, two basic geometric transformations are used in morphological operations. The translation of a region by a vector t is defined as

$$R_t = \{p \mid p - t \in R\} = \{q \mid q = p + t \text{ for } p \in R\} \tag{9.71}$$

Finally, the transposition of a region is defined as a mirroring about the origin:

$$\check{R} = \{-p \mid p \in R\} \tag{9.72}$$

Note that this is the only operation where a special point (the origin) is singled out. All the other operations do not depend on the origin of the coordinate system, that is, they are translation-invariant.

With these building blocks, we can now take a look at the morphological operations. They typically involve two regions. One of these is the region we want to process, which will be denoted by R in the following. The other region has a special meaning. It is called the structuring element, and will be denoted by S. The structuring element is the means by which we can describe the shapes we are interested in.

The first morphological operation we consider is the Minkowski addition, which is defined by

$$R \oplus S = \{r + s \mid r \in R, s \in S\} = \bigcup_{s \in S} R_s = \bigcup_{r \in R} S_r = \{t \mid R \cap (\check{S})_t \neq \emptyset\} \tag{9.73}$$

It is interesting to interpret the formulas. The first formula says that, to get the Minkowski addition of R with S, we take every point in R and every point in S and compute the vector sum of the points. The result of the Minkowski addition is the set of all points thus obtained. If we single out S, this can also be interpreted as taking all points in S, translating the region R by the vector corresponding to the point s from S, and computing the union of all the translated regions. Thus, we obtain the second formula. By symmetry, we can also translate S by all points in R to obtain the third formula. Another way to look at the Minkowski addition is the fourth formula. It tells us that we move the transposed structuring element around in the plane. Whenever the translated, transposed structuring element and the region have at least one point in common, we copy the translated reference point into the output. Figure 9.41 shows an example of the Minkowski addition.

While the Minkowski addition has a simple formula, it has one small drawback. Its geometric criterion is that the transposed structuring element has at least one point in common with the region. Ideally, we would like to have an operation that returns all translated reference points for which the structuring element itself has

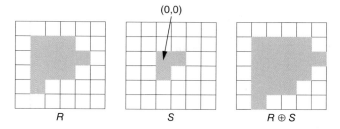

Figure 9.41 Example of the Minkowski addition $R \oplus S$.

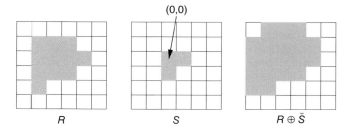

Figure 9.42 Example of the dilation $R \oplus \check{S}$.

at least one point in common with the region. To achieve this, we only need to use the transposed structuring element in the Minkowski addition. This operation is called a dilation, and is defined by

$$R \oplus \check{S} = \{t \mid R \cap S_t \neq \emptyset\} = \bigcup_{s \in S} R_{-s} \qquad (9.74)$$

Figure 9.42 shows an example of the dilation. Note that the results of the Minkowski addition and dilation are different. This is true whenever the structuring element is not symmetric with respect to the origin. If the structuring element is symmetric, the results of the Minkowski addition and dilation are identical. Be aware that this is assumed in many discussions about and implementations of the morphology. Therefore, the dilation is often defined without the transposition, which is technically incorrect.

The implementation of the Minkowski addition for binary images is straightforward. As suggested by the second formula in equation (9.73), it can be implemented as a nonlinear filter with logical OR operations. The runtime complexity is proportional to the size of the image times the number of pixels in the structuring element. The second factor can be reduced to roughly the number of boundary pixels in the structuring element [15]. Also, for binary images represented with 1 bit per pixel, very efficient algorithms can be developed for special structuring elements [36]. Nevertheless, in both cases the runtime complexity is proportional to the number of pixels in the image. To derive an implementation for the run-length representation of the regions, we first need to examine some algebraic properties of the Minkowski addition. It is commutative: $R \oplus S = S \oplus R$. Furthermore, it is distributive with respect to the union: $(R \cup S) \oplus$

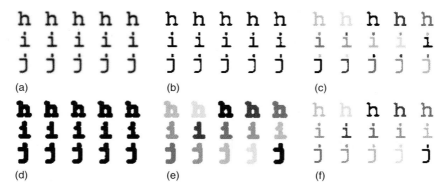

Figure 9.43 (a) Image of a print of several characters. (b) Result of thresholding (a). (c) Connected components of (b) displayed with six different gray values. Note that the characters and their dots are separate connected components, which is undesirable. (d) Result of dilating the region in (b) with a circle of diameter 5. (e) Connected components of (d). Note that each character is now a single connected component. (f) Result of intersecting the connected components in (e) with the original segmentation in (b). This transforms the connected components into the correct shape.

$T = R \oplus T \cup S \oplus T$. Since a region can be regarded as the union of its runs, we can use the commutativity and distributivity to transform the Minkowski addition as follows:

$$R \oplus S = \left(\bigcup_{i=1}^{n} \mathbf{r}_i \right) \oplus \left(\bigcup_{j=1}^{m} \mathbf{s}_j \right) = \bigcup_{j=1}^{m} \left(\left(\bigcup_{i=1}^{n} \mathbf{r}_i \right) \oplus \mathbf{s}_j \right) = \bigcup_{i=1}^{n} \bigcup_{j=1}^{m} \mathbf{r}_i \oplus \mathbf{s}_j$$

(9.75)

Thus, the Minkowski addition can be implemented as the union of nm dilations of single runs, which are trivial to compute. Since the union of the runs can be computed easily, the runtime complexity is $O(mn)$, which is better than for binary images.

As we have seen, the dilation and Minkowski addition enlarge the input region. This can be used, for example, to merge separate parts of a region into a single part, and thus to obtain the correct connected components of objects. One example of this is shown in Figure 9.43. Here, we want to segment each character as a separate connected component. If we compute the connected components of the thresholded region in Figure 9.43b, we can see that the characters and their dots are separate components (Figure 9.43c). To solve this problem, we first need to connect the dots with their characters. This can be achieved using a dilation with a circle of diameter 5 (Figure 9.43d). With this, the correct connected components are obtained (Figure 9.43e). Unfortunately, they have the wrong shape because of the dilation. This can be corrected by intersecting the components with the originally segmented region. Figure 9.43f shows that with these simple steps we have obtained one component with the correct shape for each character.

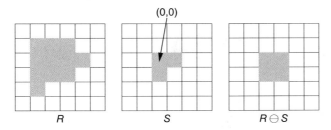

Figure 9.44 Example of the Minkowski subtraction $R \ominus S$.

The dilation is also very useful for constructing ROIs based on regions that were extracted from the image. We will see an example of this in Section 9.7.3.

The second type of morphological operation is the Minkowski subtraction. It is defined by

$$R \ominus S = \bigcap_{s \in S} R_s = \{r \mid \forall \ s \in S : r - s \in R\} = \{t \mid (\check{S})_t \subseteq R\} \quad (9.76)$$

The first formula is similar to the second formula in equation (9.73) with the union having been replaced by an intersection. Hence, we can still think about moving the region R by all vectors s from S. However, now the points must be contained in all translated regions (instead of at least one translated region). This is what the second formula in equation (9.76) expresses. Finally, if we look at the third formula, we see that we can also move the transposed structuring element around in the plane. If it is completely contained in the region R, we add its reference point to the output. Again, note the similarity to the Minkowski addition, where the structuring element had to have at least one point in common with the region. For the Minkowski subtraction, it must lie completely within the region. Figure 9.44 shows an example of the Minkowski subtraction.

The Minkowski subtraction has the same small drawback as the Minkowski addition: its geometric criterion is that the transposed structuring element must lie completely within the region. As for the dilation, we can use the transposed structuring element. This operation is called an erosion and is defined by

$$R \ominus \check{S} = \bigcap_{s \in S} R_{-s} = \{t \mid S_t \subseteq R\} \quad (9.77)$$

Figure 9.45 shows an example of the erosion. Again, note that the Minkowski subtraction and erosion produce identical results only if the structuring element is symmetric with respect to the origin. Be aware that this is often silently assumed, and the erosion is defined as a Minkowski subtraction, which is technically incorrect.

As we have seen from the small examples, the Minkowski subtraction and erosion shrink the input region. This can, for example, be used to separate objects that are attached to each other. Figure 9.46 shows an example of this. Here, the goal is to segment the individual globular objects. The result of thresholding the image is shown in Figure 9.46b. If we compute the connected components of

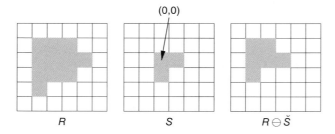

Figure 9.45 Example of the erosion $R \ominus \check{S}$.

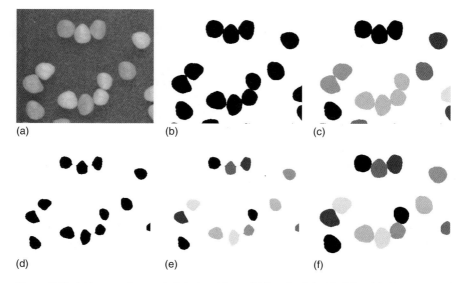

Figure 9.46 (a) Image of several globular objects. (b) Result of thresholding (a). (c) Connected components of (b) displayed with six different gray values. Note that several objects touch each other and hence are in the same connected component. (d) Result of eroding the region in (b) with a circle of diameter 15. (e) Connected components of (d). Note that each object is now a single connected component. (f) Result of dilating the connected components in (e) with a circle of diameter 15. This transforms the correct connected components into approximately the correct shape.

this region, an incorrect result is obtained because several objects touch each other (Figure 9.46c). The solution is to erode the region with a circle of diameter 15 (Figure 9.46d) before computing the connected components (Figure 9.46e). Unfortunately, the connected components have the wrong shape. Here, we cannot use the same strategy that we used for the dilation (intersecting the connected components with the original segmentation) because the erosion has shrunk the region. To approximately get the original shape back, we can dilate the connected components with the same structuring element that we used for the erosion (Figure 9.46f).

We can see another use of the erosion if we remember its definition: it returns the translated reference point of the structuring element S for every translation

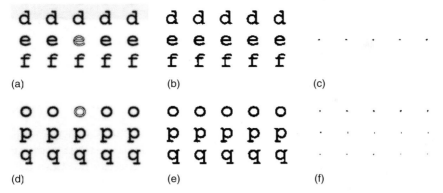

Figure 9.47 (a) Image of a print of several characters with the structuring element used for the erosion overlaid in white. (b) Result of thresholding (a). (c) Result of the erosion of (b) with the structuring element in (a). Note that the reference point of all letters "e" has been found. (d) A different set of characters with the structuring element used for the erosion overlaid in white. (e) Result of thresholding (d). (f) Result of the erosion of (e) with the structuring element in (d). Note that the reference point of the letter "o" has been identified correctly. In addition, the circular parts of the letters "p" and "q" have been extracted.

for which S_t completely fits into the region R. Hence, the erosion acts like a template matching operation. An example of this use of the erosion is shown in Figure 9.47. In Figure 9.47a, we can see an image of a print of several letters, with the structuring element used for the erosion overlaid in white. The structuring element corresponds to the center line of the letter "e." The reference point of the structuring element is its center of gravity. The result of eroding the thresholded letters (Figure 9.47b) with the structuring element is shown in Figure 9.47c. Note that all letters "e" have been correctly identified. In Figure 9.47d–f, the experiment is repeated with another set of letters. The structuring element is the center line of the letter "o." Note that the erosion correctly finds the letters "o." However, additionally the circular parts of the letters "p" and "q" are found, since the structuring element completely fits into them.

An interesting property of the Minkowski addition and subtraction as well as the dilation and erosion is that they are dual to each other with respect to the complement operation. For the Minkowski addition and subtraction, we have

$$R \oplus S = \overline{\overline{R} \ominus S} \quad \text{and} \quad R \ominus S = \overline{\overline{R} \oplus S} \qquad (9.78)$$

The same identities hold for the dilation and erosion. Hence, a dilation of the foreground is identical to an erosion of the background, and vice versa. We can make use of the duality whenever we want to avoid computing the complement explicitly, and hence to speed up some operations. Note that the duality holds only if the complement can be infinite. Hence, it does not hold for binary images, where the complemented region needs to be clipped to a certain image size.

One extremely useful application of the erosion and dilation is the calculation of the boundary of a region. The algorithm to compute the true boundary as a linked list of contour points is quite complicated [22]. However, an approximation to the boundary can be computed very easily. If we want to compute the inner boundary, we simply need to erode the region appropriately and to subtract the eroded region from the original region:

$$\partial R = R \backslash (R \ominus S) \tag{9.79}$$

By duality, the outer boundary (the inner boundary of the background) can be computed with a dilation:

$$\partial R = (R \oplus S) \backslash R \tag{9.80}$$

To get a suitable boundary, the structuring element S must be chosen appropriately. If we want to obtain an 8-connected boundary, we must use the structuring element S_8 in Figure 9.48. If we want a 4-connected boundary, we must use S_4.

Figure 9.49 displays an example of the computation of the inner boundary of a region. A small part of the input region is shown in Figure 9.49a. The boundary of the region computed by equation (9.79) with S_8 is shown in Figure 9.49b, while the result with S_4 is shown in Figure 9.49c. Note that the boundary is only approximately 8- or 4-connected. For example, in the 8-connected boundary there are occasional 4-connected pixels. Finally, the boundary of the region as computed by an algorithm that traces around the boundary of the region and links the boundary points into contours is shown in Figure 9.49d. Note that this is the true boundary of the region. Also note that, since only part of the region is displayed, there is no boundary at the bottom of the displayed part.

As we have seen, the erosion can be used as a template matching operation. However, sometimes it is not selective enough and returns too many matches. The reason for this is that the erosion does not take into account the background. For this reason, an operation that explicitly models the background is needed. This operation is called the hit-or-miss transform. Since the foreground and background should be taken into account, it uses a structuring element that consists of two parts: $S = (S^f, S^b)$ with $S^f \cap S^b = \emptyset$. With this, the hit-or-miss transform is defined as

$$R \otimes S = (R \ominus \check{S}^f) \cap (\overline{R} \ominus \check{S}^b) = (R \ominus \check{S}^f) \backslash (R \oplus \check{S}^b) \tag{9.81}$$

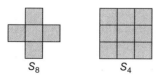

Figure 9.48 Structuring elements for computing the boundary of a region with 8-connectivity (S_8) and 4-connectivity (S_4).

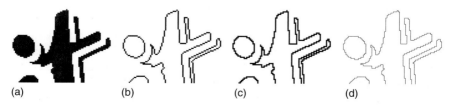

Figure 9.49 (a) Detail of a larger region. (b) The 8-connected boundary of (a) computed by equation (9.79). (c) The 4-connected boundary of (a). (d) Linked contour of the boundary of (a).

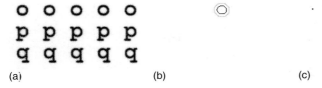

(a) (b) (c)

Figure 9.50 (a) Image of a print of several characters. (b) The structuring element used for the hit-or-miss transform. The black part is the foreground structuring element and the light gray part is the background structuring element. (c) Result of the hit-or-miss transform of the thresholded image (see Figure 9.47e) with the structuring element in (b). Note that only the reference point of the letter "o" has been identified, in contrast to the erosion (see Figure 9.47f).

Hence, the hit-or-miss transform returns those translated reference points for which the foreground structuring element S^f completely lies within the foreground and the background structuring element S^b completely lies within the background. The second equation is especially useful from an implementation point of view since it avoids having to compute the complement. The hit-or-miss transform is dual to itself if the foreground and background structuring elements are exchanged: $R \otimes S = \overline{R} \otimes S'$, where $S' = (S^b, S^f)$.

Figure 9.50 shows the same image as Figure 9.47d. The goal here is to match only the letters "o" in the image. To do so, we can define a structuring element that crosses the vertical strokes of the letters "p" and "q" (and also "b" and "d"). One possible structuring element for this purpose is shown in Figure 9.50b. With the hit-or-miss transform, we are able to remove the found matches for the letters "p" and "q" from the result, as can be seen from Figure 9.50c.

We now turn our attention to operations in which the basic operations we have discussed so far are executed in succession. The first such operation is the opening:

$$R \circ S = (R \ominus \check{S}) \oplus S = \bigcup_{S_t \subseteq R} S_t \tag{9.82}$$

Hence, the opening is an erosion followed by a Minkowski addition with the same structuring element. The second equation tells us that we can visualize the opening by moving the structuring element around the plane. Whenever the structuring element completely lies within the region, we add the entire translated structuring element to the output region (and not just the translated reference point as in the erosion). The opening's definition causes the location of the reference point to cancel out, which can be seen from the second equation. Therefore, the opening is translation-invariant with respect to the structuring element. In contrast to the erosion and dilation, the opening is idempotent, that is, applying it multiple times has the same effect as applying it once: $(R \circ S) \circ S = R \circ S$.

Like the erosion, the opening can be used as a template matching operation. In contrast to the erosion and hit-or-miss transform, it returns all points of the input region into which the structuring element fits. Hence it preserves the shape of the object to find. An example of this is shown in Figure 9.51, where the same input images and structuring elements as in Figure 9.47 are used. Note that the opening has found the same instances of the structuring elements as the erosion but has

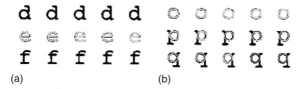

(a) (b)

Figure 9.51 (a) Result of applying an opening with the structuring element in Figure 9.47a to the segmented region in Figure 9.47b. (b) Result of applying an opening with the structuring element in Figure 9.47d to the segmented region in Figure 9.47e. The result of the opening is overlaid in light gray onto the input region, displayed in black. Note that the opening finds the same instances of the structuring elements as the erosion but preserves the shape of the matched structuring elements.

preserved the shape of the matched structuring elements. Hence, in this example it also finds the letters "p" and "q." To find only the letters "o," we could combine the hit-or-miss transformation with a Minkowski addition to get a hit-or-miss opening: $R \odot S = (R \otimes S) \oplus S^f$.

Another very useful property of the opening results if structuring elements like circles or rectangles are used. If an opening with these structuring elements is performed, parts of the region that are smaller than the structuring element are removed from the region. This can be used to remove unwanted appendages from the region and to smooth the boundary of the region by removing small protrusions. Furthermore, small bridges between object parts can be removed, which can be used to separate objects. Finally, the opening can be used to suppress small objects. Figure 9.52 shows an example of using the opening to remove unwanted appendages and small objects from the segmentation. In Figure 9.52a, an image of a ball-bonded die is shown. The goal is to segment the balls on the pads. If the

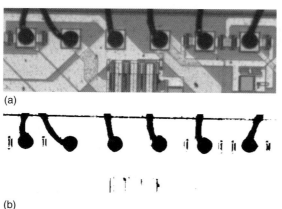

Figure 9.52 (a) Image of a ball-bonded die. The goal is to segment the balls. (b) Result of thresholding (a). The segmentation includes the wires that are bonded to the pads. (c) Result of performing an opening with a circle of diameter 31. The wires and the other extraneous segmentation results have been removed by the opening, and only the balls remain.

image is thresholded (Figure 9.52b), the wires that are attached to the balls are also extracted. Furthermore, there are extraneous small objects in the segmentation. By performing an opening with a circle of diameter 31, the wires and small objects are removed, and only smooth region parts that correspond to the balls are retained.

The second interesting operation in which the basic morphological operations are executed in succession is the closing:

$$R \bullet S = (R \oplus \check{S}) \ominus S = \overline{\bigcup_{S_t \subseteq \overline{R}} S_t} \tag{9.83}$$

Hence, the closing is a dilation followed by a Minkowski subtraction with the same structuring element. There is, unfortunately, no simple formula that tells us how the closing can be visualized. The second formula is actually defined by the duality of the opening and the closing, namely a closing on the foreground is identical to an opening on the background, and vice versa:

$$R \bullet S = \overline{\overline{R} \circ S} \quad \text{and} \quad R \circ S = \overline{\overline{R} \bullet S} \tag{9.84}$$

Like the opening, the closing is translation-invariant with respect to the structuring element. Furthermore, it is also idempotent.

Since the closing is dual to the opening, it can be used to merge objects that are separated by gaps that are smaller than the structuring element. If structuring elements like circles or rectangles are used, the closing can be used to close holes and to remove indentations that are smaller than the structuring element. The second property enables us to smooth the boundary of the region.

Figure 9.53 shows how the closing can be used to remove indentations in a region. In Figure 9.53a, a molded plastic part with a protrusion is shown. The goal is to detect the protrusion because it is a production error. Since the actual object is circular, if the entire part were visible, the protrusion could be detected by performing an opening with a circle that is almost as large as the object and then subtracting the opened region from the original segmentation. However, only a part of the object is visible, so the erosion in the opening would create artifacts or remove the object entirely. Therefore, by duality we can pursue the opposite approach: we can segment the background and perform a closing on it. Figure 9.53b shows the result of thresholding the background. The protrusion is now an indentation in the background. The result of performing a closing with a circle of diameter 801 is shown in Figure 9.53c. The diameter of the circle was set to 801 because it is large enough to completely fill the indentation and to recover the circular shape of the object. If much smaller circles were used, for example, with a diameter of 401, the indentation would not be filled completely. To detect the error itself, we can compute the difference between the closing and the original segmentation. To remove some noisy pixels that result because the boundary of the original segmentation is not as smooth as the closed region, the difference can be postprocessed with an opening, for example, with a 5×5 rectangle, to remove the noisy pixels. The resulting error region is shown in Figure 9.53d.

The operations we have discussed so far have been mostly concerned with the region as a 2D object. The only exception has been the calculation of the boundary

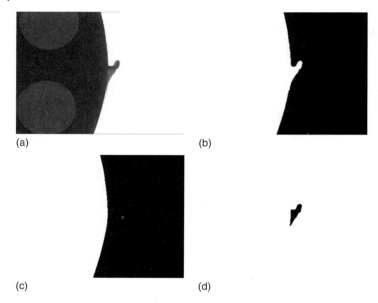

Figure 9.53 (a) Image of size 768 × 576 showing a molded plastic part with a protrusion. (b) Result of thresholding the background of (a). (c) Result of a closing on (b) with a circle of diameter 801. Note that the protrusion (the indentation in the background) has been filled in and the circular shape of the plastic part has been recovered. (d) Result of computing the difference between (c) and (b) and performing an opening with a 5 × 5 rectangle on the difference to remove small parts. The result is the erroneous protrusion of the mold.

of a region, which reduces a region to its 1D outline, and hence gives a more condensed description of the region. If the objects are mostly linear, that is, are regions that have a much greater length than width, a more salient description of the object would be obtained if we could somehow capture its one-pixel-wide center line. This center line is called the skeleton or medial axis of the region. Several definitions of a skeleton can be given [35]. One intuitive definition can be obtained if we imagine that we try to fit circles that are as large as possible into the region. More precisely, a circle C is maximal in the region R if there is no other circle in R that is a superset of C. The skeleton then is defined as the set of the centers of the maximal circles. Consequently, a point on the skeleton has at least two different points on the boundary of the region to which it has the same shortest distance. Algorithms to compute the skeleton are given in [35, 37]. They basically can be regarded as sequential hit-or-miss transforms that find points on the boundary of the region that cannot belong to the skeleton and delete them. The goal of the skeletonization is to preserve the homotopy of the region, that is, the number of connected components and holes. One set of structuring elements for computing an 8-connected skeleton is shown in Figure 9.54 [35]. These structuring elements are used sequentially in all four possible orientations to find pixels with the hit-or-miss transform that can be deleted from the region. The iteration is continued until no changes occur. It should be noted

Figure 9.54 Structuring elements for computing an 8-connected skeleton of a region. These structuring elements are used sequentially in all four possible orientations to find pixels that can be deleted.

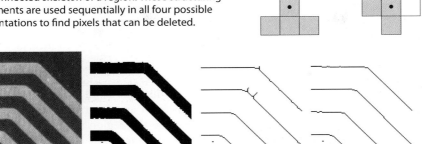

Figure 9.55 (a) Image showing a part of a PCB with several tracks. (b) Result of thresholding (a). (c) The 8-connected skeleton computed with an algorithm that uses the structuring elements in Figure 9.54 [35]. (d) Result of computing the skeleton with an algorithm that produces fewer skeleton branches [38].

that skeletonization is an example of an algorithm that can be implemented more efficiently on binary images than on the run-length representation.

Figure 9.55a shows a part of an image of a PCB with several tracks. The image is thresholded (Figure 9.55b), and the skeleton of the thresholded region is computed with the above algorithm (Figure 9.55c). Note that the skeleton contains several undesirable branches on the upper two tracks. For this reason, many different skeletonization algorithms have been proposed. One algorithm that produces relatively few unwanted branches is described in [38]. The result of this algorithm is shown in Figure 9.55d. Note that there are no undesirable branches in this case.

The final region morphology operation that we will discuss is the distance transform, which returns an image instead of a region. This image contains, for each point in the region R, the shortest distance to a point outside the region (i.e., to $\overline{R}$). Consequently, all points on the inner boundary of the region have a distance of 1. Typically, the distance of the other points is obtained by considering paths that must be contained in the pixel grid. Thus, the chosen connectivity defines which paths are allowed. If the 4-connectivity is used, the corresponding distance is called the city-block distance. Let (r_1, c_1) and (r_2, c_2) be two points. Then the city-block distance is given by

$$d_4 = |r_2 - r_1| + |c_2 - c_1| \tag{9.85}$$

Figure 9.56a shows the city-block distance between two points. In the example, the city-block distance is 5. On the other hand, if 8-connectivity is used, the

Figure 9.56 (a) City-block distance between two points. (b) Chessboard distance. (c) Euclidean distance.

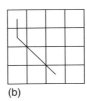
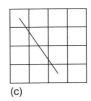

(a) (b) (c)

corresponding distance is called the chessboard distance. It is given by

$$d_8 = \max\{|r_2 - r_1|, |c_2 - c_1|\} \tag{9.86}$$

In the example in Figure 9.56b, the chessboard distance between the two points is 3. Both these distances are approximations to the Euclidean distance, given by

$$d_e = \sqrt{(r_2 - r_1)^2 + (c_2 - c_1)^2} \tag{9.87}$$

For the example in Figure 9.56c, the Euclidean distance is $\sqrt{13}$.

Algorithms to compute the distance transform are described in [39]. They work by initializing the distance image outside the region with 0 and within the region with a suitably chosen maximum distance, that is, $2^b - 1$, where b is the number of bits in the distance image, for example, $2^{16} - 1$. Then, two sequential line-by-line scans through the image are performed, one from the top left to the bottom right corner, and the second in the opposite direction. In each case, a small mask is placed at the current pixel, and the minimum over the elements in the mask of the already computed distances plus the elements in the mask is computed. The two masks are shown in Figure 9.57. If $d_1 = 1$ and $d_2 = \infty$ are used (i.e., d_2 is ignored), the city-block distance is computed. For $d_1 = 1$ and $d_2 = 1$, the chessboard distance results. Interestingly, if $d_1 = 3$ and $d_2 = 4$ is used and the distance image is divided by 3, a very good approximation to the Euclidean distance results, which can be computed solely with integer operations. This distance is called the chamfer-3 − 4 distance [39]. With slight modifications, the true Euclidean distance can be computed [40]. The principle is to compute the number of horizontal and vertical steps to reach the boundary using masks similar to the ones in Figure 9.57, and then to compute the Euclidean distance from the number of steps.

The skeleton and the distance transform can be combined to compute the width of linear objects very efficiently. In Figure 9.58a, a PCB with tracks that have several errors is shown. The protrusions on the tracks are called spurs, while the indentations are called mouse bites [41]. They are deviations from the correct track width. Figure 9.58b shows the result of computing the distance transform with the chamfer-3 − 4 distance on the segmented tracks. The errors are clearly visible in the distance transform. To extract the width of the tracks, we need to calculate the skeleton of the segmented tracks (Figure 9.58c). If the skeleton is used as the ROI for the distance image, each point on the skeleton will have the corresponding distance to the border of the track. Since the skeleton is the center line of the track, this distance is the width of the track. Hence, to detect errors, we simply need to threshold the distance image within the skeleton. Note that in this example it is extremely useful that we have defined that images can have an

Figure 9.57 Masks used in the two sequential scans to compute the distance transform. The left mask is used in the left-to-right, top-to-bottom scan. The right mask is used in the scan in the opposite direction.

9.6 Morphology | 575

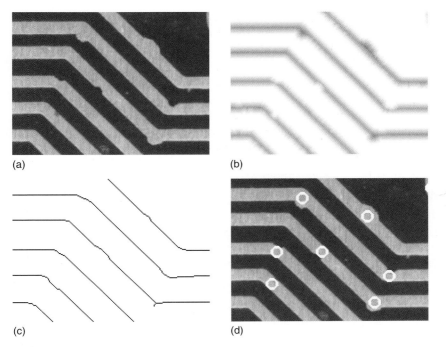

(a) (b)

(c) (d)

Figure 9.58 (a) Image showing a part of a PCB with several tracks that have spurs and mouse bites. (b) Distance transform of the result of thresholding (a). The distance image is visualized inverted (dark gray values correspond to large distances). (c) Skeleton of the segmented region. (d) Result of extracting too narrow or too wide parts of the tracks by using (c) as the ROI for (b) and thresholding the distances. The errors are visualized by drawing circles at the centers of gravity of the connected components of the error region.

arbitrary ROI. Figure 9.58d shows the result of drawing circles at the centers of gravity of the connected components of the error region. All major errors have been detected correctly.

9.6.2 Gray Value Morphology

Because morphological operations are very versatile and useful, the question of whether they can be extended to gray value images arises quite naturally. This can indeed be done. In analogy to the region morphology, let $g(r, c)$ denote the image that should be processed, and let $s(r, c)$ be an image with ROI S. Like in the region morphology, the image s is called the structuring element. The gray value Minkowski addition is then defined as

$$g \oplus s = (g \oplus s)_{r,c} = \max_{(i,j) \in S} \{g_{r-i, c-j} + s_{i,j}\} \tag{9.88}$$

This is a natural generalization because the Minkowski addition for regions is obtained as a special case if the characteristic function of the region is used as the gray value image. If, additionally, an image with gray value 0 within the ROI S is used as the structuring element, the Minkowski addition becomes

$$g \oplus s = \max_{(i,j) \in S} \{g_{r-i,c-j}\} \tag{9.89}$$

For characteristic functions, the maximum operation corresponds to the union. Furthermore, $g_{r-i,c-j}$ corresponds to the translation of the image by the vector (i, j). Hence, equation (9.89) is equivalent to the second formula in equation (9.73).

Like in the region morphology, the dilation can be obtained by transposing the structuring element. This results in the following definition:

$$g \oplus \check{s} = (g \oplus \check{s})_{r,c} = \max_{(i,j) \in S} \{g_{r+i,c+j} + s_{i,j}\} \tag{9.90}$$

The typical choice for the structuring element in the gray value morphology is the flat structuring element that was already used previously: $s(r, c) = 0$ for $(r, c) \in S$. With this, the gray value dilation has a similar effect as the region dilation: it enlarges the foreground, that is, parts in the image that are brighter than their surroundings, and shrinks the background, that is, parts in the image that are darker than their surroundings. Hence, it can be used to connect disjoint parts of a bright object in the gray value image. This is sometimes useful if the object cannot be segmented easily using region operations alone. Conversely, the dilation can be used to split dark objects.

The Minkowski subtraction for gray value images is given by

$$g \ominus s = (g \ominus s)_{r,c} = \min_{(i,j) \in S} \{g_{r-i,c-j} - s_{i,j}\} \tag{9.91}$$

As above, by transposing the structuring element we obtain the gray value erosion:

$$g \ominus \check{s} = (g \ominus \check{s})_{r,c} = \min_{(i,j) \in S} \{g_{r+i,c+j} - s_{i,j}\} \tag{9.92}$$

Like the region erosion, the gray value erosion shrinks the foreground and enlarges the background. Hence, the erosion can be used to split touching bright objects and to connect disjoint dark objects. In fact, the dilation and erosion, as well as the Minkowski addition and subtraction, are dual to each other, like for regions. For the duality, we need to define what the complement of an image should be. If the images are stored with b bits, the natural definition for the complement operation is $\overline{g}_{r,c} = 2^b - 1 - g_{r,c}$. With this, it can be easily shown that the erosion and dilation are dual:

$$g \oplus s = \overline{\overline{g} \ominus s} \quad \text{and} \quad g \ominus s = \overline{\overline{g} \oplus s} \tag{9.93}$$

Therefore, all the properties that hold for one operation for bright objects hold for the other operation for dark objects, and vice versa.

Note that the dilation and erosion can also be regarded as two special rank filters (see Section 9.2.3) if flat structuring elements are used. They select the minimum and maximum gray values within the domain of the structuring element, which can be regarded as the filter mask. Therefore, the dilation and erosion are sometimes referred to as the maximum and minimum filters (or max and min filters).

Efficient algorithms to compute the dilation and erosion are given in [15]. Their runtime complexity is $O(whn)$, where w and h are the dimensions of the image, while n is roughly the number of points on the boundary of the domain of the structuring element for flat structuring elements. For rectangular structuring elements, algorithms with a runtime complexity of $O(wh)$, that is, with a constant number of operations per pixel, can be found [42]. This is similar to the recursive implementation of a linear filter.

With these building blocks, we can define a gray value opening like for regions as an erosion followed by a Minkowski addition: that is

$$g \circ s = (g \ominus \check{s}) \oplus s \qquad (9.94)$$

and the closing as a dilation followed by a Minkowski subtraction: that is

$$g \bullet s = (g \oplus \check{s}) \ominus s \qquad (9.95)$$

The gray value opening and closing have properties similar to those of their region counterparts. In particular, with the above definition of the complement for images, they are dual to each other:

$$g \circ s = \overline{\overline{g} \bullet s} \quad \text{and} \quad g \bullet s = \overline{\overline{g} \circ s} \qquad (9.96)$$

Like the region operations, they can be used to fill in small holes or, by duality, to remove small objects. Furthermore, they can be used to join or separate objects and to smooth the inner and outer boundaries of objects in the gray value image.

Figure 9.59 shows how the gray value opening and closing can be used to detect errors in the tracks on a PCB. We have already seen in Figure 9.58 that some of these errors can be detected by looking at the width of the tracks with the distance transform and the skeleton. This technique is very useful because it enables us to detect relatively large areas with errors. However, small errors are harder to detect with this technique because the distance transform and skeleton are only pixel-precise, and consequently the width of the track can be determined reliably with a precision of only two pixels. Smaller errors can be detected more reliably with the gray value morphology. Figure 9.59a shows a part of a PCB with several tracks that have spurs, mouse bites, pinholes, spurious copper, and open and short circuits [41]. The results of performing a gray value opening and closing with an octagon of diameter 11 are shown in Figure 9.59b,c. Because of the horizontal, vertical, and diagonal layout of the tracks, using an octagon as the structuring element is preferable. It can be seen that the opening smooths out the spurs, while the closing smooths out the mouse bites. Furthermore, the short circuit and spurious copper are removed by the opening, while the pinhole and open circuit are removed by the closing. To detect these errors, we can require that the opened and closed images should not differ too much. If there were no errors, the differences would solely be caused by the texture on the tracks. Since the gray values of the opened image are always smaller than those of the closed image, we can use the dynamic threshold operation for bright objects (Equation (9.46)) to perform the required segmentation. Every pixel that has a gray value difference greater than g_{diff} can be considered as an error. Figure 9.59d shows the result of segmenting the errors using a dynamic threshold $g_{\text{diff}} = 60$. This detects all the errors on the board.

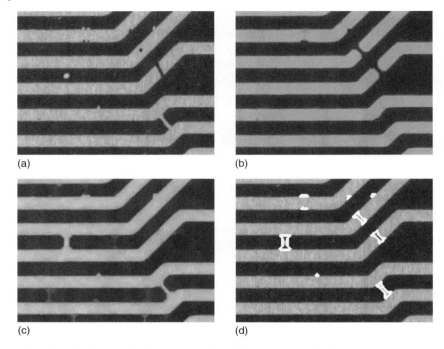

Figure 9.59 (a) Image showing a part of a PCB with several tracks that have spurs, mouse bites, pinholes, spurious copper, and open and short circuits. (b) Result of performing a gray value opening with an octagon of diameter 11 on (a). (c) Result of performing a gray value closing with an octagon of diameter 11 on (a). (d) Result of segmenting the errors in (a) by using a dynamic threshold operation with the images of (b) and (c).

We conclude this section with an operator that computes the range of gray values that occur within the structuring element. This can be obtained easily by calculating the difference between the dilation and erosion:

$$g \diamond s = (g \oplus \check{s}) - (g \ominus \check{s}) \tag{9.97}$$

Since this operator produces results similar to those of a gradient filter (see Section 9.7), it is sometimes called the morphological gradient.

Figure 9.60 shows how the gray range operator can be used to segment punched serial numbers. Because of the scratches, texture, and illumination, it is difficult to segment the characters in Figure 9.60a directly. In particular, the scratch next to the upper left part of the "2" cannot be separated from the "2" without splitting several of the other numbers. The result of computing the gray range within a 9×9 rectangle is shown in Figure 9.60b. With this, it is easy to segment the numbers (Figure 9.60c) and to separate them from other segmentation results (Figure 9.60d).

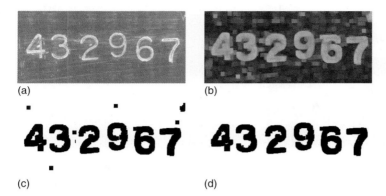

Figure 9.60 (a) Image showing a punched serial number. Because of the scratches, texture, and illumination, it is difficult to segment the characters directly. (b) Result of computing the gray range within a 9 × 9 rectangle. (c) Result of thresholding (b). (d) Result of computing the connected components of (c) and selecting the characters based on their size.

9.7 Edge Extraction

In Section 9.4, we discussed several segmentation algorithms. They have in common that they are based on thresholding the image, with either pixel or subpixel accuracy. It is possible to achieve very good accuracies with these approaches, as we saw in Section 9.5. However, in most cases the accuracy of the measurements that we can derive from the segmentation result critically depends on choosing the correct threshold for the segmentation. If the threshold is chosen incorrectly, the extracted objects typically become larger or smaller because of the smooth transition from the foreground to the background gray value. This problem is especially grave if the illumination can change, since in this case the adaptation of the thresholds to the changed illumination must be very accurate. Therefore, a segmentation algorithm that is robust with respect to illumination changes is extremely desirable. From the above discussion, we see that the boundary of the segmented region or subpixel-precise contour moves if the illumination changes or the thresholds are chosen inappropriately. Therefore, the goal of a robust segmentation algorithm must be to find the boundary of the objects as robustly and accurately as possible. The best way to describe the boundaries of the objects robustly is by regarding them as edges in the image. Therefore, in this section we will examine methods to extract edges.

9.7.1 Definition of Edges in One and Two Dimensions

To derive an edge extraction algorithm, we need to define what edges actually are. For the moment, let us make the simplifying assumption that the gray values in the object and in the background are constant. In particular, we assume that

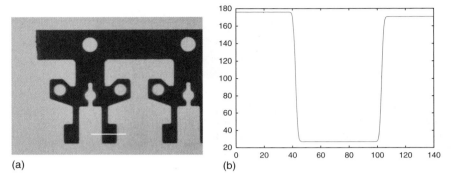

Figure 9.61 (a) Image of a back-lit workpiece with a horizontal line that indicates the location of the idealized gray value profile in (b).

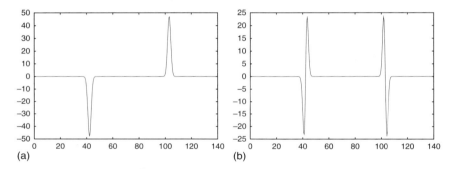

Figure 9.62 (a) First derivative $f'(x)$ of the ideal gray value profile in Figure 9.61b. (b) Second derivative $f'(x)$.

the image contains no noise. Furthermore, let us assume that the image is not discretized, that is, it is continuous. To illustrate this, Figure 9.61b shows an idealized gray value profile across the part of a workpiece that is indicated in Figure 9.61a.

From the above example, we can see that edges are areas in the image in which the gray values change significantly. To formalize this, let us regard the image for the moment as a 1D function $f(x)$. From elementary calculus we know that the gray values change significantly if the first derivative of $f(x)$ differs significantly from 0, that is, $|f'(x)| \gg 0$. Unfortunately, this alone is insufficient to define a unique edge location because there are typically many connected points for which this condition is true since the transition between the background and foreground gray values is smooth. This can be seen in Figure 9.62a, where the first derivative $f'(x)$ of the ideal gray value profile in Figure 9.61b is displayed. Note, for example, that there is an extended range of points for which $|f'(x)| \geq 20$. Therefore, to obtain a unique edge position, we must additionally require that the absolute value of the first derivative $|f'(x)|$ is locally maximal. This is called non-maximum suppression.

From elementary calculus we know that, at the points where $|f'(x)|$ is locally maximal, the second derivative vanishes: $f''(x) = 0$. Hence, edges are given by the locations of inflection points of $f(x)$. To remove flat inflection points, we would additionally have to require that $f'(x)f'''(x) < 0$. However, this restriction is seldom observed. Therefore, in one dimension, an alternative and equivalent definition to the maxima of the absolute value of the first derivative is to define edges as the locations of the zero-crossings of the second derivative. Figure 9.62b displays the second derivative $f''(x) = 0$ of the ideal gray value profile in Figure 9.61b. Clearly, the zero-crossings are in the same positions as the maxima of the absolute value of the first derivative in Figure 9.62a.

From Figure 9.62a, we can also see that in one dimension we can easily associate a polarity with an edge based on the sign of $f'(x)$. We speak of a positive edge if $f'(x) > 0$ and of a negative edge if $f'(x) < 0$.

We now turn to edges in continuous 2D images. Here, the edge itself is a curve $s(t) = (r(t), c(t))$, which is parameterized by a parameter t, for example, its arc length. At each point of the edge curve, the gray value profile perpendicular to the curve is a 1D edge profile. With this, we can adapt the first 1D edge definition above for the 2D case: we define an edge as the points in the image where the directional derivative in the direction perpendicular to the edge is locally maximal. From differential geometry, we know that the direction $n(t)$ perpendicular to the edge curve $s(t)$ is given by $n(t) = s'(t)^\perp \parallel s''(t)$. Unfortunately, the edge definition seemingly requires us to know the edge position $s(t)$ already to obtain the direction perpendicular to the edge, and hence looks like a circular definition. Fortunately, the direction $n(t)$ perpendicular to the edge can be determined easily from the image itself. It is given by the gradient vector of the image, which points in the direction of steepest ascent of the image function $f(r, c)$. The gradient of the image is given by the vector of its first partial derivatives:

$$\nabla f = \nabla f(r, c) = \left(\frac{\partial f(r, c)}{\partial r}, \frac{\partial f(r, c)}{\partial c} \right) = (f_r, f_c) \qquad (9.98)$$

In the last equation, we have used a subscript to denote the partial derivative with respect to the subscripted variable. We will use this convention throughout this section. The Euclidean length

$$\parallel \nabla f \parallel_2 = \sqrt{f_r^2 + f_c^2} \qquad (9.99)$$

of the gradient vector is the equivalent of the absolute value of the first derivative $|f'(x)|$ in one dimension. We will also call the length of the gradient vector its magnitude. It is also often called the amplitude. The gradient direction is, of course, directly given by the gradient vector. We can also convert it to an angle by calculating $\phi = -\arctan(f_r/f_c)$. Note that ϕ increases in the mathematically positive direction (counterclockwise), starting at the column axis. This is the usual convention. With the above definitions, we can define edges in two dimensions as the points in the image where the gradient magnitude is locally maximal in the direction of the gradient. To illustrate this definition, Figure 9.63a shows a plot of the gray values of an idealized corner. The corresponding gradient magnitude is shown in Figure 9.63b. The edges are the points at the top of the ridge in the gradient magnitude.

In one dimension, we have seen that the second edge definition (the zero-crossings of the second derivative) is equivalent to the first definition.

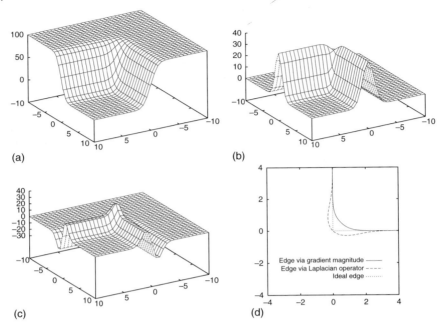

Figure 9.63 (a) Image of an idealized corner, for example, one of the corners at the bottom of the workpiece in Figure 9.61a. (b) Gradient magnitude of (a). (c) Laplacian of (a). (d) Comparison of the edges that result from the two definitions in two dimensions.

Therefore, it is natural to ask whether this definition can be adapted for the 2D case. Unfortunately, there is no direct equivalent for the second derivative in two dimensions, since there are three partial derivatives of order two. A suitable definition for the second derivative in two dimensions is the Laplacian operator (Laplacian for short), defined by

$$\Delta f = \Delta f(r,c) = \frac{\partial^2 f(r,c)}{\partial r^2} + \frac{\partial^2 f(r,c)}{\partial c^2} = f_{rr} + f_{cc} \qquad (9.100)$$

With this, the edges can be defined as the zero-crossings of the Laplacian: $\Delta f(r,c) = 0$. Figure 9.63c shows the Laplacian of the idealized corner in Figure 9.63a. The results of the two edge definitions are shown in Figure 9.63d. It can be seen that, unlike for the 1D edges, the two definitions do not result in the same edge positions. The edge positions are identical only for straight edges. Whenever the edge is significantly curved, the two definitions return different results. It can be seen that the definition via the maxima of the gradient magnitude always lies inside the ideal corner, whereas the definition via the zero-crossings of the Laplacian always lies outside the corner and passes directly through the ideal corner. The Laplacian edge also is in a different position from the true edge for a larger part of the edge. Therefore, in two dimensions the definition via the maxima of the gradient magnitude is usually preferred. However, in some applications the fact that the Laplacian edge passes through the corner can be used to measure objects with sharp corners more accurately.

9.7.2 1D Edge Extraction

We now turn our attention to edges in real images, which are discrete and contain noise. In this section, we will discuss how to extract edges from 1D gray value profiles. This is a very useful operation that is used frequently in machine vision applications because it is extremely fast. It is typically used to determine the position or diameter of an object.

The first problem we have to address is how to compute the derivatives of the discrete 1D gray value profile. Our first idea might be to use the differences of consecutive gray values on the profile: $f'_i = f_i - f_{i-1}$. Unfortunately, this definition is not symmetric. It would compute the derivative at the "half-pixel" positions $f_{i-(1/2)}$. A symmetric way to compute the first derivative is given by

$$f'_i = \tfrac{1}{2}(f_{i+1} - f_{i-1}) \tag{9.101}$$

This formula is obtained by fitting a parabola through three consecutive points of the profile and computing the derivative of the parabola at the center point. The parabola is uniquely defined by the three points. With the same mechanism, we can also derive a formula for the second derivative:

$$f''_i = \tfrac{1}{2}(f_{i+1} - 2f_i + f_{i-1}) \tag{9.102}$$

Note that the above methods to compute the first and second derivatives are linear filters, and hence can be regarded as the following two convolution masks:

$$\tfrac{1}{2} \cdot (1\ 0\ -1) \quad \text{and} \quad \tfrac{1}{2} \cdot (1\ -2\ 1) \tag{9.103}$$

Note that the -1 is the last element in the first derivative mask because the elements of the mask are mirrored in the convolution (see equation (9.18)).

Figure 9.64a displays the true gray value profile taken from the horizontal line in the image in Figure 9.61a. Its first derivative, computed with equation (9.101), is shown in Figure 9.64b. We can see that the noise in the image causes a very large number of local maxima in the absolute value of the first derivative, and consequently also a large number of zero-crossings in the second derivative. The salient edges can easily be selected by thresholding the absolute value of the first derivative: $|f'_i| \geq t$. For the second derivative, the edges cannot be selected

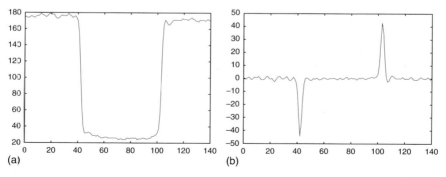

Figure 9.64 (a) Gray value profile taken from the horizontal line in the image in Figure 9.61a. (b) First derivative f'_i of the gray value profile.

as easily. In fact, we have to resort to calculating the first derivative as well to be able to select the relevant edges. Hence, the edge definition via the first derivative is preferable because it can be done with one filter operation instead of two, and consequently the edges can be extracted much faster.

The gray value profile in Figure 9.64a already contains relatively little noise. Nevertheless, in most cases it is desirable to suppress the noise even further. If the object we are measuring has straight edges in the part in which we are performing the measurement, we can use the gray values perpendicular to the line along which we are extracting the gray value profile and average them in a suitable manner. The simplest way to do this is to compute the mean of the gray values perpendicular to the line. If, for example, the line along which we are extracting the gray value profile is horizontal, we can calculate the mean in the vertical direction as follows:

$$f_i = \frac{1}{2m+1} \sum_{j=-m}^{m} f_{r+j,c+i} \tag{9.104}$$

This acts like a mean filter in one direction. Hence, the noise variance is reduced by a factor of $2m + 1$. Of course, we could also use a 1D Gaussian filter to average the gray values. However, since this would require larger filter masks for the same noise reduction, and consequently would lead to longer execution times, in this case the mean filter is preferable.

If the line along which we want to extract the gray value profile is horizontal or vertical, the calculation of the profile is simple. If we want to extract the profile from inclined lines or from circles or ellipses, the computation is slightly more difficult. To enable meaningful measurements for distances, we must sample the line with a fixed distance, typically one pixel. Then, we need to generate lines perpendicular to the curve along which we want to extract the profile. This procedure is shown for an inclined line in Figure 9.65. Because of this, the points from which we must extract the gray values typically do not lie on pixel centers. Therefore, we will have to interpolate them. This can be done with the techniques discussed in Section 9.3.3, that is, with nearest-neighbor or bilinear interpolation.

Figure 9.66 shows a gray value profile and its first derivative obtained by vertically averaging the gray values along the line shown in Figure 9.61a. The size of the 1D mean filter was 21 pixels in this case. If we compare this with Figure 9.64, which shows the profile obtained from the same line without averaging, we can see that the noise in the profile has been reduced significantly. Because of this, the salient edges are even easier to select than without the averaging.

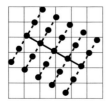

Figure 9.65 Creation of the gray value profile from an inclined line. The line is shown by the heavy solid line. The circles indicate the points that are used to compute the profile. Note that they do not lie on the pixel centers. The direction in which the 1D mean is computed is shown by the dashed lines.

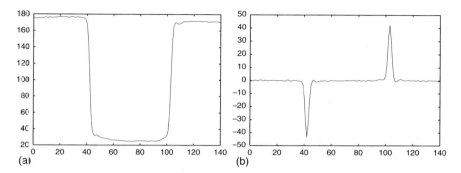

Figure 9.66 (a) Gray value profile taken from the horizontal line in the image in Figure 9.61a and averaged vertically over 21 pixels. (b) First derivative f'_i of the gray value profile.

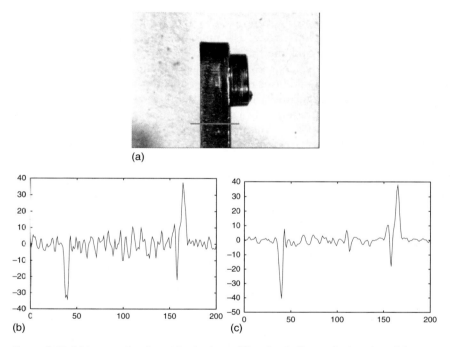

Figure 9.67 (a) Image of a relay with a horizontal line that indicates the location of the gray value profile. (b) First derivative of the gray value profile without averaging. (c) First derivative of the gray value profile with vertical averaging over 21 pixels.

Unfortunately, the averaging perpendicular to the curve along which the gray value profile is extracted is sometimes insufficient to smooth the profiles enough to enable us to extract the relevant edges easily. One example is shown in Figure 9.67. Here, the object to be measured has a significant amount of texture, which is not as random as noise and consequently does not average out completely. Note that, on the right side of the profile, there is a negative edge with an amplitude almost as large as the edges we want to extract. Another reason for the noise not to cancel out completely may be that we cannot choose the size of the averaging large enough, for example, because the object's boundary is curved.

To solve these problems, we must smooth the gray value profile itself to suppress the noise even further. This is done by convolving the profile with a smoothing filter: $f_s = f * h$. We can then extract the edges from the smoothed profile via its first derivative. This would involve two convolutions: one for the smoothing filter, and the other for the derivative filter. Fortunately, the convolution has a very interesting property that we can use to save one convolution. The derivative of the smoothed function is identical to the convolution of the function with the derivative of the smoothing filter: $(f * h)' = f * h'$. We can regard h' as an edge filter.

Like for the smoothing filters, the natural question to ask is which edge filter is optimal. This problem was addressed by Canny [43]. He proposed three criteria that an edge detector should fulfill. First of all, it should have a good detection quality, that is, it should have a low probability of falsely detecting an edge point and also a low probability of erroneously missing an edge point. This criterion can be formalized as maximizing the signal-to-noise ratio of the output of the edge filter. Second, the edge detector should have good localization quality, that is, the extracted edges should be as close as possible to the true edges. This can be formalized by minimizing the variance of the extracted edge positions. Finally, the edge detector should return only a single edge for each true edge, that is, it should avoid multiple responses. This criterion can be formalized by maximizing the distance between the extracted edge positions. Canny then combined these three criteria into one optimization criterion and solved it using the calculus of variations. To do so, he assumed that the edge filter has a finite extent (mask size). Since adapting the filter to a particular mask size involves solving a relatively complex optimization problem, Canny looked for a simple filter that could be written in closed form. He found that the optimal edge filter can be approximated very well with the first derivative of the Gaussian filter:

$$g'_\sigma(x) = \frac{-x}{\sqrt{2\pi}\,\sigma^3}\, e^{-x^2/(2\sigma^2)} \qquad (9.105)$$

One drawback of using the true derivative of the Gaussian filter is that the edge amplitudes become progressively smaller as σ is increased. Ideally, the edge filter should return the true edge amplitude independent of the smoothing. To achieve this for an idealized step edge, the output of the filter must be multiplied with $\sqrt{2\pi}\,\sigma$.

Note that the optimal smoothing filter would be the integral of the optimal edge filter, that is, the Gaussian smoothing filter. It is interesting to note that, like the criteria in Section 9.2.3, Canny's formulation indicates that the Gaussian filter is the optimal smoothing filter.

Since the Gaussian filter and its derivatives cannot be implemented recursively (see Section 9.2.3), Deriche used Canny's approach to find optimal edge filters that can be implemented recursively [44]. He derived the following two filters:

$$d'_\alpha(x) = -\alpha^2 x\, e^{-\alpha|x|}$$
$$e'_\alpha(x) = -2\alpha \sin(\alpha x)\, e^{-\alpha|x|} \qquad (9.106)$$

The corresponding smoothing filters are

$$d_\alpha(x) = \tfrac{1}{4}\alpha(\alpha|x| + 1)\, e^{-\alpha|x|}$$
$$e_\alpha(x) = \tfrac{1}{2}\alpha[\sin(\alpha|x|) + \cos(\alpha|x|)]\, e^{-\alpha|x|} \qquad (9.107)$$

Note that, in contrast to the Gaussian filter, where larger values for σ indicate more smoothing, in the Deriche filters smaller values for α indicate more smoothing. The Gaussian filter has similar effects to the first Deriche filter for $\sigma = \sqrt{\pi}/\alpha$. For the second Deriche filter, the relation is $\sigma = \sqrt{\pi}/(2\alpha)$. Note that the Deriche filters are significantly different from the Canny filter. This can also be seen from Figure 9.68, which compares the Canny and Deriche smoothing and edge filters with equivalent filter parameters.

Figure 9.69 shows the result of using the Canny edge detector with $\sigma = 1.5$ to compute the smoothed first derivative of the gray value profile in Figure 9.67a. Like in Figure 9.67c, the profile was obtained by averaging over 21 pixels vertically. Note that the amplitude of the unwanted edge on the right side of the profile has been reduced significantly. This enables us to select the salient edges more easily.

To extract the edge position, we need to perform the non-maximum suppression. If we are only interested in the edge positions with pixel accuracy, we can

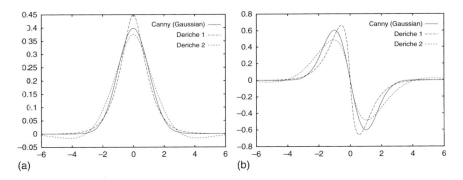

Figure 9.68 Comparison of the Canny and Deriche filters. (a) Smoothing filters. (b) Edge filters.

Figure 9.69 Result of applying the Canny edge filter with $\sigma = 1.5$ to the gray value profile in Figure 9.67a with vertical averaging over 21 pixels.

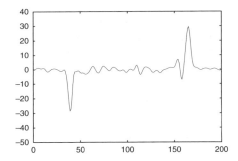

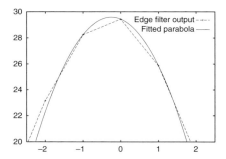

Figure 9.70 Principle of extracting edge points with subpixel accuracy. The local maximum of the edge amplitude is detected. Then, a parabola is fitted through the three points around the maximum. The maximum of the parabola is the subpixel-accurate edge location. The edge amplitude was taken from the right edge in Figure 9.69.

proceed as follows. Let the output of the edge filter be denoted by $e_i = |f * h'|_i$, where h' denotes one of the above edge filters. Then, the local maxima of the edge amplitude are given by the points for which $e_i > e_{i-1} \wedge e_i > e_{i+1} \wedge e_i \geq t$, where t is the threshold to select the relevant edges.

Unfortunately, extracting the edges with pixel accuracy is often not accurate enough. To extract edges with subpixel accuracy, we can note that around the maximum the edge amplitude can be approximated well with a parabola. Figure 9.70 illustrates this by showing a zoomed part of the edge amplitude around the right edge in Figure 9.69. If we fit a parabola through three points around the maximum edge amplitude and calculate the maximum of the parabola, we can obtain the edge position with subpixel accuracy. If an ideal camera system is assumed, this algorithm is as accurate as the precision with which the floating-point numbers are stored in the computer [45].

We conclude the discussion of the 1D edge extraction by showing the results of edge extraction on the two examples we have used so far. Figure 9.71a shows the edges that have been extracted along the line shown in Figure 9.61a with the Canny filter with $\sigma = 1.0$. From the two zoomed parts around the extracted edge

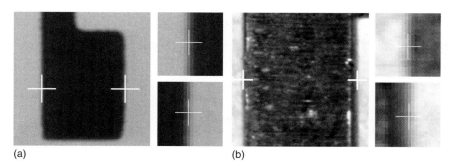

Figure 9.71 (a) Result of extracting 1D edges along the line shown in Figure 9.61a. The two small images show a zoomed part around the edge positions. In this case, they both lie very close to the pixel centers. The distance between the two edges is 60.95 pixels. (b) Result of extracting 1D edges along the line shown in Figure 9.67a. Note that the left edge, shown in detail in the upper right image, is almost exactly in the middle between two pixel centers. The distance between the two edges is 125.37 pixels.

positions, we can see that, by coincidence, both edges lie very close to the pixel centers. Figure 9.71b displays the result of extracting edges along the line shown in Figure 9.67a with the Canny filter with $\sigma = 1.5$. In this case, the left edge is almost exactly in the middle of two pixel centers. Hence, we can see that the algorithm is successful in extracting the edges with subpixel precision.

9.7.3 2D Edge Extraction

As discussed in Section 9.7.1, there are two possible definitions for edges in two dimensions, which are not equivalent. Like in the 1D case, the selection of salient edges will require us to perform a thresholding based on the gradient magnitude. Therefore, the definition via the zero-crossings of the Laplacian requires us to compute more partial derivatives than the definition via the maxima of the gradient magnitude. Consequently, we will concentrate on the maxima of the gradient magnitude for the 2D case. We will add some comments on the zero-crossings of the Laplacian at the end of this section.

As in the 1D case, the first question we need to answer is how to compute the partial derivatives of the image that are required to calculate the gradient. Similar to equation (9.101), we could use finite differences to calculate the partial derivatives. In two dimensions, they would be

$$f_{r;i,j} = \tfrac{1}{2}(f_{i+1,j} - f_{i-1,j}) \quad \text{and} \quad f_{c;i,j} = \tfrac{1}{2}(f_{i,j+1} - f_{i,j-1}) \tag{9.108}$$

However, as we have seen previously, typically the image must be smoothed to obtain good results. For time-critical applications, the filter masks should be as small as possible, that is, 3×3. All 3×3 edge filters can be brought into the following form by scaling the coefficients appropriately (note that the filter masks are mirrored in the convolution):

$$\begin{pmatrix} 1 & 0 & -1 \\ a & 0 & -a \\ 1 & 0 & -1 \end{pmatrix} \quad \begin{pmatrix} 1 & a & 1 \\ 0 & 0 & 0 \\ -1 & -a & -1 \end{pmatrix} \tag{9.109}$$

If we use $a = 1$, we obtain the Prewitt filter. Note that it performs as a mean filter perpendicular to the derivative direction. For $a = \sqrt{2}$, the Frei filter is obtained, and for $a = 2$ we obtain the Sobel filter, which performs an approximation to a Gaussian smoothing perpendicular to the derivative direction. Of the above three filters, the Sobel filter returns the best results because it uses the best smoothing filter.

Ando [46] has proposed a 3×3 edge filter that tries to minimize the artifacts that invariably are obtained with small filter masks. In our notation, his filter would correspond to $a = 2.435\,101$. Unfortunately, like the Frei filter, it requires floating-point calculations, which makes it unattractive for time-critical applications.

The 3×3 edge filters are primarily used to quickly find edges with moderate accuracy in images of relatively good quality. Since speed is important and the calculation of the gradient magnitude via the Euclidean length (the 2-norm) of the gradient vector ($\|\nabla f\|_2 = \sqrt{f_r^2 + f_c^2}$) requires an expensive square root calculation, the gradient magnitude is typically computed by one of the following norms: the 1-norm $\|\nabla f\|_1 = |f_r| + |f_c|$ or the maximum norm $\|\nabla f\|_\infty = \max(|f_r|, |f_c|)$. Note that the first norm corresponds to the city-block distance in the distance transform, while the second norm corresponds to the chessboard distance (see Section 9.6.1). Furthermore, the non-maximum suppression also is relatively expensive and is often omitted. Instead, the gradient magnitude is simply thresholded. Because this results in edges that are wider than one pixel, the thresholded edge regions are skeletonized. Note that this implicitly assumes that the edges are symmetric.

Figure 9.72 shows an example where this simple approach works quite well because the image is of good quality. Figure 9.72a displays the edge amplitude around the leftmost hole of the workpiece in Figure 9.61a computed with the Sobel filter and the 1-norm. The edge amplitude is thresholded (Figure 9.72b) and the skeleton of the resulting region is computed (Figure 9.72c). Since the assumption that the edges are symmetric is fulfilled in this example, the resulting edges are in the correct location.

This approach fails to produce good results on the more difficult image of the relay in Figure 9.67a. As can be seen from Figure 9.73a, the texture on the relay causes many areas with high gradient magnitude, which are also present in the segmentation (Figure 9.73b) and the skeleton (Figure 9.73c). Another interesting thing to note is that the vertical edge at the right corner of the top edge of the relay is quite blurred and asymmetric. This produces holes in the segmented edge region, which are exacerbated by the skeletonization.

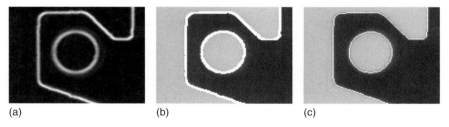

(a)   (b)   (c)

Figure 9.72 (a) Edge amplitude around the leftmost hole of the workpiece in Figure 9.61a computed with the Sobel filter and the 1-norm. (b) Thresholded edge region. (c) Skeleton of (b).

(a)   (b)   (c)

Figure 9.73 (a) Edge amplitude around the top part of the relay in Figure 9.67a computed with the Sobel filter and the 1-norm. (b) Thresholded edge region. (c) Skeleton of (b).

Because the 3 × 3 filters are not robust against noise and other disturbances, for example, textures, we need to adapt the approach to optimal 1D edge extraction described in the previous section to the 2D case. In two dimensions, we can derive the optimal edge filters by calculating the partial derivatives of the optimal smoothing filters, since the properties of the convolution again allow us to move the derivative calculation into the filter. Consequently, Canny's optimal edge filters in two dimensions are given by the partial derivatives of the Gaussian filter. Because the Gaussian filter is separable, so are its derivatives:

$$g_r = \sqrt{2\pi}\sigma g'_\sigma(r)g_\sigma(c) \quad \text{and} \quad g_c = \sqrt{2\pi}\sigma g_\sigma(r)g'_\sigma(c) \qquad (9.110)$$

(see the discussion following equation (9.105) for the factors of $\sqrt{2\pi}\sigma$). To adapt the Deriche filters to the 2D case, the separability of the filters is postulated. Hence, the optimal 2D Deriche filters are given by $d'_\alpha(r)d_\alpha(c)$ and $d_\alpha(r)d'_\alpha(c)$ for the first Deriche filter, and by $e'_\alpha(r)e_\alpha(c)$ and $e_\alpha(r)e'_\alpha(c)$ for the second Deriche filter (see equation (9.106)).

The advantage of the Canny filter is that it is isotropic, that is, rotation-invariant (see Section 9.2.3). Its disadvantage is that it cannot be implemented recursively. Therefore, the execution time depends on the amount of smoothing specified by σ. The Deriche filters, on the other hand, can be implemented recursively, and hence their runtime is independent of the smoothing parameter α. However, they are anisotropic, that is, the edge amplitude they calculate depends on the angle of the edge in the image. This is undesirable because it makes the selection of the relevant edges harder. Lanser has shown that the anisotropy of the Deriche filters can be corrected [47]. We will refer to the isotropic versions of the Deriche filters as the Lanser filters.

Figure 9.74 displays the result of computing the edge amplitude with the second Lanser filter with $\alpha = 0.5$. Compared to the the Sobel filter, the Lanser filter was able to suppress the noise and texture significantly better. This can be seen from the edge amplitude image (Figure 9.74a) as well as the thresholded edge region (Figure 9.74b). Note, however, that the edge region still contains a hole for the vertical edge that starts at the right corner of the topmost edge of the relay. This happens because the edge amplitude only has been thresholded and the important step of the non-maximum suppression has been omitted to compare the results of the Sobel and Lanser filters.

As we saw in the above examples, thresholding the edge amplitude and then skeletonizing the region sometimes does not yield the desired results. To obtain

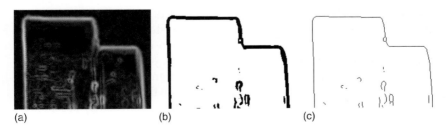

(a)   (b)   (c)

Figure 9.74 (a) Edge amplitude around the top part of the relay in Figure 9.67a computed with the second Lanser filter with $\alpha = 0.5$. (b) Thresholded edge region. (c) Skeleton of (b).

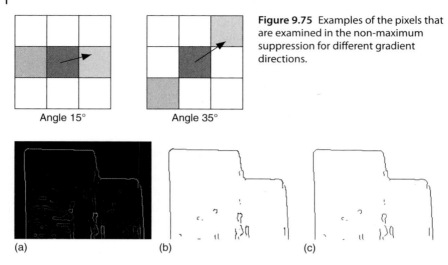

Figure 9.75 Examples of the pixels that are examined in the non-maximum suppression for different gradient directions.

Figure 9.76 (a) Result of applying the non-maximum suppression to the edge amplitude image in Figure 9.74a. (b) Thresholded edge region. (c) Skeleton of (b).

the correct edge locations, we must perform the non-maximum suppression (see Section 9.7.1). In the 2D case, this can be done by examining the two neighboring pixels that lie closest to the gradient direction. Conceptually, we can think of transforming the gradient vector into an angle. Then, we divide the angle range into eight sectors. Figure 9.75 shows two examples of this. Unfortunately, with this approach, diagonal edges often are still two pixels wide. Consequently, the output of the non-maximum suppression must still be skeletonized.

Figure 9.76 shows the result of applying the non-maximum suppression to the edge amplitude image in Figure 9.74a. From the thresholded edge region in Figure 9.76b, it can be seen that the edges are now in the correct locations. In particular, the incorrect hole in Figure 9.74 is no longer present. We can also see that the few diagonal edges are sometimes two pixels wide. Therefore, their skeleton is computed and displayed in Figure 9.76c.

Up to now, we have been using simple thresholding to select the salient edges. This works well as long as the edges we are interested in have roughly the same contrast or have a contrast that is significantly different from the contrast of noise, texture, or other irrelevant objects in the image. In many applications, however, we face the problem that, if we select the threshold so high that only the relevant edges are selected, they are often fragmented. If, on the other hand, we set the threshold so low that the edges we are interested in are not fragmented, we end up with many irrelevant edges. These two situations are illustrated in Figure 9.77a,b. A solution to this problem was proposed by Canny [43]. He devised a special thresholding algorithm for segmenting edges: hysteresis thresholding. Instead of a single threshold, it uses two thresholds. Points with an edge amplitude greater than the higher threshold are immediately accepted as safe edge points. Points with an edge amplitude smaller than the lower threshold are immediately rejected. Points with an edge amplitude between the two thresholds are accepted only if they are connected to safe edge points via a path

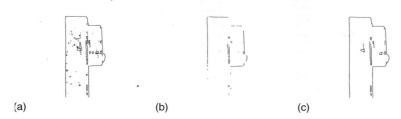

(a) (b) (c)

Figure 9.77 (a) Result of thresholding the edge amplitude for the entire relay image in Figure 9.67a with a threshold of 60. This causes many irrelevant texture edges to be selected. (b) Result of thresholding the edge amplitude with a threshold of 140. This selects only the relevant edges. However, they are severely fragmented and incomplete. (c) Result of hysteresis thresholding with a low threshold of 60 and a high threshold of 140. Only the relevant edges are selected, and they are complete.

in which all points have an edge amplitude above the lower threshold. We can also think of this operation as first selecting the edge points with an amplitude above the upper threshold, and then extending the edges as far as possible while remaining above the lower threshold. Figure 9.77c shows that hysteresis thresholding enables us to select only the relevant edges without fragmenting them or missing edge points.

Like in the 1D case, the pixel-accurate edges we have extracted so far are often not accurate enough. We can use a similar approach as for 1D edges to extract edges with subpixel accuracy: we can fit a 2D polynomial to the edge amplitude and extract its maximum in the direction of the gradient vector [45, 48]. The fitting of the polynomial can be done with convolutions with special filter masks (the so-called facet model masks) [22, 49]. To illustrate this, Figure 9.78a shows a 7×7 part of an edge amplitude image. The fitted 2D polynomial obtained from the central 3×3 amplitudes is shown in Figure 9.78b, along with an arrow that indicates the gradient direction. Furthermore, contour lines of the polynomial are shown. They indicate that the edge point is offset by approximately a quarter of a pixel in the direction of the arrow.

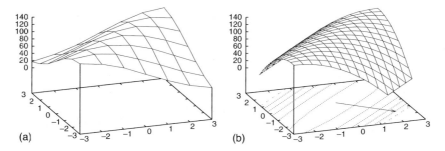

Figure 9.78 (a) A 7×7 part of an edge amplitude image. (b) Fitted 2D polynomial obtained from the central 3×3 amplitudes in (a). The arrow indicates the gradient direction. The contour lines in the plot indicate that the edge point is offset by approximately a quarter of a pixel in the direction of the arrow.

The above procedure gives us one subpixel-accurate edge point per non-maximum suppressed pixel. These individual edge points must be linked into subpixel-precise contours. This can be done by repeatedly selecting the first unprocessed edge point to start the contour and then successively finding adjacent edge points until the contour closes, reaches the image border, or reaches an intersection point.

Figure 9.79 illustrates the subpixel edge extraction along with a very useful strategy to increase the processing speed. The image in Figure 9.79a is the same workpiece as in Figure 9.61a. Because the subpixel edge extraction is relatively costly, we want to reduce the search space as much as possible. Since the workpiece is back-lit, we can threshold it easily (Figure 9.79b). If we calculate the inner boundary of the region with equation (9.79), the resulting points are close to the edge points we want to extract. We only need to dilate the boundary slightly, for example, with a circle of diameter 5 (Figure 9.79c), to obtain an ROI for the edge extraction. Note that the ROI is only a small fraction of the entire image. Consequently, the edge extraction can be done an order of magnitude faster than in the entire image, without any loss of information. The resulting subpixel-accurate edges are shown in Figure 9.79d for the part of the image indicated by the rectangle in Figure 9.79a. Note how well they capture the shape of the hole.

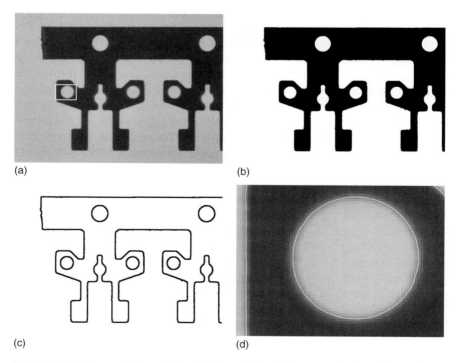

Figure 9.79 (a) Image of the workpiece in Figure 9.61a with a rectangle that indicates the image part shown in (d). (b) Thresholded workpiece. (c) Dilation of the boundary of (b) with a circle of diameter 5. This is used as the ROI for the subpixel edge extraction. (d) Subpixel-accurate edges of the workpiece extracted with the Canny filter with $\sigma = 1$.

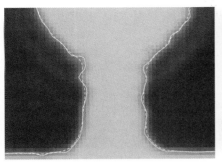 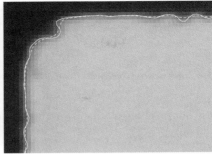

Figure 9.80 Comparison of the subpixel-accurate edges extracted via the maxima of the gradient magnitude in the gradient direction (dashed lines) and the edges extracted via the subpixel-accurate zero-crossings of the Laplacian. In both cases, a Gaussian filter with $\sigma = 1$ was used. Note that, since the Laplacian edges must follow the corners, they are much more curved than the gradient magnitude edges.

We conclude this section with a look at the second edge definition via the zero crossings of the Laplacian. Since the zero-crossings are just a special threshold, we can use the subpixel-precise thresholding operation, defined in Section 9.4.3, to extract edges with subpixel accuracy. To make this as efficient as possible, we must first compute the edge amplitude in the entire ROI of the image. Then, we threshold the edge amplitude and use the resulting region as the ROI for the computation of the Laplacian and for the subpixel-precise thresholding. The resulting edges for two parts of the workpiece image are compared to the gradient magnitude edge in Figure 9.80. Note that, since the Laplacian edges must follow the corners, they are much more curved than the gradient magnitude edges, and hence are more difficult to process further. This is another reason why the edge definition via the gradient magnitude is usually preferred.

Despite the above arguments, the property that the Laplacian edge exactly passes through corners in the image can be used advantageously in some applications. Figure 9.81a shows an image of a bolt for which the depth of the thread must be measured. Figure 9.81b–d display the results of extracting the border of the bolt with subpixel-precise thresholding, the gradient magnitude

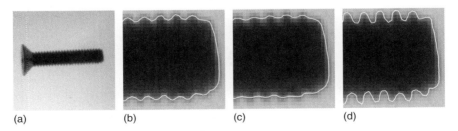

(a) (b) (c) (d)

Figure 9.81 (a) Image of a bolt for which the depth of the thread must be measured. (b) Result of performing a subpixel-precise thresholding operation. (c) Result of extracting the gradient magnitude edges with a Canny filter with $\sigma = 0.7$. (d) Result of extracting the Laplacian edges with a Gaussian filter with $\sigma = 0.7$. Note that for this application the Laplacian edges return the most suitable result.

edges with a Canny filter with $\sigma = 0.7$, and the Laplacian edges with a Gaussian filter with $\sigma = 0.7$. Note that in this case the most suitable results are obtained with the Laplacian edges.

9.7.4 Accuracy of Edges

In the previous two sections, we have seen that edges can be extracted with subpixel resolution. We have used the terms "subpixel-accurate" and "subpixel-precise" to describe these extraction mechanisms without actually justifying the use of the words "accurate" and "precise." Therefore, in this section we will examine whether the edges we can extract are actually subpixel-accurate and subpixel-precise.

Since the words "accuracy" and "precision" are often confused or used interchangeably, let us first define what we mean by them. By precision, we denote how close on average an extracted value is to its mean value [50, 51]. Hence, precision measures how repeatably we can extract the value. By accuracy, on the other hand, we denote how close on average the extracted value is to its true value [50, 51]. Note that the precision does not tell us anything about the accuracy of the extracted value. The measurements could, for example, be offset by a systematic bias, but still be very precise. Conversely, the accuracy does not necessarily tell us how precise the extracted value is. The measurement could be quite accurate, but not very repeatable. Figure 9.82 shows the different situations that can occur. Also note that accuracy and precision are statements about the average distribution of the extracted values. From a single value, we cannot tell whether the measurements are accurate or precise.

If we adopt a statistical point of view, the extracted values can be regarded as random variables. With this, the precision of the values is given by the variance of the values: $V[x] = \sigma_x^2$. If the extracted values are precise, they have a small variance. On the other hand, the accuracy can be described by the difference of the expected value $E[x]$ from the true value T: $|E[x] - T|$. Since we typically do not know anything about the true probability distribution of the extracted values, and consequently cannot determine $E[x]$ and $V[x]$, we must estimate them with the empirical mean and variance of the extracted values.

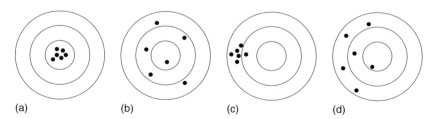

Figure 9.82 Comparison of accuracy and precision. The center of the circles indicates the true value of the feature. The dots indicate the outcome of the measurements of the feature. (a) Accurate and precise. (b) Accurate but not precise. (c) Not accurate but precise. (d) Neither accurate nor precise.

The accuracy and precision of edges is analyzed extensively in [45, 52]. The precision of ideal step edges extracted with the Canny filter can be derived analytically. If we denote the true edge amplitude by a and the noise variance in the image by σ_n^2, it can be shown that the variance of the edge positions σ_e^2 is given by

$$\sigma_e^2 = \frac{3}{8} \frac{\sigma_n^2}{a^2} \tag{9.111}$$

Even though this result was derived analytically for continuous images, it also holds in the discrete case. This result has also been verified empirically in [45, 52]. Note that it is quite intuitive: the larger the noise in the image, the less precisely the edges can be located; furthermore, the larger the edge amplitude, the higher is the precision of the edges. Note also that, possibly contrary to our intuition, increasing the smoothing does not increase the precision. This happens because the noise reduction achieved by the larger smoothing cancels out exactly with the weaker edge amplitude that results from the smoothing. From equation (9.111), we can see that the Canny filter is subpixel-precise ($\sigma_e \leq 1/2$) if the signal-to-noise ratio $a^2/\sigma_n^2 \geq 3/2$. This can, of course, be easily achieved in practice. Consequently, we see that we were justified in calling the Canny filter subpixel-precise.

The same derivation can also be performed for the Deriche and Lanser filters. For continuous images, the following variances result:

$$\sigma_e^2 = \frac{5}{64} \frac{\sigma_n^2}{a^2} \quad \text{and} \quad \sigma_e^2 = \frac{3}{16} \frac{\sigma_n^2}{a^2} \tag{9.112}$$

Note that the Deriche and Lanser filters are more precise than the Canny filter. Like for the Canny filter, the smoothing parameter α has no influence on the precision. In the discrete case, this is, unfortunately, no longer true because of the discretization of the filter. Here, less smoothing (larger values of α) leads to slightly worse precision than predicted by equation (9.112). However, for practical purposes, we can assume that the smoothing for all the edge filters that we have discussed has no influence on the precision of the edges. Consequently, if we want to control the precision of the edges, we must maximize the signal-to-noise ratio by using proper lighting and cameras. Furthermore, if analog cameras are used, the frame grabber should have a high signal-to-noise ratio and a line jitter that is as small as possible.

For ideal step edges, it is also easy to convince oneself that the expected position of the edge under noise corresponds to its true position. This happens because both the ideal step edge and the above filters are symmetric with respect to the true edge positions. Therefore, the edges that are extracted from noisy, ideal step edges must be distributed symmetrically around the true edge position. Consequently, their mean value is the true edge position. This is also verified empirically for the Canny filter in [45, 52]. Of course, it can also be verified for the Deriche and Lanser filters.

While it is easy to show that edges are very accurate for ideal step edges, we must also perform experiments on real images to test the accuracy on real data.

This is important because some of the assumptions that are used in the edge extraction algorithms may not hold in practice. Because these assumptions are seldom stated explicitly, we should examine them carefully here. Let us focus on straight edges because, as we have seen from the discussion in Section 9.7.1, especially Figure 9.63, sharply curved edges will necessarily lie in incorrect positions. See also [53] for a thorough discussion on the positional errors of the Laplacian edge detector for ideal corners of two straight edges with varying angles. Because we concentrate on straight edges, we can reduce the edge detection to the 1D case, which is simpler to analyze. From Section 9.7.1, we know that 1D edges are given by the inflection points of the gray value profiles. This implicitly assumes that the gray value profile and, consequently, its derivatives are symmetric with respect to the true edge. Furthermore, to obtain subpixel positions, the edge detection implicitly assumes that the gray values at the edge change smoothly and continuously as the edge moves in subpixel increments through a pixel. For example, if an edge covers 25% of a pixel, we would assume that the gray value in the pixel is a mixture of 25% of the foreground gray value and 75% of the background gray value. We will see whether these assumptions hold in real images.

To test the accuracy of the edge extraction on real images, it is instructive to repeat the experiments in [45, 52] with a different camera. In [45, 52], a print of an edge is mounted on an xy-stage and shifted in 50 μm increments, which corresponds to approximately 1/10 of a pixel, for a total of 1mm. The goals are to determine whether the shifts of 1/10 of a pixel can be detected reliably and to obtain information about the absolute accuracy of the edges. Figure 9.83a shows an image used in this experiment. We are not going to repeat the test to see whether the subpixel shifts can be detected reliably here. The 1/10 pixel shifts can be detected with a very high confidence (more than 99.99 999%). What is more interesting is to look at the absolute accuracy. Since we do not know the true edge position, we must get an estimate for it. Because the edge was shifted in linear increments in the test images, such an estimate can be obtained by fitting a straight line through the extracted edge positions and subtracting the line from the measured edge positions.

Figure 9.83b displays the result of extracting the edge in Figure 9.83a along a horizontal line with the Canny filter with $\sigma = 1$. The edge position error is shown in Figure 9.83c. We can see that there are errors of up to $\approx 1/22$ pixel. What causes these errors? As we discussed previously, for ideal cameras no error occurs, so one of the assumptions must be violated. In this case, the assumption that is violated is that the gray value is a mixture of the foreground and background gray values that is proportional to the area of the pixel covered by the object. This happens because the camera did not have a fill factor of 100%, that is, the light-sensitive area of a pixel on the sensor was much smaller than the total area of the pixel. Consider what happens when the edge moves across the pixel and the image is perfectly focused. In the light-sensitive area of the pixel, the gray value changes as expected when the edge moves across the pixel because the sensor integrates the incoming light. However, when the edge enters the light-insensitive area, the gray value no longer changes [54]. Consequently, the edge does not move in the image. In the real image, the focus is not perfect. Hence, the light is spread slightly over adjacent sensor elements. Therefore, the

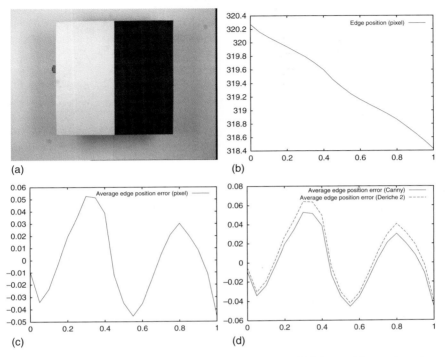

Figure 9.83 (a) Edge image used in the accuracy experiment. (b) Edge position extracted along a horizontal line in the image with the Canny filter. The edge position is given in pixels as a function of the true shift in millimeters. (c) Error of the edge positions obtained by fitting a line through the edge positions in (b) and subtracting the line from (b). (d) Comparison of the errors obtained with the Canny and second Deriche filters.

edges do not jump as they would in a perfectly focused image but shift continuously. Nevertheless, the poor fill factor causes errors in the edge positions. This can be seen very clearly from Figure 9.83c. Recall that the shift of 50 µm corresponds to 1/10 of a pixel. Consequently, the entire shift of 1mm corresponds to two pixels. This is why we see a sine wave with two periods in Figure 9.83c. Each period corresponds exactly to one pixel. That these effects are caused by the fill factor can also be seen if the lens is defocused. In this case, the light is spread over more sensor elements. This helps to create an artificially increased fill factor, which causes smaller errors.

From the above discussion, it would appear that the edge position can be extracted with an accuracy of 1/22 of a pixel. To check whether this is true, let us repeat the experiment with the second Deriche filter. Figure 9.83d shows the result of extracting the edges with $\alpha = 1$ and computing the errors with the line fitted through the Canny edge positions. The last part is done to make the errors comparable. We can see, surprisingly, that the Deriche edge positions are systematically shifted in one direction. Does this mean that the Deriche filter is less accurate than the Canny filter? Of course, it does not, since on ideal data both filters return the same result. It shows that another assumption must be

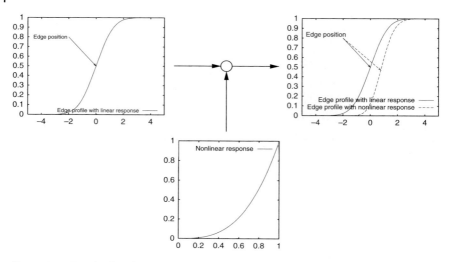

Figure 9.84 Result of applying a nonlinear gray value response curve to an ideal symmetric edge profile. The ideal edge profile is shown in the upper left graph and the nonlinear response in the bottom graph. The upper right graph shows the modified gray value profile along with the edge positions on the profiles. Note that the edge position is affected substantially by the nonlinear response.

violated. In this case, it is the assumption that the edge profile is symmetric with respect to the true edge position. This is the only reason why the two filters, which are symmetric themselves, can return different results.

There are many reasons why edge profiles may become asymmetric. One reason is that the gray value responses of the camera (and analog frame grabber, if used) are nonlinear. Figure 9.84 illustrates that an originally symmetric edge profile becomes asymmetric by a nonlinear gray value response function. It can be seen that the edge position accuracy is severely degraded by the nonlinear response. To correct the nonlinear response of the camera, it must be calibrated radiometrically with the methods described in Section 9.2.2.

Unfortunately, even if the camera has a linear response or is calibrated radiometrically, other factors may cause the edge profiles to become asymmetric. In particular, lens aberrations like coma, astigmatism, and chromatic aberrations may cause asymmetric profiles (see Section 4.5.3). Since lens aberrations cannot be corrected easily with image processing algorithms, they should be as small as possible.

While all the error sources discussed above influence the edge accuracy, we have so far neglected the largest source of errors. If the camera is not calibrated geometrically, extracting edges with subpixel accuracy is pointless because the lens distortions alone are sufficient to render any subpixel position meaningless. Let us, for example, assume that the lens has a distortion that is smaller than 1% in the entire field of view. At the corners of the image, this means that the edges are offset by four pixels for a 640×480 image. We can see that extracting edges with subpixel accuracy is an exercise in futility if the lens distortions are not corrected,

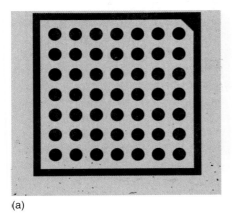 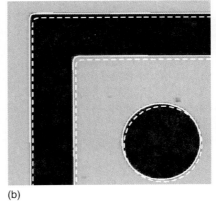

(a) (b)

Figure 9.85 (a) Image of a calibration target. (b) Extracted subpixel-accurate edges (solid lines) and edges after the correction of the lens distortions (dashed lines). Note that the lens distortions cause an error of approximately three pixels.

even for this relatively small distortion. This is illustrated in Figure 9.85, where the result of correcting the lens distortions after calibrating the camera as described in Section 9.9 is shown. Note that, despite the fact that the application used a very high quality lens, the lens distortions cause an error of approximately three pixels.

Another detrimental influence on the accuracy of the extracted edges is caused by the perspective distortions in the image. They happen whenever we cannot mount the camera perpendicular to the objects we want to measure. Figure 9.86a shows the result of extracting the 1D edges along the ruler markings on a caliper. Because of the severe perspective distortions, the distances between the ruler markings vary greatly throughout the image. If the camera is calibrated, that is, its interior orientation and the exterior orientation of the plane in which the objects to measure lie have been determined with the approach described in Section 9.9, the measurements in the image can be converted into measurements in world coordinates in the plane determined by the calibration. This is done by intersecting the optical ray that corresponds to each edge point in the image with the plane in the world. Figure 9.86b displays the results of converting the measurements in Figure 9.86a into millimeters with this approach. Note that the measurements are extremely accurate even in the presence of severe perspective distortions.

From the above discussion, we can see that extracting edges with subpixel accuracy relies on careful selection of the hardware components. First of all, the gray value response of the camera (and analog frame grabber, if used) should be linear. To ensure this, the camera should be calibrated radiometrically. Furthermore, lenses with very small aberrations (such as coma and astigmatism) should be chosen. Furthermore, monochromatic light should be used to avoid the effects of chromatic aberrations. In addition, the fill factor of the camera should be as large as possible to avoid the effects of "blind spots." Finally, the camera should be calibrated geometrically to obtain meaningful results. All these requirements for

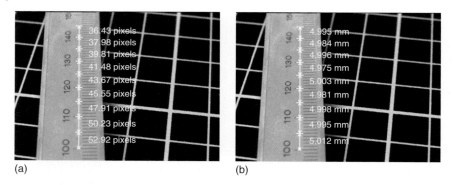

Figure 9.86 Result of extracting 1D edges along the ruler markings on a caliper. (a) Pixel distances between the markings. (b) Distances converted to world units using camera calibration.

the hardware components are, of course, also valid for other subpixel algorithms, for example, the subpixel-precise thresholding (see Section 9.4.3), the gray value moments (see Section 9.5.2), and the contour features (see Section 9.5.3).

9.8 Segmentation and Fitting of Geometric Primitives

In Sections 9.4 and 9.7, we have seen how to segment images by thresholding and edge extraction. In both cases, the boundary of objects either is returned explicitly or can be derived by some postprocessing (see Section 9.6.1). Therefore, for the purposes of this section, we can assume that the result of the segmentation is a contour with the points of the boundary, which may be subpixel-accurate. This approach often creates an enormous amount of data. For example, the subpixel-accurate edge of the hole in the workpiece in Figure 9.79d contains 172 contour points. However, we are typically not interested in such a large amount of information. For example, in the application in Figure 9.79d, we would probably be content with knowing the position and radius of the hole, which can be described with just three parameters. Therefore, in this section we will discuss methods to fit geometric primitives to contour data. We will only examine the most relevant geometric primitives: lines, circles, and ellipses. Furthermore, we will examine how contours can be segmented automatically into parts that correspond to the geometric primitives. This will enable us to substantially reduce the amount of data that needs to be processed, while also providing us with a symbolic description of the data. Furthermore, the fitting of the geometric primitives will enable us to reduce the influence of incorrectly or inaccurately extracted points (the so-called outliers). We will start by examining the fitting of the geometric primitives in Sections 9.8.1–9.8.3. In each case, we will assume that the contour or part of the contour we are examining corresponds to the primitive we are trying to fit, that is, we are assuming that the segmentation into the different primitives has already been performed. The segmentation itself will be discussed in Section 9.8.4.

9.8.1 Fitting Lines

If we want to fit lines, we first need to think about the representation of lines. In images, lines can occur in any orientation. Therefore, we have to use a representation that enables us to represent all lines. For example, the common representation $y = mx + b$ does not allow us to do this. One representation that can be used is the Hessian normal form of the line, given by

$$\alpha r + \beta c + \gamma = 0 \tag{9.113}$$

This is actually an over-parameterization, since the parameters (α, β, γ) are homogeneous [20, 21]. Therefore, they are defined only up to a scale factor. The scale factor in the Hessian normal form is fixed by requiring that $\alpha^2 + \beta^2 = 1$. This has the advantage that the distance of a point to the line can simply be obtained by substituting its coordinates into equation (9.113).

To fit a line through a set of points $(r_i, c_i), i = 1, \ldots, n$, we can minimize the sum of the squared distances of the points to the line:

$$\varepsilon^2 = \sum_{i=1}^{n} (\alpha r_i + \beta c_i + \gamma)^2 \tag{9.114}$$

While this is correct in principle, it does not work in practice, because we can achieve a zero error if we select $\alpha = \beta = \gamma = 0$. This is caused by the over-parameterization of the line. Therefore, we must add the constraint $\alpha^2 + \beta^2 = 1$ as a Lagrange multiplier, and hence must minimize the following error:

$$\varepsilon^2 = \sum_{i=1}^{n} (\alpha r_i + \beta c_i + \gamma)^2 - \lambda(\alpha^2 + \beta^2 - 1)n \tag{9.115}$$

The solution to this optimization problem is derived in [22]. It can be shown that (α, β) is the eigenvector corresponding to the smaller eigenvalue of the following matrix:

$$\begin{pmatrix} \mu_{2,0} & \mu_{1,1} \\ \mu_{1,1} & \mu_{0,2} \end{pmatrix} \tag{9.116}$$

With this, γ is given by $\gamma = -(\alpha n_{1,0} + \beta n_{0,1})$. Here, $\mu_{2,0}$, $\mu_{1,1}$, and $\mu_{0,2}$ are the second-order central moments of the point set (r_i, c_i), while $n_{1,0}$ and $n_{0,1}$ are the normalized first-order moments (the center of gravity) of the point set. If we replace the area a of a region with the number n of points and sum over the points in the point set instead of the points in the region, the formulas to compute these moments are identical to the region moments of equations (9.55) and 9.56 in Section 9.5.1. It is interesting to note that the vector (α, β) thus obtained, which is the normal vector of the line, is the minor axis that would be obtained from the ellipse parameters of the point set. Consequently, the major axis of the ellipse is the direction of the line. This is a very interesting connection between the ellipse parameters and the line fitting, because the results were derived using different approaches and models.

Figure 9.87b illustrates the line-fitting procedure for an oblique edge of the workpiece shown in Figure 9.87a. Note that, by fitting the line, we were able

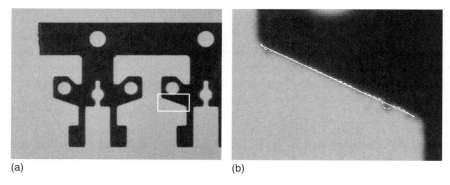

Figure 9.87 (a) Image of a workpiece with the part shown in (b) indicated by the white rectangle. (b) Extracted edge within a region around the inclined edge of the workpiece (dashed line) and straight line fitted to the edge (solid line).

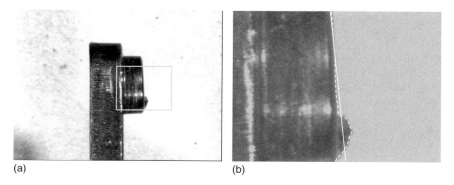

Figure 9.88 (a) Image of a relay with the part shown in (b) indicated by the light gray rectangle. (b) Extracted edge within a region around the vertical edge of the relay (dashed line) and straight line fitted to the edge (solid line). To provide a better visibility of the edge and line, the contrast of the image has been reduced in (b).

to reduce the effects of the small protrusion on the workpiece. As mentioned previously, by inserting the coordinates of the edge points into the line equation (9.113), we can easily calculate the distances of the edge points to the line. Therefore, by thresholding the distances the protrusion can be detected easily.

As can be seen from the above example, the line fit is robust to small deviations from the assumed model (small outliers). However, Figure 9.88 shows that large outliers severely affect the quality of the fitted line. In this example, the line is fitted through the straight edge as well as the large arc caused by the relay contact. Since the line fit must minimize the sum of the squared distances of the contour points, the fitted line has a direction that deviates from that of the straight edge.

The least-squares line fit is not robust to large outliers since points that lie far from the line have a very large weight in the optimization because of the squared distances. To reduce the influence of distant points, we can introduce a weight w_i for each point. The weight should be $\ll 1$ for distant points. Let us assume for the moment that we have a way to compute these weights. Then, the minimization becomes

$$\varepsilon^2 = \sum_{i=1}^{n} w_i(\alpha r_i + \beta c_i + \gamma)^2 - \lambda(\alpha^2 + \beta^2 - 1)n \qquad (9.117)$$

The solution of this optimization problem is again given by the eigenvector corresponding to the smaller eigenvalue of a moment matrix like in equation (9.116) [55]. The only difference is that the moments are computed by taking the weights w_i into account. If we interpret the weights as gray values, the moments are identical to the gray value center of gravity and the second-order central gray value moments (see equations (9.63) and (9.64) in Section 9.5.2). As above, the fitted line corresponds to the major axis of the ellipse obtained from the weighted moments of the point set. Hence, there is an interesting connection to the gray value moments.

The only remaining problem is how to define the weights w_i. Since we want to give smaller weights to points with large distances, the weights must be based on the distances $\delta_i = |\alpha r_i + \beta c_i + \gamma|$ of the points to the line. Unfortunately, we do not know the distances without fitting the line, so this seems an impossible requirement. The solution is to fit the line in several iterations. In the first iteration, $w_i = 1$ is used, that is, a normal line fit is performed to calculate the distances δ_i. They are used to define weights for the following iterations by using a weight function $w(\delta)$. This method is called iteratively reweighted least-squares (IRLS) [56, 57]. In practice, often one of the following two weight functions is used. They both work very well. The first weight function was proposed by Huber [55, 58]. It is given by

$$w(\delta) = \begin{cases} 1, & |\delta| \leq \tau \\ \tau/|\delta|, & |\delta| > \tau \end{cases} \qquad (9.118)$$

The parameter τ is the clipping factor. It defines which points should be regarded as outliers. We will see how it is computed below. For now, note that all points with a distance $\leq \tau$ receive a weight of 1. This means that, for small distances, the squared distance is used in the minimization. Points with a distance $> \tau$, on the other hand, receive a progressively smaller weight. In fact, the weight function is chosen such that points with large distances use the distance itself and not the squared distance in the optimization. Sometimes, these weights are not small enough to suppress outliers completely. In this case, the Tukey weight function can be used [55, 59]. It is given by

$$w(\delta) = \begin{cases} (1 - (\delta/\tau)^2)^2, & |\delta| \leq \tau \\ 0, & |\delta| > \tau \end{cases} \qquad (9.119)$$

Again, τ is the clipping factor. Note that this weight function completely disregards points that have a distance $> \tau$. For distances $\leq \tau$, the weight changes smoothly from 1 to 0.

In the above two weight functions, the clipping factor specifies which points should be regarded as outliers. Since the clipping factor is a distance, it could simply be set manually. However, this would ignore the distribution of the noise and the outliers in the data, and consequently would have to be adapted for each

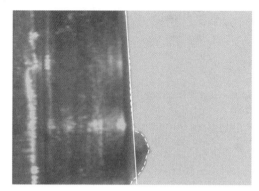

Figure 9.89 Straight line (solid line) fitted robustly to the vertical edge (dashed line). In this case, the Tukey weight function with a clipping factor of $\tau = 2\sigma_\delta$ with five iterations was used. Compared to Figure 9.88b, the line is now fitted to the straight-line part of the edge.

application. It is more convenient to derive the clipping factor from the data itself. This is typically done based on the standard deviation of the distances to the line. Since we expect outliers in the data, we cannot use the normal standard deviation, but must use a standard deviation that is robust to outliers. Typically, the following formula is used to compute the robust standard deviation:

$$\sigma_\delta = \frac{\text{median}|\delta_i|}{0.6745} \tag{9.120}$$

The constant in the denominator is chosen such that, for normally distributed distances, the standard deviation of the normal distribution is computed. The clipping factor is then set to a small multiple of σ_δ, for example, $\tau = 2\sigma_\delta$.

In addition to the Huber and Tukey weight functions, other weight functions can be defined. Several other possibilities are discussed in [20].

Figure 9.89 displays the result of fitting a line robustly to the edge of the relay using the Tukey weight function with a clipping factor of $\tau = 2\sigma_\delta$ with five iterations. If we compare this with the standard least-squares line fit in Figure 9.88b, we see that with the robust fit the line is now fitted to the straight-line part of the edge and the outliers caused by the relay contact have been suppressed.

It should also be noted that the above approach to outlier suppression by weighting down the influence of points with large distances can sometimes fail because the initial fit, which is a standard least-squares fit, can produce a solution that is dominated by the outliers. Consequently, the weight function will drop inliers. In this case, other robust methods must be used. The most important approach is the random sample consensus (RANSAC) algorithm, proposed by Fischler and Bolles [60]. Instead of dropping outliers successively, it constructs a solution (e.g., a line fit) from the minimum number of points (e.g., two for lines), which are selected randomly, and then checks how many points are consistent with the solution. The process of randomly selecting points, constructing the solution, and checking the number of consistent points is continued until a certain probability of having found the correct solution, for example, 99%, is achieved. At the end, the solution with the largest number of consistent points is selected.

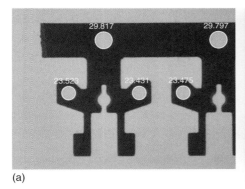 

(a) (b)

Figure 9.90 (a) Image of a workpiece with circles fitted to the edges of the holes in the workpiece. (b) Details of the upper right hole with the extracted edge (dashed line) and the fitted circle (solid line).

9.8.2 Fitting Circles

Fitting circles or circular arcs to a contour uses the same idea as fitting lines: that is, we want to minimize the sum of the squared distances of the contour points to the circle:

$$\varepsilon^2 = \sum_{i=1}^{n} \left(\sqrt{(r_i - \alpha)^2 + (c_i - \beta)^2} - \rho \right)^2 \qquad (9.121)$$

Here, (α, β) is the center of the circle and ρ is its radius. Unlike the line fitting, this leads to a nonlinear optimization problem, which can only be solved iteratively using nonlinear optimization techniques. Details can be found in [22, 61, 62].

Figure 9.90a shows the result of fitting circles to the edges of the holes of a workpiece, along with the extracted radii in pixels. In Figure 9.90b, details of the upper right hole are shown. Note how well the circle fits the extracted edges.

Like the least-squares line fit, the least-squares circle fit is not robust to outliers. To make the circle fit robust, we can use the same approach that we used for the line fitting: we can introduce a weight that is used to reduce the influence of the outliers. Again, this requires that we perform a normal least-squares fit first and then use the distances that result from it to calculate the weights in later iterations. Since it is possible that large outliers prevent this algorithm from converging to the correct solution, a RANSAC approach might be necessary in extreme cases.

Figure 9.91 compares the standard circle fitting with the robust circle fitting using the BGA example of Figure 9.34. With the standard fitting (Figure 9.91b), the circle is affected by the error in the pad, which acts like an outlier. This is corrected with the robust fitting (Figure 9.91c).

To conclude this section, we should give some thought to what happens when a circle is fitted to a contour that only represents a part of a circle (a circular arc). In this case, the accuracy of the parameters becomes progressively worse as the

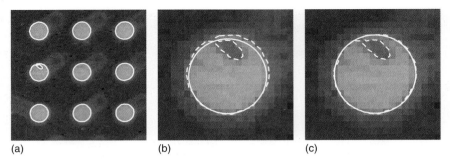

Figure 9.91 (a) Image of a BGA with pads extracted by subpixel-precise thresholding (see also Figure 9.34). (b) Circle fitted to the left pad in the center row of (a). The fitted circle is shown as a solid line, while the extracted contour is shown as a dashed line. The fitted circle is affected by the error in the pad, which acts like an outlier. (c) Result of robustly fitting a circle. The fitted circle corresponds to the true boundary of the pad.

angle of the circular arc becomes smaller. An excellent analysis of this effect is given in [61]. This effect is obvious from the geometry of the problem. Simply think about a contour that only represents a 5° arc. If the contour points are disturbed by noise, we have a very large range of radii and centers that lead to almost the same fitting error. On the other hand, if we fit to a complete circle, the geometry of the circle is much more constrained. This effect is caused by the geometry of the fitting problem and not by a particular fitting algorithm, that is, it will occur for all fitting algorithms.

9.8.3 Fitting Ellipses

To fit an ellipse to a contour, we would like to use the same principles as for lines and circles: that is, minimize the distance of the contour points to the ellipse. This requires us to determine the closest point to each contour point on the ellipse. While this can be determined easily for lines and circles, for ellipses it requires finding the roots of a fourth-degree polynomial. Since this is quite complicated and expensive, ellipses are often fitted by minimizing a different kind of distance. The principle is similar to the line fitting approach: we write down an implicit equation for ellipses (for lines, the implicit equation is given by equation (9.113)), and then substitute the point coordinates into the implicit equation to get a distance measure for the points to the ellipse. For the line-fitting problem, this procedure returns the true distance to the line. For the ellipse fitting, it only returns a value that has the same properties as a distance, but is not the true distance. Therefore, this distance is called the algebraic distance. Ellipses are described by the following implicit equation:

$$\alpha r^2 + \beta rc + \gamma c^2 + \delta r + \zeta c + \eta = 0 \qquad (9.122)$$

Like for lines, the set of parameters is a homogeneous quantity, that is, only defined up to scale. Furthermore, equation (9.122) also describes hyperbolas and parabolas. Ellipses require $\beta^2 - 4\alpha\gamma < 0$. We can solve both problems by requiring $\beta^2 - 4\alpha\gamma = -1$. An elegant solution to fitting ellipses by minimizing the algebraic error with a linear method was proposed by Fitzgibbon.

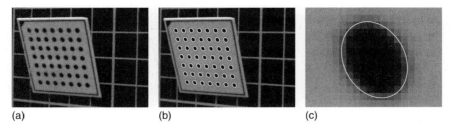

Figure 9.92 (a) Image of a calibration target. (b) Ellipses fitted to the extracted edges of the circular marks of the calibration target. (c) Detail of the center mark of the calibration target with the fitted ellipse.

The interested reader is referred to [63] for details. Unfortunately, minimizing the algebraic error can result in biased ellipse parameters. Therefore, if the ellipse parameters should be determined with maximum accuracy, the geometric error should be used. A nonlinear approach for fitting ellipses based on the geometric error is proposed in [62]. It is significantly more complicated than the linear approach in [63].

Like the least-squares line and circle fits, fitting ellipses via the algebraic or geometric distance is not robust to outliers. We can again introduce weights to create a robust fitting procedure. If the ellipses are fitted with the algebraic distance, this again results in a linear algorithm in each iteration of the robust fit [55]. In applications with a very large number of outliers or with very large outliers, a RANSAC approach might be necessary.

The ellipse fitting is very useful in camera calibration, where often circular marks are used on the calibration targets (see Section 9.9 and [54, 64, 65]). Since circles project to ellipses, fitting ellipses to the edges in the image is the natural first step in the calibration process. Figure 9.92a displays an image of a calibration target. The ellipses fitted to the extracted edges of the calibration marks are shown in Figure 9.92b. In Figure 9.92c, a detailed view of the center mark with the fitted ellipse is shown. Since the subpixel edge extraction is very accurate, there is hardly any visible difference between the edge and the ellipse, and consequently the edge is not shown in the figure.

To conclude this section, we should note that, if ellipses are fitted to contours that only represent a part of an ellipse, the same comments that were made for circular arcs at the end of the last section apply: the accuracy of the parameters will become worse as the angle that the arc subtends becomes smaller. The reason for this behavior lies in the geometry of the problem and not in the fitting algorithms we use.

9.8.4 Segmentation of Contours into Lines, Circles, and Ellipses

So far, we have assumed that the contours to which we are fitting the geometric primitives correspond to a single primitive of the correct type, for example, a line segment. Of course, a single contour may correspond to multiple primitives of different types. Therefore, in this section we will discuss how contours can be segmented into the different primitives.

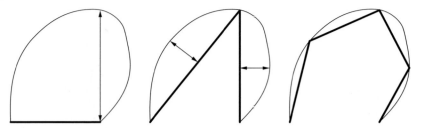

Figure 9.93 Example of the recursive subdivision that is performed in the Ramer algorithm. The contour is displayed as a thin line, while the approximating polygon is displayed as a thick line.

We will start by examining how a contour can be segmented into lines. To do so, we would like to find a polygon that approximates the contour sufficiently well. Let us call the contour points $p_i = (r_i, c_i)$, for $i = 1, \ldots, n$. Approximating the contour by a polygon means that we want to find a subset p_{i_j}, for $j = 1, \ldots, m$ with $m \leq n$, of the control points of the contour that describes the contour reasonably well. Once we have found the approximating polygon, each line segment $(p_{i_j}, p_{i_{j+1}})$ of the polygon is a part of the contour that can be approximated well with a line. Hence, we can fit lines to each line segment afterward to obtain a very accurate geometric representation of the line segments.

The question we need to answer is this: How do we define whether a polygon approximates the contour sufficiently well? A large number of different definitions have been proposed over the years. A very good evaluation of many polygonal approximation methods has been carried out by Rosin [66, 67]. In both cases, it was established that the algorithm proposed by Ramer [68], which curiously enough is one of the oldest algorithms, is the best overall method.

The Ramer algorithm performs a recursive subdivision of the contour until the resulting line segments have a maximum distance to the respective contour segments that is lower than a user-specified threshold d_{max}. Figure 9.93 illustrates how the Ramer algorithm works. We start out by constructing a single line segment between the first and last contour points. If the contour is closed, we construct two segments: one from the first point to the point with index $n/2$, and the second one from $n/2$ to n. We then compute the distances of all the contour points to the line segment and find the point with the maximum distance to the line segment. If its distance is larger than the threshold we have specified, we subdivide the line segment into two segments at the point with the maximum distance. Then, this procedure is applied recursively to the new segments until no more subdivisions occur, that is, until all segments fulfill the maximum distance criterion.

Figure 9.94 illustrates the use of the polygonal approximation in a real application. In Figure 9.94a, a back-lit cutting tool is shown. In the application, the dimensions and angles of the cutting tool must be inspected. Since the tool consists of straight edges, the obvious approach is to extract edges with subpixel accuracy (Figure 9.94b) and to approximate them with a polygon using the Ramer algorithm. From Figure 9.94c we can see that the Ramer algorithm

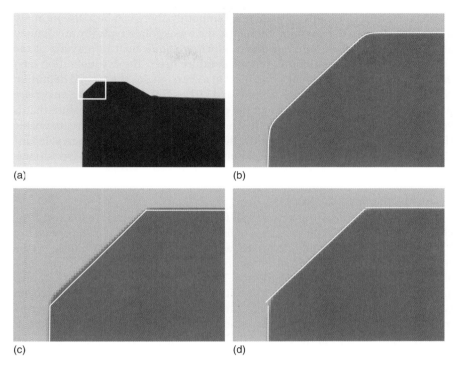

Figure 9.94 (a) Image of a back-lit cutting tool with the part that is shown in (b)–(d) overlaid as a white rectangle. To provide a better visibility of the results, the contrast of the image has been reduced in (b)–(d). (b) Subpixel-accurate edges extracted with the Lanser filter with $\alpha = 0.7$. (c) Polygons extracted with the Ramer algorithm with $d_{max} = 2$. (d) Lines fitted robustly to the polygon segments using the Tukey weight function.

splits the edges correctly. We can also see the only slight drawback of the Ramer algorithm: it sometimes places the polygon control points into positions that are slightly offset from the true corners. In this application, this poses no problem, since to achieve maximum accuracy we must fit lines to the contour segments robustly anyway (Figure 9.94d). This enables us to obtain a concise and very accurate geometric description of the cutting tool. With the resulting geometric parameters, it can easily be checked whether the tool has the required dimensions.

While lines are often the only geometric primitive that occurs for the objects that should be inspected, in several cases the contour must be split into several types of primitives. For example, machined tools often consist of lines and circular arcs or lines and elliptic arcs. Therefore, we will now discuss how such a segmentation of the contours can be performed.

The approaches to segment contours into lines and circles can be classified into two broad categories. The first type of algorithm tries to identify breakpoints on the contour that correspond to semantically meaningful entities. For example, if two straight lines with different angles are next to each other, the tangent direction of the curve will contain a discontinuity. On the other hand, if two circular arcs with different radii meet smoothly, there will be a discontinuity in the curvature of the contour. Therefore, the breakpoints typically are defined as discontinuities in the contour angle, which are equivalent to maxima of the curvature, and as discontinuities in the curvature itself. The first definition covers straight lines or circular arcs that meet at a sharp angle. The second definition covers smoothly joining circles or lines and circles [69, 70]. Since the curvature depends on the second derivative of the contour, it is an unstable feature that is very prone to even small errors in the contour coordinates. Therefore, to enable these algorithms to function properly, the contour must be smoothed substantially. This, in turn, can cause the breakpoints to shift from their desired positions. Furthermore, some breakpoints may be missed. Therefore, these approaches are often followed by an additional splitting and merging stage and a refinement of the breakpoint positions [70, 71].

While the above algorithms work well for splitting contours into lines and circles, they are quite difficult to extend to lines and ellipses because ellipses do not have constant curvature like circles. In fact, the two points on the ellipse on the major axis have locally maximal curvature and consequently would be classified as breakpoints by the above algorithms. Therefore, if we want to have a unified approach to segmenting contours into lines and circles or ellipses, the second type of algorithm is more appropriate. This type of algorithm is characterized by initially performing a segmentation of the contour into lines only. This produces an over-segmentation in the areas of the contour that correspond to circles and ellipses since here many line segments are required to approximate the contour. Therefore, in a second phase the line segments are examined as to whether they can be merged into circles or ellipses [55, 72]. For example, the algorithm in [55] initially performs a polygonal approximation with the Ramer algorithm. Then, it checks each pair of adjacent line segments to see whether it can be better approximated by an ellipse (or, alternatively, a circle). This is done by fitting an ellipse to the part of the contour that corresponds to the two line segments. If the fitting error of the ellipse is smaller than the maximum error of the two lines, the two line segments are marked as candidates for merging. After examining all pairs of line segments, the pair with the smallest fitting error is merged. In the following iterations, the algorithm also considers pairs of line and ellipse segments. The iterative merging is continued until there are no more segments that can be merged.

Figure 9.95 illustrates the segmentation into lines and circles. Like in the previous example, the application is the inspection of cutting tools. Figure 9.95a displays a cutting tool that consists of two linear parts and a circular part. The result of the initial segmentation into lines with the Ramer algorithm is shown in Figure 9.95b. Note that the circular arc is represented by four contour parts. The iterative merging stage of the algorithm successfully merges these four contour parts into a circular arc, as shown in Figure 9.95c. Finally, the angle between the linear parts of the tool is measured by fitting lines to the corresponding contour parts, while the radius of the circular arc is determined by fitting a circle to the circular arc part. Since the camera is calibrated in this application, the fitting is actually performed in world coordinates. Hence, the radius of the arc is calculated in millimeters.

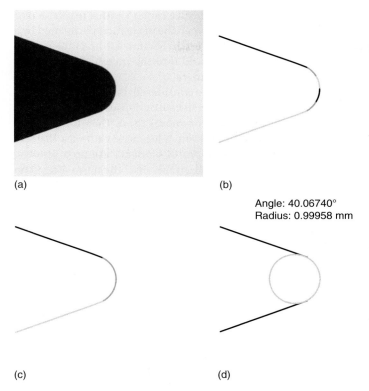

Figure 9.95 (a) Image of a back-lit cutting tool. (b) Contour parts corresponding to the initial segmentation into lines with the Ramer algorithm. The contour parts are displayed in three different gray values. (c) Result of the merging stage of the line and circle segmentation algorithm. In this case, two lines and one circular arc are returned. (d) Geometric measurements obtained by fitting lines to the linear parts of the contour and a circle to the circular part. Because the camera was calibrated, the radius is calculated in millimeters.

9.9 Camera Calibration

At the end of Section 9.7.4, we already discussed briefly that camera calibration is essential to obtain accurate measurements of objects. Chapter 5 discusses the approach that is used in close-range photogrammetry to calibrate camera setups with one or more pinhole cameras for multiview three-dimensional (3D) reconstruction applications. In this section, we will extend the discussion of the camera calibration to different types of camera and lens combinations that are used in machine vision applications. Furthermore, we will describe how metric results (e.g., object coordinates in meters or millimeters) can be obtained from single images.

To calibrate a camera, a model for the mapping of the 3D points of the world to the 2D image generated by the camera, lens, and frame grabber (if used) is necessary. Two different types of lenses are relevant for machine vision tasks: regular and telecentric lenses (see Chapter 4). Regular lenses perform a perspective projection of the world into the image. We will call a camera with a regular lens a pinhole camera because of the connection between the projection performed by a regular lens and a pinhole camera that is described in Section 4.2.12.4. Telecentric lenses perform a parallel projection of the world into the image. We will call a camera with a telecentric lens a telecentric camera.

Furthermore, two types of sensors need to be considered: line sensors and area sensors. For area sensors, regular as well as telecentric lenses are in common use. For line sensors, only regular lenses are commonly used. Therefore, we will not introduce additional labels for the pinhole and telecentric cameras. Instead, it will be silently assumed that these two types of cameras use area sensors. For line sensors with regular lenses, we will simply use the term line scan camera.

For all three camera models, the mapping from three to two dimensions performed by the camera can be described by a certain number of parameters:

$$p = \pi(P_w, c_1, \ldots, c_n) \qquad (9.123)$$

Here, p is the 2D image coordinate of the 3D point P_w produced by the projection π. Camera calibration is the process of determining the camera parameters $c_1, \ldots, c_n$.

9.9.1 Camera Models for Area Scan Cameras

Figure 9.96 displays the perspective projection performed by a pinhole camera. The world point P_w is projected through the projection center of the lens to the point p in the image plane. If there were no lens distortions present, p would lie on a straight line from P_w through the projection center, indicated by the dotted line. Lens distortions cause the point p to lie at a different position.

The image plane is located at a distance of f behind the projection center. As explained at the end of Section 4.2.12.4, f is the camera constant or principal

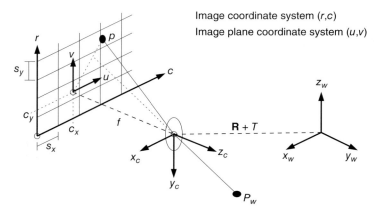

Camera coordinate system (x_c, y_c, z_c)
World coordinate system (x_w, y_w, z_w)

Figure 9.96 Camera model for a pinhole camera.

Figure 9.97 Image plane and virtual image plane.

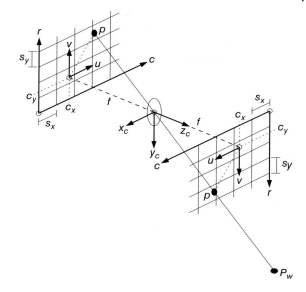

distance, and not the focal length of the lens. Nevertheless, we will use the letter f to denote the principal distance for the purposes of this section.

Although the image plane in reality lies behind the projection center of the lens, it is easier to pretend that it lies at a distance of f in front of the projection center, as shown in Figure 9.97. This causes the image coordinate system to be aligned with the pixel coordinate system (row coordinates increase downward and column coordinates to the right) and simplifies many calculations.

We are now ready to describe the mapping of objects in 3D world coordinates to the 2D image plane and the corresponding camera parameters. First, we should note that the world points P_w are given in a world coordinate system (WCS). To make the projection into the image plane possible, they need to be transformed into the camera coordinate system (CCS). The CCS is defined such that its x- and y-axis are parallel to the column and row axes of the image, respectively, and the z-axis is perpendicular to the image plane and is oriented such that points in front of the camera have positive z coordinates. The transformation from the WCS to the CCS is a rigid transformation, that is, a rotation followed by a translation. Therefore, the point $P_w = (x_w, y_w, z_w)^\top$ in the WCS is given by the point $P_c = (x_c, y_c, z_c)^\top$ in the CCS, where

$$P_c = RP_w + T \tag{9.124}$$

Here, $T = (t_x, t_y, t_z)^\top$ is a translation vector and $R = R(\alpha, \beta, \gamma)$ is a rotation matrix, which is determined by the three rotation angles γ (around the z-axis of the CCS), β (around the y-axis), and α (around the x-axis):

$$R(\alpha, \beta, \gamma) = \begin{pmatrix} 1 & 0 & 0 \\ 0 & \cos\alpha & -\sin\alpha \\ 0 & \sin\alpha & \cos\alpha \end{pmatrix} \begin{pmatrix} \cos\beta & 0 & \sin\beta \\ 0 & 1 & 0 \\ -\sin\beta & 0 & \cos\beta \end{pmatrix} \begin{pmatrix} \cos\gamma & -\sin\gamma & 0 \\ \sin\gamma & \cos\gamma & 0 \\ 0 & 0 & 1 \end{pmatrix} \tag{9.125}$$

The six parameters $(\alpha, \beta, \gamma, t_x, t_y, t_z)$ of R and T are called the exterior camera parameters, exterior orientation, or camera pose, because they determine the position of the camera with respect to the world.

The next step of the mapping is the projection of the 3D point P_c into the image plane coordinate system (IPCS). For the pinhole camera model, the projection is a perspective projection, which is given by

$$\begin{pmatrix} u \\ v \end{pmatrix} = \frac{f}{z_c} \begin{pmatrix} x_c \\ y_c \end{pmatrix} \quad (9.126)$$

For the telecentric camera model, the projection is a parallel projection, which is given by

$$\begin{pmatrix} u \\ v \end{pmatrix} = \begin{pmatrix} x_c \\ y_c \end{pmatrix} \quad (9.127)$$

As can be seen, there is no focal length f for telecentric cameras. Furthermore, the distance z_c of the object to the camera has no influence on the image coordinates.

After the projection to the image plane, lens distortions cause the coordinates $(u, v)^\top$ to be modified. Lens distortions are a transformation that can be modeled in the image plane alone, that is, 3D information is unnecessary. For many lenses, the distortion can be approximated sufficiently well by a radial distortion using the division model, which is given by [54, 55, 64]

$$\begin{pmatrix} \tilde{u} \\ \tilde{v} \end{pmatrix} = \frac{2}{1 + \sqrt{1 - 4\kappa(u^2 + v^2)}} \begin{pmatrix} u \\ v \end{pmatrix} = \frac{2}{1 + \sqrt{1 - 4\kappa r^2}} \begin{pmatrix} u \\ v \end{pmatrix} \quad (9.128)$$

where $r^2 = u^2 + v^2$. The parameter κ models the magnitude of the radial distortions. If κ is negative, the distortion is barrel-shaped; while for positive κ it is pincushion-shaped. Figure 9.98 shows the effect of κ for an image of a calibration target, which we will use in the following to calibrate the camera.

The division model has the great advantage that the rectification of the distortion can be calculated analytically by

$$\begin{pmatrix} u \\ v \end{pmatrix} = \frac{1}{1 + \kappa(\tilde{u}^2 + \tilde{v}^2)} \begin{pmatrix} \tilde{u} \\ \tilde{v} \end{pmatrix} = \frac{1}{1 + \kappa \tilde{r}^2} \begin{pmatrix} \tilde{u} \\ \tilde{v} \end{pmatrix} \quad (9.129)$$

where $\tilde{r}^2 = \tilde{u}^2 + \tilde{v}^2$. This will be important when we compute world coordinates from image coordinates.

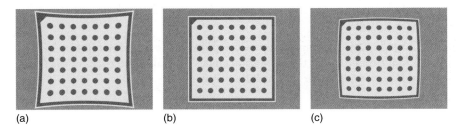

(a)   (b)   (c)

Figure 9.98 Effects of the distortion coefficient κ in the division model. (a) Pincushion distortion: $\kappa > 0$. (b) No distortion: $\kappa = 0$. (c) Barrel distortion: $\kappa < 0$.

If the division model is not sufficiently accurate for a particular lens, a polynomial distortion model that is able to model radial as well as decentering distortions can be used. Here, the rectification of the distortion is modeled by [65, 73, 74]

$$\begin{pmatrix} u \\ v \end{pmatrix} = \begin{pmatrix} \tilde{u}(1 + K_1\tilde{r}^2 + K_2\tilde{r}^4 + K_3\tilde{r}^6 + \cdots) \\ +(2P_1\tilde{u}\tilde{v} + P_2(\tilde{r}^2 + 2\tilde{u}^2))(1 + P_3\tilde{r}^2 + \cdots) \\ \tilde{v}(1 + K_1\tilde{r}^2 + K_2\tilde{r}^4 + K_3\tilde{r}^6 + \cdots) \\ +(P_1(\tilde{r}^2 + 2\tilde{v}^2) + 2P_2\tilde{u}\tilde{v})(1 + P_3\tilde{r}^2 + \cdots) \end{pmatrix} \quad (9.130)$$

The terms K_i describe a radial distortion, while the terms P_i describe a decentering distortion, which may occur if the optical axes of the individual lenses are not aligned perfectly with each other. In practice, the terms K_1, K_2, K_3, P_1, and P_2 are typically used, while higher order terms are neglected.

Note that (9.130) models the rectification of the distortion, that is, the analog of (9.129). In the polynomial model, the distortion (the analog of (9.128)) cannot be computed analytically. Instead, it must be computed numerically by a root-finding algorithm. This is no drawback since in applications we are typically interested in transforming image coordinates to measurements in the world (see Sections 9.9.4 and 9.10). Therefore, it is advantageous if the rectification can be computed analytically.

Figure 9.99 shows the effect of the parameters of the polynomial model on the distortion. In contrast to the division model, where $\kappa > 0$ leads to a pincushion distortion and $\kappa < 0$ to a barrel distortion, in the polynomial model $K_i > 0$ leads to a barrel distortion and $K_i < 0$ to a pincushion distortion. Furthermore, higher order terms lead to very strong distortions at the edges of the image, while they have a progressively smaller effect in the center of the image (if the distortions at the corners of the image are approximately the same). Decentering distortions cause an effect that is somewhat similar to a perspective distortion. However, they additionally bend the image in the horizontal or vertical direction.

There is a deeper connection between the radial distortion coefficients in the division and polynomial models, which can be seen by expanding the rectification

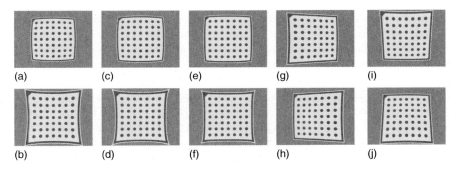

Figure 9.99 Effects of the distortion coefficients in the polynomial model. Coefficients that are not explicitly mentioned are 0. (a) $K_1 > 0$. (b) $K_1 < 0$. (c) $K_2 > 0$. (d) $K_2 < 0$. (e) $K_3 > 0$. (f) $K_3 < 0$. (g) $P_1 > 0$. (h) $P_1 < 0$. (i) $P_2 > 0$. (j) $P_2 < 0$.

factor $1/(1 + \kappa \tilde{r}^2)$ in (9.129) into a geometric series:

$$\frac{1}{1 + \kappa \tilde{r}^2} = \sum_{i=0}^{\infty} (-\kappa \tilde{r}^2)^i = 1 - \kappa \tilde{r}^2 + \kappa^2 \tilde{r}^4 - \kappa^3 \tilde{r}^6 + \cdots \quad (9.131)$$

Therefore, the division model corresponds to the polynomial model without decentering distortions and with infinitely many radial distortion terms K_i that all depend functionally on the single distortion coefficient κ: $K_i = (-\kappa)^i$.

Because of the complexity of the polynomial model, we will only use the division model in the discussion below. However, everything that will be discussed also holds if the division model is replaced by the polynomial model.

Finally, the point $(u, v)^\top$ is transformed from the IPCS into the image coordinate system (ICS):

$$\begin{pmatrix} r \\ c \end{pmatrix} = \begin{pmatrix} \dfrac{\tilde{v}}{s_y} + c_y \\ \dfrac{\tilde{u}}{s_x} + c_x \end{pmatrix} \quad (9.132)$$

Here, s_x and s_y are scaling factors. For pinhole cameras, they represent the horizontal and vertical pixel pitch on the sensor. For telecentric cameras, they represent the horizontal and vertical pixel pitch divided by the magnification factor of the lens (not taking into account the distortions of the lens). The point $(c_x, c_y)^\top$ is the principal point of the image. For pinhole cameras, this is the perpendicular projection of the projection center onto the image plane, that is, the point in the image from which a ray through the projection center is perpendicular to the image plane. It also defines the center of the distortions. For telecentric cameras, no projection center exists. Therefore, the principal point is solely defined by the distortions.

The six parameters $(f, \kappa, s_x, s_y, c_x, c_y)$ of the pinhole camera and the five parameters $(\kappa, s_x, s_y, c_x, c_y)$ of the telecentric camera are called the interior camera parameters or interior orientation, because they determine the projection from three dimensions to two dimensions performed by the camera.

9.9.2 Camera Model for Line Scan Cameras

Line scan cameras must move with respect to the object to acquire a useful image. The relative motion between the camera and the object is part of the interior orientation. By far the most frequent motion is a linear motion of the camera, that is, the camera moves with constant velocity along a straight line relative to the object, the orientation of the camera is constant with respect to the object, and the motion is equal for all images [75]. In this case, the motion can be described by the motion vector $V = (v_x, v_y, v_z)^\top$, as shown in Figure 9.100. The vector V is best described in units of meters per scan line in the camera coordinate system. As shown in Figure 9.100, the definition of V assumes a moving camera and a fixed object. If the camera is stationary and the object is moving, for example, on a conveyor belt, we can simply use $-V$ as the motion vector.

The camera model for a line scan camera is displayed in Figure 9.101. The origin of the CCS is the projection center. The z-axis is identical to the optical axis and

Figure 9.100 Principle of line scan image acquisition.

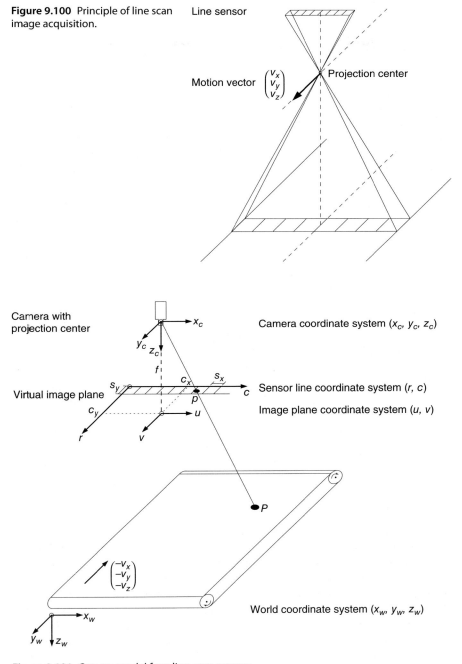

Figure 9.101 Camera model for a line scan camera.

is oriented such that points in front of the camera have positive z coordinates. The y-axis is perpendicular to the sensor line and to the z-axis. It is oriented such that the motion vector has a positive y component: that is, if a fixed object is assumed, the y-axis points in the direction in which the camera is moving. The x-axis is perpendicular to the y- and z-axis, so that the x, y, and z axes form a right-handed coordinate system.

Similar to area scan cameras, the projection of a point given in world coordinates into the image is modeled in two steps. First, the point is transformed from the WCS into the CCS. Then, it is projected into the image.

As the camera moves over the object during the image acquisition, the CCS moves with respect to the object, that is, each image is imaged from a different position. This means that each line has a different pose. To make things easier, we can use the fact that the motion of the camera is linear. Hence, it suffices to know the transformation from the WCS to the CCS for the first line of the image. The poses of the remaining lines can be computed from the motion vector, that is, the motion vector V is taken into account during the projection of P_c into the image. With this, the transformation from the WCS to the CCS is identical to equation (9.124). Like for area scan cameras, the six parameters $(\alpha, \beta, \gamma, t_x, t_y, t_z)$ are called the exterior camera parameters or exterior orientation, because they determine the position of the camera with respect to the world.

To obtain a model for the interior geometry of a line scan camera, we can regard a line sensor as one particular line of an area sensor. Therefore, like in area scan cameras, there is an IPCS that lies at a distance of f (the principal distance) behind the projection center. Again, the computations can be simplified if we pretend that the image plane lies in front of the projection center, as shown in Figure 9.101. We will defer the description of the projection performed by the line scan camera until later, since it is more complicated than for area scan cameras.

Let us assume that the point P_c has been projected to the point $(u, v)^\top$ in the IPCS. Like for area scan cameras, the point is now distorted by the radial distortion (9.128), which results in a distorted point $(\tilde{u}, \tilde{v})^\top$.

Finally, like for area scan cameras, $(\tilde{u}, \tilde{v})^\top$ is transformed into the ICS, resulting in the coordinates $(r, c)^\top$. Since we want to model the fact that the line sensor may not be mounted exactly behind the projection center, which often occurs in practice, we again have to introduce a principal point $(c_x, c_y)^\top$ that models how the line sensor is shifted with respect to the projection center, that is, it describes the relative position of the principal point with respect to the line sensor. Since $(\tilde{u}, \tilde{v})^\top$ is given in metric units, for example, meters, we need to introduce two scale factors s_x and s_y that determine how the IPCS units are converted to ICS units (i.e., pixels). Like for area scan cameras, s_x represents the horizontal pixel pitch on the sensor. As we will see in the following, s_y only serves as a scaling factor that enables us to specify the principal point in pixel coordinates. The values of s_x and s_y cannot be calibrated and must be set to the pixel size of the line sensor in the horizontal and vertical directions, respectively.

To determine the projection of the point $P_c = (x_c, y_c, z_c)^\top$ (specified in the CCS), we first consider the case where there are no radial distortions ($\kappa = 0$), the line sensor is mounted precisely behind the projection center ($c_y = 0$), and the motion is purely in the y direction of the CCS ($V = (0, v_y, 0)^\top$). In this case, the row coordinate of the projected point p is proportional to the time it takes for the point P_c to appear directly under the sensor, that is, to appear in the xz-plane of the CCS. To determine this, we must solve $x_c - tv_y = 0$ for the "time" t (since V is specified in meters per scan line, the units of t are actually scan lines, i.e., pixels). Hence, $r = t = x_c/v_y$. Since $v_x = 0$, we also have $u = fx_c/z_c$ and $c = u/s_x + c_x$. Therefore, the projection is a perspective projection in the direction of the line sensor and a parallel projection perpendicular to the line sensor (i.e., in the special motion direction $(0, v_y, 0)^\top$).

For general motion vectors (i.e., $v_x \neq 0$ or $v_z \neq 0$), non-perfectly aligned line sensors ($c_y \neq 0$), and radial distortions ($\kappa \neq 0$), the equations become significantly more complicated. As above, we need to determine the "time" t when the point P_c appears in the "plane" spanned by the projection center and the line sensor. We put "plane" in quotes since the radial distortion will cause the back-projection of the line sensor to be a curved surface in space whenever $c_y \neq 0$ and $\kappa \neq 0$. To solve this problem, we construct the optical ray through the projection center and the projected point $p = (r, c)^\top$. Let us assume that we have transformed $(r, c)^\top$ into the distorted IPCS, where we have coordinates $(\tilde{u}, \tilde{v})^\top$. Here, $\tilde{v} = s_y c_y$ is the coordinate of the principal point in metric units. Then, we rectify $(\tilde{u}, \tilde{v})^\top$ by equation (9.129), that is, $(u, v)^\top = d(\tilde{u}, \tilde{v})^\top$, where $d = 1/(1 + \kappa(\tilde{u}^2 + \tilde{v}^2))$ is the rectification factor from equation (9.129). The optical ray is now given by the line equation $\lambda(u, v, f)^\top = \lambda(d\tilde{u}, d\tilde{v}, f)^\top$. The point P_c moves along the line given by $(x_c, y_c, z_c)^\top - t(v_x, v_y, v_z)^\top$ during the acquisition of the image. If p is the projection of P_c, both lines must intersect. Therefore, to determine the projection of P_c, we must solve the following nonlinear set of equations:

$$\lambda d\tilde{u} = x_c - tv_x$$
$$\lambda d\tilde{v} = y_c - tv_y \qquad (9.133)$$
$$\lambda f = z_c - tv_z$$

for λ, $\tilde{u}$, and t, where d and $\tilde{v}$ are defined above. From $\tilde{u}$ and t, the pixel coordinates can be computed by

$$\begin{pmatrix} r \\ c \end{pmatrix} = \begin{pmatrix} t \\ \dfrac{\tilde{u}}{s_x} + c_x \end{pmatrix} \qquad (9.134)$$

The nine parameters $(f, \kappa, s_x, s_y, c_x, c_y, v_x, v_y, v_z)$ of the line scan camera are called the interior orientation because they determine the projection from three dimensions to two dimensions performed by the camera.

Although the line scan camera geometry is conceptually simply a mixture of a perspective and a telecentric lens, precisely this mixture makes the camera geometry much more complex than the area scan geometries. Figure 9.102 displays some of the effects that can occur. In Figure 9.102a, the pixels are non-square because the motion is not tuned to the line frequency of the camera. In this example, either the line frequency would need to be increased or the motion speed would need to be decreased in order to obtain square pixels. Figure 9.102b shows the effect of a motion vector of the form $V = (v_x, v_y, 0)$ with $v_x = v_y/10$. We

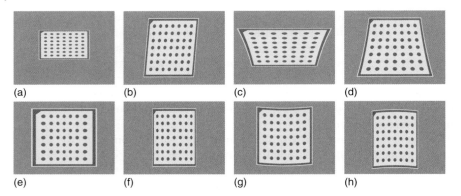

Figure 9.102 Some effects that occur for the line scan camera geometry. (a) Non-square pixels due to the not motion being tuned to the line frequency of the camera. (b) Skewed pixels due to the motion not being parallel to the y-axis of the CCS. (c) Straight lines can project to hyperbolic arcs, even if the line sensor is perpendicular to the motion. (d) This effect is more pronounced if the motion has a nonzero z component. Note that hyperbolic arcs occur even if the lens has no distortions ($\kappa = 0$). (e) Pincushion distortion ($\kappa > 0$) for $c_y = 0$. (f) Barrel distortion for $c_y = 0$. (g) Pincushion distortion ($\kappa > 0$) for $c_y > 0$. (h) Barrel distortion for $c_y > 0$.

obtain skew pixels. In this case, the camera would need to be better aligned with the motion vector. Figure 9.102c,d shows that straight lines can be projected to hyperbolic arcs [75], even if the lens has no distortions ($\kappa = 0$). This effect occurs even if $V = (0, v_y, 0)$, that is, if the line sensor is perfectly aligned perpendicular to the motion vector. The hyperbolic arcs are more pronounced if the motion vector has nonzero v_z. Figure 9.102e–h shows the effect of a lens with distortions ($\kappa \neq 0$) for the case where the sensor is located perfectly behind the projection center ($c_y = 0$) and for the case where the sensor is not perfectly aligned (here $c_y > 0$). For $c_y = 0$, the pincushion and barrel distortions only cause distortions within each row of the image. For $c_y \neq 0$, the rows are also bent.

9.9.3 Calibration Process

From the above discussion, we can see that camera calibration is the process of determining the interior and exterior camera parameters. To perform the calibration, it is necessary to know the location of a sufficiently large number of 3D points in world coordinates, and to be able to determine the correspondence between the world points and their projections in the image. To meet the first requirement, usually objects or marks that are easy to extract, for example, circles or linear grids, must be placed at known locations. If the location of a camera is to be known with respect to a given coordinate system, for example, with respect to the building plan of, say, a factory building, then each mark location must be measured very carefully within this coordinate system. Fortunately, it is often sufficient to know the position of a reference object with respect to the camera to be able to measure the object precisely, since the absolute position of the object in world coordinates is unimportant. Therefore, a movable calibration target that has been measured accurately can be used to calibrate the camera. This has the advantage that the calibration can be performed with the camera in place, for example, already mounted in the machine. Furthermore, the position of the camera with respect to the objects can be recalibrated if required, for example, if the object type to be inspected changes.

The second requirement, that is, the necessity to determine the correspondence of the known world points and their projections in the image, is in general a hard problem. Therefore, calibration targets are usually constructed in such a way that this correspondence can be determined easily. For example, a planar calibration target with $m \times n$ circular marks within a rectangular border can be used. We have already seen examples of this kind of calibration target in Figures 9.85, 9.92, 9.98, and 9.102. Planar calibration targets have several advantages. First of all, they can be handled easily. Second, they can be manufactured very accurately. Finally, they can be used for back-light applications easily if a transparent medium is used as the carrier for the marks. A rectangular border around the calibration target allows the inner part of the calibration target to be found easily. A small orientation mark in one of the corners of the border enables the camera calibration algorithm to uniquely determine the orientation of the calibration target. Circular marks are used because their center point can be determined with high accuracy. Finally, the regular matrix layout of the rows and columns of the circles enables the camera calibration algorithm to determine the correspondence between the marks and their image points easily.

To extract the calibration target, we can make use of the fact that the border separates the inner part of the calibration target from the background. Consequently, the inner part can be found by a simple threshold operation (see Section 9.4.1). Since the correct threshold depends on the brightness of the calibration target in the image, different thresholds can be tried automatically until a region with $m \times n$ holes (corresponding to the calibration marks) has been found.

Once the region of the inner part of the calibration target has been found, the borders of the calibration marks can be extracted with subpixel-accurate edge extraction (see Section 9.7.3). Since the projections of the circular marks are ellipses, ellipses can then be fitted to the extracted edges with the algorithms described in Section 9.8.3 to obtain robustness against outliers in the edge points and to increase the accuracy. An example of the extraction of the calibration marks was already shown in Figure 9.92.

Finally, the correspondence between the calibration marks and their projections in the image can be determined easily based on the smallest enclosing quadrilateral of the extracted ellipses. Furthermore, the orientation of the marks can be determined uniquely based on the small triangular orientation mark. If it were not present, the orientation can only be determined modulo 90° for square calibration targets and modulo 180° for rectangular targets. It should be noted that the orientation of the calibration target is important only if the distances between the marks are not identical in both axes or in applications where the orientation must be determined uniquely across multiple images. One such example is stereo with cameras that are rotated significantly with respect to each other around their respective optical axes.

After the correspondence between the marks and their projections has been determined, the camera can be calibrated. Let us denote the 3D positions of the centers of the marks by M_i. Since the calibration target is planar, we can place the calibration target in the plane $z = 0$. However, what we describe in the following is completely general and can be used for arbitrary calibration targets. Furthermore, let us denote the projections of the centers of the marks in the image by m_i. Here, we must take into account that the projection of the center of the circle is not the center of the ellipse [65, 76]. Finally, let us denote the camera parameters by a vector c. As described previously, c consists of the interior and exterior orientation parameters of the respective camera model. For example, $c = (f, \kappa, s_x, s_y, c_x, c_y, \alpha, \beta, \gamma, t_x, t_y, t_z)$ for pinhole cameras. Here, it should be noted that the exterior orientation is determined by attaching the WCS to the calibration target, for example, to the center mark, in such a way that the x- and y-axis of the WCS are aligned with the row and column directions of the marks on the calibration target and the z-axis points in the same direction as the optical axis if the calibration target is parallel to the image plane. Then, the camera parameters can be determined by minimizing the distance of the extracted mark centers m_i and their projections $\pi(M_i, c)$:

$$d(c) = \sum_{i=1}^{k} \| m_i - \pi(M_i, c) \|^2 \to \min \qquad (9.135)$$

Here, $k = mn$ is the number of calibration marks. This is a difficult nonlinear optimization problem. Therefore, good starting values are required for the parameters. The interior orientation parameters can be determined from the specifications of the image sensor and the lens. The starting values for the exterior orientation are in general harder to obtain. For the planar calibration target described above, good starting values can be obtained based on the geometry and size of the projected circles [55, 64].

The optimization in equation (9.135) cannot determine all camera parameters because the physically motivated camera models we have chosen are over-parameterized. For example, for the pinhole camera, f, s_x, and s_y cannot be determined uniquely since they contain a common scale factor, as shown in Figure 9.103. For example, making the pixels twice as large and increasing the principal distance by a factor of 2 results in the same image. The solution to this problem is to keep s_y fixed in the optimization since the image is transmitted row-synchronously for all kinds of video signals. This fixes the common scale factor. On the other hand, s_x cannot be kept fixed in general since the video signal may not be sampled pixel-synchronously, at least for analog video signals. A similar effect happens for line scan cameras. Here, s_x and f cannot be determined uniquely. Consequently, s_x must be kept fixed in the calibration. Furthermore, as described in Section 9.9.2, s_y cannot be determined for line scan cameras and therefore also must be kept fixed.

Even if the above problem is solved, some degeneracies remain because we use a planar calibration target. For example, as shown in Figure 9.104, if the calibration target is parallel to the image plane, f and t_z cannot be determined uniquely since they contain a common scale factor. This problem also occurs if the calibration target is not parallel to the image plane. Here, f and a combination of parameters from the exterior orientation can be determined only up to a one-parameter

Figure 9.103 For pinhole cameras, f, s_x, and s_y cannot be determined uniquely.

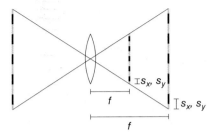

Figure 9.104 For pinhole cameras, f and t_z cannot be determined uniquely.

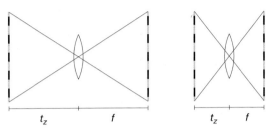

ambiguity. For example, if the calibration target is rotated around the x-axis, f, t_z, and α cannot be determined at the same time. For telecentric cameras, it is generally impossible to determine s_x, s_y, and the rotation angles from a single image. For example, a rotation of the calibration target around the x-axis can be compensated by a corresponding change in s_x. For line scan cameras, there are similar degeneracies as the ones described above plus degeneracies that include the motion vector.

To prevent the above degeneracies, the camera must be calibrated from multiple images in which the calibration target is positioned to avoid the degeneracies. For example, for pinhole cameras, the calibration targets must not be parallel to each other in all images; while for telecentric cameras, the calibration target must be rotated around all of its axes to avoid the above degeneracies. Suppose we use image l for the calibration. Then, we also have l sets of exterior orientation parameters $(\alpha_l, \beta_l, \gamma_l, t_{x,l}, t_{y,l}, t_{z,l})$ that must be determined. As above, we collect the interior orientation parameters and the l sets of exterior orientation parameters into the camera parameter vector c. Then, to calibrate the camera, we must solve the following optimization problem:

$$d(c) = \sum_{j=1}^{l} \sum_{i=1}^{k} \| m_{i,j} - \pi(M_i, c) \|^2 \to \min \tag{9.136}$$

Here, $m_{i,j}$ denotes the projection of the ith calibration mark in the jth image. If the calibration targets are placed and oriented suitably in the images, this will determine all the camera parameters uniquely. To ensure high accuracy of the camera parameters so determined, the calibration target should be placed at all four corners of the image. Since the distortion is largest in the corners, this will facilitate the determination of the distortion coefficient(s) with the highest possible accuracy.

To conclude this section, we mention that a flexible calibration algorithm will enable one to specify a subset of the parameters that should be determined.

For example, from the mechanical setup, some of the parameters of the exterior orientation may be known. One frequently encountered example is that the mechanical setup ensures with high accuracy that the calibration target is parallel to the image plane. In this case, we should set $\alpha = \beta = 0$, and the camera calibration should leave these parameters fixed. Another example is a camera with square pixels that transmits the video signal digitally. Here, $s_x = s_y$, and for pinhole cameras both parameters should be kept fixed. Finally, we will see in the next section that the calibration target determines the world plane in which measurements from a single image can be performed. In some applications, there is not enough space for the calibration target to be turned in three dimensions if the camera is mounted in its final position. Here, a two-step approach can be used. First, the interior orientation of the camera is determined with the camera not mounted in its final position. This ensures that the calibration target can be moved freely. (Note that this also determines the exterior orientation of the calibration target; however, this information is discarded.) Then, the camera is mounted in its final position. Here, it must be ensured that the focus and iris diaphragm settings of the lens are not changed, since this will change the interior orientation. In the final position, a single image of the calibration target is taken, and only the exterior orientation is optimized to determine the pose of the camera with respect to the measurement plane.

9.9.4 World Coordinates from Single Images

As mentioned previously and at the end of Section 9.7.4, if the camera is calibrated, it is possible in principle to obtain undistorted measurements in world coordinates. In general, this can be done only if two or more images of the same object are taken at the same time with cameras at different spatial positions. This is called stereo reconstruction. With this approach, discussed in Section 9.10, the reconstruction of 3D positions for corresponding points in the two images is possible because the two optical rays defined by the two optical centers of the cameras and the points in the image plane defined by the two image points can be intersected in 3D space to give the 3D position of that point. In some applications, however, it is impossible to use two cameras, for example, because there is not enough space to mount two cameras. Nevertheless, it is possible to obtain measurements in world coordinates for objects acquired through telecentric lenses and for objects that lie in a known plane, for example, on a conveyor belt, for pinhole and line scan cameras. Both of these problems can be solved by intersecting an optical ray (also called the line of sight) with a plane. With this, it is possible to measure objects that lie in a plane, even if the plane is tilted with respect to the optical axis.

Let us first look at the problem of determining world coordinates for telecentric cameras. In this case, the parallel projection in equation (9.127) discards any depth information completely. Therefore, we cannot hope to discover the distance of the object from the camera, that is, its z coordinate in the CCS. What we can recover, however, are the x and y coordinates of the object in the CCS (x_c and y_c in equation (9.127)), that is, the dimensions of the object in world units. Since the z coordinate of P_c cannot be recovered, in most cases it is unnecessary to transform P_c into world coordinates by inverting equation (9.124). Instead, the point P_c is regarded as a point in world coordinates. To recover P_c, we can start by inverting equation (9.132) to transform the coordinates from the ICS into the IPCS:

$$\begin{pmatrix} \tilde{u} \\ \tilde{v} \end{pmatrix} = \begin{pmatrix} s_x(c - c_x) \\ s_y(r - c_y) \end{pmatrix} \tag{9.137}$$

Then, we can rectify the lens distortions by applying equation (9.129) or (9.130) to obtain the rectified coordinates $(u, v)^\top$ in the image plane. Finally, the coordinates of P_c are given by

$$P_c = (x_c, y_c, z_c)^\top = (u, v, 0)^\top \tag{9.138}$$

Note that the above procedure is equivalent to intersecting the optical ray given by the point $(u, v, 0)^\top$ and the direction perpendicular to the image plane, that is, $(0, 0, 1)^\top$, with the plane $z = 0$.

The determination of world coordinates for pinhole cameras is slightly more complicated, but uses the same principle of intersecting an optical ray with a known plane. Let us look at this problem by using the application where this procedure is most useful. In many applications, the objects to be measured lie in a plane in front of the camera, for example, a conveyor belt. Let us assume for the moment that the location and orientation of this plane (its pose) are known. We will describe below how to obtain this pose. The plane can be described by its origin and a local coordinate system, that is, three orthogonal vectors, one of which is perpendicular to the plane. To transform the coordinates in the coordinate system of the plane (the WCS) into the CCS, a rigid transformation given by equation (9.124) must be used. Its six parameters $(\alpha, \beta, \gamma, t_x, t_y, t_z)$ describe the pose of the plane. If we want to measure objects in this plane, we need to determine the object coordinates in the WCS defined by the plane. Conceptually, we need to intersect the optical ray corresponding to an image point with the plane. To do so, we need to know two points that define the optical ray. Recalling Figures 9.96 and 9.97, obviously the first point is given by the projection center, which has the coordinates $(0, 0, 0)^\top$ in the CCS. To obtain the second point, we need to transform the point $(r, c)^\top$ from the ICS into the IPCS. This transformation is given by equations (9.137) and (9.129) or (9.130). To obtain the 3D point that corresponds to this point in the image plane, we need to take into account that the image plane lies at a distance of f in front of the optical center. Hence, the coordinates of the second point on the optical ray are given by $(u, v, f)^\top$. Therefore, we can describe the optical ray in the CCS by

$$L_c = (0, 0, 0)^\top + \lambda(u, v, f)^\top \tag{9.139}$$

To intersect this line with the plane, it is best to express the line L_c in the WCS of the plane, since in the WCS the plane is given by the equation $z = 0$. Therefore, we need to transform the two points $(0, 0, 0)^\top$ and $(u, v, f)^\top$ into the WCS. This can be done by inverting equation (9.124) to obtain

$$P_w = R^{-1}(P_c - T) = R^\top(P_c - T) \tag{9.140}$$

Here, $R^{-1} = R^\top$ is the inverse of the rotation matrix R in equation (9.124). Let us call the transformed optical center O_w, that is, $O_w = R^\top((0, 0, 0)^\top - T) = -R^\top T$, and the transformed point in the image plane I_w, that is, $I_w = R^T((u, v, f)^T - T)$. With this, the optical ray is given by

$$L_w = O_w + \lambda(I_w - O_w) = O_w + \lambda D_w \qquad (9.141)$$

in the WCS. Here, D_w denotes the direction vector of the optical ray. With this, it is a simple matter to determine the intersection of the optical ray in equation (9.141) with the plane $z = 0$. The intersection point is given by

$$P_w = \begin{pmatrix} o_x - o_z\, d_x/d_z \\ o_y - o_z\, d_y/d_z \\ 0 \end{pmatrix} \qquad (9.142)$$

where $O_w = (o_x, o_y, o_z)^T$ and $D_w = (d_x, d_y, d_z)^T$.

Up to now, we have assumed that the pose of the plane in which we want to measure objects is known. Fortunately, the camera calibration gives us this pose almost immediately since a planar calibration target is used. If the calibration target is placed on the plane, for example, the conveyor belt, in one of the images used for calibration, the exterior orientation of the calibration target in that image almost defines the pose of the plane we need in the above derivation. The pose would be the true pose of the plane if the calibration target were infinitely thin. To take the thickness of the calibration target into account, the WCS defined by the exterior orientation must be moved by the thickness of the calibration target in the positive z direction. This modifies the transformation from the WCS to the CCS in equation (9.124) as follows: the translation T simply becomes $RD + T$, where $D = d(0, 0, 1)^T$, and d is the thickness of the calibration target. This is the pose that must be used in equation (9.140) to transform the optical ray into the WCS. An example of computing edge positions in world coordinates for pinhole cameras is given at the end of Section 9.7.4 (see Figure 9.86).

For line scan cameras, the procedure to obtain world coordinates in a given plane is conceptually similar to the approaches described above. First, the optical ray is constructed from equations (9.134) and (9.133). Then, it is transformed into the WCS and intersected with the plane $z = 0$.

In addition to transforming image points, for example, 1D edge positions or subpixel-precise contours, into world coordinates, sometimes it is also useful to transform the image itself into world coordinates. This creates an image that would have resulted if the camera had looked perfectly perpendicularly without distortions onto the world plane. This image rectification is useful for applications that must work on the image data itself, for example, region processing, template matching, or OCR. It can be used whenever the camera cannot be mounted perpendicular to the measurement plane. To rectify the image, we conceptually cut out a rectangular region of the world plane $z = 0$ and sample it with a specified distance, for example, 200 µm. We then project each sample point into the image with the equations of the relevant camera model, and obtain the gray value through interpolation, for example, bilinear interpolation. Figure 9.105 shows an example of this process. In Figure 9.105a, the image of a caliper together with the calibration target that defines the world plane is shown. The unrectified and rectified images of the caliper are shown in Figure 9.105b,c, respectively.

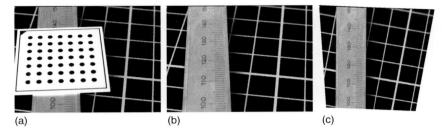

Figure 9.105 (a) Image of a caliper with a calibration target. (b) Unrectified image of the caliper. (c) Rectified image of the caliper.

Note that the rectification has removed the perspective and radial distortions from the image.

9.9.5 Accuracy of the Camera Parameters

We conclude the discussion of camera calibration by discussing two different aspects: the accuracy of the camera parameters, and the changes in the camera parameters that result from adjusting the focus and iris diaphragm settings on the lens.

As was already noted in Section 9.9.3, there are some cases where an inappropriate placement of the calibration target can result in degenerate configurations where one of the camera parameters or a combination of some of the parameters cannot be determined. These configurations must obviously be avoided if the camera parameters should be determined with high accuracy. Apart from this, the main influencing factor for the accuracy of the camera parameters is the number of images that are used to calibrate the camera. This is illustrated in Figure 9.106, where the standard deviations of the principal distance f, the radial distortion coefficient κ, and the principal point (c_x, c_y) are plotted as functions of the number of images that are used for calibration. To obtain this data, 20 images of a calibration target were taken. Then, every possible subset of l images ($l = 2, \ldots, 19$) from the 20 images was used to calibrate the camera. The standard deviations were calculated from the resulting camera parameters when l of the 20 images were used for the calibration. From Figure 9.106 it is obvious that the accuracy of the camera parameters increases significantly as the number of images l increases. This is not surprising when we consider that each image serves to constrain the parameters. If the images were independent measurements, we could expect the standard deviation to decrease proportionally to $l^{-0.5}$. In this particular example, f decreases roughly proportionally to $l^{-1.5}$, κ decreases roughly proportionally to $l^{-1.1}$, and c_x and c_y decrease roughly proportionally to $l^{-1.2}$, that is, much faster than $l^{-0.5}$.

From Figure 9.106, it can also be seen that a comparatively large number of calibration images is required to determine the camera parameters accurately. This happens because there are nonnegligible correlations between the camera parameters, which can only be resolved through multiple independent measurements. To obtain accurate camera parameters, it is important that the calibration target covers the entire field of view and that it tries to cover the range of

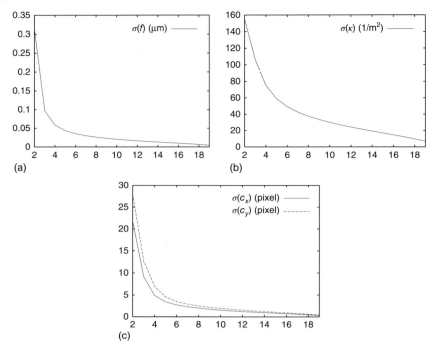

Figure 9.106 Standard deviations of (a) the principal distance f, (b) the radial distortion coefficient κ, and (c) the principal point (c_x, c_y) as functions of the number of images that are used for calibration.

exterior orientations as well as possible. In particular, κ can be determined more accurately if the calibration target is placed into each corner of the image. Furthermore, all parameters can be determined more accurately if the calibration target covers a large depth range. This can be achieved by turning the calibration target around its x- and y-axes, and by placing it at different depths relative to the camera.

We now turn to a discussion of whether changes in the lens settings change the camera parameters. Figure 9.107 displays the effect of changing the focus

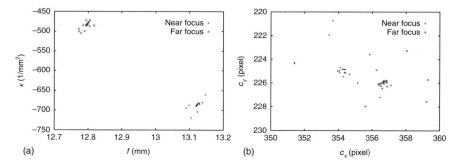

Figure 9.107 (a) Principal distances and radial distortion coefficients and (b) principal points for a lens with two different focus settings.

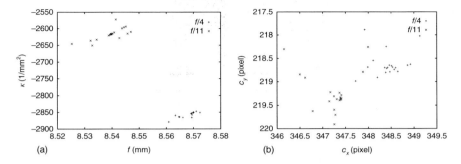

Figure 9.108 (a) Principal distances and radial distortion coefficients and (b) principal points for a lens with two different iris diaphragm settings (f-numbers: $f/4$ and $f/11$).

setting of the lens. Here, a 12.5 mm lens with a 1mm extension tube was used. The lens was set to the nearest and farthest focal settings. In the near focus setting, the camera was calibrated with a calibration target of size 1 cm × 1 cm, while for the far focus setting a calibration target of size 3 cm × 3 cm was used. This resulted in the same size of the calibration target in the focusing plane for both settings. Care was taken to use images of calibration targets with approximately the same range of depths and positions in the images. For each setting, 20 images of the calibration target were taken. To be able to evaluate statistically whether the camera parameters are different, all 20 subsets of 19 of the 20 images were used to calibrate the camera. As can be expected from the discussion in Section 4.2, changing the focus will change the principal distance. From Figure 9.107a, we can see that this clearly is the case. Furthermore, the radial distortion coefficient κ also changes significantly. From Figure 9.107b, it is also obvious that the principal point changes. The probability that the two means of the respective principal points are identical is less than 10^{-7}.

Finally, we examine what can happen when the iris diaphragm on the lens is changed. To test this, a similar setup as above was used. The camera was set to f-numbers $f/4$ and $f/11$. For each setting, 20 images of a 3 cm × 3 cm calibration target were taken. Care was taken to position the calibration targets in similar positions for the two settings. The lens is an 8.5mm lens with a 1mm extension tube. Again, all 20 subsets of 19 of the 20 images were used to calibrate the camera. Figure 9.108a displays the principal distance and radial distortion coefficient. Clearly, the two parameters change in a statistically significant way. Figure 9.108b also shows that the principal point changes significantly. All parameters have a probability of being equal that is less than 10^{-7}. The changes in the parameters mean that there is an overall difference in the point coordinates across the image diagonal of ≈ 1.5 pixels. Therefore, we can see that changing the f-number on the lens requires a recalibration, at least for some lenses.

9.10 Stereo Reconstruction

In Sections 9.9 and 9.7.4, we have seen that we can perform very accurate measurements from a single image by calibrating the camera and by determining its exterior orientation with respect to a plane in the world. We could then convert the image measurements to world coordinates within the plane by intersecting optical rays with the plane. Note, however, that these measurements are still 2D measurements within the world plane. In fact, from a single image we cannot reconstruct the 3D geometry of the scene because we can only determine the optical ray for each point in the image. We do not know at which distance on the optical ray the point lies in the world. In the approach in Section 9.9.4, we had to assume a special geometry in the world to be able to determine the distance of a point along the optical ray. Note that this is not a true 3D reconstruction. To perform a 3D reconstruction, we must use at least two images of the same scene taken from different positions. Typically, this is done by simultaneously taking the images with two cameras. This process is called stereo reconstruction. In this section, we will examine the case of binocular stereo, that is, we will concentrate on the two-camera case. Throughout this section, we will assume that the cameras have been calibrated, that is, their interior orientations and relative orientation are known. While uncalibrated reconstruction is also possible [20, 21], the corresponding methods have not yet been used in industrial applications.

9.10.1 Stereo Geometry

Before we can discuss the stereo reconstruction, we must examine the geometry of two cameras, as shown in Figure 9.109. Since the cameras are assumed to be calibrated, we know their interior orientations, that is, their principal points, focal lengths (more precisely, their principal distances, that is, the distance between the image plane and the projection center), pixel size, and distortion coefficient(s). In Figure 9.109, the principal points are shown by the points C_1 and C_2 in the first and second image, respectively. Furthermore, the projection centers are shown by the points O_1 and O_2. The dashed line between the projection centers and principal points shows the principal distances. Note that, since the image planes physically lie behind the projection centers, the image is turned upside down. Consequently, the origin of the ICS lies in the lower right corner, with the row

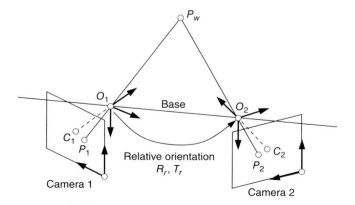

Figure 9.109 Stereo geometry of two cameras.

axis pointing upward and the column axis pointing leftward. The CCS axes are defined such that the x-axis points to the right, the y-axis points downwards, and the z-axis points forward from the image plane, that is, along the viewing direction. The position and orientation of the two cameras with respect to each other are given by the relative orientation, which is a rigid 3D transformation specified by the rotation matrix R_r and the translation vector T_r. It can be interpreted either as the transformation of the camera coordinate system of the first camera into the CCS of the second camera or as a transformation that transforms point coordinates in the camera coordinate system of the second camera into point coordinates of the CCS of the first camera: $P_{c1} = R_r P_{c2} + T_r$. The translation vector T_r, which specifies the translation between the two projection centers, is also called the base. With this, we can see that a point P_w in the world is mapped to a point P_1 in the first image and to a point P_2 in the second image. If there are no lens distortions (which we will assume for the moment), the points P_w, O_1, O_2, P_1, and P_2 all lie in a single plane.

To calibrate the stereo system, we can extend the method of Section 9.9.3 as follows. Let M_i denote the positions of the calibration marks. We extract their projections in both images with the methods described in Section 9.9.3. Let us denote the projection of the centers of the marks in the first set of calibration images by $m_{i,j,1}$ and in the second set by $m_{i,j,2}$. Furthermore, let us denote the camera parameters by a vector c. The camera parameters c include the interior orientation of the first and second camera, the exterior orientation of the l calibration targets in the second image, and the relative orientation of the two cameras. From the above discussion of the relative orientation, it follows that these parameters determine the mappings $\pi_1(M_i, c)$ and $\pi_2(M_i, c)$ into the first and second images completely. Hence, to calibrate the stereo system, the following optimization problem must be solved:

$$d(c) = \sum_{j=1}^{l} \sum_{i=1}^{k} \| m_{i,j,1} - \pi_1(M_i, c) \|^2 + \| m_{i,j,2} - \pi_2(M_i, c) \|^2 \to \min \quad (9.143)$$

To illustrate the relative orientation and the stereo calibration, Figure 9.110 shows an image pair taken from a sequence of 15 image pairs that were used to calibrate a binocular stereo system. The calibration returns a translation vector of (0.1534 m, − 0.0037 m, 0.0449 m) between the cameras, that is, the second camera is 15.34 cm to the right, 0.37 cm above, and 4.49 cm in front of the first camera, expressed in the camera coordinates of the first camera. Furthermore, the calibration returns a rotation angle of 40.1139° around the axis (−0.0035, 1.0000, 0.0008), that is, almost around the vertical y-axis of the CCS. Hence, the cameras are verging inward, like in Figure 9.109.

To reconstruct 3D points, we must find the corresponding points in the two images. "Corresponding" means that the two points P_1 and P_2 in the images belong to the same point P_w in the world. At first, it might seem that, given a point P_1 in the first image, we would have to search in the entire second image for the corresponding point P_2. Fortunately, this is not the case. In Figure 9.109, we already noted that the points P_w, O_1, O_2, P_1, and P_2 all lie in a single plane. The situation of trying to find a corresponding point for P_1 is shown in Figure 9.111.

Figure 9.110 One image pair taken from a sequence of 15 image pairs that are used to calibrate a binocular stereo system. The calibration returns a translation vector (base) of (0.1534 m, −0.0037 m, 0.0449 m) between the cameras and a rotation angle of 40.1139° around the axis (−0.0035, 1.0000, 0.0008), that is, almost around the y-axis of the camera coordinate system. Hence, the cameras are verging inward.

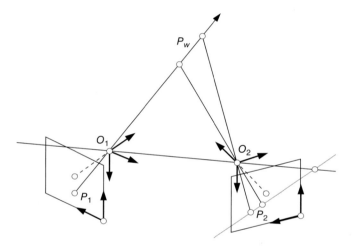

Figure 9.111 Epipolar geometry of two cameras. Given the point P_1 in the first image, the point P_2 in the second image can only lie on the epipolar line of P_1, which is the projection of the epipolar plane spanned by P_1, O_1, and O_2 onto the second image.

We can note that we know P_1, O_1, and O_2. We do not know at which distance the point P_w lies on the optical ray defined by P_1 and O_1. However, we know that P_w is coplanar with the plane spanned by P_1, O_1, and O_2 (the epipolar plane). Hence, we can see that the point P_2 can only lie on the projection of the epipolar plane onto the second image. Since O_2 lies on the epipolar plane, the projection of the epipolar plane is a line called the epipolar line.

It is obvious that the above construction is symmetric for both images, as shown in Figure 9.112. Hence, given a point P_2 in the second image, the corresponding point can only lie on the epipolar line in the first image. Furthermore, from Figure 9.112, we can see that different points typically define different epipolar lines. We can also see that all epipolar lines of one image intersect at a single point called the epipole. The epipoles are the projections of the opposite projective centers onto the respective image. Note that, since all epipolar planes contain

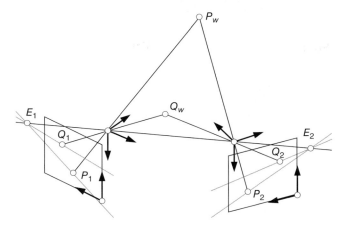

Figure 9.112 The epipolar geometry is symmetric between the two images. Furthermore, different points typically define different epipolar lines. All epipolar lines intersect at the epipoles E_1 and E_2, which are the projections of the opposite projective centers onto the respective image.

O_1 and O_2, the epipoles lie on the line defined by the two projection centers (the base line).

Figure 9.113 shows an example of the epipolar lines. The stereo geometry is identical to Figure 9.110. The images show a PCB. In Figure 9.113a, four points are marked. They have been selected manually to lie at the tips of the triangles on the

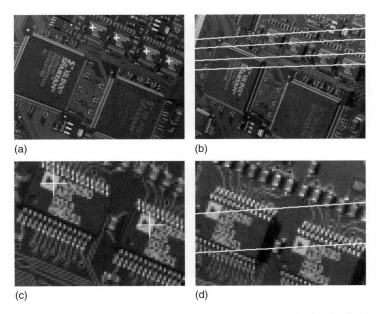

Figure 9.113 Stereo image pair of a PCB. (a) Four points marked in the first image. (b) Corresponding epipolar lines in the second image. (c) Detail of (a). (d) Detail of (b). The four points in (a) have been selected manually at the tips of the triangles on the four small ICs. Note that the epipolar lines pass through the tips of the triangles in the second image.

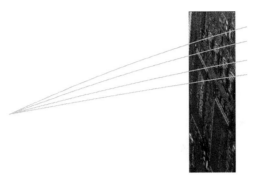

Figure 9.114 Because of lens distortions, the epipolar lines are generally not straight. The image shows the same image as Figure 9.113b. The zoom has been set so that the epipole is shown in addition to the image. The aspect ratio has been chosen so that the curvature of the epipolar lines is clearly visible.

four small ICs, as shown in the detailed view in Figure 9.113c. The corresponding epipolar lines in the second image are shown in Figure 9.113b,d. Note that the epipolar lines pass through the tips of the triangles in the second image.

As noted previously, we have so far assumed that the lenses have no distortions. In reality, this is very rarely true. In fact, by looking closely at Figure 9.113b, we can already perceive a curvature in the epipolar lines because the camera calibration has determined the radial distortion coefficient for us. If we set the displayed image part as in Figure 9.114, we can clearly see the curvature of the epipolar lines in real images. Furthermore, we can see the epipole of the image clearly.

From the above discussion, we can see that the epipolar lines are different for different points. Furthermore, because of lens distortions, they typically are not even straight. This means that, when we try to find corresponding points, we must compute a new, complicated epipolar line for each point that we are trying to match, typically for all points in the first image. The construction of the curved epipolar lines would be much too time consuming for real-time applications. Hence, we can ask ourselves whether the construction of the epipolar lines can be simplified for particular stereo geometries. This is indeed the case for the stereo geometry shown in Figure 9.115. Here, both image planes lie in the same plane and are vertically aligned. Furthermore, it is assumed that there

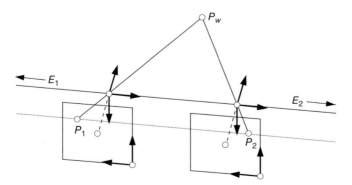

Figure 9.115 The epipolar standard geometry is obtained if both image planes lie in the same plane and are vertically aligned. Furthermore, it is assumed that there are no lens distortions. In this geometry, the epipolar line for a point is simply the line that has the same row coordinate as the point, that is, the epipolar lines are horizontal and vertically aligned.

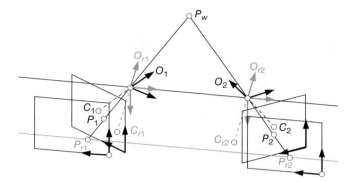

Figure 9.116 Transformation of a stereo configuration into the epipolar standard geometry.

are no lens distortions. Note that this implies that the two principal distances are identical, that the principal points have the same row coordinate, that the images are rotated such that the column axis is parallel to the base, and that the relative orientation contains only a translation in the x direction and no rotation. Since the image planes are parallel to each other, the epipoles lie infinitely far away on the base line. It is easy to see that this stereo geometry implies that the epipolar line for a point is simply the line that has the same row coordinate as the point, that is, the epipolar lines are horizontal and vertically aligned. Hence, they can be computed without any overhead at all. Since almost all stereo matching algorithms assume this particular geometry, we can call it the epipolar standard geometry.

While the epipolar standard geometry results in very simple epipolar lines, it is extremely difficult to align real cameras into this configuration. Furthermore, it is quite difficult and expensive to obtain distortion-free lenses. Fortunately, almost any stereo configuration can be transformed into the epipolar standard geometry, as indicated in Figure 9.116 [77]. The only exceptions are if an epipole happens to lie within one of the images. This typically does not occur in practical stereo configurations. The process of transforming the images to the epipolar standard geometry is called image rectification. To rectify the images, we need to construct two new image planes that lie in the same plane. To keep the 3D geometry identical, the projective centers must remain at the same positions in space, that is, $O_{r1} = O_1$ and $O_{r2} = O_2$. Note, however, that we need to rotate the CCSs such that their x-axes become identical to the base line. Furthermore, we need to construct two new principal points C_{r1} and C_{r2}. Their connecting vector must be parallel to the base. Furthermore, the vectors from the principal points to the projection centers must be perpendicular to the base. This leaves us two degrees of freedom. First of all, we must choose a common principal distance. Second, we can rotate the common plane in which the image planes lie around the base. These parameters can be chosen by requiring that the image distortion should be minimized [77]. The image dimensions are then typically chosen such that the original images are completely contained within the rectified images. Of course, we must also remove the lens distortions in the rectification.

To obtain the gray value for a pixel in the rectified image, we construct the optical ray for this pixel and intersect it with the original image plane. This is shown,

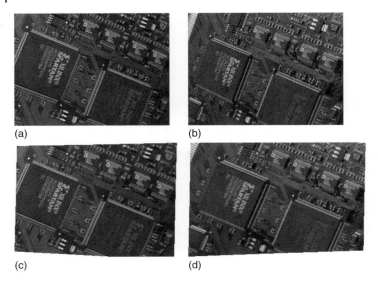

Figure 9.117 Example of the rectification of a stereo image pair. The images in (a) and (b) have the same relative orientation as those in Figure 9.110. The rectified images are shown in (c) and (d). Note the trapezoidal shape of the rectified images, which is caused by the verging cameras. Also note that the rectified images are slightly wider than the original images.

for example, for the points P_{r1} and P_1 in Figure 9.116. Since this typically results in subpixel coordinates, the gray values must be interpolated with the techniques described in Section 9.3.3.

While it may seem that image rectification is a very time-consuming process, the entire transformation can be computed once offline and stored in a table. Hence, images can be rectified very efficiently online.

Figure 9.117 shows an example of image rectification. The input image pair is shown in Figure 9.117a,b. The images have the same relative orientation as the images in Figure 9.110. The principal distances of the cameras are 13.05 mm and 13.16 mm, respectively. Both images have dimensions 320×240. Their principal points are (155.91, 126.72) and (163.67, 119.20), that is, they are very close to the image center. Finally, the images have a slight barrel-shaped distortion. The rectified images are shown in Figure 9.117c,d. Their relative orientation is given by the translation vector (0.1599 m, 0 m, 0 m). As expected, the translation is solely along the x-axis. Of course, the length of the translation vector is identical to that in Figure 9.110, since the position of the projective centers has not changed. The new principal distance of both images is 12.27 mm. The new principal points are given by $(-88.26, 121.36)$ and $(567.38, 121.36)$. As can be expected from Figure 9.116, they lie well outside the rectified images. Also, as expected, the row coordinates of the principal points are identical. The rectified images have dimensions 336×242 and 367×242, respectively. Note that they exhibit a trapezoidal shape that is characteristic of the verging camera configuration. The barrel-shaped distortion has been removed from the images. Clearly, the epipolar lines are horizontal in both images.

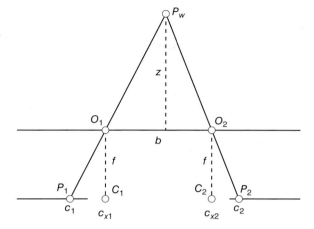

Figure 9.118 Reconstruction of the depth z of a point depends only on the disparity $d = c_2 - c_1$ of the points, that is, the difference of the column coordinates in the rectified images.

Apart from the fact that rectifying the images results in a particularly simple structure for the epipolar lines, it also results in a very simple reconstruction of the depth, as shown in Figure 9.118. In this figure, the stereo configuration is displayed as viewed along the direction of the row axis of the images, that is, the y-axis of the camera coordinate system. Hence, the image planes are shown as the lines at the bottom of the figure. The depth of a point is quite naturally defined as its z coordinate in the camera coordinate system. By examining the similar triangles $O_1 O_2 P_w$ and $P_1 P_2 P_w$, we can see that the depth of P_w depends only on the difference of the column coordinates of the points P_1 and P_2 as follows. From the similarity of the triangles, we have $z/b = (z+f)/(d_w + b)$. Hence, the depth is given by $z = bf/d_w$. Here, b is the length of the base, f is the principal distance, and d_w is the sum of the signed distances of the points P_1 and P_2 to the principal points C_1 and C_2. Since the coordinates of the principal points are given in pixels, but d_w is given in world units, for example, meters, we have to convert d_w to pixel coordinates by scaling it with the size of the pixels in the x direction: $d_p = d_w/s_x$. Now, we can easily see that $d_p = (c_{x1} - c_1) + (c_2 - c_{x2})$, where c_1 and c_2 denote the column coordinates of the points P_1 and P_2, while c_{x1} and c_{x2} denote the column coordinates of the principal points. Rearranging the terms, we find

$$d_p = (c_{x1} - c_{x2}) + (c_2 - c_1) \tag{9.144}$$

Since $c_{x1} - c_{x2}$ is constant for all points and known from the calibration and rectification, we can see that the depth z depends only on the difference of the column coordinates $d = c_2 - c_1$. This difference is called the disparity. Hence, we can see that, to reconstruct the depth of a point, we must determine its disparity.

9.10.2 Stereo Matching

As we have seen in the previous section, the main step in the stereo reconstruction is the determination of the disparity of each point in one of the images, typically the first image. Since one calculates, or at least attempts to calculate, a disparity for each point, these algorithms are called dense reconstruction algorithms. It should be noted that there is another class of algorithms that only try to reconstruct the depth for selected features, for example, straight lines or points. Since these algorithms typically require expensive feature extraction, they are seldom used in industrial applications. Therefore, we will concentrate on dense reconstruction algorithms.

Reviews of dense stereo reconstruction algorithms published until 2002 are given in [78, 79]. Since then, many new stereo algorithms have been published. Evaluations of newly proposed algorithms are constantly updated on various stereo vision benchmark web sites (see, e.g., [80, 81]). While many of these algorithms offer stereo reconstructions of somewhat better quality than the algorithms we will discuss in the following, they also often are much too slow or have too demanding memory requirements for industrial applications.

Since the goal of dense reconstruction is to find the disparity for each point in the image, the determination of the disparity can be regarded as a template matching problem. Given a rectangular window of size $(2n + 1) \times (2n + 1)$ around the current point in the first image, we must find the most similar window along the epipolar line in the second image. Hence, we can use the techniques that will be described in greater detail in Section 9.11 to match a point. The gray value matching methods described in Section 9.11.1 are of particular interest because they do not require a costly model generation step, which would have to be performed for each point in the first image. Therefore, the gray value matching methods typically are the fastest methods for stereo reconstruction. The simplest similarity measures are the SAD (sum of absolute gray value differences) and SSD (sum of squared gray value differences) measures described later (see equations (9.149) and (9.150)). For the stereo matching problem, they are given by

$$\text{SAD}(r, c, d) = \frac{1}{(2n+1)^2} \sum_{i=-n}^{n} \sum_{j=-n}^{n} |g_1(r+i, c+j) - g_2(r+i, c+j+d)|$$

(9.145)

and

$$\text{SSD}(r, c, d) = \frac{1}{(2n+1)^2} \sum_{i=-n}^{n} \sum_{j=-n}^{n} (g_1(r+i, c+j) - g_2(r+i, c+j+d))^2$$

(9.146)

As will be discussed in Section 9.11.1, these two similarity measures can be computed very quickly. Fast implementations for stereo matching using the SAD are given in [82, 83]. Unfortunately, these similarity measures have the disadvantage that they are not robust against illumination changes, which frequently happen in stereo reconstruction because of the different viewing angles along the optical rays. One way to deal with this problem is to perform a suitable preprocessing of the stereo images to remove illumination variations [84]. The preprocessing, however, is rarely invariant to arbitrary illumination changes. Consequently, in some applications it may be necessary to use the normalized cross-correlation (NCC) described later (see equation (9.151)) as the similarity measure, which has been shown to be robust to a very large range of illumination changes that can occur in stereo reconstruction [84]. For the stereo matching problem, it is given by

$$\text{NCC}(r, c, d) = \frac{1}{(2n+1)^2} \sum_{i=-n}^{n} \sum_{j=-n}^{n} \frac{g_1(r+i, c+j) - m_1(r+i, c+j)}{\sqrt{s_1^2(r+i, c+j)}}$$

$$\cdot \frac{g_2(r+i, c+j+d) - m_2(r+i, c+j+d)}{\sqrt{s_2^2(r+i, c+j+d)}} \qquad (9.147)$$

Here, m_i and s_i ($i = 1, 2$) denote the mean and standard deviation of the window in the first and second images. They are calculated similar to their template matching counterparts in equations (9.152) and (9.153). The advantage of NCC is that it is invariant against linear illumination changes. However, it is more expensive to compute.

From the above discussion, it might appear that, to match a point, we would have to compute the similarity measure along the entire epipolar line in the second image. Fortunately, this is not the case. Since the disparity is inversely related to the depth of a point, and we typically know in which range of distances the objects we are interested in occur, we can restrict the disparity search space to a much smaller interval than the entire epipolar line. Hence, we have $d \in [d_{\min}, d_{\max}]$, where $d_{\min}$ and $d_{\max}$ can be computed from the minimum and maximum expected distance in the images. Therefore, the length of the disparity search space is given by $l = d_{\max} - d_{\min} + 1$.

After we have computed the similarity measure for the disparity search space for a point to be matched, we might be tempted to simply use the disparity with the minimum (SAD and SSD) or maximum (NCC) similarity measure as the match for the current point. However, this typically will lead to many false matches, since some windows may not have a good match in the second image. In particular, this happens if the current point is occluded because of perspective effects in the second image. Therefore, it is necessary to threshold the similarity measure, that is, to accept matches only if their similarity measure is below (SAD and SSD) or above (NCC) a threshold. Obviously, if we perform this thresholding, some points will not have a reconstruction, and consequently the reconstruction will not be completely dense.

With the above search strategy, the matching process has a complexity of $O(whln^2)$. This is much too expensive for real-time performance. Fortunately, it can be shown that with a clever implementation the above similarity measures can be computed recursively. With this, the complexity can be made independent of the window size n, and becomes $O(whl)$. With this, real-time performance becomes possible. The interested reader is referred to [85] for details.

Once we have computed the match with an accuracy of one disparity step from the extremum (minimum or maximum) of the similarity measure, the accuracy can be refined with an approach similar to the subpixel extraction of matches that will be described in Section 9.11.3. Since the search space is one dimensional in the stereo matching, a parabola can be fitted through the three points around the extremum, and the extremum of the parabola can be extracted analytically.

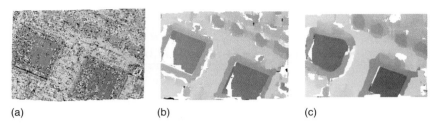

(a) (b) (c)

Figure 9.119 Distance reconstructed for the rectified image pair in Figure 9.117c,d with the NCC. (a) Window size 3 × 3. (b) Window size 17 × 17. (c) Window size 31 × 31. White areas correspond to the points that could not be matched because the similarity was too small.

Obviously, this will also result in a more accurate reconstruction of the depth of the points.

To perform stereo matching, we need to set one parameter: the size of the gray value windows n. It has a major influence on the result of the matching, as shown by the reconstructed depths in Figure 9.119. Here, window sizes of 3×3, 17×17, and 31×31 have been used with the NCC as the similarity measure. We can see that, if the window size is too small, many erroneous results will be found, despite the fact that a threshold of 0.4 has been used to select good matches. This happens because the matching requires a sufficiently distinctive texture within the window. If the window is too small, the texture is not distinctive enough, leading to erroneous matches. From Figure 9.119b, we see that the erroneous matches are mostly removed by the 17×17 window. However, because there is no texture in some parts of the image, especially in the lower left corners of the two large ICs, some parts of the image cannot be reconstructed. Note also that the areas of the leads around the large ICs are broader than in Figure 9.119a. This happens because the windows now straddle height discontinuities in a larger part of the image. Since the texture of the leads is more significant than the texture on the ICs, the matching finds the best matches at the depth of the leads. To fill the gaps in the reconstruction, we could try to increase the window size further, since this leads to more positions in which the windows have a significant texture. The result of setting the window size to 31×31 is shown in Figure 9.119c. Note that now most of the image can be reconstructed. Unfortunately, the lead area has broadened even more, which is undesirable.

From the above example, we can see that too small window sizes lead to many erroneous matches. In contrast, larger window sizes generally lead to fewer erroneous matches and a more complete reconstruction in areas with little texture. Furthermore, larger window sizes lead to a smoothing of the result, which may sometimes be desirable. However, larger window sizes lead to worse results at height discontinuities, which effectively limits the window sizes that can be used in practice.

Despite the fact that larger window sizes generally lead to fewer erroneous matches, they typically cannot be excluded completely based on the window size alone. Therefore, additional techniques are sometimes desirable to reduce the number of erroneous matches even further. An overview of methods to detect unreliable and erroneous matches is given in [86].

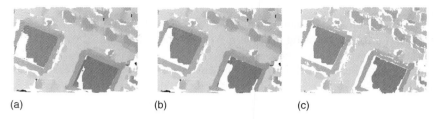

(a) (b) (c)

Figure 9.120 Increasing levels of robustness of the stereo matching. (a) Standard matching from the first to the second image with a window size of 17 × 17 using the NCC. (b) Result of requiring that the standard deviations of the windows is ≥5. (c) Result of performing the check where matching from the second to the first image results in the same disparity.

Erroneous matches occur mainly for two reasons: weak texture and occlusions. Erroneous matches caused by weak texture can sometimes be eliminated based on the matching score. However, in general it is best to exclude windows with weak texture *a priori* from the matching. Whether a window contains a weak texture can be decided on the basis of the output of a texture filter. Typically, the standard deviation of the gray values within the window is used as the texture filter. It has the advantage that it is computed in the NCC anyway, while it can be computed with just a few extra operations in the SAD and SSD. Therefore, to exclude windows with weak textures, we require that the standard deviation of the gray values within the window should be large.

The second reason why erroneous matches can occur are perspective occlusions, which, for example, occur at height discontinuities. To remove these errors, we can perform a consistency check that works as follows. First, we find the match from the first to the second image as usual. We then check whether matching the window around the match in the second image results in the same disparity, that is, finds the original point in the first image. If this is implemented naively, the runtime increases by a factor of 2. Fortunately, with a little extra bookkeeping the disparity consistency check can be performed with very few extra operations, since most of the required data have already been computed during the matching from the first to the second image.

Figure 9.120 shows the results of the different methods to increase robustness. For comparison, Figure 9.120a displays the result of the standard matching from the first to the second image with a window size of 17 × 17 using the NCC. The result of applying a texture threshold of 5 is shown in Figure 9.120b. It mainly removes untextured areas on the two large ICs. Figure 9.120c shows the result of applying the disparity consistency check. Note that it mainly removes matches in the areas where occlusions occur.

9.11 Template Matching

In the previous sections, we have discussed various techniques that can be combined to write algorithms to find objects in an image. While these techniques can in principle be used to find any kind of object, writing a robust recognition algorithm for a particular type of object can be quite cumbersome. Furthermore, if the objects to be recognized change frequently, a new algorithm must be developed for each type of object. Therefore, a method to find any kind of object that can be configured simply by showing the system a prototype of the class of objects to be found would be extremely useful.

The above goal can be achieved by template matching. Here, we describe the object to be found by a template image. Conceptually, the template is found in the image by computing the similarity between the template and the image for all relevant poses of the template. If the similarity is high, an instance of the template has been found. Note that the term "similarity" is used here in a very general sense. We will see below that it can be defined in various ways, for example, based on the gray values of the template and the image, or based on the closeness of template edges to image edges.

Template matching can be used for several purposes. First of all, it can be used to perform completeness checks. Here, the goal is to detect the presence or absence of the object. Furthermore, template matching can be used for object discrimination, that is, to distinguish between different types of objects. In most cases, however, we already know which type of object is present in the image. In these cases, template matching is used to determine the pose of the object in the image. If the orientation of the objects can be fixed mechanically, the pose is described by a translation. In most applications, however, the orientation cannot be fixed completely, if at all. Therefore, often the orientation of the object, described by rotation, must also be determined. Hence, the complete pose of the object is described by a translation and a rotation. This type of transformation is called a rigid transformation. In some applications, additionally, the size of the objects in the image can change. This can happen if the distance of the objects to the camera cannot be kept fixed, or if the real size of the objects can change. Hence, a uniform scaling must be added to the pose in these applications. This type of pose (translation, rotation, and uniform scaling) is called a similarity transformation. If even the 3D orientation of the camera with respect to the objects can change and the objects to be recognized are planar, the pose is described by a projective transformation (see Section 9.3.2). Consequently, for the purposes of this chapter, we can regard the pose of the objects as a specialization of an affine or projective transformation.

In most applications, a single object is present in the search image. Therefore, the goal of template matching is to find this single instance. In some applications, more than one object is present in the image. If we know *a priori* how many objects are present, we want to find exactly this number of objects. If we do not have this knowledge, we typically must find all instances of the template in the image. In this mode, one of the goals is also to determine how many objects are present in the image.

9.11.1 Gray-Value-Based Template Matching

In this section, we will examine the simplest kind of template matching algorithms, which are based on the raw gray values in the template and the image. As mentioned previously, template matching is based on computing a similarity between the template and the image. Let us formalize this notion. For the moment, we will assume that the object's pose is described by a translation. The template is specified by an image $t(r, c)$ and its corresponding ROI T. To perform the template matching, we can visualize moving the template over all positions in the image and computing a similarity measure **s** at each position. Hence, the similarity measure **s** is a function that takes the gray values in the template $t(r, c)$ and the gray values in the shifted ROI of the template at the current position in the image $f(r + u, c + v)$ and calculates a scalar value that measures the similarity based on the gray values within the respective ROI. With this approach, a similarity measure is returned for each point in the transformation space, which for translations can be regarded as an image. Hence, formally, we have

$$s(r, c) = \mathbf{s}\{t(u, v), f(r + u, c + v); \ (u, v) \in T\} \tag{9.148}$$

To make this abstract notation concrete, we will discuss several possible gray-value-based similarity measures [87].

The simplest similarity measures are to sum the absolute or squared gray value differences between the template and the image (SAD and SSD). They are given by

$$\text{SAD}(r, c) = \frac{1}{n} \sum_{(u,v) \in T} |t(u, v) - f(r + u, c + v)| \tag{9.149}$$

and

$$\text{SSD}(r, c) = \frac{1}{n} \sum_{(u,v) \in T} (t(u, v) - f(r + u, c + v))^2 \tag{9.150}$$

In both cases, n is the number of points in the template ROI, that is, $n = |T|$. Note that both similarity measures can be computed very efficiently with just two operations per pixel. These similarity measures have similar properties: if the template and the image are identical, they return a similarity measure of 0. If the image and template are not identical, a value greater than 0 is returned. As the dissimilarity increases, the value of the similarity measure increases. Hence, in this case the similarity measure should probably be better called a dissimilarity measure. To find instances of the template in the search image, we can threshold the similarity image $\text{SAD}(r, c)$ with a certain upper threshold. This typically gives us a region that contains several adjacent pixels. To obtain a unique location for the template, we must select the local minima of the similarity image within each connected component of the thresholded region.

Figure 9.121 shows a typical application for template matching. Here, the goal is to locate the position of a fiducial mark on a PCB. The ROI used for the template is displayed in Figure 9.121a. The similarity computed with the sum of the SAD, given by equation (9.149), is shown in Figure 9.121b. For this example, the SAD was computed with the same image from which the template was generated. If the similarity is thresholded with a threshold of 20, only a region around the position of the fiducial mark is returned (Figure 9.121c). Within this region, the local minimum of the SAD must be computed (not shown) to obtain the position of the fiducial mark.

The SAD and SSD similarity measures work very well as long as the illumination can be kept constant. However, if the illumination can change, they both return

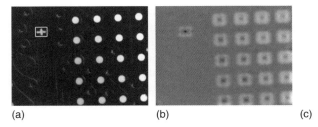

(a) (b) (c)

Figure 9.121 (a) Image of a PCB with a fiducial mark, which is used as the template (indicated by the white rectangle). (b) SAD computed with the template in (a) and the image in (a). (c) Result of thresholding (b) with a threshold of 20. Only a region around the fiducial is selected.

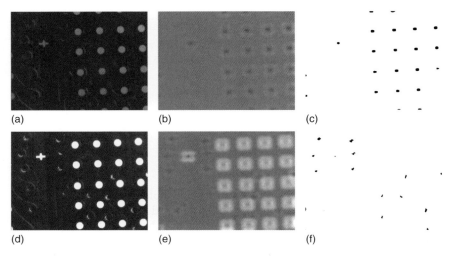

Figure 9.122 (a) Image of a PCB with a fiducial mark with a lower contrast. (b) SAD computed with the template in Figure 9.121a and the image in (a). (c) Result of thresholding (b) with a threshold of 35. (d) Image of a PCB with a fiducial mark with higher contrast. (e) SAD computed with the template of Figure 9.121a and the image in (d). (f) Result of thresholding (e) with a threshold of 35. In both cases, it is impossible to select a threshold that returns only the region of the fiducial mark.

larger values, even if the same object is contained in the image, because the gray values are no longer identical. This effect is illustrated in Figure 9.122. Here, a darker and brighter image of the fiducial mark are shown. They were obtained by adjusting the illumination intensity. The SAD computed with the template of Figure 9.121a is displayed in Figure 9.122b,e. The result of thresholding them with a threshold of 35 is shown in Figure 9.122c,f. The threshold was chosen such that the true fiducial mark is extracted in both cases. Note that, because of the contrast change, many extraneous instances of the template have been found.

As we can see from the above examples, the SAD and SSD similarity measures work well as long as the illumination can be kept constant. In applications where this cannot be ensured, a different kind of similarity measure is required. Ideally, this similarity measure should be invariant to all linear illumination changes (see Section 9.2.1). A similarity measure that achieves this is the NCC, given by

$$\mathrm{NCC}(r,c) = \frac{1}{n} \sum_{(u,v) \in T} \frac{t(u,v) - m_t}{\sqrt{s_t^2}} \cdot \frac{f(r+u,c+v) - m_f(r,c)}{\sqrt{s_f^2(r,c)}} \qquad (9.151)$$

Here, m_t is the mean gray value of the template and s_t^2 is the variance of the gray values, that is,

$$\begin{aligned} m_t &= \frac{1}{n} \sum_{(u,v) \in T} t(u,v) \\ s_t^2 &= \frac{1}{n} \sum_{(u,v) \in T} (t(u,v) - m_t)^2 \end{aligned} \qquad (9.152)$$

Analogously, $m_f(r,c)$ and $s_f^2(r,c)$ are the mean value and variance in the image at a shifted position of the template ROI:

$$\begin{aligned} m_f(r,c) &= \frac{1}{n} \sum_{(u,v) \in T} f(r+u,c+v) \\ s_f^2(r,c) &= \frac{1}{n} \sum_{(u,v) \in T} (f(r+u,c+v) - m_f(r,c))^2 \end{aligned} \qquad (9.153)$$

The NCC has a very intuitive interpretation. First of all, we should note that $-1 \leq \mathrm{NCC}(r,c) \leq 1$. Furthermore, if $\mathrm{NCC}(r,c) = \pm 1$, the image is a linearly scaled version of the template:

$$\mathrm{NCC}(r,c) = \pm 1 \quad \Leftrightarrow \quad f(r+u,c+v) = at(u,v) + b \qquad (9.154)$$

For $\mathrm{NCC}(r,c) = 1$, we have $a > 0$, that is, the template and the image have the same polarity; while $\mathrm{NCC}(r,c) = -1$ implies that $a < 0$, that is, the polarity of the template and image are reversed. Note that this property of the NCC implies the desired invariance against linear illumination changes. The invariance is achieved by explicitly subtracting the mean gray values, which cancels additive changes, and by dividing by the standard deviation of the gray values, which cancels multiplicative changes.

While the template matches the image perfectly only if $\mathrm{NCC}(r,c) = \pm 1$, large absolute values of the NCC generally indicate that the template closely corresponds to the image part under examination, while values close to zero indicate that the template and image do not correspond well.

Figure 9.123 displays the results of computing the NCC for the template in Figure 9.121a (reproduced in Figure 9.123a). The NCC is shown in Figure 9.123b, while the result of thresholding the NCC with a threshold of 0.75 is shown in Figure 9.123c. This selects only a region around the fiducial mark. In this region, the local maximum of the NCC must be computed to derive the location of the fiducial mark (not shown). The results for the darker and brighter images in Figure 9.122 are not shown because they are virtually indistinguishable from the results in Figure 9.123b,c.

In the above discussion, we have assumed that the similarity measures must be evaluated completely for every translation. This is, in fact, unnecessary, since the result of calculating the similarity measure will be thresholded with a threshold

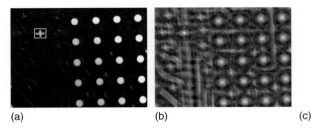

(a)   (b)   (c)

Figure 9.123 (a) Image of a PCB with a fiducial mark, which is used as the template (indicated by the white rectangle). This is the same image as in Figure 9.121a. (b) NCC computed with the template in (a) and the image in (a). (c) Result of thresholding (b) with a threshold of 0.75. The results for the darker and brighter images in Figure 9.122 are not shown because they are virtually indistinguishable from the results in (b) and (c).

t_s later on. For example, thresholding the SAD in equation (9.149) means that we require

$$\text{SAD}(r,c) = \frac{1}{n} \sum_{i=1}^{n} |t(u_i, v_i) - f(r + u_i, c + v_i)| \leq t_s \qquad (9.155)$$

Here, we have explicitly numbered the points $(u, v) \in T$ by (u_i, v_i). We can multiply both sides by n to obtain

$$\text{SAD}'(r,c) = \sum_{i=1}^{n} |t(u_i, v_i) - f(r + u_i, c + v_i)| \leq n t_s \qquad (9.156)$$

Suppose we have already evaluated the first j terms in the sum in equation (9.156). Let us call this partial result $\text{SAD}'_j(r, c)$. Then, we have

$$\text{SAD}'(r,c) = \text{SAD}'_j(r,c) + \underbrace{\sum_{i=j+1}^{n} |t(u_i, v_i) - f(r + u_i, c + v_i)|}_{\geq 0} \leq n t_s \qquad (9.157)$$

Hence, we can stop the evaluation as soon as $\text{SAD}'_j(r, c) > n t_s$, because we are certain that we can no longer achieve the threshold. If we are looking for a maximum number of m instances of the template, we can even adapt the threshold t_s based on the instance with the mth best similarity found so far. For example, if we are looking for a single instance with $t_s = 20$ and we have already found a candidate with $\text{SAD}(r, c) = 10$, we can set $t_s = 10$ for the remaining poses that need to be checked. Of course, we need to calculate the local minima of $\text{SAD}(r, c)$ and use the corresponding similarity values to ensure that this approach works correctly if more than one instance should be found.

For the NCC, there is no simple criterion to stop the evaluation of the terms. Of course, we can use the fact that the mean m_t and standard deviation $\sqrt{s_t^2}$ of the template can be computed once offline because they are identical for every translation of the template. The only other optimization we can make, analogous to the SAD, is that we can adapt the threshold t_s based on the matches we have found so far [88].

The above stopping criteria enable us to stop the evaluation of the similarity measure as soon as we are certain that the threshold can no longer be reached. Hence, they prune unwanted parts of the space of allowed poses. It is interesting to note that improvements for the pruning of the search space are still actively being investigated. For example, in [88] further optimizations for the pruning of the search space when using the NCC are discussed. In [89] and [90], strategies for pruning the search space when using SAD or SSD are discussed. They rely on transforming the image into a representation in which a large portion of the SAD and SSD can be computed with very few evaluations so that the above stopping criteria can be reached as soon as possible.

9.11.2 Matching Using Image Pyramids

The evaluation of the similarity measures on the entire image is very time consuming, even if the stopping criteria discussed above are used. If they are not used, the runtime complexity is $O(whn)$, where w and h are the width and height of the image and n is the number of points in the template. The stopping criteria typically result in a constant factor for the speed-up, but do not change the complexity. Therefore, a method to further speed up the search is necessary to be able to find the template in real time.

To derive a faster search strategy, we note that the runtime complexity of the template matching depends on the number of translations, that is, poses, that need to be checked. This is the $O(wh)$ part of the complexity. Furthermore, it depends on the number of points in the template. This is the $O(n)$ part. Therefore, to gain a speed-up, we can try to reduce the number of poses that need to be checked as well as the number of template points. Since the templates typically are large, one way to do this would be to take into account only every ith point of the image and template in order to obtain an approximate pose of the template, which could later be refined by a search with a finer step size around the approximate pose. This strategy is identical to subsampling the image and template. Since subsampling can cause aliasing effects (see Sections 9.2.4 and 9.3.3), this is not a very good strategy because we might miss instances of the template because of the aliasing effects. We have seen in Section 9.3.3 that we must smooth the image to avoid the aliasing effects. Furthermore, typically it is better to scale the image down multiple times by a factor of 2 than only once by a factor of $i > 2$. Scaling down the image (and template) multiple times by a factor of 2 creates a data structure that is called an image pyramid. Figure 9.124 displays why the name was chosen: we can visualize the smaller versions of the image stacked on top of each other. Since their width and height are halved in each step, they form a pyramid.

When constructing the pyramid, speed is essential. Therefore, the smoothing is performed by applying a 2×2 mean filter, that is, by averaging the gray value of each 2×2 block of pixels [91]. The smoothing could also be performed by a Gaussian filter [92]. Note, however, that, in order to avoid the introduction of unwanted shifts into the image pyramid, the Gaussian filter must have an even mask size. Therefore, the smallest mask size would be a 4×4 filter. Hence, using the Gaussian filter would incur a severe speed penalty in the construction of the image pyramid. Furthermore, the 2×2 mean filter does not have the frequency

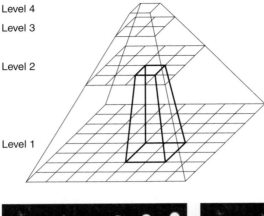

Figure 9.124 An image pyramid is constructed by successively halving the resolution of the image and combining 2 × 2 blocks of pixels in a higher resolution into a single pixel at the next lower resolution.

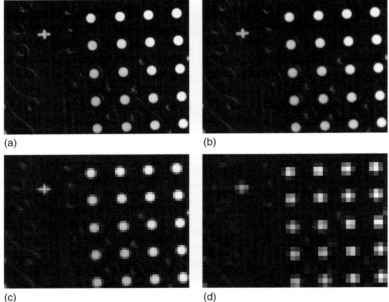

Figure 9.125 (a)–(d) Image pyramid levels 2–5 of the image in Figure 9.121a. Note that in level 5 the fiducial mark can no longer be discerned from the BGA pads.

response problems that the larger versions of the filter have (see Section 9.2.3). In fact, it drops off smoothly toward a zero response for the highest frequencies, like the Gaussian filter. Finally, it simulates the effects of a perfect camera with a fill factor of 100%. Therefore, the mean filter is the preferred filter for constructing image pyramids.

Figure 9.125 displays the image pyramid levels 2–5 of the image in Figure 9.121a. We can see that on levels 1–4 the fiducial mark can still be discerned from the BGA pads. This is no longer the case on level 5. Therefore, if we want to find an approximate location of the template, we can start the search on level 4.

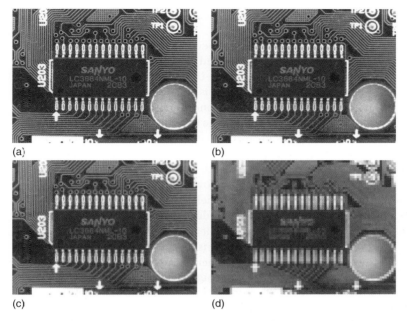

Figure 9.126 (a)–(d) Image pyramid levels 1–4 of an image of a PCB. Note that in level 4 all the tracks are merged into large components with identical gray values because of the smoothing that is performed when the pyramid is constructed.

The above example produces the expected result: the image is progressively smoothed and subsampled. The fiducial mark we are interested in can no longer be recognized as soon as the resolution becomes too low. Sometimes, however, creating an image pyramid can produce results that are unexpected at first glance. One example of this behavior is shown in Figure 9.126. Here, the image pyramid levels 1–4 of an image of a PCB are shown. We can see that on pyramid level 4 all the tracks are suddenly merged into large components with identical gray values. This happens because of the smoothing that is performed when the pyramid is constructed. Here, the neighboring thin lines start to interact with each other once the smoothing is large enough, that is, once we reach a pyramid level that is large enough. Hence, we can see that sometimes valuable information is destroyed by the construction of the image pyramid. If we were interested in matching, say, the corners of the tracks, we could only go as high as level 3 in the image pyramid.

Based on the image pyramids, we can define a hierarchical search strategy as follows. First, we calculate an image pyramid on the template and search image with an appropriate number of levels. How many levels can be used is mainly defined by the objects we are trying to find. On the highest pyramid level, the relevant structures of the object must still be discernible. Then, a complete matching is performed on the highest pyramid level. Here, of course, we take the appropriate stopping criterion into account. What gain does this give us? In each pyramid level, we reduce the number of image points and template points by a factor of 4. Hence, each pyramid level results in a speed-up of a factor of 16. Therefore, if we perform the complete matching, for example, on level 4, we reduce the amount of computations by a factor of 4096.

All instances of the template that have been found on the highest pyramid level are then tracked to the lowest pyramid level. This is done by projecting the match to the next lower pyramid level, that is, by multiplying the coordinates of the found match by 2. Since there is an uncertainty in the location of the match, a search area is constructed around the match in the lower pyramid level, for example, a 5×5 rectangle. Then, the matching is performed within this small ROI, that is, the similarity measure is computed and thresholded, and the local extrema are extracted. This procedure is continued until the match is lost or tracked to the lowest level. Since the search spaces for the larger templates are very small, tracking the match down to the lowest level is very efficient.

While matching the template on the higher pyramid levels, we need to take the following effect into account: the gray values at the border of the object can change substantially on the highest pyramid level depending on where the object lies on the lowest pyramid level. This happens because a single pixel shift of the object translates to a subpixel shift on higher pyramid levels, which manifests itself as a change in the gray values on the higher pyramid levels. Therefore, on the higher pyramid levels we need to be more lenient with the matching threshold to ensure that all potential matches are being found. Hence, for the SAD and SSD similarity measures we need to use slightly higher thresholds, and for the NCC similarity measure we need to use slightly lower thresholds on the higher pyramid levels.

The hierarchical search is seen in Figure 9.127. The template is the fiducial mark shown in Figure 9.121a. The template is searched in the same image from which the template was created. As discussed previously, four pyramid levels are used in this case. The search starts on level 4. Here, the ROI is the entire image. The NCC and found matches on level 4 are displayed in Figure 9.127a. As we can see, 12 potential matches are initially found. They are tracked down to level 3 (Figure 9.127b). The ROIs created from the matches on level 4 are shown in white. For visualization purposes, the NCC is displayed for the entire image. In reality, it is, of course, only computed within the ROIs, that is, for a total of $12 \times 25 = 300$ translations. Note that at this level the true match turns out to be the only viable match. It is tracked down through levels 2 and 1 (Figure 9.127c,d). In both cases, only 25 translations need to be checked. Therefore, the match is found extremely efficiently. The zoomed part of the NCC in Figure 9.127b–d also shows that the pose of the match is progressively refined as the match is tracked down the pyramid.

9.11.3 Subpixel-Accurate Gray-Value-Based Matching

So far, we have located the pose of the template with pixel precision. This has been done by extracting the local minima (SAD, SSD) or maxima (NCC) of the similarity measure. To obtain the pose of the template with higher accuracy, the local minima or maxima can be extracted with subpixel precision. This can be done in a manner that is analogous to the method we have used in edge extraction (see Section 9.7.3): we simply fit a polynomial to the similarity measure in a 3×3

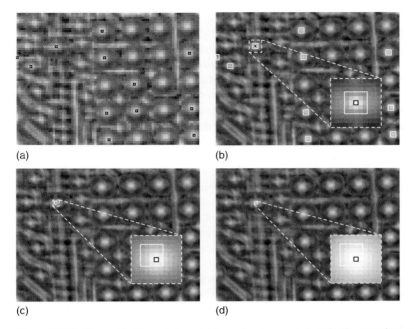

Figure 9.127 Hierarchical template matching using image pyramids. The template is the fiducial mark shown in Figure 9.121a. To provide a better visualization, the NCC is shown for the entire image on each pyramid level. In reality, however, it is only calculated within the appropriate ROI on each level, shown in white. The found matches are displayed in black. (a) On pyramid level 4, the matching is performed in the entire image. Here, 12 potential matches are found. (b) The matching is continued within the white ROIs on level 3. Only one viable match is found in the 12 ROIs. The similarity measure and ROI around the match are displayed zoomed in the lower right corner. (c,d) The match is tracked through pyramid levels 2 and 1.

neighborhood around the local minimum or maximum. Then, we extract the local minimum or maximum of the polynomial analytically. Another approach is to perform a least-squares matching of the gray values of the template and the image [93]. Since the least-squares matching of the gray values is not invariant to illumination changes, the illumination changes must be modeled explicitly, and their parameters must be determined in the least-squares fitting in order to achieve robustness to illumination changes [94].

9.11.4 Template Matching with Rotations and Scalings

Up to now, we have implicitly restricted the template matching to the case where the object must have the same orientation and scale in the template and the image, that is, the space of possible poses was assumed to be the space of translations. The similarity measures we have discussed previously can tolerate only small rotations and scalings of the object in the image. Therefore, if the object does not have the same orientation and size as the template, the object will not be found. If we want to be able to handle a larger class of transformations, for example, rigid or similarity transformations, we must modify the matching approach. For simplicity, we will only discuss rotations, but the method can be extended to scalings and even more general classes of transformations in an analogous manner.

To find a rotated object, we can create the template in multiple orientations, that is, we discretize the search space of rotations in a manner that is analogous to the discretization of the translations that is imposed by the pixel grid [95]. Unlike for the translations, the discretization of the orientations of the template depends on the size of the template, since the similarity measures are less tolerant to small angle changes for large templates. For example, a typical value is to use an angle step size of 1° for templates with a radius of 100 pixels. Larger templates must use smaller angle steps, while smaller templates can use larger angle steps. To find the template, we simply match all rotations of the template with the image. Of course, this is done only on the highest pyramid level. To make the matching in the pyramid more efficient, we can also use the fact that the templates become smaller by a factor of 2 on each pyramid level. Consequently, the angle step size can be increased by a factor of 2 for each pyramid level. Hence, if an angle step size of 1° is used on the lowest pyramid level, a step size of 8° can be used on the fourth pyramid level.

While tracking potential matches through the pyramid, we also need to construct a small search space for the angles in the next lower pyramid level, analogous to the small search space that we already use for the translations. Once we have tracked the match to the lowest pyramid level, we typically want to refine the pose to an accuracy that is higher than the resolution of the search space we have used. In particular, if rotations are used, the pose should consist of a subpixel translation and an angle that is more accurate than the angle step size we have chosen. The techniques for subpixel-precise localization of the template described above can easily be extended for this purpose.

9.11.5 Robust Template Matching

The above template matching algorithms have served for many years as the methods of choice to find objects in machine vision applications. Over time, however, there has been an increasing demand to find objects in images even if they are occluded or disturbed in other ways so that parts of the object are missing. Furthermore, the objects should be found even if there are a large number of disturbances on the object itself. These disturbances are often referred to as clutter. Finally, objects should be found even if there are severe nonlinear illumination changes. The gray-value-based template matching algorithms we have discussed so far cannot handle these kinds of disturbances. Therefore, in the remainder of this section, we will discuss several approaches that have been designed to find objects in the presence of occlusion, clutter, and nonlinear illumination changes.

We have already discussed a feature that is robust to nonlinear illumination changes in Section 9.7: edges are not (or at least very little) affected by illumination changes. Therefore, they are frequently used in robust matching algorithms. The only problem when using edges is the selection of a suitable threshold to segment the edges. If the threshold is chosen too low, there will be many clutter edges in the image. If it is chosen too high, important edges of the object will be missing. This has the same effect as if parts of the object are occluded. Since the

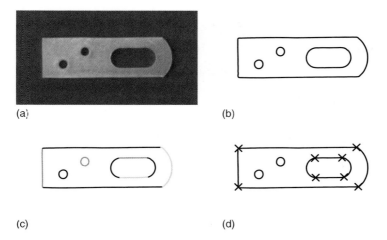

Figure 9.128 (a) Image of a model object. (b) Edges of (a). (c) Segmentation of (b) into lines and circles. (d) Salient points derived from the segmentation in (c).

threshold can never be chosen perfectly, this is another reason why the matching must be able to handle occlusions and clutter robustly.

To match objects using edges, several strategies exist. First of all, we can use the raw edge points, possibly augmented with some features per edge point, for the matching (see Figure 9.128b). Another strategy is to derive geometric primitives by segmenting the edges with the algorithms discussed in Section 9.8.4, and to match these to segmented geometric primitives in the image (see Figure 9.128c). Finally, based on a segmentation of the edges, we can derive salient points and match them to salient points in the image (see Figure 9.128d). It should be noted that the salient points can also be extracted directly from the image without extracting edges first [96, 97].

A large class of algorithms for edge matching is based on the distance of the edges in the template to the edges in the image. These algorithms typically use the raw edge points for the matching. One natural similarity measure based on this idea is to minimize the mean squared distance between the template edge points and the closest image edge points [98]. Hence, it appears that we must determine the closest image edge point for every template edge point, which would be extremely costly. Fortunately, since we are only interested in the distance to the closest edge point and not in which point is the closest point, this can be done in an efficient manner by calculating the distance transform of the complement of the segmented edges in the search image [98]. See Figure 9.129b,d for examples of the distance transform. A model is considered as being found if the mean distance of the template edge points to the image edge points is below a threshold. Of course, to obtain a unique location of the template, we must calculate the local minimum of this similarity measure. If we want to formalize this similarity measure, we can denote the edge points in the model by T and the distance transform of the complement of the segmented edge region in the search image by $d(r, c)$. Hence, the mean squared edge distance (SED) for the case of

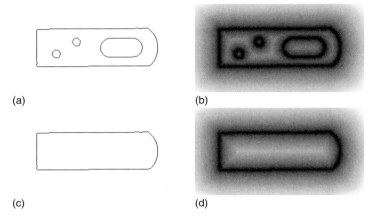

Figure 9.129 (a) Template edges. (b) Distance transform of the complement of (a). For better visualization, a square root look-up table (LUT) is used. (c) Search image with missing edges. (d) Distance transform of the complement of (c). If the template in (a) is matched to a search image in which the edges are complete and which possibly contains more edges than the template, the template will be found. If the template in (a) is matched to a search image in which template edges are missing, the template may not be found because a missing edge will have a large distance to the closest existing edge.

translations is given by

$$\text{SED}(r, c) = \frac{1}{n} \sum_{(u,v) \in T} d(r + u, c + v)^2 \qquad (9.158)$$

Note that this is very similar to the SSD similarity measure in equation (9.150) if we set $t(u, v) = 0$ there and use the distance transform image for $f(u, v)$. Consequently, the SED matching algorithm can be implemented very easily if we already have an implementation of the SSD matching algorithm. Of course, if we use the mean distance instead of the mean squared distance, we could use an existing implementation of the SAD matching, given by equation (9.149), for the edge matching.

We can now ask ourselves whether the SED fulfills the above criteria for robust matching. Since it is based on edges, it is robust to arbitrary illumination changes. Furthermore, since clutter, that is, extra edges in the search image, can only decrease the distance to the closest edge in the search image, it is robust to clutter. However, if edges are missing in the search image, the distance of the missing template edges to the closest image edges may become very large, and consequently the model may not be found. This is illustrated in Figure 9.129. Imagine what happens when the model in Figure 9.129a is searched in a search image in which some of the edges are missing (Figure 9.129c,d). Here, the missing edges will have a very large squared distance, which will increase the SED significantly. This will make it quite difficult to find the correct match.

Because of the above problems of the SED, edge matching algorithms using a different distance have been proposed. They are based on the Hausdorff distance of two point sets. Let us call the edge points in the template T and the edge points in the image E. Then, the Hausdorff distance of the two point sets is given by

$$H(T, E) = \max(h(T, E), h(E, T)) \tag{9.159}$$

where

$$h(T, E) = \max_{t \in T} \min_{e \in E} \| t - e \| \tag{9.160}$$

and $h(E, T)$ is defined symmetrically. Hence, the Hausdorff distance consists of determining the maximum of two distances: the maximum distance of the template edges to the closest image edges, and the maximum distance of the image edges to the closest template edges [99]. It is immediately clear that, to achieve a low overall distance, every template edge point must be close to an image edge point, and vice versa. Therefore, the Hausdorff distance is robust to neither occlusion nor clutter. With a slight modification, however, we can achieve the desired robustness. The reason for the bad performance for occlusion and clutter is that in equation (9.160) the maximum distance of the template edges to the image edges is calculated. If we want to achieve robustness to occlusion, instead of computing the largest distance, we can compute a distance with a different rank, for example, the fth largest distance, where $f = 0$ denotes the largest distance. With this, the Hausdorff distance will be robust to $100 \, f/n \, \%$ occlusion, where n is the number of edge points in the template. To make the Hausdorff distance robust to clutter, we can similarly modify $h(E, T)$ to use the rth largest distance. However, normally the model covers only a small part of the search image. Consequently, typically there are many more image edge points than template edge points, and hence r would have to be chosen very large to achieve the desired robustness against clutter. Therefore, $h(E, T)$ must be modified to be calculated only within a small ROI around the template. With this, the Hausdorff distance can be made robust to $100 \, r/m \, \%$ clutter, where m is the number of edge points in the ROI around the template [99]. Like the SED, the Hausdorff distance can be computed based on distance transforms: one for the edge region in the image and one for each pose (excluding translations) of the template edge region. Therefore, we must compute either a very large number of distance transforms offline, which requires an enormous amount of memory, or the distance transforms of the model during the search, which requires a large amount of computation.

As we can see, one of the drawbacks of the Hausdorff distance is the enormous computational load that is required for the matching. In [99], several possibilities are discussed to reduce the computational load, including pruning regions of the search space that cannot contain the template. Furthermore, a hierarchical subdivision of the search space is proposed. This is similar to the effect that is achieved with image pyramids. However, the method in [99] only subdivides the search space, but does not scale the template or image. Therefore, it is still very slow. A Hausdorff distance matching method using image pyramids is proposed in [100].

The major drawback of the Hausdorff distance, however, is that, even with very moderate amounts of occlusion, many false instances of the template will be detected in the image [101]. To reduce the false detection rate, in [101] a modification of the Hausdorff distance is proposed that takes the orientation of the edge pixels into account. Conceptually, the edge points are augmented with a third coordinate that represents the edge orientation. Then, the distance of these augmented 3D points and the corresponding augmented 3D image points is calculated as the modified Hausdorff distance. Unfortunately, this requires the calculation of a 3D distance transform, which makes the algorithm too expensive for machine vision applications. A further drawback of all approaches based on the Hausdorff distance is that it is quite difficult to obtain the pose with subpixel accuracy based on the interpolation of the similarity measure.

Another algorithm to find objects that is based on the edge pixels themselves is the generalized Hough transform proposed by Ballard [102]. The original Hough transform [103, 104] is a method that was designed to find straight lines in segmented edges. It was later extended to detect other shapes that can be described analytically, for example, circles or ellipses. The principle of the generalized Hough transform can be best explained by looking at a simple case. Let us try to find circles with a known radius in an edge image. Since circles are rotationally symmetric, we only need to consider translations in this case. If we want to find the circles as efficiently as possible, we can observe that, for circles that are brighter than the background, the gradient vector of the edge of the circle is perpendicular to the circle. This means that it points in the direction of the center of the circle. If the circle is darker than its background, the negative gradient vector points toward the center of the circle. Therefore, since we know the radius of the circle, we can theoretically determine the center of the circle from a single point on the circle. Unfortunately, we do not know which points lie on the circle (this is actually the task we would like to solve). However, we can detect the circle by observing that all points on the circle will have the property that, based on the gradient vector, we can construct the circle center. Therefore, we can accumulate evidence provided by all edge points in the image to determine the circle. This can be done as follows. Since we want to determine the circle center (i.e., the translation of the circle), we can set up an array that accumulates the evidence that a circle is present as a particular translation. We initialize this array with zeros. Then, we loop through all the edge points in the image and construct the potential circle center based on the edge position, the gradient direction, and the known circle radius. With this information, we increment the accumulator array at the potential circle center by one. After we have processed all the edge points, the accumulator array should contain a large amount of evidence, that is, a large number of votes, at the locations of the circle centers. We can then threshold the accumulator array and compute the local maxima to determine the circle centers in the image.

An example of this algorithm is shown in Figure 9.130. Suppose we want to locate the circle on top of the capacitor in Figure 9.130a and that we know that it has a radius of 39 pixels. The edges extracted with a Canny filter with $\sigma = 2$ and hysteresis thresholds of 80 and 20 are shown in Figure 9.130b. Furthermore, for every eighth edge point, the gradient vector is shown. Note that for the circle they all point toward the circle center. The accumulator array that is obtained with the algorithm described above is displayed in Figure 9.130c. Note that there is only one significant peak. In fact, most of the cells in the accumulator array have received so few votes that a square root LUT had to be used to visualize

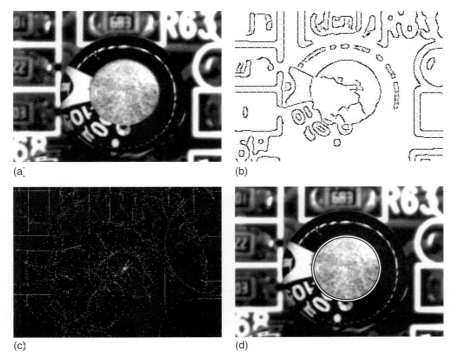

Figure 9.130 Using the Hough transform to detect a circle. (a) Image of a PCB showing a capacitor. (b) Detected edges. For every eighth edge point, the corresponding orientation is visualized by displaying the gradient vector. (c) Hough accumulator array obtained by performing the Hough transform using the edge points and orientations. A square root LUT is used to make the less populated regions of the accumulator space more visible. If a linear LUT were used, only the peak would be visible. (d) Circle detected by thresholding (c) and computing the local maxima.

whether there are any votes at all in the rest of the accumulator array. If the accumulator array is thresholded and the local maxima are calculated, the circle in Figure 9.130d is obtained.

From the above example, we can see that we can find circles in the image extremely efficiently. If we know the polarity of the circle, that is, whether it is brighter or darker than the background, we only need to perform a single increment of the accumulator array per edge point in the image. If we do not know the polarity of the edge, we need to perform two increments per edge point. Hence, the runtime is proportional to the number of edge points in the image and not to the size of the template, that is, the size of the circle. Ideally, we would like to find an algorithm that is equally efficient for arbitrary objects.

What can we learn from the above example? First of all, it is clear that, for arbitrary objects, the gradient direction does not necessarily point to a reference point of the object like it did for circles. Nevertheless, the gradient direction of the edge point provides a constraint where the reference point of the object can be, even for arbitrarily shaped objects. This is shown in Table 9.2. Suppose we have singled out the reference point o of the object. For the circle, the natural choice

Table 9.2 Principle of constructing the R-table in the generalized Hough transform (GHT). The R-table (on the right) is constructed based on the gradient angle ϕ_i of each edge point of the model object and the vector r_i from each edge point to the reference point o of the template.

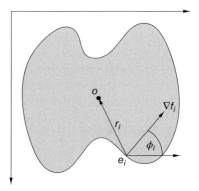

j	ϕ_j	r_i
0	0	$\{r_i \mid \phi_i = 0\}$
1	$\Delta\phi$	$\{r_i \mid \phi_i = \Delta\phi\}$
2	$2\Delta\phi$	$\{r_i \mid \phi_i = 2\Delta\phi\}$
⋮	⋮	⋮

would be its center. For an arbitrary object, we can, for example, use the center of gravity of the edge points. Now consider an edge point e_i. We can see that the gradient vector ∇f_i and the vector r_i from e_i to o always enclose the same angle, no matter how the object is translated, rotated, and scaled. For simplicity, let us consider only translations for the moment. Then, if we find an edge point in the image with a certain gradient direction or gradient angle ϕ_i, we could calculate the possible location of the template with the vector r_i and increment the accumulator array accordingly. Note that for circles the gradient vector ∇f_i has the same direction as the vector r_i. For arbitrary shapes this no longer holds. From Table 9.2, we can also see that the edge direction does not necessarily uniquely constrain the reference point, since there may be multiple points on the edges of the template that have the same orientation. For circles, this is not the case. For example, in the lower left part of the object in Table 9.2, there is a second point that has the same gradient direction as the point labeled e_i, which has a different offset vector than the reference point. Therefore, in the search we have to increment all accumulator array elements that correspond to the edge points in the template with the same edge direction. Hence, during the search we must be able to quickly determine all the offset vectors that correspond to a given edge direction in the image. This can be achieved in a preprocessing step in the template generation that is performed offline. Basically, we construct a table, called the R-table, that is indexed by the gradient angle ϕ. Each table entry contains all the offset vectors r_i of the template edges that have the gradient angle ϕ. Since the table must be discrete to enable efficient indexing, the gradient angles are discretized with a certain step size $\Delta\phi$. The concept of the R-table is also shown in Table 9.2. With the R-table, it is very simple to find the offset vectors for incrementing the accumulator array in the search: we simply calculate the gradient angle in the image and use it as an index into the R-table. After the construction of the accumulator array, we threshold the array and calculate the local maxima to find the possible locations of the object. This approach can also be extended easily to deal with rotated and scaled objects [102]. In real images, we also need to consider that there are uncertainties in the location of the edges in the image and in the edge orientations. We have already seen in equation (9.111) that the precision of the Canny edges depends on the signal-to-noise ratio. Using similar techniques, it can be shown that the precision of the edge angle ϕ for the Canny filter is given by $\sigma_\phi^2 = \sigma_n^2/(4\sigma^2 a^2)$. These values must be used in the online phase to determine a range of cells in the accumulator array that must be incremented to ensure that the cell corresponding to the true reference point is incremented.

The generalized Hough transform described previously is already quite efficient. On average, it increments a constant number of accumulator cells. Therefore, its runtime depends only on the number of edge points in the image. However, it is still not fast enough for machine vision applications because the accumulator space that must be searched to find the objects can quickly become very large, especially if rotations and scalings of the object are allowed. Furthermore, the accumulator uses an enormous amount of memory. Consider, for example, an object that should be found in a 640×480 image with an angle range of $360°$, discretized in $1°$ steps. Let us suppose that two bytes are sufficient to store the accumulator array entries without overflow. Then, the accumulator array requires $640 \times 480 \times 360 \times 2 = 221\,184\,000$ bytes of memory, that is, 211 MB. This is unacceptably large for most applications. Furthermore, it means that initializing this array alone will require a significant amount of processing time. For this reason, a hierarchical generalized Hough transform is proposed in [105]. It uses image pyramids to speed up the search and to reduce the size of the accumulator array by using matches found on higher pyramid levels to constrain the search on lower pyramid levels. The interested reader is referred to [105] for details of the implementation. With this hierarchical generalized Hough transform, objects can be found in real time even under severe occlusions, clutter, and almost arbitrary illumination changes.

The algorithms we have discussed so far were based on matching edge points directly. Another class of algorithms is based on matching geometric primitives, for example, points, lines, and circles. These algorithms typically follow the hypothesize-and-test paradigm, that is, they hypothesize a match, typically from a small number of primitives, and then test whether the hypothetical match has enough evidence in the image.

The biggest challenge that this type of algorithm must solve is the exponential complexity of the correspondence problem. Let us, for the moment, suppose that we are only using one type of geometric primitive, for example, lines. Furthermore, let us suppose that all template primitives are visible in the image, so that potentially there is a subset of the primitives in the image that corresponds exactly to the primitives in the template. If the template consists of m primitives and there are n primitives in the image, there are $\binom{n}{m}$, that is, $O(n^m)$, potential correspondences between the template and image primitives. If the objects in the search image can be occluded, the number of potential matches is even larger, since we must allow that multiple primitives in the image can match a single primitive in the template, because a single primitive in the template may break up into several pieces, and that some primitives in the template are not present in the search image. It is clear that, even for moderately large values of m and n, the cost of exhaustively checking all possible correspondences is prohibitive. Therefore, geometric constraints and strong heuristics must be used to perform the matching in an acceptable time.

One approach to perform the matching efficiently is called geometric hashing [106]. It was originally described for points as primitives, but can equally well be used with lines. Furthermore, the original description uses affine transformations as the set of allowable transformations. We will follow the original presentation and will note where modifications are necessary for other classes of transformations and lines as primitives. Geometric hashing is based on the observation that three points define an affine basis of the 2D plane. Thus, once we select three points e_{00}, e_{10}, and e_{01} in general position, that is, not collinear, we can represent every other point as a linear combination of these three points:

$$q = e_{00} + \alpha(e_{10} - e_{00}) + \beta(e_{01} - e_{00}) \tag{9.161}$$

The interesting property of this representation is that it is invariant to affine transformations, that is, (α, β) depend only on the three basis points (the basis triplet), but not on the affine transformation, that is, they are affine invariants. With this, the values (α, β) can be regarded as the affine coordinates of the point q. This property holds equally well for lines: three nonparallel lines that do not intersect in a single point can be used to define an affine basis. If we use a more restricted class of transformations, fewer points are sufficient to define a basis. For example, if we restrict the transformations to similarity transformations, two points are sufficient to define a basis. Note, however, that two lines are sufficient to determine only a rigid transformation.

The aim of geometric hashing is to reduce the amount of work that has to be performed to establish the correspondences between the template and image points. Therefore, it constructs a hash table that enables the algorithm to determine quickly the potential matches for the template. This hash table is constructed as follows. For every combination of three noncollinear points in the template, the affine coordinates (α, β) of the remaining $m - 3$ points of the template are calculated. The affine coordinates (α, β) serve as the index into the hash table. For every point, the index of the current basis triplet is stored in the hash table. If more than one template should be found, additionally the template index is stored; however, we will not consider this case further, so for our purposes only the index of the basis triplet is stored.

To find the template in the image, we randomly select three points in the image and construct the affine coordinates (α, β) of the remaining $n - 3$ points. We then use (α, β) as an index into the hash table. This returns us the index of the basis triplet. With this, we obtain a vote for the presence of a particular basis triplet in the image. If the randomly selected points do not correspond to a basis triplet of the template, the votes of all the points will not agree. However, if they correspond to a basis triplet of the template, many of the votes will agree and will indicate the index of the basis triplet. Therefore, if enough votes agree, we have a strong indication for the presence of the model. The presence of the model is then verified as described in the following. Since there is a certain probability that we have selected an inappropriate basis triplet in the image, the algorithm iterates until it has reached a certain probability of having found the correct match. Here, we can make use of the fact that we only need to find one correct basis triplet to find the model. Therefore, if k of the m template points are present in the image, the probability of having selected at least one correct basis triplet in t trials is approximately

$$p = 1 - \left(1 - \left(\frac{k}{n}\right)^3\right)^t \qquad (9.162)$$

If similarity transforms are used, only two points are necessary to determine the affine basis. Therefore, the inner exponent will change from 3 to 2 in this case. For example, if the ratio of visible template points to image points k/n is 0.2 and we want to find the template with a probability of 99% (i.e., $p = 0.99$), 574 trials are sufficient if affine transformations are used. For similarity transformations, 113 trials would suffice. Hence, geometric hashing can be quite efficient in finding the correct correspondences, depending on how many extra features are present in the image.

After a potential match has been obtained with the algorithm described above, it must be verified in the image. In [106], this is done by establishing point correspondences for the remaining template points based on the affine transformation given by the selected basis triplet. Based on these correspondences, an improved affine transformation is computed by a least-squares minimization over all corresponding points. This, in turn, is used to map all the edge points of the template, that is, not only the characteristic points that were used for the geometric hashing, to the pose of the template in the image. The transformed edges are compared to the image edges. If there is sufficient overlap between the template and image edges, the match is accepted and the corresponding points and edges are removed from the segmentation. Should more than one instance of the template be found, the entire process is repeated.

The algorithm described so far works well as long as the geometric primitives can be extracted with sufficient accuracy. If there are errors in the point coordinates, an erroneous affine transformation will result from the basis triplet. Therefore, all the affine coordinates (α, β) will contain errors, and hence the hashing in the online phase will access the wrong entry in the hash table. This is probably the largest drawback of the geometric hashing algorithm in practice. To circumvent this problem, the template points must be stored in multiple adjacent entries of the hash table. Which hash table entries must be used can in theory be derived through error propagation [106]. However, in practice, the accuracy of the geometric primitives is seldom known. Therefore, estimates have to be used, which must be well on the safe side for the algorithm not to miss any matches in the online phase. This, in turn, makes the algorithm slightly less efficient because more votes will have to be evaluated during the search.

The final class of algorithms we will discuss tries to match geometric primitives themselves to the image. Most of these algorithms use only line segments as the primitives [107–109]. One of the few exceptions to this rule is the approach in [110], which uses line segments and circular arcs. Furthermore, in 3D object recognition, sometimes line segments and elliptic arcs are used [111]. As we already discussed, exhaustively enumerating all potential correspondences between the template and image primitives is prohibitively slow. Therefore, it is interesting to look at examples of different strategies that are employed to make the correspondence search tractable.

The approach in [107] segments the contours of the model object and the search image into line segments. Depending on the lighting conditions, the contours are obtained by thresholding or by edge detection. The 10 longest line segments in the template are singled out as privileged. Furthermore, the line segments in the model are ordered by adjacency as they trace the boundary of the model object. To generate a hypothesis, a privileged template line segment is matched to a line segment in the image. Since the approach is designed to handle similarity transforms, the angle, which is invariant under these transforms, to the preceding line segment in the image is compared with the angle to the preceding line segment in the template. If they are not close enough, the potential match is rejected. Furthermore, the length ratio of these two segments, which also is invariant, is used to check the validity of the hypothesis. The algorithm generates a certain number of hypotheses in this manner. These hypotheses are then verified by trying to match additional segments. The quality of the hypotheses, including the additionally matched segments, is then evaluated based on the ratio of the lengths of the matched segments to the length of the segments in the template. The matching is stopped once a high-quality match has been found or if enough hypotheses have been evaluated. Hence, we can see that the complexity is kept manageable by using privileged segments in conjunction with their neighboring segments.

In [109], a similar method is proposed. In contrast to [107], corners (combinations of two adjacent line segments of the boundary of the template that enclose a significant angle) are matched first. To generate a matching hypothesis, two corners must be matched to the image. Geometric constraints between the corners are used to reject false matches. The algorithm then attempts to extend the hypotheses with other segments in the image. The hypotheses are evaluated based on a dissimilarity criterion. If the dissimilarity is below a threshold, the match is accepted. Hence, the complexity of this approach is reduced by matching features that have distinctive geometric characteristics first.

The approach in [108] also generates matching hypotheses and tries to verify them in the image. Here, a tree of possible correspondences is generated and evaluated in a depth-first search. This search tree is called the interpretation tree. A node in the interpretation tree encodes a correspondence between a model line segment and an image line segment. Hence, the interpretation tree would exhaustively enumerate all correspondences, which would be prohibitively expensive. Therefore, the interpretation tree must be pruned as much as possible. To do this, the algorithm uses geometric constraints between the template line segments and the image line segments. Specifically, the distances and angles between pairs of line segments in the image and in the template must be consistent. This angle is checked by using normal vectors of the line segments that take the polarity of the edges into account. This consistency check prunes a large number of branches of the interpretation tree. However, since a large number of possible matchings still remain, a heuristic is used to explore the most promising hypotheses first. This is useful because the search is terminated once an acceptable match has been found. This early search termination is criticized in [112], and various strategies

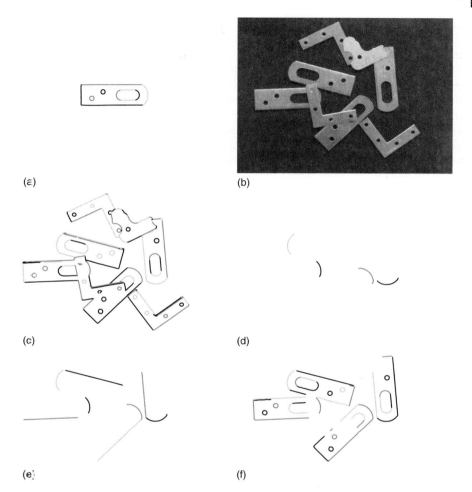

Figure 9.131 Example of matching an object in the image using geometric primitives. (a) The template consists of five line segments and five circular arcs. The model has been generated from the image in Figure 9.128a. (b) The search image contains four partially occluded instances of the template along with four clutter objects. (c) Edges extracted in (b) with a Canny filter with $\sigma = 1$ and split into line segments and circular arcs. (d) The matching in this case first tries to match the largest circular arc of the model and finds four hypotheses. (e) The hypotheses are extended with the lower of the long line segments in (a). These two primitives are sufficient to estimate a rigid transform that aligns the template with the features in the image. (f) The remaining primitives of the template are matched to the image. The resulting matched primitives are displayed.

to speed up the search for all instances of the template in the image are discussed. The interested reader is referred to [112] for details.

To make the principles of the geometric matching algorithms clearer, let us examine a prototypical matching procedure on an example. The template to be found is shown in Figure 9.131a. It consists of five line segments and five circular arcs. They were segmented automatically from the image in Figure 9.128a using a subpixel-precise Canny filter with $\sigma = 1$ and and by splitting the edge contours into line segments and circular arcs using the method described in Section 9.8.4. The template consists of the geometric parameters of these primitives as well as the segmented contours themselves. The image in which the template should be found is shown in Figure 9.131b. It contains four partially occluded instances of the model along with four clutter objects. The matching starts by extracting edges in the search image and by segmenting them into line segments and circular arcs (Figure 9.131c). Like for the template, the geometric parameters of the image primitives are calculated. The matching now determines possible matches for all of the primitives in the template. Of these, the largest circular arc is examined first because of a heuristic that rates moderately long circular arcs as more distinctive than even long line segments. The resulting matching hypotheses are shown in Figure 9.131d. Of course, the line segments could also have been examined first. Because in this case only rigid transformations are allowed, the matching of the circular arcs uses the radii of the circles as a matching constraint.

Since the matching should be robust to occlusions, the opening angle of the circular arcs is not used as a constraint. Because of this, the matched circles are not sufficient to determine a rigid transformation between the template and the image. Therefore, the algorithm tries to match an adjacent line segment (the long lower line segment in Figure 9.131a) to the image primitives while using the angle of intersection between the circle and the line as a geometric constraint. The resulting matches are shown in Figure 9.131e. With these hypotheses, it is possible to compute a rigid transformation that transforms the template to the image. Based on this, the remaining primitives can be matched to the image based on the distances of the image primitives and the transformed template primitives. The resulting matches are shown in Figure 9.131f. Note that, because of specular reflections, sometimes multiple parallel line segments are matched to a single line segment in the template. This could be fixed by taking the polarity of the edges into account. To obtain the rigid transformation between the template and the matches in the image as accurately as possible, a least-squares optimization of the distances between the edges in the template and the edges in the image can be used. An alternative is the minimal tolerance error zone optimization described in [110]. Note that the matching has already found the four correct instances of the template. For the algorithm, the search is not finished, however, since there might be more instances of the template in the image, especially instances for which the large circular arc is occluded more than in the leftmost instance in the image. Hence, the search is continued with other primitives as the first primitives to try. In this case, however, the search does not discover new viable matches.

After having discussed some of the approaches for robustly finding templates in an image, the question as to which of these algorithms should be used in practice naturally arises. We will say more on this topic in the following. From the above discussion, however, we can see that the effectiveness of a particular approach greatly depends on the shape of the template itself. Generally, the geometric matching algorithms have an advantage if the template and image contain only a few salient geometric primitives, like in the example in Figure 9.131. Here, the combinatorics of the geometric matching algorithms can work to their

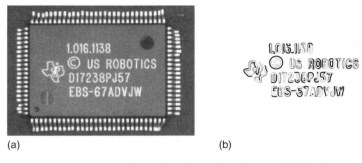

(a)   (b)

Figure 9.132 (a) Image of a template object that is not suitable for the geometric matching algorithms. Although the segmentation of the template into line segments and circular arcs in (b) only contains approximately 3 times as many edge points as the template in Figure 9.131, it contains 35 times as many geometric primitives, that is, 350.

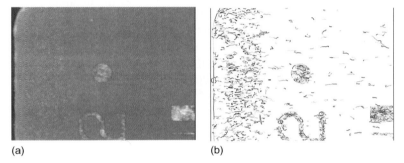

(a)   (b)

Figure 9.133 (a) A search image that is difficult for the geometric matching algorithms. Here, because of the poor contrast of the circular fiducial mark, the segmentation threshold must be chosen very low so that the relevant edges of the fiducial mark are selected. Because of this, the segmentation in (b) contains a very large number of primitives that must be examined in the search.

advantage. On the other hand, they work to their disadvantage if the template or search image contains a large number of geometric primitives.

A difficult model image is shown in Figure 9.132. The template contains fine structures that result in 350 geometric primitives, which are not particularly salient. Consequently, the search would have to examine an extremely large number of hypotheses that could be dismissed only after examining a large number of additional primitives. Note that the model contains 35 times as many primitives as the model in Figure 9.131, but only approximately 3 times as many edge points. Consequently, it could be easily found with pixel-based approaches like the generalized Hough transform.

A difficult search image is shown in Figure 9.133. Here, the goal is to find the circular fiducial mark. Since the contrast of the fiducial mark is very low, a small segmentation threshold must be used in the edge detection to find the relevant edges of the circle. This causes a very large number of edges and broken fragments that must be examined. Again, pixel-based algorithms will have little trouble with this image.

From the above examples, we can see that the pixel-based algorithms have the advantage that they can represent arbitrarily shaped templates without problems. Geometric matching algorithms, on the other hand, are restricted to relatively simple shapes that can be represented with a very small number of primitives. Therefore, in the remainder of this section, we will discuss a pixel-based robust template matching algorithm called shape-based matching [113–117] that works very well in practice [118, 119].

One of the drawbacks of all the algorithms that we have discussed so far is that they segment the edge image. This makes the object recognition algorithm invariant only against a narrow range of illumination changes. If the image contrast is lowered, progressively fewer edge points will be segmented, which has the same effect as progressively larger occlusion. Consequently, the object may not be found for low-contrast images. To overcome this problem, a similarity measure that is robust against occlusion, clutter, and nonlinear illumination changes must be used. This similarity measure can then be used in the pyramid-based recognition strategy described in Sections 9.11.2 and 9.11.4.

To define the similarity measure, we first define the model of an object as a set of points $p_i = (r_i, c_i)^\top$ and associated direction vectors $d_i = (t_i, u_i)^\top$, with $i = 1, \ldots, n$. The direction vectors can be generated by a number of different image processing operations. However, typically edge extraction (see Section 9.7.3) is used. The model is generated from an image of the object, where an arbitrary ROI specifies the part of the image in which the object is located. It is advantageous to specify the coordinates p_i relative to the center of gravity of the ROI of the model or to the center of gravity of the points of the model.

The image in which the model should be found can be transformed into a representation in which a direction vector $e_{r,c} = (v_{r,c}, w_{r,c})^\top$ is obtained for each image point (r, c). In the matching process, a transformed model must be compared with the image at a particular location. In the most general case considered here, the transformation is an arbitrary affine transformation (see Section 9.3.1). It is useful to separate the translation part of the affine transformation from the linear part. Therefore, a linearly transformed model is given by the points $p'_i = \mathrm{A} p_i$ and the accordingly transformed direction vectors $d'_i = (\mathrm{A}^{-1})^\top d_i$, where

$$\mathrm{A} = \begin{pmatrix} a_{11} & a_{12} \\ a_{21} & a_{22} \end{pmatrix} \tag{9.163}$$

As discussed previously, the similarity measure by which the transformed model is compared with the image must be robust to occlusions, clutter, and illumination changes. One such measure is to sum the (unnormalized) dot product of the direction vectors of the transformed model and the image over all points of the model to compute a matching score at a particular point $q = (r, c)^\top$ of the image. That is, the similarity measure of the transformed model at the point q, which corresponds to the translation part of the affine transformation, is computed as follows:

$$s = \frac{1}{n} \sum_{i=1}^{n} d'^\top_i e_{q+p'} = \frac{1}{n} \sum_{i=1}^{n} t'_i \, v_{r+r'_i, c+c'_i} + u'_i \, w_{r+r'_i, c+c'_i} \tag{9.164}$$

If the model is generated by edge filtering and the image is preprocessed in the same manner, this similarity measure fulfills the requirements of robustness to occlusion and clutter. If parts of the object are missing in the image, there will be no edges at the corresponding positions of the model in the image, that is, the direction vectors will have a small length and hence contribute little to the sum. Likewise, if there are clutter edges in the image, there will either be no point in the model at the clutter position or it will have a small length, which means it will contribute little to the sum.

The similarity measure in equation (9.164) is not truly invariant against illumination changes however, because the length of the direction vectors depends on the brightness of the image if edge detection is used to extract the direction vectors. However, if a user specifies a threshold on the similarity measure to determine whether the model is present in the image, a similarity measure with a well-defined range of values is desirable. The following similarity measure achieves this goal:

$$s = \frac{1}{n}\sum_{i=1}^{n} \frac{d_i'^{\mathrm{T}} e_{q+p'}}{\|d_i'\| \|e_{q+p'}\|} = \frac{1}{n}\sum_{i=1}^{n} \frac{t_i' v_{r+r_i',c+c_i'} + u_i' w_{r+r_i',c+c_i'}}{\sqrt{t_i'^2 + u_i'^2}\sqrt{v_{r+r_i',c+c_i'}^2 + w_{r+r_i',c+c_i'}^2}} \quad (9.165)$$

Because of the normalization of the direction vectors, this similarity measure is additionally invariant to arbitrary illumination changes, since all vectors are scaled to a length of 1. What makes this measure robust against occlusion and clutter is the fact that, if a feature is missing, either in the model or in the image, noise will lead to random direction vectors, which, on average, will contribute nothing to the sum.

The similarity measure in equation (9.165) will return a high score if all the direction vectors of the model and the image align, that is, point in the same direction. If edges are used to generate the model and image vectors, this means that the model and image must have the same contrast direction for each edge. Sometimes it is desirable to be able to detect the object even if its contrast is reversed. This is achieved by

$$s = \left| \frac{1}{n}\sum_{i=1}^{n} \frac{d_i'^{\mathrm{T}} e_{q+p'}}{\|d_i'\| \|e_{q+p'}\|} \right| \quad (9.166)$$

In rare circumstances, it might be necessary to ignore even local contrast changes. In this case, the similarity measure can be modified as follows:

$$s = \frac{1}{n}\sum_{i=1}^{n} \frac{|d_i'^{\mathrm{T}} e_{q+p'}|}{\|d_i'\| \|e_{q+p'}\|} \quad (9.167)$$

The normalized similarity measures in equations (9.165)–(9.167) have the property that they return a number smaller than 1 as the score of a potential match. In all cases, a score of 1 indicates a perfect match between the model and the image. Furthermore, the score roughly corresponds to the portion of the model that is visible in the image. For example, if the object is 50% occluded, the score (on average) cannot exceed 0.5. This is a highly desirable property, because it gives the user the means to select an intuitive threshold for when an object should be considered as recognized.

A desirable feature of the above similarity measures in equations (9.165)–(9.167) is that they do not need to be evaluated completely when object recognition is based on a user-defined threshold s_{min} for the similarity measure that a potential match must achieve. Let s_j denote the partial sum of the dot products up to the jth element of the model. For the match metric that uses the sum of the normalized dot products, this is

$$s_j = \frac{1}{n} \sum_{i=1}^{j} \frac{d_i'^\mathsf{T} e_{q+p'}}{\| d_i' \| \| e_{q+p'} \|} \tag{9.168}$$

Obviously, all the remaining terms of the sum are ≤ 1. Therefore, the partial score can never achieve the required score s_{min} if $s_j < s_{min} - 1 + j/n$, and hence the evaluation of the sum can be discontinued after the jth element whenever this condition is fulfilled. This criterion speeds up the recognition process considerably.

As mentioned previously, to recognize the model, an image pyramid is constructed for the image in which the model should be found (see Section 9.11.2). For each level of the pyramid, the same filtering operation that was used to generate the model, for example, edge filtering, is applied to the image. This returns a direction vector for each image point. Note that the image is not segmented, that is, thresholding or other operations are not performed. This results in true robustness to illumination changes.

As discussed in Sections 9.11.2 and 9.11.4, to identify potential matches, an exhaustive search is performed for the top level of the pyramid, that is, all possible poses of the model are used on the top level of the image pyramid to compute the similarity measure via equations (9.165), (9.166), or (9.167). A potential match must have a score larger than s_{min}, and the corresponding score must be a local maximum with respect to neighboring scores. The threshold s_{min} is used to speed up the search by terminating the evaluation of the similarity measure as early as possible. Therefore, this seemingly brute-force strategy actually becomes extremely efficient.

After the potential matches have been identified, they are tracked through the resolution hierarchy until they are found at the lowest level of the image pyramid. Once the object has been recognized on the lowest level of the image pyramid, its pose is extracted with a resolution better than the discretization of the search space with the approach described in Section 9.11.3.

While the pose obtained by the extrapolation algorithm is accurate enough for most applications, in some applications an even higher accuracy is desirable. This can be achieved through a least-squares adjustment of the pose parameters. To achieve a better accuracy than the extrapolation, it is necessary to extract the model points as well as the feature points in the image with subpixel accuracy. Then, the algorithm finds the closest image point for each model point, and then minimizes the sum of the squared distances of the image points to a line defined by their corresponding model point and the corresponding tangent to the model point, that is, the directions of the model points are taken to be correct and are assumed to describe the direction of the object's border. If an edge detector is used, the direction vectors of the model are perpendicular to the object boundary, and hence the equation of a line through a model point tangent to the object boundary is given by

$$t_i(r - r_i) + u_i(c - c_i) = 0 \qquad (9.169)$$

Let $q_i = (r'_i, c'_i)^\top$ denote the matched image points corresponding to the model points p_i. Then, the following function is minimized to refine the pose a:

$$d(a) = \sum_{i=1}^{n} (t_i(r'_i(a) - r_i) + u_i(c'_i(a) - c_i))^2 \to \min \qquad (9.170)$$

The potential corresponding image points in the search image are obtained without thresholding by a non-maximum suppression and are extrapolated to sub-pixel accuracy. By this, a segmentation of the search image is avoided, which is important to preserve the invariance against arbitrary illumination changes. For each model point, the corresponding image point in the search image is chosen as the potential image point with the smallest Euclidian distance using the pose obtained by the extrapolation to transform the model to the search image. Since the point correspondences may change by the refined pose, an even higher accuracy can be gained by iterating the correspondence search and pose refinement. Typically, after three iterations the accuracy of the pose no longer improves.

Figure 9.134 shows six examples in which the shape-based matching algorithm finds the print on the IC shown in Figure 9.132. Note that the object is found despite severe occlusions and clutter.

Extensive tests with shape-based matching have been carried out in [118, 119]. The results show that shape-based matching provides extremely high recognition rates in the presence of severe occlusion and clutter as well as in the presence of nonlinear illumination changes. Furthermore, accuracies better than 1/30 of a pixel and better than 1/50 degree can be achieved.

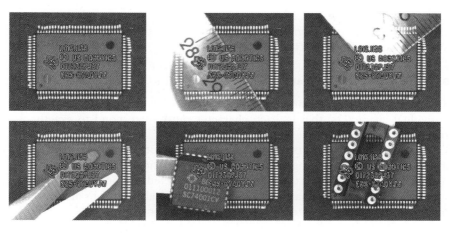

Figure 9.134 Six examples in which the shape-based matching algorithm finds an object (the print on the IC shown in Figure 9.132) despite severe occlusions and clutter.

The basic principle of the shape-based matching algorithm can be extended in various ways to handle larger classes of deformations and objects. For example, a method to recognize objects that consist of multiple parts that can move with respect to each other by rigid 2D transformations is described in [120–122]. An extension that is able to recognize planar objects under perspective transformations is proposed in [123, 124], while recognizing the 3D pose of planar objects is described in [124, 125]. A further extension that is able to handle smooth local deformations is presented in [124, 126]. Finally, the basic principle of the shape-based matching is also the foundation for a sophisticated algorithm that is able to recognize the 3D pose of objects from single images [127–130].

From the above discussion, we can see that the basic algorithms for implementing a robust template matching already are fairly complex. In reality, however, the complexity additionally resides in the time and effort that needs to be spent in making the algorithms very robust and fast. Additional complexity comes from the fact that, on one hand, templates with arbitrary ROIs should be possible to exclude undesired parts from the template, while, on the other, for speed reasons, it should also be possible to specify arbitrarily shaped ROIs for the search space in the search images. Consequently, these algorithms cannot be implemented easily. Therefore, wise machine vision users rely on standard software packages to provide this functionality rather than attempting to implement it themselves.

9.12 Optical Character Recognition

In quite a few applications, we face the challenge of having to read characters on the object we are inspecting. For example, traceability requirements often lead to the fact that the objects to be inspected are labeled with a serial number and that we have to read this serial number (see, e.g., Figures 9.22–9.24). In other applications, reading a serial number might be necessary to control the production flow.

OCR is the process of reading characters in images. It consists of two tasks: segmentation of the individual characters, and the classification of the segmented characters, that is, the assignment of a symbolic label to the segmented regions. We will examine these two tasks in this section.

9.12.1 Character Segmentation

The classification of the characters requires that we have segmented the text into individual characters, that is, each character must correspond to exactly one region.

To segment the characters, we can use all the methods that we have discussed in Section 9.4: thresholding with fixed and automatically selected thresholds, dynamic thresholding, and the extraction of connected components.

Furthermore, we might have to use the morphological operations of Section 9.6 to connect separate parts of the same character, for example, the dot of the character "i" to its main part (see Figure 9.43) or parts of the same character that are disconnected, for example, because of bad print quality. For characters on difficult surfaces, for example, punched characters on a metal surface, gray value morphology may be necessary to segment the characters (see Figure 9.60).

Additionally, in some applications it may be necessary to perform a geometric transformation of the image to transform the characters into a standard position, typically such that the text is horizontal. This process is called image rectification. For example, the text may have to be rotated (see Figure 9.18), perspectively rectified (see Figure 9.20), or rectified with a polar transformation (see Figure 9.21).

Even though we have many segmentation strategies at our disposal, in some applications it may be difficult to segment the individual characters because the characters actually touch each other, either in reality or in the resolution at which we are looking at them in the image. Therefore, special methods to segment touching characters are sometimes required.

The simplest such strategy is to define a separate ROI for each character we are expecting in the image. This strategy sometimes can be used in industrial applications because the fonts typically have a fixed pitch (width) and we know *a priori* how many characters are present in the image, for example, if we are trying to read serial numbers with a fixed length. The main problem with this approach is that the character ROIs must enclose the individual characters we are trying to separate. This is difficult if the position of the text can vary in the image. If this is the case, we first need to determine the pose of the text in the image based on another strategy, for example, template matching to find a distinct feature in the vicinity of the text we are trying to read, and to use the pose of the text either to rectify the text to a standard position or to move the character ROIs to the appropriate position.

While defining separate ROIs for each character works well in some applications, it is not very flexible. A better method can be derived by realizing that the characters typically touch only with a small number of pixels. An example of this is shown in Figure 9.135a,b. To separate these characters, we can simply count the number of pixels per column in the segmented region. This is shown in Figure 9.135c. Since the touching part is only a narrow bridge between the characters, the number of pixels in the region of the touching part only has a very small number of pixels per column. In fact, we can simply segment the characters by splitting them vertically at the position of the minimum in Figure 9.135c. The result is shown in Figure 9.135d. Note that in Figure 9.135c the optimal splitting point is the global minimum of the number of pixels per column. However, in general, this may not be the case. For example, if the strokes between the vertical bars of the letter "m" were slightly thinner, the letter "m" might be split erroneously. Therefore, to make this algorithm more robust, it is typically necessary to define a search space for the splitting of the characters based on the expected width of the characters. For example, in this application the characters are approximately 20 pixels wide. Therefore, we could restrict the search space for the optimal splitting point to a range of ± 4 pixels (20% of the expected width) around the expected width of the characters. This simple splitting method works very well in practice. Further approaches for segmenting characters are discussed in [131].

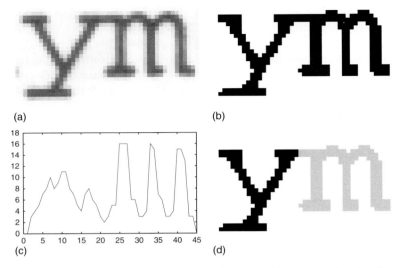

Figure 9.135 (a) An image of two touching characters. (b) Segmented region. Note that the characters are not separated. (c) Plot of the number of pixels in each column of (b). (d) The characters have been split at the minimum of (c) at position 21.

9.12.2 Feature Extraction

As mentioned previously, the reading of the characters corresponds to the classification of the regions, that is, the assignment of a class ω_i to a region. For the purposes of OCR, the classes ω_i can be thought of as the interpretation of the character, that is, the string that represents the character. For example, if an application must read serial numbers, the classes $\{\omega_1, \ldots, \omega_{10}\}$ are simply the strings $\{0, \ldots, 9\}$. If numbers and uppercase letters must be read, the classes are $\{\omega_1, \ldots, \omega_{36}\} = \{0, \ldots, 9, A, \ldots, Z\}$. Hence, classification can be thought of as a function f that maps to the set of classes $\Omega = \{\omega_i, i = 1, \ldots, m\}$. What is the input of this function? First of all, to make the above mapping well defined and easy to handle, we require that the number n of input values to the function f is constant. The input values to f are called features. Typically they are real numbers. With this, the function f that performs the classification can be regarded as a mapping $f : \mathbb{R}^n \mapsto \Omega$.

For OCR, the features that are used for the classification are features that we extract from the segmented characters. Any of the region features described in Section 9.5.1 and the gray value features described in Section 9.5.2 can be used as features. The main requirement is that the features enable us to discern the different character classes. Figure 9.136 illustrates this point. The input image is shown in Figure 9.136a. It contains examples of lowercase letters. Suppose that we want to classify the letters based on the region features anisometry and compactness. Figure 9.136b,c shows that the letters "c" and "o" as well as "i" and "j" can be distinguished easily based on these two features. In fact, they can be distinguished solely based on their compactness. As Figure 9.136d,e shows, however, these two features are not sufficient to distinguish between the classes "p" and "q" as well as "h" and "k."

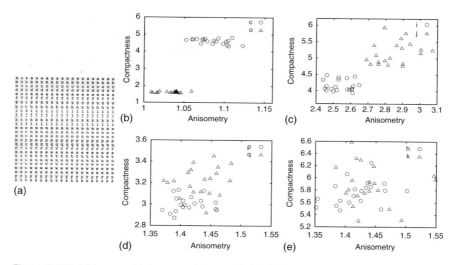

Figure 9.136 (a) Image with lowercase letters. (b)–(e) The features anisometry and compactness plotted for the letters "c" and "o" (b), "i" and "j" (c), "p" and "q" (d), and "h" and "k" (e). Note that the letters in (b) and (c) can be easily distinguished based on the selected features, while the letters in (d) and (e) cannot be distinguished.

From the above example, we can see that the features we use for the classification must be sufficiently powerful to enable us to classify all relevant classes correctly. The region and gray value features described in Sections 9.5.1 and 9.5.2, unfortunately, are often not powerful enough to achieve this. A set of features that is sufficiently powerful to distinguish all classes of characters is the gray values of the image themselves. Using the gray values directly, however, is not possible because the classifier requires a constant number of input features. To achieve this, we can use the smallest enclosing rectangle around the segmented character, enlarge it slightly to include a suitable amount of background of the character in the features (e.g., by one pixel in each direction), and then zoom the gray values within this rectangle to a standard size, for example, 8×10 pixels. While transforming the image, we must take care to use the interpolation and smoothing techniques discussed in Section 9.3.3. Note, however, that by zooming the image to a standard size based on the surrounding rectangle of the segmented character, we lose the ability to distinguish characters like "−" (minus sign) and "I" (upper case I in fonts without serifs). The distinction can easily be done based on a single additional feature: the ratio of the width and height of the smallest surrounding rectangle of the segmented character.

Unfortunately, the gray value features defined above are not invariant to illumination changes in the image. This makes the classification very difficult. To achieve invariance to illumination changes, two options exist. The first option is to perform a robust normalization of the gray values of the character, as described in Section 9.2.1, before the character is zoomed to the standard size. The second option is to convert the segmented character into a binary image before the character is zoomed to the standard size. Since the gray values generally contain more information, the first strategy is preferable in most cases. The second strategy can

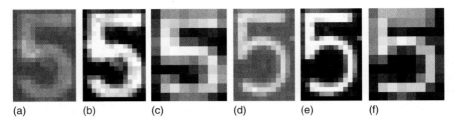

Figure 9.137 Gray value feature extraction for OCR. (a) Image of the letter "5" taken from the second row of characters in the image in Figure 9.23a. (b) Robust contrast normalization of (a). (c) Result of zooming (b) to a size of 8×10 pixels. (d) Image of the letter "5" taken from the second row of characters in the image in Figure 9.23b. (e) Robust contrast normalization of (d). (f) Result of zooming (e) to a size of 8×10 pixels.

be used whenever there is significant texture in the background of the segmented characters, which would make the classification more difficult.

Figure 9.137 displays two examples of the gray value feature extraction for OCR. Figure 9.137a,d displays two instances of the letter "5," taken from images with different contrast (Figure 9.23a,b). Note that the characters have different sizes (14×21 and 13×20 pixels, respectively). The result of the robust contrast normalization is shown in Figure 9.137b,e. Note that both characters now have full contrast. Finally, the result of zooming the characters to a size of 8×10 pixels is shown in Figure 9.137c,f. Note that this feature extraction automatically makes the OCR scale-invariant because of the zooming to a standard size.

To conclude the discussion about feature extraction, some words about the standard size are necessary. The discussion above has used the size 8×10. A large set of tests has shown that this size is a very good size to use for most industrial applications. If there are only a small number of classes to distinguish, for example, only numbers, it may be possible to use slightly smaller sizes. For some applications involving a larger number of classes, for example, numbers and uppercase and lowercase characters, a slightly larger size may be necessary (e.g., 10×12). On the other hand, using much larger sizes typically does not lead to better classification results because the features become progressively less robust against small segmentation errors if a large standard size is chosen. This happens because larger standard sizes imply that a segmentation error will lead to progressively larger position inaccuracies in the zoomed character as the standard size becomes larger. Therefore, it is best not to use a standard size that is much larger than the above recommendations. One exception to this rule is the recognition of an extremely large set of classes, for example, ideographic characters like the Japanese Kanji characters. Here, much larger standard sizes are necessary to distinguish the large number of different characters.

9.12.3 Classification

As we saw in the previous section, classification can be regarded as a mapping from the feature space to the set of possible classes, that is, $f : \mathbb{R}^n \mapsto \Omega$. We will now take a closer look at how the mapping can be constructed.

First of all, we can note that the feature vector x that serves as the input to the mapping can be regarded as a random variable because of the variations that the characters exhibit. In the application, we are observing this random feature vector for each character we are trying to classify. It can be shown that, to minimize the probability of erroneously classifying the feature vector, we should maximize the probability that the class ω_i occurs under the condition that we observe the feature vector x, that is, we should maximize $P(\omega_i|x)$ over all classes ω_i, for $i = 1, \ldots, m$ [132, 133]. The probability $P(\omega_i|x)$ is also called the *a posteriori* probability because of the above property that it describes the probability of class ω_i given that we have observed the feature vector x. This decision rule is called the Bayes decision rule. It yields the best classifier if all errors have the same weight, which is a reasonable assumption for OCR.

We now face the problem of how to determine the *a posteriori* probability. Using the Bayes theorem, $P(\omega_i|x)$ can be computed as follows:

$$P(\omega_i|x) = \frac{P(x|\omega_i)P(\omega_i)}{P(x)} \qquad (9.171)$$

Hence, we can compute the *a posteriori* probability based on the *a priori* probability $P(x|\omega_i)$ that the feature vector x occurs given that the class of the feature vector is ω_i, the probability $P(\omega_i)$ that the class ω_i occurs, and the probability $P(x)$ that the feature vector x occurs. To simplify the calculations, we can note that the Bayes decision rule only needs to maximize $P(\omega_i|x)$ and that $P(x)$ is a constant if x is given. Therefore, the Bayes decision rule can be written as

$$x \in \omega_i \Leftrightarrow P(x|\omega_i)P(\omega_i) > P(x|\omega_j)P(\omega_j), \quad j = 1, \ldots, m, j \neq i \qquad (9.172)$$

What do we gain by this transformation? As we will see in the following, the probabilities $P(x|\omega_i)$ and $P(\omega_i)$ can, in principle, be determined from training samples. This enables us to evaluate $P(\omega_i|x)$, and hence to classify the feature vector x. Before we examine this point in detail, however, let us assume that the probabilities in equation (9.172) are known. For example, let us assume that the feature space is one dimensional ($n = 1$) and that there are two classes ($m = 2$). Furthermore, let us assume that $P(\omega_1) = 0.3$, $P(\omega_2) = 0.7$, and that the features of the two classes have a normal distribution $N(\mu, \sigma)$ such that $P(x|\omega_1) \sim N(-3, 1.5)$ and $P(x|\omega_2) \sim N(3, 2)$. The corresponding likelihoods $P(x|\omega_i)P(\omega_i)$ are shown in Figure 9.138. Note that features to the left of $x \approx -0.7122$ are classified as belonging to ω_1, while features to the right are classified as belonging to ω_2. Hence, there is a dividing point $x \approx -0.7122$ that separates the classes from each other.

As a further example, consider a 2D feature space with three classes that have normal distributions with different means and covariances, as shown in Figure 9.139a. Again, there are three regions in the 2D feature space in which the respective class has the highest probability, as shown in Figure 9.139b. Note that now there are 1D curves that separate the regions in the feature space from each other.

As the above examples suggest, the Bayes decision rule partitions the feature space into mutually disjoint regions. This is obvious from the definition in equation (9.172): each region corresponds to the part of the feature space in which the class ω_i has the highest *a posteriori* probability. As also suggested by

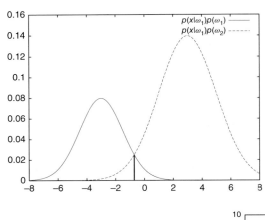

Figure 9.138 Example of a two-class classification problem in a 1D feature space in which $P(\omega_1) = 0.3$, $P(\omega_2) = 0.7$, $P(x|\omega_1) \sim N(-3,1.5)$, and $P(x|\omega_2) \sim N(3,2)$. Note that features to the left of $x \approx -0.7122$ are classified as belonging to ω_1, while features to the right are classified as belonging to ω_2.

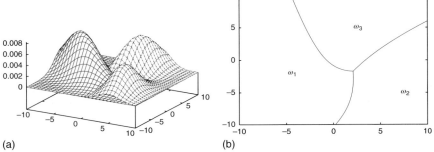

Figure 9.139 Example of a three-class classification problem in a 2D feature space in which the three classes have normal distributions with different means and covariances. (a) The *a posteriori* probabilities of the occurrence of the three classes. (b) Regions in the 2D feature space in which the respective class has the highest probability.

the above examples, the regions are separated by $(n - 1)$-dimensional hypersurfaces (points for $n = 1$ and curves for $n = 2$, as in Figures 9.138 and 9.139). The hypersurfaces that separate the regions from each other are given by the points at which two classes are equally probable, that is, by $P(\omega_i|x) = P(\omega_j|x)$, for $i \neq j$.

Accordingly, we can identify two different types of classifiers. The first type of classifier tries to estimate the *a posteriori* probabilities, typically via the Bayes theorem, from the *a priori* probabilities of the different classes. In contrast, the second type of classifier tries to construct the separating hypersurfaces between the classes. In the following, we will examine representatives for both types of classifier.

All classifiers require a method with which the probabilities or separating hypersurfaces are determined. To do this, a training set is required. The training set is a set of sample feature vectors x_k with corresponding class labels ω_k. For OCR, the training set is a set of character samples from which the corresponding feature vectors can be calculated, along with the interpretation of the respective character. The training set should be representative of the data that can be expected in the application. In particular, for OCR the characters in the training set should contain the variations that will occur later, for example, different character sets, stroke widths, noise, and so on. Since it is often difficult to obtain a training set with all variations, the image processing system must provide means to extend the training set over time with samples that are collected in the field, and should optionally also provide means to artificially add variations to the training set. Furthermore, to evaluate the classifier, in particular how well it has generalized the decision rule from the training samples, it is indispensable to have a test set that is independent of the training set. This test set is essential to determine the error rate that the classifier is likely to have in the application. Without the independent test set, no meaningful statement about the quality of the classifier can be made.

The classifiers that are based on estimating the probabilities, more precisely the probability densities, are called Bayes classifiers because they try to implement the Bayes decision rule via the probability densities. The first problem they have to solve is how to obtain the probabilities $P(\omega_i)$ of the occurrence of the class ω_i. There are two basic strategies for this purpose. The first strategy is to estimate $P(\omega_i)$ from the training set. Note that, for this, the training set must be representative not only in terms of the variations of the feature vectors but also in terms of the frequencies of the classes. Since this second requirement is often difficult to ensure, an alternative strategy for the estimation of $P(\omega_i)$ is to assume that each class is equally likely to occur, and hence to use $P(\omega_i) = 1/m$. Note that, in this case, the Bayes decision rule reduces to the classification according to the *a priori* probabilities since $P(\omega_i|x) \sim P(x|\omega_i)$ should now be maximized.

The remaining problem is how to estimate $P(x|\omega_i)$. In principle, this could be done by determining the histogram of the feature vectors of the training set in the feature space. To do so, we could subdivide each dimension of the feature space into b bins. Hence, the feature space would be divided into b^n bins in total. Each bin would count the number of occurrences of the feature vectors in the training set that lie within this bin. If the training set and b are large enough, the histogram would be a good approximation to the probability density $P(x|\omega_i)$. Unfortunately, this approach cannot be used in practice because of the so-called curse of dimensionality: the number of bins in the histogram is b^n, that is, its size grows exponentially with the dimension of the feature space. For example, if we use the 81 features described in the previous section and subdivide each dimension into a modest number of bins, for example, $b = 10$, the histogram would have 10^{81} bins, which is much too large to fit into any computer memory.

To obtain a classifier that can be used in practice, we can note that in the histogram approach the size of the bin is kept constant, while the number of samples in the bin varies. To get a different estimate for the probability of a feature vector, we can keep the number k of samples of class ω_i constant while varying the volume $v(x, \omega_i)$ of the region in space around the feature vector x that contains the k samples. Then, if there are t feature vectors in the training set, the probability of occurrence of the class ω_i is approximately given by

$$P(x|\omega_i) \approx \frac{k}{tv(x, \omega_i)} \qquad (9.173)$$

Since the volume $v(x, \omega_i)$ depends on the k nearest neighbors of class ω_i, this type of density estimation is called the k nearest-neighbor density estimation.

In practice, this approach is often modified as follows. Instead of determining the k nearest neighbors of a particular class and computing the volume $v(x, \omega_i)$, the k nearest neighbors in the training set of any class are determined. The feature vector x is then assigned to the class that has the largest number of samples among the k nearest neighbors. This classifier is called the k nearest-neighbor classifier (kNN classifier). For $k = 1$, we obtain the nearest-neighbor classifier (NN classifier). It can be shown that the NN classifier has an error probability that is at most twice as large as the error probability of the optimal Bayes classifier that uses the correct probability densities [132], that is, $P_B \leq P_{NN} \leq 2P_B$. Furthermore, if P_B is small, we have $P_{NN} \approx 2P_B$ and $P_{3NN} \approx P_B + 3P_B^2$. Hence, the 3NN classifier is almost as good as the optimal Bayes classifier. Nevertheless, kNN classifiers are difficult to use in practice because they require that the entire training set is stored with the classifier (which can easily contain several hundred thousands of samples). Furthermore, the search for the k nearest neighbors is time consuming even if optimized data structures are used to find exact [134] or approximate nearest neighbors [135, 136].

As we have seen from the above discussion, direct estimation of the probability density function is not practicable, either because of the curse of dimensionality for the histograms or because of efficiency considerations for the kNN classifier. To obtain an algorithm that can be used in practice, we can assume that $P(x|\omega_i)$ follows a certain distribution, for example, an n-dimensional normal distribution:

$$P(x|\omega_i) = \frac{1}{(2\pi)^{n/2}|\Sigma_i|^{1/2}} \exp\left(-\frac{1}{2}(x - \mu_i)^\top \Sigma_i^{-1}(x - \mu_i)\right) \qquad (9.174)$$

With this, estimating the probability density function reduces to the estimation of the parameters of the probability density function. For the normal distribution, the parameters are the mean vector μ_i and the covariance matrix Σ_i of each class. Since the covariance matrix is symmetric, the normal distribution has $(n^2 + 3n)/2$ parameters in total. They can, for example, be estimated via the standard maximum likelihood estimators

$$\mu_i = \frac{1}{n_i} \sum_{j=1}^{n_i} x_{i,j} \quad \text{and} \quad \Sigma_i = \frac{1}{n_i - 1} \sum_{j=1}^{n_i} (x_{i,j} - \mu_i)(x_{i,j} - \mu_i)^\top \qquad (9.175)$$

Here, n_i is the number of samples for class ω_i, while $x_{i,j}$ denotes the samples for class ω_i.

While the Bayes classifier based on the normal distribution can be quite powerful, often the assumption that the classes have a normal distribution does not hold in practice. In OCR applications, this happens frequently if characters in different fonts are to be recognized with the same classifier. One striking example of this is the shapes of the letters "a" and "g" in different fonts. For these letters, two basic shapes exist: a versus *a* and g versus g. It is clear that a single normal distribution is insufficient to capture these variations. In these cases, each font will typically lead to a different distribution. Hence, each class consists of a mixture of l_i different densities $P(x|\omega_i, k)$, each of which occurs with probability $P_{i,k}$:

$$P(x|\omega_i) = \sum_{k=1}^{l_i} P(x|\omega_i, k) P_{i,k} \qquad (9.176)$$

Typically, the mixture densities $P(x|\omega_i, k)$ are assumed to be normally distributed. In this case, equation (9.176) is called a Gaussian mixture model. If we knew to which mixture density each sample belongs, we could easily estimate the parameters of the normal distribution with the above maximum likelihood estimators. Unfortunately, in real applications we typically do not have this knowledge, that is, we do not know k in equation (9.176). Hence, determining the parameters of the mixture model requires the estimation of not only the parameters of the mixture densities but also the mixture density labels k. This is a much harder problem, which can be solved by the expectation maximization algorithm (EM algorithm). The interested reader is referred to [132] for details. Another problem in the mixture model approach is that we need to specify how many mixture densities there are in the mixture model, that is, we need to specify l_i in equation (9.176). This is quite cumbersome to do manually. To solve this problem, algorithms that compute l_i automatically have been proposed. The interested reader is referred to [137, 138] for details.

Let us now turn our attention to classifiers that construct the separating hypersurfaces between the classes. Of all possible surfaces, the simplest ones are planes. Therefore, it is instructive to consider this special case first. Planes in the n-dimensional feature space are given by

$$w^\top x + b = 0 \tag{9.177}$$

Here, x is an n-dimensional vector that describes a point, while w is an n-dimensional vector that describes the normal vector to the plane. Note that this equation is linear. Because of this, classifiers based on separating hyperplanes are called linear classifiers.

Let us first consider the problem of classifying two classes with the plane. We can assign a feature vector to the first class ω_1 if x lies on one side of the plane, while we can assign it to the second class ω_2 if it lies on the other side of the plane. Mathematically, the test on which side of the plane a point lies is performed by looking at the sign of $w^\top x + b$. Without loss of generality, we can assign x to ω_1 if $w^\top x + b > 0$, while we assign x to ω_2 if $w^\top x + b < 0$.

For classification problems with more than two classes, we construct m separating planes (w_i, b_i) and use the following classification rule [132]:

$$x \in \omega_i \Leftrightarrow w_i^\top x + b_i > w_j^\top x + b_j, \quad j = 1, \ldots, m, j \neq i \tag{9.178}$$

Note that, in this case, the separating planes do not have the same meaning as in the two-class case, where the plane actually separates the data. The interpretation of equation (9.178) is that the plane is chosen such that the feature vectors of the correct class have the largest positive distance of all feature vectors from the plane.

Linear classifiers can also be regarded as neural networks, as shown in Figure 9.140 for the two-class and n-class cases. The neural network has processing units (neurons) that are visualized by circles. They first compute the linear combination of the feature vector x and the weights w: $w^\top x + b$. Then, a nonlinear activation function f is applied. For the two-class case, the activation function simply is $\text{sgn}(w^\top x + b)$, that is, the side of the hyperplane on which the feature vector lies. Hence, the output is mapped to its essence: -1 or $+1$.

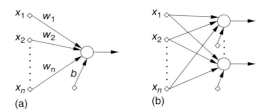

Figure 9.140 Architecture of a linear classifier expressed as a neural network (single-layer perceptron). (a) A two-class neural network. (b) An n-class neural network. In both cases, the neural network has a single layer of processing units that are visualized by circles. They first compute the linear combination of the feature vector and the weights. After this, a nonlinear activation function is computed, which maps the output to -1 or $+1$ (two-class neural network) or 0 or 1 (n-class neural network).

Note that this type of activation function essentially thresholds the input value. For the n-class case, the activation function f is typically chosen such that input values $\ll 0$ are mapped to 0, while input values ≥ 0 are mapped to 1. The goal in this approach is that a single processing unit returns the value 1, while all other units return the value 0. The index of the unit that returns 1 indicates the class of the feature vector. Note that the plane in equation (9.178) needs to be modified for this activation function to work since the plane is chosen such that the feature vectors have the largest distance from the plane. Therefore, $w_j^\top x + b_j$ is not necessarily <0 for all values that do not belong to the class. Nevertheless, the two definitions are equivalent. Note that, because the neural network has one layer of processing units, this type of neural network is also called a single-layer perceptron.

While linear classifiers are simple and easy to understand, they have very limited classification capabilities. By construction, the classes must be linearly separable, that is, separable by a hyperplane, for the classifier to produce the correct output. Unfortunately, this is rarely the case in practice. In fact, linear classifiers are unable to represent a simple function like the XOR function, as illustrated in Figure 9.141, because there is no line that can separate the two classes. Furthermore, for n-class linear classifiers, there is often no separating hyperplane for each class against all the other classes, although each pair of classes can be separated by a hyperplane. This happens, for example, if the samples of one class lie completely within the convex hull of all the other classes.

To get a classifier that is able to construct more general separating hypersurfaces, one approach is simply to add more layers to the neural network, as shown in Figure 9.142. Each layer first computes the linear combination of the feature

Figure 9.141 A linear classifier is not able to represent the XOR function because the two classes, corresponding to the two outputs of the XOR function, cannot be separated by a single line.

Figure 9.142 Architecture of a multilayer perceptron. The neural network has multiple layers of processing units that are visualized by circles. They compute the linear combination of the results of the previous layer and the network weights, and then pass the results through a nonlinear activation function.

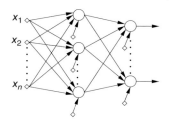

vector or the results from the previous layer:

$$a_j^{(l)} = \sum_{i=1}^{n_l} w_{ji}^{(l)} x_i^{(l-1)} + b_j^{(l)} \tag{9.179}$$

Here, $x_i^{(0)}$ is simply the feature vector, while $x_i^{(l)}$, with $l \geq 1$, is the result vector of layer l. The coefficients $w_{ji}^{(l)}$ and $b_j^{(l)}$ are the weights of layer l. Then, the results are passed through a nonlinear activation function

$$x_j^{(l)} = f(a_j^{(l)}) \tag{9.180}$$

Let us assume for the moment that the activation function in each processing unit is the threshold function that is also used in the single-layer perceptron, that is, the function that maps input values <0 to 0 while mapping input values ≥ 0 to 1. Then, it can be seen that the first layer of processing units maps the feature space to the corners of the hypercube $\{0, 1\}^p$, where p is the number of processing units in the first layer. Hence, the feature space is subdivided by hyperplanes into half-spaces [132]. The second layer of processing units separates the points on the hypercube by hyperplanes. This corresponds to intersections of half-spaces, that is, convex polyhedra. Hence, the second layer is capable of constructing the boundaries of convex polyhedra as the separating hypersurfaces [132]. This is still not general enough however, since the separating hypersurfaces might need to be more complex than this. If a third layer is added, the network can compute unions of the convex polyhedra [132]. Hence, three layers are sufficient to approximate any separating hypersurface arbitrarily closely if the threshold function is used as the activation function.

In practice, the above threshold function is rarely used because it has a discontinuity at $x = 0$, which is very detrimental for the determination of the network weights by numerical optimization. Instead, often a sigmoid activation function is used, for example, the logistic function (see Figure 9.143a)

$$f(x) = \frac{1}{1 + e^x} \tag{9.181}$$

Similar to the hard threshold function, it maps its input to a value between 0 and 1. However, it is continuous and differentiable, which is a requirement for most numerical optimization algorithms. Another choice for the activation functions is to use the hyperbolic tangent function (see Figure 9.143b)

$$f(x) = \tanh(x) = \frac{e^x - e^{-x}}{e^x + e^{-x}} \tag{9.182}$$

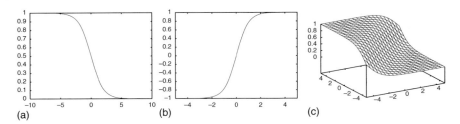

Figure 9.143 (a) Logistic activation function (9.181). (b) Hyperbolic tangent activation function (9.182). (c) Softmax activation function (9.183) for two classes.

in all layers except the output layer, in which the softmax activation function is used [139] (see Figure 9.143c)

$$f(x) = \frac{e^{x_i}}{\sum_{j=1}^{m} e^{x_j}} \qquad (9.183)$$

The hyperbolic tangent function behaves similar to the logistic function. The major difference is that it maps its input to values between −1 and +1. There is experimental evidence that the hyperbolic tangent function leads to a faster training of the network [139]. In the output layer, the softmax function maps the input to the range [0,1], as desired. Furthermore, it ensures that the output values sum to 1, and hence have the same properties as a probability density [139]. With any of these choices of the activation function, it can be shown that two layers are sufficient to approximate any separating hypersurface and, in fact, any output function with values in [0,1], arbitrarily closely [139]. The only requirement for this is that there is a sufficient number of processing units in the first layer (the "hidden layer").

After having discussed the architecture of the multilayer perceptron, we can now examine how the network is trained. Training the network means that the weights $w_{ji}^{(l)}$ and $b_j^{(l)}$, with $l = 1, 2$, of the network must be determined. Let us denote the number of input features by n_i, the number of hidden units (first layer units) by n_h, and the number of output units (second layer units) by n_o. Note that n_i is the dimensionality of the feature vector, while n_o is the number of classes in the classifier. Hence, the only free parameter is the number n_h of units in the hidden layer. Note that there are $(n_i + 1)n_h + (n_h + 1)n_o$ weights in total. For example, if $n_i = 81$, $n_h = 40$, and $n_o = 10$, there are 3690 weights that must be determined. It is clear that this is a very complex problem and that we can hope to determine the weights uniquely only if the number of training samples is of the same order of magnitude as the number of weights.

As described previously, the training of the network is performed based on a training set, which consists of sample feature vectors x_k with corresponding class labels ω_k, for $k = 1, \ldots, l$. The sample feature vectors can be used as they are. The class labels, however, must be transformed into a representation that can be used in an optimization procedure. As described previously, ideally we would like to have the multilayer perceptron return a 1 in the output unit that corresponds to the class of the sample. Hence, a suitable representation of the classes is a target vector $y_k \in \{0, 1\}^{n_o}$, chosen such that there is a 1 at the index that corresponds to the class of the sample and a 0 in all other positions. With this, we can train the network by minimizing, for example, the squared error of the outputs of the network on all the training samples [139]. In the notation of equation (9.180), we would like to minimize

$$\varepsilon = \sum_{k=1}^{l} \sum_{j=1}^{n_o} (x_j^{(2)} - y_{k,j})^2 \qquad (9.184)$$

Here, $y_{k,j}$ is the jth element of the target vector y_k. Note that $x_j^{(2)}$ implicitly depends on all the weights $w_{ji}^{(l)}$ and $b_j^{(l)}$ of the network. Hence, minimization of equation (9.184) determines the optimum weights. To minimize equation (9.184), for a long time the back-propagation algorithm was used, which successively inputs each training sample into the network, determines the output error, and derives a correction term for the weights from the error. It can be shown that this procedure corresponds to the steepest descent minimization algorithm, which is well known to converge extremely slowly [18]. Currently, the minimization of equation (9.184) is typically being performed by sophisticated numerical minimization algorithms, such as the conjugate gradient algorithm [18, 139] or the scaled conjugate gradient algorithm [139].

Another approach to obtain a classifier that is able to construct arbitrary separating hypersurfaces is to transform the feature vector into a space of higher dimension, in which the features are linearly separable, and to use a linear classifier in the higher dimensional space. Classifiers of this type have been known for a long time as generalized linear classifiers [132]. One instance of this approach is the polynomial classifier, which transforms the feature vector by a polynomial of degree $\leq d$. For example, for $d = 2$ the transformation is

$$\Phi(x_1, \ldots, x_n) = (x_1, \ldots, x_n, x_1^2, \ldots, x_1 x_n, x_2^2 \cdots, x_2 x_n, \ldots, x_n^2) \qquad (9.185)$$

The problem with this approach is again the curse of dimensionality: the dimension of the feature space grows exponentially with the degree d of the polynomial. In fact, there are $\binom{d+n-1}{d}$ monomials of degree $= d$ alone. Hence, the dimension of the transformed feature space is

$$n' = \sum_{i=1}^{d} \binom{i+n-1}{i} = \binom{d+n}{d} - 1 \qquad (9.186)$$

For example, if $n = 81$ and $d = 5$, the dimension is 34 826 301. Even for $d = 2$, the dimension already is 3402. Hence, transforming the features into the larger feature space seems to be infeasible, at least from an efficiency point of view. Fortunately, however, there is an elegant way to perform the classification with generalized linear classifiers that avoids the curse of dimensionality. This is achieved by support vector machine (SVM) classifiers [140, 141].

Before we can take a look at how SVMs avoid the curse of dimensionality, we have to take a closer look at how the optimal separating hyperplane can be constructed. Let us consider the two-class case. As described in equation (9.177) for linear classifiers, the separating hyperplane is given by $w^\top x + b = 0$. As noted previously, the classification is performed based on the sign of $w^\top x + b$. Hence, the

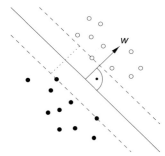

Figure 9.144 Optimal separating hyperplane between two classes. The samples of the two classes are represented by the filled and unfilled circles. The hyperplane is shown by the solid line. The margin is shown by the dotted line between the two dashed lines that show the hyperplanes in which samples are on the margin, that is, attain the minimum distance between the classes. The samples on the margin define the separating hyperplane. Since they "support" the margin hyperplanes, they are called support vectors.

classification function is

$$f(x) = \text{sgn}(w^\top x + b) \tag{9.187}$$

Let the training samples be denoted by x_i and their corresponding class labels by $y_i = \pm 1$. Then, a feature is classified correctly if $y_i(w^\top x_i + b) > 0$. However, this restriction is not sufficient to determine the hyperplane uniquely. This can be achieved by requiring that the margin between the two classes be as large as possible. The margin is defined as the closest distance of any training sample to the separating hyperplane.

Let us look at a small example of the optimal separating hyperplane, shown in Figure 9.144. Note that, if we want to maximize the margin (shown as a dotted line), there will be samples from both classes that attain the minimum distance to the separating hyperplane defined by the margin. These samples "support" the two hyperplanes that have the margin as the distance to the separating hyperplane (shown as the dashed lines). Hence, the samples are called the support vectors.

In fact, the optimal separating hyperplane is defined entirely by the support vectors, that is, a subset of the training samples: $w = \sum_{i=1}^{l} \alpha_i y_i x_i$, for $\alpha_i \geq 0$, where $\alpha_i > 0$ if and only if the training sample is a support vector [140]. With this, the classification function can be written as

$$f(x) = \text{sgn}(w^\top x + b) = \text{sgn}\left(\sum_{i=1}^{l} \alpha_i y_i x_i^\top x + b\right) \tag{9.188}$$

Hence, to determine the optimal hyperplane, the coefficients α_i of the support vectors must be determined. This can be achieved by solving the following quadratic programming problem [140]: maximize

$$\sum_{i=1}^{l} \alpha_i - \frac{1}{2} \sum_{i=1}^{l} \sum_{j=1}^{l} \alpha_i \alpha_j y_i y_j x_i^\top x_j \tag{9.189}$$

subject to

$$\alpha_i \geq 0, \quad i = 1, \ldots, l, \quad \text{and} \quad \sum_{i=1}^{l} \alpha_i y_i = 0 \tag{9.190}$$

Note that in both the classification function (9.188) and the optimization function (9.189), the feature vectors x, x_i, and x_j only are present in the dot product.

We now turn our attention back to the case in which the feature vector x is first transformed into a higher dimensional space by a function $\Phi(x)$, for example, by the polynomial function in equation (9.185). Then, the only change in the above discussion is that we substitute the feature vectors x, x_i, and x_j by their transformations $\Phi(x)$, $\Phi(x_i)$, and $\Phi(x_j)$. Hence, the dot products are simply computed in the higher dimensional space. The dot products become functions of two input feature vectors: $\Phi(x)^\top \Phi(x')$. These dot products of transformed feature vectors are called kernels in the SVM literature and are denoted by $k(x, x') = \Phi(x)^\top \Phi(x')$. Hence, the decision function becomes a function of the kernel $k(x, x')$:

$$f(x) = \text{sgn}\left(\sum_{i=1}^{l} \alpha_i y_i k(x_i, x) + b\right) \quad (9.191)$$

The same happens with the optimization function equation (9.189).

So far, it seems that we do not gain anything from the kernel because we still have to transform the data into a feature space of a prohibitively large dimension. The ingenious trick of the SVM classification is that, for a large class of kernels, the kernel can be evaluated efficiently without explicitly transforming the features into the higher dimensional space, thus making the evaluation of the classification function (9.191) feasible. For example, if we transform the features by a polynomial of degree d, it can be easily shown that

$$k(x, x') = (x^\top x')^d \quad (9.192)$$

Hence, the kernel can be evaluated solely based on the input features without going to the higher dimensional space. This kernel is called a homogeneous polynomial kernel. As another example, the transformation by a polynomial of degree $\leq d$ can simply be evaluated as

$$k(x, x') = (x^\top x' + 1)^d \quad (9.193)$$

This kernel is called an inhomogeneous polynomial kernel. Further examples of possible kernels include the Gaussian radial basis function kernel

$$k(x, x') = \exp\left(-\frac{\|x - x'\|^2}{2\sigma^2}\right) \quad (9.194)$$

and the sigmoid kernel

$$k(x, x') = \tanh(\kappa x^\top x' + \vartheta) \quad (9.195)$$

Note that this is the same function that is also used in the hidden layer of the multilayer perceptron. With any of the above four kernels, SVMs can approximate any separating hypersurface arbitrarily closely.

Note that the above training algorithm that determines the support vectors still assumes that the classes can be separated by a hyperplane in the higher dimensional transformed feature space. This may not always be achievable. Fortunately, the training algorithm can be extended to handle overlapping classes. The reader is referred to [140] for details.

By its nature, the SVM classification can handle only two-class problems. To extend the SVM to multiclass problems, two basic approaches are possible.

The first strategy is to perform a pairwise classification of the feature vector against all pairs of classes and to use the class that obtains the most votes, that is, is selected most often as the result of the pairwise classification. Note that this implies that $m(m-1)/2$ classifications have to be performed if there are m classes. The second strategy is to perform m classifications of one class against the union of the rest of the classes. From an efficiency point of view, the second strategy may be preferable since it depends linearly on the number of classes. Note, however, that in the second strategy, typically there will be a larger number of support vectors than in the pairwise classification. Since the runtime depends linearly on the number of support vectors, this number must grow less than quadratically for the second strategy to be faster.

After having discussed the different types of classifiers, the natural question to ask is which of the classifiers should be used in practice. First of all, it must be noted that the quality of the classification results of all the classifiers depends to a large degree on the size and quality of the training set. Therefore, to construct a good classifier, the training set should be as large and as representative as possible.

If the main criterion for comparing classifiers is the classification accuracy, that is, the error rate on an independent test set, classifiers that construct the separating hypersurfaces, that is, the multilayer perceptron or the SVM, should be preferred. Of these two, the SVM is portrayed to have a slight advantage [140]. This advantage, however, is achieved by building certain invariances into the classifier that do not generalize to other classification tasks apart from OCR and a particular set of gray value features. The invariances built into the classifier in [140] are translations of the character by one pixel, rotations, and variations of the stroke width of the character. With the features in Section 9.12.2, the translation invariance is automatically achieved. The remaining invariances could also be achieved by extending the training set by systematically modified training samples. Therefore, neither the multilayer perceptron nor the SVM has a definite advantage in terms of classification accuracy.

Another criterion is the training speed. Here, SVMs have some advantage over the multilayer perceptron because the training times are often shorter. Therefore, if the speed in the training phase is important, SVMs currently should be preferred. Unfortunately, the picture is reversed in the online phase when unknown features must be classified. As noted previously, the classification time for the SVMs depends linearly on the number of support vectors, which usually is a substantial fraction of the training samples (typically, between 10% and 40%). Hence, if the training set consists of several hundred thousands of samples, tens of thousands of support vectors must be evaluated with the kernel in the online phase. In contrast, the classification time of the multilayer perceptron depends only on the topology of the net, that is, the number of processing units per layer. Therefore, if the speed in the online classification phase is important, the multilayer perceptron currently should be preferred.

A final criterion is whether the classifier provides a simple means to decide whether the feature vector to be classified should be rejected because it does not belong to any of the trained classes. For example, if only digits have been trained, but the segmented character is the letter "M," it is important in some applications to be able to reject the character as being no digit. Another example is an erroneous segmentation, that is, a segmentation of an image part that corresponds to no character at all. Here, classifiers that construct the separating

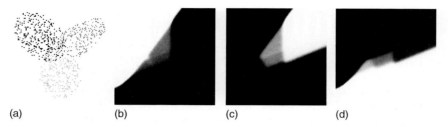

(a)   (b)   (c)   (d)

Figure 9.145 (a) Samples in a 2D feature space for three classes, which are visualized by three gray levels. (b) Likelihood for class 1 determined in a square region of the feature space with a multilayer perceptron with five hidden units. (c) Likelihood for class 2. (d) Likelihood for class 3. Note that all classes have a very high likelihood for feature vectors that are far away from the training samples of each class. For example, class 3 has a very high likelihood in the lower corners of the displayed portion of the feature space. This high likelihood continues to infinity because of the architecture of the multilayer perceptron.

hypersurfaces provide no means to tell whether the feature vector is close to a class in some sense, since the only criterion is on which side of the separating hypersurface the feature lies. For the SVMs, this behavior is obvious from the architecture of the classifier. For the multilayer perceptron, this behavior is not immediately obvious since, as we have noted, the softmax activation function (9.183) has the same properties as a probability density. Hence, one could assume that the output reflects the likelihood of each class, and can thus be used to threshold unlikely classes. In practice, however, the likelihood is very close to 1 or 0 everywhere, except in areas in which the classes overlap in the training samples, as shown by the example in Figure 9.145. Note that all classes have a very high likelihood for feature vectors that are far away from the training samples of each class.

As can be seen from the above discussion, the behaviors of the multilayer perceptron and the SVMs are identical with respect to samples that lie far away from the training samples: they provide no means to evaluate the closeness of a sample to the training set. In applications where it is important that feature vectors can be rejected as not belonging to any class, there are two options. First, we can train an explicit rejection class. The problem with this approach is how to obtain or construct the samples for the rejection class. Second, we can use a classifier that provides a measure of closeness to the training samples, such as the Gaussian mixture model classifier. However, in this case we have to be prepared to accept slightly higher error rates for feature vectors that are close to the training samples.

We conclude this section with an example that uses the ICs that we have already used in Section 9.4. In this application, the goal is to read the characters in the last two lines of the print in the ICs. Figure 9.146a,b shows images of two sample ICs. The segmentation is performed with a threshold that is selected automatically based on the gray value histogram (see Figure 9.23). After this, the last two lines of characters are selected based on the smallest surrounding rectangle of the characters. For this, the character with the largest row coordinate is determined and characters lying within an interval above this character are selected. Furthermore, irrelevant characters like the "−" are suppressed based on the height of the characters. The characters are classified with a multilayer perceptron that has been trained with several tens of thousands of samples of characters on electronic components, which do not include the characters on the

(a)   (b)

```
    M5I8222 30              CXD1175AM
     6285352                 648E10E
    M5 I822 2 30            CXD1175AM
    6 2853 52               6 4 8 E1 0 E
```

(c)   (d)

Figure 9.146 (a,b) Images of prints on ICs. (c,d) Result of the segmentation of the characters (light gray) and the OCR (black). The images are segmented with a threshold that is selected automatically based on the gray value histogram (see Figure 9.23). Furthermore, only the last two lines of characters are selected. Additionally, irrelevant characters like the "–" are suppressed based on the height of the characters.

ICs in Figure 9.146. The result of the segmentation and classification is shown in Figure 9.146c,d. Note that all characters have been read correctly.

References

1 Hagen, N. and Kudenov, M.W. (2013) Review of snapshot spectral imaging technologies. *Opt. Eng.*, **52** (9), 090 901-1–090 901-23.
2 Lapray, P.J., Wang, X., Thomas, J.B., and Gouton, P. (2014) Multispectral filter arrays: recent advances and practical implementation. *Sensors*, **14** (11), 21 626–21 659.
3 ISO 14524:2009. (2009) Photography – Electronic Still-Picture Cameras – Methods for Measuring Opto-Electronic Conversion Functions (OECFs), ISO, Geneva.
4 Mann, S. and Mann, R. (2001) Quantigraphic imaging: estimating the camera response and exposures from differently exposed images. Computer Vision and Pattern Recognition, vol. **I**, pp. 842–849.
5 Mitsunaga, T. and Nayar, S.K. (1999) Radiometric self calibration. Computer Vision and Pattern Recognition, vol. **I**, pp. 374–380.
6 Papoulis, A. (1991) *Probability, Random Variables, and Stochastic Processes*, 3rd edn, McGraw-Hill, New York.
7 Deriche, R. (1990) Fast algorithms for low-level vision. *IEEE Trans. Pattern Anal. Mach. Intell.*, **12** (1), 78–87.

8 Lindeberg, T. (1994) *Scale-Space Theory in Computer Vision*, Kluwer Academic, Dordrecht.
 9 Witkin, A.P. (1983) Scale-space filtering. 8th International Joint Conference on Artificial Intelligence, vol. **2**, pp. 1019–1022.
10 Babaud, J., Witkin, A.P., Baudin, M., and Duda, R.O. (1986) Uniqueness of the Gaussian kernel for scale-space filtering. *IEEE Trans. Pattern Anal. Mach. Intell.*, **8** (1), 26–33.
11 Florack, L.M.J., ter Haar Romeny, B.M., Koenderink, J.J., and Viergever, M.A. (1992) Scale and the differential structure of images. *Image Vision Comput.*, **10** (6), 376–388.
12 Deriche, R. (1993) Recursively Implementing the Gaussian and its Derivatives. Rapport de Recherche 1893, INRIA, Sophia Antipolis.
13 Young, I.T. and Lucas van Vliet, J. (1995) Recursive implementation of the Gaussian filter. *Signal Process.*, **44**, 139–151.
14 Huang, T.S., Yang, G.J., and Tang, G.Y. (1979) A fast two-dimensional median filtering algorithm. *IEEE Trans. Acoust. Speech Signal Process.*, **27** (1), 13–18.
15 Van Droogenbroeck, M. and Talbot, H. (1996) Fast computation of morphological operations with arbitrary structuring elements. *Pattern Recognit. Lett.*, **17** (14), 1451–1460.
16 Perreault, S. and Hébert, P. (2007) Median filtering in constant time. *IEEE Trans. Image Process.*, **16** (9), 2389–2394.
17 Brigham, E.O. (1988) *The Fast Fourier Transform and its Applications*, Prentice-Hall, Upper Saddle River, NJ.
18 Press, W.H., Teukolsky, S.A., Vetterling, W.T., and Flannery, B.P. (1992) *Numerical Recipes in C: The Art of Scientific Computing*, 2nd edn, Cambridge University Press, Cambridge.
19 Frigo, M. and Johnson, S.G. (2005) The design and implementation of FFTW3. *Proc. IEEE*, **93** (2), 216–231.
20 Hartley, R. and Zisserman, A. (2003) *Multiple View Geometry in Computer Vision*, 2nd edn, Cambridge University Press, Cambridge.
21 Faugeras, O. and Luong, Q.T. (2001) *The Geometry of Multiple Images: The Laws That Govern the Formation of Multiple Images of a Scene and Some of Their Applications*, MIT Press, Cambridge, MA.
22 Haralick, R.M. and Shapiro, L.G. (1992) *Computer and Robot Vision*, vol. **I**, Addison-Wesley, Reading, MA.
23 Jain, R., Kasturi, R., and Schunck, B.G. (1995) *Machine Vision*, McGraw-Hill, New York.
24 Otsu, N. (1979) A threshold selection method from gray-level histograms. *IEEE Trans. Syst. Man Cybern.*, **9** (1), 62–66.
25 Sedgewick, R. (1990) *Algorithms in C*, Addison-Wesley, Reading, MA.
26 Hu, M.K. (1962) Visual pattern recognition by moment invariants. *IRE Trans. Inf. Theory*, **8**, 179–187.
27 Flusser, J. and Suk, T. (1993) Pattern recognition by affine moment invariants. *Pattern Recognit.*, **26** (1), 167–174.

28 Mamistvalov, A.G. (1998) n-dimensional moment invariants and conceptual mathematical theory of recognition n-dimensional solids. *IEEE Trans. Pattern Anal. Mach. Intell.*, **20** (8), 819–831.
29 Toussaint, G. (1983) Solving geometric problems with the rotating calipers. Proceedings of IEEE MELECON '83, IEEE Press, Los Alamitos, CA, pp. A10.02/1–4.
30 Welzl, E. (1991) Smallest enclosing disks (balls and ellipsoids), in *New Results and Trends in Computer Science*, Lecture Notes in Computer Science, vol. **555** (ed. H. Maurer), Springer-Verlag, Berlin, pp. 359–370.
31 de Berg, M., van Kreveld, M., Overmars, M., and Schwarzkopf, O. (2000) *Computational Geometry: Algorithms and Applications*, 2nd edn, Springer-Verlag, Berlin.
32 O'Rourke, J. (1998) *Computational Geometry in C*, 2nd edn, Cambridge University Press, Cambridge.
33 Mendel, J.M. (1995) Fuzzy logic systems for engineering: a tutorial. *Proc. IEEE*, **83** (3), 345–377.
34 Steger, C. (1996) On the Calculation of Arbitrary Moments of Polygons. Technical Report FGBV–96–05, Forschungsgruppe Bildverstehen (FG BV), Informatik IX, Technische Universität München.
35 Soille, P. (2003) *Morphological Image Analysis*, 2nd edn, Springer-Verlag, Berlin.
36 Bloomberg, D.S. (2002) Implementation efficiency of binary morphology. International Symposium on Mathematical Morphology VI, pp. 209–218.
37 Lam, L., Lee, S.W., and Suen, C.Y. (1992) Thinning methodologies – a comprehensive survey. *IEEE Trans. Pattern Anal. Mach. Intell.*, **14** (9), 869–885.
38 Eckhardt, U. and Maderlechner, G. (1993) Invariant thinning. *Int. J. Pattern Recognit. Artif. Intell.*, **7** (5), 1115–1144.
39 Borgefors, G. (1984) Distance transformation in arbitrary dimensions. *Comput. Vision Graph. Image Process.*, **27**, 321–345.
40 Danielsson, P.E. (1980) Euclidean distance mapping. *Comput. Graph. Image Process.*, **14**, 227–248.
41 Moganti, M., Ercal, F., Dagli, C.H., and Tsunekawa, S. (1996) Automatic PCB inspection algorithms: a survey. *Comput. Vision Image Understanding*, **63** (2), 287–313.
42 Gil, J. and Kimmel, R. (2002) Efficient dilation, erosion, opening, and closing algorithms. *IEEE Trans. Pattern Anal. Mach. Intell.*, **24** (12), 1606–1617.
43 Canny, J. (1986) A computational approach to edge detection. *IEEE Trans. Pattern Anal. Mach. Intell.*, **8** (6), 679–698.
44 Deriche, R. (1987) Using Canny's criteria to derive a recursively implemented optimal edge detector. *Int. J. Comput. Vision*, **1**, 167–187.
45 Steger, C. (1998) Unbiased extraction of curvilinear structures from 2D and 3D images. PhD thesis. Fakultät für Informatik, Technische Universität München. Herbert Utz Verlag, München.
46 Ando, S. (2000) Consistent gradient operators. *IEEE Trans. Pattern Anal. Mach. Intell.*, **22** (3), 252–265.

47 Lanser, S. and Eckstein, W. (1992) A modification of Deriche's approach to edge detection. 11th International Conference on Pattern Recognition, vol. **III**, pp. 633–637.
48 Steger, C. (2000) Subpixel-precise extraction of lines and edges. International Archives of Photogrammetry and Remote Sensing, vol. **XXXIII**, Part B3, pp. 141–156.
49 Haralick, R.M., Watson, L.T., and Laffey, T.J. (1983) The topographic primal sketch. *Int. J. Rob. Res.*, **2** (1), 50–72.
50 Haralick, R.M. and Shapiro, L.G. (1993) *Computer and Robot Vision*, vol. **II**, Addison-Wesley, Reading, MA.
51 JCGM 200:2012. (2012) International vocabulary of metrology – Basic and general concepts and associated terms (VIM), 3rd edition, JCGM.
52 Steger, C. (1998) Analytical and empirical performance evaluation of subpixel line and edge detection, in *Empirical Evaluation Methods in Computer Vision* (eds K.J. Bowyer and P.J. Phillips), IEEE Computer Society Press, Los Alamitos, CA, pp. 188–210.
53 Berzins, V. (1984) Accuracy of Laplacian edge detectors. *Comput. Vision Graph. Image Process.*, **27**, 195–210.
54 Lenz, R. and Fritsch, D. (1990) Accuracy of videometry with CCD sensors. *ISPRS J. Photogramm. Remote Sens.*, **45** (2), 90–110.
55 Lanser, S. (1997) Modellbasierte Lokalisation gestützt auf monokulare Videobilder. PhD thesis. Forschungs- und Lehreinheit Informatik IX, Technische Universität München. Shaker Verlag, Aachen.
56 Holland, P.W. and Welsch, R.E. (1977) Robust regression using iteratively reweighted least-squares. *Commun. Stat. Theory Methods*, **6** (9), 813–827.
57 Stewart, C.V. (1999) Robust parameter estimation in computer vision. *SIAM Rev.*, **41** (3), 513–537.
58 Huber, P.J. (1981) *Robust Statistics*, John Wiley & Sons, Inc., New York.
59 Mosteller, F. and Tukey, J.W. (1977) *Data Analysis and Regression*, Addison-Wesley, Reading, MA.
60 Fischler, M.A. and Bolles, R.C. (1981) Random sample consensus: a paradigm for model fitting with applications to image analysis and automated cartography. *Commun. ACM*, **24** (6), 381–395.
61 Joseph, S.H. (1994) Unbiased least squares fitting of circular arcs. *CVGIP: Graph. Models Image Process.*, **56** (5), 424–432.
62 Ahn, S.J., Rauh, W., and Warnecke, H.J. (2001) Least-squares orthogonal distances fitting of circle, sphere, ellipse, hyperbola, and parabola. *Pattern Recognit.*, **34** (12), 2283–2303.
63 Fitzgibbon, A., Pilu, M., and Fisher, R.B. (1999) Direct least square fitting of ellipses. *IEEE Trans. Pattern Anal. Mach. Intell.*, **21** (5), 476–480.
64 Lanser, S., Zierl, C., and Beutlhauser, R. (1995) Multibildkalibrierung einer CCD-Kamera, in *Mustererkennung, Informatik aktuell* (eds G. Sagerer, S. Posch, and F. Kummert), Springer-Verlag, Berlin, pp. 481–491.
65 Heikkilä, J. (2000) Geometric camera calibration using circular control points. *IEEE Trans. Pattern Anal. Mach. Intell.*, **22** (10), 1066–1077.
66 Rosin, P.L. (1997) Techniques for assessing polygonal approximations of curves. *IEEE Trans. Pattern Anal. Mach. Intell.*, **19** (6), 659–666.

67 Rosin, P.L. (2003) Assessing the behaviour of polygonal approximation algorithms. *Pattern Recognit.*, **36** (2), 508–518.

68 Ramer, U. (1972) An iterative procedure for the polygonal approximation of plane curves. *Comput. Graph. Image Process.*, **1**, 244–256.

69 Wuescher, D.M. and Boyer, K.L. (1991) Robust contour decomposition using a constant curvature criterion. *IEEE Trans. Pattern Anal. Mach. Intell.*, **13** (1), 41–51.

70 Sheu, H.T. and Hu, W.C. (1999) Multiprimitive segmentation of planar curves – a two-level breakpoint classification and tuning approach. *IEEE Trans. Pattern Anal. Mach. Intell.*, **21** (8), 791–797.

71 Chen, J.M., Ventura, J.A., and Wu, C.H. (1996) Segmentation of planar curves into circular arcs and line segments. *Image Vision Comput.*, **14** (1), 71–83.

72 Rosin, P.L. and West, G.A.W. (1995) Nonparametric segmentation of curves into various representations. *IEEE Trans. Pattern Anal. Mach. Intell.*, **17** (12), 1140–1153.

73 Brown, D.C. (1971) Close-range camera calibration. *Photogramm. Eng.*, **37** (8), 855–866.

74 Gruen, A. and Huang, T.S. (eds) (2001) *Calibration and Orientation of Cameras in Computer Vision*, Springer-Verlag, Berlin.

75 Gupta, R. and Hartley, R.I. (1997) Linear pushbroom cameras. *IEEE Trans. Pattern Anal. Mach. Intell.*, **19** (9), 963–975.

76 Ahn, S.J., Warnecke, H.J., and Kotowski, R. (1999) Systematic geometric image measurement errors of circular object targets: mathematical formulation and correction. *Photogramm. Rec.*, **16** (93), 485–502.

77 Faugeras, O. (1993) *Three-Dimensional Computer Vision: A Geometric Viewpoint*, MIT Press, Cambridge, MA.

78 Scharstein, D. and Szeliski, R. (2002) A taxonomy and evaluation of dense two-frame stereo correspondence algorithms. *Int. J. Comput. Vision*, **47** (1–3), 7–42.

79 Brown, M.Z., Burschka, D., and Hager, G.D. (2003) Advances in computational stereo. *IEEE Trans. Pattern Anal. Mach. Intell.*, **25** (8), 993–1008.

80 Scharstein, D. and Szeliski, R. Middlebury stereo vision page, http://vision.middlebury.edu/stereo/ (accessed 16 February 2015).

81 Geiger, A., Lenz, P., Stiller, C., and Urtasun, R. The KITTI vision benchmark suite, http://www.cvlibs.net/datasets/kitti/ (accessed 16 February 2015).

82 Hirschmüller, H., Innocent, P.R., and Garibaldi, J. (2002) Real-time correlation-based stereo vision with reduced border errors. *Int. J. Comput. Vision*, **47** (1–3), 229–246.

83 Mühlmann, K., Maier, D., Hesser, J., and Männer, R. (2002) Calculating dense disparity maps from color stereo images, an efficient implementation. *Int. J. Comput. Vision*, **47** (1–3), 79–88.

84 Hirschmüller, H. and Scharstein, D. (2009) Evaluation of stereo matching costs on images with radiometric differences. *IEEE Trans. Pattern Anal. Mach. Intell.*, **31** (9), 1582–1599.

85 Faugeras, O., Hotz, B., Mathieu, H., Viéville, T., Zhang, Z., Fua, P., Théron, E., Moll, L., Berry, G., Vuillemin, J., Bertin, P., and Proy, C. (1993) Real Time

Correlation-based Stereo: Algorithm, Implementations and Applications. Rapport de Recherche 2013, INRIA, Sophia Antipolis.
86. Hu, X. and Mordohai, P. (2012) A quantitative evaluation of confidence measures for stereo vision. *IEEE Trans. Pattern Anal. Mach. Intell.*, **34** (11), 2121–2133.
87. Brown, L.G. (1992) A survey of image registration techniques. *ACM Comput. Surv.*, **24** (4), 325–376.
88. Di Stefano, L., Mattoccia, S., and Mola, M. (2003) An efficient algorithm for exhaustive template matching based on normalized cross correlation. 12th International Conference on Image Analysis and Processing, pp. 322–327.
89. Gharavi-Alkhansari, M. (2001) A fast globally optimal algorithm for template matching using low-resolution pruning. *IEEE Trans. Image Process.*, **10** (4), 526–533.
90. Hel-Or, Y. and Hel-Or, H. (2003) Real time pattern matching using projection kernels. 9th International Conference on Computer Vision, vol. **2**, pp. 1486–1493.
91. Tanimoto, S.L. (1981) Template matching in pyramids. *Comput. Graph. Image Process.*, **16**, 356–369.
92. Glazer, F., Reynolds, G., and Anandan, P. (1983) Scene matching by hierarchical correlation. Computer Vision and Pattern Recognition, pp. 432–441.
93. Tian, Q. and Huhns, M.N. (1986) Algorithms for subpixel registration. *Comput. Vision Graph. Image Process.*, **35**, 220–233.
94. Lai, S.H. and Fang, M. (1999) Accurate and fast pattern localization algorithm for automated visual inspection. *Real-Time Imaging*, **5** (1), 3–14.
95. Anisimov, V.A. and Gorsky, N.D. (1993) Fast hierarchical matching of an arbitrarily oriented template. *Pattern Recognit. Lett.*, **14** (2), 95–101.
96. Förstner, W. (1994) A framework for low level feature extraction, in *3rd European Conference on Computer Vision*, Lecture Notes in Computer Science, vol. **801** (ed. J.O. Eklundh), Springer-Verlag, Berlin, pp. 383–394.
97. Schmid, C., Mohr, R., and Bauckhage, C. (2000) Evaluation of interest point detectors. *Int. J. Comput. Vision*, **37** (2), 151–172.
98. Borgefors, G. (1988) Hierarchical chamfer matching: a parametric edge matching algorithm. *IEEE Trans. Pattern Anal. Mach. Intell.*, **10** (6), 849–865.
99. Rucklidge, W.J. (1997) Efficiently locating objects using the Hausdorff distance. *Int. J. Comput. Vision*, **24** (3), 251–270.
100. Kwon, O.K., Sim, D.G., and Park, R.H. (2001) Robust Hausdorff distance matching algorithms using pyramidal structures. *Pattern Recognit.*, **34**, 2005–2013.
101. Olson, C.F. and Huttenlocher, D.P. (1997) Automatic target recognition by matching oriented edge pixels. *IEEE Trans. Image Process.*, **6** (1), 103–113.
102. Ballard, D.H. (1981) Generalizing the Hough transform to detect arbitrary shapes. *Pattern Recognit.*, **13** (2), 111–122.
103. Hough, P.V.C. (1962) Method and means for recognizing complex patterns. US Patent 3 069 654.
104. Duda, R.O. and Hart, P.E. (1972) Use of the Hough transformation to detect lines and curves in pictures. *Commun. ACM*, **15** (1), 11–15.

105 Ulrich, M., Steger, C., and Baumgartner, A. (2003) Real-time object recognition using a modified generalized Hough transform. *Pattern Recognit.*, **36** (11), 2557–2570.

106 Lamdan, Y., Schwartz, J.T., and Wolfson, H.J. (1990) Affine invariant model-based object recognition. *IEEE Trans. Rob. Autom.*, **6** (5), 578–589.

107 Ayache, N. and Faugeras, O.D. (1986) HYPER: a new approach for the recognition and positioning of two-dimensional objects. *IEEE Trans. Pattern Anal. Mach. Intell.*, **8** (1), 44–54.

108 Grimson, W.E.L. and Lozano-Pérez, T. (1987) Localizing overlapping parts by searching the interpretation tree. *IEEE Trans. Pattern Anal. Mach. Intell.*, **9** (4), 469–482.

109 Koch, M.W. and Kashyap, R.L. (1987) Using polygons to recognize and locate partially occluded objects. *IEEE Trans. Pattern Anal. Mach. Intell.*, **9** (4), 483–494.

110 Ventura, J.A. and Wan, W. (1997) Accurate matching of two-dimensional shapes using the minimal tolerance error zone. *Image Vision Comput.*, **15**, 889–899.

111 Costa, M.S. and Shapiro, L.G. (2000) 3D object recognition and pose with relational indexing. *Comput. Vision Image Understanding*, **79** (3), 364–407.

112 Joseph, S.H. (1999) Analysing and reducing the cost of exhaustive correspondence search. *Image Vision Comput.*, **17**, 815–830.

113 Steger, C. (2001) Similarity measures for occlusion, clutter, and illumination invariant object recognition, in *Pattern Recognition*, Lecture Notes in Computer Science, vol. **2191** (eds B. Radig and S. Florczyk), Springer-Verlag, Berlin, pp. 148–154.

114 Steger, C. (2002) Occlusion, clutter, and illumination invariant object recognition. International Archives of Photogrammetry and Remote Sensing, vol. **XXXIV**, Part 3A, pp. 345–350.

115 Steger, C. (2005) System and method for object recognition. European Patent 1 193 642.

116 Steger, C. (2006) System and method for object recognition. Japanese Patent 3 776 340.

117 Steger, C. (2006) System and method for object recognition. US Patent 7 062 093.

118 Ulrich, M. and Steger, C. (2001) Empirical performance evaluation of object recognition methods, in *Empirical Evaluation Methods in Computer Vision* (eds H.I. Christensen and P.J. Phillips), IEEE Computer Society Press, Los Alamitos, CA, pp. 62–76.

119 Ulrich, M. and Steger, C. (2002) Performance comparison of 2D object recognition techniques. International Archives of Photogrammetry and Remote Sensing, vol. **XXXIV**, Part 3A, pp. 368–374.

120 Ulrich, M., Baumgartner, A., and Steger, C. (2002) Automatic hierarchical object decomposition for object recognition. International Archives of Photogrammetry and Remote Sensing, vol. **XXXIV**, Part 5, pp. 99–104.

121 Ulrich, M. (2003) *Hierarchical Real-Time Recognition of Compound Objects in Images, Reihe C*, vol. **569**, Deutsche Geodätische Kommission bei der Bayerischen Akademie der Wissenschaften, München.

122 Ulrich, M. and Steger, C. (2007) Hierarchical component based object recognition. US Patent 7 239 929.
123 Hofhauser, A., Steger, C., and Navab, N. (2008) Edge-based template matching and tracking for perspectively distorted planar objects, in *Advances in Visual Computing*, Lecture Notes in Computer Science, vol. **5358** (eds G. Bebis, R. Boyle, B. Parvin, D. Koracin, P. Remagnino, F. Porikli, J. Peters, J. Klosowski, L. Arns, Y.K. Chun, T.M. Rhyne, and L. Monroe), Springer-Verlag, Berlin, pp. 35–44.
124 Hofhauser, A. and Steger, C. (2012) System and method for deformable object recognition. US Patent 8 260 059.
125 Hofhauser, A., Steger, C., and Navab, N. (2009) Perspective planar shape matching, in *Image Processing: Machine Vision Applications II*, Proceedings of SPIE 7251 (eds K.S. Niel and D. Fofi), SPIE Press, Bellingham.
126 Hofhauser, A., Steger, C., and Navab, N. (2009) Edge-based template matching with a harmonic deformation model, in *Computer Vision and Computer Graphics: Theory and Applications International Conference VISIGRAPP 2008, Revised Selected Papers*, Communications in Computer and Information Science, vol. **24** (eds A.K. Ranchordas, H.J. Araujo, J.M. Pereira, and J. Braz), Springer-Verlag, Berlin, pp. 176–187.
127 Wiedemann, C., Ulrich, M., and Steger, C. (2008) Recognition and tracking of 3D objects, in *Pattern Recognition*, Lecture Notes in Computer Science, vol. **5096** (ed. G. Rigoll), Springer-Verlag, Berlin, pp. 132–141.
128 Ulrich, M., Wiedemann, C., and Steger, C. (2009) CAD-based recognition of 3D objects in monocular images. International Conference on Robotics and Automation, pp. 1191–1198.
129 Ulrich, M., Wiedemann, C., and Steger, C. (2012) Combining scale-space and similarity-based aspect graphs for fast 3D object recognition. *IEEE Trans. Pattern Anal. Mach. Intell.*, **34** (10), 1902–1914.
130 Wiedemann, C., Ulrich, M., and Steger, C. (2013) System and method for 3D object recognition. US Patent 8 379 014.
131 Casey, R.G. and Lecolinet, E. (1996) A survey of methods and strategies in character segmentation. *IEEE Trans. Pattern Anal. Mach. Intell.*, **18** (7), 690–706.
132 Theodoridis, S. and Koutroumbas, K. (1999) *Pattern Recognition*, Academic Press, San Diego, CA.
133 Webb, A. (1999) *Statistical Pattern Recognition*, Arnold Publishers, London.
134 Friedman, J.H., Bentley, J.L., and Finkel, R.A. (1977) An algorithm for finding best matches in logarithmic expected time. *ACM Trans. Math. Softw.*, **3** (3), 209–226.
135 Arya, S., Mount, D.M., Netanyahu, N.S., Silverman, R., and Wu, A.Y. (1998) An optimal algorithm for approximate nearest neighbor searching in fixed dimensions. *J. ACM*, **45** (6), 891–923.
136 Muja, M. and Lowe, D.G. (2014) Scalable nearest neighbor algorithms for high dimensional data. *IEEE Trans. Pattern Anal. Mach. Intell.*, **36** (11), 2227–2240.
137 Figueiredo, M.A.T. and Jain, A.K. (2002) Unsupervised learning of finite mixture models. *IEEE Trans. Pattern Anal. Mach. Intell.*, **24** (3), 381–396.

138 Wang, H.X., Luo, B., Zhang, Q.B., and Wei, S. (2004) Estimation for the number of components in a mixture model using stepwise split-and-merge EM algorithm. *Pattern Recognit. Lett.*, **25** (16), 1799–1809.

139 Bishop, C.M. (1995) *Neural Networks for Pattern Recognition*, Oxford University Press, Oxford.

140 Schölkopf, B. and Smola, A.J. (2002) *Learning with Kernels – Support Vector Machines, Regularization, Optimization, and Beyond*, MIT Press, Cambridge, MA.

141 Christianini, N. and Shawe-Taylor, J. (2000) *An Introduction to Support Vector Machines and Other Kernel-Based Learning Methods*, Cambridge University Press, Cambridge.

10

Machine Vision in Manufacturing
Peter Waszkewitz

Robert Bosch GmbH, Robert-Bosch-Platz 1. 70839 Gerlingen-Schillerhöhe, Germany

10.1 Introduction

The preceding chapters have given a far-reaching and detailed view of the world of machine vision, its elements, components, tools, and methods. A lot of the connections between the topics of the individual chapters have already been explored, for example, concerning the interactions of light, object surfaces, optics, and sensors. At this point, then, we have everything we need to create machine vision systems. But, of course, a machine vision system is not created in a void without relations to and constraints from the outer world, nor is it made up and determined by image processing components alone.

This chapter will try to illustrate the environment in which the tools, Technologies, and techniques presented in the previous chapters are applied and give a view of machine vision as a part of automation technology – admittedly with a certain bias toward (German) automotive applications; most of it should translate easily to other industrial environments, though.

The vast variety of existing and possible applications and solutions in this field renders any claim to completeness meaningless. This chapter will therefore try to give an idea of issues that may arise in the design of a machine vision system, what they may be related to, how they have been solved under particular circumstances, and what to watch out for. We will have to keep in mind, though, that there will always be a point where explanations and checklists end, and we will simply have to go out there and solve the problems we encounter.

10.1.1 The Machine Vision Market

Economic data changes faster than book editions. Nevertheless, they serve to underscore the dynamic development the field has undergone in recent years and will, as far as the indicators show, continue to do.

European market figures, available, for example, at [1, 2], show healthy growth of the machine vision sector, usually outstripping overall economic growth. The German market, for example, returned to its growth trajectory of the previous decade after a financial-crisis-related drop in 2009, reaching a new record volume in 2014 with further growth expected. Strongest growth took place in nonmanufacturing industries.

However, there is still growth in manufacturing, especially in the automotive industries. Not only are there the constantly increasing quality demands driving the traditional role of image processing as an inspection technology, but also the evolution of machine vision into an enabling technology, indispensable for many production processes. Vision-capable robots, be it autonomously moving robots, pick-and-place systems, or glue dispenser robots, are but one example of guiding and controlling processes through machine vision. Safety requirements are another driver of growth, for example, in the field of traceability or – again in the robotics area – for work environment surveillance and collision avoidance.

Market figures for North America paint a similar picture, exceeding expectations with double-digit growth and hitting record levels in 2014, and another record level in 2015, albeit at lower growth figures, as can be seen from press releases [3].

High labor costs in developed countries certainly remain an important factor for growth in automation technology and thus machine vision. The coupling between automation in general and machine vision in particular can be clearly seen in the connection between the increased use of industrial robots and that of machine vision. Only the combination with machine vision allows robotics to enter the field of robotic assistants, as was impressively demonstrated, for example, at the 2014 Hannover Messe Industrie with offerings from all major robotics players as well as newcomers like Rethink Robotics and Bosch [4].

In recent years, China has also become a major market for machine vision. Steadily growing labor costs in the "factory of the world" certainly play a role; another factor is the drive to achieve constant high quality ensured by tireless, objective machine vision systems. China also enjoys a disproportionate increase of robot installations, which also drives machine vision growth [1].

Despite the stagnation of CPU frequencies, computation power in PCs is still growing, allowing for increasingly sophisticated applications and achieving new speed records. The proliferation of 64-bit operating systems makes larger applications possible, that is, bigger images, higher resolution, more memory-intensive computation.

At the same time, novel small devices – typically systems-on-chip (SoC), often with integrated or easily connected cameras – enable new, powerful applications on a very small scale, with the potential to make machine vision a practically ubiquitous technology in an increasingly connected industry.

In addition, three-dimensional (3D) capturing and processing methods are gaining ground, leading in many applications to more robust and capable solutions than traditional methods based on two-dimensional (2D) images, as well as opening up new application areas – or making certain applications, like bin-picking, finally viable.

We have certainly yet to see the end of the possibilities, technologically as well as economically. From an application world largely dominated by 2D black-and-white images, machine vision has grown into a diverse area where color, depth, and motion play an increasing role leading to increasingly powerful, versatile, and cost-effective machine vision systems. Machine vision systems are already a common part of all kinds of production Environments, and it seems safe to assume that with decreasing size, increasing Power, and ever-tighter integration with robotics and automation technology, they will become a ubiquitous but nevertheless decisive element in the future of manufacturing as well as other industries.

10.2 Application Categories

Machine vision applications can be categorized in various ways. This section will introduce some terms that may help us to define a frame of reference to place machine vision systems in.

10.2.1 Types of Tasks

Many machine vision systems are highly specialized, designed to fulfill a unique and complicated task, and are thus special-purpose machines in themselves. Nevertheless, it is possible to identify some recurring types of applications, as a first frame of reference, as to what to expect from a new task.

The following categorization follows that in [5] and [6] with one exception: it seemed appropriate to make code recognition a category of its own, since code reading does not have much to do with actual characteristics of the workpiece (like size, shape, etc.), and even more so because scanners, which many users probably would not even identify as image processing systems, have come into such widespread use as specialized devices.

This leads to the following categories:

Code recognition denotes the identification of objects using markings on the objects; these are typically standardized bar codes or DataMatrix codes, but can also be custom codes. Typical applications are material flow control and logistics. Internally, methods from all areas of image processing are used, including, for example, edge detection, filtering, and positioning techniques.

Object recognition denotes the identification of objects using characteristic features like shape/geometry, dimensions, color, structure/topology, or texture. Object identification includes the distinction of object variants and has many applications, not least as an "auxiliary science" for many other tasks. For example, position recognition or completeness checks may require prior identification of the correct objects in the scene. Depending on the objects in question, this can be a simple task or an extremely complex one, especially in areas outside the manufacturing industry, like autonomous driving. Increasingly, 3D data is used for object recognition, literally adding a new dimension to this field and allowing for completely new ways of matching and evaluating object characteristics, for example, by comparison with computer-aided design (CAD) data.

Position recognition denotes the determination of position and orientation of an object – or a particular point of an object – in a predefined coordinate system, using feature computation and matching methods. Typical features are center of gravity coordinates and orientation angles. An important distinction is the dimensionality, that is, whether position and orientation have to be determined in two or three dimensions, where the term *pose* is typically used. Typical applications are robot guidance, pick-and-place operations, and insertion machines. An interesting variation is the reverse application, that is, using images to determine the location and orientation of the camera system itself, used, for example, by autonomous robots to determine their position.

Completeness check denotes a categorization of workpieces as correctly or incorrectly assembled; it checks whether all components are present and in the correct position, often as a precondition for passing the workpiece on to the next assembly step or as a final check before releasing the workpiece to be packed and delivered – or, one step later, the inspection of the package to be completely filled with products of the right type.

Shape and dimension check denotes the determination of geometrical quantities with a focus on precise and accurate measurements. The importance of this area increases in accordance with rising quality standards as products must meet ever tighter tolerance requirements. Applications can be found wherever work pieces or also tools have to be checked for compliance with nominal dimensions. Because of the required accuracy, these tasks typically impose high demands on sensor equipment as well as on the mechanical construction of the inspection station.

Surface inspection can be divided into *quantitative* surface inspection aiming at the determination of topographical features like roughness, and *qualitative* surface inspection where the focus is on the recognition of surface defects, such as dents, scratches, pollution, or deviations from desired surface characteristics, like color or texture. Quantitative measurements of geometrical properties may be required for judging the surface quality. Typical challenges in surface inspection applications are large datasets and computationally intensive algorithms, such as gray level statistics, Fourier transformation, and the like. Especially, qualitative surface inspection tasks are frequently difficult to specify formally, for example, compared to a dimensional check, and are often based on "fault catalogs" used by human inspectors. This makes this kind of surface inspection a natural field for the application of machine learning methods.

Of course, these categories are frequently mixed in real-world applications. Inspections of separate aspects of a part may belong to different categories – for example, reading a bar code with a serial number and performing a completeness check to ensure correct assembly, or the various types of applications support and enhance each other. For example, information gained from position recognition methods can be used to adapt a dimensional check to the precise location of the workpiece in the camera image.

An interesting mixture of categories are identification methods based not on codes applied to the objects but on the characteristics of the objects itself, as in [7] and [8]. Here, the purpose is the same as for code recognition; however, the objects are recognized directly, using methods from surface inspection, among others.

Sometimes, the context of the application somewhat obscures the type of the underlying task. For example, a rather new challenge is to avoid collisions of robotic assistants working with humans in the same area. On closer scrutiny, however, this is nothing but a sophisticated form of position recognition, coupled with a considerable amount of domain knowledge, for example, about the relative mobility of human limbs in relation to the torso, which may be identified as individual objects with a separate, but nevertheless related, pose.

10.2.2 Types of Production

Another important point for designing a machine vision system is the type of production the system is to work in. Dorf [9] lists three basic types of manufacturing:

Job-shop and batch production which produces in small lots or batches. Examples are tool and die making or casting in a foundry.

Mass production typically – but not necessarily – involving machines or assembly lines that manufacture discrete units repetitively. Volumes are high, and flexibility is comparatively low. Typically, assembly lines require at least partial stoppage for changeovers between different products.

Continuous production, which produces in a continuous flow. Examples are paper mills, refineries, or extrusion processes. Product volumes are typically very high, and the variety and flexibility possibly even lower than with mass production.

Of course, these types rarely occur in a pure form in real-world production. Mass production frequently requires parts made in job-shop style supplied to the assembly line, or raw materials for continuous flow production are prepared in batches. There are also gray areas, where, for example, production of very small parts is organized like continuous production although discrete units are produced.

Different types of manufacturing pose different demands on machine vision systems. Obviously there will not be a 1 : 1 assignment of requirements to particular production types, but some general tendencies can be noted.

10.2.2.1 Discrete Unit Production Versus Continuous Flow

As we will see in more detail in Section 10.8, it makes sense to contrast the first two categories from above as *discrete unit production* with *continuous flow production*.

In discrete unit production, it will typically be necessary to capture individual workpieces in an image. This will require some sort of trigger. In relatively slow production lines, for example, using a work-piece carrier transport system, it may suffice to have the control system bring the workpiece in position in front of the camera, possibly wait for some time to let remaining movement or vibrations decay, and then start the machine vision system.

In faster production lines – say bottling lines running at several bottles per second – appropriate sensors, for example, light barriers, will be required to determine the precise moment when the part is in the correct position for capturing.

As this type of fast mass production approximates continuous production, in that the parts are continually in motion, additional measures such as electronic shuttering and strobe lights may have to be taken to avoid motion blur in the image.

In the gray area of small parts produced in an almost continuous flow (like screws on a conveyor belt), we have the typical robot vision task of picking up the pieces fast enough. Obviously, a discrete unit trigger is very difficult to implement here. Rather, the image processing has to trigger itself, and perform the detection of objects within its field of view fast enough to allow the robot to clear the belt completely.

There is another important distinction. Actual continuous flow production – often called endless material production which is, of course, a fiction, nothing man-made is ever endless – requires appropriate algorithms. For example, when looking for surface defects exceeding a certain size, we cannot arbitrarily stop the image at some line, and then start acquiring a new image to have the convenience of evaluating individual rectangular images. This could lead to a defect cut in half and thus be missed. Either a strategy has to be devised to handle this with subsequent rectangular images, or algorithms have to be used that can handle continuous images efficiently, that is, images where continuously the first line is thrown away and a new line is added at the other end, without inefficient re-evaluation of the entire image section currently in view.

10.2.2.2 Job-Shop Production Versus Mass Production

There are mass-produced items coming in more than 1000 variants. However, new types can usually be introduced much faster in job-shop production. Mass-producing a new variant of a product will require many alterations and adjustments to a production line, a lot of test runs, and so forth, so that there is considerable time to adapt a machine vision system. Reliability and run-time diagnosis, as well as optimization features, are called for here.

The possibility to start producing new types – or even entirely new products – quite rapidly in job-shop production, on the other hand, puts more emphasis on the ease and speed with which a vision system can be reconfigured and adapted to perform a new task. Interactivity is much more of a concern here, so the type of production in this case may have a decisive influence on system design.

10.2.3 Types of Evaluations

Image processing can assume quite different roles in the manufacturing process.

It can be used for *inspection*, that is, checking after the production process whether the workpiece is correct. This used to be the case for most image processing systems.

Inspection usually denotes checking for defects such as dents, scratches, wrong dimensions, and so on. It merges fluently into *verification*, where the vision system verifies that an expected state actually exists. This can be the state of the workpiece being assembled completely with all parts at the right place – which can just as well be seen as an inspection task – or the correspondence of an identification, for example, a serial number string, with an expected value. This application contains another role, that of *recognition*; however, verification can actually be easier than pure recognition because *a priori* knowledge may be used to guide the process. In other words, it is easier to verify that a known serial number is actually present than reading just any number that happens to be on the part.

Another role is that of *monitoring*, that is, observing during the production process whether it is carried out correctly: for example, having a camera look at a laser welding process to see whether the melt pool has the correct size during welding.

This role may be further extended to *control*, that is, using the results of the machine vision system to change – read, improve – or control the process; this is possible as statistical process control or as direct feedback control, for example, when using contour measurements from a vision system to guide a gantry robot dispensing glue or sealant along the measured contour.

As usual, the roles can mix. For example, a machine vision system placed after the nozzle in an aluminum extrusion process does not technically look *inside* the process. The effect, however, is that of a monitoring system. Deviations in the tube profile can be used immediately to take care of a production problem instead of waiting for the tube to cool down and be cut into the final work pieces.

Or, the quantitative measurements an inspection system uses to make the correctness decision for each individual workpiece need not be thrown away after the workpiece leaves the system, but can be statistically evaluated to determine the current characteristics and quality of the manufacturing process. For example, a system checking whether a groove is completely filled with sealant (a typical 3D-application nowadays) may record the height of the sealant in the groove to monitor the machine for over- or underfilling; it also may evaluate the number of waists in the sealant to draw conclusions about the viscosity of the sealant.

On the other hand, monitoring systems can be used for verification as well as control purposes. A system guiding a robot to apply a sealing agent along a part contour can at the same time check the sealing material for interruptions or overflowing.

10.2.4 Value-Adding Machine Vision

Traditionally, machine vision systems destroy value.

This is certainly a controversial statement in a handbook of machine vision. But it holds for every system that is used to find defects on finished or semifinished products. If a defect is found and the part has to be scrapped, the value already added to the original materials is gone. Even if the components can be salvaged, the effort spent on them is lost. In addition, the system itself, its maintenance, and operation cost money, and false rejects may cost even more, either by scrapping a perfectly good part or by rechecking.

Of course, it is a little more complicated than that. Allowing a defective part to reach the customer will probably destroy much more value than finding and scrapping the part. Also, increasing use of inspection systems early in the process – instead of only as a final check – will filter out defective parts before additional effort is wasted on them. But it is still a game of minimizing losses instead of maximizing gains.

However, machine vision systems increasingly play a value-adding role. Sometimes they just show where the potential for process improvement lies. But they can do more than that, particularly in the control-type applications mentioned in Section 10.2.3. Using machine vision systems to help machines do their job well instead of finding parts where they did not, to increase process quality instead of detecting process flaws, to improve precision instead of throwing out imprecise pieces – in short, enabling production to manufacture better parts instead of just selecting the good ones – adds value.

Even further, machine vision has developed into an enabling technology, a decisive factor without which certain applications and processes would not be possible at all. Vision-guided laser structuring or dispensing as well as robotic assistants capable of bin-picking and handling of imprecisely positioned workpieces are inconceivable without sophisticated (3D) image processing methods.

10.3 System Categories

Like applications, machine vision systems can also be categorized in various ways. This section will introduce some important distinctions that affect cost as well as performance, operation, and handling of the system. There are many criteria that can be used to differentiate machine vision systems, some of which are as follows:

- *Dimensionality*[1]: 0D, 1D, 2D, 2.5D[2], and 3D systems.
- *Flexibility*: from simple, hardwired sensors to systems with limited or full configurability and freely programmable systems.
- *System basis*: ranging from large parallel computers to common PCs, as well as digital signal processor (DSP)-based smart cameras, custom single-purpose chips, and, increasingly, freely programmable standard system-on chip (SoC), all of these frequently enhanced by field-programmable gate arrays (FPGAs) for special-purpose algorithms and control tasks.
- *Manufacturing depth*: how much of the system is built from commercial off-the-shelf (COTS) components, especially in the software area, how much is (or needs to be) custom-developed.

All these categories – and certainly quite a few more – can be of importance for a system decision. The number of possible configurations far exceeds the scope of this chapter and is only partly of interest from an integration point of view. Therefore, we will restrict ourselves to some typical categories, which are important for their widespread use as well as for the different approaches they represent.

---

1 Note that we use dimensionality here in a purely geometrical sense; from a physical or informational point of view, systems may have much higher dimensionality, for example, in the case of multispectral imagery or the combination of coordinates, time, color, and so on.
2 Commonly, if not very scientifically, used for systems evaluating height maps, gray level images where the brightness encodes height.

10.3.1 Common Types of Systems

There is little common terminology in this area. For example, some companies call a vision sensor what for others is an intelligent camera; others use the term vision controller for a configurable system much like a smart camera – only without the camera built in – others for a specialized DSP-based computer, and so on. The following list therefore introduces several terms for different types of systems that we will try to use consistently in the remainder of this chapter. Those who are used to these terms in a different meaning, please bear with us.

Sensors for small, single-purpose, hardwired systems usually giving a binary yes/no result and working in 0D or 1D; we will treat these only very briefly.

Vision sensors representing a middle-ground between traditional sensors and simple image processing systems.

Compact systems for want of a better word, although there are so many for this type of system: intelligent camera, smart camera, smart sensor, or vision sensor (not the one from above!).

Vision controllers for small, configurable, multipurpose units; these are essentially small computers specialized on machine vision tasks and equipped with communication interfaces for automation purposes.

PC-based systems, naming the most common hardware basis for systems built using general-purpose computers. Thanks to the rapid development of the hardware over the last decade and the flexible programmability, these systems lend themselves readily to parallelization on the system as well as over the network for cloud-based processing – as exemplified by the face recognition capabilities of Google and Facebook.

In the following sections, we will try to characterize these systems mainly from an automation point of view.

10.3.2 Sensors

A sensor is, from the point of view of automation, a very simple thing. It is fixed somewhere and gives a signal, indicating some state. There are all kinds of sensors using all conceivable physical quantities: force, distance, pressure, and so on. We are most interested, naturally, in optical sensors.

Typical optical sensors are light barriers (retroreflective or through-beam) and color sensors. A light sensor can recognize the presence of an object, either by the interruption of its beam or by the reflection from the part. A color sensor can recognize the color of the light spot created on the object by the illumination of the sensor.

These sensors are essentially zero dimensional, and they have a very small field of view; basically, they evaluate a single spot. It is obvious that effects like position tolerances or variations across the part's surface pose real problems to such a system. Applied appropriately, they are very useful, of course; in fact, they are indispensable for high-speed image processing as trigger indicators, as we will see in Section 10.8. One has to be clear about their limitations, however.

We will not go any deeper into the subject of these sensors. From an integration point of view, they are basically components that are fixed and adjusted in some place and then deliver a yes/no signal, like any binary switch, or a numerical value, for example, as with a brightness sensor.

10.3.3 Vision Sensors

The term *vision sensor* has been coined for systems that use areal sensors and machine vision methods for performing specific tasks.

Thanks to the areal sensors, they have some advantages over basic sensors. They can take a larger field of view into account and thus cope, for example, with irregular reflexions created by structured surfaces (like foil packaging), and color and brightness variations across surface areas.

Together with machine vision algorithms, the areal sensors enable these systems to perform evaluations not possible with basic sensors. Many applications are feasible using such systems, from very simple tasks, such as computing the average brightness over a surface area, to counting, sorting, and character recognition.

The main point is that this type of system is built for a single, particular purpose. Perhaps the best known systems of this kind are DataMatrix code scanners – although they are not typically seen as vision systems at all by the end users; so we see that with the DataMatrix scanner, there is already a type of system where the underlying technology is retreating behind the application as it should be with a mature technology.

Vision sensors in this sense of the term will certainly take some market share from more complex, more expensive systems that used to be required for these applications. Even more, however, they may expand the market as a whole, making applications economically viable that have simply not been done before.

Being considerably more complex, especially in their algorithms, than simple sensors, these systems allow for – and require – more configuration than these. Nevertheless, doing an application with this kind of system is still usually less complex than with a full-fledged vision system. Being single-purpose systems makes them easier to set up and operate for the end users.

From an integration point of view, they can be as simple as a basic sensor, delivering a yes/no signal according to their configuration. They may also provide numerical or string-type results that DataMatrix scanners necessarily do, but usually with little variation. Vision systems, on the other hand, being used for all kinds of applications produce very different types of results and thus may have very complex information interfaces (cf. Section 10.7).

To sum up, vision sensors in this sense of the term can deliver very cost-effective solutions to a range of applications that exceed the capabilities of simple sensors and are not economically viable using fully flexible vision systems. Integration effort will largely lie with the automation system, as vision sensors will typically have only limited flexibility in their communication protocols. For a system integrator, standardization will therefore be important: finding a range of sensors that meet the application requirements and provide long-term solutions.

10.3.4 Compact Systems

This is, admittedly, not a common term in this field. some companies call this type of system a vision sensor, and others an intelligent or smart camera.[3] The term *compact system* reflects the fact that the entire vision system hardware, namely camera sensor, digitization, processing, and communication, is integrated into a small space, typically contained in a single unit. The original compact system therefore is nothing but a digital camera with a built-in computer.

Compact systems come in very different forms and with different application methods. There are central units coordinating several such compact systems, as well as systems with a separate camera head or an additional camera input. Area-scan sensors dominate the field, but line-scan systems are also available and increasingly also 3D data acquisition. The time-of-flight principle (see Section 10.10.2.2) lends itself naturally to compact, stand-alone Units, and is used, for example, in logistics and security applications.

Many systems come with a configuration program, typically running on a PC and communicating with the unit over Ethernet or other suitable interfaces, for conveniently setting up a built-in vision functionality, which can be quite sophisticated. However, DSP-based systems programmed using a cross-compiler and a library of machine vision routines, as well as systems with a standard CPU and operating system – typically some flavor of Linux or Windows – are also common, sometimes supported by FPGAs to speed up typical image processing algorithms as well as carry out control tasks like light switching, camera triggering, and so on.

Naturally, compared with a PC, there will be restrictions on some or all of the aspects of processing power, RAM and permanent storage space, number of sensor connections, and extensibility of hardware as well as software.

On the other hand, a closed system – regarding hardware as well as software – has undeniable advantages. System security is easier to achieve than for PC-based systems, and configuration management is also simpler: hardware type and firmware version will usually be sufficient to reconstruct a system that will behave identically with the same vision software configuration. This can be much harder with PCs.

The ready availability of SoCs, like the well-known Raspberry Pi or alternatives like BeagleBone or Hummingboard[4] running standard operating systems will yield another boost to this segment. Already there are industrial cameras on the market with an integrated SoC, also sometimes coupled with an FPGA, so we can assume that their small footprint, flexible programmability, and low price tag will have an impact on the industry as they had on the hobbyist area, especially since they are often touted as the building blocks of the Internet of Things due to their inherent connectivity.

---

3 The term *smart camera* is increasingly used for cameras built into smart phones, which tend to have more and more sophisticated processing capabilities, like face recognition, and so on. They are built and programmed for other ends and to quite different specifications than cameras for industrial vision systems; therefore we will use the term *intelligent camera* instead.

4 There is no claim to completeness here and certainly no recommendation intended; these are just some often-heard examples of this system category.

10.3.5 Vision Controllers

In the preceding sections, we have characterized vision controllers as small, special-purpose computers with a camera and communication connections. From an integration point of view, they are similar to PC-based systems, except that the units are typically smaller, thus easier to accommodate, use a 24 V DC power supply, and no standard operating system. Otherwise, with camera, communication, and power supply connections, they are integrated in much the same way as PCs.

From an application point of view, they are not much different from compact systems. They usually have built-in image processing algorithms, which are set up using a configuration program, determining the sequence and parameters of the algorithms.

Vision controllers are typically less expensive than PC-based solutions and appear convenient because of their small size. They are also less flexible, for example, with regard to communication, so this cost advantage has to be carefully calculated. A one-shot application of such a system will probably not be cost effective, as it will require a lot of nonstandard expenditure; if one can use such units as a standard for a considerable number of applications, calculations will be much different, of course.

10.3.6 PC-Based Systems

In this context, a PC-based system denotes systems based on general-purpose computers with a standard operating system. The term is not restricted to the combination most commonly encountered in offices, namely a PC with an Intel architecture and a Windows operating system. It may just as well be a PowerPC or ARM system with a Linux operating system or other variations.

There are mixtures, as has already been mentioned, for example, compact systems built upon such a CPU and running a standard operating system. Under the aspect of *how* an application is carried out, this does not make too big a difference. However, there is a crucial difference, namely the extensibility of standard PCs. They can be equipped with different interface cards for various bus systems, with different frame grabbers for all kinds of cameras, with additional RAM and hard disk space, and so on.

In addition, the standard operating systems on these machines offer a wide range of services, for data management, networking, display, communication, and so on, and the variety of software, including development systems and machine vision software, is overwhelming. Add to this the emphasis on multi-core systems in recent years, supplemented by many-core graphics processing units and the relative ease of combining such machines to computing clusters, and it is obvious that flexibility and performance can hardly be greater than with such a system.

This does come at a price however: the hardware is relatively expensive, at least for a single-camera system; configuration management is difficult, considering that standard PC components sometimes are available for hardly more than half a year on the market and that there is such an inexhaustible variety of hardware and software components which may or may not work together. Also, PC systems are usually equipped with hard disks that are not always capable of running 24/7 under production conditions. Alternatives, such as solid-state drives (SSDs), have secured a foothold in the market and are standard with some systems; however, their long-term behavior is not yet well understood and they are still more expensive. Especially when traceability is a requirement or the convenience to have a large back storage of images for optimizing the system, size does matter.

And, of course, there is the security risk posed by malware, and shutting the systems off from the network is not really a solution, especially in the times of the Industrial Internet of Things. Even if the system does not really have an actual internet connection, viruses may be introduced into the system in a variety of ways that are not easy to close completely.

We can further differentiate PC-based systems based on the way the machine vision software solution is created: library-based and application-package-based systems.

10.3.6.1 Library-Based Systems

In a library-based system, functionality from a machine vision library is in some way incorporated into an executable program that represents (the software-part of) the vision system. There are many ways to do that; most libraries today come with a rapid-prototyping tool, which allows a sequence of machine vision functions to be set up rapidly and supplied with initial parameters. This sequence can be exported as source code and compiled into a larger overall program; or a complete prototype setup is loaded by an executable dynamic link library (DLL); or the library has a built-in interpreter executing a script connecting the library functions.

The common element is that library-based systems involve a programmer in the creation of a vision system, someone who provides the necessary framework to control the execution of the vision algorithms, take care of data handling and communications, provide a user interface, and so on. Since a programmer is not necessarily a specialist in lighting or optics, this will often mean an additional person in the project, and hence additional cost and organizational complexity, especially with regard to system maintenance.

The programming work to be done for such systems can be considerable, and there is the danger that after carrying out several applications there will be several diverse executables to be maintained. On the other hand, this approach offers the ultimate flexibility. The way the application is executed is under your control; you can adapt to any automation environment, provide every user interface the customer wants, include any functionality you need, and so on. We do not want to get carried away here, and there will always be limitations and be it that some libraries do not work well with each other, but the fact is that with this approach, the system integrator is also the system designer.

For systems that are identically duplicated many times – for example, driver assistance systems, video surveillance systems, or standard machines – and/or that have specific requirements on performance, integration with the environment, user interface, and so on, this approach is very effective, allowing exactly the required system to be built and distributing the development cost on a large number of copies. For one-shot systems, the development and maintenance effort will often be hard to justify.

10.3.6.2 Application-Package-Based Systems

Here, an application-package means a piece of software used to configure a machine vision routine which can then be loaded and executed by the same (or another, that does not really matter) piece of software *without* modifying source code or compiling anything in between. So, ideally, if the machine vision functionality built into the application package suffices, no programmer is part of the application loop. The application engineer alone sets up the solution and everything that belongs to it, and deploys the solution using the application package.

The basic idea behind the application-package approach is that there are many things outside and above the level of machine vision functionality incorporated in a library that are identical between vision systems and that productivity and quality of program development can be improved by uncoupling programming from the application process. This can lead to rapid and cost-effective solutions for a large class of problems. For a company with a fast-changing product spectrum, this can be a very effective approach.

The downside is that some degrees of freedom are lost in comparison with the library-based approach. Here, the system integrator is no longer the master of the execution environment, of the overall application logic; depending on the architecture of the package, they may not be master of the communication taking place between the system and their (or their customers') automation environment. This *can* be a problem. And the distinction still holds even if the same company creates the application package and the application because if every application is allowed to feedback immediately into the package development and have its specific requirements fulfilled, we are back with the library-based approach, extended to a somewhat standardized framework.

Also, in many cases, some functionality may be missing from the application package, a small one to make the customer happy, or a crucial one to solve the application at all. In any case, a method to extend the package's functionality is essential. How easily and how well this is possible depends on the extension interfaces provided by the application package vendor.

For machine vision companies making a considerable number of systems, it may prove worthwhile to create their own application package, if they cannot find one on the market meeting their needs – or simply want to avoid dependencies and keep their freedom of adaptation. When they build many basically similar systems, encapsulating that similarity in a configurable base application can be useful. Or, they have such an application turnaround that there is a return on the investment to provide the resources to create such a package. There are, in fact, machine vision companies that act as turn-key system builders, but use self-developed libraries and application packages internally, which they do not sell on the market.

10.3.6.3 Library-Based Application Packages

To extend this last thought, building one's own application package on the basis of a well-established library of image processing (and possibly other) functions can have several benefits. Not only does it further standardization and reduce the implementation effort for the package itself considerably, but it can also ease application work for each individual project – especially in the case of a scriptable library with a built-in interpreter which was described above, as this allows fast turnaround between development, testing, and deployment.

10.3.7 Excursion: Embedded Image Processing

Embedded image processing systems are a category that in some respects runs crosswise to the system types discussed so far in this section. In terms of their implementation in hardware and/or software, embedded image processing systems can belong to practically all of the above categories. So, in a sense, we have already covered this area.

Nevertheless, some remarks appear appropriate, as this area is often cited recently as being poised for immense growth in the near to medium future. Since it is also a diversified topic with several emerging lines of development and a not-yet-quite-clear direction, we will restrict ourselves to some general remarks here.

In general, an embedded system denotes a computer integrated into some sort of technical context, from something as simple as the controller of a dishwasher up to the avionics of an aircraft. In that general sense, almost every industrial image processing system is "embedded," as it plays some role within a larger technical context – a machining station, a manufacturing line, or an entire plant.

However, in most installations, we still observe clearly separated roles between sensors and actuators and between control and measuring or inspection systems. In that sense, the image processing systems are not embedded but stand-alone subsystems. On the other hand, there is an emerging trend to integrate these functions into one system.

We can distinguish two main lines of development, both of which will probably continue to grow in their respective functions.

On one hand, compact vision systems, such as smart cameras, are equipped with limited control and actuator functions, for example, the ability to control valves to sort or expel parts. Therefore, for example, feeders with selectivity for type and quality of the parts can be based solely on a smart camera system without the need for a programmable logic controller (PLC). Of course, this has its limits, for example, in safety functionality.

On the other hand, the increasing computational power of PC-based control systems, especially multicore systems, makes it possible to integrate machine vision functions into the control system. Various degrees of integration are conceivable, from having distinct software entities running on the same hardware to image acquisition and processing functions within the PLC software.

Again, the different principles have different advantages and limitations. Keep in mind that a control system is typically – and necessarily – a real-time system, meaning that it has to guarantee certain reaction times (real time is often equated with speed, but that is not quite accurate; the computational throughput of a machine vision system is usually far higher than that of a PLC system, and it will in general achieve its task fast enough, but it does not guarantee reaction times). Vast demands on memory and computational power may exceed the limits of a real-time system. For example, real-time processes on a Windows system are typically implemented at a kernel-driver level where dynamic memory allocation and exception handling – which are usually taken for granted in modern image processing software – are not possible.

Therefore, the potential for advanced solutions will be greater outside the restrictions of the real-time process; however, latencies will of course be larger than with integration into the real-time PLC run-time process. So for certain applications, integration into the real-time process is a must.

The up-and-coming SoC we mentioned in Section 10.3.4 will be a major factor in this area. Their small footprint, free programmability, and input/output versatility will allow many applications to be realized that where hitherto uneconomical or not possible within space or power constraints.

All these systems can and increasingly are supported by FPGAs integrated into cameras, frame grabbers, and SoCs, for speed-up of algorithms and other special tasks. Moore's law may be reaching its limits, but clever combination of the capabilities of diverse components will still increase performance.

10.3.8 Summary

Naturally, there can be no fixed rules as to what system to use for what purpose, nor is there a single right answer to the question of the system approach. However, one thing is clear: the more powerful and the more common the hardware platform is, the more flexible the system will be and the wider its range of applications. At the same time, it will often be more difficult to set up and more difficult to troubleshoot – not very surprising, actually.

Systems based on general-purpose computers provide the greatest flexibility due to their extensibility and the richness and variety of the development environments, libraries, and application packages available. Vision controllers and compact systems may fare better in ease of use and purchasing costs but may come up against limiting factors like computation power and flexibility, since neither hardware nor software is usually built for being extended. Special-purpose computers, like parallel DSP systems, for example, may offer the best performance and be indispensable for very demanding applications, but require highly specialized programmers. Finally, vision sensors are by definition limited in their range of applications, but within that range, they are often hard to beat with respect to price–performance relation and ease of use.

Where there are several ways to solve an image processing task – for example, when a PC system and a compact system are both capable of doing the inspection – the decisive factors may actually be outside the area of image processing itself: communication requirements, for example, may rule out some systems which simply do not have the required interfaces, or production organization may rule out others which cannot cover the product spectrum and the type diversity. Cost and space constraints, as well as competent personnel, may impose different restrictions.

Again, there can be no single right systems approach. The following sections will cover many of these topics outside actual machine vision. Hopefully, this will give some insight into the questions to be answered when making such a decision.

10.4 Integration and Interfaces

The development of technology and market in recent years (see Section 10.1.1) clearly shows that machine vision has become a standard tool of automation technology and will continue to gain importance in the foreseeable future.

Increasing capabilities of hardware and software will make more applications technically feasible, and improving price–performance ratio will help from the economics point of view. However, the ability of integrating this technology into the production environment and the organization will probably be even more important. Together with product complexity and quality requirements, production systems become more complex also; manufacturing stations are already crammed with technology, equipped with various measuring and inspection devices in addition to the actual production processes. Production and maintenance personnel have to manage this complexity and to operate and service all those devices.

Especially smaller companies – or smaller locations of large companies – will not be able to afford several machine vision experts, if at all. To further the use of machine vision systems, it is therefore necessary, among other things, to facilitate integration, operation, and maintenance by nonspecialists.

Take PLCs as an example. Every PLC fulfills a unique task, specialized for its production station, and it is *programmed* to do so by a specialist, a PLC programmer. However, normal production operation as well as many maintenance operations – up to, for example, the complete reinstallation of the system after a hardware failure – can be carried out by nonprogrammers. This requires providing (nonspecialist) end-user personnel with the right information and means of intervention to operate the system, to diagnose and remedy problems, to exchange system components without breaking functionality, and to adapt the system within the limits of its original specification.

It should not be overlooked, however, that the physics of part surface, light, optics, and sensor introduces an additional complexity, which is typically not considered in the area of PLCs. There, work usually starts with a directly usable sensor signal; making that signal usable is typically left to a specialist, unless the sensor is very simple. Here, in machine vision, it is just the point: making the system usable as a whole, including the sensor chain.

10.4.1 Standardization

Before we come to the various interfacing requirements of vision systems, a word on standardization is appropriate. There used to be little or no standardization in the field of machine vision beyond video signals. Today, several (digital camera) interface standards (such as CameraLink, GigE Vision,, etc.) have emerged, as well as some software interface standards (such as the GenICam interface specification), mostly in the area of image acquisition [10].

Beyond that, there is still very little standardization, which is due, in part, to the comparative youth of the field, and also to the structure of the industry. The machine vision market is dominated by component suppliers, offering cameras, framegrabbers, software libraries, and vertical solution providers offering complete solutions, turn-key machine vision systems. Most vertical solution providers make their own software or use a few selected products, but far fewer make their own cameras and frame grabbers, so the primary area of standardization is that of interfaces to components bought by system integrators on the market.

Internally, the vertical solution providers, of course, do standardize; we already mentioned that there are system integrators who use self-developed application packages. As yet, these providers do not see a clear benefit from higher level standardization, spanning companies, but the increasing importance of integration into a highly digitized and networked manufacturing environment may change the equation. In particular, to reap the expected benefits of Industry 4.0 or the Industrial Internet of Things) standardization will have to go much further.

Extensive use of machine vision systems will make it worthwhile to standardize in some or all of the areas mentioned here. This will be an effort, to be sure; it may make some systems more expensive than strictly necessary. Overall, however, it will prove valuable, especially when considering maintenance, service, and spare part costs over the lifetime of the systems – which can be surprisingly long.

10.4.2 Interfaces

As outlined previously, a major factor for the ongoing success of machine vision is its integration into the automation technology environment; integration can be understood as interfacing with other systems. The following sections will take a look at some of the interfaces that play a role in the integration of machine vision systems:

- *mechanical* integration into the production line in Section 10.5;
- *electrical* connections in Section 10.6;
- *information* exchange in Section 10.7;
- *synchronization* aspects in Section 10.8;
- *user interfaces* in Section 10.9.

10.5 Mechanical Interfaces

It may sound trivial, but it is one of the first things to be dealt with: a machine vision system including all its components must find its place(s) inside a production station and must be mounted and fixed there.

Everywhere we find miniaturization: sensors, parts, and computers become smaller. This continues in machine vision, of course. Simply compare current cameras with those 5 years ago. However, we cannot miniaturize the laws of optics. A telecentric lens for a part of certain dimensions also needs to have a certain size. Light does not change its way of propagation, so working distances have to be kept to capture clear, sharp images with sufficient field of view as well as depth of focus, and so on. Not that there has been no progress in this area, with liquid lenses and active optics, for example, but physics still rules.

So machine vision has its particular demands on the mechanical setup, and although a mechanical designer may have knowledge of geometrical optics, we cannot necessarily expect specific knowledge about the types and characteristics of particular optical setups, lighting, cameras – much less an ingrained feel of these things – which will lead to a suitable mechanical design. So, it is the duty of the machine vision specialist, as well as to his advantage, to explain all these things to the mechanical designer, discussing them as early and as often as possible so that the requirements of the vision system are incorporated into the machine design.

Such information includes (as usual, without any claim to completeness) the following:

- component dimensions (i.e., cameras, optics, lights, computers, always including connectors!) and means of fixation;
- working distances for lights and optics;
- position tolerances with respect to translation as well as rotation;
- forced constraints, for example, for telecentric lenses and illumination (see the following for an example);
- additional sensor requirements (e.g., the need for a light barrier as a triggering device. Even though wiring and setting up such a sensor is the responsibility of electrical engineers, the mechanical designer has to provide the space and mounting for it);
- additional motion requirements;
- environmental conditions.

Note that there is no inherent difference between 2D and 3D machine vision in this respect. If anything, a 3D system will have more components and tighter constraints than a 2D system.

10.5.1 Dimensions and Fixation

As with every component to be built into a production station, the first thing the mechanical designer needs to know is the dimensions as well as the means of fixation.

Speaking of dimensions, it should not be forgotten that vision system components – cameras as well as lighting and processing units – usually have cables connected to them! The connectors have a certain size and the cables have certain minimum bending radii. These are factors the designer has to take into account.

All the components used in imaging vary considerably in size and shape. Just look at all the various forms of LED illumination available today or at the vastly different cameras. These differences, unfortunately, continue in the means of fastening the components. Cameras may have screw threads in all possible places and may use all kinds of different screws – which may be impractically small for mounting the cameras reliably in a production environment.

Standardization is an important means of handling this variety. Restricting oneself to a minimum number of components – easier for cameras and optics than for the often highly project-specific lighting – and trying to convince the manufacturer or distributor to provide these components with practical and consistent means of fastening is a good strategy to make life easier for the mechanical designer as well as one's own and that of the maintenance personnel later on.

For example, precise, unvarying, reproducible geometrical relations (first between the workpiece and optics/camera) are of prime importance, especially for gauging applications. Software can support this, for example, by providing comparison of a stored calibration image with the current image. Mechanically, accuracy can be improved in such applications by pinning the cameras to ensure a good fixation as well as precise reproducibility of the position. This requires, of course, that the manufacturer or distributor equipped the camera accordingly.

10.5.2 Working Distances

Closely related to the dimensions are the working distances. Optics as well as illumination has to be in certain positions relative to the piece to be inspected. The tolerances for these working distances may be rather small, especially in situations where little light is available, for example, when very short exposure times are required, leading to small depth of focus, or where the angle of incidence is of prime importance, like in certain surface inspection applications.

The working distances and their tolerances are among the most important parameters to the mechanical designer because they strongly influence the overall design of the system and they are absolutely not obvious to a nonspecialist unless he or she has considerable experience designing visual inspection stations.

10.5.3 Position Tolerances

Most machine vision systems have some means to handle variations of the object position or orientation in the image. However, there are limits to this capability. Most obviously, of course, the features to be inspected need to be completely visible in the image, giving an absolute upper limit to positional variations. But the practical limit may be much smaller. For example, the quality of the image may decrease toward the borders due to optical effects; lens distortion typically increases with distance from the lens center, so gauge capability may be lost or require complicated calibration methods; or the incident angle of the light may change, rendering certain features less distinct, and so on.

Therefore, the effects of positional variations should be estimated and an upper limit given to the mechanical designer – and it should be conservative.

Product design may be relevant here also. For example, if a part to be inspected from top has a height tolerance of 0.8 mm and the required resolution leads to an optical system with a depth of focus of just 1 mm, the vertical position tolerance for the mechanical setup is reduced to only 0.2 mm (Figure 10.1). Rarely does the

Figure 10.1 Addition of part and setup tolerances.

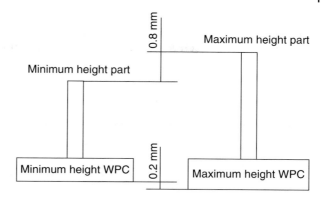

chance of influencing product design for better "inspectability" present itself, but if it does, use it.

10.5.4 Forced Constraints

Sometimes there are relationships between components that are not obvious for a nonspecialist. These need to be explained and communicated.

Take the example of a system equipped with cameras with telecentric lenses and corresponding telecentric lights. As the optics can only see parallel rays and the lighting only send parallel rays, there is a forced constraint, namely that the lens and the corresponding light always need to be parallel and preferably exactly opposite to each other. Neglecting to inform the mechanical designer about this fact can, and most probably will, result in a design where the opposite partners are not forcibly parallelized, causing a lot of unnecessary adjustment work (Figure 10.2). In a similar way, certain types of 3D acquisition, like photometric or deflectometric methods, may have a strong dependence on the angle between incident light and the optical axis of the camera.

10.5.5 Additional Sensor Requirements

A vision system may require additional sensors, for example, to detect the presence of a part in the first place – this signal might go to the PLC, which in turn starts the vision system inspection; or light barriers that are used to trigger image capturing of moving objects at a precise point in time, often connected with

Figure 10.2 Correctly aligned, translated, and rotated telecentric components.

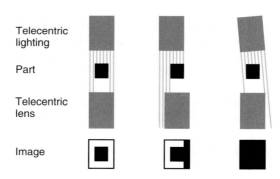

triggering a strobe light to freeze the motion in the image; or rotary encoders to synchronize capturing by line-scan cameras with motion of the workpiece to achieve constant scale and geometrical properties over the entire image.

From the mechanical point of view, these are simply additional components that the mechanical designer has to know about, including dimensions and possible restrictions to mounting and position – like the maximum signal cable length.

10.5.6 Additional Motion Requirements

There are various reasons why a manufacturing station may require capabilities for additional movements because of a vision system. According to the frequency of the movement, we can distinguish between the following:

- *Adjustment movements* are required only rarely, often only in the first stages of an application. Not everything can be tested or calculated in advance, so some means of adjustment, for example, slides or rotating joints for mounting cameras or lighting, may be required during tryouts until an optimum position is found. Then the position may be fixed, or the adjustment means kept in place for later changes.
  Adjustment means should be easily accessible and they should have a method for fixation and also for marking the setting – such as digital counters – so that a setting can be easily reproduced, for example, in case the system has to be partly disassembled.
- *Changeover movements* may be required when the type of product being inspected is changed. Different part geometries may require not only changes to software procedures or parameters but also changes in, for example, distances or angles between part and optics, or part and lighting, or both. Changeover movements occur outside the area of machine vision also and can be manual or automated.
  Sometimes, however, an additional set of sensor equipment (camera, optics, illumination, etc.) will be less expensive than a moving axis, which requires not only purchasing but also mounting and – in the automated case – control system programming.
  If changeover movements are carried out manually, the means for easy and precise reproduction, such as digital counters, are even more important than for adjustment, as personnel may be required to switch frequently between the settings for different types and do so quickly and precisely.
- *Process movements* are carried out for every single piece. There are many reasons why process movements may be required. Here are a few examples:
  - A line-scan camera always requires moving (be it a translatory or rotatory movement) either the part or the camera – preferably the part to avoid tracking camera cables.
  - Insertion sensors – such as endoscopes – or lights have to be moved into the part cavity and back out again.
  - Space constraints may require lights, optics, cameras, or the part to be moved into position for inspection and removed afterwards. For example, the sensor may be in the path of part transportation: if a part has to be inspected in a backlit situation in a conveyor-belt setup, you obviously

cannot mount the sensor equipment over the belt at the height of the workpiece, as it would have to move *through* them; mounting the camera and light on both sides of the conveyor belt may lead to undesired width of the workstation. A typical solution would be to lift the part from the conveyor belt level up to the camera level for the inspection (Figure 10.3).
- Working distances are also a frequent reason for moving pieces of equipment. For example, diffuse on-axis lighting typically works best close to the illuminated surface. There, however, it may again be in the way of part transportation.
- There can be mechanical changes to optical situations. For example, moving ambient light shielding in place for inspection and out of place for transportation of the parts.
- Mechanical autofocus: part tolerances may exceed the optics' depth of focus, which may be overcome by moving the part or optics into the optimum position.

10.5.7 Environmental Conditions

Typical cases of environmental conditions that cause mechanical requirements are the following:

Vibrations, which may require mechanical decoupling or other measures, for example, to protect sensitive computer equipment or to avoid adverse effects on image quality.

Heat, which may also cause damage to equipment; possible remedies are additional cooling means or "spatial decoupling," that is, placing computers further away from heat sources.

Light shielding comes in two varieties: shielding the vision system against ambient light, and shielding the environment against particular light sources.

With the exception of ambient light shielding, these requirements do not differ from other systems where computer equipment is employed in a production environment, so designers should be familiar with this problem. It may be good, however, to point out the possible sensitivities of the system. Especially, the effect of vibration on image quality may not be immediately obvious.

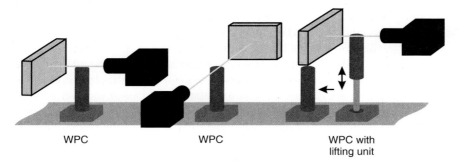

Figure 10.3 Impossible, too wide, and workable arrangement of light and camera with respect to part transportation.

Light shielding, on the other hand, is a point that should always be taken into account when discussing the (mechanical) requirements of a vision system.

Ambient light is, of course, potentially a major disturbance for a machine vision system, which typically depends upon particular and stable illumination conditions. This is especially true if the level, direction, or other characteristics of the ambient light vary, as may be the case in a production hall with windows letting in daylight. Light shields, however, are a major obstruction in a production station and may cause additional motion requirements if they have to be moved for transporting the part.

Protecting the environment against the vision system's illumination is basically no different from ambient light shielding as far as the mechanical requirements are concerned. Only the reasons differ. These shields are typically needed because of safety requirements, for example, when using lasers or other high-intensity light sources (e.g., strobes). Infrared or ultraviolet lighting is also a cause of concern, as our eyes do not have a natural protection strategy against these as they have against visible light. The same holds for light sources producing ultra-short light pulses, which are much faster than the protective reactions of our eyes. So, when using high-intensity or invisible radiation sources, consult a safety engineer to discuss the protection requirements.

10.5.8 Reproducibility

It has been mentioned in the context of mechanical movements for adjustment or changeover, but the importance of reproducibility deserves to be stressed explicitly.

Software engineers sometimes tend to forget considering reproducibility since software is so easy to reproduce perfectly (although software problems sometimes are not), but to reproduce mechanical setups precisely, a little extra work and thinking is required.

Mechanical reproducibility is naturally a prime concern in measuring systems where accuracy often directly depends on the mechanical setup, but it is important in every machine vision system. Machines *are* disassembled sometimes, and components do fail and have to be exchanged; in all these situations, it must be possible to re-create the original setup of lighting and optics to achieve the same image conditions as before, and with as little effort as possible. Preferably, re-creating these conditions should be possible without the help of a machine vision specialist who may not be at hand then.

Of course, this also applies to changeover movements. If these are not executed automatically but adjusted manually, appropriate limit stops and indicators are required so that the various setups can be easily reconstructed. Preferably, software, either on the PLC or the vision system, should assist the user here by indicating clearly the adjustments to be made and possibly offer means of checking these adjustments – like reference images for checking the camera field of view, for example.

Standardization also helps in reproducibility. It is much easier to re-create a particular optical situation if only a few different components are involved, and if these components have unvarying standard fixations and long-term availability. The difficulties of camera fixations have already been mentioned in Section 10.5.1. The rapid technological development does not help either, as there is a good chance that exactly the same camera will not be available when an exchange or a duplicate system is needed. Standard fixations, used consistently and refitted on subsequent camera models, help to meet the end user's reasonable expectation that, after replacing a camera, the same image should result as before. The end user, after all, is usually not interested in the camera as such but in the result the system delivers.

Pinning, as mentioned in Section 10.5.1, is a possible method to create a reproducible setup. It can also be used for retrofitting after finding an optimal setup in try-outs. If the system cannot be built for accurate reproducibility in such a way – for example, because adjustment possibilities must be maintained – then position and orientation of the components may be recorded to allow for re-creating the setup, or a specialized jig may be designed and manufactured as an assembly aid to assist a mechanic in readjusting or duplicating the setup.

The above remarks are equally valid, of course, for all parts of an optical setup. Actually, since lenses, especially telecentric lenses, are often considerably larger than modern cameras, the lens is sometimes the main object to fasten while the camera becomes more of an attachment.

That lenses should be lockable with respect to focus and aperture is a matter of course. That does not help much, however, with exchanging lenses (or duplicating a system which is no different in principle from exchanging a lens). Again, standardization is very helpful since lens sizes and characteristics vary so much even for lenses with basically identical imaging properties.

Light sources also have to be considered. They have a limited life-span – even LEDs do – and they may change their characteristics over time, especially close to the end. Depending on the application, methods to detect this change and to compensate for it may be necessary, for example, automatic monitoring of well-defined image areas for brightness changes and adjustments to the light source power supply can help keep the brightness stable. Exchanging the light source can lead to sudden drastic changes. In addition to brightness changes, changes in wavelength are also very critical, since the exact point of focus changes with the wavelength, so the imaging characteristics may be altered considerably.

In all these cases, software tools can be very helpful to aid the user in re-creating a particular optical setup. For example, the system may provide a means to store reference images for various cameras, possibly several per camera to account for different lighting situations, combined with tools to compare the current image with the stored one. Such tools may be markers identifying particular points in the image to compare the field of view, brightness computation in prescribed areas to compare lighting levels, or gradient computation to estimate the focus quality. Without such tools, comparing live images is basically the only – and not very precise – way of re-creating a particular imaging situation.

10.5.9 Gauge Capability

Gauge capability is a difficult topic to place. It touches all areas of a machine vision system that has to perform dimensional measuring: lighting and optics, quality of sensor and signal transmission, accuracy of algorithms, and so on. All these are treated in depth in other chapters of this volume.

Of the subjects in this chapter, the most important one for gauging accuracy is the mechanics of the system. It has to guarantee the stable conditions required for precise and accurate measurements – just as with non-optical measuring systems.

The automotive industry has long followed strict guidelines concerning the capability of measuring systems to deliver precise and accurate results,[5] one of the most prominent results of this process being the *Guide to the Expression of Uncertainty in Measurement* [11].

We will leave the theoretical aspects of gauge capability to these guidelines as well as to works on statistical process control and the like. Suffice to say that gauge capability is a much stricter requirement than simply having sufficient resolution to measure a value with a given tolerance. And these requirements affect all parts of a machine vision system.

We can see the effect on the mechanics of a system using a simple example. Suppose we had a vision system intended to measure the diameter of a cylindrical part, a fairly easy task, or so it seems.

We will back-light the part, using all the available tools for accurate imaging, namely telecentric lighting, telecentric optics, and so on. Then we could have the system measure the width of the part's shadow. However, the diameter has to be measured parallel to the cylinder's base. What if the cylinder is not precisely horizontal? Can we simply ignore the inclination and measure horizontally anyway?

Let us assume a tolerance of ±0.04 mm for the nominal diameter of 10 mm and an evenly distributed stochastic measuring error with an amplitude of 0.006 mm. This gauge would be capable, according to evaluation methods common in the automotive industry.

Now, what would be the effect of an inclination? As Figure 10.4 shows, the horizontally measured diameter is $d/\cos(\alpha)$, which is the actual diameter divided by the cosine of the inclination. At 3° of inclination, this amounts to a measuring error of 0.14%, corresponding to 14 µm on the nominal length of 10 mm. Although considerably smaller than the part tolerance of 40 µm, this error does, however, significantly reduce the *usable* tolerance range: if inclinations up to 3° have to be tolerated, a part measured at 9.973 mm has to be scrapped, since its actual value could be 9.959 mm, which is just outside of tolerance.

Although this particular error will reduce the tolerance range only on one side – as it will always result in increasing the measurement value – it still reduces the usable tolerance range from 0.08 to 0.066 mm, only 82.5% of its original value. An evenly distributed random inclination with an amplitude of 2° would cause the system to lose its gauge capability according to common evaluation methods in the automotive industry. If the construction of the workpiece and the receptacle is such that the part falls with equal probability

---

5 The distinction may not be obvious to non-native speakers of the English language: precision denotes the capability of a measuring system to produce stable measurement results (for the same part) within a narrow range of variation; accuracy denotes the capability to deliver a result that is close to the correct value.

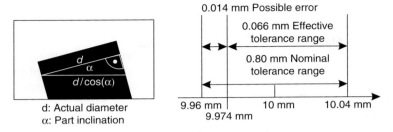

Figure 10.4 Effect of part inclination on measurement value and tolerance range.

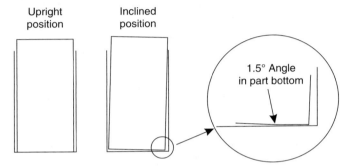

Figure 10.5 Part with two possible inclinations, due to construction of part and receptacle.

into one of two orientations, either vertical or inclined, the effect is even worse. In that situation, an amplitude of 1.5° is already sufficient to make the system lose its gauge capability without any other source of errors.[6] Mechanical inaccuracy therefore has a severe effect on the capability of the system (Figure 10.5).

This example clearly illustrates the importance of outside factors for the capabilities of a vision system. Especially for systems required to be gauge capable, the quality of the mechanical handling of the parts is very often a decisive factor. Expensive measuring systems with all kinds of fancy sensor equipment and software have been known to fail because of an unsuitable mechanical design.

10.6 Electrical Interfaces

Like most other automation systems of some complexity, machine vision systems require the following:

- Power supply connections for processing units and other vision system components;
- "Internal" data connections between processing units and other vision system components;
- "External" data connections to the automation environment.

Note that "data" does not necessarily mean "digital" in this context.

---

[6] Of course, the inclination could be measured and used for compensation. However, this measurement would be subject to error also. It is better, therefore, to prevent the problem in the first place.

Data connections typically have two aspects or dimensions: an informational one, describing what information is exchanged, what the timing behavior is, what the communication protocol looks like, and so on; and an electrical one, which is concerned with the actual wiring, voltages, and the like. There is little intrinsically specific about the electrical interfaces of machine vision systems compared to other automation components; nevertheless, some points are worth mentioning.

10.6.1 Wiring and Movement

If possible, avoid moving cameras and other vision system parts; if not possible, design and wire in such a way that there is as little stress on the connectors as possible. Many of the connectors used today in vision systems are not really designed for regular mechanical strain; just think of Ethernet RJ45 connectors common on DataMatrix scanners and some intelligent cameras, or of FireWire connectors. Screw-fixed connectors, as used for CameraLink, can certainly tolerate some movement, but they are probably not made for the stress of, say, robot movements. Appropriate cables and mechanisms for this type of application will be a major cost factor.

This applies also to line-scan camera applications, where a relative motion between part and camera is always required. Here, also, the part should be moving – which it often does anyway due to the transport requirements of the production process, the motion just needs to be controlled to create good image-capturing conditions.

10.6.2 Power Supply

Machine vision systems use the same types of power supply as other electrical devices used in automation technology. In that respect, electrical interfaces are less varied and easier to handle than the mechanical ones. Typical power supply characteristics are 230 V AC (or 110, depending on the country) and 24 V DC.

24 V DC is usually readily available in a manufacturing station; it is less dangerous than higher voltage AC and therefore less heavily regulated. However, the power consumption of high-performance PCs of around 400 W would require impractical current ratings for the cabling. Therefore, 24 V DC is mostly limited to systems of the vision sensor or intelligent camera type, although it is also available in some types of PCs. These are typically less powerful, often fan-less, systems that, because of their lower power consumption and therefore heat-generation, can be operated in closed housings or inside switch cabinets. Very demanding applications, however, will typically be outside the performance range of these systems. However, this threshold is constantly moving upward, mainly due to the demands of mobile computing, that is, notebooks and even more so smartphones whose CPUs deliver unprecedented performance-to-power ratios.

Whether 24 V DC or 230 V AC, a system running a modern general-purpose operating system like Windows, Linux, or others, in general requires a controlled system shutdown to avoid data corruption. Production stations, however, are often powered down by their mains switch without regard to specific requirements of individual devices. Therefore, these systems will usually need an uninterruptible power supply (UPS) to either help the system over a short power outage or – more frequently – supply it with power during a controlled shutdown initiated by the UPS's controlling software.

A UPS can be integrated within the system. The main disadvantage is that the electrical storage to keep the system running for some time without the external supply is rather limited and difficult to exchange in case of failure. The advantage is that control of the UPS can be encapsulated in the system and there is a very simple interface to the outside, namely the usual power supply connector.

A UPS can also be built into the switch cabinet. The advantage is that it can be larger, last longer, and be more readily accessible. The disadvantage is the additional cabling required, as the UPS requires not only a power supply connection but also a communication connection to signal to the vision system when it has to initiate shutdown due to loss of power.

Also in use are central UPS systems, possibly backed by emergency generators, for an entire production line or plant, obviating the need for communication connections to shutdown systems and keeping all systems permanently running.

Other power-consuming components are lighting and cameras. They do not require shutdown, hence they can in principle be connected like any other electrical component. They may, however, require a higher quality of supplied power than many other devices. This should be checked with the manufacturer.

It is also common that the central unit of the vision system supplies cameras and/or lighting with power itself, enabling the system, for example, to switch and regulate light sources.

Cameras can be supplied with power through their signal cables. This is the case with modern analog cameras using multiwire cables, often with standardized connectors, and the popular digital camera interfaces USB 2.0 and IEEE1394. The CameraLink interface of high-end cameras, however, does not have this capability, so these cameras require an additional power supply.

10.6.3 Internal Data Connections

By internal data connections we mean those between components of the vision system itself (note that "internal" is a purely logical term here, such a connection may well run over the standard factory network and thus be external to the vision system physically).

The first such connection that comes to mind is naturally that between the processing unit and the cameras (excluding, of course, systems of the smart camera type where this connection is physically internal and hence of no further concern for machine building). It is certainly unnecessary to elaborate on camera/computer interfaces after all that has already been said in previous chapters – at least about the informational aspect. What should be kept in mind, however, is that the signal in these wires has to carry enormous amounts of data. A standard analog video signal carries almost 90 Mbit/s information[7] at a typical frequency of 15 MHz, close to the data rate of Fast Ethernet; the IEEE1394a bus has a maximum bandwidth of 400 Mbit/s at a strobe frequency

---

7 Assuming 25 full frames of 768 × 576 pixels at 8-bit depth; of course, this is not directly comparable to digital data transmission.

of approximately 49 MHz. USB uses similar values. CameraLink is available in various configurations, supporting 1.2–3.5 Gbit/s at 85 MHz. Signal lines of such capacity are naturally susceptible to interference.

We also have to keep in mind that – in comparison to the 24 V digital I/O standard of automation systems – the signals have fairly low amplitudes: analog video has a signal amplitude of 700 mV, and CameraLink (as a low-voltage differential signal application) has 350 mV. Electromagnetic noise can have a severe detrimental effect on the signals.

It is therefore not recommended to run video cables parallel to power cables, or to cables carrying fast communication (like bus cables), or close to strong electrical devices, like motors. One will not often have to go so far as to put all camera cables into stainless steel tubes, but sometimes there are environments requiring such extreme shielding measures. In any case, the quality of cables, connectors, shields, and the connections between them is very important for lines of such bandwidth.

It is often necessary to control lighting during image processing. This can be as simple as switching certain lights off, others on between capturing successive images. It can also mean controlling their brightness levels and LED patterns online. This becomes more common with 3D systems using structured lighting to make topological structures visible.

Traditionally – and this remains a good, simple, and reliable solution – digital I/O connections have been used to switch brightness levels and/or preprogrammed lighting patterns; or lighting controllers have been used with serial interfaces. Of course, these can also be connected to field buses using appropriate converters, for example, bus terminals to set analog voltages for controlling brightness levels.

Recently, lighting equipment has become available using USB or Ethernet interfaces to program and control the illumination patterns. The amount of data required is naturally much smaller than for a camera connection, posing no challenge to modern bus systems. The interesting point, however, is that using the same bus for more and more devices and applications requires more and more addresses, increasing the bandwidth and affecting real-time behavior. This is as true for Ethernet as it is for field buses.

We should certainly not forget connections between individual vision systems; this is very common for certain types of intelligent cameras that communicate with each other or with a specialized central unit. These connections typically use some proprietary protocol embedded in TCP/IP over Ethernet connections – again increasing the required bandwidth and the number of addresses.

So, as devices become more and more flexible and use of digital (bus) interfaces more and more common, requirements on these interfaces also grow, and it remains to be seen what the typical bus topology of an automated manufacturing cell with a machine vision system will look like in the future – for example, with GigabitEthernet for camera signals, some kind of real-time Ethernet for control and data connections, USB for slower devices, converters for legacy devices, and so on (Figure 10.6).

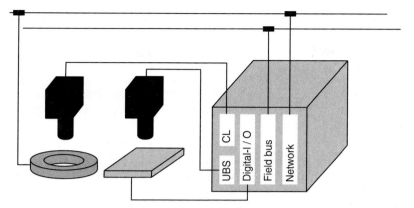

Figure 10.6 Possible system setup with USB and CameraLink camera, Ethernet and digital I/O controlled lighting, and field bus connection.

10.6.4 External Data Connections

Finally, there are data connections between the machine vision system and its environment. Typically, these will connect the processing unit of the machine vision system with superior systems, such as the station PLC or a supervisory-level computer.

Traditionally, such connections have been made by digital I/O and/or serial interface, and these are indeed still used, though less frequently. Field bus connections are basically standard today, and there is hardly a vision system (software or product) that does not support at least one field bus flavor. And, of course, Ethernet is making progress in this area as in all other areas of automation technology. Actually, especially in the area of intelligent cameras and vision sensors, there is a growing number of devices whose *only* connection to the outside world is Ethernet – TCP/IP; parameters are set via TCP/IP, and results and images are transmitted via TCP/IP. The various flavors of industrial, or real-time, Ethernet are increasingly gaining ground here.

All these connections are standard to automation technology, and as far as electrics, wiring, and so on, are concerned, they are no different than for any other device – including sensitivity to electromagnetic noise, of course. The interesting parts are the communication protocols and the information interfaces, discussed in Section 10.7.

10.7 Information Interfaces

A vision system needs to exchange data with its environment – be it just receiving a trigger and setting a yes/no result. Usually, it is a lot more complicated. For this, a vision system needs data interfaces. In the following, some information on the two closely intertwined topics of data and interfaces is presented – unfortunately the medium of writing allows for a sequential representation only.

There are various developments that increase the amount and importance of information exchange between vision systems and other systems. Among these is the spread of small cooperating units, for example, networked intelligent cameras, increasing the demand on the availability of actual feature values – instead of just yes/no decisions – for statistical process control, tighter integration of vision systems with the automation environment, for example, with the use of common type data, traceability requirements, and so on. Therefore, we will deal at some length with information exchange interfaces. What this section can only hint at, however, is the diversity – not to say, disorder – to be found in this area. Therefore, a few words on standardization first.

10.7.1 Interfaces and Standardization

Many machine vision systems or software packages offer support for various interfaces, including all those mentioned in the following: digital I/O, serial interface, field bus, network, and files. This does not necessarily mean support for a standardized protocol or format – or any protocol at all. Often it is reduced to a system having some means of accessing corresponding hardware, like selected digital I/O or field bus boards, or operating system functions for data transfer.

This leaves questions of protocol in the hands of the user. For example, the communication partner – usually a PLC – can be programmed to understand a proprietary protocol of the vision system manufacturer – causing expenses for every type of system supported. On the other hand, having the manufacturer of the system tailor its communication to the requirements of PLC and automation environment may not be free of costs either.

The fact that every machine vision system is essentially a piece of special machinery in itself, producing specific results and requiring specific parameters, will make it difficult to eliminate custom programming completely from communication with vision systems. However, recent developments, especially in connection with Industry 4.0 or the Industrial Internet of Things (to name the German and the American term), are driving emerging standards. We will see more about that in Section 10.7.10.2.

10.7.2 Traceability

Many machine vision systems exist solely because of the traceability requirements of certain products; the rise in DataMatrix code usage – and correspondingly DataMatrix code readers – is partly due to the need or desire to be able to trace back every single part to its origins, to the place, time, shift, even the individual worker, who produced it.

Traceability may be a safety requirement on the product, or it may be useful for reasons of production organization. For example, subsequent manufacturing steps may need data from previous steps, which, of course, have to be assignable to the individual workpiece.

If the machine vision system itself stores data that needs to be connected to the individual workpiece – for example, images that are subject to mandatory archiving – then it needs to do so in a traceability-aware manner. A typical method would be to use the serial number of the workpiece as the (base) name for the image(s). The serial number itself is very often nowadays marked on the part in the form of a DataMatrix code. This code can be read by the machine vision system itself, or it can be provided by a DataMatrix code reader. In the latter case, either the vision system needs a communication connection to the scanner, or the information is handled through the control system which keeps this essential information central to the workstation.

If the vision system itself is not capable of working in such a traceability-aware manner, then outside means have to be designed, like removing and renaming the data created by the vision system for the individual workpiece – which may be inelegant and possibly expensive.

10.7.3 Types of Data and Data Transport

On one side, we can distinguish different types of data to be exchanged:

- Control signals
- Result/parameter data
- Mass data (typically images).

On the other side, there are different ways of transporting data and signals:

- Digital I/O
- Field bus (e.g., PROFIBUS, CAN-Bus, Interbus-S, etc.)
- Serial interfaces
- Network (e.g., Ethernet, and real-time variations like EtherCAT, Ethernet/IP, Profinet)[8], which is an extremely wide field because of the various protocols and services that can be built on top of the network transport layer
- Files (images, statistical data files, etc.).

Note that all of these interfaces with the exception of digital I/O are actually message-based, that is, distinct data packages are serialized into bit sequences, transmitted over the signal line, and deserialized again (that also holds for files that are essentially a sequence of bytes that has to be interpreted). Field buses sometimes hide this fact from the user by presenting themselves as quasistatic I/O connections, but it should be kept in mind that they actually function in this way.

10.7.4 Control Signals

Here, control signals denote signals that remote-control the run-time behavior of the vision system. Typical input and output signals (from the point of view of the control system[9]) are as follows:

- Output signals: *Start*, (for a normal inspection run) *Changeover* (to change inspection programs), *Adjust*, *Calibrate*[10], *Reset*, and so on.
- Input signals: *Ready, Busy, Done, OK, Not OK*, and so on.

---

8 As usual without claim to completeness nor any recommendation or endorsement.
9 Agreeing on a single way of looking at the data flow is very helpful when designing a communication, and as the control system is typically the master in an automation system and has to handle the data flow with a lot of peripheral systems, it is frequently easier to assume the point of view of the control system programmer.
10 As defined in [12], calibration is a "set of operations that establish ...the relationship between the values of quantities indicated by a ...measuring system ...and the corresponding values realised

These are only some possible examples, of course; additional signals can be defined in a given system as circumstances require. A doubling of reciprocal signals like *OK* and *Not OK* is typically required when using interfaces – such as digital I/O – without data consistency. One, and only one, of the signals must be TRUE, otherwise something is wrong, for example, a wire interruption.

On message-based interfaces, these control signals can be represented in different ways. Commands, from the PLC to the vision system, may be encoded as numbers: "1," for example, may indicate a start signal, "2" a changeover command, and so on. This method automatically avoids sending more than one command at a time.

The system status of the vision system, however, is frequently encoded in the form of individual bits in a status byte or word, because the system may have several statuses at once. For example, it can at the same time have the statuses Done and OK, indicating that it has completed the most recent task and did so with an OK result. For the purpose of a clean software representation, it may be worthwhile to think about a representation in clearly distinct numerical states with defined transitions.

10.7.5 Result and Parameter Data

Results transferred from the vision system to the environment and parameters received by the vision system from the environment are typically alphanumeric data of considerable, but not exactly overwhelming, size. Results may be, for example, individual measurement values, or strings identified by optical character recognition (OCR) or bar code/DataMatrix code functions. Parameters may be nominal values for measurement evaluation, search area coordinates, part identification numbers for storing traceability data, and so forth.

The size of this data, be it results or parameters, varies typically between a few bytes and a few hundred bytes. In very simple cases – for example, a single small integer number – digital I/O is suitable for transferring such data. It will be rather more typical to use message-based interfaces.

It should not be overlooked that in many cases file transfer is a perfectly suitable method to exchange such data. This is especially true for result data, which are to be archived for long-term traceability or statistical analysis and for type-dependent parameters.

Type-dependent parameters play an important role for efficiently adapting test programs for different types of a product. Often, the structure of the tests is completely or mostly identical for different types of the same product, but certain parameters differ; for example, nominal measurement values may vary, colors or text markings may be different, and so forth. Having separate test programs for each type, differing only in a few parameter values, would not be very efficient and difficult for maintenance.

A possible solution is, of course, to have the PLC transmit the pertaining values to the vision system in connection with a changeover to the type in question.

---

by Standards," whereas adjustment is the "operation of bringing a measuring instrument into a state of performance suitable for its use." The term *calibration* is, however, frequently used to mean adjustment.

Or, the parameters may be embedded in the data describing the type, which is often available in the form of a file anyway, and have the vision system read the relevant parameters directly from the type data[11] file. An example of such a setup is presented in Section 10.11.6.

10.7.6 Mass Data

Mass data, in the case of a vision system, is typically images, be it raw camera images or "decorated" images showing the results of processing steps, such as segmented objects, measuring lines, values, and the like.

Some systems use serial interfaces for this kind of data; even field bus is possible theoretically, but the typical interface is the network. Especially, intelligent camera systems often make their live images available only through an Ethernet connection, thus saving the cost and size requirements for a monitor interface.

Note that Ethernet, even in connection with TCP/IP, can mean very different things. See the following section on network connections for various methods to access and transmit mass data over Ethernet.

10.7.7 Digital I/O

This type of interface provides a limited number of discrete signal lines; typical numbers are 4 for small systems, like certain types of intelligent cameras, or 16 or 32 for PC interface cards. A high voltage level on a line is interpreted as 1 or TRUE, a low level as 0 or FALSE, so every line can carry a single bit of information. Digital I/O interfaces usually operate either in the 5 V TTL range or in the 24 V range. In automation technology, the 24 V range is usually preferred, as it offers much more robust signal transmission in the electromagnetically noisy production environment.

It is in principle possible, but cumbersome and rarely done, to use digital I/O for actual data transmission. The typical use of digital I/O is for control signals. There, its strength lies in the speed of practically instantaneous transmission and in the static availability of status signals. Expensive cabling – one line per bit – and the risk of wire breaks are equally obvious weaknesses, making digital I/O less and less desirable in modern production environments. Increasingly, the use of digital I/O is being restricted to the direct switching of illumination setups by the vision system, avoiding handshaking with the PLC during image acquisition, whereas all other signals tend to be passed over field buses or network.

As for protocol, there is no standard assignment of signals to the digital I/O channels; this is up to the system manufacturer and/or the user to define – and to deal with, for example, with custom programming on the PLC side when using a device with limited flexibility.

10.7.8 Field Bus

Field bus systems, like PROFIBUS, Interbus-S, CAN Bus, and others, have mostly replaced digital I/O in the automation environment. They fill a middle ground

---

11 Another common term for this data in the PLC world is "recipes," derived from its typical use in the chemical industry.

between digital I/O and networks: they are message-based bus systems, like networks; on the other hand, they have a deterministic time behavior and can often be used like large digital I/Os.

For example, the DP[12] communication profile of PROFIBUS represents the contents of a PROFIBUS message as a process image, which is automatically updated between the master (usually the PLC) and the slave (any other device) within each bus cycle. The bus cycle time differs between installations, depending on the data rate of the bus and the size of the process images to be exchanged, but it is fixed and guaranteed for this system – at least, as long as the number of devices using asynchronous messages does not get out of hand. The automatic update lets the process image appear to applications much like the static signal levels of digital I/O.

The possible size of the process images, (small devices may use just a few bytes, but 200 bytes and more are possible), allows for the exchange of result and parameter data, while the quasistatic, deterministic behavior is well suited for control signals.

Though differing considerable in detail, all the various field bus systems available combine real-time behavior with message sizes far exceeding the width of digital I/O. Built-in data consistency and a much better ratio of bytes to wires are further advantages.

As with digital I/O, the protocol, that is, the assignment of bits and bytes in the process image to control signals and data, is up to the system supplier and/or the user to define and handle.

We will deal with network-based field buses in Section 10.7.10.

10.7.9 Serial Interfaces

The classical RS232 serial interface as a means of run-time communication with machine vision systems is more or less dying out. It is still used for the integration of certain sensors, like DataMatrix or bar code scanners, and for the configuration of cameras, but is being gradually replaced by either field bus or network connections. Interestingly, USB – although well established in signal acquisition and metrology, as well as for camera signals – has not made much of an impact in this area.

10.7.10 Network

In this context, network practically always means Ethernet as the hardware basis and TCP/IP as the protocol family.

10.7.10.1 Standard Ethernet–TCP/IP

Currently, the most prominent use of Ethernet-TCP/IP by machine vision systems is to transfer mass data, that is, images, although there are systems that are completely controlled via Ethernet. This is often the case with smart sensors, DataMatrix scanners, and the like, which are completely configured and programmed over network connections.

---

12 Decentralized peripherals.

Various methods are used to make (live) images available over the network. Sometimes, especially with smart sensor systems, proprietary protocols are used for which the manufacturer provides decoding software – for example, browser applets or ActiveX controls. FTP download is used as well as built-in web servers, providing the image via HTTP directly to a standard browser.

The web server paradigm has the advantage that it allows easy handling of different kinds of data, not only images, without having to install proprietary software and is prevalent in a lot of other devices; network printers, for example, are capable of delivering status data via HTTP as web pages. This method thus enables easy access to various systems using only a familiar web browser, including configuration pages, and so on.

For data communication with a PLC, however, text-based HTTP is not necessarily the best option, as handling text is not a particular strength of PLC programming languages. So for TCP/IP communication with a PLC, a binary protocol is probably better suited. These protocols used to be and still largely are proprietary, but standardized alternatives are emerging. We will see more of that a little later.

Even with an efficient binary protocol, handling image data through a PLC is typically not very useful and could be severely detrimental to the performance of the PLC (having a human–machine interface (HMI) common to a vision system and PLC to display the images is quite a different matter; we will come to that in Section 10.9).

10.7.10.2 OPC UA and Industry 4.0

Especially in connection with the developments in the area of Industry 4.0/Industrial Internet of Things, network communication is taking on a dominant role in automation systems.

To facilitate easy integration of diverse systems and the exchange of semantically meaningful, rich data, OPC UA[13] has been adopted as the standard for communication in the Industry 4.0 reference architecture [13]. OPC UA offers binary as well as textual protocols, and can transport a rich and extendable set of data types together with meta-data so that the data can be made self-descriptive.

OPC UA has the notion of profiles whereby a vendor or an organization can use the information modeling capabilities of OPC UA to define a set of data specifications for a particular use or a specific type of system. In 2015, talks started to define such a profile for machine vision systems [14]. So we may yet end up with a flexible, widely supported standard.

10.7.10.3 Ethernet-Based Field Bus/Real-Time Ethernet

Ethernet–TCP/IP has some distinct advantages over traditional field bus systems, especially in that it handles large amounts of data very well and is comparatively very fast. Speed alone, however, can be completely useless without a defined time behavior. Therefore, many efforts have been underway for some time to establish real-time behavior based on Ethernet.

---

13 OPC Unified Architecture; follow-up specification to OPC as the dominant way to communicate between HMIs and supervisory control and data acquisition (SCADA) systems on the one side and PLCs on the other side.

Real-time Ethernet specifications occupy a middle ground between traditional field bus systems and networking. Systems like Profinet, Ethernet/IP, or EtherCAT[14] offer communication protocols equivalent to field bus systems, only transported over standard Ethernet, as well as the capability to transport normal network protocols with their mass data.

Compact systems, such as intelligent cameras (see Section 10.3.4) typically feature standard Ethernet interfaces, for example, for setting up through their configuration programs. This makes it relatively easy to equip these systems with a real-time Ethernet interface and thus integrate it directly as a fieldbus device.

In the frame of this chapter, we cannot go into the particulars and differences of the various real-time Ethernet implementations. Here, we have to refer the reader to the individual specifications. In any case, the decision for a particular implementation will be only partly based on the comparison of technical specifications and performance, unless one is building a complete automation system. A large and probably dominant part will be played by the availability of components and by the preferences of the customer in whose automation system the vision application has to be integrated.

10.7.11 Files

This section may at first not seem to fit here really well. Files are not what we commonly understand by an interface. In fact, they are on a different hierarchical level, since they may, for example, be transported over an Ethernet–TCP/IP connection in the case of a file on a network share. Nevertheless, files are an important method of transferring data. We have already mentioned result and type data files for storing statistical or traceability information as well as information describing characteristics of product types.

Another very important use of files in machine vision system is of course to store images. The capability of storing "error images," that is, images of parts inspected with a "not OK" result, is very helpful for the efficient optimization of machine vision systems as well as for the documentation of production problems. Error images enable us to reconstruct the chain of processing steps that led the vision system to the "not OK" decision, so that we can judge whether the system was right or needs to be optimized.

Of course, there are also systems that store not only error images but also every single image they capture. This is often done in a start-up phase where one wants to collect as much data as possible to have a basis for setting up the system. But it may also be necessary for safety-critical parts to store every single image and to mark the image in such a way that it can later be associated with the specific part being inspected, for example, by deriving the image file name from a part identification number or by embedding binary tags with the part identification in an image file with a suitable format to make manipulation more difficult.

10.7.12 Time and Integrity Considerations

Time and status integrity are important factors for the way data, especially control signals, is exchanged.

---

14 As usual without claim to completeness or any intention of recommendation or endorsement.

PLC output: start

PLC input: ready

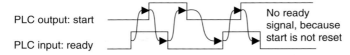

No ready signal, because start is not reset

Figure 10.7 Handshaking scheme requiring reciprocal signal changes.

Take the handling of *Start* and *Ready* signals, for example. If the system is to operate with maximum speed, a practical method is to have the system react to the status of the *Start* signal and forego actual handshaking. That is, as long as the *Start* signal is on a HIGH level, the system will immediately restart itself. This method is often used in continuous motion production (see Section 10.8.2) where the actual start is given by the camera trigger. On the other hand, this gives the PLC very little control about the actual status of the vision system.

When more control over the temporal sequence is desired, for example, to be able to determine whether the system actually did check every single part, then a rigid handshaking is usually employed where the system reacts on signal edges or state changes and all state transitions are signaled to and checked by the PLC. Of course, this takes some time, as every handshake requires at least one PLC cycle (Figure 10.7).[15]

As far as status data is concerned, there is an important difference between (quasi)static (see Sections 10.7.7 and 10.7.8) interfaces on one hand, and message-based (Ethernet, serial interface) communication on the other.

On a (quasi)static interface, the PLC can get the status data at any time. A digital I/O line has its level, independent of what the vision system is currently executing; on a field bus system, the bus logic itself takes care of the permanent exchange of status data, so again the PLC has permanent access to the status.

On a (pure) message-based interface, this is not possible. There, the status has to be explicitly sent by the vision system – either automatically (when the status changes), cyclically, or explicitly upon request. This means that the vision system has to be able to receive a request and to communicate its status at any given time. This may seem a matter of course, but is not actually, as it requires multitasking of some kind (Figure 10.8).

A program running under the Windows operating system, for example, has at least one thread of execution, and, by default, exactly one. If this thread is busy, for example, computing a filtering operation, it will not be able to react to communication requests. The typical solution is to open another thread in the program that listens permanently for communication requests and answers them. This thread will need access to status, or possibly result data computed by the main thread. This data needs to be locked against simultaneous access by the two, lest one of them changes the data while the other is trying to retrieve it.

Of course, these are standard tasks in multithreaded programming, but it is surprising how difficult it can be in practice to ensure data integrity and correct

---

15 A PLC cycle, or more precisely "scan cycle", denotes one run of the PLC through its program. The length of the scan cycle is correctly called the scan time, but sometimes the term "cycle time" is used, which usually denotes the time required to process a single workpiece. Scan times of modern PLCs are in the range of a few milliseconds or even less than a millisecond, and cycle times typically vary from 100 ms in packaging applications to several seconds.

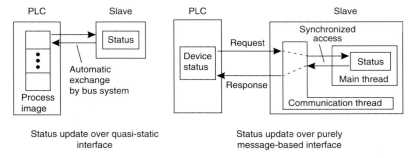

Figure 10.8 Status data exchange methods.

sequencing at all times. There are authorities in the field of programming who take the view that today's programming languages and methods are not capable of producing multithreaded programs that are correct under all circumstances [15], and it is definitely not a trivial task.

Other types of systems, such as intelligent cameras, must meet the same requirements, of course, but these often have dedicated communication processors that can simplify the handling of such issues.

The OPC UA specification with its subscription and subsampling mechanisms may make this a lot easier for the implementers, as OPC UA servers can offer such capabilities "out of the box" so that the application does not have to take care of the handling of the data. It just has to provide the status for the OPC UA server.

10.8 Temporal Interfaces

The term *temporal interface* is perhaps a little surprising at first. What does it mean? In Section 10.2.2, production systems were distinguished by the way in which the product moves through the production system as discrete or continuous; these are essentially temporal categories. In both categories, speed can of course vary considerably: 10 units per second is quite normal for bottling systems in the beverage or pharmaceutical industry, whereas in the production of discrete, complex, products 3 s and more per unit is rather more typical. In continuous production, we have 20–30 m s^{-1} for paper production, 2–3 m s^{-1} for flat steel mill entry speed, and more than 100 m s^{-1} for steel rod finishing. These differences naturally result in different requirements on machine vision systems and different technical solutions.

Much depends on the way production itself is carried out through time, and therefore the following is organized by different types of production.

10.8.1 Discrete Motion Production

The term *discrete motion production* shall denote here types of production where individual parts are produced and – most importantly – handled individually. This can be either job-shop, batch, or mass production; the salient point is that the part handling and the time constraints are such that each part can be presented separately to the camera system and, typically, at rest. This mode of production is often found for complicated parts that need to be assembled from other parts or subassemblies, for example, in the automotive supplier industry or in the production of electrical devices. In contrast, simple parts, like screws or washers, are usually produced as bulk goods, not handled individually.

Cycle times for these parts can be in the range of minutes for very large parts down to seconds. Below a cycle time of somewhat less than 1 s, there is a practical limit due to the time required for the separate handling of the parts. Below that limit, we reach the area of continuous motion discussed in Section 10.8.2.

From a temporal point of view, this type of production sounds comparatively simple in contrast to parts that are in continuous fast motion, or even endless material. But it does have its own difficulties.

First of all, cycle time can be quite misleading. In a 3-s production – meaning one part every 3 s – the time actually available for inspection can be much shorter. For a workpiece carrier system in which the parts need to be lifted out of the workpiece carrier for inspection and replaced afterward, the 3 s may shrink to something between 0.7 and 1.5 s depending on how the part handling is designed.

Also, mechanical movements need damping periods. A part is not immediately at rest after the movement has been technically stopped. Capturing the part during that time may introduce motion blur and other image artifacts due to vibration of the part. Sometimes, this is difficult to calculate or even estimate in advance, putting additional time pressure on the image processing once the required lengths of the decay periods is clear.

A typical method to gain some time is to inform the environment – that is, usually, the station control system in that case – that all required images have been taken. The control system is then free to start moving the part while the vision system is still working on calculating the result. So the vision system has time to finish its task until the next part comes in, instead of just until the time when the present part has to be moved out of the inspection position.

This results in a rather typical sequence of events, which, from the point of view of the control system, include the following (Figure 10.9):

1) Carry out movement (e.g., move workpiece carrier in position, lift part from carrier, etc.)
2) Wait for stable conditions (e.g., wait for vibrations to decay)
3) Start capturing
4) Wait for end of capturing
5) Carry out movement (e.g., move part out of the capturing position).

Obviously, this requires more communication between the vision system and the control system than just setting a start signal and retrieving a final result. At the very least, some handshaking is required to ensure that the image capturing is complete before the part is moved.

And it is not always as simple as that. For example, a vision system in a station with an indexing table hosting several production processes suddenly exhibited a marked increase in false alarms. Investigation of error images showed apparent unfocusing, but with a preferred direction. It turned out that this was motion

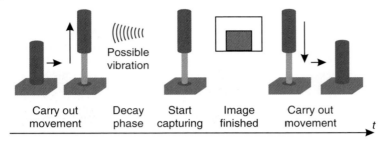

Figure 10.9 Discrete motion production phases for image capturing.

blur, caused by a recent cycle-time optimization of the entire station, which had placed a powerful press-in process so close in time to the image capturing that sometimes the vibration created by that process had not yet decayed when the image was captured.

This example serves to illustrate that the concentration of many, often Complicated, processes in the deceptively slow unit production stations can result in complicated temporal relationships; the individual stations of fast continuous motion systems typically contain less and also less complicated individual processes. It is also a good example for the importance of being able to reconstruct inspection errors using error images. Without these, it would have been a lot more difficult to identify that particular problem.

10.8.2 Continuous Motion Production

In this type of production, discrete parts are produced – in contrast to continuous flow production of "endless" materials – but the production is too fast to stop individual parts for capturing their images(or it is simply not desired to do so). This means, parts have to be captured in motion. A typical example is systems in the beverage industry where we have a constant, never-stopping stream of bottles passing the camera.

Timing conditions are completely different from those of discrete motion production. On one hand, no part will be at rest in front of the camera. On the other hand, the time-consuming cycle illustrated above of starting and stopping movements is eliminated. Nevertheless, continuous motion systems will usually be a lot faster than discrete motion systems.

First of all, though, there is the issue of capturing a sharp image of a single part in the first place. And there we already have the two aspects of this task: *single* part and *sharp* image.

To capture a single part, or more accurately a particular part (i.e., the next to be inspected), image capturing must take place in a very narrow time window. Suppose we have a system for checking the fill level and the presence of caps in bottle necks. The bottles may have a diameter of 80 mm with bottle necks of 20 mm diameter. The system processes five bottles per second, which means that the bottles are moving at a speed of 400 mm s^{-1}.

As Figure 10.10 shows, a camera field of view of 60 mm and a required distance between bottle neck and image border of at least 10 mm leave a range of 20 mm

Figure 10.10 Capturing window and motion blur for moving bottles.

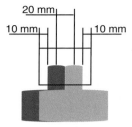

for the position of the bottle at the moment of image capturing. This corresponds to a time window of 0.05 s.

A typical solution is to use some kind of simple sensor, for example, a light barrier, to detect the part, for example, when it enters the field of view, and use this sensor signal to trigger the image capturing – directly on the camera or through a frame grabber. The camera should be triggered when the bottle is in the center of the image. If the sensor detects the bottle neck when it enters the camera's field of view, the bottle has to travel 40 mm to the ideal capturing position – or 0.1 s. It will be in the prescribed capturing area of the 0.05 s time window already mentioned, so there has to be a circuitry that delays the trigger by 0.1 ± 0.025 s – or somewhat less depending on the speed with which the camera reacts to the trigger.

So triggering solves the first task, namely acquiring an image of a particular, single part. However, of course, the movement has an additional effect: it blurs the image. Using Equation 10.1, we can compute motion blur in millimeters, or using Equations 10.2 or 10.3 in fractions of image pixels.

$$b_{mm} = v\Delta t \tag{10.1}$$

$$b_{pix} = \frac{v}{res}\Delta t \tag{10.2}$$

$$= \frac{v * pix}{fov}\Delta t \tag{10.3}$$

where

b_{mm} is the motion blur in millimeters
b_{pix} is the motion blur in fractions of an image pixel
v is the velocity of the part moving past the camera in millimeters per second
res is the geometrical resolution of the image, in other words, the size of a pixel in real-world coordinates in millimeters per pixel, in the direction of movement
pix is the number of pixels along a given coordinate direction
fov is the size of the field of view along the same coordinate direction in millimeters
Δt is the exposure time in seconds.

Note that the last relation holds only if the part moves along the coordinate direction in which the number of pixels and the size of the field of view were taken.

For a standard video camera with normal exposure time (40 ms), an image size of 768 pixels (horizontal), and a horizontal field of view of 60 mm, we have a motion blur of 16 mm or 204.8 pixels; this is clearly out of the question.

It is debatable how small the motion blur should be to have no impact on the image processing and is, in fact, dependent on the application, as different algorithms will react differently to motion blur. As a first orientation, Equations 10.4 and 10.5 give the exposure time that will create a motion blur exactly the size of an image pixel. They are derived from Equations 10.2 and 10.3, respectively:

$$\exp_{\text{pix}} = \frac{\text{res}}{v} \tag{10.4}$$

$$= \frac{\text{fov}}{v * \text{pix}} \tag{10.5}$$

With the values above, we find that an exposure time of 0.195 ms gives a motion blur of one pixel. With a shutter speed of 1/10 000, that is, an exposure time of 0.1 ms, we should be fairly on the safe side for checking the fill level and the presence of the cap.

Of course, at such exposure times, very little light reaches the sensor, resulting in poor contrast, poor depth of focus, and all the other disadvantages of low light conditions. To get a sufficient amount of light into the image during this short time span, strobe lights are typically used. The trigger signal can be used for both the camera and the strobe, possibly with different delays.

By the way, the quick light pulses that can be achieved with strobe lights make the shuttering actually unnecessary as far as the reduction of motion blur is concerned. This is the strobe effect well known from either physical experiments or visiting discotheques: the motion appears frozen. Shutters are nevertheless frequently used to reduce the influence ambient light might have if the sensor were exposed for longer periods. Of course, using the shutter and strobe together requires increased precision of the triggering delays, as the strobe must fall precisely into the shutter interval.

We see that there is considerable additional logic, circuitry, and wiring expenses connected with a continuous motion system. Therefore, some companies offer readymade "trigger boxes" where you can connect cameras, strobe lights, and also adjust delay times.

Finally, there is the question of processing speed. In our example, we have five bottles per second. The system thus has at most 200 ms for delivering the result after the bottle has entered its field of view. Actually, it will be somewhat less since the peripheral systems may require some time to react. The available processing time is further reduced by the time required for image transmission (capturing is almost negligible when shuttered).

Figure 10.11 shows that less than 160 ms – since supervisory systems will need some reaction time and the vision system needs to prepare itself for the next trigger in time – are available for processing the image and computing the results. Depending on what has to be checked, this can be ample time, barely sufficient, or simply too short.

There is one frequently used device to win some time back from the process, namely performing image capturing in parallel with running the computation. Figure 10.12 shows that now there is 200 ms for processing one image (again, a little less for overhead). In effect, the time for the image transmission has been recovered from the process since, during the transmission process, the system

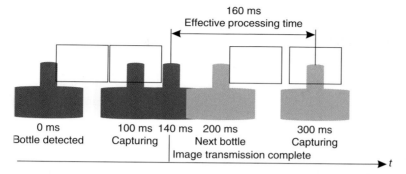

Figure 10.11 Processing time with computation and capturing in sequence.

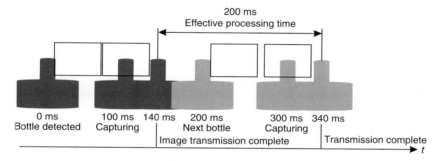

Figure 10.12 Processing time with computation in parallel with capturing.

can continue to process the *previous* image. And that is important when using this method: it always processes the image of the previous part, so there is a one-part offset of the result to the image trigger. This is not particularly difficult to handle, but will have to be kept in mind.

10.8.3 Line-Scan Processing

Line-scan camera systems require a relative motion between the object and the camera since the camera captures only a single line. This entails particular characteristics of the time behavior. We can distinguish three different types of line-scan processing [16]:

Line-wise processing immediately evaluates the current line and makes a statement on that line; this can be seen as a kind of sophisticated light barrier, for example, to monitor the width of elongated parts or continuous materials.

Piece-wise processing scans the surface of a single workpiece (or a surface section of a material) into a rectangular image, which is then processed as usual (apart from the fact that it is typically a lot larger than matrix camera images).

Continuous processing looks at the material surface as through a sliding window: a portion of the surface is present in the image and, by continuously adding new lines as they come in from the camera and throwing out old lines, the image size stays the same and the image practically moves along the surface. This is the typical processing method for endless materials where it is important not to cut a possible defect (e.g., a knothole in the wood industry) accidentally in half as could happen with piece-wise processing.

A similar effect could be achieved by acquiring discrete rectangular images with sufficient overlap to avoid cutting the objects of interest. This would allow the use of standard algorithms made for rectangular images, but it is not applicable in all situations and also requires continuous capturing and buffering capabilities.

Line-wise processing is of relatively little interest as far as time behavior goes. The system simply has to be fast enough to make the required statement before the next line is acquired and waiting to be processed. Since the evaluations – possible on a single line of pixels – are fairly limited anyway, this is typically not a problem. In fact, there are vision sensors working exactly in this way as intelligent, cost-effective light barriers.

More interesting is the relationship between camera speed, speed of the required relative motion, and image characteristics for the other types of processing.

Along the sensor line, the resolution can be calculated from the characteristics of the optics and the sensor in the same way as for a rectangular sensor.

Now we will assume that the direction of the relative motion is perpendicular to the sensor line, which is the typical case and avoids some additional complications. What geometrical resolution do we have in the direction of motion then?

For simplicity's sake, we assume that the part in Figure 10.13 has a circumference of 10 mm and completes a full rotation in 1 s. When the camera uses a line frequency of 1 kHz, the result is an image of 1000 lines acquired in that one second, covering a length of 10 mm, so every pixel corresponds to 10 μm (note that this does not say anything about the pixel resolution given by the optical setup, pixel size, field of view, etc.). This may or may not be equal to the resolution in the direction of the sensor line, so pixels could be square or rectangular. And that relation can easily be changed: for example, doubling the line frequency results in 2000 lines, each corresponding to 5 μm of the surface *in that direction*. This is a marked difference to a rectangular sensor where the aspect ratio of the pixels is fixed by the geometrical characteristics of the sensor elements.

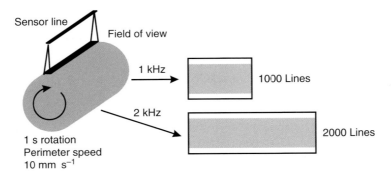

Figure 10.13 Line scan of a rotating part.

There is more to it, however. Camera clocks are typically more stable than the rotation of an electrical motor. The motor will have an acceleration ramp at the beginning of the movement, and a deceleration ramp at its end. These we can get rid of by starting image capturing some time after starting the motor, and stopping the motor only after capturing has ended. Still, variations in the motor speed during rotation will change the geometrical resolution in the direction of motion. The typical solution to this problem is using a shaft encoder measuring the actual speed of the axis and deriving from the encoder signal a line-trigger signal for the camera. Then, the camera acquisition speed will always match the speed of the motor.

Note that tying the exposure time to the line frequency will result in varying exposure – and hence brightness – when the line frequency changes because of variations in the motor speed. Exposure time will therefore have to be shorter than the typical line frequency.

Incidentally, the acceleration/deceleration ramp example again shows the importance of synchronizing various processes in the inspection station with the image capturing. The sequence here is a variation of the typical pattern for discrete motion production (cf. Section 10.8.1):

1) Start movement (here: accelerate motor);
2) Wait for stable conditions (here: stable rotation speed);
3) Start capturing;
4) Wait for end of capturing;
5) Start movement (here: decelerate motor).

Exploring all possible interactions of sensor, optics, speed, line frequency, and exposure time affecting actual image resolution is beyond the scope of this chapter. One effect is clear, however: If the optical resolution is smaller than the geometrical resolution resulting from the relation between speed and line frequency, then the camera will not see the entire surface of the part. For example, an optical resolution of 5 μm and a geometrical increment of 10 μm will result in an undersampling effect, where the camera will see a field of 5 μm every 10 μm, that is, only half the surface.

10.9 Human–Machine Interfaces

Machine vision systems are made by humans, and they are also operated by humans. Therefore, they must interface with humans in different situations and at different times.

There are many differences between working with vision systems during engineering and at runtime. Environments differ, tasks differ, and typically persons differ, in their goals as well as in their qualifications. Requirements on the HMI differ correspondingly.

What the actual requirements are on a particular system depends very much on what the system has to do, how complicated the task is, how wide the variations expected at runtime are, and so on. It does also depend on the production organization, availability of skilled staff, and many other factors, some of which will be discussed in this section.

10.9.1 Interfaces for Engineering Vision Systems

There are some typical common activities in creating a vision system, such as

- taking samples for setting up lighting and optics;
- arranging and configuring machine vision functionality to solve the inspection task (be they built into a vision sensor, part of an application package, or a machine vision library);
- programming of required (algorithmic) extensions (provided the system can be extended);
- interfacing with the environment;
- creating a runtime HMI.

Although these are typical use cases, there are many different concepts or interface designs for carrying out these activities. For instance, how many HMIs are we talking about here? That of a single tool, which is the working environment of the machine vision engineer from taking the first images up to putting the system into operation? Or those of five specialized tools? It is not even necessarily clear which approach is superior, the all-encompassing general tool or the specialized ones.

What constitutes a "good" HMI anyway? Is that the same HMI for every user and for every task?

An integrated working environment is very convenient, as it eliminates the need to switch between programs and presents a single unified user interface to be learned. For a company, for example, whose product spectrum varies considerably – and can undergo extensions at any moment due to customer demands – the rapid deployment and reconfiguration possible with integrated packages can be a decisive factor. If such a company employs a vision specialist at each location to create vision systems for their own production, this person will usually be available for fine-tuning the system, working directly with the development interface. There will be no great need for a sophisticated runtime interface.

However, for a manufacturer of standard machines, built in series, all equipped with the same machine vision system for the same purpose, the investment in a specially programmed single-purpose solution that is then duplicated again and again may well be worthwhile. There will probably not be any specialists for the vision system at the customers' sites, so a well-designed runtime HMI can be a major success factor. A custom-programmed system gives the manufacturer the freedom to create exactly the solution his customers need. In that case, the HMI for the engineering phase is actually a standard program development environment.

Too different are the needs and circumstances of various users for a single right answer as to how a user interface, or the overall package, for the development of machine vision systems should be designed. And since this chapter is supposed to be about machine vision in *manufacturing* not in the vision laboratory, we will turn to runtime HMIs in a moment.

There is one thing, however, which can be said with a high degree of certainty: just as installed machine vision systems will be integrated more and more with their automation environment, so will the engineering work on machine vision systems be integrated more and more with other engineering processes in automation technology. Many automation technology suppliers provide engineering frameworks, building upon progress in software interoperability and interprocess communication. Sooner or later, machine vision will be expected to become part of the engineering processes carried out within such frameworks. Activities occurring at the interfaces between vision system and the automation world will be affected first by this development, but there is no saying where it may end.

As a simple example, instead of the tedious and error-prone procedure of defining type data (see Sections 10.7.5 and 10.11.6) structures on each system individually and tracking changes on each system individually, type data structures would be defined in the framework and used alike by all systems involved, machine vision, PLC, and SCADA. The framework becomes the central authority for this information, avoiding redundancy and thus reducing the required work and the possibilities for errors.

10.9.2 Runtime Interface

This section is concerned with the HMI of a vision system that has successfully undergone its engineering phase and its deployment and is now running in production. We will call this an *installed* vision system.

For the installed system, the degree of variation of *how* to perform the required activities through the HMI is usually smaller than for the engineering environment; on the other hand, the variation of *what* to do may actually be quite large, at least when comparing different companies. The fundamental question remains: what tasks have to be performed using the (runtime) HMI, and where is the line to be drawn between tasks to be done through the runtime HMI and tasks that require a specialist to delve into the depths of the system and deal with the full complexity of the test program.

The answer to that question may differ considerably between production organizations. Every organization has its particular ideas about the tasks to be performed by production personnel and about the borders between production, maintenance, technical assistance, and specialist staff. So activities that are in one company performed by maintenance may in others be the duty of the production personnel directly – or, the other way round, of a specialist.

Therefore, the requirements of what the HMI should allow the user to do, down to what level of the system it lets him reach, and what level of assistance it gives, vary greatly. Nevertheless, we can list some typical activities that may have to be performed on or with an installed vision system. They are roughly sorted according to increasing involvement and interaction with the system.

Monitoring, that is, watching the vision system do its work; typically this is not an activity pursued for lengthy periods. But watching the screen display of a vision system may lead to discovering trends in the production and emerging anomalies. For this to be effective, the system display has to convey a clear idea of what is going on in the system, where it stopped in case of an error and also, if possible, why – especially when the system can be used to analyze stored error images.

Changing over, that is, changing the system setup for inspecting different types of products. It is usually an automatic process, initiated by a command from the PLC and carried out by loading a different test program or a different parameter set; nevertheless, confirmation of certain steps by the operator may be required, for example, when the changeover involves mechanical changes, and this may be done either on the PLC or on the vision system, whichever seems more appropriate.

Adjustment and calibration are essential tasks, at least for gauging systems, which may have to be performed periodically using specially manufactured calibration pieces under a "testing device administration regime," and of course every time a change occurs on the system that may affect the relationship between camera and world coordinates, for example, a mechanical changeover. Often, calibration is a special mode of operation on the PLC, which automatically initiates calibration on the vision system. As with changeover, operator input may nevertheless be required, either on the PLC or the vision system. And, obviously, in PLC-less systems, the operator will have to initiate the calibration him/herself.

Troubleshooting refers to the task of finding out why the vision system is not functioning as expected and removing the cause of the problem. For this task, meaningful messages are essential, in particular, messages that people can relate to observable circumstances. For example, a message like "Image of top-view camera is too dark" is probably more helpful than "No object in image 2," as it will induce the operator to check a particular camera and the corresponding illumination. Admittedly, thinking up and managing messages for all possible combinations of errors is a tall order, especially for low-cost systems. But the fundamental idea holds that the system should give a clear indication of what went wrong and possibly why.

Also useful are easy-to-use test functions, starting with a live image function to check the operation of the cameras, and not ending with functions to execute communication processes for testing interfaces.

Tweaking, that is, making small changes to parameters during production in order to compensate for batch variations in the appearance of parts, for example. It is essential that there are sanity checks for the parameter changes – that is, the operator is limited in what he can change – and that there is some method to check that parameter changes do not break existing inspections, that is, regression testing.

Re-teaching, like optimizing, is a borderline case. Re-teaching means adapting the test program to a new type of product, usually involving more than just changes to numerical parameters. The typical example is that of recognizing a new type in a RobotVision application, which is a position recognition type of application often based on contour/edge features; the distinctive feature here is the shape of the part, which has to be made known to the system.

Re-teaching may necessitate changes to a test program that go deep into the engineering area; ideally, however, the system should be designed in such a way that plant personnel can initiate a process by which the system "learns" the characteristic features of the new part and stores them as a new type. This process should not require plant personnel to deal with the full internal complexity of the machine vision program, be it source code or the configuration mode of an application package.

Optimizing as opposed to *tweaking* is typically an offline activity, where stacks of images – for example, error images, of parts considered faulty by the system – are re-evaluated to find out why the system evaluated the part the way it did and if it was correct in doing so. Here, it is important that the system is capable of storing and loading data in such a way that an inspection cycle for a part can be completely reconstructed. This, though, is less a requirement on the HMI than on the overall system architecture. The changes needed to optimize the system may require reverting to the engineering environment, but the runtime HMI can offer means of analyzing and changing the system behavior using stored images. So this is clearly an activity on the borderline between runtime and engineering.

So what general requirements can we distill from these typical activities?

Obviously, an HMI must be capable of conveying an idea of the current system state and how that state was reached, using display of images as well as results and protocols. Images can either be "naked," that is pure camera images, or "decorated," that is, containing visible results of the image processing, like detected objects, measuring lines, and so on. This decoration should enable the user, together with results and protocols, to understand why a particular situation occurred.

Meaningful messages are an important requirement. It is increasingly required and becoming state of the art in the PLC world to have these messages in local language. In fact, the European Union's Machine Directive requires that for all essential runtime messages and interactions.

The ability to get and set parameters of the test program and/or the vision system itself is required for tweaking and optimizing. Ideally, visual feedback should be given on the effects of parameter changes, but this can be quite difficult. More important is that it is not foreseeable which parameter may be useful to change in a given system and situation. Therefore, the underlying system *itself* should not impose restrictions on the parameters that can be set at runtime. This restriction should be the responsibility of the application engineer, production lead technician, plant vision specialist, or whoever is responsible for maintaining the system.

Incidentally, these requirements are often easier met with library-based approaches than with application packages, since there you can program everything just the way you need it. Note, however, that easier does not necessarily mean simpler or cheaper.

10.9.2.1 Using the PLC HMI for Machine Vision

Today's production stations are highly complicated setups. Sometimes they are so densely packed with technology that a screw falling into the station from top would never reach the ground. Many different systems, manufacturing processes, as well as measuring and inspection devices are built into the stations, each with its own user interface, its own operating philosophy, data formats, displays, and so on. This diversity is hard to handle for the production personnel. They cannot possibly be intimately familiar with all these devices, and therefore measures must be taken to make the operation of the station as easy and streamlined as possible.

One way of doing this is to enrich the data flow between the station's subsystems and the PLC of the station such that normal production operation can be carried out completely from the PLC. Automating changeover and calibration are steps in that direction. Remote setting of parameters for tweaking the vision system could be another. Troubleshooting is a very important point. Production staff is typically used to error messages on the PLC clearly indicating what device is malfunctioning in what way, like jammed stop gates, failed end switches, and so on. This can also be approximated only by a rich information flow between the vision system and the PLC.

Somewhere in the area of optimizing and re-teaching is probably where the line for further integration is currently to be drawn. We forgot, however, the monitoring aspect.

In many setups, HMI and PLC are actually separate systems, though in the case of PC-based PLCs they may run on the same hardware. If sufficiently powerful information channels are provided (that means hardware, i.e., bandwidth, as well as software, i.e., protocol), there is no fundamental obstacle to using the same HMI for PLC and machine vision. The HMI could then display not only numerical but also iconic results of the image processing system – perhaps not permanently since screen real estate is always at a premium – but switchable, whenever the user feels the need to see the output of the vision system.

Using the same display for PLC and vision system has a number of advantages; it saves a monitor, it saves the space and construction effort of stowing the additional monitor; and it saves the user the trouble to watch two systems.

Naturally, there is a strong case for a separate display for the vision system. Performance, especially for large images, and the possibility to watch the system permanently at work are definitive advantages. Even then, however, the ability to display iconic results on the PLC makes sense.

Moving many operating steps, like setting parameters for tweaking the vision system, to the PLC is useful because the user interface of the PLC is familiar to the production personnel, and integrating devices in this way gives some degree of uniformity to the handling of various systems. Also, these activities can then be integrated into a user authorization management on the station and an activity logging that will not have to be duplicated on the vision system side. But many parameters of a vision system require a visual feedback to check their correct setting. Displaying iconic results on the PLC would allow that and thus further the transfer of operating activities and responsibility to the PLC as the central system.

Integrating the vision system runtime more and more with the PLC in this way is a trend visible in the offerings of large automation system and component suppliers, and it resonates well with today's drive toward an increasingly digitized and connected production environment.

10.9.3 Remote Maintenance

Modern production is a global undertaking. All around the world, we expect to be able to manufacture the same products, meeting the same quality standards everywhere. Inevitably, machine vision systems of all kinds and degrees of complexity are also proliferating throughout the world – including locations where no vision specialist may be available or affordable. The tasks that production or maintenance personnel can carry out are always limited by their skills in such a specialized area as well as by the interface a particular system provides for them in the production environment.

Transporting vision specialists around the globe to set up systems or solve problems is sometimes necessary, but not always desired. Ideally, any work on a vision system that can be done without actually having to touch the system hardware should be possible from everywhere in the world – and sometimes even more if you have someone on site who can do the touching for you.

This requirement is easily fulfilled with smart sensors that are configured over the network anyway. There is no essential difference as to the location of the system, apart from a possibly inconvenient lack of speed when working on locations with less highly developed infrastructure. Clearly, any system that requires other means than an Ethernet–TCP/IP connection to be configured – such as, for example, a serial connection or a memory card – is at a clear disadvantage here.

Also at a disadvantage, perhaps surprisingly, are PC-based systems (or other systems on general-purpose computers). The machine vision software on these systems is rarely designed in such a way as to allow every operation over a remote connection also – and even then, there may be limits due to necessary interactions with the operating system. The only way to work remotely with such a system, then, is to remote-control the entire operating system using appropriate software. Since this software must at least transmit changes to the system display, it requires considerable network bandwidth and may be unwieldy over slow connections. Also it may be considered a security risk by network administrators, blocked by firewalls, or downright forbidden.

The very power and versatility of general-purpose computers running a modern operating system is actually the problem here; single-purpose systems designed for a particular task are much easier to handle remotely. They have a limited set of possible actions, and hence they can be controlled by a limited set of commands.

10.9.3.1 Safety Precaution: No Movements

A word of caution with regard to remote maintenance: Machine vision systems seldom do cause movements in a machine, but there are cases where a vision system does initiate axis or cylinder movements, for example, by digital I/O signals. It is a matter of course in control system programming but may not be so well known or deeply ingrained in a machine vision programmer: *Never ever* initiate a movement on a machine that you do not have directly in your sight. You, yourself, personally, may be responsible for severe injuries.

10.9.4 Offline Setup

The ability to set up a vision system (software) offline, that is, without actually using the target system, is particularly useful in connection with remote maintenance; consider a lengthy optimization job, looking at loads of error images, fine-tuning parameters, and so on. Doing that online, on the production system, is most likely an unpopular method, as it would cause a lengthy production stop and possibly further disturbances.

Therefore, it is highly desirable to be able to carry out any configuration of a system also offline, without direct access to the target system. In a maintenance or optimization situation, this means configuring – or even creating – a complete test routine which can then be downloaded to the target system and without further changes executed there in automatic operation mode.

Obviously, this requires that the system software can work from stored images as well as from camera images, since the required production parts will not be available at the maintenance location nor are the necessary lighting and imaging setup, and optimization is typically done on error images anyway. PC-based application packages or libraries are usually capable of this (specific library-based programs only if it was considered during their development, however); with vision sensor setup programs, it depends on the overall architecture of the program: whether it is capable of working without the sensor hardware or, otherwise, whether the sensor hardware is capable of storing images or receiving stored images for processing. This is an area where PC-based systems are usually superior, though not necessarily so, because the clearly defined hardware of the smart sensors makes it in principle easier to simulate them than the endless variations possible in PC systems.

This relates to another not-so-obvious requirement: the problem of hardware-related parameters. Some settings cannot really be made without at least knowing what hardware there is in the system. For example, how do you select the correct camera for image capturing in a particular test subroutine if you have no idea how many cameras there are in the system? How do you set up image section sizes if the size of the camera image is not available? How do you configure digital I/O handshakes without the information how many input/output lines are available?

Now it is obviously economically – and also often technically – infeasible to have duplicates of all target systems likely to be in need of remote configuration; even having a complete selection of all possible hardware would not help much, as configurations would have to be changed back and forth permanently, which is clearly impractical if not actually impossible.

To solve this problem, a system would have to be able to completely simulate all machine-vision-related hardware possibly available in the target system. Here we can see the advantage of smart sensors. They *are* specialized, stand-alone hardware, and the setup program is typically dedicated to that hardware. Therefore, the manufacturer has complete control over the entire system and can provide his configuration program with the ability to simulate the image capturing, processing, and communication abilities of his hardware. Such systems actually do exist and are very convenient to use especially in distributed environments.

Hardware simulation is much more difficult for a PC-based system because of the variety of possible hardware setups. There are helpful approaches in some software packages, but a system capable of overall hardware simulation is currently unknown (which does not necessarily mean that it does not exist, of course).

10.10 3D Systems

This section is somewhat outside the overall line of this discussion, as it singles out systems on the basis of the structure of the sensor data. Although there are quite a few remarks on 3D systems elsewhere in this chapter, it seems appropriate to sum up a few points on this class of systems in one place.

The majority of applications in industrial image processing still relies on just that: images, that is, 2D renderings of a single view of the test piece. When several images are used, then in most cases it is to analyze different aspects of the test piece without actually exploiting relationships between the images.

This situation is changing, however. The increase in computational power in recent years has made it possible to use 3D data acquisition and evaluation methods in industrial applications and makes 3D image processing the prospective next strong driver for the growth of the machine vision market [17].

Obviously, we are just beginning to explore the possibilities, but it is already clear that there is immense potential for robust and highly significant inspection applications in these methods. There is still a lot of research going on, and new data acquisition and evaluation methods are invented constantly, making it difficult to get an overview of the methods and their best use.

Before discussing a few points of interest with regard to 3D systems in this section, we would like to stress first that everything said elsewhere in this chapter – about the importance of mechanical interfacing, calibration, characteristics of data interfaces, integration, and so on – equally holds for 3D systems, and sometimes more so. For example, 3D systems often have more sensory elements than 2D systems. Instead of a single camera and illumination, we may have two cameras for a stereo setup, which need to be carefully aligned and calibrated, or one camera and three to four light sources at precise angles, switched in sequence for photometric stereo. Space has to be found for all these components, they need to be exactly placed, connected, interfaced, and so on.

10.10.1 Dimensionality and Representation

Generating and processing a full 3D model of a test piece requires some work, but many applications do not actually need the full model. This leads to a distinction that is quite useful in practice.

10.10.1.1 Dimensionality

We already mentioned briefly in Section 10.3 that dimensionality can be viewed in different ways.

We typically use the term "2D systems" for vision systems working with traditional images, that is, 2D grids of brightness or color values. This corresponds to the mathematical concept of 2D functions, that is, functions of two independent variables. In that sense, the graylevels of an image are a function of two variables $g = f(x, y)$. In the case of a color image, we then have three 2D functions, one for each of the basic colors red, green, blue (or for variables in a different color system, like hue, saturation, and intensity).

From a physical point of view, these systems are actually three or five dimensional, as each point is described by two geometrical and one or three intensity coordinates.

Accordingly, we speak of 3D systems when the data points represent a function of three variables x, y, z. Most systems that actually process data based on three geometrical coordinates take into account only the simple presence or absence of a point. For example, a cube may be represented by a more or less dense set of points on its six surfaces, as they would result from scanning the cube with a 3D data acquisition system. In that case, we are only interested in the fact that at certain coordinates a point has been registered.

A traditional 2D image assigns a value to the coordinates, representing a physical quality, namely the brightness of the scene at that coordinate. The 3D analogy to these pixels would be voxels representing a physical characteristic of a – typically cube-shaped – area of 3D space. Such an "image" would result, for example, from a computer-aided tomography (CAT) scan where the physical quality is the density of the tissue.

And there is an interesting special case, which we deal with in the next section.

10.10.1.2   2.5D and 3D

The term 2.5D or $2\frac{1}{2}$D is probably not all too scientific but nevertheless in widespread use. It has several different meanings, depending on the field of use. In machine vision, it denotes data models that do not contain full 3D positional information but instead treat the third dimension only as a function or mapping of the 2D position.

This is basically identical to a traditional 2D image, except that the gray values do not represent brightness or reflectance but height – or more precisely the distance, from the sensor. So at every x, y coordinate of a 2.5D image, a single numerical height information is encoded as a gray value. Such images are often generated by methods based on gradient data, that is, the slope of the surface. One such example is photometric stereo, which is shown in more detail in Figure 10.20.

This approach has several advantages. Compared to "true" 3D data (i.e., point clouds which we will encounter in Section 10.10.1.3), height maps have clear neighborhood relationships and allow the use of traditional image processing algorithms which are well understood and typically show very good performance.

Compared to 2D images of surfaces captured in incident light (images in backlight do not show surface information anyway), the big advantage is that the surface features are depicted on the basis of their topology instead of their reflectance. Many disturbances impeding feature recognition and segmentation under incident lighting, like pollution, discoloration, reflections, and so on, simply go away.

First of all, the topological information often enables much more robust and reliable segmentation. Depending on the acquisition method, it may even be possible to perform the segmentation in a 2.5D image and superimpose it on a congruent 2D image to examine the segmented features under incident lighting. In addition, it is often possible to evaluate other quality criteria than under incident light.

Figure 10.14 Basic part, perspective (generated by Blender) and theoretical height map (generated by OpenCV with NumPy).

But there are, of course, significant shortcomings in 2.5D. As has been mentioned previously, it treats the topology as a function of the 2D coordinate, meaning there is only a single height value for any given x–y coordinate. The representation of vertical parts, like side walls of a testpiece, cavities, overhangs, and undercuts, is not possible with 2.5D models. For this, you need actual 3D data.

Figure 10.14 illustrates this using a fairly simple 3D object, basically a truncated pyramid with a door-like opening and a depression in the center of the top plane. For the sake of precision and simplicity, the object has been created digitally using a 3D modeling program. The figure also shows the theoretical, that is, exact, not computed from samples, height map of the object. Obviously, even the exact height map does not tell us everything about the shape of the object: there is no information about the area beneath the "door" lintel. For this, we need actual 3D data.

10.10.1.3 Point Clouds and Registration

There are various representations of 3D data. The most basic is the point cloud, a collection of data points, each usually defined by its x-, y-, and z-coordinates. A point cloud created by a 3D scan of a real-world object will contain only points on the surface of the object – and only the surface areas visible from the point of view of the scanner, at that.

Therefore, a nontrivial object cannot be sampled as a point cloud by a single scan. Let us assume a very simple setup: a brick on a table. Even neglecting the bottom of the brick, we will need more than one scan. From directly above, we will not be able to scan the sides[16], and from a side angle we cannot scan the side behind the brick from the point of view of the scanner. So we will need at least two scans, creating point clouds of different aspects of the brick.

In a real-world setup with more complicated objects, the situation will likely become more complex, involve more scans, with different areas of the object

---

16 With a hypercentric or pericentric lens, it is possible to show the top and all sides in a single image; however, the sides are depicted with severe perspective foreshortening, and such a lens can only capture objects that are considerably smaller than the front opening of the lens.

Figure 10.15 Series of point cloud scans from various angles (simulated by Blender).

missing in the scans, for example, due to undercuts and the like. Figure 10.15 shows point clouds of the object in Figure 10.14 from four different perspectives. It is obvious that some features are visible only from certain angles and that some areas, for example, the depression on the top plane, are difficult to sample at all due to shadowing effects. It is clear that obtaining a 3D representation of an object will be increasingly difficult the more complex the shape of the object is.

As Figure 10.15 shows, we will need more than one single 3D scan to obtain a complete representation of an object. Each scan yields its own point cloud, and regardless how carefully we build and calibrate the scan setup, there will never be an exact correspondence of the points in these clouds. So we will have to form a coherent whole from the disparate point clouds. This process is called "registration."[17] As there will be no exact match, that is, placing points directly at the same positions, this is basically an optimization problem. Over time, many specific algorithms have been developed. The most widely used one (according to [18]) is the iterative closest point (ICP) method, introduced in [19].

The ICP algorithm is based on the assumption that every point in one point cloud corresponds to the closest point in the other point cloud, and then finds the least squares rigid (i.e., point-distance-preserving) transformation between the two point clouds. Because of its basic assumption, it works best if the two poses are relatively close to begin with or if some *a priori* knowledge from a calibration process can be utilized.

Registration is still an active research topic, so it is difficult to say what the optimal algorithm for a given problem will be. ICP is a good starting point, however, at least for industrial inspection data, as we will typically have a fairly well controlled data acquisition situation, allowing a good initial estimate.

There are many variations of the ICP algorithm, and also other methods, specialized for various applications, such as real-time tracking of multiple objects, useful for the orientation of robots in 3D space. In practice, trying out the optimal algorithm and implementing it – possibly in hardware – will probably be cost-effective only when developing a product for widespread distribution. In the area of industrial quality inspection, where new applications and thus requirement changes are daily routine, one will be more or less restricted to the methods provided by the (software) platform used. A robust, broadly applicable algorithm will be preferable here, even if it is not perfectly optimized for the given task.

---

17 For non-native readers of English, this term may be somewhat surprising; at least it was for the author. One of the meanings of the verb "to register" is "to make or adjust so as to correspond exactly"; this is where this use of the term "registration" derives from, and it is not only used for the case of 3D point clouds but generally when two or more disparate sets of data are brought into correspondence.

An overview of ICP variants can be found in [20]. Pears *et al.* [21] contains an extensive introduction into the algorithm as well as many remarks and citations on variations of it. Many papers and application hints on ICP can also be found in [22], and [23] gives a comparison of the performance of ICP variants on real-world datasets, whereas [24] compare ICP with a variational approach.

10.10.1.4 Representation

Point clouds are ill suited for direct processing. To derive information about the object, like its surface area, volume, integrity, and other numeric or symbolic information, the point cloud will typically be converted into a polygon or triangle mesh so that there are connected vertices, closed surfaces, surface normals, and so on. To this end, the point cloud will be locally – that is, piecewise – fitted to algorithmic surfaces. The surface will thus also become "smoother" in comparison to the often rather ragged points obtained directly from the scan.

One difficulty in the conversion of point clouds to other representations is that – in contrast to the equidistant grid of 2D images or height maps – the points in the set do not have "natural" neighborhood relationships, that is, it is not immediately and unambiguously clear which points are situated on the same surface, where vertices and edges are, and so on. Considering Figure 10.15 again, even for the human visual apparatus, honed through million years of evolution, it is not always easy to derive the actual shape from the point cloud. For various methods of surface representation and their derivation from point clouds, see, for example, [21].

10.10.2 3D Data Acquisition

It would far exceed the scope of this chapter to explore the variety of methods to acquire 3D information about an object in detail with respect to equipment or algorithms, so we will restrict ourselves to some general remarks and common methods.

The basic methods for 3D data acquisition are far from new. For example, photometric stereo was introduced in 1980 [25], and laser triangulation is even older. Of course, many variations on these basic methods have been invented, improved, and refined over the years. As is the case with many image processing methods in traditional 2D image processing, many methods were impractical to use before the widespread availability of cheap computational power.

There are different ways to categorize 3D image acquisition methods. We follow here the categorization by Pears *et al.* [21] with the exception of the photometric stereo technique. Pears *et al.* [21] distinguish at the first level between passive and active methods. Passive methods use the ambient-lit scene only, whereas active methods apply some form of controlled lighting.

Table 10.1 lists several popular 3D data acquisition methods and their characteristics, based on [21] and [26]. These methods are introduced in more detail later in this section – without any claim to completeness.

For the purpose of this categorization, laser beam and sheet-of-light methods have been subsumed under structured light. Also note that mixtures of methods are possible. For example, structured light may be used to aid in finding correspondence points for stereo vision, turning it into an active method.

Table 10.1 List of popular 3D data acquisition methods.

Method	Lighting	Based on	Result
Shape from focus	Passive	Monocular images	Range data
Shape from shading	Passive	Monocular images	Surface orientation
Shape from texture	Passive	Monocular images	Surface orientation
Shape from disparity (stereo)	Passive	Triangulation	Range data
Structured light	Active	Triangulation	Range data
Deflectometry	Active	Triangulation	Surface orientation
Photometric stereo	Active	Monocular images	Surface orientation
Time of flight	Active	Time delay	Range data
Interferometry	Active	Time delay	Range data

The terms in the "Based on" column are used as follows:

Monocular images: Calculation is based on variations within a single or between several images taken from the same point of view;

Triangulation: Calculation is based on triangles of light rays (in the sense of geometrical optics), stereo imaging being the case of classical triangulation;

Time delay: Calculation is based on the different times of flight of light from different points in the scene or along different paths, usually measured by means of the light phase.

The methods have been further distinguished by delivering range data, that is, distance from the sensor directly, or surface orientation. From the surface orientation, the topology of the surface, that is, a height map, can be computed by integrating over the surface.

In the following, we will describe the principle of the methods briefly. Further details can easily be found from the exhaustive list of [21, 26], and other overview articles and books cited in Section 10.10.4 or a web search.

It should be noted that combinations of these "pure" methods are possible and in use. We will not go into that in detail, however. One example is the combination of stereo imaging with structured light, where the projection of a (random) light pattern onto the scene increases its texturing and thus the number and quality of correspondence points for the triangulation.

10.10.2.1 Passive Methods

The passive methods derive shape information from several different characteristics of the scene (resp. the object) in question:

Focus: By varying the distance between camera and object or the focal characteristics of the lens and measuring focus-related characteristics of the scene (e.g., sharpness of edges), it is possible to establish a map of the relative distances of parts of the scene from the camera and thus a height map. The method acquires dense height maps with a relatively low height resolution and accuracy.

Shading: Shape is deduced from the reflectance of the various parts of the image. Pears *et al.* [21] mention photometric stereo as a related technique using several images with different illuminations. Other authors subsume shape from shading and photometric stereo in a single method. We list the latter here as an active technique in Section 10.10.2.2 because of the necessary change in illumination between images, that is, the application of controlled illumination.

Texture: Shape is deduced from the perspective appearance of a (known) regular pattern on the object's surface.

Disparity: This is typically referred to as stereo imaging. Images are taken from two different viewpoints with a known spatial relationship to each other. Typically, these are two cameras with parallel optical axes mounted at a fixed, known distance, the so-called baseline. The two images are searched for corresponding points, and from the apparent distance of the points in the two images and the known baseline, the distance of the points from the camera setup can be computed trigonometrically. The technique can be extended to multiple images.

The main problem of stereo imaging is finding good correspondences between the images. Stereo imaging in general does not generate dense distance maps because the distance can be computed only for the corresponding points and not for all points in the image. Significant texturing of surfaces is advantageous for stereo methods, as the texture creates many candidate points for finding correspondences. Stereo imaging is therefore sometimes combined with structured light methods to increase the texturing on the surface artificially.

A variation on stereo imaging is *structure from motion*, where the two images are not taken simultaneously by two cameras but sequentially by a single moving camera. From the speed and direction of the movement, the distance between the two points of view can be determined to form essentially the same as the baseline in stereo imaging (Figure 10.16).

10.10.2.2 Active Methods

Active methods use some kind of controlled lighting to influence the characteristics of the image scene from which shape or distance can be computed.

10.10.2.2.1 Time-of-Flight TOF cameras are based on the principle of sending out a light pulse and measuring for each pixel the time from pulse to reflection.

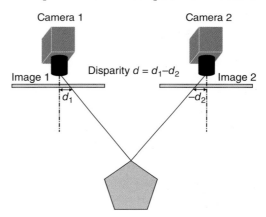

Figure 10.16 Principle of stereo imaging.

The complexity of the required circuitry results in large pixels and hence low spatial resolution; on the other hand, these cameras deliver complete depth maps of the scene with each shot at a relatively high frame rate. They are therefore rather more suited to applications involving motion (like gaming, gesture recognition, robotics) than to quality inspection tasks. Usually, infrared light is used in order not to disturb the environment by the light pulses and to make the measurements less sensitive to ambient lighting. See, for example, [27] for more detail on the principles and application of TOF cameras.

Another example of this principle are the well-known LIDAR[18] systems traditionally used in the geosciences (geography, forestry, seismology, remote sensing, meteorology, etc.) which uses a laser to create a depth map of the scene by measuring the time of flight of the reflection point by point. First mentioned in 1963, an early high-profile application was mapping the surface of the moon by the Apollo 15 mission in 1971 [28]. Today, LIDAR systems are also used for traffic speed controls, distance measuring on construction sites, and so on.

10.10.2.2.2 Structured Light In [21], this is referred to as *triangulation*, based on the mathematical principle used to compute the depth. The term structured light is probably more recognizable in today's application world.

In its simplest form, the spot scanner, a single beam of light, for example, a spot laser, is projected onto the surface to be measured. From the known distance and angle between camera and illumination and from the angle of the reflection of the spot on the part's surface, as perceived by the camera, the distance between camera and surface can be calculated by triangulation. By moving the spot in a scanning motion across the surface, a complete height map of the surface can be derived.

The method can be extended to use a sheet of light, so that only a scanning motion in one direction is required (Figure 10.17), and to structured light, which in principle allows for deriving a height map with a single shot.

The points of the (known) projected pattern are displaced in the image with respect to the original pattern because of the topology of the illuminated surface.

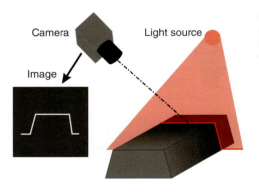

Figure 10.17 Principle of sheet-of-light scanning. Either the object or the sensor setup needs to be moved to capture a complete surface topology.

---

18 Capitalization varies. It is not actually an acronym but a composite formed from light and radar; in military use it stands for "Laser Illuminated Detection and Ranging."

Figure 10.18 Modulated lighting pattern on geometrical shape (generated by Blender).

Figure 10.18 shows the displacement clearly. It also shows that this technique suffers from shadowing effects, too.

An unambiguous correspondence between the points in the pattern and the image requires in principle a nonrepeating pattern over the area. This can also be achieved by capturing a sequence of images synchronized with a time-modulated pattern.

There are many variations on the method; Salvi *et al.* [29] lists, for example, spatial multiplexing by color stripes, random maps of dots of different brightness, or brightness gradients, as well as time multiplexing by binary codes – gray codes are frequently used – and phase shifting using sinusoidal patterns. Sometimes, a coding method is developed specifically for a particular task to be solved.

Structured lighting can also be used to increase the texturing of a surface artificially to improve the chances of stereo imaging to find correspondence points for the triangulation, typically with random patterns.

In general, structured lighting requires the surface to have sufficient reflectance (i.e., is not completely black in the sense that it reflects very little light), preferably homogeneous, diffuse reflection (because an ideal mirror would, in that setup, reflect the light completely away from the camera). The surfaces should not exhibit strong texturing, as this may distort the pattern.

Also note that there is a trade-off between the baseline of the system – determined by the angle between light source (resp. pattern projector) and camera – and the occlusion problem. Since the computational method is triangulation-based, the larger the baseline, the more accurate the height data. On the other hand, a large baseline leads to more missing parts in the picture because, figuratively speaking, the shadows grow longer, that is, there are more areas where the camera will not be able to see the pattern because it is occluded by surface features. In particular, steep slopes and undercuts cannot be scanned.

10.10.2.2.3 Deflectometry This is the equivalent of structured light scanning for surfaces with specular reflection, that is, shiny or mirror-like surfaces; it is used, for example, to characterize optical surfaces, such as mirrors or lenses, or glossy technical surfaces, like car body parts. A geometrical pattern is projected onto the surface and the reflected pattern checked for deviations.

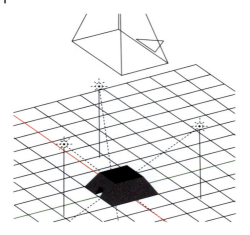

Figure 10.19 Principle of photometric stereo (actual setup in Blender).

10.10.2.2.4 Photometric Stereo Here, height information is derived from brightness measurements, hence the term "photometric." It is basically a shape from shading method, but as it uses controlled lighting situations, we list it under the active methods here. The characteristic controlled here is the direction of the light, that is, its angle of incidence (Figure 10.19).

The principle of photometric stereo is to take several congruent images of the scene lighted from different directions. From the different shading of the images, the slope (in x and y) can be computed at every point in the image. By integrating over the slope, a height map is obtained.

The method is originally [25] based on a reflection model assuming, among other prerequisites, pure Lambertian reflectance, that is, an ideal matte or diffusely reflecting surface. Variations of the method have been introduced for surfaces exhibiting other reflection characteristics.

At least three lighting directions are required for the computation. This setup is shown in Figure 10.19 with a single camera giving a top view of the object and three light sources spaced around it at regular intervals (this is not a requirement, as the light direction enters into the computation).

Additional lighting directions allow for the exploitation of symmetry and other properties to ease the computation. Using four directions is also a common setup, described, for example, in [30].

Just as with structured lighting, the surface needs sufficient reflectance and a significant amount of diffuse reflection, as mirror-like surfaces would reflect the light away from the camera.

Compared with the theoretical height map shown in Figure 10.14, there are some notable differences. Most Striking is that the depression in the middle of the top plane is missing. The reason is that the height map in a photometric stereo application – indeed in all applications based on measuring surface direction – is determined by integrating over the slope of the surface in the x and y directions. The walls of the depression are vertical, that is, the gradient on the edges is infinite, so the surface is not integrable over the edges (Figure 10.20).

We will not go into the mathematical details here. There are many papers on surface reconstruction from gradient fields, for example, the classic [31] and the

Figure 10.20 Geometric object under different lighting directions (generated by Blender), slopes in *x* and *y* directions and the height map (computed by NumPy, SciPy, and OpenCV).

seminal paper by Agrawal *et al.* [32] which is the basis of many implementations in practical use. Note that it may not be always possible to achieve a globally "correct" reconstruction of the surface, but for the purposes of industrial machine vision it may also not be necessary. For the typical application of looking for defects, for example, a local deviation in the smoothness of the surface is significant, so it is sufficient to have a *locally* correct reconstruction. The actual overall height may not be of importance at all.

We take with us the message that one may have to be careful in interpreting the results of 3D data acquisition and reconstruction methods. This holds not only for photometric stereo. Every technique has particular weaknesses leading to possibly erroneous results, like shadowing, occlusion, and so on.

10.10.2.2.5 Interferometry Here the controlled characteristic of the illumination is its phase. The most widely used method in industrial quality control is actually a special case of general interferometry, namely *white light interferometry*. The basic setup is that of a microscope: a broad-spectrum (hence the term *white light*) beam of light is split into a reference beam, reflected by a mirror, and a measurement beam, reflected by the part to be measured; both fall on the camera where they generate an interference pattern. A phase shift is achieved by changing the length of the measurement beam relative to the length of the reference beam – typically using a high-accuracy piezoelectric stage – changing the interference pattern. For each pixel, the modulation is measured; it reaches its maximum when the beam lengths are identical. Height resolutions in the sub-nanometer range are achievable – at the price of a relatively long measuring time due to the scanning through an axial measuring range (Figure 10.21).

There are different types of white light interferometers, and some of them are described in [33]. White light interferometry is suitable for plane, smooth

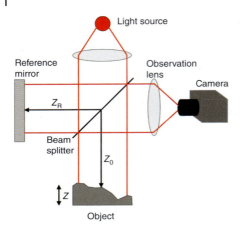

Figure 10.21 Principle of white light interferometry.

surfaces only, as its accuracy is limited among other effects by speckle noise generated by rough surfaces. There are variations on the method suitable for optically rough surfaces also.

White light interferometry is actually a fairly old technique; it was proposed in 1972 for measuring the thickness of thin films [34]. A typical application of white light interferometry is measuring the roughness of high-quality technical surfaces. It is interesting to note that an important requirement was to show the correspondence to traditional stylus measurements [35]. The capabilities of interferometers increased with the computational power available to evaluate the interference patterns so that there is a broad range of applications today, for example, defect inspection of mirrors, as in [36], semiconductor wafers in [37], microelectromechanical systems (MEMS) in [38], to name but a few.

10.10.3 Applications

From a machine integration point of view, there are no fundamental differences between 2D and 3D applications but only gradual distinctions: possibly somewhat more complicated mechanical integration due to a greater number and complexity of sensor equipment; possibly higher demands on data transfer for 3D data; likely more interesting visualization for the user – nothing revolutionary in *this* respect.

On the other hand, the application areas for 3D image processing are currently evolving at an astonishing pace. New, often more robust, solutions are found for traditional machine vision tasks; other tasks that were considered nonsolvable are becoming feasible, while at the same time completely new application possibilities are being discovered. A lot of it is still quite experimental, and solutions are therefore possibly even more specialized than in the more mature field of 2D image processing.

Anything that can be written here will thus of necessity be a preliminary, incomplete snapshot. Therefore, it does not seem appropriate to go into great depth; instead, a number of published applications will be listed to give an idea of what is already possible in this field and encourage the reader to probe further and develop new fascinating combinations of methods, test pieces, and objectives.

In order to avoid any hint of favoring particular companies or products, company publications have been excluded – regrettably sometimes, as they give some detailed explanations of particular technologies – and citations are thus restricted to articles from scientific and general industrial journals and publications from research institutions and professional associations. However, in following up the citations, especially from industrial journals, you will find that some authors have company affiliations and that some articles directly mention specific companies and their proprietary technology. It should be emphasized that no endorsement is implied thereby.

To make it easier for the reader to assess the changes brought about by 3D image processing, the presentation broadly follows the application types outlined in Section 10.2.1; we will see, however, that the emerging new capabilities challenge the boundaries of these task categorizations even more than traditional machine vision does.

10.10.3.1 Identification

The first task category in Section 10.2.1 was actually code recognition because of the special role played by purpose-built code scanners. Here we chose the broader term "identification," instead.

UKIVA [39] describes a solution to a long-standing machine vision Challenge, namely the identification of characters on tires (which, being made from black rubber, are basically contrast-free) using laser line-scanning and preprocessing in a camera-integrated FPGA. The 3D acquisition renders the lack of contrast between the raised characters and the tire rim meaningless.

The principle is, of course, also applicable to other surfaces and types of writing. Chen *et al.* [40] demonstrates the use of photometric stereo for the segmentation of embossed characters on a metallic surface using texture algorithms. Adding a fourth light source to the mandatory three for photometric stereo allows for the compensation of specular reflection (remember that photometric stereo was formulated for pure Lambertian reflection only) – as had been shown in [30].

In an interesting non-industrial application [41] demonstrates the possibility of extracting handwriting from severely textured or cluttered background by detecting the indentations of the ball-pen point in the paper using photometric stereo.

In all three cases, 3D data acquisition serves to make a fundamentally well-known application – character recognition – more robust, or at all possible, by providing more robust and significant data than 2D imaging. The segmentation of the characters is greatly improved, whereas the rest of the application can remain more or less unchanged.

10.10.3.2 Completeness Check

Checking assemblies for completeness, correct positioning of all parts, and so on, as we have briefly described in Section 10.2.1, is an important and widespread application of machine vision. It is obvious that it will, in many cases, be much more robust and easier to solve with 3D information. For example, determining the exact position of a (black) IC on a (dark-green) circuit board can be a challenge due to low contrast, making segmentation difficult; using a height map, segmentation becomes trivial.

Heizmann [42] describes fill level measuring in blister packages using laser stripe projection, and Wöhler [22] shows the verification of a glue line using a stereo vision system. The latter is a prime example of the improvement brought about by 3D vision: contrast between glue lines and the casing or car body parts they are applied to is typically poor and unreliable, whereas the topology is easily reconstructed. This application also underlines how application areas are merging into each other. Instead of a completeness check, this could with equal justification be regarded as a shape check or a pose recognition, albeit of a nonrigid object. In the same vein, the inspection of solder joints – a notoriously difficult problem due to the varying reflection of the solder material and thus much easier in 3D – could just as well be classified as a completeness or as a shape check.

Many more examples of this application category can be found on company web sites, marketing material, press releases, whitepapers, and so on.

10.10.3.3 Object and Pose Recognition

In Section 10.2.1, we spoke of object recognition and position recognition. In 3D applications, the more general term "pose recognition" is commonly used, referring to the combination of position and orientation in space.

The distinction between object and position (or pose) recognition tasks becomes more blurry in 3D applications. Pose can be used for object recognition, for example, in gesture recognition where constraints on the relative pose of upper arm, forearm, and digits can be used for identification.

Wöhler [22] cites several applications in robot–human interaction, based on multicamera setups, from collision avoidance and safety barriers – that is, separating humans and robots or stopping the robot in the proximity of a human – to the use of gesture recognition methods and tracking of body parts for actual interaction. In a similar vein, [43] presents a collision-avoidance approach for human–robot coexistence based on depth images derived by a coded-light method.

Then, of course, there is the vast field of pick-and-place tasks, where a part is to be picked from a source location and placed into a destination location. Of course, this is not a machine vision task alone but a combination of object and pose recognition tasks on both sides, so to speak, with a handling task.

Industrial pick-and-place tasks are often well defined. For example, the source location may be a blister or some other type of packaging that keeps the parts in well-defined positions. And, almost by definition, the destination location is rather precisely defined. Frequently, the task will be to put the part directly into its intended place of assembly, as shown in Section 10.11.5.

The source location will frequently contain several parts, whereas the destination location will (in assembly applications) usually accept only a single part. But of course there are also repackaging tasks, where the parts are to be relocated, for example, from a bin into a blister.

The difficulty of the task and the degree of support by machine vision vary with the degree of structuring and precision in the source location as well as the destination location.

On the source side, we may have, sorted by increasing difficulty and without claim to completeness, the following:

- *Precisely defined location*: the parts' locations may be so well defined that they can be picked up by a handling device, for example, an industrial robot or a gantry, without any further guidance.
- *Sufficiently precise relative location*: the parts may be so precisely placed in their receptacles that it is sufficient to determine its location and then compute the location of the individual parts from there. Machine vision support is required here when the overall location of the receptacle is not sufficiently well known for the handling system, and will often not require 3D methods at all. In many cases, it will be sufficient to have a camera capture the entire receptacle, calculate its overall position, and from there compute the individual positions of the parts.
- *Unstructured but separated locations*: parts may be transported on a conveyor belt or some other feeding device where, within the physical restrictions of the device, they may be in any location. Typically, one will try to separate at least some of the parts, for example, by a brush across the conveyor, letting parts through one by one, identify these by image processing methods, and transmit their coordinates to the handling system for picking them up. Whether 3D methods are required for this task mainly depends on the parts. If their height or, more generally, 3D topology is significant for distinguishing between part types or for determining their pose in order to pick them up, then 3D methods will be necessary. For example, it may be that only the 3D topology allows distinguishing whether a part is lying upside down. On the other hand, if the part's silhouette alone is sufficient for locating them well enough to be picked, 2D methods will suffice.
- *Unstructured locations*: an example of this is the famous "bin-picking" task where parts are lying more or less haphazardly within a bin and have to be taken out one by one for assembly or other purposes. This task, trivial for a human, has kept machine vision busy for a long time. It is in general not solvable without 3D methods. We will say more about that in Section 10.10.3.6.

The destination side will be typically well structured. It may be that the part is directly placed into its final assembly destination (as in the example in Section 10.11.5); it may also be that the part is put into a receptacle, for example, parts may be picked from a bin and put into blisters. Both cases will frequently require vision guidance, but 3D methods will usually not be required, as the height of the destination position is usually well controlled. This is not without exceptions, however; we may think of placing boxes on storage shelves, possibly on top of other boxes, where a 3D model may be required. Or one could think of bin-placing, where parts have to be stacked inside a bin. Here also, 3D methods will be necessary, to derive a model of where to put the next part safely.

10.10.3.4 Shape and Dimension Applications

This category has been renamed here from "check" to "application" because there is an increasing number of applications where shapes and dimensions are measured but not checked against nominal values, for example, re-engineering applications.

In the realm of 3D machine vision, this category sometimes overlaps with the following one, surface inspection, because certain 3D acquisition methods enable us to actually measure the topological features of surface characteristics and defects, such as roughness, depth of dents and scratches, and so on. For example, does checking an automotive body part for minute deformations before – or after – paint work, classify it as a shape check or a surface inspection? So, for some examples from this section and the next, the classification may be somewhat arbitrary.

Shape checks quite literally reach a new dimension with 3D acquisition methods, demonstrated, for example, in [39] with pleat detection in aluminum bottles using laser light scans and in [44] with the inspection of plastic cups for shape defects and the measuring of axle diameters, also using laser line profiling.

Somewhat larger are the automotive body parts inspected for dents and other defects using fringe projection, that is, calculating the deformation of a periodic grid, shown in [45]. Cost savings are immense when such defects are found before paintwork, especially right in the pressing plant.

Remember that it was noted in Section 10.10.2.2 that structured light methods such as fringe projection in general require diffuse reflection. After paintwork, automotive body parts are typically glossy, so the method of choice is therefore deflectometry, as shown in [46].

In the above examples, local discontinuities were taken as candidates for defects, indicated by an "insufficient smoothness" of the surface. The ubiquitous use of 3D CAD software makes it possible to take shape and dimension checks one step further. Bosche and Haas [47] proposes the comparison of point clouds derived by laser scanning to point clouds computed from CAD models for dimensional quality control of the parts. A similar approach is used in [48] for defect detection in pressed parts. An important step is the alignment of scanned data and CAD model for which an ICP algorithm (see Section 10.10.1.3) is used.

Advancing from inspection for local deviations and comparison with given CAD models, another step takes us into an area very much concerned with dimensional measuring, although not a *check* in the strict sense of the word, namely reverse engineering, that is, the derivation of a model of the part from 3D scanning data.

Sansoni *et al.* [26] shows stereo vision and structured light approaches for the measurement of large free-form objects, as well as combinations with mechanical methods especially for the high-precision measurements required for reverse engineering of parts.

An interesting nonindustrial application area they illustrate is "cultural heritage applications," that is, the preservation of cultural artifacts, such as sculptures, buildings, and so on, in the form of 3D data. Structured light and laser scanning methods are typical here, depending on the size of the objects and the required resolution. Another interesting nonindustrial field is forensic investigations, including postmortem analysis of bodies as well as crime scene documentation where TOF methods and laser scanning systems have started to replace traditional photographic methods.

Flisch *et al.* [49] describes several re-engineering applications based on point cloud data derived by a method we have not discussed so far because it is rarely used in production, namely computer tomography. It requires an X-ray source and is typically rather time consuming, making it awkward to use in inline inspection. It is, however, an important tool in re-engineering as well as in sample checks of individual, usually complex, parts taken from production.

Istook and Hwang [50] show the application of 3D body scanners to the apparel industry.

10.10.3.5 Surface Inspection

For industrial surface quality control, [26] mentions interferometry, focus methods, and laser triangulation, depending on the type of surface and the required resolution.

Wöhler [22] cites several application examples where photometric methods, sometimes in combination with measurements of the angle and degree of polarization of the reflected light, lead to 3D reconstruction results of metallic surfaces comparable to those of coded structured light approaches. Albedo variations of the surface, such as discolorations, pollution, and so on, which can be very confusing for segmentation in 2D images, are eliminated in the 3D reconstruction. They also show that combinations of methods – for example, photometric and structured light approaches or stereo disparity and photopolarimetric methods – can improve the reconstruction result by compensating weaknesses of one method by strengths of the other.

Heizmann [42] demonstrates the application of photometric stereo for the continuous inspection of floor covering for defects and the use of deflectometry for the detection of defects on highly glossy porcelain and polished pressing dies.

Bauer [45] shows the inspection of micro weld seams for blow holes using confocal microscopy, that is, a specialization of shape from focus. The same principle is used for the characterization of fine-machined surfaces such as camshafts and cylinder liners for wear prognosis and analysis. Larger weld seams, as occurring in car body manufacturing, can be inspected using laser scan systems.

Another example in [45] is the use of photometric stereo for the detection of air pockets in copper laminates in line-scan camera images. We already mentioned the inspection of automotive body parts – before paint work, that is, when they are still matte – for dents and other shape defects using a structured light approach in Section 10.10.3.4. For the surface inspection of cylindrical parts, a laser-line sensor is used to derive a surface profile of the rotating part.

For the inspection of shiny metal surfaces, as are common as sealing surfaces on automotive parts, for surface defects, such as dents and scratches, [45] describes an approach using relief images derived by a patented shape-from-shading approach. This method allows for the elimination of optical surface variations, such as corrosion and cleaning residue. UK Industrial Vision Association [39] describes the same approach for the inspection of high-precision metal–plastic composite parts for defects down to a depth of a few micrometers using a patented shape-from-shading technology.

Pernkopf and O'Leary [51] show the application of laser-line profiling and photometric stereo for the detection of topological surface features, such as indentations, on metal surfaces.

Scholz-Reiter et al. [52] describe a prototypical system applying classical image processing techniques to height maps, derived by digital holographic microscopy, for the detection of cracks, dents, and scratches on micro deep-drawn components.

Landström and Thurley [53] present a method for the detection of cracks in steel slabs based on morphological processing of 3D profiles derived by laser triangulation. Note that in this application, as in many others here, well-known and proven image processing methods can be used to analyze and evaluate the defects, that is, by measuring their area, length, orientation, position, and so on. This illustrates one of the great benefits of 2.5D methods: most of the application remains unchanged with respect to a traditional incident light application.

In [54], color photometric stereo in line-scan images is used for the inspection of small corner cracks in cast steel.

Heizmann [55] shows the evaluation of groove marks, for example, on projectile shells for forensic purposes, as a 2.5D application based on laser triangulation, white light interferometry, and confocal microscopy as well as a technique called "shadow modulation," which bears some similarity to photometric stereo.

Speck et al. [56] describe the use of phase-measuring deflectometry, which projects a sinusoidal pattern on the parts, for the detection of defects in plastic molded eyewear, that is, glossy transparent objects.

Pears et al. [21] give overviews of nonindustrial application areas, such as face recognition using data from 3D scanners, geosciences (elevation models, forest sensing) on InSAR,[19] LiDAR,[20] and stereoscopic data, and medical imaging, based on X-ray data.

In Section 10.10.2.2, we have already mentioned the application of white light interferometry to the inspection of high-quality surfaces such as mirrors [36], semiconductor wafers [37], and MEMS [38].

10.10.3.6 Robotics

Robotic applications have already been mentioned several times in this section. Most of the 3D acquisition and processing methods covered here can be used in different types of robotic applications.

The main applications of image processing in connection with robots are as follows:

Navigation: A mobile robot may move in a known environment for which, for example, a map or a CAD model exists; machine vision can then be used to identify features in the environment, map them to the model, and thus determine location and pose of the robot. TOF cameras, laser scanning, and stereo vision are methods that come to mind here. When moving in an unknown environment, we often speak of simultaneous localization and mapping (SLAM), meaning that the robot has at the same time to build a map or model of its environment and keep track of its own location within it. This is a very broad topic, so we cannot go into it here, but it is of course of utmost importance for autonomous robots and vehicles.

---

19 Interferometric Synthetic Aperture Radar.
20 Light Detection and Ranging, see Section 10.10.2.2.

Collision avoidance: This is not only important for mobile robots but also for classical industrial robots intended to interact with humans. It can simply mean the detection of the presence of a person within a prescribed volume around the robot (which may be far from simple, by the way), or it can require breaking down the detected shape into articulated parts and tracking their movement, for example, to avoid collision with a human arm – or even to cooperate with said arm by passing some object to it. Methods used here must be capable of covering a large volume so again stereo, laser scanning, and TOF are the methods of choice (of course, laser scanning has to be done at safe intensity levels).

Pick-and-Place: This refers to the use of machine vision to detect, Identify, and locate objects – the objects to be picked up as well as the locations where to place them. The objects may initially be inside a blister, which makes localization simpler as there are only defined positions or they may be stored in an unstructured way, for example, thrown haphazardly into a box of some kind which is the proverbial "bin-picking" application. The choice of the acquisition method strongly depends on these environmental conditions. For a structured environment, 2D imaging may actually be sufficient, or stereo – possibly supported by pattern projection to increase texture – may be a good choice as the scene structure is fairly well known, making it easier to find point matches. In bin-picking, we will typically want to pick up the top objects, so a more or less complete topography of the box contents will be necessary.

Pochyly *et al.* [57] describe a bin-picking system based on 3D scanning with two laser lines, whereas Kim *et al.* [58] propose a fusion of 3D and 2D data to improve detection in the presence of noise and occlusions. Oh *et al.* [59] use a structured light approach with projected gray codes in connection with geometrical object matching, and [60] work with stereoimages and neural networks to isolate objects from the height image. Buchholz *et al.* [61] again use laser line scanning and concentrate on the matching to CAD data. Laser line scanning is also used in a nontechnical application, such as the bin-picking of sausages – as "featureless" cylindrical objects – described in [39].

This is but a small sample of articles on the subject, but it shows that despite the long history of research on the bin-picking task, there is no general solution yet. Laser-line or structured light scanning is the common approach, but every application requires fine-tuning to the objects and environment in question. Matching to CAD data helps make systems more generally applicable and can also be used to determine places where the robot gripper can securely hold the part.

10.10.4 Conclusion

In the space of this section, we could do no more than scratch the surface of this vast and rapidly developing field of 3D industrial image processing. Several entire books on this topic alone could easily be written, and that has of course already been done (e.g., [21] for an overview of acquiring and processing 3D shapes with a section on (nonindustrial) applications, [22] for the combination of acquisition and processing methods and applications in industrial quality inspection and robotics, [62] for a projective geometry approach, [63] with an emphasis on registration, [64] with a focus on stereo imaging, and [65] with a broad overview of the acquisition and processing techniques).

Over time, standard approaches will certainly emerge, much like in 2D image processing, and we made some remarks on that throughout the introduction of acquisition methods in Section 10.10.2.1. For the time being, however, following the relevant publications will be necessary to keep up-to-date with acquisition and processing methods as well as their application.

The industrial solution potential of 3D image processing is immense, ranging from all kinds of quality inspection tasks to advanced robotics and HMI topics. This is certain to be a very interesting field of research for a long time.

10.11 Industrial Case Studies

This section will present several actual industrial applications. Despite the necessary discretion with respect to product – and even more, nowadays, production – information, they will hopefully raise a few interesting ideas, reinforce some of the points made in this chapter, and lead the reader to some novel solutions and applications in her/his own environment.

At the end of each application description, a brief description of equipment and important algorithms is given. The equipment description is most detailed in Section 10.11.1, but in the following only a brief overview is given.

The case studies have not been altered with respect to the first edition, which may make the equipment lists appear somewhat outdated. Today, we would have USB or GigE cameras instead of analog cameras on framegrabbers, LED lights instead of fluorescents or cold-light sources, and also, of course, current PCs and operating systems. However, all this is just "implementation details," irrelevant for the salient points of the examples, and therefore we have decided to leave them as they are.

10.11.1 Glue Check Under UV Light

By kind permission of Robert Bosch GmbH, Eisenach plant, Germany.

10.11.1.1 Task

The application presented here falls into the *completeness check* category, and it is a typical verification inspection, that is, the part is checked for correctness after some manufacturing process has been carried out.

The part in question (see Figure 10.22) is an automotive sensor element, and the process is the application of glue on the part's lid. The part has to meet stringent quality requirements with respect to sealing and resistance against chemically aggressive media. The casing therefore has to be tightly and securely closed. This is achieved by using a special glue.

To ensure strength and sealing properties of the joint, an image processing system is used to verify the amount and shape of glue before connecting the pieces. The vision system also checks whether there is glue outside the prescribed spots.

Figure 10.22 Section of sensor component with glue spots (marked).

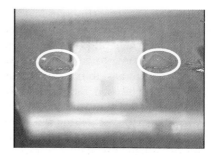

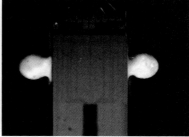

Figure 10.23 Glue spots of different quality under UV illumination.

10.11.1.2 Solution

The most interesting part of this application is the illumination. In visible light, the glue exhibits almost no contrast to the part. Under UV light, however, the glue is fluorescent, resulting in an image with excellent contrast properties (see Figure 10.23).

10.11.1.3 Equipment

Except for the UV illumination, the application was mostly solved with standard components and methods. A standard charge-coupled device (CCD) matrix camera with a 50 mm lens and a UV filter to avoid saturating the sensor with reflection of the UV illumination from the component was used to capture the image. The speed of the production line did not require specific triggering mechanisms, and image capture is done directly after the start signal from the control system has been received.

On the computer side, a custom-built fanless PC was used with a 24 V DC power supply, a standard frame grabber, a PROFIBUS board for control system communication, and an Ethernet connection for remote maintenance. Since 24 V is a standard voltage in automation technology systems, and also used for digital I/O connections or to supply lighting equipment, using such a power supply makes the cabling easy (and makes the mandatory CE certification process less costly in terms of work as well as money).

As for the software, a configurable Windows-based image processing system was used running under Windows 2000 Professional. Interfacing to the control system was done with a configurable protocol on top of PROFIBUS DP. In addition to permanently available control signals (such as Start, Change Program,

Ready, Done, etc.), this protocol uses the PROFIBUS DP process image for the transmission of user-definable data structures, which can contain practically any information generated by an image processing system. It would therefore be possible at any time to enhance the system not only to evaluate the quality of the glue spots but also to transmit actual measurement values to the control system. These could be used, for example, to adapt dispenser settings based on statistical process control results.

10.11.1.4 Algorithms

Because of the excellent contrast of the fluorescent glue under the UV illumination, the system can rely mostly on thresholding for segmentation. Template matching is also used, mainly for position determination. Of course, various feature computation algorithms are used to describe the characteristics of the glue spots and thus determine their correctness.

10.11.1.5 Key Points

This application holds some points of interest: first of all, it proves once more that finding a suitable illumination is a key issue in most vision applications. The rest is structurally simple – which does not mean that it does not involve a lot of effort and is trivial. And we see what makes a suitable illumination: one that is capable of clearly and consistently emphasizing the salient features of the inspection task.

The second point is very much related to the first. It shows the importance of the knowledge, help, and commitment of the people from the product development and manufacturing side for the vision system engineer. The solution to use UV illumination to make the glue visible can only be found by either receiving the information that the glue used is fluorescent or by influencing production to use such glue – or, in some cases, to have one developed. Only by talking to the people who know about the product and about the process, by asking questions and making suggestions, by using all available knowledge, can good solutions be found.

10.11.2 Completeness Check

By kind permission of Robert Bosch GmbH, Nuremberg plant, Germany.

10.11.2.1 Task

The application presented here is a *completeness check* of the verification inspection type, meaning that the part is checked for correctness after execution of a particular manufacturing step.

The part in question is an automotive control component. For protection against the environmental conditions prevalent in the engine space, the component is encased in injection-molded plastic. Before that process, the presence and correct position of various components are checked – which are then encased in layers of plastic. Afterward, several features of the finished molding are checked. Figure 10.24 shows an image of the part in background illumination.

10.11.2.2 Solution

The parts are captured by standard cameras in front of diffuse infrared backlights. In the clear-cut contour image, a number of prescribed areas are checked to see

Figure 10.24 Backlit image of controller component before and after molding.

whether they contain the required components; other areas are checked for being free of obstacles. This ensures not only the completeness of the required components but also that no other material is present inside the injection-molding volume and that the components are actually in their required positions (because unacceptable deviations from these positions would result in nominally free areas to be at least partially covered). The position checks are augmented by edge-based measurements to verify certain geometrical features with the required accuracy.

10.11.2.3 Key Point: Mechanical Setup

A very interesting feature of the application is the mechanical setup. A four-position indexing table is used to transport the parts. The parts are checked at three of the four positions. Figure 10.25 shows a sketch of the indexing table and the setup of cameras and illumination. Note that nowhere a camera is placed directly beside any of the lighting components providing the illumination for a different camera to avoid problems with stray light.

Also interesting is the complexity of the check sequence and data management on the control system for the round-table check. Since a single computer is responsible for the checks at the loading and unloading positions, it receives several start signals per indexing table step. Each time, a different test program is executed and the control system has to assign the correct results to the various parts in the different positions.

10.11.2.4 Equipment

The system uses standard-format CCD cameras, one 24 V industrial PC for the loading and unloading position, one for the premolding position, both equipped with standard frame grabbers for up to four cameras and PROFIBUS boards for communication with the control system.

All illuminations are diffuse LED area lights. Since there are no particular requirements on gauge capability in this application, standard 35 and 50 mm lenses are used.

As for the software, a configurable Windows-based image processing system running under Windows 2000 Professional was used in combination with a custom-developed standard protocol for control system communication.

10.11.2.5 Algorithms

The excellent contrast properties of the backlit images allow the application to rely almost completely on thresholding segmentation. For the dimensional

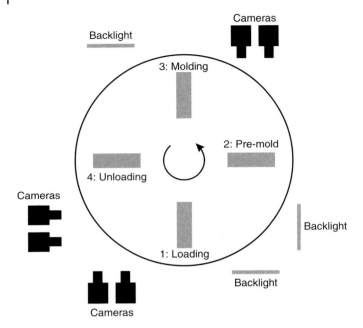

Figure 10.25 Camera and illumination arrangement on indexing table.

checks, where particular component positions are checked, edge detection is used for increased accuracy.

10.11.3 Multiple Position and Completeness Check

By kind permission of Robert Bosch Espana Fca. Madrid, S.A. This application has been implemented in cooperation with the technical functions department of Robert Bosch Espana, RBEM/TEF3, and the vision group of the special machinery department of Robert Bosch GmbH, PA-ATMO1/EES22.

10.11.3.1 Task

The application presented here is a *completeness check* of the verification inspection type, that is, a part (in this case 42 parts) is checked for presence and correctness, combined with position recognition.

The actual part in question is a small hybrid circuit. Several components on this circuit have to be checked for presence and position; in addition, the type has to be verified by reading and checking a character. So far, the process is basic. The interesting thing about the application is that production logistics puts up to 42 of these circuits on a single foil, and still the resolution has to be sufficient to check the distances between individual components with considerable accuracy. Figure 10.26 shows such a foil.

10.11.3.2 Solution

The size versus resolution obstacle can be overcome in different ways; one would be to use a sufficient number of cameras – large enough cameras at that – or a

Figure 10.26 Fully occupied foil with 42 hybrid circuits.

line-scan camera to capture a single high-resolution image of the entire foil. In the end, neither of these two options came to be used.

Increasing the number of cameras ran into a cost barrier, and led to a difficult – or space-consuming – mechanical design which had to find room for all the cameras and would have complicated the application insofar as it would have been necessary to check images for overlap; otherwise, components might have been checked twice or entirely overlooked.[21]

The large line-scan camera image would have required, naturally, a line-scan camera and a mechanical setup capable of smoothly moving either the foil or camera. In addition, it would have resulted in a very large image and, advances in computer hardware notwithstanding, it is always nicer to work with images of "normal" size.

So in the end, it was decided to use a single camera and do a separate check for each of the 42 components. This made the image processing programs simpler – the same procedure every time for 42 hybrids – moving some of the complexity toward the interface between vision system and control system. The test procedure was realized in the following way:

- For a new foil, the control system gives a reset message to the vision system, indicating precisely that: "delete all current results, positions, and statistics data, we are starting a new foil."
- For each hybrid, the control system proceeds as follows:
  – Bring the camera into position;
  – Transmit the position number to the vision system;
  – Start the evaluation.

The vision system carries out the following steps:

- Capture an image with backlighting through the foil;
- Execute the evaluation of the distances of the circuit to its neighbors;
- Capture an image with IR top-lighting;
- Capture an image with red top-lighting;
- Execute the evaluation of the components on the circuit;
- Visualize the result at the appropriate overall position (this is the main purpose of the reset signal, namely clearing the visualization);

---

21 Of course, current image processing packages provide support for stitching images, but it is usually easier to be able to do without it.

- Transmit the results for the given position to the control system (including the position itself as a cross-check).

10.11.3.3 Key Point: Cycle Time

Incidentally, this procedure solved another requirement, namely that a foil is not be fully occupied, that is, any position on a given foil could be empty. Only the control system would have this knowledge, and could thus simply skip the position without any additional communication overhead or logic on the vision system side.

A note on the result itself: the specification called for a detailed result, not merely yes or no but a yes/no on a number of properties, namely the presence and position of several individual components as well as the presence and correctness of the type mark. This communication was also very easy to handle using the above procedure.

Obviously, the procedure is easily scalable – in principle – but as always in life, there is no free lunch. Of course, the separate positioning and execution for each individual hybrid takes time. For each hybrid, three high-resolution images are captured. Together with switching the LED illumination, this takes ~0.7 s. Then the camera has to be moved from one position to the next: fortunately, these are only about 20 mm apart. Since even the tiniest movement by the most simple axis requires an acceleration and a braking phase, there is clearly a limit on the achievable cycle time.

On the current system, there is ample time for this procedure. If the timeframe tightens, there are two measures that can immediately be taken to keep the cycle time:

- Immediately after acquiring the images, the vision system could set a handshake signal on the PROFIBUS, indicating to the control system that the camera can be moved to the next position. So the control system does not have to wait for the actual evaluation result to move the camera. Of course, it does have to wait for the evaluation to be finished before giving the next start signal.
- Assume that one row of circuits has been processed from left to right; then it is of course faster to move the camera merely to the next row and start the row from right to left than to move the camera the entire way back to the beginning of the line. Thanks to the transmission of the position number to the vision system, it can nevertheless assign and visualize its results correctly.

10.11.3.4 Equipment

The system uses a high-resolution CCD camera and an appropriate frame grabber. For the three images, the system switches between an infrared diffuse light below the foil and an infrared directed light above the foil and a red directed light above the foil. The light beneath the foil gives a good backlit image of the circuit in question and parts of its neighbors, so distances between a circuit and its neighbors can be measured with high accuracy. The directed lights above the foil enhance different features to be checked on the circuits.

The system was implemented using a configurable vision software package running under Windows 2000 on an 19″ IPC. The rather product-specific requirements on the management of results (i.e., visualizing and transmitting the separate feature results for the individual circuits) made some custom programming necessary; the control system interface itself, however, is a standardized protocol on top of PROFIBUS DP that allows for the transmission of configurable data structures in addition to the usual control signals.

10.11.3.5 Algorithms

The system has to check distances between each circuit and its neighbors. With a single circuit in the center of the image and just the borders of its neighbors visible (for maximum resolution), these distances necessarily reach far into the border areas of the image and thus into the areas of maximum lens distortion. An algorithm for calibrating the measured lengths according to the distance from the center proved to be helpful for reaching gauge capability here.

Also, subpixel edge detection techniques and corresponding distance and angle measuring algorithms played an important role. For the distinction between the type characters, template matching is used. Template matching is usually better at finding things than at distinguishing between them, but with only two clearly distinct characters this is no problem at all.

10.11.4 Pin-Type Verification

By kind permission of Robert Bosch GmbH, Bamberg plant.

10.11.4.1 Task

The purpose of this application is to check the type of contact fed into the station before actually attaching it to the product, in itself a fairly simple *object recognition* problem. It is interesting because constraints imposed by the mechanical setup of the machine prevented the optimal solution from being implemented, so an indirect solution had to be found.

10.11.4.2 Solution

The contact pins are distinguished by the following main characteristics:

- length and width
- angle to the horizontal and bending points.

Figure 10.27 shows some of the different types of pins. Obviously, the width can only be seen from top (or bottom), whereas the angle and bending points are best determined in a side view. The length could be determined from both aspects. Both images should ideally be taken in backlight. Unfortunately, the geometry of the machine did not allow for such a lighting and capturing setup. A side view could not be achieved at all, and for the top view a back light was not possible.

It was impossible, therefore, to measure all the distinguishing features directly. An indirect method had to be found. Figure 10.28 shows its principle. The parts are illuminated from top at such an angle that the flat surfaces reflect maximum light into the camera, whereas the bend reflects the light in a completely different direction. This makes it possible to deduce the position of the bends from the position of dark areas interrupting the reflexion of the pins. Of course, in reality,

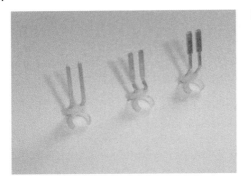

Figure 10.27 Different types of pins.

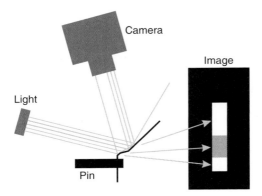

Figure 10.28 Basic lighting and camera setup.

Figure 10.29 Different types of pins under top lighting.

the light and lens are much larger in relation to the pin than in the sketch, and there is also diffuse reflexion on the pin so that the entire length of the pin will appear bright to the camera.

In this way, it was possible to distinguish between all required types of pins. Figure 10.29 shows some different types. The check then becomes relatively easy: at certain type-dependent positions in the image, the presence of dark and light areas is checked.

10.11.4.3 Key Point: Self-Test

There are, of course, limits to this setup. It is very difficult, if not impossible, to distinguish pins whose only difference is their angle to the horizontal. If the bends are not in different places, this is practically not visible. More important, however, is that changes to the position of the checked regions would lead to a high proportion of false alarms and could, in principle, lead to different types being confused – which is very unlikely with the existing types, but nevertheless possible.

Therefore, the system was equipped with a "self-test capability." This self-test uses stored reference images of each type to check whether a test program performs as expected after a change to the program. To this end, all the images are loaded into the test program one by one – instead of camera images – and the result is determined and compared to the expected result for the image. Only for images of the correct type should the program yield OK, but for all other images it is "not OK." Thus it can easily be seen whether a particular change led to the program accepting the wrong type or rejecting the correct type.

10.11.4.4 Equipment

The system uses a standard CCD matrix camera and a 50 mm lens to capture the image. The camera is connected to a high-precision frame grabber in a custom-built fanless 24 V IPC with a PROFIBUS board for control system communication and an Ethernet connection for remote maintenance.

As for the software, a configurable Windows-based image processing system was used running under Windows 2000 Professional. Interfacing to the control system was done with a configurable protocol on top of PROFIBUS DP. The protocol would allow at any time enhancing the system not only to evaluate the type of the pins internally but also to transmit actual measurement values to the control system.

10.11.4.5 Algorithms

Because of the excellent contrast of the illuminated parts of the pins, the system can rely mostly on thresholding for segmentation to check the required bright and dark areas of the pins. For measuring the width and distance of the pins, additional edge detection algorithms are used.

Note that this application is not a measuring application by nature but a type verification with considerable distances between the nominal measurements of the different types of pins. Therefore, the system has not been designed for gauge capability requirements.

10.11.5 Robot Guidance

By kind permission of Robert Bosch GmbH.

10.11.5.1 Task

The goal of this application is *position recognition* with the added requirement of transmitting this position so that a robot can take the component and automatically join it with its counterpart.

The part in question is a plastic lid that is glued onto a metal casing. The robot has to take the lid from the feeder, gripping it at the correct points, turn and move it into the required end position, and press it onto the glue-covered casing to fix it securely and precisely into place.

10.11.5.2 Solution

To this end, the original position of the part coming from the feeder must be recognized with sufficient accuracy so that the robot gripper can take hold of it and can turn and move it precisely into the required end position. The feeder places the lid on an LED backlight, as shown in Figure 10.30, where it is captured by a high-resolution camera mounted at a fixed position inside the manufacturing cell (which means that we have a fixed camera coordinate system as well as a fixed robot coordinate system).

Using a geometrical matching algorithm, the position and orientation of the lid can be accurately determined. The frame of reference for these coordinates is of course the camera coordinate system. Subsequently, a coordinate transformation into the robot coordinate system is carried out. The transformed coordinates are then transmitted to the robot control system.

A geometrical matching algorithm – in contrast to a gray-level template matching method – correlates the position of geometrical features (such as corners, straight edges, curves, etc.) found in the image with those in the matching model. It can thus achieve a high degree of accuracy and can also be made independent of orientation and scaling of the part in the image.

10.11.5.3 Key Point: Calibration

A calibration is required to enable the system to transform between the two coordinate systems. Because of the geometrical and optical characteristics of the system, no image rectification is needed to achieve the required accuracy. Therefore, a three-point calibration is sufficient.

Calibration is requested by the operator through the control system. The operator has to insert a calibration part, which in this case is a part similar to the actual production part but made with particularly high accuracy and – for

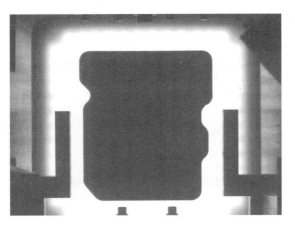

Figure 10.30 Plastic lid on LED backlight.

durability – of a metal. This part is then presented to the vision system in three different positions, involving a rotation of the part (which should therefore not be symmetrical). In each position, a handshaking takes place (i.e., the robot control system transmits a message to the vision system that it has reached the position), and the vision system captures the image of the part and in turn transmits a message to the robot control system to indicate that it has captured the image and the part can be moved again.

The robot coordinates of this procedure are predetermined and are transmitted to the vision system. The vision system compares the coordinates of the part in the three images with the robot coordinates and determines and stores the transformation parameters.

The coordinates thus determined refer to the tool center point of the robot, because that is what the predetermined coordinates refer to. Suppose we had different types of lids with different sizes so that the tool center point is at a different distance from the border of the parts. In that case, the robot control system needs a corrective offset in order to place all types at the correct position. This corrective factor could have been set to a fixed value in the robot control program but it is incorporated into the vision system programs for two reasons:

- Changing the calibration of the vision system may affect the correction factors.
- The vision system will need different matching models for the different lids since their geometrical features will be different; it is thus quite natural to place the correction factors together with the different models. The robot can then – in principle for simple movements, but it may not be practical in all circumstances – use the same program for all types.

The correction factors are determined by a similar procedure as the calibration. Instead of a calibration part, however, a part of the pertaining type is used to determine the correction factor.

10.11.5.4 Key Point: Communication

Finally, a word on communication in this application. There are three components talking to each other in this setup:

1) The station control system, which is the overall master. It controls the feeder as well as all the glue dispensers, the safety equipment, and so on.
2) The robot control system, which is slave to the station control system but is in itself the master for the vision system.
3) The vision system as slave to the robot control system.

Figure 10.31 shows the relationship between the three components. The vision system receives its start commands, handshake signals, and other information (like type numbers and calibration coordinates) from the robot control system and sends its handshake responses and results to the robot control system. This entire communication is carried out over Ethernet in the TCP/IP protocol. The robot control system in turn is controlled also via Ethernet from the station control system.

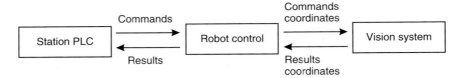

Figure 10.31 Communication partners in robot vision application.

10.11.5.5 Equipment

The system uses a high-resolution (1392 × 1040) camera on an appropriate frame grabber in a 24 V industrial PC. A large LED area backlight is used to render the contours of the lid for the positioning algorithm.

10.11.5.6 Algorithms

The most prominent algorithm here is geometrical pattern matching, which enables the system to find the different part types reliably and accurately. Also important is the three-point calibration and the offset adjustment algorithm for processing the different types of lids.

Another key factor is the close interaction between vision system and robot control carried out through the TCP/IP-based protocol.

10.11.6 Type and Result Data Management

By kind permission of Robert Bosch GmbH, Bamberg plant.

10.11.6.1 Task

Modern spark plugs are specifically optimized for particular gasoline engines. Therefore, a practically endless variety of different spark plug types is produced nowadays, potentially more than 1000 in a single plant. Figure 10.32 shows a few of them. Accordingly, there is a large number of features to check. Some of these checks are quite basic, and others are extremely difficult, but that is not our main concern here. The data management for such a number of variants is a challenge in itself.

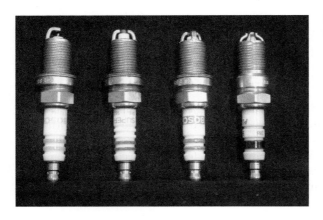

Figure 10.32 Various types of spark plugs.

10.11.6.2 Solution

It is clearly not possible to have a completely separate check routine for every single type. Assume that all these routines have some common procedure and parameters. Now, someone develops an optimization of these parameters. Imagine the work and cost required to upgrade all the check routines, and the necessary configuration management!

Fortunately, spark plugs are made from several basic building blocks which in themselves occur in several variants but not as many as with the overall spark plug. Its variants are to a large extent created by assembling different varieties of the basic components; so, clearly, the way to go is by using separate subroutines for these basic components and reconfigure those according to the type currently manufactured.

10.11.6.3 Key Point: Type Data

The problem of variety concerns parameters as well as nominal values and result data. Obviously, when there are spark plugs with different dimensions that have to be checked, there will be different nominal values and tolerances for those dimensions. At the same time, however, basic parameters of an algorithm may depend on this dimension. Take, for example, a high-precision edge detection as the basis for a geometrical check. This edge detection needs to take place in the correct location for the given type of spark plug. Thus, the region of interest, search direction, as well as parameters of the edge model may change with the type of spark plug being checked.

To meet these requirements, the software has been designed using subroutines corresponding to the various checks on the individual building blocks of the spark plugs. Each of these subroutines has been implemented in a generic way so that its detailed behavior is actually controlled by parameters set externally.

The parameters, on the other hand, are managed in a type database, which contains data describing the type of product currently manufactured and inspected. Inspection parameters thus become part of the characteristics of the part type being produced.

Here, type data is centrally managed on a supervisory level server. From this server, the type data relevant for the type currently produced is handed down to the inspection stations. During initialization or changeover, the inspection programs read the type data and adjust their parameters for the type to be inspected. This scheme would also naturally allow for central optimization of the parameters of various inspection stations doing the same type of inspection.

10.11.6.4 Key Point: Result Data

Another interesting point in this inspection system is also related to the management of data, in this case result data. For each inspected workpiece, a considerable amount of results is produced. What we are typically used to is the situation where the vision system itself draws the conclusion as to whether the part is good or not and submits its decision to the control system. This decision has been broken down here to the level of individual inspection features. For some features, the actual value is transmitted, but for most, a good/faulty decision of the vision system – but referring only to this feature, not the overall part – is made.

The reason for this is that different things may be done with the part subsequently. For example, there may be defects on a part that can be remedied by rework; or a particular fault occurs with a higher than normal frequency so that the production management may deem it appropriate to investigate this type of fault by sending workpieces exhibiting that fault to parts analysis. What parts to send for rework and parts analysis and what parts to actually scrap is a question of the manufacturing strategy and therefore not necessarily appropriate to be decided by a machine vision system.

It is, of course, always a question of overall production organization and strategy as to how to distribute responsibilities between various systems. In this case, the decision about how to handle these "borderline parts" was placed in the hands of the control system, for several reasons; one is that this is the tool the line personnel are most familiar with. Also, the actions required to steer the parts to the appropriate places are carried out by the control system anyway. Most importantly, however, because it was perceived as the appropriate way to assign the responsibility, the vision system delivers results, that is, data, like any other measuring system; the control system controls the handling of the parts and what is to be done with them.

10.11.6.5 Equipment

There are various image processing systems for this product. All use high-performance industrial PCs to meet the cycle-time requirements. The different algorithms run inside a shell program providing communication to the PLC via PROFIBUS, loading of type data provided by the PLC via Ethernet, and visualizing and providing statistics for the operator.

PROFIBUS communication is used for control signals (Start, Ready, etc.) as well as for communicating result data as described above in a configurable protocol, enabling the transmission of practically arbitrary data structures through the PROFIBUS process image.

10.11.7 Dimensional Check for Process Control

By kind permission of Robert Bosch GmbH, Bamberg plant.

10.11.7.1 Task

This application is a *shape and dimension check* as far as the image processing is concerned. However, the point that concerns us here is the use that is made of the measured dimensions, not the method of obtaining these measurements in a gauge-capable manner in the first place. Although some of the measurements are used to evaluate the correctness of the part, the main application of these values lies in controlling the production process.

The part in question is a spark plug, and the dimension concerned is the shearing point, that is the height where the ground electrode (on the side of the spark plug) has to be sheared off prior to bending it over the middle electrode. The correct geometrical arrangement of the middle electrode and ground electrode is critical for the performance of the spark plug and hence for the quality of the combustion process and therefore fuel consumption and pollution immission levels of the engine. Since inevitable part tolerances will cause the middle electrode to have slightly different heights, the shearing point must be determined for every spark plug individually to compensate for these tolerances and achieve a stable distance between the two electrodes.

10.11.7.2 Solution

Figure 10.33 shows the backlit image of the top of a spark plug with the ground electrode not yet sheared off and bent.

The ideal height where the ground electrode is to be sheared off is a type parameter. The practical height depends, among other things, on the exact shape and dimensions of the middle electrode, which will of course be subject to small variations as in every production process. Therefore, the exact position, height, surface slope, and other geometric characteristics of the middle electrode have to be determined with great accuracy. Although the basic structure of the check appears simple – some sizes and angles are to be measured and some additional geometrical features to be computed – reaching the required accuracy is not trivial. Excellent image properties, a good mechanical setup, and sophisticated algorithms to handle the possible effects on the edges of the electrodes have to work together to achieve that result.

The result is then transmitted to the control system using a data exchange protocol on top of PROFIBUS DP. There it is used to control the shearing process. Here we have then a combined control and inspection application as well as an example of a control application that does not have a monitoring structure (cf. Section 10.2.3).

10.11.7.3 Equipment

The system uses a high-resolution (1376 × 1024 pixel) camera on a high-accuracy frame grabber. Telecentric lenses together with telecentric illumination are used to achieve maximum accuracy and quality for capturing the edges. On the computer side, high-performance industrial PCs are used to meet the cycle-time requirements.

The software uses standard image processing algorithms as well as highly product specific algorithms; they are combined in an architecture that allows reconfiguration of the algorithms depending on the current type data.

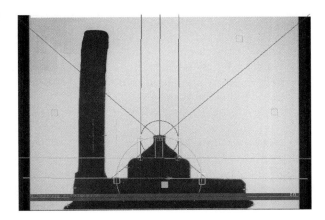

Figure 10.33 Backlit top of spark plug for determination of shearing point.

10.11.7.4 Algorithms

Important algorithms in this application are high-precision edge-detection together with Hough-based line-fitting to precisely determine the height of the center electrode, angles of the center electrode surfaces, and distance to the ground electrode.

You may ask what happens with these distances if the spark plug is rotated slightly around its central axis: this does, of course, affect the measurements and is compensated by a product-specific algorithm.

10.11.8 Ceramic Surface Check

By kind permission of Robert Bosch GmbH, Bamberg plant.

10.11.8.1 Task

This application is a qualitative *surface inspection.* The part in question is a ceramic isolator with a circular cross-section. The entire surface has to be checked for various possible defects such as cracks and holes at the head and edges, pollution, and so forth.

10.11.8.2 Solution

The typical solution for checking the surface of a cylindrical part is to use a line-scan camera and to rotate the part in front of the camera. Together with the movement of the part, the property of a line-scan camera to capture one single line of the image at a time creates an image where the entire surface is unrolled into a flat, rectangular area. Figure 10.34 shows such a surface with a clearly visible crack.

As usual, the evaluation is not quite as straightforward as it may appear at first glance. The image already shows some of the potential problems: there are the vertical stripes that are due to the shape of the isolator body and have to be distinguished from actual defects. There is also some harmless discoloration to be seen, which in turn has to be distinguished from actual pollution.

It is difficult to say anything in general about how to handle such issues. Too different and too individual are the visual appearances of surface defects on different parts. For example, holes in this type of material show themselves as a

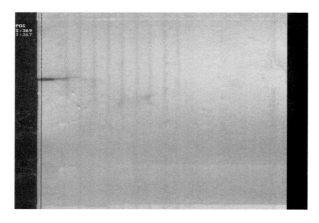

Figure 10.34 Ceramic isolator surface with crack.

characteristic dark-and-light combination because part of the hole will reflect the light whereas another part will be in the shadow. Thus, knowledge about the part, the possible defects, the material, the illumination, and the way light and material interact is necessary to find suitable algorithms, which will nevertheless need to be fine-tuned using a large number of samples.

Here, for example, a shading correction based on an average of the images of several good parts is used to lessen the influence of the part's shape (in the form of the vertical stripes and other systematic effects). Also, segmentation thresholds are recursively adapted to changes in the average brightness that can occur because of minute difference in the angle between the light source and the part surface in order to avoid breaking objects apart by such effects.

10.11.8.3 Equipment

The system was implemented using a 1024 pixel line-scan camera and a cold-light source with a fiber-optic linelight. LED lights are beginning to enter the area of line-scan camera applications, but cold-light sources are still widely used there because of their high light density. The main problem of line-scan cameras is that the exposure time is typically a lot shorter – since they work line by line – than for the entire image of a matrix camera, therefore requiring more light.

The hardware basis of the application is a multiprocessor system on VMEbus basis, connected to the PLC via digital I/O.

10.12 Constraints and Conditions

The previous sections have given some information on various kinds of machine vision applications you may encounter in practice, different types of systems, and aspects of their integration into the automation technology environment.

The next chapter will focus on the question of how to proceed when designing a machine vision system, from requirements to realization, so we need not go into this in too much detail. Nevertheless, this section will explore, given the background from this chapter, some aspects of approaching machine vision applications.

An idea of how various constraints and conditions influence the operation of a machine vision system is important for determining the technology to be used. Having a clear view of the task in question, the environment in which it is to be carried out, the requirements and constraints under which it is to be performed is the first step of a strategy to design a machine vision system.

There are various constraints that are of importance for making a system decision. Obvious constraints are speed, resolution, and cost. Equally important, however, may be the technical and organizational structure of the production, the personnel, as well as the technical environment.

10.12.1 Inspection Task Requirements

The actual requirements on the inspection to be performed are obviously the starting point for designing a vision system. There are many requirements that can be systematically checked, and several check lists have been designed for that purpose. Typical requirements are, for example, resolution, type spectrum, cycle time or speed of motion; all these can be quantified or categorized.

In an ideal world, this would describe the problem completely and there would be sufficient samples – from actual production, of course, not pre-series parts from model making – to test the entire range of variation the parts' appearance may have. Alas, this is not an ideal world, and so we frequently have to deal with small sets of samples that are not at all representative of series production on one hand, and incomplete and sometimes indescribable requirements on the other.

Often, machine vision systems are installed to eliminate human visual inspection. Frequently, these human inspectors work using a "defect catalog," containing examples of what constitutes a good part and what constitutes a bad part. They do not typically use many numerical or objective criteria. Sometimes, the possible defects may not even be known, at least not completely. This is frequently the case with surface inspection tasks. Often, it is quite well known what a good surface looks like, but no one knows all the defects that could possibly occur.

Even considering the remarkable progress made in the area of pattern recognition in recent years, at present such methods still require significant training effort as well as computational power beyond the capacity of typical industrial applications in order to approach human capabilities even in small application segments. We will come back to this in Section 10.12.4.

So the task of finding out what the system actually has to do is not as trivial as it may seem at first. After the obvious quantitative requirements mentioned above have been covered, it will be necessary to keep close contact with the customer, mechanical designers, and all other people involved to make sure that you really are building the system that is required.

It is important to get some understanding of the manufacturing process that produces the part to be inspected. This will give you a better idea of what defects there can be – or should not be – and also perhaps of better indirect ways to check a feature that is not immediately obvious. The process engineer – the one responsible for the manufacturing process whose outcome has to be checked – is a very important contact for the vision engineer. He usually knows much more about the part and the possible problems than there will ever be on paper.

10.12.2 Circumstantial Requirements

Even when all the direct requirements are known, when it is clear how lighting and optics have to be set up to render the salient features visible, and when the algorithms have been found that can solve the task, there is still considerable freedom of design.

It may be equally feasible, technically, to implement the solution in an intelligent camera- or a PC-based system. You may have a choice between using a distributed system of less powerful networked units, or a single powerful machine. What factors affect such design decisions if the fundamental feasibility does not?

An area we will not cover here are legal requirements. Of course, a vision system, like any other part of a machine, underlies various legal requirements, ruling all kinds of things, but this is no different from other areas of machine building.

10.12.2.1 Cost

Cost is a very obvious factor, but it is not always obvious what has to be taken into account. Cost is more than the money required to buy the system. It has to be installed and integrated, and that may cost more with a less flexible low-cost unit than with a – at first glance more expensive – PC-based system. This, of course, depends very much on the overall way of building machines and integrating subsystems.

But neither the task nor expenses are finished after buying the system and getting it up and running. It will in many cases be necessary to optimize the system after initial start of operation, for example, because the actual range of appearance of the series parts becomes clear only after the systems starts operation. A system that can store and re-evaluate error images is clearly superior in this respect than one that cannot. The cost factor of an efficient way of reducing false alarm rates should not be underestimated. A lower rate of false alarms can easily achieve amortization of a higher system price within half a year.

Another important cost factor are spare parts. Using many different systems requires managing and holding a corresponding number of spare parts. Therefore, using a particular system just once because of its price will most certainly not pay off in the long run. Although possibly more expensive at first glance, a standard system that has the flexibility to be used frequently in many applications will probably win out in the end. In every company, such considerations depend, of course, on internal calculation conditions and therefore cannot be generalized.

These are but a few examples which show that the price of purchase is not the only measure of the cost of a system. Ease of use, hard though it is to measure, reliability, flexibility, extensibility, and standardization to reduce training as well as spare parts cost – in short, the total cost of ownership – will in the long run prove more important.

10.12.2.2 Automation Environment

Not every system can be integrated with the same ease into every environment, and every machine builder typically has his particular style of building work stations. Here are just a few examples, as we have covered the various interfaces between machine vision systems and their environment already in some depth.

On the geometrical side, for example, when switch cabinets are commonly used, which do not accommodate 19in. PCs, then it may be difficult to find space for such a system and it will cause extra costs. On the other hand, intelligent cameras are typically larger than normal cameras, so if space is at a premium inside the station, only systems with normal cameras – or intelligent cameras with a separate sensor head – can be used.

On the information side, if, for example, PROFIBUS is the communication medium of choice in the facilities, then systems with other interfaces will cause additional cost for converters. Control system programmers are used to adapting their systems to proprietary protocols of device manufacturers since flexibility is typically higher on the control system side; if, however, the communication protocol of the device is not powerful enough to transmit the desired information, then a compromise in functionality may be necessary.

In the same vein, the automation style of a machine builder may require master – slave behavior from a vision system (as an "inferior" device with respect to the control system), and not every vision system may be equally well suited for that. For example, some vision systems initiate communication by themselves at – from the control system's point of view – arbitrary moments in time: whenever they have a result available, they send it out. This can lead to considerable effort on the PLC side to handle the communication.

We could go on like this for a while, but the general idea should be clear: the physical as well as informational interfaces of the system, which we already have covered in some detail previously, must fit the automation environment. Depending on whether the vision system is mostly compiled from off-the-shelf components or programmed from scratch, this is either a requirement on component selection or on system development or both.

10.12.2.3 Organizational Environment

The environment that the organization provides for the vision system to work in covers a wide range of topics, reaching from the type of production to the departmental and personnel structure of the company.

Some questions that can arise in this area are the following:

- What is the type of production? We have covered that in some detail in Sections 10.2.2 and 10.8.
- What is the product spectrum of the company? Are there few similar products or very different ones? Are product life cycles long or do products change frequently? This question is most interesting when a decision about a standardized machine vision system, applied throughout the company, has to be made, because it indicates, for example, whether there is a focus on rapid reconfiguration capabilities or not. A system integrator building machine vision systems for other companies will have to ask similar questions about his customer base.
- How are the production and maintenance personnel organized? What are their tasks? For example, it makes a big difference whether there is a technical function or maintenance group that will take care of the vision systems, or whether this is part of the responsibilities of the direct production personnel, who will have much less time to devote to these tasks.
- What are the skills of the personnel working with the system? This refers to the people responsible for tuning and troubleshooting the system as well as to those who solely operate it – or even less, in whose production area the system is operating. Design of visualization, message texts, available parameters, and how to set them, all can be affected by the question *who* are the people working with the system and what is their way to work.

  It can be an extremely enlightening experience for a machine vision programmer to work in production for some time, for example, putting into operation one of his own systems and answering questions of production personnel. This may lead to completely new ways of looking at software features and user interfaces.
- For a large organization, a question may be how much optimization and maintenance work is to be done by people onsite and how much by a centralized

vision specialist group. For an independent builder of machine vision systems, the question is similar from the technical point of view, but the economical aspect may be quite different: how much service work is to be provided by the system builder, to what extent can (or should) the customer be enabled to do this work him/herself.

This is less a technical question than one of business model, but it has technical consequences. If the provider of the system (be it an independent company or an internal vision specialist group) also provides service and optimization work, his employees will have either to travel a lot or powerful means of remote maintenance and setup will be necessary – or both.

We could prolong this list more or less indefinitely. The main point is that a technically feasible – even excellent – solution may be impractical under the conditions at a particular manufacturing location.

10.12.3 Refinements

In addition to all the advances in image processing algorithms, machine learning, camera and computer technology, and so on, there are important aspects in system design and integration where we will hopefully see significant improvements in the not-so-far future.

This includes the following:

- Condition monitoring as the capability of a system to monitor and report important indicators of its state. These can be values that are a normal part of the evaluation process, or they can be specifically determined. For example, a system may check particular image areas for their brightness to get information about the health of the illumination, it can check edge contrast as an indicator of focus, or it can also report the temperature of its CPU by accessing the corresponding operating system interfaces.
- Self-adjustment is the capability of a system to react to changes in its environment or its own state to maintain its level of operation. For example, a system may discover a brightness reduction of the illumination through condition monitoring and – within certain limits – compensate by boosting the power supply; or it may detect that surface reflectance in the current batch of work pieces deviates from the expected average and change lighting or processing parameters as a reaction. All this works, of course, only within certain limits, which have to be carefully defined.
- Self-retooling as the capability of a system to change its operation according to the type of workpiece or task. For example, the first step in an inspection may be reading of a DMC on the part containing type information. According to this type information, the system may load the appropriate parameter set. This corresponds to the Industry 4.0/Industrial Internet of Things idea of the part itself controlling the way it is processed or manufactured to facilitate variant management.
- Robustness and regression tests as methods to determine, on one hand, the capability of the system to achieve stable results under changing conditions, for example, for changes in part reflectance, illumination brightness, camera

focus, part scale (when working distances vary), and so on, and, on the other hand, the reaction of the system to parameter changes. This is the classic regression test in software development: does the system still solve all its prescribed tasks correctly after a change; in this case, typically does it yield the same results for the same reference images?

These advances can be partly found in current systems. Comprehensive and widespread implementation will not be easy, and standardization even harder. But they will do a lot for the user experience of machine vision systems and for the stability of their operation.

It is to be expected that the advancement of Industry 4.0/Industrial Internet of Things with its goal of autonomous, intelligent subsystems, which configure themselves for the current workpiece and allow for stable and efficient production down to batch sizes of one, will be a huge driver of such enhancements and also of their standardization at least in terms of information interfaces.

10.12.4 Limits and Prospects

Ten years ago, for the first edition of this book, I wrote at this point in essence that we had seen many years of remarkable growth in machine vision and that there was no sign of this trend ending soon. I talked about the increasing performance of hardware and software, of improving cost–performance relationships, of compact sensors moving into the domain of PC-based systems and PC applications, at the same time upscaling to more demanding applications that were not technically or economically feasible earlier.

All these statements are still true, perhaps even more so than they were 10 years ago. In fact, the advances in hardware and software during this time are nothing short of astonishing. We have seen the rise of general-purpose computing on graphics processing units (GPUs), as well as the incorporation of FPGAs into frame grabbers. On one end of the size scale, multicore PC systems are a matter of course today; on the other end, we have a class of new, formerly inconceivable devices based on SoCs allowing for machine vision to be used virtually everywhere. These include object recognition as a focusing aid and augmented reality in smart phone cameras, and visually guided robots scanning the world around them with 3D vision technology – it is a bit like a science fiction movie having come true around us.

But still there are limits to what the technology can do and what people will be able or willing to do with the technology.

The technology is there to solve even complex, weakly specified tasks; face recognition is a reality, and from there the leap to systems that can do what human visual inspectors do, spot arbitrary deviations from the normal appearance of a test piece, does not seem all too far. Keep in mind, though, that these feats of recognition are computationally still enormously expensive. When Facebook runs face recognition, they do so on large server clusters. So there is still quite some way to go before we see this technology in everyday industrial applications.

Not to forget that face recognition is basically a single – if very complex – task for which there is an overwhelming market. Our industrial tasks may not be quite as complex, regarded in isolation, but they are quite diverse, and resources are much more limited. Therefore, the goal of a self-learning system on a level of semantic understanding with a human is still far away.

It is thus still true, so probably somewhat less than it was 10 years ago, that weakly specified, example-based, non-quantifiable tasks, especially tasks of detecting "anything unusual," remain a difficult topic.

And it is also still true that in many industrial applications, it is absolutely necessary – due to legal requirements, customer procedure, product liability topics, and so on – to be certain that a system delivers a reproducible result that can be plausibly explained, preferably by quantifiable criteria. This is often difficult with systems that try to achieve human-like cognitive abilities. So, we as vision engineers still have the responsibility to design our systems carefully and putting all the knowledge we have about the task at hand into the systems. The tools we have available, however, have matured a lot and grown immensely in power and performance, allowing us to tackle tasks we did not even need to think about 10 years ago.

This also holds for the "integration" topics. We have more powerful communication interfaces now, and we have new ways of interacting with the user, making their tasks much easier – just take a look at the various means of teaching collaborative robots by easy-to-use software wizards or even guiding them by hand – we have a whole bunch of new, powerful technology on our hands to help further the use of machine vision.

Naturally, user expectations grow in lock-step with technological possibilities. Smart-phone-like multitouch user interfaces will soon be a matter of course, putting new demands on system developers, requiring them to learn new skills. So the life of the system designer is not necessarily made easier by all this new technology – although probably more interesting.

As a final point, I would like to mention the impact of the Industry 4.0/Industrial Internet of Things topic: not because of the hype surrounding it, but because of the reality it partly already is and the possibilities it will grow into. IIoT revolves around information; information about products, and information about machine conditions, and machine vision systems are one of the great information providers in a production system. There is a great deal of as-yet-unused information in machine vision systems and even more information additional – or appropriately adapted – vision systems can deliver. Therefore, IIoT will become another driver of the growth of machine vision. On the other hand, it will make high demands on vision systems, their interoperability, their communication abilities, their flexibility, and their ease of use. This development is just beginning.

Ten years ago, I summed up the future development of industrial machine vision in the four points below, and it seems, I actually do not need to change them. It looks like all these drivers will continue to shape machine vision in the years to come.

- Solid growth, increasing coverage in low-cost areas as well as in demanding applications;
- Development of new fields of use in addition to the traditional quality control;
- Continuing improvement of technology as well as usability;
- Increasing integration into automation technology.

Of course, we are starting at a much higher level now, in every respect: sheer number of installations, performance, capabilities, complexity, integration, usability, and thus we will, naturally, be aiming at an even higher and more demanding level.

We have come far in these 10 years, and machine vision looks set to stay a dynamic, rapidly evolving, and growing field, which will certainly continue to surprise us with its developments in the next 10 years.

And possibly the biggest surprise would be if the last statement I made in this chapter 10 years ago were no longer true 10 years from now: that we are still waiting for widespread, company-spanning standards outside the area of acquisition interfaces.

References

1 Wendel, A. (2014) *Machine Vision - Approaching New Records*, VDMA, Frankfurt a. Main, http://ibv.vdma.org (last visited April 2016).
2 Wendel, A. (2015) *Machine Vision Showing Strong Growth*, VDMA, Frankfurt a. Main, http://ibv.vdma.org (last visited April 2016).
3 Automated Imaging Assocation. http://www.machinevisiononline.org (last visited April 2016).
4 Kaiser, A. (2014) Acht Roboter auf die Sie achten sollten. Manager Magazine Online, 10 April 2014, http://www.manager-magazin.de/unternehmen/industrie/roboter-fuer-industrie-4-0-auf-hannover-messe-a-963636.html (last visited May 2015).
5 Jähne, B., Massen, R., Nickolay, B., and Scharfenberg, H. (1995) *Technische Bildverarbeitung – Maschinelles Sehen*, Springer-Verlag, Berlin, Heidelberg, New York.
6 Bauer, N. (2001) *Leitfaden zur Industriellen Bildverarbeitung*, Fraunhofer Allianz Vision, Erlangen.
7 Diephuis, M. and Voloshynovskiy, S. (2013) Physical object identification based on FAMOS microstructure fingerprinting: comparison of templates versus invariant features. 8th International Symposium on Image and Signal Processing and Analysis (ISPA), IEEE.
8 Ulrich, M. and Kreutzer, L. (2013) Sample-based identification eases object recognition tasks. *Vision Syst. Des.*, **18** (4), http://www.vision-systems.com/articles/print/volume-18/issue-4/features/sample-based-identification-eases-object-recognition-tasks.html (last visited May 2015).
9 Dorf, R.C. (ed.) (1996) *The Engineering Handbook*, CRC Press, Boca Raton, FL.
10 AIA, EMVA, and JIIA (2013) Global Machine Vision Interface Standards, http://www.emva.org/cms/upload/ Marketing_edocs_download/FSF_Vision_Standards_Brochure_A4_screen.pdf (last visited May 2015).
11 BIPM, IEC, IFCC, ISO, IUPAC, IUPAP and OIML (1995) Guide to the Expression of Uncertainty in Measurement.
12 ISO (1995) International Vocabulary of Basic and General Terms in Metrology, ISO/IEC Guide 99:2007.

13 OPC. (2015) Platform Industrie 4.0 Propose Reference Architecture Model of Industrie 4.0, Press release of the OPC Foundation Available at https://opcfoundation.org/news/press-releases/platform-industrie-4-0-propose-reference-architecture-model-industrie-4-0/ (accessed 31 October 2016).
14 News item available at http://www.invision-news.de/artikel/105431 (accessed 7 October 2016).
15 Sutter, H. (2005) The Concurrency Revolution, C/C++ Users' Journal, 2005/02.
16 Demant, C., Streicher-Abel, B., and Waszkewitz, P. (eds) (1998) *Industrial Image Processing*, Springer-Verlag, Berlin Heidelberg, New York.
17 Hardin, W. (2014) 3D Vision Options Drive Machine Vision Growth, Automated Imaging Association, https://www.coherent.com/downloads/VisionOnlineApril2014.pdf (last visited May 2015).
18 Szeliski, R. (2011) *Computer Vision*, Springer-Verlag, London.
19 Besl, P.J. and McKay, N.D. (1992) A method for registration of 3-D shapes. *IEEE Trans. Pattern Anal. Mach. Intell.*, **14** (2), 239–256.
20 Rusinkiewicz, S. and Levoy, M. (2001) Efficient variants of the ICP algorithm. 3rd International Conference on 3-D Digital Imaging and Modeling IEEE.
21 Pears, N., Liu, Y., and Bunting, P. (eds) (2012) *3D Imaging, Analysis and Applications*, Springer-Verlag, London.
22 Wöhler, C. (2009, 2013) *3D Computer Vision*, Springer-Verlag, London.
23 Pomerleau, F., Colas, F., Siegwart, R., and Magnenat, S. (2013) Comparing ICP variants on real-world data sets. *Auton. Rob.*, **34** (3), 133–148.
24 Rosenhahn, B., Brox, T., Cremers, D., and Seidel, H.P. (2006) A comparison of shape matching methods for contour based pose estimation, in *Combinatorial Image Analysis* (eds R. Reulke et al.), Springer-Verlag, Berlin Heidelberg.
25 Woodham, R.J. (1980) Photometric method for determining surface orientation from multiple images. *Opt. Eng.*, **19** (I), 139–144.
26 Sansoni, G., Trebeschi, M., and Docchio, F. (2009) State-of-the-art and applications of 3D imaging sensors in industry, cultural heritage, medicine, and criminal investigation. *Sensors*, **9**, 568–601.
27 Hansard, M., Lee, S., Choi, O., and Horaud, R.P. (2012) *Time of Flight Cameras: Principles, Methods, and Applications*, Springer Briefs in Computer Science, Springer-Verlag.
28 Sun, X. (2012) Space-based lidar systems. Conference on Lasers and Electro-Optics 2012 OSA Technical Digest, paper JW3C.5.
29 Salvi, J., Fernandez, S., Pribanic, T., and Llado, X. (2010) A state of the art in structured light patterns for surface profilometry. *Pattern Recognit.*, **43**, 2666–2680.
30 Barsky, S. and Petrou, M. (2003) The 4-source photometric stereo technique for three-dimensional surfaces in the presence of highlights and shadows. *IEEE Trans. Pattern Anal. Mach. Intell.*, **25** (10), 1239–1252.
31 Frankot, R.T. and Chellappa, R. (1988) A method for enforcing integrability in shape from shading algorithms. *IEEE Trans. Pattern Anal. Mach. Intell.*, **10** (4), 439–451.
32 Agrawal, A., Raskar, R., and Chellappa, R. (2006) What is the range of surface reconstructions from a gradient field?, in *Computer Vision - ECCV 2006*,

Lecture Notes in Computer Science, vol. **3951** (eds A. Leonardis, H. Bischof, and A. Pinz), Springer-Verlag.

33 Wyant, J.C. (2002) White light interferometry, in *Holography: A Tribute to Yuri Denisyuk and Emmett Leith*, 98 Proceedings of SPIE, vol. 4737 (ed. H.J. Caulfield), SPIE.

34 Lin, C. and Sullivan, R.F. (1972) An application of white light interferometry in thin film measurements. *IBM J. Res. Dev.*, **16** (3), 269–276.

35 Windecker, R. and Tiziani, H.J. (1999) Optical roughness measurements using extended white-light interferometry. *Opt. Eng.*, **38** (6), 1081–1087.

36 Jiang, X., Tang, D., and Gao, F. (2015) In-situ surface inspection using white light channelled spectrum interferometer. 15th International Conference on Metrology and Properties of Engineering Surfaces, 2-5 March, Charlotte, NC, in press.

37 Blunt, R.T. (2006) White Light Interferometry - a production worthy technique for measuring surface roughness on semiconductor wafers. CS MANTECH Conference, April 24-27, Vancouver.

38 O'Mahony, C., Hill, M., Brunet, M., Duane, R., and Mathewson, A. (2003) Characterization of micromechanical structures using white-light interferometry. *Meas. Sci. Technol.*, **14** (10), 1807–1814.

39 Newsletter of the UK Industrial Vision Association, (ed. D. Bulgin) 2014.

40 Chen, W., Lu, C., and Zhao, S. (2012) Segmentation of embossed characters pressed on metallic label based on surface normal texture. *Int. J. Adv. Comput. Technol. (IJACT)*, **4** (19), 332–340.

41 McGunnigle, G. and Chantler, M.J. (2003) Resolving handwriting from background printing using photometric stereo. *Pattern Recognit.*, **36** (8), 1869–1879.

42 Heizmann, M. (2008) Moderne Methoden für die bildaufnehmende 3-D-Inspektion von Oberflächen, 37. Heidelberger Bildverarbeitungsforum.

43 Flacco, F., Kröger, T., De Luca, A., and Khatib, O. (2012) A depth space approach to human-robot collision avoidance. IEEE International Conference on Robotics and Automation.

44 Wilson, A. (ed.) (2015) Using 3D imaging in machine vision, Vision Systems Design Editorial Digest, PennWell.

45 Bauer, N. (ed.) (2006) *Leitfaden zur Inspektion von Oberflächen mit Bildverarbeitung*, Fraunhofer Gesellschaft zur Förderung der angewandten Forschung e.V.

46 Kammel, S. and León, F.P. (2008) Deflectometric measurement of specular surfaces. *IEEE Trans. Instrum. Meas.*, **57** (4), 763–769.

47 Bosche, F.N. and Haas, C.T. (2008) Automated retrieval of project three-dimensional CAD objects in range point clouds to support automated dimensional QA/QC. *J. Inf. Technol. Constr.*, **13**, 71–85.

48 Hong-Seok, P. and Mani, T.U. (2013) Development of an inspection system for defect detection in pressed parts using laser scanned data. 24th DAAAM International Symposium on Intelligent Manufacturing and Automation, Elsevier.

49 Flisch, A., Wirth, J., Zanini, R., Breitenstein, M., Rudin, A., Wendt, F., Mnich, F., and Golz, R. (1999) Industrial computed tomography in reverse engineering applications. Computerized Tomography for Industrial Applications and Image Processing in Radiology, DGZfP-Proceedings BB67-CD, Berlin.
50 Istook, C.L. and Hwang, S.-J. (2001) 3D body scanning systems with application to the apparel industry. *J. Fashion Mark. Manage.*, **5** (2), 120–132.
51 Pernkopf, F. and O'Leary, P. (2003) Image acquisition techniques for automatic visual inspection of metallic surfaces. *NDT&E Int.*, **36** (8), 609–617.
52 Scholz-Reiter, B., Thamer, H., and Lütjen, M. (2010) Optical quality assurance in micro production. Proceedings of the International MultiConference of Engineers and Computer Scientists 2010, vol. III, IMECS.
53 Landström, A. and Thurley, M.J. (2012) Morphology-based crack detection for steel slabs. *IEEE J. Sel. Top. Sign. Process.* **6** (7), 866–875.
54 Landström, A., Thurley, M.J., and Jonsson, H. (2013) Sub-millimeter crack detection in casted steel using color photometric stereo. 2013 International Conference on Digital Image Computing: Techniques and Applications (DICTA), IEEE.
55 Heizmann, M. (2004) *Auswertung von forensischen Riefenspuren mittels automatischer Sichtprüfung*, universitätsverlag karlsruhe.
56 Speck, A., Zelzer, B., Langenbucher, A., and Eppig, T. (2014) Quality control of injection molded eyewear by non-contact deflectometry. *J. Eur. Opt. Soc.*, **9**, 14027-1–14027-8.
57 Pochyly, A., Kubela, T., Kozak, M., and Cihak, P. (2010) Robotic vision for bin-picking applications of various objects. Robotics (ISR), 2010 41st International Symposium on and 2010 6th German Conference on Robotics, VDE.
58 Kim, K., Kim, J., Kang, S., Kim, J., and Lee, J. (2012) Vision-based bin picking system for industrial robotics applications. 9th International Conference on Ubiquitous Robots and Ambient Intelligent (URAI).
59 Oh, J.-K., Baek, K.K., Kim, D., and Lee, S. (2009) Development of structured light based bin picking system using primitive models. Proceedings of 2009 IEEE International Symposium on Assembly and Manufacturing.
60 Hema, C.R., Paulraj, M.P., Nagarajan, R., and Yaacob, S. (2007) Segmentation and location computation of bin objects. *Int. J. Adv. Rob. Syst.*, **4** (1), 57–62.
61 Buchholz, D., Winkelbach, S., and Wahl, F.M. (2010) RANSAM for industrial bin-picking. Robotics (ISR), 2010 41st International Symposium on and 2010 6th German Conference on Robotics, VDE.
62 Wang, G. and Wu, Q.M.J. (2011) *Guide to Three Dimensional Structure and Motion Factorization*, Springer-Verlag, London.
63 Argyriou, V., Del Rincon, J.M., Villarini, B., and Roche, A. (2015) *Image, Video and 3D Data Registration: Medical, Satellite and Video Processing Applications with Quality Metrics*, John Wiley & Sons, Inc., Hoboken, NJ.
64 Cyganek, B. and Siebert, J.P. (2009) *An Introduction to 3D Computer Vision Techniques and Algorithms*, John Wiley & Sons, Inc., Hoboken, NJ.
65 Zhang, S. (ed.) (2013) *Handbook of 3D Machine Vision: Optical Metrology and Imaging*, Series in Optics and Optoelectronics, CRC Press.

Appendix

Checklist for designing a machine vision system

General

Date   _____
Company   _____
Contact person   _____
Department   _____
City   _____
Zip code   _____
Street   _____
Phone   _____
E-mail   _____

Task

Description of task and benefit

_____

_____

Size of the smallest feature to be detected   ____

Required accuracy   ____

100% Inspection   ____   Random control   ____

Offline inspection   ____   In-line inspection   ____

Retrofit   ____   New design   ____

Parts

Description of parts

Discrete parts	___	Endless material	___
Dimensions (min, max)		to	
		to	
		to	
Color		Surface finish	

Corrosion, adhesives
Changes due to handling

Number of part types
Difference of parts: _____
Batch production   ___
Can production change be addressed   ___

Part Presentation

Indexed positioning	___	Time of nonmovement	___
Manual positioning	___	Time of nonmovement	___
Continuous positioning	___	Speed	___
Tolerances in positioning	x		
	y		
	z		
	Rotation about x		
	Rotation about y		
	Rotation about z		

Number of parts in view
Overlapping parts	___	Touching parts	___

Time Requirements

Maximum processing time   ___
Processing time is variable in tolerances   ___

Information Interfaces

Triggering manual ____   automatic   ____

What information has to be passed by the interfaces?
_____

What interfaces are necessary?

Digital I/O   ____
TCP/IP   ____
Fieldbus   ____
RS-232   ____

Requirements for user interface
_____

Miscellaneous

Installation space

x
y
z

Maximum distance between camera and PC
Ambient light   ____
Protection class   ____
Dirt or dust   ____
Shock or vibration   ____
Variations in temperature   ____
Electromagnetic influences   ____
Availability of power supply

Index

a

aberrations   185, 277
absolute sum of normalized dot products   669
absorbance   97, 98, 111
absorbing filter   124
absorption   97
acceptance test   49
accommodation   3, 5, 25
accumulator array   658, 660, 661
accuracy   596, 702, 718, 724, 725, 778, 782, 787
   camera parameters   629–631
   contour moments   560
   edges   512, 597–602
   gray value features   512
   gray value moments   557–558, 560
   hardware requirements   601–602
   region moments   557–558
   subpixel-precise threshold   512
achromatic axis   10
acquisition   371
action commands   361, 371, 372, 375–377
action potentials   16
active optical cables (AOC)   381
active pixel sensor   331
adaptation   12, 14, 17, 26
   contrast   26
   ligth/dark   26
   motion   26
   to optical aberrations   26
   to scaling   26
   tilt   26
adaptive lighting   118, 171

A/D conversion   357
additive mixed illumination colors   103
additive noise   272
additivity   253
adjustment   719, 720, 722, 723, 732
   vs. calibration   732
affine transformation   532–533, 555, 644, 662, 668
afocal system   229
aging   88
Airy disk   244, 246
algebraic distance   608
algebraic error   608
aliasing   529–530, 537–538, 649
   effect   267, 269
   function   276
   potential   276
   ratio   276
alignment   532, 544, 545
Altera Cyclone V series   405
amacrine cells   17, 20
amplitude distribution in the image plane   242
analog cameras   435
analog connectors   439
analog front end (AFE)   357, 358
analog image acquisition   437
analog processing   356
analog-to-digital converter (ADC)   329, 330, 336, 366, 388
analog video signal   436
analyzer   108
Ando filter   589
angel kappa   3
anisometry   554, 557, 559, 674

Index

anterior chamber   2
anti-reflective coating (AR)   126, 283
aperture   206
　correction   354
　stop   206, 514
a posteriori probability   677
application-package, *see* systems, application-package   699
Application Programming Interface (API)   475
applications
　code recognition   701
　completeness check   701, 702, 772, 774, 776
　object recognition   701, 779
　position recognition   701, 781
　shape and dimensioncheck   702
　surface inspection   702, 788
　types   702
application-specific integrated circuits (ASICs)   345, 402
a priori probability   677, 679
Aptina   337
area   552, 557–560
　of interest   329, 348
　MT   22
　sensor   319, 614
artificial astigmatism   124
aspect ratio   744
astigmatism   5, 11, 600
attention   22, 23
Automated Imaging Association (AIA)   454
axial magnification ratio   200, 233
axons   3, 11, 16, 17, 19

b

backlight (ing)   44, 138, 174
back side illumination (BSI)   337, 338
band-limited system   269
bandpass filter (BP)   125
bandwidth   122, 395 *see also* signal, bandwidth, 699
bar codes, *see* codes, bar codes   699
batch production, *see* production, batch   699
Bayer color encoding   485

Bayer Color Filter Array (CFA)   485
BAYER pattern   351, 359
Bayes decision rule   677
Bayes theorem   677
beam converging lens   193
beam diverging lens   193
Bessel function   244
bilateral telecentric systems   229
bilinear   359, 367
binary image   507, 549, 552, 561, 563, 567, 573
binning   338, 345, 347
binocular stereo reconstruction   631–643
bin-picking   767, 771
bipolar cells   16
　OFF   13
　ON   13
black light   107
blob analysis   60
blobs   22, 23
block diagram   350, 354
blooming   326
boundary   550, 556, 567–568
　condition   239
bounding box   555, 560, 675
bright field   45
　illumination   138
brightness   206
　behavior   90
　control   166
　perception   74
b/w   338

c

C-Mount   318, 350
C-Mount lens   43
calcium   13
calibration   731, 748, 750, 782–784
　vs. adjustment   732
　geometric   600, 601, 613–632
　　accuracy of interior orientation   629–631
　　binocular stereo calibration   633
　　calibration target   622–623

camera constant, *see* calibration, geometric, principal distance 690
camera coordinate system 615–616, 618–620, 633
camera motion vector 618
distortion coefficient (division model) 616–632, 636
distortion coefficients (polynomial model) 616, 618, 632
exterior orientation 601, 623–626
focal length 614–615, 632
image coordinate system 618, 620
image plane coordinate system 616, 620
interior orientation 601, 623–626, 632
pixel size 618, 620, 632
principal distance 614–616, 620, 629–632
principal point 618, 620, 629–632
projection center 614, 632, 633, 635, 637
relative orientation 632, 633
world coordinate system 615–616, 620
radiometric 512–517, 600
  calibration target 513
  chart-based 513
  chart-less 514–517
  defining equation for chart-less calibration 514
  discretization of inverse response function 514, 515
  gamma responsefunction 513, 516
  inverse response function 514
  normalization of inverse response function 515, 516
  polynomial inverse response function 516
  response function 513, 514, 516
  smoothness constraint 516
camera (s) 505–506
  bus
    analog cameras 435
    analog connectors 439

analog image acquisition 437
analog video signal 436
bandwidth 459
cables 460
Camera Link 449
Camera Link HS 432, 451
Camera Link signals 450
CoaXPress 432, 452
differential signaling 441
digital video transmission 439
FireWire/IEEE 1394, 432
frame grabber 432
frame rate 460
G3 433
GenICam 433
Gigabit Ethernet for machine vision 455, 456
GigE Vision 432
IEEE 1394 (FireWire) (Legacy) 442
IEEE 1394 for machine vision 445
IIDC2 standard 434
interlaced video transfer 436
LCD inspection 462
line scan 441, 460
manufacturing inspection 461
parallel digital camera buses 439
parallel digital connectors 441
progressive scan video 437
reliability 460
resolution 459
RGB 438
security 463
S-Video 438
taps 440
timing signals 437
USB 452
USB for machine vision 454
USB3 Vision standards 432, 433
calibration
  accident photography 313
  additional object information 304
  affinity and non-orthogonality 299
  applications with simultaneous calibration 309
  architecture 313

camera (s) (*contd.*)
  camera model   295
  camera system   292
  car safety applications   312
  central projection   295
  coordinate systems   292
  direct linear transformation   308
  distortion and affinity   297
  extended system calibration   307
  exterior orientation   293
  focal length and principal point   297
  image information   302
  image rectification   628–629
  interior orientation   293
  in the laboratory   302
  optical system   293
  plumb-line method   307
  radial asymmetrical and tangential distortion   299
  radial symmetrical distortion   297
  sensor flatness   301
  sensor stability   294
  signal processing and transfer   294
  system calibration   293
  tube measurement   311
  variant camera parameters   299
  verification   308
  whitelight scanners   312
  world coordinates from single image   601, 626–628
  world coordinates from stereo reconstruction   631, 643
constant   182
exposuretime   514
electrical design   46, 58
fill factor   558, 598, 601
gamma response function   513, 516
gray value response   512–513
  linear   512, 600, 601
  nonlinear   512, 600
inverse response function   514
line scan   614, 618–622, 628
mechanical design   46, 58
model   32, 37, 39, 40
pinhole   614–618, 627–628
resolution   39
response function   513, 514, 516
sensor
  aspect ratio   37, 39, 51
  resolution   37, 38
  telecentric   614–618, 626–627
Camera Link   345, 395, 432, 449, 716
  connector   451
  HS   432, 451
  signals   450
candela   110
Canny filter   586, 591, 597
  edge accuracy   597, 598
  edge precision   597
cardinal elements   191
center of gravity   552–554, 557, 558, 560, 603, 605
center of perspective   182
center wavelength   83, 122
central disk   244, 248
central moments   553–554, 557, 560, 603
central projection   182, 219
chamfer-3-4 distance   574
changeover   720, 748, 750
channel capacity   11, 16
characteristic function   507, 557, 575
charge   328, 345
  transfer   321
charge-coupled device (CCD)   317, 320–322, 324–328, 334, 336, 337, 339–342, 345, 348–351, 353–357, 359, 360, 369, 375, 391, 392, 394, 397
chessboard distance   574
chief ray   207
chroma   351
chromatic aberration   6, 10, 600
  longitudinal   10
  transverse   10
chrominance   351
circle fitting   607–608
  outlier suppression   607
  robust   607
circle of confusion   211, 214
  permissible size   218
circular aperture   243
city-block distance   573, 574

classification   674, 676–690
  Bayes classifier   679–681
  classification accuracy   688
  classifier types   678
  curse of dimensionality   679, 685
  decision theory   676–678
    Bayes decision rule   677
    Bayes theorem   677
  error rate   679
  expectation maximization algorithm   681
  features   674
  Gaussian mixture model classifier   680–681, 689
  generalized linear classifier   685
  k nearest-neighbor classifier   679–680
  linear classifier   681–682
  neural network   681–685, 688–689
    hyperbolic tangent activation function   683
    logistic activation function   683
    multilayer perceptron training   682–685, 688–689
    sigmoid activation function   683–684
    single-layer perceptron   681–682
    softmax activation function   684
    threshold activation function   682, 683
    universal approximator   683, 684
  nonlinear classifier   682–689
  polynomial classifier   685
  a posteriori probability   677
  a priori probability   677, 679
  rejection   688–689
  support vector machine   685–689
    Gaussian radial basis function kernel   687
    homogeneous polynomial kernel   687
    inhomogeneous polynomial kernel   687
    kernel   687
    margin   686
    separating hyperplane   685–686
    sigmoid kernel   687
    universal approximator   687
  test set   679
  training set   678, 684
  training speed   688
Closed Circuit TeleVision (CCTV)   317–319
closing   571, 577
cloudy day illumination   150
cluster   710
clutter   654, 657, 661, 668
CMOSIS   328, 335, 336
coaxial diffuse light   140
coaxial directed light   142
coaxial telecentric light   143
CoaXPress   432, 452
coded light   145
code recognition, see codes, recognition   699
codes
  bar codes   701
  DataMatrix   701, 708, 730, 731, 734
  recognition   701
coherent light   85
cold light source   78
collision avoidance   771
color   338
  alias   367
  Burst   437
  constancy   23, 25
  contrast   23, 25
  correction   368
  difference   354
  filter   130
  information   367
  interpolation   367
  color perception   73
  color space   371
ColorChecker   369
column parallel readout   330
coma   11, 600
  horizontal   5
combined lighting technique   162
compact systems, see systems, compact systems   699
Compact Vision System (CVS)   41, 423
compactness   556, 674

complement   561–562
complementary color   101, 322, 351, 353
complementary metal-oxide-semiconductor (CMOS)   317, 320, 328, 329, 331, 332, 335–337, 339–342, 348, 351, 354, 355, 357, 359, 375, 382, 391, 392, 394
completeness check, *see* applications, completeness check   699
complex cells   22
component labeling   549
computer bus
   cost   471
   ISA/EISA   463
   machine vision applications   463
   PCI/CompactPCI/PXI   464
   PCI Express/CompactPCI Express/PXI Express   467
   PCI-X   466
   prevalence and lifetime   471
   throughput   469
   throughput requirements application   473
   throughput requirements determination   471
   timeline   464
condition monitoring   793
cone pedicle   16
cones   6, 12, 16, 24, 26, 27
configuration management   709, 710, 785
confocal frontlight   45
connected components   548–549, 672
connectivity   548–549, 562, 568, 573
constancy of luminance   113
Consultative Committee for International Radio (CCIR)   338, 435
Consulting Team Machine Vision (CTMV)   55
continuous production, *see* production, continuous   699
contour   508–509
   feature, *see* features, contour   690
   length   556

segmentation   609–612, 655
   lines   609–611
   lines and circles   611–612
   lines and ellipses   611–612
contour-based algorithms   34
contrast   44, 118
   adaptation   11
   enhancement   510–512
   normalization   511–512
   robust   511–512, 676
   sensitivity function   17, 18
   threshold   17
control, *see* evaluation, control   699
controlled lighting   167
control signals, *see* data, control signals   699
convex hull   555–556, 560
convexity   555–556
convolution   522–523, 528–529
   integral   256
   kernel   522
   theorem   259, 267
coordinates
   homogeneous   533, 534
   inhomogeneous   533, 534
   polar   538
cornea   1–3, 5
correct perspective viewing distance   213
correction data   365
Correlated Double Sampling (CDS)   334, 348, 349, 357, 359, 392
correlation   529, *see also* normalized cross-correlation, 690
$\cos^4$-law   283
counters   372, 376
CPU load   367, 368, 379, 380, 396
crosstalk   269
CRT   322, 363
crystalline lens   1
CS-Mount   318
CS-Mount camera   43
cumulative histogram   511, 557
cutoff spatial frequency   6
cutoff wavelength   122
cuton wavelength   122

Index | 811

cycle time, 34, *see* production, cycle
    time   699, 737
Cyclic Redundancy Check (CRC) error
    checking   454

d

dark current noise   391
darkfield illumination   139
dark field lighting   45, 152
dark noise   16, 364, 366
data
    control signals   731, 736
    images   733, 734
    packets   378
    rate, *see* signal, data rate   699
    structures
        images   505–506
        regions   506–508
        subpixel-precise contours
            508–509
    type data   733, 785, 786
    valid signal   450
DataMatrix code, *see* codes, DataMatrix
    699
daylight suppression filter   128
decision theory   676–678
    Bayes decisionrule   677
    Bayes theorem   677
    a posteriori probability   677
    a priori probability   677, 679
defocused image plane   248
delay time   167
deltaE   370
demosaicing   367, 368
depth-first search   549
depth of field   214, 215, 234
depth of field T 216
depth of focus, *see* focus, depth of   699
depth of focus T 216
Deriche filter   586–587, 591, 597
    edge accuracy   597, 599
    edge precision   597
derivative
    directional   581
    first   580, 583
    gradient   581
    Laplacian   582

partial   581, 582, 589, 591
second   580, 583
deterministic system   253
deviation from telecentricity   284
dichromatic   24
difference   561
differential signaling   441
diffraction   99, 235
diffraction integral   236, 237
diffraction-limited   3, 241
    depth of focus   247
    MTF   3
diffuse area lighting   141
diffuse bright field incident light   140
diffuse bright field transmitted lighting
    155
diffuse dark field incident light   152
diffuse directed partial bright field
    incident light   148
diffuse lights (ing)   45, 136
diffuse on axis light   140
diffuse transmitted dark field lighting
    161
digital I/O, *see* interface, digital I/O
    699
digital signal processor (DSP)   351, 404
Digital Video Interface (DVI) connector
    413, 443
digital video transmission   439
dilation   562–565, 567–568, 576, 594
dimension check, *see* applications,
    dimension check   699
DIN   1335, 204
DIN   19040, 202
diplopia   25
Dirac comb   266, 269
directed bright field incident light   142
directed bright field transmitted lighting
    157
directed dark field incident light   152
directed light (ing)   45, 136
directed on axis light   142
directed reflection   93
directed transmission   97
directed transmitted dark field lighting
    161
directional properties of the light   135

direction of light   192
direct linear transformation (DLT)   308
Direct Memory Access (DMA)   380, 396, 474, 478
discharging lamp   76, 78
discrete Fourier transform (DFT)   270, 529–532, *see also* discrete Fourier transform, 690
disparity   25, 27, 638–639
dispersion   102
dispersion of light   184
distance
   chamfer-3–4   574
   chessboard   574
   city-block   573, 574
   Euclidean   574
   transform   573–575, 655, 657
distortion   280, 600, 616–618, 620
   barrel   616–618, 620
   division model   616
   pincushion   616–618, 620
   polynomial model   616–618
distribution of illuminance   115
DL-Cutfilter   355
DNL   357
dorsal stream   22, 25
drift   78, 84, 88
driver software
   acquisition mode   479
   API   475
   Bayer color encoding   485
   display modes   488
   image display   488
   image representation on disk   482, 487
   layers of   474
   nondestructive overlays   490
   palettes   489
   performance   477
   supported platforms   477
   utility functions   478
duality
   dilation–erosion   567, 576
   hit-or-miss transform   569
   opening–closing   571, 577
dynamic   336, 375, 387, 393
   range   328, 393
   thresholding   542–544, 577, 672

e

edge
   amplitude   548, 581, 590
   definition
      1D   580–581
      2D   581–582
   gradient magnitude   548, 581, 590
   gradient vector   581
   Laplacian   582, 594–596
   non-maximum suppression   580, 587, 591–592
   polarity   581
   spread function   278
edge extraction   579–602, 655
   1D   583–589
      Canny filter   586
      Deriche filter   586–587
      derivative   580, 583
      gray value profile   584
      non-maximum suppression   587
      subpixel-accurate   588
   2D   548, 589–596
      Ando filter   589
      Canny filter   591, 597
      Deriche filter   591, 597
      Frei filter   589
      gradient   581
      hysteresis thresholding   592–593
      Lanser filter   591, 597
      Laplacian   582, 594–596
      non-maximum suppression   591–592
      Prewitt filter   589
      Sobel filter   589
      subpixel-accurate   593–596
edge filter   586–587
   Ando   589
   Canny   586, 591, 597
      edge accuracy   597, 598
      edge precision   597
   Deriche   586–587, 591, 597
      edge accuracy   597, 599
      edge precision   597
   Frei   589

Lanser   591, 597
    edge accuracy   597
    edge precision   597
    optimal   586–587, 590–591
    Prewitt   589
    Sobel   589
edge spread function (ESF)   278
effective f-number   216
Eikonal equation   180
electromagnetic compatibilty (EMC)   80
electromagnetic wave   179
Electronic Industries Association (EIA) RS-170   338, 435
electronic shutter   323
ellipse fitting   608–609
    algebraic error   608
    geometric error   609
    outlier suppression   609
    robust   609
ellipse parameters   553–555, 557, 559, 560, 603, 605, 608, 609
embedded image processing   713
embedded MultiMediaCard (eMMC)   407
embedded vision systems
    better shock and vibration ratings and testing   423
    built-in hardware   423
    closed loop control applications   424
    definition   401
    environment   425
    fanless design and greater temperature range specifications   423
    flexibility in component selection   422
    flexibility in system integration   422
    full bus bandwidth   423
    higher performance processing   421
    I/O set   422
    multi-camera applications   424
    multi-camera connectivity   421
    programming and configuration   425
    SLC vs. MLC memory solid state memory   423
emmetropia   3

EMVA1288   386–388, 394
enclosing circle   555, 560
enclosing rectangle   555, 560, 675
engineering framework   747
entocentric perspective   222
entrance pupil   198, 208
entrance window   209
epipolar image rectification   637–638
epipolar line   634
epipolar plane   634
epipolar standard geometry   636–637
epipole   634
erosion   565–568, 576
error of second order   159
error signal   61
errors of the first order   160
Ethernet, see interface, Ethernet   699
Euclidean distance   574
evaluation
    control   705, 706, 781, 786, 787
    inspection   704, 772, 774, 776, 787
    monitoring   705
    recognition   705
    verification   704, 705, 772, 774, 776, 779
exit pupil   198, 208
exit window   209
exposure   115, 120, 318, 327, 329, 332, 335, 345, 359, 361, 371, 372, 374, 375, 383, 384, 387
    time   120, 514
Extended Industry Standard Architecture (EISA) bus   464
extensibility   710, 714, 791
exterior orientation   601, 615–616, 620, 623–626
    world coordinate system   615–616, 620
extraneous light   175
ExViewHAD   325
eye lens   1
eye movement   10, 12, 27
eye protection   106

f

face-distortion aftereffect   26
face recognition   707, 794

facet model   593
far cells   25
far point   214, 223
fast Fourier transform   530, *see also* Fourier transform, 690
feature extraction   552–560
features
   contour   552, 559–560
      area   560
      center of gravity   560
      central moments   560
      contour length   559
      ellipse parameters   560
      major axis   560
      minor axis   560
      moments   560
      normalized moments   560
      orientation   560
      smallest enclosing circle   560
      smallest enclosing rectangle   560
   gray value   552, 556–559
      α-quantile   557
      anisometry   557, 559
      area, 557–559
      center of gravity   557, 558
      central moments   557
      ellipse parameters   557, 559
      major axis   557, 559
      maximum   511, 556
      mean   556
      median   557
      minimum   511, 556
      minor axis   557, 559
      moments   557–559
      normalized moments   557
      orientation   557
      standard deviation   556
      variance   556
   region   552–556
      anisometry   554, 674
      area   552, 558
      center of gravity   552–554, 558
      central moments   553–554
      compactness   556, 674
      contour length   556
      convexity   555–556
      ellipse parameters   553–555
      major axis   553–554
      minor axis   553–554
      moments   552–555
      normalized moments   552–553
      orientation   553–555
      smallest enclosing circle   555
      smallest enclosing rectangle   555, 675
Fermat's principle   180
FFT, *see* fast Fourier transform   690
fields   322, 323, 345
   angle, object side   202
   buses, 411*see* interface, field bus   699
   integration, 321–323
   readout   351
   stop   206
field-programmable gate array (FPGA)   354, 361, 365–367, 402, 405, 709, 714, 794
files, *see* interface, files   699
fill factor   321, 322, 334, 558, 598, 601
filter
   anisotropic   524, 591
   border treatment   520–521
   combination   131
   convolution   522–523, 528–529
      kernel   522
   definition   522
   edge   586–587
      Ando   589
      Canny   586, 591, 597
      Deriche   586–587, 591, 597
      Frei   589
      Lanser   591, 597
      optimal   586–587, 590–591
      Prewitt   589
      Sobel   589
   factor   123
   Gaussian   524–526, 538, 542, 543, 586, 591, 649
      frequency response   525, 529
   isotropic   524, 525, 591
   linear   522–523, 583
   mask   522
   maximum, *see* morphology, gray value, dilation   690

mean   519–522, 526, 538, 543, 584, 649
  frequency response   523–524, 528, 650
  median   526–527, 543
  minimum, *see* morphology, gray value, erosion   690
  nonlinear   526–527, 576
  rank   527, 576
  recursive   522, 523, 525, 577
  runtime complexity   521–522
  separable   521, 523, 525
  smoothing   517–527
    optimal   524–525, 586, 591
  spatial averaging   519–522
  temporal averaging   518–519, 545
finite extension of ray pencils   205
FireWire, 361, 449, *see* interface, FireWire   699
FireWire/IEEE   1394, 432
first Bessel function   18
first in–first out (FIFO)   362
fitting
  circles   607–608
    outlier suppression   607
    robust   607
  ellipses   608–609
    algebraic error   608
    geometric error   609
    outlier suppression   609
    robust   609
  lines   603–606
    outlier suppression   604–606
    robust   604–606
fixation   717, 718, 722, 723
fixed pattern noise   334, 392
flash   322, 323, 327, 332, 335, 350
  duration   80
  lighting   84, 167
  mode   167
  repeating frequency   167
  time   170
fluorescent lamp   81
fluorescent tubes   45
f-number   210, 514
focal length   42, 614–615, 632
  image side   192
  object side   192
focal point
  image side   189
  object side   189
focus depth of   718, 742
focusing plane   211, 214
Fourier transform   240, 523, 528–532
  continuous   528–529
  convolution   528–529
  discrete   529–532
    inverse   530
  fast   530
  frequency domain   528
  Nyquist frequency   529
  1D   528
    inverse   528
  real-valued   530
  spatial domain   528
  texture removal   530–532
  2D   528
    inverse   528
fovea   3, 10
FPGA counter   59
FPN   392
frame   4, 37
  averaging   366
  frame grabber   350
    analog, line jitter   597
  integration   321, 323, 324
  memory   361
  rates   336, 382
  transfer   321
  work, *see* engineering framework   699
FrameBurstStart   373
Fraunhofer approximation   240
Frei filter   589
frequency, 183, *see* signal, frequency   699
  domain   528
Fresnel's approximation   239
FTP, *see* interface, network   699
Full frame   321
Full well   336
fuzzy membership   557–559
fuzzy set   557–559
FX3   384

g

G3   433
gage capability   718, 724
Gamma function   362
gamma response function   513, 516
gamut   351, 369, 370
ganglion cells   11, 17, 18, 20–22, 24, 27
gauge capability   724, 779
Gaussian filter   524–526, 538, 542, 543, 586, 591, 649
  frequency response   525, 529
Gaussian optics   185, 235
GenAPI   378
generalized Hough transform   658–661
  accumulatorarray   658, 660, 661
  R-table   660
Generic Application Programming Interface (GenApi)   434
Generic Control Protocol (GenCP)   434
Generic Transport Layer (GenTL)   434
GenICam, 354, 371, 378, 380, 384, 394–396   433, 457, 716
GenTL   378
geometrical optics   179, 180
geometrical path   180
geometric camera calibration   600, 601, 613–631, 632
  binocular stereo calibration   633
  calibration target   622–623
  exterior orientation   601, 615–616, 620, 623–626
    world coordinate system   615–616, 620
  interior orientation   601, 614–618, 623–626, 632
    accuracy   629–631
    camera coordinate system   615–618, 633
    camera motion vector   618
    camera constant, *see* geometric camera calibration, interior
    distortion coefficient (division model)   632, 636
    distortion coefficients (polynomial model)   632
    focal length   632
    pixel size   632
    principal distance   632
    projection center   614, 632, 633, 635, 637
  orientation, principal distance   690
    camera coordinate system   616, 620
    distortion coefficient (division model)   616–629, 631
    distortion coefficients (polynomial model)   616, 618
    focal length   614, 615
    image coordinate system   618–620
    image plane coordinate system   616–620
    pixel size   618–620
    principal distance   614–629, 631
    principal point   618–632
  relative orientation   632, 633
    base   633
    base line   635
geometric error   609
geometric hashing   662–663
geometric matching   661–671
gesture recognition   766
Gigabit Ethernet for machine vision   456
Gigabit Ethernet (GigE Vision)   340, 341, 345, 354, 361, 363, 375, 377–380, 384, 385, 394–396, 432, 455, 716
GigE Vision Control Protocol (GVCP)   378, 456
GigE Vision device discovery   456
GigE Vision Stream Protocol (GVSP)   378, 379, 457
Global Machine Vision Interface Standards   433
Global Reset Release Shutter   332
global shutter   332, 334
glutamate   13
grab acquisition   480
gradient   581, 754, 762
  algorithm   119
  amplitude   548, 581, 590
  angle   581, 660
  direction   581, 658, 660

index lens   5
length   581
magnitude   548, 581, 590
morphological   577–578
graphics processing unit (GPU)   404
    see also GPU, 699, 710, 794
grating acuity   8, 18
gray value   506
    α-quantile   557
    camera response   512–513
        linear   512, 600, 601
        nonlinear   512, 600
    difference   118
    feature, see features, gray value   690
    maximum   511, 556
    mean   556
    median   557
    minimum   511, 556
    normalization   511–512
        robust   511–512, 676
    1D histogram   511–512, 541–542
        cumulative   511, 557
        maximum   541–542
        minimum   541–542
        peak   541–542
    profile   584
    robust normalization   675
    scaling   510
    standard deviation   556
    transformation   510–512, 556, 559
    2D histogram   515
    variance   556
GretagMacbeth   369
grey filter   129

h

H264   318
half-power points   122
half-width   82
halogen and xenon lamps   45
halogen lamp   77
handling, see production, part handling   699
handshaking, see interface, handshaking   699
hardware trigger   371
harmonic wave   258

Hausdorff distance   656–658
HD   343, 350
height map   754, 755, 757, 758, 760, 762, 765, 770, 771
Helmholtz equation   237
Hessian normal form   603
HF-ballast   81
High-Definition Multimedia Interface (HDMI) connector   413
higher order aberrations   5
high dynamic range (HDR)   328, 331
high speed imaging   331
high-speed inspection   168
HiRose   350, 382
histogram   361
    1D   511–512, 541–542, 557
        cumulative   511, 557
        maximum   541–542
        minimum   541–542
        peak   541–542
    2D   515
hit-or-miss opening   570
hit-or-miss transform   568–569, 572
HMI, see human machine interface   699
hole accumulation diode   325
homocentric pencil   180, 185
homogeneity   253
homogeneous coordinates   533, 534
homogeneous lighting   151
horizon line   223
Horizontal Synchronization (Hsync) pulse   437
HSL color space   500
Hsync signal   439
HTTP, see interface, network   699
Huber weight function   605
human machine interfaces   34, 735, 745–747, 749, 750
human perception   119
100-pin SCSI connector   443
hyper acuity   25
hyper centric perspective   226
hyper column   23
hyper focal depth, near limit   217

hyper focal distance   217
hyper polarization   13, 14
hypothesize-and-test paradigm   661
hysteresis thresholding   592–593

i

ICP   756, 757, 768
ideal lens transformation   242
idealized impulse   253
IEEE 1394, *see* interface, IEEE   1394, 699
IEEE 1394 (FireWire) (Legacy)   442
IEEE 1394 for machine vision   445
IIDC   371, 378
IIDC Isochronous video packet   448
IIDC2 standard   434
IIoT   716, 730, 735, 793–795
illuminances   110, 111, 113, 169
  at image sensor   114
  choice of   44, 52, 58
  component   67
imaging equations   195
  general   198
  Newtonian   197
imaging optics   134
images   505–506 *see also* data, images, 699
  acquisition time   34
  binary   507, 549, 552, 561, 563, 567, 573
  bit depth   506
  circle diameter   211, 256
  complement   576
  construction, graphical   195
  domain, *see* region of interest   690
  edges   37
  enhancement   509–527
  function   506–507
  gray value   506
    scaling   510
    transformation   510–512
  gray value normalization   511–512
    robust   511–512, 676
  label   507, 549
  multichannel   506
  noise, *see* noise   690
  orientation   186

  plane   632, 636, 637, 639
  processing library   53, 385
  pyramid   649–652, 670
  quality   49, 277
  real   187
  rectification   535, 538, 628–629, 637–638, 673
  representation on disk   482, 487
  RGB   506
  segmentation, *see* segmentation   690
  sensors   409
  side focal length   192
  single-channel   506
  space   191, 200
  smoothing   517–527
  spatial averaging   519–522
  temporal averaging   518–519, 545
  transformation   534–539, 544
  virtual   187
impact acquire   370
impulse response   238, 241, 242
incandescent emission   76
incandescent lamp   77
incident light (ing)   138, 150, 174
incoherent imaging   243
incoherent light   137
incoherent transmission chain   267
incoming light   93
Industrial Internet of Things, *see* IIoT   699
industrial lighting   67
Industry   4.0, 716, 730, 735, 793–795
Industry Standard Architecture (ISA) bus   463
information interfaces   56
information theoretical aspect   252
Infrared Light (IR)   70, 322, 325, 340, 341, 348, 355
  cut filter   348, 355
  suppression filter   128
inhomogeneous coordinates   533, 534
INL   357
inline tubing inspection   55
input   382
inspection, *see* evaluation, inspection   699
inspection protocol   56

installation space   56
integration time   14, 17
intelligent camera, *see* systems, compact systems   699
intensity distribution near focus   246
interface
  comparison   396
  digital I/O   728, 729, 732–734
  Ethernet   727–729, 733–735, 737, 751, 783
  field bus   728, 729, 733–735
  files   736
  hand shaking   737, 739, 783
  multi threading   737, 738
  network   734
  real-time Ethernet   735
  serial   733
  USB   727–729, 734
interference filter   125
interfering lighting   46
interior orientation   614–626
  accuracy   629–631
  camera constant, *see* interior orientation, camera constant   690
  camera coordinate system   615–616, 618–620, 633
  camera motion vector   618
  distortion coefficient (division model)   616–631, 632, 636
  distortion coefficients (polynomial model)   616, 618, 632
  focal length   614–615, 632
  image plane coordinate system   616, 620
  image plane system   618, 620
  pixel size   618, 620, 632
  principal distance   614–616, 620, 629–631, 632
  principal point   618, 620, 629–632
  projection center   614, 632, 633, 635, 637
interlaced   321–324, 345, 350, 351
  scan   321, 322
  transfer   321
  video transfer   436
intermediate pupil   208

International System of Units   110
interpolation   359, 367, 380
  bilinear   536–537, 550, 584
  nearest-neighbor   535, 584
interrupt moderation   379
interrupt service routine (ISR)   478
intersection   561
invariant moments   555
IoT   709
irregular diffuse reflection   93
irregular diffuse transmission   97
ISO   361
ISO9001:2000   70
Isochronous   378
isoplanasie condition   256
isoplanatic region   256
Iterative Closest Point, *see* ICP   699
iteratively reweighted least-squares   605

j

jitter   318, 371, 375, 377
job-shop production, *see* production, job-shop   699
Journaling Flash File System (JFFS / JFFS2)   407
JPEG   318
jumbo packets   361, 379
junction   509

k

Keplerian telescope   230
kernel, *see* convolution, kernel *and* support vectormachine, kernel   690
knee   328–331
koniocellular pathway   21, 24
kT/C noise   349

l

label image   507, 549
labeling   549
LabVIEW   475
LAG   379
Lambert radiator   116, 136
Lanser filter   591, 597
  edge accuracy   597

Lanser filter (*contd.*)
  edge precision   597
Laplacian   582, 594–596
laser   76, 85
laser protection classes   85
latency   362, 367, 368, 371, 375, 377, 395
law of reflection   181
law of refraction   181, 183
LCD inspection   462
L cone   10, 24, 26
LED lights   45, 76, 82
lens
  aperture stop   514
  design   41, 52, 58
  diameter   43
  extension   43
  f-number   514
  magnification factor   618
  quality   43
  vignetting   513
lens aberrations
  astigmatism   600
  chromatic aberration   600
  coma   600
  distortion   600, 616–618, 620
    barrel   616–618, 620
    pincushion   616–618, 620
LGN, *see* lateral genicalate nucleus   17, 18, 21
LIDAR   760, 770
lifetime   77–80, 82, 84, 86, 357
light   70, 179
  color   101
  deflection   175
  distribution   115
  emitting diode   82
  filter   121
  guides   337
  infrared   70
  perception   73
  propagation   71
  ray   71, 179
  shielding   721, 722
  source   76
    life-span   723
    wavelength   723

  ultraviolet   70
  visible   70
light-slit method   147
lighting control   163
lighting systematic   135
lighting technique   131, 135
lighting with through-camera view   149
line
  frequency   744, 745
  fitting   603–606
    outlier suppression   604–606
    robust   604–606
  Hessian normalform   603
  line jitter   597
  scan   320, 441
  scan camera   39, 614, 618–622, 628
  sensor   319, 614
  spread function   264
linea camera model   212
linearity   357, 387, 388
linear system   253
line-scan processing   743
line spread function (LSF)   278
link aggregation grouping   379
Linux®kernel   407
local deformation   672
Lommel functions   244, 245
long-wavelength pass filter (LWP)   125
look-up table (LUT)   362–364, 497, 510, 514
low-pass filter   260
low-voltage differential signaling (LVDS)   330, 384
luminance   110, 351
  channel   21, 24
  distribution   116
  indicatrix   116
  of the object   113
luminescence radiator   76
luminous efficiency   76
luminous intensity   110
LUT, *see* look-up table   690

m
M12   355, 382
machine learning   793

machine vision 317, 324
  acquisition architectures 431
  hardware 134
  software 134
  system 31, 32
  accuracy 34
    color space conversion 499
  designing desi 36
  different part types types 33
    image reconstruction 491
    look-up table 497
    memory handling 494
  part presentation perf 33
  parts 33
    region of interest 499
    shading correction 501
  task and benefit 32
  time performance 34
  timing and triggering 492
magnification factor 618
magnification ratio 186
magnocellular pathway 21, 24
maintenance modus 48
major axis 553–554, 557, 559, 560, 603, 605
manufacturing tolerances 284
marginal ray 207
mass production, *see* production, mass 699
material flow 701
mathematical operator 253
maximum filter, *see* morphology, gray value, dilation 690
maximum likelihood estimator 680
maximum transmission unit (MTU) 361, 375, 378
M cone 10, 24, 26
MDR connector 443
mean filter 519–522, 526, 538, 543, 584, 649
  frequency response 523–524, 528, 650
mean squared edge distance 655–656
measurement accuracy 38
measuring error 159
median filter 526–527, 543
mesh 757

metal vapor lamp 78
Microlens 325
minimum filter, *see* morphology, gray value, erosion 690
Minkowski addition 562–564, 567, 575–576
Minkowski subtraction 565, 567, 576
minor axis 553–554, 557, 559, 560, 603
mirror 175
miscellaneous points 41
missing codes 357
modulation transfer function (MTF) 6, 17, 281
  semiconductor imaging device 265
Moiré pattern 7
moments 552–555, 557–559
  invariant 555
monitoring, *see* evaluation, monitoring 699
monochromatic aberration 10
monochromatic light 82, 85, 101
monocular images 758, 762
morphological adaptation 10
morphology 560–578, 672
  duality
    dilation–erosion 567, 576
    hit-or-miss transform 569
    opening–closing 571, 577
  gray value
    closing 577
    complement 576
    dilation 576
    erosion 576
    gradient 577–578
    Minkowski addition 575–576
    Minkowski subtraction 576
    opening 577
    range 577–578
  region 561–575
    boundary 567–568
    closing 571
    complement 561–562
    difference 561
    dilation 562–565, 567–568, 594
    distance transform 573–575, 655, 657
    erosion 565–568

morphology (*contd.*)
   hit-or-miss opening   570
   hit-or-miss transform   568–569, 572
   intersection   561
   Minkowski addition   562–564, 567
   Minkowski subtraction   565, 567
   opening   569–571
   skeleton   571–573
   translation   562
   transposition   562
   union   561
  structuring element   562, 568, 575, 576
motional blurring   121, 169
motion blur   704, 739–742
  computation   741, 742
motion sensitivity   3, 21
movements   720, 726, 739, 740, 751, 783
  adjustment   720
  changeover   720, 722
  process   720
MPEG   318
multi-coated lens   126
multi-core   710, 713
multi-drop bus configuration   465
multi-tap   324
MultiMediaCard (MMC)   407
multithreading, *see* interface, multithreading   699
mvPropView   329
MVTec's Embedded HALCON   414
myopia   3

n

National Instruments Compact Vision System (NI CVS)   52
National Television Systems Committee (NTSC)   435
natural light   107
natural vignetting   114, 283
near cells   25
near limit   217
near point   214
negative principal points   198

neighborhood   548–549, 568, 573
neural network   681–685, 688–689
  activation function
    hyperbolictangent   683
    logistic   683
    sigmoid   683–684
    softmax   684
    threshold   682, 683
  multilayer perceptron   682–685, 688–689
    training   684–685
  single-layer perceptron   681–682
  universal approximator   683, 684
neutral density filter   125, 129
neutral filter   129
noise   330, 334–336, 338, 347–349, 357, 366, 386, 387, 391–393, 517–518
  floor   393
  suppression   518–527
  variance   517, 519, 520, 525, 584, 597
nondestructive overlays   490
nonhomogeneous illumination scenes   47
non-maximum suppression   580, 587, 591–592
normal distribution   680
normalized cross-correlation   640, 646–648
normalized moments   552–553, 557, 560, 603, 605
null direction   20
numerical aperture   210
  image side   229
Nyquist bandpass   272
Nyquist frequency   277, 281, 529
Nyquist limit   7
Nyquist sampling theorem   269

o

object
  virtual   187
  field angle   202
  field stop   209
  plane   138
  recognition, *see* applications   699
  side field angle   210

side focal length   192
side telecentric perspective   226
side telecentric system   228
space   191, 200
object-side field angle   202
obliquity factor   238
occlusion   654, 657, 661, 668
OCR, *see* optical character recognition   690
ocular dominance column   23
OmniVision   337
ON and OFF channels   18
one-chip   359
1-D   319
one-dimensional representation   262
$1/f$ noise   392
OneShot   375
on-the-go (OTG) interface   412
OPC Unified Architecture   735, 738 *see also* OPC UA, 699
opening   569–571, 577
Open Source Automation Development Lab (OSADL)   408
"Open Source Computer Vision" (OpenCV)   416
operating system   41
optical axis   3, 185
   eye   3
optical character recognition   512, 532, 533, 552, 672–690
   character segmentation   672–673
      touching characters   673
   classification, *see* classification   690
   features   674–676
   image rectification   535, 538, 673
optical density   123
optical path difference   240
optical path length   123
optical transfer function (OTF)   260
   multiplication rule   276
optic nerve   10–12, 27
   head   3
optimum setup   45
orientation   553–555, 557, 560
   exterior   601, 615–616, 620, 623–626
      world coordinate system   615–616, 620

      column   23
   interior   601, 614–626, 632
      accuracy   629–631
      camera constant, *see* orientation, interior, principal distance   690
      camera coordinate system   615–616, 618–620, 633
      camera motion vector   618
      distortion coefficient (division model)   616–631, 632, 636
      distortion coefficients (polynomial model)   616, 618, 632
      focal length   614–615, 632
      image plane coordinate system   616, 620
      image plane system   618, 620
      pixel size   618, 620, 632
      principal distance   614–616, 620, 629–631, 632
      principal point   618, 620, 629–632
      projection center   614, 632, 633, 635, 637
   relative   632, 633
      base   633
      base line   635
outlier   602, 604
outlier suppression   604–607, 609
   Huberweight function   605
   iteratively reweighted least-squares   605
   random sample consensus   606
   RANSAC   606
   Tukey weight function   605
output   382
overtemperature   88

p

parallax   25
parallel capturing   742
parallel digital camera buses   439
parallel digital connectors   441
parallel lighting   137
parallel offset   124
parameter data, *see* data, parameters   699
paraxial region   185

part handling, *see* production, part handling   699
partial bright field illumination   139
parvocellular pathway   21, 24
pattern recognition   790
PC-based systems, *see* systems, PC-based   699
PCI/CompactPCI/PXI   464
PCI Express/CompactPCI Express/PXI Express   467
PCI-X   466
Peripheral Component Interconnect (PCI) bus   464
permissible defocusing tolerance   247
permissible size for the circle of confusion   218
perspective   219
   transformation   533–534, 538, 672, 673
PFNC   378, 380
pharoid ray   207
phase-lock loop (PLL)   350
photogrammetry   291
photometric inverse square law   111
photometric quantity   110
photon   12, 14, 71
   counter   23
   noise   16, 19, 391
   shot noise   366, 386
   transfer   387, 388
   receptor   1, 3, 6, 7, 11, 12, 23, 25, 26
   response non uniformity   392
Photo Response Non Uniformity (PRNU)   392
phototransduction   12, 26
photovoltaic effect   328
pick-and-place   766–767, 771
pinhole camera   181, 221, 614–618, 627–628
   projectioncenter   614, 632, 633, 635, 637
pinning, cameras   718
pipelined global shutter   334
pixels   265, 267, 318–326, 328–332, 334–338, 345, 347, 349, 351, 357, 359, 363, 365–368, 371, 375, 378, 380, 384, 386, 391, 392, 505–506

clock signal   439
   internal sensor   38
   rate   40
   resolution, calculation of   39
   sensitivity function   265
plane wave   237
PLC cycle   737
PLS   335, 336
point cloud   754–757, 768
point spread extension   250
point spread function (PSF)   256
Poisson distribution   391
Poisson statistics   14
polar coordinates   538
polarization   107
   effect of   44
   filter   125, 130
   phenomena   236
polarized light   107
   circular   107
   elliptical   107
   linear   107
   unpolarized   107
polarizer   107
polar transformation   538–539, 673
polygonal approximation   609–611
   Ramer algorithm   610–611
pose   532, 615–616, 620, 644, 672, 702
   recognition   766
position recognition, *see* applications, position recognition   699
position variation   718
Power-over-Ethernet (PoE)   355, 375, 381, 382, 396
power supply   726, 727, 773
   uninterruptible   727
precision   596, 724
   edge angle   661
   edges   596–597
   hardwarerequirements   597
preferred direction   19, 20, 22, 27
Pregius   336, 382
presynaptic   13
Prewitt filter   589
primary colors   351, 359, 360, 367
principle of triangulation   146
principal plane   190

image side   190
object side   190
principal point   618, 620, 629–632
principal ray   207
print inspection   544–548
prism   175
processing load   41
processing parameters   48
processing speed   56
processing time   119
production
    batch   703
    continuous   703, 704, 738, 740
    continuous motion   737, 740
    cycle time   739, 778
    discrete motion   738, 745
    discrete unit   703, 740
    job-shop   704
    mass   703, 704
    part handling   739
programmable logic controller (PLC)
        715, 730, 732–735, 737, 748–750,
        786
progressive scan   321, 324, 344, 345
    video   437
projection   159
    center   182, 212, 213, 222, 614, 632,
        633, 635, 637
projective transformation   182,
        533–534, 538, 644, 672, 673
PropView   363, 370
pulse-duty-factor   84, 90
pulse mode   167
pupil   3, 10, 12, 27
    function   243
    magnification ratio   200, 211, 234

q
quantization noise   392

r
radial spatial frequency   264
radiant intensity   110
radii of curvature   192
radiometric camera calibration
        512–517, 600
    calibration target   513

chart-based   513
chart-less   514–517
    defining equation   514
    gamma response function   513, 516
    inverse response function   514
        discretization   514, 515
        normalization   515, 516
        polynomial   516
        smoothness constraint   516
    response function   513, 514, 516
radiometric quantity   110
Ramer algorithm   610–611
rank filter   527, 576
rapid-prototyping   711
RAW   367, 368, 380
RBG to YUV   370
real object   187
real-time   714
    operating systems   408
receptive field   17–22, 27
recipes, *see* data, type data   699
reciprocity equation   196
recognition, *see* evaluation, recognition
        699
reduced coordinates   244
reflectance   92, 98, 111
reflection   92, 179
    directed   93
    irregular diffuse   93
    regular diffuse   93
    law   92
refraction   100, 179
    law   72
refractive index   183
region   506–508
    as binary image   507, 549, 552, 561,
        563, 567, 573
    boundary   556, 567–568
    characteristic function   507, 557, 575
    complement   561–562
    connected components   548–549,
        672
    convex hull   555–556
    definition   506
    difference   561
    feature, *see* features, region   690
    intersection   561

region (*contd.*)
    run-length representation   507–508, 549, 552, 561, 563, 573
    translation   562
    transposition   562
    union   561
regions of interest (ROIs)   47, 506, 532, 534, 565, 575, 594, 645
registration   756, 772
regression testing   793
regular diffuse reflection   93
relative illumination   283
relative irradiance   283
relative orientation   632, 633
    base   633
    base line   635
remote maintenance   751, 793
removal of surface reflexes   108
repeatability, *see* precision   690
representation space   258
reproducibility   718, 722, 723
reserved signal   450
reset noise   392
resolution   319, 323, 324, 338, 343, 351, 354, 359
    limit   281
    resolution   336, 338–340, 342
result data, *see* data, results   699
retina   2, 3, 6, 11, 12, 19, 26, 27
reverse engineering   768
RGB cameras   438
RGB color space   500
rhodopsin   14
rigid transformation   615, 644, 653, 662, 672
ring acquisition   481
ring light   149
rivet image   54
RJ-45 Ethernet connector   455
robot   700
    assistant   700
    collaborative   795
    navigation   770
rod photoreceptor   12
rods   6, 12, 14, 16, 18, 26
ROI, *see* region of interest   690
rolling (curtain) shutter   332
rotary encoders   372
rotation   533, 535, 555, 644, 653, 673
RS-170 video standard   437
RS-232   382, *see also* interface, serial, 699
RS-422   345, 441
RS-644 Low Voltage Differential Signaling (LVDS)   441
R-table   660
run-length encoding   507–508, 549, 552, 561, 563, 573

S

sampling interval   6
sampling theorem   7
saturation   12, 26, 119, 335, 388, 391
scaling   533, 537–538, 555, 644, 654
scan camera   36
scan cycle   737
scattering   92
Scheduled Action Command   377
S cone   10, 24
secondary wavelet   235
Secure Digital (SD)   407
security, *see* systems, security   699
segmentation   540–552
    connected components   548–549, 672
    dynamic thresholding   542–544, 577, 672
    hysteresis thresholding   592–593
    subpixel-precise thresholding   550–552, 595
    thresholding   540–542, 672
        automatic threshold selection   541–542, 672
    variation model   544–548
self-adjustment   793
self-retooling   793
sensitivity   338, 393
sensor   319, 339, 340, 342, 344, 369, 375, 382, 505–506
    resolution   43, 52
    size   43
sequencer   374
sequences   372

acquisition   480
SG-pulse   345
shading correction   365
shading images   365
Shannon   7
shape-based matching   667–671
shape check, *see* applications, shape check   699
shifting property   254
shift register   322, 324, 326, 345
shift theorem   275
short-wavelength pass filter   125
shutter   318, 321–323, 326, 331–337, 345, 349, 350, 371
   efficiency   335
   speed   742
   time   120, 170
signal
   bandwidth   727, 728, 750, 751
   frequency   727, 728, 744, 745, 786
signal-to-noise ratio   357, 393, 586, 597, 661
similarity measure   644–649, 668–670
   absolute sum of normalized dot products   669
   normalized cross-correlation   640, 646–648
   sum of absolute gray value differences   640, 645–648
   sum of absolute normalized dot products   669
   sum of normalized dot products   669
   sum of squared gray value differences   640, 645–646
   sum of unnormalized dot products   668–669
similarity transformation   644, 653, 662
simple cells   22
simultaneous location and mapping, *see* SLAM   699
62-pin high-density DSUB connector   443
skeleton   571–573
skew   533
SLAM   770
slant   533
slope, *see* gradient   699

smallest enclosing circle   555, 560
smallest enclosing rectangle   555, 560, 675
smart cameras, 41, *see* systems, compact systems   699
   applications   403
   block diagram   404
   cross-compiling   414
   definition   401
   design parameters   403
   field buses   411
   FPGA processing   406
   image sensors   409
   ingress protection   417
   Java and .NET   414
   memory and storage   407
   on-the-go interface   412
   power dissipation   416
   processors   404
   real-time operating systems   408
   scripting   413
   third-party tools   416
   timers and counters   413
   updates   409
   USB host interface   412
   visual programming   415
Smear   326
smoothing filter   517–527
   Gaussian   524–526, 538, 542, 543, 586, 591, 649
      frequency response   525, 529
   mean   519–522, 526, 538, 543, 584, 649
      frequency response   523–524, 528, 650
   median   526–527, 543
   optimal   524–525, 586, 591
   spatial averaging   519–522
   temporal averaging   518–519, 545
SNR   336, 357, 366, 387, 393, 394
Sobel filter   589
SoC   709, 714, 794
software library software   47
software structure str   47
solid angle   111
solid state disk (SSD)   407
solid state material   83

SONY HAD 325
SONY SuperHAD 325
space invariance 255
space variant nature of aliasing 274
spatial averaging 519–522
spatial depth 219
spatial domain 528
spatial frequencies 3, 6, 7, 11, 27, 240, 260
   components 261
spatial resolution 38, 57
SPC, *see* statistical process control 699
speckle 137
   pattern 85
spectral band 79
spectral opponency 21
spectral response 73, 123
   Gaussian filter 525, 529
   mean filter 523–524, 528, 650
   sensor 505
spectral sensitivity 348, 351, 356, 360
spectral transmittance 283
spectrum 78
spectrum of light 71
spherical aberration 5
spherical wave 237
spikes 16, 17
spontaneous spike activity 17
spurious resolution 6
square pixels 38, 321
stabilization 78
Standard Feature Naming Convention (SFNC) 371, 378, 434
standardization 708, 715, 716, 723, 730, 791
standardized viewing distance 219
standoff distance 42
static lighting 167
statistical process control 705
statistics engine 361
stereo geometry 632–639
   corresponding points 633
   disparity 638–639
   epipolar line 634
   epipolar standard geometry 636–637
   epipolar plane 634

epipole 634
image rectification 637–638
stereo matching 639–643
   robust 642–643
      disparity consistency check 643
      excluding weakly textured areas 642–643
   similarity measure
      normalized cross-correlation 640
      sum of squared gray value differences 640
   subpixel-accurate 641–642
   window size 642
stereopsis 25, 27
stereo reconstruction 631–643
stochastic process 517, 519
   ergodic 520
   stationary 517
streaking light 154
Strehl ratio 247
strongly translucent part 161
structured bright field incident light 145
structured lighting 137, 145, 728
structuring element 562, 568, 575, 576
subpixeling 38
subpixel-precise contour 508–509
   convex hull 560
   features, *see* features, contour 690
subpixel-precise thresholding 550–552, 595
sub-pixel region 265
SUB pulse 345
sub sampling 338
sum of absolute gray value differences 640, 645–648
sum of absolute normalized dot products 669
sum of normalized dot products 669
sum of squared gray value differences 640, 645–646
sum of unnormalized dot products 668–669
superdiffuse ring lights and shadow-free lighting 150
Super HAD 325
superposition integral 238

support vector machine 685–689
    kernel 687
        Gaussian radial basis function 687
        homogeneous polynomial 687
        inhomogeneous polynomial 687
        sigmoid 687
    margin 686
    separating hyperplane 685–686
    universal approximator 687
surface inspection, *see* applications, surface inspection 699
surface orientation 758
SVGA 338
S-Video 438
SVM, *see* support vector machine 690
SWP 125
synaptic plasticity 26
synchronization of flash lighting 170
sync pulse 349
system of lenses 202
System of Units (SI) 110
systems
    application-package 711, 712
    compact systems 709, 710, 714, 727–729, 733
    library-based 711
    PC-based 709–711, 751, 752
    security 709, 711, 751
    types of 706–715
    vision controllers 710
    vision sensors 708, 714, 729, 744
systems-on-chip, *see* SoC 699

t

tangential spatial frequency 264
taps 440
TCP/IP 35, 728, 729, 733–735, 751, 783, 784
telecentric bright field incident light 143
telecentric bright field transmitted lighting 158
telecentric camera 614–618, 626–627
telecentric lighting 136, 159
telecentric objective 137
telecentric on axis light 143

telecentric path 44
telecentric perspective 228
telecentric system 219
    object side 228
telescope magnification 231
television 317
temperature compensation 166
temperature radiator 76
template matching 544, 643–673
    clutter 654, 657, 661, 668
    erosion 567
    generalized Hough transform 658–661
        accumulator array 658, 660, 661
        R-table 660
    generalized Hough transform
        accumulator array 658, 660
    geometric hashing 662–663
    geometric matching 661–671
    Hausdorff distance 656–658
    hierarchical search 651–652, 670
    hit-or-miss transform 568
    hypothesize-and-test paradigm 661
    image pyramid 649–652, 670
    linear illumination changes 646
    matching geometric primitives 663–666
    mean squared edge distance 655–656
    nonlinear illumination changes 654, 661, 668–669
    occlusion 654, 657, 661, 668
    opening 569
    robust 654–672
    rotation 653–654
    scaling 653–654
    shape-based matching 667–671
    similarity measure 644–649, 668–670
        absolute sum of normalized dot products 669
        normalized cross-correlation 640, 646–648
        sum of absolute gray value differences 640, 645–648
        sum of absolute normalized dot products 669

template matching (*contd.*)
    sum of normalized dot products 669
    sum of squared gray value differences 640, 645–646
    sum of unnormalized dot products 668, 669
    stopping criterion 647–649
        normalized cross-correlation 648
        sum of absolute gray value differences 647–648
        sum of normalized dot products 670
    subpixel-accurate 652–653, 670–671
    translation 644–652
temporal averaging 518–519, 545
temporal control 167
test object 91, 134
texture, removal 530–532
TFT 363, 375
thermal noise 14
thicklens
    of the lens 192
    magnification factor 618
thin films 126
thin lens 193
    model 42
1394a 395
1394b 395
3D data acquisition
    active 757, 759–764
    computer tomography 769
    deflectometry 757, 761, 768–770
    interferometry 757, 763, 764, 769, 770
    laser triangulation 760, 765, 766, 768–771
    passive 757–759
    photometric stereo 753, 754, 757, 758, 762, 763, 765, 769, 770
    shape from disparity 757, 759, 769
    shape from focus 757, 758, 769
    shape from shading 757, 758, 762, 769
    shape from texture 757, 759
    sheet of light 760
    stereo 753, 757–759, 761, 766, 768–772
    structured light 757–761, 768, 769, 771
    structure from motion 759
    time-of-flight 709, 757, 759, 760, 768, 770, 771
3D reconstruction 631–643
3D-Systems 753, 772
thresholded image 54
thresholding 540–542, 672
    automatic threshold selection 541–542, 672
    subpixel-precise 550–552, 595
tilt rule 188
timed 371
time-invariant system 255
time response 375
timers 372, 376
time stamp 361, 377
timing signals 437
tolerances 34, 47, 54
topography 147
total reflection 95
traceability 730–732, 736
transfer function 259
    of the pixel 267
transformation
    affine 532–533, 555, 644, 662, 668
    geometric 532–539, 673
    gray value 510–512
    image 534–539, 544
    local deformation 672
    perspective 533–534, 538, 672, 673
    polar 538–539, 673
    projective 533–534, 538, 644, 672, 673
    rigid 615, 644, 653, 662, 672
    rotation 533, 535, 555, 644, 653, 673
    scaling 533, 537–538, 555, 644, 654
    similarity 644, 653, 662
    skew 533
    slant 533
    translation 533, 555, 562, 644, 653
Transistor-Transistor Logic (TTL)
    signaling 441
translation 533, 555, 562, 644, 653

Index | 831

transmission   96, 98, 122, 123
　chain   267
　diffuse   97
　directed   97
　irregular diffuse   97
　through the lens   114
transmittance   96, 111
transmitted lighting   138
transposition   562
triangulation   757–761, 769, 770
trichromatic   24
trigger   371, 703, 704, 707, 719, 720, 737, 741–743, 745
triggering pulse   167
trigger width   371
Tristimulus theory   359
Tukey weight function   605
12-pin Hirose connector   443
2-D   319
2.5D   754, 770
type data, *see* data, type data   699

U

UBS3 Vision   377
UDP   378
ultra-short light pulse   722
ultraviolet (UV)   70, 106, 348
　blocking filter   127
　light   106
uninterruptible power supply, *see* power supply, uninterruptible   699
union   561
unit production, *see* production, discrete unit   699
Universal Asynchronous Receiver–Transmitter (UART)   450
Universal Serial Bus (USB)   345, 452, *see also* interface, USB, 699
　host interface   412
　for machine vision   454
unpolarized light   107
UPS, *see* power supply, uninterruptible   699
USB   2.0, 395
USB 3 Vision standards   342, 345, 378, 380, 385, 394–396, 432, 433

USB   3.0, 345, 395, 396
User Datagram Protocol   378
user interface, *see* human machine interface   699

V

variable height acquisition (VHA)   494
variance   387, 392
variation model   544–548
VD   350
veiling glare   283
velocity of light   180
ventral stream   22
verification, *see* evaluation, verification   699
Vertical Synchronization (Vsync) pulse   437
vertices   192
VHDCI connector   443
vibrations   739
Video Graphic Array (VGA)   338, 413
　camera   52
video signal   267
vignetting   116, 513
visible light (VIS)   70, 101, 103
vision controllers, *see* systems, vision controllers   699
vision sensors, *see* systems, vision sensors   699
　applications   419
　component parts   420
　definition   401
　description   418
　environmental considerations   421
　programming and configuring   420
vision system design   399
visual cortex   12, 22, 23, 25
vitreous chamber   2
$V(\lambda)$-curve   73
Vsync signal   439

W

wave–particle dualism   71
wave equation   179
wavefront
　aberration   247
　plane   180

wavefront (*contd.*)
  spherical   180
waveguides   8
wavelength, 183, *see* light source,
        wavelength   699
wave nature of light   235
wave number   237
web server, *see* interface, network   699
weight function
  Huber   605
  Tukey   605
WEN   350
white light   103
  scanners   312
windows   209
wiring   729, 742
wood effect   106
working distance   123, 717, 718
world coordinates
  from single image   601, 626–628
  line scan camera   628
  pinhole camera   627–628
  telecentric camera   626–627
  from stereo reconstruction   631–643
the world is grey   361

x
Xenon flash lamp   79, 80
Xilinx Zynq®   405
XML   378

y
Y'CbCr   371
Yet Another Flash File System (YAFFS)   407
YUV   370, 371

z
zero copy mechanism   380
zero-crossing   581, 582, 595